CRIMINAL LAW AND PROCEDURE HANDBOOK OF ILLINOIS

–Including–

CHAPTERS 720, 725, 730
and Related Sections from
CHAPTERS 20, 30, 45, 410, 415, 430,
705, 735, 740, 750, 815
OF THE ILLINOIS COMPILED STATUTES
and
SUPREME COURT RULES
Articles IV, V, VI

1993

GOULD PUBLICATIONS
199/300 State Street
Binghamton, New York 13901-2782

Published by
GOULD PUBLICATIONS
199/300 State Street
Binghamton, NY 13901-2782
(607) 724-3000

ISBN 0-87526-199-X

Every attempt has been made to ensure the accuracy and the completeness of the law contained herein. No express or implied guarantees or warranties are made.

Since laws change very often and vary from jurisdiction to jurisdiction, it is very important to check the timeliness and applicability of the laws contained herein.

FOREWORD

The material presented herewith in convenient form is the **Illinois Criminal Law and Procedure Handbook**, known as **Chapter 720, 725** and **730** of the Illinois Compiled Statutes, as currently amended to include the enactments of the 87th General Assembly through Public Act 87-1276, for use in 1993. All changes to these laws have been incorporated in text, and effective dates have been added where applicable. Also included is a comprehensive index.

Some sections of the law were affected by several Public Acts which were issued concurrently or consecutively during the same legislative session. If no summary bill was passed, all changes, additions and deletions were incorporated into the changed section. Please consult all Public Acts from the same legislative session affecting sections of the law.

To make this volume more useful, related Supreme Court Rules and certain sections of the following chapters have been included herein:

(1) Chapter 20 — Executive Branch
(2) Chapter 30 — Finance
(3) Chapter 45 — Interstate Compacts
(4) Chapter 410 — Public Health
(5) Chapter 415 — Environmental Safety
(6) Chapter 430 — Public Safety
(7) Chapter 705 — Courts
(8) Chapter 735 — Civil Procedure
(9) Chapter 740 — Civil Liabilities
(10) Chapter 750 — Families
(11) Chapter 815 — Business Transactions

At the end of this volume is Gould's handy "Quick Find Locator" which helps you find the law you need.

Updated pages are supplied periodically to keep your book current. Please send back the "Important" card at the front of this book to ensure that you are on our subscription list.

Comments from users of this book and ways to improve it to facilitate its use would be appreciated by the publisher.

This page intentionally left blank.

1992 Legislative Changes to the CRIMINAL LAW AND PROCEDURE HANDBOOK OF ILLINOIS (for use in 1993)

ILCS Act/Section	*Ill. Rev. Stat. Former Section*	*Change*	*Public Act*	*Effective Date*
		Chapter 20		
305/1-102	111½, §6351-2	Amend	87-895(2-60)	8/14/92
305/1-103	111½, §6351-3	Amend	87-895(2-60)	8/14/92
305/1-109	111½, §6351-9	Renumber	87-895(2-60)	8/14/92
305/1-109	111½, §6351-9	Amend	87-895(2-60)	8/14/92
305/4-101	111½, §6354-1	Amend	87-895(2-60)	8/14/92
305/4-101	111½, §6354-1	Amend	87-1054(2)	9/11/92
305/4-101(d)	111½, §6354-1(d)	Amend	87-860(80)	7/1/92
305/4-101(e)	111½, §6354-1(e)	Amend	87-860(80)	7/1/92
305/4-103	111½, §6354-3	Amend	87-895(3-76)	8/14/92
305/4-103	111½, §6354-3	Amend	87-1054(2)	9/11/92
305/5-103.1	111½, §6355-3.1	Amend	87-1054(2)	9/11/92
—	111½, §§6357-1 to 6357-3	Repeal	87-860(81)	7/1/92
2210/3.2	40, §2403.2	Amend	87-895(2-23)	8/14/92
2630/5	38, §206-5	Amend	87-895(2-21)	8/14/92
2630/5	38, §206-5	Amend	87-963(1)	8/28/92
2630/5	38, §206-5	Amend	87-1230(5)	7/1/93
2640/1	—	New	87-932(1-1)	1/1/93
2640/5	—	New	87-932(1-5)	1/1/93
2640/10	—	New	87-932(1-10)	1/1/93
2640/15	—	New	87-932(1-15)	1/1/93
		Chapter 430		
65/8.1	38, §83-8.1	Amend	87-905(2)	8/14/92
		Chapter 705		
405/1-4.1	37, §801-4.1	New	87-1154(1)	1/1/93
405/1-7	37, §801-7	Amend	87-927(1)	1/1/93
405/1-7	37, §801-7	Amend	87-1198(1)	9/25/92
405/1-8	37, §801-8	Amend	87-927(1)	1/1/93
405/1-8	37, §801-8	Amend	87-928(5)	1/1/93
405/1-8.1	37, §801-8.1	New	87-928(5)	1/1/93
405/1-8.2	37, §801-8.2	New	87-928(5)	1/1/93
405/1-17	37, §801-17	New	87-1147(1)	9/17/92
405/2-19	37, §802-19	Amend	87-1148(2)	1/1/93

(continued)

1992 Legislative Changes to the CRIMINAL LAW AND PROCEDURE HANDBOOK OF ILLINOIS
(Continued)

ILCS Act / Section	*Ill. Rev. Stat. Former Section*	*Change*	*Public Act*	*Effective Date*
		Chapter 705 *(Continued)*		
405/3-4	37, §803-4	Amend	87-1154(1)	1/1/93
405/3-7	37, §803-7	Amend	87-1154(1)	1/1/93
405/4-4	37, §804-4	Amend	87-1154(1)	1/1/93
405/5-4	37, §805-4	Amend	87-895(2-18)	8/14/92
405/5-4	37, §805-4	Amend	87-931(1)	1/1/93
405/5-5	37, §805-5	Amend	87-1154(1)	1/1/93
405/5-23	37, §805-23	Amend	87-895(3-22)	8/14/92
405/5-23	37, §805-23	Amend	87-1173(1)	9/18/92
		Chapter 720		
5/2-10.1	38, §2-10.1	Amend	87-1198(2)	9/25/92
5/8-4(c)(1)	38, §8-4(c)(1)	Amend	87-921(1)	1/1/93
5/9-1	38, §9-1	Amend	87-921(1)	1/1/93
5/9-3	38, §9-3	Amend	87-1198(2)	9/25/92
5/9-3.3	38, §9-3.3	Amend	87-1198(2)	9/25/92
5/11-9.1	38, §11-9.1	New	87-1198(2)	9/25/92
5/11-20.1	38, §11-20.1	Amend	87-1069(1)	1/1/93
5/11-20.1	38, §11-20.1	Amend	87-1070(1)	9/13/92
5/12-2	38, §12-2	Amend	87-921(1)	1/1/93
5/12-4	38, §12-4	Amend	87-921(1)	1/1/93
5/12-4	38, §12-4	Amend	87-1083(1)	1/1/93
5/12-4.2	38, §12-4.2	Amend	87-921(1)	1/1/93
5/12-4.2(a)	38, §12-4.2(a)	Amend	87-1256(2)	7/1/93
5/12-4.7	38, §12-4.7	Amend	87-1198(2)	9/25/92
5/12-7.1	38, §12-7.1	Amend	87-1048(1)	1/1/93
5/12-7.1	38, §12-7.1	Amend	87-1170(1)	1/1/93
5/12-7.3	38, §12-7.3	New	87-870(1)	7/12/92
5/12-7.3	38, §12-7.3	New	87-871(1)	7/12/92
5/12-7.4	38, §12-7.4	New	87-870(1)	7/12/92
5/12-7.4	38, §12-7.4	New	87-871(1)	7/12/92
5/12-17	38, §12-17	Amend	87-895(2-19)	8/14/92
5/12-21	38, §12-21	Amend	87-1072(1)	1/1/93
5/12-31	38, §12-31	Amend	87-1167(1)	1/1/93
5/12-33	38, §12-33	New	87-1167(1)	1/1/93
5/16B-2	38, §16B-2	Amend	87-898(1)	1/1/93
5/17A-1	38, §17A-1	Amend	87-895(3-23)	8/14/92
5/24-1	38, §24-1	Amend	87-930(1)	1/1/93
5/24-1.2	38, §24-1.2	Amend	87-921(1)	1/1/93
5/24-2	38, §24-2	Amend	87-895(2-19)	8/14/92
5/24-6	38, §24-6	Amend	87-895(3-23)	8/14/92

(continued)

1992 Legislative Changes to the CRIMINAL LAW AND PROCEDURE HANDBOOK OF ILLINOIS

(Continued)

ILCS Act / Section	*Ill. Rev. Stat. Former Section*	*Change*	*Public Act*	*Effective Date*
		Chapter 720 *(Continued)*		
5/26-4	38, §26-4	New	87-970(1)	7/1/93
5/28-2(a)(4)	38, §28-2(a)(4)	New	87-855(2)	5/8/92
5/31-1	38, §31-1	Amend	87-1198(2)	9/25/92
5/31A-1.2	38, §31A-1.2	Amend	87-905(1)	8/14/92
5/33E-13	38, §33E-13	New	87-855(2)	7/1/92
5/42-2	38, §42-2	Amend	87-1170(1)	1/1/93
5/45-1	38, §45-1	New	87-1134(1)	1/1/93
5/45-2	38, §45-2	New	87-1134(1)	1/1/93
5/45-3	38, §45-3	New	87-1134(1)	1/1/93
5/45-4	38, §45-4	New	87-1134(1)	1/1/93
5/45-5	38, §45-5	New	87-1134(1)	1/1/93
250/17.03	17, §5930.3	New	87-1150(1)	9/17/92
275/118	73, §1101	Repeal	87-1134(2)	1/1/93
375/1.5	121½, §157.32	Amend	87-895(4-24)	8/14/92
525/4.1	40, §1704.1	New	87-1129(3)	1/1/93
550/12	56½, §712	Amend	87-993(1)	9/1/92
570/303.1	56½, §1303.1	Amend	87-1031(2)	1/1/93
570/407	56½, §1407	Amend	87-895(2-29)	8/14/92
570/407	56½, §1407	Amend	87-1225(1)	12/22/92
570/413	56½, §1413	Amend	87-993(2)	9/1/92
		Chapter 725		
5/106-2.5	38, §106-2.5	New	87-932(2-100)	1/1/93
5/106C-1	38, §106C-1	Renumber	87-895(2-20)	8/14/92
5/106C-1	38, §106C-1	Amend	87-895(2-20)	8/14/92
5/106C-2	38, §106C-2	Renumber	87-895(2-20)	8/14/92
5/106C-2	38, §106C-2	Amend	87-895(2-20)	8/14/92
5/108-8	38, §108-8	Amend	87-895(3-24)	8/14/92
5/110-4	38, §110-4	Amend	87-870(2)	7/12/92
5/110-4	38, §110-4	Amend	87-871(2)	7/12/92
5/110-6	38, §110-6	Amend	87-870(2)	7/12/92
5/110-6	38, §110-6	Amend	87-871(2)	7/12/92
5/110-6.3	38, §110-6.3	New	87-870(2)	7/12/92
5/110-6.3	38, §110-6.3	New	87-871(2)	7/12/92
5/110-10	38, §110-10	Amend	87-1186(1)	1/1/93
5/112A-2	38, §112A-2	Amend	87-1186(1)	1/1/93
5/112A-3	38, §112A-3	Amend	87-1186(1)	1/1/93
5/112A-4	38, §112A-4	Amend	87-1186(1)	1/1/93
5/112A-5	38, §112A-5	Amend	87-1186(1)	1/1/93
5/112A-6	38, §112A-6	Amend	87-1186(1)	1/1/93

(continued)

1992 Legislative Changes to the CRIMINAL LAW AND PROCEDURE HANDBOOK OF ILLINOIS
(Continued)

ILCS Act / Section	*Ill. Rev. Stat. Former Section*	*Change*	*Public Act*	*Effective Date*
		Chapter 725 *(Continued)*		
5/112A-7	38, §112A-7	Amend	87-895(3-24)	8/14/92
5/112A-7	38, §112A-7	Amend	87-1186(1)	1/1/93
5/112A-10	38, §112A-10	Amend	87-1186(1)	1/1/93
5/112A-12	38, §112A-12	Amend	87-1186(1)	1/1/93
5/112A-14	38, §112A-14	Amend	87-1186(1)	1/1/93
5/112A-15	38, §112A-15	Amend	87-1186(1)	1/1/93
5/112A-17	38, §112A-17	Amend	87-1186(1)	1/1/93
5/112A-18	38, §112A-18	Amend	87-1186(1)	1/1/93
5/112A-20	38, §112A-20	Amend	87-1186(1)	1/1/93
5/112A-21	38, §112A-21	Amend	87-1186(1)	1/1/93
5/112A-22	38, §112A-22	Amend	87-1186(1)	1/1/93
5/112A-23	38, §112A-23	Amend	87-1186(1)	1/1/93
5/112A-24	38, §112A-24	Amend	87-1186(1)	1/1/93
5/112A-26	38, §112A-26	New	87-1186(1)	1/1/93
5/112A-27	38, §112A-27	New	87-1186(1)	1/1/93
5/112A-28	38, §112A-28	New	87-1186(1)	1/1/93
5/112A-29	38, §112A-29	New	87-1186(1)	1/1/93
5/112A-30	38, §112A-30	New	87-1186(1)	1/1/93
5/112A-31	38, §112A-31	New	87-1186(1)	1/1/93
5/115-7	38, §115-7	Amend	87-1068(1)	1/1/93
5/115-7.2	38, §115-7.2	Amend	87-1167(2)	1/1/93
5/119-5	38, §119-5	Amend	87-1198(3)	9/25/92
5/122-2.1	38, §122-2.1	Amend	87-904(1)	1/1/93
prec. 145/1	70, prec. §401	Amend	87-1157(1)	9/18/92
145/1	70, §401	Amend	87-1157(1)	9/18/92
145/2.2	70, §402.2	Repeal	87-1157(4)	9/18/92
145/3	70, §403	Amend	87-1157(1)	9/18/92
145/4 to 14	70, §404 to 414	Repeal	87-1157(4)	9/18/92
175/5	56½, §1655	Amend	87-895(2-30)	8/14/92
175/5	56½, §1655	Amend	87-1013(1)	9/3/92
240/10	70, §510	Amend	87-895(3-35)	8/14/92
		Chapter 730		
5/3-8-2	38, §1003-8-2	Amend	87-1256(3)	7/1/93
5/3-10-5	38, §1003-10-5	Amend	87-1158(1)	9/18/92
5/3-14-2(c)	38, §1003-14-2(c)	Amend	87-855(3)	5/8/92
5/3-14-5	38, §1003-14-5	New	87-870(3)	7/12/92
5/3-14-5	38, §1003-14-5	New	87-871(3)	7/12/92
5/3-15-2	38, §1003-15-2	Amend	87-860(23)	7/1/92
5/5-3-4	38, §1005-3-4	Amend	87-900(1)	1/1/93

(continued)

1992 Legislative Changes to the CRIMINAL LAW AND PROCEDURE HANDBOOK OF ILLINOIS

(Continued)

ILCS Act/Section	*Ill. Rev. Stat. Former Section*	*Change*	*Public Act*	*Effective Date*
		Chapter 730 *(Continued)*		
5/5-4-3	38, §1005-4-3	Amend	87-963(2)	8/28/92
5/5-4-3.1	38, §1005-4-3.1	New	87-900(1)	1/1/93
5/5-5-3	38, §1005-5-3	Amend	87-1167(3)	1/1/93
5/5-5-3	38, §1005-5-3	Amend	87-1190(1)	9/24/92
5/5-5-3.2	38, §1005-5-3.2	Amend	87-895(2-22)	8/14/92
5/5-5-3.2	38, §1005-5-3.2	Amend	87-921(2)	1/1/93
5/5-5-3.2	38, §1005-5-3.2	Amend	87-1067(1)	1/1/93
5/5-5-3.2	38, §1005-5-3.2	Amend	87-1167(3)	1/1/93
5/5-5-6	38, §1005-5-6	Amend	87-895(2-22)	8/14/92
5/5-5-6	38, §1005-5-6	Amend	87-1170(2)	1/1/93
5/5-5-6	38, §1005-5-6	Amend	87-1230(6)	7/1/93
5/5-5-9	38, §1005-5-9	New	87-907(1)	1/1/93
5/5-6-1	38, §1005-6-1	Amend	87-1074(1)	1/1/93
5/5-6-2	38, §1005-6-2	Amend	87-895(3-25)	8/14/92
5/5-6-3	38, §1005-6-3	Amend	87-895(2-22)	8/14/92
5/5-6-3	38, §1005-6-3	Amend	87-1198(4)	9/25/92
5/5-6-3.1	38, §1005-6-3.1	Amend	87-895(2-22)	8/14/92
5/5-8-1	38, §1005-8-1	Amend	87-921(2)	1/1/93
5/5-8A-3	38, §1005-8A-3	Amend	87-860(23)	7/1/92
5/5-8A-3	38, §1005-8A-3	Amend	87-890(1)	7/1/92
5/5-8A-5(c)	38, §1005-8A-5(c)	Amend	87-890(1)	7/1/92
5/5-8A-5(c)	38, §1005-8A-5(c)	Amend	87-860(23)	7/1/92
5/5-9-1.5	38, §1005-9-1.5	Amend	87-1072(2)	1/1/93
5/5-9-1.6	38, §1005-9-1.6	Renumber and Amend	87-895(2-22)	8/14/92
5/5-9-1.7	38, §1005-9-1.7	New	87-1070(2)	9/13/92
5/5-9-1.7	38, §1005-9-1.7	New	87-1072(2)	1/1/93
125/11	75, §111	Amend	87-899	1/1/93
130/3	75, §32	Amend	87-1198(5)	9/25/92
135/3	38, §1103	Amend	87-860(25)	7/1/92
prec. 50/1	38, prec. §221	Amend	87-1064(2)	1/1/93
150/1	38, §221	Amend	87-1064(1)	1/1/93
150/2	38, §222	Amend	87-1064(1)	1/1/93
150/3	38, §223	Amend	87-1064(1)	1/1/93
150/4	38, §224	Amend	87-1064(1)	1/1/93
150/5	38, §225	Amend	87-1064(1)	1/1/93
150/7	38, §227	Amend	87-1064(1)	1/1/93
150/8	38, §228	Amend	87-1065(2)	9/13/92

(continued)

1992 Legislative Changes to the CRIMINAL LAW AND PROCEDURE HANDBOOK OF ILLINOIS

(Continued)

ILCS Act/Section	*Ill. Rev. Stat. Former Section*	*Change*	*Public Act*	*Effective Date*
		Chapter 740		
45/2	70, §72	Amend	87-895(2-35)	8/14/92
45/2	70, §72	Amend	87-1186(4)	1/1/93
147/1	—	New	87-932(2-1)	1/1/93
147/5	—	New	87-932(2-5)	1/1/93
147/10	—	New	87-932(2-10)	1/1/93
147/15	—	New	87-932(2-15)	1/1/93
147/20	—	New	87-932(2-20)	1/1/93
147/25	—	New	87-932(2-25)	1/1/93
147/30	—	New	87-932(2-30)	1/1/93
147/35	—	New	87-932(2-35)	1/1/93
		Chapter 750		
60/102	40, §2311-2	Amend	87-1186(3)	1/1/93
60/103	40, §2311-3	Amend	87-1186(3)	1/1/93
60/201	40, §2312-1	Amend	87-1186(3)	1/1/93
60/202	40, §2312-2	Amend	87-1186(3)	1/1/93
60/203	40, §2312-3	Amend	87-1186(3)	1/1/93
60/204	40, §2312-4	Amend	87-1186(3)	1/1/93
60/205	40, §2312-5	Amend	87-1186(3)	1/1/93
60/205	40, §2312-5	Amend	87-1255(2)	1/7/93
60/206	40, §2312-6	Amend	87-1186(3)	1/1/93
60/209	40, §2312-9	Amend	87-1186(3)	1/1/93
60/210	40, §2312-10	Amend	87-1186(3)	1/1/93
60/210.1	40, §2312-10.1	New	87-1186(3)	1/1/93
60/211	40, §2312-11	Amend	87-1186(3)	1/1/93
60/212	40, §2312-12	Amend	87-1186(3)	1/1/93
60/213	40, §2312-13	Amend	87-1186(3)	1/1/93
60/214	40, §2312-14	Amend	87-1186(3)	1/1/93
60/214(b)(1)	40, §2312-14(b)(1)	Amend	87-870(4)	7/12/92
60/214(b)(1)	40, §2312-14(b)(1)	Amend	87-871(4)	7/12/92
60/215	40, §2312-15	Amend	87-1186(3)	1/1/93
60/217	40, §2312-17	Amend	87-1186(3)	1/1/93
60/218	40, §2312-18	Amend	87-1186(3)	1/1/93
60/220	40, §2312-20	Amend	87-1186(3)	1/1/93
60/221	40, §2312-21	Amend	87-1186(3)	1/1/93
60/222	40, §2312-22	Amend	87-1186(3)	1/1/93
60/223	40, §2312-23	Amend	87-1186(3)	1/1/93
60/224	40, §2312-24	Amend	87-1186(3)	1/1/93
60/225	40, §2312-25	Amend	87-1186(3)	1/1/93
60/226	40, §2312-26	Amend	87-1186(3)	1/1/93
60/227	40, §2312-27	Amend	87-1186(3)	1/1/93

(continued)

1992 Legislative Changes to the CRIMINAL LAW AND PROCEDURE HANDBOOK OF ILLINOIS
(Continued)

ILCS Act/Section	*Ill. Rev. Stat. Former Section*	*Change*	*Public Act*	*Effective Date*

Chapter 750
(Continued)

ILCS Act/Section	*Ill. Rev. Stat. Former Section*	*Change*	*Public Act*	*Effective Date*
60/227.1	40, §2312-27.1	New	87-1186(3)	1/1/93
60/301.1	40, §2313-1.1	New	87-1186(3)	1/1/93
60/302	40, §2313-2	Amend	87-1186(3)	1/1/93
60/303	40, §2313-3	Amend	87-1186(3)	1/1/93
60/304	40, §2313-4	Amend	87-1186(3)	1/1/93
60/306	40, §2313-6	New	87-1255(2)	1/7/93

Supreme Court Rules

Rule	*Change*	*Effective Date*
501(a)	Amend	7/1/92
503(a)	Amend	7/1/92
526	Amend	7/1/92
527(a)	Amend	7/1/92
527(i)	Repeal	7/1/92
528	Amend	7/1/92
529(a)	Amend	1/20/93
529(b)	Amend	7/1/92
530	Amend	7/1/92
551(e)	Amend	7/1/92
553(e)	Amend	7/1/92
604(d)	Amend	8/1/92
605(b)	Amend	8/1/92

This page intentionally left blank.

TABLE OF CONTENTS
CRIMINAL LAW AND PROCEDURE HANDBOOK OF ILLINOIS

This page intentionally left blank.

CHAPTER 20
EXECUTIVE BRANCH

ILLINOIS ALCOHOLISM AND OTHER DRUG DEPENDENCY ACT

ARTICLE I. GENERAL PROVISIONS

305/1-101. Short title.

§1-101. Short title. This Act shall be known and may be cited as the Illinois Alcoholism and Other Drug Dependency Act.
(Source: P.A. 85-965.) [Formerly Ill. Rev. Stat. 111½ §6351-1.]

305/1-102. Legislative declaration.

§1-102. Legislative Declaration. The human suffering and social and economic loss caused by the illness of alcoholism, addiction to controlled substances, the use of cannabis, and the abuse and misuse of alcohol and other drugs are public health problems of grave concern to the people of the State of Illinois. It is imperative that a comprehensive and coordinated strategy be developed through the leadership of a State agency, and implemented through the facilities of Federal and local government and private agencies, to the end that persons and their spouses and children, if any, who abuse or misuse alcohol or other drugs be restored to good health and become productive citizens in the community. The human, social, and economic benefits of preventing alcohol and other drug abuse and dependence are great, and it is imperative that there be interagency cooperation in the planning and delivery of alcohol and other drug abuse prevention, intervention, and treatment efforts in Illinois.

The provisions of this Act shall be liberally construed to enable the Department to carry out these objectives and purposes.
(Source: P.A. 86-1004; 87-540; 87-719; 87-895.) [Formerly Ill. Rev. Stat. 111½ §6351-2.]

305/1-103. Definitions.

§1-103. Definitions. As used in this Act, unless the context clearly indicates otherwise, the following words and terms have the following meanings:

"Abuse" means a pattern of use of alcohol or other drugs with the potential of leading to immediate functional problems or to addiction or the use of alcohol or other drugs solely for purposes of intoxication.

"Act" means the Illinois Alcoholism and Other Drug Dependency Act.

"Addict" means an individual who habitually uses any chemical or substance other than alcohol so as to endanger the individual or the public health, safety or welfare or who is so dependent on this use as to have lost the power of self-control with reference to it and to be subject to continued use or relapse.

"Addiction" means an illness characterized by preoccupation with alcohol or other drugs which is typically associated with physical disability and impaired emotional, occupational or social adjustments or a combination thereof as a direct consequence of loss of control over consumption leading to periodic or chronic intoxication; tendency to increase the dose; tendency toward relapse; a psychological and, sometimes, a physical dependence on the effects of the alcohol or other drugs; and a detrimental effect on the individual, his or her family and on society.

"Administrator" means a person responsible for administration of a facility.

"Alcoholic" means a person who suffers from an illness characterized by preoccupation with alcohol which is typically associated with physical disability and impaired emotional, occupational or social adjustments as a direct consequence of loss of control over consumption of alcohol and demonstrated by persistent and excessive use of alcohol such as usually leads to intoxication if drinking is begun; by chronicity; by progression; and by tendency toward relapse.

"Alcoholism" means an illness characterized by preoccupation with alcohol which is typically associated with physical disability and impaired emotional, occupational or social adjustments as a direct consequence of loss of control over consumption of alcohol, and demonstrated by persistent and excessive use of alcohol such as usually leads to intoxication if drinking is begun; by chronicity; by progression; and by tendency toward relapse. Alcoholism is a family illness which harms the physical and emotional health of each person in the family.

"Children of alcoholics and other drug addicts or abusers" means the minor or adult children of individuals who are, or have been addicted to alcohol or other drugs. These children may or may not become addicted themselves, however they are physically, psychologically, and behaviorally at high risk of developing the illness. Children of alcoholics and other drug abusers experience emotional and other problems, and benefit from prevention and treatment services provided by Department funded and Department licensed agencies.

"Co-dependents" means individuals who are involved in the lives of, and are affected by, people who are addicted to alcohol and other drugs. Co-dependents compulsively engage in behaviors that cause them to suffer adverse physical, emotional, familial, social, behavioral, vocational, and legal consequences as they attempt to cope with the alcohol or drug addicted person. People who become co-dependents include spouses, parents, siblings, and friends of alcohol or drug addicted people. Co-dependents benefit from prevention and treatment services provided by Department funded and Department licensed agencies.

"Controlled substance" means any substance or immediate precursor which is enumerated in the schedules of Article II of the Illinois Controlled Substances Act [720 ILCS 570/201 et seq.] or the Cannabis Control Act, as now or hereafter amended [720 ILCS 550/1 et seq.].

"Crime of violence" means any of the following crimes: treason, murder, voluntary manslaughter, criminal sexual assault, aggravated criminal sexual assault, armed robbery, arson, kidnapping, aggravated battery, aggravated arson, or any other felony which involves the use or threat of physical force or violence against another individual.

"Deaf person" means a person with a disability which precludes successful processing of speech through hearing with or without a hearing aid.

"Department" means the Illinois Department of Alcoholism and Substance Abuse.

"Designated program" means a program designated by the Department to provide intervention services described in paragraph (B)(1)(b) of Section 2-101 of this Act [20 ILCS 305/2-101] whose primary function is screening, assessing, referring and tracking clients identified by the criminal justice system and which agrees to apply standard, uniform criteria and procedures established by the Department Statewide pursuant to such designation.

"Detoxification" means the process of cessation of substance use by persons who abuse or are dependent on alcohol or other drugs.

"Director" means the Director of the Illinois Department of Alcoholism and Substance Abuse or his designee.

"D.U.I." means driving under the influence of alcohol or other substance.

"Educational Service Region" means any geographical Educational Service Region established pursuant to The School Code [105 ILCS 5/1-1 et seq.].

"Facility" means a public or private home, institution, building, residence or any other place which provides, through its ownership or management, alcoholism and other drug abuse dependency treatment services or intervention services as specified in Section 2-101 of this Act, or conducts research activities with controlled substances as specified in Section 2-101 of this Act.

"Hearing impaired person" means a person with some degree of hearing impairment.

"Incapacitated" means that a person is unconscious or otherwise exhibits by overt behavior or by extreme physical debilitation an inability to care for his own needs or to recognize the obvious danger of his situation or to make rational decisions with respect to his need for treatment.

"Incompetent person" means a person who has been adjudged incompetent by the Circuit Court.

"Intermediary person" means a person with expertise relative to addiction, alcoholism and other drug abuse who may be called on to assist the police in carrying on activities with respect to persons who abuse or are dependent on alcohol or other drugs.

"Intervention" means activities which are readily accessible to assist individuals and their partners or family members to cope with the immediate problems of alcohol and other drug abuse or dependency, to reduce their alcohol and other drug use, and to facilitate emotional and social stability, referring people for further treatment as needed, and as specified in Section 2-101 of this Act.

"Intoxicated person" means a person whose mental or physical functioning is substantially impaired as a result of the use of alcohol or other drugs.

"Person" means any individual, firm, group, association, partnership, corporation, trust, government or governmental subdivision or agency.

"Relapse" means a process that occurs in an individual which manifests itself in a progressive pattern of behavior that reactivates the symptoms of a disease or creates debilitating conditions in an individual who has experienced remission from addiction or alcoholism.

"Regional prevention groups" means an alcohol and substance abuse prevention body established in Educational Service Regions in the State.

"Research" means research done for legitimate purposes and involving the possession, dispensing, use, or administration of controlled substances, as defined in the Illinois Controlled Substances Act, or cannabis, as defined in the Cannabis Control Act.

"Satellite facility" means a facility at which treatment services, intervention services, or research activities are conducted for less than 16 hours per week, and which is under the supervision of the administrator of a licensed facility.

"Treatment" means the broad range of emergency, outpatient, intermediate and residential services and care, including diagnosis, medical, psychiatric, psychological and social service care and counseling, which may be extended to individuals who abuse or are dependent on alcohol or other drugs.

(Source: P.A. 86-848; 86-1004; 86-1342; 87-503; 87-540; 87-895.) [Formerly Ill. Rev. Stat. 111½ §6351-3.]

305/1-104. Creation of the Department.

§1-104. Creation of the Department. There is created the Department of Alcoholism and Substance Abuse, which shall assume the various rights, powers, duties and functions herein described, in addition to the powers, duties and functions provided by other laws of this State.

It is declared to be the public policy of this State, pursuant to paragraphs (h) and (i) of Section 6 of Article VII of the Illinois Constitution of 1970, that the powers and functions set forth in this Act and expressly delegated to the Illinois Department of Alcoholism and Substance Abuse are exclusive State powers and functions. Nothing herein prohibits the exercise of any power or the performance of any function, including the power to regulate, for the protection of the public health, safety, morals and welfare, by any unit of local government, other than the powers and functions set forth in this Act and expressly delegated to the Department to be exclusive State powers and functions.
(Source: P.A. 85-965.) [Formerly Ill. Rev. Stat. 111½ §6351-4.]

305/1-105. Applicability.

§1-105. Applicability. It is unlawful for any person to provide treatment for alcoholism and other drug abuse or dependency, or to provide intervention services as specified in Section 2-101 of this Act [20 ILCS 305/2-101], or to conduct research relating to alcoholism and other drug abuse or dependency as specified in Section 2-101 of this Act, unless such person is licensed by the Illinois Department of Alcoholism and Substance Abuse. The performance of these activities by any person in violation of this Act is declared to be inimical to the public health and welfare, and to be a public nuisance.

Nothing in this Act shall be construed to require any hospital, as defined by the Hospital Licensing Act, that is required to have a license from the Department of Public Health pursuant to the Hospital Licensing Act [210 ILCS 85/1 et seq.], to obtain any license under this Act for any alcoholism and other drug dependency treatment services offered through or operated from the licensed premises of the hospital, provided that such services are covered within the scope of the Hospital Licensing Act. No person or facility required to be licensed under this Act shall be required to obtain a license pursuant to the Hospital Licensing Act or the Child Care Act of 1969 [225 ILCS 10/1 et seq.].

Nothing in this Act shall be construed to require an individual employee of a licensed program to be licensed under this Act.

Nothing in this Act shall be construed to require any private professional practice, whether by an individual practitioner, by a partnership, or by a duly incorporated professional service corporation, that provides outpatient treatment for alcoholism and other drug abuse to be licensed under this Act, if the treatment is done personally by the professional, in his own name, and the professional is authorized by individual professional licensure or registration from the Department of Professional Regulation to do such treatment unsupervised. This exemption shall not apply to such private professional practice which specializes exclusively in the treatment of alcoholism and other drug abuse. This exemption shall also not apply to intervention services, research, or residential treatment services as defined in this Act or by rule.

Nothing in this Act shall be construed to require any employee assistance program operated by an employer or any intervenor program operated by a professional association to obtain any license pursuant to this Act to perform services that do not constitute treatment, intervention, or research as defined in this Act.

Before any violation of this Act is reported by the Department or any of its agents to any State's Attorney for the institution of a criminal proceeding, the person against whom such proceeding is contemplated shall be given appropriate notice and an opportunity to present his views before the Department or its designated agent, either orally or in writing, in person or by an attorney, with regard to such contemplated proceeding. Nothing in this Act shall be construed as requiring the Department to report minor violations of this Act whenever the Department believes that the public interest would be adequately served by a suitable written notice or warning.
(Source: P.A. 86-848; 86-1342.) [Formerly Ill. Rev. Stat. 111½ §6351-5.]

305/1-106. Application of Administrative Procedure Act.

§1-106. Application of Administrative Procedure Act. The Illinois Administrative Procedure Act [5 ILCS 100/1-1 et seq.] is incorporated herein as if all of its provisions were included in this Act.
(Source: P.A. 85-965.) [Formerly Ill. Rev. Stat. 111½ §6351-6.]

305/1-107. Transition.

§1-107. Transition. All persons who were licensed in good standing on the effective date of this Act to engage in activities requiring licensure will be deemed to qualify, upon payment of the appropriate fee, for licensure under this Act. The Department shall establish by regulation a procedure for issuance of such licenses under this Act, and a schedule of compliance with any regulations applicable to such license holders.

On the effective date of this Act, all materials, records, papers, documents, books, correspondence and other resources of the Illinois Department of Public Health relating to the administration of the Alcoholism Treatment Licensing Act shall be transferred to the Illinois Department of Alcoholism and Substance Abuse.

On the effective date of this Act, rules adopted by the Illinois Department of Public Health under the Alcoholism Treatment Licensing Act shall remain in effect until amended or rescinded under this Act by the Illinois Department of Alcoholism and Substance Abuse.

All licenses issued by the Illinois Department of Public Health permitting the holder thereof to establish or maintain an alcoholism treatment facility or program and valid and in effect on the effective date of this Act shall have the same force, and be subject to the same authority of the Illinois Department of Alcoholism and Substance Abuse to revoke or suspend them as licenses issued under this Act.
(Source: P.A. 85-965; 86-1342.) [Formerly Ill. Rev. Stat. 111½ §6351-7.]

305/1-108. Youth Drug Abuse Prevention Fund checkoff.

§1-108. Youth Drug Abuse Prevention Fund Checkoff. (a) Each Illinois individual income tax return form issued under the Illinois Income Tax Act [35 ILCS 5/101 et seq.] for taxable years ending December 31, 1991 and thereafter, shall contain a designation regarding an Income Tax Checkoff for the Youth Drug Abuse Prevention Fund, in the form and manner prescribed by Section 507C [35 ILCS 5/507C].

(b) All monies collected pursuant to this Section shall be deposited into the Youth Drug Abuse Prevention Fund, and shall be appropriated to the Department of Alcoholism and Substance Abuse for grants to community based agencies or non-profit organizations providing residential or nonresidential drug treatment or prevention programs or any combination thereof.
(Source: P.A. 87-342.) [Formerly Ill. Rev. Stat. 111½ §6351-8.]

305/1-109. Designation of lead agency.

§1-109. Designation of lead agency. The Governor shall designate a lead agency to coordinate a Statewide strategy among State agencies for the prevention, intervention, and treatment of substance abuse, that shall include the development, in consultation with other State agencies, of an interagency Statewide comprehensive plan. Each State agency that funds alcohol or drug prevention, intervention, and treatment efforts shall prepare an agency plan that shall be used by the designated lead agency in preparing the comprehensive Statewide plan. The designated lead agency shall review all State agency applications for federal funds for consistency with the comprehensive Statewide plan. The designated lead agency shall also convene interagency meetings; foster cooperation among federal, State, and local prevention, intervention, and

treatment providers; provide training recommendations to other State agencies that fund alcohol or drug abuse prevention, intervention, and treatment services; and provide technical assistance to other State agencies, as required, in the development of their agency plans.
(Source: P.A. 87-719; 87-895.) [Formerly Ill. Rev. Stat. 111½ §6351-9.]

ARTICLE II. LICENSURE

Sec.

305/2-101. Licensure categories.

§2-101. Licensure Categories. Licensure is required for the categories of activities set forth in this Section. The Department shall provide requirements for each such category by regulation as follows:

TYPE A: TREATMENT

(1) Licenses for persons providing residential treatment for alcoholism and other drug abuse and dependency.

(2) Licenses for persons providing outpatient treatment for alcoholism and other drug abuse and dependency.

TYPE B: INTERVENTION

(1) Identification Functions

(a) Licenses for persons providing D.U.I. evaluation services for Illinois courts and the Secretary of State.

(b) Licenses for persons who screen, assess, refer or track clients identified by the criminal justice system as having indications of alcoholism or other drug abuse or dependency.

(2) Education and Training

(a) Licenses for persons providing D.U.I. remedial education services for Illinois courts or the Secretary of State.

(b) Licenses for persons providing beverage alcohol servers and sellers education and training, as defined by the Department.

TYPE C: RESEARCH

Licenses for persons conducting research activities that involve the possession, dispensing, use or administration of controlled substances as enumerated in the Illinois Controlled Substances Act [720 ILCS 570/100 et seq.], or the possession, dispensing, use, or administration of cannabis as defined in the Cannabis Control Act [720 ILCS 550/1 et seq.].
(Source: P.A. 85-965; 86-1342.) [Formerly Ill. Rev. Stat. 111½ §6352-1.]

305/2-102. Licensure process.

§2-102. Licensure process. Each application for licensure under this Act shall be in writing and on forms provided by the Department. Such application shall be accompanied by the required fee, which shall be non-refundable, and shall be signed by the applicant. In the case of corporate applicants, the application shall be signed by at least 2 officers. In the case of partnership or association applicants, the application shall be signed by all partners or associates.

Upon receipt of a completed application for licensure and the appropriate fee, the Director shall issue a license if he finds that the applicant meets the requirements established by regulation for the particular license.
(Source: P.A. 85-965.) [Formerly Ill. Rev. Stat. 111½ §6352-2.]

305/2-103. Fees.

§2-103. Fees. The fee for each licensure category shall be $200 for each site at which activities requiring licensure are to be conducted except for satellite facilities and facilities operated by units of government. All license fees collected under this Act shall be paid into the State Treasury and placed in the General Revenue Fund.
(Source: P.A. 86-848.) [Formerly Ill. Rev. Stat. 111½ §6352-3.]

305/2-104. Renewal.

§2-104. Renewal. The expiration date and renewal period for each license issued under this Act shall be set by regulation. The Department may establish procedures to extend the usual expiration date of a license upon a satisfactory showing of compliance with applicable standards. Licenses issued on the effective date of this Act will expire no earlier than December 31, 1989.
(Source: P.A. 85-965.) [Formerly Ill. Rev. Stat. 111½ §6352-4.]

305/2-105. Transfer of ownership, management or location.

§2-105. Transfer of ownership, management or location. Each license issued by the Department shall be valid only for the premises and persons named in the application, and shall not be transferable.

Any transfer of 10% or less in the aggregate ownership interest within a one year period shall not be deemed a transfer for purposes of this section.
(Source: P.A. 85-965.) [Formerly Ill. Rev. Stat. 111½ §6352-5.]

305/2-106. Cessation of operations.

§2-106. Cessation of Operations. The Department shall promulgate regulations to establish a procedure to be followed by a licensee who ceases operations.
(Source: P.A. 85-965.) [Formerly Ill. Rev. Stat. 111½ §6352-6.]

305/2-107. Display of the license.

§2-107. Display of the license. Licenses shall be posted in a conspicuous place on the licensed premises.
(Source: P.A. 85-965.) [Formerly Ill. Rev. Stat. 111½ §6352-7.]

305/2-108. Notice.

§2-108. Notice. For the purposes of this Act, the notice required under Section 10 of The Illinois Administrative Procedure Act [5 ILCS 100/10-25] is deemed sufficient when mailed to the last known address of a party.
(Source: P.A. 85-965.) [Formerly Ill. Rev. Stat. 111½ §6352-8.]

ARTICLE III. COMPLIANCE

Sec.

305/3-101. Inspections.

§3-101. Inspections. (a) Employees or officers of the Department are authorized to enter, at reasonable times and upon presentation of credentials, the premises on which any licensed or funded activity is conducted, in order to inspect all pertinent property, records, personnel and business data which relate to such activity.

(b) When authorized by an administrative inspection warrant issued pursuant to this Act, any officer or employee may execute the inspection warrant according to its terms. Entries, inspections and seizures of property may be made without a warrant:

(1) if the person in charge of the premises consents;

(2) in situations presenting imminent danger to health or safety;

(3) in situations involving inspections of conveyances if there is reasonable cause to believe that the mobility of the conveyance makes it impracticable to obtain a warrant; or

(4) in any other exceptional or emergency circumstances where time or opportunity to apply for a warrant is lacking.

(c) Issuance and execution of administrative inspection warrants shall be as follows:

(1) A judge of the Circuit Court, upon proper oath or affirmation showing probable cause, may issue administrative inspection warrants for the purpose of conducting inspections and seizing property. Probable cause exists upon showing a valid public interest in the effective enforcement of this Act or regulations promulgated hereunder, sufficient to justify inspection or seizure of property.

(2) An inspection warrant shall be issued only upon an affidavit of a person having knowledge of the facts alleged, sworn to before the circuit judge and established as grounds for issuance of a warrant. If the circuit judge is satisfied that probable cause exists, he shall issue an inspection warrant identifying the premises to be inspected, the property, if any, to be seized, and the purpose of the inspection or seizure.

(3) The inspection warrant shall state the grounds for its issuance, the names of persons whose affidavits have been taken in support thereof, and any items or types of property to be seized.

(4) The inspection warrant shall be directed to a person authorized by the Director to execute it, shall command the person to inspect or seize the property, direct that it be served at any time of day or night, and designate a circuit judge to whom it shall be returned.

(5) The inspection warrant must be executed and returned within 10 days of the date of issuance unless the court orders otherwise.

(6) If property is seized, an inventory shall be made. A copy of the inventory of the seized property shall be given to the person from whom the property was taken, or if no person is available to receive the inventory, it shall be left at the premises.

(7) No warrant shall be quashed nor evidence suppressed because of technical irregularities not affecting the substantive rights of the persons affected.

The Department shall have exclusive jurisdiction for the enforcement of this Act and for violations thereof.

(Source: P.A. 85-965.) [Formerly Ill. Rev. Stat. 111½ §6353-1.]

305/3-102. Investigations.

§3-102. Investigations. The Department may on its own motion, and shall upon the sworn complaint in writing of any person setting forth charges which, if proved, would constitute grounds for sanction pursuant to this Act, investigate the actions of any person licensed or funded by the Department, or of any person whose activities are alleged to require licensure under this Act.

The Department shall cooperate with all agencies charged with enforcement of the laws of the United States, or of any state, concerning matters pertaining to this Act.

The Department may request the cooperation of the State Fire Marshal, county and municipal health departments, or municipal boards of health to assist in determining whether a person has violated this Act.

(Source: P.A. 85-965.) [Formerly Ill. Rev. Stat. 111½ §6353-2.]

305/3-103. Recordkeeping and reporting.

§3-103. Recordkeeping and reporting. The Department shall promulgate regulations providing for recordkeeping and reporting requirements.

(Source: P.A. 85-965.) [Formerly Ill. Rev. Stat. 111½ §6353-3.]

305/3-104. Denial of license or other sanction.

§3-104. Denial of license or other sanction. The Department may deny an application for licensure or for renewal of licensure, or may suspend, revoke or place on probation or impose a financial penalty upon any licensee, upon a finding that the applicant or licensee:

(a) has violated any provision of this Act or any rule promulgated hereunder;

(b) is owned, managed or operated by any person who has been convicted within the previous 2 years in any court of law of operating a motor vehicle while under the influence of alcohol or any drug;

(c) has furnished false or fraudulent information to the Department;

(d) is owned, operated or managed by any person who has had suspended or revoked a Federal registration to distribute or dispense methadone, or any governmental license relating to operation of the facility;

(e) has failed to provide effective controls against the diversion of controlled substances in other than legitimate medical, scientific or industrial channels;

(f) has demonstrated unprofessional conduct or dishonesty in conducting licensed activities;

(g) is owned, managed or operated by any person who has been convicted of a felony under any law of the United States or any state within the previous 2 years; or

(h) has failed to provide information requested by the Department within 30 days of a formal written request.

The Department shall promulgate regulations setting forth provisions for the imposition of financial penalties. Proceeds from any financial penalties imposed shall be deposited into the Youth Drug Abuse Prevention Fund administered by the Department.

Any penalty imposed for any violation of this Act shall be in addition to, and not in lieu of, any criminal, civil or administrative penalty or sanction otherwise authorized by this Act or any other law.

(Source: P.A. 87-342.) [Formerly Ill. Rev. Stat. 111½ §6353-4.]

305/3-105. Hearings.

§3-105. Hearings. Except as otherwise provided herein, before denying an application for licensure or an application for renewal of licensure, or suspending, revoking, placing on probation or imposing a financial penalty upon any licensee, the Department shall serve upon the applicant or licensee a notice of opportunity for hearing to determine why licensure should not be denied, refused, suspended, revoked, placed on probation or financially sanctioned.

Opportunity shall be afforded to the applicant or licensee to respond and present evidence. Except as otherwise provided herein, proceedings to suspend, revoke or refuse to renew an existing license shall not abate the existing license until the Department has conducted the hearing and ordered that the license shall no longer remain in effect.

Hearings shall be conducted by hearing officers appointed by the Department, in accordance with the Department's regulations.

Nothing in this Section shall be construed to limit the authority of the Department to sanction or deny a license if a licensee or applicant waives his right to a hearing by failing to request a hearing within the prescribed time after notice is served. In such a case, the determination of the Department shall be conclusively presumed to be correct.
(Source: P.A. 85-965.) [Formerly Ill. Rev. Stat. 111½ §6353-5.]

305/3-106. Summary suspension.

§3-106. Summary suspension. If the Department finds that there is an imminent danger to the public health or safety which requires emergency action, and if the Department incorporates a finding to that effect in its order, summary suspension of a license may be ordered pending proceedings which shall be instituted within 14 days to determine whether the summary suspension shall remain in effect until conclusion of a formal hearing on the merits.
(Source: P.A. 85-965.) [Formerly Ill. Rev. Stat. 111½ §6353-6.]

305/3-107. Unlicensed practice.

§3-107. Unlicensed practice. If any unlicensed person engages in activities requiring licensure under this Act, the Director may, in the name of the people of the State of Illinois, through the Attorney General of the State of Illinois, or through the State's Attorney of any county, petition for a court order enjoining such activities.

If it is established that such person has violated the order the court may punish the offender for contempt of court. Proceedings under this Section shall be in addition to, and not in lieu of, all other remedies and penalties provided under this Act. Any unlicensed person who engages in activities requiring licensure under this Act commits a Class A misdemeanor.
(Source: P.A. 85-965.) [Formerly Ill. Rev. Stat. 111½ §6353-7.]

305/3-108. Review of administrative decisions.

§3-108. Review of administrative decisions. The Department shall preserve a record of all proceedings at any formal hearing conducted by the Department involving refusal or sanction of a license. Final administrative decisions of the Department are subject to judicial review pursuant to provisions of the Administrative Review Law [735 ILCS 5/3-101 et seq.].
(Source: P.A. 85-965.) [Formerly Ill. Rev. Stat. 111½ §6353-8.]

305/3-109. Subpoena; administration of oaths.

§3-109. Subpoena; administration of oaths. The Department is empowered to subpoena and bring before it any person in this State and to take testimony, upon payment of the same fees and in the same manner as is prescribed by law for judicial proceedings in civil cases in the courts of this State.

The Director and any hearing officer designated by him are empowered to administer oaths at any proceeding which the Department is authorized to conduct.
(Source: P.A. 85-965.) [Formerly Ill. Rev. Stat. 111½ §6353-9.]

305/3-110. Attendance of witnesses and production of documents.

§3-110. Attendance of witnesses and production of documents. Any circuit court, upon the application of the Department or any licensee, may order the attendance of witnesses and the production of documents before the hearing officer in any hearing. The court may compel compliance with its order by proceedings for contempt.
(Source: P.A. 85-965.) [Formerly Ill. Rev. Stat. 111½ §6353-10.]

305/3-111. Powers and duties of designated agents.

§3-111. Powers and duties of designated agents. It is hereby made the sole and exclusive duty of the Department, and its designated agents, officers and investigators, to investigate all violations of this Act, and to cooperate with all agencies charged with enforcement of the laws of the United States, or any state, concerning matters pertaining to this Act. Nothing in this Act shall bar a grand jury from conducting an investigation of any alleged violation of this Act. Any agent, officer, investigator or peace officer designated by the Department may:

(a) execute and serve administrative inspection warrants and subpoenas under the authority of this State;

(b) make seizures of property pursuant to the provisions of this Act; and

(c) perform such other duties as the Department may designate.

The Director may appoint such investigators as is deemed necessary to carry out the provisions of this Act. It shall be the duty of such investigators to investigate and report violations of the provisions of this Act. With respect to the enforcement of the provisions of this Act, such investigators shall have the authority to serve subpoenas, summonses and administrative inspection warrants. They shall be conservators of the peace and, as such, they shall have and may exercise during the course of an inspection or investigation all the powers possessed by policemen in the cities and sheriffs in the counties of this State, except that they may exercise such powers anywhere in the State.

The Department or its designated agents, either before or after the issuance of a license, may request and shall receive the cooperation of the Illinois Department of State Police, county and multiple county health departments, or municipal boards of health to make investigations to determine if the applicant or licensee is complying with minimum standards prescribed by the Department.

(Source: P.A. 85-965.) [Formerly Ill. Rev. Stat. 111½ §6353-11.]

ARTICLE IV. POWERS AND DUTIES AND FUNCTIONS OF DEPARTMENT

Sec.

305/4-101. Powers, duties and functions of the Department.

§4-101. Powers, duties and functions of the Department. In addition to the powers, duties and functions vested in the Department by this Act, or by other laws of this State, the Department shall have the powers, duties and functions enumerated below:

(a) To promulgate regulations to provide appropriate standards for programs and levels of payment for governmentally funded health and disability programs which provide care prevention, intervention or treatment for alcoholism and other drug abuse or dependency.

(b) To promulgate regulations as may be necessary to carry out the purposes and enforce the provisions of this Act.

(c) To the extent made possible by appropriations, to fund a comprehensive and coordinated array of services throughout the State for prevention, intervention, treatment, and relapse prevention that is accessible to, and meets the needs of, at risk or addicted individuals and their families.

(d) (Blank)

(e) To develop an annual comprehensive State plan for the provision of intervention, treatment, rehabilitation, prevention, education, including education of the elderly, and other services and activities to alleviate alcoholism and other drug abuse and dependency. The plan shall include identification of problems, needs priorities, services and other pertinent information, including the needs of minorities and other specific populations in each region of the State and in the entire State. The plan shall also include a statement of the need for services to reduce the spread of AIDS and to provide treatment and care for people with AIDS or AIDS-related complex whose infections were related to intravenous drug use. Additionally, the plan shall contain a report of the activities and progress of the program established under Section 4-103 of this Act [20 ILCS 305/4-103]. In the development of the plan, input shall be sought from providers, parent groups, associations and interested citizens.

(f) To establish a clearinghouse and central repository for the development and maintenance of a centralized data collection and dissemination system and a management information system for all alcoholism and other drug abuse and dependency functions.

(g) To review all State health, welfare and treatment services proposals submitted for Federal funding under legislation that includes provisions relating to alcoholism and other drug abuse and dependency.

(h) To cooperate with public and private agencies, organizations and individuals in the development of programs, and to provide technical assistance and consultation services for this purpose.

(i) To specify a uniform statistical methodology for use by agencies, organizations and individuals, and to collect and disseminate statistical information, including the number of persons treated, frequency of admission and readmission, and duration of treatment.

(j) To receive data and assistance from federal, State and local governmental agencies, and to obtain copies of identification and arrest data from all federal, State and local law enforcement agencies for use in carrying out the purposes and functions of the Department.

(k) To coordinate the funding of programs relating to alcoholism and other drug abuse and dependency, to accept gifts or grants, and to act as the exclusive State agency to accept, receive and expend funds, grants and services from the Federal government or its agents, and to deposit such funds into the Alcoholism and Substance Abuse Fund in the State Treasury which is hereby created, except funds received from the Federal Alcohol, Drug Abuse and Mental Health Block Grant, which shall be deposited as elsewhere provided, and except funds deposited in the Youth Drug Abuse Prevention Fund. Obligation and expenditure of public funds may be made by the Department subject to appropriations by the General Assembly.

(*l*) To make such agreements, grants-in-aid and purchase-care arrangements with any other Department, authority or commission of this State, or any other state or the Federal Government or with any public or private agency, including the disbursement of funds and furnishing of staff, to effectuate the purposes of this Act.

(m) To designate and maintain medical examination and other facilities for measuring alcoholism and other drug abuse and dependency.

(n) To designate, coordinate and assist rehabilitation centers and other necessary facilities for the treatment of alcoholism and other drug abuse and dependency.

(*o*) To assign or transfer any person placed under the treatment supervision of the Department pursuant to this Act to any person providing facilities or services approved by the Department, and who agrees to provide the necessary services, provided that any person so transferred shall continue to be under the treatment supervision of the Department or its designee.

(p) To cooperate with the Department of Corrections in establishing and conducting programs relating to alcoholism and other drug abuse and dependency.

(q) To cooperate with the State Superintendent of Education, boards of education, schools, police departments, courts and other public and private agencies and individuals in establishing programs for prevention and preparing curriculum materials for use at all levels of education, and to establish prevention programs in all Educational Service Regions in the State and to enter into an agreement with the State Superintendent of Education to establish such programs.

(r) To prepare, publish, evaluate and disseminate educational materials dealing with the nature and effects of alcoholism and other drug abuse and dependency.

(s) To develop and coordinate, with regional and local agencies, education and training programs for persons engaged in the treatment and detoxification of persons having alcoholism or other drug abuse and dependency problems, which programs shall include specific AIDS education and training for program personnel.

(t) To cooperate with and assist in the development of education, prevention and treatment programs for employees of State and local governments and businesses in the State.

(u) To utilize the support and assistance of interested persons in the community, particularly recovered addicts and alcoholics, to encourage clients to voluntarily undergo treatment.

(v) To promote, conduct, assist and sponsor basic clinical, epidemiological and statistical research in alcoholism and other drug abuse and dependency, either individually or in conjunction with any public or private agency.

(w) To encourage service providers who receive financial assistance in any form from the State to assess and collect fees for services rendered; provided, however, that no person shall be denied services by any program licensed or funded under this Act because of inability to pay. Services shall be afforded to such persons on the same terms and conditions as services afforded to persons who are able to pay.

(x) To cooperate with the Illinois Department of Public Aid in the development and provision of services offered to recipients of public assistance for the treatment and prevention of alcoholism and other drug abuse and dependency.

(y) To encourage all health and disability insurance programs to include alcoholism and other drug abuse and dependency as a covered illness.

(z) To promulgate regulations to provide appropriate standards for programs for privately funded health and disability programs which provide care or treatment for alcoholism and other drug abuse or dependency.

(aa) The Department may establish and maintain 2 State-wide toll-free telephone numbers, or may contract with a private agency for the establishment and maintenance of such telephone numbers. One telephone number shall be used to provide information and referrals in relation to alcohol and drug abuse by adults, and the other telephone number shall be used to provide information and referrals in relation to alcohol and drug abuse by juveniles. In conjunction with the establishment of the toll-free telephone numbers, the Department may, with the assistance of the news media, produce and actively market television and radio announcements and billboard advertising using the theme "drug usage and addiction is a crippling disease" and encouraging the public to avoid the use of alcohol and illegal drugs and to seek the help of parents, teachers and professional counselors.

(bb) To promulgate rules in relation to service plans and rehabilitative services to be provided to persons upon referral by the Department of Children and Family Services pursuant to Section 8.2 of the Abused and Neglected Child Reporting Act, as now or hereafter amended [325 ILCS 5/8.2].

(cc) To submit to the General Assembly not later than November 1 of each year a report of the uses to which funds from the Youth Drug Abuse Prevention Fund were applied during the previous fiscal year.

(dd) To cooperate with the Illinois Department of Public Health in the establishment, funding and operation of programs for the prevention and treatment of acquired immunodeficiency syndrome (AIDS), especially with respect to those persons who may abuse drugs by intravenous injection, or may have been sexual partners of drug abusers, or may have abused substances so that their immune systems are impaired, making them high-risk.

(ee) To require all programs supported by the Department to include an education component to inform participants regarding the causes and means of transmission and methods of reducing the risk of acquiring or transmitting AIDS, and to include funding for such education component in its support of the program.

(ff) The Department shall provide training in the recognition of symptoms and side effects of anabolic steroid abuse. Training shall be made available to physicians, other health care professionals, educators, persons engaged in the coaching and supervision of high school and college athletics, and other groups determined by the Department to be likely to come into contact with anabolic steroid abusers. The training shall also include information concerning education and appropriate referral of persons identified as probable or actual anabolic steroid abusers.

The Department is hereby authorized to develop and implement a Statewide steroid education program to alert the public, and particularly Illinois student athletes, athletic trainers, coaches, practitioners, and health club personnel, to the dangers and adverse effects of abusing anabolic steroids. The program shall be developed with the advice of the Illinois Advisory Council established by Section 5-101 of this Act [20 ILCS 305/5-101].

(gg) To develop and publish pamphlets that describe the causes and effects of fetal alcohol syndrome and distribute the pamphlets free of charge to each county clerk in sufficient quantities that the county clerk may provide a pamphlet to the recipients of all marriage licenses issued in the county.

(hh) To fund intervention services including the identification of substance abuse problems in an individual and within a family, the assessment and impact of that substance abuse on the individual's health and social, economic, and family well-being, and the development of a plan to prevent the increased or continued use of alcohol or other addictive drugs or substances.

(ii) To fund services to help, first, children of alcohol or drug addicted parents, and then partners, parents, family members, and other co-dependents who are adversely affected by their relationship with an alcohol or other drug abuser.

(jj) To make grants with funds appropriated from the Drug Treatment Fund in accordance with Section 7 of the Controlled Substance and Cannabis Nuisance Act [740 ILCS 40/7].

(Chgd. by P.A. 87-1054, §2, eff. 9/11/92.)

(Source: P.A. 86-829; 86-832; 86-1028; 87-342; 87-503; 87-754; 87-765; 87-860; 87-895.) [Formerly Ill. Rev. Stat. 111½ §6354-1.]

305/4-102. Grants to reimburse DUI programs.

§4-102. The Department may make grants to reimburse DUI evaluation and remedial education programs licensed by the Department for the costs of providing indigent persons with free or reduced-cost services relating to a charge of driving under the influence of alcohol or other drugs. Such grants may be made from funds appropriated to the Department for that purpose from the

Drunk and Drugged Driving Prevention Fund, which is hereby established as a special fund in the State treasury. The Department may adopt such rules as it may deem appropriate for the administration of such grants. Monies in the Drunk and Drugged Driving Prevention Fund may also be used to enhance and support regulatory inspections and investigations conducted by the Department under Article III of the Illinois Alcoholism and Other Drug Dependency Act [20 ILCS 305/3-101 et seq.]. The balance of the Fund on June 30 of each fiscal year, less the amount of any expenditures attributable to that fiscal year during the lapse period, shall be transferred by the Treasurer to the General Revenue Fund by the following October 10.

(Source: P.A. 85-1304.) [Formerly Ill. Rev. Stat. 111½ §6354-2.]

305/4-103. Treatment programs for addicted women and their children.

§4-103. From funds appropriated expressly for the purposes of this Section, the Department shall contract with licensed, certified agencies to develop one model program for the care and treatment of addicted pregnant women, addicted mothers and their children. The program shall be in Cook County in an area of high density population having a disproportionate number of addicted women and a high infant mortality rate.

From funds appropriated expressly for the purposes of this Section, the Department shall contract with licensed, certified agencies to develop one model program for the care and treatment of low income pregnant women. The program shall be located anywhere in the State outside of Cook County in an area of high density population having a disproportionate number of low income pregnant women.

The programs shall include but not be limited to the following services: individual medical care, including prenatal care, under the supervision of a physician and temporary, residential shelter for pregnant women, mothers and children when necessary.

(Chgd. by P.A. 87-1054, §2, eff. 9/11/92.)
(Source: P.A. 86-877; 87-324; 87-895.) [Formerly Ill. Rev. Stat. 111½ §6354-3.]

305/4-104. Listing of substance abuse service providers.

§4-104. The Department shall supply to the Department of Public Health and prenatal care providers a list of all substance abuse service providers for addicted pregnant women in this State.

(Source: P.A. 86-1004.) [Formerly Ill. Rev. Stat. 111½ §6354-4.]

ARTICLE V. ADVISORY COUNCILS AND COMMITTEES

Sec.

305/5-101. Illinois Advisory Council.

§5-101. Illinois Advisory Council. There is established the Illinois Advisory Council on Alcoholism and Other Drug Dependency. The members of the Council shall receive no compensation for their service but shall be reimbursed for all expenses actually and necessarily incurred by them in the performance of their duties under this Act, and within the amounts made available to them by the Department. The Council shall annually elect a presiding officer from its membership. The Council shall meet from time to time at the call of the Department, or at the call of its presiding officer, or upon the request of any 4

of its members. The Department shall provide space and secretarial and consulting services to the Council.
(Source: P.A. 85-965.) [Formerly Ill. Rev. Stat. 111½ §6355-1.]

305/5-102. Powers and duties of the Council.

§5-102. Powers and duties of the Council. The Council shall:

(a) advise the Department on ways to encourage public understanding and support of the Department's programs;

(b) advise the Department on regulations and licensure proposed by the Department;

(c) advise the Department in the formulation, preparation and implementation of the comprehensive State plan for intervention, prevention and treatment of alcoholism and other drug abuse and dependency;

(d) advise the Department on implementation of alcoholism and other drug abuse and dependency education and prevention programs in all Educational Service Regions in the State; and

(e) perform such other duties as requested by the Director.

With the advice and consent of the Director, the presiding officer shall annually appoint a Special Committee on Licensure, who shall advise the Director on particular cases on which the Department intends to take action which is adverse to an applicant or licenseholder, and shall review an annual report submitted by the Director summarizing all licensure sanctions imposed by the Department.
(Source: P.A. 85-965.) [Formerly Ill. Rev. Stat. 111½ §6355-2.]

305/5-103. Qualification and appointment of members.

§5-103. Qualification and appointment of members. The membership of the Illinois Advisory Council shall consist of:

(a) a State's Attorney designated by the President of the Illinois State's Attorneys Association;

(b) a judge designated by the Chief Justice of the Illinois Supreme Court;

(c) a Public Defender appointed by the President of the Illinois Public Defenders Association;

(d) a local law enforcement officer appointed by the Governor;

(e) a labor representative appointed by the Governor;

(f) an educator appointed by the Governor;

(g) a physician licensed to practice medicine in all its branches appointed by the Governor with due regard for the appointee's knowledge of the field of alcoholism and other drug abuse and dependency;

(h) four members of the Illinois House of Representatives, 2 each appointed by the Speaker and Minority Leader;

(i) four members of the Illinois Senate, 2 each appointed by the President and Minority Leader;

(j) the President of the Illinois Alcohol and Drug Dependency Association;

(k) an advocate for the needs of youth appointed by the Governor;

(*l*) the President of the Illinois State Medical Society;

(m) the President of the Illinois Hospital Association;

(n) the President of the Illinois Nurses Association or a registered nurse designated by the President;

(*o*) the President of the Illinois Pharmacists Association or a licensed pharmacist designated by the President;

(p) the President of the Illinois Chapter of the Association of Labor Management Administrators and Consultants on Alcoholism;

(q) the Attorney General or his or her designee;

(r) the State Comptroller or his or her designee; and

(s) twenty public members, 8 appointed by the Governor, 3 of whom shall be representatives of alcoholism or other drug abuse and dependency treatment programs and one of whom shall be a representative of a manufacturer or importing distributor of alcoholic liquor licensed by the State of Illinois, and 3 public members appointed by each of the President and Minority Leader of the Senate and the Speaker and Minority Leader of the House. The public members may not be officers or employees of the executive branch of State government; however, the public members may be officers or employees of a State college or University or of any law enforcement agency. In appointing members, due consideration shall be given to the experience of appointees in the fields of medicine, law, prevention, correctional activities, and social welfare. Vacancies in the public membership shall be filled for the unexpired term by appointment in like manner as for original appointments, and the appointive members shall serve until their successors are appointed and have qualified. Vacancies among the public members appointed by the legislative leaders shall be filled by the leader of the same House and of the same political party as the leader who originally appointed the member.

Each non-appointive member may designate a representative to serve in his place by written notice to the Department. All General Assembly members shall serve until their respective successors are appointed or until termination of their legislative service, whichever occurs first.

The terms of office for each of the members appointed by the Governor shall be for 3 years, except that of the members first appointed, 3 shall be appointed for a term of one year, and 4 shall be appointed for a term of 2 years. The terms of office of each of the public members appointed by the legislative leaders shall be for 2 years.

(Source: P.A. 87-325.) [Formerly Ill. Rev. Stat. 111½ §6355-3.]

305/5-103.1. Subcommittee on Women's Alcohol and Substance Abuse Treatment.

§5-103.1. Subcommittee on Women's Alcohol and Substance Abuse Treatment. (a) Subcommittee on Women's Alcohol and Substance Abuse Treatment. There is established a Subcommittee on Women's Alcohol and Substance Abuse Treatment of the Illinois Advisory Council on Alcoholism and Other Drug Dependency. Members shall serve without compensation but shall be reimbursed for any ordinary and necessary expenses incurred in the performance of their duties. The Subcommittee shall annually elect a chair from its public members. The Subcommittee shall meet no less often than quarterly and at other times at the call of its chair or any 5 members.

(b) Powers and Duties of the Subcommittee. The Subcommittee shall have the following powers and duties:

(1) Advise the Council and the Director in the development of intervention, prevention and treatment objectives and standards, educational and outreach programs, and support services specific to the needs of women.

(2) Advise the Council and the Director in the formulation, preparation and implementation of a State plan for intervention, prevention and treatment of alcoholism and other drug abuse and dependency targeted to women.

(3) Advise the Council and the Director regarding strategies to enhance service delivery to women.

(4) Advise the Council and the Director in the development and implementation of a State plan, in conjunction with the Department of Children and Family Services, to provide child care services, at no or low cost, to addicted mothers with children who are receiving substance abuse treatment services.

(5) Perform other duties as requested by the Council or the Director.

(c) Membership. The Subcommittee shall be composed of individuals from the medical and substance abuse treatment communities who have expertise and experience in women-specific programming and representatives of appropriate public agencies. Members may be but need not be members of the Council.

(d) By January 1, 1995, and by January 1 of every third year thereafter, the Council shall, in cooperation with the Subcommittee, submit to the Governor and General Assembly a planning document specific to the female population. The document shall contain, but need not be limited to, interagency information concerning the types of services funded, the client population served, the support services available and provided during the preceding 3 year period, and the goals, objectives, proposed methods of achievement, client projections and cost estimate for the upcoming 3 year period. The document shall include, if deemed necessary and appropriate, recommendations regarding the reorganization of the Department to enhance and increase prevention, treatment and support services available to women.

(Chgd. by P.A. 87-1054, §2, eff. 9/11/92.)
(Source: P.A. 86-1316; 87-742.) [Formerly Ill. Rev. Stat. 111½ §6355-3.1.]

305/5-104. Medical Advisory Committee.

§5-104. Medical Advisory Committee. The Director shall appoint a Medical Advisory Committee to the Department consisting of 15 physicians licensed to practice medicine in all of its branches in Illinois who shall serve in an advisory capacity to the Director. The membership of the Medical Advisory Committee shall reasonably reflect representation from the geographic areas and the range of alcoholism and other drug abuse and dependency service providers of this State. In making appointments, the Director shall give consideration to recommendations made by the Illinois State Medical Society and other appropriate professional organizations. All appointments shall be made with regard to the interest and expertise of the individual with regard to alcoholism and other drug abuse and dependency services. At a minimum, members shall represent the following specializations: 2 members shall be Board-certified psychiatrists, 2 members shall be affiliated with community based alcoholism or other drug dependency treatment programs, 2 members shall be affiliated with hospital based alcoholism or other drug dependency treatment programs, 2 members shall be from the faculty of Illinois medical schools, and 1 member shall be chief Medical Consultant to the Department. Members shall serve 3-year terms and until their successors are appointed and qualified except that of the initial appointments, 5 members shall be appointed for one year, 5 members shall be appointed for 2 years, and 5 members shall be appointed for 3 years and until their successors are appointed and qualified. Appointments to fill vacancies shall be made in the same manner as original appointments, for the unexpired portion of the vacated term. Initial terms shall begin on July 1, 1988. Members shall elect a chairperson annually from their membership.

(Source: P.A. 85-965.) [Formerly Ill. Rev. Stat. 111½ §6355-4.]

305/5-105. Powers and duties of the Medical Advisory Committee.

§5-105. Powers and Duties of the Medical Advisory Committee. The Medical Advisory Committee shall consult with and advise the Department on clinical procedures, medical technology, medical practice and standards, and such other matters as the Director may from time to time assign to it. The members of the Medical Advisory Committee shall receive no compensation for their services but shall be reimbursed for their actual and necessary travel and subsistence expenses incurred in the performance of their duties as members of the Medical Advisory Committee. The Medical Advisory Committee shall meet as frequently as the Director deems necessary. Upon the request of 4 or more members, the Director shall call a meeting of the Medical Advisory Committee.

(Source: P.A. 85-965.) [Formerly Ill. Rev. Stat. 111½ §6355-5.]

ARTICLE VI. INTERAGENCY BOARD

305/6-101. Interagency Alcoholism and Other Drug Dependency Board.

§6-101. Interagency Alcoholism and Other Drug Dependency Board. There is created the Interagency Alcoholism and Other Drug Dependency Board. The members of the Board shall receive no compensation for service, but shall be reimbursed for all expenses actually and necessarily incurred by them in performance of their duties under this Act. The Board shall meet from time to time at the request of the Department, or at the call of the chairman, or upon the request of any 3 of its members. The Director or his designee shall serve as secretary. The Department shall provide necessary staff to assist the Board in the performance of is functions.
(Source: P.A. 85-965.) [Formerly Ill. Rev. Stat. 111½ §6356-1.]

305/6-102. Membership.

§6-102. Membership. The Board shall consist of 18 members:
(a) the Director of Aging,
(b) the State Superintendent of Education,
(c) the Director of Corrections,
(d) the Director of State Police,
(e) the Director of Professional Regulation,
(f) the Director of Mental Health and Developmental Disabilities,
(g) the Director of Children and Family Services,
(h) the Director of Rehabilitation Services,
(i) the Director of Public Aid,
(j) the Director of Public Health,
(k) the Secretary of State,
(*l*) the Secretary of Transportation,
(m) the Director of Insurance,
(n) the Director of the Administrative Office of Illinois Courts,
(*o*) the Chairman of the Board of Higher Education,
(p) the Director of Revenue,
(q) the Executive Director of Criminal Justice Information Authority, and
(r) a chairman who shall be appointed by the Governor for a term of 3 years.

Each member may designate a representative to serve in his place by written notice to the Department.
(Source: P.A. 86-825.) [Formerly Ill. Rev. Stat. 111½ §6356-2.]

305/6-103. Powers and duties of the Board.

§6-103. Powers and duties of the Board. The Board shall advise and assist the Director in the planning, development and coordination of programs among all agencies and Departments of State government, including prevention and programs to discourage abuse and misuse of alcohol and other drugs. The Board shall:

(a) promote and encourage participation by the private sector, including business, industry, labor and the media, in programs to prevent alcoholism and other drug abuse and dependency;

(b) encourage the implementation of programs to prevent alcoholism and other drug abuse and dependency in the public and private schools and educational institutions, including establishment of alcoholism and other drug abuse and dependency programs in all Educational Service Regions in the State;

(c) gather information, conduct hearings and make recommendations to the Director concerning additions, deletions or rescheduling of substances under the Illinois Controlled Substances Act [720 ILCS 570/100 et seq.]; and

(d) perform other duties and functions as the Director may assign to it.

(Source: P.A. 85-965.) [Formerly Ill. Rev. Stat. 111½ §6356-3.]

ARTICLE VII. ILLINOIS ADDICTIONS RESEARCH INSTITUTE

(Former Ill. Rev. Stat. 111½ §§6357-1 to 6357-3 repealed by P.A. 87-860, §81, eff. 7/1/92.)

ARTICLE VIII. CLIENTS' RIGHTS

305/8-101. Right to treatment.

§8-101. Right to treatment. A person shall not be denied treatment solely because he has withdrawn from treatment against medical advice on a prior occasion or because he has relapsed after earlier treatment, or because of inability to pay.

A person who is in need of treatment may apply for voluntary admission to a treatment facility in the manner and with the rights provided for under regulations promulgated by the Department. If a person is refused admission to a licensed treatment facility, the administrator of the facility, subject to rules promulgated by the Department, shall refer the person to another treatment facility.

Upon the written request of any person who has been denied treatment at any facility, the Department shall review such decision. The determination of the Department whether such person is in need of treatment shall be final, and not subject to review.

(Source: P.A. 85-965.) [Formerly Ill. Rev. Stat. 111½ §6358-1.]

305/8-102. Confidentiality.

§8-102. Confidentiality. Records of the identity, diagnosis, prognosis or treatment of any client which are maintained in connection with the performance of any alcoholism or other drug abuse or dependency prevention or treatment service or function authorized or assisted by any Department or agency of this State or under any provision of this Act shall be confidential and may be disclosed only for the purposes and under the circumstances expressly authorized by this Section.

The contents of any record referred to in this Section may be disclosed in accordance with the prior written consent of the patient with respect to whom such record is maintained, but only to such extent, under such circumstances and for such purposes as may be allowed under regulations prescribed by the Department.

Whether or not the patient, with respect to whom any given record referred to in this Section is maintained, gives his written consent, the content of such record may be disclosed as follows:

(1) To medical personnel to the extent necessary to meet a bona fide medical emergency.

(2) To qualified personnel for the purpose of conducting scientific research, management audits, financial audits or program evaluation, but such personnel may not identify, directly or indirectly, any individual patient in any report of such research, audit or evaluation, or otherwise disclose patient identities in any manner.

(3) If authorized by an appropriate order of a court of competent jurisdiction granted after application showing good cause therefor. In assessing good cause the court shall weigh the public interest and the need for disclosure against the injury to the patient, to the practitioner-patient relationship, and to the treatment services. Upon the granting of such order, the court, in determining the extent to which such disclosure of all or any part of any record is necessary, shall impose appropriate safeguards against unauthorized disclosure.

The content of any record referred to in this Section may be disclosed in accordance with the provisions of federal law and regulations concerning the confidentiality of Alcohol and Drug Abuse Patient Records as contained in Title 21 of the United States Code, Section 1175; Title 42 of the United States Code, Section 4582; and 42 C.F.R. Part 2, all as now or hereafter amended, except where such disclosure is expressly prohibited by this Section or by regulation prescribed by the Department. Except as authorized by a court order granted under this Section, no record referred to in this Section may be used to initiate or substantiate any charges against a patient or to conduct any investigation of a patient.

The prohibitions of this Section shall apply to records concerning any individual who has been a patient, regardless of whether or when he ceases to be a patient.

Except as authorized, any person who discloses the contents of any record referred to in this section shall, upon conviction, be guilty of a Class A misdemeanor.

The Department shall prescribe regulations to carry out the purposes of this Section. These regulations may contain such definitions, and may provide for such safeguards and procedures, including procedures and criteria for the issuance and scope of court orders, as in the judgment of the Department are necessary or proper to effectuate the purposes of this Section to prevent circumvention or evasion thereof, or to facilitate compliance therewith.

Notwithstanding any provision of this Section to the contrary, personnel of any program performing any alcoholism or other drug abuse or dependency function, including personnel of the Department, may disclose the contents of any record referred to in this Section to a law enforcement or prosecutorial agency, but only to the extent necessary to seek the assistance of such agency, or to report and prosecute the commission of a crime on the premises of such program or against personnel of any such program.

Nothing in this Section shall be construed to abridge or deny any right or guarantee to a criminal defendant under the Constitution or laws of the United States or the State of Illinois.

(Source: P.A. 85-965.) [Formerly Ill. Rev. Stat. 111½ §6358-2.]

305/8-103. Specific rights.

§8-103. Specific rights. No client or resident of any treatment program shall be deprived of any rights, benefits or privileges guaranteed by law solely on account of his status as a client or resident of a program.

Persons who abuse or are dependent on alcohol or other drugs who are also suffering from medical conditions shall not be discriminated against in admission or treatment by any hospital which receives support in any form from any program supported in whole or in part by funds appropriated to any State department or agency.

(Source: P.A. 85-965.) [Formerly Ill. Rev. Stat. 111½ §6358-3.]

ARTICLE IX. SPECIAL SERVICES

Sec.

305/9-101. Special services.

§9-101. Special services. The Department shall adopt regulations for acceptance of persons for treatment, taking into consideration available resources and facilities, for the purpose of early and effective treatment of alcoholism and other drug abuse and dependency.

The Department shall create or contract with existing residences or recovery homes in areas having a disproportionate number of women who are substance abusers needing residential treatment and counseling. Priority shall be women who:

(1) are pregnant,

(2) have minor children,

(3) are both pregnant and have minor children, or

(4) are referred by medical personnel because they either gave birth to a baby addicted to cocaine, or will give birth to a baby addicted to cocaine.

The services provided by the home shall include, but need not be limited to:

(1) a range of educational or counseling services,

(2) coordinated social services, including:

(a) substance abuse therapy groups,

(b) family therapy groups,

(c) programs to develop positive self-awareness,

(d) parent-child therapy, and

(e) residential support groups.

An intoxicated person may come voluntarily to a treatment facility for emergency treatment. A person who appears to be intoxicated in a public place and may be a danger to himself or others, if he consents to the proffered help, may be assisted to his home, a treatment facility or other health facility either directly by the police or through an intermediary person.

A person who appears to be unconscious or in immediate need of emergency medical services while in a public place and who shows symptoms of alcoholism or other drug abuse or dependency may be taken into protective custody by the police and forthwith brought to an emergency medical service. A person who is otherwise incapacitated while in a public place and who shows symptoms of alcoholism or other drug abuse or dependency may be taken into custody and forthwith brought to a facility available for detoxification. The police in detaining the person shall take him into protective custody only; the taking into protective custody shall not constitute an arrest. No entry or other record shall be made to indicate that the person has been arrested or charged with a crime. The detaining officer may take reasonable steps to protect himself from harm.

No intermediary person acting in good faith and without negligence in connection with the preparation of petitions, applications, certificates or other documents for apprehension, transportation, examination, treatment, detention or discharge or the taking into protective custody of an individual under the provisions of this Act shall incur any civil or criminal liability by reason of these acts.

No county, municipality or political subdivision may adopt or enforce any law that includes being intoxicated as the sole basis of the offense, nor interpret or apply any law to circumvent the provisions of this Section. However, nothing in this Section affects any law, ordinance, resolution or rule against driving under the influence of alcohol or other drugs, or any similar offense involving operation of a vehicle, aircraft, boat, machinery, or the use of firearms or other equipment. Nothing in this Section affects any law regarding the sale, purchase, use, possession or dispensing of drugs or alcohol at stated places, at stated times or by particular classes of persons.

(Source: P.A. 86-1004.) [Formerly Ill. Rev. Stat. 111½ §6359-1.]

ARTICLE X. TREATMENT ALTERNATIVES

305/10-101. Election of treatment.

§10-101. Election of treatment. An addict or alcoholic who is charged with or convicted of a crime may elect treatment under the supervision of a licensed program designated by the Department (hereinafter in this Article referred to as "designated program") unless (a) the crime is a crime of violence; (b) the crime is a violation of Section 401, 402(a), 405 or 407 of the Illinois Controlled Substances Act [720 ILCS 570/401, 570/402, 570/405 or 570/407], or Sections 4(d), 4(e), 5 (d), 5(e), 7 or 9 of the Cannabis Control Act [720 ILCS 550/4, 550/5, 550/7 or 550/9]; (c) the person has a record of 2 or more convictions of a crime of violence; (d) other criminal proceedings alleging commission of a felony are pending against the person; (e) the person is on probation or parole and the appropriate parole or probation authority does not consent to that election; (f) the person elected and was admitted to a designated program on 2 prior occasions within any consecutive 2-year period; (g) the person has been convicted of residential burglary and has a record of one or more felony convictions; (h) the crime is a violation of Section 11-501 of the Illinois Vehicle Code, as now or hereafter amended [625 ILCS 5/11-501], or a similar provision of a local ordinance; or (i) the crime is a reckless homicide or a reckless homicide of an unborn child, as defined in Section 9-3 or 9-3.2 of the Criminal Code of 1961, as now or hereafter amended [720 ILCS 5/9-3 or 5/9-3.2], in which the cause of death consists of the driving of a motor vehicle by a person under the influence of alcohol or any other drug or drugs at the time of the violation.
(Source: P.A. 86-848.) [Formerly Ill. Rev. Stat. 111½ §6360-1.]

305/10-102. Treatment as a condition of probation.

§10-102. Treatment as a condition of probation. If a court has reason to believe that an individual who is charged with or convicted of a crime is an addict or alcoholic and the court finds that he is eligible to make the election provided for under Section 10-101 [20 ILCS 305/10-101], the court shall advise him that he may be placed on probation if he elects to submit to treatment and is accepted for treatment by a designated program. The court shall further advise him that: (a) if he elects to submit to treatment and is accepted he may be placed on probation and under the supervision of the designated program for a period not to exceed the maximum sentence that could be imposed for his conviction or 5 years, whichever is less; (b) during probation he may be treated at the discretion of the designated program; and (c) if he adheres to the requirements of the designated program and fulfills the other conditions of probation, he will be discharged, but any failure to adhere to the requirements of the designated program is a breach of probation. The court may certify an individual for treatment while on probation under the supervision of a designated program and probation authorities regardless of the election of the individual.

If the individual elects to undergo treatment or is certified for treatment, the court shall order an examination by a designated program to determine whether he is an addict or alcoholic and is likely to be rehabilitated through treatment. The designated program shall report to the court the results of the examination and recommend whether the individual should be placed for treatment. If the court, on the basis of the report and other information, finds that such an individual is an addict or alcoholic and is likely to be rehabilitated through treatment, the individual shall be placed on probation and under the supervision of a designated program for treatment and under the supervision of the proper probation authorities for probation supervision unless, giving consideration to the nature and circumstances of the offense and to the history, character and condition of the individual, the court is of the opinion that no significant relationship exists between the addiction or alcoholism of the individual and the crime committed, or that his imprisonment or periodic imprisonment is necessary for the protection of the public, and the court specifies on the record the particular evidence, information or other reasons that form the basis of such opinion. However, under no circumstances shall the individual be placed under the supervision of a designated program for treatment before the entry of a judgment of conviction.

If the court, on the basis of the report or other information, finds that the individual is not an addict or an alcoholic likely to be rehabilitated through treatment, or that his addiction or alcoholism and the crime committed are not significantly related, or that his imprisonment or periodic imprisonment is necessary for the protection of the public, the court shall impose sentence as in other cases. The court may require such progress reports on the individual from the probation officer and designated program as the court finds necessary. No individual may be placed under treatment supervision unless a designated program accepts him for treatment.

Failure of an individual placed on probation and under the supervision of a designated program to observe the requirements set down by the designated program shall be considered a probation violation. Such failure shall be reported by the designated program to the probation officer in charge of the individual and treated in accordance with probation regulations.

Upon successful fulfillment of the terms and conditions of probation the court shall discharge the person from probation. If the person has not previously been convicted of any felony offense and has not previously been granted a vacation of judgment under this Section, upon motion, the court shall vacate the judgment of conviction and dismiss the criminal proceedings against him unless, having considered the nature and circumstances of the offense and to the history, character and condition of the individual, the court finds that the motion should not be granted. Unless good cause is shown, such motion to vacate must be filed within 30 days of the entry of the judgment.
(Source: P.A. 86-848.) [Formerly Ill. Rev. Stat. 111½ §6360-2.]

305/10-103. Acceptance for treatment as parole condition.

§10-103. Acceptance for treatment as parole condition. Acceptance for treatment for addiction or alcoholism under the supervision of a designated program may be made a condition of parole, and failure to comply with such treatment may be treated as a violation of parole. A designated program shall establish the conditions under which a parolee is accepted for treatment. No parolee may be placed under the supervision of a designated program for treatment unless the designated program accepts him for treatment. The designated program shall make periodic progress reports regarding each such parolee to the appropriate parole authority and shall report failures to comply with the prescribed treatment program.
(Source: P.A. 85-965.) [Formerly Ill. Rev. Stat. 111½ §6360-3.]

305/10-104. Minors; treatment supervision.

§10-104. Minors; treatment supervision. A minor may be placed under the treatment supervision of the Department pursuant to Section 4-21 of the Juvenile Court Act of 1987 [705 ILCS 405/4-21].
(Source: P.A. 85-1209.) [Formerly Ill. Rev. Stat. 111½ §6360-4.]

ARTICLE XI. JUVENILE EDUCATION AND PREVENTION

305/11-101. Juvenile initiative.

§11-101. Juvenile initiative. (a) As part of the Department's comprehensive and coordinated strategy, a Statewide juvenile alcoholism and other drug abuse and dependency initiative shall be implemented. In doing so, the Department shall account for local requirements and involve as much as possible of the local community. The initiative shall include the following objectives:

(1) decrease the incidence prevalence of alcoholism and other drug abuse and dependency by school-age youth;

(2) implement a statewide program of education in all public and private schools;

(3) provide programs to improve the competence of Illinois teachers to present alcohol and substance abuse education effectively;

(4) encourage cooperation among all agencies and groups having an interest in the welfare of youth;

(5) establish and provide Regional Prevention Groups in Educational Service Regions to assist and coordinate local community education and prevention programs; and

(6) provide financial and technical assistance to units of local government, Educational Service Regions and other community organizations for establishment of local community education and prevention programs.

(b) There is created in the State treasury a fund to be known as the Youth Alcoholism and Substance Abuse Prevention Fund. The Department shall use monies from the fund to help support and establish community based alcohol and substance abuse prevention programs directed at youth.

(Source: P.A. 86-983.) [Formerly Ill. Rev. Stat. 111½ §6361-1.]

305/11-102. Regional Prevention Groups.

§11-102. Regional Prevention Groups. (a) Each Regional Prevention Group shall be established under the direction of the Department, may apply to the Department for financial assistance to promote coordinated education and prevention programming, and may engage in, but shall not be limited to, the following activities:

(1) establish and conduct programs to educate parents, children and communities in ways to prevent alcoholism and other drug abuse and dependency among juveniles;

(2) conduct training programs and distribute materials on the dangers of alcoholism and other drug abuse and dependency;

(3) draft and implement plans for the most efficient use of available resources to publicize the dangers of alcoholism and other drug abuse and dependency; and

(4) coordinate local programs of alcoholism and other drug abuse and dependency education and prevention.

(b) A Regional Prevention Group shall be eligible to receive grants from the Department if the Department determines that the program meets the following minimum criteria:

(1) Contains membership which includes, at a minimum, school district and Educational Service Region representatives, local alcohol and substance abuse prevention providers, parent groups and other appropriate voluntary alcohol and substance abuse prevention organizations;

(2) Designates a primary agency which shall serve as the representative to the Department;

(3) Designates a single corporation from among participating organizations in the Regional Prevention Group to act as the financial officer for the grant and to receive funds from the Department;

(4) Limits its operations to alcohol and drug abuse education and prevention;

(5) Cooperates with the Department in order to assure compliance with this Act and to enable the Department to fulfill its duties under this Act, and supplies the Department with all information the Department deems necessary; and

(6) Complies with such other alcohol and substance abuse education and prevention criteria as may be established by the Department.

(Source: P.A. 85-965.) [Formerly Ill. Rev. Stat. 111½ §6361-2.]

305/11-103. Financial assistance.

§11-103. Financial assistance. (a) Units of local government, Educational Service Regions and other eligible community organizations may apply to the Department for financial assistance to promote coordinated education and prevention programs and may engage in, but shall not be limited to, the following activities:

(1) establish and maintain programs to educate parents, children and communities in ways to prevent alcoholism and other drug abuse and dependency among juveniles;

(2) conduct training programs and distribute materials on the dangers of alcoholism and other drug abuse and dependency; and

(3) compile, maintain and make available data upon the request of entities deemed appropriate by the Department in order to assist communities and law enforcement agencies in preventing illegal sale or distribution of alcohol and other drugs to juveniles.

(b) A unit of local government, Educational Service Region or other community organization shall be eligible to receive grants from the Department if the Department determines that the program meets the following criteria:

(1) Contains membership which includes, at a minimum, school district representatives, local alcohol and substance abuse prevention providers, parent groups and other appropriate voluntary alcohol and substance abuse prevention organizations and representatives of units of local government;

(2) Designates a primary agency which shall serve as the representative to the Department;

(3) Designates a single corporation or unit of local government from among participating organizations to act as the financial officer for the grant and to receive funds from the Department;

(4) Cooperates with the Department, and Regional Prevention Group where appropriate, in order to assure compliance with this Act and to enable the Department to fulfill its duties under this Act, and supplies the Department with all information the Department deems necessary; and

(5) Complies with such other alcohol and substance abuse education and prevention criteria as may be established by the Department.

(Source: P.A. 85-965.) [Formerly Ill. Rev. Stat. 111½ §6361-3.]

ARTICLE XII. SERVICES FOR DEAF AND HEARING IMPAIRED PERSONS

(Added by P.A. 86-1004, §11, eff. 7/1/90.)

Sec.

305/12-101. Implementation of programs.

§12-101. The Department shall implement programs to provide education, treatment and other services in relation to alcoholism and other drug abuse and dependency for deaf and hearing impaired persons. Such services may include the following:

(a) A 10-bed residential treatment program in an existing program licensed by the Department which shall be developed specifically for deaf persons who are alcoholics or addicts.

(b) Other services initiated or adapted to meet the specific needs of deaf and hearing impaired persons in the following areas related to alcoholism and other drug abuse and dependency: education and prevention, outreach, detoxification, outpatient care, aftercare and transitional living.

(Source: P.A. 86-1004.) [Formerly Ill. Rev. Stat. 111½ §6362-1.]

305/12-102. Appointment of coordinator.

§12-102. The Department shall appoint a coordinator of services for deaf and hearing impaired persons. In hiring this coordinator, every consideration shall be given to qualified deaf or hearing impaired individuals. The coordinator shall monitor the residential treatment program established under Section 12-101. The coordinator shall also serve as the Department's liaison to providers of treatment or intervention services for alcoholism and other drug abuse and dependency.

(Source: P.A. 86-1004.) [Formerly Ill. Rev. Stat. 111½ §6362-2.]

305/12-103. Licensing requirements for providers of services.

§12-103. Providers of services under this Article shall, in addition to meeting all licensing requirements under this Act and rules and regulations adopted by the Department, have demonstrated ability, knowledge and expertise in the provision of services to deaf and hearing impaired persons.

(Source: P.A. 86-1004.) [Formerly Ill. Rev. Stat. 111½ §6362-3.]

ARTICLE XIII. SERVICES FOR PREGNANT WOMEN AND MOTHERS

(Added by P.A. 87-742, §2, eff. 9/26/91.)

Sec.

305/13-101. Department responsibility for the coordination of services among all State agencies and service providers.

§13-101. Department responsibility for the coordination of services among all State agencies and service providers. (a) In order to promote a comprehensive, Statewide, and multidisciplinary approach to addicted pregnant women and addicted mothers and their children, including addicted pregnant women and addicted mothers who are minors, the lead agency, as designated by the Governor, shall have the responsibility for ongoing exchange of referral information, as set forth in subsection (b) and (c) of this Section, among the following:

(1) Medical and social service providers that provide services to pregnant women, mothers and their children, whether or not substance abuse is evident, including providers in the Drug Free Families with a Future program, the Families with a Future program, the Prenatal Care Programs, the Parents Too Soon program, and any other State funded medical or social service program that provides services to pregnant women.

(2) Substance abuse treatment providers that provide services to addicted women.

(b) The lead agency, as designated by the Governor may, in conjunction with the Department and Departments of Children and Family Services, Public Health, and Public Aid, develop and maintain an updated and comprehensive list of medical and social service providers, that shall be arranged by geographic region. The lead agency may periodically send this comprehensive list of medical and social service providers to all substance abuse treatment providers identified under Section 13-102 of this Article [20 ILCS 305/13-102], so that appropriate referrals can be made. The Department shall obtain the specific consent of each provider of services before publishing, distributing, verbally making information available for purposes of referral, or otherwise utilizing or publicizing the availability of services from a provider. The Department may make available to recipients information concerning availability of services, but may not require recipients to utilize specific sources of care.

(c) The lead agency may, on an ongoing basis, keep all medical and social service providers identified under subsection (b) of this Section informed about any relevant changes in any laws relating to substance abuse, about services that are available from any State agencies for addicted pregnant women and addicted mothers and their children, and about any other developments that the Department finds to be informative.

(d) All substance abuse treatment providers may receive information from the lead agency or other agency designated by the Governor on the availability of services under the Drug Free Families with a Future or any comparable program providing case management services for addicted women, including information on appropriate referrals for other services that may be needed by addicted women in addition to treatment for addiction.

(e) The lead agency may implement the policies and programs set forth in this Article with the advice of the Subcommittee on Women's Alcohol and Substance Abuse Treatment created under Section 5-103.1 of this Act [20 ILCS 305/5-103.1].

(Source: P.A. 87-742.) [Formerly Ill. Rev. Stat. 111½ §6363-1.]

305/13-102. Directory of substance abuse treatment providers.

§13-102. Directory of substance abuse treatment providers. The Department shall develop and maintain an updated and comprehensive directory of service providers that provide substance abuse treatment services to pregnant women, mothers, and their children in this State. The Department shall disseminate an updated directory, as often as is necessary, to the list of medical and social service providers compiled under Section 13-101 of this Article [20 ILCS 305/13-101]. The Department shall obtain the specific consent of each provider of services before publishing, distributing, verbally making information available for purposes of referral or otherwise utilizing or publicizing the availability of services from a provider. The Department may make available to recipients information concerning availability of services, but may not require recipients to utilize specific sources of care.

(Source: P.A. 87-742.) [Formerly Ill. Rev. Stat. 111½ §6363-2.]

305/13-103. Standards for substance abuse treatment programs for addicted women.

§13-103. Standards for substance abuse treatment programs for addicted women. (a) The Department shall require, as a condition of any State grant or contract, that any substance abuse treatment program for addicted women provide services, either by its own staff or by contracting with other agencies or individuals, that include, but need not be limited to the following:

(1) Coordination with the Drug Free Families with a Future or any comparable program providing case management services to assure ongoing monitoring and coordination of services after the addicted woman has returned home.

(2) Coordination with medical services for individual medical care of addicted pregnant women, including prenatal care under the supervision of a physician.

(3) Coordination with child care services under any State plan developed pursuant to subsection (b) of Section 5-103.1 of this Act [20 ILCS 305/5-103.1].

(b) The Department shall require, as a condition of any State grant or contract, that any nonresidential substance abuse treatment program receiving any funding for treatment services for women shall accept women who are pregnant. Failure to comply with this Section shall result in termination of the grant or contract and loss of State funding.

(Source: P.A. 87-742.) [Formerly Ill. Rev. Stat. 111½ §6363-3.]

305/13-104. Model programs.

§13-104. Model programs. (a) The Department shall continue the model program established under Section 4-103 of this Act [20 ILCS 305/4-103]. The Department shall, in continuing the existing program established under Section 4-103 of this Act, contract with existing residencies or recovery homes in areas having a disproportionate number of women who are substance abusers needing residential treatment and counseling. Priority shall be given to the following:

(1) Women who are pregnant, or have minor children, or are both pregnant and have minor children.

(2) Women who are referred by medical personnel because they either gave birth to a baby addicted to cocaine, or will give birth to a baby addicted to cocaine.

Model recovery homes shall provide comprehensive social services, including a range of educational and counseling services, substance abuse therapy groups, family therapy groups, programs to develop positive self-awareness, parent-child therapy, and residential support groups, and shall conform with the standards set forth in Section 13-103 of this Article [20 ILCS 305/13-103].

(b) From funds appropriated expressly for the purposes of this Section, the Department shall contract with licensed, certified agencies to develop one model program for the care and treatment of addicted pregnant women, addicted mothers and their children. The program shall be in Cook County in an area of high density population having a disproportionate number of addicted women and a high infant mortality rate. The model program shall conform with the standards set forth in Section 13-103 of this Article and shall include, but not be limited to, the following services:

(1) On-site individual medical care, including prenatal care under the supervision of a physician.

(2) Temporary, residential shelters for pregnant women, mothers and children, when necessary.

(c) The Department shall report to the Governor and the General Assembly by December 31 of each year upon the activities and progress of the model programs established under this Section.

(Source: P.A. 87-742.) [Formerly Ill. Rev. Stat. 111½ §6363-4.]

305/13-105. Multidisciplinary guidelines.

§13-105. Multidisciplinary guidelines. (a)* The lead agency or other agency designated by the Governor, may publish a manual to assist medical and social service providers in identifying addiction and coordinating the multidisciplinary delivery of services to addicted pregnant women, addicted mothers and their children. The manual shall be used to assist providers only by providing specified information and may not be used by the Department to establish practice standards. The Department may not require recipients to use specific providers nor may they require providers to refer recipients to specific providers. The manual shall include, but not be limited to, the following:

(1) Information concerning risk assessments of women seeking prenatal, natal, and postnatal medical care.

(2) Information concerning risk assessments of infants who may be substance-affected.

(3) Protocols that have been adopted by the Illinois Department of Children and Family Services for the reporting and investigation of allegations of child abuse or neglect under the Abused and Neglected Child Reporting Act [325 ILCS 5/1 et seq.].

(4) Summary of procedures utilized in juvenile court in cases of children born to addicted women alleged or found to be abused or neglected.

(5) Information concerning referral of addicted pregnant women, addicted mothers and their children by medical, social service, and substance abuse treatment providers, by the Department of Alcoholism and Substance Abuse and by the Department of Children and Family Services.

(6) Effects of substance abuse on infants and guidelines on the symptoms, care, and comfort of drug-withdrawing infants.

(7) Responsibilities of the Department to maintain statistics on the number of children in Illinois addicted at birth.

**So in original. No subsec. (b) has been enacted.*

(Source: P.A. 87-742.) [Formerly Ill. Rev. Stat. 111½ §6363-5.]

DOMESTIC VIOLENCE SHELTERS ACT

Sec.

2210/0.01. Short title.

§0.01. Short title. This Act may be cited as the Domestic Violence Shelters Act.

(Source: P.A. 86-1324.) [Formerly Ill. Rev. Stat. 40 §2400.]

2210/1. Definitions.

§1. The terms used in this Act shall have the following meanings ascribed to them:

(a) "Domestic violence" means attempting to cause or causing abuse of a family or household member or high-risk adult with disabilities, or attempting to cause or causing neglect or exploitation of a high-risk adult with disabilities which threatens the adult's health and safety, as defined in Section 103 of the Illinois Domestic Violence Act of 1986 [750 ILCS 60/103].

(b) "Family or household member" means a spouse, person living as a spouse, parent, or other adult person related by consanguinity or affinity, who is residing or has resided with the person committing domestic violence. "Family or household member" includes a high-risk adult with disabilities who resides with or receives care from any person who has the responsibility for a high-risk adult as a result of a family relationship or who has assumed responsibility for all or a portion of the care of an adult with disabilities voluntarily, by express or implied contract, or by court order.

(c) "Shelter" means a facility including, but not limited to, a facility providing temporary residential facilities to family or household members who are victims of domestic violence and their children and to high-risk adults with disabilities.

(d) "High-risk adult with disabilities" means a person aged 18 or over whose physical or mental disability impairs his or her ability to seek or obtain protection from abuse, neglect, or exploitation.
(Source: P.A. 86-542.) [Formerly Ill. Rev. Stat. 40 §2401.]

2210/2. Service programs—Administration.

§2. The Department of Public Aid shall administer domestic violence shelters and service programs, or shall provide for their administration by not-for-profit corporations with whom the Department has contracts, for adults and their dependents who are the subjects of domestic violence.
(Source: P.A. 82-645.) [Formerly Ill. Rev. Stat. 40 §2402.]

2210/3. Domestic Violence Shelter and Service Fund.

§3. The Department of Public Aid shall provide for the funding of domestic violence shelters and service programs in part from the Domestic Violence Shelter and Service Fund and in part from the General Revenue Fund. In allotting monies from such fund, the Department shall give priority to shelters or programs offering or proposing to offer the broadest range of services and referrals to the community served. Such shelters or programs may be operated by community-based organizations or units of local government. The Department shall require shelters or programs eligible for funding under this Act to provide matching funds in such percentage as the Department shall by rule determine and such percentage shall be uniform throughout the State.
(Source: P.A. 84-1480.) [Formerly Ill. Rev. Stat. 40 §2403.]

2210/3.2. Domestic Violence Shelter and Service Fund—Deposits.

§3.2. All funds collected pursuant to P.A. 82-645, which are held in escrow for refund and for which a refund is not approved by September 1, 1988, shall be forwarded to the State Treasurer for deposit into the Domestic Violence Shelter and Service Fund. The Domestic Violence Shelter and Service Fund shall also include fines received by the State Treasurer from circuit clerks in accordance with Section 5-9-1.5 of the Unified Code of Corrections [730 ILCS 5/5-9-1.5]. Monies deposited in the Fund pursuant to this Section and the income tax check-off for the Domestic Violence Shelter and Service Fund authorized by Section 507F of the Illinois Income Tax Act [35 ILCS 5/507F] shall be appropriated to the Department of Public Aid for the purpose of providing services specified by this Act; however, the Department may waive the matching funds requirement of this Act with respect to such monies. Any such waiver shall be uniform throughout the State. This amendatory Act of 1987 applies to all funds collected pursuant to PA 82-645, held in escrow and for which no refund is approved by September 1, 1988, whether those funds are administered by the State, a county, a court, or any other unit or agency of government.
(Source: P.A. 86-559; 87-342; 87-791; 87-895.) [Formerly Ill. Rev. Stat. 40 §2403.2.]

CRIMINAL IDENTIFICATION ACT

Sec.

2630/0.01. Short title.

§0.01. Short title. This Act may be cited as the Criminal Identification Act.
(Source: P.A. 86-1324.) [Formerly Ill. Rev. Stat. 38 §206.]

2630/1. Powers of Department of State Police.

§1. The Department of State Police hereinafter referred to as the "Department", is hereby empowered to cope with the task of criminal identification and investigation.

The Director of the Department of State Police shall, from time to time, appoint such employees or assistants as may be necessary to carry out this work. Employees or assistants so appointed shall receive salaries subject to the standard pay plan provided for in the "Personnel Code", approved July 18, 1955, as amended [20 ILCS 415/1 et seq.].
(Source: P.A. 84-25.) [Formerly Ill. Rev. Stat. 38 §206-1.]

2630/2. Convicted persons; records.

§2. The Department shall procure and file for record, as far as can be procured from any source, photographs, all plates, outline pictures, measurements, descriptions and information of all persons who have been arrested on a charge of violation of a penal statute of this State and such other information as is necessary and helpful to plan programs of crime prevention, law enforcement and criminal justice, and aid in the furtherance of those programs.
(Source: P.A. 76-444.) [Formerly Ill. Rev. Stat. 38 §206-2.]

2630/2.1. Criminal case information.

§2.1. For the purpose of maintaining complete and accurate criminal records of the Department of State Police, it is necessary for all policing bodies of this State, the clerk of the circuit court, the Illinois Department of Corrections, the sheriff of each county, and State's Attorney of each county to submit certain criminal arrest, charge, and disposition information to the Department for filing at the earliest time possible. Unless otherwise noted herein, it shall be the duty of all policing bodies of this State, the clerk of the circuit court, the Illinois Department of Corrections, the sheriff of each county, and the State's Attorney of each county to report such information as provided in this Section, both in the form and manner required by the Department and within 30 days of the criminal history event. Specifically:

(a) Arrest Information. All agencies making arrests for offenses which are required by statute to be collected, maintained or disseminated by the Department of State Police shall be responsible for furnishing daily to the Department fingerprints, charges and descriptions of all persons who are arrested for such offenses. All such agencies shall also notify the Department of all decisions not to refer such arrests for prosecution. An agency making such arrests may enter into arrangements with other agencies for the purpose of furnishing daily such fingerprints, charges and descriptions to the Department upon its behalf.

(b) Charge Information. The State's Attorney of each county shall notify the Department of all charges filed, including all those added subsequent to the filing of a case, and whether charges were not filed in cases for which the Department has received information required to be reported pursuant to paragraph (a) of this Section.

(c) Disposition Information. The clerk of the circuit court of each county shall furnish the Department, in the form and manner required by the Supreme Court, with all final dispositions of cases for which the Department has received information required to be reported pursuant to paragraphs (a) or (d) of this Section. Such information shall include, for each charge, all (1) judgments of not guilty, judgments of guilty including the sentence pronounced by the court, discharges and dismissals in the court; (2) reviewing court orders filed with the clerk of the circuit court which reverse or remand a reported conviction or vacate or modify a sentence; (3) continuances to a date certain in furtherance of an order of supervision granted under Section 5-6-1 of the Unified Code of Corrections [730 ILCS 5/5-6-1] or an order of probation granted under Section 10 of the Cannabis Control Act [720 ILCS 550/10], Section 410 of the Illinois Controlled Substances Act [720 ILCS 570/410], Section 12-4.3 of the Criminal Code of 1961 [720 ILCS 5/12-4.3], Section 10-102 of the Illinois Alcoholism and Other Drug Dependency Act [20 ILCS 305/10-102], or Section 10 of the Steroid Control Act [repealed]; and (4) judgments terminating or revoking a sentence to probation, supervision or conditional discharge and any resentencing after such revocation.

(d) Fingerprints After Sentencing.

(1) After the court pronounces sentence, or issues an order of supervision or an order of probation granted under Section 10 of the Cannabis Control Act, Section 410 of the Illinois Controlled Substances Act, Section 12-4.3 of the Criminal Code of 1961, Section 10-102 of the Illinois Alcoholism and Other Drug Dependency Act, or Section 10 of the Steroid Control Act, for any offense which is required by statute to be collected, maintained, or disseminated by the Department of State Police, the State's Attorney of each county shall ask the court to order a law enforcement agency to fingerprint immediately all persons appearing before the court who have not previously been fingerprinted for the same case. The court shall so order the requested fingerprinting, if it determines that any such person has not previously been fingerprinted for the same case. The law enforcement agency shall submit such fingerprints to the Department daily.

(2) After the court pronounces sentence for any offense which is not required by statute to be collected, maintained, or disseminated by the Department of State Police, the prosecuting attorney may ask the court to order a law enforcement agency to fingerprint immediately all persons appearing before the court who have not previously been fingerprinted for the same case. The court may so order the requested fingerprinting, if it determines that any so sentenced person has not previously been fingerprinted for the same case. The law enforcement agency may retain such fingerprints in its files.

(e) Corrections Information. The Illinois Department of Corrections and the sheriff of each county shall furnish the Department with all information concerning the receipt, escape, execution, death, release, pardon, parole, commutation of sentence, granting of executive clemency or discharge of an individual who has been sentenced to the agency's custody for any offenses which are mandated by statute to be collected, maintained or disseminated by the Department of State Police. For an individual who has been charged with any such offense and who escapes from custody or dies while in custody, all information concerning the receipt and escape or death, whichever is appropriate, shall also be so furnished to the Department.

(Source: P.A. 86-575; 86-1269.) [Formerly Ill. Rev. Stat. 38 §206-2.1.]

2630/3. Information furnished to peace officers.

§3. (A) The Department shall file or cause to be filed all plates, photographs, outline pictures, measurements, descriptions and information which shall be received by it by virtue of its office and shall make a complete and systematic record and index of the same, providing thereby a method of convenient reference and comparison. The Department shall furnish, upon application, all information pertaining to the identification of any person or persons, a plate, photograph, outline picture, description, measurements, or any data of which there is a record in its office. Such information shall be furnished to peace officers of the United States, of other states or territories, of the Insular possessions of the United States, of foreign countries duly authorized to receive the same, to all peace officers of the State of Illinois and, conviction information only, to units of local government, school districts and private organizations, under the provisions of Section 55a of The Civil Administrative Code of Illinois [20 ILCS 2605/55a]. Applications shall be in writing and accompanied by a certificate, signed by the peace officer or chief administrative officer or his designee making such application, to the effect that the information applied for is necessary in the interest of and will be used solely in the due administration of the criminal laws or for the purpose of evaluating the qualifications and character of employees or prospective employees of units of local government and school districts and of employees, prospective employees, volunteers or prospective volunteers of such private organizations.

For the purposes of this subsection, "chief administrative officer" is defined as follows:

a) The city manager of a city or, if a city does not employ a city manager, the mayor of the city.

b) The manager of a village or, if a village does not employ a manager, the president of the village.

c) The chairman or president of a county board or, if a county has adopted the county executive form of government, the chief executive officer of the county.

d) The president of the school board of a school district.

e) The supervisor of a township.

f) The official granted general administrative control of a special district, an authority, or organization of government establishment by law which may issue obligations and which either may levy a property tax or may expend funds of the district, authority, or organization independently of any parent unit of government.

g) The executive officer granted general administrative control of a private organization defined in subsection 27 of Section 55a of The Civil Administrative Code of Illinois.

(B) Upon written application and payment of fees authorized by this subsection, State agencies and units of local government, not including school districts, are authorized to submit fingerprints of employees, prospective employees and license applicants to the Department for the purpose of obtaining conviction information maintained by the Department and the Federal Bureau of Investigation about such persons. The Department shall submit such fingerprints to the Federal Bureau of Investigation on behalf of such agencies and units of local government. The Department shall charge an application fee, based on actual costs, for the dissemination of conviction information pursuant to this subsection. The Department is empowered to establish this fee and shall prescribe the form and manner for requesting and furnishing conviction information pursuant to this subsection.

(C) Upon payment of fees authorized by this subsection, the Department shall furnish to the commanding officer of a military installation in Illinois having an arms storage facility, upon written request of such commanding officer or his designee, and in the form and manner prescribed by the Department, all criminal history record information pertaining to any individual seeking access to such a storage facility, where such information is sought pursuant to a federally-mandated security or criminal history check.

The Department shall establish and charge a fee, not to exceed actual costs, for providing information pursuant to this subsection.
(Source: P.A. 85-293; 85-921.) [Formerly Ill. Rev. Stat. 38 §206-3.]

2630/3.1. Dissemination of records.

§3.1. (a) The Department may furnish, pursuant to positive identification, records of convictions to the Department of Professional Regulation for the purpose of meeting registration or licensure requirements under The Private Detective, Private Alarm, and Private Security Act of 1983 [225 ILCS 445/1 et seq.].

(b) The Department may furnish, pursuant to positive identification, records of convictions to policing bodies of this State for the purpose of assisting local liquor control commissioners in carrying out their duty to refuse to issue licenses to persons specified in paragraphs (4), (5) and (6) of Section 6-2 of The Liquor Control Act of 1934 [235 ILCS 5/6-2].

(c) The Department shall charge an application fee, based on actual costs, for the dissemination of records pursuant to this Section. Fees received for the dissemination of records pursuant to this Section shall be deposited in the State Police Services Fund. The Department is empowered to establish this fee and to prescribe the form and manner for requesting and furnishing conviction information pursuant to this Section.

(d) Any dissemination of any information obtained pursuant to this Section to any person not specifically authorized hereby to receive or use it for the purpose for which it was disseminated shall constitute a violation of Section 7 [20 ILCS 2630/7].
(Source: P.A. 85-1440.) [Formerly Ill. Rev. Stat. 38 §206-3.1.]

2630/3.2. Firearm injury; notification of treatment.

§3.2. It is the duty of any person conducting or operating a medical facility, or any physician or nurse as soon as treatment permits to notify the local law enforcement agency of that jurisdiction upon the application for treatment of a person who is not accompanied by a law enforcement officer, when it reasonably appears that the person requesting treatment has received:

(1) any injury resulting from the discharge of a firearm; or

(2) any injury sustained in the commission of or as a victim of a criminal offense.

Any hospital, physician or nurse shall be forever held harmless from any civil liability for their reasonable compliance with the provisions of this Section.
(Source: P.A. 86-1475.) [Formerly Ill. Rev. Stat. 38 §206-3.2.]

2630/4. Identification systems.

§4. The Department may use the following systems of identification: The Bertillion system, the finger print system, and any system of measurement or identification that may be adopted by law or rule in the various penal institutions or bureaus of identification wherever located.

The Department shall make a record consisting of duplicates of all measurements, processes, operations, signalletic cards, plates, photographs, outline pictures, measurements, descriptions of and data relating to all persons confined in penal institutions wherever located, so far as the same are obtainable, in accordance with whatever system or systems may be found most efficient and practical.
(Source: Laws 1957, p. 1422.) [Formerly Ill. Rev. Stat. 38 §206-4.]

2630/5. Records of arrest furnished to Department; expungement; correction; serving of notice of petition.

§5. (a) All policing bodies of this State shall furnish to the Department, daily, in the form and detail the Department requires, fingerprints and descriptions, of all persons who are arrested on charges of violating any penal statute of this State, for offenses that are classified as felonies and Class A or B misdemeanors, of all minors who have been arrested or taken into custody before their 17th birthday for an offense that if committed by an adult would constitute the offense of unlawful use of weapons under Section 24-1 of the Criminal Code of 1961 [720 ILCS 5/24-1] or a forcible felony as defined in Section 2-8 of the Criminal Code of 1961 [720 ILCS 5/2-8]. Moving or nonmoving traffic violations under the Illinois Vehicle Code [625 ILCS 5/1-100 et seq.] shall not be reported except for violations of Chapter 4 and Section 11-204.1 of that Code [625 ILCS 5/1-100 et seq. and 5/11-204.1]. In addition, conservation offenses, as defined in the Supreme Court Rule 501(c), that are classified as Class B misdemeanors shall not be reported. Whenever an adult or minor prosecuted as an adult, not having previously been convicted of any criminal offense or municipal ordinance violation, charged with a violation of a municipal ordinance or a felony or misdemeanor, is acquitted or released without being convicted, whether the acquittal or release occurred before, on, or after the effective date of this amendatory Act of 1991, the Chief Judge of the circuit wherein the charge was brought, any judge of that circuit designated by the Chief Judge, or in counties of less than 3,000,000 inhabitants, the presiding trial judge at the defendant's trial may upon verified petition of the defendant order the record of arrest expunged from the official records of the arresting authority and the Department and order that the records of the clerk of the circuit court be [impounded until further order of the court upon good cause shown] *sealed until further order of the court upon good cause shown and the name of the defendant obliterated on the official index required to be kept by the circuit court clerk under Section 16 of the Clerks of Courts Act [705 ILCS 105/16], but the order shall not affect any index issued by the circuit court clerk before the entry of the order.* The Department may charge the petitioner a fee equivalent to the cost of processing any order to expunge or seal the records, and the fee shall be deposited into the State Police Services Fund. The records of those arrests, however, that result in a disposition of (i) supervision for any offense shall not be expunged from the records of the arresting authority or the Department nor impounded by the court until 2 years after discharge and dismissal of supervision; and (ii) those records that result from a supervision for a violation of Section 3-707, 3-708, 3-710, 5-401.3, 11-501 or 11-503 of the Illinois Vehicle Code [625 ILCS 5/3-707, 5/3-708, 5/3-710, 5/5-401.3, 5/11-501 or 5/11-503] or a similar provision of a local ordinance, or for a violation of Section 12-3.2, 12-15 or 16A-3 of the Criminal Code of 1961 [720 ILCS 5/12-3.2, 5/12-15 or 5/16A-3], or probation under Section 10 of the Cannabis Control Act [720 ILCS 550/10], Section 410 of the Illinois Controlled Substances Act [720 ILCS 570/410], Section 12-4.3 b(1) and (2) of the Criminal Code of 1961 [720 ILCS 5/12-4.3], Section 10-102 of the Illinois Alcoholism and Other Drug Dependency Act [720 ILCS 305/10-102] when the judgment of conviction has been vacated, or Section 10 of the Steroid Control Act [repealed] shall not be expunged from the records of the arresting authority nor impounded by the court until 5 years after termination of probation or supervision. All records set out above may be ordered by the court to be expunged from the records of the arresting authority and impounded by the court after 5 years, but shall not be expunged by the Department, but shall, on court order be sealed by the Department and may be disseminated by the Department only as required by law or to the arresting authority, the State's Attorney, and the court upon a later arrest for the same or a similar offense or for the purpose of sentencing for any subsequent felony. Upon conviction for any offense, the Department of Corrections shall have access to all sealed records of the Department pertaining to that individual.

(b) Whenever a person has been convicted of a crime or of the violation of a municipal ordinance, in the name of a person whose identity he has stolen or otherwise come into possession of, the aggrieved person from whom the identity was stolen or otherwise obtained without authorization, upon learning of the person having been arrested using his identity, may, upon verified petition to the chief judge of the circuit wherein the arrest was made, have a court order entered nunc pro tunc by the chief judge to correct the arrest record, conviction record, if any, and all official records of the arresting authority, the Department, other criminal justice agencies, the prosecutor, and the trial court concerning such arrest, if any, by removing his name from all such records in connection with the arrest and conviction, if any, and by inserting in the records the name of the offender, if known or ascertainable, in lieu of the aggrieved's name. *The records of the clerk of the circuit court clerk* shall be sealed until further order of the court upon good cause shown and the name of the aggrieved person obliterated on the official index required to be kept by the circuit court clerk under Section 16 of the Clerks of Courts Act, but the order shall not affect any index issued by the circuit court clerk before the entry of the order.* Nothing in this Section shall limit the Department of State Police or other criminal justice agencies or prosecutors from listing under an offender's name the false names he or she has used. For purposes of this Section, convictions for moving and nonmoving traffic violations other than convictions for violations of Chapter 4 and Section 11-204.1 of the Illinois Vehicle Code shall not be a bar to expunging the record of arrest and court records for violation of a misdemeanor or municipal ordinance.

**So in original.*

(c) Whenever a person who has been convicted of an offense is granted a pardon by the Governor which specifically authorizes expungement, he may, upon verified petition to the chief judge of the circuit where the person had been convicted, any judge of the circuit designated by the Chief Judge, or in counties of less than 3,000,000 inhabitants, the presiding trial judge at the defendant's trial, may have a court order entered expunging the record of arrest from the official records of the arresting authority and order that the records of the clerk of the circuit court and the Department be sealed until further order of the court upon good cause shown or as otherwise provided herein, and the name of the defendant obliterated from the official index requested to be kept by the circuit court clerk under Section 16 of the Clerks of Courts Act in connection with the arrest and conviction for the offense for which he had been pardoned but the order shall not affect any index issued by the circuit court clerk before the entry of the order. All records sealed by the Department may be disseminated by the Department only as required by law or to the arresting authority, the States Attorney, and the court upon a later arrest for the same or similar offense or for the purpose of sentencing for any subsequent felony. Upon conviction for any subsequent offense, the Department of Corrections shall have access to all sealed records of the Department pertaining to that individual. Upon entry of the order of expungement, the clerk of the circuit court shall promptly mail a copy of the order to the person who was pardoned.*

**So in original. Probably should be "State's".*

[(c)] *(d)* Notice of the petition for subsections (a), [and] (b), *and (c)* shall be served upon the State's Attorney or prosecutor charged with the duty of prosecuting the offense, the Department of State Police, the arresting agency and the chief legal officer of the unit of local government affecting the arrest. Unless the State's Attorney or prosecutor, the Department of State Police, the arresting agency or such chief legal officer objects to the petition within 30 days from the date of the notice, the court shall enter an order granting or denying the petition. The clerk of the court shall promptly mail a copy of the order to the person, the arresting agency, the prosecutor, the Department of State Police and such other criminal justice agencies as may be ordered by the judge.

[(d)] *(e)* Nothing herein shall prevent the Department of State Police from maintaining all records of any person who is admitted to probation upon terms and conditions and who fulfills those terms and conditions pursuant to Section 10 of the Cannabis Control Act, Section 410 of the Illinois Controlled Substances Act, Section 12-4.3 of the Criminal Code of 1961, Section 10-102 of the Illinois Alcoholism and Other Drug Dependency Act, or Section 10 of the Steroid Control Act.

[(e)] *(f)* No court order issued pursuant to the expungement provisions of this Section shall become final for purposes of appeal until 30 days after notice is received by the Department. Any court order contrary to the provisions of this Section is void.

(Chgd. by P.A. 87-963, §1, eff. 8/28/92; P.A. 87-1230, §5, eff. 7/1/93. Matter in brackets eff. only until 7/1/93. Matter in italics eff. 7/1/93.)

(Source: P.A. 86-575; 86-1269; 87-448; 87-548; 87-761; 87-895.) [Formerly Ill. Rev. Stat. 38 §206-5.]

2630/5.1. Reporting of domestic crime.

§5.1. Reporting of domestic crime. All law enforcement agencies in Illinois which have received complaints and had its officers investigate any alleged commission of a domestic crime, shall indicate the incidence of any alleged commission of said crime with the Department through the Illinois Uniform Crime Reporting System as part of the data reported pursuant to Section 8 of this Act [20 ILCS 2630/8].

Domestic crime for the purposes of this Section means any crime attempted or committed between husband and wife or between members of the same family or household.

(Source: P.A. 81-921.) [Formerly Ill. Rev. Stat. 38 §206-5.1.]

2630/7. Release of records restricted.

§7. No file or record of the Department hereby created shall be made public, except as provided in the "Illinois Uniform Conviction Information Act" [20 ILCS 2635/1 et seq.] or other Illinois law or as may be necessary in the identification of persons suspected or accused of crime and in their trial for offenses committed after having been imprisoned for a prior offense; and no information of any character relating to its records shall be given or furnished by said Department to any person, bureau or institution other than as provided in this Act or other State law, or when a governmental unit is required by state or federal law to consider such information in the performance of its duties. Violation of this Section shall constitute a Class A misdemeanor.

However, if an individual requests the Department to release information as to the existence or nonexistence of any criminal record he might have, the Department shall do so upon determining that the person for whom the record is to be released is actually the person making the request. The Department shall establish reasonable fees and rules to allow an individual to review and correct any criminal history record information the Department may hold concerning that individual upon verification of the identity of the individual. Such rulemaking is subject to the provisions of the Illinois Administrative Procedure Act [5 ILCS 100/1-1 et seq.].

(Source: P.A. 85-922.) [Formerly Ill. Rev. Stat. 38 §206-7.]

2630/8. Crime statistics.

§8. The Department shall be a central repository and custodian of crime statistics for the State and it shall have all power incident thereto to carry out the purposes of this Act, including the power to demand and receive cooperation in the submission of crime statistics from all units of government. On an annual basis, the Illinois Criminal Justice Information Authority shall make available compilations published by the Authority of crime statistics required to be reported by each policing body of the State, the clerks of the circuit court of each county, the Illinois Department of Corrections, the Sheriff of each county, and the State's Attorney of each county, including, but not limited to, criminal arrest, charge and disposition information.

(Source: P.A. 86-701.) [Formerly Ill. Rev. Stat. 38 §206-8.]

2630/9. Dental records for identification purposes.

§9. (a) Every county medical examiner and coroner shall, in every death investigation where the identity of a dead body cannot be determined by visual means, fingerprints, or other identifying data, have a qualified dentist, as determined by the county medical examiner or coroner, conduct a dental examination of the dead body. If the county medical examiner or coroner, with the aid of the dental examination and other identifiers, is still unable to establish the identity of the dead body, the medical examiner or coroner shall forthwith submit the dental records to the Department.

(b) If a person reported missing has not been found within 30 days, the law enforcement agency to whom the person was reported missing shall, within the next 5 days, make all necessary efforts to locate and request from the family or next of kin of the missing person written consent to contact and receive from the dentist of the missing person that person's dental records and shall forthwith make every reasonable effort to acquire such records. Within 5 days of the receipt of the missing person's dental records, the law enforcement agency shall submit such records to the Department.

(c) The Department shall be the State central repository for all dental records submitted pursuant to this Section. The Department may promulgate rules for the form and manner of submission of dental records, reporting of the location or identification of persons for whom dental records have been submitted and other procedures for program operations.

(d) When a person who has been reported missing is located and that person's dental records have been submitted to the Department, the law enforcement agency which submitted that person's dental records to the Department shall report that fact to the Department and the Department shall expunge the dental records of that person from the Department's file. The Department shall also expunge from its files the dental records of those dead and missing persons who are positively identified as a result of comparisons made with its files, the files maintained by other states, territories, insular possessions of the United States, or the United States.

(Source: P.A. 84-255.) [Formerly Ill. Rev. Stat. 38 §206-9.]

2630/10. Judicial remedies.

§10. Judicial Remedies. The Attorney General or a State's Attorney may bring suit in the circuit courts to prevent and restrain violations of the Illinois Uniform Conviction Information Act [20 ILCS 2635/1 et seq.], enacted by the 85th General Assembly and to enforce the reporting provisions of Section 2.1 of this Act [20 ILCS 2630/2.1]. The Department of State Police may request the Attorney General to bring any such action authorized by this subsection.

(Source: P.A. 85-922.) [Formerly Ill. Rev. Stat. 38 §206-10.]

ILLINOIS UNIFORM CONVICTION INFORMATION ACT

2635/1. Short title.

§1. Short Title. This Act shall be known and may be cited as the "Illinois Uniform Conviction Information Act."
(Source: P.A. 85-922.) [Formerly Ill. Rev. Stat. 38 §1601.]

2635/2. Legislative findings and purposes.

§2. Legislative Findings and Purposes. (A) The legislature finds and hereby declares that conviction information maintained by the Illinois Department of State Police shall be publicly available in the State of Illinois.

(B) The purpose of this Act is: (1) to establish uniform policy for gaining access to and disseminating conviction information maintained by the State of Illinois; (2) to establish guidelines and priorities which fully support effective law enforcement and ongoing criminal investigations and which ensure that conviction information is made accessible within appropriate time frames; (3) to ensure the accuracy and completeness of conviction information in the State of Illinois; and (4) to establish procedures for effectively correcting errors and providing individuals with redress of grievances in the event that inaccurate or incomplete information may be disseminated about them.
(Source: P.A. 85-922.) [Formerly Ill. Rev. Stat. 38 §1602.]

2635/3. Definitions.

§3. Definitions. Whenever used in this Act, and for the purposes of this Act, unless the context clearly indicates otherwise:

(A) "Accurate" means factually correct, containing no mistake or error of a material nature.

(B) The phrase "administer the criminal laws" includes any of the following activities: intelligence gathering, surveillance, criminal investigation, crime detection and prevention (including research), apprehension, detention, pretrial or post-trial release, prosecution, the correctional supervision or rehabilitation of accused persons or criminal offenders, criminal identification activities, or the collection, maintenance or dissemination of criminal history record information.

(C) "The Authority" means the Illinois Criminal Justice Information Authority.

(D) "Automated" means the utilization of computers, telecommunication lines, or other automatic data processing equipment for data collection or storage, analysis, processing, preservation, maintenance, dissemination, or display and is distinguished from a system in which such activities are performed manually.

(E) "Complete" means accurately reflecting all the criminal history record information about an individual that is required to be reported to the Department pursuant to Section 2.1 of "An Act in relation to criminal identification and investigation", approved July 2, 1931, as amended [20 ILCS 2630/2.1].

(F) "Conviction information" means data reflecting a judgment of guilt or nolo contendere. The term includes all prior and subsequent criminal history events directly relating to such judgments, such as, but not limited to: (1) the notation of arrest; (2) the notation of charges filed; (3) the sentence imposed; (4) the fine imposed; and (5) all related probation, parole, and release information. Information ceases to be "conviction information" when a judgment of guilt is reversed or vacated.

For purposes of this Act, continuances to a date certain in furtherance of an order of supervision granted under Section 5-6-1 of the Unified Code of Corrections [730 ILCS 5/5-6-1] or an order of probation granted under either Section 10 of the Cannabis Control Act [720 ILCS 550/10], Section 410 of the Illinois Controlled Substances Act [720 ILCS 570/410], Section 12-4.3 of the Criminal Code of 1961 [720 ILCS 5/12-4.3], Section 10-102 of the Illinois Alcoholism and Other Drug Dependency Act [20 ILCS 305/10-102], or Section 10 of the Steroid Control Act [repealed] shall not be deemed "conviction information".

(G) "Criminal history record information" means data identifiable to an individual and consisting of descriptions or notations of arrests, detentions, indictments, informations, pretrial proceedings, trials, or other formal events in the criminal justice system or descriptions or notations of criminal charges (including criminal violations of local municipal ordinances) and the nature of any disposition arising therefrom, including sentencing, court or correctional supervision, rehabilitation and release. The term does not apply to statistical records and reports in which individual are not identified and from which their identities are not ascertainable, or to information that is for criminal investigative or intelligence purposes.

(H) "Criminal justice agency" means (1) a government agency or any subunit thereof which is authorized to administer the criminal laws and which allocates a substantial part of its annual budget for that purpose, or (2) an agency supported by public funds which is authorized as its principal function to administer the criminal laws and which is officially designated by the Department as a criminal justice agency for purposes of this Act.

(I) "The Department" means the Illinois Department of State Police.

(J) "Director" means the Director of the Illinois Department of State Police.

(K) "Disseminate" means to disclose or transmit conviction information in any form, oral, written, or otherwise.

(L) "Exigency" means pending danger or the threat of pending danger to an individual or property.

(M) "Non-criminal justice agency" means a State agency, Federal agency, or unit of local government that is not a criminal justice agency. The term does not refer to private individuals, corporations, or non-governmental agencies or organizations.

(N) "Requester" means any private individual, corporation, organization, employer, employment agency, labor organization, or non-criminal justice agency that has made a written application pursuant to this Act to obtain conviction information maintained in the files of the Department of State Police regarding a particular individual.

(O) "Statistical information" means data from which the identity of an individual cannot be ascertained, reconstructed, or verified and to which the identity of an individual cannot be linked by the recipient of the information.
(Source: P.A. 85-922; 86-1269.) [Formerly Ill. Rev. Stat. 38 §1603.]

2635/4. Applicability.

§4. Applicability. (A) The provisions of this Act shall apply only to conviction information mandated by statute to be reported to or to be collected, maintained, or disseminated by the Department of State Police.

(B) The provisions of this Act shall not apply to statistical information.

(C) In the event of conflict between the application of this Act and the statutes listed in paragraphs (1), (2), (3), (4), or (5) below, the statutes listed below, as hereafter amended, shall control unless specified otherwise:

(1) The Juvenile Court Act [see 705 ILCS 405/1-1 et seq.]; or

(2) Section 5-3-4 of the Unified Code of Corrections [730 ILCS 5/5-3-4]; or

(3) Paragraph (4) of Section 12 of "An Act providing for a system of probation, for the appointment and compensation of probation officers, and authorizing the suspension of final judgment and the imposition of sentence upon persons found guilty of certain defined crimes and offenses, an legalizing their ultimate discharge without punishment", approved June 10, 1911, as amended [730 ILCS 110/12]; or

(4) Section 2.1 of "An Act in relation to criminal identification and investigation", approved July 2, 1931, as amended [20 ILCS 2630/2.1]; or

(5) "An Act in relation to pretrial services" [725 ILCS 185/0.01 et seq.], certified January 5, 1987.
(Source: P.A. 85-922.) [Formerly Ill. Rev. Stat. 38 §1604.]

2635/5. Public availability of conviction information.

§5. Public Availability of Conviction Information. All conviction information mandated by statute to be collected and maintained by the Department of State Police shall be open to public inspection in the State of Illinois. All persons, state agencies and units of local government shall have access to inspect, examine and reproduce such information, in accordance with this Act, and shall have the right to take memoranda and abstracts concerning such information, except to the extent that the provisions of this Act or other Illinois statutes might create specific restrictions on the use or disclosure of such information.
(Source: P.A. 85-922.) [Formerly Ill. Rev. Stat. 38 §1605.]

2635/6. Dissemination time frames and priorities.

§6. Dissemination Time Frames and Priorities. (A) The Department's duty and obligation to furnish criminal history record information to peace officers and criminal justice agencies shall take precedence over any requirement of this Act to furnish conviction information to non-criminal justice agencies or to the public. When, in the judgment of the Director, such duties and obligations are being fulfilled in a timely manner, the Department shall furnish conviction information to requesters in accordance with the provisions of this Act. The Department may give priority to requests for conviction information from non-criminal justice agencies over other requests submitted pursuant to this Act.

(B) The Department shall attempt to honor requests for conviction information made pursuant to this Act in the shortest time possible. Subject to the dissemination priorities of subsection (A) of this Section, the Department shall respond to a request for conviction information within 2 weeks from receipt of a request.
(Source: P.A. 85-922.) [Formerly Ill. Rev. Stat. 38 §1606.]

2635/7. Restrictions on the use of conviction information.

§7. Restrictions on the Use of Conviction Information. (A) The following provisions shall apply to requests submitted pursuant to this Act for employment or licensing purposes or submitted to comply with the provisions of subsection (B) of this Section:

(1) A requester shall, in the form and manner prescribed by the Department, submit a written application to the Department, signed by the individual to whom the information request pertains. The Department shall furnish the requester with 2 copies of its response.

(2) Each requester of conviction information furnished by the Department shall provide the individual named in the request with a copy of the response furnished by the Department. Within 7 working days of receipt of such copy, the individual shall have the obligation and responsibility to notify the requester if the information is inaccurate or incomplete.

(3) Unless notified by the individual named in the request or by the Department that the information furnished is inaccurate or incomplete, no requester of conviction information shall be liable for damages to any person to whom the information pertains for actions the requester may reasonably take in reliance on the accuracy and completeness of conviction information received from the Department pursuant to this act, if: (a) the requester in good faith believes the conviction information furnished by the Department to be accurate and complete; (b) the requester has complied with the requirements of paragraphs (1) and (2) of this subsection (A); and (c) the identifying information submitted by the requester to the Department is accurate with respect to the individual about whom the information was requested.

(4) Consistent with rules adopted by the Department pursuant to Section 7 of "An Act in relation to criminal identification and investigation", approved July 2, 1931, as amended [20 ILCS 2630/7], the individual to whom the conviction information pertains may initiate proceedings directly with the Department to challenge or correct a record furnished by the Department pursuant to this subsection (A). Such correction proceedings shall be given priority over other individual record review and challenges filed with the Department.

(B) Regardless of the purpose of the request, no requester of conviction information shall be liable for damages to any person to whom the information pertains for actions the requester may reasonably take in reliance on the accuracy and completeness of conviction information received from the Department pursuant to this Act, if: (1) the requester in good faith believes the conviction information furnished by the Department to be accurate and complete; (2) the requester has complied with the requirements of paragraphs (1) and (2) of subsection (A) of this Section; and (3) the identifying information submitted by the requester to the Department is accurate with respect to the individual about whom the information was requested.

(Source: P.A. 85-922.) [Formerly Ill. Rev. Stat. 38 §1607.]

2635/8. Form, manner and fees for requesting and obtaining conviction information.

§8. Form, Manner and Fees for Requesting and Obtaining Conviction Information. (A) The Department shall prescribe the form and manner for requesting and furnishing conviction information pursuant to this Act. The Department shall prescribe the types of identifying information that must be submitted by written application to the Department in order to process any request for conviction information and the form and manner for making such application, consistent with this Act.

(B) The Department shall establish the maximum fee it shall charge and assess for processing requests for conviction information, and the Authority

shall establish the maximum fee that other criminal justice agencies shall charge and assess for processing requests for conviction information pursuant to this Act. Such fees shall include the general costs associated with performing a search for all information about each person for which a request is received including classification, search, retrieval, reproduction, manual and automated data processing, telecommunications services, supplies, mailing and those general costs associated with the inquiries required by subsection (B) of Section 9 and Section 13 of this Act [20 ILCS 2635/9 and 2635/13], and, when applicable, such fees shall provide for the direct payment to or reimbursement of a criminal justice agency for assisting the requester or the Department pursuant to this Act. In establishing the fees required by this Section, the Department and the Authority may also take into account the costs relating to multiple or automated requests and the costs relating to any other special factors or circumstances required by statute or rule. The maximum fees established by the Authority pursuant to this Section shall be reviewed annually, and may be waived or reduced at the discretion of a criminal justice agency.
(Source: P.A. 85-922.) [Formerly Ill. Rev. Stat. 38 §1608.]

2635/9. Procedural requirements for disseminating conviction information.

§9. Procedural Requirements for Disseminating Conviction Information. (A) In accordance with the time parameters of Section 6 [20 ILCS 2635/6] and the requirements of subsections (B) and (C) of this Section 9, the Department shall either: (1) transmit conviction information to the requester, including an explanation of any code or abbreviation; (2) explain to the requester why the information requested cannot be transmitted; or (3) inform the requester of any deficiency in the request.

(B) Before disseminating conviction information pursuant to this Act, the Department shall first conduct a formal update inquiry and review to make certain that the information to be disseminated is complete, except (1) in cases of exigency, (2) upon request by another criminal justice agency, (3) for conviction information that is less than 30 days old, or (4) for information intentionally fabricated upon the express written authorization of the Director of State Police to support undercover law enforcement efforts.

(C) It shall be the responsibility of the Department to retain a record of every extra-agency dissemination of conviction information for a period of not less than 3 years. Such records shall be subject to audit by the Department, and shall, upon request, be supplied to the individual to whom the information pertains for requests from members of the general public, corporations, organizations, employers, employment agencies, labor organizations and non-criminal justice agencies. At a minimum, the following information shall be recorded and retained by the Department:

(1) The name of the individual to whom the disseminated information pertains;

(2) The name of the individual requesting the information;

(3) The date of the request;

(4) The name and address of the private individual, corporation, organization, employer, employment agency, labor organization or non-criminal justice agency receiving the information;

(5) The date of the dissemination; and

(6) The name of the Department employee releasing the information.

(Source: P.A. 85-922.) [Formerly Ill. Rev. Stat. 38 §1609.]

2635/10. Dissemination requests based upon fingerprint identification.

§10. Dissemination requests Based Upon Fingerprint Identification. When fingerprint identification accompanies a request for conviction information maintained by the Department, an appropriate statement shall be issued by the Department indicating that the information furnished by the Department positively pertains to the individual whose fingerprints were submitted and that the response contains all the conviction information that has been reported to the Department pursuant to Section 2.1 of "An Act in relation to criminal identification and investigation", approved July 2, 1931, as amended [20 ILCS 2630/2.1].

(Source: P.A. 85-922.) [Formerly Ill. Rev. Stat. 38 §1610.]

2635/11. Dissemination requests not based upon fingerprint identification.

§11. Dissemination requests Not Based Upon Fingerprint Identification. (A) When a requester is not legally mandated to submit positive fingerprint identification to the Department or when a requester is precluded from submitting positive fingerprint identification to the Department due to exigency, an appropriate warning shall be issued by the Department indicating that the information furnished cannot be identified with certainty as pertaining to the individual named in the request and may only be relied upon as being accurate and complete if the requester has first complied with the requirements of subsection (B) of Section 7 [20 ILCS 2635/7].

(B) If the identifying information submitted by the requester to the Department corresponds to more than one individual found in the files maintained by the Department, the Department shall not disclose the information to the requester, unless it is determined by the Department that dissemination is still warranted due to exigency or to administer the criminal laws. In such instances, the Department may require the requester to submit additional identifying information or fingerprints in the form and manner prescribed by the Department.

(Source: P.A. 85-922.) [Formerly Ill. Rev. Stat. 38 §1611.]

2635/12. Error notification and correction procedure.

§12. Error Notification and Correction Procedure. It is the duty and responsibility of the Department to maintain accurate and complete criminal history record information and to correct or update such information after determination by audit, individual review and challenge procedures, or by other verifiable means, that it is incomplete or inaccurate. Except as may be required for a longer period of time by Illinois law, the Department shall notify a requester if a subsequent disposition of conviction or a subsequent modification of conviction information has been reported to the Department within 30 days of responding to the requester.

(Source: P.A. 85-922.) [Formerly Ill. Rev. Stat. 38 §1612.]

2635/13. Limitation on further dissemination.

§13. Limitation on Further Dissemination. Unless otherwise permitted by law or in the case of exigency, the subsequent dissemination of conviction information furnished by the Department pursuant to this Act shall only be permitted by a requester for the 30 day period immediately following receipt of the information. Except as permitted in this Section, any requester still wishing to further disseminate or to rely on the accuracy and completeness of conviction information more than 30 days from receipt of the information from the Department shall request that the Department conduct a formal update inquiry

and review to verify that the information originally provided is still accurate and complete.
(Source: P.A. 85-922.) [Formerly Ill. Rev. Stat. 38 §1613.]

2635/14. Judicial remedies.

§14. Judicial Remedies. (A) The Attorney General or a State's Attorney may bring suit in the circuit courts to prevent and restrain violations of this Act and to enforce the reporting provisions of Section 2.1 of "An Act in relation to criminal identification and investigation", approved July 2, 1931, as amended [20 ILCS 2630/2.1]. The Department may request the Attorney General to bring any such action authorized by this subsection.

(B) An individual aggrieved by a violation of this Act by a State agency or unit of local government shall have the right to pursue a civil action for damages or other appropriate legal or equitable remedy, including an action to compel the Department to disclose or correct conviction information in its files, once administrative remedies have been exhausted.

(C) Any civil action for damages alleging the negligent dissemination of inaccurate or incomplete conviction information by a State agency or by a unit of local government in violation of this Act may only be brought against the State agency or unit of local government and shall not be brought against any employee or official thereof.

(D) Civil remedies authorized by this Section may be brought in any circuit court of the State of Illinois in the county in which the violation occurs or in the county where the State agency or unit of local government is situated; except all damage claims against the State of Illinois for violations of this Act shall be determined by the Court of Claims.
(Source: P.A. 85-922.) [Formerly Ill. Rev. Stat. 38 §1614.]

2635/15. Civil damages.

§15. Civil Damages. (A) In any action brought pursuant to this Act, an individual aggrieved by any violation of this Act shall be entitled to recover actual and general compensatory damages for each violation, together with costs and attorney's fees reasonably incurred, consistent with Section 16 of this Act [20 ILCS 2635/16]. In addition, an individual aggrieved by a willful violation of this Act shall be entitled to recover $1,000. In addition, an individual aggrieved by a non-willful violation of this Act for which there has been dissemination of inaccurate or incomplete conviction information shall be entitled to recover $200; provided, however, if conviction information is determined to be incomplete or inaccurate, by audit, by individual review and challenge procedures, or by other verifiable means, then the individual aggrieved shall only be entitled to recover such amount if the Department fails to correct the information within 30 days.

(B) For the purposes of this Act, the State of Illinois shall be liable for damages as provided in this Section and for attorney's fees and litigation costs as provided in Section 16 of this Act. All damage claims against the State of Illinois or any of its agencies for violations of this Act shall be determined by the Court of Claims.

(C) For purposes of limiting the amount of civil damages that may be assessed against the State of Illinois or a unit of local government pursuant to this Section, a State agency, a unit of local government, and the officials or employees of a State agency or a unit of local government may in good faith rely upon the assurance of another State agency or unit of local government that conviction information is maintained or disseminated in compliance with the provisions of this Act. However, such reliance shall not constitute a defense with respect to equitable or declaratory relief.

(D) For purposes of limiting the amount of damages that may be assessed against the State of Illinois pursuant to this Section, the Department may in good faith presume that the conviction information reported to it by a clerk of the circuit court or a criminal justice agency is accurate. However, such presumption shall not constitute a defense with respect to equitable or declaratory relief.
(Source: P.A. 85-922.) [Formerly Ill. Rev. Stat. 38 §1615.]

2635/16. Attorney's fees and costs.

§16. Attorney's Fees and Costs. (A) Attorney's fees and other costs shall be awarded to any plaintiff who obtains declaratory, equitable, or injunctive relief. The amount awarded shall represent the reasonable value of the services rendered, taking into account all the surrounding circumstances, including but not limited to: the amount of attorney time and other disbursements determined by the court to be reasonably required by the nature of the case; the benefit rendered to the public; the skill demanded by the novelty or complexity of the issues; and the need to encourage the enforcement of this Act.

(B) Attorney's fees and other costs shall, consistent with subsection (A) of this Section, also be awarded to any plaintiff who obtains monetary relief for damages. However, in no event shall such an award exceed the actual amount of monetary damages awarded to the plaintiff.

(C) The court shall, consistent with subsection (A) of this Section, assess attorney's fees and litigation costs reasonably incurred by the State, a unit of local government, or government official or employee to defend against any private party or parties bringing an action pursuant to this Act, upon the court's determination that the action was brought in bad faith or is malicious, vexatious, or frivolous in nature.
(Source: P.A. 85-922.) [Formerly Ill. Rev. Stat. 38 §1616.]

2635/17. Administrative sanctions.

§17. Administrative Sanctions. The Department shall refuse to comply with any request to furnish conviction information maintained in its files, if the requester has not acted in accordance with the requirements of this Act or rules and regulations issued pursuant thereto. The requester may appeal such a refusal by the Department to the Director. Upon written application by the requester, the Director shall hold a hearing to determine whether dissemination of the requested information would be in violation of this Act or rules and regulations issued pursuant to it or other federal or State law pertaining to the collection, maintenance or dissemination of criminal history record information. When the Director finds such a violation, the Department shall be prohibited from disseminating conviction information to the requester, under such terms and conditions and for such periods of time as the Director deems appropriate.
(Source: P.A. 85-922.) [Formerly Ill. Rev. Stat. 38 §1617.]

2635/18. Criminal penalties.

§18. Criminal Penalties. Any person who intentionally and knowingly (A) requests, obtains, or seeks to obtain conviction information under false pretenses, or (B) disseminates inaccurate or incomplete conviction information in violation of this Act, or (C) fails to disseminate or make public conviction information as required under this Act, or (D) fails to correct or update a conviction record after it is determined by audit, by individual review and challenge procedures, or by other verifiable means to be inaccurate or incomplete for the purpose of causing harm to the individual named in the request or to whom the information pertains, or (E) violates any other provision of this Act, shall for each offense be guilty of a Class A misdemeanor.
(Source: P.A. 85-922.) [Formerly Ill. Rev. Stat. 38 §1618.]

2635/19. Coordinating and implementing policy.

§19. Coordinating and Implementing Policy. The Department shall adopt rules to prescribe the appropriate form, manner and fees for complying with the requirements of this Act. The Authority shall adopt rules to prescribe form, manner and maximum fees which the Authority is authorized to establish pursuant to subsection (B) of Section 8 of this Act [20 ILCS 2635/8]. Such rulemaking is subject to the provisions of the Illinois Administrative Procedure Act [5 ILCS 100/1-1 et seq.].

(Source: P.A. 85-922.) [Formerly Ill. Rev. Stat. 38 §1619.]

2635/20. State liability and indemnification of units of local government.

§20. State Liability and Indemnification of Units of Local Government. (A) The State of Illinois shall guarantee the accuracy and completeness of conviction information disseminated by the Department that is based upon fingerprint identification. The State of Illinois shall not be liable for the accuracy and completeness of any information disseminated upon identifying information other than fingerprints.

(B) The State of Illinois shall indemnify a clerk of the circuit court, a criminal justice agency, and their employees and officials from, and against, all damage claims brought by others due to dissemination by the Department of inaccurate or incomplete conviction information based upon positive fingerprint identification, provided that the conviction information in question was initially reported to the Department accurately and in the timely manner mandated by Section 2.1 of "An Act in relation to criminal identification and investigation", approved July 2, 1931, as amended [20 ILCS 2630/2.1].

(Source: P.A. 85-922.) [Formerly Ill. Rev. Stat. 38 §1620.]

2635/21. Audits.

§21. Audits. The Department shall regularly conduct representative audits of the criminal history record keeping and criminal history record reporting policies, practices, and procedures of the repositories for such information in Illinois to ensure compliance with the provisions of this Act and Section 2.1 of "An Act in relation to criminal identification and investigation", approved July 2, 1931, as amended [20 ILCS 2630/2.1]. The findings of such audits shall be reported to the Governor, General Assembly, and, upon request, to members of the general public.

(Source: P.A. 85-922.) [Formerly Ill. Rev. Stat. 38 §1621.]

2635/22. Supplementary remedies.

§22. Supplementary Remedies. The remedies provided in this Act are supplementary to, and in no way modify or supplant, any other applicable causes of action arising under the Constitution, statutes, or common law of the State of Illinois.

(Source: P.A. 85-922.) [Formerly Ill. Rev. Stat. 38 §1622.]

2635/23. Construction.

§23. Construction. (A) The provisions of this Act shall be construed to afford the maximum feasible protection to the individual's right to privacy and enjoyment of his good name and reputation and shall be construed to apply to both manual and automated criminal history record information systems wherever possible.

(B) The provisions of this Act shall be construed to make government agencies accountable to individuals in the collection, use, and dissemination of conviction information based upon positive fingerprint identification relating to them.

(C) Nothing in this Act shall be construed as restricting or prohibiting the dissemination of criminal history record information to a requesting criminal justice agency or peace officer or the dissemination of local criminal history record information maintained by criminal justice agencies on behalf of units of local government to members of the general public requesting such information.
(Source: P.A. 85-922.) [Formerly Ill. Rev. Stat. 38 §1623.]

2635/24. Statute of limitations.
§24. Statute of Limitations. Any cause of action arising under this Act shall be barred unless brought within 3 years from the date of the violation of the Act or within 3 years from the date the plaintiff should reasonably have known of its violation, whichever is later.
(Source: P.A. 85-922.) [Formerly Ill. Rev. Stat. 38 §1624.]

STATEWIDE ORGANIZED GANG DATABASE ACT

(Added by P.A. 87-932, §§1-1 to 1-15, eff. 1/1/93.)

2640/1. Short title.
§1. Short title. This Article may be cited as the Statewide Organized Gang Database Act.
(Added by P.A. 87-932, §1-1, eff. 1/1/93.)

2640/5. Definitions.
§5. Definitions. As used in this Act:
"Department" means the Department of State Police.
"Director" means the Director of State Police.
A "SWORD terminal" is an interactive computerized communication and processing unit that permits a direct on-line communication with the Department of State Police's central data repository, the Statewide Organized Gang Database (SWORD).
(Added by P.A. 87-932, §1-5, eff. 1/1/93.)

2640/10. Duties of the Department.
§10. Duties of the Department. The Department may:
(a) provide a uniform reporting format for the entry of pertinent information regarding the report of an arrested organized gang member or organized gang affiliate into SWORD;
(b) notify all law enforcement agencies that reports of arrested organized gang members or organized gang affiliates shall be entered into the database as soon as the minimum level of data specified by the Department is available to the reporting agency, and that no waiting period for the entry of that data exists;
(c) develop and implement a policy for notifying law enforcement agencies of the emergence of new organized gangs, or the change of a name or other identifying sign by an existing organized gang;
(d) compile and retain information regarding organized gangs and their members and affiliates, in a manner that allows the information to be used by law enforcement and other agencies, deemed appropriate by the Director, for investigative purposes;
(e) compile and maintain a historic data repository relating to organized gangs and their members and affiliates in order to develop and improve

techniques utilized by law enforcement agencies and prosecutors in the investigation, apprehension, and prosecution of members and affiliates of organized gangs;

(f) create a quality control program regarding confirmation of organized gang membership and organized gang affiliation data, timeliness and accuracy of information entered into SWORD, and performance audits of all entering agencies;

(g) locate all law enforcement agencies that could, in the opinion of the Director, benefit from access to SWORD, and notify them of its existence; and

(h) cooperate with all law enforcement agencies wishing to gain access to the SWORD system, and facilitate their entry into the system and their continued maintenance of access to it.

(Added by P.A. 87-932, §1-10, eff. 1/1/93.)

2640/15. Duties of local law enforcement agencies.

§15. Duties of local law enforcement agencies. Local law enforcement agencies who are members of the SWORD system may:

(a) after carrying out any arrest of any individual whom they believe to be a member or affiliate of an organized gang, create or update that individual's electronic file within the SWORD system; and

(b) notify the prosecutor of the accused of the accused individual's gang membership or gang affiliate status.

(Added by P.A. 87-932, §1-15, eff. 1/1/93.)

ANTI-CRIME ADVISORY COUNCIL ACT

Sec.

3910/0.01. Short title.

§0.01. Short title. This Act may be cited as the Anti-Crime Advisory Council Act.

(Source: P.A. 86-1324.) [Formerly Ill. Rev. Stat. 38 §1300.]

3910/1. Creation—Membership—Tenure—Vacancies.

§1. Creation—Membership—Tenure—Vacancies. There is created the Illinois Anti-Crime Advisory Council, called the Council, consisting of 11 members. Of the 11 members, 4 shall be chosen from the General Assembly, 2 are to be Senators, 1 appointed by the President of the Senate and 1 by the Senate Minority Leader, and 2 are to be Representatives, 1 appointed by the Speaker of the House of Representatives and 1 by the House Minority Leader. The remaining 7 members shall be chosen as follows: 2 appointed by the President of the Senate and 1 by the Senate Minority Leader and 2 appointed by the Speaker of the House of Representatives and 1 by the House Minority Leader and 1 appointed by the Governor. Council members are to be appointed prior to July 1 of each odd-numbered year for a 2-year term commencing July 1, and until their respective successors are appointed and qualified, except that General Assembly members are to serve that term or until the termination of their legislative service, whichever first occurs. Vacancies are to be filled for the unexpired term in the same manner as original appointments. All appointments must be in writing and filed with the Secretary of State as a public record.

(Source: P.A. 83-829.) [Formerly Ill. Rev. Stat. 38 §1301.]

3910/2. Compensation.

§2. Compensation. Members of the Council shall receive no compensation but shall be reimbursed for expenses necessarily incurred in the performance of their duties.

(Source: P.A. 83-829) [Formerly Ill. Rev. Stat. 38 §1302.]

3910/3. Meeting—Selection of chairman and vice-chairman—Quorum.

§3. Meeting—Selection of chairman and vice-chairman—Quorum. The Council shall meet at least quarterly and at other times on call of the chairman or any 6 members at such place as shall be designated by the chairman. Notice of the time and place of each meeting shall be given by the secretary of the Council to each member at least 7 days prior to the date of the meeting.

The Council at its first meeting in each year shall select a chairman and vice-chairman from among its membership who shall serve until their successors are selected.

Six members of the Council shall constitute a quorum and a majority of a quorum shall have authority to act in any matter within the jurisdiction of the Council.

(Source: P.A. 83-829.) [Formerly Ill. Rev. Stat. 38 §1303.]

3910/4. Employees.

§4. Employees. The Council may, without regard to any law relating to public employment, employ a director and such stenographic staff and other assistants as it deems necessary.

(Source: P.A. 83-829.) [Formerly Ill. Rev. Stat. 38 §1304.]

3910/5. Duties.

§5. Duties. The Council shall have the following powers and duties:

(a) to advise and assist in the creation of local anti-crime programs, such as Crime Stoppers, We-Tip and similar programs designed to solve crimes;

(b) to foster the detection of crime and encourage persons through the program and otherwise to come forward with information about criminal activity;

(c) to encourage the news media to promote local anti-crime programs and to inform the public of the functions of the Council;

(d) to assist local anti-crime programs in channeling information reported to those programs concerning criminal activity to the appropriate law enforcement agencies; and

(e) to assist local anti-crime programs in promoting the private funding of local anti-crime programs.

(Source: P.A. 83-829.) [Formerly Ill. Rev. Stat. 38 §1305.]

3910/6. Powers.

§6. Powers. The Council is empowered to prepare and cause to be printed any and all drafts of bills intended to carry out its recommendations, as well as any and all reports, memoranda or other papers necessary or incidental to the performance of its tasks. Its members, with a view to obtaining information and suggestions which will aid in the attainment of its objects, are authorized to visit and observe local anti-crime programs and to attend meetings of professional bodies and of associations and groups engaged in study or research other work relating to such local anti-crime programs.

(Source: P.A. 83-829.) [Formerly Ill. Rev. Stat. 38 §1306.]

3910/7. Definition.

§7. Definition. For the purposes of this Act, "local anti-crime program" means a plan established in various regions of this State which is designed to

encourage the public to report incidences of crime to law enforcement agencies and to assist such agencies in the apprehension of criminal offenders.
(Source: P.A. 83-829.) [Formerly Ill. Rev. Stat. 38 §1307.]

3910/8. Reports.

§8. Reports. The Council shall submit a report of the results of its study together with its recommendations and drafts of bills to each General Assembly within 30 days after the convening board.
(Source: P.A. 83-829.) [Formerly Ill. Rev. Stat. 38 §1308.]

ILLINOIS CRIMINAL JUSTICE INFORMATION ACT

Sec.

3930/1. Short title.

§1. Short Title. This Act shall be known and may be cited as the "Illinois Criminal Justice Information Act".
(Source: P.A. 82-1039.) [Formerly Ill. Rev. Stat. 38 §210-1.]

3930/2. Purpose of Act.

§2. Purpose of Act. The purpose of this Act is to coordinate the use of information in the criminal justice system; to promulgate effective criminal justice information policy; to encourage the improvement of criminal justice agency procedures and practices with respect to information; to provide new information technologies; to permit the evaluation of information practices and programs; to stimulate research and development of new methods and uses of criminal justice information for the improvement of the criminal justice system and the reduction of crime; and to protect the integrity of criminal history record information, while protecting the citizen's right to privacy.
(Source: P.A. 82-1039.) [Formerly Ill. Rev. Stat. 38 §210-2.]

3930/3. Definitions.

§3. Definitions. Whenever used in this Act, and for the purposes of this Act unless the context clearly denotes otherwise:

(a) The term "criminal justice system" includes all activities by public agencies pertaining to the prevention or reduction of crime or enforcement of the criminal law, and particularly, but without limitation, the prevention, detection, and investigation of crime; the apprehension of offenders; the protection of victims and witnesses; the administration of juvenile justice; the prosecution and defense of criminal cases; the trial, conviction, and sentencing of offenders; as well as the correction and rehabilitation of offenders, which includes imprisonment, probation, parole and treatment.

(b) The term "Authority" means the Illinois Criminal Justice Information Authority created by this Act.

(c) The term "criminal justice information" means any and every type of information that is collected, transmitted, or maintained by the criminal justice system.

(d) The term "criminal history record information" means data identifiable to an individual and consisting of descriptions or notations of arrests, detentions, indictments, informations, pre-trial proceedings, trials, or other formal events in the criminal justice system or descriptions or notations of criminal charges (including criminal violations of local municipal ordinances) and the nature of any disposition arising therefrom, including sentencing, court or correctional supervision, rehabilitation, and release. The term does not apply to statistical records and reports in which individuals are not identified and from which their identities are not ascertainable, or to information that is for criminal investigative or intelligence purposes.

(e) The term "unit of general local government" means any county, municipality or other general purpose political subdivision of this State.

(Source: P.A. 85-653.) [Formerly Ill. Rev. Stat. 38 §210-3.]

3930/4. Illinois Criminal Justice Information Authority—Creation, membership and meetings.

§4. Illinois Criminal Justice Information Authority—Creation, membership and meetings. There is created an Illinois Criminal Justice Information Authority consisting of 15 members. The membership of the Authority shall consist of the Illinois Attorney General, or his designee, the Director of the Illinois Department of Corrections, the Director of the Illinois Department of State Police, the Sheriff of Cook County, the State's Attorney of Cook County, the Superintendent of the Chicago Police Department, the Director of the Office of the State's Attorneys Appellate Prosecutor, and the following additional members, each of whom shall be appointed by the Governor: a sheriff and a state's attorney of a county other than Cook, a chief of police, and 5 members of the general public.

The Governor from time to time shall designate a Chairman of the Authority from the membership. All members of the Authority appointed by the Governor shall serve at the pleasure of the Governor for a term not to exceed 4 years. The initial appointed members of the Authority shall serve from January, 1983 until the third Monday in January, 1987 or until their successors are appointed.

The Authority shall meet at least quarterly, and all meetings of the Authority shall be called by the Chairman.

(Source: P.A. 84-1308; 84-1438.) [Formerly Ill. Rev. Stat. 38 §210-4.]

3930/5. No compensation—Expenses.

§5. No Compensation—Expenses. Members of the Authority, other than the Chairman, shall serve without compensation. All members shall be reimbursed for reasonable expenses incurred in connection with their duties.

(Source: P.A. 82-1039.) [Formerly Ill. Rev. Stat. 38 §210-5.]

3930/6. Executive Director.

§6. Executive Director. The Governor shall appoint an Executive Director of the Authority with the advice and consent of the Senate. The Executive Director shall employ, in accordance with the provisions of the Illinois Personnel Code [20 ILCS 415/1 et seq.], such administrative, professional, clerical, and other personnel as may be required. The Executive Director may organize the staff of the Authority as he may deem appropriate.

(Source: P.A. 82-1039.) [Formerly Ill. Rev. Stat. 38 §210-6.]

3930/7. Powers and duties.

§7. Powers and Duties. The Authority shall have the following powers, duties and responsibilities:

(a) To develop and operate comprehensive information systems for the improvement and coordination of all aspects of law enforcement, prosecution and corrections;

(b) To define, develop, evaluate and correlate State and local programs and projects associated with the improvement of law enforcement and the administration of criminal justice;

(c) To act as a central repository and clearing house for federal, state and local research studies, plans, projects, proposals and other information relating to all aspects of criminal justice system improvement and to encourage educational programs for citizen support of State and local efforts to make such improvements;

(d) To undertake research studies to aid in accomplishing its purposes;

(e) To monitor the operation of existing criminal justice information systems in order to protect the constitutional rights and privacy of individuals about whom criminal history record information has been collected;

(f) To provide an effective administrative forum for the protection of the rights of individuals concerning criminal history record information;

(g) To issue regulations, guidelines and procedures which ensure the privacy and security of criminal history record information consistent with State and federal laws;

(h) To act as the sole administrative appeal body in the State of Illinois to conduct hearings and make final determinations concerning individual challenges to the completeness and accuracy of criminal history record information;

(i) To act as the sole, official, criminal justice body in the State of Illinois to conduct annual and periodic audits of the procedures, policies, and practices of the State central repositories for criminal history record information to verify compliance with federal and state laws and regulations governing such information;

(j) To advise the Authority's Statistical Analysis Center;

(k) To apply for, receive, establish priorities for, allocate, disburse and spend grants of funds that are made available by and received on or after January 1, 1983 from private sources or from the United States pursuant to the federal Crime Control Act of 1973, as amended [42 U.S.C. §3701 et seq.], and similar federal legislation, and to enter into agreements with the United States government to further the purposes of this Act, or as may be required as a condition of obtaining federal funds;

(*l*) To receive, expend and account for such funds of the State of Illinois as may be made available to further the purposes of this Act;

(m) To enter into contracts and to cooperate with units of general local government or combinations of such units, State agencies, and criminal justice system agencies of other states for the purpose of carrying out the duties of the Authority imposed by this Act or by the federal Crime Control Act of 1973, as amended;

(n) To enter into contracts and cooperate with units of general local government outside of Illinois, other states' agencies, and private organizations outside of Illinois to provide computer software or design that has been developed for the Illinois criminal justice system, or to participate in the cooperative development or design of new software or systems to be used by the Illinois criminal justice system. Revenues received as a result of such arrangements shall be deposited in the Criminal Justice Information Systems Trust Fund.

(*o*) To establish general policies concerning criminal justice information systems and to promulgate such rules, regulations and procedures as are necessary to the operation of the Authority and to the uniform consideration of appeals and audits;

(p) To advise and to make recommendations to the Governor and the General Assembly on policies relating to criminal justice information systems;

(q) To direct all other agencies under the jurisdiction of the Governor to provide whatever assistance and information the Authority may lawfully require to carry out its functions;

(r) To exercise any other powers that are reasonable and necessary to fulfill the responsibilities of the Authority under this Act and to comply with the requirements of applicable federal law or regulation;

(s) To exercise the rights, powers and duties which have been vested in the Authority by the "Illinois Uniform Conviction Information Act", enacted by the 85th General Assembly, as hereafter amended [20 ILCS 2635/1 et seq.]; and

(t) To exercise the rights, powers and duties which have been vested in the Authority by the Illinois Motor Vehicle Theft Prevention Act [20 ILCS 4005/1 et seq.].

The requirement for reporting to the General Assembly shall be satisfied by filing copies of the report with the Speaker, the Minority Leader and the Clerk of the House of Representatives and the President, the Minority Leader and the Secretary of the Senate and the Legislative Research Unit, as required by Section 3.1 of "An Act to revise the law in relation to the General Assembly", approved February 25, 1874, as amended [25 ILCS 5/3.1], and filing such additional copies with the State Government Report Distribution Center for the General Assembly as is required under paragraph (t) of Section 7 of the State Library Act [15 ILCS 320/7].

(Subd. (t) added by P.A. 86-1408, §9, eff. 1/1/91 only until 1/1/96.)
(Source: P.A. 85-922; 86-1408.) [Formerly Ill. Rev. Stat. 38 §210-7.]

3930/8. Criminal justice agency.

§8. Criminal Justice Agency. The Authority shall be deemed a criminal justice agency under all federal and State laws and regulations, and as such shall have access to any information available to criminal justice agencies.
(Source: P.A. 82-1039.) [Formerly Ill. Rev. Stat. 38 §210-8.]

3930/9. Criminal Justice Information Systems Trust Fund.

§9. Criminal Justice Information Systems Trust Fund. The special fund in the State Treasury known as the Criminal Justice Information Systems Trust Fund shall be funded in part from users' fees collected from criminal justice agencies that are the users of information systems developed and operated for them by the Authority. The users' fees shall be based on pro rated shares according to the share of operating cost that is attributed to each agency, as determined by the Authority. The General Assembly shall make an appropriation from the Criminal Justice Information Systems Trust Fund for the operating expenses of the Authority incident to providing the services described in this Section.
(Source: P.A. 86-1227.) [Formerly Ill. Rev. Stat. 38 §210-9.]

3930/10. Supersedure and transfer.

§10. Supersedure and Transfer. The Illinois Criminal Justice Information Authority created by this Act supersedes and shall assume, exercise and administer all rights, powers, duties and responsibilities vested in the Illinois Law Enforcement Commission by "An Act creating an Illinois Law Enforcement Commission and defining its powers and duties", approved September 20, 1977, as amended [see 20 ILCS 3930/1 et seq.], except:

(a) those rights, powers, duties and responsibilities created by that Act with respect to the operation or administration of juvenile justice programs pursuant to applicable State or federal laws or regulations; and

(b) the right, power, duty and responsibility to allocate, disburse and account for grants of funds actually received by the Illinois Law Enforcement

Commission prior to January 1, 1983 from the United States pursuant to the federal Crime Control Act of 1973, as amended [42 U.S.C. §3701 et seq.], or pursuant to other similar federal legislation.

The transfer to the Illinois Criminal Justice Information Authority of the rights, powers, duties and responsibilities of the Illinois Law Enforcement Commission as provided in this Section shall not be deemed to abolish or diminish the exercise, by the Illinois Law Enforcement Commission or as otherwise provided by law, of those rights, powers, duties and responsibilities described in paragraphs (a) and (b) of this Section which are not transferred to the Authority pursuant to this Section.

Personnel previously assigned to programs transferred pursuant to this Section from the Illinois Law Enforcement Commission to the Authority, other than the Executive Director of the Illinois Law Enforcement Commission, are hereby transferred to the Authority. Effective April 1, 1983, personnel of the Illinois Law Enforcement Commission previously assigned to the function and responsibility described in paragraph (b) above of this Section—except such of those personnel who, immediately prior to April 1, 1983, were either performing such function and responsibility for the primary benefit of, or who were also assigned to the operation or administration of the juvenile justice programs referred to in paragraph (a) above of this Section—shall be transferred to the Authority. The rights of the employees or the State under the "Personnel Code" [20 ILCS 415/1 et seq.] or under any other contract or plan, however, shall not be affected thereby.

All books, records, papers, documents, real or personal property, unexpended appropriations and pending business in any way pertaining to the rights, powers, duties and responsibilities transferred by this Section shall be delivered and transferred to the Authority. Effective April 1, 1983, all books, records, papers, documents, real or personal property, unexpended appropriations, undisbursed grant moneys, if any, and pending business pertaining to the rights, powers, duties and responsibilities described in paragraph (b) of this Section—except such of said items as pertain primarily to the juvenile justice programs referred to in paragraph (a) above of this Section—shall be transferred to the Authority.

All rights, powers, duties and responsibilities transferred pursuant to this Act to the Illinois Criminal Justice Information Authority shall be vested in and shall be exercised by that Authority subject to the provisions of this Act. Each act done in the exercise of such rights, powers and duties shall be exercised by that Authority subject to the provisions of this Act. Each act done in the exercise of such rights, powers and duties shall have the same legal effect as if done by the Illinois Law Enforcement Commission or divisions, officers or employees thereof.

Every person or corporation shall be subject to the same obligations and duties and any penalties, civil or criminal, arising therefrom, and shall have the same rights arising from the exercise of such rights, powers and duties as if such rights, powers and duties had been exercised by the Illinois Law Enforcement Commission or divisions, officers or employees thereof.

Every officer and employee of the Illinois Criminal Justice Information Authority shall, for any offense, be subject to the same penalty or penalties, civil or criminal, as are prescribed by existing law for the same offense by any officer or employee whose powers or duties were transferred to him by this Act.

Whenever reports or notices are required to be made or given or paper or documents furnished or served by any person to or upon the Illinois Law Enforcement Commission or divisions, officers or employees thereof with respect to any rights, powers, duties or responsibilities transferred pursuant to this Act, the same shall be made, given, furnished or served in the same manner to or upon the Illinois Criminal Justice Information Authority.

This Act shall not affect any act done, ratified or cancelled or any right occurring or established or any action or proceeding had or commenced in an administrative, civil, or criminal cause before this Act takes effect; but such actions or proceedings may be prosecuted and continued by the Illinois Criminal Justice Information Authority.

No rule or regulation promulgated by the Illinois Law Enforcement Commission pursuant to an exercise of right, power or duty which has been transferred to the Illinois Criminal Justice Information Authority shall be affected by this Act, and all such rules and regulations shall become the rules and regulations of the Illinois Criminal Justice Information Authority.

(Source: P.A. 82-1039.) [Formerly Ill. Rev. Stat. 38 §210-10.]

3930/11. Other functions.

§11. Other Functions. Effective April 1, 1983, if any of the functions relating to the rights, powers, duties and responsibilities described in paragraph (b) of Section 10 of this Act [20 ILCS 3930/10]—other than such of said functions, if any, as pertain primarily to the juvenile justice programs referred to in paragraph (a) of Section 10 of this Act—have not been fully completed and performed by the Illinois Law Enforcement Commission, the same shall be transferred to and assumed by the Authority.

(Source: P.A. 82-1039.) [Formerly Ill. Rev. Stat. 38 §210-11.]

3930/12. Administrative action and review.

§12. Administrative Action and Review. The Illinois Administrative Procedure Act, as amended [5 ILCS 100/1-1 et seq.], and the rules and regulations adopted thereunder shall apply to and govern all administrative actions taken by the Authority, where applicable, unless otherwise prescribed by this Act. Judicial review of final administrative decisions may be had in accordance with the Administrative Review Law [735 ILCS 5/3-101 et seq.], as now or hereafter amended.

(Source: P.A. 82-1039.) [Formerly Ill. Rev. Stat. 38 §210-12.]

3930/13. Construction of Act.

§13. Construction of Act. This Act shall be liberally construed to achieve the purposes set forth in Section 2 of this Act [20 ILCS 3930/2].

Sections 1 through 13 of this Act [20 ILCS 3930/1 through 3930/13] shall in no respect be considered as a repeal of, nor, except as herein provided with respect to the transfer to the Authority of certain rights, powers, duties and responsibilities of the Illinois Law Enforcement Commission under "An Act creating an Illinois Law Enforcement Commission and defining its powers and duties" [see 20 ILCS 3930/1 et seq.], as a limitation of the provisions of any existing law of this State concerning law enforcement or criminal justice, but shall be construed as supplemental thereto.

(Source: P.A. 82-1039.) [Formerly Ill. Rev. Stat. 38 §210-13.]

3930/14. Illinois Law Enforcement Commission.

§14. Illinois Law Enforcement Commission. Effective April 1, 1983:

(a) The position of Executive Director of the Illinois Law Enforcement Commission is abolished;

(b) The Illinois Law Enforcement Commission is abolished, and the terms and appointments of its members and Chairman are terminated; and

(c) "An Act creating an Illinois Law Enforcement Commission and defining its powers and duties", approved September 20, 1977, as now or hereafter amended [see 20 ILCS 3930/1 et seq.], is repealed.

(Source: P.A. 82-1039.) [Formerly Ill. Rev. Stat. 38 §210-14.]

This page intentionally left blank.

CHAPTER 30
FINANCE

INTERGOVERNMENTAL DRUG LAWS ENFORCEMENT ACT

715/1. Short title.

§1. This Act shall be known and may be cited as the "Intergovernmental Drug Laws Enforcement Act".
(Source: P.A. 80-617.) [Formerly Ill. Rev. Stat. 56½ §1701.]

715/2. Definitions.

§2. As used in this Act, unless the context otherwise requires, the terms specified in Section 2.01 through 2.04 [30 ILCS 715/2.01 through 715/2.04] have the meanings ascribed to them in those Sections.
(Source: P.A. 80-617.) [Formerly Ill. Rev. Stat. 56½ §1702.]

715/2.01. Department; director; definitions.

§2.01. "Department" means the Department of State Police and "Director" means the Director of State Police.
(Source: P.A. 84-25.) [Formerly Ill. Rev. Stat. 56½ §1702.01.]

715/2.02. Metropolitan Enforcement Group; definition.

§2.02. "Metropolitan Enforcement Group" or "MEG" means a combination of units of local government established under this Act to enforce the drug laws of this State.
(Source: P.A. 80-617.) [Formerly Ill. Rev. Stat. 56½ §1702.02.]

715/2.03. Unit of local government; definition.

§2.03. "Unit of local government" is defined as in Article VII, Sec. 1 of the Constitution, and includes both home rule units and units which are not home rule units.
(Source: P.A. 80-617.) [Formerly Ill. Rev. Stat. 56½ §1702.03.]

715/2.04. Drug laws; definition.

§2.04. "Drug laws" means all laws regulating the production, sale, prescribing, manufacturing, administering, transporting, having in possession, dispensing, delivering, distributing or use of "controlled substances", as defined in the Illinois Controlled Substances Act [720 ILCS 570/100 et seq.], and "cannabis", as defined in the Cannabis Control Act [720 ILCS 550/1 et seq.].
(Source: P.A. 80-617.) [Formerly Ill. Rev. Stat. 56½ §1702.04.]

715/3. State grants.

§3. A Metropolitan Enforcement Group which meets the minimum criteria established in this Section is eligible to receive State grants to help defray the costs of operation. To be eligible a MEG must:

(1) Be established and operating pursuant to intergovernmental contracts written and executed in conformity with the Intergovernmental Cooperation Act [5 ILCS 220/1 et seq.], and involve 2 or more units of local government.

(2) Establish a MEG Policy Board composed of an elected official, or his designee, and the chief law enforcement officer, or his designee, from each participating unit of local government to oversee the operations of the MEG and make such reports to the Department of State Police as the Department may require.

(3) Designate a single appropriate elected official of a participating unit of local government to act as the financial officer of the MEG for all participating units of local government and to receive funds for the operation of the MEG.

(4) Limit its operations to enforcement of drug laws.

(5) Cooperate with the Department of State Police in order to assure compliance with this Act and to enable the Department to fulfill its duties under this Act, and supply the Department with all information the Department deems necessary therefor.

(6) Receive funding of at least 50% of the total operating budget of the MEG from the participating units of local government.

(Source: P.A. 84-25.) [Formerly Ill. Rev. Stat. 56½ §1703.]

715/4. Eligibility.

§4. The Department of State Police shall monitor the operations of all MEG units and determine their eligibility to receive State grants under this Act. From the moneys appropriated annually by the General Assembly for this purpose, the Director shall determine and certify to the Comptroller the amount of the grant to be made to each designated MEG financial officer. The amount of the State grant which a MEG may receive hereunder may not exceed 50% of the total operating budget of that MEG.

(Source: P.A. 84-25.) [Formerly Ill. Rev. Stat. 56½ §1704.]

715/5. Rules and regulations.

§5. The Department of State Police shall coordinate the operations of all MEG units and may establish such reasonable rules and regulations and conduct those investigations the Director deems necessary to carry out its duties under this Act, including the establishment of forms for reporting by each MEG to the Department.

(Source: P.A. 84-25.) [Formerly Ill. Rev. Stat. 56½ §1705.]

715/5.1. Functions and duties; assignment.

§5.1. The Director may assign the functions and duties created under this Act to be administered by the Department of State Police, Division of Investigation.

(Source: P.A. 84-25.) [Formerly Ill. Rev. Stat. 56½ §1705.1.]

715/6. Annual reports.

§6. The Director shall report annually, no later than February 1, to the Governor and the General Assembly on the operations of the Metropolitan Enforcement Groups, including a breakdown of the appropriation for the current fiscal year indicating the amount of the State grant each MEG received or will receive.

The requirement for reporting to the General Assembly shall be satisfied by filing copies of the report with the Speaker, the Minority Leader and the Clerk of the House of Representatives and the President, the Minority Leader and the Secretary of the Senate and the Legislative Research Unit, as required by Section 3.1 of "An Act to revise the law in relation to the General Assembly", approved February 25, 1874, as amended [25 ILCS 5/3.1], and filing such additional copies with the State Government Report Distribution Center for the General Assembly as is required under paragraph (t) of Section 7 of the State Library Act [15 ILCS 320/7].

(Source: P.A. 84-1438.) [Formerly Ill. Rev. Stat. 56½ §1706.]

CHAPTER 45
INTERSTATE COMPACTS

INTERSTATE AGREEMENTS ON SEXUALLY DANGEROUS PERSONS ACT

20/0.01. Short title.

§0.01. Short title. This Act may be cited as the Interstate Agreements on Sexually Dangerous Persons Act.

(Source: P.A. 86-1324.) [Formerly Ill. Rev. Stat. 38 §205.]

20/1. Authority of governor in interstate agreements regarding transfers.

§1. The Governor is hereby authorized to enter into reciprocal agreements with other states regarding the interstate transfer and out of state residence of conditionally released persons who are classified as sexually dangerous under the provisions of "An Act in relation to sexually dangerous persons, and providing for their commitment, detention and supervision", approved July 6, 1938, as amended [725 ILCS 205/1.01 et seq.] or so classified under the provisions of "An Act in relation to the Illinois State Penitentiary and to repeal certain parts of designated Acts", approved June 30, 1933, as amended [see 730 ILCS 1003-2-2(c)].

(Source: Laws 1963, p. 3083.) [Formerly Ill. Rev. Stat. 38 §205-1.]

This page intentionally left blank.

CHAPTER 410
PUBLIC HEALTH

SMOKELESS TOBACCO OUTDOOR ADVERTISING ACT

75/0.01. Short title.

§0.01. Short title. This Act may be cited as the Smokeless Tobacco Outdoor Advertising Act.

(Source: P.A. 86-1324.) [Formerly Ill. Rev. Stat. 23 §2358-30.]

75/1. Definition.

§1. As used in this Act, "smokeless tobacco" means any loose, cut, shredded, ground, powdered, compressed or leaf tobacco that is intended to be placed in the mouth without being smoked.

(Source: P.A. 85-518.) [Formerly Ill. Rev. Stat. 23 §2358-31.]

75/2. Billboard advertisement—Smokeless tobacco—Warnings.

§2. All outdoor billboard advertisement for smokeless tobacco shall bear one of the following statements:

WARNING: THIS PRODUCT MAY CAUSE MOUTH CANCER.

WARNING: THIS PRODUCT MAY CAUSE GUM DISEASE AND TOOTH LOSS.

WARNING: THIS PRODUCT IS NOT A SAFE ALTERNATIVE TO CIGARETTES.

The warnings shall be rotated every 4 months by the manufacturer, packager or importer of snuff and chewing tobacco products in an alternating sequence in the advertisement for each brand of such tobacco product. Such warning shall appear in the format and type style prescribed under 15 U.S.C. 1333 (b) (3), as amended.

No other warning, format, or type style in any outdoor billboard advertisement shall be required by any State or local statute or regulation.

Any outdoor billboard advertisement that does not conform to the provisions of this Section shall be deemed a nuisance affecting the public health.

(Source: P.A. 85-518.) [Formerly Ill. Rev. Stat. 23 §2358-32.]

ILLINOIS CLEAN INDOOR AIR ACT

80/1. Short title.

§1. This Act shall be known and may be cited as the "Illinois Clean Indoor Air Act".

(Source: P.A. 86-1018.) [Formerly Ill. Rev. Stat. 111½ §8201.]

80/2. Findings.

§2. The General Assembly finds that tobacco smoke is annoying, harmful and dangerous to human beings and a hazard to public health.
(Source: P.A. 86-1018.) [Formerly Ill. Rev. Stat. 111½ §8202.]

80/3. Definitions.

§3. For the purposes of this Act, the following terms have the meanings ascribed to them in this Section unless different meanings are plainly indicated by the context:

(a) "Department" means the Department of Public Health.

(b) "Proprietor" means any individual or his designated agent who by virtue of his office, position, authority or duties has legal or administrative responsibility for the use or operation of property.

(c) "Public Place" means any enclosed indoor area used by the public or serving as a place of work including, but not limited to, hospitals, restaurants, retail stores, offices, commercial establishments, elevators, indoor theaters, libraries, art museums, concert halls, public conveyances, educational facilities, nursing homes, auditoriums, arenas and meeting rooms, but excluding bowling establishments and excluding places whose primary business is the sale of alcoholic beverages for consumption on the premises and excluding rooms rented for the purpose of living quarters or sleeping or housekeeping accommodations from a hotel, as defined in The Hotel Operators' Occupation Tax Act [35 ILCS 145/1 et seq.] and private, enclosed offices occupied exclusively by smokers even though such offices may be visited by nonsmokers.

(d) "Smoking" means the act of inhaling the smoke from or possessing a lighted cigarette, cigar, pipe or any other form of tobacco or similar substance used for smoking.

(e) "State agency" has the meaning ascribed to it in subsection (a) of Section 3 of The Illinois Purchasing Act [30 ILCS 505/1 et seq.].

(f) "Unit of local government" has the meaning ascribed to it in Section 1 of Article VII of the Illinois Constitution of 1970.
(Source: P.A. 86-1018.) [Formerly Ill. Rev. Stat. 111½ §8203.]

80/4. Restricted areas.

§4. No person shall smoke in a public place except in that portion of a public place which may be established and posted under Section 5 [410 ILCS 80/5] as a smoking area. This prohibition does not apply in cases in which an entire room or hall is used for a private social function and seating arrangements are under the control of the sponsor of the function and not of the proprietor or person in charge of the place. Furthermore, this prohibition shall not apply to factories, warehouses and similar places of work not usually frequented by the general public.
(Source: P.A. 86-1018.) [Formerly Ill. Rev. Stat. 111½ §8204.]

80/5. Establishment of smoking areas.

§5. The elected and appointed officials of the State of Illinois and of any unit of local government and of any school district, or their designee, having control over property of the State or of a unit of local government or of a school district which includes a public place, and the proprietor of a structure which includes a public place may establish an area on the premises as a smoking area where smoking shall be permitted, unless otherwise prohibited by law or ordinance. When establishing an area as a smoking area, a person establishing such area shall utilize existing physical barriers, ventilation systems, and other physical elements of the premises to minimize the intrusion of smoke into areas where smoking is not permitted. When a public place is a single room or enclosure, a person establishing such area may satisfy the purposes and provisions of this

Act by establishing a reasonable portion of the room or enclosure as a smoking area.
(Source: P.A. 86-1018.) [Formerly Ill. Rev. Stat. 111½ §8205.]

80/6. Smoking outside established areas.
§6. The State or unit of local government or school district official or their designee or a proprietor and his agents in control of a place which includes a public place shall make reasonable efforts to prevent smoking in the public place outside established smoking areas by posting appropriate signs or contacting a law enforcement officer, or other appropriate means.
(Source: P.A. 86-1018.) [Formerly Ill. Rev. Stat. 111½ §8206.]

80/7. Violation of Section 80/4.
§7. A person, corporation, partnership, association or other entity, who violates Section 4 of this Act [410 ILCS 80/4] is guilty of a petty offense.
(Source: P.A. 86-1018.) [Formerly Ill. Rev. Stat. 111½ §8207.]

80/8. Violations of Act; court action.
§8. The Department, a local board of health, or any individual personally affected by repeated violations may institute, in a circuit court, an action to enjoin violations of this Act.
(Source: P.A. 86-1018.) [Formerly Ill. Rev. Stat. 111½ §8208.]

80/9. Discrimination not allowed.
§9. No individual may be discriminated against in any manner because of the exercise of any rights afforded by this Act.
(Source: P.A. 86-1018.) [Formerly Ill. Rev. Stat. 111½ §8209.]

80/10. Effect of invalid provisions.
§10. If any provision, clause or paragraph of this Act shall be held invalid by a court of competent jurisdiction, such validity shall not affect the other provisions of this Act.
(Source: P.A. 86-1018.) [Formerly Ill. Rev. Stat. 111½ §8210.]

80/11. Limitations of local governments.
§11. A home rule or non-home rule unit of local government in this State shall not have the power and authority, after the effective date of this Act, to regulate smoking in public places. Pursuant to Article VII, Section 6, paragraph (h) of the Illinois Constitution of 1970, it is declared to be the law of this State that the regulation of smoking as provided by this Act is a power which pre-empts home rule units from exercising such power subject to the limitations provided in the Act, provided that any home rule unit that has passed an ordinance concerning the regulation of smoking prior to October 1, 1989 is exempt from pre-emption.
(Source: P.A. 86-1018.) [Formerly Ill. Rev. Stat. 111½ §8211.]

This page intentionally left blank.

CHAPTER 415
ENVIRONMENTAL SAFETY

LITTER CONTROL ACT

105/1. Short title.

§1. This Act shall be known and may be cited as the "Litter Control Act".
(Source: P.A. 78-837.) [Formerly Ill. Rev. Stat. 38 §86-1.]

105/2. Legislative findings.

§2. The General Assembly finds and determines that:

(i) rapid population growth, the ever increasing mobility of the population and improper and abusive discard habits cause the existence, proliferation and accumulation of litter upon public and private property in this State;

(ii) litter is detrimental to the welfare of the people of this State; and

(iii) while there has been a collective failure by government, industry and the public to develop and accomplish effective litter control, there is a need to educate the public with respect to the problem of litter and to provide for strict enforcement of litter control measures.

This Act is, therefore, necessary to provide for uniform prohibition throughout the State of any and all littering on public or private property so as to protect the health, safety and welfare of the people of this State.
(Source: P.A. 78-837.) [Formerly Ill. Rev. Stat. 38 §86-2.]

105/3. Definitions.

§3. As used in this Act, unless the context otherwise requires:

(a) "Litter" means any discarded, used or unconsumed substance or waste. "Litter" may include, but is not limited to, any garbage, trash, refuse, debris, rubbish, grass clippings or other lawn or garden waste, newspaper, magazines, glass, metal, plastic or paper containers or other packaging construction material, abandoned vehicle (as defined in Section 4-100 of The Illinois Vehicle Code [625 ILCS 5/4-100]), motor vehicle parts, furniture, oil, carcass of a dead animal, any nauseous or offensive matter of any kind, any object likely to injure any person or create a traffic hazard, or anything else of an unsightly or unsanitary nature, which has been discarded, abandoned or otherwise disposed of improperly.

(b) "Motor vehicle" has the meaning ascribed to that term in Section 1-146 of The Illinois Vehicle Code [625 ILCS 5/1-146].

(c) "Person" means any individual, partnership, copartnership, firm, company, corporation, association, joint stock company, trust, estate, or any other legal entity, or their legal representative, agent or assigns.
(Source: P.A. 86-1475.) [Formerly Ill. Rev. Stat. 38 §86-3.]

105/4. Dumping; exemptions.

§4. No person shall dump, deposit, drop, throw, discard, leave, cause or permit the dumping, depositing, dropping, throwing, discarding or leaving of litter upon any public or private property in this State, or upon or into any river, lake, pond, or other stream or body of water in this State, unless:

(a) the property has been designated by the State or any of its agencies, political subdivisions, units of local government or school districts for the disposal of litter, and the litter is disposed of on that property in accordance with the applicable rules and regulations of the Pollution Control Board;

(b) the litter is placed into a receptacle or other container intended by the owner or tenant in lawful possession of that property for the deposit of litter;

(c) the person is the owner or tenant in lawful possession of the property or has first obtained the consent of the owner or tenant in lawful possession, or unless the act is done under the personal direction of the owner or tenant and does not create a public health or safety hazard, a public nuisance, or a fire hazard;

(d) the person is acting under the direction of proper public officials during special cleanup days; or

(e) the person is lawfully acting in or reacting to an emergency situation where health and safety is threatened, and removes and properly disposes of such litter when the emergency situation no longer exists.

(Source: P.A. 78-837.) [Formerly Ill. Rev. Stat. 38 §86-4.]

105/5. Dumping from motor vehicle prohibited.

§5. No person shall dump, deposit, drop, throw, discard or otherwise dispose of litter from any motor vehicle upon any public highway, upon any public or private property or upon or into any river, lake, pond, stream or body of water in this State except as permitted under any of paragraphs (a) through (e) of Section 4 [415 ILCS 105/4]. Nor shall any person transport by any means garbage or refuse from any dwelling, residence, place of business, farm or other site to and deposit such material in, around or on top of trash barrels or other receptacles placed along public highways or at roadside rest areas.

(Source: P.A. 78-837.) [Formerly Ill. Rev. Stat. 38 §86-5.]

105/6. Accumulation of litter.

§6. No person shall allow litter to accumulate upon real property, of which the person charged is the owner or tenant in control, in such a manner as to constitute a public nuisance or in such a manner that the litter may be blown or otherwise carried by the natural elements on to the real property of another person.

(Source: P.A. 78-837.) [Formerly Ill. Rev. Stat. 38 §86-6.]

105/7. Abandonment of motor vehicle.

§7. No person shall abandon a motor vehicle on any highway, on any public property or on any private property of which he is not the owner or tenant in lawful possession in this State. The person to whom last was issued the certificate of title to the vehicle by the Secretary of State is presumed to be the person to have abandoned that vehicle, but such presumption may be rebutted.

(Source: P.A. 78-837.) [Formerly Ill. Rev. Stat. 38 §86-7.]

105/8. Violations.

§8. Persons who violate any of Sections 4 through 7 are subject to the penalties set out in this Section.

(a) Any person convicted of a violation of Section 4, 5, 6 or 7 [415 ILCS 105/4, 105/5, 105/6 or 105/7] is guilty of a Class B misdemeanor. A second conviction for an offense committed after the first conviction is a Class A misdemeanor. A third or subsequent violation, committed after a second conviction is a Class 4 felony.

(b) In addition to any fine imposed under this Act, the court may order that the person convicted of such a violation remove and properly dispose of the litter, may employ special bailiffs to supervise such removal and disposal, and may tax the costs of such supervision as costs against the person so convicted.

(c) The penalties prescribed in this Section are in addition to, and not in lieu of, any penalties, rights, remedies, duties or liabilities otherwise imposed or conferred by law.

(Source: P.A. 85-1410.) [Formerly Ill. Rev. Stat. 38 §86-8.]

105/9. Presumption of violation by operator.

§9. Whenever litter is thrown, deposited, dropped or dumped from any motor vehicle not carrying passengers for hire, the presumption is created that the operator of that motor vehicle has violated Section 5 [415 ILCS 105/5], but that presumption may be rebutted.

(Source: P.A. 78-837.) [Formerly Ill. Rev. Stat. 38 §86-9.]

105/10. Placing and maintaining receptacles for litter.

§10. In order to assist the public in complying with this Act, the owner or person in control of any property which is held out to the public as a place for assemblage, the transaction of business, recreation or as a public way shall cause to be placed and maintained receptacles for the deposit of litter, of sufficient volume and in sufficient numbers to meet the needs of the numbers of people customarily coming on or using the property.

For purposes of this Section, "property held out to the public for the transaction of business" includes, but is not limited to, commercially-operated parks, campgrounds, drive-in restaurants, automobile service stations, business parking lots, car washes, shopping centers, marinas, boat launching areas, industrial parking lots, boat moorage and fueling stations, piers, beaches and bathing areas, airports, roadside rest stops, drive-in movies, and shopping malls; and "property held out to the public for assemblage, recreation or as a public way" includes, but is not limited to, any property that is publicly owned or operated for any of the purposes stated in the definition in this paragraph for "property held out to the public for the transaction of business" but excludes State highway rights-of-way and rest areas located thereon.

The Secretary of Transportation and the Director of Conservation shall prescribe the type or types of litter receptacles to be placed on property under the jurisdiction of the Department of Transportation and of the Department of Conservation, respectively. The Secretary of Transportation shall also promulgate rules and regulations governing the placement of receptacles on property under the jurisdiction of the Department of Transportation.

If no litter receptacles are placed on property described in this Section, the owner or person in control of the property may be convicted of a petty offense and fined $100 for violating this Section. If the owner or person in control of such property has placed litter receptacles on his property but the number or size of such receptacles has proved inadequate to meet the needs of the numbers of people coming on or using his property as indicated by the condition and appearance of that property, and the owner or person in control has failed to provide sufficient or adequate receptacles within 10 days after being made aware of that fact by written notice from the appropriate law enforcement agency, he may be convicted of a petty offense and fined $25 for each receptacle not so provided and maintained.

(Source: P.A. 78-837.) [Formerly Ill. Rev. Stat. 38 §86-10.]

105/11. Enforcement of act.

§11. This Act shall be enforced by all law enforcement officers in their respective jurisdictions, whether employed by the State or by any unit of local government. Prosecutions for violation of this Act shall be conducted by the State attorneys of the several counties and by the Attorney General of this State.

(Source: P.A. 78-837.) [Formerly Ill. Rev. Stat. 38 §86-11.]

105/13. Severability.

§13. If any provision of this Act, or the application of such provision to any person or circumstance is held invalid, such invalidity shall not affect other provisions or applications of the Act which can be given effect without the invalid provision or application, and to this end the provisions of this Act are declared to be severable.

(Source: P.A. 78-837.) [Formerly Ill. Rev. Stat. 38 §86-13.]

105/14. Effective date.

§14. This Act takes effect January 1, 1974.

(Source: P.A. 78-837.) [Formerly Ill. Rev. Stat. 38 §86-14.]

CHAPTER 430
PUBLIC SAFETY

FIREARM OWNERS IDENTIFICATION CARD ACT

65/0.01. Short title.

§0.01. Short title. This Act may be cited as the Firearm Owners Identification Card Act.
(Source: P.A. 86-1324.) [Formerly Ill. Rev. Stat. 38 §83-0.1.]

65/1. Declaration of legislative determination.

§1. It is hereby declared as a matter of legislative determination that in order to promote and protect the health, safety and welfare of the public, it is necessary and in the public interest to provide a system of identifying persons who are not qualified to acquire or possess firearms and firearm ammunition within the State of Illinois by the establishment of a system of Firearm Owner's Identification Cards, thereby establishing a practical and workable system by which law enforcement authorities will be afforded an opportunity to identify those persons who are prohibited by Section 24-3.1 of the "Criminal Code of 1961", as amended [720 ILCS 5/24-3.1], from acquiring or possessing firearms and firearm ammunition.
(Source: Laws 1967, p. 2600.) [Formerly Ill. Rev. Stat. 38 §83-1.]

65/1.1. Definitions.

§1.1. For purposes of this Act: "Firearm" means any device, by whatever name known, which is designed to expel a projectile or projectiles by the action of an explosion, expansion of gas or escape of gas; excluding, however:

(1) any pneumatic gun, spring gun, paint ball gun or B-B gun which either expels a single globular projectile not exceeding .18 inch in diameter and which has a maximum muzzle velocity of less than 700 feet per second or breakable paint balls containing washable marking colors;

(2) any device used exclusively for signalling or safety and required or recommended by the United States Coast Guard or the Interstate Commerce Commission; or

(3) any device used exclusively for the firing of stud cartridges, explosive rivets or similar industrial ammunition;

(4) an antique firearm (other than a machine-gun) which, although designed as a weapon, the Department of State Police finds by reason of the date of its manufacture, value, design, and other characteristics is primarily a collector's item and is not likely to be used as a weapon.

"Firearm Ammunition" means any self-contained cartridge or shotgun shell, by whatever name known, which is designed to be used or adaptable to use in a firearm; excluding, however:

(1) any ammunition exclusively designed for use with a device used exclusively for signalling or safety and required or recommended by the United States Coast Guard or the Interstate Commerce Commission; or

(2) any ammunition designed exclusively for use with a stud or rivet driver or other similar industrial ammunition.

(Source: P.A. 86-349; 86-1265.) [Formerly Ill. Rev. Stat. 38 §83-1.1.]

65/2. Firearm Owner's Identification Card required; exceptions.

§2. Firearm Owner's Identification Card required; exceptions. (a) No person may acquire or possess any firearm or any firearm ammunition within this State without having in his possession a Firearm Owner's Identification Card previously issued in his name by the Department of State Police under the provisions of this Act.

(b) The provisions of this Section regarding the possession of firearms and firearm ammunition do not apply to:

(1) United States Marshals, while engaged in the operation of their official duties;

(2) Members of the Armed Forces of the United States or the National Guard, while engaged in the operation of their official duties;

(3) Federal officials required to carry firearms, while engaged in the operation of their official duties;

(4) Members of bona fide veterans organizations which receive firearms directly from the armed forces of the United States, while using the firearms for ceremonial purposes with blank ammunition;

(5) Nonresident hunters during hunting season, with valid nonresident hunting licenses and while in an area where hunting is permitted; however, at all other times and in all other places these persons must have their firearms unloaded and enclosed in a case;

(6) Those hunters exempt from obtaining a hunting license who are required to submit their Firearm Owner's Identification Card when hunting on Department of Conservation owned or managed sites;

(7) Nonresidents while on a firing or shooting range recognized by the Department of State Police; however, these persons must at all other times and in all other places have their firearms unloaded and enclosed in a case;

(8) Nonresidents while at a firearm showing or display recognized by the Department of State Police; however, at all other times and in all other places these persons must have their firearms unloaded and enclosed in a case;

(9) Nonresidents whose firearms are unloaded and enclosed in a case;

(10) Nonresidents who are currently licensed or registered to possess a firearm in their resident state;

(11) Unemancipated minors while in the custody and immediate control of their parent or legal guardian or other person in loco parentis to the minor if the parent or legal guardian or other person in loco parentis to the minor has a currently valid Firearm Owner's Identification Card;

(12) Color guards of bona fide veterans organizations or members of bona fide American Legion bands while using firearms for ceremonial purposes with blank ammunition;

(13) Nonresident hunters whose state of residence does not require them to be licensed or registered to possess a firearm and only during hunting season, with valid hunting licenses, while accompanied by, and using a firearm owned by, a person who possesses a valid Firearm Owner's Identification Card and while in an area within a commercial club licensed under the Wildlife Code [520 ILCS 5/1.1 et seq.] where hunting is permitted and controlled, but in no instance upon sites owned or managed by the Department of Conservation; and

(14) Resident hunters who are properly authorized to hunt and, while accompanied by a person who possesses a valid Firearm Owner's Identification Card, hunt in an area within a commercial club licensed under the Wildlife Code where hunting is permitted and controlled.

(c) The provisions of this Section regarding the acquisition and possession of firearms and firearm ammunition do not apply to law enforcement officials of this or any other jurisdiction, while engaged in the operation of their official duties.

(Source: P.A. 87-240.) [Formerly Ill. Rev. Stat. 38 §83-2.]

65/3. Transfer of firearm.

§3. (a) Except as provided in Section 3a [430 ILCS 65/3a], no person within this State may knowingly transfer, or cause to be transferred, any firearm or any firearm ammunition to any person within this State unless the transferee with whom he deals displays a currently valid Firearm Owner's Identification Card which has previously been issued in his name by the Department of State Police under the provisions of this Act. In addition, all firearm transfers by federally licensed firearm dealers are subject to Section 3.1 [430 ILCS 65/3.1].

(b) Any person within this State who transfers or causes to be transferred any firearm shall keep a record of such transfer for a period of 10 years from the date of transfer. Such record shall contain the date of the transfer; the description, serial number or other information identifying the firearm if no serial number is available; and, if the transfer was completed within this State, the transferee's Firearm Owner's Identification Card number. On demand of a peace officer such transferor shall produce for inspection such record of transfer.

(c) The provisions of this Section regarding the transfer of firearm ammunition shall not apply to those persons specified in paragraph (b) of Section 2 of this Act [430 ILCS 65/2].

(Source: P.A. 87-299.) [Formerly Ill. Rev. Stat. 38 §83-3.]

65/3a. Firearms; owner's identification cards; purchase: reciprocity.

§3a. (a) Any resident of Illinois who has obtained a firearm owner's identification card pursuant to this Act and who is not otherwise prohibited from obtaining, possessing or using a firearm may purchase or obtain a rifle or shotgun or ammunition for a rifle or shotgun in Iowa, Missouri, Indiana, Wisconsin or Kentucky.

(b) Any resident of Iowa, Missouri, Indiana, Wisconsin or Kentucky, who is 18 years of age or older and who is not prohibited by the laws of Illinois, the state of his domicile, or the United States from obtaining, possessing or using a firearm, may purchase or obtain a rifle, shotgun or ammunition for a rifle or shotgun in Illinois.

(c) Any transaction under this Section is subject to the provisions of the Gun Control Act of 1968 (18 U.S.C. 922 (b)(3)).

(Source: P.A. 84-442; 84-819.) [Formerly Ill. Rev. Stat. 38 §83-3a.]

65/3.1. Dial up system.

§3.1. Dial up system. The Department of State Police shall provide a dial up telephone system which shall be used by any federally licensed firearm dealer who is to transfer a firearm under the provisions of this Act. The

Department of State Police shall utilize existing technology which allows the caller to be charged a fee equivalent to the cost of providing this service but not to exceed $2. Fees collected by the Department of State Police shall be deposited in the State Police Services Fund and used to provide the service.

Upon receiving a request from a federally licensed firearm dealer, the Department of State Police shall immediately approve, or within the time period established by Section 24-3 of the Criminal Code of 1961 [720 ILCS 5/24-3] regarding the delivery of firearms, notify the inquiring dealer of any objection that would disqualify the transferee from acquiring or possessing a firearm. In conducting the inquiry, the Department of State Police shall initiate and complete an automated search of its criminal history record information files and those of the Federal Bureau of Investigation and of the files of the Department of Mental Health and Developmental Disabilities to obtain any felony conviction or patient hospitalization information which would disqualify a person from obtaining or require revocation of a currently valid Firearm Owner's Identification Card.

The Department of State Police shall promulgate rules to implement this system.

The Governor shall appoint a 9 member Committee that shall consist of the following: the Director of the Department of State Police, who shall serve as its chairman; the Mayor of Chicago, or his representative; a State's Attorney; an individual representing a private organization that opposes strict regulation of firearms; an individual representing a private organization that supports strict regulation of firearms; 4 members of the General Assembly, one each nominated by the President and Minority Leader of the Senate and the Speaker and Minority Leader of the House of Representatives. The Committee shall study and make recommendations to the Governor and the General Assembly regarding the continuation or abolition of the "dial up system" or the "Firearm Owners Identification Card Act" [430 ILCS 65/0.01 et seq.] or any combination thereof, no later than December 31, 1993. The Committee shall submit an interim report, which shall be due no later than December 31, 1992, at which time a recommendation may be made, if appropriate.

This Section is repealed September 1, 1994.

(Source: P.A. 87-299.) [Formerly Ill. Rev. Stat. 38 §83-3.1.]

65/4. Application for Firearm Owner's Identification Card.

§4. (a) Each applicant for a Firearm Owner's Identification Card shall:

(1) Make application on blank forms prepared and furnished at convenient locations throughout the State by the Department of State Police; and

(2) Submit evidence under penalty of perjury to the Department of State Police that:

(i) He is 21 years of age or over, or if he is under 21 years of age that he has the written consent of his parent or legal guardian to possess and acquire firearms and firearm ammunition and that he has never been convicted of a misdemeanor other than a traffic offense or adjudged delinquent, provided, however, that such parent or legal guardian is not an individual prohibited from having a Firearm Owner's Identification Card and files an affidavit with the Department as prescribed by the Department stating that he is not an individual prohibited from having a Card;

(ii) He has not been convicted of a felony under the laws of this or any other jurisdiction;

(iii) He is not addicted to narcotics;

(iv) He has not been a patient in a mental institution within the past 5 years; and

(v) He is not mentally retarded.

(b) Each application form shall include the following statement printed in bold type: "Warning: False statements of the applicant shall result in prosecution for perjury in accordance with Section 32-2 of the Criminal Code of 1961." [720 ILCS 5/32-2].

(c) Upon such written consent, pursuant to Section 4, paragraph (a) (2) (i), the parent or legal guardian giving the consent shall be liable for any damages resulting from the applicant's use of firearms or firearm ammunition.
(Source: P.A. 84-25.) [Formerly Ill. Rev. Stat. 38 §83-4.]

65/5. Approval or denial of application, fees.

§5. The Department of State Police shall either approve or deny all applications within 30 days from the date they are received, and every applicant found qualified pursuant to Section 8 of this Act [430 ILCS 65/8] by the Department shall be entitled to a Firearm Owner's Identification Card upon the payment of a $5 fee. $3 of each fee derived from the issuance of Firearm Owner's Identification Cards, or renewals thereof, shall be deposited in the Wildlife and Fish Fund in the State Treasury; $1 of such fee shall be deposited in the General Revenue Fund in the State Treasury and $1 of such fee shall be deposited in the Firearm Owner's Notification Fund. Monies in the Firearm Owner's Notification Fund shall be used exclusively to pay for the cost of sending notices of expiration of Firearm Owner's Identification Cards under Section 13.2 of this Act [430 ILCS 65/13.2]. Excess monies in the Firearm Owner's Notification Fund shall be used to ensure the prompt and efficient processing of applications received under Section 4 of this Act [430 ILCS 65/4].
(Source: P.A. 84-1426.) [Formerly Ill. Rev. Stat. 38 §83-5.]

65/6. Contents.

§6. A Firearm Owner's Identification Card, issued by the Department of State Police at such places as the Director of the Department shall specify, shall contain the applicant's name, residence, date of birth, sex, physical description, recent photograph and such other personal identifying information as may be required by the Director. Each Firearm Owner's Identification Card must have printed on it the following: "CAUTION - This card does not permit bearer to UNLAWFULLY carry or use firearms."
(Source: P.A. 84-25.) [Formerly Ill. Rev. Stat. 38 §83-6.]

65/7. Duration.

§7. Except as provided in Section 8 of this Act [430 ILCS 65/8], a Firearm Owner's Identification Card issued under the provisions of this Act shall be valid for the person to whom it is issued for a period of 5 years from the date of issuance.
(Source: Laws 1967, p. 2600.) [Formerly Ill. Rev. Stat. 38 §83-7.]

65/8. Notice of denial of application or revocation or seizure of card.

§8. The Department of State Police has authority to deny an application for or to revoke and seize a Firearm Owner's Identification Card previously issued under this Act only if the Department finds that the applicant or the person to whom such card was issued is or was at the time of issuance:

(a) A person under 21 years of age who has been convicted of a misdemeanor other than a traffic offense or adjudged delinquent;

(b) A person under 21 years of age who does not have the written consent of his parent or guardian to acquire and possess firearms and firearm ammunition, or whose parent or guardian has revoked such written consent, or where such parent or guardian does not qualify to have a Firearm Owner's Identification Card;

(c) A person convicted of a felony under the laws of this or any other jurisdiction;

(d) A person addicted to narcotics;

(e) A person who has been a patient of a mental institution within the past 5 years; or

(f) A person whose mental condition is of such a nature that it poses a clear and present danger to the applicant, any other person or persons or the community.

For the purposes of this Section, "mental condition" means a state of mind manifested by violent, suicidal, threatening or assaultive behavior.

(g) A person who is mentally retarded; or

(h) A person who intentionally makes a false statement in the Firearm Owner's Identification Card application.

(Source: P.A. 86-882.) [Formerly Ill. Rev. Stat. 38 §83-8.]

65/8.1. Convictions—Notification to Department.

§8.1. The Circuit Clerk shall, in the form and manner required by the Supreme Court, notify the Department of State Police of all final dispositions of cases for which the Department has received information reported to it under Section 2.1 of the Criminal Identification Act [20 ILCS 2630/2.1].

(Chgd. by P.A. 87-905, §2, eff. 8/14/92.)

(Source: P.A. 84-25.) [Formerly Ill. Rev. Stat. 38 §83-8.1.]

65/9. Notification of grounds for denial of application, revocation or seizure of card.

§9. Every person whose application for a Firearm Owner's Identification Card is denied, and every holder of such a Card before his Card is revoked or seized, shall receive a written notice from the Department of State Police stating specifically the grounds upon which his application has been denied or upon which his Identification Card has been revoked.

(Source: P.A. 84-25.) [Formerly Ill. Rev. Stat. 38 §83-9.]

65/10. Appeal.

§10. (a) Whenever an application for a Firearm Owner's Identification Card is denied, whenever the Department fails to act on an application within 30 days of its receipt, or whenever such a Card is revoked or seized as provided for in Section 8 of this Act [430 ILCS 65/8], the aggrieved party may appeal to the Director of the Department of State Police for a hearing upon such denial, revocation or seizure.

(b) Whenever, upon the receipt of such an appeal for a hearing, the Director is satisfied that substantial justice has not been done, he may order a hearing to be held by the Department upon the denial or revocation.

(c) Any person prohibited from possessing a firearm under Sections 24-1.1 or 24-3.1 of the Criminal Code of 1961 [720 ILCS 5/24-1.1 or 5/24-3.1] or acquiring a Firearm Owner's Identification Card under Section 8 of this Act may apply to the Director of the Department of State Police requesting relief from such prohibition and the Director may grant such relief if it is established by the applicant to the Director's satisfaction that:

(1) the applicant has not been convicted of a forcible felony under the laws of this State or any other jurisdiction within 20 years of the applicant's application for a Firearm Owner's Identification Card, or at least 20 years have passed since the end of any period of imprisonment imposed in relation to that conviction,

(2) the circumstances regarding a criminal conviction, where applicable, the applicant's criminal history and his reputation are such that the applicant will not be likely to act in a manner dangerous to public safety; and

(3) granting relief would not be contrary to the public interest.

(Source: P.A. 85-920.) [Formerly Ill. Rev. Stat. 38 §83-10.]

65/11. Judicial review.

§11. All final administrative decisions of the Department under this Act shall be subject to judicial review under the provisions of the Administrative Review Law, and all amendments and modifications thereof [735 ILCS 5/3-101 et seq.], and the rules adopted pursuant thereto. The term "administrative decision" is defined as in Section 3-101 of the Code of Civil Procedure [735 ILCS 5/3-101].

The Director of State Police shall submit a report to the General Assembly on March 1 of each year, beginning March 1, 1991, listing all final decisions by a court of this State upholding, reversing, or reversing in part any administrative decision made by the Department of State Police.

(Source: P.A. 86-882.) [Formerly Ill. Rev. Stat. 38 §83-11.]

65/12. Death of owner.

§12. The provisions of this Act shall not apply to the passing or transfer of any firearm or firearm ammunition upon the death of the owner thereof to his heir or legatee or to the passing or transfer of any firearm or firearm ammunition incident to any legal proceeding or action until 60 days after such passing or transfer.

(Source: Laws 1967, p. 2600.) [Formerly Ill. Rev. Stat. 38 §83-12.]

65/13. Acquisition or possession of firearms prohibited by law.

§13. Nothing in this Act shall make lawful the acquisition or possession of firearms or firearm ammunition which is otherwise prohibited by law.

(Source: Laws 1967, p. 2600.) [Formerly Ill. Rev. Stat. 38 §83-13.]

65/13.1. Municipal ordinance unaffected where more restrictive or where imposing further limitations.

§13.1. The provisions of any ordinance enacted by any municipality which requires registration or imposes greater restrictions or limitations on the acquisition, possession and transfer of firearms than are imposed by this Act, are not invalidated or affected by this Act.

(Source: P.A. 76-1939.) [Formerly Ill. Rev. Stat. 38 §83-13.1.]

65/13.2. Firearm Owner's Identification Card—Notification of expiration.

§13.2. The Department of State Police shall, 30 days prior to the expiration of a Firearm Owner's Identification Card, forward each person whose card is to expire a notification of the expiration of the card and an application which may be used to apply for renewal of the card.

(Source: P.A. 84-25.) [Formerly Ill. Rev. Stat. 38 §83-13.2.]

65/14. Sentence.

§14. Sentence. Violation of this Act is a Class A misdemeanor.

(Source: P.A. 77-2644.) [Formerly Ill. Rev. Stat. 38 §83-14.]

65/15. Severability.

§15. If any provision of this Act or application thereof to any person or circumstance is held invalid, such invalidity does not affect other provisions or applications of this Act which can be given effect without the invalid application or provision, and to this end the provisions of this Act are declared to be severable.

(Source: Laws 1967, p. 2600.) [Formerly Ill. Rev. Stat. 38 §83-15.]

65/15a. Transfer of records.

§15a. When this amendatory Act enacted by the Seventy-Sixth General Assembly takes effect the records of the Department of Public Safety relating to the administration of the Act amended shall be transferred to the Department

of State Police. All Firearm Owner's Identification Cards issued by the Department of Public Safety shall be valid for the period for which they were issued unless revoked or seized in the manner provided in the Act amended. The Department of State Police as the successor to the Department of Public Safety shall have the rights, powers and duties provided in, and be subject to the provisions of sections 32, 33 and 34 of "The Civil Administrative Code of Illinois" [20 ILCS 5/32, 5/33 and 5/34].
(Source: P.A. 84-25.) [Formerly Ill. Rev. Stat. 38 §83-15a.]

65/16. Referendum.
§16. When 2% of the number of registered voters in the State desire to pass upon the question of whether the General Assembly should repeal this Act regulating the acquisition, possession and transfer of firearms and firearm ammunition, they shall, at least 78 days before a regular election to be held throughout the State, file in the office of the State Board of Elections, a petition directed to the Board in accordance with the general election law. The petition shall be composed of county petitions from each of the counties throughout the State and each county petition shall contain the signatures of at least 2% of the number of registered voters in the county. The petition shall request that the question "Should the General Assembly repeal the Act entitled 'An Act relating to the acquisition, possession and transfer of firearms and firearm ammunition, to provide a penalty for the violation thereof and to make an appropriation in connection therewith,' approved August 3, 1967, as amended?" [430 ILCS 65/1 et seq.] be submitted to the voters of the State at the next ensuing State-wide election at which such question may be acted upon.
(Source: P.A. 81-1489.) [Formerly Ill. Rev. Stat. 38 §83-16.]

65/16.1. Form of petition for referendum.
§16.1. A petition for the submission of the proposition shall be in substantially the following form:

To the State Board of Elections

The undersigned, residents and registered voters of the State of Illinois, respectfully petition that you cause to be submitted, in the manner provided by the general election law to the voters of the State of Illinois, at the next State-wide election, the proposition "Should the General Assembly repeal an Act entitled 'An Act relating to the acquisition, possession and transfer of firearms and firearm ammunition, to provide a penalty for the violation thereof and to make an appropriation in connection therewith', approved August 3, 1967, as amended?" [430 ILCS 65/1 et seq.]

Such petition shall conform to the requirements of the general election law. The Board shall certify the question to the proper election officials who shall submit the question at an election in accordance with the general election law. Upon request of any citizen for a reproduced copy of the petition and paying or tendering to the State Board of Elections the costs of making the copy, the Board shall immediately make, or cause to be made a reproduced copy of such petition. The Board shall also deliver to such person his official certification that such copy is a true copy of the original, stating the day when such original was filed in its office.
(Source: P.A. 81-1489.) [Formerly Ill. Rev. Stat. 38 §83-16.1.]

65/16.3. Ballot.
§16.3. The Secretary of State shall cause the question to be plainly printed upon separate ballots as follows:

Should the General Assembly repeal the Act entitled "An Act relating to the acquisition, possession and transfer of firearms and firearm ammunition, to provide a penalty for the violation thereof and to make an appropriation in connection therewith", approved August 3, 1967, as amended?	YES	
	NO	

(Source: P.A. 77-1819.) [Formerly Ill. Rev. Stat. 38 §83-16.3.]

ILLINOIS PUBLIC DEMONSTRATIONS LAW

70/1. Short title.

§1. Short title. This Act shall be known as the "Illinois Public Demonstrations Law".
(Source: Laws 1967, p. 3613.) [Formerly Ill. Rev. Stat. 38 §85-1.]

70/2. Declaration of purpose.

§2. Declaration of purpose. It is declared to be the public policy of this State: That the maintenance of good order on highways, as defined in Section 2-202 of the "Illinois Highway Code" [605 ILCS 5/2-202], is a paramount responsibility of democratic government;

That the public health, welfare and safety of the community require that the movement of vehicular traffic on such roadways be lawfully conducted with a minimum of disruption;

That the practice of unhindered or unrestrained picketing or demonstrating on such roadways has caused disruption of police, fire and emergency services, and injury to persons regardless of participation in the march, assembly or demonstration;

That the practice of multiple demonstrations on the same day in different locations in municipalities and unincorporated areas of counties has unreasonably deprived the citizens of the police, fire and emergency services; and

That the provisions herein enacted are necessary for the protection of the health, welfare and safety of the public.
(Source: P.A. 81-840.) [Formerly Ill. Rev. Stat. 38 §85-2.]

70/3. Unlawful action—Parade permit.

§3. Unlawful action—Parade permit. It is unlawful for any person, group or organization to conduct or participate in any march, assembly, meeting or gathering on roadways in more than one specific area of or location in, any municipality or the unincorporated area of a county, on any given day, unless it is acting under authority of a duly issued municipal or county parade or demonstration permit if local ordinance or regulation requires such permit, or, if not, with permission of the principal law enforcement officer for such area.
(Source: Laws 1967, p. 3613.) [Formerly Ill. Rev. Stat. 38 §85-3.]

70/4. Acting with other groups—Size of assemblage.

§4. Acting with other groups—Size of assemblage. It is unlawful for any group or organization or any individual acting with such group or organization,

to conduct or participate in any march, assembly, meeting or gathering on roadways unless such march, assembly, meeting, or gathering is limited to such numbers as, in the opinion of the principal law enforcement officer, will not obstruct pedestrian or vehicular traffic in an unreasonable manner. The principal law enforcement officer shall, within 12 hours of receiving the notice required by Section 5 [430 ILCS 70/5], inform the group or organization as to the limitation on number of persons allowed to participate.
(Source: Laws 1967, p. 3613.) [Formerly Ill. Rev. Stat. 38 §85-4.]

70/5. Notice of assemblage in writing—Contents.

§5. Notice of assemblage in writing—Contents. It is unlawful for any group or organization to conduct or participate in any march, assembly, meeting or gathering on roadways unless the principal law enforcement officer has been given notice in writing of the location, the maximum number of persons participating, and the names and addresses of the organizers of any such march, assembly, meeting or gathering, its route, and its time of inception and duration at least 24 hours before such inception.
(Source: Laws 1967, p. 3613.) [Formerly Ill. Rev. Stat. 38 §85-5.]

70/6. Time of holding.

§6. Time of holding. It is unlawful for any group, organization, or any individual to conduct or participate in any march, assembly, meeting or gathering on roadways during peak traffic periods unless authorized by the principal law enforcement officer for the area in which the march, assembly, meeting or gathering is to be held. Peak traffic periods, unless otherwise set by municipal or county authority, are for the purposes of this Act declared to be 7:30 a.m. o'clock to 9:00 a.m. o'clock in the forenoon, and from 4:30 p.m. o'clock to 6:00 p.m. o'clock in the afternoon, Monday through Friday except for State and National holidays.
(Source: Laws 1967, p. 3613.) [Formerly Ill. Rev. Stat. 38 §85-6.]

70/7. Conflict with municipal ordinance.

§7. Conflict with municipal ordinance. Nothing in this Act shall be construed to invalidate or repeal by inference any local or municipal enactment in regard to parades or demonstrations, but if there is an unreconcilable conflict this Act shall prevail as to such portion or portions that are in direct conflict, except as to duly designated peak hours of traffic within its boundaries.
(Source: Laws 1967, p. 3613.) [Formerly Ill. Rev. Stat. 38 §85-7.]

70/8. Sentence.

§8. Sentence. Violation of this Act is a Class A misdemeanor.
(Source: P.A. 77-2646.) [Formerly Ill. Rev. Stat. 38 §85-8.]

70/9. Severability.

§9. Severability. If any provision or term of this Act, or any application thereof, is held invalid, the invalidity shall not affect other applications of the provisions or terms, or other provisions or terms of this Act, which reasonably can be given effect without the invalid provision or term, or the application thereof.
(Source: Laws 1967, p. 3613.) [Formerly Ill. Rev. Stat. 38 §85-9.]

CHAPTER 705
COURTS

CHILD WITNESS TRAUMA REDUCTION ACT

80/1. Education programs for circuit judges.

The Illinois Supreme Court is hereby authorized to establish programs to educate Illinois circuit and associate circuit judges on the techniques and methods of reducing or eliminating the trauma of testifying at trial for children who are witnesses or victims in criminal sexual offense cases. The cost of conducting such programs shall be paid from funds appropriated for that purpose.
(Source: P.A. 84-1426.) [Formerly Ill. Rev. Stat. 37 §801.]

JUVENILE COURT ACT OF 1987

ARTICLE I. GENERAL PROVISIONS

405/1-1. Short title.

§1-1. Short title. This Act shall be known and may be cited as the Juvenile Court Act of 1987.
(Source: P.A. 85-601.) [Formerly Ill. Rev. Stat. 37 §801-1.]

405/1-2. Purpose and policy.

§1-2. Purpose and policy. (1) The purpose of this Act is to secure for each minor subject hereto such care and guidance, preferably in his or her own home, as will serve the moral, emotional, mental, and physical welfare of the minor and the best interests of the community; to preserve and strengthen the minor's family ties whenever possible, removing him or her from the custody of his or her parents only when his or her welfare or safety or the protection of the public cannot be adequately safeguarded without removal; and, when the minor is removed from his or her own family, to secure for him or her custody, care and discipline as nearly as possible equivalent to that which should be given by his or her parents, and in cases where it should and can properly be done to place the minor in a family home so that he or she may become a member of the family by legal adoption or otherwise.

(2) In all proceedings under this Act the court may direct the course thereof so as promptly to ascertain the jurisdictional facts and fully to gather information bearing upon the current condition and future welfare of persons subject to this Act. This Act shall be administered in a spirit of humane concern, not only for the rights of the parties, but also for the fears and the limits of understanding of all who appear before the court.

(3) In all procedures under this Act, the following shall apply:

(a) The procedural rights assured to the minor shall be the rights of adults unless specifically precluded by laws which enhance the protection of such minors.

(b) Every child has a right to services necessary to his or her proper development, including health, education and social services.

(c) The parents' right to the custody of their child shall not prevail when the court determines that it is contrary to the best interests of the child.

(4) This Act shall be liberally construed to carry out the foregoing purpose and policy.

(Source: P.A. 85-601.) [Formerly Ill. Rev. Stat. 37 §801-2.]

405/1-3. Definitions.

§1-3. Definitions. Terms used in this Act, unless the context otherwise requires, have the following meanings ascribed to them:

(1) Adjudicatory hearing. "Adjudicatory hearing" means a hearing to determine whether the allegations of a petition under Section 2-13, 3-15 or 4-12 [705 ILCS 405/2-13, 405/3-15 or 405/4-12] that a minor under 18 years of age is abused, neglected or dependent, or requires authoritative intervention, or addicted, respectively, are supported by a preponderance of the evidence or whether the allegations of a petition under Section 5-13 [705 ILCS 405/5-13] that a minor is delinquent are proved beyond a reasonable doubt.

(2) Adult. "Adult" means a person 21 years of age or older.

(3) Agency. "Agency" means a public or private child care facility legally authorized or licensed by this State for placement or institutional care or for both placement and institutional care.

(4) Association. "Association" means any organization, public or private, engaged in welfare functions which include services to or on behalf of children but does not include "agency" as herein defined.

(4.1) Chronic truant. "Chronic truant" shall have the definition ascribed to it in Section 26-2a of The School Code [105 ILCS 5/26-2a].

(5) Court. "Court" means the circuit court in a session or division assigned to hear proceedings under this Act.

(6) Dispositional hearing. "Dispositional hearing" means a hearing to determine whether a minor should be adjudged to be a ward of the court, and to determine what order of disposition should be made in respect to a minor adjudged to be a ward of the court.

(7) Emancipated minor. "Emancipated minor" means any minor 16 years of age or over who has been completely or partially emancipated under the "Emancipation of Mature Minors Act", enacted by the Eighty-First General Assembly [750 ILCS 30/1 et seq.], or under this Act [705 ILCS 405/1-1 et seq.].

(8) Guardianship of the person. "Guardianship of the person" of a minor means the duty and authority, subject to residual parental rights and responsibilities, to make important decisions in matters having a permanent effect on the life and development of the minor and to be concerned with his or her general welfare. It includes but is not necessarily limited to:

(a) the authority to consent to marriage, to enlistment in the armed forces of the United States, or to a major medical, psychiatric, and surgical treatment; to represent the minor in legal actions; and to make other decisions of substantial legal significance concerning the minor;

(b) the authority and duty of reasonable visitation, except to the extent that these have been limited by court order;

(c) the rights and responsibilities of legal custody except where legal custody has been vested in another person or agency; and

(d) the power to consent to the adoption of the minor, but only if expressly conferred on the guardian in accordance with Section 2-29, 3-30, 4-27 or 5-31 [705 ILCS 405/2-29, 405/3-30, 405/4-27 or 405/5-31].

(9) Legal custody. "Legal custody" means the relationship created by an order of court which imposes on the custodian the responsibility of physical possession of a minor and the duty to protect, train and discipline him and to provide him with food, shelter, education and ordinary medical care, except as these are limited by residual parental rights and responsibilities and the rights and responsibilities of the guardian of the person, if any.

(10) Minor. "Minor" means a person under the age of 21 years subject to this Act.

(11) Parents. "Parent" means the father or mother of a child and includes any adoptive parent. It also includes the father whose paternity is presumed or has been established under the law of this or another jurisdiction. It does not include a parent whose rights in respect to the minor have been terminated in any manner provided by law.

(12) Petition. "Petition" means the petition provided for in Section 2-13, 3-15, 4-12 or 5-13, including any supplemental petitions thereunder.

(13) Residual parental rights and responsibilities. "Residual parental rights and responsibilities" means those rights and responsibilities remaining with the parent after the transfer of legal custody or guardianship of the person, including, but not necessarily limited to, the right to reasonable visitation, the right to consent to adoption, the right to determine the minor's religious affiliation, and the responsibility for his support.

(14) Shelter. "Shelter" means the temporary care of a minor in physically unrestricting facilities pending court disposition or execution of court order for placement.

(15) Station adjustment. "Station adjustment" means the informal handling of an alleged offender by a juvenile police officer.

(16) Ward of the court. "Ward of the court" means a minor who is so adjudged under Section 2-22, 3-23, 4-20 or 5-22 [705 ILCS 405/2-22, 405/3-23, 405/4-20 or 405/5-22], after a finding of the requisite jurisdictional facts, and thus is subject to the dispositional powers of the court under this Act.

(Source: P.A. 86-820.) [Formerly Ill. Rev. Stat. 37 §801-3.]

405/1-4. Limitations of scope of Act.

§1-4. Limitations of scope of Act. Nothing in this Act shall be construed to give: (a) any guardian appointed hereunder the guardianship of the estate of the minor or to change the age of minority for any purpose other than those expressly stated in this Act; or (b) any court jurisdiction, except as provided in Sections 2-7, 3-6, 3-9, 4-6 and 5-7 [705 ILCS 405/2-7, 405/3-6, 405/3-9, 405/4-6 and 405/5-7], over any minor solely on the basis of the minor's (i) misbehavior which does not violate any federal or state law or municipal ordinance, (ii) refusal to obey the orders or directions of a parent, guardian or custodian, (iii) absence from home without the consent of his or her parent, guardian or custodian, or (iv) truancy, until efforts and procedures to address and resolve such actions by a law enforcement officer during a period of limited custody, by crisis intervention services under Section 3-5 [705 ILCS 405/3-5], and by alternative voluntary residential placement or other disposition as provided by Section 3-6 [705 ILCS 405/3-6] have been exhausted without correcting such actions.

(Source: P.A. 85-601.) [Formerly Ill. Rev. Stat. 37 §801-4.]

405/1-4.1. Acts illegal only if committed by minors; imprisonment prohibited.

§1-4.1. Except for minors accused of violation of an order of the court, any minor accused of any act under federal or State law, or a municipal ordinance that would not be illegal if committed by an adult, cannot be placed in a jail, municipal lockup, detention center or secure correctional facility.

(Added by P.A. 87-1154, §1, eff. 1/1/93.)

[Formerly Ill Rev. Stat. 37 §801-4.1.]

405/1-5. Rights of parties to proceedings.

§1-5. Rights of parties to proceedings. (1) Except as provided in this Section and paragraph (2) of Sections 2-22, 3-23, 4-20 or 5-22 [705 ILCS 405/2-22, 405/3-23, 405/4-20 or 405/5-22], the minor who is the subject of the proceeding and his parents, guardian, legal custodian or responsible relative who are parties respondent have the right to be present, to be heard, to present evidence material to the proceedings, to cross-examine witnesses, to examine pertinent court files and records and also, although proceedings under this Act are not intended to be adversary in character, the right to be represented by counsel. At the request of any party financially unable to employ counsel, the court shall appoint the Public Defender or such other counsel as the case may require.

No hearing on any petition filed under this Act may be commenced unless the minor who is the subject of the proceeding is represented by counsel. Each adult respondent shall be furnished a written "Notice of Rights" at or before the first hearing at which he or she appears.

(2) Though not appointed guardian or legal custodian or otherwise made a party to the proceeding, any current or previously appointed foster parent or representative of an agency or association interested in the minor has the right to be heard by the court, but does not thereby become a party to the proceeding.

In addition to the foregoing right to be heard by the court, any current foster parent of a minor and the agency designated by the court or the Department of Children and Family Services as custodian of the minor who has been adjudicated an abused or neglected minor under Section 2-3 [705 ILCS 405/2-3] or a dependent minor under Section 2-4 of this Act [705 ILCS 405/2-4] has the right to and shall be given adequate notice at all stages of any hearing or proceeding under this Act wherein the custody or status of the minor may be changed. Such notice shall contain a statement regarding the nature and denomination of the hearing or proceeding to be held, the change in custody or status of the minor sought to be obtained at such hearing or proceeding, and the date, time and place of such hearing or proceeding. The clerk shall mail the notice by certified mail marked for delivery to addressee only. The regular return receipt for certified mail is sufficient proof of service.

(3) Parties respondent are entitled to notice in compliance with Sections 2-15 and 2-16, 3-17 and 3-18, 4-14 and 4-15 or 5-15 and 5-16 [705 ILCS 405/2-15 and 405/2-16, 405/3-17 and 405/3-18, 405/4-14 and 405/4-15 or 405/5-15 and 405/5-16], as appropriate. At the first appearance before the court by the minor, his parents, guardian, custodian or responsible relative, the court shall explain the nature of the proceedings and inform the parties of their rights under the first 2 paragraphs of this Section. Upon an adjudication of wardship of the court under Sections 2-22, 3-23, 4-20 or 5-22, the court shall inform the parties of their right to appeal therefrom as well as from any other final judgment of the court.

(4) No sanction may be applied against the minor who is the subject of the proceedings by reason of his refusal or failure to testify in the course of any hearing held prior to final adjudication under Section 2-22, 3-23, 4-20 or 5-22.

(5) In the discretion of the court, the minor may be excluded from any part or parts of a dispositional hearing and, with the consent of the parent or parents,

guardian, counsel or a guardian ad litem, from any part or parts of an adjudicatory hearing.

(6) The general public except for the news media and the victim shall be excluded from any hearing and, except for the persons specified in this Section only persons, including representatives of agencies and associations, who in the opinion of the court have a direct interest in the case or in the work of the court shall be admitted to the hearing. However, the court may, for the minor's protection and for good cause shown, prohibit any person or agency present in court from further disclosing the minor's identity.

(Source: P.A. 87-759.) [Formerly Ill. Rev. Stat. 37 §801-5.]

405/1-6. State's Attorney.

§1-6. State's Attorney. The State's Attorneys of the several counties shall represent the people of the State of Illinois in proceedings under this Act in their respective counties.

(Source: P.A. 85-601.) [Formerly Ill. Rev. Stat. 37 §801-6.]

405/1-7. Confidentiality of law enforcement records.

§1-7. Confidentiality of law enforcement records. (A) Inspection and copying of law enforcement records maintained by law enforcement agencies which relate to a minor who has been arrested or taken into custody before his 17th birthday shall be restricted to the following:

(1) Any local, State or federal law enforcement officers of any jurisdiction or agency when necessary for the discharge of their official duties during the investigation or prosecution of a crime or relating to a minor who has been adjudicated delinquent and there has been a previous finding that the act which constitutes the previous offense was committed in furtherance of criminal activities by a criminal street gang. For purposes of this Section, "criminal street gang" means any ongoing organization, association, or group of 3 or more persons, whether formal or informal, having as one of its primary activities the commission of one or more criminal acts and that has a common name or common identifying sign, symbol or specific color apparel displayed, and whose members individually or collectively engage in or have engaged in a pattern of criminal activity.

(2) Prosecutors, probation officers, social workers, or other individuals assigned by the court to conduct a pre-adjudication or pre-disposition investigation, and individuals responsible for supervising or providing temporary or permanent care and custody for minors pursuant to the order of the juvenile court, when essential to performing their responsibilities.

(3) Prosecutors and probation officers:

(a) in the course of a trial when institution of criminal proceedings has been permitted under Section 5-4 [705 ILCS 405/5-4] or required under Section 5-4; or

(b) when institution of criminal proceedings has been permitted under Section 5-4 or required under Section 5-4 and such minor is the subject of a proceeding to determine the amount of bail; or

(c) when criminal proceedings have been permitted under Section 5-4 or required under Section 5-4 and such minor is the subject of a pre-trial investigation, pre-sentence investigation, fitness hearing, or proceedings on an application for probation.

(4) Adult and Juvenile Prisoner Review Board.

(5) Authorized military personnel.

(6) Persons engaged in bona fide research, with the permission of the Presiding Judge of the Juvenile Court and the chief executive of the respective law enforcement agency; provided that publication of such research results in

no disclosure of a minor's identity and protects the confidentiality of the minor's record.

(B) (1) Except as provided in paragraph (2), no law enforcement officer or other person or agency may knowingly transmit to the Department of Corrections, Adult Division or the Department of State Police or to the Federal Bureau of Investigation any fingerprint or photograph relating to a minor who has been arrested or taken into custody before his 17th birthday, unless the court in proceedings under this Act authorizes the transmission or enters an order under Section 5-4 permitting or requiring the institution of criminal proceedings.

(2) Law enforcement officers or other persons or agencies shall transmit to the Department of State Police copies of fingerprints and descriptions of all minors who have been arrested or taken into custody before their 17th birthday for the offense of unlawful use of weapons under Section 24-1 of the Criminal Code of 1961 [720 ILCS 5/24-1] or a forcible felony as defined in Section 2-8 of the Criminal Code of 1961 [720 ILCS 5/2-8], pursuant to Section 5 of the Criminal Identification Act [20 ILCS 2630/5]. Information reported to the Department pursuant to this Section may be maintained with records that the Department files pursuant to Section 2.1 of the Criminal Identification Act [20 ILCS 2630/2.1].

(C) The records of law enforcement officers concerning all minors under 17 years of age must be maintained separate from the records of arrests and may not be open to public inspection or their contents disclosed to the public except by order of the court or when the institution of criminal proceedings has been permitted under Section 5-4 or required under Section 5-4 or such a person has been convicted of a crime and is the subject of pre-sentence investigation or proceedings on an application for probation or when provided by law.

(D) Nothing contained in subsection (C) of this Section shall prohibit the inspection or disclosure to victims and witnesses of photographs contained in such records of law enforcement agencies when such inspection and disclosure is conducted in the presence of a law enforcement officer for the purpose of the identification or apprehension of any person subject to the provisions of this Act or for the investigation or prosecution of any crime.

(E) Law enforcement officers may not disclose the identity of any minor in releasing information to the general public as to the arrest, investigation or disposition of any case involving a minor.

(F) Nothing contained in this Section shall prohibit law enforcement agencies from communicating with each other by letter, memorandum, teletype or intelligence alert bulletin or other means the identity or other relevant information pertaining to a person under 17 years of age if there are reasonable grounds to believe that the person poses a real and present danger to the safety of the public or law enforcement officers. The information provided under this subsection (F) shall remain confidential and shall not be publicly disclosed, except as otherwise allowed by law.

(Chgd. by P.A. 87-927, §1, eff. 1/1/93; P.A. 87-1198, §1, eff. 9/25/92.)
(Source: P.A. 85-1209; 85-1433; 86-820.) [Formerly Ill. Rev. Stat. 37 §801-7.]

405/1-8. Confidentiality and accessibility of juvenile court records.

§1-8. Confidentiality and accessibility of juvenile court records. (A) Inspection and copying of juvenile court records relating to a minor who is the subject of a proceeding under this Act shall be restricted to the following:

(1) The minor who is the subject of record, his parents, guardian and counsel.

(2) Law enforcement officers and law enforcement agencies when such information is essential to executing an arrest or search warrant or other compulsory process, or to conducting an ongoing investigation or relating to a minor who has been adjudicated delinquent and there has been a previous

finding that the act which constitutes the previous offense was committed in furtherance of criminal activities by a criminal street gang.

For purposes of this Section, "criminal street gang" means any ongoing organization, association, or group of 3 or more persons, whether formal or informal, having as one of its primary activities the commission of one or more criminal acts and that has a common name or common identifying sign, symbol or specific color apparel displayed, and whose members individually or collectively engage in or have engaged in a pattern of criminal activity.

(3) Judges, prosecutors, probation officers, social workers or other individuals assigned by the court to conduct a pre-adjudication or predisposition investigation, and individuals responsible for supervising or providing temporary or permanent care and custody for minors pursuant to the order of the juvenile court when essential to performing their responsibilities.

(4) Judges, prosecutors and probation officers:

(a) in the course of a trial when institution of criminal proceedings has been permitted under Section 5-4 [705 ILCS 405/5-4] or required under Section 5-4; or

(b) when criminal proceedings have been permitted under Section 5-4 or required under Section 5-4 and a minor is the subject of a proceeding to determine the amount of bail; or

(c) when criminal proceedings have been permitted under Section 5-4 or required under Section 5-4 and a minor is the subject of a pre-trial investigation, pre-sentence investigation or fitness hearing, or proceedings on an application for probation; or

(d) when a minor becomes 17 years of age or older, and is the subject of criminal proceedings, including a hearing to determine the amount of bail, a pre-trial investigation, a pre-sentence investigation, a fitness hearing, or proceedings on an application for probation.

(5) Adult and Juvenile Prisoner Review Boards.

(6) Authorized military personnel.

(7) Victims, their subrogees and legal representatives; however, such persons shall have access only to the name and address of the minor and information pertaining to the disposition or alternative adjustment plan of the juvenile court.

(8) Persons engaged in bona fide research, with the permission of the presiding judge of the juvenile court and the chief executive of the agency that prepared the particular records; provided that publication of such research results in no disclosure of a minor's identity and protects the confidentiality of the record.

(9) The Secretary of State to whom the Clerk of the Court shall report the disposition of all cases, as required in Section 6-204 of The Illinois Vehicle Code [625 ILCS 5/6-204]. However, information reported relative to these offenses shall be privileged and available only to the Secretary of State, courts, and police officers.

(10) The administrator of a bonafide substance abuse student assistance program with the permission of the presiding judge of the juvenile court.

(B) A minor who is the victim in a juvenile proceeding shall be provided the same confidentiality regarding disclosure of identity as the minor who is the subject of record.

(C) Juvenile court records shall not be made available to the general public but may be inspected by representatives of agencies, associations and news media or other properly interested persons by general or special order of the court. The State's Attorney, the minor, his parents, guardian and counsel shall at all times have the right to examine court files and records.

(D) Pending or following any adjudication of delinquency for any offense defined in Sections 12-13 through 12-16 of the Criminal Code of 1961 [720 ILCS 5/12-13 through 5/12-16], the victim of any such offense shall receive the rights set out in Sections 4 and 6 of the Bill of Rights for Victims and Witnesses of Violent Crime Act [725 ILCS 120/4 and 120/6]; and the juvenile who is the subject of the adjudication, notwithstanding any other provision of this Act, shall be treated as an adult for the purpose of affording such rights to the victim.

(E) Nothing in this Section shall affect the right of a Civil Service Commission or appointing authority examining the character and fitness of an applicant for a position as a law enforcement officer to ascertain whether that applicant was ever adjudicated to be a delinquent minor and, if so, to examine the records of disposition or evidence which were made in proceedings under this Act.

(F) Following any adjudication of delinquency for a crime which would be a felony if committed by an adult, the State's Attorney shall ascertain whether the minor respondent is enrolled in school and, if so, shall provide a copy of the dispositional order to the principal or chief administrative officer of the school. Access to such juvenile records shall be limited to the principal or chief administrative officer of the school and any guidance counselor designated by him.

(G) Nothing contained in this Act prevents the sharing or disclosure of information or records relating or pertaining to juveniles subject to the provisions of the Serious Habitual Offender Comprehensive Action Program when that information is used to assist in the early identification and treatment of habitual juvenile offenders.

(Chgd. by P.A. 87-927, §1, eff. 1/1/93; P.A. 87-928, §5, eff. 1/1/93.)
(Source: P.A. 86-1450; 87-353; 87-614.) [Formerly Ill. Rev. Stat. 37 §801-8.]

405/1-8.1. Legislative findings.

§1-8.1. Legislative findings. (a) The General Assembly finds that a substantial and disproportionate amount of serious crime is committed by a relatively small number of juvenile offenders, otherwise known as serious habitual offenders. By this amendatory Act of 1992, the General Assembly intends to support the efforts of the juvenile justice system comprised of law enforcement, state's attorneys, probation departments, juvenile courts, social service providers, and schools in the early identification and treatment of habitual juvenile offenders. The General Assembly further supports increased interagency efforts to gather comprehensive data and actively disseminate the data to the agencies in the juvenile justice system to produce more informed decisions by all entites in that system.

(b) The General Assembly finds that the establishment of a Serious Habitual Offender Comprehensive Action Program throughout the State of Illinois is necessary to effectively intensify the supervision of serious habitual juvenile offenders in the community and to enhance current rehabilitative efforts. A cooperative and coordinated multi-disciplinary approach will increase the opportunity for success with juvenile offenders and assist in the development of early intervention strategies.

(Added by P.A. 87-928, §5, eff. 1/1/93.)
[Formerly Ill. Rev. Stat. 37 §801-8.1.]

405/1-8.2. Cooperation of agencies; Serious Habitual Offender Comprehensive Action Program.

§1-8.2. Cooperation of agencies; Serious Habitual Offender Comprehensive Action Program. (a) The Serious Habitual Offender Comprehensive Action Program (SHOCAP) is a multi-disciplinary interagency case management and information sharing system that enables the juvenile justice system, schools, and social service agencies to make more informed decisions regarding a small number of juveniles who repeatedly commit serious delinquent acts.

(b) Each county in the State of Illinois may establish a multi-disciplinary agency (SHOCAP) committee. The committee shall consist of representatives from the following agencies: local law enforcement, area school district, state's attorney's office, and court services (probation).

The chairman may appoint additional members to the committee as deemed appropriate to accomplish the goals of this program, including, but not limited to, representatives from the juvenile detention center, mental health, the Illinois Department of Children and Family Services, and community representatives at large.

(c) The SHOCAP committee shall adopt, by a majority of the members:

(1) criteria that will identify those who qualify as a serious habitual juvenile offender; and

(2) a written interagency information sharing agreement to be signed by the chief executive officer of each of the agencies represented on the committee. The interagency information sharing agreement shall include a provision that requires that all records pertaining to a serious habitual offender (SHO) shall be confidential. Disclosure of information may be made to other staff from member agencies as authorized by the SHOCAP committee for the furtherance of case management and tracking of the SHO. Staff from the member agencies who receive this information shall be governed by the confidentiality provisions of this Act. The staff from the member agencies who will qualify to have access to the SHOCAP information must be limited to those individuals who provide direct services to the SHO or who provide supervision of the SHO.

(d) The Chief Juvenile Circuit Judge, or the Chief Circuit Judge, or his designee, may issue a comprehensive information sharing court order. The court order shall allow agencies who are represented on the SHOCAP committee and whose chief executive officer has signed the interagency information sharing agreement to provide and disclose information to the SHOCAP committee. The sharing of information will ensure the coordination and cooperation of all agencies represented in providing case management and enhancing the effectiveness of the SHOCAP efforts.

(e) Any person or agency who is participating in good faith in the sharing of SHOCAP information under this Act shall have immunity from any liability, civil, criminal, or otherwise, that might result by reason of the type of information exchanged. For the purpose of any proceedings, civil or criminal, the good faith of any person or agency permitted to share SHOCAP information under this Act shall be presumed.

(f) All reports concerning SHOCAP clients made available to members of the SHOCAP committee and all records generated from these reports shall be confidential and shall not be disclosed, except as specifically authorized by this Act or other applicable law. It is a Class A misdemeanor to permit, assist, or encourage the unauthorized release of any information contained in SHOCAP reports or records.

(Added by P.A. 87-928, §5, eff. 1/1/93.)
[Formerly Ill. Rev. Stat. 37 §801-8.2.]

405/1-9. Expungement of law enforcement and juvenile court records.

§1-9. Expungement of law enforcement and juvenile court records. (1) Whenever any person has attained the age of 17 or whenever all juvenile court proceedings relating to that person have been terminated, whichever is later, the person may petition the court to expunge law enforcement records relating to incidents occurring before his 17th birthday or his juvenile court records, or both, but only in the following circumstances:

(a) the minor was arrested and no petition for delinquency was filed with the clerk of the circuit court; or

(b) the minor was charged with an offense and was found not delinquent of that offense; or

(c) the minor was placed under supervision pursuant to Sections 2-20, 3-21, 4-18 or 5-19 [705 ILCS 405/2-20, 405/3-21, 405/4-18 or 405/5-19], and such order of supervision has since been successfully terminated.

(2) Any person may petition the court to expunge all law enforcement records relating to any incidents occurring before his 17th birthday and not resulting in criminal proceedings and all juvenile court records relating to any adjudications for any crimes committed before his 17th birthday, except first degree murder, if he has had no convictions for any crime since his 17th birthday and:

(a) 10 years have elapsed since his 17th birthday; or

(b) 10 years have elapsed since all juvenile court proceedings relating to him have been terminated or his commitment to the Department of Corrections pursuant to this Act has been terminated; whichever is later of (a) or (b).

(3) The chief judge of the circuit in which an arrest was made or a charge was brought or any judge of that circuit designated by the chief judge may, upon verified petition of a person who is the subject of an arrest or a juvenile court proceeding pursuant to subsection (1) or (2) of this Section, order the law enforcement records or juvenile court records, or both, to be expunged from the official records of the arresting authority and the clerk of the circuit court. Notice of the petition shall be served upon the State's Attorney and upon the arresting authority which is the subject of the petition for expungement.

(Source: P.A. 85-601.) [Formerly Ill. Rev. Stat. 37 §801-9.]

405/1-10. Admissibility of evidence and adjudications in other proceedings.

§1-10. Admissibility of evidence and adjudications in other proceedings. (1) Evidence and adjudications in proceedings under this Act shall be admissible:

(a) in subsequent proceedings under this Act concerning the same minor; or

(b) in criminal proceedings when the court is to determine the amount of bail, fitness of the defendant or in sentencing under the Unified Code of Corrections [730 ILCS 5/1-1-1 et seq.]; or

(c) in proceedings under this Act or in criminal proceedings in which anyone who has been adjudicated delinquent under Section 5-3 [705 ILCS 405/5-3] is to be a witness, and then only for purposes of impeachment and pursuant to the rules of evidence for criminal trials; or

(d) in civil proceedings concerning causes of action arising out of the incident or incidents which initially gave rise to the proceedings under this Act.

(2) No adjudication or disposition under this Act shall operate to disqualify a minor from subsequently holding public office nor shall operate as a forfeiture of any right, privilege or right to receive any license granted by public authority.

(3) The court which adjudicated that a minor has committed any offense relating to motor vehicles prescribed in Sections 4-102 and 4-103 of The Illinois Vehicle Code [625 ILCS 5/4-102 and 5/4-103] shall notify the Secretary of State of such adjudication and such notice shall constitute sufficient grounds for revoking that minor's driver's license or permit as provided in Section 6-205 of The Illinois Vehicle Code [625 ILCS 5/6-205]; no minor shall be considered a criminal by reason thereof, nor shall any such adjudication be considered a conviction.

(Source: P.A. 85-601.) [Formerly Ill. Rev. Stat. 37 §801-10.]

405/1-11. Designation of special courtrooms.

§1-11. Designation of special courtrooms. Special courtrooms may be provided in any county for the hearing of all cases under this Act.
(Source: P.A. 85-601.) [Formerly Ill. Rev. Stat. 37 §801-11.]

405/1-12. Liability—Person performing public or community service.

§1-12. Neither the State, any unit of local government, probation department, public or community service program or site, nor any official or employee thereof acting in the course of their official duties shall be liable for any injury or loss a person might receive while performing public or community service as ordered by the court, nor shall they be liable for any tortious acts of any person performing public or community service, except for wilful, wanton misconduct or gross negligence on the part of such governmental unit, official or employee.
(Source: P.A. 85-1209.) [Formerly Ill. Rev. Stat. 37 §801-12.]

405/1-13. Compensation to minors.

§1-13. No minor assigned to a public or community service program shall be considered an employee for any purpose, nor shall the county board be obligated to provide any compensation to such minor.
(Source: P.A. 85-1209.) [Formerly Ill. Rev. Stat. 37 §801-13.]

405/1-14. Confiscation of weapons possessed by minor.

§1-14. Any weapon in possession of a minor found to be a delinquent under Section 5-3 [705 ILCS 405/5-3] for an offense involving the use of a weapon or for being in possession of a weapon during the commission of an offense shall be confiscated and disposed of by the juvenile court whether the weapon is the property of the minor or his parent or guardian. Disposition of the weapon by the court shall be in accordance with Section 24-6 of the Criminal Code of 1961, as now or hereafter amended [720 ILCS 5/24-6].
(Source: P.A. 86-980.) [Formerly Ill. Rev. Stat. 37 §801-14.]

405/1-15. Wrong venue or inadequate service.

§1-15. Wrong Venue or Inadequate Service. (a) All objections of improper venue are waived by a party respondent unless a motion to transfer to a proper venue is made by that party respondent before the start of an adjudicatory hearing conducted under any Article of this Act. No order or judgment is void because of a claim that it was rendered in the wrong venue unless that claim is raised in accordance with this Section.

(b) A party respondent who either has been properly served, or who appears before the court personally or by counsel at the adjudicatory hearing or at any earlier proceeding on a petition for wardship under this Act leading to that adjudicatory hearing, and who wishes to object to the court's jurisdiction on the ground that some necessary party either has not been served or has not been properly served must raise that claim before the start of the adjudicatory hearing conducted under any Article of this Act. No order or judgment is void because of a claim of inadequate service unless that claim is raised in accordance with this Section.
(Source: P.A. 86-1012; 86-1475.) [Formerly Ill. Rev. Stat. 37 §801-15.]

405/1-16. Order of protection; status.

§1-16. Order of protection; status. Whenever relief is sought regarding any type of custody matter under this Act, the court, before granting relief, shall determine whether any order of protection has previously been entered in the instant proceeding or any other proceeding in which any party, or a child of any party, or both, if relevant, has been designated as either a respondent or a protected person.
(Source: P.A. 87-743.) [Formerly Ill. Rev. Stat. 37 §801-16.]

405/1-17. Designation of private agency to give factual testimony.

§1-17. With respect to any minor for whom the Department of Children and Family Services Guardianship Administrator is appointed the temporary custodian or guardian, the Guardianship Administrator may designate in writing a private agency or an employee of a private agency to appear at court proceedings and testify as to the factual matters contained in the casework files and recommendations involving the minor. The private agency or the employee of a private agency must have personal and thorough knowledge of the facts of the case in which the appointment is made. The designated private agency or employee shall appear at the proceedings. If the Court finds that it is in the best interests of the minor that an employee or employees of the Department appear in addition to the private agency or employee of a private agency, the Court shall set forth the reasons in writing for their required appearance.
(Added by P.A. 87-1147, §1, eff. 9/17/92.)
[Formerly Ill. Rev. Stat. 37 §801-17.]

ARTICLE II. ABUSED, NEGLECTED OR DEPENDENT MINORS

Sec.

405/2-1. Jurisdictional facts.

§2-1. Jurisdictional facts. Proceedings may be instituted under the provisions of this Article concerning boys and girls who are abused, neglected or dependent, as defined in Sections 2-3 or 2-4 [705 ILCS 405/2-3 or 405/2-4].
(Source: P.A. 85-601.) [Formerly Ill. Rev. Stat. 37 §802-1.]

405/2-2. Venue.

§2-2. Venue. (1) Venue under this Article lies in the county where the minor resides or is found.

(2) If proceedings are commenced in any county other than that of the minor's residence, the court in which the proceedings were initiated may at any time before or after adjudication of wardship transfer the case to the county of the minor's residence by transmitting to the court in that county an authenticated copy of the court record, including all documents, petitions and orders filed therein, and the minute orders and docket entries of the court. Transfer in like manner may be made in the event of a change of residence from one county to another of a minor concerning whom proceedings are pending.
(Source: P.A. 85-601.) [Formerly Ill. Rev. Stat. 37 §802-2.]

405/2-3. Neglected or abused minor.

§2-3. Neglected or abused minor. (1) Those who are neglected include:

(a) any minor under 18 years of age whose parent or other person responsible for the minor's welfare does not provide the proper or necessary support, education as required by law, or medical or other remedial care recognized under State law as necessary for a minor's well-being, or other care necessary for his or her well-being, including adequate food, clothing and shelter, or who is abandoned by his or her parents or other person responsible for the minor's welfare; or

(b) any minor under 18 years of age whose environment is injurious to his or her welfare; or

(c) any newborn infant whose blood or urine contains any amount of a controlled substance as defined in subsection (f) of Section 102 of the Illinois Controlled Substances Act [720 ILCS 570/102], as now or hereafter amended, or a metabolite of a controlled substance, with the exception of controlled substances or metabolites of such substances, the presence of which in the newborn infant is the result of medical treatment administered to the mother or the newborn infant.

(2) Those who are abused include any minor under 18 years of age whose parent or immediate family member, or any person responsible for the minor's welfare, or any person who is in the same family or household as the minor, or any individual residing in the same home as the minor, or a paramour of the minor's parent:

(i) inflicts, causes to be inflicted, or allows to be inflicted upon such minor physical injury, by other than accidental means, which causes death, disfigurement, impairment of physical or emotional health, or loss or impairment of any bodily function;

(ii) creates a substantial risk of physical injury to such minor by other than accidental means which would be likely to cause death, disfigurement, impairment of emotional health, or loss or impairment of any bodily function;

(iii) commits or allows to be committed any sex offense against such minor, as such sex offenses are defined in the Criminal Code of 1961 [720 ILCS 5/1-1 et seq.], as amended, and extending those definitions of sex offenses to include minors under 18 years of age;

(iv) commits or allows to be committed an act or acts of torture upon such minor; or

(v) inflicts excessive corporal punishment.

(3) This Section does not apply to a minor who would be included herein solely for the purpose of qualifying for financial assistance for himself, his parents, guardian or custodian.
(Source: P.A. 86-275; 86-659.) [Formerly Ill. Rev. Stat. 37 §802-3.]

405/2-4. Dependent minor.

§2-4. Dependent minor. (1) Those who are dependent include any minor under 18 years of age (a) who is without a parent, guardian or legal custodian;

(b) who is without proper care because of the physical or mental disability of his parent, guardian or custodian; or

(c) who is without proper medical or other remedial care recognized under State law or other care necessary for his or her well being through no fault, neglect or lack of concern by his parents, guardian or custodian, provided that no order may be made terminating parental rights, nor may a minor be removed from the custody of his or her parents for longer than 6 months, pursuant to an adjudication as a dependent minor under this subsection (c); or

(d) who has a parent, guardian or legal custodian who with good cause wishes to be relieved of all residual parental rights and responsibilities, guardianship or custody, and who desires the appointment of a guardian of the person with power to consent to the adoption of the minor under Section 2-29 [705 ILCS 405/2-29].

(2) This Section does not apply to a minor who would be included herein solely for the purpose of qualifying for financial assistance for himself, his parents, guardian or custodian.

(Source: P.A. 85-601.) [Formerly Ill. Rev. Stat. 37 §802-4.]

405/2-5. Taking into custody.

§2-5. Taking into custody. (1) A law enforcement officer may, without a warrant, take into temporary custody a minor (a) whom the officer with reasonable cause believes to be a person described in Section 2-3 or 2-4 [705 ILCS 405/2-3 or 405/2-4]; (b) who has been adjudged a ward of the court and has escaped from any commitment ordered by the court under this Act; or (c) who is found in any street or public place suffering from any sickness or injury which requires care, medical treatment or hospitalization.

(2) Whenever a petition has been filed under Section 2-13 [705 ILCS 405/2-13] and the court finds that the conduct and behavior of the minor may endanger the health, person, welfare, or property of himself or others or that the circumstances of his home environment may endanger his health, person, welfare or property, a warrant may be issued immediately to take the minor into custody.

(3) The taking of a minor into temporary custody under this Section is not an arrest nor does it constitute a police record.

(Source: P.A. 85-601.) [Formerly Ill. Rev. Stat. 37 §802-5.]

405/2-6. Duty of officer.

§2-6. Duty of officer. (1)* A law enforcement officer who takes a minor into custody under Section 2-5 [705 ILCS 405/2-5] shall immediately make a reasonable attempt to notify the parent or other person legally responsible for the minor's care or the person with whom the minor resides that the minor has been taken into custody and where he or she is being held.

(a) A law enforcement officer who takes a minor into custody with a warrant shall without unnecessary delay take the minor to the nearest juvenile police officer designated for such purposes in the county of venue.

(b) A law enforcement officer who takes a minor into custody without a warrant shall place the minor in temporary protective custody and shall immediately notify the Department of Children and Family Services by contacting either the central register established under 7.7 of the Abused and Neglected Child Reporting Act [325 ILCS 5/7.7] or the nearest Department of Children and Family Services office. If there is reasonable cause to suspect that a minor has died as a result of abuse or neglect, the law enforcement officer shall immediately report such suspected abuse or neglect to the appropriate medical examiner or coroner.

**So in original. No subsec. (2) has been enacted.*

(Source: P.A. 85-601.) [Formerly Ill. Rev. Stat. 37 §802-6.]

405/2-7. Temporary custody.

§2-7. Temporary custody. "Temporary custody" means the temporary placement of the minor out of the custody of his or her guardian or parent, and includes the following:

(1) "Temporary protective custody" means custody within a hospital or other medical facility or a place previously designated for such custody by the Department of Children and Family Services, subject to review by the court, including a licensed foster home, group home, or other institution. However, such place shall not be a jail or other place for the detention of the criminal or juvenile offenders.

(2) "Shelter care" means a physically unrestrictive facility designated by the Department of Children and Family Services or a licensed child welfare agency, or other suitable place designated by the court for a minor who requires care away from his or her home.

(Source: P.A. 85-601.) [Formerly Ill. Rev. Stat. 37 §802-7.]

405/2-8. Investigation; release.

§2-8. Investigation; release. When a minor is delivered to the court, or to the place designated by the court under Section 2-7 of this Act [705 ILCS 405/2-7], a probation officer or such other public officer designated by the court shall immediately investigate the circumstances of the minor and the facts surrounding his or her being taken into custody. The minor shall be immediately released to the custody of his or her parent, guardian, legal custodian or responsible relative, unless the probation officer or such other public officer designated by the court finds that further temporary protective custody is necessary, as provided in Section 2-7.

(Source: P.A. 85-601.) [Formerly Ill. Rev. Stat. 37 §802-8.]

405/2-9. Setting of temporary custody hearing; notice; release.

§2-9. Setting of temporary custody hearing; notice; release. (1) Unless sooner released, a minor as defined in Section 2-3 or 2-4 of this Act [705 ILCS 405/2-3 or 405/2-4] taken into temporary protective custody must be brought before a judicial officer within 48 hours, exclusive of Saturdays, Sundays and court-designated holidays, for a temporary custody hearing to determine whether he shall be further held in custody.

(2) If the probation officer or such other public officer designated by the court determines that the minor should be retained in custody, he shall cause a petition to be filed as provided in Section 2-13 of this Article [705 ILCS 405/2-13], and the clerk of the court shall set the matter for hearing on the temporary custody hearing calendar. When a parent, guardian, custodian or responsible relative is present and so requests, the temporary custody hearing shall be held immediately if the court is in session, otherwise at the earliest feasible time. The petitioner through counsel or such other public officer designated by the court shall insure notification to the minor's parent, guardian, custodian or responsible relative of the time and place of the hearing by the best practicable notice, allowing for oral notice in place of written notice only if provision of written notice is unreasonable under the circumstances.

(3) The minor must be released from temporary protective custody at the expiration of the 48 hour period specified by this Section if not brought before a judicial officer within that period.

(Source: P.A. 87-759.) [Formerly Ill. Rev. Stat. 37 §802-9.]

405/2-10. Temporary custody hearing.

§2-10. Temporary custody hearing. At the appearance of the minor before the court at the temporary custody hearing, all witnesses present shall be examined before the court in relation to any matter connected with the allegations made in the petition.

(1) If the court finds that there is not probable cause to believe that the minor is abused, neglected or dependent it shall release the minor and dismiss the petition.

(2) If the court finds that there is probable cause to believe that the minor is abused, neglected or dependent, the minor, his or her parent, guardian, custodian and other persons able to give relevant testimony shall be examined before the court. The Department of Children and Family Services shall give testimony concerning indicated reports of abuse and neglect, of which they are aware of through the central registry, involving the minor's parent, guardian or custodian. After such testimony, the court may enter an order that the minor shall be released upon the request of parent, guardian or custodian if the parent, guardian or custodian appears to take custody. Custodian shall include any agency of the State which has been given custody or wardship of the child. The Court shall require documentation by representatives of the Department of Children and Family Services or the probation department as to the reasonable efforts that were made to prevent or eliminate the necessity of removal of the minor from his or her home, and shall consider the testimony of any person as to those reasonable efforts. If the court finds that it is a matter of immediate and urgent necessity for the protection of the minor or of the person or property of another that the minor be placed in a shelter care facility or that he or she is likely to flee the jurisdiction of the court, and further finds that reasonable efforts have been made or good cause has been shown why reasonable efforts cannot prevent or eliminate the necessity of removal of the minor from his or her home, the court may prescribe shelter care and order that the minor be kept in a suitable place designated by the court or in a shelter care facility designated by the Department of Children and Family Services or a licensed child welfare agency; otherwise it shall release the minor from custody. When a minor is placed in the home of a close relative, the Department of Children and Family Services shall complete a preliminary background review of the members of the minor's custodian's household in accordance with Section 4.3 of the Child Care Act of 1969 [225 ILCS 10/4.3] within 90 days of that placement, and information required by Section 4.1 and Section 4.2 of the Child Child Care Act of 1969 [225 ILCS 10/4.1 and 10/4.2] will be evaluated within 180 days. If the minor is ordered placed in a shelter care facility of the Department of Children and Family Services or a licensed child welfare agency, the court shall, upon request of the appropriate Department or other agency, appoint the Department of Children and Family Services Guardianship Administrator or other appropriate agency executive temporary custodian of the minor and the court may enter such other orders related to the temporary custody as it deems fit and proper, including the provision of services to the minor or his family to ameliorate the causes contributing to the finding of probable cause or to the finding of the existence of immediate and urgent necessity. Acceptance of services shall not be considered an admission of any allegation in a petition made pursuant to this Act, nor may a referral of services be considered as evidence in any proceeding pursuant to this Act, except where the issue is whether the Department has made reasonable efforts to reunite the family. In making its findings that reasonable efforts have been made or that good cause has been shown why reasonable efforts cannot prevent or eliminate the necessity of removal of the minor from his or her home, the court shall state in writing its findings concerning the nature of the services that were offered or the efforts that were made to prevent removal of the child and the apparent reasons that such services or efforts could not prevent the need for removal. The parents, guardian, custodian, temporary custodian and minor shall each be furnished a

copy of such written findings. The temporary custodian shall maintain a copy of the court order and written findings in the case record for the child. The order together with the court's findings of fact in support thereof shall be entered of record in the court.

Once the court finds that it is a matter of immediate and urgent necessity for the protection of the minor that the minor be placed in a shelter care facility, the minor shall not be returned to the parent, custodian or guardian until the court finds that such placement is no longer necessary for the protection of the minor.

(3) If prior to the shelter care hearing for a minor described in Sections 2-3, 2-4, 3-3 and 4-3 [705 ILCS 405/2-3, 405/2-4, 405/3-3 and 405/4-3] the moving party is unable to serve notice on the party respondent, the shelter care hearing may proceed ex-parte. A shelter care order from an ex-parte hearing shall be endorsed with the date and hour of issuance and shall be filed with the clerk's office and entered of record. The order shall expire after 10 days from the time it is issued unless before its expiration it is renewed, at a hearing upon appearance of the party respondent, or upon an affidavit of the moving party as to all diligent efforts to notify the party respondent by notice as herein prescribed. The notice prescribed shall be in writing and shall be personally delivered to the minor or the minor's attorney and to the last known address of the other person or persons entitled to notice. The notice shall also state the nature of the allegations, the nature of the order sought by the State, including whether temporary custody is sought, and the consequences of failure to appear; and shall explain the right of the parties and the procedures to vacate or modify a shelter care order as provided in this Section. The notice for a shelter care hearing shall be substantially as follows:

NOTICE TO PARENTS AND CHILDREN OF
SHELTER CARE HEARING

On .... at ...., before the Honorable ...., (address:) ...., the State of Illinois will present evidence (1) that (name of child or children) .... are abused, neglected or dependent for the following reasons: .... and (2) that there is "immediate and urgent necessity" to remove the child or children from the responsible relative.

YOUR FAILURE TO APPEAR AT THE HEARING MAY RESULT IN PLACEMENT of the child or children in foster care until a trial can be held. A trial may not be held for up to 90 days.

At the shelter care hearing, parents have the following rights:

1. To ask the court to appoint a lawyer if they cannot afford one.
2. To ask the court to continue the hearing to allow them time to prepare.
3. To present evidence concerning:

a. Whether or not the child or children were abused, neglected or dependent.

b. Whether or not there is "immediate and urgent necessity" to remove the child from home (including: their ability to care for the child, conditions in the home, alternative means of protecting the child other than removal).

c. The best interests of the child.

4. To cross examine the State's witnesses.

The Notice for rehearings shall be substantially as follows:

NOTICE OF PARENT'S AND CHILDREN'S RIGHTS TO REHEARING ON
TEMPORARY CUSTODY

If you were not present at and did not have adequate notice of the Shelter Care Hearing at which temporary custody of .... was awarded to ...., you have the right to request a full rehearing on whether the State should have temporary custody of .... To request this rehearing, you must file with the Clerk of the Juvenile Court (address): ...., in person or by mailing a statement (affidavit) setting forth the following:

1. That you were not present at the shelter care hearing.

2. That you did not get adequate notice (explaining how the notice was inadequate).

3. Your signature.

4. Signature must be notarized.

The rehearing should be scheduled within one day of your filing this affidavit.

At the rehearing, your rights are the same as at the initial shelter care hearing. The enclosed notice explains those rights.

At the Shelter Care Hearing, children have the following rights:

1. To have a guardian ad litem appointed.

2. To be declared competent as a witness and to present testimony concerning:

a. Whether they are abused, neglected or dependent.

b. Whether there is "immediate and urgent necessity" to be removed from home.

c. Their best interests.

3. To cross examine witnesses for other parties.

4. To obtain an explanation of any proceedings and orders of the court.

(4) If the parent, guardian, legal custodian, responsible relative, minor age 8 or over, or counsel of the minor did not have actual notice of or was not present at the shelter care hearing, he or she may file an affidavit setting forth these facts, and the clerk shall set the matter for rehearing not later than 48 hours, excluding Sundays and legal holidays, after the filing of the affidavit. At the rehearing, the court shall proceed in the same manner as upon the original hearing.

(5) Only when there is reasonable cause to believe that the minor taken into custody is a person described in Section 5-3 [705 ILCS 405/5-3] may the minor be kept or detained in a detention home or county or municipal jail. This Section shall in no way be construed to limit subsection (6).

(6) No minor under 16 years of age may be confined in a jail or place ordinarily used for the confinement of prisoners in a police station. Minors under 17 years of age must be kept separate from confined adults and may not at any time be kept in the same cell, room, or yard with adults confined pursuant to the criminal law.

(7) If the minor is not brought before a judicial officer within the time period as specified in Section 2-9 [705 ILCS 405/2-9], the minor must immediately be released from custody.

(8) If neither the parent, guardian or custodian appears within 24 hours to take custody of a minor released upon request pursuant to subsection (2) of this Section, then the clerk of the court shall set the matter for rehearing not later than 7 days after the original order and shall issue a summons directed to the parent, guardian or custodian to appear. At the same time the probation department shall prepare a report on the minor. If a parent, guardian or custodian does not appear at such rehearing, the judge may enter an order prescribing that the minor be kept in a suitable place designated by the Department of Children and Family Services or a licensed child welfare agency.

(9) Notwithstanding any other provision of this Section any interested party, including the State, the temporary custodian, an agency providing services to the minor or family under a service plan pursuant to Section 8.2 of the Abused and Neglected Child Reporting Act [325 ILCS 5/8.2], foster parent, or any of their representatives, on notice to all parties entitled to notice, may

file a motion to modify or vacate a temporary custody order on any of the following grounds:

(a) It is no longer a matter of immediate and urgent necessity that the minor remain in shelter care; or

(b) There is a material change in the circumstances of the natural family from which the minor was removed; or

(c) A person not a party to the alleged abuse, neglect or dependency, including a parent, relative or legal guardian, is capable of assuming temporary custody of the minor; or

(d) Services provided by the Department of Children and Family Services or a child welfare agency or other service provider have been successful in eliminating the need for temporary custody.

The clerk shall set the matter for hearing not later than 14 days after such motion is filed. In the event that the court modifies or vacates a temporary custody order but does not vacate its finding of probable cause, the court may order that appropriate services be continued or initiated in behalf of the minor and his or her family.

(Source: P.A. 86-1482; 87-759.) [Formerly Ill. Rev. Stat. 37 §802-10.]

405/2-10.1. Minor in shelter care.

§2-10.1. Whenever a minor is placed in shelter care with the Department or a licensed child welfare agency in accordance with Section 2-10 [705 ILCS 405/2-10], the Department or agency, as appropriate, shall prepare and file with the court within 30 days of placement under Section 2-10 a case plan which complies with the federal Adoption Assistance and Child Welfare Act of 1980 [42 U.S.C. §§602 et seq., 1305 et seq.] and is in the best interests of the minor.

(Source: P.A. 86-1293.) [Formerly Ill. Rev. Stat. 37 §802-10.1.]

405/2-11. Medical and dental treatment and care.

§2-11. Medical and dental treatment and care. At all times during temporary custody or shelter care, the court may authorize a physician, a hospital or any other appropriate health care provider to provide medical, dental or surgical procedures if such procedures are necessary to safeguard the minor's life or health.

With respect to any minor for whom the Department of Children and Family Services Guardianship Administrator is appointed the temporary custodian, the Guardianship Administrator or his designee shall be deemed the minor's legally authorized representative for purposes of consenting to an HIV test and obtaining and disclosing information concerning such test pursuant to the AIDS Confidentiality Act [410 ILCS 305/1 et seq.] and for purposes of consenting to the release of information pursuant to the Illinois Sexually Transmissible Disease Control Act [410 ILCS 325/1 et seq.].

Any person who administers an HIV test upon the consent of the Department of Children and Family Services Guardianship Administrator or his designee, or who discloses the results of such tests to the Department's Guardianship Administrator or his designee, shall have immunity from any liability, civil, criminal or otherwise, that might result by reason of such actions. For the purpose of any proceedings, civil or criminal, the good faith of any persons required to administer or disclose the results of tests, or permitted to take such actions, shall be presumed.

(Source: P.A. 86-904.) [Formerly Ill. Rev. Stat. 37 §802-11.]

405/2-12. Preliminary conferences.

§2-12. Preliminary conferences. (1) The court may authorize the probation officer to confer in a preliminary conference with any person seeking to file a petition under Section 2-13 [705 ILCS 405/2-13], the prospective respondents and other interested persons concerning the advisability of filing the petition, with a view to adjusting suitable cases without the filing of a petition.

The probation officer should schedule a conference promptly except where the State's Attorney insists on court action or where the minor has indicated that he or she will demand a judicial hearing and will not comply with an informal adjustment.

(2) In any case of a minor who is in temporary custody, the holding of preliminary conferences does not operate to prolong temporary custody beyond the period permitted by Section 2-9 [705 ILCS 405/2-9].

(3) This Section does not authorize any probation officer to compel any person to appear at any conference, produce any papers, or visit any place.

(4) No statement made during a preliminary conference may be admitted into evidence at an adjudicatory hearing or at any proceeding against the minor under the criminal laws of this State prior to his or her conviction thereunder.

(5) The probation officer shall promptly formulate a written, non-judicial adjustment plan following the initial conference.

(6) Non-judicial adjustment plans include but are not limited to the following:

(a) up to 6 months informal supervision within family;

(b) up to 6 months informal supervision with a probation officer involved;

(c) up to 6 months informal supervision with release to a person other than parent;

(d) referral to special educational, counseling or other rehabilitative social or educational programs;

(e) referral to residential treatment programs; and

(f) any other appropriate action with consent of the minor and a parent.

(7) The factors to be considered by the probation officer in formulating a non-judicial adjustment plan shall be the same as those limited in subsection (4) of Section 5-6 [705 ILCS 405/5-6].

(Source: P.A. 86-639.) [Formerly Ill. Rev. Stat. 37 §802-12.]

405/2-13. Petition; supplemental petitions.

§2-13. Petition; supplemental petitions. (1) Any adult person, any agency or association by its representative may file, or the court on its own motion may direct the filing through the State's Attorney of a petition in respect of a minor under this Act. The petition and all subsequent court documents shall be entitled "In the interest of.........., a minor".

(2) The petition shall be verified but the statements may be made upon information and belief. It shall allege that the minor is abused, neglected or dependent, and set forth (a) facts sufficient to bring the minor under Section 2-3 or 2-4 [705 ILCS 405/2-3 or 405/2-4]; (b) the name, age and residence of the minor; (c) the names and residences of his parents; (d) the name and residence of his legal guardian or the person or persons having custody or control of the minor, or of the nearest known relative if no parent or guardian can be found; and (e) if the minor upon whose behalf the petition is brought is sheltered in custody, the date on which such temporary custody was ordered by the court or the date set for a temporary custody hearing. If any of the facts herein required are not known by the petitioner, the petition shall so state.

(3) The petition must allege that it is in the best interests of the minor and of the public that he be adjudged a ward of the court and may pray generally for relief available under this Act. The petition need not specify any proposed disposition following adjudication of wardship.

(4) If appointment of a guardian of the person with power to consent to adoption of the minor under Section 2-29 [705 ILCS 405/2-29] is sought, the petition shall so state.

(5) At any time before dismissal of the petition or before final closing and discharge under Section 2-31 [705 ILCS 405/2-31], one or more supplemental petitions may be filed in respect of the same minor.
(Source: P.A. 85-1209.) [Formerly Ill. Rev. Stat. 37 §802-13.]

405/2-14. Date for adjudicatory hearing.

§2-14. Date for Adjudicatory Hearing. (a) Purpose and policy. The legislature recognizes that serious delay in the adjudication of abuse, neglect, or dependency cases can cause grave harm to the child and the family and that it frustrates the effort to establish permanent homes for children in need. The purpose of this Section is to insure that, consistent with the federal Adoption Assistance and Child Welfare Act of 1980, Public Law 96-272, as amended [42 U.S.C. §§602 et seq., 1305 et seq.], and the intent of this Act, the State of Illinois will act in a just and speedy manner to determine families in need, reunify families where appropriate and, if reunification is inappropriate, find other permanent homes for children.

(b) When a petition is filed alleging that the minor is abused, neglected or dependent, an adjudicatory hearing shall be held within 90 days of the date of service of process upon the minor, parents, any guardian and any legal custodian.

(c) Upon written motion of a party filed no later than 10 days prior to hearing, or upon the court's own motion and only for good cause shown, the Court may continue the hearing for a period not to exceed 30 days, and only if the continuance is in the best interests of the minor. Only one such continuance shall be granted. A period of continuance for good cause as described in this Section shall temporarily suspend as to all parties, for the time of the delay, the period within which a hearing must be held. On the day of the expiration of the delay, the period shall continue at the point at which it was suspended.

The term "good cause" as applied in this Section shall be strictly construed and be in accordance with Supreme Court Rule 231 (a) through (f). Neither stipulation by counsel nor the convenience of any party constitutes good cause. Where the court grants a continuance, it shall enter specific factual findings to support its order. If the adjudicatory hearing is not heard within the time limits required by subsection (b) or (c) of this Section, upon motion by any party the petition shall be dismissed without prejudice.

(d) The time limits of this Section may be waived only by consent of all parties and approval by the court.

(e) For all cases filed before July 1, 1991, an adjudicatory hearing must, be held within 180 days of July 1, 1991.
(Source: P.A. 85-1440; 86-1293.) [Formerly Ill. Rev. Stat. 37 §802-14.]

405/2-15. Summons.

§2-15. Summons. (1) When a petition is filed, the clerk of the court shall issue a summons with a copy of the petition attached. The summons shall be directed to the minor's legal guardian or custodian and to each person named as a respondent in the petition, except that summons need not be directed to a minor respondent under 8 years of age for whom the court appoints a guardian ad litem if the guardian ad litem appears on behalf of the minor in any proceeding under this Act.

(2) The summons must contain a statement that the minor or any of the respondents is entitled to have an attorney present at the hearing on the petition, and that the clerk of the court should be notified promptly if the minor or any other respondent desires to be represented by an attorney but is financially unable to employ counsel.

(3) The summons shall be issued under the seal of the court, attested in and signed with the name of the clerk of the court, dated on the day it is issued, and

shall require each respondent to appear and answer the petition on the date set for the adjudicatory hearing.

(4) The summons may be served by any county sheriff, coroner or probation officer, even though the officer is the petitioner. The return of the summons with endorsement of service by the officer is sufficient proof thereof.

(5) Service of a summons and petition shall be made by: (a) leaving a copy thereof with the person summoned at least 3 days before the time stated therein for appearance; (b) leaving a copy at his usual place of abode with some person of the family, of the age of 10 years or upwards, and informing that person of the contents thereof, provided the officer or other person making service shall also send a copy of the summons in a sealed envelope with postage fully prepaid, addressed to the person summoned at his usual place of abode, at least 3 days before the time stated therein for appearance; or (c) leaving a copy thereof with the guardian or custodian of a minor, at least 3 days before the time stated therein for appearance. If the guardian or custodian is an agency of the State of Illinois, proper service may be made by leaving a copy of the summons and petition with any administrative employee of such agency designated by such agency to accept service of summons and petitions. The certificate of the officer or affidavit of the person that he has sent the copy pursuant to this Section is sufficient proof of service.

(6) When a parent or other person, who has signed a written promise to appear and bring the minor to court or who has waived or acknowledged service, fails to appear with the minor on the date set by the court, a bench warrant may be issued for the parent or other person, the minor, or both.

(7) The appearance of the minor's legal guardian or custodian, or a person named as a respondent in a petition, in any proceeding under this Act shall constitute a waiver of service of summons and submission to the jurisdiction of the court, except that the filing of a special appearance authorized under Section 2-301 of the Code of Civil Procedure [735 ILCS 5/2-301] does not constitute an appearance under this subsection. A copy of the summons and petition shall be provided to the person at the time of his appearance.

(Source: P.A. 86-441.) [Formerly Ill. Rev. Stat. 37 §802-15.]

405/2-16. Notice by certified mail or publication.

§2-16. Notice by certified mail or publication. (1) If service on individuals as provided in Section 2-15 [705 ILCS 405/2-15] is not made on any respondent within a reasonable time or if it appears that any respondent resides outside the State, service may be made by certified mail. In such case the clerk shall mail the summons and a copy of the petition to that respondent by certified mail marked for delivery to addressee only. The court shall not proceed with the adjudicatory hearing until 5 days after such mailing. The regular return receipt for certified mail is sufficient proof of service.

(2) If service upon individuals as provided in Section 2-15 is not made on any respondents within a reasonable time or if any person is made a respondent under the designation of "All whom it may Concern", or if service cannot be made because the whereabouts of a respondent are unknown, service may be made by publication. The clerk of the court as soon as possible shall cause publication to be made once in a newspaper of general circulation in the county where the action is pending. Notice by publication is not required in any case when the person alleged to have legal custody of the minor has been served with summons personally or by certified mail, but the court may not enter any order or judgment against any person who cannot be served with process other than by publication unless notice by publication is given or unless that person appears. When a minor has been sheltered under Section 2-10 of this Act [705 ILCS 405/2-10] and summons has not been served personally or by certified mail within 20 days from the date of the order of court directing such shelter

care, the clerk of the court shall cause publication. Notice by publication shall be substantially as follows:

"A, B, C, D, (here giving the names of the named respondents, if any) and to All Whom It May Concern (if there is any respondent under that designation):

Take notice that on the .... day of......., 19... a petition was filed under the Juvenile Court Act by .... in the circuit court of........ county entitled 'In the interest of........., a minor', and that in .... courtroom at .... on the .... day of........ at the hour of...., or as soon thereafter as this cause may be heard, an adjudicatory hearing will be held upon the petition to have the child declared to be a ward of the court under that Act. The court has authority in this proceeding to take from you the custody and guardianship of the minor, (and if the petition prays for the appointment of a guardian with power to consent to adoption) and to appoint a guardian with power to consent to adoption of the minor.

Now, unless you appear at the hearing and show cause against the petition, the allegations of the petition may stand admitted as against you and each of you, and an order or judgment entered.

....
Clerk

Dated (the date of publication)"

(3) The clerk shall also at the time of the publication of the notice send a copy thereof by mail to each of the respondents on account of whom publication is made at his or her last known address. The certificate of the clerk that he or she has mailed the notice is evidence thereof. No other publication notice is required. Every respondent notified by publication under this Section must appear and answer in open court at the hearing. The court may not proceed with the adjudicatory hearing until 10 days after service by publication on any parent, guardian or legal custodian in the case of a minor described in Section 2-3 or 2-4 [705 ILCS 405/2-3 or 405/2-4].

(4) If it becomes necessary to change the date set for the hearing in order to comply with Section 2-14 [705 ILCS 405/2-14] or with this Section, notice of the resetting of the date must be given, by certified mail or other reasonable means, to each respondent who has been served with summons personally or by certified mail.

(Source: P.A. 85-601.) [Formerly Ill. Rev. Stat. 37 §802-16.]

405/2-17. Guardian ad litem.

§2-17. Guardian ad litem. (1) Immediately upon the filing of a petition alleging that the minor is a person described in Sections 2-3 or 2-4 of this Article [705 ILCS 405/2-3 or 405/2-4], the court shall appoint a guardian ad litem for the minor if:

(a) such petition alleges that the minor is an abused or neglected child; or

(b) such petition alleges that charges alleging the commission of any of the sex offenses defined in Article 11 [720 ILCS 5/11-6 et seq.] or in Sections 12-13, 12-14, 12-15 or 12-16 of the Criminal Code of 1961, as amended [720 ILCS 5/12-13, 5/12-14, 5/12-15 or 5/12-16, have been filed against a defendant in any court and that such minor is the alleged victim of the acts of defendant in the commission of such offense.

Unless the guardian ad litem appointed pursuant to this paragraph (1) is an attorney at law he shall be represented in the performance of his duties by counsel.

(2) Before proceeding with the hearing, the court shall appoint a guardian ad litem for the minor if

(a) no parent, guardian, custodian or relative of the minor appears at the first or any subsequent hearing of the case;

(b) the petition prays for the appointment of a guardian with power to consent to adoption; or

(c) the petition for which the minor is before the court resulted from a report made pursuant to the Abused and Neglected Child Reporting Act [325 ILCS 5/1 et seq.].

(3) The court may appoint a guardian ad litem for the minor whenever it finds that there may be a conflict of interest between the minor and his parents or other custodian or that it is otherwise in the minor's interest to do so.

(4) Unless the guardian ad litem is an attorney, he shall be represented by counsel.

(5) The reasonable fees of a guardian ad litem appointed under this Section shall be fixed by the court and charged to the parents of the minor, to the extent they are able to pay. If the parents are unable to pay those fees, they shall be paid from the general fund of the county.

Whenever the petition alleges that the minor is neglected or abused because of physical abuse inflicted by the parent or guardian the guardian ad litem must have at least one face to face interview with the minor before the beginning of the adjudicatory hearing.

(6) A guardian ad litem appointed under this Section, shall receive copies of any and all classified reports of child abuse and neglect made under the Abused and Neglected Child Reporting Act in which the minor who is the subject of a report under the Abused and Neglected Child Reporting Act, is also the minor for whom the guardian ad litem is appointed under this Section.
(Source: P.A. 86-1167; 87-649.) [Formerly Ill. Rev. Stat. 37 §802-17.]

405/2-18. Evidence.

§2-18. Evidence. (1) At the adjudicatory hearing, the court shall first consider only the question whether the minor is abused, neglected or dependent. The standard of proof and the rules of evidence in the nature of civil proceedings in this State are applicable to proceedings under this Article.

(2) In any hearing under this Act, the following shall constitute prima facie evidence of abuse or neglect, as the case may be:

(a) Proof that a minor has a medical diagnosis of battered child syndrome is prima facie evidence of abuse;

(b) Proof that a minor has a medical diagnosis of failure to thrive syndrome is prima facie evidence of neglect;

(c) Proof that a minor has a medical diagnosis of fetal alcohol syndrome is prima facie evidence of neglect;

(d) Proof that a minor has a medical diagnosis at birth of withdrawal symptoms from narcotics or barbiturates is prima facie evidence of neglect;

(e) Proof of injuries sustained by a minor or of the condition of a minor of such a nature as would ordinarily not be sustained or exist except by reason of the acts or omissions of the parent, custodian or guardian of such minor shall be prima facie evidence of abuse or neglect, as the case may be;

(f) Proof that a parent, custodian or guardian of a minor repeatedly used a drug, to the extent that it has or would ordinarily have the effect of producing in the user a substantial state of stupor, unconsciousness, intoxication, hallucination, disorientation or incompetence, or a substantial impairment of judgment, or a substantial manifestation of irrationality, shall be prima facie evidence of neglect.

(3) In any hearing under this Act, proof of the abuse, neglect or dependency of one minor shall be admissible evidence on the issue of the abuse, neglect or dependency of any other minor for whom the respondent is responsible.

(4) (a) Any writing, record, photograph or x-ray of any hospital or public or private agency, whether in the form of an entry in a book or otherwise, made as a memorandum or record of any condition, act, transaction, occurrence or

event relating to a minor in an abuse, neglect or dependency proceeding, shall be admissible in evidence as proof of that condition, act, transaction, occurrence or event, if the court finds that the document was made in the regular course of the business of the hospital or agency and that it was in the regular course of such business to make it, at the time of the act, transaction, occurrence or event, or within a reasonable time thereafter. A certification by the head or responsible employee of the hospital or agency that the writing, record, photograph or x-ray is the full and complete record of the condition, act, transaction, occurrence or event and that it satisfies the conditions of this paragraph shall be prima facie evidence of the facts contained in such certification. A certification by someone other than the head of the hospital or agency shall be accompanied by a photocopy of a delegation of authority signed by both the head of the hospital or agency and by such other employee. All other circumstances of the making of the memorandum, record, photograph or x-ray, including lack of personal knowledge of the maker, may be proved to affect the weight to be accorded such evidence, but shall not affect its admissibility.

(b) Any indicated report filed pursuant to the Abused and Neglected Child Reporting Act [325 ILCS 5/1 et seq.] shall be admissible in evidence.

(c) Previous statements made by the minor relating to any allegations of abuse or neglect shall be admissible in evidence. However, no such statement, if uncorroborated and not subject to cross-examination, shall be sufficient in itself to support a finding of abuse or neglect.

(d) There shall be a rebuttable presumption that a minor is competent to testify in abuse or neglect proceedings. The court shall determine how much weight to give to the minor's testimony, and may allow the minor to testify in chambers with only the court, the court reporter and attorneys for the parties present.

(e) The privileged character of communication between any professional person and patient or client, except privilege between attorney and client, shall not apply to proceedings subject to this Article.

(f) Proof of the impairment of emotional health or impairment of mental or emotional condition as a result of the failure of the respondent to exercise a minimum degree of care toward a minor may include competent opinion or expert testimony, and may include proof that such impairment lessened during a period when the minor was in the care, custody or supervision of a person or agency other than the respondent.

(5) In any hearing under this Act alleging neglect for failure to provide education as required by law under subsection (1) of Section 2-3 [705 ILCS 405/2-3], proof that a minor under 13 years of age who is subject to compulsory school attendance under The School Code is a chronic truant as defined under The School Code shall be prima facie evidence of neglect by the parent or guardian in any hearing under this Act and proof that a minor who is 13 years of age or older who is subject to compulsory school attendance under The School Code [105 ILCS 5/1-1 et seq.] is a chronic truant shall raise a rebuttable presumption of neglect by the parent or guardian. This subsection (5) shall not apply in counties with 2,000,000 or more inhabitants.

(Source: P.A. 86-883.) [Formerly Ill. Rev. Stat. 37 §802-18.]

405/2-19. Preliminary orders after filing a petition.

§2-19. Preliminary orders after filing a petition. In all cases involving physical abuse the court shall order, and in all cases involving neglect or sexual abuse the court may order, an examination of the child under Section 2-11 of this Act [705 ILCS 405/2-11] or by a physician appointed or designated for this purpose by the court. As part of the examination, the physician shall arrange to have color photographs taken, as soon as practical, of areas of trauma visible on the child and may, if indicated, arrange to have a radiological examination

performed on the child. The physician, on the completion of the examination, shall forward the results of the examination together with the color photographs to the State's Attorney of the county of the court ordering such examination. The court may dispense with the examination in those cases which were commenced on the basis of a physical examination by a physician. Unless color photographs have already been taken or unless there are no areas of visible trauma, the court shall arrange to have color photographs taken if no such examination is conducted.
(Chgd. by P.A. 87-1148, §2, eff. 1/1/93.)
(Source: P.A. 85-601.) [Formerly Ill. Rev. Stat. 37 §802-19.]

405/2-20. Continuance under supervision.

§2-20. Continuance under supervision. (1) The court may enter an order of continuance under supervision (a) upon an admission or stipulation by the appropriate respondent or minor respondent of the facts supporting the petition and before proceeding to findings and adjudication, or after hearing the evidence at the adjudicatory hearing but before noting in the minutes of proceeding a finding of whether or not the minor is abused, neglected or dependent; and (b) in the absence of objection made in open court by the minor, his parent, guardian, custodian, responsible relative, defense attorney or the State's Attorney.

(2) If the minor, his parent, guardian, custodian, responsible relative, defense attorney or the State's Attorney, objects in open court to any such continuance and insists upon proceeding to findings and adjudication, the court shall so proceed.

(3) Nothing in this Section limits the power of the court to order a continuance of the hearing for the production of additional evidence or for any other proper reason.

(4) When a hearing where a minor is alleged to be abused, neglected or dependent is continued pursuant to this Section, the court may permit the minor to remain in his home subject to such conditions concerning his conduct and supervision as the court may require by order.

(5) If a petition is filed charging a violation of a condition of the continuance under supervision, the court shall conduct a hearing. If the court finds that such condition of supervision has not been fulfilled the court may proceed to findings and adjudication and disposition. The filing of a petition for violation of a condition of the continuance under supervision shall toll the period of continuance under supervision until the final determination of the charge, and the term of the continuance under supervision shall not run until the hearing and disposition of the petition for violation; provided where the petition alleges conduct that does not constitute a criminal offense, the hearing must be held within 15 days of the filing of the petition unless a delay in such hearing has been occasioned by the minor, in which case the delay shall continue the tolling of the period of continuance under supervision for the period of such delay.
(Source: P.A. 85-601.) [Formerly Ill. Rev. Stat. 37 §802-20.]

405/2-21. Findings and adjudication.

§2-21. Findings and adjudication. (1) After hearing the evidence the court shall make and note in the minutes of the proceeding a finding of whether or not the minor is abused, neglected or dependent. If it finds that the minor is not such a person, the court shall order the petition dismissed and the minor discharged.

(2) If the court finds and notes in its findings that the minor is either abused or neglected or dependent, the court shall then set a time not later than 30 days after the entry of the finding for a dispositional hearing to be conducted under Section 2-22 [705 ILCS 405/2-22] at which hearing the court shall determine

whether it is in the best interests of the minor and the public that he be made a ward of the court. To assist the court in making this and other determinations at the dispositional hearing, the court may order that an investigation be conducted and a dispositional report be prepared concerning the minor's physical and mental history and condition, family situation and background, economic status, education, occupation, history of delinquency or criminality, personal habits, and any other information that may be helpful to the court. The dispositional hearing may be continued once for a period not to exceed 30 days if the court finds that such continuance is necessary to complete the dispositional report.

If the court finds that the minor is abused, neglected or dependent, the court shall then find whether such abuse, neglect or dependency is the result of physical abuse to the minor inflicted by a parent, guardian or legal custodian and such finding shall appear in the order of the court.

(3) The time limits of this Section may be waived only by consent of all parties and approval by the court.

(4) For all cases adjudicated prior to July 1, 1991, for which no dispositional hearing has been held prior to that date, a dispositional hearing under Section 2-22 shall be held within 90 days of July 1, 1991.

(Source: P.A. 85-601; 86-1293.) [Formerly Ill. Rev. Stat. 37 §802-21.]

405/2-22. Dispositional hearing; evidence; continuance.

§2-22. Dispositional hearing; evidence; continuance. (1) At the dispositional hearing, the court shall determine whether it is in the best interests of the minor and the public that he be made a ward of the court, and, if he is to be made a ward of the court, the court shall determine the proper disposition best serving the interests of the minor and the public. All evidence helpful in determining these questions, including oral and written reports, may be admitted and may be relied upon to the extent of its probative value, even though not competent for the purposes of the adjudicatory hearing.

(2) Notice in compliance with Sections 2-15 and 2-16 [705 ILCS 405/2-15 and 405/2-16] must be given to all parties-respondents prior to proceeding to a dispositional hearing. Before making an order of disposition the court shall advise the State's Attorney, the parents, guardian, custodian or responsible relative or their counsel of the factual contents and the conclusions of the reports prepared for the use of the court and considered by it, and afford fair opportunity, if requested, to controvert them. The court may order, however, that the documents containing such reports need not be submitted to inspection, or that sources of confidential information need not be disclosed except to the attorneys for the parties. Factual contents, conclusions, documents and sources disclosed by the court under this paragraph shall not be further disclosed without the express approval of the court pursuant to an in camera hearing.

(3) A record of a prior continuance under supervision under Section 2-20 [705 ILCS 405/2-20], whether successfully completed or not, is admissible at the dispositional hearing.

(4) On its own motion or that of the State's Attorney, a parent, guardian, custodian, responsible relative or counsel, the court may adjourn the hearing for a reasonable period to receive reports or other evidence. In scheduling investigations and hearings, the court shall give priority to proceedings in which a minor has been removed from his or her home before an order of disposition has been made.

(Source: P.A. 85-601.) [Formerly Ill. Rev. Stat. 37 §802-22.]

405/2-23. Kinds of dispositional orders.

§2-23. Kinds of dispositional orders. (1) The following kinds of orders of disposition may be made in respect of wards of the court:

(a) A minor under 18 years of age found to be neglected or abused under Section 2-3 [705 ILCS 405/2-3] may be (1) continued in the custody of his or her parents, guardian or legal custodian; (2) placed in accordance with Section 2-27 [705 ILCS 405/2-27]; or (3) ordered partially or completely emancipated in accordance with the provisions of the "Emancipation of Mature Minors Act", approved September 19, 1979, as now or hereafter amended [750 ILCS 30/1 et seq.].

However, in any case in which a minor is found by the court to be neglected or abused under Section 2-3 of this Act, custody of the minor shall not be restored to any parent, guardian or legal custodian found by the court to have caused the neglect or to have inflicted the abuse on the minor until such time as a hearing is held on the issue of the fitness of such parent, guardian or legal custodian to care for the minor and the court enters an order that such parent, guardian or legal custodian is fit to care for the minor.

(b) A minor under 18 years of age found to be dependent under Section 2-4 [705 ILCS 405/2-4] may be (1) placed in accordance with Section 2-27 or (2) ordered partially or completely emancipated in accordance with the provisions of the "Emancipation of Mature Minors Act", approved September 19, 1979, as now or hereafter amended.

However, in any case in which a minor is found by the court to be dependent under Section 2-4 of this Act and the court has made a further finding under paragraph (2) of Section 2-21 [705 ILCS 405/2-21] that such dependency is the result of physical abuse, custody of the minor shall not be restored to any parent, guardian or legal custodian found by the court to have inflicted physical abuse on the minor until such time as a hearing is held on the issue of the fitness of such parent, guardian or legal custodian to care for the minor and the court enters an order that such parent, guardian or legal custodian is fit to care for the minor.

(2) Any order of disposition may provide for protective supervision under Section 2-24 [705 ILCS 405/2-24] and may include an order of protection under Section 2-25 [705 ILCS 405/2-25].

(3) Unless the order of disposition expressly so provides, it does not operate to close proceedings on the pending petition, but is subject to modification until final closing and discharge of the proceedings under Section 2-31 [705 ILCS 405/2-31].

(4) In addition to any other order of disposition, the court may order any minor adjudicated neglected with respect to his or her own injurious behavior to make restitution, in monetary or non-monetary form, under the terms and conditions of Section 5-5-6 of the "Unified Code of Corrections" [730 ILCS 5/5-5-6], except that the "presentence hearing" referred to therein shall be the dispositional hearing for purposes of this Section. The parent, guardian or legal custodian of the minor may pay some or all of such restitution on the minor's behalf.

(5) Any order for disposition where the minor is committed or placed in accordance with Section 2-27 shall provide for the parents or guardian of the estate of such minor to pay to the legal custodian or guardian of the person of the minor such sums as are determined by the custodian or guardian of the person of the minor as necessary for the minor's needs. Such payments may not exceed the maximum amounts provided for by Section 5.1 of "An Act creating the Department of Children and Family Services, codifying its powers and duties and repealing certain Acts and Sections herein named", approved June 4, 1963, as amended [see 20 ILCS 505/9.1].

(6) Whenever the order of disposition requires the minor to attend school or participate in a program of training, the truant officer or designated school

official shall regularly report to the court if the minor is a chronic or habitual truant under Section 26-2a of The School Code [105 ILCS 5/26-2a].
(Source: P.A. 85-601.) [Formerly Ill. Rev. Stat. 37 §802-23.]

405/2-24. Protective supervision.

§2-24. Protective supervision. If the order of disposition releases the minor to the custody of his parents, guardian or legal custodian, or continues him in such custody, the court may place the person having custody of the minor, except for representatives of private or public agencies or governmental departments, under supervision of the probation office. Rules or orders of court shall define the terms and conditions of protective supervision, which may be modified or terminated when the court finds that the best interests of the minor and the public will be served thereby.
(Source: P.A. 85-601.) [Formerly Ill. Rev. Stat. 37 §802-24.]

405/2-25. Order of protection.

§2-25. Order of protection. (1) The court may make an order of protection in assistance of or as a condition of any other order authorized by this Act. The order of protection may set forth reasonable conditions of behavior to be observed for a specified period. Such an order may require a person:

(a) To stay away from the home or the minor;

(b) To permit a parent to visit the minor at stated periods;

(c) To abstain from offensive conduct against the minor, his parent or any person to whom custody of the minor is awarded;

(d) To give proper attention to the care of the home;

(e) To cooperate in good faith with an agency to which custody of a minor is entrusted by the court or with an agency or association to which the minor is referred by the court;

(f) To prohibit and prevent any contact whatsoever with the respondent minor by a specified individual or individuals who are alleged in either a criminal or juvenile proceeding to have caused injury to a respondent minor or a sibling of a respondent minor;

(g) To refrain from acts of commission or omission that tend to make the home not a proper place for the minor.

(2) The court shall enter an order of protection to prohibit and prevent any contact between a respondent minor or a sibling of a respondent minor and any person named in a petition seeking an order of protection who has been convicted of heinous battery under Section 12-4.1, aggravated battery of a child under Section 12-4.3, criminal sexual assault under Section 12-13, aggravated criminal sexual assault under Section 12-14, criminal sexual abuse under Section 12-15, or aggravated criminal sexual abuse under Section 12-16 of the Criminal Code of 1961 [720 ILCS 5/12-4.1, 5/12-4.3, 5/12-13, 5/12-14, 5/12-15 or 5/12-16], or has been convicted of an offense that resulted in the death of a child, or has violated a previous order of protection under this Section.

(3) When the court issues an order of protection against any person as provided by this Section, the court shall direct a copy of such order to the Sheriff of that county. The Sheriff shall furnish a copy of the order of protection to the Department of State Police with 24 hours of receipt, in the form and manner required by the Department. The Department of State Police shall maintain a complete record and index of such orders of protection and make this data available to all local law enforcement agencies.

(4) After notice and opportunity for hearing afforded to a person subject to an order of protection, the order may be modified or extended for a further specified period or both or may be terminated if the court finds that the best interests of the minor and the public will be served thereby.

(5) An order of protection may be sought at any time during the course of any proceeding conducted pursuant to this Act. Any person against whom an order of protection is sought may retain counsel to represent him at a hearing, and has rights to be present at the hearing, to be informed prior to the hearing in writing of the contents of the petition seeking a protective order and of the date, place and time of such hearing, and to cross examine witnesses called by the petitioner and to present witnesses and argument in opposition to the relief sought in the petition.

(6) Diligent efforts shall be made by the petitioner to serve any person or persons against whom any order of protection is sought with written notice of the contents of the petition seeking a protective order and of the date, place and time at which the hearing on the petition is to be held. When a protective order is being sought in conjunction with a temporary custody hearing, if the court finds that the person against whom the protective order is being sought has been notified of the hearing or that diligent efforts have been made to notify such person, the court may conduct a hearing. If a protective order is sought at any time other than in conjunction with a temporary custody hearing, the court may not conduct a hearing on the petition in the absence of the person against whom the order is sought unless the petitioner has notified such person by personal service at least 3 days before the hearing or has sent written notice by first class mail to such person's last known address at least 5 days before the hearing.

(7) A person against whom an order of protection is being sought who is neither a parent, guardian, legal custodian or responsible relative as described in Section 1-5 [705 ILCS 405/1-5] is not a party or respondent as defined in that Section and shall not be entitled to the rights provided therein. Such person does not have a right to appointed counsel or to be present at any hearing other than the hearing in which the order of protection is being sought or a hearing directly pertaining to that order. Unless the court orders otherwise, such person does not have a right to inspect the court file.

(8) All protective orders entered under this Section shall be in writing. Unless the person against whom the order was obtained was present in court when the order was issued, the sheriff, other law enforcement official or special process server shall promptly serve that order upon that person and file proof of such service, in the manner provided for service of process in civil proceedings. The person against whom the protective order was obtained may seek a modification of the order by filing a written motion to modify the order within 7 days after actual receipt by the person of a copy of the order.
(Source: P.A. 85-1209.) [Formerly Ill. Rev. Stat. 37 §802-25.]

405/2-26. Enforcement of orders of protective supervision or of protection.

§2-26. Enforcement of orders of protective supervision or of protection. (1) Orders of protective supervision and orders of protection may be enforced by citation to show cause for contempt of court by reason of any violation thereof and, where protection of the welfare of the minor so requires, by the issuance of a warrant to take the alleged violator into custody and bring him before the court.

(2) In any case where an order of protection has been entered, the clerk of the court may issue to the petitioner, to the minor or to any other person affected by the order a certificate stating that an order of protection has been made by the court concerning such persons and setting forth its terms and requirements. The presentation of the certificate to any peace officer authorizes him to take into custody a person charged with violating the terms of the order of protection, to bring such person before the court and, within the limits of his legal authority

as such peace officer, otherwise to aid in securing the protection the order is intended to afford.
(Source: P.A. 85-601.) [Formerly Ill. Rev. Stat. 37 §802-26.]

405/2-27. Placement; legal custody or guardianship.

§2-27. Placement; legal custody or guardianship. (1) If the court finds that the parents, guardian or legal custodian of a minor adjudged a ward of the court are unfit or are unable, for some reason other than financial circumstances alone, to care for, protect, train or discipline the minor or are unwilling to do so, and that appropriate services aimed at family preservation and family reunification have been unsuccessful in rectifying the conditions which have led to a finding of unfitness or inability to care for, protect, train or discipline the minor, and that it is in the best interest of the minor to take him from the custody of his parents, guardian or custodian, the court may:

(a) place him in the custody of a suitable relative or other person;

(b) place him under the guardianship of a probation officer;

(c) commit him to an agency for care or placement, except an institution under the authority of the Department of Corrections or of the Department of Children and Family Services;

(d) commit him to the Department of Children and Family Services for care and service. The Department shall be given due notice of the pendency of the action and the Guardianship Administrator of the Department of Children and Family Services shall be appointed guardian of the person of the minor. Whenever the Department discharges a minor from its care and service, the Guardianship Administrator shall petition the court for an order terminating guardianship. The Guardianship Administrator may designate one or more other officers of the Department, appointed as Department officers by administrative order of the Department Director, authorized to affix the signature of the Guardianship Administrator to documents affecting the guardian-ward relationship of children for whom he has been appointed guardian at such times as he is unable to perform the duties of his office. The signature authorization shall include but not be limited to matters of consent of marriage, enlistment in the armed forces, legal proceedings, adoption, major medical and surgical treatment and application for driver's license. Signature authorizations made pursuant to the provisions of this paragraph shall be filed with the Secretary of State and the Secretary of State shall provide upon payment of the customary fee, certified copies of the authorization to any court or individual who requests a copy.

(2) When making a placement, the court, wherever possible, shall select a person holding the same religious belief as that of the minor or a private agency controlled by persons of like religious faith of the minor. In addition, whenever alternative plans for placement are available, the court shall ascertain and consider, to the extent appropriate in the particular case, the views and preferences of the minor.

(3) When a minor is placed with a suitable relative or other person, the court shall appoint him the legal custodian or guardian of the person of the minor. When a minor is committed to any agency, the court shall appoint the proper officer or representative thereof as legal custodian or guardian of the person of the minor. Legal custodians and guardians of the person of the minor have the respective rights and duties set forth in subsection (9) of Section 1-3 [705 ILCS 405/1-3] except as otherwise provided by order of court; but no guardian of the person may consent to adoption of the minor unless that authority is conferred upon him in accordance with Section 2-29 [705 ILCS 405/2-29]. An agency whose representative is appointed guardian of the person or legal custodian of the minor may place him in any child care facility, but the facility must be licensed

under the Child Care Act of 1969 [225 ILCS 10/1 et seq.] or have been approved by the Department of Children and Family Services as meeting the standards established for such licensing. No agency may place a minor adjudicated under Sections 2-3 or 2-4 [705 ILCS 405/2-3 or 405/2-4] in a child care facility unless the placement is in compliance with the rules and regulations for placement under this Section promulgated by the Department of Children and Family Services under Section 5 of the Children and Family Services Act [20 ILCS 505/5]. Like authority and restrictions shall be conferred by the court upon any probation officer who has been appointed guardian of the person of a minor.

(4) No placement by any probation officer or agency whose representative is appointed guardian of the person or legal custodian of a minor may be made in any out of State child care facility unless it complies with the Interstate Compact on the Placement of Children [45 ILCS 15/0.01 et seq.].

(5) The clerk of the court shall issue to the legal custodian or guardian of the person a certified copy of the order of court, as proof of his authority. No other process is necessary as authority for the keeping of the minor.

(6) Custody or guardianship granted under this Section continues until the court otherwise directs, but not after the minor reaches the age of 19 years except as set forth in Section 2-31.

(Source: P.A. 87-14.) [Formerly Ill. Rev. Stat. 37 §802-27.]

405/2-28. Court review.

§2-28. Court review. (1) The court may require any legal custodian or guardian of the person appointed under this Act to report periodically to the court or may cite him into court and require him or his agency, to make a full and accurate report of his or its doings in behalf of the minor. The custodian or guardian, within 10 days after such citation, shall make the report, either in writing verified by affidavit or orally under oath in open court, or otherwise as the court directs. Upon the hearing of the report the court may remove the custodian or guardian and appoint another in his stead or restore the minor to the custody of his parents or former guardian or custodian. However, custody of the minor shall not be restored to any parent, guardian or legal custodian in any case in which the minor is found to be neglected or abused under Section 2-3 of this Act [705 ILCS 405/2-3] and such neglect or abuse is found by the court under paragraph (2) of Section 2-21 of this Act [705 ILCS 405/2-21] to be the result of physical abuse inflicted on the minor by such parent, guardian or legal custodian, until such time as an investigation is made as provided in paragraph (4) and a hearing is held on the issue of the fitness of such parent, guardian or legal custodian to care for the minor and the court enters an order that such parent, guardian or legal custodian is fit to care for the minor.

(2) A guardian or custodian appointed by the court pursuant to this Act shall file updated case plans with the court every 6 months. Every agency which has guardianship of a child shall file a supplemental petition for court review, or review by an administrative body appointed or approved by the court and further order within 18 months of an order for shelter care pursuant to Section 2-10 [705 ILCS 405/2-10] and each 18 months thereafter. Such petition shall state facts relative to the child's present condition of physical, mental and emotional health as well as facts relative to his present custodial or foster care. The petition shall be set for hearing and the clerk shall mail 10 days notice of the hearing by certified mail return receipt requested to the person or agency having the physical custody of the child, the minor and other interested parties unless a written waiver of notice is filed with the petition.

Rights of wards of the court under this Act are enforceable against any public agency by complaints for relief by mandamus filed in any proceedings brought under this Act.

(3) The minor or any person interested in the minor may apply to the court for a change in custody of the minor and the appointment of a new custodian or guardian of the person or for the restoration of the minor to the custody of his parents or former guardian or custodian. However, custody of the minor shall not be restored to any parent, guardian or legal custodian in any case in which the minor is found to be neglected or abused under Section 2-3 of this Act and such neglect or abuse is found by the court under paragraph (2) of Section 2-21 of this Act to be the result of physical abuse inflicted on the minor by such parent, guardian or legal custodian, until such time as an investigation is made as provided in paragraph (4) and a hearing is held on the issue of the fitness of such parent, guardian or legal custodian to care for the minor and the court enters an order that such parent, guardian or legal custodian is fit to care for the minor. In the event that the minor has attained 18 years of age and the guardian or custodian petitions the court for an order terminating his guardianship or custody, guardianship or custody shall terminate automatically 30 days after the receipt of the petition unless the court orders otherwise. No legal custodian or guardian of the person may be removed without his consent until given notice and an opportunity to be heard by the court.

(4) Whenever a parent, guardian, or legal custodian petitions for restoration of custody of the minor, and the minor was adjudicated neglected or abused as a result of physical abuse, the court shall cause to be made an investigation as to whether the petitioner has ever been charged with or convicted of any criminal offense which would indicate the likelihood of any further physical abuse to the minor. Evidence of such criminal convictions shall be taken into account in determining fitness of the parent, guardian, or legal custodian.

(a) Any agency of this State or any subdivision thereof shall co-operate with the agent of the court in providing any information sought in the investigation.

(b) The information derived from the investigation and any conclusions or recommendations derived from the information shall be provided to the parent, guardian, or legal custodian seeking restoration of custody prior to the hearing on fitness and the petitioner shall have an opportunity at the hearing to refute the information or contest its significance.

(c) No information obtained from any investigation may be placed in any automated information system. All information shall be confidential as provided in Section 1-10 of this Act [705 ILCS 405/1-10].

(Source: P.A. 85-1235.) [Formerly Ill. Rev. Stat. 37 §802-28.]

405/2-29. Adoption; appointment of guardian with power to consent.

§2-29. Adoption; appointment of guardian with power to consent. (1) A ward of the court under this Act, with the consent of the court, may be the subject of a petition for adoption under "An Act in relation to the adoption of persons, and to repeal an Act therein named", approved July 17, 1959, as now or hereafter amended [750 ILCS 50/0.01 et seq.], or with like consent his or her parent or parents may, in the manner required by such Act, surrender him or her for adoption to an agency legally authorized or licensed to place children for adoption.

(2) If the petition prays and the court finds that it is in the best interest of the minor that a guardian of the person be appointed and authorized to consent to the adoption of the minor, the court with the consent of the parents, if living, or after finding, based upon clear and convincing evidence, that a non-consenting parent is an unfit person as defined in Section 1 of "An Act in relation to the adoption of persons, and to repeal an Act therein named", approved July 17, 1959, as amended [750 ILCS 50/0.01], may empower the guardian of the person of the minor, in the order appointing him or her as such guardian, to appear in court where any proceedings for the adoption of the minor may at any time be pending and to consent to the adoption. Such consent is sufficient to

authorize the court in the adoption proceedings to enter a proper order or judgment of adoption without further notice to, or consent by, the parents of the minor. An order so empowering the guardian to consent to adoption terminates parental rights, deprives the parents of the minor of all legal rights as respects the minor and relieves them of all parental responsibility for him or her, and frees the minor from all obligations of maintenance and obedience to his or her natural parents.

If the minor is over 14 years of age, the court may, in its discretion, consider the wishes of the minor in determining whether the best interests of the minor would be promoted by the finding of the unfitness of a non-consenting parent.

(3) Parental consent to the order authorizing the guardian of the person to consent to adoption of the minor shall be given in open court whenever possible and otherwise must be in writing and signed in the form provided in "An Act in relation to the adoption of persons, and to repeal an Act therein named", approved July 17, 1959, as now or hereafter amended, but no names of petitioners for adoption need be included. A finding of the unfitness of a nonconsenting parent must be made in compliance with that Act and be based upon clear and convincing evidence. Provisions of that Act relating to minor parents and to mentally ill or mentally deficient parents apply to proceedings under this Section and any findings with respect to such parents shall be based upon clear and convincing evidence.

(Source: P.A. 85-601.) [Formerly Ill. Rev. Stat. 37 §802-29.]

405/2-30. Notice to putative father; service.

§2-30. Notice to putative father; service. Upon the written request to any clerk of any circuit court by any interested party, including persons intending to adopt a child, a child welfare agency with whom the mother has placed or has given written notice of her intention to place a child for adoption, the mother of a child, or any attorney representing an interested party, a notice may be served on a putative father in the same manner as Summons is served in other proceedings under this Act, or in lieu of personal service, service may be made as follows:

(a) The person requesting notice shall furnish to the clerk an original and one copy of a notice together with an affidavit setting forth the putative father's last known address. The original notice shall be retained by the clerk.

(b) The clerk forthwith shall mail to the putative father, at the address appearing in the affidavit, the copy of the notice, certified mail, return receipt requested; the envelope and return receipt shall bear the return address of the clerk. The receipt for certified mail shall state the name and address of the addressee, and the date of mailing, and shall be attached to the original notice.

(c) The return receipt, when returned to the clerk, shall be attached to the original notice, and shall constitute proof of service.

(d) The clerk shall note the fact of service in a permanent record.

2.* The notice shall be signed by the clerk, and may be served on the putative father at any time after conception, and shall read as follows:

**So in original. No subsec. 1 has been designated.*

"IN THE MATTER OF NOTICE TO . . . . , PUTATIVE FATHER.

You have been identified as the father of a child (born on the . . . . . day of . . . . . , 19 . . .), or (expected to be born on or about the . . . . . day of . . . . . , 19. . .). The mother of said child is . . . .

The mother has indicated she intends to place the child for adoption or otherwise have a judgment entered terminating her rights with respect to such child.

As the alleged father of said child, you have certain legal rights with respect to said child, including the right to notice of the filing of proceedings instituted for the termination of your parental rights regarding said child. If you wish to retain your rights with respect to said child, you must file with the Clerk of this Circuit Court of . . . . . , County, Illinois, whose address is . . . . . , ... , Illinois, within 30 days after the date of receipt of this notice, a declaration of paternity stating that you are, in fact, the father of said child and that you intend to retain your legal rights with respect to said child, or request to be notified of any further proceedings with respect to custody, termination of parental rights or adoption of the child.

If you do not file such a declaration of paternity, or a request for notice, then whatever legal rights you have with respect to said child, including the right to notice of any future proceedings for the adoption of said child, may be terminated without any further notice to you. When your legal rights with respect to said child are so terminated, you will not be entitled to notice of any proceeding instituted for the adoption of said child.

If you are not the father of said child, you may file with the Clerk of this Court, a disclaimer of paternity which will be noted in the Clerk's file and you will receive no further notice with respect to said child".

The disclaimer of paternity shall be substantially as follows:

"IN THE CIRCUIT COURT OF THE
.... JUDICIAL CIRCUIT, ILLINOIS
.... County

____)
)
) No.
)
____)

DENIAL OF PATERNITY WITH ENTRY OF APPEARANCE AND CONSENT TO ADOPTION

I, ... , state as follows:

(1) That I am . . . . . years of age; and I reside at . . . . in the County of . . . . , State of . . . .

(2) That I have been advised that . . . . is the mother of a . . . . . male child named . . . . born or expected to be born on or about . . . . and that such mother has stated that I am the father of this child.

(3) I deny that I am the father of this child.

(4) I further understand that the mother of this child wishes to consent to the adoption of the child. I hereby consent to the adoption of this child, and waive any rights, remedies and defenses that I may now or in the future have as a result of the mother's allegation of the paternity of this child. This consent is being given in order to facilitate the adoption of the child and so that the court may terminate what rights I may have to the child as a result of being named the father by the mother. This consent is not in any manner an admission of paternity.

(5) I hereby enter my appearance in the above entitled cause and waive service of summons and other pleading and consent to an immediate hearing on a petition TO TERMINATE PARENTAL RIGHTS AND TO APPOINT A GUARDIAN WITH THE POWER TO CONSENT TO THE ADOPTION OF THIS CHILD.

OATH

I have been duly sworn and I say under oath that I have read and understood this Denial of Paternity With Entry of Appearance and Consent to Adoption.

The facts it contains are true and correct to the best of my knowledge, and I understand that by signing this document I have not admitted paternity. I have signed this document as my free and voluntary act in order to facilitate the adoption of the child.

. . . .
(signature)

Dated this . . . . . day of . . . . . , 19. . .
Signed and Sworn Before Me This . . . . . day of . . . . . , 19. . .

. . . .
(notary public)".

The names of adoptive parents, if any, shall not be included in the notice.

3. If the putative father files a disclaimer of paternity, he shall be deemed not to be the father of the child with respect to any adoption or other proceeding held to terminate the rights of parents as respects such child.

4. In the event the putative father does not file a declaration of paternity of the child or request for notice within 30 days of service of the above notice, he need not be made a party to or given notice of any proceeding brought for the adoption of the child. An order or judgment may be entered in such proceeding terminating all of his rights with respect to said child without further notice to him.

5. If the putative father files a declaration of paternity or a request for notice in accordance with subsection 2 with respect to the child, he shall be given notice in the event any proceeding is brought for the adoption of the child or for termination of parents' rights of the child.

6. The Clerk shall maintain separate numbered files and records of requests and proofs of service and all other documents filed pursuant to this article. All such records shall be impounded.

(Source: P.A. 85-601.) [Formerly Ill. Rev. Stat. 37 §802-30.]

405/2-31. Duration of wardship and discharge of proceedings.

§2-31. Duration of wardship and discharge of proceedings. (1) All proceedings under this Act in respect of any minor for whom a petition was filed after the effective date of this amendatory Act of 1991 automatically terminate upon his attaining the age of 19 years, except that a court may continue the wardship of a minor until age 21 for good cause when there is satisfactory evidence presented to the court that the best interest of the minor and the public require the continuation of the wardship.

(2) Whenever the court finds that the best interests of the minor and the public no longer require the wardship of the court, the court shall order the wardship terminated and all proceedings under this Act respecting that minor finally closed and discharged. The court may at the same time continue or terminate any custodianship or guardianship theretofore ordered but the termination must be made in compliance with Section 2-28 [705 ILCS 405/2-28].

(3) The wardship of the minor and any custodianship or guardianship respecting the minor for whom a petition was filed after the effective date of this amendatory Act of 1991 automatically terminates when he attains the age of 19 years except as set forth in subsection (1) of this Section. The clerk of the court shall at that time record all proceedings under this Act as finally closed and discharged for that reason.

(Source: P.A. 87-14.) [Formerly Ill. Rev. Stat. 37 §802-31.]

ARTICLE III. MINORS REQUIRING AUTHORITATIVE INTERVENTION

Sec.

405/3-1. Jurisdictional facts.

§3-1. Jurisdictional facts. Proceedings may be instituted under this Article concerning boys and girls who require authoritative intervention as defined in Section 3-3 [705 ILCS 405/3-3] or who are truant minors in need of supervision as defined in Section 3-33 [705 ILCS 405/3-33].
(Source: P.A. 85-1235.) [Formerly Ill. Rev. Stat. 37 §803-1.]

405/3-2. Venue.

§3-2. (1) Venue under this Article lies in the county where the minor resides or is found.

(2) If proceedings are commenced in any county other than that of the minor's residence, the court in which the proceedings were initiated may at any time before or after adjudication of wardship transfer the case to the county of the minor's residence by transmitting to the court in that county an authenticated copy of the court record, including all documents, petitions and orders filed therein, and the minute orders and docket entries of the court. Transfer in like manner may be made in the event of a change of residence from one county to another of a minor concerning whom proceedings are pending.
(Source: P.A. 85-601.) [Formerly Ill. Rev. Stat. 37 §803-2.]

405/3-3. Minor requiring authoritative intervention.

§3-3. Minor requiring authoritative intervention. Those requiring authoritative intervention include any minor under 18 years of age (1) who is (a) absent from home without consent of parent, guardian or custodian, or (b) beyond the control of his or her parent, guardian or custodian, in circumstances which constitute a substantial or immediate danger to the minor's physical safety; and (2) who, after being taken into limited custody for the period provided for in this Section and offered interim crisis intervention services, where available, refuses to return home after the minor and his or her parent, guardian or

custodian cannot agree to an arrangement for an alternative voluntary residential placement or to the continuation of such placement. Any minor taken into limited custody for the reasons specified in this Section may not be adjudicated a minor requiring authoritative intervention until the following number of days have elapsed from his or her having been taken into limited custody: 21 days for the first instance of being taken into limited custody and 5 days for the second, third, or fourth instances of being taken into limited custody. For the fifth or any subsequent instance of being taken into limited custody for the reasons specified in this Section, the minor may be adjudicated as requiring authoritative intervention without any specified period of time expiring after his or her being taken into limited custody, without the minor's being offered interim crisis intervention services, and without the minor's being afforded an opportunity to agree to an arrangement for an alternative voluntary residential placement. Notwithstanding any other provision of this Section, for the first instance in which a minor is taken into limited custody where one year has elapsed from the last instance of his having been taken into limited custody, the minor may not be adjudicated a minor requiring authoritative intervention until 21 days have passed since being taken into limited custody.
(Source: P.A. 85-601.) [Formerly Ill. Rev. Stat. 37 §803-3.]

405/3-4. Taking into limited custody.

§3-4. Taking into limited custody. (a) A law enforcement officer may, without a warrant, take into limited custody a minor who the law enforcement officer reasonably determines is (i) absent from home without consent of the minor's parent, guardian or custodian, or (ii) beyond the control of his or her parent, guardian or custodian, in circumstances which constitute a substantial or immediate danger to the minor's physical safety.

(b) A law enforcement officer who takes a minor into limited custody shall (i) immediately inform the minor of the reasons for such limited custody, and (ii) make a prompt, reasonable effort to inform the minor's parents, guardian, or custodian that the minor has been taken into limited custody and where the minor is being kept.

(c) If the minor consents, the law enforcement officer shall make a reasonable effort to transport, arrange for the transportation of or otherwise release the minor to the parent, guardian or custodian. Upon release of a minor who is believed to need or would benefit from medical, psychological, psychiatric or social services, the law enforcement officer may inform the minor and the person to whom the minor is released of the nature and location of appropriate services and shall, if requested, assist in establishing contact between the family and an agency or association providing such services.

(d) If the law enforcement officer is unable by all reasonable efforts to contact a parent, custodian, relative or other responsible person; or if the person contacted lives an unreasonable distance away; or if the minor refuses to be taken to his or her home or other appropriate residence; or if the officer is otherwise unable despite all reasonable efforts to make arrangements for the safe release of the minor taken into limited custody, the law enforcement officer shall take or make reasonable arrangements for transporting the minor to an agency or association providing crisis intervention services, or, where appropriate, to a mental health or developmental disabilities facility for screening for voluntary or involuntary admission under Section 3-500 et seq. of the Illinois Mental Health and Developmental Disabilities Code [405 ILCS 5/3-500 et seq.]; provided that where no crisis intervention services exist, the minor may be transported for services to court service departments or probation departments under the court's administration.

(e) No minor shall be involuntarily subject to limited custody for more than 6 hours from the time of the minor's initial contact with the law enforcement officer.

(f) No minor taken into limited custody shall be placed in a jail, municipal lockup, detention center or secure correctional facility.

(g) The taking of a minor into limited custody under this Section is not an arrest nor does it constitute a police record; and the records of law enforcement officers concerning all minors taken into limited custody under this Section shall be maintained separate from the records of arrest and may not be inspected by or disclosed to the public except by order of the court. However, such records may be disclosed to the agency or association providing interim crisis intervention services for the minor.

(h) Any law enforcement agency, juvenile officer or other law enforcement officer acting reasonably and in good faith in the care of a minor in limited custody shall be immune from any civil or criminal liability resulting from such custody.

(Chgd. by P.A. 87-1154, §1, eff. 1/1/93.)
(Source: P.A. 85-601.) [Formerly Ill. Rev. Stat. 37 §803-4.]

405/3-5. Interim crisis intervention services.

§3-5. Interim crisis intervention services. (a) Any minor who is taken into limited custody, or who independently requests or is referred for assistance, may be provided crisis intervention services by an agency or association, as defined in this Act, provided the association or agency staff (i) immediately investigate the circumstances of the minor and the facts surrounding the minor being taken into custody and promptly explain these facts and circumstances to the minor, and (ii) make a reasonable effort to inform the minor's parent, guardian or custodian of the fact that the minor has been taken into limited custody and where the minor is being kept, and (iii) if the minor consents, make a reasonable effort to transport, arrange for the transportation of, or otherwise release the minor to the parent, guardian or custodian. Upon release of the child who is believed to need or benefit from medical, psychological, psychiatric or social services, the association or agency may inform the minor and the person to whom the minor is released of the nature and location ofappropriate services and shall, if requested, assist in establishing contact between the family and other associations or agencies providing such services. If the agency or association is unable by all reasonable efforts to contact a parent, guardian or custodian, or if the person contacted lives an unreasonable distance away, or if the minor refuses to be taken to his or her home or other appropriate residence, or if the agency or association is otherwise unable despite all reasonable efforts to make arrangements for the safe return of the minor, the minor may be taken to a temporary living arrangement which is in compliance with the Child Care Act of 1969 [225 ILCS 10/1 et seq.] or which is with persons agreed to by the parents and the agency or association.

(b) An agency or association is authorized to permit a minor to be sheltered in a temporary living arrangement provided the agency seeks to effect the minor's return home or alternative living arrangements agreeable to the minor and the parent, guardian or custodian as soon as practicable. If the parent, guardian or custodian refuses to permit the minor to return home, and no other living arrangement agreeable to the minor and the parent, guardian, or custodian can be made, the agency shall file a petition alleging that the minor is neglected or abused as described in Section 2-3 of this Act [705 ILCS 405/2-3]. No minor shall be sheltered in a temporary living arrangement for more than 48 hours, excluding Saturdays, Sundays and court-designated holidays, without parental consent unless the agency documents its unsuccessful efforts to contact a parent or guardian, including recording the date and time and staff involved in all telephone calls, telegrams, letters, and personal contacts to obtain the consent or authority, in which case the minor may be so sheltered for not more than 21 days.

(c) Any agency or association or employee thereof acting reasonably and in good faith in the care of a minor being provided interim crisis intervention services and shelter care shall be immune from any civil or criminal liability resulting from such care.

(Source: P.A. 85-601.) [Formerly Ill. Rev. Stat. 37 §803-5.]

405/3-6. Alternative voluntary residential placement.

§3-6. Alternative voluntary residential placement. (a) A minor and his or her parent, guardian or custodian may agree to an arrangement for alternative voluntary residential placement, in compliance with the "Child Care Act of 1969" [225 ILCS 10/1 et seq.], without court order. Such placement may continue as long as there is agreement.

(b) If the minor and his or her parent, guardian or custodian cannot agree to an arrangement for alternative voluntary residential placement in the first instance, or cannot agree to the continuation of such placement, and the minor refuses to return home, the minor or his or her parent, guardian or custodian, or a person properly acting at the minor's request, may file with the court a petition alleging that the minor requires authoritative intervention as described in Section 3-3 [705 ILCS 405/3-3].

(Source: P.A. 85-601.) [Formerly Ill. Rev. Stat. 37 §803-6.]

405/3-7. Taking into temporary custody.

§3-7. Taking into temporary custody. (1) A law enforcement officer may, without a warrant, take into temporary custody a minor (a) whom the officer with reasonable cause believes to be a minor requiring authoritative intervention; (b) who has been adjudged a ward of the court and has escaped from any commitment ordered by the court under this Act; or (c) who is found in any street or public place suffering from any sickness or injury which requires care, medical treatment or hospitalization.

(2) Whenever a petition has been filed under Section 3-15 [705 ILCS 405/3-15] and the court finds that the conduct and behavior of the minor may endanger the health, person, welfare, or property of himself or others or that the circumstances of his home environment may endanger his health, person, welfare or property, a warrant may be issued immediately to take the minor into custody.

(3) The taking of a minor into temporary custody under this Section is not an arrest nor does it constitute a police record.

(4) No minor taken into temporary custody shall be placed in a jail, municipal lockup, detention center, or secure correctional facility.

(Chgd. by P.A. 87-1154, §1, eff. 1/1/93.)
(Source: P.A. 85-601.) [Formerly Ill. Rev. Stat. 37 §803-7.]

405/3-8. Duty of officer; admissions by minor.

§3-8. Duty of officer; admissions by minor. (1) A law enforcement officer who takes a minor into custody with a warrant shall immediately make a reasonable attempt to notify the parent or other person legally responsible for the minor's care or the person with whom the minor resides that the minor has been taken into custody and where he or she is being held; and the officer shall without unnecessary delay take the minor to the nearest juvenile police officer designated for such purposes in the county of venue or shall surrender the minor to a juvenile police officer in the city or village where the offense is alleged to have been committed.

The minor shall be delivered without unnecessary delay to the court or to the place designated by rule or order of court for the reception of minors. The court may not designate a place of detention for the reception of minors, unless the minor is alleged to be a person described in Section 5-3 [705 ILCS 405/5-3].

(2) A law enforcement officer who takes a minor into custody without a warrant under Section 3-7 [705 ILCS 405/3-7] shall, if the minor is not released, immediately make a reasonable attempt to notify the parent or other person legally responsible for the minor's care or the person with whom the minor resides that the minor has been taken into custody and where the minor is being held; and the law enforcement officer shall without unnecessary delay take the minor to the nearest juvenile police officer designated for such purposes in the county of venue or shall surrender the minor to a juvenile police officer in the city or village where the offense is alleged to have been committed.

(3) The juvenile police officer may take one of the following actions:

(a) station adjustment with release of the minor;

(b) station adjustment with release of the minor to a parent;

(c) station adjustment, release of the minor to a parent, and referral of the case to community services;

(d) station adjustment, release of the minor to a parent, and referral of the case to community services with informal monitoring by a juvenile police officer;

(e) station adjustment and release of the minor to a third person pursuant to agreement of the minor and parents;

(f) station adjustment, release of the minor to a third person pursuant to agreement of the minor and parents, and referral of the case to community services;

(g) station adjustment, release of the minor to a third person pursuant to agreement of the minor and parent, and referral to community services with informal monitoring by a juvenile police officer;

(h) release of the minor to his or her parents and referral of the case to a county juvenile probation officer or such other public officer designated by the court;

(i) release of the minor to school officials of his school during regular school hours;

(j) if the juvenile police officer reasonably believes that there is an urgent and immediate necessity to keep the minor in custody, the juvenile police officer shall deliver the minor without unnecessary delay to the court or to the place designated by rule or order of court for the reception of minors; and

(k) any other appropriate action with consent of the minor and a parent.

(Source: P.A. 86-628.) [Formerly Ill. Rev. Stat. 37 §803-8.]

405/3-9. Temporary custody; shelter care.

§3-9. Temporary custody; shelter care. Any minor taken into temporary custody pursuant to this Act who requires care away from his or her home but who does not require physical restriction shall be given temporary care in a foster family home or other shelter facility designated by the court. In the case of a minor alleged to be a minor requiring authoritative intervention, the court may order, with the approval of the Department of Children and Family Services, that custody of the minor be with the Department of Children and Family Services for designation of temporary care as the Department determines. No such child shall be ordered to the Department without the approval of the Department.

(Source: P.A. 85-601.) [Formerly Ill. Rev. Stat. 37 §803-9.]

405/3-10. Investigation; release.

§3-10. Investigation; release. When a minor is delivered to the court, or to the place designated by the court under Section 3-9 of this Act [705 ILCS 405/3-9], a probation officer or such other public officer designated by the court shall immediately investigate the circumstances of the minor and the facts

surrounding his or her being taken into custody. The minor shall be immediately released to the custody of his or her parent, guardian, legal custodian or responsible relative, unless the probation officer or such other public officer designated by the court finds that further shelter care is necessary as provided in Section 3-7 [705 ILCS 405/3-7]. This Section shall in no way be construed to limit Section 1-7 [705 ILCS 405/1-7].
(Source: P.A. 85-601.) [Formerly Ill. Rev. Stat. 37 §803-10.]

405/3-11. Setting of shelter care hearing; notice; release.

§3-11. Setting of shelter care hearing; notice; release. (1) Unless sooner released, a minor requiring authoritative intervention, taken into temporary custody, must be brought before a judicial officer within 48 hours, exclusive of Saturdays, Sundays and court-designated holidays, for a shelter care hearing to determine whether he shall be further held in custody.

(2) If the probation officer or such other public officer designated by the court determines that the minor should be retained in custody, he shall cause a petition to be filed as provided in Section 3-15 of this Act [705 ILCS 405/3-15], and the clerk of the court shall set the matter for hearing on the shelter care hearing calendar. When a parent, guardian, custodian or responsible relative is present and so requests, the shelter care hearing shall be held immediately if the court is in session, otherwise at the earliest feasible time. The petitioner through counsel or such other public officer designated by the court shall insure notification to the minor's parent, guardian, custodian or responsible relative of the time and place of the hearing by the best practicable notice, allowing for oral notice in place of written notice only if provision of written notice is unreasonable under the circumstances.

(3) The minor must be released from custody at the expiration of the 48 hour period, if not brought before a judicial officer within that period.
(Source: P.A. 87-759.) [Formerly Ill. Rev. Stat. 37 §803-11.]

405/3-12. Shelter care hearing.

§3-12. Shelter care hearing. At the appearance of the minor before the court at the shelter care hearing, all witnesses present shall be examined before the court in relation to any matter connected with the allegations made in the petition.

(1) If the court finds that there is not probable cause to believe that the minor is a person requiring authoritative intervention, it shall release the minor and dismiss the petition.

(2) If the court finds that there is probable cause to believe that the minor is a person requiring authoritative intervention, the minor, his or her parent, guardian, custodian and other persons able to give relevant testimony shall be examined before the court. After such testimony, the court may enter an order that the minor shall be released upon the request of a parent, guardian or custodian if the parent, guardian or custodian appears to take custody. Custodian shall include any agency of the State which has been given custody or wardship of the child. The Court shall require documentation by representatives of the Department of Children and Family Services or the probation department as to the reasonable efforts that were made to prevent or eliminate the necessity of removal of the minor from his or her home, and shall consider the testimony of any person as to those reasonable efforts. If the court finds that it is a matter of immediate and urgent necessity for the protection of the minor or of the person or property of another that the minor be placed in a shelter care facility, or that he or she is likely to flee the jurisdiction of the court, and further finds that reasonable efforts have been made or good cause has been shown why reasonable efforts cannot prevent or eliminate the necessity of removal of the minor from his or her home, the court may prescribe shelter

care and order that the minor be kept in a suitable place designated by the court or in a shelter care facility designated by the Department of Children and Family Services or a licensed child welfare agency; otherwise it shall release the minor from custody. If the minor is ordered placed in a shelter care facility of the Department of Children and Family Services or a licensed child welfare agency, the court shall, upon request of the Department or other agency, appoint the Department of Children and Family Services Guardianship Administrator or other appropriate agency executive temporary custodian of the minor and the court may enter such other orders related to the temporary custody as it deems fit and proper, including the provision of services to the minor or his family to ameliorate the causes contributing to the finding of probable cause or to the finding of the existence of immediate and urgent necessity. Acceptance of services shall not be considered an admission of any allegation in a petition made pursuant to this Act, nor may a referral of services be considered as evidence in any proceeding pursuant to this Act, except where the issue is whether the Department has made reasonable efforts to reunite the family. In making its findings that reasonable efforts have been made or that good cause has been shown why reasonable efforts cannot prevent or eliminate the necessity of removal of the minor from his or her home, the court shall state in writing its findings concerning the nature of the services that were offered or the efforts that were made to prevent removal of the child and the apparent reasons that such services or efforts could not prevent the need for removal. The parents, guardian, custodian, temporary custodian and minor shall each be furnished a copy of such written findings. The temporary custodian shall maintain a copy of the court order and written findings in the case record for the child.

The order together with the court's findings of fact and support thereof shall be entered of record in the court.

Once the court finds that it is a matter of immediate and urgent necessity for the protection of the minor that the minor be placed in a shelter care facility, the minor shall not be returned to the parent, custodian or guardian until the court finds that such placement is no longer necessary for the protection of the minor.

(3) If prior to the shelter care hearing for a minor described in Sections 2-3, 2-4, 3-3 and 4-3 [705 ILCS 405/2-3, 405/2-4, 405/3-3 and 405/4-3] the petitioner is unable to serve notice on the party respondent, the shelter care hearing may proceed ex-parte. A shelter care order from an ex-parte hearing shall be endorsed with the date and hour of issuance and shall be filed with the clerk's office and entered of record. The order shall expire after 10 days from the time it is issued unless before its expiration it is renewed, at a hearing upon appearance of the party respondent, or upon an affidavit of the moving party as to all diligent efforts to notify the party respondent by notice as herein prescribed. The notice prescribed shall be in writing and shall be personally delivered to the minor or the minor's attorney and to the last known address of the other person or persons entitled to notice. The notice shall also state the nature of the allegations, the nature of the order sought by the State, including whether temporary custody is sought, and the consequences of failure to appear; and shall explain the right of the parties and the procedures to vacate or modify a shelter care order as provided in this Section. The notice for a shelter care hearing shall be substantially as follows:

NOTICE TO PARENTS AND CHILDREN OF SHELTER CARE HEARING

On . . . . at . . . . , before the Honorable . . . . , (address:) . . . . , the State of Illinois will present evidence (1) that (name of child or children) . . . . are abused, neglected or dependent for the following reasons: . . . .

. . . . and (2) that there is "immediate and urgent necessity" to remove the child or children from the responsible relative.

YOUR FAILURE TO APPEAR AT THE HEARING MAY RESULT IN PLACEMENT of the child or children in foster care until a trial can be held. A trial may not be held for up to 90 days.

At the shelter care hearing, parents have the following rights:

1. To ask the court to appoint a lawyer if they cannot afford one.
2. To ask the court to continue the hearing to allow them time to prepare.
3. To present evidence concerning:

a. Whether or not the child or children were abused, neglected or dependent.

b. Whether or not there is "immediate and urgent necessity" to remove the child from home (including: their ability to care for the child, conditions in the home, alternative means of protecting the child other than removal).

c. The best interests of the child.

4. To cross examine the State's witnesses.

The Notice for rehearings shall be substantially as follows:

NOTICE OF PARENT'S AND CHILDREN'S RIGHTS TO REHEARING ON TEMPORARY CUSTODY

If you were not present at and did not have adequate notice of the Shelter Care Hearing at which temporary custody of . . . . was awarded to . . . . , you have the right to request a full rehearing on whether the State should have temporary custody of . . . . To request this rehearing, you must file with the Clerk of the Juvenile Court (address): . . . . , in person or by mailing a statement (affidavit) setting forth the following:

1. That you were not present at the shelter care hearing.
2. That you did not get adequate notice (explaining how the notice was inadequate).
3. Your signature.
4. Signature must be notarized.

The rehearing should be scheduled within one day of your filing this affidavit.

At the rehearing, your rights are the same as at the initial shelter care hearing. The enclosed notice explains those rights.

At the Shelter Care Hearing, children have the following rights:

1. To have a guardian ad litem appointed.
2. To be declared competent as a witness and to present testimony concerning:

a. Whether they are abused, neglected or dependent.

b. Whether there is "immediate and urgent necessity" to be removed from home.

c. Their best interests.

3. To cross examine witnesses for other parties.
4. To obtain an explanation of any proceedings and orders of the court.

(4) If the parent, guardian, legal custodian, responsible relative, or counsel of the minor did not have actual notice of or was not present at the shelter care hearing, he or she may file an affidavit setting forth these facts, and the clerk shall set the matter for rehearing not later than 48 hours, excluding Sundays and legal holidays, after the filing of the affidavit. At the rehearing, the court shall proceed in the same manner as upon the original hearing.

(5) Only when there is reasonable cause to believe that the minor taken into custody is a person described in Section 5-3 [705 ILCS 405/5-3] may the minor be kept or detained in a detention home or county or municipal jail. This Section shall in no way be construed to limit subsection (6).

(6) No minor under 16 years of age may be confined in a jail or place ordinarily used for the confinement of prisoners in a police station. Minors under 17 years of age must be kept separate from confined adults and may not at any time be kept in the same cell, room, or yard with adults confined pursuant to the criminal law.

(7) If the minor is not brought before a judicial officer within the time period specified in Section 3-11 [705 ILCS 405/3-11], the minor must immediately be released from custody.

(8) If neither the parent, guardian or custodian appears within 24 hours to take custody of a minor released upon request pursuant to subsection (2) of this Section, then the clerk of the court shall set the matter for rehearing not later than 7 days after the original order and shall issue a summons directed to the parent, guardian or custodian to appear. At the same time the probation department shall prepare a report on the minor. If a parent, guardian or custodian does not appear at such rehearing, the judge may enter an order prescribing that the minor be kept in a suitable place designated by the Department of Children and Family Services or a licensed child welfare agency.

(9) Notwithstanding any other provision of this Section, any interested party, including the State, the temporary custodian, an agency providing services to the minor or family under a service plan pursuant to Section 8.2 of the Abused and Neglected Child Reporting Act [325 ILCS 5/8.2], foster parent, or any of their representatives, on notice to all parties entitled to notice, may file a motion to modify or vacate a temporary custody order on any of the following grounds:

(a) It is no longer a matter of immediate and urgent necessity that the minor remain in shelter care; or

(b) There is a material change in the circumstances of the natural family from which the minor was removed; or

(c) A person, including a parent, relative or legal guardian, is capable of assuming temporary custody of the minor; or

(d) Services provided by the Department of Children and Family Services or a child welfare agency or other service provider have been successful in eliminating the need for temporary custody.

The clerk shall set the matter for hearing not later than 14 days after such motion is filed. In the event that the court modifies or vacates a temporary custody order but does not vacate its finding of probable cause, the court may order that appropriate services be continued or initiated in behalf of the minor and his or her family.

(Source: P.A. 87-759.) [Formerly Ill. Rev. Stat. 37 §803-12.]

405/3-13. Medical and dental treatment and care.

§3-13. Medical and dental treatment and care. At all times during temporary custody or shelter care, the court may authorize a physician, a hospital or any other appropriate health care provider to provide medical, dental or surgical procedures if such procedures are necessary to safeguard the minor's life or health.

(Source: P.A. 85-1209.) [Formerly Ill. Rev. Stat. 37 §803-13.]

405/3-14. Preliminary conferences.

§3-14. Preliminary conferences. (1) The court may authorize the probation officer to confer in a preliminary conference with any person seeking to file a petition under Section 3-15 [705 ILCS 405/3-15], the prospective respondents and other interested persons concerning the advisability of filing the petition, with a view to adjusting suitable cases without the filing of a petition.

The probation officer should schedule a conference promptly except where the State's Attorney insists on court action or where the minor has indicated that he or she will demand a judicial hearing and will not comply with an informal adjustment.

(2) In any case of a minor who is in temporary custody, the holding of preliminary conferences does not operate to prolong temporary custody beyond the period permitted by Section 3-11 [705 ILCS 405/3-11].

(3) This Section does not authorize any probation officer to compel any person to appear at any conference, produce any papers, or visit any place.

(4) No statement made during a preliminary conference may be admitted into evidence at an adjudicatory hearing or at any proceeding against the minor under the criminal laws of this State prior to his or her conviction thereunder.

(5) The probation officer shall promptly formulate a written, non-judicial adjustment plan following the initial conference.

(6) Non-judicial adjustment plans include but are not limited to the following:

(a) up to 6 months informal supervision within family;

(b) up to 6 months informal supervision with a probation officer involved;

(c) up to 6 months informal supervision with release to a person other than parent;

(d) referral to special educational, counseling or other rehabilitative social or educational programs;

(e) referral to residential treatment programs; and

(f) any other appropriate action with consent of the minor and a parent.

(7) The factors to be considered by the probation officer in formulating a written non-judicial adjustment plan shall be the same as those limited in subsection (4) of Section 5-6 [705 ILCS 405/5-6].

(Source: P.A. 86-639.) [Formerly Ill. Rev. Stat. 37 §803-14.]

405/3-15. Petition; supplemental petitions.

§3-15. Petition; supplemental petitions. (1) Any adult person, any agency or association by its representative may file, or the court on its own motion may direct the filing through the State's Attorney of a petition in respect to a minor under this Act. The petition and all subsequent court documents shall be entitled "In the interest of . . . . , a minor".

(2) The petition shall be verified but the statements may be made upon information and belief. It shall allege that the minor requires authoritative intervention and set forth (a) facts sufficient to bring the minor under Section 3-3 or 3-33 [705 ILCS 405/3-3 or 405/3-33]; (b) the name, age and residence of the minor; (c) the names and residences of his parents; (d) the name and residence of his legal guardian or the person or persons having custody or control of the minor, or of the nearest known relative if no parent or guardian can be found; and (e) if the minor upon whose behalf the petition is brought is sheltered in custody, the date on which shelter care was ordered by the court or the date set for a shelter care hearing. If any of the facts herein required are not known by the petitioner, the petition shall so state.

(3) The petition must allege that it is in the best interests of the minor and of the public that he be adjudged a ward of the court and may pray generally for relief available under this Act. The petition need not specify any proposed disposition following adjudication of wardship.

(4) If appointment of a guardian of the person with power to consent to adoption of the minor under Section 3-30 [705 ILCS 405/3-30] is sought, the petition shall so state.

(5) At any time before dismissal of the petition or before final closing and discharge under Section 3-32 [705 ILCS 405/3-32], one or more supplemental petitions may be filed in respect to the same minor.

(Source: P.A. 85-1209; 85-1235; 86-1440.) [Formerly Ill. Rev. Stat. 37 §803-15.]

405/3-16. Date for adjudicatory hearing.

§3-16. Date for adjudicatory hearing. (a) Until January 1, 1988:

(1) When a petition has been filed alleging that the minor requires authoritative intervention, an adjudicatory hearing shall be held within 120 days. The 120 day period in which an adjudicatory hearing shall be held is tolled by: (A) delay occasioned by the minor; (B) a continuance allowed pursuant to Section 114-4 of the Code of Criminal Procedure of 1963 [725 ILCS 5/114-4] after a court's determination of the minor's physical incapacity for trial; or (C) an interlocutory appeal. Any such delay shall temporarily suspend for the time of the delay the period within which the adjudicatory hearing must be held. On the day of expiration of the delay, the said period shall continue at the point at which it was suspended. Where no such adjudicatory hearing is held within 120 days, the court may, on written motion of a minor's guardian ad litem, dismiss the petition with respect to such minor. Such dismissal shall be without prejudice.

Where the court determines that the State exercised, without success, due diligence to obtain evidence material to the case, and that there are reasonable grounds to believe that such evidence may be obtained at a later date, the court may, upon written motion by the State, continue the matter for not more than 30 additional days.

(2) In the case of a minor ordered held in shelter care, the hearing on the petition must be held within 10 judicial days from the date of the order of the court directing shelter care or the earliest possible date in compliance with the notice provisions of Sections 3-17 and 3-18 [705 ILCS 405/3-17 and 405/3-18] as to the custodial parent, guardian or legal custodian, but no later than 30 judicial days from the date of the order of the court directing shelter care. Delay occasioned by the respondent shall temporarily suspend, for the time of the delay, the period within which a respondent must be tried pursuant to this Section.

Upon failure to comply with the time limits specified in this subsection (a)(2), the minor shall be immediately released. The time limits specified in subsection (a)(1) shall still apply.

(3) Nothing in this Section prevents the minor's exercise of his or her right to waive any time limits set forth in this Section.

(b) Beginning January 1, 1988:

(1) (A) When a petition has been filed alleging that the minor requires authoritative intervention, an adjudicatory hearing shall be held within 120 days of a demand made by any party, except that when the court determines that the State, without success, has exercised due diligence to obtain evidence material to the case and that there are reasonable grounds to believe that such evidence may be obtained at a later date, the court may, upon motion by the State, continue the adjudicatory hearing for not more than 30 additional days.

The 120 day period in which an adjudicatory hearing shall be held is tolled by: (i) delay occasioned by the minor; or (ii) a continuance allowed pursuant to Section 114-4 of the Code of Criminal Procedure of 1963 after a court's determination of the minor's physical incapacity for trial; or (iii) an interlocutory appeal. Any such delay shall temporarily suspend, for the time of the delay, the period within which the adjudicatory hearing must be held. On the day of expiration of the delay, the said period shall continue at the point at which it was suspended.

(B) When no such adjudicatory hearing is held within the time required by paragraph (b)(1)(A) of this Section, the court shall, upon motion by any party, dismiss the petition with prejudice.

(2) Without affecting the applicability of the tolling and multiple prosecution provisions of paragraph (b)(1) of this Section, when a petition has been filed

alleging that the minor requires authoritative intervention and the minor is in shelter care, the adjudicatory hearing shall be held within 10 judicial days after the date of the order directing shelter care, or the earliest possible date in compliance with the notice provisions of Sections 3-17 and 3-18 as to the custodial parent, guardian or legal custodian, but no later than 30 judicial days from the date of the order of the court directing shelter care.

(3) Any failure to comply with the time limits of paragraph (b)(2) of this Section shall require the immediate release of the minor from shelter care, and the time limits of paragraph (b)(1) shall apply.

(4) Nothing in this Section prevents the minor or the minor's parents or guardian from exercising their respective rights to waive the time limits set forth in this Section.

(Source: P.A. 85-601.) [Formerly Ill. Rev. Stat. 37 §803-16.]

405/3-17. Summons.

§3-17. Summons. (1) When a petition is filed, the clerk of the court shall issue a summons with a copy of the petition attached. The summons shall be directed to the minor's legal guardian or custodian and to each person named as a respondent in the petition, except that summons need not be directed to a minor respondent under 8 years of age for whom the court appoints a guardian ad litem if the guardian ad litem appears on behalf of the minor in any proceeding under this Act.

(2) The summons must contain a statement that the minor or any of the respondents is entitled to have an attorney present at the hearing on the petition, and that the clerk of the court should be notified promptly if the minor or any other respondent desires to be represented by an attorney but is financially unable to employ counsel.

(3) The summons shall be issued under the seal of the court, attested to and signed with the name of the clerk of the court, dated on the day it is issued, and shall require each respondent to appear and answer the petition on the date set for the adjudicatory hearing.

(4) The summons may be served by any county sheriff, coroner or probation officer, even though the officer is the petitioner. The return of the summons with endorsement of service by the officer is sufficient proof thereof.

(5) Service of a summons and petition shall be made by: (a) leaving a copy thereof with the person summoned at least 3 days before the time stated therein for appearance; (b) leaving a copy at his usual place of abode with some person of the family, of the age of 10 years or upwards, and informing that person of the contents thereof, provided the officer or other person making service shall also send a copy of the summons in a sealed envelope with postage fully prepaid, addressed to the person summoned at his usual place of abode, at least 3 days before the time stated therein for appearance; or (c) leaving a copy thereof with the guardian or custodian of a minor, at least 3 days before the time stated therein for appearance. If the guardian or custodian is an agency of the State of Illinois, proper service may be made by leaving a copy of the summons and petition with any administrative employee of such agency designated by such agency to accept service of summons and petitions. The certificate of the officer or affidavit of the person that he has sent the copy pursuant to this Section is sufficient proof of service.

(6) When a parent or other person, who has signed a written promise to appear and bring the minor to court or who has waived or acknowledged service, fails to appear with the minor on the date set by the court, a bench warrant may be issued for the parent or other person, the minor, or both.

(7) The appearance of the minor's legal guardian or custodian, or a person named as a respondent in a petition, in any proceeding under this Act shall constitute a waiver of service of summons and submission to the jurisdiction of

the court. A copy of the summons and petition shall be provided to the person at the time of his appearance.
(Source: P.A. 86-441.) [Formerly Ill. Rev. Stat. 37 §803-17.]

405/3-18. Notice by certified mail or publication.

§3-18. Notice by certified mail or publication. (1) If service on individuals as provided in Section 3-17 [705 ILCS 405/3-17] is not made on any respondent within a reasonable time or if it appears that any respondent resides outside the State, service may be made by certified mail. In such case the clerk shall mail the summons and a copy of the petition to that respondent by certified mail marked for delivery to addressee only. The court shall not proceed with the adjudicatory hearing until 5 days after such mailing. The regular return receipt for certified mail is sufficient proof of service.

(2) If service upon individuals as provided in Section 3-17 is not made on any respondents within a reasonable time or if any person is made a respondent under the designation of "All whom it may Concern", or if service cannot be made because the whereabouts of a respondent are unknown, service may be made by publication. The clerk of the court as soon as possible shall cause publication to be made once in a newspaper of general circulation in the county where the action is pending. Notice by publication is not required in any case when the person alleged to have legal custody of the minor has been served with summons personally or by certified mail, but the court may not enter any order or judgment against any person who cannot be served with process other than by publication unless notice by publication is given or unless that person appears. When a minor has been sheltered under Section 3-12 of this Act [705 ILCS 405/3-12] and summons has not been served personally or by certified mail within 20 days from the date of the order of the court directing such shelter care, the clerk of the court shall cause publication. Notice by publication shall be substantially as follows:

"A, B, C, D, (here giving the names of the named respondents, if any) and to All Whom It May Concern (if there is any respondent under that designation):

Take notice that on the .... day of ...., 19... a petition was filed under the Juvenile Court Act by .... in the circuit court of .... county entitled 'In the interest of ...., a minor', and that in .... courtroom at .... on the .... day of .... at the hour of ...., or as soon thereafter as this cause may be heard, an adjudicatory hearing will be held upon the petition to have the child declared to be a ward of the court under that Act. The court has authority in this proceeding to take from you the custody and guardianship of the minor, (and if the petition prays for the appointment of a guardian with power to consent to adoption) and to appoint a guardian with power to consent to adoption of the minor.

Now, unless you appear at the hearing and show cause against the petition, the allegations of the petition may stand admitted as against you and each of you, and an order or judgment entered.

....
Clerk

Dated (the date of publication)"

(3) The clerk shall also at the time of the publication of the notice send a copy thereof by mail to each of the respondents on account of whom publication is made at his or her last known address. The certificate of the clerk that he or she has mailed the notice is evidence thereof. No other publication notice is required. Every respondent notified by publication under this Section must appear and answer in open court at the hearing. The court may not proceed with the adjudicatory hearing until 10 days after service by publication on any custodial parent, guardian or legal custodian in the case of a minor requiring authoritative intervention.

(4) If it becomes necessary to change the date set for the hearing in order to comply with Section 3-17 or with this Section, notice of the resetting of the date must be given, by certified mail or other reasonable means, to each respondent who has been served with summons personally or by certified mail.
(Source: P.A. 85-601.) [Formerly Ill. Rev. Stat. 37 §803-18.]

405/3-19. Guardian ad litem.

§3-19. Guardian ad litem. (1) Immediately upon the filing of a petition alleging that the minor requires authoritative intervention, the court may appoint a guardian ad litem for the minor if

(a) such petition alleges that the minor is the victim of sexual abuse or misconduct; or

(b) such petition alleges that charges alleging the commission of any of the sex offenses defined in Article 11 [720 ILCS 5/11-6 et seq.] or in Sections 12-13, 12-14, 12-15 or 12-16 of the Criminal Code of 1961, as amended [720 ILCS 5/12-13, 5/12-14, 5/12-15 or 5/12-16], have been filed against a defendant in any court and that such minor is the alleged victim of the acts of the defendant in the commission of such offense.

(2) Unless the guardian ad litem appointed pursuant to paragraph (1) is an attorney at law he shall be represented in the performance of his duties by counsel.

(3) Before proceeding with the hearing, the court shall appoint a guardian ad litem for the minor if

(a) no parent, guardian, custodian or relative of the minor appears at the first or any subsequent hearing of the case;

(b) the petition prays for the appointment of a guardian with power to consent to adoption; or

(c) the petition for which the minor is before the court resulted from a report made pursuant to the Abused and Neglected Child Reporting Act [325 ILCS 5/1 et seq.].

(4) The court may appoint a guardian ad litem for the minor whenever it finds that there may be a conflict of interest between the minor and his parents or other custodian or that it is otherwise in the minor's interest to do so.

(5) The reasonable fees of a guardian ad litem appointed under this Section shall be fixed by the court and charged to the parents of the minor, to the extent they are able to pay. If the parents are unable to pay those fees, they shall be paid from the general fund of the county.
(Source: P.A. 85-601.) [Formerly Ill. Rev. Stat. 37 §803-19.]

405/3-20. Evidence.

§3-20. Evidence. At the adjudicatory hearing, the court shall first consider only the question whether the minor is a person requiring authoritative intervention. The standard of proof and the rules of evidence in the nature of civil proceedings in this State are applicable to Section 3-3 [705 ILCS 405/3-3].
(Source: P.A. 85-601.) [Formerly Ill. Rev. Stat. 37 §803-20.]

405/3-21. Continuance under supervision.

§3-21. Continuance under supervision. (1) The court may enter an order of continuance under supervision (a) upon an admission or stipulation by the appropriate respondent or minor respondent of the facts supporting the petition and before proceeding to findings and adjudication, or after hearing the evidence at the adjudicatory hearing but before noting in the minutes of proceedings a finding of whether or not the minor is a person requiring authoritative intervention; and (b) in the absence of objection made in open court by the minor, his parent, guardian, custodian, responsible relative, defense attorney or the State's Attorney.

(2) If the minor, his parent, guardian, custodian, responsible relative, defense attorney or State's Attorney, objects in open court to any such continuance and insists upon proceeding to findings and adjudication, the court shall so proceed.

(3) Nothing in this Section limits the power of the court to order a continuance of the hearing for the production of additional evidence or for any other proper reason.

(4) When a hearing where a minor is alleged to be a minor requiring authoritative intervention is continued pursuant to this Section, the court may permit the minor to remain in his home subject to such conditions concerning his conduct and supervision as the court may require by order.

(5) If a petition is filed charging a violation of a condition of the continuance under supervision, the court shall conduct a hearing. If the court finds that such condition of supervision has not been fulfilled the court may proceed to findings and adjudication and disposition. The filing of a petition for violation of a condition of the continuance under supervision shall toll the period of continuance under supervision until the final determination of the charge, and the term of the continuance under supervision shall not run until the hearing and disposition of the petition for violation; provided where the petition alleges conduct that does not constitute a criminal offense, the hearing must be held within 15 days of the filing of the petition unless a delay in such hearing has been occasioned by the minor, in which case the delay shall continue the tolling of the period of continuance under supervision for the period of such delay.
(Source: P.A. 85-601.) [Formerly Ill. Rev. Stat. 37 §803-21.]

405/3-22. Findings and adjudication.

§3-22. Findings and adjudication. (1) After hearing the evidence the court shall make and note in the minutes of the proceeding a finding of whether or not the person is a minor requiring authoritative intervention. If it finds that the minor is not such a person, the court shall order the petition dismissed and the minor discharged from any restriction previously ordered in such proceeding.

(2) If the court finds that the person is a minor requiring authoritative intervention, the court shall note in its findings that he or she does require authoritative intervention. The court shall then set a time for a dispositional hearing to be conducted under Section 3-23 [705 ILCS 405/3-23] at which hearing the court shall determine whether it is in the best interests of the minor and the public that he be made a ward of the court. To assist the court in making this and other determinations at the dispositional hearing, the court may order that an investigation be conducted and a dispositional report be prepared concerning the minor's physical and mental history and condition, family situation and background, economic status, education, occupation, history of delinquency or criminality, personal habits, and any other information that may be helpful to the court.
(Source: P.A. 85-601.) [Formerly Ill. Rev. Stat. 37 §803-22.]

405/3-23. Dispositional hearing; evidence; continuance.

§3-23. Dispositional hearing; evidence; continuance. (1) At the dispositional hearing, the court shall determine whether it is in the best interests of the minor and the public that he be made a ward of the court, and, if he is to be made a ward of the court, the court shall determine the proper disposition best serving the interests of the minor and the public. All evidence helpful in determining these questions, including oral and written reports, may be admitted and may be relied upon to the extent of its probative value, even though not competent for the purposes of the adjudicatory hearing.

(2) Notice in compliance with Sections 3-17 and 3-18 [705 ILCS 405/3-17 and 405/3-18] must be given to all parties-respondent prior to proceeding to a dispositional hearing. Before making an order of disposition the court shall advise the State's Attorney, the parents, guardian, custodian or responsible relative or their counsel of the factual contents and the conclusions of the reports prepared for the use of the court and considered by it, and afford fair opportunity, if requested, to controvert them. The court may order, however, that the documents containing such reports need not be submitted for inspection, or that sources of confidential information need not be disclosed except to the attorneys for the parties. Factual contents, conclusions, documents and sources disclosed by the court under this paragraph shall not be further disclosed without the express approval of the court pursuant to an in camera hearing.

(3) A record of a prior continuance under supervision under Section 3-21 [705 ILCS 405/3-21], whether successfully completed or not, is admissible at the dispositional hearing.

(4) On its own motion or that of the State's Attorney, a parent, guardian, custodian, responsible relative or counsel, the court may adjourn the hearing for a reasonable period to receive reports or other evidence. In scheduling investigations and hearings, the court shall give priority to proceedings in which a minor has been removed from his or her home before an order of disposition has been made.

(Source: P.A. 85-601.) [Formerly Ill. Rev. Stat. 37 §803-23.]

405/3-24. Kinds of dispositional orders.

§3-24. Kinds of dispositional orders. (1) The following kinds of orders of disposition may be made in respect to wards of the court: A minor found to be requiring authoritative intervention under Section 3-3 [705 ILCS 405/3-3] may be (a) committed to the Department of Children and Family Services, subject to Section 5 of "An Act creating the Department of Children and Family Services, codifying its powers and duties, and repealing certain Acts and Sections herein named" [20 ILCS 505/5]; (b) placed under supervision and released to his or her parents, guardian or legal custodian; (c) placed in accordance with Section 3-28 [705 ILCS 405/3-28] with or without also being placed under supervision. Conditions of supervision may be modified or terminated by the court if it deems that the best interests of the minor and the public will be served thereby; or (d) ordered partially or completely emancipated in accordance with the provisions of the "Emancipation of Mature Minors Act", approved September 19, 1979, as now or hereafter amended [750 ILCS 30/1 et seq.].

(2) Any order of disposition may provide for protective supervision under Section 3-25 [705 ILCS 405/3-25] and may include an order of protection under Section 3-26 [705 ILCS 405/3-26].

(3) Unless the order of disposition expressly so provides, it does not operate to close proceedings on the pending petition, but is subject to modification until final closing and discharge of the proceedings under Section 3-32 [705 ILCS 405/3-32].

(4) In addition to any other order of disposition, the court may order any person found to be a minor requiring authoritative intervention under Section 3-3 to make restitution, in monetary or non-monetary form, under the terms and conditions of Section 5-5-6 of the "Unified Code of Corrections" [730 ILCS 5/5-5-6], except that the "presentence hearing" referred to therein shall be the dispositional hearing for purposes of this Section. The parent, guardian or legal custodian of the minor may pay some or all of such restitution on the minor's behalf.

(5) Any order for disposition where the minor is committed or placed in accordance with Section 3-28 shall provide for the parents or guardian of the

estate of such minor to pay to the legal custodian or guardian of the person of the minor such sums as are determined by the custodian or guardian of the person of the minor as necessary for the minor's needs. Such payments may not exceed the maximum amounts provided for by Section 5.1 of "An Act creating the Department of Children and Family Services, codifying its powers and duties and repealing certain Acts and Sections herein named", approved June 4, 1963, as amended [see 20 ILCS 505/9.1].

(6) Whenever the order of disposition requires the minor to attend school or participate in a program of training, the truant officer or designated school official shall regularly report to the court if the minor is a chronic or habitual truant under Section 26-2a of The School Code [105 ILCS 5/26-2a].

(Source: P.A. 85-1209.) [Formerly Ill. Rev. Stat. 37 §803-24.]

405/3-25. Protective supervision.

§3-25. Protective supervision. If the order of disposition releases the minor to the custody of his parents, guardian or legal custodian, or continues him in such custody, the court may place the person having custody of the minor, except for representatives of private or public agencies or governmental departments, under supervision of the probation office. Rules or orders of court shall define the terms and conditions of protective supervision, which may be modified or terminated when the court finds that the best interests of the minor and the public will be served thereby.

(Source: P.A. 85-601.) [Formerly Ill. Rev. Stat. 37 §803-25.]

405/3-26. Order of protection.

§3-26. Order of protection. (1) The court may make an order of protection in assistance of or as a condition of any other order authorized by this Act. The order of protection may set forth reasonable conditions of behavior to be observed for a specified period. Such an order may require a person:

(a) To stay away from the home or the minor;

(b) To permit a parent to visit the minor at stated periods;

(c) To abstain from offensive conduct against the minor, his parent or any person to whom custody of the minor is awarded;

(d) To give proper attention to the care of the home;

(e) To cooperate in good faith with an agency to which custody of a minor is entrusted by the court or with an agency or association to which the minor is referred by the court;

(f) To prohibit and prevent any contact whatsoever with the respondent minor by a specified individual or individuals who are alleged in either a criminal or juvenile proceeding to have caused injury to a respondent minor or a sibling of a respondent minor;

(g) To refrain from acts of commission or omission that tend to make the home not a proper place for the minor.

(2) The court shall enter an order of protection to prohibit and prevent any contact between a respondent minor or a sibling of a respondent minor and any person named in a petition seeking an order of protection who has been convicted of heinous battery under Section 12-4.1, aggravated battery of a child under Section 12-4.3, criminal sexual assault under Section 12-13, aggravated criminal sexual assault under Section 12-14, criminal sexual abuse under Section 12-15, or aggravated criminal sexual abuse under Section 12-16 of the Criminal Code of 1961 [720 ILCS 5/12-4.1, 5/12-4.3, 5/12-13, 5/12-14, 5/12-15 or 5/12-16], or has been convicted of an offense that resulted in the death of a child, or has violated a previous order of protection under this Section.

(3) When the court issues an order of protection against any person as provided by this Section, the court shall direct a copy of such order to the Sheriff of that county. The Sheriff shall furnish a copy of the order of protection to the

Department of State Police with 24 hours of receipt, in the form and manner required by the Department. The Department of State Police shall maintain a complete record and index of such orders of protection and make this data available to all local law enforcement agencies.

(4) After notice and opportunity for hearing afforded to a person subject to an order of protection, the order may be modified or extended for a further specified period or both or may be terminated if the court finds that the best interests of the minor and the public will be served thereby.

(5) An order of protection may be sought at any time during the course of any proceeding conducted pursuant to this Act. Any person against whom an order of protection is sought may retain counsel to represent him at a hearing, and has rights to be present at the hearing, to be informed prior to the hearing in writing of the contents of the petition seeking a protective order and of the date, place and time of such hearing, and to cross examine witnesses called by the petitioner and to present witnesses and argument in opposition to the relief sought in the petition.

(6) Diligent efforts shall be made by the petitioner to serve any person or persons against whom any order of protection is sought with written notice of the contents of the petition seeking a protective order and of the date, place and time at which the hearing on the petition is to be held. When a protective order is being sought in conjunction with a shelter care hearing, if the court finds that the person against whom the protective order is being sought has been notified of the hearing or that diligent efforts have been made to notify such person, the court may conduct a hearing. If a protective order is sought at any time other than in conjunction with a shelter care hearing, the court may not conduct a hearing on the petition in the absence of the person against whom the order is sought unless the petitioner has notified such person by personal service at least 3 days before the hearing or has sent written notice by first class mail to such person's last known address at least 5 days before the hearing.

(7) A person against whom an order of protection is being sought who is neither a parent, guardian, legal custodian or responsible relative as described in Section 1-5 [705 ILCS 405/1-5] is not a party or respondent as defined in that Section and shall not be entitled to the rights provided therein. Such person does not have a right to appointed counsel or to be present at any hearing other than the hearing in which the order of protection is being sought or a hearing directly pertaining to that order. Unless the court orders otherwise, such person does not have a right to inspect the court file.

(8) All protective orders entered under this Section shall be in writing. Unless the person against whom the order was obtained was present in court when the order was issued, the sheriff, other law enforcement official or special process server shall promptly serve that order upon that person and file proof of such service, in the manner provided for service of process in civil proceedings. The person against whom the protective order was obtained may seek a modification of the order by filing a written motion to modify the order within 7 days after actual receipt by the person of a copy of the order.

(Source: P.A. 85-1209.) [Formerly Ill. Rev. Stat. 37 §803-26.]

405/3-27. Enforcement of orders of protective supervision or of protection.

§3-27. Enforcement of orders of protective supervision or of protection. (1) Orders of protective supervision and orders of protection may be enforced by citation to show cause for contempt of court by reason of any violation thereof and, where protection of the welfare of the minor so requires, by the issuance of a warrant to take the alleged violator into custody and bring him before the court.

(2) In any case where an order of protection has been entered, the clerk of the court may issue to the petitioner, to the minor or to any other person affected by the order a certificate stating that an order of protection has been made by the court concerning such persons and setting forth its terms and requirements. The presentation of the certificate to any peace officer authorizes him to take into custody a person charged with violating the terms of the order of protection, to bring such person before the court and, within the limits of his legal authority as such peace officer, otherwise to aid in securing the protection the order is intended to afford.

(Source: P.A. 85-601.) [Formerly Ill. Rev. Stat. 37 §803-27.]

405/3-28. Placement; legal custody or guardianship.

§3-28. Placement; legal custody or guardianship. (1) If the court finds that the parents, guardian or legal custodian of a minor adjudged a ward of the court are unfit or are unable, for some reason other than financial circumstances alone, to care for, protect, train or discipline the minor or are unwilling to do so, and that appropriate services aimed at family preservation and family reunification have been unsuccessful in rectifying the conditions which have led to such a finding of unfitness or inability to care for, protect, train or discipline the minor, and that it is in the best interest of the minor to take him from the custody of his parents, guardian or custodian, the court may:

(a) place him in the custody of a suitable relative or other person;

(b) place him under the guardianship of a probation officer;

(c) commit him to an agency for care or placement, except an institution under the authority of the Department of Corrections or of the Department of Children and Family Services;

(d) commit him to some licensed training school or industrial school; or

(e) commit him to any appropriate institution having among its purposes the care of delinquent children, including a child protective facility maintained by a Child Protection District serving the county from which commitment is made, but not including any institution under the authority of the Department of Corrections or of the Department of Children and Family Services.

(2) When making such placement, the court, wherever possible, shall select a person holding the same religious belief as that of the minor or a private agency controlled by persons of like religious faith of the minor. In addition, whenever alternative plans for placement are available, the court shall ascertain and consider, to the extent appropriate in the particular case, the views and preferences of the minor.

(3) When a minor is placed with a suitable relative or other person, the court shall appoint him the legal custodian or guardian of the person of the minor. When a minor is committed to any agency, the court shall appoint the proper officer or representative thereof as legal custodian or guardian of the person of the minor. Legal custodians and guardians of the person of the minor have the respective rights and duties set forth in paragraph (9) of Section 1-3 [705 ILCS 405/1-3] except as otherwise provided by order of the court; but no guardian of the person may consent to adoption of the minor unless that authority is conferred upon him in accordance with Section 3-30 [705 ILCS 405/3-30]. An agency whose representative is appointed guardian of the person or legal custodian of the minor may place him in any child care facility, but such facility must be licensed under the Child Care Act of 1969 [225 ILCS 10/1 et seq.] or have been approved by the Department of Children and Family Services as meeting the standards established for such licensing. No agency may place such minor in a child care facility unless such placement is in compliance with the rules and regulations for placement under this Section promulgated by the Department of Children and Family Services under Section 5 of "An Act creating the Department of Children and Family Services, codifying its powers and

duties, and repealing certain Acts and Sections herein named" [20 ILCS 505/5]. Like authority and restrictions shall be conferred by the court upon any probation officer who has been appointed guardian of the person of a minor.

(4) No placement by any probation officer or agency whose representative is appointed guardian of the person or legal custodian of a minor may be made in any out of State child care facility unless it complies with the Interstate Compact on the Placement of Children.

(5) The clerk of the court shall issue to such legal custodian or guardian of the person a certified copy of the order of the court, as proof of his authority. No other process is necessary as authority for the keeping of the minor.

(6) Custody or guardianship granted hereunder continues until the court otherwise directs, but not after the minor reaches the age of 19 years except as set forth in Section 3-32 [705 ILCS 405/3-32].

(Source: P.A. 86-820; 87-14.) [Formerly Ill. Rev. Stat. 37 §803-28.]

405/3-29. Court review.

§3-29. Court review. (1) The court may require any legal custodian or guardian of the person appointed under this Act to report periodically to the court or may cite him into court and require him or his agency, to make a full and accurate report of his or its doings in behalf of the minor. The custodian or guardian, within 10 days after such citation, shall make the report, either in writing verified by affidavit or orally under oath in open court, or otherwise as the court directs. Upon the hearing of the report the court may remove the custodian or guardian and appoint another in his stead or restore the minor to the custody of his parents or former guardian or custodian.

(2) A guardian or custodian appointed by the court pursuant to this Act shall file updated case plans with the court every 6 months. Every agency which has guardianship of a child shall file a supplemental petition for court review, or review by an administrative body appointed or approved by the court and further order within 18 months of dispositional order and each 18 months thereafter. Such petition shall state facts relative to the child's present condition of physical, mental and emotional health as well as facts relative to his present custodial or foster care. The petition shall be set for hearing and the clerk shall mail 10 days notice of the hearing by certified mail, return receipt requested, to the person or agency having the physical custody of the child, the minor and other interested parties unless a written waiver of notice is filed with the petition.

Rights of wards of the court under this Act are enforceable against any public agency by complaints for relief by mandamus filed in any proceedings brought under this Act.

(3) The minor or any person interested in the minor may apply to the court for a change in custody of the minor and the appointment of a new custodian or guardian of the person or for the restoration of the minor to the custody of his parents or former guardian or custodian.

In the event that the minor has attained 18 years of age and the guardian or custodian petitions the court for an order terminating his guardianship or custody, guardianship or custody shall terminate automatically 30 days after the receipt of the petition unless the court orders otherwise. No legal custodian or guardian of the person may be removed without his consent until given notice and an opportunity to be heard by the court.

(Source: P.A. 85-601.) [Formerly Ill. Rev. Stat. 37 §803-29.]

405/3-30. Adoption; appointment of guardian with power to consent.

§3-30. Adoption; appointment of guardian with power to consent. (1) A ward of the court under this Act, with the consent of the court, may be the subject of a petition for adoption under "An Act in relation to the adoption of persons, and to repeal an Act therein named", approved July 17, 1959, as amended [750 ILCS 50/0.01 et seq.], or with like consent his or her parent or parents may, in the manner required by such Act, surrender him or her for adoption to an agency legally authorized or licensed to place children for adoption.

(2) If the petition prays and the court finds that it is in the best interests of the minor that a guardian of the person be appointed and authorized to consent to the adoption of the minor, the court with the consent of the parents, if living, or after finding, based upon clear and convincing evidence, that a non-consenting parent is an unfit person as defined in Section 1 of "An Act in relation to the adoption of persons, and to repeal an Act therein named", approved July 17, 1959, as amended [750 ILCS 50/0.01], may empower the guardian of the person of the minor, in the order appointing him or her as such guardian, to appear in court where any proceedings for the adoption of the minor may at any time be pending and to consent to the adoption. Such consent is sufficient to authorize the court in the adoption proceedings to enter a proper order or judgment of adoption without further notice to, or consent by, the parents of the minor. An order so empowering the guardian to consent to adoption terminates parental rights, deprives the parents of the minor of all legal rights as respects the minor and relieves them of all parental responsibility for him or her, and frees the minor from all obligations of maintenance and obedience to his or her natural parents.

If the minor is over 14 years of age, the court may, in its discretion, consider the wishes of the minor in determining whether the best interests of the minor would be promoted by the finding of the unfitness of a non-consenting parent.

(3) Parental consent to the order authorizing the guardian of the person to consent to adoption of the Minor shall be given in open court whenever possible and otherwise must be in writing and signed in the form provided in "An Act in relation to the adoption of persons, and to repeal an Act therein named", approved July 17, 1959, as amended, but no names of petitioners for adoption need be included. A finding of the unfitness of a nonconsenting parent must be made in compliance with that Act and be based upon clear and convincing evidence. Provisions of that Act relating to minor parents and to mentally ill or mentally deficient parents apply to proceedings under this Section and shall be based upon clear and convincing evidence.

(Source: P.A. 85-601.) [Formerly Ill. Rev. Stat. 37 §803-30.]

405/3-31. Notice to putative father; service.

§3-31. Notice to putative father; service. 1. Upon the written request to any Clerk of any Circuit Court by any interested party, including persons intending to adopt a child, a child welfare agency with whom the mother has placed or has given written notice of her intention to place a child for adoption, the mother of a child, or any attorney representing an interested party, a notice may be served on a putative father in the same manner as Summons is served in other proceedings under this Act, or in lieu of personal service, service may be made as follows:

(a) The person requesting notice shall furnish to the Clerk an original and one copy of a notice together with an Affidavit setting forth the putative father's last known address. The original notice shall be retained by the Clerk.

(b) The Clerk forthwith shall mail to the putative father, at the address appearing in the Affidavit, the copy of the notice, certified mail, return receipt requested; the envelope and return receipt shall bear the return address of the Clerk. The receipt for certified mail shall state the name and address of the addressee, and the date of mailing, and shall be attached to the original notice.

(c) The return receipt, when returned to the Clerk, shall be attached to the original notice, and shall constitute proof of service.

(d) The Clerk shall note the fact of service in a permanent record.

2. The notice shall be signed by the Clerk, and may be served on the putative father at any time after conception, and shall read as follows:

"IN THE MATTER OF NOTICE TO . . . ., PUTATIVE FATHER.

You have been identified as the father of a child (born on the . . . . . day of . . . , 19. . .), or (expected to be born on or about the . . . . . day of . . . . . , 19. . .). The mother of said child is . . . .

The mother has indicated she intends to place the child for adoption or otherwise have a judgment entered terminating her rights with respect to such child.

As the alleged father of said child, you have certain legal rights with respect to said child, including the right to notice of the filing of proceedings instituted for the termination of your parental rights regarding said child. If you wish to retain your rights with respect to said child, you must file with the Clerk of this Circuit Court of . . . . . , County, Illinois, whose address is . . . . . , ... , Illinois, within 30 days after the date of receipt of this notice, a declaration of paternity stating that you are, in fact, the father of said child and that you intend to retain your legal rights with respect to said child, or request to be notified of any further proceedings with respect to custody, termination of parental rights or adoption of the child.

If you do not file such a declaration of paternity, or a request for notice, then whatever legal rights you have with respect to said child, including the right to notice of any future proceedings for the adoption of said child, may be terminated without any further notice to you. When your legal rights with respect to said child are so terminated, you will not be entitled to notice of any proceeding instituted for the adoption of said child.

If you are not the father of said child, you may file with the Clerk of this Court, a disclaimer of paternity which will be noted in the Clerk's file and you will receive no further notice with respect to said child".

The disclaimer of paternity shall be substantially as follows:

"IN THE CIRCUIT COURT OF THE
.... JUDICIAL CIRCUIT, ILLINOIS
.... County

____
)
)
) No.
)
______________________________)

DENIAL OF PATERNITY WITH ENTRY OF APPEARANCE AND CONSENT TO ADOPTION

I, ... , state as follows:

(1) That I am . . . . . years of age; and I reside at . . . . in the County of . . . . , State of . . . .

(2) That I have been advised that . . . . is the mother of a . . . . .male child named . . . . born or expected to be born on or about . . . . . and that such mother has stated that I am the father of this child.

(3) I deny that I am the father of this child.

(4) I further understand that the mother of this child wishes to consent to the adoption of the child. I hereby consent to the adoption of this child, and waive any rights, remedies and defenses that I may now or in the future have as a result of the mother's allegation of the paternity of this child. This consent is being given in order to facilitate the adoption of the child and so that the court

may terminate what rights I may have to the child as a result of being named the father by the mother. This consent is not in any manner an admission of paternity.

(5) I hereby enter my appearance in the above entitled cause and waive service of summons and other pleading and consent to an immediate hearing on a petition TO TERMINATE PARENTAL RIGHTS AND TO APPOINT A GUARDIAN WITH THE POWER TO CONSENT TO THE ADOPTION OF THIS CHILD.

OATH

I have been duly sworn and I say under oath that I have read and understood this Denial of Paternity With Entry of Appearance and Consent to Adoption. The facts it contains are true and correct to the best of my knowledge, and I understand that by signing this document I have not admitted paternity. I have signed this document as my free and voluntary act in order to facilitate the adoption of the child.

....

(signature)

Dated this ..... day of ....., 19...
Signed and Sworn Before Me This ..... day of ....., 19...

....

(notary public)".

The names of adoptive parents, if any, shall not be included in the notice.

3. If the putative father files a disclaimer of paternity, he shall be deemed not to be the father of the child with respect to any adoption or other proceeding held to terminate the rights of parents as respects such child.

4. In the event the putative father does not file a declaration of paternity of the child or request for notice within 30 days of service of the above notice, he need not be made a party to or given notice of any proceeding brought for the adoption of the child. An Order or Judgment may be entered in such proceeding terminating all of his rights with respect to said child without further notice to him.

5. If the putative father files a declaration of paternity or a request for notice in accordance with subsection 2 with respect to the child, he shall be given notice in the event any proceeding is brought for the adoption of the child or for termination of parents' rights of the child.

6. The Clerk shall maintain separate numbered files and records of requests and proofs of service and all other documents filed pursuant to this article. All such records shall be impounded.

(Source: P.A. 85-601.) [Formerly Ill. Rev. Stat. 37 §803-31.]

405/3-32. Duration of wardship and discharge of proceedings.

§3-32. Duration of wardship and discharge of proceedings. (1) All proceedings under this Act in respect to any minor for whom a petition was filed after the effective date of this amendatory Act of 1991 automatically terminate upon his attaining the age of 19 years, except that a court may continue the wardship of a minor until age 21 for good cause when there is satisfactory evidence presented to the court that the best interest of the minor and the public require the continuation of the wardship.

(2) Whenever the court finds that the best interests of the minor and the public no longer require the wardship of the court, the court shall order the wardship terminated and all proceedings under this Act respecting that minor finally closed and discharged. The court may at the same time continue or terminate any custodianship or guardianship theretofore ordered but termination must be made in compliance with Section 3-29 [705 ILCS 405/3-29].

(3) The wardship of the minor and any custodianship or guardianship respecting the minor for whom a petition was filed after the effective date of this amendatory Act of 1991 automatically terminates when he attains the age of 19 years except as set forth in subsection (1) of this Section. The clerk of the court shall at that time record all proceedings under this Act as finally closed and discharged for that reason.
(Source: P.A. 87-14.) [Formerly Ill. Rev. Stat. 37 §803-32.]

405/3-33. Truant minor in need of supervision.

§3-33. Truant Minor in Need of Supervision. (a) Definition. Any minor who is reported by a regional superintendent of schools, in a county of less than 2,000,000 inhabitants, as a chronic truant (i) to whom prevention, diagnostic, intervention and remedial services and alternative programs and other school and community resources have been provided and have failed to result in the cessation of chronic truancy, or (ii) to whom such services, programs and resources have been offered and have been refused, shall be adjudged a truant minor in need of supervision.

(b) Kinds of dispositional orders. A minor found to be a truant minor in need of supervision may be:

(1) committed to the appropriate regional superintendent of schools for a multi-disciplinary case staffing, individualized educational plan or service plan, or referral to comprehensive community-based youth services;

(2) required to comply with an individualized educational plan or service plan as specifically provided by the appropriate regional superintendent of schools;

(3) ordered to obtain counseling or other supportive services;

(4) subject to a fine in an amount in excess of $5, but not exceeding $100, and each day of absence without valid cause as defined in Section 26-2a of The School Code [105 ILCS 5/26-2a] is a separate offense;

(5) required to perform some reasonable public service work such as, but not limited to, the picking up of litter in public parks or along public highways or the maintenance of public facilities; or

(6) subject to having his or her driver's license or privilege suspended.
(Source: P.A. 85-1235.) [Formerly Ill. Rev. Stat. 37 §803-33.]

ARTICLE IV. ADDICTED MINORS

Sec.

405/4-1. Jurisdictional facts.

§4-1. Jurisdictional facts. Proceedings may be instituted under the provisions of this Article concerning boys and girls who are addicted as defined in Section 4-3 [705 ILCS 405/4-3].
(Source: P.A. 85-601.) [Formerly Ill. Rev. Stat. 37 §804-1.]

405/4-2. Venue.

§4-2. Venue. (1) Venue under this Article lies in the county where the minor resides or is found.

(2) If proceedings are commenced in any county other than that of the minor's residence, the court in which the proceedings were initiated may at any time before or after adjudication of wardship transfer the case to the county of the minor's residence by transmitting to the court in that county an authenticated copy of the court record, including all documents, petitions and orders filed therein, and the minute orders and docket entries of the court. Transfer in like manner may be made in the event of a change of residence from one county to another of a minor concerning whom proceedings are pending.
(Source: P.A. 85-601.) [Formerly Ill. Rev. Stat. 37 §804-2.]

405/4-3. Addicted minor.

§4-3. Addicted minor. Those who are addicted include any minor who is an addict or an alcoholic as defined in the Illinois Alcoholism and Other Drug Dependency Act [20 ILCS 305/1-101 et seq.] as now or hereafter amended.
(Source: P.A. 85-1209.) [Formerly Ill. Rev. Stat. 37 §804-3.]

405/4-4. Taking into custody.

§4-4. Taking into custody. (1) A law enforcement officer may, without a warrant, take into temporary custody a minor (a) whom the officer with reasonable cause believes to be an addicted minor; (b) who has been adjudged a ward of the court and has escaped from any commitment ordered by the court under this Act; or (c) who is found in any street or public place suffering from any sickness or injury which requires care, medical treatment or hospitalization.

(2) Whenever a petition has been filed under Section 4-12 [705 ILCS 405/4-12] and the court finds that the conduct and behavior of the minor may endanger the health, person, welfare, or property of himself or others or that the circumstances of his home environment may endanger his health, person, welfare or property, a warrant may be issued immediately to take the minor into custody.

(3) The taking of a minor into temporary custody under this Section is not an arrest nor does it constitute a police record.

(4) Minors taken into temporary custody under this Section are subject to the provisions of Section 1-4.1 [705 ILCS 405/1-4.1].
(Chgd. by P.A. 87-1154, §1, eff. 1/1/93.)
(Source: P.A. 85-601.) [Formerly Ill. Rev. Stat. 37 §804-4.]

405/4-5. Duty of officer; admissions by minor.

§4-5. Duty of officer; admissions by minor. (1) A law enforcement officer who takes a minor into custody with a warrant shall immediately make a reasonable attempt to notify the parent or other person legally responsible for the minor's care or the person with whom the minor resides that the minor has been taken into custody and where he or she is being held; and the officer shall without unnecessary delay take the minor to the nearest juvenile police officer designated for such purposes in the county of venue or shall surrender the minor to a juvenile police officer in the city or village where the offense is alleged to have been committed.

The minor shall be delivered without unnecessary delay to the court or to the place designated by rule or order of court for the reception of minors, provided that the court may not designate a place of detention.

(2) A law enforcement officer who takes a minor into custody without a warrant under Section 4-4 [705 ILCS 405/4-4] shall, if the minor is not released, immediately make a reasonable attempt to notify the parent or other person legally responsible for the minor's care or the person with whom the minor resides that the minor has been taken into custody and where the minor is being held; and the law enforcement officer shall without unnecessary delay take the minor to the nearest juvenile police officer designated for such purposes in the county of venue.

(3) The juvenile police officer may take one of the following actions:

(a) station adjustment with release of the minor;

(b) station adjustment with release of the minor to a parent;

(c) station adjustment, release of the minor to a parent, and referral of the case to community services;

(d) station adjustment, release of the minor to a parent, and referral of the case to community services with informal monitoring by a juvenile police officer;

(e) station adjustment and release of the minor to a third person pursuant to agreement of the minor and parents;

(f) station adjustment, release of the minor to a third person pursuant to agreement of the minor and parents, and referral of the case to community services;

(g) station adjustment, release of the minor to a third person pursuant to agreement of the minor and parents, and referral to community services with informal monitoring by a juvenile police officer;

(h) release of the minor to his or her parents and referral of the case to a county juvenile probation officer or such other public officer designated by the court;

(i) if the juvenile police officer reasonably believes that there is an urgent and immediate necessity to keep the minor in custody, the juvenile police officer shall deliver the minor without unnecessary delay to the court or to the place designated by rule or order of the court for the reception of minors; and

(j) any other appropriate action with consent of the minor and a parent.

(Source: P.A. 85-601.) [Formerly Ill. Rev. Stat. 37 §804-5.]

405/4-6. Temporary custody.

§4-6. Temporary custody. "Temporary custody" means the temporary placement of the minor out of the custody of his or her guardian or parent.

(a) "Temporary protective custody" means custody within a hospital or other medical facility or a place previously designated for such custody by the Department, subject to review by the Court, including a licensed foster home, group home, or other institution; but such place shall not be a jail or other place for the detention of criminal or juvenile offenders.

(b) "Shelter care" means a physically unrestrictive facility designated by Department of Children and Family Services or a licensed child welfare agency or other suitable place designated by the court for a minor who requires care away from his or her home.

(Source: P.A. 85-601.) [Formerly Ill. Rev. Stat. 37 §804-6.]

405/4-7. Investigation; release.

§4-7. Investigation; release. When a minor is delivered to the court, or to the place designated by the court under Section 4-6 of this Act [705 ILCS 405/4-6], a probation officer or such other public officer designated by the court shall immediately investigate the circumstances of the minor and the facts surrounding his or her being taken into custody. The minor shall be immediately released to the custody of his or her parent, guardian, legal custodian or responsible relative, unless the probation officer or such other public officer designated by the court finds that further temporary custody is necessary, as provided in Section 4-6.

(Source: P.A. 85-601.) [Formerly Ill. Rev. Stat. 37 §804-7.]

405/4-8. Setting of shelter care hearing.

§4-8. Setting of shelter care hearing. (1) Unless sooner released, a minor alleged to be addicted taken into temporary protective custody must be brought before a judicial officer within 48 hours, exclusive of Saturdays, Sundays and holidays, for a shelter care hearing to determine whether he shall be further held in custody.

(2) If the probation officer or such other public officer designated by the court determines that the minor should be retained in custody, he shall cause a petition to be filed as provided in Section 4-12 of this Act [705 ILCS 405/4-12], and the clerk of the court shall set the matter for hearing on the shelter care hearing calendar. When a parent, guardian, custodian or responsible relative is present and so requests, the shelter care hearing shall be held immediately if the court is in session, otherwise at the earliest feasible time. The probation officer or such other public officer designated by the court shall notify the minor's parent, guardian, custodian or responsible relative of the time and place of the hearing. The notice may be given orally.

(3) The minor must be released from custody at the expiration of the 48 hour period, as the case may be, specified by this Section, if not brought before a judicial officer within that period.

(Source: P.A. 85-601.) [Formerly Ill. Rev. Stat. 37 §804-8.]

405/4-9. Shelter care hearing.

§4-9. Shelter care hearing. At the appearance of the minor before the court at the shelter care hearing, all witnesses present shall be examined before the court in relation to any matter connected with the allegations made in the petition.

(1) If the court finds that there is not probable cause to believe that the minor is addicted, it shall release the minor and dismiss the petition.

(2) If the court finds that there is probable cause to believe that the minor is addicted, the minor, his or her parent, guardian, custodian and other persons able to give relevant testimony shall be examined before the court. After such testimony, the court may enter an order that the minor shall be released upon the request of a parent, guardian or custodian if the parent, guardian or custodian appears to take custody. Custodian shall include any agency of the State which has been given custody or wardship of the child.

The Court shall require documentation by representatives of the Department of Children and Family Services or the probation department as to the reasonable efforts that were made to prevent or eliminate the necessity of removal of the minor from his or her home, and shall consider the testimony of any person as to those reasonable efforts. If the court finds that it is a matter of immediate and urgent necessity for the protection of the minor or of the person or property of another that the minor be or placed in a shelter care facility or that he or she is likely to flee the jurisdiction of the court, and further, finds that reasonable efforts have been made or good cause has been shown why reasonable efforts cannot prevent or eliminate the necessity of removal of the minor from his or her home, the court may prescribe shelter care and order that the minor be kept in a suitable place designated by the court or in a shelter care facility designated by the Department of Children and Family Services or a licensed child welfare agency, or, in a facility or program designated by the Department of Alcoholism and Substance Abuse for shelter and treatment services; otherwise it shall release the minor from custody. If the minor is ordered placed in a shelter care facility of the Department of Children and Family Services or a licensed child welfare agency, or, in a facility or program designated by the Department of Alcoholism and Substance Abuse for shelter and treatment services, the court shall, upon request of the appropriate Department or other agency, appoint the Department of Children and Family Services Guardianship Administrator or other appropriate agency executive temporary custodian of the minor and the court may enter such other orders related to the temporary custody as it deems fit and proper, including the provision of services to the minor or his family to ameliorate the causes contributing to the finding of probable cause or to the finding of the existence of immediate and urgent necessity. Acceptance of services shall not be considered an admission of any allegation in a petition made pursuant to this Act, nor may a referral of services be considered as evidence in any proceeding pursuant to this Act, except where the issue is whether the Department has made reasonable efforts to reunite the family. In making its findings that reasonable efforts have been made or that good cause has been shown why reasonable efforts cannot prevent or eliminate the necessity of removal of the minor from his or her home, the court shall state in writing its findings concerning the nature of the services that were offered or the efforts that were made to prevent removal of the child and the apparent reasons that such services or efforts could not prevent the need for removal. The parents, guardian, custodian, temporary custodian and minor shall each be furnished a copy of such written findings. The temporary custodian shall maintain a copy of the court order and written findings in the case record for the child. The order together with the court's findings of fact in support thereof shall be entered of record in the court.

Once the court finds that it is a matter of immediate and urgent necessity for the protection of the minor that the minor be placed in a shelter care facility, the minor shall not be returned to the parent, custodian or guardian until the court finds that such placement is no longer necessary for the protection of the minor.

(3) If neither the parent, guardian, legal custodian, responsible relative nor counsel of the minor has had actual notice of or is present at the shelter care hearing, he or she may file his or her affidavit setting forth these facts, and the clerk shall set the matter for rehearing not later than 24 hours, excluding Sundays and legal holidays, after the filing of the affidavit. At the rehearing, the court shall proceed in the same manner as upon the original hearing.

(4) If the minor is not brought before a judicial officer within the time period as specified in Section 4-8 [705 ILCS 405/4-8], the minor must immediately be released from custody.

(5) Only when there is reasonable cause to believe that the minor taken into custody is a person described in Section 5-3 [705 ILCS 405/5-3] may the minor be kept or detained in a detention home or county or municipal jail. This Section shall in no way be construed to limit subsection (6).

(6) No minor under 16 years of age may be confined in a jail or place ordinarily used for the confinement of prisoners in a police station. Minors under 17 years of age must be kept separate from confined adults and may not at any time be kept in the same cell, room or yard with adults confined pursuant to the criminal law.

(7) If neither the parent, guardian or custodian appears within 24 hours to take custody of a minor released upon request pursuant to subsection (2) of this Section, then the clerk of the court shall set the matter for rehearing not later than 7 days after the original order and shall issue a summons directed to the parent, guardian or custodian to appear. At the same time the probation department shall prepare a report on the minor. If a parent, guardian or custodian does not appear at such rehearing, the judge may enter an order prescribing that the minor be kept in a suitable place designated by the Department of Children and Family Services or a licensed child welfare agency.

(8) Any interested party, including the State, the temporary custodian, an agency providing services to the minor or family under a service plan pursuant to Section 8.2 of the Abused and Neglected Child Reporting Act [325 ILCS 5/8.2], foster parent, or any of their representatives, may file a motion to modify or vacate a temporary custody order on any of the following grounds:

(a) It is no longer a matter of immediate and urgent necessity that the minor remain in shelter care; or

(b) There is a material change in the circumstances of the natural family from which the minor was removed; or

(c) A person, including a parent, relative or legal guardian, is capable of assuming temporary custody of the minor; or

(d) Services provided by the Department of Children and Family Services or a child welfare agency or other service provider have been successful in eliminating the need for temporary custody.

The clerk shall set the matter for hearing not later than 14 days after such motion is filed. In the event that the court modifies or vacates a temporary custody order but does not vacate its finding of probable cause, the court may order that appropriate services be continued or initiated in behalf of the minor and his or her family.

(Source: P.A. 85-1209.) [Formerly Ill. Rev. Stat. 37 §804-9.]

405/4-10. Medical and dental treatment and care.

§4-10. Medical and dental treatment and care. At all times during temporary custody or shelter care, the court may authorize a physician, a hospital or any other appropriate health care provider to provide medical, dental or surgical procedures if such procedures are necessary to safeguard the minor's life or health.

(Source: P.A. 85-1209.) [Formerly Ill. Rev. Stat. 37 §804-10.]

405/4-11. Preliminary conferences.

§4-11. Preliminary conferences. (1) The court may authorize the probation officer to confer in a preliminary conference with any person seeking to file a petition under this Article, the prospective respondents and other interested persons concerning the advisability of filing the petition, with a view to adjusting suitable cases without the filing of a petition as provided for herein.

The probation officer should schedule a conference promptly except where the State's Attorney insists on court action or where the minor has indicated that he or she will demand a judicial hearing and will not comply with an informal adjustment.

(2) In any case of a minor who is in temporary custody, the holding of preliminary conferences does not operate to prolong temporary custody beyond the period permitted by Section 4-8 [705 ILCS 405/4-8].

(3) This Section does not authorize any probation officer to compel any person to appear at any conference, produce any papers, or visit any place.

(4) No statement made during a preliminary conference may be admitted into evidence at an adjudicatory hearing or at any proceeding against the minor under the criminal laws of this State prior to his or her conviction thereunder.

(5) The probation officer shall promptly formulate a written non-judicial adjustment plan following the initial conference.

(6) Non-judicial adjustment plans include but are not limited to the following:

(a) up to 6 months informal supervision within the family;

(b) up to 6 months informal supervision with a probation officer involved;

(c) up to 6 months informal supervision with release to a person other than a parent;

(d) referral to special educational, counseling or other rehabilitative social or educational programs;

(e) referral to residential treatment programs; and

(f) any other appropriate action with consent of the minor and a parent.

(7) The factors to be considered by the probation officer in formulating a written non-judicial adjustment plan shall be the same as those limited in subsection (4) of Section 5-6 [705 ILCS 405/5-6].
(Source: P.A. 86-639.) [Formerly Ill. Rev. Stat. 37 §804-11.]

405/4-12. Petition; supplemental petitions.

§4-12. Petition; supplemental petitions. (1) Any adult person, any agency or association by its representative may file, or the court on its own motion may direct the filing through the State's Attorney of a petition in respect to a minor under this Act. The petition and all subsequent court documents shall be entitled "In the interest of . . . . , a minor".

(2) The petition shall be verified but the statements may be made upon information and belief. It shall allege that the minor is addicted, as the case may be, and set forth (a) facts sufficient to bring the minor under Section 4-1 [705 ILCS 405/4-1]; (b) the name, age and residence of the minor; (c) the names and residences of his parents; (d) the name and residence of his legal guardian or the person or persons having custody or control of the minor, or of the nearest known relative if no parent or guardian can be found; and (e) if the minor upon whose behalf the petition is brought is sheltered in custody, the date on which shelter care was ordered by the court or the date set for a shelter care hearing. If any of the facts herein required are not known by the petitioner, the petition shall so state.

(3) The petition must allege that it is in the best interests of the minor and of the public that he or she be adjudged a ward of the court and may pray generally for relief available under this Act. The petition need not specify any proposed disposition following adjudication of wardship.

(4) If appointment of a guardian of the person with power to consent to adoption of the minor under Section 4-27 [705 ILCS 405/4-27] is sought, the petition shall so state.

(5) At any time before dismissal of the petition or before final closing and discharge under Section 4-29 [705 ILCS 405/4-29], one or more supplemental petitions may be filed in respect to the same minor.
(Source: P.A. 85-1209.) [Formerly Ill. Rev. Stat. 37 §804-12.]

405/4-13. Date for adjudicatory hearing.

§4-13. Date for adjudicatory hearing. (a) Until January 1, 1988:

(1) When a petition has been filed alleging that the minor is an addict under this Article, an adjudicatory hearing shall be held within 120 days. The 120 day period in which an adjudicatory hearing shall be held is tolled by: (A) delay occasioned by the minor; (B) a continuance allowed pursuant to Section 114-4 of the Code of Criminal Procedure of 1963 [725 ILCS 5/114-4] after a court's determination of the minor's physical incapacity for trial; or (C) an interlocutory appeal. Any such delay shall temporarily suspend for the time of the delay the period within which the adjudicatory hearing must be held. On the day of

expiration of the delay, the said period shall continue at the point at which it was suspended. Where no such adjudicatory hearing is held within 120 days the court may, upon written motion of such minor's guardian ad litem, dismiss the petition with respect to such minor. Such dismissal shall be without prejudice.

Where the court determines that the State has exercised, without success, due diligence to obtain evidence material to the case, and that there are reasonable grounds to believe that such evidence may be obtained at a later date the court may, upon written motion by the state, continue the matter for not more than 30 additional days.

(2) In the case of a minor ordered held in shelter care, the hearing on the petition must be held within 10 judicial days from the date of the order of the court directing shelter care, or the earliest possible date in compliance with the notice provisions of Sections 4-14 and 4-15 [705 ILCS 405/4-14 and 405/4-15] as to the custodial parent, guardian or legal custodian, but no later than 30 judicial days from the date of the order of the court directing shelter care. Delay occasioned by the respondent shall temporarily suspend, for the time of the delay, the period within which a respondent must be brought to an adjudicatory hearing pursuant to this Section.

Any failure to comply with the time limits of this subsection must require the immediate release of the minor and the time limits of subsection (a) (1) shall apply.

(3) Nothing in this Section prevents the minor's exercise of his or her right to waive the time limits set forth in this Section.

(b) Beginning January 1, 1988:

(1) (A) When a petition has been filed alleging that the minor is an addict under this Article, an adjudicatory hearing shall be held within 120 days of a demand made by any party, except that when the court determines that the State, without success, has exercised due diligence to obtain evidence material to the case and that there are reasonable grounds to believe that such evidence may be obtained at a later date, the court may, upon motion by the State, continue the adjudicatory hearing for not more than 30 additional days.

The 120 day period in which an adjudicatory hearing shall be held is tolled by: (i) delay occasioned by the minor; or (ii) a continuance allowed pursuant to Section 114-4 of the Code of Criminal Procedure of 1963 after a court's determination of the minor's physical incapacity for trial; or (iii) an interlocutory appeal. Any such delay shall temporarily suspend for the time of the delay the period within which the adjudicatory hearing must be held. On the day of expiration of the delay, the said period shall continue at the point at which it was suspended.

(B) When no such adjudicatory hearing is held within the time required by paragraph (b)(1)(A) of this Section, the court shall, upon motion by any party, dismiss the petition with prejudice.

(2) Without affecting the applicability of the tolling and multiple prosecution provisions of paragraph (b) (1) of this Section, when a petition has been filed alleging that the minor is an addict under this Article and the minor is in shelter care, the adjudicatory hearing shall be held within 10 judicial days after the date of the order directing shelter care, or the earliest possible date in compliance with the notice provisions of Sections 4-14 and 4-15 as to the custodial parent, guardian or legal custodian, but no later than 30 judicial days from the date of the order of the court directing shelter care.

(3) Any failure to comply with the time limits of paragraph (b)(2) of this Section shall require the immediate release of the minor from shelter care, and the time limits of paragraph (b)(1) shall apply.

(4) Nothing in this Section prevents the minor or the minor's parents or guardian from exercising their respective rights to waive the time limits set forth in this Section.

(Source: P.A. 85-601.) [Formerly Ill. Rev. Stat. 37 §804-13.]

405/4-14. Summons.

§4-14. Summons. (1) When a petition is filed, the clerk of the court shall issue a summons with a copy of the petition attached. The summons shall be directed to the minor's legal guardian or custodian and to each person named as a respondent in the petition, except that summons need not be directed to a minor respondent under 8 years of age for whom the court appoints a guardian ad litem if the guardian ad litem appears on behalf of the minor in any proceeding under this Act.

(2) The summons must contain a statement that the minor or any of the respondents is entitled to have an attorney present at the hearing on the petition, and that the clerk of the court should be notified promptly if the minor or any other respondent desires to be represented by an attorney but is financially unable to employ counsel.

(3) The summons shall be issued under the seal of the court, attested to and signed with the name of the clerk of the court, dated on the day it is issued, and shall require each respondent to appear and answer the petition on the date set for the adjudicatory hearing.

(4) The summons may be served by any county sheriff, coroner or probation officer, even though the officer is the petitioner. The return of the summons with endorsement of service by the officer is sufficient proof thereof.

(5) Service of a summons and petition shall be made by: (a) leaving a copy thereof with the person summoned at least 3 days before the time stated therein for appearance; (b) leaving a copy at his usual place of abode with some person of the family, of the age of 10 years or upwards, and informing that person of the contents thereof, provided that the officer or other person making service shall also send a copy of the summons in a sealed envelope with postage fully prepaid, addressed to the person summoned at his usual place of abode, at least 3 days before the time stated therein for appearance; or (c) leaving a copy thereof with the guardian or custodian of a minor, at least 3 days before the time stated therein for appearance. If the guardian or custodian is an agency of the State of Illinois, proper service may be made by leaving a copy of the summons and petition with any administrative employee of such agency designated by such agency to accept service of summons and petitions. The certificate of the officer or affidavit of the person that he has sent the copy pursuant to this Section is sufficient proof of service.

(6) When a parent or other person, who has signed a written promise to appear and bring the minor to court or who has waived or acknowledged service, fails to appear with the minor on the date set by the court, a bench warrant may be issued for the parent or other person, the minor, or both.

(7) The appearance of the minor's legal guardian or custodian, or a person named as a respondent in a petition, in any proceeding under this Act shall constitute a waiver of service of summons and submission to the jurisdiction of the court. A copy of the summons and petition shall be provided to the person at the time of his appearance.

(Source: P.A. 86-441.) [Formerly Ill. Rev. Stat. 37 §804-14.]

405/4-15. Notice by certified mail or publication.

§4-15. Notice by certified mail or publication. (1) If service on individuals as provided in Section 4-14 [705 ILCS 405/4-14] is not made on any respondent within a reasonable time or if it appears that any respondent resides outside the State, service may be made by certified mail. In such case the clerk shall mail the summons and a copy of the petition to that respondent by certified mail marked for delivery to addressee only. The court shall not proceed with the adjudicatory hearing until 5 days after such mailing. The regular return receipt for certified mail is sufficient proof of service.

(2) If service upon individuals as provided in Section 4-14 is not made on any respondents within a reasonable time or if any person is made a respondent under the designation of "All whom it may Concern", or if service cannot be made because the whereabouts of a respondent are unknown, service may be made by publication. The clerk of the court as soon as possible shall cause publication to be made once in a newspaper of general circulation in the county where the action is pending. Notice by publication is not required in any case when the person alleged to have legal custody of the minor has been served with summons personally or by certified mail, but the court may not enter any order or judgment against any person who cannot be served with process other than by publication unless notice by publication is given or unless that person appears. When a minor has been sheltered under Section 4-6 of this Act [705 ILCS 405/4-6] and summons has not been served personally or by certified mail within 20 days from the date of the order of court directing such shelter care, the clerk of the court shall cause publication. Notice by publication shall be substantially as follows:

"A, B, C, D, (here giving the names of the named respondents, if any) and to All Whom It May Concern (if there is any respondent under that designation):

Take notice that on the .... day of ...., 19... a petition was filed under the Juvenile Court Act by .... in the circuit court of .... county entitled 'In the interest of............., a minor', and that in ..... courtroom at .... on the .... day of .... at the hour of ...., or as soon thereafter as this cause may be heard, an adjudicatory hearing will be held upon the petition to have the child declared to be a ward of the court under that Act. The court has authority in this proceeding to take from you the custody and guardianship of the minor, (and if the petition prays for the appointment of a guardian with power to consent to adoption) and to appoint a guardian with power to consent to adoption of the minor.

Now, unless you appear at the hearing and show cause against the petition, the allegations of the petition may stand admitted as against you and each of you, and an order or judgment entered.

....
Clerk

Dated (the date of publication)"

(3) The clerk shall also at the time of the publication of the notice send a copy thereof by mail to each of the respondents on account of whom publication is made at his or her last known address. The certificate of the clerk that he or she has mailed the notice is evidence thereof. No other publication notice is required. Every respondent notified by publication under this Section must appear and answer in open court at the hearing. The court may not proceed with the adjudicatory hearing until 10 days after service by publication on any custodial parent, guardian or legal custodian.

(4) If it becomes necessary to change the date set for the hearing in order to comply with Section 4-14 or with this Section, notice of the resetting of the date must be given, by certified mail or other reasonable means, to each respondent who has been served with summons personally or by certified mail.

(Source: P.A. 85-601.) [Formerly Ill. Rev. Stat. 37 §804-15.]

405/4-16. Guardian ad litem.

§4-16. Guardian ad litem. (1) Immediately upon the filing of a petition alleging that the minor is a person described in Section 4-3 of this Act [705 ILCS 405/4-3], the court may appoint a guardian ad litem for the minor if:

(a) such petition alleges that the minor is the victim of sexual abuse or misconduct; or

(b) such petition alleges that charges alleging the commission of any of the sex offenses defined in Article 11 [720 ILCS 5/11-6 et seq.] or in Sections 12-13, 12-14, 12-15 or 12-16 of the Criminal Code of 1961, as amended [720 ILCS 5/12-13, 5/12-14, 5/12-15 or 5/12-16], have been filed against a defendant in any court and that such minor is the alleged victim of the acts of the defendant in the commission of such offense.

Unless the guardian ad litem appointed pursuant to this paragraph (1) is an attorney at law he shall be represented in the performance of his duties by counsel.

(2) Before proceeding with the hearing, the court shall appoint a guardian ad litem for the minor if

(a) no parent, guardian, custodian or relative of the minor appears at the first or any subsequent hearing of the case;

(b) the petition prays for the appointment of a guardian with power to consent to adoption; or

(c) the petition for which the minor is before the court resulted from a report made pursuant to the Abused and Neglected Child Reporting Act [325 ILCS 5/1 et seq.].

(3) The court may appoint a guardian ad litem for the minor whenever it finds that there may be a conflict of interest between the minor and his parents or other custodian or that it is otherwise in the minor's interest to do so.

(4) Unless the guardian ad litem is an attorney, he shall be represented by counsel.

(5) The reasonable fees of a guardian ad litem appointed under this Section shall be fixed by the court and charged to the parents of the minor, to the extent they are able to pay. If the parents are unable to pay those fees, they shall be paid from the general fund of the county.

(Source: P.A. 85-601.) [Formerly Ill. Rev. Stat. 37 §804-16.]

405/4-17. Evidence.

§4-17. Evidence. At the adjudicatory hearing, the court shall first consider only the question whether the minor is a person described in Section 4-3 [705 ILCS 405/4-3]. The standard of proof and the rules of evidence in the nature of civil proceedings in this State are applicable to proceedings under this Article.

(Source: P.A. 85-601.) [Formerly Ill. Rev. Stat. 37 §804-17.]

405/4-18. Continuance under supervision.

§4-18. Continuance under supervision. (1) The court may enter an order of continuance under supervision (a) upon an admission or stipulation by the appropriate respondent or minor respondent of the facts supporting the petition and before proceeding to findings and adjudication, or after hearing the evidence at the adjudicatory hearing but before noting in the minutes of the proceeding a finding of whether or not the minor is an addict, and (b) in the absence of objection made in open court by the minor, his parent, guardian, custodian, responsible relative, defense attorney or the State's Attorney.

(2) If the minor, his parent, guardian, custodian, responsible relative, defense attorney or State's Attorney, objects in open court to any such continuance and insists upon proceeding to findings and adjudication, the court shall so proceed.

(3) Nothing in this Section limits the power of the court to order a continuance of the hearing for the production of additional evidence or for any other proper reason.

(4) When a hearing is continued pursuant to this Section, the court may permit the minor to remain in his home subject to such conditions concerning his conduct and supervision as the court may require by order.

(5) If a petition is filed charging a violation of a condition of the continuance under supervision, the court shall conduct a hearing. If the court finds that such condition of supervision has not been fulfilled the court may proceed to findings and adjudication and disposition. The filing of a petition for violation of a condition of the continuance under supervision shall toll the period of continuance under supervision until the final determination of the charge, and the term of the continuance under supervision shall not run until the hearing and disposition of the petition for violation; provided where the petition alleges conduct that does not constitute a criminal offense, the hearing must be held within 15 days of the filing of the petition unless a delay in such hearing has been occasioned by the minor, in which case the delay shall continue the tolling of the period of continuance under supervision for the period of such delay.
(Source: P.A. 85-601.) [Formerly Ill. Rev. Stat. 37 §804-18.]

405/4-19. Findings and adjudication.

§4-19. Findings and adjudication. (1) After hearing the evidence the court shall make and note in the minutes of the proceeding a finding of whether or not the minor is an addict. If it finds that the minor is not an addict, the court shall order the petition dismissed and the minor discharged from any restriction previously ordered in such proceeding.

(2) If the court finds that the minor is an addict, the court shall set a time for a dispositional hearing to be conducted under Section 4-20 [705 ILCS 405 4-20] at which hearing the court shall determine whether it is in the best interests of the minor and the public that he be made a ward of the court. To assist the court in making this and other determinations at the dispositional hearing, the court may order that an investigation be conducted and a dispositional report be prepared concerning the minor's physical and mental history and condition, family situation and background, economic status, education, occupation, history of delinquency or criminality, personal habits, and any other information that may be helpful to the court.
(Source: P.A. 85-601.) [Formerly Ill. Rev. Stat. 37 §804-19.]

405/4-20. Dispositional hearing; evidence; continuance.

§4-20. Dispositional hearing; evidence; continuance. (1) At the dispositional hearing, the court shall determine whether it is in the best interests of the minor and the public that he be made a ward of the court, and, if he is to be made a ward of the court, the court shall determine the proper disposition best serving the interests of the minor and the public. All evidence helpful in determining these questions, including oral and written reports, may be admitted and may be relied upon to the extent of its probative value, even though not competent for the purposes of the adjudicatory hearing.

(2) Notice in compliance with Sections 4-14 and 4-15 [705 ILCS 405/4-14 and 405/4-15] must be given to all parties-respondents prior to proceeding to a dispositional hearing. Before making an order of disposition the court shall advise the State's Attorney, the parents, guardian, custodian or responsible relative or their counsel of the factual contents and the conclusions of the reports prepared for the use of the court and considered by it, and afford fair opportunity, if requested, to controvert them. The court may order, however, that the documents containing such reports need not be submitted to inspection, or that sources of confidential information need not be disclosed except to the attorneys for the parties. Factual contents, conclusions, documents and sources disclosed by the court under this paragraph shall not be further disclosed without the express approval of the court pursuant to an in camera hearing.

(3) A record of a prior continuance under supervision under Section 4-18 [705 ILCS 405/4-18], whether successfully completed or not, is admissible at the dispositional hearing.

(4) On its own motion or that of the State's Attorney, a parent, guardian, custodian, responsible relative or counsel, the court may adjourn the hearing for a reasonable period to receive reports or other evidence. In scheduling investigations and hearings, the court shall give priority to proceedings in which a minor has been removed from his or her home before an order of disposition has been made.

(Source: P.A. 85-601.) [Formerly Ill. Rev. Stat. 37 §804-20.]

405/4-21. Kinds of dispositional orders.

§4-21. Kinds of dispositional orders. (1) A minor found to be addicted under Section 4-3 [705 ILCS 405/4-3] may be (a) committed to the Department of Children and Family Services, subject to Section 5 of "An Act creating the Department of Children and Family Services, codifying its powers and duties, and repealing certain Acts and Sections herein named" [20 ILCS 505/5]; (b) placed under supervision and released to his or her parents, guardian or legal custodian; (c) placed in accordance with Section 4-25 [705 ILCS 405/4-25] with or without also being placed under supervision. Conditions of supervision may be modified or terminated by the court if it deems that the best interests of the minor and the public will be served thereby; (d) placed under the treatment supervision of the Illinois Department of Alcoholism and Substance Abuse or required to attend an approved alcohol or drug abuse treatment or counseling program on an inpatient or outpatient basis instead of or in addition to the disposition otherwise provided for in this paragraph; or (e) ordered partially or completely emancipated in accordance with the provisions of the "Emancipation of Mature Minors Act", approved September 19, 1979, as now or hereafter amended [750 ILCS 30/1 et seq.]. No disposition under this subsection shall provide for the minor's placement in a secure facility.

(2) Any order of disposition may provide for protective supervision under Section 4-22 [705 ILCS 405/4-22] and may include an order of protection under Section 4-23 [705 ILCS 405/4-23].

(3) Unless the order of disposition expressly so provides, it does not operate to close proceedings on the pending petition, but is subject to modification until final closing and discharge of the proceedings under Section 4-29 [705 ILCS 405/4-29].

(4) In addition to any other order of disposition, the court may order any minor found to be addicted under this Article as neglected with respect to his or her own injurious behavior, to make restitution, in monetary or non-monetary form, under the terms and conditions of Section 5-5-6 of the "Unified Code of Corrections" [730 ILCS 5/5-5-6], except that the "presentence hearing" referred to therein shall be the dispositional hearing for purposes of this Section. The parent, guardian or legal custodian of the minor may pay some or all of such restitution on the minor's behalf.

(5) Any order for disposition where the minor is placed in accordance with Section 4-25 shall provide for the parents or guardian of the estate of such minor to pay to the legal custodian or guardian of the person of the minor such sums as are determined by the custodian or guardian of the person of the minor as necessary for the minor's needs. Such payments may not exceed the maximum amounts provided for by Section 5.1 of "An Act creating the Department of Children and Family Services, codifying its powers and duties and repealing certain Acts and Sections herein named", approved June 4, 1963, as amended [see 20 ILCS 505/9.1].

(6) Whenever the order of disposition requires the minor to attend school or participate in a program of training, the truant officer or designated school

official shall regularly report to the court if the minor is a chronic or habitual truant under Section 26-2a of The School Code [105 ILCS 5/26-2a].
(Source: P.A. 85-601.) [Formerly Ill. Rev. Stat. 37 §804-21.]

405/4-22. Protective supervision.

§4-22. Protective supervision. If the order of disposition releases the minor to the custody of his parents, guardian or legal custodian, or continues him in such custody, the court may place the person having custody of the minor, except for representatives of private or public agencies or governmental departments, under supervision of the probation office. Rules or orders of the court shall define the terms and conditions of protective supervision, which may be modified or terminated when the court finds that the best interests of the minor and the public will be served thereby.
(Source: P.A. 85-601.) [Formerly Ill. Rev. Stat. 37 §804-22.]

405/4-23. Order of protection.

§4-23. Order of protection. (1) The court may make an order of protection in assistance of or as a condition of any other order authorized by this Act. The order of protection may set forth reasonable conditions of behavior to be observed for a specified period. Such an order may require a person:

(a) To stay away from the home or the minor;

(b) To permit a parent to visit the minor at stated periods;

(c) To abstain from offensive conduct against the minor, his parent or any person to whom custody of the minor is awarded;

(d) To give proper attention to the care of the home;

(e) To cooperate in good faith with an agency to which custody of a minor is entrusted by the court or with an agency or association to which the minor is referred by the court;

(f) To prohibit and prevent any contact whatsoever with the respondent minor by a specified individual or individuals who are alleged in either a criminal or juvenile proceeding to have caused injury to a respondent minor or a sibling of a respondent minor;

(g) To refrain from acts of commission or omission that tend to make the home not a proper place for the minor.

(2) The court shall enter an order of protection to prohibit and prevent any contact between a respondent minor or a sibling of a respondent minor and any person named in a petition seeking an order of protection who has been convicted of heinous battery under Section 12-4.1, aggravated battery of a child under Section 12-4.3, criminal sexual assault under Section 12-13, aggravated criminal sexual assault under Section 12-14, criminal sexual abuse under Section 12-15, or aggravated criminal sexual abuse under Section 12-16 of the Criminal Code of 1961 [720 ILCS 5/12-4.1, 5/12-4.3, 5/12-13, 5/12-14, 5/12-15 or 5/12-16], or has been convicted of an offense that resulted in the death of a child, or has violated a previous order of protection under this Section.

(3) When the court issues an order of protection against any person as provided by this Section, the court shall direct a copy of such order to the Sheriff of that county. The Sheriff shall furnish a copy of the order of protection to the Department of State Police with* 24 hours of receipt, in the form and manner required by the Department. The Department of State Police shall maintain a complete record and index of such orders of protection and make this data available to all local law enforcement agencies.

**So in original. Probably should be "within".*

(4) After notice and opportunity for hearing afforded to a person subject to an order of protection, the order may be modified or extended for a further specified period or both or may be terminated if the court finds that the best interests of the minor and the public will be served thereby.

(5) An order of protection may be sought at any time during the course of any proceeding conducted pursuant to this Act. Any person against whom an order of protection is sought may retain counsel to represent him at a hearing, and has rights to be present at the hearing, to be informed prior to the hearing in writing of the contents of the petition seeking a protective order and of the date, place and time of such hearing, and to cross examine witnesses called by the petitioner and to present witnesses and argument in opposition to the relief sought in the petition.

(6) Diligent efforts shall be made by the petitioner to serve any person or persons against whom any order of protection is sought with written notice of the contents of the petition seeking a protective order and of the date, place and time at which the hearing on the petition is to be held. When a protective order is being sought in conjunction with a shelter care hearing, if the court finds that the person against whom the protective order is being sought has been notified of the hearing or that diligent efforts have been made to notify such person, the court may conduct a hearing. If a protective order is sought at any time other than in conjunction with a shelter care hearing, the court may not conduct a hearing on the petition in the absence of the person against whom the order is sought unless the petitioner has notified such person by personal service at least 3 days before the hearing or has sent written notice by first class mail to such person's last known address at least 5 days before the hearing.

(7) A person against whom an order of protection is being sought who is neither a parent, guardian, legal custodian or responsible relative as described in Section 1-5 [705 ILCS 405/1-5] is not a party or respondent as defined in that Section and shall not be entitled to the rights provided therein. Such person does not have a right to appointed counsel or to be present at any hearing other than the hearing in which the order of protection is being sought or a hearing directly pertaining to that order. Unless the court orders otherwise, such person does not have a right to inspect the court file.

(8) All protective orders entered under this Section shall be in writing. Unless the person against whom the order was obtained was present in court when the order was issued, the sheriff, other law enforcement official or special process server shall promptly serve that order upon that person and file proof of such service, in the manner provided for service of process in civil proceedings. The person against whom the protective order was obtained may seek a modification of the order by filing a written motion to modify the order within 7 days after actual receipt by the person of a copy of the order.

(Source: P.A. 85-1209.) [Formerly Ill. Rev. Stat. 37 §804-23.]

405/4-24. Enforcement of orders of protective supervision or of protection.

§4-24. Enforcement of orders of protective supervision or of protection. (1) Orders of protective supervision and orders of protection may be enforced by citation to show cause for contempt of court by reason of any violation thereof and, where protection of the welfare of the minor so requires, by the issuance of a warrant to take the alleged violator into custody and bring him before the court.

(2) In any case where an order of protection has been entered, the clerk of the court may issue to the petitioner, to the minor or to any other person affected by the order a certificate stating that an order of protection has been made by the court concerning such persons and setting forth its terms and requirements. The presentation of the certificate to any peace officer authorizes him to take into custody a person charged with violating the terms of the order of protection, to bring such person before the court and, within the limits of his legal authority as such peace officer, otherwise to aid in securing the protection the order is intended to afford.

(Source: P.A. 85-601.) [Formerly Ill. Rev. Stat. 37 §804-24.]

405/4-25. Placement; legal custody or guardianship.

§4-25. Placement; legal custody or guardianship. (1) If the court finds that the parents, guardian or legal custodian of a minor adjudged a ward of the court are unfit or are unable, for some reason other than financial circumstances alone, to care for, protect, train or discipline the minor or are unwilling to do so, and that appropriate services aimed at family preservation and family reunification have been unsuccessful in rectifying the conditions which have led to a finding of unfitness or inability to care for, protect, train or discipline the minor, and that it is in the best interest of the minor to take him from the custody of his parents, guardian or custodian, the court may:

(a) place him in the custody of a suitable relative or other person;

(b) place him under the guardianship of a probation officer;

(c) commit him to an agency for care or placement, except an institution under the authority of the Department of Corrections or of the Department of Children and Family Services;

(d) commit him to some licensed training school or industrial school; or

(e) commit him to any appropriate institution having among its purposes the care of delinquent children, including a child protective facility maintained by a Child Protection District serving the county from which commitment is made, but not including any institution under the authority of the Department of Corrections or of the Department of Children and Family Services.

(2) When making such placement, the court, wherever possible, shall select a person holding the same religious belief as that of the minor or a private agency controlled by persons of like religious faith of the minor. In addition, whenever alternative plans for placement are available, the court shall ascertain and consider, to the extent appropriate in the particular case, the views and preferences of the minor.

(3) When a minor is placed with a suitable relative or other person, the court shall appoint him the legal custodian or guardian of the person of the minor. When a minor is committed to any agency, the court shall appoint the proper officer or representative thereof as legal custodian or guardian of the person of the minor. Legal custodians and guardians of the person of the minor have the respective rights and duties set forth in subsection (9) of Section 1-3 [705 ILCS 405/1-3] except as otherwise provided by order of the court; but no guardian of the person may consent to adoption of the minor unless that authority is conferred upon him in accordance with Section 4-27 [705 ILCS 405/4-27]. An agency whose representative is appointed guardian of the person or legal custodian of the minor may place him in any child care facility, but such facility must be licensed under the Child Care Act of 1969 [225 ILCS 10/1 et seq.] or have been approved by the Department of Children and Family Services as meeting the standards established for such licensing. After June 30, 1981, no agency may place a minor, if the minor is under age 13, in a child care facility unless such placement is in compliance with the rules and regulations for placement under Section 4-25 of this Act promulgated by the Department of Children and Family Services under Section 5 of the Children and Family Services Act [20 ILCS 505/5]. Like authority and restrictions shall be conferred by the court upon any probation officer who has been appointed guardian of the person of a minor.

(4) No placement by any probation officer or agency whose representative is appointed guardian of the person or legal custodian of a minor may be made in any out of State child care facility unless it complies with the Interstate Compact on the Placement of Children.

(5) The clerk of the court shall issue to the legal custodian or guardian of the person a certified copy of the order of the court, as proof of his authority. No other process is necessary as authority for the keeping of the minor.

(6) Custody or guardianship granted under this Section continues until the court otherwise directs, but not after the minor reaches the age of 19 years except as set forth in Section 4-29 [705 ILCS 405/4-29].
(Source: P.A. 87-14.) [Formerly Ill. Rev. Stat. 37 §804-25.]

405/4-26. Court review.

§4-26. Court Review. (1) The court may require any legal custodian or guardian of the person appointed under this Act to report periodically to the court or may cite him into court and require him or his agency, to make a full and accurate report of his or its doings in behalf of the minor. The custodian or guardian, within 10 days after such citation, shall make the report, either in writing verified by affidavit or orally under oath in open court, or otherwise as the court directs. Upon the hearing of the report the court may remove the custodian or guardian and appoint another in his stead or restore the minor to the custody of his parents or former guardian or custodian.

(2) A guardian or custodian appointed by the court pursuant to this Act shall file updated case plans with the court every 6 months. Every agency which has guardianship of a child shall file a supplemental petition for court review, or review by an administrative body appointed or approved by the court and further order within 18 months of dispositional order and each 18 months thereafter. Such petition shall state facts relative to the child's present condition of physical, mental and emotional health as well as facts relative to his present custodial or foster care. The petition shall be set for hearing and the clerk shall mail 10 days notice of the hearing by certified mail, return receipt requested, to the person or agency having the physical custody of the child, the minor and other interested parties unless a written waiver of notice is filed with the petition.

Rights of wards of the court under this Act are enforceable against any public agency by complaints for relief by mandamus filed in any proceedings brought under this Act.

(3) The minor or any person interested in the minor may apply to the court for a change in custody of the minor and the appointment of a new custodian or guardian of the person or for the restoration of the minor to the custody of his parents or former guardian or custodian. In the event that the minor has attained 18 years of age and the guardian or custodian petitions the court for an order terminating his guardianship or custody, guardianship or custody shall terminate automatically 30 days after the receipt of the petition unless the court orders otherwise. No legal custodian or guardian of the person may be removed without his consent until given notice and an opportunity to be heard by the court.
(Source: P.A. 85-601.) [Formerly Ill. Rev. Stat. 37 §804-26.]

405/4-27. Adoption; appointment of guardian with power to consent.

§4-27. Adoption; appointment of guardian with power to consent. (1) A ward of the court under this Act, with the consent of the court, may be the subject of a petition for adoption under "An Act in relation to the adoption of persons, and to repeal an Act therein named", approved July 17, 1959, as amended [750 ILCS 50/1 et seq.], or with like consent his or her parent or parents may, in the manner required by such Act, surrender him or her for adoption to an agency legally authorized or licensed to place children for adoption.

(2) If the petition prays and the court finds that it is in the best interests of the minor that a guardian of the person be appointed and authorized to consent to the adoption of the minor, the court with the consent of the parents, if living, or after finding, based upon clear and convincing evidence, that a non-consenting parent is an unfit person as defined in Section 1 of "An Act in relation to

the adoption of persons, and to repeal an Act therein named", approved July 17, 1959, as amended [750 ILCS 50/1], may empower the guardian of the person of the minor, in the order appointing him or her as such guardian, to appear in court where any proceedings for the adoption of the minor may at any time be pending and to consent to the adoption. Such consent is sufficient to authorize the court in the adoption proceedings to enter a proper order or judgment of adoption without further notice to, or consent by, the parents of the minor. An order so empowering the guardian to consent to adoption terminates parental rights, deprives the parents of the minor of all legal rights as respects the minor and relieves them of all parental responsibility for him or her, and frees the minor from all obligations of maintenance and obedience to his or her natural parents.

If the minor is over 14 years of age, the court may, in its discretion, consider the wishes of the minor in determining whether the best interests of the minor would be promoted by the finding of the unfitness of a non-consenting parent.

(3) Parental consent to the order authorizing the guardian of the person to consent to adoption of the Minor shall be given in open court whenever possible and otherwise must be in writing and signed in the form provided in "An Act in relation to the adoption of persons, and to repeal an Act therein named", approved July 17, 1959, as amended, but no names of petitioners for adoption need be included. A finding of the unfitness of a nonconsenting parent must be made in compliance with that Act and be based upon clear and convincing evidence. Provisions of that Act relating to minor parents and to mentally ill or mentally deficient parents apply to proceedings under this Section and shall be based upon clear and convincing evidence.

(Source: P.A. 85-601.) [Formerly Ill. Rev. Stat. 37 §804-27.]

405/4-28. Notice to putative father.

§4-28. Notice to putative father. Upon the written request to any Clerk of any Circuit Court by any interested party, including persons intending to adopt a child, a child welfare agency with whom the mother has placed or has given written notice of her intention to place a child for adoption, the mother of a child, or any attorney representing an interested party, a notice may be served on a putative father in the same manner as Summons is served in other proceedings under this Act, or in lieu of personal service, service may be made as follows:

(a) The person requesting notice shall furnish to the Clerk an original and one copy of a notice together with an Affidavit setting forth the putative father's last known address. The original notice shall be retained by the Clerk.

(b) The Clerk forthwith shall mail to the putative father, at the address appearing in the Affidavit, the copy of the notice, certified mail, return receipt requested; the envelope and return receipt shall bear the return address of the Clerk. The receipt for certified mail shall state the name and address of the addressee, and the date of mailing, and shall be attached to the original notice.

(c) The return receipt, when returned to the Clerk, shall be attached to the original notice, and shall constitute proof of service.

(d) The Clerk shall note the fact of service in a permanent record.

2.* The notice shall be signed by the Clerk, and may be served on the putative father at any time after conception, and shall read as follows:

**So in original. No subsec. 1 has been designated.*

"IN THE MATTER OF NOTICE TO . . . . , PUTATIVE FATHER.

You have been identified as the father of a child (born on the . . . . . day of . . . . . , 19. . .), or (expected to be born on or about the . . . . . day of . . . . . , 19. . .). The mother of said child is . . . .

The mother has indicated she intends to place the child for adoption or otherwise have a judgment entered terminating her rights with respect to such child.

As the alleged father of said child, you have certain legal rights with respect to said child, including the right to notice of the filing of proceedings instituted for the termination of your parental rights regarding said child. If you wish to retain your rights with respect to said child, you must file with the Clerk of this Circuit Court of . . . . . , County, Illinois, whose address is . . . ., ... , Illinois, within 30 days after the date of receipt of this notice, a declaration of paternity stating that you are, in fact, the father of said child and that you intend to retain your legal rights with respect to said child, or request to be notified of any further proceedings with respect to custody, termination of parental rights or adoption of the child.

If you do not file such a declaration of paternity, or a request for notice, then whatever legal rights you have with respect to said child, including the right to notice of any future proceedings for the adoption of said child, may be terminated without any further notice to you. When your legal rights with respect to said child are so terminated, you will not be entitled to notice of any proceeding instituted for the adoption of said child.

If you are not the father of said child, you may file with the Clerk of this Court, a disclaimer of paternity which will be noted in the Clerk's file and you will receive no further notice with respect to said child".

The disclaimer of paternity shall be substantially as follows:

"IN THE CIRCUIT COURT OF THE
.... JUDICIAL CIRCUIT, ILLINOIS
.... County

______________________________)
)
) No.
)
______________________________)

DENIAL OF PATERNITY WITH ENTRY OF APPEARANCE AND CONSENT TO ADOPTION

I, ... , state as follows:

(1) That I am . . . . . years of age; and I reside at . . . . in the County of . . . . , State of . . . .

(2) That I have been advised that . . . . is the mother of a . . male child named . . . . . born or expected to be born on or about . . . . . and that such mother has stated that I am the father of this child.

(3) I deny that I am the father of this child.

(4) I further understand that the mother of this child wishes to consent to the adoption of the child. I hereby consent to the adoption of this child, and waive any rights, remedies and defenses that I may now or in the future have as a result of the mother's allegation of the paternity of this child. This consent is being given in order to facilitate the adoption of the child and so that the court may terminate what rights I may have to the child as a result of being named the father by the mother. This consent is not in any manner an admission of paternity.

(5) I hereby enter my appearance in the above entitled cause and waive service of summons and other pleading and consent to an immediate hearing on a petition TO TERMINATE PARENTAL RIGHTS AND TO APPOINT A

GUARDIAN WITH THE POWER TO CONSENT TO THE ADOPTION OF THIS CHILD.

OATH

I have been duly sworn and I say under oath that I have read and understood this Denial of Paternity With Entry of Appearance and Consent to Adoption. The facts it contains are true and correct to the best of my knowledge, and I understand that by signing this document I have not admitted paternity. I have signed this document as my free and voluntary act in order to facilitate the adoption of the child.

.... (signature)

Dated this ..... day of ....., 19...
Signed and Sworn Before Me This ..... day of ....., 19...

.... (notary public)".

The names of adoptive parents, if any, shall not be included in the notice.

3. If the putative father files a disclaimer of paternity, he shall be deemed not to be the father of the child with respect to any adoption or other proceeding held to terminate the rights of parents as respects such child.

4. In the event the putative father does not file a declaration of paternity of the child or request for notice within 30 days of service of the above notice, he need not be made a party to or given notice of any proceeding brought for the adoption of the child. An Order or Judgment may be entered in such proceeding terminating all of his rights with respect to said child without further notice to him.

5. If the putative father files a declaration of paternity or a request for notice in accordance with subsection 2 with respect to the child, he shall be given notice in the event any proceeding is brought for the adoption of the child or for termination of parents' rights of the child.

6. The Clerk shall maintain separate numbered files and records of requests and proofs of service and all other documents filed pursuant to this article. All such records shall be impounded.

(Source: P.A. 85-601.) [Formerly Ill. Rev. Stat. 37 §804-28.]

405/4-29. Duration of wardship and discharge of proceedings.

§4-29. Duration of wardship and discharge of proceedings. (1) All proceedings under this Act in respect to any minor for whom a petition was filed after the effective date of this amendatory Act of 1991 automatically terminate upon his attaining the age of 19 years, except that a court may continue the wardship of a minor until age 21 for good cause when there is satisfactory evidence presented to the court that the best interest of the minor and the public require the continuation of the wardship.

(2) Whenever the court finds that the best interests of the minor and the public no longer require the wardship of the court, the court shall order the wardship terminated and all proceedings under this Act respecting that minor finally closed and discharged. The court may at the same time continue or terminate any custodianship or guardianship theretofore ordered but such termination must be made in compliance with Section 4-26 [705 ILCS 405/4-26].

(3) The wardship of the minor and any custodianship or guardianship respecting of* the minor for whom a petition was filed after the effective date of this amendatory Act of 1991 automatically terminates when he attains the age of 19 years except as set forth in subsection (1) of this Section. The clerk of the court shall at that time record all proceedings under this Act as finally closed and discharged for that reason.

**So in original. Probably "of" should be deleted.*

(Source: P.A. 87-14.) [Formerly Ill. Rev. Stat. 37 §804-29.]

ARTICLE V. DELINQUENT MINORS

405/5-1. Jurisdictional facts.

§5-1. Jurisdictional facts. Proceedings may be instituted under the provisions of this Article concerning boys and girls who are delinquent as defined in Section 5-3 [705 ILCS 405/5-3].
(Source: P.A. 85-601.) [Formerly Ill. Rev. Stat. 37 §805-1.]

405/5-2. Venue.

§5-2. Venue. (1) Venue under this Article lies in the county where the minor resides or is found. Venue also lies in the county where the alleged attempt to violate or violation of federal, state or local law occurred or in the county where the order of the court, alleged to have been violated by such minor, was made unless subsequent to the order the proceedings have been transferred to another county.

(2) If proceedings are commenced in any county other than that of the minor's residence, the court in which the proceedings were initiated may at any time before or after adjudication of wardship transfer the case to the county of the minor's residence by transmitting to the court in that county an authenticated copy of the court record, including all documents, petitions and orders filed therein, and the minute orders and docket entries of the court. Transfer in like manner may be made in the event of a change of residence from one county to another of a minor concerning whom proceedings are pending.
(Source: P.A. 85-601.) [Formerly Ill. Rev. Stat. 37 §805-2.]

405/5-3. Definitions.

§5-3. Definitions. (1) "Delinquent minor" means any minor who prior to his 17th birthday has violated or attempted to violate, regardless of where the act occurred, any federal or state law or municipal ordinance.

(2) "Detention" means the temporary care of a minor alleged or adjudicated as a person described in subsection (1) of this Section who requires secure custody for his or her own or the community's protection in a facility designed to physically restrict his or her movements, pending disposition by the court or execution of an order of the court for placement or commitment. Design features which physically restrict movement include, but are not limited to, locked rooms and the secure handcuffing of a minor to a rail or other stationary object.

(3) "Juvenile detention home" means a public facility with specially trained staff that conforms to the county juvenile detention standards promulgated by the Department of Corrections.

(4) "Non-secure custody" means confinement where the minor is not physically restricted by being placed in a locked cell or room, by being handcuffed or by other means. Non-secure custody may include, but is not limited to, foster home placement, home confinement, group home placement, or physical restriction of movement or activity solely through facility staff.

(5) "Public or community service" means uncompensated labor for a non-profit organization or public body whose purpose is to enhance physical or mental stability, environmental quality or the social welfare and which agrees to accept public or community service from offenders and to report on the progress of the public or community service to the court.

(6) "Site" means a non-profit organization or public body agreeing to accept community service from offenders and to report on the progress of ordered public or community service to the court or its delegate.

(Source: P.A. 85-601; 85-1443; 86-1475.) [Formerly Ill. Rev. Stat. 37 §805-3.]

405/5-4. Criminal prosecutions limited.

§5-4. Criminal prosecutions limited. (1) Except as provided in this Section, no minor who was under 17 years of age at the time of the alleged offense may be prosecuted under the criminal laws of this State or for violation of an ordinance of any political subdivision of this State.

(2) Subject to subsection (5) of Section 5-10 [705 ILCS 405/5-10], any minor alleged to have committed a traffic, boating or fish and game law violation, whether or not the violation is punishable by imprisonment or an offense punishable by fine only, may be prosecuted for the violation and if found guilty punished under any statute or ordinance relating to the violation, without reference to the procedures set out in this Act, except that detention, if any, must be in compliance with this Act.

For the purpose of this Section, "traffic violation" shall include a violation of Section 9-3 of the Criminal Code of 1961 [720 ILCS 5/9-3] relating to the offense of reckless homicide, or Section 11-501 of the Illinois Vehicle Code [625 ILCS 5/11-501], or any similar provision of a local ordinance.

(3) (a) If a petition alleges commission by a minor 13 years of age or over of an act that constitutes a crime under the laws of this State and, on motion of the State's Attorney, a Juvenile Judge designated by the Chief Judge of the Circuit to hear and determine those motions, after investigation and hearing but before commencement of the adjudicatory hearing, finds that it is not in the best interests of the minor or of the public to proceed under this Act, the court may enter an order permitting prosecution under the criminal laws.

(b) In making its determination on a motion to permit prosecution under the criminal laws, the court shall consider among other matters: (i) whether there is sufficient evidence upon which a grand jury may be expected to return an indictment; (ii) whether there is evidence that the alleged offense was committed in an aggressive and premeditated manner; (iii) the age of the minor; (iv) the previous history of the minor; (v) whether there are facilities particularly available to the Juvenile Court for the treatment and rehabilitation of the minor; (vi) whether the best interest of the minor and the security of the public may require that the minor continue in custody or under supervision for a period extending beyond his minority; and (vii) whether the minor possessed a deadly weapon when committing the alleged offense. The rules of evidence shall be the same as under Section 5-22 of this Act [705 ILCS 405/5-22], but no hearing on the motion may be commenced unless the minor is represented in court by counsel.

(c) If criminal proceedings are instituted, the petition shall be dismissed insofar as the act or acts involved in the criminal proceedings are concerned. Taking of evidence in an adjudicatory hearing in any such case is a bar to criminal proceedings based upon the conduct alleged in the petition.

(3.1) If a petition alleges commission by a minor 15 years of age or older of an act that constitutes a forcible felony under the laws of this State, and if a motion by the State's Attorney to prosecute the minor under the criminal laws of Illinois for the alleged forcible felony alleges that (i) the minor has previously been adjudicated delinquent for commission of an act that constitutes a felony under the laws of this State or any other state and (ii) the act that constitutes the offense was committed in furtherance of criminal activity by an organized gang, the Juvenile Judge designated to hear and determine those motions shall, upon determining that there is probable cause that both allegations are true, enter an order permitting prosecution under the criminal laws of Illinois.

(3.2) If a petition alleges commission by a minor 15 years of age or older of an act that constitutes a felony under the laws of this State, and if a motion by a State's Attorney to prosecute the minor under the criminal laws of Illinois for the alleged felony alleges that (i) the minor has previously been adjudicated delinquent for commission of an act that constitutes a forcible felony under the laws of this State or any other state and (ii) the act that constitutes the offense was committed in furtherance of criminal activities by an organized gang, the Juvenile Judge designated to hear and determine those motions shall, upon determining that there is probable cause that both allegations are true, enter an order permitting prosecution under the criminal laws of Illinois.

For purposes of subsections (3.1) and (3.2), "organized gang" means an association of 5 or more persons, with an established hierarchy, that encourages members of the association to perpetrate crimes or provides support to members of the association who do commit crimes.

(4) Nothing in this Act prohibits or limits the prosecution of any minor for an offense committed on or after his or her 17th birthday even though he or she is at the time of the offense a ward of the court.

(5) If an original petition for adjudication of wardship alleges the commission by a minor 13 years of age or over of an act that constitutes a crime under the laws of this State, the minor, with the consent of his or her counsel, may, at any time before commencement of the adjudicatory hearing, file with the court a motion that criminal prosecution be ordered and that the petition be dismissed insofar as the act or acts involved in the criminal proceedings are concerned. If such a motion is filed as herein provided, the court shall enter its order accordingly.

(6) (a) The definition of delinquent minor under Section 5-3 of this Act [705 ILCS 405/5-3] shall not apply to any minor who at the time of an offense was at least 15 years of age and who is charged with first degree murder, aggravated criminal sexual assault, armed robbery when the armed robbery was committed with a firearm, or violation of the provisions of paragraph (12) of subsection (a) of Section 24-1 of the Criminal Code of 1961 [720 ILCS 5/24-1]. These charges

and all other charges arising out of the same incident shall be prosecuted under the Criminal Code of 1961 [720 ILCS 5/1-1 et seq.].

(b) If before trial or plea an information or indictment is filed which does not charge an offense specified in paragraph (a) of this subsection (6), the State's Attorney may proceed on the lesser charge or charges, but only in Juvenile Court under the other provisions of this Act, unless before trial the minor defendant knowingly and with advice of counsel waives, in writing, his or her right to have the matter proceed in Juvenile Court. If before trial or plea an information or indictment is filed that includes one or more charges specified in paragraph (a) of this subsection (6) and additional charges that are not specified in that paragraph, all of the charges arising out of the same incident shall be prosecuted under the Criminal Code of 1961.

(c) If after trial or plea the minor is only convicted of an offense not covered by paragraph (a) of this subsection (6), the conviction shall not invalidate the verdict or the prosecution of the minor under the criminal laws of this State; however, the court must thereafter proceed under Sections 5-22 and 5-23 of this Act [705 ILCS 405/5-22 and 405/5-23]. In all other circumstances, in sentencing the court shall have available any or all dispositions prescribed for that offense under Chapter V of the Unified Code of Corrections [730 ILCS 5/5-1-1 et seq.].

(7) (a) The definition of delinquent minor under Section 5-3 of this Act shall not apply to any minor who at the time of an offense was at least 15 years of age and who is charged with an offense under Section 401 of the Illinois Controlled Substances Act [720 ILCS 570/401] while in a school, regardless of the time of day or the time of year, or any conveyance owned, leased or contracted by a school to transport students to or from school or a school related activity, or residential property owned, operated and managed by a public housing agency, on the real property comprising any school, regardless of the time of day or the time of year, or residential property owned, operated and managed by a public housing agency, or on a public way within 1,000 feet of the real property comprising any school, regardless of the time of day or the time of year, or residential property owned, operated and managed by a public housing agency. School is defined, for the purposes of this Section, as any public or private elementary or secondary school, community college, college, or university. These charges and all other charges arising out of the same incident shall be prosecuted under the Illinois Controlled Substances Act [720 ILCS 570/100 et seq.].

(b) If before trial or plea an information or indictment is filed that does not charge an offense specified in paragraph (a) of this subsection (7), the State's Attorney may proceed on the lesser charge or charges, but only under the other provisions of this Act, unless before trial the minor defendant knowingly and with advice of counsel waives, in writing, his or her right to have the matter proceed in Juvenile Court. If before trial or plea an information or indictment is filed that includes one or more charges specified in paragraph (a) of this subsection (7) and additional charges that are not specified in that paragraph, all of the charges arising out of the same incident shall be prosecuted under the Illinois Controlled Substances Act or the Criminal Code of 1961.

(c) If after trial or plea the minor is only convicted of an offense not covered by paragraph (a) of this subsection (7), the conviction shall not invalidate the verdict or the prosecution of the minor under the criminal laws of this State; however, the court must thereafter proceed under Sections 5-22 and 5-23 of this Act. In all other circumstances, in sentencing the court shall have available any or all dispositions prescribed for that offense under Chapter V of the Unified Code of Corrections.

(8) (a) The definition of delinquent minor under Section 5-3 of this Act shall not apply to any minor who is charged with a violation of subsection (a) of

Section 31-6 or Section 32-10 of the Criminal Code of 1961 [720 ILCS 5/31-6 or 5/32-10] when the minor is subject to prosecution under the Criminal Code of 1961 as a result of the application of the provisions of paragraph (a) of subsection (3); subsection (5); paragraph (a) of subsection (6); or paragraph (a) of subsection (7) of this Section. These charges and all other charges arising out of the same incident shall be prosecuted under the Criminal Code of 1961.

(b) If before trial or plea an information or indictment is filed that does not charge an offense specified in paragraph (a) of this subsection (8), the State's Attorney may proceed on the lesser charge or charges, but only in Juvenile Court under the other provisions of this Act, unless before trial the minor defendant knowingly and with advice of counsel waives, in writing, his or her right to have the matter proceed in Juvenile Court. If before trial or plea an information or indictment is filed that includes one or more charges specified in paragraph (a) of this subsection (8) and additional charges that are not specified in that paragraph, all of the charges arising out of the same incident shall be prosecuted under the Criminal Code of 1961.

(c) If after trial or plea the minor is only convicted of an offense not covered by paragraph (a) of this subsection (8), the conviction shall not invalidate the verdict or the prosecution of the minor under the criminal laws of this State; however, the court must thereafter proceed under Sections 5-22 and 5-23 of this Act. In all other circumstances, in sentencing the court shall have available any or all dispositions prescribed for that offense under Chapter V of the Unified Code of Corrections.

(Chgd. by P.A. 87-931, §1, eff. 1/1/93.)

(Source: P.A. 86-371; 86-820; 86-946; 86-1028; 87-524; 87-541; 87-895.) [Formerly Ill. Rev. Stat. 37 §805-4.]

405/5-5. Taking into custody.

§5-5. Taking into custody. (1) A law enforcement officer may, without a warrant, take into temporary custody a minor (a) whom the officer with reasonable cause believes to be a delinquent minor; or (b) who has been adjudged a ward of the court and has escaped from any commitment ordered by the court under this Act.

(2) Whenever a petition has been filed under Section 5-13 [705 ILCS 405/5-13] and the court finds that the conduct and behavior of the minor may endanger the health, person, welfare, or property of himself or others or that the circumstances of his home environment may endanger his health, person, welfare or property, a warrant may be issued immediately to take the minor into custody.

(3) The taking of a minor into temporary custody under this Section is not an arrest nor does it constitute a police record.

(4) Except for minors accused of violation of an order of the court, any minor accused of any act under federal or State law, or a municipal ordinance that would not be illegal if committed by an adult, cannot be placed in a jail, municipal lockup, detention center, or secure correctional facility. Juveniles accused with underage consumption and underage possession of alcohol cannot be placed in a jail, municipal lockup, detention center, or correctional facility.

(Chgd. by P.A. 87-1154, §1, eff. 1/1/93.)

(Source: P.A. 85-601.) [Formerly Ill. Rev. Stat. 37 §805-5.]

405/5-6. Duty of officer; admissions by minor.

§5-6. Duty of officer; admissions by minor. (1) A law enforcement officer who takes a minor into custody with a warrant shall immediately make a reasonable attempt to notify the parent or other person legally responsible for the minor's care or the person with whom the minor resides that the minor has been taken into custody and where he or she is being held; and the officer shall without unnecessary delay take the minor to the nearest juvenile police officer designated for such purposes in the county of venue or shall surrender the minor to a juvenile police officer in the city or village where the offense is alleged to have been committed.

The minor shall be delivered without unnecessary delay to the court or to the place designated by rule or order of court for the reception of minors.

(2) A law enforcement officer who takes a minor into custody without a warrant under Section 5-5 [705 ILCS 405/5-5] shall, if the minor is not released, immediately make a reasonable attempt to notify the parent or other person legally responsible for the minor's care or the person with whom the minor resides that the minor has been taken into custody and where the minor is being held; and the law enforcement officer shall without unnecessary delay take the minor to the nearest juvenile police officer designated for such purposes in the county of venue or shall surrender the minor to a juvenile police officer in the city or village where the offense is alleged to have been committed.

(3) The juvenile police officer may take one of the following actions:

(a) station adjustment with release of the minor;

(b) station adjustment with release of the minor to a parent;

(c) station adjustment, release of the minor to a parent, and referral of the case to community services;

(d) station adjustment, release of the minor to a parent, and referral of the case to community services with informal monitoring by a juvenile police officer;

(e) station adjustment and release of the minor to a third person pursuant to agreement of the minor and parents;

(f) station adjustment, release of the minor to a third person pursuant to agreement of the minor and parents, and referral of the case to community services;

(g) station adjustment, release of the minor to a third person pursuant to agreement of the minor and parent, and referral to community services with informal monitoring by a juvenile police officer;

(h) release of the minor to his or her parents and referral of the case to a county juvenile probation officer or such other public officer designated by the court;

(i) if the juvenile police officer reasonably believes that there is an urgent and immediate necessity to keep the minor in custody, the juvenile police officer shall deliver the minor without unnecessary delay to the court or to the place designated by rule or order of court for the reception of minors;

(j) if the minor and a parent or guardian consent in writing, the juvenile police officer may condition the minor's release upon his or her agreement to perform public or community service subject to Sections 1-12 and 1-13 of this Act [705 ILCS 405/1-12 and 405/1-13] or to make restitution for damages; and

(k) any other appropriate action with consent of the minor and a parent.

(4) The factors to be considered in determining whether to release or keep a minor in custody shall include:

(a) the nature of the allegations against the minor;

(b) the minor's history and present situation;

(c) the history of the minor's family and the family's present situation;

(d) the educational and employment status of the minor;

(e) the availability of special resource or community services to aid or counsel the minor;

(f) the minor's past involvement with and progress in social programs;

(g) the attitude of complainant and community toward the minor; and

(h) the present attitude of the minor and family.

(5) The records of law enforcement officers concerning all minors taken into custody under this Act shall be maintained separate from the records of arrests

and may not be inspected by or disclosed to the public except by order of the court.

(Source: P.A. 85-1209.) [Formerly Ill. Rev. Stat. 37 §805-6.]

405/5-7. Temporary custody.

§5-7. Temporary Custody. (1) Shelter care. Any minor taken into temporary custody pursuant to this Act who requires care away from his or her home but who does not require physical restriction shall be given temporary care in a foster family home or other shelter facility designated by the court.

(2) Detention.

(A) Any minor 10 years of age or older taken into temporary custody pursuant to this Act where there is reasonable cause to believe that the minor is a delinquent minor and that (a) secured custody is a matter of immediate and urgent necessity for the protection of the minor or of the person or property of another, (b) the minor is likely to flee the jurisdiction of the court, or (c) the minor was taken into custody under a warrant, may be kept or detained in an authorized detention facility.

(B) The written authorization of the probation officer (or such other public officer designated by the court in a county having more than 3 million inhabitants) constitutes authority for the superintendent of any juvenile detention home to detain and keep a minor for up to 36 hours, excluding Saturdays, Sundays and court-designated holidays. This Section shall in no way be construed to limit Section 1-7 [705 ILCS 405/1-7].

(C) Confinement in a county jail or municipal lockup. Except as otherwise provided in paragraph (D), no minor shall be detained in a county jail or municipal lockup for more than 6 hours. (i) The period of detention is deemed to have begun once the minor has been placed in a locked room or cell or handcuffed to a stationary object in a building housing a county jail or municipal lockup. Time spent transporting a minor is not considered to be time in detention or secure custody. (ii) Any minor so confined shall be under periodic supervision and shall not be permitted to come into or remain in contact with adults in custody in the building. (iii) Upon placement in secure custody in a jail or lockup, the minor shall be informed of the purpose of the detention, the time it is expected to last and the fact that it cannot exceed 6 hours. (iv) A log shall be kept which shows the offense which is the basis for the detention, the reasons and circumstances for the decision to detain and the length of time the minor was in detention. (v) Violation of the 6-hour time limit on detention in a county jail or municipal lockup shall not, in and of itself, render inadmissible evidence obtained as a result of the violation of this 6-hour time limit. (vi) No minor under 16 years of age may be confined in a jail or place ordinarily used for the confinement of prisoners in a police station. Minors under 17 years of age shall be kept separate from confined adults and may not at any time be kept in the same cell, room or yard with adults confined pursuant to criminal law.

(D) When a minor who is at least 15 years of age is prosecuted under the Criminal Code of 1961 [720 ILCS 5/1-1 et seq.], the court may enter an order directing that the juvenile be confined in the county jail. However, any juvenile confined in the county jail under this provision shall be separated from adults who are confined in the county jail in such a manner that there will be no contact by sight, sound or otherwise between the juvenile and adult prisoners. This subsection (2)(D) shall not apply in a county having more than 3 million inhabitants.

(3) Non-secure custody. If the probation officer (or such other public officer designated by the court in a county having more than 3 million inhabitants) determines that the minor may be a delinquent minor as described in Section 5-3 [705 ILCS 405/5-3], and should be retained in custody but does not require

physical restriction, the minor may be placed in non-secure custody for up to 36 hours pending a detention hearing.

(4) Home confinement. Any minor taken into temporary custody, not requiring secure detention, may, however, be detained in the home of his or her parent or guardian subject to such conditions as the court may impose.

(Source: P.A. 86-636; 86-1003; 86-1028; 86-1163.) [Formerly Ill. Rev. Stat. 37 §805-7.]

405/5-8. Investigation; release.

§5-8. Investigation; release. When a minor is delivered to the court, or to the place designated by the court under Section 5-7 of this Act [705 ILCS 405/5-7], a probation officer or such other public officer designated by the court shall immediately investigate the circumstances of the minor and the facts surrounding his or her being taken into custody. The minor shall be immediately released to the custody of his or her parent, guardian, legal custodian or responsible relative, unless the probation officer or such other public officer designated by the court finds that further detention is a matter of immediate and urgent necessity for the protection of the minor or of the person or property of another, that he is likely to flee the jurisdiction of the court or that the minor was taken into custody under a warrant.

This Section shall in no way be construed to limit Section 1-7 [705 ILCS 405/1-7].

(Source: P.A. 85-601.) [Formerly Ill. Rev. Stat. 37 §805-8.]

405/5-9. Setting of detention or shelter care hearing; notice; release.

§5-9. Setting of detention or shelter care hearing; notice; release. (1) Unless sooner released, a minor alleged to be a delinquent minor taken into temporary custody must be brought before a judicial officer within 36 hours, exclusive of Saturdays, Sundays and court-designated holidays, for a detention or shelter care hearing to determine whether he shall be further held in custody.

(2) If the probation officer (or such other public officer designated by the court in a county having more than 3 million inhabitants) determines that the minor should be retained in custody, he shall cause a petition to be filed as provided in Section 5-13 of this Act [705 ILCS 405/5-13], and the clerk of the court shall set the matter for hearing on the detention or shelter care hearing calendar. When a parent, guardian, custodian or responsible relative is present and so requests, the detention or shelter care hearing shall be held immediately if the court is in session, otherwise at the earliest feasible time. The probation officer (or such other public officer designated by the court in a county having more than 3 million inhabitants) shall notify the minor's parent, guardian, custodian or responsible relative of the time and place of the hearing. The notice may be given orally.

(3) The minor must be released from custody at the expiration of the 36 hour period specified by this Section if not brought before a judicial officer within that period.

(Source: P.A. 85-1443.) [Formerly Ill. Rev. Stat. 37 §805-9.]

405/5-10. Detention or shelter care hearing.

§5-10. Detention or shelter care hearing. At the appearance of the minor before the court at the detention or shelter care hearing, all witnesses present shall be examined before the court in relation to any matter connected with the allegations made in the petition. No hearing may be held unless the minor is represented by counsel.

(1) If the court finds that there is not probable cause to believe that the minor is a delinquent minor it shall release the minor and dismiss the petition.

(2) If the court finds that there is probable cause to believe that the minor is a delinquent minor, the minor, his or her parent, guardian, custodian and

other persons able to give relevant testimony shall be examined before the court. After such testimony, the court may enter an order that the minor shall be released upon the request of a parent, guardian or custodian if the parent, guardian or custodian appears to take custody. Custodian shall include any agency of the State which has been given custody or wardship of the child.

If the court finds that it is a matter of immediate and urgent necessity for the protection of the minor or of the person or property of another that the minor be detained or placed in a shelter care facility or that he or she is likely to flee the jurisdiction of the court, the court may prescribe detention or shelter care and order that the minor be kept in a suitable place designated by the court or in a shelter care facility designated by the Department of Children and Family Services or a licensed child welfare agency; otherwise it shall release the minor from custody. In making the determination of the existence of immediate and urgent necessity, the court shall consider among other matters: (a) the nature and seriousness of the alleged offense; (b) the minor's record of delinquency offenses, including whether the minor has delinquency cases pending; (c) the minor's record of willful failure to appear following the issuance of a summons or warrant; and (d) the availability of non-custodial alternatives, including the presence of a parent, guardian or other responsible relative able and willing to provide supervision and care for the minor and to assure his or her compliance with a summons. If the minor is ordered placed in a shelter care facility of the Department of Children and Family Services or a licensed child welfare agency, the court shall, upon request of the Department or other agency, appoint the Department of Children and Family Services Guardianship Administrator or other appropriate agency executive temporary custodian of the minor and the court may enter such other orders related to the temporary custody of the minor as it deems fit and proper.

The order together with the court's findings of fact in support thereof shall be entered of record in the court.

Once the court finds that it is a matter of immediate and urgent necessity for the protection of the minor that the minor be placed in a shelter care facility, the minor shall not be returned to the parent, custodian or guardian until the court finds that such placement is no longer necessary for the protection of the minor.

(3) If neither the parent, guardian, legal custodian, responsible relative nor counsel of the minor has had actual notice of or is present at the detention or shelter care hearing, he or she may file his or her affidavit setting forth these facts, and the clerk shall set the matter for rehearing not later than 24 hours, excluding Sundays and legal holidays, after the filing of the affidavit. At the rehearing, the court shall proceed in the same manner as upon the original hearing.

(4) Only when there is reasonable cause to believe that the minor taken into custody is a delinquent minor may the minor be kept or detained in a juvenile detention home. This Section shall in no way be construed to limit subsection (5).

(5) No minor under 16 years of age may be confined in a jail or place ordinarily used for the confinement of prisoners in a police station. Minors under 17 years of age must be kept separate from confined adults and may not at any time be kept in the same cell, room, or yard with adults confined pursuant to the criminal law.

(6) If the minor is not brought before a judicial officer within the time period as specified in Section 5-9 [705 ILCS 405/5-9], the minor must immediately be released from custody.

(7) If neither the parent, guardian or custodian appears within 24 hours to take custody of a minor released upon request pursuant to subsection (2) of this Section, then the clerk of the court shall set the matter for rehearing not later than 7 days after the original order and shall issue a summons directed to the parent, guardian or custodian to appear. At the same time the probation department shall prepare a report on the minor. If a parent, guardian or custodian does not appear at such rehearing, the judge may enter an order prescribing that the minor be kept in a suitable place designated by the Department of Children and Family Services or a licensed child welfare agency. The time during which a minor is in custody after being released upon the request of a parent, guardian or custodian shall be considered as time spent in detention.

(8) Any interested party, including the State, the temporary custodian, an agency providing services to the minor or family under a service plan pursuant to Section 8.2 of the Abused and Neglected Child Reporting Act [325 ILCS 5/8.2], foster parent, or any of their representatives, may file a motion to modify or vacate a temporary custody order on any of the following grounds:

(a) It is no longer a matter of immediate and urgent necessity that the minor remain in detention or shelter care; or

(b) There is a material change in the circumstances of the natural family from which the minor was removed; or

(c) A person, including a parent, relative or legal guardian, is capable of assuming temporary custody of the minor; or

(d) Services provided by the Department of Children and Family Services or a child welfare agency or other service provider have been successful in eliminating the need for temporary custody.

The clerk shall set the matter for hearing not later than 14 days after such motion is filed. In the event that the court modifies or vacates a temporary custody order but does not vacate its finding of probable cause, the court may order that appropriate services be continued or initiated in behalf of the minor and his or her family.

(Source: P.A. 86-636; 86-820; 86-1028.) [Formerly Ill. Rev. Stat. 37 §805-10.]

405/5-11. Medical and dental treatment and care.

§5-11. Medical and dental treatment and care. At all times during temporary custody, detention or shelter care, the court may authorize a physician, a hospital or any other appropriate health care provider to provide medical, dental or surgical procedures if such procedures are necessary to safeguard the minor's life or health.

(Source: P.A. 85-1209.) [Formerly Ill. Rev. Stat. 37 §805-11.]

405/5-12. Preliminary conferences.

§5-12. Preliminary conferences. (1) The court may authorize the probation officer to confer in a preliminary conference with any person seeking to file a petition under Section 5-13 [705 ILCS 405/5-13], the prospective respondents and other interested persons concerning the advisability of filing the petition, with a view to adjusting suitable cases without the filing of a petition as provided for herein.

The probation officer should schedule a conference promptly except where the State's Attorney insists on court action or where the minor has indicated that he or she will demand a judicial hearing and will not comply with an informal adjustment.

(2) In any case of a minor who is in temporary custody, the holding of preliminary conferences does not operate to prolong temporary custody beyond the period permitted by Section 5-9 [705 ILCS 405/5-9].

(3) This Section does not authorize any probation officer to compel any person to appear at any conference, produce any papers, or visit any place.

(4) No statement made during a preliminary conference may be admitted into evidence at an adjudicatory hearing or at any proceeding against the minor under the criminal laws of this State prior to his or her conviction thereunder.

(5) The probation officer shall promptly formulate a written, non-judicial adjustment plan following the initial conference.

(6) Non-judicial adjustment plans include but are not limited to the following:

(a) up to 6 months informal supervision within family;

(b) up to 6 months informal supervision with a probation officer involved;

(c) up to 6 months informal supervision with release to a person other than parent;

(d) referral to special educational, counseling or other rehabilitative social or educational programs;

(e) referral to residential treatment programs;

(f) participation in a public or community service program or activity; and

(g) any other appropriate action with consent of the minor and a parent.

(7) The factors to be considered by the probation officer in formulating a non-judicial adjustment plan shall be the same as those limited in subsection (4) of Section 5-6 [705 ILCS 405/5-6].

(Source: P.A. 85-1209.) [Formerly Ill. Rev. Stat. 37 §805-12.]

405/5-13. Petition; supplemental petitions.

§5-13. Petition; supplemental petitions. (1) Any adult person, any agency or association by its representative may file, or the court on its own motion may direct the filing through the State's Attorney of a petition in respect to a minor under this Act. The petition and all subsequent court documents shall be entitled "In the interest of . . . . , a minor".

(2) The petition shall be verified but the statements may be made upon information and belief. It shall allege that the minor is delinquent and set forth (a) facts sufficient to bring the minor under Section 5-1 [705 ILCS 405/5-1]; (b) the name, age and residence of the minor; (c) the names and residences of his parents; (d) the name and residence of his legal guardian or the person or persons having custody or control of the minor, or of the nearest known relative if no parent or guardian can be found; and (e) if the minor upon whose behalf the petition is brought is detained or sheltered in custody, the date on which detention or shelter care was ordered by the court or the date set for a detention or shelter care hearing. If any of the facts herein required are not known by the petitioner, the petition shall so state.

(3) The petition must allege that it is in the best interests of the minor and of the public that he be adjudged a ward of the court and may pray generally for relief available under this Act. The petition need not specify any proposed disposition following adjudication of wardship.

(4) If appointment of a guardian of the person with power to consent to adoption of the minor under Section 5-31 [705 ILCS 405/5-31] is sought, the petition shall so state.

(5) At any time before dismissal of the petition or before final closing and discharge under Section 5-34 [705 ILCS 405/5-34], one or more supplemental petitions may be filed in respect of the same minor.

(Source: P.A. 85-1209.) [Formerly Ill. Rev. Stat. 37 §805-13.]

405/5-14. Date for adjudicatory hearing.

§5-14. Date for adjudicatory hearing. (a) Until July 1, 1988:

(1) When a petition has been filed alleging that the minor is a delinquent minor, an adjudicatory hearing must be held within 120 days of a written

demand for such hearing made by any party. The 120 day period in which an adjudicatory hearing shall be held is tolled by: (A) delay occasioned by the minor; (B) a continuance allowed pursuant to Section 114-4 of the Code of Criminal Procedure of 1963 [725 ILCS 5/114-4] after a court's determination of the minor's physical incapacity for trial; (C) an interlocutory appeal; (D) an examination for fitness ordered pursuant to Section 104-13 of the Code of Criminal Procedure of 1963 [725 ILCS 5/104-13]; (E) a fitness hearing; or (F) an adjudication of unfitness for trial. Any such delay shall temporarily suspend, for the time of the delay, the period within which an adjudicatory hearing must be held. On the day of expiration of the delay, the said period shall continue at the point at which it was suspended. Where no such adjudicatory hearing is held within 120 days, the court shall, upon written motion on behalf of the minor, dismiss the petition with respect to such minor. Such dismissal shall be with prejudice.

If a minor respondent has multiple delinquency petitions pending against him in the same county or simultaneously demands an adjudicatory hearing upon more than one delinquency petition pending against him in the same county, he shall receive an adjudicatory hearing or have a finding after waiver of adjudicatory hearing, upon at least one such petition before expiration relative to any of such pending petitions of the period described by this Section. All remaining petitions thus pending against the minor respondent shall be adjudicated within 160 days from the date on which a finding relative to the first petition thus prosecuted is rendered pursuant to Section 5-20 of this Act [705 ILCS 405/5-20], or, if such adjudicatory hearing upon the first petition is terminated without a finding and there is no subsequent adjudicatory hearing, or adjudication after waiver of adjudicatory hearing, on the first petition within a reasonable time, the minor shall receive an adjudicatory hearing upon all of the remaining petitions within 160 days from the date on which such adjudicatory hearing, or finding after waiver of adjudicatory hearing, on the first petition is concluded. If either such period of 160 days expires without the commencement of adjudicatory hearing, or adjudication after waiver of adjudicatory hearing, of any of such remaining pending petitions, such petition or petitions shall be dismissed and barred for want of prosecution unless such delay is occasioned by any of the reasons described in this Section.

Where the court determines that the State has exercised, without success, due diligence to obtain evidence material to the case, and that there are reasonable grounds to believe that such evidence may be obtained at a later date the court may, upon written motion by the state, continue the matter for not more than 30 additional days.

(2) In the case of a minor ordered held in detention or shelter care, the hearing on the petition must be held within 10 judicial days from the date of the order of the court directing detention or shelter care, or the earliest possible date in compliance with the notice provisions of Section 5-15 and 5-16 [705 ILCS 405/5-15 and 405/5-16] as to the custodial parent, guardian or legal custodian, but no later than 30 judicial days from the date of the order of the court directing detention or shelter care. Delay occasioned by the respondent shall temporarily suspend, for the time of the delay the period within which a respondent must be brought to an adjudicatory hearing pursuant to this Section. Whenever a minor is held in detention or shelter care and the petition alleges that he or she committed a crime of violence, the State's Attorney may by written motion filed before the date set for the adjudicatory hearing, request that the adjudicatory hearing be postponed. The State's Attorney shall cause notice of such motion to be made to the minor's attorney, parent or guardian in the same form and manner provided in Section 5-15, or, if any of these individuals is not a resident of this State, in accordance with the manner provided in Section 5-16. For good cause in support of such motion, which may include, but is not limited to, delay

in obtaining medical or other scientific evidentiary reports or similar evidence or the unavailability of witnesses, the court may postpone the adjudicatory hearing up to 20 judicial days from the date of the order of the court directing detention or shelter care.

As used in this Section "crime of violence" means all offenses defined as forcible felonies in Section 2-8 of the Criminal Code of 1961 [720 ILCS 5/2-8], as now or hereafter amended, except for burglary, and includes the offense of unlawful use of a firearm as defined in Section 24-1 of the Criminal Code of 1961, as now or hereafter amended [720 ILCS 5/24-1].

Any failure to comply with the time limits of this subsection must require the immediate release of the minor and the time limits of subsection (a)(1) shall apply.

(3) Nothing in this Section prevents the minor's exercise of his or her right to waive the time limits set forth in this Section.

(b) Beginning July 1, 1988:

(1) (A) When a petition has been filed alleging that the minor is a delinquent, an adjudicatory hearing must be held within 120 days of a demand for such hearing made by any party, except that when the State, without success, has exercised due diligence to obtain evidence material to the case and there are reasonable grounds to believe that such evidence may be obtained at a later date, the court may, upon motion by the State, continue the adjudicatory hearing for not more than 30 additional days.

The 120 day period in which an adjudicatory hearing shall be held is tolled by: (i) delay occasioned by the minor; (ii) a continuance allowed pursuant to Section 114-4 of the Code of Criminal Procedure of 1963 after a court's determination of the minor's physical incapacity for trial; (iii) an interlocutory appeal; (iv) an examination for fitness ordered pursuant to Section 104-13 of the Code of Criminal Procedure of 1963; (v) a fitness hearing; or (vi) an adjudication of unfitness for trial. Any such delay shall temporarily suspend, for the time of the delay, the period within which an adjudicatory hearing must be held. On the day of expiration of the delay, the said period shall continue at the point at which it was suspended.

(B) If a minor respondent has multiple delinquency petitions pending against him in the same county or simultaneously demands an adjudicatory hearing upon more than one delinquency petition pending against him in the same county, he shall receive an adjudicatory hearing or have a finding, after waiver of adjudicatory hearing, upon at least one such petition before expiration relative to any of such pending petitions of the period described by this Section. All remaining petitions thus pending against the minor respondent shall be adjudicated within 160 days from the date on which a finding relative to the first petition thus prosecuted is rendered pursuant to Section 5-20 of this Act, or, if such adjudicatory hearing upon the first petition is terminated without a finding and there is no subsequent adjudicatory hearing, or adjudication after waiver of adjudicatory hearing, on the first petition within a reasonable time, the minor shall receive an adjudicatory hearing upon all of the remaining petitions within 160 days from the date on which such adjudicatory hearing, or finding after waiver of adjudicatory hearing, on the first petition is concluded. If either such period of 160 days expires without the commencement of adjudicatory hearing, or adjudication after waiver of adjudicatory hearing, of any of such remaining pending petitions, such petition or petitions shall be dismissed and barred for want of prosecution unless such delay is occasioned by any of the reasons described in this Section.

(C) When no such adjudicatory hearing is held within the time required by paragraphs (b)(1)(A) and (b)(1)(B) of this Section, the court shall, upon motion by any party, dismiss the petition with prejudice.

(2) Without affecting the applicability of the tolling and multiple prosecution provisions of paragraph (b) (1) of this Section when a petition has been filed alleging that the minor is a delinquent and the minor is in detention or shelter care, the adjudicatory hearing shall be held within 10 judicial days after the date of the order directing detention or shelter care, or the earliest possible date in compliance with the notice provisions of Section 5-15 and 5-16 as to the custodial parent, guardian or legal custodian, but no later than 30 judicial days from the date of the order of the court directing detention or shelter care, except that when the petition alleges the minor has committed a forcible felony as defined in Section 2-8 of the Criminal Code of 1961, other than burglary, or has committed the offense of unlawful use of a weapon as defined in Section 24-1 of that Code, the court may, upon motion of the State and for good cause, continue the adjudicatory hearing for not more than 20 judicial days after the date of the order directing detention or shelter care.

Any failure to comply with the time limits of paragraph (b) (2) of this Section shall require the immediate release of the minor from detention or shelter care, and the time limits of paragraph (b) (1) shall apply.

Nothing in this Section prevents the minor or the minor's parents or guardian from exercising their respective rights to waive the time limits set forth in this Section.

(Source: P.A. 85-1209.) [Formerly Ill. Rev. Stat. 37 §805-14.]

405/5-15. Summons.

§5-15. Summons. (1) When a petition is filed, the clerk of the court shall issue a summons with a copy of the petition attached. The summons shall be directed to the minor's legal guardian or custodian and to each person named as a respondent in the petition, except that summons need not be directed to a minor respondent under 8 years of age for whom the court appoints a guardian ad litem if the guardian ad litem appears on behalf of the minor in any proceeding under this Act.

(2) The summons must contain a statement that the minor or any of the respondents is entitled to have an attorney present at the hearing on the petition, and that the clerk of the court should be notified promptly if the minor or any other respondent desires to be represented by an attorney but is financially unable to employ counsel.

(3) The summons shall be issued under the seal of the court, attested in and signed with the name of the clerk of the court, dated on the day it is issued, and shall require each respondent to appear and answer the petition on the date set for the adjudicatory hearing.

(4) The summons may be served by any county sheriff, coroner or probation officer, even though the officer is the petitioner. The return of the summons with endorsement of service by the officer is sufficient proof thereof.

(5) Service of a summons and petition shall be made by: (a) leaving a copy thereof with the person summoned at least 3 days before the time stated therein for appearance; (b) leaving a copy at his usual place of abode with some person of the family, of the age of 10 years or upwards, and informing that person of the contents thereof, provided the officer or other person making service shall also send a copy of the summons in a sealed envelope with postage fully prepaid, addressed to the person summoned at his usual place of abode, at least 3 days before the time stated therein for appearance; or (c) leaving a copy thereof with the guardian or custodian of a minor, at least 3 days before the time stated therein for appearance. If the guardian or custodian is an agency of the State of Illinois, proper service may be made by leaving a copy of the summons and petition with any administrative employee of such agency designated by such agency to accept service of summons and petitions. The certificate of the officer

or affidavit of the person that he has sent the copy pursuant to this Section is sufficient proof of service.

(6) When a parent or other person, who has signed a written promise to appear and bring the minor to court or who has waived or acknowledged service, fails to appear with the minor on the date set by the court, a bench warrant may be issued for the parent or other person, the minor, or both.

(7) The appearance of the minor's legal guardian or custodian, or a person named as a respondent in a petition, in any proceeding under this Act shall constitute a waiver of service of summons and submission to the jurisdiction of the court. A copy of the summons and petition shall be provided to the person at the time of his appearance.

(Source: P.A. 86-441.) [Formerly Ill. Rev. Stat. 37 §805-15.]

405/5-16. Notice by certified mail or publication.

§5-16. Notice by certified mail or publication. (1) If service on individuals as provided in Section 5-15 [705 ILCS 405/5-15] is not made on any respondent within a reasonable time or if it appears that any respondent resides outside the State, service may be made by certified mail. In such case the clerk shall mail the summons and a copy of the petition to that respondent by certified mail marked for delivery to addressee only. The court shall not proceed with the adjudicatory hearing until 5 days after such mailing. The regular return receipt for certified mail is sufficient proof of service.

(2) If service upon individuals as provided in Section 5-15 is not made on any respondents within a reasonable time or if any person is made a respondent under the designation of "All whom it may Concern", or if service cannot be made because the whereabouts of a respondent are unknown, service may be made by publication. The clerk of the court as soon as possible shall cause publication to be made once in a newspaper of general circulation in the county where the action is pending. Notice by publication is not required in any case when the person alleged to have legal custody of the minor has been served with summons personally or by certified mail, but the court may not enter any order or judgment against any person who cannot be served with process other than by publication unless notice by publication is given or unless that person appears. When a minor has been detained or sheltered under Section 5-10 of this Act [705 ILCS 405/5-10] and summons has not been served personally or by certified mail within 20 days from the date of the order of court directing such detention or shelter care, the clerk of the court shall cause publication. Notice by publication shall be substantially as follows:

"A, B, C, D, (here giving the names of the named respondents, if any) and to All Whom It May Concern (if there is any respondent under that designation):

Take notice that on the .... day of ...., 19... a petition was filed under the Juvenile Court Act by .... in the circuit court of .... county entitled 'In the interest of ...., a minor', and that in .... courtroom at .... on the .... day of .... at the hour of ..., or as soon thereafter as this cause may be heard, an adjudicatory hearing will be held upon the petition to have the child declared to be a ward of the court under that Act. The court has authority in this proceeding to take from you the custody and guardianship of the minor, (and if the petition prays for the appointment of a guardian with power to consent to adoption) and to appoint a guardian with power to consent to adoption of the minor.

Now, unless you appear at the hearing and show cause against the petition, the allegations of the petition may stand admitted as against you and each of you, and an order or judgment entered.

....
Clerk

Dated (the date of publication)"

(3) The clerk shall also at the time of the publication of the notice send a copy thereof by mail to each of the respondents on account of whom publication is made at his or her last known address. The certificate of the clerk that he or she has mailed the notice is evidence thereof. No other publication notice is required. Every respondent notified by publication under this Section must appear and answer in open court at the hearing. The court may not proceed with the adjudicatory hearing until 10 days after service by publication on any custodial parent, guardian or legal custodian of a minor alleged to be delinquent.

(4) If it becomes necessary to change the date set for the hearing in order to comply with Section 5-15 or with this Section, notice of the resetting of the date must be given, by certified mail or other reasonable means, to each respondent who has been served with summons personally or by certified mail.

(Source: P.A. 85-601.) [Formerly Ill. Rev. Stat. 37 §805-16.]

405/5-17. Guardian ad litem.

§5-17. Guardian ad litem. (1) The court may appoint a guardian ad litem for the minor whenever it finds that there may be a conflict of interest between the minor and his parents or other custodian or that it is otherwise in the minor's interest to do so.

(2) Unless the guardian ad litem is an attorney, he shall be represented by counsel.

(3) The reasonable fees of a guardian ad litem appointed under this Section shall be fixed by the court and charged to the parents of the minor, to the extent they are able to pay. If the parents are unable to pay those fees, they shall be paid from the general fund of the county.

(Source: P.A. 85-601.) [Formerly Ill. Rev. Stat. 37 §805-17.]

405/5-18. Evidence.

§5-18. Evidence. At the adjudicatory hearing, the court shall first consider only the question whether the minor is delinquent. The standard of proof and the rules of evidence in the nature of criminal proceedings in this State are applicable to such consideration.

(Source: P.A. 85-601; 86-1475.) [Formerly Ill. Rev. Stat. 37 §805-18.]

405/5-19. Continuance under supervision.

§5-19. Continuance under supervision. (1) The court may enter an order of continuance under supervision (a) upon an admission or stipulation by the appropriate respondent or minor respondent of the facts supporting the petition and before proceeding to adjudication, or after hearing the evidence at the adjudicatory hearing, and (b) in the absence of objection made in open court by the minor, his parent, guardian, custodian, responsible relative, defense attorney or the State's Attorney.

(2) If the minor, his parent, guardian, custodian, responsible relative, defense attorney or State's Attorney objects in open court to any continuance and insists upon proceeding to findings and adjudication, the court shall so proceed.

(3) Nothing in this Section limits the power of the court to order a continuance of the hearing for the production of additional evidence or for any other proper reason.

(4) When a hearing where a minor is alleged to be a delinquent is continued pursuant to this Section, the period of continuance under supervision may not exceed 24 months. The court may terminate a continuance under supervision at any time if warranted by the conduct of the minor and the ends of justice.

(5) When a hearing where a minor is alleged to be delinquent is continued pursuant to this Section, the court may, as conditions of the continuance under supervision, require the minor to do any of the following:

(a) not violate any criminal statute of any jurisdiction;

(b) make a report to and appear in person before any person or agency as directed by the court;

(c) work or pursue a course of study or vocational training;

(d) undergo medical or psychotherapeutic treatment rendered by a therapist licensed under the provisions of the Medical Practice Act of 1987 [225 ILCS 60/1 et seq.], the Clinical Psychologist Licensing Act [225 ILCS 15/1 et seq.], or the Clinical Social Work and Social Work Practice Act [225 ILCS 20/1 et seq.], or treatment for drug addiction or alcoholism;

(e) attend or reside in a facility established for the instruction or residence of persons on probation;

(f) support his dependents, if any;

(g) pay costs;

(h) refrain from possessing a firearm or other dangerous weapon, or an automobile;

(i) permit the probation officer to visit him at his home or elsewhere;

(j) reside with his parents or in a foster home;

(k) attend school;

(*l*) attend a non-residential program for youth;

(m) contribute to his own support at home or in a foster home;

(n) perform some reasonable public or community service;

(*o*) make restitution to the victim, in the same manner and under the same conditions as provided in subsection (3) of Section 5-23 [705 ILCS 405/5-23], except that the "dispositional hearing" referred to in that Section shall be the adjudicatory hearing for purposes of this Section;

(p) comply with curfew requirements as designated by the court;

(q) refrain from entering into a designated geographic area except upon terms as the court finds appropriate. The terms may include consideration of the purpose of the entry, the time of day, other persons accompanying the minor, and advance approval by a probation officer;

(r) refrain from having any contact, directly or indirectly, with certain specified persons or particular types of persons, including but not limited to members of street gangs and drug users or dealers; or

(s) comply with any other conditions as may be ordered by the court.

(6) A minor whose case is continued under supervision under subsection (5) shall be given a certificate setting forth the conditions imposed by the court. Those conditions may be reduced, enlarged, or modified by the court on motion of the probation officer or on its own motion, or that of the State's Attorney, or, at the request of the minor after notice and hearing.

(7) If a petition is filed charging a violation of a condition of the continuance under supervision, the court shall conduct a hearing. If the court finds that a condition of supervision has not been fulfilled the court may proceed to findings and adjudication and disposition. The filing of a petition for violation of a condition of the continuance under supervision shall toll the period of continuance under supervision until the final determination of the charge, and the term of the continuance under supervision shall not run until the hearing and disposition of the petition for violation; provided where the petition alleges conduct that does not constitute a criminal offense, the hearing must be held within 15 days of the filing of the petition unless a delay in the hearing has been occasioned by the minor, in which case the delay shall continue the tolling of the period of continuance under supervision for the period of the delay.

(Source: P.A. 86-1012; 87-530.) [Formerly Ill. Rev. Stat. 37 §805-19.]

405/5-20. Findings and adjudication.

§5-20. Findings and adjudication. After hearing the evidence the court shall make and note in the minutes of the proceeding a finding of whether or

not the minor is delinquent. If it finds that the minor is not such a person, the court shall order the petition dismissed and the minor discharged from any detention or restriction previously ordered in such proceeding. If the court finds that the minor is a person described in Section 5-3 [705 ILCS 405/5-3], the court shall then set a time for a dispositional hearing to be conducted under Section 5-22 [705 ILCS 405/5-22] at which hearing the court shall determine whether it is in the best interests of the minor and the public that he be made a ward of the court. To assist the court in making this and other determinations at the dispositional hearing, the court may order that an investigation be conducted and a social investigation report be prepared.
(Source: P.A. 85-601.) [Formerly Ill. Rev. Stat. 37 §805-20.]

405/5-21. Social investigation report.

§5-21. Social investigation report. Upon the order of the court, a social investigation report shall be prepared. The written report of social investigation shall include an investigation and report of the minor's physical and mental history and condition, family situation and background, economic status, education, occupation, personal habits, minor's history of delinquency or criminality or other matters which have been brought to the attention of the juvenile court, information about special resources known to the person preparing the report which might be available to assist in the minor's rehabilitation, and any other matters which may be helpful to the court or which the court directs to be included.
(Source: P.A. 85-601.) [Formerly Ill. Rev. Stat. 37 §805-21.]

405/5-22. Dispositional hearing; evidence; continuance.

§5-22. Dispositional hearing; evidence; continuance. (1) At the dispositional hearing, the court shall determine whether it is in the best interests of the minor and the public that he be made a ward of the court, and, if he is to be made a ward of the court, the court shall determine the proper disposition best serving the interests of the minor and the public. All evidence helpful in determining these questions, including oral and written reports, may be admitted and may be relied upon to the extent of its probative value, even though not competent for the purposes of the adjudicatory hearing. A record of a prior continuance under supervision under Section 5-19 [705 ILCS 405/5-19], whether successfully completed or not, is admissible at the dispositional hearing. No order of commitment to the Department of Corrections, Juvenile Division, shall be entered against a minor before a written report of social investigation, which has been completed within the previous 60 days, is presented to and considered by the court.

(2) Notice in compliance with Sections 5-15 and 5-16 [705 ILCS 405/5-15 and 405/5-16] must be given to all parties-respondents prior to proceeding to a dispositional hearing. Before making an order of disposition the court shall advise the State's Attorney, the parents, guardian, custodian or responsible relative or their counsel of the factual contents and the conclusions of the reports prepared for the use of the court and considered by it, and afford fair opportunity, if requested, to controvert them. The court may order, however, that the documents containing such reports need not be submitted to inspection, or that sources of confidential information need not be disclosed except to the attorneys for the parties. Factual contents, conclusions, documents and sources disclosed by the court under this paragraph shall not be further disclosed without the express approval of the court pursuant to an in camera hearing.

(3) On its own motion or that of the State's Attorney, a parent, guardian, custodian, responsible relative or counsel, the court may adjourn the hearing for a reasonable period to receive reports or other evidence and, in such event, shall make an appropriate order for detention of the minor or his release from

detention subject to supervision by the court during the period of the continuance. In the event the court shall order detention hereunder,the period of the continuance shall not exceed 15 court days. At the end of such time, the court shall release the minor from detention unless notice is served at least 3 days prior to the hearing on the continued date that the State will be seeking an extension of the period of detention, which notice shall state the reason for the request for such extension. The extension of detention may be for a maximum period of an additional 15 court days or a lesser number of days at the discretion of the court. However, at the expiration of the period of extension, the court shall release the minor from detention if a further continuance is granted. In scheduling investigations and hearings, the court shall give priority to proceedings in which a minor is in detention or has otherwise been removed from his home before an order of disposition has been made.

(4) When commitment to the Department of Corrections, Juvenile Division, is ordered, the court shall state the basis for selecting the particular disposition, and the court shall prepare such a statement for inclusion in the record.
(Source: P.A. 85-601.) [Formerly Ill. Rev. Stat. 37 §805-22.]

405/5-23. Kinds of dispositional orders.

§5-23. Kinds of dispositional orders. (1) The following kinds of orders of disposition may be made in respect of wards of the court:

(a) A minor found to be a delinquent under Section 5-3 [705 ILCS 405/5-3] may be (1) put on probation or conditional discharge and released to his or her parents, guardian or legal custodian, provided, however, that any such minor who is not committed to the Department of Corrections, Juvenile Division under this subsection and who is found to be a delinquent for an offense which is a Class X felony shall be placed on probation; (2) placed in accordance with Section 5-29 [705 ILCS 405/5-29], with or without also being put on probation or conditional discharge; (3) where authorized under the Illinois Alcoholism and Other Drug Dependency Act [20 ILCS 305/1-101 et seq.], ordered admitted for treatment for drug addiction by the Illinois Department of Alcoholism and Substance Abuse; (4) committed to the Department of Children and Family Services subject to Section 5 of the Children and Family Services Act [20 ILCS 505/5], except that the limitations of that Section 5 shall not apply to a delinquent minor under 13 years of age; (5) placed in detention for a period not to exceed 30 days, either as the exclusive order of disposition or, where appropriate, in conjunction with any other order of disposition issued under this paragraph, provided that any such detention shall be in a juvenile detention home and the minor so detained shall be 10 years of age or older, and the minor shall be given credit on the dispositional order of detention for time spent in detention under Sections 5-10(2), 5-14(b)(2), 5-23(1)(b), or 5-25(2) of this Act as a result of the offense for which the dispositional order was imposed. The court may grant credit on a dispositional order of detention entered under a violation of probation or violation of conditional discharge under Section 5-25 of this Act for time spent in detention before the filing of the petition alleging the violation. A minor shall not be deprived of credit for time spent in detention before the filing of a violation of probation or conditional discharge alleging the same or related act(s); or (6) ordered partially or completely emancipated in accordance with the provisions of the Emancipation of Mature Minors Act [750 ILCS 30/1 et seq.].

(b) A minor found to be delinquent may be committed to the Department of Corrections, Juvenile Division, under Section 5-33 [705 ILCS 405/5-33] if the minor is 13 years of age or older, provided that the commitment to the Department of Corrections, Juvenile Division, shall be made only if a term of incarceration is permitted by law for adults found guilty of the offense for which the minor was adjudicated delinquent. The time during which a minor is in custody before being released upon the request of a parent, guardian or custodian shall be considered as time spent in detention.

(1.1) When a minor is found to be delinquent for an offense which is a violation of the Illinois Controlled Substances Act [720 ILCS 570/100 et seq.] or the Cannabis Control Act [720 ILCS 550/1 et seq.] and made a ward of the court, the court may enter a disposition order requiring the minor to undergo assessment, counseling or treatment in a substance abuse program approved by the Department of Alcoholism and Substance Abuse.

(2) Any order of disposition other than commitment to the Department of Corrections, Juvenile Division, may provide for protective supervision under Section 5-26 [705 ILCS 405/5-26] and may include an order of protection under Section 5-27 [705 ILCS 405/5-27].

(3) Unless the order of disposition expressly so provides, it does not operate to close proceedings on the pending petition, but is subject to modification until final closing and discharge of the proceedings under Section 5-34 [705 ILCS 405/5-34].

(4) In addition to any other order of disposition, the court may order any minor found to be delinquent to make restitution, in monetary or non-monetary form, under the terms and conditions of Section 5-5-6 of the Unified Code of Corrections [730 ILCS 5/5-5-6], except that the "presentence hearing" referred to therein shall be the dispositional hearing for purposes of this Section. The parent, guardian or legal custodian of the minor may pay some or all of such restitution on the minor's behalf, pursuant to the Parental Responsibility Law, as now or hereafter amended [740 ILCS 115/1 et seq.]. The State's Attorney is authorized to act on behalf of any victim in seeking restitution in proceedings under this Section up to the maximum amount allowed in Section 5 of the Parental Responsibility Law [740 ILCS 115/5].

(5) Any order for disposition where the minor is committed or placed in accordance with Section 5-29 shall provide for the parents or guardian of the estate of such minor to pay to the legal custodian or guardian of the person of the minor such sums as are determined by the custodian or guardian of the person of the minor as necessary for the minor's needs. Such payments may not exceed the maximum amounts provided for by Section 5.1 of the Children and Family Services Act [see 20 ILCS 505/9.1].

(6) Whenever the order of disposition requires the minor to attend school or participate in a program of training, the truant officer or designated school official shall regularly report to the court if the minor is a chronic or habitual truant under Section 26-2a of the School Code [105 ILCS 5/26-2a].

(7) In no event shall a delinquent minor be committed for a period of time in excess of that period for which an adult could be committed for the same act.

(Chgd. by P.A. 87-1173, §1, eff. 9/18/92.)

(Source: P.A. 86-321; 86-915; 86-1028; 87-259; 87-895.) [Formerly Ill. Rev. Stat. 37 §805-23.]

405/5-24. Probation.

§5-24. Probation. (1) The period of probation or conditional discharge shall not exceed 5 years or until the minor has attained the age of 19 years, whichever is less, except as provided in this Section for a minor who is found to be delinquent for an offense which is a Class X felony. The juvenile court may terminate probation or conditional discharge and discharge the minor at any time if warranted by the conduct of the minor and the ends of justice; provided, however, that the period of probation for a minor who is found to be a delinquent for an offense which is a Class X felony shall be at least 5 years.

(2) The court may as a condition of probation or of conditional discharge require that the minor:

(a) not violate any criminal statute of any jurisdiction;

(b) make a report to and appear in person before any person or agency as directed by the court;

(c) work or pursue a course of study or vocational training;

(d) undergo medical or psychiatric treatment, rendered by a psychiatrist or psychological treatment rendered by a clinical psychologist or social work services rendered by a clinical social worker, or treatment for drug addiction or alcoholism;

(e) attend or reside in a facility established for the instruction or residence of persons on probation;

(f) support his dependents, if any;

(g) refrain from possessing a firearm or other dangerous weapon, or an automobile;

(h) permit the probation officer to visit him at his home or elsewhere;

(i) reside with his parents or in a foster home;

(j) attend school;

(k) attend a non-residential program for youth;

(*l*) make restitution under the terms of subsection (3) of Section 5-23 [705 ILCS 405/5-23];

(m) contribute to his own support at home or in a foster home;

(n) perform some reasonable public or community service;

(o) participate with community corrections programs including unified delinquency intervention services administered by the Department of Children and Family Services subject to Section 5 of the Children and Family Services Act [20 ILCS 505/5];

(p) pay costs;

(q) serve a term of home confinement. In addition to any other applicable condition of probation or conditional discharge, the conditions of home confinement shall be that the minor:

(i) remain within the interior premises of the place designated for his confinement during the hours designated by the court;

(ii) admit any person or agent designated by the court into the minor's place of confinement at any time for purposes of verifying the minor's compliance with the conditions of his confinement; and

(iii) use an approved electronic monitoring device if ordered by the court subject to Article 8A of Chapter V of the Unified Code of Corrections [730 ILCS 5/5-8A-1 et seq.];

(r) refrain from entering into a designated geographic area except upon terms as the court finds appropriate. The terms may include consideration of the purpose of the entry, the time of day, other persons accompanying the minor, and advance approval by a probation officer, if the minor has been placed on probation, or advance approval by the court, if the minor has been placed on conditional discharge;

(s) refrain from having any contact, directly or indirectly, with certain specified persons or particular types of persons, including but not limited to members of street gangs and drug users or dealers;

(t) comply with other conditions as may be ordered by the court; or

(u) refrain from having in his or her body the presence of any illicit drug prohibited by the Cannabis Control Act [720 ILCS 550/1 et seq.] or the Illinois Controlled Substances Act [720 ILCS 570/100 et seq.], unless prescribed by a physician, and shall submit samples of his or her blood or urine or both for tests to determine the presence of any illicit drug.

(3) The court may as a condition of probation or of conditional discharge require that a minor adjudicated delinquent on any alcohol, cannabis or controlled substance violation, refrain from acquiring a driver's license during the period of probation or conditional discharge. If the minor is in possession of a permit or license, the court may require that the minor refrain from driving or operating any motor vehicle during the period of probation or conditional discharge, except as may be necessary in the course of the minor's lawful employment.

(4) A minor on probation or conditional discharge shall be given a certificate setting forth the conditions upon which he is being released.

(Source: P.A. 86-766; 86-856; 86-1012; 86-1028; 86-1281; 87-14; 87-271; 87-530.) [Formerly Ill. Rev. Stat. 37 §805-24.]

405/5-25. Probation revocation.

§5-25. Probation Revocation. (1) If a petition is filed charging a violation of a condition of probation or of conditional discharge, the court shall:

(a) order the minor to appear; or

(b) order the minor's detention where the court finds that the detention is a matter of immediate and urgent necessity for the protection of the minor or of the person or property of another or that the minor is likely to flee the jurisdiction of the court, provided that any such detention shall be in a juvenile detention home and the minor so detained shall be 10 years of age or older; and

(c) notify the persons named in the petition under Section 5-13 [705 ILCS 405/5-13].

The filing of a petition for violation of a condition of probation or of conditional discharge shall toll the period of probation or of conditional discharge until the final determination of the charge, and the term of probation or conditional discharge shall not run until the hearing and disposition of the petition for violation.

(2) The court shall conduct a hearing of the alleged violation of probation or of conditional discharge. The minor shall not be held in detention longer than 15 days pending the determination of the alleged violation.

(3) At the hearing, the State shall have the burden of going forward with the evidence and proving the violation by a preponderance of the evidence. Such evidence shall be presented in court with the right of confrontation, cross-examination and representation by counsel.

(4) After a hearing, the court may modify or enlarge the conditions of probation or of conditional discharge. If the court finds that the minor has violated a condition at any time prior to the expiration or termination of the period of probation or conditional discharge, it may continue him on the existing disposition, with or without modifying or enlarging the conditions, or may revoke probation or conditional discharge and impose any other disposition that was available under Section 5-23 [705 ILCS 405/5-23] at the time of the initial disposition.

(5) The conditions of probation and of conditional discharge may be reduced or enlarged by the court on motion of the probation officer or on its own motion or at the request of the minor after notice and hearing under this Section.

(6) Disposition after revocation of probation or of conditional discharge shall be under Section 5-22 [705 ILCS 405/5-22].

(7) Rules or orders of court must specify the term and conditions of supervision ordered under this Act. When the court finds that the best interests of the minor and the public will be served thereby, the court may modify or terminate the order of supervision.

(Source: P.A. 85-1443.) [Formerly Ill. Rev. Stat. 37 §805-25.]

405/5-26. Protective supervision.

§5-26. Protective supervision. If the order of disposition releases the minor to the custody of his parents, guardian or legal custodian, or continues him in such custody, the court may place the person having custody of the minor, except for representatives of private or public agencies or governmental departments, under supervision of the probation office. Rules or orders of court shall define the terms and conditions of protective supervision, which may be modified or terminated when the court finds that the best interests of the minor and the public will be served thereby.

(Source: P.A. 85-601.) [Formerly Ill. Rev. Stat. 37 §805-26.]

405/5-27. Order of protection.

§5-27. Order of protection. (1) The court may make an order of protection in assistance of or as a condition of any other order authorized by this Act. The order of protection may set forth reasonable conditions of behavior to be observed for a specified period. Such an order may require a person:

(a) to stay away from the home or the minor;

(b) to permit a parent to visit the minor at stated periods;

(c) to abstain from offensive conduct against the minor, his parent or any person to whom custody of the minor is awarded;

(d) to give proper attention to the care of the home;

(e) to cooperate in good faith with an agency to which custody of a minor is entrusted by the court or with an agency or association to which the minor is referred by the court;

(f) to prohibit and prevent any contact whatsoever with the respondent minor by a specified individual or individuals who are alleged in either a criminal or juvenile proceeding to have caused injury to a respondent minor or a sibling of a respondent minor;

(g) to refrain from acts of commission or omission that tend to make the home not a proper place for the minor.

(2) The court shall enter an order of protection to prohibit and prevent any contact between a respondent minor or a sibling of a respondent minor and any person named in a petition seeking an order of protection who has been convicted of heinous battery under Section 12-4.1, aggravated battery of a child under Section 12-4.3, criminal sexual assault under Section 12-13, aggravated criminal sexual assault under Section 12-14, criminal sexual abuse under Section 12-15, or aggravated criminal sexual abuse under Section 12-16 of the Criminal Code of 1961 [720 ILCS 5/12-4.1, 5/12-4.3, 5/12-13, 5/12-14, 5/12-15 or 5/12-16], or has been convicted of an offense that resulted in the death of a child, or has violated a previous order of protection under this Section.

(3) When the court issues an order of protection against any person as provided by this Section, the court shall direct a copy of such order to the Sheriff of that county. The Sheriff shall furnish a copy of the order of protection to the Department of State Police within 24 hours of receipt, in the form and manner required by the Department. The Department of State Police shall maintain a complete record and index of such orders of protection and make this data available to all local law enforcement agencies.

(4) After notice and opportunity for hearing afforded to a person subject to an order of protection, the order may be modified or extended for a further specified period or both or may be terminated if the court finds that the best interests of the minor and the public will be served thereby.

(5) An order of protection may be sought at any time during the course of any proceeding conducted pursuant to this Act. Any person against whom an order of protection is sought may retain counsel to represent him at a hearing, and has rights to be present at the hearing, to be informed prior to the hearing in writing of the contents of the petition seeking a protective order and of the date, place and time of such hearing, and to cross examine witnesses called by the petitioner and to present witnesses and argument in opposition to the relief sought in the petition.

(6) Diligent efforts shall be made by the petitioner to serve any person or persons against whom any order of protection is sought with written notice of the contents of the petition seeking a protective order and of the date, place and time at which the hearing on the petition is to be held. When a protective order is being sought in conjunction with a shelter care or detention hearing, if the court finds that the person against whom the protective order is being sought has been notified of the hearing or that diligent efforts have been made to notify such person, the court may conduct a hearing. If a protective order is sought at any time other than in conjunction with a shelter care or detention hearing, the court may not conduct a hearing on the petition in the absence of the person

against whom the order is sought unless the petitioner has notified such person by personal service at least 3 days before the hearing or has sent written notice by first class mail to such person's last known address at least 5 days before the hearing.

(7) A person against whom an order of protection is being sought who is neither a parent, guardian, legal custodian or responsible relative as described in Section 1-5 [705 ILCS 405/1-5] is not a party or respondent as defined in that Section and shall not be entitled to the rights provided therein. Such person does not have a right to appointed counsel or to be present at any hearing other than the hearing in which the order of protection is being sought or a hearing directly pertaining to that order. Unless the court orders otherwise, such person does not have a right to inspect the court file.

(8) All protective orders entered under this Section shall be in writing. Unless the person against whom the order was obtained was present in court when the order was issued, the sheriff, other law enforcement official or special process server shall promptly serve that order upon that person and file proof of such service, in the manner provided for service of process in civil proceedings. The person against whom the protective order was obtained may seek a modification of the order by filing a written motion to modify the order within 7 days after actual receipt by the person of a copy of the order.

(Source: P.A. 85-1209; 86-1475.) [Formerly Ill. Rev. Stat. 37 §805-27.]

405/5-28. Enforcement of orders of protective supervision or of protection.

§5-28. Enforcement of orders of protective supervision or of protection. (1) Orders of protective supervision and orders of protection may be enforced by citation to show cause for contempt of court by reason of any violation thereof and, where protection of the welfare of the minor so requires, by the issuance of a warrant to take the alleged violator into custody and bring him before the court.

(2) In any case where an order of protection has been entered, the clerk of the court may issue to the petitioner, to the minor or to any other person affected by the order a certificate stating that an order of protection has been made by the court concerning such persons and setting forth its terms and requirements. The presentation of the certificate to any peace officer authorizes him to take into custody a person charged with violating the terms of the order of protection, to bring such person before the court and, within the limits of his legal authority as such peace officer, otherwise to aid in securing the protection the order is intended to afford.

(Source: P.A. 85-601.) [Formerly Ill. Rev. Stat. 37 §805-28.]

405/5-29. Placement; legal custody or guardianship.

§5-29. Placement; legal custody or guardianship. (1) If the court finds that the parents, guardian or legal custodian of a minor adjudged a ward of the court are unfit or are unable, for some reason other than financial circumstances alone, to care for, protect, train or discipline the minor or are unwilling to do so, and that appropriate services aimed at family preservation and family reunification have been unsuccessful in rectifying the conditions which have led to a finding of unfitness or inability to care for, protect, train or discipline the minor, and that it is in the best interest of the minor to take him from the custody of his parents, guardian or custodian, the court may:

(a) place him in the custody of a suitable relative or other person;

(b) place him under the guardianship of a probation officer;

(c) commit him to an agency for care or placement, except an institution under the authority of the Department of Corrections or of the Department of Children and Family Services;

(d) commit him to some licensed training school or industrial school; or

(e) commit him to any appropriate institution having among its purposes the care of delinquent children, including a child protective facility maintained by a Child Protection District serving the county from which commitment is made, but not including any institution under the authority of the Department of Corrections or of the Department of Children and Family Services.

(2) When making such placement, the court, wherever possible, shall select a person holding the same religious belief as that of the minor or a private agency controlled by persons of like religious faith of the minor. In addition, whenever alternative plans for placement are available, the court shall ascertain and consider, to the extent appropriate in the particular case, the views and preferences of the minor.

(3) When a minor is placed with a suitable relative or other person, the court shall appoint him the legal custodian or guardian of the person of the minor. When a minor is committed to any agency, the court shall appoint the proper officer or representative thereof as legal custodian or guardian of the person of the minor. Legal custodians and guardians of the person of the minor have the respective rights and duties set forth in subsection (9) of Section 1-3 [705 ILCS 405/1-3] except as otherwise provided by order of court; but no guardian of the person may consent to adoption of the minor unless that authority is conferred upon him in accordance with Section 5-31 [705 ILCS 405/5-31]. An agency whose representative is appointed guardian of the person or legal custodian of the minor may place him in any child care facility, but such facility must be licensed under the Child Care Act of 1969 [225 ILCS 10/1 et seq.] or have been approved by the Department of Children and Family Services as meeting the standards established for such licensing. No agency may place a minor adjudicated delinquent, if the minor is under age 13, in a child care facility unless such placement is in compliance with the rules and regulations for placement under this Section promulgated by the Department of Children and Family Services under Section 5 of the Children and Family Services Act [20 ILCS 505/5]. Like authority and restrictions shall be conferred by the court upon any probation officer who has been appointed guardian of the person of a minor.

(4) No placement by any probation officer or agency whose representative is appointed guardian of the person or legal custodian of a minor may be made in any out of State child care facility unless it complies with the Interstate Compact on the Placement of Children.

(5) The clerk of the court shall issue to the legal custodian or guardian of the person a certified copy of the order of court, as proof of his authority. No other process is necessary as authority for the keeping of the minor.

(6) Custody or guardianship granted under this Section continues until the court otherwise directs, but not after the minor reaches the age of 19 years except as set forth in Section 5-34 [705 ILCS 405/5-34].

(Source: P.A. 87-14.) [Formerly Ill. Rev. Stat. 37 §805-29.]

405/5-30. Court review.

§5-30. Court review. (1) The court may require any legal custodian or guardian of the person appointed under this Act to report periodically to the court or may cite him into court and require him or his agency, to make a full and accurate report of his or its doings in behalf of the minor. The custodian or guardian, within 10 days after such citation, shall make the report, either in writing verified by affidavit or orally under oath in open court, or otherwise as the court directs. Upon the hearing of the report the court may remove the custodian or guardian and appoint another in his stead or restore the minor to the custody of his parents or former guardian or custodian.

(2) A guardian or custodian appointed by the court pursuant to this Act shall file updated case plans with the court every 6 months. Every agency which has

guardianship of a child shall file a supplemental petition for court review, or review by an administrative body appointed or approved by the court and further order within 18 months of dispositional order and each 18 months thereafter. Such petition shall state facts relative to the child's present condition of physical, mental and emotional health as well as facts relative to his present custodial or foster care. The petition shall be set for hearing and the clerk shall mail 10 days notice of the hearing by certified mail, return receipt requested, to the person or agency having the physical custody of the child, the minor and other interested parties unless a written waiver of notice is filed with the petition.

Rights of wards of the court under this Act are enforceable against any public agency by complaints for relief by mandamus filed in any proceedings brought under this Act.

(3) The minor or any person interested in the minor may apply to the court for a change in custody of the minor and the appointment of a new custodian or guardian of the person or for the restoration of the minor to the custody of his parents or former guardian or custodian. In the event that the minor has attained 18 years of age and the guardian or custodian petitions the court for an order terminating his guardianship or custody, guardianship or custody shall terminate automatically 30 days after the receipt of the petition unless the court orders otherwise. No legal custodian or guardian of the person may be removed without his consent until given notice and an opportunity to be heard by the court.

(Source: P.A. 85-601.) [Formerly Ill. Rev. Stat. 37 §805-30.]

405/5-31. Adoption; appointment of guardian with power to consent.

§5-31. Adoption; appointment of guardian with power to consent. (1) A ward of the court under this Act, with the consent of the court, may be the subject of a petition for adoption under "An Act in relation to the adoption of persons, and to repeal an Act therein named", approved July 17, 1959, as amended [750 ILCS 50/0.01 et seq.], or with like consent his or her parent or parents may, in the manner required by such Act, surrender him or her for adoption to an agency legally authorized or licensed to place children for adoption.

(2) If the petition prays and the court finds that it is in the best interests of the minor that a guardian of the person be appointed and authorized to consent to the adoption of the minor, the court with the consent of the parents, if living, or after finding, based upon clear and convincing evidence, that a non-consenting parent is an unfit person as defined in Section 1 of "An Act in relation to the adoption of persons, and to repeal an Act therein named", approved July 17, 1959, as amended [750 ILCS 50/1], may empower the guardian of the person of the minor, in the order appointing him or her as such guardian, to appear in court where any proceedings for the adoption of the minor may at any time be pending and to consent to the adoption. Such consent is sufficient to authorize the court in the adoption proceedings to enter a proper order or judgment of adoption without further notice to, or consent by, the parents of the minor. An order so empowering the guardian to consent to adoption terminates parental rights, deprives the parents of the minor of all legal rights as respects the minor and relieves them of all parental responsibility for him or her, and frees the minor from all obligations of maintenance and obedience to his or her natural parents.

If the minor is over 14 years of age, the court may, in its discretion, consider the wishes of the minor in determining whether the best interests of the minor would be promoted by the finding of the unfitness of a non-consenting parent.

(3) Parental consent to the order authorizing the guardian of the person to consent to adoption of the Minor shall be given in open court whenever possible

and otherwise must be in writing and signed in the form provided in "An Act in relation to the adoption of persons, and to repeal an Act therein named", approved July 17, 1959, as amended, but no names of petitioners for adoption need be included. A finding of the unfitness of a nonconsenting parent must be made in compliance with that Act and be based upon clear and convincing evidence. Provisions of that Act relating to minor parents and to mentally ill or mentally deficient parents apply to proceedings under this Section and shall be based upon clear and convincing evidence.
(Source: P.A. 85-601.) [Formerly Ill. Rev. Stat. 37 §805-31.]

405/5-32. Notice to putative father; service.

§5-32. Notice to putative father; service. 1. Upon the written request to any Clerk of any Circuit Court by any interested party, including persons intending to adopt a child, a child welfare agency with whom the mother has placed or has given written notice of her intention to place a child for adoption, the mother of a child, or any attorney representing an interested party, a notice may be served on a putative father in the same manner as Summons is served in other proceedings under this Act, or in lieu of personal service, service may be made as follows:

(a) The person requesting notice shall furnish to the Clerk an original and one copy of a notice together with an Affidavit setting forth the putative father's last known address. The original notice shall be retained by the Clerk.

(b) The Clerk forthwith shall mail to the putative father, at the address appearing in the Affidavit, the copy of the notice, certified mail, return receipt requested; the envelope and return receipt shall bear the return address of the Clerk. The receipt for certified mail shall state the name and address of the addressee, and the date of mailing, and shall be attached to the original notice.

(c) The return receipt, when returned to the Clerk, shall be attached to the original notice, and shall constitute proof of service.

(d) The Clerk shall note the fact of service in a permanent record.

2. The notice shall be signed by the Clerk, and may be served on the putative father at any time after conception, and shall read as follows:

"IN THE MATTER OF NOTICE TO . . . . . , PUTATIVE FATHER.

You have been identified as the father of a child (born on the . . . . . day of . . . . . ., 19. . .), or (expected to be born on or about the . . . . . day of . . . . . ., 19. . .). The mother of said child is . . . .

The mother has indicated she intends to place the child for adoption or otherwise have a judgment entered terminating her rights with respect to such child.

As the alleged father of said child, you have certain legal rights with respect to said child, including the right to notice of the filing of proceedings instituted for the termination of your parental rights regarding said child. If you wish to retain your rights with respect to said child, you must file with the Clerk of this Circuit Court of . . . . . , County, Illinois, whose address is . . . . . , ... , Illinois, within 30 days after the date of receipt of this notice, a declaration of paternity stating that you are, in fact, the father of said child and that you intend to retain your legal rights with respect to said child, or request to be notified of any further proceedings with respect to custody, termination of parental rights or adoption of the child.

If you do not file such a declaration of paternity, or a request for notice, then whatever legal rights you have with respect to said child, including the right to notice of any future proceedings for the adoption of said child, may be terminated without any further notice to you. When your legal rights with respect to said child are so terminated, you will not be entitled to notice of any proceeding instituted for the adoption of said child.

If you are not the father of said child, you may file with the Clerk of this Court, a disclaimer of paternity which will be noted in the Clerk's file and you will receive no further notice with respect to said child".

The disclaimer of paternity shall be substantially as follows:

"IN THE CIRCUIT COURT OF THE
.... JUDICIAL CIRCUIT, ILLINOIS
.... County

______________________________)
)
) No.
)
______________________________)

DENIAL OF PATERNITY WITH ENTRY OF APPEARANCE AND CONSENT TO ADOPTION

I, ... , state as follows:

(1) That I am . . . . . . years of age; and I reside at . . . . in the County of . . . . , State of . . . .

(2) That I have been advised that . . . . is the mother of a . . . . . male child named . . . . born or expected to be born on or about . . . . . . and that such mother has stated that I am the father of this child.

(3) I deny that I am the father of this child.

(4) I further understand that the mother of this child wishes to consent to the adoption of the child. I hereby consent to the adoption of this child, and waive any rights, remedies and defenses that I may now or in the future have as a result of the mother's allegation of the paternity of this child. This consent is being given in order to facilitate the adoption of the child and so that the court may terminate what rights I may have to the child as a result of being named the father by the mother. This consent is not in any manner an admission of paternity.

(5) I hereby enter my appearance in the above entitled cause and waive service of summons and other pleading and consent to an immediate hearing on a petition TO TERMINATE PARENTAL RIGHTS AND TO APPOINT A GUARDIAN WITH THE POWER TO CONSENT TO THE ADOPTION OF THIS CHILD.

OATH

I have been duly sworn and I say under oath that I have read and understood this Denial of Paternity With Entry of Appearance and Consent to Adoption. The facts it contains are true and correct to the best of my knowledge, and I understand that by signing this document I have not admitted paternity. I have signed this document as my free and voluntary act in order to facilitate the adoption of the child.

. . . .
(signature)

Dated this . . . . . day of . . . . , 19. . .
Signed and Sworn Before Me This . . . . . day of . . . . , 19. . .

. . . .
(notary public)".

The names of adoptive parents, if any, shall not be included in the notice.

3. If the putative father files a disclaimer of paternity, he shall be deemed not to be the father of the child with respect to any adoption or other proceeding held to terminate the rights of parents as respects such child.

4. In the event the putative father does not file a declaration of paternity of the child or request for notice within 30 days of service of the above notice, he need not be made a party to or given notice of any proceeding brought for the adoption of the child. An Order or Judgment may be entered in such proceeding terminating all of his rights with respect to said child without further notice to him.

5. If the putative father files a declaration of paternity or a request for notice in accordance with subsection 2 with respect to the child, he shall be given notice in the event any proceeding is brought for the adoption of the child or for termination of parents' rights of the child.

6. The Clerk shall maintain separate numbered files and records of requests and proofs of service and all other documents filed pursuant to this article. All such records shall be impounded.

(Source: P.A. 85-601.) [Formerly Ill. Rev. Stat. 37 §805-32.]

405/5-33. Commitment to Department of Corrections, Juvenile Division.

§5-33. Commitment to Department of Corrections, Juvenile Division. (1) When any delinquent has been adjudged a ward of the court under this Act, the court may commit him to the Department of Corrections, Juvenile Division, if it finds that (a) his parents, guardian or legal custodian are unfit or are unable, for some reason other than financial circumstances alone, to care for, protect, train or discipline the minor, or are unwilling to do so, and the best interests of the minor and the public will not be served by placement under Section 5-29 [705 ILCS 405/5-29]; or (b) it is necessary to ensure the protection of the public from the consequences of criminal activity of the delinquent.

(2) The commitment of a delinquent to the Department of Corrections shall be for an indeterminate term which shall automatically terminate upon the delinquent attaining the age of 21 years unless the delinquent is sooner discharged from parole or custodianship is otherwise terminated in accordance with this Act or as otherwise provided for by law.

(3) When the court commits a minor to the Department of Corrections, it shall order him conveyed forthwith to the appropriate reception station or other place designated by the Department of Corrections, and shall appoint the Assistant Director of Corrections, Juvenile Division, legal custodian of the minor. The clerk of the court shall issue to the Assistant Director of Corrections, Juvenile Division, a certified copy of the order, which constitutes proof of his authority. No other process need issue to warrant the keeping of the minor.

(4) If a minor is committed to the Department of Corrections, Juvenile Division, the clerk of the court shall forward to the Department:

(a) the disposition ordered;

(b) all reports;

(c) the court's statement of the basis for ordering the disposition; and

(d) all additional matters which the court directs the clerk to transmit.

(5) Whenever the Department of Corrections lawfully discharges from its custody and control a minor committed to it, the Assistant Director of Corrections, Juvenile Division, shall petition the court for an order terminating his custodianship. The custodianship shall terminate automatically 30 days after receipt of the petition unless the court orders otherwise.

(Source: P.A. 85-601.) [Formerly Ill. Rev. Stat. 37 §805-33.]

405/5-34. Duration of wardship and discharge of proceedings.

§5-34. Duration of wardship and discharge of proceedings. (1) All proceedings under this Act in respect of any minor for whom a petition was filed after the effective date of this amendatory Act of 1991 automatically terminate upon his attaining the age of 19 years, except that a court may continue the wardship of a minor until age 21 for good cause when there is satisfactory evidence presented to the court that the best interests of the minor and the public require the continuation of the wardship.

(2) Whenever the court finds that the best interests of the minor and the public no longer require the wardship of the court, the court shall order the wardship terminated and all proceedings under this Act respecting that minor finally closed and discharged. The court may at the same time continue or terminate any custodianship or guardianship theretofore ordered but such termination must be made in compliance with Section 5-30 [705 ILCS 405/5-30].

(3) The wardship of the minor and any custodianship or guardianship respecting the minor for whom a petition was filed after the effective date of this amendatory Act of 1991 automatically terminates when he attains the age of 19 years except as set forth in subsection (1) of this Section. The clerk of the court shall at that time record all proceedings under this Act as finally closed and discharged for that reason.

(Source: P.A. 87-14.) [Formerly Ill. Rev. Stat. 37 §805-34.]

405/5-35. Habitual Juvenile Offender.

§5-35. Habitual Juvenile Offender. (a) Definition. Any minor having been twice adjudicated a delinquent minor for offenses which, had he been prosecuted as an adult, would have been felonies under the laws of this State, and who is thereafter adjudicated a delinquent minor for a third time shall be adjudged an Habitual Juvenile Offender where:

1. the third adjudication is for an offense occurring after adjudication on the second; and
2. the second adjudication was for an offense occurring after adjudication on the first; and
3. the third offense occurred after January 1, 1980; and
4. the third offense was based upon the commission of or attempted commission of the following offenses: first degree murder, second degree murder or involuntary manslaughter; criminal sexual assault or aggravated criminal sexual assault; aggravated or heinous battery involving permanent disability or disfigurement or great bodily harm to the victim; burglary of a home or other residence intended for use as a temporary or permanent dwelling place for human beings; home invasion; robbery or armed robbery; or aggravated arson.

Nothing in this section shall preclude the State's Attorney from seeking to prosecute a minor as an adult as an alternative to prosecution as an habitual juvenile offender.

A continuance under supervision authorized by Section 5-19 of this Act [705 ILCS 405/5-19] shall not be permitted under this section.

(b) Notice to minor. The State shall serve upon the minor written notice of intention to prosecute under the provisions of this Section within 5 judicial days of the filing of any delinquency petition, adjudication upon which would mandate the minor's disposition as an Habitual Juvenile Offender.

(c) Petition; service. A notice to seek adjudication as an Habitual Juvenile Offender shall be filed only by the State's Attorney.

The petition upon which such Habitual Juvenile Offender notice is based shall contain the information and averments required for all other delinquency petitions filed under this Act and its service shall be according to the provisions of this Act.

No prior adjudication shall be alleged in the petition.

(d) Trial. Trial on such petition shall be by jury unless the minor demands, in open court and with advice of counsel, a trial by the court without jury.

Except as otherwise provided herein, the provisions of this Act concerning delinquency proceedings generally shall be applicable to Habitual Juvenile Offender proceedings.

(e) Proof of prior adjudications. No evidence or other disclosure of prior adjudications shall be presented to the court or jury during any adjudicatory hearing provided for under this Section unless otherwise permitted by the issues properly raised in such hearing. In the event the minor who is the subject of these proceedings elects to testify on his own behalf, it shall be competent to introduce evidence, for purposes of impeachment, that he has previously been adjudicated a delinquent minor upon facts which, had he been tried as an adult, would have resulted in his conviction of a felony. Introduction of such evidence shall be according to the rules and procedures applicable to the impeachment of an adult defendant by prior conviction.

After an admission of the facts in the petition or adjudication of delinquency, the State's Attorney may file with the court a verified written statement signed by the State's Attorney concerning any prior adjudication of an offense set forth in subsection (a) of this Section which offense would have been a felony had the minor been tried as an adult.

The court shall then cause the minor to be brought before it; shall inform him of the allegations of the statement so filed, and of his right to a hearing before the court on the issue of such prior adjudication and of his right to counsel at such hearing; and unless the minor admits such adjudication, the court shall hear and determine such issue, and shall make a written finding thereon.

A duly authenticated copy of the record of any such alleged prior adjudication shall be prima facie evidence of such prior adjudication.

Any claim that a previous adjudication offered by the State's Attorney is not a former adjudication of an offense which, had the minor been prosecuted as an adult, would have resulted in his conviction of a felony, is waived unless duly raised at the hearing on such adjudication, or unless the State's Attorney's proof shows that such prior adjudication was not based upon proof of what would have been a felony.

(f) Disposition. If the court finds that the prerequisites established in subsection (a) of this Section have been proven, it shall adjudicate the minor an Habitual Juvenile Offender and commit him to the Department of Corrections, Juvenile Division, until his 21st birthday, without possibility of parole, furlough, or non-emergency authorized absence. However, the minor shall be entitled to earn one day of good conduct credit for each day served as reductions against the period of his confinement. Such good conduct credits shall be earned or revoked according to the procedures applicable to the allowance and revocation of good conduct credit for adult prisoners serving determinate sentences for felonies.

For purposes of determining good conduct credit, commitment as an Habitual Juvenile Offender shall be considered a determinate commitment, and the difference between the date of the commitment and the minor's 21st birthday shall be considered the determinate period of his confinement.
(Source: P.A. 85-601.) [Formerly Ill. Rev. Stat. 37 §805-35.]

ARTICLE VI. ADMINISTRATION OF JUVENILE SERVICES

405/6-1. Probation departments; functions and duties.

§6-1. Probation departments; functions and duties. (1) The chief judge of each circuit shall make provision for probation services for each county in his or her circuit. The appointment of officers to probation or court services departments and the administration of such departments shall be governed by the provisions of "An Act providing for a system of probation, for the appointment and compensation of probation officers, and authorizing the suspension of final judgment and the imposition of sentence upon persons found guilty of certain defined crimes and offenses, and legalizing their ultimate discharge without punishment", approved June 10, 1911, as now or hereafter amended [730 ILCS 110/0.01 et seq.].

(2) Every county or every group of counties constituting a probation district shall maintain a Court Services or a Probation Department subject to the provisions of "An Act providing for a system of probation, for the appointment and compensation of probation officers, and authorizing the suspension of final judgment and the imposition of sentence upon persons found guilty of certain defined crimes and offenses, and legalizing their ultimate discharge without punishment", approved June 10, 1911, as amended. For the purposes of this Act such a Court Services or Probation Department has, but is not limited to, the following powers and duties:

(a) When authorized or directed by the court, to receive, investigate and evaluate complaints indicating dependency, requirement of authoritative intervention, addiction or delinquency within the meaning of Sections 2-3, 2-4, 3-3, 4-3 or 5-3 [705 ILCS 405/2-3, 405/2-4, 405/3-3, 405/4-3 or 405/5-3], respectively; to determine or assist the complainant in determining whether a petition should be filed under Sections 2-13, 3-15, 4-12 or 5-13 [705 ILCS 405/2-13, 405/3-15, 405/4-12 or 405/5-13] or whether referral should be made to an agency, association or other person or whether some other action is advisable; and to see that the indicating filing, referral or other action is accomplished. However, no such investigation, evaluation or supervision by such court services or probation department is to occur with regard to complaints indicating only that a minor may be a chronic or habitual truant.

(b) When a petition is filed under Section 2-13, 3-15, 4-15 or 5-13 [705 ILCS 405/2-13, 405/3-15, 405/4-15 or 405/5-13], to make pre-hearing investigations and formulate recommendations to the court when the court has authorized or directed the department to do so.

(c) To counsel and, by order of the court, to supervise minors referred to the court; to conduct indicated programs of casework, including referrals for medical and mental health service, organized recreation and job placement for wards of the court and, when appropriate, for members of the family of a ward; to act as liaison officer between the court and agencies or associations to which minors are referred or through which they are placed; when so appointed, to serve as guardian of the person of a ward of the court; to provide probation supervision and protective supervision ordered by the court; and to provide like services to wards and probationers of courts in other counties or jurisdictions who have lawfully become local residents.

(d) To arrange for placements pursuant to court order.

(e) To assume administrative responsibility for such detention, shelter care and other institutions for minors as the court may operate.

(f) To maintain an adequate system of case records, statistical records, and financial records related to juvenile detention and shelter care and to make reports to the court and other authorized persons, and to the Supreme Court pursuant to "An Act providing for a system of probation, for the appointment and compensation of probation officers, and authorizing the suspension of final judgment and the imposition of sentence upon persons found guilty of certain defined crimes and offenses, and legalizing their ultimate discharge without punishment", approved June 10, 1911, as amended.

(g) To perform such other services as may be appropriate to effectuate the purposes of this Act or as may be directed by any order of court made under this Act.

(3) The Court Services or Probation Department in any probation district or county having less than 1,000,000 inhabitants, or any personnel of the Department, may be required by the circuit court to render services to the court in other matters as well as proceedings under this Act.

(4) In any county or probation district, a Probation Department may be established as a separate division of a more inclusive department of court services, with any appropriate divisional designation. The organization of any such department of court services and the appointment of officers and other personnel must comply with "An Act providing for a system of probation, for the appointment and compensation of probation officers, and authorizing the suspension of final judgment and the imposition of sentence upon persons found guilty of certain defined crimes and offenses, and legalizing their ultimate discharge without punishment", approved June 10, 1911, as amended.
(Source: P.A. 86-639; 86-659; 86-1028.) [Formerly Ill. Rev. Stat. 37 §806-1.]

405/6-2. Probation districts; informal cooperation.

§6-2. Probation districts; informal cooperation. (1) Any 2 or more counties in the same judicial circuit may form a joint probation district for the maintenance of a Probation Department or of both a Probation Department and a Psychiatric Department of the circuit court in those counties. The determination and agreement to form such a probation district shall be made by the county boards of the counties desiring to form it. Any such agreement is binding on the respective counties for 4 years.

(2) The budget for such Probation Department and Psychiatric Department, if any, maintained by any probation district shall be prepared by the respective Departments and submitted for review and appropriate action to a committee representative of all county boards within the district. The budget committee shall meet annually and as many additional times as it finds necessary. All such financial information must be shared with the Supreme Court at its request.

(3) The financial burden of maintaining each such Department shall be borne by each county in the district on a pro rata system based upon the ratio that the value of property in that county, as equalized or assessed by the Department of Revenue, bears to the total value of all the property in the district, as equalized or assessed by the Department of Revenue, subject to the limitations and regulations imposed by law on the authority of any county to levy taxes.

(4) This Section does not exclude informal cooperation between any 2 or more counties with respect to the rendering of probation or psychiatric services, or prohibit the formation of a probation district by any 2 or more counties in the same circuit on any mutually acceptable basis.
(Source: P.A. 85-601.) [Formerly Ill. Rev. Stat. 37 §806-2.]

405/6-3. Court Services Departments; counties over 1,000,000.

§6-3. Court Services Departments; counties over 1,000,000. (1) Any county having more than 1,000,000 inhabitants shall maintain a Court Services

Department, which shall be under the authority and supervision of the chief judge of the circuit or of some other judge designated by him.

(2) The functions and duties of probation personnel of the Court Services Department include, but are not limited to, those described in Section 6-1 [705 ILCS 405/6-1]. Neither the Court Services Department nor any of its personnel must supervise the probation of any person over 18 years of age convicted under the criminal laws, except that the court may order the Department to supervise the probation of an adult convicted of the crime of contributing to the dependency and neglect of children or of contributing to the delinquency of children.

(3) The Court Services Department in any such county shall provide psychiatric clinical services relating to the purposes of this Act when so requested, authorized or ordered by the court. The Department may be required by the circuit court to render psychiatric clinical services to the court in other matters as well as in proceedings under this Act.

(Source: P.A. 85-601.) [Formerly Ill. Rev. Stat. 37 §806-3.]

405/6-4. Psychiatric Departments; counties under 1,000,000.

§6-4. Psychiatric Departments; counties under 1,000,000. (1) Any county having less than 1,000,000 inhabitants or any group of counties constituting a probation district may maintain a Psychiatric Department to render clinical services requested, authorized or ordered by the court. The Psychiatric Department may be required by the circuit court to render services to the court in other matters as well as in proceedings under this Act. In any county or probation district the Psychiatric Department may be established as a separate division of a more inclusive psychiatric department or of a comprehensive department of court services, with any appropriate divisional designation.

(2) The chief judge of the circuit court shall appoint a professionally qualified person as Director of the Psychiatric Department established for any county or probation district in the circuit, to serve at his pleasure, and may authorize the Director to appoint such other personnel of the Department as the chief judge from time to time may determine are needed, to serve at the pleasure of the Director. The Director shall have general charge of the Department under the supervision of the chief judge or of some other judge designated by the chief judge for that purpose.

(3) Appointments to any professional position in the Psychiatric Department must be made in accordance with standards prescribed by the chief judge in consultation with an advisory committee of his selection, composed of persons of recognized and outstanding ability in the practice of psychiatry or psychology or in the teaching or practice of social service and public welfare work.

(Source: P.A. 85-601.) [Formerly Ill. Rev. Stat. 37 §806-4.]

405/6-5. Compensation and expenses of personnel.

§6-5. Compensation and expenses of personnel. (1) The compensation of the several officers or grades of officers and other personnel of the Probation Department and the Psychiatric Department, if any, or the Court Services Department, shall be determined by the county board of any county not within a probation district or by the budget committee representative of all county boards of counties within any probation district. Department personnel shall also be paid their actual and necessary expenses incurred in the performance of their duties. The compensation and actual and necessary expenses shall be paid at least monthly out of the county treasury upon proper certification by the court.

(2) For the purpose of paying the compensation and expenses of personnel of any Probation, Psychiatric or Court Services Department maintained by a probation district, the county treasurer of each of the less populous counties of the district shall pay its monthly pro rata share to the county treasurer of the

county in the district having the largest population according to the most recent Federal census, who shall add his county's share to the amounts so received and pay the compensation and expenses due to such personnel.

(3) Personnel required to render Services to the circuit court in other matters in addition to proceedings under this Act may be separately compensated therefor under any applicable law. In the case of personnel of the Probation Departments required by this Act, the amount of compensation for services under this Act shall be specified by the county board or the budget committee of the probation district, as the case may be.

(Source: P.A. 85-601.) [Formerly Ill. Rev. Stat. 37 §806-5.]

405/6-6. State share of compensation of probation personnel.

§6-6. State share of compensation of probation Personnel. (1) Before the 15th day of each month, beginning with August, 1966, there shall be filed with the Supreme Court an itemized statement of the amounts paid, by the county, probation district or counties cooperating informally under Section 6-2 [705 ILCS 405/6-2], as compensation for Services rendered under this Act pursuant to "An Act providing for a system of probation, for the appointment and compensation of probation officers, and authorizing the suspension of final judgment and the imposition of sentence upon persons found guilty of certain defined crimes and offenses, and legalizing their ultimate discharge without punishment", approved June 10, 1911, as amended [730 ILCS 110/0.01 et seq.].

(2) Such itemized statement shall be filed by the county treasurer, or, in the case of a probation district or of counties cooperating informally under Section 6-2, by the county treasurer of the most populous county, and shall be certified as to amounts by such county treasurer and the Supreme Court or its designee shall establish a means of verifying compliance with this Section in the manner of appointment or reappointment of and the percentage of time spent by such personnel.

(3) The Supreme Court or its designee shall verify that conditions contained in this Section have been met and transmit the statements to the Comptroller who shall examine and audit the monthly statement and, upon finding it correct, shall voucher for payment to the county treasurer filing the same, for his county, probation district or group of co-operating counties the amount of $1,000 per month for salaries of qualified probation officers who are paid at least at the annual rate of $17,000.

(4) To qualify for State reimbursement under this Section, county probation departments or probation districts must conform to the provisions of "An Act providing for a system of probation, for the appointment and compensation of probation officers, and authorizing the suspension of final judgment and the imposition of sentence upon persons found guilty of certain defined crimes and offenses, and legalizing their ultimate discharge without punishment", approved June 10, 1911, as amended. Whether or not a county probation department or probation district applies for State reimbursement, such department or district must abide by the personnel qualifications and hiring procedures promulgated by the Supreme Court pursuant to "An Act providing for a system of probation, for the appointment and compensation of probation officers, and authorizing the suspension of final judgment and the imposition of sentence upon persons found guilty of certain defined crimes and offenses, and legalizing their ultimate discharge without punishment", approved June 10, 1911, as amended.

(Source: P.A. 85-601.) [Formerly Ill. Rev. Stat. 37 §806-6.]

405/6-7. Financial responsibility of counties.

§6-7. Financial responsibility of counties. (1) Each county board shall provide in its annual appropriation ordinance or annual budget, as the case may be, a reasonable sum for payments for the care and support of minors, and for payments for court appointed counsel in accordance with orders entered under this Act in an amount which in the judgment of the county board may be needed for that purpose. Such appropriation or budget item constitutes a separate fund into which shall be paid not only the moneys appropriated by the county board, but also all reimbursements by parents and other persons and by the State.

(2) No county may be charged with the care and support of any minor who is not a resident of the county unless his parents or guardian are unknown or the minor's place of residence cannot be determined.

(3) No order upon the county for care and support of a minor may be entered until the president or chairman of the county board has had due notice that such a proceeding is pending.

(Source: P.A. 85-1235; 85-1443; 86-820.) [Formerly Ill. Rev. Stat. 37 §806-7.]

405/6-8. Orders on county for care and support.

§6-8. Orders on county for care and support. (1) Whenever a minor has been ordered held in detention or placed in shelter care under Sections 2-7, 3-9, 4-6 or 5-7 [705 ILCS 405/2-7, 405/3-9, 405/4-6 or 405/5-7], the court may order the county to make monthly payments from the fund established pursuant to Section 6-7 [705 ILCS 405/6-7] in an amount necessary for his care and support, but not for a period in excess of 90 days.

(2) Whenever a ward of the court is placed under Section 2-27, 3-28, 4-25 or 5-29 [705 ILCS 405/2-27, 405/3-28, 405/4-25 or 405/5-29], the court may order the county to make monthly payments from the fund established pursuant to Section 6-7 in an amount necessary for his care and support to the guardian of the person or legal custodian appointed under this Act, or to the agency which such guardian or custodian represents.

(3) The court may, when the health or condition of any minor subject to this Act requires it, order the minor placed in a public hospital, institution or agency for treatment or special care, or in a private hospital, institution or agency which will receive him without charge to the public authorities. If such treatment or care cannot be procured without charge, the court may order the county to pay an amount for such treatment from the fund established pursuant to Section 6-7. If the placement is to a hospital or institution, the amount to be paid shall not exceed that paid by the county department of public aid for the care of minors under like conditions, or, if an agency, not more than that established by the Department of Children and Family Services for the care of minors under like conditions. On like order, the county shall pay, from the fund established pursuant to Section 6-7, medical, surgical, dental, optical and other fees and expenses which the court finds are not within the usual scope of charges for the care and support of any minor provided for under this Section.

(Source: P.A. 85-1235; 85-1443; 86-820.) [Formerly Ill. Rev. Stat. 37 §806-8.]

405/6-9. Enforcement of liability of parents and others.

§6-9. Enforcement of liability of parents and others. (1) If parentage is at issue in any proceeding under this Act, the Illinois Parentage Act of 1984 [750 ILCS 45/1 et seq.] shall apply and the court shall enter orders consistent with that Act. If it appears at any hearing that a parent or any other person named in the petition, liable under the law for the support of the minor, is able to contribute to his support, the court shall enter an order requiring that parent or other person to pay the clerk of the court, or to the guardian or custodian appointed under Sections 2-27, 3-28, 4-25 or 5-29 [705 ILCS 405/2-27, 405/3-28, 405/4-25 or 405/5-29], a reasonable sum from time to time for the care, support and necessary special care or treatment, of the minor. The court may require reasonable security for the payments. Upon failure to pay, the court may enforce obedience to the order by a proceeding as for contempt of court. On application and with the notice as it may direct, the court may alter the payment or may compromise or waive arrearages in such a manner as appears reasonable and proper.

If it appears that the person liable for the support of the minor is able to contribute to legal fees for representation of the minor, the court shall enter an order requiring that person to pay a reasonable sum for the representation, to the attorney providing the representation or to the clerk of the court for deposit in the appropriate account or fund. The sum may be paid as the court directs, and the payment thereof secured and enforced as provided in this Section for support.

(2) When a person so ordered to pay for the care and support of a minor is employed for wages, salary or commission, the court may order him to make the support payments for which he is liable under this Act out of his wages, salary or commission and to assign so much thereof as will pay the support. The court may also order him to make discovery to the court as to his place of employment and the amounts earned by him. Upon his failure to obey the orders of court he may be punished as for contempt of court.

(3) If the minor is a recipient of public aid under the Illinois Public Aid Code [305 ILCS 5/1-1 et seq.], the court shall order that payments made by a parent or through assignment of his wages, salary or commission be made directly to (a) the Illinois Department of Public Aid if the minor is a recipient of aid under Articles IV or V of the Code [305 ILCS 5/4-1 et seq.], or (b) the local governmental unit responsible for the support of the minor if he is a recipient under Articles VI or VII of the Code [305 ILCS 5/6-1 et seq.]. The order shall permit the Illinois Department of Public Aid or the local governmental unit, as the case may be, to direct that subsequent payments be made directly to the guardian or custodian of the minor, or to some other person or agency in the minor's behalf, upon removal of the minor from the public aid rolls; and upon such direction and removal of the minor from the public aid rolls, the Illinois Department or local governmental unit, as the case requires, shall give written notice of such action to the court. Payments received by the Illinois Department of Public Aid or local governmental unit are to be covered, respectively, into the General Revenue Fund of the State Treasury or General Assistance Fund of the governmental unit, as provided in Section 10-19 of the Public Aid Code [305 ILCS 5/10-19].

(Source: P.A. 87-759.) [Formerly Ill. Rev. Stat. 37 §806-9.]

405/6-10. State reimbursement of funds.

§6-10. State reimbursement of funds. Before the 15th day of each month, the clerk of the court shall itemize all payments received by him under Section 6-9 [705 ILCS 405/6-9] during the preceding month and shall pay such amounts to the county treasurer. Before the 20th day of each month, the county treasurer shall file with the Department of Children and Family Services an itemized statement of the amount of money for the care and shelter of a minor placed in shelter care under Sections 2-7, 3-9, 4-6 or 5-7 [705 ILCS 405/2-7, 405/3-9, 405/4-6 or 405/5-7] or placed under Sections 2-27, 3-28, 4-25 or 5-29 [705 ILCS 405/2-27, 405/3-28, 405/4-25 or 405/5-29] before July 1, 1980 and after June 30, 1981, paid by the county during the last preceding month pursuant to court order entered under Section 6-8 [705 ILCS 405/6-8], certified by the court, and an itemized account of all payments received by the clerk of the court under Section 6-9 during the preceding month and paid over to the county treasurer, certified by the county treasurer. The Department of Children and Family Services shall examine and audit the monthly statement and account, and upon finding them correct, shall voucher for payment to the county a sum equal to the amount so paid out by the county less the amount received by the clerk of the court under Section 6-9 and paid to the county treasurer but not more than

an amount equal to the current average daily rate paid by the Department of Children and Family Services for similar services pursuant to Section 5a of "An Act creating the Department of Children and Family Services, codifying its powers and duties, and repealing certain Acts and Sections herein named", approved June 4, 1963, as amended [20 ILCS 505/5a]. Reimbursement to the counties under this Section for care and support of minors in licensed child caring institutions must be made by the Department of Children and Family Services only for care in those institutions which have filed with the Department a certificate affirming that they admit minors on the basis of need without regard to race or ethnic origin.
(Source: P.A. 85-601.) [Formerly Ill. Rev. Stat. 37 §806-10.]

405/6-11. Annual expenditures; limitation.

§6-11. Annual expenditures; limitation. Reimbursements under Section 6-10 [705 ILCS 405/6-10] for any fiscal year may not exceed 3% of the annual appropriation from the General Revenue Fund to the Department of Children and Family Services for its ordinary and contingent expenses for that fiscal year.
(Source: P.A. 85-601.) [Formerly Ill. Rev. Stat. 37 §806-11.]

ARTICLE VII. SAVINGS; REPEALER

405/7-1. Savings.

§7-1. Savings. Notwithstanding the repeal provided for in Section 7-2 [P.A. 85-601, Art. VII, §7-2]:

(1) Any offense under the provisions of the Act thereby repealed which has been committed before the effective date of this Act may be prosecuted and punished after the effective date hereof in accordance with the provisions of that Act.

(2) All civil proceedings instituted under the former Act and pending on the effective date hereof shall be considered and treated as pending under this Act and shall be conducted insofar as possible under the provisions of this Act, without the necessity of amending petitions or other papers filed therein, but to the extent considered appropriate by the court may be conducted under the provisions of the former Act.

(3) Every order of court made by authority of the former Act and in force immediately prior to the effective date hereof remains in force in accordance with its terms until modified or terminated by further order of the court.

(4) Probation districts made up of counties in more than one circuit, created under the former Act, may continue in existence for the remainder of the terms for which they were created, in accordance with the provisions of that Act.

(5) A child welfare tax authorized to be levied in any county under authority of the former Act, and not abandoned as provided in that Act, shall continue to be levied until abandoned in the manner provided in this Act.

(6) References to the former Act contained in other Acts in force on the effective date hereof shall whenever appropriate be considered to be references to this Act.
(Source: P.A. 85-601.) [Formerly Ill. Rev. Stat. 37 §807-1.]

This page intentionally left blank.

CHAPTER 720
CRIMINAL OFFENSES

CRIMINAL CODE OF 1961

TITLE I. GENERAL PROVISIONS

ARTICLE 1. TITLE AND CONSTRUCTION OF ACT; STATE JURISDICTION

5/1-1. Short title.

§1-1. Short title. This Act shall be known and may be cited as the "Criminal Code of 1961".

(Source: Laws 1961, p. 1983.) [Formerly Ill. Rev. Stat. 38 §1-1.]

5/1-2. General purposes.

§1-2. General purposes. The provisions of this Code shall be construed in accordance with the general purposes hereof, to:

(a) Forbid and prevent the commission of offenses;

(b) Define adequately the act and mental state which constitute each offense, and limit the condemnation of conduct as criminal when it is without fault;

(c) Prescribe penalties which are proportionate to the seriousness of offenses and which permit recognition of differences in rehabilitation possibilities among individual offenders;

(d) Prevent arbitrary or oppressive treatment of persons accused or convicted of offenses.

(Source: Laws 1961, p. 1983.) [Formerly Ill. Rev. Stat. 38 §1-2.]

5/1-3. Applicability of common law.

§1-3. Applicability of common law. No conduct constitutes an offense unless it is described as an offense in this Code or in another statute of this State. However, this provision does not affect the power of a court to punish for contempt or to employ any sanction authorized by law for the enforcement of an order or civil judgment.

(Source: P.A. 79-1360.) [Formerly Ill. Rev. Stat. 38 §1-3.]

5/1-4. Civil remedies preserved.

§1-4. Civil remedies preserved. This Code does not bar, suspend, or otherwise affect any right or liability to damages, penalty, forfeiture, or other remedy authorized by law to be recovered or enforced in a civil action, for any conduct which this Code makes punishable; and the civil injury is not merged in the offense.

(Source: Laws 1961, p. 1983.) [Formerly Ill. Rev. Stat. 38 §1-4.]

5/1-5. State criminal jurisdiction.

§1-5. State criminal jurisdiction. (a) A person is subject to prosecution in this State for an offense which he commits, while either within or outside the State, by his own conduct or that of another for which he is legally accountable, if:

(1) The offense is committed either wholly or partly within the State; or

(2) The conduct outside the State constitutes an attempt to commit an offense within the State; or

(3) The conduct outside the State constitutes a conspiracy to commit an offense within the State, and an act in furtherance of the conspiracy occurs in the State; or

(4) The conduct within the State constitutes an attempt, solicitation or conspiracy to commit in another jurisdiction an offense under the laws of both this State and such other jurisdiction.

(b) An offense is committed partly within this State, if either the conduct which is an element of the offense, or the result which is such an element, occurs within the State. In a prosecution pursuant to paragraph (3) of subsection (a) of Section 9-1, the attempt or commission of a forcible felony other than second degree murder within this State is conduct which is a* element of the offense for which a person is subject to prosecution in this State. In homicide, the "result" is either the physical contact which causes death, or the death itself; and if the body of a homicide victim is found within the State, the death is presumed to have occurred within the State.

**So in original. Probably should be "an".*

(c) An offense which is based on an omission to perform a duty imposed by the law of this State is committed within the State, regardless of the location of the offender at the time of the omission.

(Source: P.A. 85-740.) [Formerly Ill. Rev. Stat. 38 §1-5.]

5/1-6. Place of trial.

§1-6. Place of trial. (a) Generally.

Criminal actions shall be tried in the county where the offense was committed, except as otherwise provided by law. All objections of improper place of trial are waived by a defendant unless made before trial.

(b) Assailant and Victim in Different Counties.

If a person committing an offense upon the person of another is located in one county and his victim is located in another county at the time of the commission of the offense, trial may be had in either of said counties.

(c) Death and Cause of Death in Different Places or Undetermined.

If cause of death is inflicted in one county and death ensues in another county, the offender may be tried in either county. If neither the county in which the cause of death was inflicted nor the county in which death ensued are known before trial, the offender may be tried in the county where the body was found.

(d) Offense Commenced Outside the State.

If the commission of an offense commenced outside the State is consummated within this State, the offender shall be tried in the county where the offense is consummated.

(e) Offenses Committed in Bordering Navigable Waters.

If an offense is committed on any of the navigable waters bordering on this State, the offender may be tried in any county adjacent to such navigable water.

(f) Offenses Committed while in Transit.

If an offense is committed upon any railroad car, vehicle, watercraft or aircraft passing within this State, and it cannot readily be determined in which county the offense was committed, the offender may be tried in any county through which such railroad car, vehicle, watercraft or aircraft has passed.

(g) Theft.

A person who commits theft of property may be tried in any county in which he exerted control over such property.

(h) Bigamy.

A person who commits the offense of bigamy may be tried in any county where the bigamous marriage or bigamous cohabitation has occurred.

(i) Kidnaping.

A person who commits the offense of kidnaping may be tried in any county in which his victim has traveled or has been confined during the course of the offense.

(j) Pandering.

A person who commits the offense of pandering may be tried in any county in which the prostitution was practiced or in any county in which any act in furtherance of the offense shall have been committed.

(k) Treason.

A person who commits the offense of treason may be tried in any county.

(*l*) Criminal Defamation.

If criminal defamation is spoken, printed or written in one county and is received or circulated in another or other counties, the offender shall be tried in the county where the defamation is spoken, printed or written. If the defamation is spoken, printed or written outside this state, or the offender resides outside this state, the offender may be tried in any county in this state in which the defamation was circulated or received.

(m) Inchoate Offenses.

A person who commits an inchoate offense may be tried in any county in which any act which is an element of the offense, including the agreement in conspiracy, is committed.

(n) Accountability for Conduct of Another.

Where a person in one county solicits, aids, abets, agrees, or attempts to aid another in the planning or commission of an offense in another county, he may be tried for the offense in either county.

(*o*) Child Abduction.

A person who commits the offense of child abduction may be tried in any county in which his victim has traveled, been detained, concealed or removed to during the course of the offense. Notwithstanding the foregoing, unless for good cause shown, the preferred place of trial shall be the county of the residence of the lawful custodian.

(p) A person who commits the offense of narcotics racketeering may be tried in any county where cannabis or a controlled substance which is the basis for the charge of narcotics racketeering was used; acquired; transferred or distributed to, from or through; or any county where any act was performed to further the use; acquisition, transfer or distribution of said cannabis or controlled substance; any money, property, property interest, or any other asset generated by narcotics activities was acquired, used, sold, transferred or distributed to, from or through; or, any enterprise interest obtained as a result of narcotics racketeering was acquired, used, transferred or distributed to, from or through, or where any activity was conducted by the enterprise or any conduct to further the interests of such an enterprise.

(q) A person who commits the offense of money laundering may be tried in any county where any part of a financial transaction in criminally derived property took place or in any county where any money or monetary instrument which is the basis for the offense was acquired, used, sold, transferred or distributed to, from or through.

(r) A person who commits the offense of cannabis trafficking or controlled substance trafficking may be tried in any county.

(Source: P.A. 87-466.) [Formerly Ill. Rev. Stat. 38 §1-6.]

5/1-8. Order of protection; status.

§1-8. Order of protection; status. Whenever relief sought under this Code is based on allegations of domestic violence, as defined in the Illinois Domestic Violence Act of 1986 [750 ILCS 60/101 et seq.], the court, before granting relief, shall determine whether any order of protection has previously been entered in the instant proceeding or any other proceeding in which any party, or a child

of any party, or both, if relevant, has been designated as either a respondent or a protected person.
(Source: P.A. 87-743.) [Formerly Ill. Rev. Stat. 38 §1-8.]

ARTICLE 2. GENERAL DEFINITIONS

5/2-.5. Definitions of words and phrases.

§2-.5. For the purposes of this Code, the words and phrases described in this Article have the meanings designated in this Article, except when a particular context clearly requires a different meaning.
(Source: Laws 1961, p. 1983.) [Formerly Ill. Rev. Stat. 38 §2-.5.]

5/2-1. "Acquittal".

§2-1. "Acquittal". "Acquittal" means a verdict or finding of not guilty of an offense, rendered by a legally constituted jury or by a court of competent jurisdiction authorized to try the case without a jury.
(Source: Laws 1961, p. 1983.) [Formerly Ill. Rev. Stat. 38 §2-1.]

5/2-2. "Act".

§2-2. "Act". "Act" includes a failure or omission to take action.
(Source: Laws 1961, p. 1983.) [Formerly Ill. Rev. Stat. 38 §2-2.]

5/2-3. "Another".

§2-3. "Another". "Another" means a person or persons as defined in this Code other than the offender.
(Source: Laws 1961, p. 1983.) [Formerly Ill. Rev. Stat. 38 §2-3.]

5/2-4. "Conduct".

§2-4. "Conduct". "Conduct" means an act or a series of acts, and the accompanying mental state.
(Source: Laws 1961, p. 1983.) [Formerly Ill. Rev. Stat. 38 §2-4.]

5/2-5. "Conviction".

§2-5. "Conviction". "Conviction" means a judgment of conviction or sentence entered upon a plea of guilty or upon a verdict or finding of guilty of an offense,

rendered by a legally constituted jury or by a court of competent jurisdiction authorized to try the case without a jury.
(Source: Laws 1961, p. 1983.) [Formerly Ill. Rev. Stat. 38 §2-5.]

5/2-6. "Dwelling".

§2-6. "Dwelling". (a) Except as otherwise provided in subsection (b) of this Section, "dwelling" means a building or portion thereof, a tent, a vehicle, or other enclosed space which is used or intended for use as a human habitation, home or residence.

(b) For the purposes of Section 19-3 of this Code, "dwelling" means a house, apartment, mobile home, trailer, or other living quarters in which at the time of the alleged offense the owners or occupants actually reside or in their absence intend within a reasonable period of time to reside.
(Source: P.A. 84-1289.) [Formerly Ill. Rev. Stat. 38 §2-6.]

5/2-7. "Felony".

§2-7. "Felony". "Felony" means an offense for which a sentence to death or to a term of imprisonment in a penitentiary for one year or more is provided.
(Source: P.A. 77-2638.) [Formerly Ill. Rev. Stat. 38 §2-7.]

5/2-8. "Forcible felony".

§2-8. "Forcible felony". "Forcible felony" means treason, first degree murder, second degree murder, aggravated criminal sexual assault, criminal sexual assault, robbery, burglary, arson, aggravated kidnaping, kidnaping, aggravated battery resulting in great bodily harm or permanent disability or disfigurement and any other felony which involves the use or threat of physical force or violence against any individual.
(Source: P.A. 85-1447; 86-291.) [Formerly Ill. Rev. Stat. 38 §2-8.]

5/2-9. "Included offense".

§2-9. "Included offense". "Included offense" means an offense which

(a) Is established by proof of the same or less than all of the facts or a less culpable mental state (or both), than that which is required to establish the commission of the offense charged, or

(b) Consists of an attempt to commit the offense charged or an offense included therein.
(Source: Laws 1961, p. 1983.) [Formerly Ill. Rev. Stat. 38 §2-9.]

5/2-10. "Includes".

§2-10. "Includes". "Includes" or "including" means comprehending among other particulars, without limiting the generality of the foregoing word or phrase.
(Source: Laws 1961, p. 1983.) [Formerly Ill. Rev. Stat. 38 §2-10.]

5/2-10.1. "Institutionalized severely or profoundly mentally retarded person".

§2-10.1. "Institutionalized severely or profoundly mentally retarded person" means a person who is institutionalized in a developmental disability facility, nursing home facility, or long term care facility and either (i) the person's intelligence quotient does not exceed 40 or (ii) the person's intelligence quotient does not exceed 55 and the person suffers from significant mental illness to the extent that the person's ability to exercise rational judgment is impaired. In any proceeding in which the defendant is charged with committing a violation of Section 10-2, 10-5, 11-15.1, 11-19.1, 11-19.2, 11-20.1, 12-4.3, 12-14, or 12-16 of this Code against a victim who is alleged to be an institutionalized severely or profoundly mentally retarded person, any findings concerning the victim's status as an institutionalized severely or profoundly mentally retarded person, made by a court after a judicial admission hearing concerning the victim under

Articles V and VI of Chapter 4 of the Mental Health and Developmental Disabilities Code [405 ILCS 5/4-500 et seq.] shall be admissible.
(Chgd. by P.A. 87-1198, §2, eff. 9/25/92.)
(Source: P.A. 85-1392.) [Formerly Ill. Rev. Stat. 38 §2-10.1.]

5/2-11. "Misdemeanor".

§2-11. "Misdemeanor". "Misdemeanor" means any offense for which a sentence to a term of imprisonment in other than a penitentiary for less than one year may be imposed.
(Source: P. A. 77-2638.) [Formerly Ill. Rev. Stat. 38 §2-11.]

5/2-12. "Offense".

§2-12. "Offense". "Offense" means a violation of any penal statute of this State.
(Source: Laws 1961, p. 1983.) [Formerly Ill. Rev. Stat. 38 §2-12.]

5/2-13. "Peace officer".

§2-13. "Peace officer". "Peace officer" means any person who by virtue of his office or public employment is vested by law with a duty to maintain public order or to make arrests for offenses, whether that duty extends to all offenses or is limited to specific offenses.

For purposes of Sections concerning unlawful use of weapons, officers, agents or employees of the federal government commissioned by federal statute to make arrests for violations of federal criminal laws shall be considered "peace officers" under this Code, including, but not limited to all criminal investigators of:

(1) The United States Department of Justice, The Federal Bureau of Investigation, The Drug Enforcement Agency and The Department of Immigration and Naturalization;

(2) The United States Department of the Treasury, The Secret Service, The Bureau of Alcohol, Tobacco and Firearms and The Customs Service;

(3) The United States Internal Revenue Service;

(4) The United States General Services Administration;

(5) The United States Postal Service; and

(6) all United States Marshalls or Deputy United States Marshalls whose duties involve the enforcement of federal criminal laws.
(Source: P.A. 84-906.) [Formerly Ill. Rev. Stat. 38 §2-13.]

5/2-14. "Penal institution".

§2-14. "Penal institution". "Penal institution" means a penitentiary, state farm, reformatory, prison, jail, house of correction, or other institution for the incarceration or custody of persons under sentence for offenses or awaiting trial or sentence for offenses.
(Source: Laws 1961, p. 1983.) [Formerly Ill. Rev. Stat. 38 §2-14.]

5/2-15. "Person".

§2-15. "Person". "Person" means an individual, public or private corporation, government, partnership, or unincorporated association.
(Source: Laws 1961, p. 1983.) [Formerly Ill. Rev. Stat. 38 §2-15.]

5/2-15a. "Physically handicapped person".

§2-15a. "Physically handicapped person". "Physically handicapped person" means a person who suffers from a permanent and disabling physical characteristic, resulting from disease, injury, functional disorder, or congenital condition.
(Source: P.A. 85-691.) [Formerly Ill. Rev. Stat. 38 §2-15a.]

5/2-16. "Prosecution".

§2-16. "Prosecution". "Prosecution" means all legal proceedings by which a person's liability for an offense is determined, commencing with the return of

the indictment or the issuance of the information, and including the final disposition of the case upon appeal.
(Source: Laws 1961, p. 1983.) [Formerly Ill. Rev. Stat. 38 §2-16.]

5/2-17. "Public employee".
§2-17. "Public employee". "Public employee" means a person, other than a public officer, who is authorized to perform any official function on behalf of, and is paid by, the State or any of its political subdivisions.
(Source: Laws 1961, p. 1983.) [Formerly Ill. Rev. Stat. 38 §2-17.]

5/2-18. "Public officer".
§2-18. "Public officer". "Public officer" means a person who is elected to office pursuant to statute, or who is appointed to an office which is established, and the qualifications and duties of which are prescribed, by statute, to discharge a public duty for the State or any of its political subdivisions.
(Source: Laws 1961, p. 1983.) [Formerly Ill. Rev. Stat. 38 §2-18.]

5/2-19. "Reasonable belief".
§2-19. "Reasonable belief". "Reasonable belief" or "reasonably believes" means that the person concerned, acting as a reasonable man, believes that the described facts exist.
(Source: Laws 1961, p. 1983.) [Formerly Ill. Rev. Stat. 38 §2-19.]

5/2-20. "Solicit".
§2-20. "Solicit". "Solicit" or "solicitation" means to command, authorize, urge, incite, request, or advise another to commit an offense.
(Source: Laws 1961, p. 1983.) [Formerly Ill. Rev. Stat. 38 §2-20.]

5/2-21. "State".
§2-21. "State". "State" or "this State" means the State of Illinois, and all land and water in respect to which the State of Illinois has either exclusive or concurrent jurisdiction, and the air space above such land and water. "Other state" means any state or territory of the United States, the District of Columbia and the Commonwealth of Puerto Rico.
(Source: Laws 1961, p. 1983.) [Formerly Ill. Rev. Stat. 38 §2-21.]

5/2-22. "Statute".
§2-22. "Statute". "Statute" means the Constitution or an Act of the General Assembly of this State.
(Source: Laws 1961, p. 1983.) [Formerly Ill. Rev. Stat. 38 §2-22.]

ARTICLE 3. RIGHTS OF DEFENDANT

5/3-1. Presumption of innocence and proof of guilt.
§3-1. Presumption of innocence and proof of guilt. Every person is presumed innocent until proved guilty. No person shall be convicted of any offense unless his guilt thereof is proved beyond a reasonable doubt.
(Source: Laws 1961, p. 1983.) [Formerly Ill. Rev. Stat. 38 §3-1.]

5/3-2. Affirmative defense.

§3-2. Affirmative defense. (a) "Affirmative defense" means that unless the State's evidence raises the issue involving the alleged defense, the defendant, to raise the issue, must present some evidence thereon.

(b) If the issue involved in an affirmative defense, other than insanity, is raised then the State must sustain the burden of proving the defendant guilty beyond a reasonable doubt as to that issue together with all the other elements of the offense. If the affirmative defense of insanity is raised, the defendant bears the burden of proving by a preponderance of evidence his insanity at the time of the offense.

(Source: P.A. 83-288.) [Formerly Ill. Rev. Stat. 38 §3-2.]

5/3-3. Multiple prosecutions for same act.

§3-3. Multiple prosecutions for same act. (a) When the same conduct of a defendant may establish the commission of more than one offense, the defendant may be prosecuted for each such offense.

(b) If the several offenses are known to the proper prosecuting officer at the time of commencing the prosecution and are within the jurisdiction of a single court, they must be prosecuted in a single prosecution, except as provided in Subsection (c), if they are based on the same act.

(c) When 2 or more offenses are charged as required by Subsection (b), the court in the interest of justice may order that one or more of such charges shall be tried separately.

(Source: Laws 1961, p. 1983.) [Formerly Ill. Rev. Stat. 38 §3-3.]

5/3-4. Effect of former prosecution.

§3-4. Effect of former prosecution. (a) A prosecution is barred if the defendant was formerly prosecuted for the same offense, based upon the same facts, if such former prosecution:

(1) Resulted in either a conviction or an acquittal or in a determination that the evidence was insufficient to warrant a conviction; or

(2) Was terminated by a final order or judgment, even if entered before trial, which required a determination inconsistent with any fact or legal proposition necessary to a conviction in the subsequent prosecution; or

(3) Was terminated improperly after the jury was impaneled and sworn or, in a trial before a court without a jury, after the first witness was sworn but before findings were rendered by the trier of facts, or after a plea of guilty was accepted by the court.

A conviction of an included offense is an acquittal of the offense charged.

(b) A prosecution is barred if the defendant was formerly prosecuted for a different offense, or for the same offense based upon different facts, if such former prosecution:

(1) Resulted in either a conviction or an acquittal, and the subsequent prosecution is for an offense of which the defendant could have been convicted on the former prosecution; or was for an offense with which the defendant should have been charged on the former prosecution, as provided in Section 3-3 of this Code (unless the court ordered a separate trial of such charge); or was for an offense which involves the same conduct, unless each prosecution requires proof of a fact not required on the other prosecution, or the offense was not consummated when the former trial began; or

(2) Was terminated by a final order or judgment, even if entered before trial, which required a determination inconsistent with any fact necessary to a conviction in the subsequent prosecution; or

(3) Was terminated improperly under the circumstances stated in Subsection (a), and the subsequent prosecution is for an offense of which the defendant

could have been convicted if the former prosecution had not been terminated improperly.

(c) A prosecution is barred if the defendant was formerly prosecuted in a District Court of the United States or in a sister State for an offense which is within the concurrent jurisdiction of this State, if such former prosecution:

(1) Resulted in either a conviction or an acquittal, and the subsequent prosecution is for the same conduct, unless each prosecution requires proof of a fact not required in the other prosecution, or the offense was not consummated when the former trial began; or

(2) Was terminated by a final order or judgment, even if entered before trial, which required a determination inconsistent with any fact necessary to a conviction in the prosecution in this State.

(d) However, a prosecution is not barred within the meaning of this Section 3-4 if the former prosecution:

(1) Was before a court which lacked jurisdiction over the defendant or the offense; or

(2) Was procured by the defendant without the knowledge of the proper prosecuting officer, and with the purpose of avoiding the sentence which otherwise might be imposed; or if subsequent proceedings resulted in the invalidation, setting aside, reversal, or vacating of the conviction, unless the defendant was thereby adjudged not guilty.

(Source: Laws 1961, p. 1983.) [Formerly Ill. Rev. Stat. 38 §3-4.]

5/3-5. General limitations.

§3-5. General Limitations. (a) A prosecution for first degree murder, second degree murder, involuntary manslaughter, reckless homicide, treason, arson, or forgery may be commenced at any time.

(b) Unless the statute describing the offense provides otherwise, or the period of limitation is extended by Section 3-6, a prosecution for any offense not designated in Subsection (a) must be commenced within 3 years after the commission of the offense if it is a felony, or within one year and 6 months after its commission if it is a misdemeanor.

(Source: P.A. 85-636; 85-673.) [Formerly Ill. Rev. Stat. 38 §3-5.]

5/3-6. Extended limitations.

§3-6. Extended limitations. The period within which a prosecution must be commenced under the provisions of Section 3-5 or other applicable statute is extended under the following conditions:

(a) A prosecution for theft involving a breach of a fiduciary obligation to the aggrieved person may be commenced as follows:

(1) If the aggrieved person is a minor or a person under legal disability, then during the minority or legal disability or within one year after the termination thereof.

(2) In any other instance, within one year after the discovery of the offense by an aggrieved person, or by a person who has legal capacity to represent an aggrieved person or has a legal duty to report the offense, and is not himself or herself a party to the offense; or in the absence of such discovery, within one year after the proper prosecuting officer becomes aware of the offense. However, in no such case is the period of limitation so extended more than 3 years beyond the expiration of the period otherwise applicable.

(b) A prosecution for any offense based upon misconduct in office by a public officer or employee may be commenced within one year after discovery of the offense by a person having a legal duty to report such offense, or in the absence of such discovery, within one year after the proper prosecuting officer becomes aware of the offense. However, in no such case is the period of limitation so extended more than 3 years beyond the expiration of the period otherwise applicable.

(c) A prosecution for any offense involving sexual conduct or sexual penetration, as defined in Section 12-12 of this Code, where the victim and defendant are family members, as defined in Section 12-12 of this Code, may be commenced within one year of the victim attaining the age of 18 years.

(d) A prosecution for child pornography, indecent solicitation of a child, soliciting for a juvenile prostitute, juvenile pimping or exploitation of a child may be commenced within one year of the victim attaining the age of 18 years. However, in no such case shall the time period for prosecution expire sooner than 3 years after the commission of the offense. When the victim is under 18 years of age, a prosecution for criminal sexual assault, aggravated criminal sexual assault, criminal sexual abuse or aggravated criminal sexual abuse may be commenced within one year of the victim attaining the age of 18 years. However, in no such case shall the time period for prosecution expire sooner than 3 years after the commission of the offense.

(e) A prosecution for any offense involving sexual conduct or sexual penetration, as defined in Section 12-12 of this Code, where the defendant was within a professional or fiduciary relationship or a purported professional or fiduciary relationship with the victim at the time of the commission of the offense may be commenced within one year after the discovery of the offense by the victim.

(f) A prosecution for any offense set forth in Section 44 of the "Environmental Protection Act", approved June 29, 1970, as amended [415 ILCS 5/44], may be commenced within 5 years after the discovery of such an offense by a person or agency having the legal duty to report the offense or in the absence of such discovery, within 5 years after the proper prosecuting officer becomes aware of the offense.

(Source: P.A. 85-1344.) [Formerly Ill. Rev. Stat. 38 §3-6.]

5/3-7. Periods excluded from limitation.

§3-7. Periods excluded from limitation. The period within which a prosecution must be commenced does not include any period in which:

(a) The defendant is not usually and publicly resident within this State; or

(b) The defendant is a public officer and the offense charged is theft of public funds while in public office; or

(c) A prosecution is pending against the defendant for the same conduct, even if the indictment or information which commences the prosecution is quashed or the proceedings thereon are set aside, or are reversed on appeal.

(Source: Laws 1961, p. 1983.) [Formerly Ill. Rev. Stat. 38 §3-7.]

5/3-8. Limitation on offense based on series of acts.

§3-8. Limitation on offense based on series of acts. When an offense is based on a series of acts performed at different times, the period of limitation prescribed by this Article starts at the time when the last such act is committed.

(Source: Laws 1961, p. 1983.) [Formerly Ill. Rev. Stat. 38 §3-8.]

TITLE II. PRINCIPLES OF CRIMINAL LIABILITY

ARTICLE 4. CRIMINAL ACT AND MENTAL STATE

5/4-1. Voluntary act.

§4-1. Voluntary act. A material element of every offense is a voluntary act, which includes an omission to perform a duty which the law imposes on the offender and which he is physically capable of performing.
(Source: Laws 1961, p. 1983.) [Formerly Ill. Rev. Stat. 38 §4-1.]

5/4-2. Possession as voluntary act.

§4-2. Possession as voluntary act. Possession is a voluntary act if the offender knowingly procured or received the thing possessed, or was aware of his control thereof for a sufficient time to have been able to terminate his possession.
(Source: Laws 1961, p. 1983.) [Formerly Ill. Rev. Stat. 38 §4-2.]

5/4-3. Mental state.

§4-3. Mental state. (a) A person is not guilty of an offense, other than an offense which involves absolute liability, unless, with respect to each element described by the statute defining the offense, he acts while having one of the mental states described in Sections 4-4 through 4-7.

(b) If the statute defining an offense prescribed a particular mental state with respect to the offense as a whole, without distinguishing among the elements thereof, the prescribed mental state applies to each such element. If the statute does not prescribe a particular mental state applicable to an element of an offense (other than an offense which involves absolute liability), any mental state defined in Sections 4-4, 4-5 or 4-6 is applicable.

(c) Knowledge that certain conduct constitutes an offense, or knowledge of the existence, meaning, or application of the statute defining an offense, is not an element of the offense unless the statute clearly defines it as such.
(Source: Laws 1961, p. 1983.) [Formerly Ill. Rev. Stat. 38 §4-3.]

5/4-4. Intent.

§4-4. Intent. A person intends, or acts intentionally or with intent, to accomplish a result or engage in conduct described by the statute defining the offense, when his conscious objective or purpose is to accomplish that result or engage in that conduct.
(Source: Laws 1961, p. 1983.) [Formerly Ill. Rev. Stat. 38 §4-4.]

5/4-5. Knowledge.

§4-5. Knowledge. A person knows, or acts knowingly or with knowledge of:

(a) The nature or attendant circumstances of his conduct, described by the statute defining the offense, when he is consciously aware that his conduct is of such nature or that such circumstances exist. Knowledge of a material fact includes awareness of the substantial probability that such fact exists.

(b) The result of his conduct, described by the statute defining the offense, when he is consciously aware that such result is practically certain to be caused by his conduct.

Conduct performed knowingly or with knowledge is performed wilfully, within the meaning of a statute using the latter term, unless the statute clearly requires another meaning.
(Source: Laws 1961, p. 1983.) [Formerly Ill. Rev. Stat. 38 §4-5.]

5/4-6. Recklessness.

§4-6. Recklessness. A person is reckless or acts recklessly, when he consciously disregards a substantial and unjustifiable risk that circumstances exist or that a result will follow, described by the statute defining the offense; and such disregard constitutes a gross deviation from the standard of care which a

reasonable person would exercise in the situation. An act performed recklessly is performed wantonly, within the meaning of a statute using the latter term, unless the statute clearly requires another meaning.
(Source: Laws 1961, p. 1983.) [Formerly Ill. Rev. Stat. 38 §4-6.]

5/4-7. Negligence.

§4-7. Negligence. A person is negligent, or acts negligently, when he fails to be aware of a substantial and unjustifiable risk that circumstances exist or a result will follow, described by the statute defining the offense; and such failure constitutes a substantial deviation from the standard of care which a reasonable person would exercise in the situation.
(Source: Laws 1961, p. 1983.) [Formerly Ill. Rev. Stat. 38 §4-7.]

5/4-8. Ignorance or mistake.

§4-8. Ignorance or mistake. (a) A person's ignorance or mistake as to a matter of either fact or law, except as provided in Section 4-3(c) above, is a defense if it negatives the existence of the mental state which the statute prescribes with respect to an element of the offense.

(b) A person's reasonable belief that his conduct does not constitute an offense is a defense if:

(1) The offense is defined by an administrative regulation or order which is not known to him and has not been published or otherwise made reasonably available to him, and he could not have acquired such knowledge by the exercise of due diligence pursuant to facts known to him; or

(2) He acts in reliance upon a statute which later is determined to be invalid; or

(3) He acts in reliance upon an order or opinion of an Illinois Appellate or Supreme Court, or a United States appellate court later overruled or reversed;

(4) He acts in reliance upon an official interpretation of the statute, regulation or order defining the offense, made by a public officer or agency legally authorized to interpret such statute.

(c) Although a person's ignorance or mistake of fact or law, or reasonable belief, described in this Section 4-8 is a defense to the offense charged, he may be convicted of an included offense of which he would be guilty if the fact or law were as he believed it to be.

(d) A defense based upon this Section 4-8 is an affirmative defense.
(Source: Laws 1961, p. 1983.) [Formerly Ill. Rev. Stat. 38 §4-8.]

5/4-9. Absolute liability.

§4-9. Absolute liability. A person may be guilty of an offense without having, as to each element thereof, one of the mental states described in Sections 4-4 through 4-7 if the offense is a misdemeanor which is not punishable by incarceration or by a fine exceeding $500, or the statute defining the offense clearly indicates a legislative purpose to impose absolute liability for the conduct described.
(Source: Laws 1961, p. 1983.) [Formerly Ill. Rev. Stat. 38 §4-9.]

ARTICLE 5. PARTIES TO CRIME

Sec.

5/5-1. Accountability for conduct of another.

§5-1. Accountability for conduct of another. A person is responsible for conduct which is an element of an offense if the conduct is either that of the person himself, or that of another and he is legally accountable for such conduct as provided in Section 5-2, or both.

(Source: Laws 1961, p. 1983.) [Formerly Ill. Rev. Stat. 38 §5-1.]

5/5-2. When accountability exists.

§5-2. When accountability exists. A person is legally accountable for the conduct of another when:

(a) Having a mental state described by the statute defining the offense, he causes another to perform the conduct, and the other person in fact or by reason of legal incapacity lacks such a mental state; or

(b) The statute defining the offense makes him so accountable; or

(c) Either before or during the commission of an offense, and with the intent to promote or facilitate such commission, he solicits, aids, abets, agrees or attempts to aid, such other person in the planning or commission of the offense. However, a person is not so accountable, unless the statute defining the offense provides otherwise, if:

(1) He is a victim of the offense committed; or

(2) The offense is so defined that his conduct was inevitably incident to its commission; or

(3) Before the commission of the offense, he terminates his effort to promote or facilitate such commission, and does one of the following: wholly deprives his prior efforts of effectiveness in such commission, or gives timely warning to the proper law enforcement authorities, or otherwise makes proper effort to prevent the commission of the offense.

(Source: Laws 1961, p. 1983.) [Formerly Ill. Rev. Stat. 38 §5-2.]

5/5-3. Separate conviction of person accountable.

§5-3. Separate conviction of person accountable. A person who is legally accountable for the conduct of another which is an element of an offense may be convicted upon proof that the offense was committed and that he was so accountable, although the other person claimed to have committed the offense has not been prosecuted or convicted, or has been convicted of a different offense or degree of offense, or is not amenable to justice, or has been acquitted.

(Source: Laws 1961, p. 1983.) [Formerly Ill. Rev. Stat. 38 §5-3.]

5/5-4. Responsibility of corporation.

§5-4. Responsibility of corporation. (a) A corporation may be prosecuted for the commission of an offense if, but only if:

(1) The offense is a misdemeanor, or is defined by Sections 11-20, 11-20.1 or 24-1 of this Code, or Section 44 of the "Environmental Protection Act", approved June 29, 1970, as amended [415 ILCS 5/44] or is defined by another statute which clearly indicates a legislative purpose to impose liability on a corporation; and an agent of the corporation performs the conduct which is an element of the offense while acting within the scope of his or her office or employment and in behalf of the corporation, except that any limitation in the defining statute, concerning the corporation's accountability for certain agents or under certain circumstances, is applicable; or

(2) The commission of the offense is authorized, requested, commanded, or performed, by the board of directors or by a high managerial agent who is acting within the scope of his or her employment in behalf of the corporation.

(b) A corporation's proof, by a preponderance of the evidence, that the high managerial agent having supervisory responsibility over the conduct which is the subject matter of the offense exercised due diligence to prevent the commission of the offense, is a defense to a prosecution for any offense to which Subsection (a) (1) refers, other than an offense for which absolute liability is imposed. This Subsection is inapplicable if the legislative purpose of the statute defining the offense is inconsistent with the provisions of this Subsection.

(c) For the purpose of this Section:

(1) "Agent" means any director, officer, servant, employee, or other person who is authorized to act in behalf of the corporation.

(2) "High managerial agent" means an officer of the corporation, or any other agent who has a position of comparable authority for the formulation of corporate policy or the supervision of subordinate employees in a managerial capacity.

(Source: P.A. 85-1440.) [Formerly Ill. Rev. Stat. 38 §5-4.]

5/5-5. Accountability for conduct of corporation.

§5-5. Accountability for conduct of corporation. (a) A person is legally accountable for conduct which is an element of an offense and which, in the name or in behalf of a corporation, he performs or causes to be performed, to the same extent as if the conduct were performed in his own name or behalf.

(b) An individual who has been convicted of an offense by reason of his legal accountability for the conduct of a corporation is subject to the punishment authorized by law for an individual upon conviction of such offense, although only a lesser or different punishment is authorized for the corporation.

(Source: Laws 1961, p. 1983.) [Formerly Ill. Rev. Stat. 38 §5-5.]

ARTICLE 6. RESPONSIBILITY

Sec.

5/6-1. Infancy.

§6-1. Infancy. No person shall be convicted of any offense unless he had attained his 13th birthday at the time the offense was committed.

(Source: Laws 1961, p. 1983.) [Formerly Ill. Rev. Stat. 38 §6-1.]

5/6-2. Insanity.

§6-2. Insanity. (a) A person is not criminally responsible for conduct if at the time of such conduct, as a result of mental disease or mental defect, he lacks substantial capacity either to appreciate the criminality of his conduct or to conform his conduct to the requirements of law.

(b) The terms "mental disease or mental defect" do not include an abnormality manifested only by repeated criminal or otherwise antisocial conduct.

(c) A person who, at the time of the commission of a criminal offense, was not insane but was suffering from a mental illness, is not relieved of criminal responsibility for his conduct and may be found guilty but mentally ill.

(d) For purposes of this Section, "mental illness" or "mentally ill" means a substantial disorder of thought, mood, or behavior which afflicted a person at the time of the commission of the offense and which impaired that person's judgment, but not to the extent that he is unable to appreciate the wrongfulness of his behavior or is unable to conform his conduct to the requirements of law.

(e) When the defense of insanity has been presented during the trial, the burden of proof is on the defendant to prove by a preponderance of the evidence that the defendant is not guilty by reason of insanity. However, the burden of proof remains on the State to prove beyond a reasonable doubt each of the elements of each of the offenses charged, and, in a jury trial where the insanity defense has been presented, the jury must be instructed that it may not consider

whether the defendant has met his burden of proving that he is not guilty by reason of insanity until and unless it has first determined that the State has proven the defendant guilty beyond a reasonable doubt of the offense with which he is charged.
(Source: P.A. 83-288.) [Formerly Ill. Rev. Stat. 38 §6-2.]

5/6-3. Intoxicated or drugged condition.

§6-3. Intoxicated or drugged condition. A person who is in an intoxicated or drugged condition is criminally responsible for conduct unless such condition either:

(a) Is so extreme as to suspend the power of reason and render him incapable of forming a specific intent which is an element of the offense; or

(b) Is involuntarily produced and deprives him of substantial capacity either to appreciate the criminality of his conduct or to conform his conduct to the requirements of law.
(Source: P.A. 85-670.) [Formerly Ill. Rev. Stat. 38 §6-3.]

5/6-4. Affirmative defense.

§6-4. Affirmative Defense. A defense based upon any of the provisions of Article 6 is an affirmative defense except that mental illness is not an affirmative defense, but an alternative plea or finding that may be accepted, under appropriate evidence, when the affirmative defense of insanity is raised or the plea of guilty but mentally ill is made.
(Source: P.A. 82-553.) [Formerly Ill. Rev. Stat. 38 §6-4.]

ARTICLE 7. JUSTIFIABLE USE OF FORCE; EXONERATION

5/7-1. Use of force in defense of person.

§7-1. Use of force in defense of person. A person is justified in the use of force against another when and to the extent that he reasonably believes that such conduct is necessary to defend himself or another against such other's imminent use of unlawful force. However, he is justified in the use of force which is intended or likely to cause death or great bodily harm only if he reasonably believes that such force is necessary to prevent imminent death or great bodily harm to himself or another, or the commission of a forcible felony.
(Source: Laws 1961, p. 1983.) [Formerly Ill. Rev. Stat. 38 §7-1.]

5/7-2. Use of force in defense of dwelling.

§7-2. Use of force in defense of dwelling. A person is justified in the use of force against another when and to the extent that he reasonably believes that such conduct is necessary to prevent or terminate such other's unlawful entry into or attack upon a dwelling. However, he is justified in the use of force which is intended or likely to cause death or great bodily harm only if:

(a) The entry is made or attempted in a violent, riotous, or tumultuous manner, and he reasonably believes that such force is necessary to prevent an assault upon, or offer of personal violence to, him or another then in the dwelling, or

(b) He reasonably believes that such force is necessary to prevent the commission of a felony in the dwelling.

(Source: Laws 1967, p. 696.) [Formerly Ill. Rev. Stat. 38 §7-2.]

5/7-3. Use of force in defense of other property.

§7-3. Use of force in defense of other property. A person is justified in the use of force against another when and to the extent that he reasonably believes that such conduct is necessary to prevent or terminate such other's trespass on or other tortious or criminal interference with either real property (other than a dwelling) or personal property, lawfully in his possession or in the possession of another who is a member of his immediate family or household or of a person whose property he has a legal duty to protect. However, he is justified in the use of force which is intended or likely to cause death or great bodily harm only if he reasonably believes that such force is necessary to prevent the commission of a forcible felony.

(Source: Laws 1961, p. 1983.) [Formerly Ill. Rev. Stat. 38 §7-3.]

5/7-4. Use of force by aggressor.

§7-4. Use of force by aggressor. The justification described in the preceding Sections of this Article is not available to a person who:

(a) Is attempting to commit, committing, or escaping after the commission of, a forcible felony; or

(b) Initially provokes the use of force against himself, with the intent to use such force as an excuse to inflict bodily harm upon the assailant; or

(c) Otherwise initially provokes the use of force against himself, unless:

(1) Such force is so great that he reasonably believes that he is in imminent danger of death or great bodily harm, and that he has exhausted every reasonable means to escape such danger other than the use of force which is likely to cause death or great bodily harm to the assailant; or

(2) In good faith, he withdraws from physical contact with the assailant and indicates clearly to the assailant that he desires to withdraw and terminate the use of force, but the assailant continues or resumes the use of force.

(Source: Laws 1961, p. 1983.) [Formerly Ill. Rev. Stat. 38 §7-4.]

5/7-5. Peace officer's use of force in making arrest.

§7-5. Peace officer's use of force in making arrest. (a) A peace officer, or any person whom he has summoned or directed to assist him, need not retreat or desist from efforts to make a lawful arrest because of resistance or threatened resistance to the arrest. He is justified in the use of any force which he reasonably believes to be necessary to effect the arrest and of any force which he reasonably believes to be necessary to defend himself or another from bodily harm while making the arrest. However, he is justified in using force likely to cause death or great bodily harm only when he reasonably believes that such force is necessary to prevent death or great bodily harm to himself or such other person, or when he reasonably believes both that:

(1) Such force is necessary to prevent the arrest from being defeated by resistance or escape; and

(2) The person to be arrested has committed or attempted a forcible felony which involves the infliction or threatened infliction of great bodily harm or is attempting to escape by use of a deadly weapon, or otherwise indicates that he will endanger human life or inflict great bodily harm unless arrested without delay.

(b) A peace officer making an arrest pursuant to an invalid warrant is justified in the use of any force which he would be justified in using if the warrant were valid, unless he knows that the warrant is invalid.
(Source: P.A. 84-1426.) [Formerly Ill. Rev. Stat. 38 §7-5.]

5/7-6. Private person's use of force in making arrest.

§7-6. Private person's use of force in making arrest. (a) A private person who makes, or assists another private person in making a lawful arrest is justified in the use of any force which he would be justified in using if he were summoned or directed by a peace officer to make such arrest, except that he is justified in the use of force likely to cause death or great bodily harm only when he reasonably believes that such force is necessary to prevent death or great bodily harm to himself or another.

(b) A private person who is summoned or directed by a peace officer to assist in making an arrest which is unlawful, is justified in the use of any force which he would be justified in using if the arrest were lawful, unless he knows that the arrest is unlawful.
(Source: Laws 1961, p. 1983.) [Formerly Ill. Rev. Stat. 38 §7-6.]

5/7-7. Private person's use of force in resisting arrest.

§7-7. Private person's use of force in resisting arrest. A person is not authorized to use force to resist an arrest which he knows is being made either by a peace officer or by a private person summoned and directed by a peace officer to make the arrest, even if he believes that the arrest is unlawful and the arrest in fact is unlawful.
(Source: P.A. 86-1475.) [Formerly Ill. Rev. Stat. 38 §7-7.]

5/7-8. Force likely to cause death or great bodily harm.

§7-8. Force likely to cause death or great bodily harm. (a)* Force which is likely to cause death or great bodily harm, within the meaning of Sections 7-5 and 7-6 includes:

(1) The firing of a firearm in the direction of the person to be arrested, even though no intent exists to kill or inflict great bodily harm; and

(2) The firing of a firearm at a vehicle in which the person to be arrested is riding.

**So in original. No subsec. (b) has been enacted.*
(Source: Laws 1961, p. 1983.) [Formerly Ill. Rev. Stat. 38 §7-8.]

5/7-9. Use of force to prevent escape.

§7-9. Use of force to prevent escape. (a) A peace officer or other person who has an arrested person in his custody is justified in the use of such force to prevent the escape of the arrested person from custody as he would be justified in using if he were arresting such person.

(b) A guard or other peace officer is justified in the use of force, including force likely to cause death or great bodily harm, which he reasonably believes to be necessary to prevent the escape from a penal institution of a person whom the officer reasonably believes to be lawfully detained in such institution under sentence for an offense or awaiting trial or commitment for an offense.
(Source: Laws 1961, p. 1983.) [Formerly Ill. Rev. Stat. 38 §7-9.]

5/7-10. Execution of death sentence.

§7-10. Execution of death sentence. A public officer who, in the exercise of his official duty, puts a person to death pursuant to a sentence of a court of competent jurisdiction, is justified if he acts in accordance with the sentence pronounced and the law prescribing the procedure for execution of a death sentence.
(Source: Laws 1961, p. 1983.) [Formerly Ill. Rev. Stat. 38 §7-10.]

5/7-11. Compulsion.

§7-11. Compulsion. (a) A person is not guilty of an offense, other than an offense punishable with death, by reason of conduct which he performs under the compulsion of threat or menace of the imminent infliction of death or great bodily harm, if he reasonably believes death or great bodily harm will be inflicted upon him if he does not perform such conduct.

(b) A married woman is not entitled, by reason of the presence of her husband, to any presumption of compulsion, or to any defense of compulsion except that stated in Subsection (a).

(Source: Laws 1961, p. 1983.) [Formerly Ill. Rev. Stat. 38 §7-11.]

5/7-12. Entrapment.

§7-12. Entrapment. A person is not guilty of an offense if his conduct is incited or induced by a public officer or employee, or agent of either, for the purpose of obtaining evidence for the prosecution of such person. However, this Section is inapplicable if a public officer or employee, or agent of either, merely affords to such person the opportunity or facility for committing an offense in furtherance of a criminal purpose which such person has originated.

(Source: Laws 1961, p. 1983.) [Formerly Ill. Rev. Stat. 38 §7-12.]

5/7-13. Necessity.

§7-13. Necessity. Conduct which would otherwise be an offense is justifiable by reason of necessity if the accused was without blame in occasioning or developing the situation and reasonably believed such conduct was necessary to avoid a public or private injury greater than the injury which might reasonably result from his own conduct.

(Source: Laws 1961, p. 1983.) [Formerly Ill. Rev. Stat. 38 §7-13.]

5/7-14. Affirmative defense.

§7-14. Affirmative defense. A defense of justifiable use of force, or of exoneration, based on the provisions of this Article is an affirmative defense.

(Source: Laws 1961, p. 1983.) [Formerly Ill. Rev. Stat. 38 §7-14.]

TITLE III. SPECIFIC OFFENSES

PART A. INCHOATE OFFENSES

ARTICLE 8. SOLICITATION, CONSPIRACY AND ATTEMPT

Sec.

5/8-1. Solicitation.

§8-1. Solicitation. (a) Elements of the offense. A person commits solicitation when, with intent that an offense be committed, other than first degree murder, he commands, encourages or requests another to commit that offense.

(b) Penalty.

A person convicted of solicitation may be fined or imprisoned or both not to exceed the maximum provided for the offense solicited: Provided, however, the penalty shall not exceed the corresponding maximum limit provided by subparagraph (c) of Section 8-4 of this Act, as heretofore and hereafter amended.

(Source: P.A. 85-1030.) [Formerly Ill. Rev. Stat. 38 §8-1.]

5/8-1.1. Solicitation of murder.

§8-1.1. Solicitation of Murder. (a) A person commits solicitation of murder when, with the intent that the offense of first degree murder be committed, he commands, encourages or requests another to commit that offense.

(b) Penalty. Solicitation of murder is a Class X felony and a person convicted of solicitation of murder shall be sentenced to a term of imprisonment for a period of not less than 15 years and not more than 30 years.

(Source: P.A. 85-1003; 85-1030; 85-1440.) [Formerly Ill. Rev. Stat. 38 §8-1.1.]

5/8-1.2. Solicitation of murder for hire.

§8-1.2. Solicitation of Murder for Hire. (a) A person commits solicitation of murder for hire when, with the intent that the offense of first degree murder be committed, he procures another to commit that offense pursuant to any contract, agreement, understanding, command or request for money or anything of value.

(b) Penalty. Solicitation of murder for hire is a Class X felony and a person convicted of solicitation of murder for hire shall be sentenced to a term of imprisonment of not less than 20 years and not more than 40 years.

(Source: P.A. 85-1003; 85-1030; 85-1440.) [Formerly Ill. Rev. Stat. 38 §8-1.2.]

5/8-2. Conspiracy.

§8-2. Conspiracy. (a) Elements of the offense. A person commits conspiracy when, with intent that an offense be committed, he agrees with another to the commission of that offense. No person may be convicted of conspiracy to commit an offense unless an act in furtherance of such agreement is alleged and proved to have been committed by him or by a co-conspirator.

(b) Co-conspirators.

It shall not be a defense to conspiracy that the person or persons with whom the accused is alleged to have conspired:

(1) Has not been prosecuted or convicted, or
(2) Has been convicted of a different offense, or
(3) Is not amenable to justice, or
(4) Has been acquitted, or
(5) Lacked the capacity to commit an offense.

(c) Sentence.

A person convicted of conspiracy may be fined or imprisoned or both not to exceed the maximum provided for the offense which is the object of the conspiracy, except that if the object is an offense prohibited by Sections 11-15, 11-16, 11-17, 11-19, 24-1 (a) (1), 24-1 (a) (7), 28-1, 28-3 and 28-4 of the "Criminal Code of 1961", approved July 28, 1961, as amended, or prohibited by Sections 404 or 406 (b) of the "Illinois Controlled Substances Act", enacted by the 77th General Assembly [720 ILCS 570/404 or 570/406], or an inchoate offense related to any of the aforesaid principal offenses, the person convicted may be sentenced for a Class 3 felony however, conspiracy to commit treason, first degree murder, or aggravated kidnapping shall not be sentenced in excess of a Class 2 felony, and conspiracy to commit any offense other than those specified in this subsection, and other than those set forth in Sections 401, 402, or 407 of the Illinois Controlled Substances Act [720 ILCS 570/401, 570/402, or 570/407], shall not be sentenced in excess of a Class 4 felony.

(Source: P.A. 86-809.) [Formerly Ill. Rev. Stat. 38 §8-2.]

5/8-3. Defense.

§8-3. Defense. It is a defense to a charge of solicitation or conspiracy that if the criminal object were achieved the accused would not be guilty of an offense.

(Source: Laws 1961, p. 1983.) [Formerly Ill. Rev. Stat. 38 §8-3.]

5/8-4. Attempt.

§8-4. Attempt. (a) Elements of the Offense. A person commits an attempt when, with intent to commit a specific offense, he does any act which constitutes a substantial step toward the commission of that offense.

(b) Impossibility.

It shall not be a defense to a charge of attempt that because of a misapprehension of the circumstances it would have been impossible for the accused to commit the offense attempted.

(c) Sentence.

A person convicted of an attempt may be fined or imprisoned or both not to exceed the maximum provided for the offense attempted but, except for an attempt to commit the offense defined in Section 33A-2 of this Act,

(1) the sentence for attempt to commit first degree murder is the sentence for a Class X felony, except that an attempt to commit first degree murder when at least one of the aggravating factors specified in paragraphs (1), (2) and (12) of subsection (b) of Section 9-1 is present is a Class X felony for which the sentence shall be a term of imprisonment of not less than 15 years and not more than 60 years;

(2) the sentence for attempt to commit a Class X felony is the sentence for a Class 1 felony;

(3) the sentence for attempt to commit a Class 1 felony is the sentence for a Class 2 felony;

(4) the sentence for attempt to commit a Class 2 felony is the sentence for a Class 3 felony; and

(5) the sentence for attempt to commit any felony other than those specified in Subsections (1), (2), (3) and (4) hereof is the sentence for a Class A misdemeanor.

(Chgd. by P.A. 87-921, §1, eff. 1/1/93.)
(Source: P.A. 84-1450.) [Formerly Ill. Rev. Stat. 38 §8-4.]

5/8-5. Multiple convictions.

§8-5. Multiple convictions. No person shall be convicted of both the inchoate and the principal offense.
(Source: Laws 1961, p. 1983.) [Formerly Ill. Rev. Stat. 38 §8-5.]

5/8-6. Offense.

§8-6. Offense. For the purposes of this Article, "offense" shall include conduct which if performed in another State would be criminal by the laws of that State and which conduct if performed in this State would be an offense under the laws of this State.
(Source: Laws 1961, p. 1983.) [Formerly Ill. Rev. Stat. 38 §8-6.]

PART B. OFFENSES DIRECTED AGAINST THE PERSON

ARTICLE 9. HOMICIDE

5/9-1. First degree murder—Death penalties—Exceptions—Separate hearings—Proof—Findings—Appellate procedures—Reversals.

§9-1. First degree Murder—Death penalties—Exceptions—Separate Hearings—Proof—Findings—Appellate procedures—Reversals. (a) A person who kills an individual without lawful justification commits first degree murder if, in performing the acts which cause the death:

(1) he either intends to kill or do great bodily harm to that individual or another, or knows that such acts will cause death to that individual or another; or

(2) he knows that such acts create a strong probability of death or great bodily harm to that individual or another; or

(3) he is attempting or committing a forcible felony other than second degree murder.

(b) Aggravating Factors. A defendant who at the time of the commission of the offense has attained the age of 18 or more and who has been found guilty of first degree murder may be sentenced to death if:

(1) the murdered individual was a peace officer or fireman killed in the course of performing his official duties, to prevent the performance of his official duties, or in retaliation for performing his official duties, and the defendant knew or should have known that the murdered individual was a peace officer or fireman; or

(2) the murdered individual was an employee of an institution or facility of the Department of Corrections, or any similar local correctional agency, killed in the course of performing his official duties, to prevent the performance of his official duties, or in retaliation for performing his official duties, or the murdered individual was an inmate at such institution or facility and was killed on the grounds thereof, or the murdered individual was otherwise present in such institution or facility with the knowledge and approval of the chief administrative officer thereof; or

(3) the defendant has been convicted of murdering two or more individuals under subsection (a) of this Section or under any law of the United States or of any state which is substantially similar to subsection (a) of this Section regardless of whether the deaths occurred as the result of the same act or of several related or unrelated acts so long as the deaths were the result of either an intent to kill more than one person or of separate acts which the defendant knew would cause death or create a strong probability of death or great bodily harm to the murdered individual or another; or

(4) the murdered individual was killed as a result of the hijacking of an airplane, train, ship, bus or other public conveyance; or

(5) the defendant committed the murder pursuant to a contract, agreement or understanding by which he was to receive money or anything of value in return for committing the murder or procured another to commit the murder for money or anything of value; or

(6) the murdered individual was killed in the course of another felony if:

(a) the murdered individual:

(i) was actually killed by the defendant, or

(ii) received physical injuries personally inflicted by the defendant substantially contemporaneously with physical injuries caused by one or more persons for whose conduct the defendant is legally accountable under Section 5-2 of this Code, and the physical injuries inflicted by either the defendant or the other person or persons for whose conduct he is legally accountable caused the death of the murdered individual; and

(b) in performing the acts which caused the death of the murdered individual or which resulted in physical injuries personally inflicted by the defendant on the murdered individual under the circumstances of subdivision (ii) of subparagraph (a) of paragraph (6) of subsection (b) of this Section, the defendant acted with the intent to kill the murdered individual or with the knowledge that his acts created a strong probability of death or great bodily harm to the murdered individual or another; and

(c) the other felony was one of the following: armed robbery, robbery, aggravated criminal sexual assault, aggravated kidnapping, forcible detention, arson, aggravated arson, burglary, residential burglary, home invasion, calculated criminal drug conspiracy as defined in Section 405 of the Illinois Controlled Substances Act [720 ILCS 570/405], or the attempt to commit any of the felonies listed in this subsection (c); or

(7) the murdered individual was under 12 years of age and the death resulted from exceptionally brutal or heinous behavior indicative of wanton cruelty; or

(8) the defendant committed the murder with intent to prevent the murdered individual from testifying in any criminal prosecution or giving material assistance to the State in any investigation or prosecution, either against the defendant or another; or the defendant committed the murder because the murdered individual was a witness in any prosecution or gave material assistance to the State in any investigation or prosecution, either against the defendant or another; or

(9) the defendant, while committing an offense punishable under Sections 401, 401.1, 401.2, 405, 407 or 407.1 or subsection (b) of Section 404 of the Illinois Controlled Substances Act [720 ILCS 570/401, 570/401.1, 570/401.2 (repealed), 570/405, 570/407 or 570/407.1], or while engaged in a conspiracy or solicitation to commit such offense, intentionally killed an individual or counseled, commanded, induced, procured or caused the intentional killing of the murdered individual; or

(10) the defendant was incarcerated in an institution or facility of the Department of Corrections at the time of the murder, and while committing an offense punishable as a felony under Illinois law, or while engaged in a conspiracy or solicitation to commit such offense, intentionally killed an individual or counseled, commanded, induced, procured or caused the intentional killing of the murdered individual; or

(11) the murder was committed in a cold, calculated and premeditated manner pursuant to a preconceived plan, scheme or design to take a human life by unlawful means, and the conduct of the defendant created a reasonable expectation that the death of a human being would result therefrom; or

(12) the murdered individual was a paramedic, ambulance driver, or other medical assistance or first aid personnel, employed by a municipality or other governmental unit, killed in the course of performing his offical duties, to prevent the performance of his official duties, or in retaliation for performing his official duties, and the defendant knew or should have known that the murdered individual was a paramedic, ambulance driver, or other medical assistance or first aid personnel.

(c) Consideration of factors in Aggravation and Mitigation.

The court shall consider, or shall instruct the jury to consider any aggravating and any mitigating factors which are relevant to the imposition of the death penalty. Aggravating factors may include but need not be limited to those factors set forth in subsection (b). Mitigating factors may include but need not be limited to the following:

(1) the defendant has no significant history of prior criminal activity;

(2) the murder was committed while the defendant was under the influence of extreme mental or emotional disturbance, although not such as to constitute a defense to prosecution;

(3) the murdered individual was a participant in the defendant's homicidal conduct or consented to the homicidal act;

(4) the defendant acted under the compulsion of threat or menace of the imminent infliction of death or great bodily harm;

(5) the defendant was not personally present during commission of the act or acts causing death.

(d) Separate sentencing hearing.

Where requested by the State, the court shall conduct a separate sentencing proceeding to determine the existence of factors set forth in subsection (b) and to consider any aggravating or mitigating factors as indicated in subsection (c). The proceeding shall be conducted:

(1) before the jury that determined the defendant's guilt; or

(2) before a jury impanelled for the purpose of the proceeding if:

A. the defendant was convicted upon a plea of guilty; or

B. the defendant was convicted after a trial before the court sitting without a jury; or

C. the court for good cause shown discharges the jury that determined the defendant's guilt; or

(3) before the court alone if the defendant waives a jury for the separate proceeding.

(e) Evidence and Argument.

During the proceeding any information relevant to any of the factors set forth in subsection (b) may be presented by either the State or the defendant under the rules governing the admission of evidence at criminal trials. Any information relevant to any additional aggravating factors or any mitigating factors indicated in subsection (c) may be presented by the State or defendant regardless of its admissibility under the rules governing the admission of evidence at criminal trials. The State and the defendant shall be given fair opportunity to rebut any information received at the hearing.

(f) Proof.

The burden of proof of establishing the existence of any of the factors set forth in subsection (b) is on the State and shall not be satisfied unless established beyond a reasonable doubt.

(g) Procedure—Jury.

If at the separate sentencing proceeding the jury finds that none of the factors set forth in subsection (b) exists, the court shall sentence the defendant to a term of imprisonment under Chapter V of the Unified Code of Corrections [730 ILCS 5/5-1-1 et seq.]. If there is a unanimous finding by the jury that one or more of the factors set forth in subsection (b) exist, the jury shall consider aggravating and mitigating factors as instructed by the court and shall determine whether the sentence of death shall be imposed. If the jury determines unanimously that there are no mitigating factors sufficient to preclude the imposition of the death sentence, the court shall sentence the defendant to death.

Unless the jury unanimously finds that there are no mitigating factors sufficient to preclude the imposition of the death sentence the court shall sentence the defendant to a term of imprisonment under Chapter V of the Unified Code of Corrections.

(h) Procedure—No Jury.

In a proceeding before the court alone, if the court finds that none of the factors found in subsection (b) exists, the court shall sentence the defendant to a term of imprisonment under Chapter V of the Unified Code of Corrections.

If the Court determines that one or more of the factors set forth in subsection (b) exists, the Court shall consider any aggravating and mitigating factors as indicated in subsection (c). If the Court determines that there are no mitigating factors sufficient to preclude the imposition of the death sentence, the Court shall sentence the defendant to death.

Unless the court finds that there are no mitigating factors sufficient to preclude the imposition of the sentence of death, the court shall sentence the defendant to a term of imprisonment under Chapter V of the Unified Code of Corrections.

(i) Appellate Procedure.

The conviction and sentence of death shall be subject to automatic review by the Supreme Court. Such review shall be in accordance with rules promulgated by the Supreme Court.

(j) Disposition of reversed death sentence.

In the event that the death penalty in this Act is held to be unconstitutional by the Supreme Court of the United States or of the State of Illinois, any person convicted of first degree murder shall be sentenced by the court to a term of imprisonment under Chapter V of the Unified Code of Corrections.

In the event that any death sentence pursuant to the sentencing provisions of this Section is declared unconstitutional by the Supreme Court of the United States or of the State of Illinois, the court having jurisdiction over a person previously sentenced to death shall cause the defendant to be brought before the court, and the court shall sentence the defendant to a term of imprisonment under Chapter V of the Unified Code of Corrections.

(Chgd. by P.A. 87-921, §1, eff. 1/1/93.)

(Source: P.A. 86-806; 86-834; 86-1012; 86-1475; 87-525.) [Formerly Ill. Rev. Stat. 38 §9-1.]

5/9-1.2. Intentional homicide of an unborn child.

§9-1.2. Intentional Homicide of an Unborn Child. (a) A person commits the offense of intentional homicide of an unborn child if, in performing acts which cause the death of an unborn child, he without lawful justification:

(1) either intended to cause the death of or do great bodily harm to the pregnant woman or her unborn child or knew that such acts would cause death or great bodily harm to the pregnant woman or her unborn child; or

(2) he knew that his acts created a strong probability of death or great bodily harm to the pregnant woman or her unborn child; and

(3) he knew that the woman was pregnant.

(b) For purposes of this Section, (1) "unborn child" shall mean any individual of the human species from fertilization until birth, and (2) "person" shall not include the pregnant woman whose unborn child is killed.

(c) This Section shall not apply to acts which cause the death of an unborn child if those acts were committed during any abortion, as defined in Section 2 of the Illinois Abortion Law of 1975, as amended [720 ILCS 510/2], to which the pregnant woman has consented. This Section shall not apply to acts which were committed pursuant to usual and customary standards of medical practice during diagnostic testing or therapeutic treatment.

(d) Penalty. The sentence for intentional homicide of an unborn child shall be the same as for first degree murder, except that the death penalty may not be imposed.

(e) The provisions of this Act shall not be construed to prohibit the prosecution of any person under any other provision of law.

(Source: P.A. 85-293.) [Formerly Ill. Rev. Stat. 38 §9-1.2.]

5/9-2. Second degree murder.

§9-2. Second Degree Murder. (a) A person commits the offense of second degree murder when he commits the offense of first degree murder as defined in paragraphs (1) or (2) of subsection (a) of Section 9-1 of this Code and either of the following mitigating factors are present:

(1) At the time of the killing he is acting under a sudden and intense passion resulting from serious provocation by the individual killed or another whom the offender endeavors to kill, but he negligently or accidentally causes the death of the individual killed; or

(2) At the time of the killing he believes the circumstances to be such that, if they existed, would justify or exonerate the killing under the principles stated in Article 7 of this Code [720 ILCS 5/7-1 et seq.], but his belief is unreasonable.

(b) Serious provocation is conduct sufficient to excite an intense passion in a reasonable person.

(c) When a defendant is on trial for first degree murder and evidence of either of the mitigating factors defined in subsection (a) of this Section has been presented, the burden of proof is on the defendant to prove either mitigating factor by a preponderance of the evidence before the defendant can be found guilty of second degree murder. However, the burden of proof remains on the State to prove beyond a reasonable doubt each of the elements of first degree murder and, when appropriately raised, the absence of circumstances at the time of the killing that would justify or exonerate the killing under the principles stated in Article 7 of this Code. In a jury trial for first degree murder in which evidence of either of the mitigating factors defined in subsection (a) of this Section has been presented and the defendant has requested that the jury be given the option of finding the defendant guilty of second degree murder, the jury must be instructed that it may not consider whether the defendant has met his burden of proof with regard to second degree murder until and unless it has first determined that the State has proven beyond a reasonable doubt each of the elements of first degree murder.

(d) Sentence.

Second Degree Murder is a Class 1 felony.

(Source: P.A. 84-1450.) [Formerly Ill. Rev. Stat. 38 §9-2.]

5/9-2.1. Voluntary manslaughter of an unborn child.

§9-2.1. Voluntary Manslaughter of an Unborn Child. (a) A person who kills an unborn child without lawful justification commits voluntary manslaughter of an unborn child if at the time of the killing he is acting under a sudden and intense passion resulting from serious provocation by another whom the offender endeavors to kill, but he negligently or accidentally causes the death of the unborn child.

Serious provocation is conduct sufficient to excite an intense passion in a reasonable person.

(b) A person who intentionally or knowingly kills an unborn child commits voluntary manslaughter of an unborn child if at the time of the killing he believes the circumstances to be such that, if they existed, would justify or exonerate the killing under the principles stated in Article 7 of this Code [720 ILCS 5/7-1 et seq.], but his belief is unreasonable.

(c) Sentence. Voluntary Manslaughter of an unborn child is a Class 1 felony.

(d) For purposes of this Section, (1) "unborn child" shall mean any individual of the human species from fertilization until birth, and (2) "person" shall not include the pregnant woman whose unborn child is killed.

(e) This Section shall not apply to acts which cause the death of an unborn child if those acts were committed during any abortion, as defined in Section 2 of the Illinois Abortion Law of 1975, as amended [720 ILCS 510/2], to which the pregnant woman has consented. This Section shall not apply to acts which were committed pursuant to usual and customary standards of medical practice during diagnostic testing or therapeutic treatment.

(Source: P.A. 84-1414.) [Formerly Ill. Rev. Stat. 38 §9-2.1.]

5/9-3. Involuntary manslaughter and reckless homicide.

§9-3. Involuntary Manslaughter and Reckless Homicide. (a) A person who unintentionally kills an individual without lawful justification commits involuntary manslaughter if his acts whether lawful or unlawful which cause the death are such as are likely to cause death or great bodily harm to some individual, and he performs them recklessly, except in cases in which the cause of the death consists of the driving of a motor vehicle, in which case the person commits reckless homicide.

(b) In cases involving reckless homicide, being under the influence of alcohol or any other drug or drugs at the time of the alleged violation shall be presumed to be evidence of a reckless act unless disproved by evidence to the contrary.

(c) For the purposes of this Section, a person shall be considered to be under the influence of alcohol or other drugs while:

1. The alcohol concentration in the person's blood or breath is 0.10 or more based on the definition of blood and breath units in Section 11-501.2 of the Illinois Vehicle Code [625 ILCS 5/11-501.2];
2. Under the influence of alcohol to a degree that renders the person incapable of safely driving;
3. Under the influence of any other drug or combination of drugs to a degree that renders the person incapable of safely driving; or
4. Under the combined influence of alcohol and any other drug or drugs to a degree which renders the person incapable of safely driving.

(d) Sentence.

(1) Involuntary manslaughter is a Class 3 felony.

(2) Reckless homicide is a Class 3 felony.

(e) In cases involving reckless homicide in which the defendant was determined to have been under the influence of alcohol or any other drug or drugs as an element of the offense, or in cases in which the defendant is proven beyond a reasonable doubt to have been under the influence of alcohol or any other drug or drugs, the penalty shall be a Class 2 felony, for which a person, if sentenced to a term of imprisonment, shall be sentenced to a term of not less than 3 years and not more than 14 years.

(Chgd. by P.A. 87-1198, §2, eff. 9/25/92.)

(Source: P.A. 86-1317; 87-274.) [Formerly Ill. Rev. Stat. 38 §9-3.]

5/9-3.1. Concealment of homicidal death.

§9-3.1. Concealment of homicidal death. (a) A person commits the offense of concealment of homicidal death when he conceals the death of any other person with knowledge that such other person has died by homicidal means.

(b) Nothing in this Section prevents the defendant from also being charged with and tried for the first degree murder, second degree murder or involuntary manslaughter of the person whose death is concealed. If a person convicted under this Section is also convicted of first degree murder, second degree murder or involuntary manslaughter, the penalty under this Section shall be imposed separately and in addition to the penalty for first degree murder, second degree murder or involuntary manslaughter.

(c) Sentence.

Concealment of homicidal death is a Class 3 felony.

(Source: P.A. 84-1308; 84-1450.) [Formerly Ill. Rev. Stat. 38 §9-3.1.]

5/9-3.2. Involuntary manslaughter and reckless homicide of an unborn child.

§9-3.2. Involuntary Manslaughter and Reckless Homicide of an Unborn Child. (a) A person who unintentionally kills an unborn child without lawful justification commits involuntary manslaughter of an unborn child if his acts whether lawful or unlawful which cause the death are such as are likely to cause death or great bodily harm to some individual, and he performs them recklessly, except in cases in which the cause of death consists of the driving of a motor vehicle, in which case the person commits reckless homicide of an unborn child.

(b) Sentence.

(1) Involuntary manslaughter of an unborn child is a Class 3 felony.

(2) Reckless homicide of an unborn child is a Class 3 felony.

(c) For purposes of this Section, (1) "unborn child" shall mean any individual of the human species from fertilization until birth, and (2) "person" shall not include the pregnant woman whose unborn child is killed.

(d) This Section shall not apply to acts which cause the death of an unborn child if those acts were committed during any abortion, as defined in Section 2 of the Illinois Abortion Law of 1975, as amended [720 ILCS 510/2], to which the pregnant woman has consented. This Section shall not apply to acts which were committed pursuant to usual and customary standards of medical practice during diagnostic testing or therapeutic treatment.

(e) The provisions of this Section shall not be construed to prohibit the prosecution of any person under any other provision of law, nor shall it be construed to preclude any civil cause of action.

(Source: P.A. 84-1414.) [Formerly Ill. Rev. Stat. 38 §9-3.2.]

5/9-3.3. Drug induced homicide.

§9-3.3. Drug induced homicide. (a) A person who violates subsection (a) or subsection (c) of Section 401 of the Illinois Controlled Substances Act [720 ILCS 570/401] by unlawfully delivering a controlled substance to another, and any person dies as a result of the injection, inhalation or ingestion of any amount of that controlled substance, commits the offense of drug induced homicide.

(b) Sentence. Drug-induced homicide is a Class X felony for which the defendant shall in addition to a sentence authorized by law, be sentenced to a term of imprisonment of not less than 15 years and not more than 30 years or an extended term of not less than 30 years and not more than 60 years.

(Chgd. by P.A. 87-1198, §2, eff. 9/25/92.)

(Source: P.A. 85-1259.) [Formerly Ill. Rev. Stat. 38 §9-3.3.]

ARTICLE 10. KIDNAPING AND RELATED OFFENSES

5/10-1. Kidnapping.

§10-1. Kidnapping. (a) Kidnapping occurs when a person knowingly:

(1) And secretly confines another against his will, or

(2) By force or threat of imminent force carries another from one place to another with intent secretly to confine him against his will, or

(3) By deceit or enticement induces another to go from one place to another with intent secretly to confine him against his will.

(b) Confinement of a child under the age of 13 years is against his will within the meaning of this Section if such confinement is without the consent of his parent or legal guardian.

(c) Sentence.

Kidnapping is a Class 2 felony.

(Source: P.A. 79-765.) [Formerly Ill. Rev. Stat. 38 §10-1.]

5/10-2. Aggravated kidnaping.

§10-2. Aggravated kidnaping. (a) A kidnaper within the definition of paragraph (a) of Section 10-1 is guilty of the offense of aggravated kidnaping when he:

(1) Kidnaps for the purpose of obtaining ransom from the person kidnaped or from any other person, or

(2) Takes as his victim a child under the age of 13 years, or an institutionalized severely or profoundly mentally retarded person, or

(3) Inflicts great bodily harm or commits another felony upon his victim, or

(4) Wears a hood, robe or mask or conceals his identity, or

(5) Commits the offense of kidnaping while armed with a dangerous weapon, as defined in Section 33A-1 of the "Criminal Code of 1961".

As used in this Section, "ransom" includes money, benefit or other valuable thing or concession.

(b) Sentence.

(1) Aggravated kidnaping for ransom is a Class X felony.

(2) Aggravated kidnaping other than for ransom is a Class 1 felony.

(Source: P.A. 85-1392.) [Formerly Ill. Rev. Stat. 38 §10-2.]

5/10-3. Unlawful restraint.

§10-3. Unlawful restraint. (a) A person commits the offense of unlawful restraint when he knowingly without legal authority detains another.

(b) Sentence.

Unlawful restraint is a Class 4 felony.

(Source: P.A. 79-840.) [Formerly Ill. Rev. Stat. 38 §10-3.]

5/10-3.1. Aggravated unlawful restraint.

§10-3.1. Aggravated Unlawful Restraint. (a) A person commits the offense of aggravated unlawful restraint when he knowingly without legal authority detains another while using a deadly weapon.

(b) Sentence. Aggravated unlawful restraint is a Class 3 felony.

(Source: P.A. 84-930.) [Formerly Ill. Rev. Stat. 38 §10-3.1.]

5/10-4. Forcible detention.

§10-4. Forcible Detention. (a) A person commits the offense of forcible detention when he holds an individual hostage without lawful authority for the purpose of obtaining performance by a third person of demands made by the person holding the hostage, and

(1) the person holding the hostage is armed with a dangerous weapon as defined in Section 33A-1 of this Code, or

(2) the hostage is known to the person holding him to be a peace officer or a correctional employee engaged in the performance of his official duties.

(b) Forcible detention is a Class 2 felony.

(Source: P.A. 79-941.) [Formerly Ill. Rev. Stat. 38 §10-4.]

5/10-5. Child abduction.

§10-5. Child Abduction. (a) For purposes of this Section, the following terms shall have the following meanings:

(1) "Child" means a person under the age of 18 or an institutionalized severely or profoundly mentally retarded person at the time the alleged violation occurred; and

(2) "Detains" means taking or retaining physical custody of a child, whether or not the child resists or objects; and

(3) "Lawful custodian" means a person or persons granted legal custody of a child or entitled to physical possession of a child pursuant to a court order. It is presumed that, when the parties have never been married to each other, the mother has legal custody of the child unless a valid court order states otherwise.

If an adjudication of paternity has been completed and the father has been assigned support obligations or visitation rights, such a paternity order should, for the purposes of this Section be considered a valid court order granting custody to the mother.

(b) A person commits child abduction when he or she:

(1) Intentionally violates any terms of a valid court order granting sole or joint custody, care or possession to another, by concealing or detaining the child or removing the child from the jurisdiction of the court; or

(2) Intentionally violates a court order prohibiting the person from concealing or detaining the child or removing the child from the jurisdiction of the court; or

(3) Intentionally conceals, detains or removes the child without the consent of the mother or lawful custodian of the child if the person is a putative father and either: (A) the paternity of the child has not been legally established or (B) the paternity of the child has been legally established but no orders relating to custody have been entered. However, notwithstanding the presumption created by paragraph (3) of subsection (a), a mother commits child abduction when she intentionally conceals or removes a child, whom she has abandoned or relinquished custody of, from an unadjudicated father who has provided sole ongoing care and custody of the child in her absence; or

(4) Intentionally conceals or removes the child from a parent after filing a petition or being served with process in an action affecting marriage or paternity but prior to the issuance of a temporary or final order determining custody; or

(5) At the expiration of visitation rights outside the State, intentionally fails or refuses to return or impedes the return of the child to the lawful custodian in Illinois; or

(6) Being a parent of the child, and where the parents of such child are or have been married and there has been no court order of custody, conceals the child for 15 days, and fails to make reasonable attempts within the 15 day period to notify the other parent as to the specific whereabouts of the child, including a means by which to contact such child, or to arrange reasonable visitation or contact with the child. It is not a violation of this Section for a person fleeing domestic violence to take the child with him or her to housing provided by a domestic violence program; or

(7) Being a parent of the child, and where the parents of the child are or have been married and there has been no court order of custody, conceals, detains, or removes the child with physical force or threat of physical force; or

(8) Conceals, detains, or removes the child for payment or promise of payment at the instruction of a person who has no legal right to custody; or

(9) Retains in this State for 30 days a child removed from another state without the consent of the lawful custodian or in violation of a valid court order of custody; or

(10) Intentionally lures or attempts to lure a child under the age of 16 into a motor vehicle, building, housetrailer, or dwelling place without the consent of the parent or lawful custodian of the child for other than a lawful purpose.

For the purposes of this subsection (b), paragraph (10), the luring or attempted luring of a child under the age of 16 into a motor vehicle, building, housetrailer, or dwelling place without the consent of the parent or lawful custodian of the child shall be prima facie evidence of other than a lawful purpose.

(c) It shall be an affirmative defense that:

(1) The person had custody of the child pursuant to a court order granting legal custody or visitation rights which existed at the time of the alleged violation; or

(2) The person had physical custody of the child pursuant to a court order granting legal custody or visitation rights and failed to return the child as a result of circumstances beyond his or her control, and the person notified and disclosed to the other parent or legal custodian the specific whereabouts of the child and a means by which such child can be contacted or made a reasonable attempt to notify the other parent or lawful custodian of the child of such circumstances and make such disclosure within 24 hours after the visitation period had expired and returned the child as soon as possible; or

(3) The person was fleeing an incidence or pattern of domestic violence; or

(4) The person lured or attempted to lure a child under the age of 16 into a motor vehicle, building, housetrailer, or dwelling place for a lawful purpose in prosecutions under subsection (b), paragraph (10).

(d) A person convicted of child abduction under this Section is guilty of a Class 4 felony. It shall be a factor in aggravation for which a court may impose a more severe sentence under Section 5-8-1 of the Unified Code of Corrections [730 ILCS 5/5-8-1], if upon sentencing the court finds evidence of any of the following aggravating factors:

(1) that the defendant abused or neglected the child following the concealment, detention or removal of the child; or

(2) that the defendant inflicted or threatened to inflict physical harm on a parent or lawful custodian of the child or on the child with intent to cause such parent or lawful custodian to discontinue criminal prosecution of the defendant under this Section; or

(3) that the defendant demanded payment in exchange for return of the child or demanded that he or she be relieved of the financial or legal obligation to support the child in exchange for return of the child; or

(4) that the defendant has previously been convicted of child abduction; or

(5) that the defendant committed the abduction while armed with a deadly weapon or the taking of the child resulted in serious bodily injury to another.

(e) The court may order the child to be returned to the parent or lawful custodian from whom the child was concealed, detained or removed. In addition to any sentence imposed, the court may assess any reasonable expense incurred in searching for or returning the child against any person convicted of violating this Section.

(f) Nothing contained in this Section shall be construed to limit the court's contempt power.

(g) Every law enforcement officer investigating an alleged incident of child abduction shall make a written police report of any bona fide allegation and the disposition of such investigation. Every police report completed pursuant to this Section shall be compiled and recorded within the meaning of Section 5.1 of "An Act in relation to criminal identification and investigation", approved July 2, 1931, as now or hereafter amended [20 ILCS 2630/5.1].

(h) Whenever a law enforcement officer has reasons to believe a child abduction has occurred, he shall provide the lawful custodian a summary of her or his rights under this Act, including the procedures and relief available to her or him.

(i) If during the course of an investigation under this Section the child is found in the physical custody of the defendant or another, the law enforcement officer shall return the child to the parent or lawful custodian from whom the child was concealed, detained or removed, unless there is good cause for the law enforcement officer or the Department of Children and Family Services to retain temporary protective custody of the child pursuant to the Abused and Neglected Child Reporting Act, as now or hereafter amended [325 ILCS 5/1 et seq.].

(Source: P.A. 85-1440; 86-312.) [Formerly Ill. Rev. Stat. 38 §10-5.]

5/10-6. Harboring a runaway.

§10-6. Harboring a runaway. (a) Any person, other than an agency or association providing crisis intervention services as defined in Section 3-5 of the Juvenile Court Act of 1987 [705 ILCS 405/3-5], or an operator of a youth emergency shelter as defined in Section 2.21 of the Child Care Act of 1969 [225 ILCS 10/2.21], who, without the knowledge and consent of the minor's parent or guardian, knowingly gives shelter to a minor, other than a mature minor who has been emancipated under the Emancipation of Mature Minors Act [750 ILCS 30/1 et seq.], for more than 48 hours without the consent of the minor's parent or guardian, and without notifying the local law enforcement authorities of the minor's name and the fact that the minor is being provided shelter commits the offense of harboring a runaway.

(b) Any person who commits the offense of harboring a runaway is guilty of a Class A misdemeanor.

(Source: P.A. 86-278; 86-386.) [Formerly Ill. Rev. Stat. 38 §10-6.]

5/10-7. Aiding and abetting child abduction.

§10-7. Aiding and abetting child abduction. (a) A person violates this Section when:

(i) Before or during the commission of a child abduction as defined in Section 10-5 and with the intent to promote or facilitate such offense, he or she intentionally aids or abets another in the planning or commission of child abduction, unless before the commission of the offense he or she makes proper effort to prevent the commission of the offense; or

(ii) With the intent to prevent the apprehension of a person known to have committed the offense of child abduction, or with the intent to obstruct or prevent efforts to locate the child victim of a child abduction, he or she knowingly destroys, alters, conceals or disguises physical evidence or furnishes false information.

(b) Sentence. A person who violates this Section commits a Class 4 felony.

(Source: P.A. 84-1308.) [Formerly Ill. Rev. Stat. 38 §10-7.]

5/10-8. Unlawful sale of a public conveyance travel ticket to a minor.

§10-8. Unlawful sale of a public conveyance travel ticket to a minor. (a) A person commits the offense of unlawful sale of a public conveyance travel ticket to a minor when the person sells a ticket for travel on any public conveyance to an unemancipated minor under 17 years of age without the consent of the minor's parents or guardian for passage to a destination outside this state and knows the minor's age or fails to take reasonable measures to ascertain the minor's age.

(b) Evidence. The fact that the defendant demanded, was shown, and reasonably relied upon written evidence of a person's age in any transaction forbidden by this Section is competent evidence, and may be considered in any criminal prosecution for a violation of this Section.

(c) Definition. "Public Conveyance", includes an airplane, boat, bus, railroad, train, taxicab or other vehicle used for the transportation of passengers for hire.

(d) Sentence. Unlawful sale of a public conveyance travel ticket to a minor is a Class C misdemeanor.

(Source: P.A. 86-336.) [Formerly Ill. Rev. Stat. 38 §10-8.]

ARTICLE 11. SEX OFFENSES

Sec.

5/11-6. Indecent solicitation of a child.

§11-6. Indecent solicitation of a child. (a) Any person of the age of 17 years and upwards who solicits a child under the age of 13 to do any act, which if done would be aggravated criminal sexual assault, criminal sexual assault, aggravated criminal sexual abuse or criminal sexual abuse, commits indecent solicitation of a child.

(b) It shall not be a defense to indecent solicitation of a child that the accused reasonably believed the child to be of the age of 13 years and upwards.

(c) Sentence.

Indecent solicitation of a child is:

(1) a Class A misdemeanor when the act, if done, would be criminal sexual abuse;

(2) a Class 4 felony when the act, if done, would be criminal sexual assault, aggravated criminal sexual assault, or aggravated criminal sexual abuse.
(Source: P.A. 84-1280.) [Formerly Ill. Rev. Stat. 38 §11-6.]

5/11-7. Adultery.

§11-7. Adultery. (a) Any person who has sexual intercourse with another not his spouse commits adultery, if the behavior is open and notorious, and

(1) The person is married and the other person involved in such intercourse is not his spouse; or

(2) The person is not married and knows that the other person involved in such intercourse is married.

A person shall be exempt from prosecution under this Section if his liability is based solely on evidence he has given in order to comply with the requirements of Section 4-1.7 of "The Illinois Public Aid Code", approved April 11, 1967, as amended [305 ILCS 5/4-1.7].

(b) Sentence.

Adultery is a Class A misdemeanor.
(Source: P.A. 86-490.) [Formerly Ill. Rev. Stat. 38 §11-7.]

5/11-8. Fornication.

§11-8. Fornication. (a) Any person who has sexual intercourse with another not his spouse commits fornication if the behavior is open and notorious.

A person shall be exempt from prosecution under this Section if his liability is based solely on evidence he has given in order to comply with the requirements of Section 4-1.7 of "The Illinois Public Aid Code", approved April 11, 1967, as amended [305 ILCS 5/4-1.7].

(b) Sentence.

Fornication is a Class B misdemeanor.

(Source: P.A. 86-490.) [Formerly Ill. Rev. Stat. 38 §11-8.]

5/11-9. Public indecency.

§11-9. Public indecency. (a) Any person of the age of 17 years and upwards who performs any of the following acts in a public place commits a public indecency:

(1) An act of sexual penetration or sexual conduct as defined in Section 12-12 of this Code; or

(2) A lewd exposure of the body done with intent to arouse or to satisfy the sexual desire of the person.

(b) "Public place" for purposes of this Section means any place where the conduct may reasonably be expected to be viewed by others.

(c) Sentence.

Public indecency is a Class A misdemeanor.

(Source: P.A. 83-1067.) [Formerly Ill. Rev. Stat. 38 §11-9.]

5/11-9.1. Sexual exploitation of a child.

§11-9.1. Sexual Exploitation of a Child. (a) Any person commits sexual exploitation of a child if in the presence of a child and with intent or knowledge that a child would view his or her acts, that person:

(1) engages in a sexual act; or

(2) exposes his or her sex organs, anus or breast for the purpose of sexual arousal or gratification of such person or the child.

(b) Definitions. As used in this Section:

"Sexual act" means masturbation, sexual conduct or sexual penetration as defined in Section 12-12 of this Code.

"Child" means a person under 17 years of age.

(c) Sentence.

(1)* Sexual exploitation of a child is a Class A misdemeanor. A second or subsequent violation of this Section is a Class 4 felony.

**So in original. No subsec. (2) has been enacted.*

(Added by P.A. 87-1198, §2, eff. 9/25/92.)
[Formerly Ill. Rev. Stat. 38 §11-9.1.]

5/11-11. Sexual relations within families.

§11-11. Sexual Relations Within Families. (a) A person commits sexual relations within families if he or she:

(1) Commits an act of sexual penetration as defined in Section 12-12 of this Code; and

(2) The person knows that he or she is related to the other person as follows: (i) Brother or sister, either of the whole blood or the half blood; or (ii) Father or mother, when the child, regardless of legitimacy and regardless of whether the child was of the whole blood or half-blood or was adopted, was 18 years of age or over when the act was committed; or (iii) Stepfather or stepmother, when the stepchild was 18 years of age or over when the act was committed.

(b) Sentence. Sexual relations within families is a Class 3 felony.

(Source: P.A. 84-1280.) [Formerly Ill. Rev. Stat. 38 §11-11.]

5/11-12. Bigamy.

§11-12. Bigamy. (a) Any person having a husband or wife who subsequently marries another or cohabits in this State after such marriage commits bigamy.

(b) It shall be an affirmative defense to bigamy that:

(1) The prior marriage was dissolved or declared invalid; or

(2) The accused reasonably believed the prior spouse to be dead; or

(3) The prior spouse had been continually absent for a period of 5 years during which time the accused did not know the prior spouse to be alive; or

(4) The accused reasonably believed that he was legally eligible to remarry.

(c) Sentence.

Bigamy is a Class 4 felony.

(Source: P.A. 81-230.) [Formerly Ill. Rev. Stat. 38 §11-12.]

5/11-13. Marrying a bigamist.

§11-13. Marrying a bigamist. (a) Any unmarried person who knowingly marries another under circumstances known to him which would render the other person guilty of bigamy under the laws of this State, or who cohabits in this State after such a marriage, commits the offense of marrying a bigamist.

(b) Sentence.

Marrying a bigamist is a Class A misdemeanor.

(Source: P. A. 77-2638.) [Formerly Ill. Rev. Stat. 38 §11-13.]

5/11-14. Prostitution.

§11-14. Prostitution. (a) Any person who performs, offers or agrees to perform any act of sexual penetration as defined in Section 12-12 of this Code for money, or any touching or fondling of the sex organs of one person by another person, for money or anything of value, for the purpose of sexual arousal or gratification commits an act of prostitution.

(b) Sentence.

Prostitution is a Class A misdemeanor. A person convicted of a third or subsequent violation of this Section, or of any combination of such number of convictions under this Section and Sections 11-15, 11-17, 11-18, 11-18.1 and 11-19 of this Code shall be guilty of a Class 4 felony. When a person has 2 or more prior convictions, the information or indictment charging that person shall state such prior convictions so as to give notice of the State's intention to treat the charge as a felony. The fact of such prior convictions is not an element of the offense and may not be disclosed to the jury during trial unless otherwise permitted by issues properly raised during such trial.

(Source: P.A. 85-1447.) [Formerly Ill. Rev. Stat. 38 §11-14.]

5/11-15. Soliciting for a prostitute.

§11-15. Soliciting for a prostitute. (a) Any person who performs any of the following acts commits soliciting for a prostitute:

(1) Solicits another for the purpose of prostitution; or

(2) Arranges or offers to arrange a meeting of persons for the purpose of prostitution; or

(3) Directs another to a place knowing such direction is for the purpose of prostitution.

(b) Sentence. Soliciting for a prostitute is a Class A misdemeanor. A person convicted of a third or subsequent violation of this Section, or of any combination of such number of convictions under this Section and Sections 11-14, 11-17, 11-18, 11-18.1 and 11-19 of this Code shall be guilty of a Class 4 felony. When a person has 2 or more prior convictions, the information or indictment charging that person shall state such prior convictions so as to give notice of the State's intention to treat the charge as a felony. The fact of such prior convictions is not an element of the offense and may not be disclosed to the jury during trial unless otherwise permitted by issues properly raised during such trial.

(Source: P.A. 85-1447.) [Formerly Ill. Rev. Stat. 38 §11-15.]

5/11-15.1. Soliciting for a juvenile prostitute.

§11-15.1. Soliciting for a Juvenile Prostitute. (a) Any person who violates any of the provisions of Section 11-15(a) of this Act commits soliciting for a juvenile prostitute where the prostitute for whom such person is soliciting is under 16 years of age or is an institutionalized severely or profoundly mentally retarded person.

(b) It is an affirmative defense to a charge of soliciting for a juvenile prostitute that the accused reasonably believed the person was of the age of 16 years or over or was not an institutionalized severely or profoundly mentally retarded person at the time of the act giving rise to the charge.

(c) Sentence.

Soliciting for a juvenile prostitute is a Class 1 felony.

(Source: P.A. 85-1392.) [Formerly Ill. Rev. Stat. 38 §11-15.1.]

5/11-16. Pandering.

§11-16. Pandering. (a) Any person who performs any of the following acts for money commits pandering:

(1) Compels a person to become a prostitute; or

(2) Arranges or offers to arrange a situation in which a person may practice prostitution.

(b) Sentence.

Pandering by compulsion is a Class 4 felony. Pandering other than by compulsion is a Class 4 felony.

(Source: P.A. 80-360.) [Formerly Ill. Rev. Stat. 38 §11-16.]

5/11-17. Keeping a place of prostitution.

§11-17. Keeping a Place of Prostitution. (a) Any person who has or exercises control over the use of any place which could offer seclusion or shelter for the practice of prostitution who performs any of the following acts keeps a place of prostitution:

(1) Knowingly grants or permits the use of such place for the purpose of prostitution; or

(2) Grants or permits the use of such place under circumstances from which he could reasonably know that the place is used or is to be used for purposes of prostitution; or

(3) Permits the continued use of a place after becoming aware of facts or circumstances from which he should reasonably know that the place is being used for purposes of prostitution.

(b) Sentence.

Keeping a place of prostitution is a Class A misdemeanor. A person convicted of a third or subsequent violation of this Section, or of any combination of such number of convictions under this Section and Sections 11-14, 11-15, 11-18, 11-18.1 and 11-19 of this Code, shall be guilty of a Class 4 felony. When a person has 2 or more prior convictions, the information or indictment charging that person shall state such prior convictions so as to give notice of the State's intention to treat the charge as a felony. The fact of such convictions is not an element of the offense and may not be disclosed to the jury during trial unless otherwise permitted by issues properly raised during such trial.

(Source: P.A. 85-1447.) [Formerly Ill. Rev. Stat. 38 §11-17.]

5/11-17.1. Keeping a place of juvenile prostitution.

§11-17.1. Keeping a Place of Juvenile Prostitution. (a) Any person who knowingly violates any of the provisions of Section 11-17 of this Act commits keeping a place of juvenile prostitution when any prostitute in the place of prostitution is under 16 years of age.

(b) It is an affirmative defense to a charge of keeping a place of juvenile prostitution that the accused reasonably believed the person was of the age of 16 years or over at the time of the act giving rise to the charge.

(c) Sentence. Keeping a place of juvenile prostitution is a Class 1 felony. A person convicted of a second or subsequent violation of this Section is guilty of a Class X felony.

(d) Forfeiture. Any person convicted under this Section is subject to the forfeiture provisions of Section 11-20.1A of this Act.

(Source: P.A. 85-1194.) [Formerly Ill. Rev. Stat. 38 §11-17.1.]

5/11-18. Patronizing a prostitute.

§11-18. Patronizing a prostitute. (a) Any person who performs any of the following acts with a person not his or her spouse commits the offense of patronizing a prostitute:

(1) Engages in an act of sexual penetration as defined in Section 12-12 of this Code with a prostitute; or

(2) Enters or remains in a place of prostitution with intent to engage in an act of sexual penetration as defined in Section 12-12 of this Code.

(b) Sentence.

Patronizing a prostitute is a Class B misdemeanor. A person convicted of a third or subsequent violation of this Section, or of any combination of such number of convictions under this Section and Sections 11-14, 11-15, 11-17, 11-18.1 and 11-19 of this Code, shall be guilty of a Class 4 felony. When a person has 2 or more prior convictions, the information or indictment charging that person shall state such prior convictions so as to give notice of the State's intention to treat the charge as a felony. The fact of such convictions is not an element of the offense and may not be disclosed to the jury during trial unless otherwise permitted by issues properly raised during such trial.

(Source: P.A. 85-1447.) [Formerly Ill. Rev. Stat. 38 §11-18.]

5/11-18.1. Patronizing a juvenile prostitute.

§11-18.1. Patronizing a juvenile prostitute. (a) Any person who engages in an act of sexual penetration as defined in Section 12-12 of this Code with a prostitute under 17 years of age commits the offense of patronizing a juvenile prostitute.

(b) It is an affirmative defense to the charge of patronizing a juvenile prostitute that the accused reasonably believed that the person was of the age of 17 years or over at the time of the act giving rise to the charge.

(c) Sentence. A person who commits patronizing a juvenile prostitute is guilty of a Class 4 felony.

(Source: P.A. 85-1447.) [Formerly Ill. Rev. Stat. 38 §11-18.1.]

5/11-19. Pimping.

§11-19. Pimping. (a) Any person who receives money or other property from a prostitute, not for a lawful consideration, knowing it was earned in whole or in part from the practice of prostitution, commits pimping.

(b) Sentence.

Pimping is a Class A misdemeanor. A person convicted of a third or subsequent violation of this Section, or of any combination of such number of convictions under this Section and Sections 11-14, 11-15, 11-17, 11-18 and 11-18.1 of this Code shall be guilty of a Class 4 felony. When a person has 2 or more prior convictions, the information or indictment charging that person shall state such prior convictions so as to give notice of the State's intention to treat the charge as a felony. The fact of such convictions is not an element of the offense and may not be disclosed to the jury during trial unless otherwise permitted by issues properly raised during such trial.

(Source: P.A. 85-1447.) [Formerly Ill. Rev. Stat. 38 §11-19.]

5/11-19.1. Juvenile pimping.

§11-19.1. Juvenile Pimping. (a) Any person who receives money or other property from a prostitute under 16 years of age or from a prostitute who is an institutionalized severely or profoundly mentally retarded person, not for a lawful consideration, knowing it was earned in whole or in part from the practice of prostitution, commits juvenile pimping.

(b) It is an affirmative defense to a charge of juvenile pimping that the accused reasonably believed the person was of the age of 16 years or over or was not an institutionalized severely or profoundly mentally retarded person at the time of the act giving rise to the charge.

(c) Sentence.

Juvenile pimping is a Class 1 felony.

(Source: P.A. 85-1392.) [Formerly Ill. Rev. Stat. 38 §11-19.1.]

5/11-19.2. Exploitation of a child.

§11-19.2. Exploitation of a Child. (A) A person commits exploitation of a child when he or she confines a child under the age of 16 or an institutionalized severely or profoundly mentally retarded person against his or her will by the infliction or threat of imminent infliction of great bodily harm, permanent disability or disfigurement or by administering to the child or an institutionalized severely or profoundly mentally retarded person without his or her consent or by threat or deception and for other than medical purposes, any alcoholic intoxicant or a drug as defined in the Controlled Substances Act [720 ILCS 570/100 et seq.] or the Cannabis Control Act [720 ILCS 550/1 et seq.] and:

(1) Compels the child or an institutionalized severely or profoundly mentally retarded person to become a prostitute; or

(2) Arranges a situation in which the child or an institutionalized severely or profoundly mentally retarded person may practice prostitution; or

(3) Receives money or other property from the child or an institutionalized severely or profoundly mentally retarded person knowing it was obtained in whole or in part from the practice of prostitution.

(B) For purposes of this Section, administering drugs, as defined in Subsection (A), or an alcoholic intoxicant to a child under the age of 13 or an institutionalized severely or profoundly mentally retarded person shall be deemed to be without consent if such administering is done without the consent of the parents or legal guardian.

(C) Exploitation of a child is a Class X felony.

(D) Any person convicted under this Section is subject to the forfeiture provisions of Section 11-20.1A of this Act.

(Source: P.A. 85-1440.) [Formerly Ill. Rev. Stat. 38 §11-19.2.]

5/11-20. Obscenity.

§11-20. Obscenity. (a) Elements of the Offense. A person commits obscenity when, with knowledge of the nature or content thereof, or recklessly failing to exercise reasonable inspection which would have disclosed the nature or content thereof, he:

(1) Sells, delivers or provides, or offers or agrees to sell, deliver or provide any obscene writing, picture, record or other representation or embodiment of the obscene; or

(2) Presents or directs an obscene play, dance or other performance or participates directly in that portion thereof which makes it obscene; or

(3) Publishes, exhibits or otherwise makes available anything obscene; or

(4) Performs an obscene act or otherwise presents an obscene exhibition of his body for gain; or

(5) Creates, buys, procures or possesses obscene matter or material with intent to disseminate it in violation of this Section, or of the penal laws or regulations of any other jurisdiction; or

(6) Advertises or otherwise promotes the sale of material represented or held out by him to be obscene, whether or not it is obscene.

(b) Obscene Defined.

Any material or performance is obscene if: (1) the average person, applying contemporary adult community standards, would find that, taken as a whole, it appeals to the prurient interest; and (2) the average person, applying contemporary adult community standards, would find that it depicts or describes, in a patently offensive way, ultimate sexual acts or sadomasochistic sexual acts, whether normal or perverted, actual or simulated, or masturbation, excretory functions or lewd exhibition of the genitals; and (3) taken as a whole, it lacks serious literary, artistic, political or scientific value.

(c) Interpretation of Evidence.

Obscenity shall be judged with reference to ordinary adults, except that it shall be judged with reference to children or other specially susceptible audiences if it appears from the character of the material or the circumstances of its dissemination to be specially designed for or directed to such an audience.

Where circumstances of production, presentation, sale, dissemination, distribution, or publicity indicate that material is being commercially exploited for the sake of its prurient appeal, such evidence is probative with respect to the nature of the matter and can justify the conclusion that the matter is lacking in serious literary, artistic, political or scientific value.

In any prosecution for an offense under this Section evidence shall be admissible to show:

(1) The character of the audience for which the material was designed or to which it was directed;

(2) What the predominant appeal of the material would be for ordinary adults or a special audience, and what effect, if any, it would probably have on the behavior of such people;

(3) The artistic, literary, scientific, educational or other merits of the material, or absence thereof;

(4) The degree, if any, of public acceptance of the material in this State;

(5) Appeal to prurient interest, or absence thereof, in advertising or other promotion of the material;

(6) Purpose of the author, creator, publisher or disseminator.

(d) Sentence.

Obscenity is a Class A misdemeanor. A second or subsequent offense is a Class 4 felony.

(e) Prima Facie Evidence.

The creation, purchase, procurement or possession of a mold, engraved plate or other embodiment of obscenity specially adapted for reproducing multiple copies, or the possession of more than 3 copies of obscene material shall be prima facie evidence of an intent to disseminate.

(f) Affirmative Defenses.

It shall be an affirmative defense to obscenity that the dissemination:

(1) Was not for gain and was made to personal associates other than children under 18 years of age;

(2) Was to institutions or individuals having scientific or other special justification for possession of such material.

(g) Forfeiture of property:

(1) Legislative Declaration. Obscenity is a far-reaching and extremely profitable crime. This crime persists despite the threat of prosecution and successful prosecution because existing sanctions do not effectively reach the

money and other assets generated by it. It is therefore necessary to supplement existing sanctions by mandating forfeiture of money and other assets generated by this crime. Forfeiture diminishes the financial incentives which encourage and sustain obscenity and secures for the State, local government and prosecutors a resource for prosecuting these crimes.

(2) Definitions.

(i) "Person" means an individual, partnership, private corporation, public, municipal, governmental or quasi-municipal corporation, unincorporated association, trustee or receiver.

(ii) "Property" means:

(a) real estate, including things growing on, affixed to and found in land, and any kind of interest therein; and

(b) tangible and intangible personal property, including rights, privileges, interests, claims and securities.

(3) Forfeiture of Property. Any person who has been convicted previously of the offense of obscenity and who shall be convicted of a second or subsequent offense of obscenity shall forfeit to the State of Illinois:

(i) Any property constituting or derived from any proceeds such person obtained, directly or indirectly, as a result of such offense; and

(ii) Any of the person's property used in any manner, wholly or in part, to commit such offense.

(4) Forfeiture Hearing. At any time following a second or subsequent conviction for obscenity, the court shall, upon petition by the Attorney General or the State's Attorney, conduct a hearing to determine whether there is any property that is subject to forfeiture as provided hereunder. At the forfeiture hearing the People shall have the burden of establishing by preponderance of the evidence that such property is subject to forfeiture.

(5) Prior Restraint.

Nothing in this subsection shall be construed as authorizing the prior restraint of any showing, performance or exhibition of allegedly obscene films, plays or other presentations or of any sale or distribution of allegedly obscene materials.

(6) Seizure, Sale and Distribution of the Property.

(i) Upon a determination under subparagraph (4) that there is property subject to forfeiture, the court shall authorize the Attorney General or the State's Attorney, except as provided in this Section, to seize all property declared forfeited upon terms and conditions as the court shall deem proper.

(ii) The Attorney General or State's Attorney is authorized to sell all property forfeited and seized pursuant to this Article, and, after the deduction of all requisite expenses of administration and sale, shall distribute the proceeds of such sale, along with any moneys forfeited or seized, in accordance with subparagraph (iii) hereof. If the Attorney General or State's Attorney believes any such property describes, depicts or portrays any of the acts or activities described in subsection (b) of this Section, he shall apply to the court for an order to destroy such property, and if the court determines the property describes, depicts or portrays such acts it shall order the Attorney General or State's Attorney to destroy such property.

(iii) All monies and the sale proceeds of all other property forfeited and seized pursuant hereto shall be distributed as follows:

(a) Fifty percent shall be distributed to the unit of local government whose officers or employees conducted the investigation into and caused the arrest or arrests and prosecution leading to the forfeiture, or, if the investigations, arrest or arrests and prosecution leading to the forfeiture were undertaken by the sheriff, this portion shall be distributed to the county for deposit in a special fund in the county treasury appropriated to the sheriff. Amounts distributed to the county for the sheriff or to the units of local government hereunder shall be used for enforcement of laws or ordinances governing obscenity and child pornography. In the event, however, that the investigation, arrest or arrests and prosecution leading to the forfeiture were undertaken solely by a State agency, the portion provided hereunder shall be paid into the State treasury to be used for enforcement of laws governing obscenity and child pornography.

(b) Twenty-five percent shall be distributed to the county in which the prosecution resulting in the forfeiture was instituted, deposited in a special fund in the county treasury and appropriated to the State's Attorney for use in the enforcement of laws governing obscenity and child pornography.

(c) Twenty-five percent shall be distributed to the Office of the State's Attorneys Appellate Prosecutor and deposited in the Obscenity Profits Forfeiture Fund, which is hereby created in the State Treasury, to be used by the Office of the State's Attorneys Appellate Prosecutor for additional expenses incurred in prosecuting appeals arising under Sections 11-20 and 11-20.1 of the Criminal Code of 1961. Any amounts remaining in the Fund after all additional expenses have been paid shall be used by the Office to reduce the participating county contributions to the Office on a pro-rated basis as determined by the board of governors of the Office of the State's Attorneys Appellate Prosecutor based on the populations of the participating counties.

(7) Construction of subsection (g).

It shall be the intent of the General Assembly that this subsection be liberally construed so as to effect its purposes. The forfeiture of property and other remedies hereunder shall be considered to be in addition, and not exclusive of any sentence or other remedy provided by law. Subsection (g) of this Section shall not apply to any property of a public library or any property of a library operated by an institution accredited by a generally recognized accrediting agency.

(Source: P.A. 85-1014.) [Formerly Ill. Rev. Stat. 38 §11-20.]

5/11-20.1. Child pornography.

§11-20.1. (a) A person commits the offense of child pornography who:

(1) films, videotapes, photographs, or otherwise depicts or portrays by means of any similar visual medium or reproduction any child whom he knows or reasonably should know to be under the age of 18 or any institutionalized severely or profoundly mentally retarded person where such child or institutionalized severely or profoundly mentally retarded person is:

(i) actually or by simulation engaged in any act of sexual intercourse with any person or animal; or

(ii) actually or by simulation engaged in any act of sexual contact involving the sex organs of the child or institutionalized severely or profoundly mentally retarded person and the mouth, anus, or sex organs of another person or animal; or which involves the mouth, anus or sex organs of the child or institutionalized severely or profoundly mentally retarded person and the sex organs of another person or animal; or

(iii) actually or by simulation engaged in any act of masturbation; or

(iv) actually or by simulation portrayed as being the object of, or otherwise engaged in, any act of lewd fondling, touching, or caressing involving another person or animal; or

(v) actually or by simulation engaged in any act of excretion or urination within a sexual context; or

(vi) actually or by simulation portrayed or depicted as bound, fettered, or subject to sadistic, masochistic, or sadomasochistic abuse in any sexual context; or

(vii) depicted or portrayed in any pose, posture or setting involving a lewd exhibition of the unclothed genitals, pubic area, buttocks, or, if such person is female, a fully or partially developed breast of the child or other person; or

(2) with the knowledge of the nature or content thereof, reproduces, disseminates, offers to disseminate, exhibits or possesses with intent to disseminate any film, videotape, photograph or other similar visual reproduction of any child or institutionalized severely or profoundly mentally retarded person whom the person knows or reasonably should know to be under the age of 18 or to be an institutionalized severely or profoundly mentally retarded person, engaged in any activity described in subparagraphs (i) through (vii) of paragraph (1) of this subsection; or

(3) with knowledge of the subject matter or theme thereof, produces any stage play, live performance, film, videotape or other similar visual portrayal which includes a child whom the person knows or reasonably should know to be under the age of 18 or an institutionalized severely or profoundly mentally retarded person engaged in any activity described in subparagraphs (i) through (vii) of paragraph (1) of this subsection; or

(4) solicits any child whom he knows or reasonably should know to be under the age of 18 or an institutionalized severely or profoundly mentally retarded person to appear in any stage play, live presentation, film, videotape, photograph or other similar visual reproduction in which the child or institutionalized severely or profoundly mentally retarded person is or will be depicted, actually or by simulation, in any act, pose or setting described in subparagraphs (i) through (vii) of paragraph (1) of this subsection; or

(5) is a parent, legal guardian or other person having care or custody of a child whom the person knows or reasonably should know to be under the age of 18 or an institutionalized severely or profoundly mentally retarded person and who knowingly permits or arranges for such child or institutionalized severely or profoundly mentally retarded person to appear in any stage play, live performance, film, videotape, photograph or other similar visual presentation, portrayal or simulation of any act or activity described in subparagraphs (i) through (vii) of paragraph (1) of this subsection; or

(6) with knowledge of the nature or content thereof, possesses any film, videotape, photograph or other similar visual reproduction of any child or institutionalized severely or profoundly mentally retarded person whom the person knows or reasonably should know to be under the age of 18 or to be an institutionalized severely or profoundly mentally retarded person, engaged in any activity described in subparagraphs (i) through (vii) of paragraph (1) of this subsection; or

(7) solicits a person to provide a child under the age of 18 or an institutionalized severely or profoundly mentally retarded person to appear in any videotape, photograph, film, stage play, live presentation, or other similar visual reproduction in which the child or an institutionalized severely or profoundly mentally retarded person will be depicted, actually or by simulation, in any act, pose, or setting described in subparagraphs (i) through (vii) of paragraph (1) of this subsection.

(b)(1) It shall be an affirmative defense to a charge of child pornography that the defendant reasonably believed, under all of the circumstances, that the child was 18 years of age or older or that the person was not an institutionalized severely or profoundly mentally retarded person but only where, prior to the act or acts giving rise to a prosecution under this Section, he took some affirmative action or made a bonafide inquiry designed to ascertain whether the child was 18 years of age or older or that the person was not an institutionalized severely or profoundly mentally retarded person and his reliance upon the information so obtained was clearly reasonable.

(2) It shall be an affirmative defense to a charge of child pornography that the defendant was employed by a public library or any library operated by an institution accredited by a generally recognized accrediting agency, at the time the act leading to the charge of child pornography took place and such act was committed during the course of employment.

(3) The charge of child pornography shall not apply to the performance of official duties by law enforcement or prosecuting officers, court personnel or attorneys, nor to bonafide treatment or professional education programs conducted by licensed physicians, psychologists or social workers.

(4) Possession by the defendant of more than one of the same film, videotape or visual reproduction in which child pornography is depicted shall raise a rebuttable presumption that the defendant possessed such materials with the intent to disseminate them.

(c) Violation of paragraph (1), (4), (5), or (7) of subsection (a) is a Class 1 felony with a mandatory minimum fine of $2,000 and a maximum fine of $100,000. Violation of paragraph (3) of subsection (a) is a Class 2 felony with a mandatory minimum fine of $1500 and a maximum fine of $100,000. Violation of paragraph (2) of subsection (a) is a Class 3 felony with a mandatory minimum fine of $1000 and a maximum fine of $100,000. Violation of paragraph (6) of subsection (a) is a Class 4 felony with a mandatory minimum fine of $1000 and a maximum fine of $100,000.

(d) If a person is convicted of a second or subsequent violation of this Section within 10 years of a prior conviction, the court shall order a presentence psychiatric examination of the person. The examiner shall report to the court whether treatment of the person is necessary.

(e) Any film, videotape, photograph or other similar visual reproduction which includes a child under the age of 18 or an institutionalized severely or profoundly mentally retarded person engaged in any activity described in subparagraphs (i) through (vii) or* paragraph 1** of subsection (a), and any material or equipment used or intended for use in photographing, filming, printing, producing, reproducing, manufacturing, projecting, exhibiting, or disseminating such material shall be seized and forfeited in the manner, method and procedure provided by Section 36-1 of this Code for the seizure and forfeiture of vessels, vehicles and aircraft.

**So in original. Probably should be "of".*

***So in original. Probably should be "(1)".*

(f) Definitions. For the purposes of this Section, the term:

(1) "Disseminate" means to sell, distribute, exchange or transfer possession, whether with or without consideration;

(2) "Produce" means to direct, promote, advertise, publish, manufacture, issue, present or show;

(3) "Reproduce" means to make a duplication or copy.

(Chgd. by P.A. 87-1069, §1, eff. 1/1/93; P.A. 87-1070, §1, eff. 9/13/92.)
(Source: P.A. 86-820; 86-1168.) [Formerly Ill. Rev. Stat. 38 §11-20.1.]

5/11-20.1A. Juvenile prostitution.

§11-20.1A. (a) A person who commits the offense of keeping a place of juvenile prostitution, exploitation of a child or child pornography under Sections 11-17.1, 11-19.2 or 11-20.1 of this Code, shall forfeit to the State of Illinois:

(1) any profits or proceeds and any interest or property he has acquired or maintained in violation of Sections 11-17.1, 11-19.2 or 11-20.1 of this Code that the sentencing court determines, after a forfeiture hearing, to have been acquired or maintained as a result of keeping a place of juvenile prostitution, exploitation of a child or child pornography; and

(2) any interest in, security of, claim against, or property or contractual right of any kind affording a source of influence over, any enterprise which he has

established, operated, controlled or conducted in violation of Sections 11-17.1, 11-19.2 or 11-20.1 of this Code that the sentencing court determines, after a forfeiture hearing, to have been acquired or maintained as a result of keeping a place of juvenile prostitution, exploitation of a child or child pornography.

(b)(1) The court shall, upon petition by the Attorney General or State's Attorney at any time following sentencing, conduct a hearing to determine whether any property or property interest is subject to forfeiture under this Section. At the forfeiture hearing the people shall have the burden of establishing, by a preponderance of the evidence, that property or property interests are subject to forfeiture under this Section.

(2) In any action brought by the People of the State of Illinois under this Section, wherein any restraining order, injunction or prohibition or any other action in connection with any property or interest subject to forfeiture under this Section is sought, the circuit court presiding over the trial of the person or persons charged with keeping a place of juvenile prostitution, exploitation of a child or child pornography shall first determine whether there is probable cause to believe that the person or persons so charged have committed the offense of keeping a place of juvenile prostitution, exploitation of a child or child pornography and whether the property or interest is subject to forfeiture pursuant to this Section. In order to make such a determination, prior to entering any such order, the court shall conduct a hearing without a jury, wherein the People shall establish that there is: (i) probable cause that the person or persons so charged have committed the offense of keeping a place of juvenile prostitution, exploitation of a child or child pornography and (ii) probable cause that any property or interest may be subject to forfeiture pursuant to this Section. Such hearing may be conducted simultaneously with a preliminary hearing, if the prosecution is commenced by information or complaint, or by motion of the People, at any stage in the proceedings. The court may accept a finding of probable cause at a preliminary hearing following the filing of an information charging the offense of keeping a place of juvenile prostitution, exploitation of a child or child pornography or the return of an indictment by a grand jury charging the offense of keeping a place of juvenile prostitution, exploitation of a child or child pornography as sufficient evidence of probable cause as provided in item (i) above. Upon such a finding, the circuit court shall enter such restraining order, injunction or prohibition, or shall take such other action in connection with any such property or other interest subject to forfeiture, as is necessary to insure that such property is not removed from the jurisdiction of the court, concealed, destroyed or otherwise disposed of by the owner of that property or interest prior to a forfeiture hearing under this Section. The Attorney General or State's Attorney shall file a certified copy of such restraining order, injunction or other prohibition with the recorder of deeds or registrar of titles of each county where any such property of the defendant may be located. No such injunction, restraining order or other prohibition shall affect the rights of any bona fide purchaser, mortgagee, judgment creditor or other lienholder arising prior to the date of such filing. The court may, at any time, upon verified petition by the defendant or an innocent owner or innocent bona fide third party lienholder who neither had knowledge of, nor consented to, the illegal act or omission, conduct a hearing to release all or portions of any such property or interest which the court previously determined to be subject to forfeiture or subject to any restraining order, injunction, or prohibition or other action. The court may release such property to the defendant or innocent owner or innocent bona fide third party lienholder who neither had knowledge of, nor consented to, the illegal act or omission for good cause shown and within the sound discretion of the court.

A forfeiture under this Section may be commenced by the Attorney General or a State's Attorney.

(3) Upon conviction of a person of keeping a place of juvenile prostitution, exploitation of a child or child pornography, the court shall authorize the Attorney General to seize all property or other interest declared forfeited under this Section upon such terms and conditions as the court shall deem proper.

(4) The Attorney General is authorized to sell all property forfeited and seized pursuant to this Section, unless such property is required by law to be destroyed or is harmful to the public, and, after the deduction of all requisite expenses of administration and sale, shall distribute the proceeds of such sale, along with any moneys forfeited or seized, in accordance with subsection (c) of this Section.

(c) All monies forfeited and the sale proceeds of all other property forfeited and seized under this Section shall be distributed as follows:

(1) One-half shall be divided equally among all units of local government whose officers or employees conducted the investigation which resulted in the forfeiture; and

(2) One-half shall be deposited in the Violent Crime Victims Assistance Fund.

(Source: P.A. 85-1194.) [Formerly Ill. Rev. Stat. 38 §11-20.1A.]

5/11-20.2. Commercial film and photographic print processor—Observations.

§11-20.2. Any commercial film and photographic print processor who has knowledge of or observes, within the scope of his professional capacity or employment, any film, photograph, videotape, negative or slide which depicts a child whom the processor knows or reasonably should know to be under the age of 18 where such child is:

(i) actually or by simulation engaged in any act of sexual intercourse with any person or animal; or

(ii) actually or by simulation engaged in any act of sexual contact involving the sex organs of the child and the mouth, anus, or sex organs of another person or animal; or which involves the mouth, anus or sex organs of the child and the sex organs of another person or animal; or

(iii) actually or by simulation engaged in any act of masturbation; or

(iv) actually or by simulation portrayed as being the object of, or otherwise engaged in, any act of lewd fondling, touching, or caressing involving another person or animal; or

(v) actually or by simulation engaged in any act of excretion or urination within a sexual context; or

(vi) actually or by simulation portrayed or depicted as bound, fettered, or subject to sadistic, masochistic, or sadomasochistic abuse in any sexual context; shall report such instance to a peace officer immediately or as soon as possible. Failure to make such report shall be a business offense with a fine of $1,000.

(Source: P.A. 84-1280.) [Formerly Ill. Rev. Stat. 38 §11-20.2.]

5/11-21. Harmful material.

§11-21. Harmful material. (a) Elements of the Offense.

A person who, with knowledge that a person is a child, that is a person under 18 years of age, or who fails to exercise reasonable care in ascertaining the true age of a child, knowingly distributes to or sends or causes to be sent to, or exhibits to, or offers to distribute or exhibit any harmful material to a child, is guilty of a misdemeanor.

(b) Definitions.

(1) Material is harmful if, to the average person, applying contemporary standards, its predominant appeal, taken as a whole, is to prurient interest, that is a shameful or morbid interest in nudity, sex, or excretion, which goes substantially beyond customary limits of candor in description or repre-

sentation of such matters, and is material the redeeming social importance of which is substantially less than its prurient appeal.

(2) Material, as used in this Section means any writing, picture, record or other representation or embodiment.

(3) Distribute means to transfer possession of, whether with or without consideration.

(4) Knowingly, as used in this section means having knowledge of the contents of the subject matter, or recklessly failing to exercise reasonable inspection which would have disclosed the contents thereof.

(c) Interpretation of Evidence.

The predominant appeal to prurient interest of the material shall be judged with reference to average children of the same general age of the child to whom such material was offered, distributed, sent or exhibited, unless it appears from the nature of the matter or the circumstances of its dissemination, distribution or exhibition that it is designed for specially susceptible groups, in which case the predominant appeal of the material shall be judged with reference to its intended or probable recipient group.

In prosecutions under this section, where circumstances of production, presentation, sale, dissemination, distribution, or publicity indicate the material is being commercially exploited for the sake of its prurient appeal, such evidence is probative with respect to the nature of the material and can justify the conclusion that the redeeming social importance of the material is in fact substantially less than its prurient appeal.

(d) Sentence.

Distribution of harmful material in violation of this Section is a Class A misdemeanor. A second or subsequent offense is a Class 4 felony.

(e) Affirmative Defenses.

(1) Nothing in this section shall prohibit any public library or any library operated by an accredited institution of higher education from circulating harmful material to any person under 18 years of age, provided such circulation is in aid of a legitimate scientific or educational purpose, and it shall be an affirmative defense in any prosecution for a violation of this section that the act charged was committed in aid of legitimate scientific or educational purposes.

(2) Nothing in this section shall prohibit any parent from distributing to his child any harmful material.

(3) Proof that the defendant demanded, was shown and acted in reliance upon any of the following documents as proof of the age of a child, shall be a defense to any criminal prosecution under this section: A document issued by the federal government or any state, county or municipal government or subdivision or agency thereof, including, but not limited to, a motor vehicle operator's license, a registration certificate issued under the Federal Selective Service Act [50 App. U.S.C. §451 et seq.] or an identification card issued to a member of the armed forces.

(4) In the event an advertisement of harmful material as defined in this section culminates in the sale or distribution of such harmful material to a child, under circumstances where there was no personal confrontation of the child by the defendant, his employees or agents, as where the order or request for such harmful material was transmitted by mail, telephone, or similar means of communication, and delivery of such harmful material to the child was by mail, freight, or similar means of transport, it shall be a defense in any prosecution for a violation of this section that the advertisement contained the following statement, or a statement substantially similar thereto, and that the defendant required the purchaser to certify that he was not under 18 years of age and that the purchaser falsely stated that he was not under 18 years of age: "NOTICE: It is unlawful for any person under 18 years of age to purchase the matter herein

advertised. Any person under 18 years of age who falsely states that he is not under 18 years of age for the purpose of obtaining the material advertised herein, is guilty of a Class B misdemeanor under the laws of the State of Illinois."

(f) Child Falsifying Age.

Any person under 18 years of age who falsely states, either orally or in writing, that he is not under the age of 18 years, or who presents or offers to any person any evidence of age and identity which is false or not actually his own for the purpose of ordering, obtaining, viewing, or otherwise procuring or attempting to procure or view any harmful material, is guilty of a Class B misdemeanor.

(Source: P.A. 77-2638.) [Formerly Ill. Rev. Stat. 38 §11-21.]

5/11-22. Tie-in sales of obscene publications to distributors.

§11-22. Tie-in sales of obscene publications to distributors. Any person, firm or corporation, or any agent, officer or employee thereof, engaged in the business of distributing books, magazines, periodicals, comic books or other publications to retail dealers, who shall refuse to furnish to any retail dealer such quantity of books, magazines, periodicals, comic books or other publications as such retail dealer normally sells because the retail dealer refuses to sell, or offer for sale, any books, magazines, periodicals, comic books or other publications which are obscene, lewd, lascivious, filthy or indecent is guilty of a petty offense. Each publication sold or delivered in violation of this Act shall constitute a separate petty offense.

(Source: P.A. 77-2638.) [Formerly Ill. Rev. Stat. 38 §11-22.]

ARTICLE 12. BODILY HARM

5/12-1. Assault.

§12-1. Assault. (a) A person commits an assault when, without lawful authority, he engages in conduct which places another in reasonable apprehension of receiving a battery.

(b) Sentence.

Assault is a Class C misdemeanor.

(Source: P.A. 77-2638.) [Formerly Ill. Rev. Stat. 38 §12-1.]

5/12-2. Aggravated assault.

§12-2. Aggravated assault. (a) A person commits an aggravated assault, when, in committing an assault, he:

(1) Uses a deadly weapon or any device manufactured and designed to be substantially similar in appearance to a firearm, other than by discharging a firearm in the direction of another person, a peace officer, a person summoned or directed by a peace officer, a correctional officer or a fireman or in the direction of a vehicle occupied by another person, a peace officer, a person summoned or directed by a peace officer, a correctional officer or a fireman while the officer or fireman is engaged in the execution of any of his official duties, or to prevent the officer or fireman from performing his official duties, or in retaliation for the officer or fireman performing his official duties;

(2) Is hooded, robed or masked in such manner as to conceal his identity or any device manufactured and designed to be substantially similar in appearance to a firearm;

(3) Knows the individual assaulted to be a teacher or other person employed in any school and such teacher or other employee is upon the grounds of a school or grounds adjacent thereto, or is in any part of a building used for school purposes;

(4) Knows the individual assaulted to be a supervisor, director, instructor or other person employed in any park district and such supervisor, director, instructor or other employee is upon the grounds of the park or grounds adjacent thereto, or is in any part of a building used for park purposes;

(5) Knows the individual assaulted to be a caseworker, investigator, or other person employed by the State Department of Public Aid or a County Department of Public Aid and such caseworker, investigator, or other person is upon the grounds of a Public Aid office or grounds adjacent thereto, or is in any part of a building used for Public Aid purposes, or upon the grounds of a home of a public aid applicant, recipient or any other person being interviewed or investigated in the employees'* discharge of his duties, or on grounds adjacent thereto, or is in any part of a building in which the applicant, recipient, or other such person resides or is located;

**So in original. Probably should be "employee's".*

(6) Knows the individual assaulted to be a peace officer, or a person summoned and directed by him or a correctional officer, or a fireman while the officer or fireman is engaged in the execution of any of his official duties, or to prevent the officer or fireman from performing his official duties, or in retaliation for the officer or fireman performing his official duties, and the assault is committed

other than by the discharge of a firearm in the direction of the officer or fireman or in the direction of a vehicle occupied by the officer or fireman;

(7) Knows the individual assaulted to be a paramedic, ambulance driver or other medical assistance or first aid personnel employed by a municipality or other governmental unit engaged in the execution of any of his official duties, or to prevent the paramedic, ambulance driver, or other medical assistance or first aid personnel from performing his official duties, or in retaliation for the paramedic, ambulance driver, or other medical assistance or first aid personnel performing his official duties;

(8) Knows the individual assaulted to be the driver, operator, employee or passenger of any transportation facility or system engaged in the business of transportation of the public for hire and the individual assaulted is then performing in such capacity or then using such public transportation as a passenger or using any area of any description designated by the transportation facility or system as a vehicle boarding, departure, or transfer location;

(9) Or the individual assaulted is on or about a public way, public property, or public place of accommodation or amusement;

(10) Knows the individual assaulted to be an employee of the State of Illinois, a municipal corporation therein or a political subdivision thereof, engaged in the performance of his authorized duties as such employee;

(11) Knowingly and without legal justification, commits an assault on a physically handicapped person;

(12) Knowingly and without legal justification, commits an assault on a person 60 years of age or older; or

(13) Discharges a firearm.

(b) Sentence.

Aggravated assault as defined in paragraphs (1) through (12) of subsection (a) of this Section is a Class A misdemeanor. Aggravated assault as defined in paragraph (13) of subsection (a) of this Section is a Class 4 felony.

(Chgd. by P.A. 87-921, §1, eff. 1/1/93.)
(Source: P.A. 85-1209; 86-1393.) [Formerly Ill. Rev. Stat. 38 §12-2.]

5/12-3. Battery.

§12-3. Battery. (a) A person commits battery if he intentionally or knowingly without legal justification and by any means, (1) causes bodily harm to an individual or (2) makes physical contact of an insulting or provoking nature with an individual.

(b) Sentence.

Battery is a Class A misdemeanor.

(Source: P.A. 77-2638.) [Formerly Ill. Rev. Stat. 38 §12-3.]

5/12-3.1. Battery of an unborn child.

§12-3.1. Battery of an Unborn Child. (a) A person commits battery of an unborn child if he intentionally or knowingly without legal justification and by any means causes bodily harm to an unborn child.

(b) For purposes of this Section, (1) "unborn child" shall mean any individual of the human species from fertilization until birth, and (2) "person" shall not include the pregnant woman whose unborn child is harmed.

(c) Sentence. Battery of an unborn child is a Class A misdemeanor.

(d) This Section shall not apply to acts which cause bodily harm to an unborn child if those acts were committed during any abortion, as defined in Section 2 of the Illinois Abortion Law of 1975, as amended [720 ILCS 510/2], to which the pregnant woman has consented. This Section shall not apply to acts which were committed pursuant to usual and customary standards of medical practice during diagnostic testing or therapeutic treatment.

(Source: P.A. 84-1414.) [Formerly Ill. Rev. Stat. 38 §12-3.1.]

5/12-3.2. Domestic battery.

§12-3.2. Domestic Battery. (a) A person commits Domestic Battery if he intentionally or knowingly without legal justification by any means:

(1) Causes bodily harm to any family or household member as defined in Subsection (3) of Section 112A-3 of the Code of Criminal Procedure of 1963, as amended [725 ILCS 5/112A-3];

(2) Makes physical contact of an insulting or provoking nature with any family or household member as defined in subsection (3) of Section 112A-3 of the Code of Criminal Procedure of 1963, as amended.

(b) Sentence. Domestic Battery is a Class A Misdemeanor. In addition to any other sentencing alternatives, for any second conviction of violating this Section within 5 years of a previous conviction for violating this Section, the offender shall be mandatorily sentenced to a minimum of 48 consecutive hours of imprisonment. The imprisonment shall not be subject to suspension, nor shall the person be eligible for probation in order to reduce the sentence.

(Source: P.A. 86-979.) [Formerly Ill. Rev. Stat. 38 §12-3.2.]

5/12-4. Aggravated battery.

§12-4. Aggravated Battery. (a) A person who, in committing a battery, intentionally or knowingly causes great bodily harm, or permanent disability or disfigurement commits aggravated battery.

(b) A person who, in committing a battery, commits aggravated battery if he:

(1) Uses a deadly weapon other than by the discharge of a firearm;

(2) Is hooded, robed or masked, in such manner as to conceal his identity;

(3) Knows the individual harmed to be a teacher or other person employed in any school and such teacher or other employee is upon the grounds of a school or grounds adjacent thereto, or is in any part of a building used for school purposes;

(4) Knows the individual harmed to be a supervisor, director, instructor or other person employed in any park district and such supervisor, director, instructor or other employee is upon the grounds of the park or grounds adjacent thereto, or is in any part of a building used for park purposes;

(5) Knows the individual harmed to be a caseworker, investigator, or other person employed by the State Department of Public Aid or a County Department of Public Aid and such caseworker, investigator, or other person is upon the grounds of a Public Aid office or grounds adjacent thereto, or is in any part of a building used for Public Aid purposes, or upon the grounds of a home of a public aid applicant, recipient, or any other person being interviewed or investigated in the employee's discharge of his duties, or on grounds adjacent thereto, or is in any part of a building in which the applicant, recipient, or other such person resides or is located;

(6) Knows the individual harmed to be a peace officer, a person summoned and directed by a peace officer, or a correctional institution employee, or a fireman while such officer, employee or fireman is engaged in the execution of any of his official duties including arrest or attempted arrest, or to prevent the officer, employee or fireman from performing his official duties, or in retaliation for the officer, employee or fireman performing his duties, and the battery is committed other than by the discharge of a firearm.*

**So in original. Probably should be a semi-colon.*

(7) Knows the individual harmed to be a paramedic, ambulance driver or other medical assistance or first aid personnel engaged in the performance of his or her duties, or to prevent the paramedic, ambulance driver, or other medical assistance or first aid personnel from performing his official duties, or in retaliation for performing his official duties;

(8) Is, or the person battered is, on or about a public way, public property or public place of accommodation or amusement;

(9) Knows the individual harmed to be the driver, operator, employee or passenger of any transportation facility or system engaged in the business of transportation of the public for hire and the individual assaulted is then performing in such capacity or then using such public transportation as a passenger or using any area of any description designated by the transportation facility or system as a vehicle boarding, departure, or transfer location;

(10) Knowingly and without legal justification and by any means causes bodily harm to an individual of 60 years of age or older;

(11) Knows the individual harmed is pregnant;

(12) Knows the individual harmed to be a judge whom the person intended to harm as a result of the judge's performance of his or her official duties as a judge;

(13) Knows the individual harmed to be an employee of the Illinois Department of Children and Family Services engaged in the performance of his authorized duties as such employee; or

(14) Knows the individual harmed to be a person who is physically handicapped.

For the purpose of paragraph (14) of subsection (b) of this Section, a physically handicapped person is a person who suffers from a permanent and disabling physical characteristic, resulting from disease, injury, functional disorder or congenital condition.

(c) A person who administers to an individual or causes him to take, without his consent or by threat or deception, and for other than medical purposes, any intoxicating, poisonous, stupefying, narcotic or anesthetic substance commits aggravated battery.

(d) A person who knowingly gives to another person any food that contains any substance or object that is intended to cause physical injury if eaten, commits aggravated battery.

(e) Sentence.

Aggravated battery is a Class 3 felony.

(Chgd. by P.A. 87-921, §1; P.A. 87-1083, §1, eff. 1/1/93.)
(Source: P.A. 86-979; 86-980; 86-1028.) [Formerly Ill. Rev. Stat. 38 §12-4.]

5/12-4.1. Heinous battery.

§12-4.1. Heinous Battery. (a) A person who, in committing a battery, knowingly causes severe and permanent disability or disfigurement by means of a caustic substance commits heinous battery.

(b) Sentence.

Heinous battery is a Class X felony.

(Source: P.A. 80-1099.) [Formerly Ill. Rev. Stat. 38 §12-4.1.]

5/12-4.2. Aggravated battery with a firearm.

§12-4.2. Aggravated Battery with a firearm. (a) A person commits aggravated battery with a firearm when he, in committing a battery, knowingly or intentionally *by means of the discharging of a firearm* (1) causes any injury to another person [by means of the discharging of a firearm], or (2) causes any injury to a person he knows to be a peace officer, a person summoned by a peace officer, a correctional institution employee or a fireman while the officer, employee or fireman is engaged in the execution of any of his official duties, or to prevent the officer, employee or fireman from performing his official duties, or in retaliation for the officer, employee or fireman performing his official duties, or (3) causes any injury to a person he knows to be a paramedic, ambulance driver, or other medical assistance or first aid personnel, employed by a municipality or other governmental unit, while the paramedic, ambulance driver, or other medical assistance or first aid personnel is engaged in the execution of any of his official duties, or to prevent the paramedic, ambulance driver, or other medical assistance or first aid personnel from performing his official duties, or in retaliation for the paramedic, ambulance driver, or other medical assistance or first aid personnel performing his official duties.

(b) A violation of subsection (a)(1) of this Section is a Class X felony. A violation of subsection (a)(2) or subsection (a)(3) of this Section is a Class X felony for which the sentence shall be a term of imprisonment of no less than 10 years and no more than 45 years.

(c) For purposes of this Section, "firearm" is defined as in "An Act relating to the acquisition, possession and transfer of firearms and firearm ammunition, to provide a penalty for the violation thereof and to make an appropriation in connection therewith", approved August 1, 1967, as amended [430 ILCS 65/1 et seq.].

(Chgd. by P.A. 87-921, §1, eff. 1/1/93; P.A. 87-1256, §2, eff. 7/1/93. Matter in brackets eff. only until 7/1/93. Matter in italics eff. 7/1/93.)
(Source: P.A. 86-980.) [Formerly Ill. Rev. Stat. 38 §12-4.2.]

5/12-4.3. Aggravated battery of a child.

§12-4.3. Aggravated Battery of a Child. (a) Any person of the age 18 years and upwards who intentionally or knowingly, and without legal justification and by any means, causes great bodily harm or permanent disability or disfigurement to any child under the age of 13 years or to any institutionalized severely or profoundly mentally retarded person, commits the offense of aggravated battery of a child.

Aggravated battery of a child is a Class 1 felony for which a person, if sentenced to a term of imprisonment, shall be sentenced to a term of no less than 5 years and no more than 30 years.

A second or subsequent offense of aggravated battery of a child committed after conviction but before 5 years have elapsed following completion of the sentence for a prior conviction of such offense or committed within a 5 year period following a discharge and dismissal under paragraph (b) of this Section is a Class X felony.

(b) Aggravated battery of a child when committed by a person engaged in the actual care of the child or institutionalized severely or profoundly mentally retarded person-special penalty provision.

(1) When a person engaged in the actual care of the victim child or institutionalized severely or profoundly mentally retarded person, as determined by the court on the facts before it, pleads guilty to, or is found guilty of the offense of aggravated battery of a child, the court may, without entering a judgment of guilt and with the consent of such person, defer further proceedings and place such person upon probation upon such reasonable terms and conditions as it may require. At least one such term of probation shall be that the person report to and cooperate with the Department of Children and Family Services at such times and in such programs as the Department of Children and Family Services may require.

(2) Upon fulfillment of the terms and conditions imposed, the court shall discharge such person and dismiss the proceedings. Discharge and dismissal under this Section shall be without court adjudication of guilt and shall not be deemed a conviction for purposes of disqualification or disabilities imposed by law upon conviction of a crime. However, a record of the disposition shall be reported by the clerk of the circuit court to the Department of State Police pursuant to Section 2.1 of "An Act in relation to criminal identification and investigation", approved July 2, 1931, as amended [20 ILCS 2630/2.1], maintained and provided to any civil authority in connection with a determination

of whether the person is an acceptable candidate for the care, custody, and supervision of children.

(3) Discharge and dismissal under this Section may occur only once.

(4) Probation under this Section shall be for not less than 2 years.

(5) In the event that the child or institutionalized severely or profoundly mentally retarded person dies of the injuries alleged, this Section shall be inapplicable.

(6) Subsection (b) is intended to be supplemental to, not in derogation of, any other proceeding available under the Juvenile Court Act of 1987 [705 ILCS 405/1-1 et seq.].

(Source: P.A. 86-575; 86-1003.) [Formerly Ill. Rev. Stat. 38 §12-4.3.]

5/12-4.4. Aggravated battery of an unborn child.

§12-4.4. Aggravated battery of an unborn child. (a) A person who, in committing battery of an unborn child, intentionally or knowingly causes great bodily harm, or permanent disability or disfigurement commits aggravated battery of an unborn child.

(b) Sentence. Aggravated battery of an unborn child is a Class 2 felony.

(Source: P.A. 84-1414.) [Formerly Ill. Rev. Stat. 38 §12-4.4.]

5/12-4.5. Tampering with food, drugs or cosmetics.

§12-4.5. Tampering with food, drugs or cosmetics. (a) Any person who knowingly puts any substance capable of causing death or great bodily harm to a human being into any food, drug or cosmetic offered for sale or consumption commits the offense of tampering with food, drugs or cosmetics.

(b) Sentence. Tampering with food, drugs or cosmetics is a Class 2 felony.

(Source: P.A. 84-1428; 84-1438.) [Formerly Ill. Rev. Stat. 38 §12-4.5.]

5/12-4.6. Aggravated battery of a senior citizen.

§12-4.6. Aggravated Battery of a Senior Citizen. (a) A person who, in committing battery, intentionally or knowingly causes great bodily harm or permanent disability or disfigurement to an individual of 60 years of age or older commits aggravated battery of a senior citizen.

(b) Sentence. Aggravated battery of a senior citizen is a Class 2 felony.

(Source: P.A. 85-1177.) [Formerly Ill. Rev. Stat. 38 §12-4.6.]

5/12-4.7. Drug induced infliction of great bodily harm.

§12-4.7. Drug induced infliction of great bodily harm. (a) Any person who violates subsection (a) or subsection (c) of Section 401 of the Illinois Controlled Substances Act [720 ILCS 570/401] by unlawfully delivering a controlled substance to another commits the offense of drug induced infliction of great bodily harm if any person experiences great bodily harm or permanent disability as a result of the injection, inhalation or ingestion of any amount of that controlled substance.

(b) Drug induced infliction of great bodily harm is a Class 1 felony.

(Chgd. by P.A. 87-1198, §2, eff. 9/25/92.)

(Source: P.A. 86-1459; 87-435.) [Formerly Ill. Rev. Stat. 38 §12-4.7.]

5/12-5. Reckless conduct.

§12-5. Reckless conduct. (a) A person who causes bodily harm to or endangers the bodily safety of an individual by any means, commits reckless conduct if he performs recklessly the acts which cause the harm or endanger safety, whether they otherwise are lawful or unlawful.

(b) Sentence.

Reckless conduct is a Class A misdemeanor.

(Source: P.A. 77-2638.) [Formerly Ill. Rev. Stat. 38 §12-5.]

5/12-5.1. Criminal housing management.

§12-5.1. Criminal housing management. (a) A person commits the offense of criminal housing management when, having personal management or control of residential real estate, whether as a legal or equitable owner or as a managing agent or otherwise, he recklessly permits the physical condition or facilities of the residential real estate to become or remain in any condition which endangers the health or safety of any person.

(b) Sentence.

Criminal housing management is a Class A misdemeanor. A subsequent conviction for a violation of subsection (a) is a Class 4 felony.

(Source: P.A. 85-341.) [Formerly Ill. Rev. Stat. 38 §12-5.1.]

5/12-5.2. Injunction.

§12-5.2. Injunction. (a) In addition to any other remedies, the State's Attorney of the county where the property described in Section 12-5.1 of this Act is located is authorized to file a complaint and apply to the circuit court for a temporary restraining order, and such circuit court shall upon hearing grant a temporary restraining order or a preliminary or permanent injunction, without bond, restraining any person who owns, manages, or has any equitable interest in the property, from collecting, receiving or benefiting from any rents or other monies available from the property, so long as the property remains in the condition described in Section 12-5.1 of this Act.

(b) The court may order any rents or other monies owed to be paid into an escrow account. The funds are to be paid out of the escrow account only to satisfy the reasonable cost of necessary repairs of the property which had been incurred or will be incurred in ameliorating the condition of the property as described in Section 12-5.1 of this Act, payment of delinquent real estate taxes on the property or payment of other legal debts relating to the property. The court may order that funds remain in escrow for a reasonable time after the completion of all necessary repairs to assure continued upkeep of the property and satisfaction of other outstanding legal debts of the property.

(c) The owner shall be responsible for contracting to have necessary repairs completed and shall be required to submit all bills, together with certificates of completion, to the manager of the escrow account within 30 days after their receipt by the owner.

(d) In contracting for any repairs required pursuant to this Section the owner of the property shall enter into a contract only after receiving bills from at least 3 independent contractors capable of making the necessary repairs. If the owner does not contract for the repairs with the lowest bidder, he shall file an affidavit with the court explaining why the lowest bid was not acceptable. At no time, under the provisions of this Act, shall the owner contract with anyone who is not a licensed contractor. The court may order release of those funds in the escrow account that are in excess of the monies that the court determines to its satisfaction are needed to correct the condition of the property as described in Section 12-5.1 of this Act.

(e) The Clerk of the Circuit Court shall maintain a separate trust account entitled "Property Improvement Trust Account", which shall serve as the depository for the escrowed funds prescribed by this Section. The Clerk of the Court shall be responsible for the receipt, disbursement, monitoring and maintenance of all funds entrusted to this account, and shall provide to the court a quarterly accounting of the activities for any property, with funds in such account, unless the court orders accountings on a more frequent basis.

The Clerk of the Circuit Court shall promulgate rules and procedures to administer the provisions of this Act.

(f) Nothing in this Section shall in any way be construed to limit or alter any existing liability incurred, or to be incurred, by the owner or manager except as expressly provided in this Act. Nor shall anything in this Section be construed to create any liability on behalf of the Clerk of the Court, the State's Attorney's office or any other governmental agency involved in this action.

Nor shall anything in this Section be construed to authorize tenants to refrain from paying rent.

(g) Costs. As part of the costs of an action under this Section, the court shall assess a reasonable fee against the defendant to be paid to the Clerk of the Court. This amount is to be used solely for the maintenance of the Property Improvement Trust Account. No money obtained directly or indirectly from the property subject to the case may be used to satisfy this cost.

(h) The municipal building department or other entity responsible for inspection of property and the enforcement of such local requirements shall, within 5 business days of a request by the State's Attorney, provide all documents requested, which shall include, but not be limited to, all records of inspections, permits and other information relating to any property.

(Source: P.A. 86-584.) [Formerly Ill. Rev. Stat. 38 §12-5.2.]

5/12-6. Intimidation.

§12-6. Intimidation. (a) A person commits intimidation when, with intent to cause another to perform or to omit the performance of any act, he communicates to another, whether in person, by telephone or by mail, a threat to perform without lawful authority any of the following acts:

(1) Inflict physical harm on the person threatened or any other person or on property; or

(2) Subject any person to physical confinement or restraint; or

(3) Commit any criminal offense; or

(4) Accuse any person of an offense; or

(5) Expose any person to hatred, contempt or ridicule; or

(6) Take action as a public official against anyone or anything, or withhold official action, or cause such action or withholding; or

(7) Bring about or continue a strike, boycott or other collective action.

(b) Sentence.

Intimidation is a Class 3 felony.

(Source: P.A. 85-1210.) [Formerly Ill. Rev. Stat. 38 §12-6.]

5/12-6.1. Compelling organization membership of persons.

§12-6.1. Compelling organization membership of persons. A person who expressly or impliedly threatens to do bodily harm or does bodily harm to an individual or to that individual's family or uses any other criminally unlawful means to solicit or cause any person to join any organization or association regardless of the nature of such organization or association, is guilty of a Class 3 felony.

Any person of the age of 18 years or older who expressly or impliedly threatens to do bodily harm or does bodily harm to a person under 18 years of age or uses any other criminally unlawful means to solicit or cause any person under 18 years of age to join any organization or association regardless of the nature of such organization or association is guilty of a Class 2 felony.

(Source: P.A. 84-1075.) [Formerly Ill. Rev. Stat. 38 §12-6.1.]

5/12-7. Compelling confession or information by force or threat.

§12-7. Compelling confession or information by force or threat. (a) A person who, with intent to obtain a confession, statement or information regarding any offense, inflicts or threatens to inflict physical harm upon the person threatened or upon any other person commits the offense of compelling a confession or information by force or threat.

(b) Sentence.

Compelling a confession or information is a Class 4 felony.

(Source: P.A. 77-2638.) [Formerly Ill. Rev. Stat. 38 §12-7.]

5/12-7.1. Hate crime.

§12-7.1. Hate crime. (a) A person commits hate crime when, by reason of the race, color, creed, religion, ancestry, gender, sexual orientation, physical or mental disability, or national origin of another individual or group of individuals, he commits assault, battery, aggravated assault, misdemeanor theft, criminal trespass to residence, misdemeanor criminal damage to property, criminal trespass to vehicle, criminal trespass to real property, mob action or disorderly conduct as these crimes are defined in Sections 12-1, 12-2, 12-3, 16-1, 19-4, 21-1, 21-2, 21-3, 25-1, and 26-1 of this Code, respectively, or harrassment by telephone as defined in Section 1-1 of the Obscene Phone Call Act [720 ILCS 135/1-1].

(b) Hate crime is a Class 4 felony for a first offense and a Class 2 felony for a second or subsequent offense. Any order of probation or conditional discharge entered following a conviction for an offense under this Section, or any order of supervision entered based on a violation of this Section, shall include, in addition to any other condition of probation, conditional discharge, or supervision the court may require, a condition that the offender perform public or community service of no less than 100 hours for a misdemeanor offense and no less than 200 hours for a felony offense.

(c) Independent of any criminal prosecution or the result thereof, any person suffering injury to his person or damage to his property as a result of hate crime may bring a civil action for damages, injunction or other appropriate relief. The court may award actual damages, including damages for emotional distress, or punitive damages. A judgment may include attorney's fees and costs. The parents or legal guardians, other than guardians appointed pursuant to the Juvenile Court Act [repealed] or the Juvenile Court Act of 1987 [705 ILCS 405/1-1 et seq.], of an unemancipated minor shall be liable for the amount of any judgment for actual damages rendered against such minor under this subsection (c) in any amount not exceeding the amount provided under Section 5 of the Parental Responsibility Law [740 ILCS 115/5].

(d) "Sexual orientation" means heterosexuality, homosexuality, or bisexuality.

(Chgd. by P.A. 87-1048, §1; 87-1170, §1, eff. 1/1/93.)
(Source: P.A. 86-1418; 87-440.) [Formerly Ill. Rev. Stat. 38 §12-7.1.]

5/12-7.2. Educational intimidation.

§12-7.2. Educational intimidation. (a) A person commits educational intimidation when he knowingly interferes with the right of any child who is or is believed to be afflicted with a chronic infectious disease to attend or participate in the activities of an elementary or secondary school in this State:

(1) by actual or threatened physical harm to the person or property of the child or the child's family; or

(2) by impeding or obstructing the child's right of ingress to, egress from, or freedom of movement at school facilities or activities; or

(3) by exposing or threatening to expose the child, or the family or friends of the child, to public hatred, contempt or ridicule.

(b) Subsection (a) does not apply to the actions of school officials or the school's infectious disease review team who are acting within the course of their professional duties and in accordance with applicable law.

(c) Educational intimidation is a Class C misdemeanor, except that a second or subsequent offense shall be a Class A misdemeanor.

(d) Independent of any criminal prosecution or the result thereof, any person suffering injury to his person or damage to his property as a result of educational intimidation may bring a civil action for damages, injunction or other appropriate relief. The court may award actual damages, including damages for emotional distress, or punitive damages. A judgment may include attorney's

fees and costs. The parents or legal guardians of an unemancipated minor, other than guardians appointed pursuant to the Juvenile Court Act [repealed] or the Juvenile Court Act of 1987 [705 ILCS 405/1-1 et seq.], shall be liable for the amount of any judgment for actual damages awarded against such minor under this subsection (d) in any amount not exceeding the amount provided under Section 5 of the Parental Responsibility Law [740 ILCS 115/5].
(Source: P.A. 86-890.) [Formerly Ill. Rev. Stat. 38 §12-7.2.]

5/12-7.3. Stalking.

§12-7.3. Stalking. (a) A person commits stalking when he or she transmits to another person a threat with the intent to place that person in reasonable apprehension of death, bodily harm, sexual assault, confinement or restraint, and in furtherance of the threat knowingly does any one or more of the following acts on at least 2 separate occasions:

(1) follows the person, other than within the residence of the defendant;

(2) places the person under surveillance by remaining present outside his or her school, place of employment, vehicle, other place occupied by the person, or residence other than the residence of the defendant.

(b) Sentence. Stalking is a Class 4 felony. A second or subsequent conviction for stalking is a Class 3 felony.

(c) Exemption. This Section does not apply to picketing occurring at the workplace that is otherwise lawful and arises out of a bona fide labor dispute.
(Source: P.A. 87-870; 87-871.) [Formerly Ill. Rev. Stat. 38 §12-7.3.]

5/12-7.4. Aggravated stalking.

§12-7.4. Aggravated stalking. (a) A person commits aggravated stalking when he or she, in conjunction with committing the offense of stalking, also does any of the following:

(1) causes bodily harm to the victim;

(2) confines or restrains the victim; or

(3) violates a temporary restraining order, an order of protection, or an injunction prohibiting the behavior described in subsection (b)(1) of Section 214 of the Illinois Domestic Violence Act of 1986 [750 ILCS 60/214].

(b) Sentence. Aggravated stalking is a Class 3 felony. A second or subsequent conviction for aggravated stalking is a Class 2 felony.

(c) Exemption. This Section does not apply to picketing occurring at the workplace that is otherwise lawful and arises out of a bona fide labor dispute.
(Source: P.A. 87-870; 87-871.) [Formerly Ill. Rev. Stat. 38 §12-7.4.]

5/12-8. Dueling.

§12-8. Dueling. (a) A person who engages in a duel commits the offense of dueling.

(b) Sentence.

Dueling is a Class A misdemeanor.
(Source: P.A. 77-2638.) [Formerly Ill. Rev. Stat. 38 §12-8.]

5/12-9. Threatening public officials.

§12-9. Threatening public officials. (a) A person commits the offense of threatening a public official when:

(1) that person knowingly and willfully delivers or conveys, directly or indirectly, to a public official any telephone communication, letter, paper, writing, print, missive, or document containing a threat to take the life of or to inflict great bodily harm upon the public official or a member of his immediate family and

(2) the threat was conveyed because of the performance or nonperformance of some public duty, because of hostility of the person making the threat toward

the status or position of the public official, or because of some other factor related to the official's public existence.

(b) For purposes of this Section: (1) "public official" means a person who is elected to office in accordance with a statute or who is appointed to an office which is established, and the qualifications and duties of which are prescribed, by statute, to discharge a public duty for the State or any of its political subdivisions or in the case of an elective office any person who has filed the required documents for nomination or election to such office; (2) "immediate family" means a public official's spouse, child or children.

(c) Threatening a public official is a Class 4 felony.

(Source: P.A. 87-238.) [Formerly Ill. Rev. Stat. 38 §12-9.]

5/12-10. Tattooing body of minor.

§12-10. Tattooing Body of Minor. Any person, other than a person licensed to practice medicine in all its branches, who tattoos or offers to tattoo a person under the age of 21 is guilty of a Class C misdemeanor.

As used in this Section, to "tattoo" means to insert pigment under the surface of the skin of a human being, by pricking with a needle or otherwise, so as to produce an indelible mark or figure visible through the skin.

(Source: P.A. 77-2638.) [Formerly Ill. Rev. Stat. 38 §12-10.]

5/12-11. Home invasion.

§12-11. Home Invasion. a) A person who is not a peace officer acting in the line of duty commits home invasion when without authority he or she knowingly enters the dwelling place of another when he or she knows or has reason to know that one or more persons is present or he or she knowingly enters the dwelling place of another and remains in such dwelling place until he or she knows or has reason to know that one or more persons is present and

1) While armed with a dangerous weapon uses force or threatens the imminent use of force upon any person or persons within such dwelling place whether or not injury occurs, or

2) Intentionally causes any injury to any person or persons within such dwelling place.

b) It is an affirmative defense to a charge of home invasion that the accused who knowingly enters the dwelling place of another and remains in such dwelling place until he or she knows or has reason to know that one or more persons is present either immediately leaves such premises or surrenders to the person or persons lawfully present therein without either attempting to cause or causing serious bodily injury to any person present therein.

c) Sentence. Home invasion is a Class X felony.

(Source: P.A. 85-1387; 85-1433; 86-820.) [Formerly Ill. Rev. Stat. 38 §12-11.]

5/12-11.1. Vehicular invasion.

§12-11.1. Vehicular invasion. (a) A person commits vehicular invasion who knowingly, by force and without lawful justification, enters or reaches into the interior of a motor vehicle as defined in The Illinois Vehicle Code [625 ILCS 5/1-100 et seq.] while such motor vehicle is occupied by another person or persons, with the intent to commit therein a theft or felony.

(b) Sentence. Vehicular invasion is a Class 1 felony.

(Source: P.A. 86-1392.) [Formerly Ill. Rev. Stat. 38 §12-11.1.]

5/12-12. Definitions.

§12-12. Definitions. For the purposes of Sections 12-13 through 12-18 of this Code, the terms used in these Sections shall have the following meanings ascribed to them:

(a) "Accused" means a person accused of an offense prohibited by Sections 12-13, 12-14, 12-15 or 12-16 of this Code or a person for whose conduct the accused is legally responsible under Article 5 of this Code [720 ILCS 5/5-1 et seq.].

(b) "Bodily harm" means physical harm, and includes, but is not limited to, sexually transmitted disease, pregnancy and impotence.

(c) "Family member" means a parent, grandparent, or child, whether by whole blood, half-blood or adoption and includes a step-grandparent, step-parent or step-child. "Family member" also means, where the victim is a child under 18 years of age, an accused who has resided in the household with such child continuously for at least one year.

(d) "Force or threat of force" means the use of force or violence, or the threat of force or violence, including but not limited to the following situations:

(1) when the accused threatens to use force or violence on the victim or on any other person, and the victim under the circumstances reasonably believed that the accused had the ability to execute that threat; or

(2) when the accused has overcome the victim by use of superior strength or size, physical restraint or physical confinement.

(e) "Sexual conduct" means any intentional or knowing touching or fondling by the victim or the accused, either directly or through clothing, of the sex organs, anus or breast of the victim or the accused, or any part of the body of a child under 13 years of age, for the purpose of sexual gratification or arousal of the victim or the accused.

(f) "Sexual penetration" means any contact, however slight, between the sex organ of one person and the sex organ, mouth or anus of another person, or any intrusion, however slight, of any part of the body of one person or of any animal or object into the sex organ or anus of another person, including but not limited to cunnilingus, fellatio or anal penetration. Evidence of emission of semen is not required to prove sexual penetration.

(g) "Victim" means a person alleging to have been subjected to an offense prohibited by Sections 12-13, 12-14, 12-15 or 12-16 of this Code.
(Source: P.A. 83-1117.) [Formerly Ill. Rev. Stat. 38 §12-12.]

5/12-13. Criminal sexual assault.

§12-13. Criminal Sexual Assault. (a) The accused commits criminal sexual assault if he or she:

(1) commits an act of sexual penetration by the use of force or threat of force; or

(2) commits an act of sexual penetration and the accused knew that the victim was unable to understand the nature of the act or was unable to give knowing consent; or

(3) commits an act of sexual penetration with a victim who was under 18 years of age when the act was committed and the accused was a family member; or

(4) commits an act of sexual penetration with a victim who was at least 13 years of age but under 18 years of age when the act was committed and the accused was 17 years of age or over and held a position of trust, authority or supervision in relation to the victim.

(b) Sentence. Criminal sexual assault is a Class 1 felony. A second or subsequent conviction for a violation of this Section or under any similar statute of this State or any other state for any offense involving criminal sexual assault that is substantially equivalent to or more serious than the sexual assault prohibited under this Section is a Class X felony. When a person has any such prior conviction, the information or indictment charging that person shall state such prior conviction so as to give notice of the State's intention to treat the charge as a Class X felony. The fact of such prior conviction is not an element of the offense and may not be disclosed to the jury during trial unless otherwise permitted by issues properly raised during such trial.
(Source: P.A. 85-1440.) [Formerly Ill. Rev. Stat. 38 §12-13.]

5/12-14. Aggravated criminal sexual assault.

§12-14. Aggravated Criminal Sexual Assault. (a) The accused commits aggravated criminal sexual assault if he or she commits criminal sexual assault and any of the following aggravating circumstances existed during the commission of the offense:

(1) the accused displayed, threatened to use, or used a dangerous weapon or any object fashioned or utilized in such a manner as to lead the victim under the circumstances reasonably to believe it to be a dangerous weapon; or

(2) the accused caused bodily harm to the victim; or

(3) the accused acted in such a manner as to threaten or endanger the life of the victim or any other person; or

(4) the criminal sexual assault was perpetrated during the course of the commission or attempted commission of any other felony by the accused; or

(5) the victim was 60 years of age or over when the offense was committed; or

(6) the victim was a physically handicapped person.

(b) The accused commits aggravated criminal sexual assault if:

(1) the accused was 17 years of age or over and commits an act of sexual penetration with a victim who was under 13 years of age when the act was committed; or

(2) the accused was under 17 years of age and (i) commits an act of sexual penetration with a victim who was under 9 years of age when the act was committed; or (ii) commits an act of sexual penetration with a victim who was at least 9 years of age but under 13 years of age when the act was committed and the accused used force or threat of force to commit the act.

(c) The accused commits aggravated criminal sexual assault if he or she commits an act of sexual penetration with a victim who was an institutionalized severely or profoundly mentally retarded person at the time the act was committed.

(d) Sentence. Aggravated criminal sexual assault is a Class X felony.

(Source: P.A. 85-1392.) [Formerly Ill. Rev. Stat. 38 §12-14.]

5/12-15. Criminal sexual abuse.

§12-15. Criminal Sexual Abuse. (a) The accused commits criminal sexual abuse if he or she:

(1) commits an act of sexual conduct by the use of force or threat of force; or

(2) commits an act of sexual conduct and the accused knew that the victim was unable to understand the nature of the act or was unable to give knowing consent.

(b) The accused commits criminal sexual abuse if the accused was under 17 years of age and commits an act of sexual penetration or sexual conduct with a victim who was at least 9 years of age but under 17 years of age when the act was committed.

(c) The accused commits criminal sexual abuse if he or she commits an act of sexual penetration or sexual conduct with a victim who was at least 13 years of age but under 17 years of age and the accused was less than 5 years older than the victim.

(d) Sentence. Criminal sexual abuse is a Class A misdemeanor. A second or subsequent conviction for a violation of subsection (a) of this Section is a Class 2 felony. For purposes of this Section it is a second or subsequent conviction if the accused has at any time been convicted under this Section or under any similar statute of this State or any other state for any offense involving sexual abuse or sexual assault that is substantially equivalent to or more serious than the sexual abuse prohibited under this Section.

(Source: P.A. 85-651.) [Formerly Ill. Rev. Stat. 38 §12-15.]

5/12-16. Aggravated criminal sexual abuse.

§12-16. Aggravated Criminal Sexual Abuse. (a) The accused commits aggravated criminal sexual abuse if he or she commits criminal sexual abuse as defined in subsection (a) of Section 12-15 of this Code and any of the following aggravating circumstances existed during the commission of the offense:

(1) the accused displayed, threatened to use or used a dangerous weapon or any object fashioned or utilized in such a manner as to lead the victim under the circumstances reasonably to believe it to be a dangerous weapon; or

(2) the accused caused great bodily harm to the victim; or

(3) the victim was 60 years of age or over when the offense was committed; or

(4) the victim was a physically handicapped person.

(b) The accused commits aggravated criminal sexual abuse if he or she commits an act of sexual conduct with a victim who was under 18 years of age when the act was committed and the accused was a family member.

(c) The accused commits aggravated criminal sexual abuse if:

(1) the accused was 17 years of age or over and (i) commits an act of sexual conduct with a victim who was under 13 years of age when the act was committed; or (ii) commits an act of sexual conduct with a victim who was at least 13 years of age but under 17 years of age when the act was committed and the accused used force or threat of force to commit the act; or

(2) the accused was under 17 years of age and (i) commits an act of sexual conduct with a victim who was under 9 years of age when the act was committed; or (ii) commits an act of sexual conduct with a victim who was at least 9 years of age but under 17 years of age when the act was committed and the accused used force or threat of force to commit the act.

(d) The accused commits aggravated criminal sexual abuse if he or she commits an act of sexual penetration or sexual conduct with a victim who was at least 13 years of age but under 17 years of age and the accused was at least 5 years older than the victim.

(e) The accused commits aggravated criminal sexual abuse if he or she commits an act of sexual conduct with a victim who was an institutionalized severely or profoundly mentally retarded person at the time the act was committed.

(f) The accused commits aggravated criminal sexual abuse if he or she commits an act of sexual conduct with a victim who was at least 13 years of age but under 18 years of age when the act was committed and the accused was 17 years of age or over and held a position of trust, authority or supervision in relation to the victim.

(g) Sentence. Aggravated criminal sexual abuse is a Class 2 felony.
(Source: P.A. 85-1440.) [Formerly Ill. Rev. Stat. 38 §12-16.]

5/12-16.2. Criminal transmission of HIV.

§12-16.2. Criminal Transmission of HIV. (a) A person commits criminal transmission of HIV when he or she, knowing that he or she is infected with HIV:

(1) engages in intimate contact with another;

(2) transfers, donates, or provides his or her blood, tissue, semen, organs, or other potentially infectious body fluids for transfusion, transplantation, insemination, or other administration to another; or

(3) dispenses, delivers, exchanges, sells, or in any other way transfers to another any nonsterile intravenous or intramuscular drug paraphernalia.

(b) For purposes of this Section:

"HIV" means the human immunodeficiency virus or any other identified causative agent of acquired immunodeficiency syndrome.

"Intimate contact with another" means the exposure of the body of one person to a bodily fluid of another person in a manner that could result in the transmission of HIV.

"Intravenous or intramuscular drug paraphernalia" means any equipment, product, or material of any kind which is peculiar to and marketed for use in injecting a substance into the human body.

(c) Nothing in this Section shall be construed to require that an infection with HIV has occurred in order for a person to have committed criminal transmission of HIV.

(d) It shall be an affirmative defense that the person exposed knew that the infected person was infected with HIV, knew that the action could result in infection with HIV, and consented to the action with that knowledge.

(e) A person who commits criminal transmission of HIV commits a Class 2 felony.

(Source: P.A. 86-897.) [Formerly Ill. Rev. Stat. 38 §12-16.2.]

5/12-17. Defenses.

§12-17. Defenses. (a) It shall be a defense to any offense under Section 12-13 through 12-16 of this Code where force or threat of force is an element of the offense that the victim consented. "Consent" means a freely given agreement to the act of sexual penetration or sexual conduct in question. Lack of verbal or physical resistance or submission by the victim resulting from the use of force or threat of force by the accused shall not constitute consent. The manner of dress of the victim at the time of the offense shall not constitute consent.

(b) It shall be a defense under subsection (b) and subsection (c) of Section 12-15 and subsection (d) of Section 12-16 of this Code that the accused reasonably believed the person to be 17 years of age or over.

(Source: P.A. 87-438; 87-457; 87-895.) [Formerly Ill. Rev. Stat. 38 §12-17.]

5/12-18. General provisions.

§12-18. General Provisions. (a) No person accused of violating Sections 12-13, 12-14, 12-15 or 12-16 of this Code shall be presumed to be incapable of committing an offense prohibited by Sections 12-13, 12-14, 12-15 or 12-16 of this Code because of age, physical condition or relationship to the victim, except as otherwise provided in subsection (c) of this Section. Nothing in this Section shall be construed to modify or abrogate the affirmative defense of infancy under Section 6-1 of this Code or the provisions of Section 5-4 of the Juvenile Court Act of 1987 [705 ILCS 405/5-4].

(b) Any medical examination or procedure which is conducted by a physician, nurse, medical or hospital personnel, parent, or caretaker for purposes and in a manner consistent with reasonable medical standards is not an offense under Sections 12-13, 12-14, 12-15 and 12-16 of this Code.

(c) No person may be charged by his or her spouse under Sections 12-15 and 12-16 of this Code.

Prosecution of a spouse of a victim under this subsection for any violation by the victim's spouse of Section 12-13 or 12-14 of this Code is barred unless the victim reported such offense to a law enforcement agency or the State's Attorney's office within 30 days after the offense was committed, except when the court finds good cause for the delay.

(d) In addition to the sentences provided for in Sections 12-13, 12-14, 12-15 and 12-16 of the Criminal Code of 1961 the Court may order any person who is convicted of violating any of those Sections to meet all or any portion of the financial obligations of treatment, including but not limited to medical, psychiatric, rehabilitative or psychological treatment, prescribed for the victim or victims of the offense.

(e) After a finding at a preliminary hearing that there is probable cause to believe that an accused has committed a violation of Section 12-13 or 12-14 of this Code, or after an indictment is returned charging an accused with a violation of Section 12-13 and 12-14 of this Code, at the request of the person who was the victim of the violation of Section 12-13 or 12-14, the prosecuting State's attorney shall seek an order from the court to compel the accused to be tested for infection with human immunodeficiency virus (HIV). The medical test shall be performed only by appropriately licensed medical practitioners, and shall consist of an enzyme-linked immunosorbent assay (ELISA) test, or such other test as may be approved by the Illinois Department of Public Health; in the event of a positive result, the Western Blot Assay or a more reliable confirmatory test shall be administered. The results of the test shall be kept strictly confidential by all medical personnel involved in the testing and must be personally delivered in a sealed envelope to the victim and to the judge who entered the order, for the judge's inspection in camera. Acting in accordance with the best interests of the victim and the public, the judge shall have the discretion to determine to whom, if anyone, the result of the testing may be revealed; however, in no case shall the identity of the victim be disclosed. The court shall order that the cost of the test shall be paid by the county, and may be taxed as costs against the accused if convicted.
(Source: P.A. 86-770; 87-763.) [Formerly Ill. Rev. Stat. 38 §12-18.]

5/12-18.1. Civil liability.

§12-18.1. Civil Liability. (a) If any person has been convicted of any offense defined in Section 12-13, 12-14, 12-15, or 12-16 of this Act, a victim of such offense has a cause of action for damages against any person or entity who, by the manufacture, production, or wholesale distribution of any obscene material which was possessed or viewed by the person convicted of the offense, proximately caused such person, through his or her reading or viewing of the obscene material, to commit the violation of Section 12-13, 12-14, 12-15, or 12-16. No victim may recover in any such action unless he or she proves by a preponderance of the evidence that: (1) the reading or viewing of the specific obscene material manufactured, produced, or distributed wholesale by the defendant proximately caused the person convicted of the violation of Section 12-13, 12-14, 12-15, or 12-16 to commit such violation and (2) the defendant knew or had reason to know that the manufacture, production, or wholesale distribution of such material was likely to cause a violation of an offense substantially of the type enumerated.

(b) The manufacturer, producer or wholesale distributor shall be liable to the victim for:

(1) actual damages incurred by the victim, including medical costs;
(2) court costs and reasonable attorneys fees;
(3) infliction of emotional distress;
(4) pain and suffering; and
(5) loss of consortium.

(c) Every action under this Section shall be commenced within 3 years after the conviction of the defendant for a violation of Section 12-13, 12-14, 12-15 or 12-16 of this Code. However, if the victim was under the age of 18 years at the time of the conviction of the defendant for a violation of Section 12-13, 12-14, 12-15 or 12-16 of this Code, an action under this Section shall be commenced within 3 years after the victim attains the age of 18 years.

(d) For the purposes of this Section:

(1) "obscene" has the meaning ascribed to it in subsection (b) of Section 11-20 of this Code;

(2) "wholesale distributor" means any individual, partnership, corporation, association, or other legal entity which stands between the manufacturer and

the retail seller in purchases, consignments, contracts for sale or rental of the obscene material;

(3) "producer" means any individual, partnership, corporation, association, or other legal entity which finances or supervises, to any extent, the production or making of obscene material;

(4) "manufacturer" means any individual, partnership, corporation, association, or other legal entity which manufacturers,* assembles or produces obscene material.

**So in original. Probably should be "manufactures,".*

(Source: P.A. 86-857.) [Formerly Ill. Rev. Stat. 38 §12-18.1.]

5/12-19. Abuse and gross neglect of a long term care facility resident.

§12-19. Abuse and Gross Neglect of a Long Term Care Facility Resident. (a) Any person or any owner or licensee of a long term care facility who abuses a long term care facility resident is guilty of a Class 3 felony. Any person or any owner or licensee of a long term care facility who grossly neglects a long term care facility resident is guilty of a Class 4 felony. However, nothing herein shall be deemed to apply to a physician licensed to practice medicine in all its branches or a duly licensed nurse providing care within the scope of his or her professional judgment and within the accepted standards of care within the community.

(b) Notwithstanding the penalties in subsections (a) and (c) and in addition thereto, if a licensee or owner of a long term care facility or his or her employee has caused neglect of a resident, the licensee or owner is guilty of a petty offense. An owner or licensee is guilty under this subsection (b) only if the owner or licensee failed to exercise reasonable care in the hiring, training, supervising or providing of staff or other related routine administrative responsibilities.

(c) Notwithstanding the penalties in subsections (a) and (b) and in addition thereto, if a licensee or owner of a long term care facility or his or her employee has caused gross neglect of a resident, the licensee or owner is guilty of a business offense for which a fine of not more than $10,000 may be imposed. An owner or licensee is guilty under this subsection (c) only if the owner or licensee failed to exercise reasonable care in the hiring, training, supervising or providing of staff or other related routine administrative responsibilities.

(d) For the purpose of this Section:

(1) "Abuse" means intentionally or knowingly causing any physical or mental injury or committing any sexual offense set forth in this Code.

(2) "Gross neglect" means recklessly failing to provide adequate medical or personal care or maintenance, which failure results in physical or mental injury or the deterioration of a physical or mental condition.

(3) "Neglect" means negligently failing to provide adequate medical or personal care or maintenance, which failure results in physical or mental injury or the deterioration of a physical or mental condition.

(4) "Resident" means a person residing in a long term care facility.

(5) "Owner" means the person who owns a long term care facility as provided under the Nursing Home Care Act [210 ILCS 45/1-101 et seq.].

(6) "Licensee" means the individual or entity licensed to operate a facility under the Nursing Home Care Act.

(7) "Facility" or "long term care facility" means a private home, institution, building, residence, or any other place, whether operated for profit or not, or a county home for the infirm and chronically ill operated pursuant to Division 5-21 or 5-22 of the Counties Code [55 ILCS 5/5-21001 et seq. or 5/5-22001 et seq.], or any similar institution operated by the State of Illinois or a political subdivision thereof, which provides, through its ownership or management, personal care, sheltered care or nursing for 3 or more persons not related to the owner by blood or marriage. The term also includes skilled nursing facilities

and intermediate care facilities as defined in Title XVIII and Title XIX of the federal Social Security Act [42 U.S.C. §§1395 et seq., 1396 et seq.].

(e) Nothing contained in this Section shall be deemed to apply to the medical supervision, regulation or control of the remedial care or treatment of residents in a facility conducted for those who rely upon treatment by prayer or spiritual means in accordance with the creed or tenets of any well recognized church or religious denomination and which is licensed in accordance with Section 3-803 of the Nursing Home Care Act [210 ILCS 45/3-803].

(Source: P.A. 86-820; 86-1475.) [Formerly Ill. Rev. Stat. 38 §12-19.]

5/12-20. Sale of body parts.

§12-20. Sale of body parts. (a) Except as provided in subsection (b), any person who knowingly buys or sells, or offers to buy or sell, a human body or any part of a human body, is guilty of a Class A misdemeanor for the first conviction and a Class 4 felony for subsequent convictions.

(b) This Section does not prohibit:

(1) An anatomical gift made in accordance with the Uniform Anatomical Gift Act [755 ILCS 50/1 et seq.].

(2) The removal and use of a human cornea in accordance with the Illinois Corneal Transplant Act [755 ILCS 55/1 et seq.].

(3) Reimbursement of actual expenses incurred by a living person in donating an organ, tissue or other body part or fluid for transplantation, implantation, infusion, injection, or other medical or scientific purpose, including medical costs, loss of income, and travel expenses.

(4) Payments provided under a plan of insurance or other health care coverage.

(5) Reimbursement of reasonable costs associated with the removal, storage or transportation of a human body or part thereof donated for medical or scientific purposes.

(6) Purchase or sale of blood, plasma, blood products or derivatives, other body fluids, or human hair.

(7) Purchase or sale of drugs, reagents or other substances made from human bodies or body parts, for use in medical or scientific research, treatment or diagnosis.

(Source: P.A. 85-191.) [Formerly Ill. Rev. Stat. 38 §12-20.]

5/12-21. Criminal neglect of an elderly or disabled person.

§12-21. Criminal Neglect of an Elderly or Disabled person. (a) A person commits the offense of criminal neglect of an elderly or disabled person when he is a caregiver and he knowingly:

(1) performs acts which cause the elderly or disabled person's life to be endangered, health to be injured, or pre-existing physical or mental condition to deteriorate; or

(2) fails to perform acts which he knows or reasonably should know are necessary to maintain or preserve the life or health of the elderly or disabled person and such failure causes the elderly or disabled person's life to be endangered, health to be injured or pre-existing physical or mental condition to deteriorate; or

(3) abandons the elderly or disabled person.

Criminal neglect of an elderly person is a Class 3 felony.

(b) For purposes of this Section:

(1) "Elderly person" means a person 60 years of age or older who is suffering from a disease or infirmity associated with advanced age and manifested by physical, mental or emotional dysfunctioning to the extent that such person is incapable of adequately providing for his own health and personal care.

(2) "Disabled person" means a person who suffers from a permanent physical or mental impairment, resulting from disease, injury, functional disorder or congenital condition which renders such person incapable of adequately providing for his own health and personal care.

(3) "Caregiver" means a person who has a duty to provide for an elderly or disabled person's health and personal care, at such person's place of residence, including but not limited to, food and nutrition, shelter, hygiene, prescribed medication and medical care and treatment.

"Caregiver" shall include:

(A) a parent, spouse, adult child or other relative by blood or marriage who resides with or resides in the same building with and regularly visits the elderly or disabled person, knows or reasonably should know of such person's physical or mental impairment and knows or reasonably should know that such person is unable to adequately provide for his own health and personal care;

(B) a person who is employed by the elderly or disabled person or by another to reside with or regularly visit the elderly or disabled person and provide for such person's health and personal care;

(C) a person who has agreed for consideration to reside with or regularly visit the elderly or disabled person and provide for such person's health and personal care; and

(D) a person who has been appointed by a private or public agency or by a court of competent jurisdiction to provide for the elderly or disabled person's health and personal care.

"Caregiver" shall not include a long-term care facility licensed or certified under the Nursing Home Care Act [210 ILCS 45/1-101 et seq.] or any administrative, medical or other personnel of such a facility, or a health care provider who is licensed under the Medical Practice Act [225 ILCS 60/1 et seq.] and renders care in the ordinary course of his profession.

(4) "Abandon" means to desert or knowingly foresake* an elderly or disabled person under circumstances in which a reasonable person would continue to provide care and custody.

**So in original. Probably should be "forsake".*

(c) Nothing in this Section shall be construed to limit the remedies available to the victim under the Illinois Domestic Violence Act [see 725 ILCS 5/112A-1 et seq., 750 ILCS 60/101 et seq.].

(d) Nothing in this Section shall be construed to impose criminal liability on a person who has made a good faith effort to provide for the health and personal care of an elderly or disabled person, but through no fault of his own has been unable to provide such care.

(e) Nothing in this Section shall be construed as prohibiting a person from providing treatment by spiritual means through prayer alone and care consistent therewith in lieu of medical care and treatment in accordance with the tenets and practices of any church or religious denomination of which the elderly or disabled person is a member.

(f) It shall not be a defense to criminal neglect of an elderly or disabled person that the accused reasonably believed that the victim was not an elderly or disabled person.

(Chgd. by P.A. 87-1072, §1, eff. 1/1/93.)
(Source: P.A. 86-153; 86-1028.) [Formerly Ill. Rev. Stat. 38 §12-21.]

5/12-30. Violation of an order of protection.

§12-30. Violation of an order of protection. (a) A person commits violation of an order of protection if he or she:

(1) Commits an act which was prohibited by a court or fails to commit an act which was ordered by a court in violation of a remedy in a valid order of protection authorized under paragraphs (1) or (2) of subsection (b) of Section

214 of the Illinois Domestic Violence Act of 1986, enacted by the 84th General Assembly [750 ILCS 60/214 et seq.].

(2) Such violation occurs after the offender has been served notice of the contents of the order, pursuant to the Illinois Domestic Violence Act, or otherwise has acquired actual knowledge of the contents of the order.

(b) For purposes of this Section, an "order of protection" may have been issued by any circuit or associate judge in the State of Illinois in a criminal or civil proceeding.

(c) Nothing in this Section shall be construed to diminish the inherent authority of the courts to enforce their lawful orders through civil or criminal contempt proceedings.

(d) Violation of an order of protection under subsection (a) of this Section is a Class A misdemeanor. The court should:

(1) increase the penalty, within the range of penalties available for a Class A misdemeanor, for the knowing violation of any order of protection over any penalty previously imposed by any court for the defendant's prior violation of an order of protection; and

(2) impose a minimum penalty of 24 hours imprisonment for defendant's second or subsequent violation of any order of protection; unless the court explicitly finds that an increased penalty or such period of imprisonment would be manifestly unjust. In addition to any other penalties, the court may order the defendant to pay a fine as authorized under Section 5-9-1 of the Unified Code of Corrections [730 ILCS 5/5-9-1] or to make restitution to the victim under Section 5-5-6 of the Unified Code of Corrections [730 ILCS 5/5-5-6].

(Source: P.A. 84-1305.) [Formerly Ill. Rev. Stat. 38 §12-30.]

5/12-31. Inducement to commit suicide.

§12-31. Inducement to Commit Suicide. (a) A person commits the offense of inducement to commit suicide when he coerces another to commit suicide and the other person commits or attempts to commit suicide as a direct result of the coercion, and he exercises substantial control over the other person through (1) control of the other person's physical location or circumstances; (2) use of psychological pressure; or (3) use of actual or ostensible religious, political, social, philosophical or other principles. For the purposes of this Section, "attempts to commit suicide" means any act done with the intent to commit suicide and which constitutes a substantial step toward commission of suicide.

(b) Sentence. Inducement to commit suicide when the other person commits suicide as a direct result of the coercion is a Class 2 felony. Inducement to commit suicide when the other person attempts to commit suicide as a direct result of the coercion is a Class 3 felony.

(Chgd. by P.A. 87-1167, §1, eff. 1/1/93.)
(Source: P.A. 86-980.) [Formerly Ill. Rev. Stat. 38 §12-31.]

5/12-32. Ritual mutilation.

§12-32. Ritual Mutilation. (a) A person commits the offense of ritual mutilation, when he mutilates, dismembers or tortures another person as part of a ceremony, rite, initiation, observance, performance or practice, and the victim did not consent or under such circumstances that the defendant knew or should have known that the victim was unable to render effective consent.

(b) Sentence. Ritual mutilation is a Class 2 felony.

(c) The offense ritual mutilation does not include the practice of circumcision or a ceremony, rite, initiation, observance, or performance related thereto.

(Source: P.A. 86-864; 86-1028.) [Formerly Ill. Rev. Stat. 38 §12-32.]

5/12-33. Ritualized abuse of a child.

§12-33. Ritualized abuse of a child. (a) A person is guilty of ritualized abuse of a child when he or she commits any of the following acts with, upon, or in the presence of a child as part of a ceremony, rite or any similar observance:

(1) actually or in simulation, tortures, mutilates, or sacrifices any warm-blooded animal or human being;

(2) forces ingestion, injection or other application of any narcotic, drug, hallucinogen or anaesthetic for the purpose of dulling sensitivity, cognition, recollection of, or resistance to any criminal activity;

(3) forces ingestion, or external application, of human or animal urine, feces, flesh, blood, bones, body secretions, nonprescribed drugs or chemical compounds;

(4) involves the child in a mock, unauthorized or unlawful marriage ceremony with another person or representation of any force or deity, followed by sexual contact with the child;

(5) places a living child into a coffin or open grave containing a human corpse or remains;

(6) threatens death or serious harm to a child, his or her parents, family, pets, or friends that instills a well-founded fear in the child that the threat will be carried out; or

(7) unlawfully dissects, mutilates, or incinerates a human corpse.

(b) The provisions of this Section shall not be construed to apply to:

(1) lawful agricultural, animal husbandry, food preparation, or wild game hunting and fishing practices and specifically the branding or identification of livestock;

(2) the lawful medical practice of circumcision or any ceremony related to circumcision;

(3) any state or federally approved, licensed, or funded research project; or

(4) the ingestion of animal flesh or blood in the performance of a religious service or ceremony.

(c) Ritualized abuse of a child is a Class 1 felony for a first offense. A second or subsequent conviction for ritualized abuse of a child is a Class X felony for which the offender may be sentenced to a term of natural life imprisonment.

(d) For the purposes of this Section, "child" means any person under 18 years of age.

(Added by P.A. 87-1167, §1, eff. 1/1/93.)
[Formerly Ill. Rev. Stat. 38 §12-33.]

ARTICLE 14. EAVESDROPPING

5/14-1. Definition.

§14-1. Definition. (a) Eavesdropping device.

An eavesdropping device is any device capable of being used to hear or record oral conversation whether such conversation is conducted in person, by telephone, or by any other means; Provided, however, that this definition shall not include devices used for the restoration of the deaf or hard-of-hearing to normal or partial hearing.

(b) Eavesdropper.

An eavesdropper is any person, including law enforcement officers, who operates or participates in the operation of any eavesdropping device contrary to the provisions of this Article.

(c) Principal.

A principal is any person who:

(1) Knowingly employs another who illegally uses an eavesdropping device in the course of such employment; or

(2) Knowingly derives any benefit or information from the illegal use of an eavesdropping device by another; or

(3) Directs another to use an eavesdropping device illegally on his behalf.

(Source: Laws 1961, p. 1983.) [Formerly Ill. Rev. Stat. 38 §14-1.]

5/14-2. Elements of the offense; affirmative defense.

§14-2. Elements of the offense; affirmative defense. A person commits eavesdropping when he:

(a) Uses an eavesdropping device to hear or record all or any part of any conversation unless he does so (1) with the consent of all of the parties to such conversation or (2) in accordance with Article 108A or Article 108B of the "Code of Criminal Procedure of 1963", approved August 14, 1963, as amended [725 ILCS 5/108A-1 et seq. or 5/108B-1 et seq.]; or

(b) Uses or divulges, except as authorized by this Article or by Article 108A or 108B of the "Code of Criminal Procedure of 1963", approved August 14, 1963, as amended, any information which he knows or reasonably should know was obtained through the use of an eavesdropping device.

(c) It is an affirmative defense to a charge brought under this Article relating to the interception of a privileged communication that the person charged:

1. was a law enforcement officer acting pursuant to an order of interception, entered pursuant to Section 108A-1 or 108B-5 of the Code of Criminal Procedure of 1963; and

2. at the time the communication was intercepted, the officer was unaware that the communication was privileged; and

3. stopped the interception within a reasonable time after discovering that the communication was privileged; and

4. did not disclose the contents of the communication.

(Source: P.A. 85-1203.) [Formerly Ill. Rev. Stat. 38 §14-2.]

5/14-3. Exemptions.

§14-3. Exemptions. The following activities shall be exempt from the provisions of this Article:

(a) Listening to radio, wireless and television communications of any sort where the same are publicly made;

(b) Hearing conversation when heard by employees of any common carrier by wire incidental to the normal course of their employment in the operation, maintenance or repair of the equipment of such common carrier by wire so long as no information obtained thereby is used or divulged by the hearer;

(c) Any broadcast by radio, television or otherwise whether it be a broadcast or recorded for the purpose of later broadcasts of any function where the public is in attendance and the conversations are overheard incidental to the main purpose for which such broadcasts are then being made;

(d) Recording or listening with the aid of any device to any emergency communication made in the normal course of operations by any federal, state or local law enforcement agency or institutions dealing in emergency services, including, but not limited to, hospitals, clinics, ambulance services, fire fighting agencies, any public utility, emergency repair facility, civilian defense establishment or military installation;

(e) Recording the proceedings of any meeting required to be open by the Open Meetings Act, as amended [5 ILCS 120/1 et seq.]; and

(f) Recording or listening with the aid of any device to incoming telephone calls of phone lines publicly listed or advertised as consumer "hotlines" by manufacturers or retailers of food and drug products. Such recordings must be destroyed, erased or turned over to local law enforcement authorities within 24 hours from the time of such recording and shall not be otherwise disseminated. Failure on the part of the individual or business operating any such recording or listening device to comply with the requirements of this subsection shall eliminate any civil or criminal immunity conferred upon that individual or business by the operation of this Section.

(Source: P.A. 86-763.) [Formerly Ill. Rev. Stat. 38 §14-3.]

5/14-4. Sentence.

§14-4. Sentence. Eavesdropping, for a first offense, is a Class 4 felony, and, for a second or subsequent offense, is a Class 3 felony.

(Source: P.A. 79-781.) [Formerly Ill. Rev. Stat. 38 §14-4.]

5/14-5. Evidence inadmissible.

§14-5. Evidence inadmissible. Any evidence obtained in violation of this Article is not admissible in any civil or criminal trial, or any administrative or legislative inquiry or proceeding, nor in any grand jury proceedings; provided, however, that so much of the contents of an alleged unlawfully intercepted, overheard or recorded conversation as is clearly relevant, as determined as a matter of law by the court in chambers, to the proof of such allegation may be admitted into evidence in any criminal trial or grand jury proceeding brought against any person charged with violating any provision of this Article.

(Source: Laws 1965, p. 3198.) [Formerly Ill. Rev. Stat. 38 §14-5.]

5/14-6. Civil remedies to injured parties.

§14-6. Civil remedies to injured parties. (1) Any or all parties to any conversation upon which eavesdropping is practiced contrary to this Article shall be entitled to the following remedies:

(a) To an injunction by the circuit court prohibiting further eavesdropping by the eavesdropper and by or on behalf of his principal, or either;

(b) To all actual damages against the eavesdropper or his principal or both;

(c) To any punitive damages which may be awarded by the court or by a jury;

(d) To all actual damages against any landlord, owner or building operator, or any common carrier by wire who aids, abets, or knowingly permits the eavesdropping concerned;

(e) To any punitive damages which may be awarded by the court or by a jury against any landlord, owner or building operator, or common carrier by wire who aids, abets, or knowingly permits the eavesdropping concerned.

(2) No cause of action shall lie in any court against any common carrier by wire or its officers, agents or employees for providing information, assistance or facilities in accordance with the terms of a court order entered under Article 108A of the Code of Criminal Procedure of 1963 [725 ILCS 5/108A-1 et seq.].

(Source: P.A. 85-868.) [Formerly Ill. Rev. Stat. 38 §14-6.]

5/14-7. Common carrier to aid in detection.

§14-7. Common carrier to aid in detection. Subject to regulation by the Illinois Commerce Commission, any common carrier by wire shall, upon request of any subscriber and upon responsible offer to pay the reasonable cost thereof, furnish whatever services may be within its command for the purpose of

detecting any eavesdropping involving its wires which are used by said subscriber. All such requests by subscribers shall be kept confidential unless divulgence is authorized in writing by the requesting subscriber.
(Source: Laws 1961, p. 1983.) [Formerly Ill. Rev. Stat. 38 §14-7.]

5/14-8. Discovery of eavesdropping device by an individual, common carrier, private investigative agency or non-governmental corporation.

§14-8. Discovery of eavesdropping device by an individual, common carrier, private investigative agency or non-governmental corporation. Any agent, officer or employee of a private investigative agency or non-governmental corporation, or of a common carrier by wire, or any individual, who discovers any physical evidence of an eavesdropping device being used which such person does not know to be a legal eavesdropping device shall, within a reasonable time after such discovery disclose the existence of such eavesdropping device to the State's Attorney of the county where such device was found. The State's Attorney shall within a reasonable time notify the person or persons apparently being eavesdropped upon of the existence of that device if the device is illegal. A violation of this Section is a Business Offense for which a fine shall be imposed not to exceed $500.
(Source: P.A. 79-984; 79-1454.) [Formerly Ill. Rev. Stat. 38 §14-8.]

5/14-9. Discovery of eavesdropping device by common carrier by wire—Disclosure to subscriber.

§14-9. Discovery of eavesdropping device by common carrier by wire—disclosure to subscriber. Any agent, officer or employee of any common carrier by wire who discovers any physical evidence of an eavesdropping device which such person does not know to be a legal eavesdropping device shall, within a reasonable time after such discovery, disclose the existence of the eavesdropping device to the State's Attorney of the County where such device was found. The State's Attorney shall within a reasonable time notify the person or persons apparently being eavesdropped upon of the existence of that device if the device is illegal. A violation of this Section is a Business Offense for which a fine shall be imposed not to exceed $500.
(Source: P.A. 79-985.) [Formerly Ill. Rev. Stat. 38 §14-9.]

PART C. OFFENSES DIRECTED AGAINST PROPERTY

ARTICLE 15. DEFINITIONS

Sec.

5/15-1. Property.

§15-1. Property. As used in this Part C, "property" means anything of value. Property includes real estate, money, commercial instruments, admission or transportation tickets, written instruments representing or embodying rights concerning anything of value, labor, or services, or otherwise of value to the owner; things growing on, affixed to, or found on land, or part of or affixed to any building; electricity, gas and water; birds, animals and fish, which ordinari-

ly are kept in a state of confinement; food and drink; samples, cultures, microorganisms, specimens, records, recordings, documents, blueprints, drawings, maps, and whole or partial copies, descriptions, photographs, computer programs or data, prototypes or models thereof, or any other articles, materials, devices, substances and whole or partial copies, descriptions, photographs, prototypes, or models thereof which constitute, represent, evidence, reflect or record a secret scientific, technical, merchandising, production or management information, design, process, procedure, formula, invention, or improvement.
(Source: P.A. 81-548.) [Formerly Ill. Rev. Stat. 38 §15-1.]

5/15-2. Owner.

§15-2. Owner. As used in this Part C, "owner" means a person, other than the offender, who has possession of or any other interest in the property involved, even though such interest or possession is unlawful, and without whose consent the offender has no authority to exert control over the property.
(Source: Laws 1961, p. 1983.) [Formerly Ill. Rev. Stat. 38 §15-2.]

5/15-3. Permanent deprivation.

§15-3. Permanent deprivation. As used in this Part C, to "permanently deprive" means to:

(a) Defeat all recovery of the property by the owner; or

(b) Deprive the owner permanently of the beneficial use of the property; or

(c) Retain the property with intent to restore it to the owner only if the owner purchases or leases it back, or pays a reward or other compensation for its return; or

(d) Sell, give, pledge, or otherwise transfer any interest in the property or subject it to the claim of a person other than the owner.
(Source: Laws 1961, p. 1983.) [Formerly Ill. Rev. Stat. 38 §15-3.]

5/15-4. Deception.

§15-4. Deception. As used in this Part C "deception" means knowingly to:

(a) Create or confirm another's impression which is false and which the offender does not believe to be true; or

(b) Fail to correct a false impression which the offender previously has created or confirmed; or

(c) Prevent another from acquiring information pertinent to the disposition of the property involved; or

(d) Sell or otherwise transfer or encumber property, failing to disclose a lien, adverse claim, or other legal impediment to the enjoyment of the property, whether such impediment is or is not valid, or is or is not a matter of official record; or

(e) Promise performance which the offender does not intend to perform or knows will not be performed. Failure to perform standing alone is not evidence that the offender did not intend to perform.
(Source: Laws 1961, p. 1983.) [Formerly Ill. Rev. Stat. 38 §15-4.]

5/15-5. Threat.

§15-5. Threat. As used in this Part C, "threat" means a menace, however communicated, to:

(a) Inflict physical harm on the person threatened or any other person or on property; or

(b) Subject any person to physical confinement or restraint; or

(c) Commit any criminal offense; or

(d) Accuse any person of a criminal offense; or

(e) Expose any person to hatred, contempt or ridicule; or

(f) Harm the credit or business repute of any person; or

(g) Reveal any information sought to be concealed by the person threatened; or

(h) Take action as an official against anyone or anything, or withhold official action, or cause such action or withholding; or

(i) Bring about or continue a strike, boycott or other similar collective action if the property is not demanded or received for the benefit of the group which he purports to represent; or

(j) Testify or provide information or withhold testimony or information with respect to another's legal claim or defense; or

(k) Inflict any other harm which would not benefit the offender.

(Source: Laws 1961, p. 1983.) [Formerly Ill. Rev. Stat. 38 §15-5.]

5/15-6. Stolen property.

§15-6. Stolen property. As used in this Part C, "stolen property" means property over which control has been obtained by theft.

(Source: Laws 1961, p. 1983.) [Formerly Ill. Rev. Stat. 38 §15-6.]

5/15-7. Obtain.

§15-7. Obtain. As used in this Part C, "obtain" means:

(a) In relation to property, to bring about a transfer of interest or possession, whether to the offender or to another, and

(b) In relation to labor or services, to secure the performance thereof.

(Source: Laws 1961, p. 1983.) [Formerly Ill. Rev. Stat. 38 §15-7.]

5/15-8. Obtains control.

§15-8. Obtains control. As used in this Part C, the phrase "obtains or exerts control" over property, includes but is not limited to the taking, carrying away, or the sale, conveyance, or transfer of title to, or interest in, or possession of property.

(Source: Laws 1961, p. 1983.) [Formerly Ill. Rev. Stat. 38 §15-8.]

5/15-9. Value.

§15-9. Value. As used in this Part C, the "value" of property consisting of any commercial instrument or any written instrument representing or embodying rights concerning anything of value, labor, or services or otherwise of value to the owner shall be:

(a) The "market value" of such instrument if such instrument is negotiable and has a market value; and

(b) The "actual value" of such instrument if such instrument is not negotiable or is otherwise without a market value. For the purpose of establishing such "actual value", the interest of any owner or owners entitled to part or all of the property represented by such instrument, by reason of such instrument, may be shown, even if another "owner" may be named in the complaint, information or indictment.

(Source: Laws 1967, p. 2849.) [Formerly Ill. Rev. Stat. 38 §15-9.]

ARTICLE 16. THEFT AND RELATED OFFENSES

Sec.

5/16-1. Theft.

§16-1. Theft. (a) A person commits theft when he knowingly:

(1) Obtains or exerts unauthorized control over property of the owner; or

(2) Obtains by deception control over property of the owner; or

(3) Obtains by threat control over property of the owner; or

(4) Obtains control over stolen property knowing the property to have been stolen or under such circumstances as would reasonably induce him to believe that the property was stolen, and

(A) Intends to deprive the owner permanently of the use or benefit of the property; or

(B) Knowingly uses, conceals or abandons the property in such manner as to deprive the owner permanently of such use or benefit; or

(C) Uses, conceals, or abandons the property knowing such use, concealment or abandonment probably will deprive the owner permanently of such use or benefit; or

(5) Obtains or exerts control over property in the custody of any law enforcement agency which is explicitly represented to him by any law enforcement officer or any individual acting in behalf of a law enforcement agency as being stolen.

The term "firearm" for the purposes of this Section has the meaning ascribed to it in Section 1.1 of "An Act relating to the acquisition, possession and transfer of firearms and firearm ammunition, to provide a penalty for the violation thereof and to make an appropriation in connection therewith", approved August 3, 1967, as amended [430 ILCS 65/1.1].

(b) Sentence.

(1) Theft of property, other than a firearm, not from the person and not exceeding $300 in value is a Class A misdemeanor.

(2) A person who has been convicted of theft of property not exceeding $300 in value, other than a firearm and not from the person, who has been previously convicted of any type of theft, robbery, armed robbery, burglary, residential burglary, possession of burglary tools or home invasion is guilty of a Class 4 felony. When a person has any such prior conviction, the information or indictment charging that person shall state such prior conviction so as to give notice of the State's intention to treat the charge as a felony. The fact of such prior conviction is not an element of the offense and may not be disclosed to the jury during trial unless otherwise permitted by issues properly raised during such trial.

(3) Theft of a firearm not from the person regardless of value is a Class 4 felony. A second or subsequent such offense is a Class 3 felony.

(4) Theft of property from the person not exceeding $300 in value, or theft of property exceeding $300 and not exceeding $10,000 in value, is a Class 3 felony.

(5) Theft of property exceeding $10,000 and not exceeding $100,000 in value is a Class 2 felony.

(6) Theft of property exceeding $100,000 in value is a Class 1 felony.

(7) Theft by deception, as described by paragraph (2) of subsection (a) of this Section, in which the offender obtained money or property valued at $5,000 or more from a victim 60 years of age or older is a Class 2 felony.

(c) When a charge of theft of property exceeding a specified value is brought, the value of the property involved is an element of the offense to be resolved by the trier of fact as either exceeding or not exceeding the specified value.
(Source: P.A. 85-1440.) [Formerly Ill. Rev. Stat. 38 §16-1.]

5/16-1.1. Theft by lessee; prima facie evidence.

§16-1.1. It shall be prima facie evidence that a person "knowingly obtains or exerts unauthorized control over property of the owner" when a lessee of the personal property of another fails to return it to the owner within 30 days after written demand from the owner for its return. A notice in writing, given after the expiration of the leasing agreement, addressed and mailed, by registered mail, to the lessee at the address given by him and shown on the leasing agreement shall constitute proper demand.
(Source: Laws 1967, p. 3509.) [Formerly Ill. Rev. Stat. 38 §16-1.1.]

5/16-1.2. Deceptive practices; prima facie evidence.

§16-1.2. It shall be prima facie evidence of intent that a person "knowingly obtains by deception control over property of the owner" when he fails to return, within 45 days after written demand from the owner, the downpayment and any additional payments accepted under a promise, oral or in writing, to perform services for the owner for consideration of $3,000 or more, and the promisor willfully without good cause failed to substantially perform pursuant to the agreement after taking a downpayment of 10% or more of the agreed upon consideration. This provision shall not apply where the owner initiated the suspension of performance under the agreement, or where the promisor responds to the notice within the 45 day notice period. A notice in writing, addressed and mailed, by registered mail, to the promisor at the last known address of the promisor, shall constitute proper demand.
(Source: P.A. 84-992.) [Formerly Ill. Rev. Stat. 38 §16-1.2.]

5/16-1.3. Financial exploitation of an elderly or disabled person.

§16-1.3. Financial Exploitation of an Elderly or Disabled Person. (a) A person commits the offense of financial exploitation of an elderly person when he stands in a position of trust and confidence with the elderly or disabled person and he knowingly and by deception or intimidation obtains control over the elderly or disabled person's property with the intent to permanently deprive the elderly or disabled person of the use, benefit, or possession of his property.

Financial exploitation of an elderly or disabled person is a Class 4 felony if the value of the property is $300 or less, a Class 3 felony if the value of the property is more than $300 but less than $5,000, a Class 2 felony if the value of the property is $5,000 or more but less than $100,000 and a Class 1 felony if the value of the property is $100,000 or more.

(b) For purposes of this Section:

(1) "Elderly person" means a person 60 years of age or older who is suffering from a disease or infirmity associated with advanced age and manifested by physical, mental or emotional dysfunctioning to the extent that such person is incapable of avoiding or preventing the commission of the offense.

(2) "Disabled person" means a person who suffers from a permanent physical or mental impairment resulting from disease, injury, functional disorder or congenital condition which renders such person incapable of avoiding or preventing the commission of the offense.

(3) "Intimidation" means the communication to an elderly or disabled person that he shall be deprived of food and nutrition, shelter, prescribed medication or medical care and treatment.

(4) "Deception" means, in addition to its meaning as defined in Section 15-4 of this Code, a misrepresentation or concealment of material fact relating to the

terms of a contract or agreement entered into with the elderly or disabled person or to the existing or pre-existing condition of any of the property involved in such contract or agreement; or the use or employment of any misrepresentation, false pretense or false promise in order to induce, encourage or solicit the elderly or disabled person to enter into a contract or agreement.

(c) For purposes of this Section, a person stands in a position of trust and confidence with an elderly or disabled person when he (1) is a parent, spouse, adult child or other relative by blood or marriage of the elderly or disabled person, (2) is a joint tenant or tenant in common with the elderly or disabled person or (3) has a legal or fiduciary relationship with the elderly or disabled person.

(d) Nothing in this Section shall be construed to limit the remedies available to the victim under the Illinois Domestic Violence Act [750 ILCS 60/101 et seq.].

(e) Nothing in this Section shall be construed to impose criminal liability on a person who has made a good faith effort to assist the elderly or disabled person in the management of his property, but through no fault of his own has been unable to provide such assistance.

(f) It shall not be a defense to financial exploitation of an elderly or disabled person that the accused reasonably believed that the victim was not an elderly or disabled person.

(g) Civil Liability. A person who is charged by information or indictment with the offense of financial exploitation of an elderly or disabled person and who fails or refuses to return the victim's property within 60 days following a written demand from the victim or the victim's legal representative shall be liable to the victim or to the estate of the victim in damages of treble the amount of the value of the property obtained, plus reasonable attorney fees and court costs. The burden of proof that the defendant unlawfully obtained the victim's property shall be by a preponderance of the evidence. This subsection shall be operative whether or not the defendant has been convicted of the offense.
(Source: P.A. 86-153.) [Formerly Ill. Rev. Stat. 38 §16-1.3.]

5/16-2. Theft of lost or mislaid property.

§16-2. Theft of lost or mislaid property. A person who obtains control over lost or mislaid property commits theft when he:

(a) Knows or learns the identity of the owner or knows, or is aware of, or learns of a reasonable method of identifying the owner, and

(b) Fails to take reasonable measures to restore the property to the owner, and

(c) Intends to deprive the owner permanently of the use or benefit of the property.

(d) Sentence.

Theft of lost or mislaid property is a petty offense.
(Source: P.A. 78-255.) [Formerly Ill. Rev. Stat. 38 §16-2.]

5/16-3. Use of property; theft of labor or services.

§16-3. (a) A person commits theft when he obtains the temporary use of property, labor or services of another which are available only for hire, by means of threat or deception or knowing that such use is without the consent of the person providing the property, labor or services.

(b) A person commits theft when after renting or leasing a motor vehicle, obtaining a motor vehicle through a "driveaway" service mode of transportation or renting or leasing any other type of personal property exceeding $500 in value, under an agreement in writing which provides for the return of the vehicle or other personal property to a particular place at a particular time, he without good cause wilfully fails to return the vehicle or other personal property to that place within the time specified, and is thereafter served or sent a written demand mailed to the last known address, made by certified mail return receipt requested, to return such vehicle or other personal property within 3 days from the mailing of the written demand, and who without good cause wilfully fails to return the vehicle or any other personal property to any place of business of the lessor within such period.

(c) Sentence.

A person convicted of theft under subsection (a) of this Section is guilty of a Class A misdemeanor. A person convicted of theft under subsection (b) of this Section is guilty of a Class 4 felony.

(Source: P.A. 84-800.) [Formerly Ill. Rev. Stat. 38 §16-3.]

5/16-3.1. False report of theft and other losses.

§16-3.1. False Report of Theft and Other Losses. (a) A person who knowingly makes a false report of a theft, destruction, damage or conversion of any property to a law enforcement agency or other governmental agency with the intent to defraud an insurer is guilty of a Class A misdemeanor.

(b) A person convicted of a violation of this Section a second or subsequent time is guilty of a Class 4 felony.

(Source: P.A. 83-1004.) [Formerly Ill. Rev. Stat. 38 §16-3.1.]

5/16-4. Offender's interest in the property.

§16-4. Offender's interest in the property. (a) It is no defense to a charge of theft of property that the offender has an interest therein, when the owner also has an interest to which the offender is not entitled.

(b) Where the property involved is that of the offender's spouse, no prosecution for theft may be maintained unless the parties were not living together as man and wife and were living in separate abodes at the time of the alleged theft.

(Source: Laws 1961, p. 1983.) [Formerly Ill. Rev. Stat. 38 §16-4.]

5/16-5. Theft from coin-operated machines.

§16-5. Theft from coin-operated machines. (a) A person commits theft from a coin-operated machine when he knowingly and without authority and with intent to commit a theft from such machine, opens, breaks into, tampers with, or damages a coin-operated machine.

(b) As used in this Section, the term "coin-operated machine" shall include any automatic vending machine or any part thereof, parking meter, coin telephone, coin laundry machine, coin dry cleaning machine, amusement machine, music machine, vending machine dispensing goods or services, money changer.

(c) Sentence. A person convicted of theft from a coin-operated machine shall be guilty of a Class A misdemeanor. A person who has been convicted of theft from a coin-operated machine and who has been previously convicted of any type of theft, robbery, armed robbery, burglary, residential burglary, possession of burglary tools or home invasion is guilty of a Class 4 felony. When a person has any such prior conviction, the information or indictment charging that person shall state such prior conviction so as to give notice of the State's intention to treat the charge as a felony. The fact of such prior conviction is not an element of the offense and may not be disclosed to the jury during trial unless otherwise permitted by issues properly raised during such trial.

(Source: P.A. 85-691.) [Formerly Ill. Rev. Stat. 38 §16-5.]

5/16-6. Coin-operated machines; possession of a key or device.

§16-6. Coin-operated machines; possession of a key or device. Whoever possesses a key, tool, instrument, explosive or device or a drawing, print or mold of a key, tool, instrument, explosive or device designed to open, break into, tamper with or damage a coin-operated machine as defined in paragraph (b) of

Section 16-5 of this Act, with intent to commit a theft from such machine, shall be guilty of a Class A misdemeanor.
(Source: P.A. 77-2830.) [Formerly Ill. Rev. Stat. 38 §16-6.]

5/16-7. Unlawful use of recorded sounds or images.

§16-7. Unlawful use of recorded sounds or images. (a) A person commits unlawful use of recorded sounds or images when he:

(1) Intentionally, knowingly or recklessly transfers or causes to be transferred without the consent of the owner, any sounds or images recorded on any sound or audio visual recording with the purpose of selling or causing to be sold, or using or causing to be used for profit the article to which such sounds or recordings of sound are transferred.

(2) Intentionally, knowingly or recklessly sells, offers for sale, advertises for sale, uses or causes to be used for profit any such article described in subsection 16-7(a)(1) without consent of the owner.

(3) Intentionally, knowingly or recklessly offers or makes available for a fee, rental or any other form of compensation, directly or indirectly, any equipment or machinery for the purpose of use by another to reproduce or transfer, without the consent of the owner, any sounds or images recorded on any sound or audio visual recording to another sound or audio visual recording or for the purpose of use by another to manufacture any sound or audio visual recording in violation of Section 16-8.

(4) Intentionally, knowingly or recklessly transfers or causes to be transferred without the consent of the owner, any live performance with the purpose of selling or causing to be sold, or using or causing to be used for profit the sound or audio visual recording to which the performance is transferred.

(b) As used in this Section and Section 16-8:

(1) "Person" means any individual, partnership, corporation, association or other entity.

(2) "Owner" means the person who owns the master sound recording on which sound is recorded and from which the transferred recorded sounds are directly or indirectly derived, or the person who owns the rights to record or authorize the recording of a live performance.

(3) "Sound or audio visual recording" means any sound or audio visual phonograph record, disc, pre-recorded tape, film, wire, magnetic tape or other object, device or medium, now known or hereafter invented, by which sounds or images may be reproduced with or without the use of any additional machine, equipment or device.

(4) "Master sound recording" means the original physical object on which a given set of sounds were first recorded and which the original object from which all subsequent sound recordings embodying the same set of sounds are directly or indirectly derived.

(5) "Unidentified sound or audio visual recording" means a sound or audio visual recording without the actual name and full and correct street address of the manufacturer, and the name of the actual performers or groups prominently and legibly printed on the outside cover or jacket and on the label of such sound or audio visual recording.

(6) "Manufacturer" means the person who actually makes or causes to be made a sound or audio visual recording.

(c) Unlawful use of recorded sounds or images is a Class 4 felony; however:

(1) If the offense involves more than 100 but not exceeding 1000 unidentified sound recordings or more than 7 but not exceeding 65 unidentified audio visual recordings during any 180 day period the authorized fine is up to $100,000; and

(2) If the offense involves more than 1,000 unidentified sound recordings or more than 65 unidentified audio visual recordings during any 180 day period the authorized fine is up to $250,000.

(d) This Section shall neither enlarge nor diminish the rights of parties in private litigation.

(e) This Section does not apply to any person engaged in the business of radio or television broadcasting who transfers, or causes to be transferred, any sounds (other than from the sound track of a motion picture) solely for the purpose of broadcast transmission.

(f) If any provision or item of this Section or the application thereof is held invalid, such invalidity shall not affect other provisions, items or applications of this Section which can be given effect without the invalid provisions, items or applications and to this end the provisions of this Section are hereby declared severable.

(g) Each and every individual manufacture, distribution or sale or transfer for a consideration of such recorded devices in contravention of this Section constitutes a separate violation of this Section.

(h) Any sound or audio visual recordings containing transferred sounds or a performance whose transfer was not authorized by the owner of the master sound recording or performance, in violation of this Section, or in the attempt to commit such violation as defined in Section 8-2, or in a solicitation to commit such offense as defined in Section 8-1, may be confiscated and destroyed upon conclusion of the case or cases to which they are relevant, except that the Court may enter an order preserving them as evidence for use in other cases or pending the final determination of an appeal.

(i) It is an affirmative defense to any charge of unlawful use of recorded sounds or images that the recorded sounds or images so used are public domain material. For purposes of this Section, recorded sounds are deemed to be in the public domain if the recorded sounds were copyrighted pursuant to the copyright laws of the United States, as the same may be amended from time to time, and the term of the copyright and any extensions or renewals thereof has expired.

(Source: P.A. 86-1210.) [Formerly Ill. Rev. Stat. 38 §16-7.]

5/16-8. Unlawful use of unidentified sound or audio visual recordings.

§16-8. Unlawful use of unidentified sound or audio visual recordings. (a) A person commits unlawful use of unidentified sound or audio visual recordings when he intentionally, knowingly, recklessly or negligently for profit manufactures, sells, distributes, vends, circulates, performs, leases or otherwise deals in and with unidentified sound or audio visual recordings or causes the manufacture, sale, distribution, vending, circulation, performance, lease or other dealing in and with unidentified sound or audio visual recordings.

(b) Unlawful use of unidentified sound or audio visual recordings is a Class 4 felony; however:

(1) If the offense involves more than 100 but not exceeding 1000 unidentified sound recordings or more than 7 but not exceeding 65 unidentified audio visual recordings during any 180 day period the authorized fine is up to $100,000; and

(2) If the offense involves more than 1,000 unidentified sound recordings or more than 65 unidentified audio visual recordings during any 180 day period the authorized fine is up to $250,000.

(c) Each and every individual manufacture, sale, distribution, vending, circulation, performance, lease or other dealing in and with an unidentified sound or audio visual recording constitutes a separate violation of this Section.

(d) If any provision or item of this Section or the application thereof is held invalid, such invalidity shall not affect other provisions, items or applications of this Section which can be given effect without the invalid provisions, items or applications and to this end the provisions of this Section are hereby declared severable.

(e) Any unidentified sound or audio visual recording used in violation of this Section, or in the attempt to commit such violation as defined in Section 8-4, or in a conspiracy to commit such violation as defined in Section 8-2, or in a solicitation to commit such offense as defined in Section 8-1, may be confiscated and destroyed upon conclusion of the case or cases to which they are relevant, except that the Court may enter an order preserving them as evidence for use in other cases or pending the final determination of an appeal.
(Source: P.A. 86-1210.) [Formerly Ill. Rev. Stat. 38 §16-8.]

5/16-10. Cable television service; unauthorized service.

§16-10. (a) 1. As used in this subsection "cable television service" means any and all services provided by or through the facilities of any cable television system or closed circuit coaxial cable communication system, or any microwave or similar transmission service used in connection with any cable television system or similar closed circuit coaxial cable communications system.

2. No person shall knowingly obtain or use cable television service without the authorization of or compensation paid to the operator of such service. The existence of any connection, wire, conductor, or other device whatsoever, which effects the use of cable television service by any person without such use being specifically authorized by, or compensation paid to the operator of the cable television service may be considered as evidence of intent to violate this Section.

3. No person shall, with intent to defraud a cable television operator, assist or instruct any other person in obtaining any cable television service.

4. No person shall, with intent to defraud a cable television operator, sell or rent, or offer to sell or rent any instrument, apparatus, equipment or device, or any plans, specifications or instructions for making or assembling any instrument, apparatus, equipment or device to any person with knowledge that the person to whom the item is sold or offered intends to use it to make unauthorized use of cable television service.

(b) Sentence.

A person convicted under subsection (a) of this Section is guilty of a Class A misdemeanor.
(Source: P.A. 81-1179; 81-1509.) [Formerly Ill. Rev. Stat. 38 §16-10.]

5/16-11. Unauthorized use of television decoding device.

§16-11. (a) A person commits the offense of the unauthorized use of a television interception or decoding device if, (1) with the intent to intercept or decode a transmission by a subscription television service without the authorization of the provider of the service, or (2) with the intent to obtain or use any cable television service without the authorization of the cable television system which provides such cable television service, the person knowingly attaches to, causes to be attached to, or incorporates in a television set, video tape recorder, or other equipment designed to receive a television transmission or cable television service, a device that intercepts or decodes the transmission or the cable television service.

(b) "Subscription television service" means a service whereby television broadcast programs intended to be received in an intelligible form by members of the public only for a fee or charge are transmitted pursuant to a grant of subscription television authority by the Federal Communications Commission.

(c) For the purposes of this Section, the term "cable television service" shall have the meaning ascribed to it in subsection (a) of Section 16-10 of this Code.

(d) The actual possession by a person of any device proscribed by this Section shall be prima facie evidence of a violation of this Section by such person; however, this presumption shall not apply unless the person charged has received the direct benefit of the reduction of the cost of the cable television service or the subscription television service or has received remuneration for the conduct proscribed in this Section.

(e) An offense under this Section is a Class B misdemeanor unless the person committed the offense for remuneration, in which event it is a Class A misdemeanor.
(Source: P.A. 83-519.) [Formerly Ill. Rev. Stat. 38 §16-11.]

5/16-12. Contributing to unauthorized use of television decoding device.

§16-12. (a) A person commits the offense of contributing to the unauthorized use of a television decoding or interception device when he knowingly manufactures, distributes, or sells, for remuneration, and with the intent to aid an offense under Section 16-11 of this Code, a device, plan or kit of parts for a device that intercepts or decodes a cable television service or a transmission by a subscription television service.

(b) For the purposes of this Section, "subscription television service" shall have the meaning ascribed to it in subsection (b) of Section 16-11 of this Code.

(c) For the purposes of this Section, "cable television service" shall have the meaning ascribed to it in subsection (c) of Section 16-11 of this Code.

(d) For purposes of this Section, the sale or distribution by a person of any device proscribed by Section 16-11 of this Code shall be prima facie evidence of a violation of this Section by such person, provided that such sale or distribution is made to a person who uses such device to intercept or decode a cable television service or a transmission by a subscription television service without the specific authorization of the provider of such cable television service or subscription television service.

(e) A person convicted of contributing to the unauthorized use of a television decoding or interception device shall be guilty of a Class A misdemeanor.
(Source: P.A. 83-519.) [Formerly Ill. Rev. Stat. 38 §16-12.]

5/16-13. Violations of Sections 16-10, 16-11, or 16-12.

§16-13. (a) Any person who violates the provisions of Sections 16-10, 16-11, or 16-12 of this Code, shall be liable to the cable television system or subscription television service whose transmission or cable television service has been intercepted or decoded for monetary damages measured by three times the amount of actual damages sustained by the plaintiff as result of the violation and any resulting profits of the person committing the violation plus an amount equal to three times the amount of services unlawfully obtained. For the purpose of this subsection, to establish "profits" the plaintiff is required to present proof only of the gross revenue of the person committing the violation, and such person is required to prove his deductible expenses and the elements of profit attributable to factors other than the violation. In addition to the foregoing, the Court may award punitive damages where the Court finds that the violation was committed for the purpose of commercial advantage.

(b) In any civil action under this Section, the court shall allow the recovery of full costs plus an award of reasonable attorney's fees to the prevailing party.

(c) In any civil action brought under this Section, the plaintiff may also bring an action to enjoin and restrain any violation of Sections 16-10, 16-11 and 16-12 of this Code without having to make a showing of special damages, irreparable harm or the inadequacy of other legal remedies, and may in the same action seek damages as provided in subsection (a). Upon the execution of a proper bond against damages for an injunction improvidently granted a temporary restraining order or a preliminary injunction may be issued in any such action before a final determination on the merits.

(d) It is not a necessary prerequisite to an action pursuant to this Section that the plaintiff has suffered, or be threatened with, actual damages.
(Source: P.A. 83-519.) [Formerly Ill. Rev. Stat. 38 §16-13.]

5/16-14. Unlawful interference with public utility services.

§16-14. (a) A person commits the offense of unlawful interference with public utility services when he knowingly, without the consent of the owner of the services, impairs or interrupts any public water, gas or power supply, or other public services, or diverts, or causes to be diverted in whole or in part, any public water, gas, or power supply, or installs or removes any device for the purpose of such diversion.

(b) The terms "public water, gas, or power supply, or other public service" mean any service subject to regulation by the Illinois Commerce Commission; any service furnished by a public utility that is owned and operated by any political subdivision, public institution of higher education or municipal corporation of this State; any service furnished by any public utility that is owned by such political subdivision, public institution of higher education, or municipal corporation and operated by any of its lessees or operating agents; and any service furnished by an electric cooperative as defined in Section 3.4 of the Electric Supplier Act [220 ILCS 30/3.4].

(c) Any instrument, apparatus, or device used in obtaining utility services without paying the full charge therefore or any meter that has been altered, tampered with, or bypassed so as to cause a lack of measurement or inaccurate measurement of utility services on premises controlled by the customer or by the person using or receiving the direct benefit of utility service at that location shall raise a rebuttable presumption of the commission of the offense described in subparagraph (a) by such person.

(d)(1) A person convicted of unlawful interference with public utility services is guilty of a Class A misdemeanor unless the offense was committed for remuneration, in which case it is a Class 4 felony.

(2) After a first conviction of unlawful interference with public utility services any subsequent conviction shall be a Class 4 felony.

(Source: P.A. 84-1444.) [Formerly Ill. Rev. Stat. 38 §16-14.]

5/16-15. Unlawful use of a theft detection shielding device.

§16-15. (a) A person commits unlawful use of a theft detection shielding device when he knowingly manufactures, sells, offers for sale or distributes any laminated or coated bag or device peculiar to and marketed for shielding and intended to shield merchandise from detection by an electronic or magnetic theft alarm sensor.

(b) A person commits unlawful possession of a theft detection shielding device when he knowingly possesses any laminated or coated bag or device peculiar to and designed for shielding and intended to shield merchandise from detection by an electronic or magnetic theft alarm sensor, with the intent to commit theft or retail theft.

(c) A person commits unlawful possession of a theft detection device remover when he knowingly possesses any tool or device designed to allow the removal of any theft detection device from any merchandise with the intent to use such tool to remove any theft detection device from any merchandise without the permission of the merchant or person owning or holding said merchandise.

(d) Any person convicted for the first time of violating the provisions of subsection (a)* (b) or (c) of this Section is guilty of a Class A misdemeanor. A second or subsequent offense is a Class 4 felony.

**So in original. Probably should be "(a),".*

(Source: P.A. 84-1094.) [Formerly Ill. Rev. Stat. 38 §16-15.]

ARTICLE 16A. RETAIL THEFT

Sec.

5/16A-1. Legislative declaration.

§16A-1. Legislative declaration. It is the public policy of this State that the substantial burden placed upon the economy of this State resulting from the rising incidence of retail theft is a matter of grave concern to the people of this State who have a right to be protected in their health, safety and welfare from the effects of this crime.
(Source: P.A. 79-840.) [Formerly Ill. Rev. Stat. 38 §16A-1.]

5/16A-2. Definitions.

§16A-2. Definitions. For the purposes of this Article, the words and phrases defined in Section 16A-2.1 through 16A-2.11 have the meanings ascribed to them in those Sections unless a contrary meaning is clear from the context.
(Source: P.A. 79-840.) [Formerly Ill. Rev. Stat. 38 §16A-2.]

5/16A-2.1. Conceal, definition.

§16A-2.1. To "conceal" merchandise means that, although there may be some notice of its presence, that merchandise is not visible through ordinary observation.
(Source: P.A. 79-840.) [Formerly Ill. Rev. Stat. 38 §16A-2.1.]

5/16A-2.2. Full retail value, definition.

§16A-2.2. "Full Retail Value" means the merchant's stated or advertised price of the merchandise.
(Source: P.A. 79-840.) [Formerly Ill. Rev. Stat. 38 §16A-2.2.]

5/16A-2.3. Merchandise, definition.

§16A-2.3. "Merchandise" means any item of tangible personal property.
(Source: P.A. 79-840.) [Formerly Ill. Rev. Stat. 38 §16A-2.3.]

5/16A-2.4. Merchant, definition.

§16A-2.4. "Merchant" means an owner or operator of any retail mercantile establishment or any agent, employee, lessee, consignee, officer, director, franchisee or independent contractor of such owner or operator.
(Source: P.A. 79-840.) [Formerly Ill. Rev. Stat. 38 §16A-2.4.]

5/16A-2.5. Minor, definition.

§16A-2.5. "Minor" means a person who is less than 19 years of age, is unemancipated and resides with his parents or legal guardian.
(Source: P.A. 79-840.) [Formerly Ill. Rev. Stat. 38 §16A-2.5.]

5/16A-2.6. Person, definition.

§16A-2.6. "Person" means any natural person or individual.
(Source: P.A. 79-840.) [Formerly Ill. Rev. Stat. 38 §16A-2.6.]

5/16A-2.7. Peace officer, definition.

§16A-2.7. "Peace officer" has the meaning ascribed to that term in Section 2-13 of this Code.
(Source: P.A. 79-840.) [Formerly Ill. Rev. Stat. 38 §16A-2.7.]

5/16A-2.8. Premises of a retail mercantile establishment, definition.

§16A-2.8. "Premises of a Retail Mercantile Establishment" includes, but is not limited to, the retail mercantile establishment; any common use areas in shopping centers and all parking areas set aside by a merchant or on behalf of a merchant for the parking of vehicles for the convenience of the patrons of such retail mercantile establishment.
(Source: P.A. 79-840.) [Formerly Ill. Rev. Stat. 38 §16A-2.8.]

5/16A-2.9. Retail mercantile establishment, definition.

§16A-2.9. "Retail Mercantile Establishment" means any place where merchandise is displayed, held, stored or offered for sale to the public.
(Source: P.A. 79-840.) [Formerly Ill. Rev. Stat. 38 §16A-2.9.]

5/16A-2.10. Shopping cart, definition.

§16A-2.10. "Shopping Cart" means those push carts of the type or types which are commonly provided by grocery stores, drug stores or other retail mercantile establishments for the use of the public in transporting commodities in stores and markets and, incidentally, from the stores to a place outside the store.
(Source: P.A. 79-840.) [Formerly Ill. Rev. Stat. 38 §16A-2.10.]

5/16A-2.11. Under-ring, definition.

§16A-2.11. "Under-ring" means to cause the cash register or other sales recording device to reflect less than the full retail value of the merchandise.
(Source: P.A. 79-840.) [Formerly Ill. Rev. Stat. 38 §16A-2.11.]

5/16A-2.12. Theft detection shielding device, definition.

§16A-2.12. "Theft detection shielding device" means any laminated or coated bag or device designed and intended to shield merchandise from detection by an electronic or magnetic theft alarm sensor.
(Source: P.A. 85-749.) [Formerly Ill. Rev. Stat. 38 §16A-2.12.]

5/16A-2.13. Theft detection device remover, definition.

§16A-2.13. "Theft detection device remover" means any tool or device specifically designed and intended to be used to remove any theft detection device from any merchandise.
(Source: P.A. 85-749.) [Formerly Ill. Rev. Stat. 38 §16A-2.13.]

5/16A-3. Offense of retail theft.

§16A-3. Offense of Retail Theft. A person commits the offense of retail theft when he or she knowingly:

(a) Takes possession of, carries away, transfers or causes to be carried away or transferred, any merchandise displayed, held, stored or offered for sale in a retail mercantile establishment with the intention of retaining such merchandise or with the intention of depriving the merchant permanently of the possession, use or benefit of such merchandise without paying the full retail value of such merchandise; or

(b) Alters, transfers, or removes any label, price tag, marking, indicia of value or any other markings which aid in determining value affixed to any merchandise displayed, held, stored or offered for sale, in a retail mercantile establishment and attempts to purchase such merchandise personally or in consort with another at less than the full retail value with the intention of depriving the merchant of the full retail value of such merchandise; or

(c) Transfers any merchandise displayed, held, stored or offered for sale, in a retail mercantile establishment from the container in or on which such merchandise is displayed to any other container with the intention of depriving the merchant of the full retail value of such merchandise; or

(d) Under-rings with the intention of depriving the merchant of the full retail value of the merchandise; or

(e) Removes a shopping cart from the premises of a retail mercantile establishment without the consent of the merchant given at the time of such removal with the intention of depriving the merchant permanently of the possession, use or benefit of such cart; or

(f) Represents to a merchant that he or another is the lawful owner of property, knowing that such representation is false, and conveys or attempts to convey that property to a merchant who is the owner of the property in exchange for money, merchandise credit or other property of the merchant; or

(g) Uses or possesses any theft detection shielding device or theft detection device remover with the intention of using such device to deprive the merchant permanently of the possession, use or benefit of any merchandise displayed, held, stored or offered for sale in a retail mercantile establishment without paying the full retail value of such merchandise. A violation of this subsection shall be a Class A misdemeanor for a first offense and a Class 4 felony for a second or subsequent offense; or

(h) Obtains or exerts unauthorized control over property of the owner and thereby intends to deprive the owner permanently of the use or benefit of the property when a lessee of the personal property of another fails to return it to the owner, or if the lessee fails to pay the full retail value of such property to the lessor in satisfaction of any contractual provision requiring such, within 30 days after written demand from the owner for its return. A notice in writing, given after the expiration of the leasing agreement, by registered mail, to the lessee at the address given by the lessee and shown on the leasing agreement shall constitute proper demand.

(Source: P.A. 86-356.) [Formerly Ill. Rev. Stat. 38 §16A-3.]

5/16A-4. Presumptions.

§16A-4. Presumptions. If any person:

(a) conceals upon his or her person or among his or her belongings, unpurchased merchandise displayed, held, stored or offered for sale in a retail mercantile establishment; and

(b) removes that merchandise beyond the last known station for receiving payments for that merchandise in that retail mercantile establishment such person shall be presumed to have possessed, carried away or transferred such merchandise with the intention of retaining it or with the intention of depriving the merchant permanently of the possession, use or benefit of such merchandise without paying the full retail value of such merchandise.

(Source: P.A. 80-352.) [Formerly Ill. Rev. Stat. 38 §16A-4.]

5/16A-5. Detention.

§16A-5. Detention. Any merchant who has reasonable grounds to believe that a person has committed retail theft may detain such person, on or off the premises of a retail mercantile establishment, in a reasonable manner and for a reasonable length of time for all or any of the following purposes:

(a) To request identification;

(b) To verify such identification;

(c) To make reasonable inquiry as to whether such person has in his possession unpurchased merchandise and, to make reasonable investigation of the ownership of such merchandise;

(d) To inform a peace officer of the detention of the person and surrender that person to the custody of a peace officer;

(e) In the case of a minor, to inform a peace officer, the parents, guardian or other private person interested in the welfare of that minor of this detention and to surrender custody of such minor to such person.

A merchant may make a detention as permitted herein off the premises of a retail mercantile establishment only if such detention is pursuant to an immediate pursuit of such person.

A merchant shall be deemed to have reasonable grounds to make a detention for the purposes of this Section if the merchant detains a person because such person has in his possession either a theft detection shielding device or a theft detection device remover.

(Source: P.A. 85-749.) [Formerly Ill. Rev. Stat. 38 §16A-5.]

5/16A-6. Affirmative defense.

§16A-6. Affirmative Defense. A detention as permitted in this Article does not constitute an arrest or an unlawful restraint, as defined in Section 10-3 of this Code, nor shall it render the merchant liable to the person so detained.

(Source: P.A. 79-840.) [Formerly Ill. Rev. Stat. 38 §16A-6.]

5/16A-7. Civil liability.

§16A-7. Civil Liability. (a) A person who commits the offense of retail theft as defined in Section 16A-3 paragraphs (a), (b) or (c) of this Code, shall be civilly liable to the merchant of the merchandise in an amount consisting of:

(i) actual damages equal to the full retail value of the merchandise as defined herein; plus

(ii) an amount not less than $100 nor more than $1,000; plus

(iii) attorney's fees and court costs.

(b) If a minor commits the offense of retail theft, the parents or guardian of said minor shall be civilly liable as provided in this Section; provided, however that a guardian appointed pursuant to the Juvenile Court Act [repealed] or the Juvenile Court Act of 1987 [705 ILCS 405/1-1 et seq.] shall not be liable under this Section. Total recovery under this Section shall not exceed the maximum recovery permitted under Section 5 of the "Parental Responsibility Law", approved October 6, 1969, as now or hereafter amended [740 ILCS 115/5].

(c) A conviction or a plea of guilty to the offense of retail theft is not a prerequisite to the bringing of a civil suit hereunder.

(d) Judgments arising under this Section may be assigned.

(Source: P.A. 85-1209.) [Formerly Ill. Rev. Stat. 38 §16A-7.]

5/16A-8. Severability.

§16A-8. If any Section, clause, sentence, paragraph or part of this Article is for any reason adjudged by any court of competent jurisdiction to be invalid, such judgment will not affect, impair or invalidate the remainder thereof, but shall be confined in its operation to the Section, clause, sentence, paragraph or part thereof directly involved in the controversy in which such judgment shall have been rendered.

(Source: P.A. 79-840.) [Formerly Ill. Rev. Stat. 38 §16A-8.]

5/16A-9. Continuation of prior law.

§16A-9. Continuation of prior law. The provisions of this Article insofar as they are the same or substantially the same as those of Article 16 of this Code [720 ILCS 5/16-1 et seq.] shall be construed as a continuation of such Article 16 and not as a new enactment.

(Source: P.A. 79-840.) [Formerly Ill. Rev. Stat. 38 §16A-9.]

5/16A-10. Sentence.

§16A-10. Sentence. (1) Retail theft of property, the full retail value of which does not exceed $150, is a Class A misdemeanor.

(2) A person who has been convicted of retail theft of property, the full retail value of which does not exceed $150, and who has been previously convicted of any type of theft, robbery, armed robbery, burglary, residential burglary, possession of burglary tools or home invasion is guilty of a Class 4 felony. When a person has any such prior conviction, the information or indictment charging that person shall state such prior conviction so as to give notice of the State's intention to treat the charge as a felony. The fact of such prior conviction is not an element of the offense and may not be disclosed to the jury during trial unless otherwise permitted by issues properly raised during such trial.

(3) Any retail theft of property, the full retail value of which exceeds $150, is a Class 3 felony. When a charge of retail theft of property, the full value of which exceeds $150, is brought, the value of the property involved is an element of the offense to be resolved by the trier of fact as either exceeding or not exceeding $150.

(Source: P.A. 85-691.) [Formerly Ill. Rev. Stat. 38 §16A-10.]

ARTICLE 16B. PROTECTION OF LIBRARY MATERIALS

Sec.

5/16B-1. Definitions.

§16B-1. Definitions. As used in this Article:

(a) "Library facility" includes any public library or museum, or any library or museum of an educational, historical or eleemosynary institution, organization or society.

(b) "Library material" includes any book, plate, picture, photograph, engraving, painting, sculpture, statue, artifact, drawing, map, newspaper, pamphlet, broadside, magazine, manuscript, document, letter, microfilm, sound recording, audiovisual material, magnetic or other tape, electronic data processing record or other documentary, written or printed material regardless of physical form or characteristics, or any part thereof, belonging to, or on loan to or otherwise in the custody of a library facility.

(c) "Premises of a library facility" means the interior of a building, structure or other enclosure in which a library facility is located and in which the library facility keeps, displays and makes available for inspection or borrowing library material, but for purposes of this Article, such premises do not include the exterior appurtenances to such building, structure or enclosure nor the land on which such building, structure or other enclosure is located.

(d) "Library card" means a card or plate issued by a library facility for purposes of identifying the person to whom the library card was issued as authorized to borrow library material, subject to all limitations and conditions imposed on such borrowing by the library facility issuing such card.

(Source: P.A. 84-1308.) [Formerly Ill. Rev. Stat. 38 §16B-1.]

5/16B-2. Library theft.

§16B-2. Library Theft. A person commits the offense of library theft when he or she:

(a) Knowingly and intentionally removes any library material from the premises of a library facility without authority to do so; or

(b) Knowingly and intentionally conceals any library material upon his or her person or among his or her belongings, while still in the premises of a library facility and in such manner that the library material is not visible through ordinary observation although there may be some notice of its presence, and removes such library material beyond the last point in the premises of that library facility at which library material may be borrowed in accordance with procedures established by that library facility for the borrowing of library material; or

(c) With the intent to deceive borrows or attempts to borrow any library material from a library facility by (i) use of a library card issued to another without the other's consent, or (ii) use of a library card knowing that it is revoked, cancelled or expired, or (iii) use of a library card knowing that it is falsely made, counterfeit or materially altered; or

(d) Borrows from a library facility library material which has an aggregate value of $50 or more pursuant to an agreement with or procedure established by the library facility for the return of such library material, and willfully without good cause fails to return the library material so borrowed in accordance with such agreement or procedure, and further willfully without good cause fails to return such library material within 30 days after receiving written notice by certified mail from the library facility demanding the return of such library material.

A person who violates this subsection (d) is liable to the library for the cost of postage and attorney fees.

(Chgd. by P.A. 87-898, §1, eff. 1/1/93.)

(Source: P.A. 84-925.) [Formerly Ill. Rev. Stat. 38 §16B-2.]

5/16B-2.1. Criminal mutilation or vandalism of library materials.

§16B-2.1. Criminal mutilation or vandalism of library materials. A person commits criminal mutilation or vandalism of library materials when he knowingly tears, marks on, maliciously renders imperfect or otherwise damages or destroys library materials.

(Source: P.A. 87-435.) [Formerly Ill. Rev. Stat. 38 §16B-2.1.]

5/16B-3. Posting of warning.

§16B-3. Posting of Warning. Each library facility shall post a copy of this Act at a location adjacent to each entrance to the premises of the library facility and at each point in the premises of the library facility at which the borrowing of library materials occurs.

(Source: P.A. 82-603.) [Formerly Ill. Rev. Stat. 38 §16B-3.]

5/16B-4. Continuation of prior law.

§16B-4. Continuation of Prior Law. The provisions of this Article insofar as they are the same or substantially the same as those of Article 16 of this Code [720 ILCS 5/16-1 et seq.] shall be construed as a continuation of such Article 16 and not as a new enactment.

(Source: P.A. 82-603.) [Formerly Ill. Rev. Stat. 38 §16B-4.]

5/16B-5. Sentence.

§16B-5. Sentence. (a) Library theft, as defined in paragraph (d) of Sec. 16B-2, is a petty offense for which the offender may be fined an amount not to exceed $500 and be ordered to reimburse the library for actual replacement costs of the materials not returned.

(b) Library theft, other than as defined in paragraph (d) of Sec. 16B-2, when the aggregate value of the library material which is the subject of such theft does not exceed $300, is a Class A misdemeanor.

(c) Any library theft, when the aggregate value of the library material which is the subject of such theft exceeds $300, is a Class 3 felony. For the purpose of sentencing under subsections (a), (b) and (c), separate transactions totalling more than $300 within a 90 day period shall be presumed to constitute a single offense.

(d) Criminal mutilation or vandalism of library materials, when the aggregate damage or loss of the library materials which are the subject of such mutilation or vandalism does not exceed $300, is a Class A misdemeanor.

(e) Criminal mutilation or vandalism of library materials, when the aggregate damage or loss of the library materials which are the subject of such mutilation or vandalism exceeds $300, is a Class 3 felony. For the purpose of sentencing under subsections (d) and (e), separate acts totalling more than $300 within a 90 day period shall be presumed to constitute a single offense.
(Source: P.A. 84-925.) [Formerly Ill. Rev. Stat. 38 §16B-5.]

ARTICLE 16C. UNLAWFUL SALE OF HOUSEHOLD APPLIANCES

Sec.

5/16C-1. Definitions.

§16C-1. Definitions. For purposes of this Article the following words and phrases have the following meaning:

(1) "commercial context" means a continuing business enterprise conducted for profit by any person whose primary business is the wholesale or retail marketing of household appliances, or a significant portion of whose business or inventory consists of household appliances kept or sold on a wholesale or retail basis.

(2) "household appliance" means any gas or electric device or machine marketed for use as home entertainment or for facilitating or expediting household tasks or chores. The term shall include but not necessarily be limited to refrigerators, freezers, ranges, radios, television sets, vacuum cleaners, toasters, dishwashers, and other similar household items.

(3) "manufacturer's identification number" means any serial number or other similar numerical or alphabetical designation imprinted upon or attached to or placed, stamped, or otherwise imprinted upon or attached to a household appliance by the manufacturer for purposes of identifying a particular appliance individually or by lot number.
(Source: P.A. 87-435.) [Formerly Ill. Rev. Stat. 38 §16C-1.]

5/16C-2. Unlawful sale of household appliances.

§16C-2. (a) A person commits the offense of unlawful sale of household appliances when he or she knowingly, with the intent to defraud or deceive another, keeps for sale, within any commercial context, any household appliance with a missing, defaced, obliterated or otherwise altered manufacturer's identification number.

(b) Violation of this Section is a Class 4 felony, if the value of the appliance or appliances exceeds $1,000 and a Class B misdemeanor if the value of the appliance or appliances is $1,000 or less.

(c) No liability shall be imposed upon any person for the unintentional failure to comply with this Section.
(Source: P.A. 87-435.) [Formerly Ill. Rev. Stat. 38 §16C-2.]

5/16C-3. Continuation of prior law.

§16C-3. Continuation of prior law. The provisions of this Article, insofar as they are the same or substantially the same as those of Article 16 of this Code [720 ILCS 5/16-1 et seq.] shall be construed as a continuation of such Article 16 and not as a new enactment.
(Source: P.A. 87-435.) [Formerly Ill. Rev. Stat. 38 §16C-3.]

ARTICLE 16D. COMPUTER CRIME

Sec.

5/16D-1. Short title.

§16D-1. Short title. This Article shall be known and may be cited as the "Computer Crime Prevention Law".
(Source: P.A. 85-926.) [Formerly Ill. Rev. Stat. 38 §16D-1.]

5/16D-2. Definitions.

§16D-2. Definitions. As used in this Article, unless the context otherwise indicates:

(a) "Computer" means a device that accepts, processes, stores, retrieves or outputs data, and includes but is not limited to auxiliary storage and telecommunications devices connected to computers.

(b) "Computer program" or "program" means a series of coded instructions or statements in a form acceptable to a computer which causes the computer to process data and supply the results of the data processing.

(c) "Data" means a representation of information, knowledge, facts, concepts or instructions, including program documentation, which is prepared in a formalized manner and is stored or processed in or transmitted by a computer. Data shall be considered property and may be in any form including but not limited to printouts, magnetic or optical storage media, punch cards or data stored internally in the memory of the computer.

(d) In addition to its meaning as defined in Section 15-1 of this Code, "property" means: (1) electronic impulses; (2) electronically produced data; (3) confidential, copyrighted or proprietary information; (4) private identification codes or numbers which permit access to a computer by authorized computer users or generate billings to consumers for purchase of goods and services, including but not limited to credit card transactions and telecommunications services or permit electronic fund transfers; (5) software or programs in either machine or human readable form; or (6) any other tangible or intangible item relating to a computer or any part thereof.

(e) "Access" means to use, instruct, communicate with, store data in, retrieve or intercept data from, or otherwise utilize any services of a computer.

(f) "Services" includes but is not limited to computer time, data manipulation or storage functions.

(g) "Vital services or operations" means those services or operations required to provide, operate, maintain, and repair network cabling, transmission, distribution, or computer facilities necessary to ensure or protect the public health, safety, or welfare. Public health, safety, or welfare include, but are not limited to, services provided by medical personnel or institutions, fire departments, emergency services agencies, national defense contractors, armed forces

or militia personnel, private and public utility companies, or law enforcement agencies.
(Source: P.A. 85-926.) [Formerly Ill. Rev. Stat. 38 §16D-2.]

5/16D-3. Computer tampering.

§16D-3. Computer Tampering. (a) A person commits the offense of computer tampering when he knowingly and without the authorization of a computer's owner, as defined in Section 15-2 of this Code, or in excess of the authority granted to him:

(1) Accesses or causes to be accessed a computer or any part thereof, or a program or data;

(2) Accesses or causes to be accessed a computer or any part thereof, or a program or data, and obtains data or services;

(3) Accesses or causes to be accessed a computer or any part thereof, or a program or data, and damages or destroys the computer or alters, deletes or removes a computer program or data;

(4) Inserts or attempts to insert a "program" into a computer or computer program knowing or having reason to believe that such "program" contains information or commands that will or may damage or destroy that computer, or any other computer subsequently accessing or being accessed by that computer, or that will or may alter, delete or remove a computer program or data from that computer, or any other computer program or data in a computer subsequently accessing or being accessed by that computer, or that will or may cause loss to the users of that computer or the users of a computer which accesses or which is accessed by such "program".

(b) Sentence.

(1) A person who commits the offense of computer tampering as set forth in subsection (a)(1) of this Section shall be guilty of a Class B misdemeanor.

(2) A person who commits the offense of computer tampering as set forth in subsection (a)(2) of this Section shall be guilty of a Class A misdemeanor and a Class 4 felony for the second or subsequent offense.

(3) A person who commits the offense of computer tampering as set forth in subsection (a)(3) or subsection (a)(4) of this Section shall be guilty of a Class 4 felony and a Class 3 felony for the second or subsequent offense.

(c) Whoever suffers loss by reason of a violation of subsection (a)(4) of this Section may, in a civil action against the violator, obtain appropriate relief. In a civil action under this Section, the court may award to the prevailing party reasonable attorney's fees and other litigation expenses.
(Source: P.A. 86-762.) [Formerly Ill. Rev. Stat. 38 §16D-3.]

5/16D-4. Aggravated computer tampering.

§16D-4. Aggravated Computer Tampering. (a) A person commits aggravated computer tampering when he commits the offense of computer tampering as set forth in subsection (a)(3) of Section 16D-3 and he knowingly:

(1) causes disruption of or interference with vital services or operations of State or local government or a public utility; or

(2) creates a strong probability of death or great bodily harm to one or more individuals.

(b) Sentence. (1) A person who commits the offense of aggravated computer tampering as set forth in subsection (a)(1) of this Section shall be guilty of a Class 3 felony.

(2) A person who commits the offense of aggravated computer tampering as set forth in subsection (a)(2) of this Section shall be guilty of a Class 2 felony.
(Source: P.A. 86-820.) [Formerly Ill. Rev. Stat. 38 §16D-4.]

5/16D-5. Computer fraud.

§16D-5. Computer Fraud. (a) A person commits the offense of computer fraud when he knowingly:

(1) Accesses or causes to be accessed a computer or any part thereof, or a program or data, for the purpose of devising or executing any scheme, artifice to defraud, or as part of a deception;

(2) Obtains use of, damages, or destroys a computer or any part thereof, or alters, deletes, or removes any program or data contained therein, in connection with any scheme, artifice to defraud, or as part of a deception; or

(3) Accesses or causes to be accessed a computer or any part thereof, or a program or data, and obtains money or control over any such money, property, or services of another in connection with any scheme, artifice to defraud, or as part of a deception.

(b) Sentence. (1) A person who commits the offense of computer fraud as set forth in subsection (a)(1) of this Section shall be guilty of a Class 4 felony.

(2) A person who commits the offense of computer fraud as set forth in subsection (a)(2) of this Section shall be guilty of a Class 3 felony.

(3) A person who commits the offense of computer fraud as set forth in subsection (a)(3) of this Section shall:

(i) be guilty of a Class 4 felony if the value of the money, property or services is $1,000 or less; or

(ii) be guilty of a Class 3 felony if the value of the money, property or services is more than $1,000 but less than $50,000; or

(iii) be guilty of a Class 2 felony if the value of the money, property or services is $50,000 or more.

(Source: P.A. 85-926.) [Formerly Ill. Rev. Stat. 38 §16D-5.]

5/16D-6. Forfeiture.

§16D-6. Forfeiture. 1. Any person who commits the offense of computer fraud as set forth in Section 16D-5 shall forfeit, according to the provisions of this Section, any monies, profits or proceeds, and any interest or property which the sentencing court determines he has acquired or maintained, directly or indirectly, in whole or in part, as a result of such offense. Such person shall also forfeit any interest in, security, claim against, or contractual right of any kind which affords him a source of influence over any enterprise which he has established, operated, controlled, conducted or participated in conducting, where his relationship to or connection with any such thing or activity directly or indirectly, in whole or in part, is traceable to any item or benefit which he has obtained or acquired through computer fraud.

Proceedings instituted pursuant to this Section shall be subject to and conducted in accordance with the following procedures:

(a) The sentencing court shall, upon petition by the prosecuting agency, whether it is the Attorney General or a State's Attorney, at any time following sentencing, conduct a hearing to determine whether any property or property interest is subject to forfeiture under this Section. At the forfeiture hearing the People of the State of Illinois shall have the burden of establishing, by a preponderance of the evidence, that the property or property interests are subject to such forfeiture.

(b) In any action brought by the People of the State of Illinois under this Section, the circuit courts of Illinois shall have jurisdiction to enter such restraining orders, injunctions or prohibitions, or to take such other action in connection with any real, personal, or mixed property or other interest subject to forfeiture, as they shall consider proper.

(c) In any action brought by the People of the State of Illinois under this Section, wherein any restraining order, injunction or prohibition or any other action in connection with any property or interest subject to forfeiture under this Section is sought, the circuit court presiding over the trial of the person or persons charged with computer fraud shall first determine whether there is probable cause to believe that the person or persons so charged have committed the offense of computer fraud and whether the property or interest is subject to forfeiture pursuant to this Section. In order to make this determination, prior to entering any such order, the court shall conduct a hearing without a jury, where the People shall establish: (1) probable cause that the person or persons so charged have committed the offense of computer fraud, and (2) probable cause that any property or interest may be subject to forfeiture pursuant to this Section. Such hearing may be conducted simultaneously with a preliminary hearing if the prosecution is commenced by information or complaint, or by motion of the People at any stage in the proceedings. The court may enter a finding of probable cause at a preliminary hearing following the filing of an information charging the offense of computer fraud or the return of an indictment by a grand jury charging the offense of computer fraud as sufficient evidence of probable cause for purposes of this Section. Upon such a finding, the circuit court shall enter such restraining order, injunction or prohibition, or shall take such other action in connection with any such property or other interest subject to forfeiture under this Section as is necessary to insure that such property is not removed from the jurisdiction of the court, concealed, destroyed or otherwise disposed of by the owner or holder of that property or interest prior to a forfeiture hearing under this Section. The Attorney General or State's Attorney shall file a certified copy of such restraining order, injunction or other prohibition with the recorder of deeds or registrar of titles of each county where any such property of the defendant may be located. No such injunction, restraining order or other prohibition shall affect the rights of any bona fide purchaser, mortgagee, judgment creditor or other lienholder arising prior to the date of such filing. The court may, at any time, upon verified petition by the defendant, conduct a hearing to release all or portions of any such property or interest which the court previously determined to be subject to forfeiture or subject to any restraining order, injunction, prohibition or other action. The court may release such property to the defendant for good cause shown and within the sound discretion of the court.

(d) Upon conviction of a person under Section 16D-5, the court shall authorize the Attorney General to seize and sell all property or other interest declared forfeited under this Act, unless such property is required by law to be destroyed or is harmful to the public. The court may order the Attorney General to segregate funds from the proceeds of such sale sufficient: (1) to satisfy any order of restitution, as the court may deem appropriate; (2) to satisfy any legal right, title, or interest which the court deems superior to any right, title, or interest of the defendant at the time of the commission of the acts which gave rise to forfeiture under this Section; or (3) to satisfy any bona-fide purchaser for value of the right, title, or interest in the property who was without reasonable notice that the property was subject to forfeiture. Following the entry of an order of forfeiture, the Attorney General shall publish notice of the order and his intent to dispose of the property. Within the 30 days following such publication, any person may petition the court to adjudicate the validity of his alleged interest in the property.

After the deduction of all requisite expenses of administration and sale, the Attorney General shall distribute the proceeds of such sale, along with any moneys forfeited or seized as follows:

(1) 50% shall be distributed to the unit of local government whose officers or employees conducted the investigation into computer fraud and caused the arrest or arrests and prosecution leading to the forfeiture. Amounts distributed to units of local government shall be used for training or enforcement purposes

relating to detection, investigation or prosecution of financial crimes, including computer fraud. In the event, however, that the investigation, arrest or arrests and prosecution leading to the forfeiture were undertaken solely by a State agency, the portion provided hereunder shall be paid into the State Police Services Fund of the Illinois Department of State Police to be used for training or enforcement purposes relating to detection, investigation or prosecution of financial crimes, including computer fraud.

(2) 50% shall be distributed to the county in which the prosecution and petition for forfeiture resulting in the forfeiture was instituted by the State's Attorney, and deposited in a special fund in the county treasury and appropriated to the State's Attorney for use in training or enforcement purposes relating to detection, investigation or prosecution of financial crimes, including computer fraud. Where a prosecution and petition for forfeiture resulting in the forfeiture has been maintained by the Attorney General, 50% of the proceeds shall be paid into the Attorney General's Financial Crime Prevention Fund. Where the Attorney General and the State's Attorney have participated jointly in any part of the proceedings, 25% of the proceeds forfeited shall be paid to the county in which the prosecution and petition for forfeiture resulting in the forfeiture occurred, and 25% shall be paid to the Attorney General's Financial Crime Prevention Fund to be used for the purposes as stated in this subsection.

2. Where any person commits a felony under any provision of this Code or another statute and the instrumentality used in the commission of the offense, or in connection with or in furtherance of a scheme or design to commit the offense, is a computer owned by the defendant or if the defendant is a minor, owned by his or her parents or legal guardian, the computer shall be subject to the provisions of this Section. However, in no case shall a computer, or any part thereof, be subject to the provisions of the Section if the computer accessed in the commission of the offense is owned or leased by the victim or an innocent third party at the time of the commission of the offense or if the rights of creditors, lienholders, or any person having a security interest in the computer at the time of the commission of the offense shall be adversely affected.
(Source: P.A. 85-1042.) [Formerly Ill. Rev. Stat. 38 §16D-6.]

5/16D-7. Rebuttable presumption—Without authority.

§16D-7. Rebuttable Presumption—without authority. In the event that a person accesses or causes to be accessed a computer, which access requires a confidential or proprietary code which has not been issued to or authorized for use by that person, a rebuttable presumption exists that the computer was accessed without the authorization of its owner or in excess of the authority granted.
(Source: P.A. 85-926.) [Formerly Ill. Rev. Stat. 38 §16D-7.]

ARTICLE 16E. DELIVERY CONTAINER CRIME
(Added by P.A. 87-613, §1, eff. 1/1/92.)

5/16E-1. Short title.

§16E-1. Short title. This Article may be cited as the Delivery Container Crime Law.
(Source: P.A. 87-613.) [Formerly Ill. Rev. Stat. 38 §16E-1.]

5/16E-2. Definitions.

§16E-2. Definitions. "Container" means any bakery basket of wire or plastic used to transport or store bread or bakery products, any dairy case of wire or plastic used to transport or store dairy products, and any dolly or cart of 2 or 4 wheels used to transport or store any bakery or dairy product. Any person who is the owner of any container upon which a trade mark has been placed or affixed, stamped, impressed, labeled, blown-in or otherwise marked on it, may file with the Secretary of State a written statement or description of the trade mark used on any container in a manner provided in Section 3 of the Registered Container Trade Mark Act [765 ILCS 1050/3].
(Source: P.A. 87-613.) [Formerly Ill. Rev. Stat. 38 §16E-2.]

5/16E-3. Offense.

§16E-3. Offense. (a) A person commits the offense of delivery container theft when he knowingly does any of the following:

(1) Uses for any purpose, when not on the premises of the owner or an adjacent parking area, a container of another person which is marked by a name or mark unless the use is authorized by the owner.

(2) Sells, or offers for sale, a container of another person which is marked by a name or mark unless the sale is authorized by the owner.

(3) Defaces, obliterates, destroys, covers up or otherwise removes or conceals a name or mark on a container of another person without the written consent of the owner.

(4) Removes the container of another person from the premises, parking area or any other area under the control of any processor, distributor or retail establishment, or from any delivery vehicle, without the consent of the owner of the container. Any person who possesses any marked or named container without the consent of the owner and while not on the premises, parking area or other area under control of a processor, distributor or retail establishment doing business with the owner shall be presumed to have removed the container in violation of this paragraph.

(b) Any common carrier or private carrier for hire, except those engaged in transporting bakery or dairy products to and from the places where they are produced, that receives or transports any container marked with a name or mark without having in its possession a bill of lading or invoice for that container commits the offense of delivery container theft.
(Source: P.A. 87-613.) [Formerly Ill. Rev. Stat. 38 §16E-3.]

5/16E-4. Sentence.

§16E-4. Sentence. (a)* Delivery container theft is a Class B misdemeanor. An offender may be sentenced to pay a fine of $150 for the first offense and $500 for a second or subsequent offense.
**So in original. No subsec. (b) has been enacted.*
(Source: P.A. 87-613.) [Formerly Ill. Rev. Stat. 38 §16E-4.]

ARTICLE 17. DECEPTION

Sec.

5/17-1. Deceptive practices.

§17-1. Deceptive practices. (A) As used in this Section:

(i) A financial institution means any bank, savings and loan association, credit union, or other depository of money, or medium of savings and collective investment.

(ii) An account holder is any person, having a checking account or savings account in a financial institution.

(iii) To act with the "intent to defraud" means to act wilfully, and with the specific intent to deceive or cheat, for the purpose of causing financial loss to another, or to bring some financial gain to oneself. It is not necessary to establish that any person was actually defrauded or deceived.

(B) General Deception

A person commits a deceptive practice when, with intent to defraud:

(a) He causes another, by deception or threat to execute a document disposing of property or a document by which a pecuniary obligation is incurred, or

(b) Being an officer, manager or other person participating in the direction of a financial institution, he knowingly receives or permits the receipt of a deposit or other investment, knowing that the institution is insolvent, or

(c) He knowingly makes or directs another to make a false or deceptive statement addressed to the public for the purpose of promoting the sale of property or services, or

(d) With intent to obtain control over property or to pay for property, labor or services of another, or in satisfaction of an obligation for payment of tax under the Retailers' Occupation Tax Act [35 ILCS 120/1 et seq.] or any other tax due to the State of Illinois, he issues or delivers a check or other order upon a real or fictitious depository for the payment of money, knowing that it will not be paid by the depository. Failure to have sufficient funds or credit with the depository when the check or other order is issued or delivered, or when such check or other order is presented for payment and dishonored on each of 2 occasions at least 7 days apart, is prima facie evidence that the offender knows that it will not be paid by the depository, and that he has the intent to defraud.

(e) He issues or delivers a check or other order upon a real or fictitious depository in an amount exceeding $150 in payment of an amount owed on any credit transaction for property, labor or services, or in payment of the entire amount owed on any credit transaction for property, labor or services, knowing that it will not be paid by the depository, and thereafter fails to provide funds or credit with the depository in the face amount of the check or order within seven days of receiving actual notice from the depository or payee of the dishonor of the check or order.

Sentence.

A person convicted of deceptive practice under paragraphs (a) through (e) of this subsection (B), except as otherwise provided by this Section, is guilty of a Class A misdemeanor.

A person convicted of a deceptive practice in violation of paragraph (d) a second or subsequent time shall be guilty of a Class 4 felony.

A person convicted of deceptive practices in violation of paragraph (d), when the value of the property so obtained, in a single transaction, or in separate transactions within a 90 day period, exceeds $150, shall be guilty of a Class 4 felony. In the case of a prosecution for separate transactions totaling more than $150 within a 90 day period, such separate transactions shall be alleged in a single charge and provided in a single prosecution.

(C) Deception on a Bank or Other Financial Institution False Statements

1) Any person who, with the intent to defraud, makes or causes to be made, any false statement in writing in order to obtain an account with a bank or other financial institution, or to obtain credit from a bank or other financial institution, knowing such writing to be false, and with the intent that it be relied upon, is guilty of a Class A misdemeanor.

For purposes of this subsection (C), a false statement shall mean any false statement representing identity, address, or employment, or the identity, address or employment of any person, firm or corporation.

Possession of Stolen or Fraudulently Obtained Checks

2) Any person who possesses, with the intent to defraud, any check or order for the payment of money, upon a real or fictitious account, without the consent of the account holder, or the issuing financial institution, is guilty of a Class A misdemeanor.

Any person who, within any 12 month period, violates this Section with respect to 3 or more checks or orders for the payment of money at the same time or consecutively, each the property of a different account holder or financial institution, is guilty of a Class 4 felony.

3) Possession of Implements of Check Fraud. Any person who possesses, with the intent to defraud, and without the authority of the account holder or financial institution any check imprinter, signature imprinter, or "certified" stamp is guilty of a Class A misdemeanor.

A person who within any 12 month period violates this subsection (C) as to possession of 3 or more such devices at the same time or consecutively, is guilty of a Class 4 felony.

Possession of Identification Card

4) Any person, who with the intent to defraud, possesses any check guarantee card or key card or identification card for cash dispensing machines without the authority of the account holder or financial institution, is guilty of a Class A misdemeanor.

A person who, within any 12 month period, violates this Section at the same time or consecutively with respect to 3 or more cards, each the property of different account holders, is guilty of a class 4 felony.

A person convicted under this Section, when the value of property so obtained, in a single transaction, or in separate transactions within any 90 day period, exceeds $150 shall be guilty of a Class 4 felony.

(Source: P.A. 84-897.) [Formerly Ill. Rev. Stat. 38 §17-1.]

5/17-1a. Civil liability for deceptive practices.

§17-1a. Civil Liability for Deceptive Practices. A person who issues a check or order to a payee in violation of Section 17-1(B)(d) and who fails to pay the amount of the check or order to the payee within 30 days following either delivery and acceptance by the addressee of a written demand by certified mail to the person's last known address or attempted delivery of a written demand sent by certified mail to the person's last known address and returned to the sender with a notation that delivery was refused by the person to whom the certified mail was addressed, shall be liable to the payee or a person subrogated to the rights of the payee for, in addition to the amount owing upon such check or order, damages of treble the amount so owing, but in no case less than $100 nor more than $500, plus attorney fees and court costs.

A cause of action under this Section may be brought in small claims court or in any other appropriate court. Prior to the hearing of any action under this Section, the defendant may tender to the plaintiff and the plaintiff shall accept as satisfaction of the claim, an amount of money equal to the sum of the amount of the check and the incurred court costs, and service and attorney fees.

(Source: P.A. 86-1012.) [Formerly Ill. Rev. Stat. 38 §17-1a.]

5/17-2. Impersonating member of police, fraternal or veterans' organization, or representative of charitable organization—Use of words "Chicago Police" etc.—Sentence.

§17-2. Impersonating Member of Police, Fraternal or Veterans' Organization, or Representative of Charitable Organization—Use of Words "Chicago Police" etc.—Sentence. (a) A person commits a false personation when he falsely represents himself to be a member of any police, fraternal or veteran's organization, including the Illinois Police Association, or a representative of any charitable organization, or when any person exhibits or uses in any manner any decal, badge or insignia of any police organization when not authorized to do so by such police organization.

(b) No person shall use the words "Chicago Police," "Chicago Police Department," "Chicago Patrolman," "Chicago Sergeant," "Chicago Lieutenant," "Chicago Peace Officer" or any other words to the same effect in the title of any organization, magazine, or other publication without the express approval of the Chicago Police Board.

(c) No person may solicit advertisements to appear in any firefighters', law enforcement or police officers' magazine, journal or other publication without first having obtained a current certificate of qualification from the Illinois Attorney General. Upon the presentation of proof that the applicant does in fact represent a legitimate and bona fide firefighters', law enforcement or police officers' publication, the Attorney General may issue to the applicant a certificate of qualification to solicit advertisements on behalf of such publication. The Attorney General shall prescribe forms and promulgate rules governing the making of applications and the certification of persons under this subsection.

(d) Sentence. False personation, unapproved use of a name or title, or solicitation in violation of subsections (a) and (b) of this Section is a Class C misdemeanor. Solicitation in violation of subsection (c) of this Section is a Class A misdemeanor. A second or subsequent conviction for a violation of subsection (c) of this Section committed after the first conviction is a Class 4 felony.
(Source: P.A. 84-956.) [Formerly Ill. Rev. Stat. 38 §17-2.]

5/17-3. Forgery.

§17-3. Forgery. (a) A person commits forgery when, with intent to defraud, he knowingly:

(1) Makes or alters any document apparently capable of defrauding another in such manner that it purports to have been made by another or at another time, or with different provisions, or by authority of one who did not give such authority; or

(2) Issues or delivers such document knowing it to have been thus made or altered; or

(3) Possesses, with intent to issue or deliver, any such document knowing it to have been thus made or altered.

(b) An intent to defraud means an intention to cause another to assume, create, transfer, alter or terminate any right, obligation or power with reference to any person or property.

(c) A document apparently capable of defrauding another includes, but is not limited to, one by which any right, obligation or power with reference to any person or property may be created, transferred, altered or terminated.

(d) Sentence.

Forgery is a Class 3 felony.
(Source: P.A. 77-2638.) [Formerly Ill. Rev. Stat. 38 §17-3.]

5/17-4. Deceptive altering or sale of coins.

§17-4. Deceptive altering or sale of coins. (a) A person commits a deceptive altering of coins when he in any manner alters any coin to increase the value of the coin to coin collectors.

(b) A person commits a deceptive sale of coins when he sells or advertises for sale any coin he knows has been deceptively altered for a higher rate or value than is indicated by the denomination of the coin.

(c) Sentence.

Deceptive altering or sale of coins is a Class A misdemeanor.

(Source: P.A. 77-2638.) [Formerly Ill. Rev. Stat. 38 §17-4.]

5/17-5. Deceptive collection practices.

§17-5. Deceptive collection practices. A collection agency as defined in the "Collection Agency Act" [225 ILCS 425/1 et seq.] or any employee of such collection agency commits a deceptive collection practice when, with the intent to collect a debt owed to a person, corporation, or other entity, he:

(a) represents falsely that he is an attorney, a policeman, a sheriff or deputy sheriff, a bailiff, a county clerk or employee of a county clerk's office, or any other person who by statute is authorized to enforce the law or any order of a court; or

(b) while attempting to collect an alleged debt, misrepresents to the alleged debtor or to his immediate family the corporate, partnership or proprietary name or other trade or business name under which the debt collector is engaging in debt collections and which he is legally authorized to use; or

(c) while attempting to collect an alleged debt, adds to the debt any service charge, interest or penalty which he is not entitled by law to add; or

(d) threatens to ruin, destroy, or otherwise adversely affect an alleged debtor's credit rating unless, at the same time, a disclosure is made in accordance with federal law that the alleged debtor has a right to inspect his credit rating; or

(e) accepts from an alleged debtor a payment which he knows is not owed.

The commission of a deceptive collection practice is a Business Offense punishable by a fine not to exceed $3,000.

(Source: P.A. 78-1248.) [Formerly Ill. Rev. Stat. 38 §17-5.]

5/17-6. State benefits fraud.

§17-6. State Benefits Fraud. (a) Any person who obtains or attempts to obtain money or benefits from the State of Illinois, from any political subdivision thereof, or from any program funded or administered in whole or in part by the State of Illinois or any political subdivision thereof through the knowing use of false identification documents or through the knowing misrepresentation of his age, place of residence, number of dependents, marital or family status, employment status, financial status, or any other material fact upon which his eligibility for or degree of participation in any benefit program might be based, is guilty of State benefits fraud.

(b) Notwithstanding any provision of State law to the contrary, every application or other document submitted to an agency or department of the State of Illinois or any political subdivision thereof to establish or determine eligibility for money or benefits from the State of Illinois or from any political subdivision thereof, or from any program funded or administered in whole or in part by the State of Illinois or any political subdivision thereof, shall be made available upon request to any law enforcement agency for use in the investigation or prosecution of State benefits fraud or for use in the investigation or prosecution of any other crime arising out of the same transaction or occurrence. Except as otherwise permitted by law, information disclosed pursuant to this subsection shall be used and disclosed only for the purposes provided herein.

The provisions of this Section shall be operative only to the extent that they do not conflict with any federal law or regulation governing federal grants to this State.

(c) Any employee of the State of Illinois or any agency or political subdivision thereof may seize as evidence any false or fraudulent document presented to him in connection with an application for or receipt of money or benefits from the State of Illinois, from any political subdivision thereof, or from any program funded or administered in whole or in part by the State of Illinois or any political subdivision thereof.

(d) State benefits fraud is a Class 4 felony except when more than $300 is obtained, in which case State benefits fraud is a Class 3 felony.

(Source: P.A. 82-999.) [Formerly Ill. Rev. Stat. 38 §17-6.]

5/17-7. Promotion of pyramid sales schemes.

§17-7. Promotion of pyramid sales schemes. (a) The term "pyramid sales scheme" means any plan or operation whereby a person, in exchange for money or other thing of value, acquires the opportunity to receive a benefit or thing of value, which is primarily based upon the inducement of additional persons, by himself or others, regardless of number, to participate in the same plan or operation and is not primarily contingent on the volume or quantity of goods, services, or other property sold or distributed or to be sold or distributed to persons for purposes of resale to consumers. For purposes of this subsection, "money or other thing of value" shall not include payments made for sales demonstration equipment and materials furnished on a nonprofit basis for use in making sales and not for resale.

(b) Any person who knowingly sells, offers to sell, or attempts to sell the right to participate in a pyramid sales scheme commits a Class A misdemeanor.

(Source: P.A. 83-808.) [Formerly Ill. Rev. Stat. 38 §17-7.]

5/17-8. Health care benefits fraud.

§17-8. Health Care Benefits Fraud. (a) A person commits health care benefits fraud if he or she with the intent to defraud or deceive any provider, other than a governmental unit or agency, obtains or attempts to obtain health care benefits.

(b) Health care benefits fraud is a Class A misdemeanor.

(Source: P.A. 84-418.) [Formerly Ill. Rev. Stat. 38 §17-8.]

5/17-9. Public aid wire fraud.

§17-9. Public aid wire fraud. (a) Whoever knowingly makes or transmits any communication by means of telephone, wire, radio or television, such communication being made, transmitted or received within the State of Illinois, intending that such communication be made or transmitted in furtherance of any plan, scheme or design to obtain, unlawfully, any benefit or payment under "The Illinois Public Aid Code", as amended [305 ILCS 5/1-1 et seq.], commits the offense of public aid wire fraud.

(b) Whoever knowingly directs or causes any communication to be made or transmitted by means of telephone, wire, radio or television, intending that such communication be made or transmitted in furtherance of any plan, scheme or design to obtain, unlawfully, any benefit or payment under "The Illinois Public Aid Code", as amended, commits the offense of public aid wire fraud.

(c) Penalty. Public aid wire fraud is a Class 4 felony.

(Source: P.A. 84-1255.) [Formerly Ill. Rev. Stat. 38 §17-9.]

5/17-10. Public aid mail fraud.

§17-10. Public aid mail fraud. (a) Whoever knowingly places any communication with the United States Postal Service, or with any private or other mail, package or delivery service or system, such communication being placed or received within the State of Illinois, intending that such communication be delivered in furtherance of any plan, scheme or design to obtain, unlawfully, any benefit or payment under "The Illinois Public Aid Code", as amended [305 ILCS 5/1-1 et seq.], commits the offense of public aid mail fraud.

(b) Whoever knowingly directs or causes any communication to be placed with the United States Postal Service, or with any private or other mail, package or delivery service or system, intending that such communication be delivered in furtherance of any plan, scheme or design to obtain, unlawfully, any benefit or payment under "The Illinois Public Aid Code", as amended, commits the offense of public aid mail fraud.

(c) Penalty. Public aid mail fraud is a Class 4 felony.

(Source: P.A. 84-1256; 84-1438.) [Formerly Ill. Rev. Stat. 38 §17-10.]

5/17-11. Odometer fraud.

§17-11. Odometer Fraud. Any person who shall, with intent to defraud another, disconnect, reset, or alter, or cause to be disconnected, reset or altered, the odometer of any used motor vehicle with the intent to conceal or change the actual miles driven shall be guilty of a Class A misdemeanor. A person convicted of a second or subsequent violation of this Section shall be guilty of a Class 4 felony. This Section shall not apply to legitimate business practices of automotive parts recyclers who recycle used odometers for resale.

(Source: P.A. 84-1391; 84-1438.) [Formerly Ill. Rev. Stat. 38 §17-11.]

ARTICLE 17A. DISQUALIFICATION FOR STATE BENEFITS

Sec.

5/17A-1. Persons subject to deportation—ineligibility for benefits.

§17A-1. An individual against whom a United States Immigration Judge has issued an order of deportation which has been affirmed by the Board of Immigration Review, as well as an individual who appeals such an order pending appeal, under paragraph 19 of Section 241(a) of the Immigration and Nationality Act [see 8 U.S.C. 1182(a)(3)(E)] relating to persecution of others on account of race, religion, national origin or political opinion under the direction of or in association with the Nazi government of Germany or its allies, shall be ineligible for the following benefits authorized by State law:

(a) The homestead exemption and homestead improvement exemption under Sections 19.23-1, 19.23-1a, 19.23-2 and 19.23-3 of the Revenue Act of 1939 [35 ILCS 205/19.23-1, 205/19.23-1a, 205/19.23-2 and 205/19.23-3].

(b) Grants under the Senior Citizens and Disabled Persons Property Tax Relief and Pharmaceutical Assistance Act [320 ILCS 25/1 et seq.].

(c) The double income tax exemption conferred upon persons 65 years of age or older by Section 204 of the Illinois Income Tax Act [35 ILCS 5/204].

(d) Grants provided by the Department on Aging.

(e) Reductions in vehicle registration fees under Section 3-806.3 of the Illinois Vehicle Code [625 ILCS 5/3-806.3].

(f) Free fishing and reduced fishing license fees under Sections 20-5 and 20-40 of the Fish and Aquatic Life Code [515 ILCS 5/20-5 and 5/20-40].

(g) Tuition free courses for senior citizens under the Senior Citizen Courses Act [110 ILCS 990/0.01 et seq.].

(h) Any benefits under the Illinois Public Aid Code [305 ILCS 5/1-1 et seq.].

(Source: P.A. 87-895.) [Formerly Ill. Rev. Stat. 38 §17A-1.]

5/17A-2. Recovery of grants.

§17A-2. Any grants awarded to persons described in Section 17A-1 of this Act may be recovered by the State of Illinois in a civil action commenced by the Attorney General in the circuit court of Sangamon County or the State's Attorney of the county of residence of the person described in Section 17A-1 of this Act.

(Source: P.A. 84-1391.) [Formerly Ill. Rev. Stat. 38 §17A-2.]

5/17A-3. Penalties for violations.

§17A-3. (a) Any person who has been found by a court to have received benefits in violation of Section 17A-1 where:

(1) the total monetary value of the benefits involved in the violation is less than $150, shall be guilty of a Class A misdemeanor;

(2) the total monetary value of the benefits involved in the violation is $150 or more but less than $1,000, shall be guilty of a Class 4 felony;

(3) the total monetary value of the benefits involved in the violation is $1,000 or more but less than $5,000, shall be guilty of a Class 3 felony;

(4) the total monetary value of the benefits involved in the violation is $5,000 or more but less than $10,000, shall be guilty of a Class 2 felony; or

(5) the total monetary value of the benefits involved in the violation is $10,000 or more, shall be guilty of a Class 1 felony.

(b) Any person who commits a subsequent violation of Section 17A-1 and:

(1) the total monetary value of the benefits involved in the subsequent violation is less than $150, shall be guilty of a Class 4 felony;

(2) the total monetary value of the benefits involved in the subsequent violation is $150 or more but less than $1,000, shall be guilty of a Class 3 felony;

(3) the total monetary value of the benefits involved in the subsequent violation is $1,000 or more but less than $5,000, shall be guilty of a Class 2 felony;

(4) the total monetary value of the benefits involved in the subsequent violation is $5,000 or more but less than $10,000, shall be guilty of a Class 1 felony.

(c) For purposes of determining the classification of offense under this Section, all of the monetary value of the benefits received as a result of the unlawful act, practice or course of conduct can be accumulated.

(Source: P.A. 84-1391.) [Formerly Ill. Rev. Stat. 38 §17A-3.]

5/17A-3.1. Restoration of benefits.

§17A-3.1. An individual described in Section 17A-1 who has been deported shall be restored to any benefits which that individual has been denied under State law pursuant to Section 17A-1 if (a) the Attorney General of the United States has issued an order cancelling deportation and has adjusted the status of the individual to that of an alien lawfully admitted for permanent residence in the United States or (b) the country to which the individual has been deported adjudicates or exonerates the individual in a judicial or administrative proceeding as not being guilty of the persecution of others on account of race, religion, national origin or political opinion under the direction of or in association with the Nazi government of Germany or its allies.

(Source: P.A. 84-1391.) [Formerly Ill. Rev. Stat. 38 §17A-3.1.]

5/17A-4. Applicability.

§17A-4. This Article shall be applicable to persons who have filed applications for benefits prior to, on or after its effective date.

(Source: P.A. 84-1391.) [Formerly Ill. Rev. Stat. 38 §17A-4.]

ARTICLE 18. ROBBERY

5/18-1. Robbery.

§18-1. Robbery. (a) A person commits robbery when he takes property from the person or presence of another by the use of force or by threatening the imminent use of force.

(b) Sentence. Robbery is a Class 2 felony. However, if the victim is 60 years of age or over or is a physically handicapped person, robbery is a Class 1 felony.
(Source: P.A. 85-691.) [Formerly Ill. Rev. Stat. 38 §18-1.]

5/18-2. Armed robbery.

§18-2. Armed robbery. (a) A person commits armed robbery when he or she violates Section 18-1 while he or she carries on or about his or her person, or is otherwise armed with a dangerous weapon.

(b) Sentence.

Armed robbery is a Class X felony.
(Source: P.A. 80-1099.) [Formerly Ill. Rev. Stat. 38 §18-2.]

ARTICLE 19. BURGLARY

5/19-1. Burglary.

§19-1. Burglary. (a) A person commits burglary when without authority he knowingly enters or without authority remains within a building, housetrailer, watercraft, aircraft, motor vehicle as defined in The Illinois Vehicle Code [625 ILCS 5/1-100 et seq.], railroad car, or any part thereof, with intent to commit therein a felony or theft. This offense shall not include the offenses set out in Section 4-102 of The Illinois Vehicle Code [625 ILCS 5/4-102], nor the offense of residential burglary as defined in Section 19-3 hereof.

(b) Sentence.

Burglary is a Class 2 felony.
(Source: P.A. 82-238.) [Formerly Ill. Rev. Stat. 38 §19-1.]

5/19-2. Possession of burglary tools.

§19-2. Possession of burglary tools. (a) A person commits the offense of possession of burglary tools when he possesses any key, tool, instrument, device, or any explosive, suitable for use in breaking into a building, housetrailer, watercraft, aircraft, motor vehicle as defined in The Illinois Vehicle Code [625 ILCS 5/1-100 et seq.], railroad car, or any depository designed for the safekeeping of property, or any part thereof, with intent to enter any such place and with intent to commit therein a felony or theft.

(b) Sentence.

Possession of burglary tools in violation of this Section is a Class 4 felony.
(Source: P.A. 78-255.) [Formerly Ill. Rev. Stat. 38 §19-2.]

5/19-3. Residential burglary.

§19-3. Residential burglary. (a) A person commits residential burglary who knowingly and without authority enters the dwelling place of another with the intent to commit therein a felony or theft.

(b) Sentence. Residential burglary is a Class 1 felony.
(Source: P.A. 84-832.) [Formerly Ill. Rev. Stat. 38 §19-3.]

5/19-4. Criminal trespass to residence.

§19-4. Criminal Trespass to Residence. (a) A person commits the offense of criminal trespass to a residence when, without authority, he knowingly enters or remains within any residence, including a house trailer. For purposes of this Section, in the case of a multi-unit residential building or complex, "residence" shall only include the portion of the building or complex which is the actual dwelling place of any person and shall not include such places as common recreational areas or lobbies.

(b) Sentence. Criminal trespass to residence is a Class A misdemeanor.
(Source: P.A. 83-1070.) [Formerly Ill. Rev. Stat. 38 §19-4.]

5/19-5. Criminal fortification of a residence or building.

§19-5. Criminal fortification of a residence or building. (a) A person commits the offense of criminal fortification of a residence or building when, with the intent to prevent the lawful entry of a law enforcement officer or another, he maintains a residence or building in a fortified condition, knowing that such residence or building is used for the manufacture, storage, delivery, or trafficking of cannabis or controlled substances as defined in the Cannabis Control Act [720 ILCS 550/1 et seq.] or Illinois Controlled Substances Act [720 ILCS 570/100 et seq.].

(b) "Fortified condition" means preventing or impeding entry through the use of steel doors, wooden planking, crossbars, alarm systems, dogs, or other similar means.

(c) Sentence. Criminal fortification of a residence or building is a Class 3 felony.
(Source: P.A. 86-760.) [Formerly Ill. Rev. Stat. 38 §19-5.]

ARTICLE 20. ARSON

Sec.

5/20-1. Arson.

§20-1. Arson. A person commits arson when, by means of fire or explosive, he knowingly:

(a) Damages any real property, or any personal property having a value of $150 or more, of another without his consent; or

(b) With intent to defraud an insurer, damages any property or any personal property having a value of $150 or more.

Property "of another" means a building or other property, whether real or personal, in which a person other than the offender has an interest which the offender has no authority to defeat or impair, even though the offender may also have an interest in the building or property.

(c) Sentence.

Arson is a Class 2 felony.
(Source: P.A. 77-2638.) [Formerly Ill. Rev. Stat. 38 §20-1.]

5/20-1.1. Aggravated arson.

§20-1.1. Aggravated Arson. (a) A person commits aggravated arson when in the course of committing arson he knowingly damages, partially or totally, any building or structure, including any adjacent building or structure, and (1) he knows or reasonably should know that one or more persons are present therein or (2) any person suffers great bodily harm, or permanent disability or disfigurement as a result of the fire or explosion or (3) a fireman or policeman who is present at the scene acting in the line of duty, is injured as a result of the fire or explosion.

(b) Sentence. Aggravated arson is a Class X felony.

(Source: P.A. 84-1100.) [Formerly Ill. Rev. Stat. 38 §20-1.1.]

5/20-2. Possession of explosives or explosive or incendiary devices.

§20-2. Possession of explosives or explosive or incendiary devices. (a) A person commits the offense of possession of explosives or explosive or incendiary devices in violation of this Section when he possesses, manufactures or transports any explosive compound, timing or detonating device for use with any explosive compound or incendiary device and either intends to use such explosive or device to commit any offense or knows that another intends to use such explosive or device to commit a felony.

(b) Sentence.

Possession of explosives or explosive or incendiary devices in violation of this Section is a Class 2 felony.

(Source: P.A. 84-1308.) [Formerly Ill. Rev. Stat. 38 §20-2.]

ARTICLE 21. DAMAGE AND TRESPASS TO PROPERTY

5/21-1. Criminal damage to property.

§21-1. Criminal damage to property. (1) A person commits an illegal act when he:

(a) knowingly damages any property of another without his consent; or

(b) recklessly by means of fire or explosive damages property of another; or

(c) knowingly starts a fire on the land of another without his consent; or

(d) knowingly injures a domestic animal of another without his consent; or

(e) knowingly deposits on the land or in the building of another, without his consent, any stink bomb or any offensive smelling compound and thereby intends to interfere with the use by another of the land or building; or

(f) damages any property, other than as described in subsection (b) of Section 20-1, with intent to defraud an insurer; or

(g) knowingly shoots a firearm at any portion of a railroad train; or

(h) knowingly damages the property of another without his consent by defacing, deforming or otherwise damaging such property by the use of paint or any other similar substance.

When the charge of criminal damage to property exceeding a specified value is brought, the extent of the damage is an element of the offense to be resolved by the trier of fact as either exceeding or not exceeding the specified value.

(2) The acts described in items (a) through (f) and item (h) are Class A misdemeanors if the damage to property does not exceed $300. The act described in item (g) is a Class 4 felony. The acts described in items (a) through (f) and in item (h) are Class 4 felonies if the damage to property exceeds $300 but does not exceed $10,000. The acts described in items (a) through (f) and in item (h) are Class 3 felonies if the damage to property exceeds $10,000 but does not exceed $100,000. The acts described in items (a) through (f) and in item (h) are

Class 2 felonies if the damage to property exceeds $100,000. If the damage to property exceeds $10,000, the court shall impose upon the offender a fine equal to the value of the damages to the property.
(Source: P.A. 86-495; 86-1254.) [Formerly Ill. Rev. Stat. 38 §21-1.]

5/21-1.1. Criminal damage of fire fighting apparatus, hydrants or equipment.

§21-1.1. Criminal Damage of Fire Fighting Apparatus, Hydrants or Equipment. Whoever wilfully and maliciously cuts, injures, damages, tampers with or destroys or defaces any fire hydrant or any fire hose or any fire engine, or other public or private fire fighting equipment, or any apparatus appertaining to such equipment, or intentionally opens any fire hydrant without proper authorization, is guilty of a Class B misdemeanor.
(Source: P.A. 78-255.) [Formerly Ill. Rev. Stat. 38 §21-1.1.]

5/21-1.2. Institutional vandalism.

§21-1.2. Institutional vandalism. (a) A person commits institutional vandalism when, by reason of the race, color, creed, religion or national origin of another individual or group of individuals, he knowingly and without consent inflicts damage to any of the following properties, provided that the damage inflicted is at least $300:

(1) Any church, synagogue or other building, structure or place used for religious worship or other religious purpose;

(2) Any cemetery, mortuary, or other facility used for the purpose of burial or memorializing the dead;

(3) Any school, educational facility or community center;

(4) The grounds adjacent to, and owned or rented by, any institution, facility, building, structure or place described in paragraphs (1), (2) or (3) above; or

(5) Any personal property contained in any institution, facility, building, structure or place described in paragraphs (1), (2) or (3) above.

(b) Institutional vandalism is a Class 3 felony.

(c) Independent of any criminal prosecution or the result thereof, any person suffering damage to property or injury to his person as a result of institutional vandalism may bring a civil action for damages, injunction or other appropriate relief. The court may award actual damages, including damages for emotional distress, or punitive damages. A judgment may include attorney's fees and costs. The parents or legal guardians of an unemancipated minor, other than guardians appointed pursuant to the Juvenile Court Act [repealed] or the Juvenile Court Act of 1987 [705 ILCS 405/1-1 et seq.], shall be liable for the amount of any judgment for actual damages rendered against such minor under this subsection (c) in any amount not exceeding the amount provided under Section 5 of the Parental Responsibility Law [740 ILCS 115/5].
(Source: P.A. 85-1209.) [Formerly Ill. Rev. Stat. 38 §21-1.2.]

5/21-2. Criminal trespass to vehicles.

§21-2. Criminal trespass to vehicles. Whoever knowingly and without authority enters any part of or operates any vehicle, aircraft, watercraft or snowmobile commits a Class A misdemeanor.
(Source: P.A. 83-488.) [Formerly Ill. Rev. Stat. 38 §21-2.]

5/21-3. Criminal trespass to real property.

§21-3. Criminal trespass to real property. (a) Whoever enters upon the land or a building, other than a residence, or any part thereof of another, after receiving, prior to such entry, notice from the owner or occupant that such entry is forbidden, or remains upon the land or in a building, other than a residence, of another after receiving notice from the owner or occupant to depart, commits a Class C misdemeanor.

(b) A person has received notice from the owner or occupant within the meaning of Subsection (a) if he has been notified personally, either orally or in writing including a valid court order as defined by subsection (7) of Section 112A-3 of the Code of Criminal Procedure of 1963 [725 ILCS 5/112A-3] granting remedy (2) of subsection (b) of Section 112A-14 of that Code [725 ILCS 5/112A-14], or if a printed or written notice forbidding such entry has been conspicuously posted or exhibited at the main entrance to such land or the forbidden part thereof.

(c) This Section does not apply to any person, whether a migrant worker or otherwise, living on the land with permission of the owner or of his agent having apparent authority to hire workers on such land and assign them living quarters or a place of accommodations for living thereon, nor to anyone living on such land at the request of, or by occupancy, leasing or other agreement or arrangement with the owner or his agent, nor to anyone invited by such migrant worker or other person so living on such land to visit him at the place he is so living upon the land.

(d) A person shall be exempt from prosecution under this Section if he beautifies unoccupied and abandoned residential and industrial properties located within any municipality. For the purpose of this subsection, "unoccupied and abandoned residential and industrial property" means any real estate (1) in which the taxes have not been paid for a period of at least 2 years; and (2) which has been left unoccupied and abandoned for a period of at least one year; and "beautifies" means to landscape, clean up litter, or to repair dilapidated conditions on or to board up windows and doors.

(e) No person shall be liable in any civil action for money damages to the owner of unoccupied and abandoned residential and industrial property which that person beautifies pursuant to subsection (d) of this Section.
(Source: P.A. 86-1300.) [Formerly Ill. Rev. Stat. 38 §21-3.]

5/21-4. Criminal damage to State supported property.

§21-4. Criminal Damage to State Supported Property. (1) Any of the following acts is a Class 4 felony when the damage to property is $500 or less, and any such act is a Class 3 felony when the damage to property exceeds $500 but does not exceed $10,000; a Class 2 felony when the damage to property exceeds $10,000 but does not exceed $100,000 and a Class 1 felony when the damage to property exceeds $100,000:

(a) Knowingly damages any property supported in whole or in part with State funds or Federal funds administered or granted through State agencies without the consent of the State; or

(b) Knowingly, by means of fire or explosive damages property supported in whole or in part with State funds or Federal funds administered or granted through State agencies; or

(c) Knowingly starts a fire on property supported in whole or in part with State funds or Federal funds administered or granted through State agencies without the consent of the State; or

(d) Knowingly deposits on land or in a building supported in whole or in part with State funds, or Federal funds administered or granted through State agencies without the consent of the State, any stink bomb or any offensive smelling compound and thereby intends to interfere with the use by another of the land or building.

(2) When the damage to property exceeds $10,000, the court shall impose upon the offender a fine equal to the value of the damages to the property.
(Source: P.A. 86-1254.) [Formerly Ill. Rev. Stat. 38 §21-4.]

5/21-5. Criminal trespass to State supported land.

§21-5. Criminal Trespass to State Supported Land. (a) Whoever enters upon land supported in whole or in part with State funds, or Federal funds administered or granted through State agencies or any building on such land, after receiving, prior to such entry, notice from the State or its representative that such entry is forbidden, or remains upon such land or in such building after receiving notice from the State or its representative to depart, and who thereby interferes with another person's lawful use or enjoyment of such building or land, commits a Class A misdemeanor.

(b) A person has received notice from the State within the meaning of sub-section (1)* if he has been notified personally, either orally or in writing, or if a printed or written notice forbidding such entry to him or a group of which he is a part, has been conspicuously posted or exhibited at the main entrance to such land or the forbidden part thereof.

**So in original. Probably should be "(a)".*

(Source: P.A. 84-1041.) [Formerly Ill. Rev. Stat. 38 §21-5.]

5/21-6. Unauthorized possession or storage of weapons.

§21-6. Unauthorized Possession or Storage of Weapons. (a) Whoever possesses or stores any weapon enumerated in Section 33A-1 on land supported in whole or in part with State funds or federal funds administered through State agencies or in any building on such land without prior written permission from the chief security officer for such land or building commits a Class A misdemeanor.

(b) The chief security officer must grant any reasonable request for permission under paragraph (a).

(Source: P.A. 77-2638.) [Formerly Ill. Rev. Stat. 38 §21-6.]

5/21-7. Criminal trespass to restricted areas and restricted landing areas at airports.

§21-7. Criminal trespass to Restricted areas and restricted Landing areas at airports. Whoever enters upon, or remains in, any restricted area or restricted landing area used in connection with an airport facility, or part thereof, in this State, after such person has received notice from the airport authority that such entry is forbidden commits a Class A misdemeanor. Notice that the area is "restricted" and entry thereto "forbidden", for purposes of this Section, means that the person or persons have been notified personally, either orally or in writing, or by a printed or written notice forbidding such entry to him or a group or an organization of which he is a member, which has been conspicuously posted or exhibited at every usable entrance to such area or the forbidden part thereof.

The terms "Restricted area" or "Restricted landing area" in this Section are defined to incorporate the meaning ascribed to those terms in Section 8 of the "Illinois Aeronautics Act", approved July 24, 1945, as amended [620 ILCS 5/8], and also include any other area of the airport that has been designated such by the airport authority.

(Source: P.A. 81-564.) [Formerly Ill. Rev. Stat. 38 §21-7.]

ARTICLE 21.1. RESIDENTIAL PICKETING

Sec.

5/21.1-1. Legislative finding and declaration.

§21.1-1. Legislative finding and declaration. The Legislature finds and declares that men in a free society have the right to quiet enjoyment of their homes; that the stability of community and family life cannot be maintained unless the right to privacy and a sense of security and peace in the home are respected and encouraged; that residential picketing, however just the cause inspiring it, disrupts home, family and communal life; that residential picketing is inappropriate in our society, where the jealously guarded rights of free speech and assembly have always been associated with respect for the rights of others. For these reasons the Legislature finds and declares this Article to be necessary.
(Source: Laws 1967, p. 940.) [Formerly Ill. Rev. Stat. 38 §21.1-1.]

5/21.1-2. Exceptions; prohibition.

§21.1-2. It is unlawful to picket before or about the residence or dwelling of any person, except when the residence or dwelling is used as a place of business. However, this Article does not apply to a person peacefully picketing his own residence or dwelling and does not prohibit the peaceful picketing of the place of holding a meeting or assembly on premises commonly used to discuss subjects of general public interest.
(Source: P.A. 81-1270.) [Formerly Ill. Rev. Stat. 38 §21.1-2.]

5/21.1-3. Sentence.

§21.1-3. Sentence. Violation of Section 21.1-2 is a Class B misdemeanor.
(Source: P.A. 77-2638.) [Formerly Ill. Rev. Stat. 38 §21.1-3.]

ARTICLE 21.2. INTERFERENCE WITH A PUBLIC INSTITUTION OF HIGHER EDUCATION

Sec.

5/21.2-1. Legislative declaration.

§21.2-1. The General Assembly, in recognition of unlawful campus disorders across the nation which are disruptive of the educational process, dangerous to the health and safety of persons, damaging to public and private property, and which divert the use of institutional facilities from the primary function of education, establishes by this Act criminal penalties for conduct declared in this Article to be unlawful. However, this Article does not modify or supersede any other law relating to damage to persons or property, nor does it prevent a public institution of higher education from establishing restrictions upon the availability or use of any building or other facility owned, operated or controlled by the institution to preserve their dedication to education, nor from establishing standards of scholastic and behavioral conduct reasonably relevant to the missions, processes and functions of the institution, nor from invoking appropriate discipline or expulsion for violations of such standards.
(Source: P.A. 76-1582.) [Formerly Ill. Rev. Stat. 38 §21.2-1.]

5/21.2-2. Public institution of higher education; interference.

§21.2-2. A person commits interference with a public institution of higher education when, on the campus of a public institution of higher education, or at or in any building or other facility owned, operated or controlled by the institution, without authority from the institution he, through force or violence, actual or threatened:

(a) willfully denies to a trustee, employee, student or invitee of the institution:

(1) Freedom of movement at such place; or

(2) Use of the property or facilities of the institution; or

(3) The right of ingress or egress to the property or facilities of the institution; or

(b) willfully impedes, obstructs, interferes with or disrupts:

(1) the performance of institutional duties by a trustee or employee of the institution; or

(2) the pursuit of educational activities, as determined or prescribed by the institution, by a trustee, employee, student or invitee of the institution; or

(c) knowingly occupies or remains in or at any building, property or other facility owned, operated or controlled by the institution after due notice to depart.

(Source: P.A. 76-1582.) [Formerly Ill. Rev. Stat. 38 §21.2-2.]

5/21.2-3. Lawful assembly.

§21.2-3. Nothing in this Article prevents lawful assembly of the trustees, employees, students or invitees of a public institution of higher education, or prevents orderly petition for redress of grievances.

(Source: P.A. 76-1582.) [Formerly Ill. Rev. Stat. 38 §21.2-3.]

5/21.2-4. Sentence.

§21.2-4. Sentence. A person convicted of violation of this Article commits a Class C misdemeanor for the first offense and for a second or subsequent offense commits a Class B misdemeanor.

(Source: P.A. 77-2638.) [Formerly Ill. Rev. Stat. 38 §21.2-4.]

5/21.2-5. Definitions.

§21.2-5. For the purposes of this Article the words and phrases described in this Section have the meanings designated in this Section, except when a particular context clearly requires a different meaning.

"Public institution of higher education" means an educational organization located in this State which provides an organized post-high school educational program, and which is supported in whole or in part by appropriations of the General Assembly.

A person has received "due notice" if he, or the group of which he is a part, has been given oral or written notice from an authorized representative of the public institution of higher education in a manner reasonably designated to inform him, or the group of which he is a part, that he or they should cease such action or depart from such premises. The notice may also be given by a printed or written notice forbidding entry conspicuously posted or exhibited at the main entrance of the building or other facility, or the forbidden part thereof.

"Force or violence" includes, but is not limited to, use of one's person, individually or in concert with others, to impede access to or movement within or otherwise to interfere with the conduct of the authorized activities of the public institution of higher education, its trustees, employees, students or invitees.

(Source: P.A. 76-1582.) [Formerly Ill. Rev. Stat. 38 §21.2-5.]

5/21.2-6. Severability.

§21.2-6. If any provision of this Act or the application thereof to any person or circumstances is held invalid, such invalidity shall not affect other provisions or applications of the Act which can be given effect without the invalid provision or application, and to this end the provisions of this Act are declared severable.

(Source: P.A. 76-1582.) [Formerly Ill. Rev. Stat. 38 §21.2-6.]

PART D. OFFENSES AFFECTING PUBLIC HEALTH, SAFETY AND DECENCY

ARTICLE 24. DEADLY WEAPONS

5/24-1. Unlawful use of weapons.

§24-1. Unlawful Use of Weapons. (a) A person commits the offense of unlawful use of weapons when he knowingly:

(1) Sells, manufactures, purchases, possesses or carries any bludgeon, black-jack, slung-shot, sand-club, sand-bag, metal knuckles, throwing star, or any knife, commonly referred to as a switchblade knife, which has a blade that opens automatically by hand pressure applied to a button, spring or other device in the handle of the knife, or a ballistic knife, which is a device that propels a knifelike blade as a projectile by means of a coil spring, elastic material or compressed gas; or

(2) Carries or possesses with intent to use the same unlawfully against another, a dagger, dirk, billy, dangerous knife, razor, stiletto, broken bottle or other piece of glass, stun gun or taser or any other dangerous or deadly weapon or instrument of like character; or

(3) Carries on or about his person or in any vehicle, a tear gas gun projector or bomb or any object containing noxious liquid gas or substance, other than an object containing a non-lethal noxious liquid gas or substance designed solely for personal defense carried by a person 18 years of age or older; or

(4) Carries or possesses in any vehicle or concealed on or about his person except when on his land or in his own abode or fixed place of business any pistol, revolver, stun gun or taser or other firearm; or

(5) Sets a spring gun; or

(6) Possesses any device or attachment of any kind designed, used or intended for use in silencing the report of any firearm; or

(7) Sells, manufactures, purchases, possesses or carries a machine gun, which shall be defined for the purposes of this subsection as any weapon, which shoots, is designed to shoot, or can be readily restored to shoot, automatically more than one shot without manually reloading by a single function of the trigger, including the frame or receiver of any such weapon, or sells, manufactures, purchases, possesses, or carries any combination of parts designed or intended for use in converting any weapon into a machine gun, or any combination or* parts from which a machine gun can be assembled if such parts are in the possession or under the control of a person, or any rifle having one or more

barrels less than 16 inches in length or a shotgun having one or more barrels less than 18 inches in length or any weapon made from a rifle or shotgun, whether by alteration, modification, or otherwise, if such a weapon as modified has an overall length of less than 26 inches or any bomb, bomb-shell, grenade, bottle or other container containing an explosive substance of over one-quarter ounce for like purposes, such as, but not limited to, black powder bombs and Molotov cocktails or artillery projectiles; or

*So in original. Probably should be "of".

(8) Carries or possesses any firearm, stun gun or taser or other deadly weapon in any place which is licensed to sell intoxicating beverages, or at any public gathering held pursuant to a license issued by any governmental body or any public gathering at which an admission is charged, excluding a place where a showing, demonstration or lecture involving the exhibition of unloaded firearms is conducted; or

(9) Carries or possesses in a vehicle or on or about his person any pistol, revolver, stun gun or taser or firearm or ballistic knife, when he is hooded, robed or masked in such manner as to conceal his identity; or

(10) Carries or possesses on or about his person, upon any public street, alley, or other public lands within the corporate limits of a city, village or incorporated town, except when an invitee thereon or therein, for the purpose of the display of such weapon or the lawful commerce in weapons, or except when on his land or in his own abode or fixed place of business, any pistol, revolver, stun gun or taser or other firearm.

A "stun gun or taser", as used in this paragraph (a) means (i) any device which is powered by electrical charging units, such as, batteries, and which fires one or several barbs attached to a length of wire and which, upon hitting a human, can send out a current capable of disrupting the person's nervous system in such a manner as to render him incapable of normal functioning or (ii) any device which is powered by electrical charging units, such as batteries, and which, upon contact with a human or clothing worn by a human, can send out current capable of disrupting the person's nervous system in such a manner as to render him incapable of normal functioning; or

(11) Sells, manufactures or purchases any explosive bullet. For purposes of this paragraph (a) "explosive bullet" means the projectile portion of an ammunition cartridge which contains or carries an explosive charge which will explode upon contact with the flesh of a human or an animal. "Cartridge" means a tubular metal case having a projectile affixed at the front thereof and a cap or primer at the rear end thereof, with the propellant contained in such tube between the projectile and the cap; or

(12) Carries or possesses on about* his person any bludgeon, black-jack, sling-shot, sand-club, sand-bag, metal knuckles, switchblade knife, ballistic knife, tear gas gun projector bomb or any object containing noxious liquid gas, pistol or revolver or other firearm, bomb, grenade, bottle or other container containing an explosive substance of over one-quarter ounce, or cartridge while in the building or on the grounds of any elementary or secondary school, community college, college or university. This paragraph (12) shall not apply to law enforcement officers or security officers of such school, college or university, nor to students carrying or possessing firearms for use in training courses, parades, hunting, target shooting on school ranges, or otherwise with the consent of school authorities and which firearms are transported unloaded and enclosed in a suitable case, box or transportation package.

*So in original. Probably should be "or about".

(b) Sentence. A person convicted of a violation of Subsection 24-1(a)(1) through (5), Subsection 24-1(a)(8), Subsection (a)(10) or of 24-1(a)(11), commits a Class A misdemeanor; a person convicted of a violation of Subsection 24-1(a)(6) or 24-1(a)(7) commits a Class 3 felony. A person convicted of a violation of Subsection 24-1(a)(9) or 24-1(a)(12) commits a Class 4 felony. A person convicted of a second or subsequent violation of Subsection 24-1(a)(4) commits a Class 4 felony.

(c) Violations on school property, or in a public park, or any conveyance owned, leased or contracted by a school to transport students to or from school or a school related activity, or residential property owned, operated and managed by a public housing agency.

(1) A person who violates Subsection 24-1(a)(6) or 24-1(a)(7) in any school, regardless of the time of day or the time of year or residential property owned, operated and managed by a public housing agency, or in a public park or on the real property comprising any school, regardless of the time of day or the time of year or residential property owned, operated and managed by a public housing agency or on the real property comprising any public park, or any conveyance owned, leased or contracted by a school to transport students to or from school or a school related activity or on any public way within 1,000 feet of the real property comprising any school or public park or residential property owned, operated, and managed by a public housing agency commits a Class 2 felony.

(2) A person who violates Subsection 24-1(a)(9) in any school, regardless of the time of day or the time of year or residential property owned, operated and managed by a public housing agency or in a public park or on the real property comprising any school, regardless of the time of day or the time of year or residential property owned, operated and managed by a public housing agency or on the real property comprising any public park or any conveyance owned, leased or contracted by a school to transport students to or from school or a school related activity or on any public way within 1,000 feet of the real property comprising any school or public park or residential property owned, operated, and managed by a public housing agency commits a Class 3 felony. School is defined as any public or private elementary or secondary school, community college, college or university.

(d) The presence in an automobile other than a public omnibus of any weapon, instrument or substance referred to in Subsection (a)(7) is prima facie evidence that it is in the possession of, and is being carried by, all persons occupying such automobile at the time such weapon, instrument or substance is found, except under the following circumstances: (i) if such weapon, instrument or instrumentality is found upon the person of one of the occupants therein; or (ii) if such weapon, instrument or substance is found in an automobile operated for hire by a duly licensed driver in the due, lawful and proper pursuit of his trade, then such presumption shall not apply to the driver.

(e) Exemptions. Crossbows, Common or Compound bows and Underwater Spearguns are exempted from the definition of ballistic knife as defined in paragraph (1) of subsection (a) of this Section.

(Chgd. by P.A. 87-930, §1, eff. 1/1/93.)

(Source: P.A. 86-465; 86-946; 86-1003; 86-1028; 86-1393; 87-524.) [Formerly Ill. Rev. Stat. 38 §24-1.]

5/24-1.1. Unlawful use or possession of weapons by felons or persons in the custody of the Department of Corrections facilities.

§24-1.1. Unlawful Use or Possession of Weapons by Felons or Persons in the Custody of the Department of Corrections Facilities. (a) It is unlawful for a person to knowingly possess on or about his person or on his land or in his own abode or fixed place of business any weapon prohibited under Section 24-1 of this Act or any firearm or any firearm ammunition if the person has been convicted of a felony under the laws of this State or any other jurisdiction. This Section shall not apply if the person has been granted relief by the Director of the Department of State Police pursuant to Section 10 of "An Act relating to the acquisition, possession, and transfer of firearms and firearm ammunition, to provide a penalty for the violation thereof and to make an appropriation in connection therewith", approved August 3, 1967, as amended [430 ILCS 65/10].

(b) It is unlawful for any person confined in a penal institution, which is a facility of the Illinois Department of Corrections, to possess any weapon prohibited under Section 24-1 of this Code or any firearm or firearm ammunition, regardless of the intent with which he possesses it.

(c) It shall be an affirmative defense to a violation of subsection (b) hereof, that such possession was specifically authorized by rule, regulation, or directive of the Illinois Department of Corrections or order issued pursuant thereto.

(d) Sentence. Violation of this Section by a person not confined in a penal institution shall be a Class 3 felony. Any person who violates this Section while confined in a penal institution, which is a facility of the Illinois Department of Corrections, is guilty of a Class 1 felony, if he possesses any weapon prohibited under Section 24-1 of this Code regardless of the intent with which he possesses it, and a Class X felony if he possesses any firearm, firearm ammunition or explosive.

(Source: P.A. 85-425; 85-736.) [Formerly Ill. Rev. Stat. 38 §24-1.1.]

5/24-1.2. Aggravated discharge of a firearm.

§24-1.2. Aggravated discharge of a firearm. (a) A person commits aggravated discharge of a firearm when he knowingly or intentionally:

(1) Discharges a firearm at or into a building he knows to be occupied and the firearm is discharged from a place or position outside that building;

(2) Discharges a firearm in the direction of another person or in the direction of a vehicle he knows to be occupied;

(3) Discharges a firearm in the direction of a person he knows to be a peace officer, a person summoned or directed by a peace officer, a correctional institution employee, or a fireman while the officer, employee or fireman is engaged in the execution of any of his official duties, or to prevent the officer, employee or fireman from performing his official duties, or in retaliation for the officer, employee or fireman performing his official duties;

(4) Discharges a firearm in the direction of a vehicle he knows to be occupied by a peace officer, a person summoned or directed by a peace officer, a correctional institution employee or a fireman while the officer, employee or fireman is engaged in the execution of any of his official duties, or to prevent the officer, employee or fireman from performing his official duties, or in retaliation for the officer, employee or fireman performing his official duties;

(5) Discharges a firearm in the direction of a person he knows to be a paramedic, ambulance driver, or other medical assistance or first aid personnel, employed by a municipality or other governmental unit, while the paramedic, ambulance driver, or other medical assistance or first aid personnel is engaged in the execution of any of his official duties, or to prevent the paramedic, ambulance driver, or other medical assistance or first aid personnel from performing his official duties, or in retaliation for the paramedic, ambulance driver, or other medical assistance or first aid personnel performing his official duties; or

(6) Discharges a firearm in the direction of a vehicle he knows to be occupied by a paramedic, ambulance driver, or other medical assistance or first aid personnel, employed by a municipality or other governmental unit, while the paramedic, ambulance driver, or other medical assistance or first aid personnel is engaged in the execution of any of his official duties, or to prevent the paramedic, ambulance driver, or other medical assistance or first aid personnel from performing his official duties, or in retaliation for the paramedic, ambulance driver, or other medical assistance or first aid personnel performing his official duties.

(b) A violation of subsection (a)(1) or subsection (a)(2) of this Section is a Class 1 felony. A violation of subsection (a)(3), (a)(4), (a)(5), or (a)(6) of this Section is a Class X felony.
(Chgd. by P.A. 87-921, §1, eff. 1/1/93.)
(Source: P.A. 86-1393.) [Formerly Ill. Rev. Stat. 38 §24-1.2.]

5/24-2. Exemptions.

§24-2. Exemptions. (a) Subsections 24-1(a)(3), 24-1(a)(4) and 24-1(a)(10) do not apply to or affect any of the following:

(1) Peace officers, and any person summoned by a peace officer to assist in making arrests or preserving the peace, while actually engaged in assisting such officer.

(2) Wardens, superintendents and keepers of prisons, penitentiaries, jails and other institutions for the detention of persons accused or convicted of an offense, while in the performance of their official duty, or while commuting between their homes and places of employment.

(3) Members of the Armed Services or Reserve Forces of the United States or the Illinois National Guard or the Reserve Officers Training Corps, while in the performance of their official duty.

(4) Special agents employed by a railroad or a public utility to perform police functions, and guards of armored car companies, while actually engaged in the performance of the duties of their employment or commuting between their homes and places of employment; and watchmen while actually engaged in the performance of the duties of their employment.

(5) Persons licensed as private security contractors, private detectives, or private alarm contractors, or employed by an agency certified by the Department of Professional Regulation, if their duties include the carrying of a weapon under the provisions of the Private Detective, Private Alarm, and Private Security Act of 1983 [225 ILCS 445/1 et seq.], while actually engaged in the performance of the duties of their employment or commuting between their homes and places of employment, provided that such commuting is accomplished within one hour from departure from home or place of employment, as the case may be. Persons exempted under this subdivision (a)(5) shall be required to have completed a course of study in firearms handling and training approved and supervised by the Department of Professional Regulation as prescribed by Section 28 of the Private Detective, Private Alarm, and Private Security Act of 1983 [225 ILCS 445/28], prior to becoming eligible for this exemption. The Department of Professional Regulation shall provide suitable documentation demonstrating the successful completion of the prescribed firearms training. Such documentation shall be carried at all times when such persons are in possession of a concealable weapon.

(6) Any person regularly employed in a commercial or industrial operation as a security guard for the protection of persons employed and private property related to such commercial or industrial operation, while actually engaged in the performance of his or her duty or traveling between sites or properties belonging to the employer, and who, as a security guard, is a member of a security force of at least 5 persons registered with the Department of Professional Regulation; provided that such security guard has successfully completed a course of study, approved by and supervised by the Department of Professional Regulation, consisting of not less than 40 hours of training that includes the theory of law enforcement, liability for acts, and the handling of weapons. A person shall be considered eligible for this exemption if he or she has completed the required 20 hours of training for a security officer and 20 hours of required firearm training, and has been issued a firearm authorization card by the Department of Professional Regulation. Conditions for the renewal of firearm authorization cards issued under the provisions of this Section shall be the same

as for those cards issued under the provisions of the Private Detective, Private Alarm and Private Security Act of 1983. Such firearm authorization card shall be carried by the security guard at all times when he or she is in possession of a concealable weapon.

(7) Agents and investigators of the Illinois Legislative Investigating Commission authorized by the Commission to carry the weapons specified in subsections 24-1(a)(3) and 24-1(a)(4), while on duty in the course of any investigation for the Commission.

(8) Persons employed by a financial institution for the protection of other employees and property related to such financial institution, while actually engaged in the performance of their duties, commuting between their homes and places of employment, or traveling between sites or properties owned or operated by such financial institution, provided that any person so employed has successfully completed a course of study, approved by and supervised by the Department of Professional Regulation, consisting of not less than 40 hours of training which includes theory of law enforcement, liability for acts, and the handling of weapons. A person shall be considered to be eligible for this exemption if he or she has completed the required 20 hours of training for a security officer and 20 hours of required firearm training, and has been issued a firearm authorization card by the Department of Professional Regulation. Conditions for renewal of firearm authorization cards issued under the provisions of this Section shall be the same as for those issued under the provisions of the Private Detective, Private Alarm and Private Security Act of 1983. Such firearm authorization card shall be carried by the person so trained at all times when such person is in possession of a concealable weapon. For purposes of this subsection, "financial institution" means a bank, savings and loan association, credit union or company providing armored car services.

(9) Any person employed by an armored car company to drive an armored car, while actually engaged in the performance of his duties.

(10) Persons who have been classified as peace officers pursuant to the Peace Officer Fire Investigation Act [20 ILCS 2910/0.01 et seq.].

(11) Investigators of the Office of the State's Attorneys Appellate Prosecutor authorized by the board of governors of the Office of the State's Attorneys Appellate Prosecutor to carry weapons pursuant to Section 7.06 of the State's Attorneys Appellate Prosecutor's Act [725 ILCS 210/7.06].

(12) Special investigators appointed by a State's Attorney under Section 3-9005 of the Counties Code [55 ILCS 5/3-9005].

(13) Manufacture, transportation, or sale of weapons to persons authorized under subdivisions (1) through (12) of this subsection to possess those weapons.

(b) Subsections 24-1(a)(4) and 24-1(a)(10) do not apply to or affect any of the following:

(1) Members of any club or organization organized for the purpose of practicing shooting at targets upon established target ranges, whether public or private, and patrons of such ranges, while such members or patrons are using their firearms on those target ranges.

(2) Duly authorized military or civil organizations while parading, with the special permission of the Governor.

(3) Licensed hunters, trappers or fishermen while engaged in hunting, trapping or fishing.

(4) Transportation of weapons that are broken down in a non-functioning state or are not immediately accessible.

(c) Subsection 24-1(a)(7) does not apply to or affect any of the following:

(1) Peace officers while in performance of their official duties.

(2) Wardens, superintendents and keepers of prisons, penitentiaries, jails and other institutions for the detention of persons accused or convicted of an offense.

(3) Members of the Armed Services or Reserve Forces of the United States or the Illinois National Guard, while in the performance of their official duty.

(4) Manufacture, transportation, or sale of machine guns to persons authorized under subdivisions (1) through (3) of this subsection to possess machine guns, if the machine guns are broken down in a non-functioning state or are not immediately accessible.

(5) Persons licensed under federal law to manufacture any weapon from which 8 or more shots or bullets can be discharged by a single function of the firing device, or ammunition for such weapons, and actually engaged in the business of manufacturing such weapons or ammunition, but only with respect to activities which are within the lawful scope of such business, such as the manufacture, transportation, or testing of such weapons or ammunition. This exemption does not authorize the general private possession of any weapon from which 8 or more shots or bullets can be discharged by a single function of the firing device, but only such possession and activities as are within the lawful scope of a licensed manufacturing business described in this paragraph.

During transportation, such weapons shall be broken down in a non-functioning state or not immediately accessible.

(6) The manufacture, transport, testing, delivery, transfer or sale, and all lawful commercial or experimental activities necessary thereto, of rifles, shotguns, and weapons made from rifles or shotguns, or ammunition for such rifles, shotguns or weapons, where engaged in by a person operating as a contractor or subcontractor pursuant to a contract or subcontract for the development and supply of such rifles, shotguns, weapons or ammunition to the United States government or any branch of the Armed Forces of the United States, when such activities are necessary and incident to fulfilling the terms of such contract.

The exemption granted under this subdivision (c)(6) shall also apply to any authorized agent of any such contractor or subcontractor who is operating within the scope of his employment, where such activities involving such weapon, weapons or ammunition are necessary and incident to fulfilling the terms of such contract.

During transportation, any such weapon shall be broken down in a non-functioning state, or not immediately accessible.

(d) Subsection 24-1(a)(1) does not apply to the purchase, possession or carrying of a black-jack or slung-shot by a peace officer.

(e) Subsection 24-1(a)(8) does not apply to any owner, manager or authorized employee of any place specified in that subsection nor to any law enforcement officer.

(f) Subsection 24-1(a)(4) and subsection 24-1(a)(10) do not apply to members of any club or organization organized for the purpose of practicing shooting at targets upon established target ranges, whether public or private, while using their firearms on those target ranges.

(g) Subsections 24-1(a)(11) and 24-3.1(a)(6) do not apply to:

(1) Members of the Armed Services or Reserve Forces of the United States or the Illinois National Guard, while in the performance of their official duty.

(2) Bonafide collectors of antique or surplus military ordinance.

(3) Laboratories having a department of forensic ballistics, or specializing in the development of ammunition or explosive ordinance.

(4) Commerce, preparation, assembly or possession of explosive bullets by manufacturers of ammunition licensed by the federal government, in connection with the supply of those organizations and persons exempted by subdivision (g)(1) of this Section, or like organizations and persons outside this State, or the

transportation of explosive bullets to any organization or person exempted in this Section by a common carrier or by a vehicle owned or leased by an exempted manufacturer.

(h) An information or indictment based upon a violation of any subsection of this Article need not negative any exemptions contained in this Article. The defendant shall have the burden of proving such an exemption.

(i) Nothing in this Article shall prohibit, apply to, or affect the transportation, carrying, or possession, of any pistol or revolver, stun gun, taser, or other firearm consigned to a common carrier operating under license of the State of Illinois or the federal government, where such transportation, carrying, or possession is incident to the lawful transportation in which such common carrier is engaged; and nothing in this Article shall prohibit, apply to, or affect the transportation, carrying, or possession of any pistol, revolver, stun gun, taser, or other firearm, not the subject of and regulated by subsection 24-1(a)(7) or subsection 24-2(c) of this Article, which is unloaded and enclosed in a case, firearm carrying box, shipping box, or other container, by the possessor of a valid Firearm Owners Identification Card.

(Source: P.A. 87-435; 87-845; 87-895.) [Formerly Ill. Rev. Stat. 38 §24-2.]

5/24-2.1. Unlawful use of metal piercing bullets.

§24-2.1. Unlawful Use of Metal Piercing Bullets. (a) A person commits the offense of unlawful use of metal piercing bullets when he knowingly manufactures, sells, purchases, possesses, or carries any metal piercing bullet.

For the purposes of this Section, "metal piercing bullet" means polytetrafluoroethylene-coated bullets; jacketed bullets with other than lead or lead alloy cores; and ammunition of which the bullet itself is wholly composed of a metal or metal alloy other than lead.

The definition contained herein shall not be construed to include shotgun shells.

(b) Exemptions. This Section does not apply to or affect any of the following:

(1) Peace officers.

(2) Wardens, superintendents and keepers of prisons, penitentiaries, jails and other institutions for the detention of persons accused or convicted of an offense.

(3) Members of the Armed Services or Reserve Forces of the United States or the Illinois National Guard while in the performance of their official duties.

(4) Federal officials required to carry firearms, while engaged in the performance of their official duties.

(5) United States Marshals, while engaged in the performance of their official duties.

(6) Persons licensed under federal law to manufacture, import, or sell firearms and firearm ammunition, and actually engaged in any such business, but only with respect to activities which are within the lawful scope of such business, such as the manufacture, transportation, or testing of such bullets or ammunition.

This exemption does not authorize the general private possession of any metal or armor piercing bullet, but only such possession and activities which are within the lawful scope of a licensed business described in this paragraph.

(7) Laboratories having a department of forensic ballistics or specializing in the development of ammunition or explosive ordnance.

(8) Manufacture, transportation or sale of metal or armor piercing bullets to persons specifically authorized under paragraphs (1) through (7) of this subsection to possess such bullets.

(c) An information or indictment based upon a violation of this Section need not negate any exemption herein contained. The defendant shall have the burden of proving such an exemption.

(d) Sentence. A person convicted of unlawful use of metal piercing bullets shall be guilty of a Class 3 felony.
(Source: P.A. 82-934.) [Formerly Ill. Rev. Stat. 38 §24-2.1.]

5/24-2.2. Manufacture, sale or transfer of bullets represented to be metal piercing bullets.

§24-2.2. Manufacture, sale or transfer of bullets represented to be metal piercing bullets. (a) Except as provided in subsection (b) of this Section, it is unlawful for any person to knowingly manufacture, sell, offer to sell, or transfer any bullet which is represented to be metal or armor piercing; to be polytetrafluoroethylene coated; to be jacketed and have a core other than lead or lead alloy; or to be wholly composed of a metal or metal alloy other than lead.

(b) Exemptions. This Section does not apply to or affect any person authorized under Section 24-2.1 to manufacture, sell, purchase, possess, or carry any metal piercing bullet with respect to activities which are within the lawful scope of the exemption therein granted.

(c) An information or indictment based upon a violation of this Section need not negate any exemption herein contained. The defendant shall have the burden of proving such an exemption and that the activities forming the basis of any criminal charge brought pursuant to this Section were within the lawful scope of such exemption.

(d) Sentence. Manufacture, sale, or transfer of bullets represented to be metal piercing bullets is a Class 4 felony.
(Source: P.A. 82-934.) [Formerly Ill. Rev. Stat. 38 §24-2.2.]

5/24-3. Unlawful sale of firearms.

§24-3. Unlawful Sale of Firearms. A person commits the offense of unlawful sale of firearms when he knowingly:

(a) Sells or gives any firearm of a size which may be concealed upon the person to any person under 18 years of age; or

(b) Sells or gives any firearm to a person under 21 years of age who has been convicted of a misdemeanor other than a traffic offense or adjudged delinquent; or

(c) Sells or gives any firearm to any narcotic addict; or

(d) Sells or gives any firearm to any person who has been convicted of a felony under the laws of this or any other jurisdiction; or

(e) Sells or gives any firearm to any person who has been a patient in a mental hospital within the past 5 years; or

(f) Sells or gives any firearms to any person who is mentally retarded; or

(g) Delivers any firearm of a size which may be concealed upon the person, incidental to a sale, without withholding delivery of such firearm for at least 72 hours after application for its purchase has been made, or delivers any rifle, shotgun or other long gun, incidental to a sale, without withholding delivery of such rifle, shotgun or other long gun for at least 24 hours after application for its purchase has been made. However, this paragraph shall not apply to: (1) the sale of a firearm to a law enforcement officer or a person who desires to purchase a firearm for use in promoting the public interest incident to his employment as a bank guard, armed truck guard, or other similar employment; or (2) a mail order sale of a firearm to a nonresident of Illinois under which the firearm is mailed to a point outside the boundaries of Illinois; or (3) the sale of a firearm to a nonresident of Illinois while at a firearm showing or display recognized by the Illinois Department of State Police; or (4) the sale of a firearm to a dealer licensed under the Federal Firearms Act of the United States [18 U.S.C. 921 et seq.]; or

(h) While holding any license under the Federal "Gun Control Act of 1968", as amended [18 U.S.C. 921 et seq.; 26 U.S.C. 5801 et seq.], as a dealer, importer, manufacturer or pawnbroker; manufactures, sells or delivers to any unlicensed person a handgun having a barrel, slide, frame or receiver which is a die casting of zinc alloy or any other nonhomogeneous metal which will melt or deform at a temperature of less than 800 degrees Fahrenheit. For purposes of this paragraph, (1) "firearm" is defined as in "An Act relating to the acquisition, possession and transfer of firearms and firearm ammunition, to provide a penalty for the violation thereof and to make an appropriation in connection therewith", approved August 3, 1967, as amended [430 ILCS 65/0.01 et seq.]; (2) "handgun" is defined as a firearm designed to be held and fired by the use of a single hand, and includes a combination of parts from which a firearm can be assembled; or

(i) Sells or gives a firearm of any size to any person under 18 years of age who does not possess a valid Firearm Owner's Identification Card.

(j) Paragraph (h) of this Section shall not include firearms sold within 6 months after enactment of this amendatory Act of 1973, nor shall any firearm legally owned or possessed by any citizen or purchased by any citizen within 6 months after the enactment of this amendatory Act of 1973 be subject to confiscation or seizure under the provisions of this amendatory Act of 1973. Nothing in this amendatory Act of 1973 shall be construed to prohibit the gift or trade of any firearm if that firearm was legally held or acquired within 6 months after the enactment of this amendatory Act of 1973.

(k) Sentence.

Any person convicted of unlawful sale of firearms in violation of paragraphs (b) through (h) commits a Class A misdemeanor.

Any person convicted of unlawful sale of firearms in violation of paragraphs (a) or (i) commits a Class 4 felony.

(Source: P.A. 84-1308.) [Formerly Ill. Rev. Stat. 38 §24-3.]

5/24-3.1. Unlawful possession of firearms and firearm ammunition.

§24-3.1. Unlawful possession of firearms and firearm ammunition. (a) A person commits the offense of unlawful possession of firearms or firearm ammunition when:

(1) He is under 18 years of age and has in his possession any firearm of a size which may be concealed upon the person; or

(2) He is under 21 years of age, has been convicted of a misdemeanor other than a traffic offense or adjudged delinquent and has any firearms or firearm ammunition in his possession; or

(3) He is a narcotic addict and has any firearms or firearm ammunition in his possession; or

(4) He has been a patient in a mental hospital within the past 5 years and has any firearms or firearm ammunition in his possession; or

(5) He is mentally retarded and has any firearms or firearm ammunition in his possession; or

(6) He has in his possession any explosive bullet.

For purposes of this paragraph "explosive bullet" means the projectile portion of an ammunition cartridge which contains or carries an explosive charge which will explode upon contact with the flesh of a human or an animal. "Cartridge" means a tubular metal case having a projectile affixed at the front thereof and a cap or primer at the rear end thereof, with the propellant contained in such tube between the projectile and the cap.

(b) Sentence.

Unlawful possession of firearms and firearm ammunition is a Class A misdemeanor.

(Source: P.A. 85-669.) [Formerly Ill. Rev. Stat. 38 §24-3.1.]

5/24-3.2. Unlawful discharge of metal piercing bullets.

§24-3.2. Unlawful Discharge of Metal Piercing Bullets. (a) A person commits the offense of unlawful discharge of metal piercing bullets when he knowingly or recklessly uses a metal piercing bullet in violation of this Section. For purposes of this Section, "metal piercing bullet" means polytetrafluoroethylene-coated bullets; jacketed bullets with other than lead or lead alloy cores; and ammunition of which the bullet itself is wholly composed of a metal or metal alloy other than lead. The definition contained herein shall not be construed to include shotgun shells.

(b) A person commits a Class X felony when he or she, knowing that a firearm, as defined in Section 1.1 of "An Act relating to the acquisition, possession and transfer of firearms and firearm ammunition, to provide a penalty for the violation thereof and to make an appropriation in connection therewith", approved August 3, 1967, as amended [430 ILCS 65/1.1], is loaded with a metal piercing bullet, intentionally or recklessly discharges such firearm and such bullet strikes any other person.

(c) Any person who possesses, concealed on or about his person, a metal piercing bullet and a firearm suitable for the discharge thereof is guilty of a Class 2 felony.

(d) This Section does not apply to or affect any of the following:

(1) Peace officers;

(2) Wardens, superintendents and keepers of prisons, penitentiaries, jails and other institutions for the detention of persons accused or convicted of an offense;

(3) Members of the Armed Services or Reserve Forces of the United States or the Illinois National Guard while in the performance of their official duties;

(4) Federal officials required to carry firearms, while engaged in the performance of their official duties;

(5) United States Marshals, while engaged in the performance of their official duties.

(Source: P.A. 82-1026.) [Formerly Ill. Rev. Stat. 38 §24-3.2.]

5/24-3.3. Unlawful sale or delivery of firearms on the premises of any school, regardless of the time of day or the time of year, or any conveyance owned, leased or contracted by a school to transport students to or from school or a school related activity, or residential property owned, operated and managed by a public housing agency.

§24-3.3. Unlawful Sale or Delivery of Firearms on the Premises of Any School, regardless of the time of day or the time of year, or any conveyance owned, leased or contracted by a school to transport students to or from school or a school related activity, or residential property owned, operated and managed by a public housing agency. Any person 18 years of age or older who sells, gives or delivers any firearm to any person under 18 years of age in any school, regardless of the time of day or the time of year or residential property owned, operated and managed by a public housing agency or on the real property comprising any school, regardless of the time of day or the time of year or residential property owned, operated and managed by a public housing agency commits a Class 3 felony. School is defined, for the purposes of this Section, as any public or private elementary or secondary school, community college, college or university. This does not apply to peace officers or to students carrying or possessing firearms for use in school training courses, parades, target shooting on school ranges, or otherwise with the consent of school authorities and which firearms are transported unloaded and enclosed in a suitable case, box or transportation package.

(Source: P.A. 86-946; 87-524.) [Formerly Ill. Rev. Stat. 38 §24-3.3.]

5/24-3.4. Unlawful sale of firearms by liquor licensee.

§24-3.4. Unlawful sale of firearms by liquor licensee. (a) It shall be unlawful for any person who holds a license to sell at retail any alcoholic liquor issued by the Illinois Liquor Control Commission or local liquor control commissioner under the Liquor Control Act of 1934 [235 ILCS 5/1-1 et seq.] or an agent or employee of the licensee to sell or deliver to any other person a firearm in or on the real property of the establishment where the licensee is licensed to sell alcoholic liquors unless the sale or delivery of the firearm is otherwise lawful under this Article and under the Firearm Owners Identification Card Act [430 ILCS 65/0.01 et seq.].

(b) Sentence. A violation of subsection (a) of this Section is a Class 4 felony.
(Source: P.A. 87-591.) [Formerly Ill. Rev. Stat. 38 §24-3.4.]

5/24-4. Register of sales by dealer.

§24-4. Register of sales by dealer. (a) Any seller of firearms of a size which may be concealed upon the person, other than a manufacturer selling to a bona fide wholesaler or retailer or a wholesaler selling to a bona fide retailer, shall keep a register of all firearms sold or given away.

(b) Such register shall contain the date of the sale or gift, the name, address, age and occupation of the person to whom the weapon is sold or given, the price of the weapon, the kind, description and number of the weapon, and the purpose for which it is purchased and obtained.

(c) Such seller on demand of a peace officer shall produce for inspection the register and allow such peace officer to inspect such register and all stock on hand.

(d) Sentence.

Violation of this Section is a Class B misdemeanor.
(Source: P.A. 77-2638.) [Formerly Ill. Rev. Stat. 38 §24-4.]

5/24-5. Defacing identification marks of firearms.

§24-5. Defacing identification marks of firearms. (a) Any person who shall change, alter, remove or obliterate the name of the maker, model, manufacturer's number or other mark of identification of any firearm commits a Class A misdemeanor.

(b) Possession of any firearm upon which any such mark shall have been changed, altered, removed or obliterated shall be prima facie evidence that the possessor has changed, altered, removed or obliterated the same.
(Source: P.A. 77-2638.) [Formerly Ill. Rev. Stat. 38 §24-5.]

5/24-6. Confiscation and disposition of weapons.

§24-6. Confiscation and disposition of weapons. (a) Upon conviction of an offense in which a weapon was used or possessed by the offender, any weapon seized shall be confiscated by the trial court.

(b) Any stolen weapon so confiscated, when no longer needed for evidentiary purposes, shall be returned to the person entitled to possession if known. After the disposition of a criminal case and when a confiscated weapon is no longer needed for evidentiary purposes, and when in due course no legitimate claim has been made for the weapon, the court may transfer the weapon to the sheriff of the county who may permit the trade or sale of the weapon for other weapons or other equipment used by a police agency for law enforcement purposes or may proceed to destroy it, or may in its discretion order the weapon preserved as property of the governmental body whose police agency seized the weapon, or may in its discretion order the weapon to be transferred to the Department of State Police for use by the crime laboratory system, for training purposes, or for any other application as deemed appropriate by the Department. If, after the disposition of a criminal case, a need still exists for the use of the confiscated weapon for evidentiary purposes, the court may transfer the weapon to the custody of the State Department of Corrections for preservation.

The provisions of this Section shall not apply to violations of the Fish and Aquatic Life Code [515 ILCS 5/1-1 et seq.] or the Wildlife Code [520 ILCS 5/1.1]. Confiscation of weapons for Fish and Aquatic Life Code and Wildlife Code violations shall be only as provided in those Codes.

(c) Any mental hospital that admits a person as an inpatient pursuant to any of the provisions of the Mental Health and Developmental Disabilities Code [405 ILCS 5/1-100 et seq.] shall confiscate any firearms in the possession of that person at the time of admission, or at any time the firearms are discovered in the person's possession during the course of hospitalization. The hospital shall, as soon as possible following confiscation, transfer custody of the firearms to the appropriate law enforcement agency. The hospital shall give written notice to the person from whom the firearm was confiscated of the identity and address of the law enforcement agency to which it has given the firearm.

The law enforcement agency shall maintain possession of any firearm it obtains pursuant to this subsection for a minimum of 90 days. Thereafter, the firearm may be disposed of pursuant to the provisions of subsection (b) of this Section.

(Source: P.A. 86-1403; 87-464; 87-895.) [Formerly Ill. Rev. Stat. 38 §24-6.]

ARTICLE 25. MOB ACTION AND RELATED OFFENSES

5/25-1. Mob action.

§25-1. Mob action. (a) Mob action consists of any of the following:

(1) The use of force or violence disturbing the public peace by 2 or more persons acting together and without authority of law; or

(2) The assembly of 2 or more persons to do an unlawful act; or

(3) The assembly of 2 or more persons, without authority of law, for the purpose of doing violence to the person or property of any one supposed to have been guilty of a violation of the law, or for the purpose of exercising correctional powers or regulative powers over any person by violence.

(b) Mob action as defined in paragraph (1) of subsection (a) is a Class 4 felony.

(c) Mob action as defined in paragraphs (2) and (3) of subsection (a) is a Class C misdemeanor.

(d) Any participant in a mob action which shall by violence inflict injury to the person or property of another commits a Class 4 felony.

(e) Any participant in a mob action who does not withdraw on being commanded to do so by any peace officer commits a Class A misdemeanor.

(Source: P.A. 86-863.) [Formerly Ill. Rev. Stat. 38 §25-1.]

5/25-2. Removal of chief of police or sheriff.

§25-2. Removal of chief of police or sheriff. (a) If a prisoner is taken from the custody of any policeman or chief of police of any city, town or village and lynched, it shall be prima facie evidence of wrong-doing on the part of such chief of police and he shall be suspended. The mayor or chief executive of such city, town or village shall appoint an acting chief of police until he has ascertained whether the suspended chief of police has done all in his power to protect the life of the prisoner. If, upon hearing all evidence and argument, the mayor or chief executive finds that the chief of police has done his utmost to protect the prisoner, he may reinstate the chief of police; but, if he finds the chief of police guilty of not properly protecting the prisoner, a new chief of police shall be appointed. Any chief of police replaced shall not be eligible to serve again in such office.

(b) If a prisoner is taken from the custody of any sheriff or his deputy and lynched, it shall be prima facie evidence of wrong-doing on the part of such sheriff and he shall be suspended. The governor shall appoint an acting sheriff until he has ascertained whether the suspended sheriff has done all in his power to protect the life of the prisoner. If, upon hearing all evidence and argument, the governor finds that the sheriff has done his utmost to protect the prisoner, he shall reinstate the sheriff; but, if he finds the sheriff guilty of not properly protecting the prisoner, a new sheriff shall be duly elected or appointed, pursuant to the existing law provided for the filling of vacancies in such office. Any sheriff replaced shall not be eligible to serve again in such office.

(Source: Laws 1961, p. 1983.) [Formerly Ill. Rev. Stat. 38 §25-2.]

ARTICLE 26. DISORDERLY CONDUCT

5/26-1. Elements of the offense.

§26-1. Elements of the Offense. (a) A person commits disorderly conduct when he knowingly:

(1) Does any act in such unreasonable manner as to alarm or disturb another and to provoke a breach of the peace; or

(2) Transmits in any manner to the fire department of any city, town, village or fire protection district a false alarm of fire, knowing at the time of such transmission that there is no reasonable ground for believing that such fire exists; or

(3) Transmits in any manner to another a false alarm to the effect that a bomb or other explosive of any nature is concealed in such place that its explosion would endanger human life, knowing at the time of such transmission that there is no reasonable ground for believing that such bomb or explosive is concealed in such place; or

(4) Transmits in any manner to any peace officer, public officer or public employee a report to the effect that an offense has been committed, knowing at the time of such transmission that there is no reasonable ground for believing that such an offense has been committed; or

(5) Enters upon the property of another and for a lewd or unlawful purpose deliberately looks into a dwelling on the property through any window or other opening in it; or

(6) While acting as a collection agency as defined in the "Collection Agency Act" [225 ILCS 425/1 et seq.] or as an employee of such collection agency, and while attempting to collect an alleged debt, makes a telephone call to the alleged debtor which is designed to harass, annoy or intimidate the alleged debtor; or

(7) Transmits a false report to the Department of Children and Family Services under Section 4 of the "Abused and Neglected Child Reporting Act" [325 ILCS 5/4]; or

(8) Transmits a false report to the Department of Public Health under the Nursing Home Care Act [210 ILCS 45/1-101 et seq.]; or

(9) Transmits in any manner to the police department or fire department of any municipality or fire protection district, or any privately owned and operated ambulance service, a false request for an ambulance, emergency medical technician-ambulance or emergency medical technician-paramedic knowing at

the time there is no reasonable ground for believing that such assistance is required; or

(10) Transmits a false report under Article II of "An Act in relation to victims of violence and abuse", approved September 16, 1984, as amended [320 ILCS 15/0.01 et seq.].

(b) Sentence.

A violation of subsection (a)(1) of this Section is a Class C misdemeanor. A violation of subsection (a)(7) or (a)(9) of this Section is a Class A misdemeanor. A violation of subsection (a)(4), (a)(5), (a)(8) or (a)(10) of this Section is a Class B misdemeanor. A violation of subsection (a)(2) or (a)(3) of this Section is a Class 4 felony.

A violation of subsection (a)(6) of this Section is a Business Offense and shall be punished by a fine not to exceed $3,000. A second or subsequent violation of (a)(7) of this Section is a Class 4 felony.

(Source: P.A. 86-407; 86-712; 86-820; 86-835; 86-1028.) [Formerly Ill. Rev. Stat. 38 §26-1.]

5/26-2. Interference with emergency communication.

§26-2. Interference with Emergency Communication. (a) A person commits the offense of interference with emergency communication when he knowingly, intentionally and without lawful justification interrupts, disrupts, impedes, or otherwise interferes with the transmission of a communication over a citizens band radio channel, the purpose of which communication is to inform or inquire about an emergency.

(b) For the purpose of this Section, "emergency" means a condition or circumstance in which an individual is or is reasonably believed by the person transmitting the communication to be in imminent danger of serious bodily injury or in which property is or is reasonably believed by the person transmitting the communication to be in imminent danger of damage or destruction.

(c) Sentence. (1) Interference with emergency communication is a Class B misdemeanor, except as otherwise provided in paragraph (2).

(2) Interference with emergency communication, where serious bodily injury or property loss in excess of $1,000 results, is a Class A misdemeanor.

(Source: P.A. 82-418.) [Formerly Ill. Rev. Stat. 38 §26-2.]

5/26-3. Use of a facsimile machine in unsolicited advertising or fund-raising.

§26-3. Use of a facsimile machine in unsolicited advertising or fund-raising. (a) Definitions:

(1) "Facsimile machine" means a device which is capable of sending or receiving facsimiles of documents through connection with a telecommunications network.

(2) "Person" means an individual, public or private corporation, unit of government, partnership or unincorporated association.

(b) No person shall knowingly use a facsimile machine to send or cause to be sent to another person a facsimile of a document containing unsolicited advertising or fund-raising material, except to a person which the sender knows or under all of the circumstances reasonably believes has given the sender permission, either on a case by case or continuing basis, for the sending of such material.

(c) Sentence. Any person who violates subsection (b) is guilty of a petty offense and shall be fined an amount not to exceed $500.

(Source: P.A. 86-555.) [Formerly Ill. Rev. Stat. 38 §26-3.]

5/26-4. Unauthorized videotaping.

§26-4. Unauthorized videotaping. (a) It is unlawful for any person to videotape, photograph, or film another person without that person's consent in a restroom, tanning bed, or tanning salon.

(b) Exemptions. The following activities shall be exempt from the provisions of this Section:

(1) Videotaping, photographing, and filming by law enforcement officers pursuant to a criminal investigation, which is otherwise lawful;

(2) Videotaping, photographing, and filming by correctional officials for security reasons or for investigation of alleged misconduct involving a person committed to the Department of Corrections.

(c) The provisions of this Section do not apply to any sound recording of an oral conversation made as the result of the videotaping or filming, and to which Article 14 of this Code [720 ILCS 5/14-1 et seq.] applies.

(d) Sentence. A violation of subsection (a) is a Class A misdemeanor.

(Added by P.A. 87-970, §1, eff. 7/1/93.)

[Formerly Ill. Rev. Stat. 38 §26-4.]

ARTICLE 28. GAMBLING AND RELATED OFFENSES

5/28-1. Gambling.

§28-1. Gambling. (a) A person commits gambling when he:

(1) Plays a game of chance or skill for money or other thing of value, unless excepted in subsection (b) of this Section; or

(2) Makes a wager upon the result of any game, contest, or any political nomination, appointment or election; or

(3) Operates, keeps, owns, uses, purchases, exhibits, rents, sells, bargains for the sale or lease of, manufactures or distributes any gambling device; or

(4) Contracts to have or give himself or another the option to buy or sell, or contracts to buy or sell, at a future time, any grain or other commodity whatsoever, or any stock or security of any company, where it is at the time of making such contract intended by both parties thereto that the contract to buy or sell, or the option, whenever exercised, or the contract resulting therefrom, shall be settled, not by the receipt or delivery of such property, but by the payment only of differences in prices thereof; however, the issuance, purchase, sale, exercise, endorsement or guarantee, by or through a person registered with the Secretary of State pursuant to Section 8 of the Illinois Securities Law of 1953 [815 ILCS 5/8], or by or through a person exempt from such registration under said Section 8, of a put, call, or other option to buy or sell securities which have been registered with the Secretary of State or which are exempt from such registration under Section 3 of the Illinois Securities Law of 1953 [815 ILCS 5/3] is not gambling within the meaning of this paragraph (4); or

(5) Knowingly owns or possesses any book, instrument or apparatus by means of which bets or wagers have been, or are, recorded or registered, or knowingly possesses any money which he has received in the course of a bet or wager; or

(6) Sells pools upon the result of any game or contest of skill or chance, political nomination, appointment or election; or

(7) Sets up or promotes any lottery or sells, offers to sell or transfers any ticket or share for any lottery; or

(8) Sets up or promotes any policy game or sells, offers to sell or knowingly possesses or transfers any policy ticket, slip, record, document or other similar device; or

(9) Knowingly drafts, prints or publishes any lottery ticket or share, or any policy ticket, slip, record, document or similar device, except for such activity related to lotteries, bingo games and raffles authorized by and conducted in accordance with the laws of Illinois or any other state or foreign government; or

(10) Knowingly advertises any lottery or policy game, except for such activity related to lotteries, bingo games and raffles authorized by and conducted in accordance with the laws of Illinois or any other state; or

(11) Knowingly transmits information as to wagers, betting odds, or changes in betting odds by telephone, telegraph, radio, semaphore or similar means; or knowingly installs or maintains equipment for the transmission or receipt of such information; except that nothing in this subdivision (11) prohibits transmission or receipt of such information for use in news reporting of sporting events or contests.

(b) Participants in any of the following activities shall not be convicted of gambling therefor:

(1) Agreements to compensate for loss caused by the happening of chance including without limitation contracts of indemnity or guaranty and life or health or accident insurance;

(2) Offers of prizes, award or compensation to the actual contestants in any bona fide contest for the determination of skill, speed, strength or endurance or to the owners of animals or vehicles entered in such contest;

(3) Pari-mutuel betting as authorized by the law of this State;

(4) Manufacture of gambling devices, including the acquisition of essential parts therefor and the assembly thereof, for transportation in interstate or foreign commerce to any place outside this State when such transportation is not prohibited by any applicable Federal law;

(5) The game commonly known as "bingo", when conducted in accordance with the Bingo License and Tax Act [230 ILCS 25/1 et seq.];

(6) Lotteries when conducted by the State of Illinois in accordance with the Illinois Lottery Law [20 ILCS 1605/1 et seq.];

(7) Possession of an antique slot machine that is neither used nor intended to be used in the operation or promotion of any unlawful gambling activity or enterprise. For the purpose of this subparagraph (b)(7), an antique slot machine is one manufactured 25 years ago or earlier;

(8) Raffles when conducted in accordance with the Raffles Act [230 ILCS 15/0.01 et seq.];

(9) Charitable games when conducted in accordance with the Charitable Games Act [230 ILCS 30/1 et seq.];

(10) Pull tabs and jar games when conducted under the Illinois Pull Tabs and Jar Games Act [230 ILCS 20/1 et seq.]; or

(11) Gambling games conducted on riverboats when authorized by the Riverboat Gambling Act [230 ILCS 10/1 et seq.].

(c) Sentence.

Gambling under subsection (a)(1) or (a)(2) of this Section is a Class A misdemeanor. Gambling under any of subsections (a)(3) through (a)(11) of this Section is a Class A misdemeanor. A second or subsequent conviction under any of subsections (a)(3) through (a)(11), is a Class 4 felony.

(d) Circumstantial evidence.

In prosecutions under subsection (a)(1) through (a)(11) of this Section circumstantial evidence shall have the same validity and weight as in any criminal prosecution.

(Source: P.A. 86-1029; 87-435.) [Formerly Ill. Rev. Stat. 38 §28-1.]

5/28-1.1. Syndicated gambling.

§28-1.1. Syndicated gambling. (a) Declaration of Purpose. Recognizing the close relationship between professional gambling and other organized crime, it is declared to be the policy of the legislature to restrain persons from engaging in the business of gambling for profit in this State. This Section shall be liberally construed and administered with a view to carrying out this policy.

(b) A person commits syndicated gambling when he operates a "policy game" or engages in the business of bookmaking.

(c) A person "operates a policy game" when he knowingly uses any premises or property for the purpose of receiving or knowingly does receive from what is commonly called "policy":

(1) money from a person other than the better* or player whose bets or plays are represented by such money; or

(2) written "policy game" records, made or used over any period of time, from a person other than the better* or player whose bets or plays are represented by such written record.

So in original. Probably should be "bettor".

(d) A person engages in bookmaking when he receives or accepts more than five bets or wagers upon the result of any trials or contests of skill, speed or power of endurance or upon any lot, chance, casualty, unknown or contingent event whatsoever, which bets or wagers shall be of such size that the total of the amounts of money paid or promised to be paid to such bookmaker on account thereof shall exceed $2,000. Bookmaking is the receiving or accepting of such bets or wagers regardless of the form or manner in which the bookmaker records them.

(e) Participants in any of the following activities shall not be convicted of syndicated gambling:

(1) Agreements to compensate for loss caused by the happening of chance including without limitation contracts of indemnity or guaranty and life or health or accident insurance; and

(2) Offers of prizes, award or compensation to the actual contestants in any bona fide contest for the determination of skill, speed, strength or endurance or to the owners of animals or vehicles entered in such contest; and

(3) Pari-mutuel betting as authorized by law of this State; and

(4) Manufacture of gambling devices, including the acquisition of essential parts therefor and the assembly thereof, for transportation in interstate or foreign commerce to any place outside this State when such transportation is not prohibited by any applicable Federal law; and

(5) Raffles when conducted in accordance with the Raffles Act [230 ILCS 15/0.01 et seq.]; and

(6) Gambling games conducted on riverboats when authorized by the Riverboat Gambling Act [230 ILCS 10/1 et seq.].

(f) Sentence. Syndicated gambling is a Class 3 felony.

(Source: P.A. 86-1029; 87-435.) [Formerly Ill. Rev. Stat. 38 §28-1.1.]

5/28-2. Definitions.

§28-2. Definitions. (a) A "gambling device" is any clock, tape machine, slot machine or other machines or device for the reception of money or other thing of value on chance or skill or upon the action of which money or other thing of value is staked, hazarded, bet, won or lost; or any mechanism, furniture, fixture, equipment or other device designed primarily for use in a gambling place. A "gambling device" does not include:

(1) A coin-in-the-slot operated mechanical device played for amusement which rewards the player with the right to replay such mechanical device, which device is so constructed or devised as to make such result of the operation thereof depend in part upon the skill of the player and which returns to the player thereof no money, property or right to receive money or property.

(2) Vending machines by which full and adequate return is made for the money invested and in which there is no element of chance or hazard.

(3) A crane game. For the purposes of this paragraph (3), a "crane game" is an amusement device involving skill, if it rewards the player exclusively with merchandise contained within the amusement device proper and limited to toys, novelties and prizes other than currency, each having a wholesale value which is not more than 7 times the cost charged to play the amusement device once or $5, whichever is less.

(4) A redemption machine. For the purposes of this paragraph (4), a "redemption machine" is a single-player or multi-player amusement device involving a game, the object of which is throwing, rolling, bowling, shooting, placing, or propelling a ball or other object into, upon, or against a hole or other target, provided that all of the following conditions are met:

(A) The outcome of the game is predominantly determined by the skill of the player.

(B) The award of the prize is based solely upon the player's achieving the object of the game or otherwise upon the player's score.

(C) Only merchandise prizes are awarded.

(D) The average wholesale value of prizes awarded in lieu of tickets or tokens for single play of the device does not exceed the lesser of $5 or 7 times the cost charged for a single play of the device.

(E) The redemption value of tickets, tokens, and other representations of value, which may be accumulated by players to redeem prizes of greater value, does not exceed the amount charged for a single play of the device.

(b) A "lottery" is any scheme or procedure whereby one or more prizes are distributed by chance among persons who have paid or promised consideration for a chance to win such prizes, whether such scheme or procedure is called a lottery, raffle, gift, sale or some other name.

(c) A "policy game" is any scheme or procedure whereby a person promises or guarantees by any instrument, bill, certificate, writing, token or other device that any particular number, character, ticket or certificate shall in the event of any contingency in the nature of a lottery entitle the purchaser or holder to receive money, property or evidence of debt.

(Source: P.A. 87-855.) [Formerly Ill. Rev. Stat. 38 §28-2.]

5/28-3. Keeping a gambling place.

§28-3. Keeping a Gambling Place. A "gambling place" is any real estate, vehicle, boat or any other property whatsoever used for the purposes of gambling other than gambling conducted in the manner authorized by the Riverboat Gambling Act [230 ILCS 10/1 et seq.]. Any person who knowingly permits any premises or property owned or occupied by him or under his control to be used as a gambling place commits a Class A misdemeanor. Each subsequent offense is a Class 4 felony. When any premises is determined by the circuit court to be a gambling place:

(a) Such premises is a public nuisance and may be proceeded against as such, and

(b) All licenses, permits or certificates issued by the State of Illinois or any subdivision or public agency thereof authorizing the serving of food or liquor on such premises shall be void; and no license, permit or certificate so cancelled shall be reissued for such premises for a period of 60 days thereafter; nor shall any person convicted of keeping a gambling place be reissued such license for one year from his conviction and, after a second conviction of keeping a gambling place, any such person shall not be reissued such license, and

(c) Such premises of any person who knowingly permits thereon a violation of any Section of this Article shall be held liable for, and may be sold to pay any unsatisfied judgment that may be recovered and any unsatisfied fine that may be levied under any Section of this Article.

(Source: P.A. 86-1029.) [Formerly Ill. Rev. Stat. 38 §28-3.]

5/28-4. Registration of federal gambling stamps.

§28-4. Registration of Federal Gambling Stamps. (a) Every person who has purchased a Federal Wagering Occupational Tax Stamp, as required by the United States under the applicable provisions of the Internal Revenue Code [repealed], or a Federal Gaming Device Tax Stamp, as required by the United States under the applicable provisions of the Internal Revenue Code, shall register forthwith such stamp or stamps with the county clerk's office in which he resides and the county clerk's office of each and every county in which he conducts any business. A violation of this Section is a Class B misdemeanor. A subsequent violation is a Class A misdemeanor.

(b) To register a stamp as required by this Section, each individual stamp purchaser and each member of a firm or association which is a stamp purchaser and, if such purchaser is corporate, the registered agent of the purchasing corporation shall deliver the stamp to the county clerk for inspection and shall under oath or affirmation complete and sign a registration form which shall state the full name and residence and business address of each purchaser and of each member of a purchasing firm or association and of each person employed or engaged in gambling on behalf of such purchaser, shall state the registered agent and registered address of a corporate purchaser, shall state each place where gambling is to be performed by or on behalf of the purchaser, and shall state the duration of validity of the stamp and the federal registration number and tax return number thereof. Any false statement in the registration form is material and is evidence of perjury.

(c) Within 3 days after such registration the county clerk shall by registered mail forward notice of such registration and a duplicate copy of each registration form to the Attorney General of this State, to the Chairman of the Illinois Liquor Control Commission, to the State's Attorney and Sheriff of each county wherein the stamp is registered, and to the principal official of the department of police of each city, village and incorporated town in this State wherein the stamp is registered or wherein the registrant maintains a business address.

(Source: P.A. 77-2638.) [Formerly Ill. Rev. Stat. 38 §28-4.]

5/28-5. Seizure of gambling devices and gambling funds.

§28-5. Seizure of gambling devices and gambling funds. (a) Every device designed for gambling which is incapable of lawful use or every device used unlawfully for gambling shall be considered a "gambling device", and shall be subject to seizure, confiscation and destruction by the Department of State Police or by any municipal, or other local authority, within whose jurisdiction the same may be found. As used in this Section, a "gambling device" includes any slot machine, and includes any machine or device constructed for the reception of money or other thing of value and so constructed as to return, or to cause someone to return, on chance to the player thereof money, property or a right to receive money or property. With the exception of any device designed for gambling which is incapable of lawful use, no gambling device shall be forfeited or destroyed unless an individual with a property interest in said device knows of the unlawful use of the device.

(b) Every gambling device shall be seized and forfeited to the county wherein such seizure occurs. Any money or other thing of value integrally related to acts of gambling shall be seized and forfeited to the county wherein such seizure occurs.

(c) If, within 60 days after any seizure pursuant to subparagraph (b) of this Section, a person having any property interest in the seized property is charged with an offense, the court which renders judgment upon such charge shall, within 30 days after such judgment, conduct a forfeiture hearing to determine whether such property was a gambling device at the time of seizure. Such hearing shall be commenced by a written petition by the State, including material allegations of fact, the name and address of every person determined by the State to have any property interest in the seized property, a representation that written notice of the date, time and place of such hearing has been mailed to every such person by certified mail at least 10 days before such date, and a request for forfeiture. Every such person may appear as a party and present evidence at such hearing. The quantum of proof required shall be a preponderance of the evidence, and the burden of proof shall be on the State. If the court determines that the seized property was a gambling device at the time of seizure, an order of forfeiture and disposition of the seized property shall be entered: a gambling device shall be received by the State's Attorney, who shall effect its destruction, except that valuable parts thereof may be liquidated and the resultant money shall be deposited in the general fund of the county wherein such seizure occurred; money and other things of value shall be received by the State's Attorney and, upon liquidation, shall be deposited in the general fund of the county wherein such seizure occurred. However, in the event that a defendant raises the defense that the seized slot machine is an antique slot machine described in subparagraph (b)(7) of Section 28-1 of this Code and therefore he is exempt from the charge of a gambling activity participant, the seized antique slot machine shall not be destroyed or otherwise altered until a final determination is made by the Court as to whether it is such an antique slot machine. Upon a final determination by the Court of this question in favor of the defendant, such slot machine shall be immediately returned to the defendant. Such order of forfeiture and disposition shall, for the purposes of appeal, be a final order and judgment in a civil proceeding.

(d) If a seizure pursuant to subparagraph (b) of this Section is not followed by a charge pursuant to subparagraph (c) of this Section, or if the prosecution of such charge is permanently terminated or indefinitely discontinued without any judgment of conviction or acquittal (1) the State's Attorney shall commence an in rem proceeding for the forfeiture and destruction of a gambling device, or for the forfeiture and deposit in the general fund of the county of any seized money or other things of value, or both, in the circuit court and (2) any person having any property interest in such seized gambling device, money or other thing of value may commence separate civil proceedings in the manner provided by law.

(e) Any gambling device displayed for sale to a riverboat gambling operation or used to train occupational licensees of a riverboat gambling operation as authorized under the Riverboat Gambling Act [230 ILCS 10/1 et seq.] is exempt from seizure under this Section.

(f) Any gambling equipment, devices and supplies provided by a licensed supplier in accordance with the Riverboat Gambling Act which are removed from the riverboat for repair are exempt from seizure under this Section.
(Source: P.A. 87-826.) [Formerly Ill. Rev. Stat. 38 §28-5.]

5/28-7. Gambling contracts void.

§28-7. Gambling contracts void. (a) All promises, notes, bills, bonds, covenants, contracts, agreements, judgments, mortgages, or other securities or conveyances made, given, granted, drawn, or entered into, or executed by any person whatsoever, where the whole or any part of the consideration thereof is for any money or thing of value, won or obtained in violation of any Section of this Article are null and void.

(b) Any obligation void under this Section may be set aside and vacated by any court of competent jurisdiction, upon a complaint filed for that purpose, by the person so granting, giving, entering into, or executing the same, or by his executors or administrators, or by any creditor, heir, legatee, purchaser or other person interested therein; or if a judgment, the same may be set aside on motion of any person stated above, on due notice thereof given.

(c) No assignment of any obligation void under this Section may in any manner affect the defense of the person giving, granting, drawing, entering into or executing such obligation, or the remedies of any person interested therein.

(d) This Section shall not prevent a licensed owner of a riverboat gambling operation from instituting a cause of action to collect any amount due and owing under an extension of credit to a riverboat gambling patron as authorized under the Riverboat Gambling Act [230 ILCS 10/1 et seq.].

(Source: P.A. 87-826.) [Formerly Ill. Rev. Stat. 38 §28-7.]

5/28-8. Gambling losses recoverable.

§28-8. Gambling losses recoverable. (a) Any person who by gambling shall lose to any other person, any sum of money or thing of value, amounting to the sum of $50 or more and shall pay or deliver the same or any part thereof, may sue for and recover the money or other thing of value, so lost and paid or delivered, in a civil action against the winner thereof, with costs, in the circuit court. No person who accepts from another person for transmission, and transmits, either in his own name or in the name of such other person, any order for any transaction to be made upon, or who executes any order given to him by another person, or who executes any transaction for his own account on, any regular board of trade or commercial, commodity or stock exchange, shall, under any circumstances, be deemed a "winner" of any moneys lost by such other person in or through any such transactions.

(b) If within 6 months, such person who under the terms of Subsection 28-8(a) is entitled to initiate action to recover his losses does not in fact pursue his remedy, any person may initiate a civil action against the winner. The court or the jury, as the case may be, shall determine the amount of the loss. After such determination, the court shall enter a judgment of triple the amount so determined.

(Source: P.A. 79-1360.) [Formerly Ill. Rev. Stat. 38 §28-8.]

5/28-9. Prosecution commenced by information.

§28-9. At the option of the prosecuting attorney any prosecution under this Article may be commenced by an information as defined in Section 102-12 of the Code of Criminal Procedure of 1963.

(Source: P.A. 76-1131.) [Formerly Ill. Rev. Stat. 38 §28-9.]

ARTICLE 29. BRIBERY IN CONTESTS

Sec.

5/29-1. Offering a bribe.

§29-1. Offering a bribe. (a) Any person who, with intent to influence any person participating in, officiating or connected with any professional or amateur athletic contest, sporting event or exhibition, gives, offers or promises any money, bribe or other thing of value or advantage to induce such participant, official or other person not to use his best efforts in connection with such contest, event or exhibition commits a Class 4 felony.

(b) Any person who, with the intent to influence the decision of any individual, offers or promises any money, bribe or other thing of value or advantage to induce such individual to attend, refrain from attending or continue to attend a particular public or private institution of secondary education or higher education for the purpose of participating or not participating in interscholastic athletic competition for such institution commits a Class A misdemeanor. This Section does not apply to the: (1) offering or awarding to an individual any type of scholarship, grant or other bona fide financial aid or employment; (2) offering of any type of financial assistance by such individual's family; or (3) offering of any item of de minimis value by such institution's authorities if such item is of the nature of an item that is commonly provided to any or all students or prospective students.

(c) Any person who gives any money, goods or other thing of value to an individual enrolled in an institution of higher education who participates in interscholastic competition and represents or attempts to represent such individual in future negotiations for employment with any professional sports team commits a Class A misdemeanor.

(Source: P.A. 85-665.) [Formerly Ill. Rev. Stat. 38 §29-1.]

5/29-2. Accepting a bribe.

§29-2. Accepting a bribe. Any person participating in, officiating or connected with any professional or amateur athletic contest, sporting event or exhibition who accepts or agrees to accept any money, bribe or other thing of value or advantage with the intent, understanding or agreement that he will not use his best efforts in connection with such contest, event or exhibition commits a Class 4 felony.

(Source: P.A. 77-2638.) [Formerly Ill. Rev. Stat. 38 §29-2.]

5/29-3. Failure to report offer of bribe.

§29-3. Failure to report offer of bribe. Any person participating, officiating or connected with any professional or amateur athletic contest, sporting event or exhibition who fails to report forthwith to his employer, the promoter of such contest, event or exhibition, a peace officer, or the local State's Attorney any offer or promise made to him in violation of Section 29-1 commits a Class A misdemeanor.

(Source: P.A. 77-2638.) [Formerly Ill. Rev. Stat. 38 §29-3.]

ARTICLE 29A. COMMERCIAL BRIBERY

Sec.

5/29A-1. Commercial bribery; offering a bribe.

§29A-1. A person commits commercial bribery when he confers, or offers or agrees to confer, any benefit upon any employee, agent or fiduciary without the consent of the latter's employer or principal, with intent to influence his conduct in relation to his employer's or principal's affairs.

(Source: P.A. 76-1129.) [Formerly Ill. Rev. Stat. 38 §29A-1.]

5/29A-2. Commercial bribery; accepting a bribe.

§29A-2. An employee, agent or fiduciary commits commercial bribe receiving when, without consent of his employer or principal, he solicits, accepts or agrees to accept any benefit from another person upon an agreement or understanding that such benefit will influence his conduct in relation to his employer's or principal's affairs.
(Source: P.A. 76-1129.) [Formerly Ill. Rev. Stat. 38 §29A-2.]

5/29A-3. Sentence.

§29A-3. Sentence. Commercial bribery or commercial bribe receiving is a business offense for which a fine shall be imposed not to exceed $5,000.
(Source: P.A. 77-2638.) [Formerly Ill. Rev. Stat. 38 §29A-3.]

ARTICLE 29B. MONEY LAUNDERING

Sec.

5/29B-1. Money laundering.

§29B-1. (a) A person commits the offense of money laundering when he knowingly engages or attempts to engage in a financial transaction in criminally derived property with either the intent to promote the carrying on of the unlawful activity from which the criminally derived property was obtained or where he knows that the financial transaction is designed in whole or in part to conceal or disguise the nature, the location, the source, the ownership or the control of the criminally derived property.

(b) As used in this Section:

(1) "Financial transaction" means the deposit, withdrawal, transfer or exchange of funds or a monetary instrument by, through or to a financial institution. The receipt by an attorney of bona fide fees for the purpose of legal representation is not a financial transaction for purposes of this Section.

(2) "Financial institution" means any bank; saving and loan association; trust company; agency or branch of a foreign bank in the United States; currency exchange; credit union, mortgage banking institution; pawnbroker; loan or finance company; operator of a credit card system; issuer, redeemer or cashier of travelers checks, checks or money orders; dealer in precious metals, stones or jewels; broker or dealer in securities or commodities; investment banker; or investment company.

(3) "Monetary instrument" means United States coins and currency; coins and currency of a foreign country; travelers checks; bearer negotiable instruments; bearer investment securities; or bearer securities and certificates of stock.

(4) "Criminally derived property" means any property constituting or derived from proceeds obtained, directly or indirectly, pursuant to a violation of the Criminal Code of 1961 [720 ILCS 5/1-1 et seq.], the Illinois Controlled Substances Act [720 ILCS 570/100 et seq.] or the Cannabis Control Act [720 ILCS 550/1 et seq.].

(c) Sentence.

(1) Laundering of criminally derived property of a value not exceeding $10,000 is a Class 3 felony;

(2) Laundering of criminally derived property of a value exceeding $10,000 but not exceeding $100,000 is a Class 2 felony;

(3) Laundering of criminally derived property of a value exceeding $100,000 is a Class 1 felony.
(Source: P.A. 85-675; 86-1459.) [Formerly Ill. Rev. Stat. 38 §29B-1.]

PART E. OFFENSES AFFECTING GOVERNMENTAL FUNCTIONS

ARTICLE 30. TREASON AND RELATED OFFENSES

5/30-1. Treason.

§30-1. Treason. (a) A person owing allegiance to this State commits treason when he or she knowingly:

(1) Levies war against this State; or

(2) Adheres to the enemies of this State, giving them aid or comfort.

(b) No person may be convicted of treason except on the testimony of 2 witnesses to the same overt act, or on his confession in open court.

(c) Sentence. Treason is a Class X felony for which an offender may be sentenced to death under Section 5-5-3 of the Unified Code of Corrections.
(Source: P.A. 80-1099.) [Formerly Ill. Rev. Stat. 38 §30-1.]

5/30-2. Misprision of treason.

§30-2. Misprision of treason. (a) A person owing allegiance to this State commits misprision of treason when he conceals or withholds his knowledge that another has committed treason against this State.

(b) Sentence.

Misprision of treason is a Class 4 felony.
(Source: P.A. 77-2638.) [Formerly Ill. Rev. Stat. 38 §30-2.]

5/30-3. Advocating overthrow of government.

§30-3. Advocating overthrow of Government. A person who advocates, or with knowledge of its contents knowingly publishes, sells or distributes any document which advocates or with knowledge of its purpose, knowingly becomes a member of any organization which advocates the overthrow or reformation of the existing form of government of this State by violence or unlawful means commits a Class 3 felony.
(Source: P.A. 77-2638.) [Formerly Ill. Rev. Stat. 38 §30-3.]

ARTICLE 31. INTERFERENCE WITH PUBLIC OFFICERS

5/31-1. Resisting or obstructing a peace officer or correctional institution employee.

§31-1. Resisting or obstructing a peace officer or correctional institution employee. (a) A person who knowingly resists or obstructs the performance by one known to the person to be a peace officer or correctional institution employee of any authorized act within his official capacity commits a Class A misdemeanor.

(b) For purposes of this Section, "correctional institution employee" means any person employed to supervise and control inmates incarcerated in a penitentiary, State farm, reformatory, prison, jail, house of correction, police

detention area, half-way house, or other institution or place for the incarceration or custody of persons under sentence for offenses or awaiting trial or sentence for offenses, under arrest for an offense, a violation of probation, a violation of parole, or a violation of mandatory supervised release, or awaiting a bail setting hearing or preliminary hearing.
(Chgd. by P.A. 87-1198, §2, eff. 9/25/92.)
(Source: P.A. 77-2638.) [Formerly Ill. Rev. Stat. 38 §31-1.]

5/31-1a. Disarming a peace officer.

§31-1a. Disarming a peace officer. A person who knowingly disarms a person known to him to be a peace officer, while the peace officer is engaged in the performance of his official duties by taking a firearm from the person of the peace officer or from an area within the peace officer's immediate presence without the peace officer's consent shall be guilty of a Class 2 felony.
(Source: P.A. 84-181.) [Formerly Ill. Rev. Stat. 38 §31-1a.]

5/31-3. Obstructing service of process.

§31-3. Obstructing service of process. Whoever knowingly resists or obstructs the authorized service or execution of any civil or criminal process or order of any court commits a Class B misdemeanor.
(Source: P.A. 77-2638.) [Formerly Ill. Rev. Stat. 38 §31-3.]

5/31-4. Obstructing justice.

§31-4. Obstructing justice. A person obstructs justice when, with intent to prevent the apprehension or obstruct the prosecution or defense of any person, he knowingly commits any of the following acts:

(a) Destroys, alters, conceals or disguises physical evidence, plants false evidence, furnishes false information; or

(b) Induces a witness having knowledge material to the subject at issue to leave the State or conceal himself; or

(c) Possessing knowledge material to the subject at issue, he leaves the State or conceals himself.

(d) Sentence.

Obstructing justice is a Class 4 felony.
(Source: P.A. 77-2638.) [Formerly Ill. Rev. Stat. 38 §31-4.]

5/31-5. Concealing or aiding a fugitive.

§31-5. Concealing or aiding a fugitive. Every person not standing in the relation of husband, wife, parent, child, brother or sister to the offender, who, with intent to prevent the apprehension of the offender, conceals his knowledge that an offense has been committed or harbors, aids or conceals the offender, commits a Class 4 felony.
(Source: P.A. 77-2638.) [Formerly Ill. Rev. Stat. 38 §31-5.]

5/31-6. Escape; failure to report to a penal institution or to report for periodic imprisonment.

§31-6. Escape; failure to report to a penal institution or to report for periodic imprisonment. (a) A person convicted of a felony, or charged with the commission of a felony who intentionally escapes from any penal institution or from the custody of an employee of that institution commits a Class 2 felony; however, a person convicted of a felony who knowingly fails to report to a penal institution or to report for periodic imprisonment at any time or knowingly fails to return from furlough or from work and day release is guilty of a Class 3 felony.

(b) A person convicted of a misdemeanor or charged with the commission of a misdemeanor who intentionally escapes from any penal institution or from the custody of an employee of that institution commits a Class A misdemeanor; however, a person convicted of a misdemeanor who knowingly fails to report to a penal institution or to report for periodic imprisonment at any time or knowingly fails to return from furlough or from work and day release is guilty of a Class B misdemeanor.

(c) A person in the lawful custody of a peace officer for the alleged commission of a felony offense and who intentionally escapes from custody commits a Class 2 felony; however, a person in the lawful custody of a peace officer for the alleged commission of a misdemeanor offense and who intentionally escapes from custody commits a Class A misdemeanor.

(d) A person who violates this Section while armed with a dangerous weapon commits a Class 1 felony.

(Source: P.A. 86-335.) [Formerly Ill. Rev. Stat. 38 §31-6.]

5/31-7. Aiding escape.

§31-7. Aiding escape. (a) Whoever, with intent to aid any prisoner in escaping from any penal institution, conveys into the institution or transfers to the prisoner anything for use in escaping commits a Class A misdemeanor.

(b) Whoever knowingly aids a person convicted of a felony, or charged with the commission of a felony in escaping from any penal institution or from the custody of any employee of that institution commits a Class 2 felony; however, whoever knowingly aids a person convicted of a felony or charged with the commission of a felony in failing to return from furlough or from work and day release is guilty of a Class 3 felony.

(c) Whoever knowingly aids a person convicted of a misdemeanor or charged with the commission of a misdemeanor in escaping from any penal institution or from the custody of an employee of that institution commits a Class A misdemeanor; however, whoever knowingly aids a person convicted of a misdemeanor or charged with the commission of a misdemeanor in failing to return from furlough or from work and day release is guilty of a Class B misdemeanor.

(d) Whoever knowingly aids a person in escaping from any public institution, other than a penal institution, in which he is lawfully detained, or from the custody of an employee of that institution, commits a Class A misdemeanor.

(e) Whoever knowingly aids a person in the lawful custody of a peace officer for the alleged commission of a felony offense in escaping from custody commits a Class 2 felony; however, whoever knowingly aids a person in the lawful custody of a peace officer for the alleged commission of a misdemeanor offense in escaping from custody commits a Class A misdemeanor.

(f) An officer or employee of any penal institution who recklessly permits any prisoner in his custody to escape commits a Class A misdemeanor.

(g) A person who violates this Section while armed with a dangerous weapon commits a Class 2 felony.

(Source: P.A. 86-335.) [Formerly Ill. Rev. Stat. 38 §31-7.]

5/31-8. Refusing to aid an officer.

§31-8. Refusing to aid an officer. Whoever upon command refuses or knowingly fails reasonably to aid a person known by him to be a peace officer in:

(a) Apprehending a person whom the officer is authorized to apprehend; or

(b) Preventing the commission by another of any offense, commits a petty offense.

(Source: P.A. 77-2638.) [Formerly Ill. Rev. Stat. 38 §31-8.]

ARTICLE 31A. INTERFERENCE WITH PENAL INSTITUTION

Sec.

5/31A-1.2. Unauthorized bringing of contraband into a penal institution by an employee; unauthorized possessing of contraband in a penal institution by an employee; unauthorized delivery of contraband in a penal institution by an employee.

5/31A-1.1. Bringing contraband into a penal institution; possessing contraband in a penal institution.

§31A-1.1. Bringing Contraband into a Penal Institution; Possessing Contraband in a Penal Institution. (a) A person commits the offense of bringing contraband into a penal institution when he knowingly and without authority of any person designated or authorized to grant such authority (1) brings an item of contraband into a penal institution or (2) causes another to bring an item of contraband into a penal institution or (3) places an item of contraband in such proximity to a penal institution as to give an inmate access to the contraband.

(b) A person commits the offense of possessing contraband in a penal institution when he possesses contraband in a penal institution, regardless of the intent with which he possesses it.

(c) For the purposes of this Section, the words and phrases listed below shall be defined as follows:

(1) "Penal institution" means any penitentiary, State farm, reformatory, prison, jail, house of correction, police detention area, half-way house or other institution or place for the incarceration or custody of persons under sentence for offenses awaiting trial or sentence for offenses, under arrest for an offense, a violation of probation, a violation of parole, or a violation of mandatory supervised release, or awaiting a bail setting hearing or preliminary hearing; provided that where the place for incarceration or custody is housed within another public building this Act shall not apply to that part of such building unrelated to the incarceration or custody of persons.

(2) "Item of contraband" means any of the following:

(i) "Alcoholic liquor" as such term is defined in Section 1-3.05 of The Liquor Control Act of 1934 as such Act may be now or hereafter amended [235 ILCS 5/1-3.05].

(ii) "Cannabis" as such term is defined in subsection (a) of Section 3 of the "Cannabis Control Act", approved August 16, 1971, as now or hereafter amended [720 ILCS 550/3].

(iii) "Controlled substance" as such term is defined in the "Illinois Controlled Substances Act", approved August 16, 1971, as now or hereafter amended [720 ILCS 570/100 et seq.].

(iv) "Hypodermic syringe" or hypodermic needle, or any instrument adapted for use of controlled substances or cannabis by subcutaneous injection.

(v) "Weapon" means any knife, dagger, dirk, billy, razor, stiletto, broken bottle, or other piece of glass which could be used as a dangerous weapon. Such term includes any of the devices or implements designated in subsections (a)(1), (a)(3) and (a)(6) of Section 24-1 of this Act, or any other dangerous weapon or instrument of like character.

(vi) "Firearm" means any device, by whatever name known, which is designed to expel a projectile or projectiles by the action of an explosion, expansion of gas or escape of gas, including but not limited to:

(A) any pneumatic gun, spring gun, or B-B gun which expels a single globular projectile not exceeding .18 inch in diameter, or;

(B) any device used exclusively for signaling or safety and required as recommended by the United States Coast Guard or the Interstate Commerce Commission; or

(C) any device used exclusively for the firing of stud cartridges, explosive rivets or industrial ammunition; or

(D) any device which is powered by electrical charging units, such as batteries, and which fires one or several barbs attached to a length of wire and which, upon hitting a human, can send out current capable of disrupting the person's nervous system in such a manner as to render him incapable of normal functioning, commonly referred to as a stun gun or taser.

(vii) "Firearm ammunition" means any self-contained cartridge or shotgun shell, by whatever name known, which is designed to be used or adaptable to use in a firearm, including but not limited to:

(A) any ammunition exclusively designed for use with a device used exclusively for signaling or safety and required or recommended by the United States Coast Guard or the Interstate Commerce Commission; or

(B) any ammunition designed exclusively for use with a stud or rivet driver or other similar industrial ammunition.

(viii) "Explosive" means, but is not limited to, bomb, bombshell, grenade, bottle or other container containing an explosive substance of over one-quarter ounce for like purposes such as black powder bombs and Molotov cocktails or artillery projectiles.

(d) Bringing alcoholic liquor into a penal institution is a Class 4 felony. Possessing alcoholic liquor in a penal institution is a Class 4 felony.

(e) Bringing cannabis into a penal institution is a Class 3 felony. Possessing cannabis in a penal institution is a Class 3 felony.

(f) Bringing any amount of a controlled substance classified in Schedules III, IV or V of Article II of the Controlled Substance Act [720 ILCS 570/201 et seq.] into a penal institution is a Class 2 felony. Possessing any amount of a controlled substance classified in Schedule III, IV, or V of Article II of the Controlled Substance Act in a penal institution is a Class 2 felony.

(g) Bringing any amount of a controlled substance classified in Schedules I or II of Article II of the Controlled Substance Act into a penal institution is a Class 1 felony. Possessing any amount of a controlled substance classified in Schedules I or II of Article II of the Controlled Substance Act in a penal institution is a Class 1 felony.

(h) Bringing an item of contraband listed in paragraph (iv) of subsection (c)(2) into a penal institution is a Class 1 felony. Possessing an item of contraband listed in paragraph (iv) of subsection (c)(2) in a penal institution is a Class 1 felony.

(i) Bringing an item of contraband listed in paragraph (v) of subsection (c)(2) into a penal institution is a Class 1 felony. Possessing an item of contraband listed in paragraph (v) of subsection (c)(2) in a penal institution is a Class 1 felony.

(j) Bringing an item of contraband listed in paragraphs (vi), (vii) or (viii) of subsection (c)(2) in a penal institution is a Class X felony. Possessing an item of contraband listed in paragraphs (vi), (vii), or (viii) of subsection (c)(2) in a penal institution is a Class X felony.

(k) It shall be an affirmative defense to subsection (b) hereof, that such possession was specifically authorized by rule, regulation, or directive of the governing authority of the penal institution or order issued pursuant thereto.

(*l*) It shall be an affirmative defense to subsection (a)(1) and subsection (b) hereof that the person bringing into or possessing contraband in a penal institution had been arrested, and that that person possessed such contraband at the time of his arrest, and that such contraband was brought into or possessed in the penal institution by that person as a direct and immediate result of his arrest.

(Source: P.A. 86-866; 86-1003.) [Formerly Ill. Rev. Stat. 38 §31A-1.1.]

5/31A-1.2. Unauthorized bringing of contraband into a penal institution by an employee; unauthorized possessing of contraband in a penal institution by an employee; unauthorized delivery of contraband in a penal institution by an employee.

§31A-1.2. Unauthorized bringing of contraband into a penal institution by an employee; unauthorized possessing of contraband in a penal institution by an employee; unauthorized delivery of contraband in a penal institution by an employee. (a) A person commits the offense of unauthorized bringing of contraband into a penal institution by an employee when a person who is an employee knowingly and without authority or any person designated or authorized to grant such authority:

(1) brings or attempts to bring an item of contraband listed in paragraphs (i) through (iv) of subsection (d)(4) into a penal institution, or

(2) causes or permits another to bring an item of contraband listed in paragraphs (i) through (iv) of subsection (d)(4) into a penal institution.

(b) A person commits the offense of unauthorized possession of contraband in a penal institution by an employee when a person who is an employee knowingly and without authority of any person designated or authorized to grant such authority possesses contraband listed in paragraphs (i) through (iv) of subsection (d)(4) in a penal institution, regardless of the intent with which he possesses it.

(c) A person commits the offense of unauthorized delivery of contraband in a penal institution by an employee when a person who is an employee knowingly and without authority of any person designated or authorized to grant such authority:

(1) delivers or possesses with intent to deliver an item of contraband to any inmate of a penal institution, or

(2) conspires to deliver or solicits the delivery of an item of contraband to any inmate of a penal institution, or

(3) causes or permits the delivery of an item of contraband to any inmate of a penal institution, or

(4) permits another person to attempt to deliver an item of contraband to any inmate of a penal institution.

(d) For purpose of this Section, the words and phrases listed below shall be defined as follows:

(1) "Penal Institution" shall have the meaning ascribed to it in subsection (c)(1) of Section 31A-1.1 of this Code;

(2) "Employee" means any elected or appointed officer, trustee or employee of a penal institution or of the governing authority of the penal institution, or any person who performs services for the penal institution pursuant to contract with the penal institution or its governing authority.

(3) "Deliver" or "delivery" means the actual, constructive or attempted transfer of possession of an item of contraband, with or without consideration, whether or not there is an agency relationship;

(4) "Item of contraband" means any of the following:

(i) "Alcoholic liquor" as such term is defined in Section 1-3.05 of the Liquor Control Act of 1934 [235 ILCS 5/1-3.05].

(ii) "Cannabis" as such term is defined in subsection 9a)* of Section 3 of the Cannabis Control Act [720 ILCS 550/3].

**So in original. Probably should be "(a)".*

(iii) "Controlled substance" as such term is defined in the Illinois Controlled Substance Act [720 ILCS 570/100 et seq.].

(iv) "Hypodermic syringe" or hypodermic needle, or any instrument adapted for use of controlled substances or cannabis by subcutaneous injection.

(v) "Weapon" means any knife, dagger, dirk, billy, razor, stiletto, broken bottle, or other piece of glass which could be used as a dangerous weapon. Such term includes any of the devices or implements designated in subsections (a)(1), (a)(3) and (a)(6) of Section 24-1 of this Act, or any other dangerous weapon or instrument of like character.

(vi) "Firearm" means any device, by whatever name known, which is designed to expel a projectile or projectiles by the action of an explosion, expansion of gas or escape of gas, including but not limited to:

(A) any pneumatic gun, spring gun, or B-B gun which expels a single globular projectile not exceeding .18 inch in diameter; or

(B) any device used exclusively for signaling or safety and required or recommended by the United States Coast Guard or the Interstate Commerce Commission; or

(C) any device used exclusively for the firing of stud cartridges, explosive rivets or industrial ammunition; or

(D) any device which is powered by electrical charging units, such as batteries, and which fires one or several barbs attached to a length of wire and which, upon hitting a human, can send out current capable of disrupting the person's nervous system in such a manner as to render him incapable of normal functioning, commonly referred to as a stun gun or taser.

(vii) "Firearm ammunition" means any self-contained cartridge or shotgun shell, by whatever name known, which is designed to be used or adaptable to use in a firearm, including but not limited to:

(A) any ammunition exclusively designed for use with a device used exclusively for signaling or safety and required or recommended by the United States Coast Guard or the Interstate Commerce Commission; or

(B) any ammunition designed exclusively for use with a stud or rivet driver or other similar industrial ammunition.

(viii) "Explosive" means, but is not limited to, bomb, bombshell, grenade, bottle or other container containing an explosive substance of over one-quarter ounce for like purposes such as black powder bombs and Molotov cocktails or artillery projectiles.

(e) A violation of paragraphs (a) or (b) of this Section involving alcohol is a Class 4 felony. A violation of paragraph (a) or (b) of this Section involving cannabis is a Class 2 felony. A violation of paragraph (a) or (b) involving any amount of a controlled substance classified in Schedules III, IV or V of Article II of the Controlled Substances Act [720 ILCS 570/201 et seq.] is a Class 1 felony. A violation of paragraph (a) or (b) of this Section involving any amount of a controlled substance classified in Schedules I or II of Article II of the Controlled Substances Act is a Class X felony. A violation of paragraph (a) or (b) involving an item of contraband listed in paragraph (iv) of subsection (d)(4) is a Class X felony. A violation of paragraph (a) or (b) involving an item of contraband listed in paragraph (v) of subsection (d)(4) is a Class 1 felony. A violation of paragraph (a) or (b) involving an item of contraband listed in paragraphs (vi), (vii) or (viii) of subsection (d)(4) is a Class X felony.

(f) A violation of paragraph (c) of this Section involving alcoholic liquor is a Class 3 felony. A violation of paragraph (c) involving cannabis is a Class 1 felony. A violation of paragraph (c) involving any amount of a controlled substance classified in Schedules III, IV or V of Article II of the Controlled Substances Act is a Class X felony. A violation of paragraph (c) involving any amount of a controlled substance classified in Schedules I or II of Article II of the Controlled Substances Act is a Class X felony for which the minimum term of imprisonment shall be 8 years. A violation of paragraph (c) involving an item of contraband listed in paragraph (iv) of subsection (d)(4) is a Class X felony for which the minimum term of imprisonment shall be 8 years. A violation of paragraph (c)

involving an item of contraband listed in paragraph (v) of subsection (d)(4) is a Class X felony for which the minimum term of imprisonment shall be 10 years. A violation of paragraph (c) involving an item of contraband listed in paragraphs (vi), (vii) or (viii) of subsection (d)(4) is a Class X felony for which the minimum term of imprisonment shall be 12 years.
(Chgd. by P.A. 87-905, §1, eff. 8/14/92.)
(Source: P.A. 86-866; 86-1003.) [Formerly Ill. Rev. Stat. 38 §31A-1.2.]

ARTICLE 32. INTERFERENCE WITH JUDICIAL PROCEDURE

5/32-1. Compounding a crime.

§32-1. Compounding a crime. (a) A person compounds a crime when he receives or offers to another any consideration for a promise not to prosecute or aid in the prosecution of an offender.

(b) Sentence. Compounding a crime is a petty offense.
(Source: P.A. 77-2638.) [Formerly Ill. Rev. Stat. 38 §32-1.]

5/32-2. Perjury.

§32-2. Perjury. (a) A person commits perjury when, under oath or affirmation, in a proceeding or in any other matter where by law such oath or affirmation is required, he makes a false statement, material to the issue or point in question, which he does not believe to be true.

(b) Proof of Falsity.

An indictment or information for perjury alleging that the offender, under oath, has made contradictory statements, material to the issue or point in question, in the same or in different proceedings, where such oath or affirmation is required, need not specify which statement is false. At the trial, the prosecution need not establish which statement is false.

(c) Admission of Falsity.

Where the contradictory statements are made in the same continuous trial, an admission by the offender in that same continuous trial of the falsity of a contradictory statement shall bar prosecution therefor under any provisions of this Code.

(d) A person shall be exempt from prosecution under subsection (a) of this Section if he is a peace officer who uses a false or fictitious name in the enforcement of the criminal laws, and such use is approved in writing as provided in Section 10-1 of "The Liquor Control Act of 1934", as amended [235 ILCS 5/10-1], Section 5 of "An Act in relation to the use of an assumed name in the conduct or transaction of business in this State", approved July 17, 1941, as amended [805 ILCS 405/5], or Section 55a of The Civil Administrative Code of Illinois, as amended [20 ILCS 2605/55a]. However, this exemption shall not apply to testimony in judicial proceedings where the identity of the peace officer is material to the issue, and he is ordered by the court to disclose his identity.

(e) Sentence.

Perjury is a Class 3 felony.

(Source: P.A. 84-1308.) [Formerly Ill. Rev. Stat. 38 §32-2.]

5/32-3. Subornation of perjury.

§32-3. Subornation of perjury. (a) A person commits subornation of perjury when he procures or induces another to make a statement in violation of Section 32-2 which the person knows to be false.

(b) Sentence.

Subornation of perjury is a Class 4 felony.

(Source: P.A. 77-2638.) [Formerly Ill. Rev. Stat. 38 §32-3.]

5/32-4. Communicating with jurors and witnesses.

§32-4. Communicating with jurors and witnesses. (a) A person who, with intent to influence any person whom he believes has been summoned as a juror, regarding any matter which is or may be brought before such juror, communicates, directly or indirectly, with such juror otherwise than as authorized by law commits a Class 4 felony.

(b) A person who, with intent to deter any party or witness from testifying freely, fully and truthfully to any matter pending in any court, or before a Grand Jury, Administrative agency or any other State or local governmental unit, forcibly detains such party or witness, or communicates, directly or indirectly, to such party or witness any knowingly false information or a threat of injury or damage to the property or person of such party or witness or to the property or person of any relative of such party or witness, or offers or delivers money or another thing of value to such party or witness or to a relative of such party or witness, commits a Class 4 felony.

(Source: P.A. 82-291.) [Formerly Ill. Rev. Stat. 38 §32-4.]

5/32-4a. Harassment of jurors and witnesses.

§32-4a. Harassment of jurors and witnesses. A person who, with intent to harass or annoy one who has served as a juror or as a witness in a legal proceeding, because of the verdict returned by the jury therein or the participation of such juror in the verdict or because of the testimony of such witness, communicates directly or indirectly with the juror or witness in such manner as to produce mental anguish or emotional distress or who conveys a threat of injury or damage to the property or person of such party or witness or to the property or person of any relative of such party or witness commits a Class 4 felony.

(Source: P.A. 82-517.) [Formerly Ill. Rev. Stat. 38 §32-4a.]

5/32-4b. Excusing persons from jury duty; bribery.

§32-4b. A jury commissioner, or any other person acting on behalf of a jury commissioner, who requests, solicits, suggests, or accepts financial compensation or any other form of consideration in exchange for a promise to excuse or for excusing any person from jury duty commits a Class 3 felony.

In addition to any other penalty provided by law, any jury commissioner convicted under this Section shall forfeit the performance bond required by Section 1 of "An Act in relation to jury commissioners and authorizing judges to appoint such commissioners and to make rules concerning their powers and duties", approved June 15, 1887, as amended [705 ILCS 310/1], and shall be excluded from further service as a jury commissioner.

(Source: P.A. 84-1428.) [Formerly Ill. Rev. Stat. 38 §32-4b.]

5/32-5. False personation of judicial or governmental officials.

§32-5. False personation of Judicial or Governmental Officials. A person who falsely represents himself to be an attorney authorized to practice law or a public officer or a public employee commits a Class B misdemeanor.
(Source: P.A. 77-2638.) [Formerly Ill. Rev. Stat. 38 §32-5.]

5/32-5.1. False personation of a peace officer.

§32-5.1. False Personation of a Peace Officer. A person who knowingly and falsely represents himself to be a peace officer of any jurisdiction commits a Class 4 felony.
(Source: P.A. 85-741.) [Formerly Ill. Rev. Stat. 38 §32-5.1.]

5/32-5.2. Aggravated false personation of a peace officer.

§32-5.2. Aggravated False Personation of a Peace Officer. A person who knowingly and falsely represents himself to be a peace officer of any jurisdiction in attempting or committing a felony commits a Class 3 felony.
(Source: P.A. 85-741.) [Formerly Ill. Rev. Stat. 38 §32-5.2.]

5/32-6. Performance of unauthorized acts.

§32-6. Performance of unauthorized acts. A person who performs any of the following acts, knowing that his performance is not authorized by law, commits a Class 4 felony:

(a) Conducts a marriage ceremony; or

(b) Acknowledges the execution of any document which by law may be recorded; or

(c) Becomes a surety for any party in any civil or criminal proceeding, before any court or public officer authorized to accept such surety.
(Source: P.A. 77-2638.) [Formerly Ill. Rev. Stat. 38 §32-6.]

5/32-7. Simulating legal process.

§32-7. Simulating legal process. A person who issues or delivers any document which he knows falsely purports to be or simulates any civil or criminal process commits a Class B misdemeanor.
(Source: P.A. 77-2638.) [Formerly Ill. Rev. Stat. 38 §32-7.]

5/32-8. Tampering with public records.

§32-8. Tampering with public records. A person who knowingly and without lawful authority alters, destroys, defaces, removes or conceals any public record commits a Class 4 felony.
(Source: P.A. 77-2638.) [Formerly Ill. Rev. Stat. 38 §32-8.]

5/32-9. Tampering with public notice.

§32-9. Tampering with public notice. A person who knowingly and without lawful authority alters, destroys, defaces, removes or conceals any public notice, posted according to law, during the time for which the notice was to remain posted, commits a petty offense.
(Source: P.A. 77-2638.) [Formerly Ill. Rev. Stat. 38 §32-9.]

5/32-10. Violation of bail bond.

§32-10. Violation of bail bond. Whoever, having been admitted to bail for appearance before any court of this State, incurs a forfeiture of the bail and willfully fails to surrender himself within 30 days following the date of such forfeiture, commits, if the bail was given in connection with a charge of felony or pending appeal or certiorari after conviction of any offense, a felony of the next lower Class or a Class A misdemeanor if the underlying offense was a Class 4 felony; or, if the bail was given in connection with a charge of committing a misdemeanor, or for appearance as a witness, commits a misdemeanor of the next lower Class, but not less than a Class C misdemeanor.

Nothing in this section shall interfere with or prevent the exercise by any court of its power to punishment for contempt. Any sentence imposed for violation of this Section shall be served consecutive to the sentence imposed for the charge for which bail had been granted and with respect to which the defendant has been convicted.
(Source: P.A. 84-945.) [Formerly Ill. Rev. Stat. 38 §32-10.]

ARTICLE 33. OFFICIAL MISCONDUCT

5/33-1. Bribery.

§33-1. Bribery. A person commits bribery when:

(a) With intent to influence the performance of any act related to the employment or function of any public officer, public employee, juror or witness, he promises or tenders to that person any property or personal advantage which he is not authorized by law to accept; or

(b) With intent to influence the performance of any act related to the employment or function of any public officer, public employee, juror or witness, he promises or tenders to one whom he believes to be a public officer, public employee, juror or witness, any property or personal advantage which a public officer, public employee, juror or witness would not be authorized by law to accept; or

(c) With intent to cause any person to influence the performance of any act related to the employment or function of any public officer, public employee, juror or witness, he promises or tenders to that person any property or personal advantage which he is not authorized by law to accept; or

(d) He receives, retains or agrees to accept any property or personal advantage which he is not authorized by law to accept knowing that such property or personal advantage was promised or tendered with intent to cause him to influence the performance of any act related to the employment or function of any public officer, public employee, juror or witness; or

(e) He solicits, receives, retains, or agrees to accept any property or personal advantage pursuant to an understanding that he shall improperly influence or attempt to influence the performance of any act related to the employment or function of any public officer, public employee, juror or witness.

(f) Sentence.

Bribery is a Class 2 felony.
(Source: P.A. 84-761.) [Formerly Ill. Rev. Stat. 38 §33-1.]

5/33-2. Failure to report a bribe.

§33-2. Failure to report a bribe. Any public officer, public employee or juror who fails to report forthwith to the local State's Attorney, or in the case of a State employee to the Department of State Police, any offer made to him in violation of Section 33-1 commits a Class A misdemeanor.

In the case of a State employee, the making of such report to the Department of State Police shall discharge such employee from any further duty under this Section. Upon receiving any such report, the Department of State Police shall forthwith transmit a copy thereof to the appropriate State's Attorney.
(Source: P.A. 84-25.) [Formerly Ill. Rev. Stat. 38 §33-2.]

5/33-3. Official misconduct.

§33-3. Official Misconduct. A public officer or employee commits misconduct when, in his official capacity, he commits any of the following acts:

(a) Intentionally or recklessly fails to perform any mandatory duty as required by law; or

(b) Knowingly performs an act which he knows he is forbidden by law to perform; or

(c) With intent to obtain a personal advantage for himself or another, he performs an act in excess of his lawful authority; or

(d) Solicits or knowingly accepts for the performance of any act a fee or reward which he knows is not authorized by law.

A public officer or employee convicted of violating any provision of this Section forfeits his office or employment. In addition, he commits a Class 3 felony.

(Source: P.A. 82-790.) [Formerly Ill. Rev. Stat. 38 §33-3.]

PART F. CERTAIN AGGRAVATED OFFENSES

ARTICLE 33A. ARMED VIOLENCE

Sec.

5/33A-1. Definitions.

§33A-1. Definitions. (a) "Armed with a dangerous weapon". A person is considered armed with a dangerous weapon for purposes of this Article, when he carries on or about his person or is otherwise armed with a category I or category II weapon. (b) A category I weapon is a pistol, revolver, rifle, shotgun, spring gun, or any other firearm, sawed-off shotgun, a stun gun or taser as defined in paragraph (a) of Section 24-1 of this Code, knife with a blade of at least 3 inches in length, dagger, dirk, switchblade knife, stiletto, or any other deadly or dangerous weapon or instrument of like character. (c) A category II weapon is a bludgeon, black-jack, slungshot, sand-bag, sandclub, metal knuckles, billy or other dangerous weapon of like character.

(Source: P.A. 80-259; 80-1099.) [Formerly Ill. Rev. Stat. 38 §33A-1.]

5/33A-2. Armed violence—Elements of the offense.

§33A-2. Armed violence—Elements of the offense. A person commits armed violence when, while armed with a dangerous weapon, he commits any felony defined by Illinois Law.

(Source: P.A. 80-1099.) [Formerly Ill. Rev. Stat. 38 §33A-2.]

5/33A-3. Sentence.

§33A-3. Sentence. (a) Violation of Section 33A-2 with a Category I weapon is a Class X felony. (b) Violation of Section 33A-2 with a Category II weapon is a Class 2 felony or the felony classification provided for the same act while unarmed, whichever permits the greater penalty. A second or subsequent violation of Section 33A-2 with a Category II weapon is a Class 1 felony or the felony classification provided for the same act while unarmed, whichever permits the greater penalty.

(Source: P.A. 80-1387.) [Formerly Ill. Rev. Stat. 38 §33A-3.]

ARTICLE 33B. MANDATORY LIFE SENTENCE A THIRD OR SUBSEQUENT FORCIBLE OFFENSE

Sec.

5/33B-1. Habitual criminals; life imprisonment—Application of article.

§33B-1. (a) Every person who has been twice convicted in any state or federal court of an offense that contains the same elements as an offense now classified in Illinois as a Class X felony, criminal sexual assault or first degree murder, and is thereafter convicted of a Class X felony, criminal sexual assault or first degree murder, committed after the 2 prior convictions, shall be adjudged an habitual criminal.

(b) The 2 prior convictions need not have been for the same offense.

(c) Any convictions which result from or are connected with the same transaction, or result from offenses committed at the same time, shall be counted for the purposes of this Section as one conviction.

(d) This Article shall not apply unless each of the following requirements are satisfied:

(1) the third offense was committed after the effective date of this Act;

(2) the third offense was committed within 20 years of the date that judgment was entered on the first conviction, provided, however, that time spent in custody shall not be counted;

(3) the third offense was committed after conviction on the second offense;

(4) the second offense was committed after conviction on the first offense.

(e) Except when the death penalty is imposed, anyone adjudged an habitual criminal shall be sentenced to life imprisonment.

(Source: P.A. 85-872.) [Formerly Ill. Rev. Stat. 38 §33B-1.]

5/33B-2. Evidence of prior convictions; waiver of exceptions.

§33B-2. (a) A prior conviction shall not be alleged in the indictment, and no evidence or other disclosure of such conviction shall be presented to the court or the jury during the trial of an offense set forth in Section 33B-1 unless otherwise permitted by the issues properly raised in such trial. After a plea or verdict or finding of guilty and before sentence is imposed, the prosecutor may file with the court a verified written statement signed by the State's Attorney concerning any former conviction of an offense set forth in Section 33B-1 rendered against the defendant. The court shall then cause the defendant to be brought before it; shall inform him of the allegations of the statement so filed, and of his right to a hearing before the court on the issue of such former conviction and of his right to counsel at such hearing; and unless the defendant admits such conviction, the court shall hear and determine such issue, and shall make a written finding thereon. If a sentence has previously been imposed, the court may vacate such sentence and impose a new sentence in accordance with Section 33B-1 of this Act.

(b) A duly authenticated copy of the record of any alleged former conviction of an offense set forth in Section 33B-1 shall be prima facie evidence of such former conviction; and a duly authenticated copy of the record of the defendant's final release or discharge from probation granted, or from sentence and parole supervision (if any) imposed pursuant to such former conviction, shall be prima facie evidence of such release or discharge.

(c) Any claim that a previous conviction offered by the prosecution is not a former conviction of an offense set forth in Section 33B-1 because of the existence of any exceptions described in this Act, is waived unless duly raised at the hearing on such conviction, or unless the prosecution's proof shows the existence of such exceptions described in this Act.

(Source: P.A. 80-1099.) [Formerly Ill. Rev. Stat. 38 §33B-2.]

5/33B-3. Pardon; release from imprisonment.

§33B-3. If the person so convicted shall show to the satisfaction of the court before whom such conviction was had that he was released from imprisonment, upon either of the sentences upon a pardon granted for the reason that he was

innocent, such conviction and sentence shall not be considered under Section 33B-1.
(Source: P.A. 80-1099.) [Formerly Ill. Rev. Stat. 38 §33B-3.]

ARTICLE 33C. DECEPTION RELATING TO CERTIFICATION OF DISADVANTAGED BUSINESS ENTERPRISES

5/33C-1. Fraudulently obtaining or retaining certification.

§33C-1. Fraudulently obtaining or retaining certification. A person who, in the course of business, fraudulently obtains or retains certification as a minority owned business or female owned business commits a Class 2 felony.
(Source: P.A. 84-192.) [Formerly Ill. Rev. Stat. 38 §33C-1.]

5/33C-2. Willfully making a false statement.

§33C-2. Willfully making a false statement. A person who, in the course of business, willfully makes a false statement whether by affidavit, report or other representation, to an official or employee of a State agency or the Minority and Female Business Enterprise Council for the purpose of influencing the certification or denial of certification of any business entity as a minority owned business or female owned business commits a Class 2 felony.
(Source: P.A. 84-192.) [Formerly Ill. Rev. Stat. 38 §33C-2.]

5/33C-3. Willfully obstructing or impeding an official or employee of any agency in his investigation.

§33C-3. Willfully obstructing or impeding an official or employee of any agency in his investigation. Any person who, in the course of business, willfully obstructs or impedes an official or employee of any State agency or the Minority and Female Business Enterprise Council who is investigating the qualifications of a business entity which has requested certification as a minority owned business or a female owned business commits a Class 2 felony.
(Source: P.A. 84-192.) [Formerly Ill. Rev. Stat. 38 §33C-3.]

5/33C-4. Fraudulently obtaining public moneys reserved for disadvantaged business enterprises.

§33C-4. Fraudulently obtaining public moneys reserved for disadvantaged business enterprises. Any person who, in the course of business, fraudulently obtains public moneys reserved for, or allocated or available to minority owned businesses or female owned businesses commits a Class 2 felony.
(Source: P.A. 84-192.) [Formerly Ill. Rev. Stat. 38 §33C-4.]

5/33C-5. Definitions.

§33C-5. Definitions. As used in this Article, "Minority owned business", "female owned business", "State agency" and "Certification" shall have the meanings ascribed to them in Section 2 of the Minority and Female Business Enterprise Act, approved September 6, 1984, as amended [30 ILCS 575/2].
(Source: P.A. 84-192.) [Formerly Ill. Rev. Stat. 38 §33C-5.]

ARTICLE 33D. CONTRIBUTING TO THE CRIMINAL DELINQUENCY OF A JUVENILE

5/33D-1. Contributing to the criminal delinquency of a juvenile.

§33D-1. (a) Contributing to the criminal delinquency of a juvenile. Any person of the age of 21 years and upwards, who with the intent to promote or facilitate the commission of a felony, solicits, compels or directs any person under the age of 17 years in the commission of such felony commits the offense of contributing to the criminal delinquency of a juvenile.

(b) Sentence. Contributing to the criminal delinquency of a juvenile is a felony one grade higher than the offense committed, except when the offense committed is first degree murder or a Class X felony. When the offense committed is first degree murder or a Class X felony, the penalty for contributing to the criminal delinquency of a juvenile is the same as the penalty for first degree murder or a Class X felony, respectively.
(Source: P.A. 85-906.) [Formerly Ill. Rev. Stat. 38 §33D-1.]

ARTICLE 33E. PUBLIC CONTRACTS

5/33E-1. Interference with public contracting.

§33E-1. Interference with public contracting. It is the finding of the General Assembly that the cost to the public is increased and the quality of goods, services and construction paid for by public monies is decreased when contracts for such goods, services or construction are obtained by any means other than through independent noncollusive submission of bids or offers by individual contractors or suppliers, and the evaluation of those bids or offers by the governmental unit pursuant only to criteria publicly announced in advance.
(Source: P.A. 85-1295.) [Formerly Ill. Rev. Stat. 38 §33E-1.]

5/33E-2. Definitions.

§33E-2. Definitions. In this Act: (a) "Public contract" means any contract for goods, services or construction let to any person with or without bid by any unit of State or local government.

(b) "Unit of State or local government" means the State or any unit of state government or agency thereof, any county or municipal government or committee or agency thereof, or any other entity which is funded by or expends tax dollars or the proceeds of publicly guaranteed bonds.

(c) "Change order" means a change in a contract term other than as specifically provided for in the contract which authorizes or necessitates any increase or decrease in the cost of the contract or the time to completion.

(d) "Person" means any individual, firm, partnership, corporation, joint venture or other entity, but does not include a unit of State or local government.

(e) "Person employed by any unit of State or local government" means any employee of a unit of State or local government and any person defined in subsection (d) who is authorized by such unit of State or local government to act on its behalf in relation to any public contract.

(f) "Sheltered market" has the meaning ascribed to it in Section 2 of the Minority and Female Business Enterprise Act, as now or hereafter amended [30 ILCS 575/2].

(g) "Kickback" means any money, fee, commission, credit, gift, gratuity, thing of value, or compensation of any kind which is provided, directly or indirectly, to any prime contractor, prime contractor employee, subcontractor, or subcontractor employee for the purpose of improperly obtaining or rewarding favorable treatment in connection with a prime contract or in connection with a subcontract relating to a prime contract.

(h) "Prime contractor" means any person who has entered into a public contract.

(i) "Prime contractor employee" means any officer, partner, employee, or agent of a prime contractor.

(j) "Subcontract" means a contract or contractual action entered into by a prime contractor or subcontractor for the purpose of obtaining goods or services of any kind under a prime contract.

(k) "Subcontractor" (1) means any person, other than the prime contractor, who offers to furnish or furnishes any goods or services of any kind under a prime contract or a subcontract entered into in connection with such prime contract; and (2) includes any person who offers to furnish or furnishes goods or services to the prime contractor or a higher tier subcontractor.

(*l*) "Subcontractor employee" means any officer, partner, employee, or agent of a subcontractor.

(Source: P.A. 86-150.) [Formerly Ill. Rev. Stat. 38 §33E-2.]

5/33E-3. Bid-rigging.

§33E-3. Bid-rigging. A person commits the offense of bid-rigging when he knowingly agrees with any person who is, or but for such agreement would be, a competitor of such person concerning any bid submitted or not submitted by such person or another to a unit of State or local government when with the intent that the bid submitted or not submitted will result in the award of a contract to such person or another and he either (1) provides such person or receives from another information concerning the price or other material term or terms of the bid which would otherwise not be disclosed to a competitor in an independent noncollusive submission of bids or (2) submits a bid that is of such a price or other material term or terms that he does not intend the bid to be accepted.

Bid-rigging is a Class 3 felony. Any person convicted of this offense or any similar offense of any state or the United States which contains the same elements as this offense shall be barred for 5 years from the date of conviction from contracting with any unit of State or local government. No corporation shall be barred from contracting with any unit of State or local government as a result of a conviction under this Section of any employee or agent of such corporation if the employee so convicted is no longer employed by the corporation and: (1) it has been finally adjudicated not guilty or (2) if it demonstrates to the governmental entity with which it seeks to contract and that entity finds that the commission of the offense was neither authorized, requested, commanded, nor performed by a director, officer or a high managerial agent in behalf of the corporation as provided in paragraph (2) of subsection (a) of Section 5-4 of this Code.

(Source: P.A. 86-150.) [Formerly Ill. Rev. Stat. 38 §33E-3.]

5/33E-4. Bid rotating.

§33E-4. Bid rotating. A person commits the offense of bid rotating when, pursuant to any collusive scheme or agreement with another, he engages in a pattern over time (which, for the purposes of this Section, shall include at least 3 contract bids within a period of 10 years, the most recent of which occurs after the effective date of this amendatory Act of 1988) of submitting sealed bids to units of State or local government with the intent that the award of such bids rotates, or is distributed among, persons or business entities which submit bids on a substantial number of the same contracts. Bid rotating is a Class 2 felony. Any person convicted of this offense or any similar offense of any state or the United States which contains the same elements as this offense shall be permanently barred from contracting with any unit of State or local government. No corporation shall be barred from contracting with any unit of State or local government as a result of a conviction under this Section of any employee or agent of such corporation if the employee so convicted is no longer employed by the corporation and: (1) it has been finally adjudicated not guilty or (2) if it demonstrates to the governmental entity with which it seeks to contract and that entity finds that the commission of the offense was neither authorized, requested, commanded, nor performed by a director, officer or a high managerial agent in behalf of the corporation as provided in paragraph (2) of subsection (a) of Section 5-4 of this Code.

(Source: P.A. 86-150.) [Formerly Ill. Rev. Stat. 38 §33E-4.]

5/33E-5. Acquisition or disclosure of bidding information by public official.

§33E-5. Acquisition or disclosure of bidding information by public official. (a) Any person who is an official of or employed by any unit of State or local government who knowingly opens a sealed bid at a time or place other than as specified in the invitation to bid or as otherwise designated by the State or unit of local government, or outside the presence of witnesses required by the applicable statute or ordinance, commits a Class 4 felony.

(b) Any person who is an official of or employed by any unit of State or local government who knowingly discloses to any interested person any information related to the terms of a sealed bid whether that information is acquired through a violation of subsection (a) or by any other means except as provided by law or necessary to the performance of such official's or employee's responsibilities relating to the bid, commits a Class 3 felony.

(c) It shall not constitute a violation of subsection (b) of this Section for any person who is an official of or employed by any unit of State or local government to make any disclosure to any interested person where such disclosure is also made generally available to the public.

(d) This Section only applies to contracts let by sealed bid.

(Source: P.A. 86-150.) [Formerly Ill. Rev. Stat. 38 §33E-5.]

5/33E-6. Interference with contract submission and award by public official.

§33E-6. Interference with contract submission and award by public official. (a) Any person who is an official of or employed by any unit of State or local government who knowingly conveys, either directly or indirectly, outside of the publicly available official invitation to bid, pre-bid conference, solicitation for contracts procedure or such procedure used in any sheltered market procurement adopted pursuant to law or ordinance by that unit of government, to any person any information concerning the specifications for such contract or the identity of any particular potential subcontractors, when inclusion of such information concerning the specifications or contractors in the bid or offer would influence the likelihood of acceptance of such bid or offer, commits a Class 4 felony. It shall not constitute a violation of this subsection to convey information intended to clarify plans or specifications regarding a public contract where such disclosure of information is also made generally available to the public.

(b) Any person who is an official of or employed by any unit of State or local government who, either directly or indirectly, knowingly informs a bidder or offeror that the bid or offer will be accepted or executed only if specified individuals are included as subcontractors commits a Class 3 felony.

(c) It shall not constitute a violation of subsection (a) of this Section where any person who is an official of or employed by any unit of State or local government follows procedures established by federal, State or local minority or female owned business enterprise programs.

(d) Any bidder or offeror who is the recipient of communications from the unit of government which he reasonably believes to be proscribed by subsections (a) or (b), and fails to inform either the Attorney General or the State's Attorney for the county in which the unit of government is located, commits a Class A misdemeanor.

(e) Any public official who knowingly awards a contract based on criteria which were not publicly disseminated via the invitation to bid, when such invitation to bid is required by law or ordinance, the pre-bid conference, or any solicitation for contracts procedure or such procedure used in any sheltered market procurement procedure adopted pursuant to statute or ordinance, commits a Class 3 felony.

(f) It shall not constitute a violation of subsection (a) for any person who is an official of or employed by any unit of State or local government to provide to any person a copy of the transcript or other summary of any pre-bid conference where such transcript or summary is also made generally available to the public.

(Source: P.A. 86-150.) [Formerly Ill. Rev. Stat. 38 §33E-6.]

5/33E-7. Kickbacks.

§33E-7. Kickbacks. (a) A person violates this Section when he knowingly either:

(1) provides, attempts to provide or offers to provide any kickback;

(2) solicits, accepts or attempts to accept any kickback; or

(3) includes, directly or indirectly, the amount of any kickback prohibited by paragraphs (1) or (2) of this subsection (a) in the contract price charged by a subcontractor to a prime contractor or a higher tier subcontractor or in the contract price charged by a prime contractor to any unit of State or local government for a public contract.

(b) Any person violates this Section when he has received an offer of a kickback, or has been solicited to make a kickback, and fails to report it to law enforcement officials, including but not limited to the Attorney General or the State's Attorney for the county in which the contract is to be performed.

(c) A violation of subsection (a) is a Class 3 felony. A violation of subsection (b) is a Class 4 felony.

(d) Any unit of State or local government may, in a civil action, recover a civil penalty from any person who knowingly engages in conduct which violates paragraph (3) of subsection (a) of this Section in twice the amount of each kickback involved in the violation. This subsection (d) shall in no way limit the ability of any unit of State or local government to recover monies or damages regarding public contracts under any other law or ordinance. A civil action shall be barred unless the action is commenced within 6 years after the later of (1) the date on which the conduct establishing the cause of action occurred or (2) the date on which the unit of State or local government knew or should have known that the conduct establishing the cause of action occurred.

(Source: P.A. 85-1295.) [Formerly Ill. Rev. Stat. 38 §33E-7.]

5/33E-8. Bribery of inspector employed by contractor.

§33E-8. Bribery of inspector employed by contractor. (a) A person commits bribery of an inspector when he offers to any person employed by a contractor or subcontractor on any public project contracted for by any unit of State or local government any property or other thing of value with the intent that such offer is for the purpose of obtaining wrongful certification or approval of the quality or completion of any goods or services supplied or performed in the course of work on such project. Violation of this subsection is a Class 4 felony.

(b) Any person employed by a contractor or subcontractor on any public project contracted for by any unit of State or local government who accepts any property or other thing of value knowing that such was intentionally offered for the purpose of influencing the certification or approval of the quality or completion of any goods or services supplied or performed under subcontract to that contractor, and either before or afterwards issues such wrongful certification, commits a Class 3 felony. Failure to report such offer to law enforcement officials, including but not limited to the Attorney General or the State's Attorney for the county in which the contract is performed, constitutes a Class 4 felony.

(Source: P.A. 85-1295.) [Formerly Ill. Rev. Stat. 38 §33E-8.]

5/33E-9. Change orders.

§33E-9. Change orders. Any change order authorized under this Section shall be made in writing. Any person employed by and authorized by any unit of State or local government to approve a change order to any public contract who knowingly grants that approval without first obtaining from the unit of State or local government on whose behalf the contract was signed, or from a designee authorized by that unit of State or local government, a determination in writing that (1) the circumstances said to necessitate the change in performance were not reasonably foreseeable at the time the contract was signed, or (2) the change is germane to the original contract as signed, or (3) the change order is in the best interest of the unit of State or local government and authorized by law, commits a Class 4 felony. The written determination and the written change order resulting from that determination shall be preserved in the contract's file which shall be open to the public for inspection. This Section shall only apply to a change order or series of change orders which authorize or necessitate an increase or decrease in either the cost of a public contract by a total of $10,000 or more or the time of completion by a total of 30 days or more.

(Source: P.A. 86-150; 87-618.) [Formerly Ill. Rev. Stat. 38 §33E-9.]

5/33E-10. Rules of evidence.

§33E-10. Rules of evidence. (a) The certified bid is prima facie evidence of the bid.

(b) It shall be presumed that in the absence of practices proscribed by this Article 33E, all persons who submit bids in response to an invitation to bid by any unit of State or local government submit their bids independent of all other bidders, without information obtained from the governmental entity outside the invitation to bid, and in a good faith effort to obtain the contract.

(Source: P.A. 85-1295.) [Formerly Ill. Rev. Stat. 38 §33E-10.]

5/33E-11. Certification.

§33E-11. (a) Every bid submitted to and public contract executed pursuant to such bid by the State or a unit of local government shall contain a certification by the prime contractor that the prime contractor is not barred from contracting with any unit of State or local government as a result of a violation of either Section 33E-3 or 33E-4 of this Article. The State and units of local government shall provide the appropriate forms for such certification.

(b) A contractor who makes a false statement, material to the certification, commits a Class 3 felony.
(Source: P.A. 86-150.) [Formerly Ill. Rev. Stat. 38 §33E-11.]

5/33E-12. Exemptions of government officials.

§33E-12. It shall not constitute a violation of any provisions of this Article for any person who is an official of or employed by a unit of State or local government to (1) disclose the name of any person who has submitted a bid in response to or requested plans or specifications regarding an invitation to bid or who has been awarded a public contract to any person or, (2) to convey information concerning acceptable alternatives or substitute to plans or specifications if such information is also made generally available to the public and mailed to any person who has submitted a bid in response to or requested plans or specifications regarding an invitation to bid on a public contract or, (3) to negotiate with the lowest responsible bidder a reduction in only the price term of the bid.
(Source: P.A. 86-150.) [Formerly Ill. Rev. Stat. 38 §33E-12.]

5/33E-13. Local Government Professional Services Selection Act unaffected.

§33E-13. Contract negotiations under the Local Government Professional Services Selection Act [50 ILCS 510/0.01 et seq.] shall not be subject to the provisions of this Article.
(Source: P.A. 87-855.) [Formerly Ill. Rev. Stat. 38 §33E-13.]

ARTICLE 33F. UNLAWFUL USE OF BODY ARMOR

Sec.

5/33F-1. Definitions.

§33F-1. Definitions. For purposes of this Article:

(a) "Body Armor" means any one of the following:

(1) A military style flak or tactical assault vest which is made of Kevlar or any other similar material or metal, fiberglass, plastic, and nylon plates and designed to be worn over one's clothing for the intended purpose of stopping not only missile fragmentation from mines, grenades, mortar shells and artillery fire but also fire from rifles, machine guns, and small arms.

(2) Soft body armor which is made of Kevlar or any other similar material or metal or any other type of insert and which is lightweight and pliable and which can be easily concealed under a shirt.

(3) A military style recon/surveillance vest which is made of Kevlar or any other similar material and which is lightweight and designed to be worn over one's clothing.

(4) Protective casual clothing which is made of Kevlar or any other similar material and which was originally intended to be used by undercover law enforcement officers or dignitaries and is designed to look like jackets, coats, raincoats, quilted or three piece suit vests.

(b) "Dangerous weapon" means a Category I or Category II weapon as defined in Section 33A-1 of this Code.
(Source: P.A. 87-521.) [Formerly Ill. Rev. Stat. 38 §33F-1.]

5/33F-2. Unlawful use of body armor.

§33F-2. Unlawful use of body armor. A person commits the offense of unlawful use of body armor when he knowingly wears body armor and is in

possession of a dangerous weapon in the commission or attempted commission of any offense.
(Source: P.A. 87-521.) [Formerly Ill. Rev. Stat. 38 §33F-2.]

5/33F-3. Sentence.

§33F-3. Sentence. A person convicted of unlawful use of body armor for a first offense shall be guilty of a Class A misdemeanor and for a second or subsequent offense shall be guilty of a Class 4 felony.
(Source: P.A. 87-521.) [Formerly Ill. Rev. Stat. 38 §33F-3.]

TITLE IV. CONSTRUCTION, EFFECTIVE DATE AND REPEAL

ARTICLE 34. CONSTRUCTION AND EFFECTIVE DATE

5/34-1. Effect of headings.

§34-1. Effect of headings. Section Article and Title headings contained herein shall not be deemed to govern, limit, modify or in any manner affect the scope, meaning or intent of the provisions of any Section, Article or Title hereof.
(Source: Laws 1961, p. 1983.) [Formerly Ill. Rev. Stat. 38 §34-1.]

5/34-2. Partial invalidity.

§34-2. Partial invalidity. The invalidity of any provision of this Code shall not affect the validity of the remainder of this Code.
(Source: Laws 1961, p. 1983.) [Formerly Ill. Rev. Stat. 38 §34-2.]

5/34-3. Savings provisions; continuation of prior Statutes.

§34-3. Savings provisions; continuation of prior Statutes. The provisions of Sections 2, 3 and 4 of "An Act to revise the law in relation to the construction of the Statutes", approved March 5, 1874, as amended, shall apply in all constructions of this Code.
(Source: Laws 1961, p. 1983.) [Formerly Ill. Rev. Stat. 38 §34-3.]

5/34-4. Effective date.

§34-4. Effective date. This Code shall take effect January 1, 1962.
(Source: Laws 1961, p. 1983.) [Formerly Ill. Rev. Stat. 38 §34-4.]

TITLE V. ADDED ARTICLES

ARTICLE 36. SEIZURE AND FORFEITURE OF VESSELS, VEHICLES AND AIRCRAFT

5/36-1. Seizure.

§36-1. Seizure. Any vessel, vehicle or aircraft used with the knowledge and consent of the owner in the commission of, or in the attempt to commit as defined in Section 8-4 of this Code, an offense prohibited by (a) Section 9-1, 10-2, 11-6, 11-15.1, 11-19.1, 11-19.2, 11-20.1, 12-13, 12-14, 18-2, 19-1, 19-2, 19-3, 20-1, 20-2,

24-1.2 or 28-1 of this Code, or paragraph (a) of Section 12-15 or paragraphs (a), (c) or (d) of Section 12-16 of this Code; (b) Section 21, 22, 23, 24 or 26 of the Cigarette Tax Act [35 ILCS 130/21, 130/22, 130/23, 130/24 or 130/26] if the vessel, vehicle or aircraft contains more than 10 cartons of such cigarettes; (c) Section 28, 29 or 30 of the Cigarette Use Tax Act [35 ILCS 135/28, 135/29 or 135/30] if the vessel, vehicle or aircraft contains more than 10 cartons of such cigarettes; or (d) Section 44 of the Environmental Protection Act [415 ILCS 5/44]; may be seized and delivered forthwith to the sheriff of the county of seizure. Within 15 days after such delivery the sheriff shall give notice of seizure to each person according to the following method: Upon each such person whose right, title or interest is of record in the office of the Secretary of State, the Secretary of Transportation, the Administrator of the Federal Aviation Agency, or any other Department of this State, or any other state of the United States if such vessel, vehicle or aircraft is required to be so registered, as the case may be, by mailing a copy of the notice by certified mail to the address as given upon the records of the Secretary of State, the Department of Aeronautics, Department of Public Works and Buildings or any other Department of this State or the United States if such vessel, vehicle or aircraft is required to be so registered. Within that 15 day period the sheriff shall also notify the State's Attorney of the county of seizure about the seizure. In addition, any mobile or portable equipment used in the commission of an act which is in violation of Section 7g of the Metropolitan Water Reclamation District Act [70 ILCS 2605/1 et seq.] shall be subject to seizure and forfeiture under the same procedures provided in this Article for the seizure and forfeiture of vessels, vehicles and aircraft, and any such equipment shall be deemed a vessel, vehicle or aircraft for purposes of this Article. When a person discharges a firearm at another individual from a vehicle with the knowledge and consent of the owner of the vehicle and with the intent to cause death or great bodily harm to that individual and as a result causes death or great bodily harm to that individual, the vehicle shall be subject to seizure and forfeiture under the same procedures provided in this Article for the seizure and forfeiture of vehicles used in violations of clauses (a), (b), (c), (d), (e) or (f) of this Section.
(Source: P.A. 86-1372; 86-1382; 86-1393; 86-1475.) [Formerly Ill. Rev. Stat. 38 §36-1.]

5/36-1a. Rights of lienholders and secured parties.

§36-1a. Rights of lienholders and secured parties. The State's Attorney shall promptly release a vessel, vehicle or aircraft seized under the provisions of this Article to any lienholder or secured party whose right, title or interest is of record as described in Section 36-1 if such lienholder or secured party shows to the State's Attorney that his lien or secured interest is bona fide and was created without actual knowledge that such vessel, vehicle or aircraft was used or to be used in the commission of the offense charged.
(Source: Laws 1965, p. 2868.) [Formerly Ill. Rev. Stat. 38 §36-1a.]

5/36-2. Action for forfeiture.

§36-2. Action for forfeiture. (a) The State's Attorney in the county in which such seizure occurs if he finds that such forfeiture was incurred without willful negligence or without any intention on the part of the owner of the vessel, vehicle or aircraft or any person whose right, title or interest is of record as described in Section 36-1, to violate the law, or finds the existence of such mitigating circumstances as to justify remission of the forfeiture, may cause the sheriff to remit the same upon such terms and conditions as the State's Attorney deems reasonable and just. The State's Attorney shall exercise his discretion under the foregoing provision of this Section 36-2(a) promptly after notice is given in accordance with Section 36-1. If the State's Attorney does not cause the forfeiture to be remitted he shall forthwith bring an action for forfeiture in the Circuit Court within whose jurisdiction the seizure and confiscation has taken place. The State's Attorney shall give notice of the forfeiture proceeding by mailing a copy of the Complaint in the forfeiture proceeding to the persons, and upon the manner, set forth in Section 36-1. The owner of the seized vessel, vehicle or aircraft or any person whose right, title, or interest is of record as described in Section 36-1, may within 20 days after the mailing of such notice file a verified answer to the Complaint and may appear at the hearing on the action for forfeiture. The State shall show at such hearing by a preponderance of the evidence, that such vessel, vehicle or aircraft was used in the commission of an offense described in Section 36-1. The owner of such vessel, vehicle or aircraft or any person whose right, title, or interest is of record as described in Section 36-1, may show by a preponderance of the evidence that he did not know, and did not have reason to know, that the vessel, vehicle or aircraft was to be used in the commission of such an offense or that any of the exceptions set forth in Section 36-3 are applicable. Unless the State shall make such showing, the Court shall order such vessel, vehicle or aircraft released to the owner. Where the State has made such showing, the Court may order the vessel, vehicle or aircraft destroyed; may order it delivered to any local, municipal or county law enforcement agency, or the Department of State Police or the Department of Revenue of the State of Illinois; or may order it sold at public auction.

(b) A copy of the order shall be filed with the sheriff of the county in which the seizure occurs and with each Federal or State office or agency with which such vessel, vehicle or aircraft is required to be registered. Such order, when filed, constitutes authority for the issuance of clear title to such vehicle, aircraft, or boat to the department or agency to whom it is delivered or any purchaser thereof. The sheriff shall comply promptly with instructions to remit received from the State's Attorney or Attorney General in accordance with Sections 36-2(a) or 36-3.

(c) The proceeds of any sale at public auction pursuant to Section 36-2 of this Act, after payment of all liens and deduction of the reasonable charges and expenses incurred by the sheriff in storing and selling such vehicle, shall be paid into the general fund of the county of seizure.

(Source: P.A. 84-25.) [Formerly Ill. Rev. Stat. 38 §36-2.]

5/36-3. Exceptions to forfeiture.

§36-3. Exceptions to forfeiture. (a) No vessel, vehicle, or aircraft used by any person as a common carrier in the transaction of business as such common carrier may be forfeited under the provisions of Section 36-2 unless it appears that (1) in the case of a railway car or engine, the owner, or (2) in the case of any other such vessel, vehicle or aircraft, the owner or the master of such vessel or the owner or conductor, driver, pilot, or other person in charge of such vehicle or aircraft was at the time of the alleged illegal act a consenting party or privy thereto.

(b) No vessel, vehicle, or aircraft shall be forfeited under the provisions of Section 36-2 by reason of any act or omission established by the owner thereof to have been committed or omitted by any person other than such owner while such vessel, vehicle, or aircraft was unlawfully in the possession of a person who acquired possession thereof in violation of the criminal laws of the United States, or of any state.

(Source: Laws 1965, p. 2868.) [Formerly Ill. Rev. Stat. 38 §36-3.]

5/36-4. Remission by Attorney General.

§36-4. Remission by Attorney General. Whenever any owner of, or other person interested in, a vessel, vehicle, or aircraft seized under the provisions of this Act files with the Attorney General before the sale or destruction of such vessel, vehicle, or aircraft, a petition for the remission of such forfeiture the

Attorney General if he finds that such forfeiture was incurred without willful negligence or without any intention on the part of the owner or any person whose right, title or interest is of record as described in Section 36-1, to violate the law, or finds the existence of such mitigating circumstances as to justify the remission of forfeiture, may cause the same to be remitted upon such terms and conditions as he deems reasonable and just, or order discontinuance of any forfeiture proceeding relating thereto.
(Source: Laws 1965, p. 2868.) [Formerly Ill. Rev. Stat. 38 §36-4.]

ARTICLE 37. PROPERTY FORFEITURE

Sec.

5/37-1. Maintaining public nuisance.

§37-1. Maintaining Public Nuisance. Any building used in the commission of offenses prohibited by Sections 9-1, 10-1, 10-2, 11-14, 11-15, 11-16, 11-17, 11-20, 11-20.1, 11-21, 11-22, 12-5.1, 16-1, 20-2, 23-1, 23-1(a)(1), 24-1(a)(7), 24-3, 28-1, 28-3, 31-5 or 39A-1 of the "Criminal Code of 1961", approved July 28, 1961, as heretofore and hereafter amended [720 ILCS 5/9-1, 5/10-1, 5/10-2, 5/11-14, 5/11-15, 5/11-16, 5/11-17, 5/11-20, 5/11-20.1, 5/11-21, 5/11-22, 5/12-5.1, 5/16-1, 5/20-2, repealed, 5/24-1, 5/24-3, 5/28-1, 5/28-3, 5/31-5 or repealed], or prohibited by the "Illinois Controlled Substances Act" [720 ILCS 570/100 et seq.], or the "Cannabis Control Act" enacted by the 77th General Assembly, as heretofore and hereafter amended [720 ILCS 550/1 et seq.], or used in the commission of an inchoate offense relative to any of the aforesaid principal offenses is a public nuisance.

(b)* Sentence. A person convicted of knowingly maintaining such a public nuisance commits a Class A misdemeanor. Each subsequent offense under this Section is a Class 4 felony.

**So in original. No subsec. (a) has been designated.*

(Source: P.A. 85-384.) [Formerly Ill. Rev. Stat. 38 §37-1.]

5/37-2. Enforcement of lien upon public nuisance.

§37-2. Enforcement of lien upon public nuisance. Any building, used in the commission of an offense specified in Section 37-1 of this Act with the intentional, knowing, reckless or negligent permission of the owner thereof, or the agent of the owner managing the building, shall, together with the underlying real estate, all fixtures and other property used to commit such an offense, be subject to a lien and may be sold to pay any unsatisfied judgment that may be recovered and any unsatisfied fine that may be levied under any Section of this Article and to pay to any person not maintaining the nuisance his damages as a consequence of the nuisance; provided, that the lien herein created shall not affect the rights of any purchaser, mortgagee, judgment creditor or other lien holder arising prior to the filing of a notice of such lien in the office of the recorder of the county in which the real estate subject to the lien is located, or in the office of the registrar of titles of such county if that real estate is registered under "An Act concerning land titles" approved May 1, 1897, as amended [765 ILCS 35/1 et seq.]; which notice shall definitely describe the real estate and property involved, the nature and extent of the lien claimed, and the facts upon which the same is based. An action to enforce such lien may be commenced in any circuit court by the State's Attorney of the county of the nuisance or by the person suffering damages or both, except that a person seeking to recover

damages must pursue his remedy within 6 months after the damages are sustained or his cause of action becomes thereafter exclusively enforceable by the State's Attorney of the county of the nuisance.
(Source: P.A. 83-358.) [Formerly Ill. Rev. Stat. 38 §37-2.]

5/37-3. Revocation of licenses, permits and certificates.

§37-3. Revocation of licenses, permits and certificates. All licenses, permits or certificates issued by the State of Illinois or any subdivision or political agency thereof authorizing the serving of food or liquor on any premises found to constitute a public nuisance as described in Section 37-1 shall be void and shall be revoked by the issuing authority; and no license, permit or certificate so revoked shall be reissued for such premises for a period of 60 days thereafter; nor shall any person convicted of knowingly maintaining such nuisance be reissued such license, permit or certificate for one year from his conviction. No license, permit or certificate shall be revoked pursuant to this Section without a full hearing conducted by the commission or agency which issued the license.
(Source: Laws 1965, p. 403.) [Formerly Ill. Rev. Stat. 38 §37-3.]

5/37-4. Abatement of nuisance.

§37-4. Abatement of nuisance. The Attorney General of this State or the State's Attorney of the county wherein the nuisance exists may commence an action to abate a public nuisance as described in Section 37-1 of this Act, in the name of the People of the State of Illinois, in the circuit court. Upon being satisfied by affidavits or other sworn evidence that an alleged public nuisance exists, the court may without notice or bond enter a temporary restraining order or preliminary injunction to enjoin any defendant from maintaining such nuisance and may enter an order restraining any defendant from removing or interfering with all property used in connection with the public nuisance. If during the proceedings and hearings upon the merits, which shall be in the manner of "An Act in relation to places used for the purpose of using, keeping or selling controlled substances or cannabis", approved July 5, 1957 [740 ILCS 40/1 et seq.], the existence of the nuisance is established, and it is found that such nuisance was maintained with the intentional, knowing, reckless or negligent permission of the owner or the agent of the owner managing the building, the court shall enter an order restraining all persons from maintaining or permitting such nuisance and from using the building for a period of one year thereafter, except that an owner, lessee or other occupant thereof may use such place if the owner shall give bond with sufficient security or surety approved by the court, in an amount between $1,000 and $5,000 inclusive, payable to the People of the State of Illinois, and including a condition that no offense specified in Section 37-1 of this Act [720 ILCS 5/37-1] shall be committed at, in or upon the property described and a condition that the principal obligor and surety assume responsibility for any fine, costs or damages resulting from such an offense thereafter.
(Source: P.A. 83-342.) [Formerly Ill. Rev. Stat. 38 §37-4.]

5/37-5. Enforcement by private person.

§37-5. Enforcement by private person. A private person may, after 30 days and within 90 days of giving the Attorney General and the State's Attorney of the county of nuisance written notice by certified or registered mail of the fact that a public nuisance as described in Section 37-1 of this Act, commence an action pursuant to Section 37-4 of this Act, provided that the Attorney General or the State's Attorney of the county of nuisance has not already commenced said action.
(Source: Laws 1965, p. 403.) [Formerly Ill. Rev. Stat. 38 §37-5.]

ARTICLE 38. CRIMINALLY OPERATED BUSINESSES

5/38-1. Forfeiture of charter and revocation of certificate.

§38-1. Forfeiture of charter and revocation of certificate. The State's Attorney is authorized to institute civil proceedings in the Circuit Court to forfeit the charter of a corporation organized under the laws of this State or to revoke the certificate authorizing a foreign corporation to conduct business in this State. The Court may order the charter forfeited or the certificate revoked upon finding (a) that a director, officer, employee, agent or stockholder acting in behalf of the corporation has, in conducting the corporation's affairs, purposely engaged in a persistent course of intimidation, coercion, bribery or other such illegal conduct with the intent to compel other persons, firms, or corporations to deal with such corporation, and (b) that for the prevention of future illegal conduct of the same character, the public interest requires the charter of the corporation to be forfeited and the corporation to be dissolved or the certificate to be revoked.
(Source: Laws 1965, p. 1222.) [Formerly Ill. Rev. Stat. 38 §38-1.]

5/38-2. Enjoining operation of a business.

§38-2. Enjoining operation of a business. The State's Attorney is authorized to institute civil proceedings in the Circuit Court to enjoin the operation of any business other than a corporation, including a partnership, joint venture or sole proprietorship. The Court may grant the injunction upon finding that (a) any person in control of any such business, who may be a partner in a partnership, a participant in a joint venture, the owner of a sole proprietorship, an employee or agent of any such business, or a person who, in fact, exercises control over the operations of any such business, has, in conducting its business affairs, purposely engaged in a persistent course of intimidation, coercion, bribery or other such illegal conduct with the intent to compel other persons, firms, or corporations to deal with such business, and (b) that for the prevention of future illegal conduct of the same character, the public interest requires the operation of the business to be enjoined.
(Source: Laws 1965, p. 1222.) [Formerly Ill. Rev. Stat. 38 §38-2.]

5/38-3. Institution and conduct of proceedings.

§38-3. Institution and conduct of proceedings. (a) The proceedings authorized by Section 38-1 may be instituted against a corporation in any county in which it is doing business and the proceedings shall be conducted in accordance with the Civil Practice Law [735 ILCS 5/2-101 et seq.] and all existing and future amendments of that Law and the Supreme Court Rules now or hereafter adopted in relation to that Law. Such proceedings shall be deemed additional to any other proceeding authorized by law for the purpose of forfeiting the charter of a corporation or revoking the certificate of a foreign corporation.

(b) The proceedings authorized by Section 38-2 may be instituted against a business other than a corporation in any county in which it is doing business and the proceedings shall be conducted in accordance with the Civil Practice Law and all existing and future amendments of that Law and the Supreme Court Rules now or hereafter adopted in relation to that Law.

(c) Whenever proceedings are instituted against a corporation or business pursuant to Section 38-1 or 38-2, the State's Attorney shall give written notice of the institution of such proceedings to the corporation or business against which the proceedings are brought.
(Source: P.A. 82-783.) [Formerly Ill. Rev. Stat. 38 §38-3.]

ARTICLE 39. CRIMINAL USURY

5/39-1. Criminal usury.

§39-1. Criminal Usury. (a) Any person commits criminal usury when, in exchange for either a loan of money or other property or forbearance from the collection of such a loan, he knowingly contracts for or receives from an individual, directly or indirectly, interest, discount or other consideration at a rate greater than 20% per annum either before or after the maturity of the loan.

(b) When a person has in his personal or constructive possession records, memoranda, or other documentary record of usurious loans it shall be prima facie evidence that he has violated Subsection 39-1(a) hereof.
(Source: P.A. 76-1879.) [Formerly Ill. Rev. Stat. 38 §39-1.]

5/39-2. Sentence.

§39-2. Sentence. Criminal usury is a Class 4 felony.
(Source: P.A. 77-2638.) [Formerly Ill. Rev. Stat. 38 §39-2.]

5/39-3. Non-application to licensed persons.

§39-3. Non-application to licensed persons. This Article does not apply to any loan authorized to be made by any person licensed under the Consumer Installment Loan Act, approved August 30, 1963, as heretofore or hereafter amended [205 ILCS 670/1 et seq.], or to any loan permitted by Sections 4, 4.2 and 4a of "An Act in relation to the rate of interest and other charges in connection with sales on credit and the lending of money", approved May 24, 1879, as heretofore or hereafter amended [815 ILCS 205/4, 205/4.2 and 205/4a], or by any other law of this State.
(Source: P.A. 84-1004.) [Formerly Ill. Rev. Stat. 38 §39-3.]

ARTICLE 42. LOOTING

5/42-1. Looting by individuals.

§42-1. Looting by individuals. A person commits looting when he knowingly without authority of law or the owner enters any home or dwelling, or upon any premises of another, or enters any commercial, mercantile, business or industrial building, plant or establishment, in which normal security of property is not present by virtue of a hurricane, fire or vis major of any kind or by virtue of a riot, mob, or other human agency and obtains or exerts control over property of the owner.
(Source: Laws 1967, p. 2598.) [Formerly Ill. Rev. Stat. 38 §42-1.]

5/42-2. Sentence.

§42-2. Sentence. Looting is a Class 4 felony. In addition to any other penalty imposed, the Court shall impose a sentence of at least 100 hours of community service as determined by the Court and shall require the defendant to make restituiton to the owner of the property looted pursuant to Section 5-5-6 of the Unified Code of Corrections.
(Chgd. by P.A. 87-1170, §1, eff. 1/1/93.)
(Source: P.A. 77-2638.) [Formerly Ill. Rev. Stat. 38 §42-2.]

ARTICLE 44. TELECOMMUNICATIONS DEVICES

5/44-1. Definitions.

§44-1. As used in this Act, "telecommunications device" or "device" means a device which is portable or which may be installed in a motor vehicle, boat or other means of transportation, and which is capable of receiving or transmitting speech, data, signals or other information, including but not limited to paging devices, cellular and mobile telephones, and radio transceivers, transmitters and receivers, but not including radios designed to receive only standard AM and FM broadcasts.
(Source: P.A. 86-811.) [Formerly Ill. Rev. Stat. 38 §44-1.]

5/44-2. Unlawful transfer to a minor.

§44-2. (a) A person commits unlawful transfer of a telecommunications device to a minor when he gives, sells or otherwise transfers possession of a telecommunications device to a person under 18 years of age with the intent that the device be used to commit any offense under this Code, the Cannabis Control Act [720 ILCS 550/1 et seq.] or the Illinois Controlled Substances Act [720 ILCS 570/100 et seq.].

(b) Unlawful transfer of a telecommunications device to a minor is a Class A misdemeanor.
(Source: P.A. 86-811.) [Formerly Ill. Rev. Stat. 38 §44-2.]

5/44-3. Forfeiture of illegal telecommunications devices.

§44-3. (a) Seizure. Any telecommunications device possessed by a person on the real property of any elementary or secondary school without the authority of the school principal, or used in the commission of an offense prohibited by this Code, the Illinois Controlled Substances Act [720 ILCS 570/100 et seq.] or the Cannabis Control Act [720 ILCS 550/1 et seq.] or which constitutes evidence of the commission of such offenses may be seized and delivered forthwith to the investigating law enforcement agency. A person who is not a student of the particular elementary or secondary school, who is on school property as an invitee of the school, and who has possession of a telecommunication device for lawful and legitimate purposes, shall not need to obtain authority from the school principal to possess the telecommunication device on school property. Such telecommunication device shall not be seized unless it was used in the commission of an offense specified above, or constitutes evidence of such an offense. Within 15 days after such delivery the investigating law enforcement agency shall give notice of seizure to any known owners, lienholders and secured parties of such property. Within that 15 day period the investigating law enforcement agency shall also notify the State's Attorney of the county of seizure about the seizure.

(b) Rights of lienholders and secured parties.

The State's Attorney shall promptly release a telecommunications device seized under the provisions of this Article to any lienholder or secured party if such lienholder or secured party shows to the State's Attorney that his lien or security interest is bona fide and was created without actual knowledge that such telecommunications device was or possessed in violation of this Section or used or to be used in the commission of the offense charged.

(c) Action for forfeiture. (1) The State's Attorney in the county in which such seizure occurs if he finds that such forfeiture was incurred without willful negligence or without any intention on the part of the owner of the telecommunications device or a lienholder or secured party to violate the law, or finds the existence of such mitigating circumstances as to justify remission of the forfeiture, may cause the investigating law enforcement agency to remit the same upon such terms and conditions as the State's Attorney deems reasonable and just. The State's Attorney shall exercise his discretion under the foregoing provision of this Section promptly after notice is given in accordance with subsection (a). If the State's Attorney does not cause the forfeiture to be remitted he shall forthwith bring an action for forfeiture in the circuit court within whose jurisdiction the seizure and confiscation has taken place. The State's Attorney shall give notice of the forfeiture proceeding by mailing a copy of the complaint in the forfeiture proceeding to the persons and in the manner set forth in subsection (a). The owner of the device or any person with any right, title, or interest in the device may within 20 days after the mailing of such notice file a verified answer to the complaint and may appear at the hearing on the action for forfeiture. The State shall show at such hearing by a preponderance of the evidence that the device was used in the commission of an offense described in subsection (a). The owner of the device or any person with any right, title, or interest in the device may show by a preponderance of the evidence that he did not know, and did not have reason to know, that the device was possessed in violation of this Section or to be used in the commission of such an offense or that any of the exceptions set forth in subsection (d) are applicable. Unless the State shall make such showing, the Court shall order the device released to the owner. Where the State has made such showing, the Court may order the device destroyed; may upon the request of the investigating law enforcement agency, order it delivered to any local, municipal or county law enforcement agency, or the Department of State Police or the Department of Revenue of the State of Illinois; or may order it sold at public auction.

(2) A copy of the order shall be filed with the investigating law enforcement agency of the county in which the seizure occurs. Such order, when filed, confers ownership of the device to the department or agency to whom it is delivered or any purchaser thereof. The investigating law enforcement agency shall comply promptly with instructions to remit received from the State's Attorney or Attorney General in accordance with paragraph (1) of this subsection or subsection (d).

(3) The proceeds of any sale at public auction pursuant to this subsection, after payment of all liens and deduction of the reasonable charges and expenses incurred by the investigating law enforcement agency in storing and selling the device, shall be paid into the general fund of the level of government responsible for the operation of the investigating law enforcement agency.

(d) Exceptions to forfeiture. (b) No device shall be forfeited under the provisions of subsection (c) by reason of any act or omission established by the owner thereof to have been committed or omitted by any person other than the owner while the device was unlawfully in the possession of a person who acquired possession thereof in violation of the criminal laws of the United States, or of any state.

(e) Remission by Attorney General. Whenever any owner of, or other person interested in, a device seized under the provisions of this Section files with the Attorney General before the sale or destruction of the device a petition for the remission of such forfeiture the Attorney General if he finds that such forfeiture was incurred without willful negligence or without any intention on the part of the owner or any person with any right, title or interest in the device to violate the law, or finds the existence of such mitigating circumstances as to justify the remission of forfeiture, may cause the same to be remitted upon such terms and conditions as he deems reasonable and just, or order discontinuance of any forfeiture proceeding relating thereto.

(Source: P.A. 86-811.) [Formerly Ill. Rev. Stat. 38 §44-3.]

ARTICLE 45. DISCLOSING LOCATION OF DOMESTIC VIOLENCE VICTIM

(Added by P.A. 87-441, §1, eff. 9/11/91. See other Article 45 below.)

5/45-1. Definitions.

§45-1. Definitions. As used in this Article:

(a) "Domestic violence" means attempting to cause or causing abuse of a family or household member or high-risk adult with disabilities, or attempting to cause or causing neglect or exploitation of a high-risk adult with disabilities which threatens the adult's health and safety.

(b) "Family or household member" means a spouse, person living as a spouse, parent, or other adult person related by consanguinity or affinity, who is residing or has resided with the person committing domestic violence. "Family or household member" includes a high-risk adult with disabilities who resides with or receives care from any person who has the responsibility for a high-risk adult as a result of a family relationship or who has assumed responsibility for all or a portion of the care of an adult with disabilities voluntarily, by express or implied contract, or by court order.

(c) "High-risk adult with disabilities" means a person aged 18 or over whose physical or mental disability impairs his or her ability to seek or obtain protection from abuse, neglect, or exploitation.

(d) "Abuse", "exploitation", and "neglect" have the meanings ascribed to those terms in Section 103 of the Illinois Domestic Violence Act of 1986 [750 ILCS 60/103].

(Source: P.A. 87-441.) [Formerly Ill. Rev. Stat. 38 §45-1.]

(See other 720 ILCS 5/45-1 in other Article 45 below.)

5/45-2. Disclosure of location of domestic violence victim.

§45-2. Disclosure of location of domestic violence victim. Any person who publishes, disseminates or otherwise discloses the location of any domestic violence victim, without the authorization of that domestic violence victim, knowing that such disclosure will result in, or has the substantial likelihood of resulting in, the threat of bodily harm, is guilty of a Class A misdemeanor. Nothing in this Section shall apply to confidential communications between an attorney and his or her client.

(Source: P.A. 87-441.) [Formerly Ill. Rev. Stat. 38 §45-2.]

(See other 720 ILCS 5/45-2 in other Article 45 below.)

ARTICLE 45. INSURANCE FRAUD AND RELATED OFFENSES

(Added by P.A. 87-1134, §1, eff. 1/1/93. See other Article 45 above.)

5/45-1. Insurance fraud.

§45.1. Insurance fraud. (a) A person who knowingly obtains, attempts to obtain, or causes to be obtained, by deception, control over the property of an insurance company by the making of a false claim on any policy of insurance issued by an insurance company, intending to deprive an insurance company permanently of the use and benefit of that property, commits insurance fraud.

(b) Sentence.

(1) A violation of this Section in which the value of the property obtained or attempted to be obtained is $300 or less is a Class A misdemeanor.

(2) A violation of the Section in which the value of the property obtained or attempted to be obtained is more than $300 but not more than $10,000 is a Class 3 felony.

(3) A violation of this Section in which the value of the property obtained or attempted to be obtained is more than $10,000 but not more than $100,000 is a Class 2 felony.

(4) A violation of this Section in which the value of the property obtained or attempted to be obtained is more than $100,000 is a Class 1 felony.

(c) For the purposes of this Section, where the exact value of property obtained or attempted to be obtained is either not alleged by the accused or not specifically set by the terms of the policy of insurance, the value of the property shall be the fair market replacement value of the property claimed to be lost, the reasonable costs of reimbursing a vendor or other claimant for services to be rendered, or both.

(Added by P.A. 87-1134, §1, eff. 1/1/93.) [Formerly Ill. Rev. Stat. 38 §45-1.]

(See other 720 ILCS 5/45-1 in other Article 45 above.)

5/45-2. Aggravated insurance fraud.

§45-2. Aggravated insurance fraud. (a) A person commits the offense of aggravated insurance fraud when he, within an 18 month period, obtains, attempts to obtain, or causes to be obtained, by deception, control over the property of an insurance company or insurance companies by the making of 3 or more false claims allegedly arising out of separate incidents or transactions on any policy or policies issued by an insurance company or insurance companies intending to deprive an insurance company or insurance companies permanently of the use and benefit of that property.

(b) Sentence. A violation of this Section is a Class 1 felony, regardless of the value of the property obtained, attempted to be obtained, or caused to be obtained.

(Added by P.A. 87-1134, §1, eff. 1/1/93.) [Formerly Ill. Rev. Stat. 38 §45-2.]

(See other 720 ILCS 5/45-2 in other Article 45 above.)

5/45-3. Insurance fraud conspiracy.

§45-3. Insurance fraud conspiracy. (a) A person commits insurance fraud conspiracy when, with the intent that a violation of Section 45-1 or 45-2 of this Code be committed, he agrees with another to violate either Section 45-1 or 45-2. No person may be convicted of insurance fraud conspiracy unless an overt act or acts in furtherance of the agreement is alleged and proved to have been committed by him or by a co-conspirator and the accused is a part of a common scheme or plan to engage in the unlawful activity. Where the offense intended to be committed is a violation of Section 45-2, the person or persons with whom the accused is alleged to have agreed to commit the 3 or more violations of Section 45-1 need not be the same person or persons for each violation, as long as the accused was a part of the common scheme or plan to engage in each of the 3 or more alleged violations.

(b) It is not a defense to insurance fraud conspiracy that the person or persons with whom the accused is alleged to have conspired:

(1) have not been prosecuted or convicted;

(2) have been convicted of a different offense;

(3) are not amenable to justice;

(4) have been acquitted; or

(5) lacked the capacity to commit an offense.

(c) Notwithstanding Section 8-5 of this Code, a person may be convicted and sentenced both for the offense of insurance fraud conspiracy and for any other offense that is the object of the conspiracy.

(d) Insurance fraud conspiracy involving a violation of Section 45-1 of this Code is a Class 2 felony. Insurance fraud conspiracy involving a violation of Section 45-2 of this Code is a Class 1 felony.

(Added by P.A. 87-1134, §1, eff. 1/1/93.)
[Formerly Ill. Rev. Stat. 38 §45-3.]

5/45-4. Organizer of an aggravated insurance fraud conspiracy.

§45-4. Organizer of an aggravated insurance fraud conspiracy. (a) A person commits organizer of an aggravated insurance fraud conspiracy when he:

(1) with the intent that a violation of Section 45-2 of this Code be committed, agrees with another to the commission of that offense; and

(2) with respect to other persons within the conspiracy, occupies a position of organizer, supervisor, financer, or other position of management.

No person may be convicted of organizer of an aggravated insurance fraud conspiracy unless an overt act or acts in furtherance of the agreement is alleged and proved to have been committed by him or by a co-conspirator and the accused is part of a common scheme or plan to engage in the unlawful activity. For the purposes of this Section, the person or persons with whom the accused is alleged to have agreed to commit the 3 or more violations of Section 45-1 of this Code need not be the same person or persons for each violation, as long as the accused occupied a position of organizer, supervisor, financer, or other position of management in each of the 3 or more alleged violations.

(b) It is not a defense to organizer of an aggravated insurance fraud conspiracy that the person or persons with whom the accused is alleged to have conspired:

(1) have not been prosecuted or convicted;
(2) have been convicted of a different offense;
(3) are not amenable to justice;
(4) have been acquitted; or
(5) lacked the capacity to commit an offense.

(c) Notwithstanding Section 8-5 of this Code, a person may be convicted and sentenced both for the offense of organizer of an aggravated insurance fraud conspiracy and for any other offense that is the object of the conspiracy.

(d) Organizer of an aggravated insurance fraud conspiracy is a Class 1 felony.

(Added by P.A. 87-1134, §1, eff. 1/1/93.)
[Formerly Ill. Rev. Stat. 38 §45-4.]

5/45-5. Civil damages for insurance fraud.

§45-5. Civil damages for insurance fraud. (a) A person who knowingly obtains, attempts to obtain, or causes to be obtained, by deception, control over the property of any insurance company by the making of a false claim on a policy of insurance issued by an insurance company, intending to deprive an insurance company permanently of the use and benefit of that property, shall be civilly liable to the insurance company that paid the claim or against whom the claim was made or to the subrogee of that insurance company in an amount equal to 3 times the value of the property wrongfully obtained or twice the value of the property attempted to be obtained, plus reasonable attorneys fees.

(b) An insurance company that brings an action against a person undr subsection (a) of this Section in bad faith shall be liable to that person for twice the value of the property claimed, plus reasonable attorneys* fees. In determining whether an insurance company acted in bad faith, the court shall relax the rules of evidence to allow for the introduction of any facts or other information on which the insurance company may have relied in bringing an action under subsection (a) of this Section.

**So in original. Probably should be "attorney's".*

(c) For the purposes of this Section, where the exact value of the property attempted to be obtained is either not alleged by the claimant or not specifically set by the terms of the policy of insurance, the value of the property shall be the fair market replacement value of the property claimed to be lost, the reasonable costs of reimbursing a vendor or other claimant for services to be rendered, or both.
(Added by P.A. 87-1134, §1, eff. 1/1/93.)
[Formerly Ill. Rev. Stat. 38 §45-5.]

OFFENSES AGAINST PERSONS

ABANDONED CHILDREN PREVENTION ACT

105/0.01. Short title.

§0.01. Short title. This Act may be cited as the Abandoned Children Prevention Act.
(Source: P.A. 86-1324.) [Formerly Ill. Rev. Stat. 23 §2358-90.]

105/1. Child abandonment.

§1. When any child under the age of fourteen years shall be abandoned by its father, mother, guardian, or by any person having legal control or custody thereof, such person or persons shall be deemed guilty of a Class 4 felony. The abandonment of a child under the age of 14 years by its father or mother, or by both such parents, shall constitute a felony and be punished as herein provided notwithstanding that any other person or persons may have legal control or custody or be in a position of loco parentis to the child as a result of such abandonment. Where more than one child has been abandoned, the abandonment of each such child shall constitute a separate offense hereunder.
(Source: P.A. 77-2349.) [Formerly Ill. Rev. Stat. 23 §2359.]

COMMUNICATIONS CONSUMER PRIVACY ACT

110/1. Short title.

§1. This Act may be cited as the Communications Consumer Privacy Act.
(Source: P.A. 86-1475.) [Formerly Ill. Rev. Stat. 38 §87-1.]

110/2. Definitions.

§2. For purposes of this Act, "Communications Company" means any person or organization which owns, controls, operates or manages any company which provides information or entertainment electronically to a household, including but not limited to a cable or community antenna television system.
(Source: P.A. 82-526.) [Formerly Ill. Rev. Stat. 38 §87-2.]

110/3. Unlawful practices; penalty.

§3. (a) It shall be unlawful for a communications company to: (1) install and use any equipment which would allow a communications company to visually observe or listen to what is occurring in an individual subscriber's household without the knowledge or permission of the subscriber; (2) provide any person or public or private organization with a list containing the name of a subscriber, unless the communications company gives notice thereof to the subscriber; (3) disclose the television viewing habits of any individual subscriber without the subscriber's consent; or (4) install or maintain a home-protection scanning device in a dwelling as part of a communication service without the express written consent of the occupant.

(b) A violation of any provision of this Section shall be a business offense, punishable by a fine not to exceed $10,000 for each violation. Any person who has been injured by a violation of this Section may commence an action in the circuit court for damages against any communications company which has committed a violation. If the court awards damages, the plaintiff shall be awarded costs.

(Source: P.A. 82-526.) [Formerly Ill. Rev. Stat. 38 §87-3.]

CRIMINAL JURISPRUDENCE ACT [CRUELTY TO CHILDREN]

115/53. Cruelty to children and others—Penalty.

§53. Any person who shall wilfully and unnecessarily expose to the inclemency of the weather, or shall in any other manner injure in health or limb, any child, apprentice, or other person under his legal control, shall be guilty of a Class 4 felony.

(Source: P.A. 77-2353.) [Formerly Ill. Rev. Stat. 23 §2368.]

HAZING ACT

120/0.01. Short title.

§0.01. Short title. This Act may be cited as the Hazing Act.

(Source: P.A. 86-1324.) [Formerly Ill. Rev. Stat. 144 §220.9.]

120/1. Penalty.

§1. Whoever shall engage in the practice of hazing in this state, whereby any one sustains an injury to his person therefrom, shall be guilty of a Class B misdemeanor.

(Source: P.A. 77-2456.) [Formerly Ill. Rev. Stat. 144 §221.]

120/2. Hazing, defined.

§2. The term "hazing" in this act shall be construed to mean any pastime or amusement, engaged in by students or other people in schools, academies, colleges, universities, or other educational institutions of this state, or by people connected with any of the public institutions of this state, whereby such pastime or amusement is had for the purpose of holding up any student, scholar or individual to ridicule for the pastime of others.

(Source: Laws 1901, p. 145.) [Formerly Ill. Rev. Stat. 144 §222.]

HUNTER INTERFERENCE PROHIBITION ACT

125/0.01. Short title.

§0.01. Short title. This Act may be cited as the Hunter Interference Prohibition Act.

(Source: P.A. 86-1324.) [Formerly Ill. Rev. Stat. 61 §300.]

125/1. Definitions.

§1. Definitions. As used in this Act:

a. "Wild animal" means any wild creature the taking of which is authorized by the fish and game laws of the State.

b. "Taking", means the capture or killing of a wild animal and includes travel, camping, and other acts preparatory to taking which occur on lands or waters upon which the affected person has the right or privilege to take such wild animal.

(Source: P.A. 83-153.) [Formerly Ill. Rev. Stat. 61 §301.]

125/2. Violations—Class C misdemeanor.

§2. Any person who performs any of the following is guilty of a Class C misdemeanor:

(a) Interferes with the lawful taking of a wild animal by another with intent to prevent the taking.

(b) Disturbs or engages in an activity that will tend to disturb wild animals, with intent to prevent their lawful taking.

(c) disturbs another person who is engaged in the lawful taking of a wild animal or who is engaged in the process of taking, with intent to dissuade or otherwise prevent the taking.

(d) enters or remains upon public lands, or upon private lands without permission of the owner or his agent, with intent to violate this Section.

(Source: P.A. 83-153.) [Formerly Ill. Rev. Stat. 61 §302.]

125/3. Violations—Class B misdemeanor.

§3. Any person who knowingly performs any of the following acts is guilty of a Class B misdemeanor:

(a)* fails to obey the order of a peace officer to desist from conduct in violation of Section 2 of this Act if the officer observes such conduct, or has reasonable grounds to believe that the person has engaged in such conduct that day or that the person plans or intends to engage in such conduct that day on a specific premises.

**So in original. No subsec. (b) has been enacted.*

(Source: P.A. 83-153.) [Formerly Ill. Rev. Stat. 61 §303.]

125/4. Violations—Injunctions—Damages.

§4. (a) Any court may enjoin conduct which would be in violation of Section 2 of this Act upon petition by a person affected or who reasonably may be affected by such conduct, upon a showing that such conduct is threatened or that it has occurred on a particular premises in the past and that it is not unreasonable to expect that under similar circumstances it will be repeated.

(b) A court may award damages to any person adversely affected by a violation of Section 2, which may include an award for punitive damages. In addition to other items of special damage, the measure of damages may include expenditures of the affected person for license and permit fees, travel, guides, special equipment and supplies, to the extent that such expenditures were rendered futile by prevention of the taking of a wild animal.

(Source: P.A. 83-153.) [Formerly Ill. Rev. Stat. 61 §304.]

NEGLECTED CHILDREN OFFENSE ACT

130/0.01. Short title.

§0.01. Short title. This Act may be cited as the Neglected Children Offense Act.
(Source: P.A. 86-1324.) [Formerly Ill. Rev. Stat. 23 §2359.9.]

130/1. Dependent or neglected child defined.

§1. For the purposes of this Act a dependent and neglected child shall mean any child who while under the age of 18 years, for any reason is destitute, homeless or abandoned; or dependent upon the public for support; or has not proper parental care or guardianship; or habitually begs or receives alms; or is found living in any house of ill fame or with any vicious or disreputable person; or has a home which by reason of neglect, cruelty or depravity on the part of its parents, guardian or any other person in whose care it may be is an unfit place for such child; and any child who while under the age of 10 years is found begging, peddling or selling any articles or singing or playing any musical instrument for gain upon the street or giving any public entertainments or accompanies or is used in aid of any person so doing.
(Source: Laws 1955, p. 1411.) [Formerly Ill. Rev. Stat. 23 §2360.]

130/1a. Delinquent child defined.

§1a. For the purposes of this Act a delinquent child is any minor who prior to his 17th birthday has violated or attempted to violate, regardless of where the act occurred, any federal or State law or municipal ordinance.
(Source: P.A. 85-573.) [Formerly Ill. Rev. Stat. 23 §2360a.]

130/2. Contributing to dependency or neglect of child.

§2. Any parent, legal guardian or person having the custody of a child under the age of 18 years, who knowingly or wilfully causes, aids or encourages such person to be or to become a dependent and neglected child as defined in section 1 [720 ILCS 130/1], who knowingly or wilfully does acts which directly tend to render any such child so dependent and neglected, or who knowingly or wilfully fails to do that which will directly tend to prevent such state of dependency and neglect is guilty of the Class A misdemeanor of contributing to the dependency and neglect of children. Instead of imposing the punishment hereinbefore provided, the court may release the defendant from custody on probation for one year upon his or her entering into recognizance with or without surety in such sum as the court directs. The conditions of the recognizance shall be such that if the defendant appears personally in court whenever ordered to do so within the year and provides and cares for such neglected and dependent child in such manner as to prevent a continuance or repetition of such state of dependency and neglect or as otherwise may be directed by the court then the recognizance shall be void, otherwise it shall be of full force and effect. If the court is satisfied by information and due proof under oath that at any time during the year the defendant has violated the terms of such order it may forthwith revoke the order and sentence him or her under the original conviction. Unless so sentenced, the defendant shall at the end of the year be discharged. In case of forfeiture on the recognizance the sum recovered thereon may in the discretion of the court be paid in whole or in part to someone designated by the court for the support of such dependent and neglected child.
(Source: P. A. 77-2350.) [Formerly Ill. Rev. Stat. 23 §2361.]

130/2a. Contributing to delinquency of child.

§2a. Any person who knowingly or wilfully causes, aids or encourages any boy or girl to be or to become a delinquent child, or who knowingly or wilfully does acts which directly tend to render any such child so delinquent is guilty of the Class A misdemeanor of contributing to the delinquency of children. Instead of imposing such punishment the court may release the defendant from custody

on probation for 1 year upon his or her entering into recognizance with or without surety in such sum as the court may direct.
(Source: P. A. 77-2350.) [Formerly Ill. Rev. Stat. 23 §2361a.]

130/3. Husband or wife competent witness.
§3. The husband or wife of the defendant shall be a competent witness to testify in any case brought under this Act and to any and all matters relevant thereto.
(Source: Laws 1915, p. 368.) [Formerly Ill. Rev. Stat. 23 §2362.]

OBSCENE PHONE CALL ACT

135/0.01. Short title.
§0.01. Short title. This Act may be cited as the Obscene Phone Call Act.
(Source: P.A. 86-1324.) [Formerly Ill. Rev. Stat. 134 §16.3h.]

135/1. Obscene messages.
§1. Any person in this State who sends messages or uses language or terms which are obscene, lewd or immoral with the intent to offend by means of or while using a telephone or telegraph facilities, equipment or wires of any person, firm or corporation engaged in the transmission of news or messages between states or within the State of Illinois is guilty of a Class B misdemeanor. The use of language or terms which are obscene, lewd or immoral is prima facie evidence of the intent to offend.
(Source: P.A. 77-2620.) [Formerly Ill. Rev. Stat. 134 §16.4.]

135/1-1. Harassment by telephone.
§1-1. Harassment by telephone. Harassment by telephone is use of telephone communication for any of the following purposes:
(1) Making any comment, request, suggestion or proposal which is obscene, lewd, lascivious, filthy or indecent with an intent to offend; or
(2) Making a telephone call, whether or not conversation ensues, with intent to abuse, threaten or harass any person at the called number; or
(3) Making or causing the telephone of another repeatedly to ring, with intent to harass any person at the called number; or
(4) Making repeated telephone calls, during which conversation ensues, solely to harass any person at the called number; or
(5) Knowingly permitting any telephone under one's control to be used for any of the purposes mentioned herein.
Every telephone directory published for distribution to members of the general public shall contain a notice setting forth a summary of the provisions of this Section. Such notice shall be printed in type which is no smaller than any other type on the same page and shall be preceded by the word "WARNING". All telephone companies in this State shall cooperate with law enforcement agencies in using their facilities and personnel to detect and prevent violations of this Act.
(Source: P.A. 80-795.) [Formerly Ill. Rev. Stat. 134 §16.4-1.]

135/2. Sentence.
§2. Sentence. Any person who violates any of the provisions of Sections 1 or 1-1 of this Act shall, upon conviction, be guilty of a Class B misdemeanor.
(Source: P.A. 80-795.) [Formerly Ill. Rev. Stat. 134 §16.5.]

TAXPREPARER DISCLOSURE OF INFORMATION ACT

140/0.01. Short title.

§0.01. Short title. This Act may be cited as the Taxpreparer Disclosure of Information Act.
(Source: P.A. 86-1324.) [Formerly Ill. Rev. Stat. 38 §65-10.]

140/1. Disclosure of information.

§1. It is a Class A misdemeanor for any person, including an individual, firm, corporation, association, partnership, joint venture, or any employee or agent thereof, to disclose, or to convey a list of names prepared on the basis of any information obtained in the business of preparing federal or state income tax returns or assisting taxpayers in preparing such returns, including the disclosure or conveyance of such information between separate departments of the same firm, corporation, association, partnership, or joint venture, unless such disclosure or conveyance is within any of the following:

(a) Consented to in writing by the taxpayer in a separate document.
(b) Expressly authorized by state or federal law.
(c) Necessary to the preparation of the return.
(d) Pursuant to court order.

(Source: P.A. 77-2830.) [Formerly Ill. Rev. Stat. 38 §65-11.]

140/2. Preparing income tax returns.

§2. For the purposes of this Act, a person is engaged in the business of preparing federal or state income tax returns or assisting taxpayers in preparing such returns if he does either of the following:

(a) Advertises, or gives publicity to the effect that he prepares or assists others in the preparation of federal income tax returns.

(b) Prepares or assists others in the preparation of state or federal income tax returns for compensation.

(Source: P.A. 77-33.) [Formerly Ill. Rev. Stat. 38 §65-12.]

140/3. Written consent of taxpayer.

§3. Contacting a taxpayer to obtain his written consent to disclosure does not constitute a violation of this Act.
(Source: P.A. 77-33.) [Formerly Ill. Rev. Stat. 38 §65-13.]

TELECOMMUNICATION LINE TAPPING ACT

145/0.01. Short title.

§0.01. Short title. This Act may be cited as the Telecommunication Line Tapping Act.
(Source: P.A. 86-1324.) [Formerly Ill. Rev. Stat. 134 §15m.]

145/1. Wrongful tapping; penalty.

§1. Any person who shall within this state wrongfully tap or connect a wire with the telegraph or telephone wires of any person, company or association engaged in the transmission of news or telegraph or telephone lines between the states or in this state for the purpose of wrongfully taking or making use of

the news dispatches of such person, company or association, or of its customers, shall be deemed guilty of a Class A misdemeanor.
(Source: P.A. 77-2617.) [Formerly Ill. Rev. Stat. 134 §16.]

WRONGS TO CHILDREN ACT

150/0.01. Short title.

§0.01. Short title. This Act may be cited as the Wrongs to Children Act.
(Source: P.A. 86-1324.) [Formerly Ill. Rev. Stat. 23 §2350.]

150/1. Unlawful employment.

§1. It shall be unlawful for any person having the care, custody or control of any child under the age of fourteen years, to exhibit, use or employ, or in any manner, or under any pretense, sell, apprentice, give away, let out, or otherwise dispose of any such child to any person in or for the vocation or occupation, service or purpose of singing, playing on musical instruments, rope or wire walking, dancing, begging, or peddling, or as a gymnast, contortionist, rider or acrobat in any place whatsoever, or for any obscene, indecent or immoral purpose, exhibition or practice whatsoever, or for, or in any business, exhibition or vocation injurious to the health or dangerous to the life or limb of such child, or cause, procure or encourage any such child to engage therein. Nothing in this section contained shall apply to or affect the employment or use of any such child as a singer or musician in any church, school or academy (or at any respectable entertainment), or the teaching or learning the science or practice of music.
(Source: Laws 1877, p. 90.) [Formerly Ill. Rev. Stat. 23 §2351.]

150/2. Unlawful to exhibit.

§2. It shall also be unlawful for any person to take, receive, hire, employ, use, exhibit, or have in custody any child under the age and for the purposes prohibited in the first section of this act.
(Source: Laws 1877, p. 90.) [Formerly Ill. Rev. Stat. 23 §2352.]

150/3. Order as to custody.

§3. When upon examination before any court it appears that any child within the age previously mentioned in this Act was engaged or used for or in any business, exhibition, vocation, or purpose prohibited in this Act; and when upon the conviction of any person of a criminal assault upon a child in his custody, the court before whom such conviction is had, shall deem it desirable for the welfare of such child, that the person so convicted should be deprived of its custody; thereafter such child shall be deemed to be in the custody of court, and such court may in its discretion, make such order as to the custody thereof as now is, or hereafter may be, provided by law in cases of vagrant, truant, disorderly, pauper, or destitute children.
(Source: P.A. 77-1274.) [Formerly Ill. Rev. Stat. 23 §2353.]

150/3.1. Required employment of single parent.

§3.1. No agency of the State or unit of local government shall require a single parent or other person having the care, custody or control of any child under the age of 6 to accept employment that would unreasonably interfere with such responsibilities to the child. It is unlawful for any person acting under color of law to require or to attempt to require such employment of a parent or other person having the care, custody or control of such a child.
(Source: P.A. 80-860.) [Formerly Ill. Rev. Stat. 23 §2353.1.]

150/4. Endangered life or health.

§4. It shall be unlawful for any person having the care or custody of any child, wilfully to cause or permit the life of such child to be endangered, or the health of such child to be injured, or wilfully cause or permit such child to be placed in such a situation that its life or health may be endangered.
(Source: Laws 1877, p. 90.) [Formerly Ill. Rev. Stat. 23 §2354.]

150/4.1. Abandonment of children by school bus drivers.

§4.1. It is unlawful for any school bus driver to wilfully abandon the school bus while it contains any children who are without other adult supervision, except in an emergency where the driver is seeking help or otherwise acting in the best interests of the children.
(Source: P.A. 87-526.) [Formerly Ill. Rev. Stat. 23 §2354.1.]

150/5. Violations.

§5. Any person convicted under the provisions of the preceding sections, shall for the first offense be guilty of a Class A misdemeanor; and for a second or any subsequent offense shall be guilty of a Class 4 felony.
(Source: P.A. 77-2346.) [Formerly Ill. Rev. Stat. 23 §2355.]

150/5.1. Offense of permitting sexual abuse of a child.

§5.1. A. A parent or step-parent who knowingly allows or permits an act of criminal sexual abuse or criminal sexual assault as defined in Section 12-13, 12-14, 12-15 or 12-16 of the "Criminal Code of 1961" [720 ILCS 5/12-13, 5/12-14, 5/12-15 or 5/12-16], upon his or her child and fails to take reasonable steps to prevent its commission or future occurrences of such acts commits the offense of permitting the sexual abuse of a child. For purposes of this Section, "child" means a minor under the age of 17 years.

B. Any person convicted of permitting the sexual abuse of a child shall be guilty of a Class A misdemeanor.
(Source: P.A. 85-1433.) [Formerly Ill. Rev. Stat. 23 §2355.1.]

OFFENSES AGAINST PROPERTY

AIRCRAFT CRASH PARTS ACT

205/0.01. Short title.

§0.01. Short title. This Act may be cited as the Aircraft Crash Parts Act.
(Source: P.A. 86-1324.) [Formerly Ill. Rev. Stat. 15½ §200.]

205/1. Carrying away aircraft parts after crash.

§1. Any person, other than a person officially investigating the crash of an aircraft or a person acting under the direction of such an investigator, who carries away from the scene of the crash parts of such aircraft, prior to the completion of the investigation, shall be guilty of a Class A misdemeanor.
(Source: P.A. 77-2317.) [Formerly Ill. Rev. Stat. 15½ §201.]

ANIMAL REGISTRATION UNDER FALSE PRETENSES ACT

210/0.01. Short title.

§0.01. Short title. This Act may be cited as the Animal Registration Under False Pretenses Act.
(Source: P.A. 86-1324.) [Formerly Ill. Rev. Stat. 8 §31.9.]

210/1. Fraudulently obtaining certificate of registration.

§1. Any person, who by any false pretense, shall obtain from any club, association, society or company for improving the breed of cattle, horses, sheep, swine, or other domestic animals, a certificate of registration of any animal in the herd register, or other register of any such club, association, society or company, or a transfer of any such registration, and every person who shall knowingly give a false pedigree of any animal, upon conviction thereof shall be guilty of a Class A misdemeanor.
(Source: P.A. 77-2663.) [Formerly Ill. Rev. Stat. 8 §32.]

ANIMAL RESEARCH AND PRODUCTION FACILITIES PROTECTION ACT

215/1. Short title.

§1. This Act shall be known and may be cited as the Animal Research and Production Facilities Protection Act.
(Source: P.A. 86-1397.) [Formerly Ill. Rev. Stat. 8 §751.]

215/2. Legislative findings.

§2. There has been an increasing number of illegal acts committed against animal research and production facilities involving injury or loss of life to humans or animals, criminal trespass and damage to property. These actions not only abridge the property rights of the owner of the facility, they may also damage the public interest by jeopardizing crucial scientific, biomedical, or agricultural research or production. These actions can also threaten the public safety by possibly exposing communities to serious public health concerns and creating traffic hazards. These actions may substantially disrupt or damage publicly funded research and can result in the potential loss of physical and intellectual property. Therefore, it is in the interest of the people of the State of Illinois to protect the welfare of humans and animals as well as productive use of public funds to require regulation to prevent unauthorized possession, alteration, destruction, or transportation of research records, test data, research materials, equipment, research and agricultural production animals.
(Source: P.A. 86-1397.) [Formerly Ill. Rev. Stat. 8 §752.]

215/3. Definitions.

§3. Definitions. a) "Animal" means every living creature, domestic or wild, but does not include man.

b) "Director" means the Director of the Illinois Department of Agriculture or the Director's authorized representative.

c) "Animal facility" means any facility engaging in legal scientific research or agricultural production of or involving the use of animals including any organization with a primary purpose of representing livestock production or processing, any organization with a primary purpose of promoting or marketing livestock or livestock products, any person licensed to practice veterinary medicine, any institution as defined in the Impounding and Disposition of Stray Animals Act, and any organization with a primary purpose of representing any such person, organization, or institution. "Animal facility" shall include the owner, operator, and employees of any animal facility and any premises where animals are located.

(Source: P.A. 86-1397.) [Formerly Ill. Rev. Stat. 8 §753.]

215/4. Prohibited acts.

§4. Prohibited Acts. It shall be unlawful for any person,

(1) to release, steal, or otherwise intentionally cause the death, injury, or loss of any animal at or from an animal facility and not authorized by that facility;

(2) to damage, vandalize, or steal any property in or on an animal facility;

(3) to obtain access to an animal facility by false pretenses for the purpose of performing acts not authorized by that facility;

(4) to enter into an animal facility with an intent to destroy, alter, duplicate, or obtain unauthorized possession of records, data, materials, equipment, or animals;

(5) by theft or deception knowingly to obtain control or to exert control over records, data, material, equipment, or animals of any animal facility for the purpose of depriving the rightful owner or animal facility of the records, material, data, equipment, or animals or for the purpose of concealing, abandoning, or destroying such records, material, data, equipment, or animals; or

(6) to enter or remain on an animal facility with the intent to commit an act prohibited under this Section.

(Source: P.A. 86-1397.) [Formerly Ill. Rev. Stat. 8 §754.]

215/5. Penalties.

§5. Penalties. (a) (1) Any person who violates any provision of Section 4 shall be guilty of a Class 4 felony for each such violation, unless the loss, theft, or damage to the animal facility property exceeds $300 in value.

(2) If the loss, theft, or damage to the animal facility property exceeds $300 in value but does not exceed $10,000 in value, the person is guilty of a Class 3 felony.

(3) If the loss, theft, or damage to the animal facility property exceeds $10,000 in value but does not exceed $100,000 in value, the person is guilty of a Class 2 felony.

(4) If the loss, theft, or damage to the animal facility property exceeds $100,000 in value, the person is guilty of a Class 1 felony.

(b) Any person who, with the intent that any violation of any provision of Section 4 be committed, agrees with another to the commission of the violation and commits an act in furtherance of this agreement is guilty of the same class of felony as provided in subsection (a) for that violation.

(c) Restitution.

(1) Court shall conduct a hearing to determine the reasonable cost of replacing materials, data, equipment, animals and records that may have been damaged, destroyed, lost or cannot be returned, and the reasonable cost of repeating any experimentation that may have been interrupted or invalidated as a result of a violation of Section 4.

(2) Any persons convicted of such violation shall be ordered jointly and severally to make restitution to the owner, operator, or both, of the animal facility in the full amount of the reasonable cost determined under paragraph (1).
(Source: P.A. 86-1397.) [Formerly Ill. Rev. Stat. 8 §755.]

215/6. Private rights of action.

§6. Private rights of action. Nothing in this Act shall preclude any animal facility injured in its business or property by a violation of this Act from seeking appropriate relief under any other provision of law or remedy including the issuance of a permanent injunction against any person who violates any provision of this Act. The animal facility owner or operator may petition the court to permanently enjoin such person from violating this Act and the court shall provide such relief.
(Source: P.A. 86-1397.) [Formerly Ill. Rev. Stat. 8 §756.]

215/7. Investigation; prosecution.

§7. The Director shall have authority to investigate any alleged violation of this Act, along with any other law enforcement agency, and may take any action within the Director's authority necessary for the enforcement of this Act. State's Attorneys, State police and other law enforcement officials shall provide any assistance required in the conduct of an investigation and prosecution. Before the Director reports a violation for prosecution he or she may give the owner or operator of the animal facility and the alleged violator an opportunity to present his or her views at an administrative hearing.
(Source: P.A. 86-1397.) [Formerly Ill. Rev. Stat. 8 §757.]

215/8. Rules and regulations.

§8. The Director may adopt any rules and regulations necessary for the enforcement of this Act.
(Source: P.A. 86-1397.) [Formerly Ill. Rev. Stat. 8 §758.]

215/9. Effective date.

§9. This Act takes effect upon becoming law.
(Source: P.A. 86-1397.) [Formerly Ill. Rev. Stat. 8 §759.]

APPLIANCE TAG ACT

Sec.

220/0.01. Short title.

§0.01. Short title. This Act may be cited as the Appliance Tag Act.
(Source: P.A. 86-1324.) [Formerly Ill. Rev. Stat. 121½ §830.]

220/1. Definitions.

§1. Definitions. As used in this Act unless the context otherwise requires, the terms specified in this Section have the meanings ascribed to them in this Section.

(a) "Demonstrator unit" means any household appliance, not sold or transferred to a consumer, utilized by a seller or dealer as a sample to demonstrate the operation of the appliance to customers.

(b) "Rebuilt" means any household appliance that has a substantial portion of its original, major parts replaced.

(c) "Reconditioned" means any household appliance which has been substantially repaired but has not been rebuilt.

(d) "Repossessed" means any household appliance purchased on credit that is offered for sale after it has been reclaimed by the seller or holder of the instrument evidencing the debt because of default.

(e) "Used" means any household appliance, previously sold, transferred to a consumer and put in service and utilized by the consumer for its intended purpose, that is not a rebuilt, reconditioned or repossessed appliance.

(f) "Household appliance" means any gas or electric appliance used in the home, such as but not limited to the following: stoves, heating devices, cooking equipment, refrigerators, air conditioners, vacuum cleaners, electric fans, clocks, radios, toasters, irons, television sets, washing machines, dryers and dishwashers.

(Source: P.A. 79-730.) [Formerly Ill. Rev. Stat. 121½ §831.]

220/2. Labeling requirements.

§2. No person shall sell, attempt to sell or offer to sell, by retail, wholesale or auction, any household appliance other than a new appliance unless there is affixed thereto a tag or label no smaller in size than 4 inches in length and 2 inches in width bearing a statement that the appliance is used, repossessed, rebuilt or reconditioned or that the appliance has been utilized as a demonstrator unit.

(Source: P.A. 79-730.) [Formerly Ill. Rev. Stat. 121½ §832.]

220/3. Exemption.

§3. Exemption. Any person who sells or offers for sale a household appliance which was obtained by the person making the sale for his own use, but who is not regularly engaged in the business of making such sales is exempted from the provisions of this Act.

(Source: P.A. 79-730.) [Formerly Ill. Rev. Stat. 121½ §833.]

220/4. Penalty; fines.

§4. Every person, who by himself, his agents or employees violates any of the provisions of this Act may for each offense be deemed guilty of a business offense, and shall, upon conviction thereof, be punished by a fine of not exceeding $100 nor less than $50 for the first offense; not exceeding $200 nor less than $100 for the second offense; and not exceeding $500 nor less than $200 for the third and each subsequent offense and all costs for each and every offense.

(Source: P.A. 79-730.) [Formerly Ill. Rev. Stat. 121½ §834.]

AUCTION SALES SIGN ACT

Sec.

225/0.01. Short title.

§0.01. Short title. This Act may be cited as the Auction Sales Sign Act.

(Source: P.A. 86-1324.) [Formerly Ill. Rev. Stat. 121½ §219.01.]

225/1. Signs, etc. prohibited unless bidding open to public.

§1. The use of any signs, billboards, flags, banners or other media commonly used to designate that an auction is being held, or is going to be held, is prohibited unless the bidding on all sales of goods in the place so designated is open to the general public.

(Source: Laws 1953, p. 1654.) [Formerly Ill. Rev. Stat. 121½ §219.1.]

225/2. Penalty.

§2. Whoever violates the provisions of this Act shall be guilty of a Class B misdemeanor.
(Source: P.A. 77-2260.) [Formerly Ill. Rev. Stat. 121½ §219.2.]

BUSINESS USE OF MILITARY TERMS ACT

Sec.

230/0.01. Short title.

§0.01. Short title. This Act may be cited as the Business Use of Military Terms Act.
(Source: P.A. 86-1324.) [Formerly Ill. Rev. Stat. 96 §8m.]

230/1. Use of terms denoting branch of government prohibited.

§1. It is unlawful for any person, concern, firm or corporation to use in the name, or description of the name, of any privately operated mercantile establishment which may or may not be engaged principally in the buying and selling of equipment or materials of the Government of the United States or any of its departments, agencies or military services, the terms "Army", "Navy", "Marine", "Coast Guard", "Government", "GI", "PX" or any terms denoting a branch of the government, either independently or in connection or conjunction with any other word or words, letter or insignia which import or imply that the products so described are or were made for the United States government or in accordance with government specifications or requirements, or of government materials, or that such products have been disposed of by the United States government as surplus or rejected stock.
(Source: Laws 1945, p. 694.) [Formerly Ill. Rev. Stat. 96 §9.]

230/2. Penalty; fines.

§2. Any person, concern, firm or corporation violating the provisions of this act is guilty of a petty offense and shall be fined not less than $25.00 nor more than $500 for the first conviction, and not less than $500 or more than $1000 for each subsequent conviction.
(Source: P.A. 77-2543.) [Formerly Ill. Rev. Stat. 96 §10.]

COIN SLUG ACT

Sec.

235/1. Unlawful operation of coin-operated devices; penalty.

§1. Any person who shall operate, or cause to be operated, or who shall attempt to operate, or attempt to cause to be operated any coin box telephone, coin operated transit turnstile or transit fare box by means of a slug, washer, disc, token, string, cord or wire or by means of any false, counterfeited, mutilated, sweated or foreign coin, or by any means, method, trick, or device whatsoever not lawfully authorized by the owner of such coin box telephone, coin operated transit turnstile or transit fare box or who shall obtain or receive from any coin box telephone, coin operated transit turnstile or transit fare box the use or enjoyment of any telephone or transit facilities or service without depositing in and surrendering to such coin box telephone, coin operated transit turnstile or transit fare box lawful coin of the United States of America to the amount required therefor by the owner of such coin box telephone, coin operated transit turnstile or transit fare box shall be guilty of a Class B misdemeanor.
(Source: P.A. 77-2619.) [Formerly Ill. Rev. Stat. 134 §16.3.]

235/1a. Short title.

§1a. Short title. This Act may be cited as the Coin Slug Act.
(Source: P.A. 86-1324.) [Formerly Ill. Rev. Stat. 134 §16.3a.]

CONDITIONAL SALES PROTECTION ACT

240/0.01. Short title.

§0.01. Short title. This Act may be cited as the Conditional Sales Protection Act.
(Source: P.A. 86-1324.) [Formerly Ill. Rev. Stat. 121½ §157.40.]

240/1. Sale before fulfillment of sales contract conditions; penalty.

§1. Any person purchasing personal property under a conditional sales contract who, during the existence of such conditional sales contract and before the conditions thereof have been fulfilled, sells, transfers, conceals or in any manner disposes of such property, or causes or allows the same to be done without the written consent of the holder of title is guilty of a Class A misdemeanor.
(Source: P.A. 84-551.) [Formerly Ill. Rev. Stat. 121½ §157.41.]

CONSTRUCTION EQUIPMENT IDENTIFICATION DEFACEMENT ACT

245/0.01. Short title.

§0.01. Short title. This Act may be cited as the Construction Equipment Identification Defacement Act.
(Source: P.A. 86-1324.) [Formerly Ill. Rev. Stat. 38 §71.]

245/1. Defacing identification marks on construction equipment.

§1. (a) Any person who shall intentionally or knowingly change, alter, remove, mutilate or obliterate a permanently affixed serial number, product identification number, part number, component identification number owner-applied identification or other mark of identification attached to or stamped, inscribed, molded or etched into a machine or other equipment, whether stationary or mobile or self-propelled, or a part of such machine or equipment used in the construction, maintenance or demolition of buildings, structures, bridges, tunnels, sewers, utility pipes or lines, ditches or open cuts, roads, highways, dams, airports or waterways or material handling for such projects commits a Class A misdemeanor.

(b) Possession of any machine or other equipment or a part of such machine or equipment used in the construction, maintenance or demolition of buildings, structures, bridges, tunnels, sewers, utility pipes or lines, ditches or open cuts, roads, highways, dams, airports or waterways or material handling for such projects upon which any such serial number, product identification number, part number, component identification number, owner-applied identification number or other mark of identification shall have been changed, altered, removed, or obliterated shall raise a rebuttable presumption that the possessor has intentionally or knowingly changed, altered, removed, or obliterated the same.
(Source: P.A. 82-578.) [Formerly Ill. Rev. Stat. 38 §71-1.]

ILLINOIS CREDIT CARD AND DEBIT CARD ACT

250/1. Short title.

§1. This Act shall be known and may be cited as the "Illinois Credit Card and Debit Card Act".
(Source: P.A. 84-486.) [Formerly Ill. Rev. Stat. 17 §5901.]

250/2. Definitions.

§2. As used in this Act, unless the context otherwise requires, the terms defined in Sections 2.01 through 2.16 [720 ILCS 250/2.01 through 250/2.16] shall have the meanings ascribed to them in those Sections.
(Source: P.A. 84-486.) [Formerly Ill. Rev. Stat. 17 §5902.]

250/2.01. Altered credit card or debit card, defined.

§2.01. "Altered credit card or debit card" means any instrument or device, whether known as a credit card or debit card, which has been changed in any respect by addition or deletion of any material, except for the signature by the person to whom the card is issued.
(Source: P.A. 84-486.) [Formerly Ill. Rev. Stat. 17 §5903.]

250/2.02. Cardholder, defined.

§2.02. "Cardholder" means the person or organization named on the face of a credit card or debit card to whom or for whose benefit the credit card or debit card is issued by an issuer.
(Source: P.A. 84-486.) [Formerly Ill. Rev. Stat. 17 §5904.]

250/2.03. Credit card, defined.

§2.03. "Credit card" means any instrument or device, whether known as a credit card, credit plate, charge plate or any other name, issued with or without fee by an issuer for the use of the cardholder in obtaining money, goods, services or anything else of value on credit or in consideration or an undertaking or guaranty by the issuer of the payment of a check drawn by the cardholder.
(Source: P.A. 78-777.) [Formerly Ill. Rev. Stat. 17 §5905.]

250/2.04. Counterfeit, defined.

§2.04. "Counterfeit" means to manufacture, produce or create, by any means, a credit card or debit card without the purported issuer's consent or authorization.
(Source: P.A. 84-486.) [Formerly Ill. Rev. Stat. 17 §5906.]

250/2.05. Expired credit card or debit card, defined.

§2.05. "Expired credit card or debit card" means a credit card or debit card which is no longer valid because the term on it has elapsed.
(Source: P.A. 84-486.) [Formerly Ill. Rev. Stat. 17 §5907.]

250/2.06. Incomplete credit card or debit card, defined.

§2.06. "Incomplete credit card or debit card" means a credit card or debit card which is missing part of the matter other than the signature of the cardholder which an issuer requires to appear on the credit card or debit card before it can be used by a cardholder, and this includes credit cards or debit cards which have not been stamped, embossed, imprinted or written on.
(Source: P.A. 84-486.) [Formerly Ill. Rev. Stat. 17 §5908.]

250/2.07. Intent to defraud, defined.

§2.07. "Intent to defraud" means an intention to wrongfully cause another to assume, create, transfer, alter or terminate any right, obligation or power with reference to any person or property.
(Source: P.A. 78-777.) [Formerly Ill. Rev. Stat. 17 §5909.]

250/2.08. Issuer, defined.

§2.08. "Issuer" means the business organization or financial institution which issues a credit card or debit card, or its duly authorized agent.
(Source: P.A. 84-486.) [Formerly Ill. Rev. Stat. 17 §5910.]

250/2.09. Person, defined.

§2.09. "Person" means any individual, corporation, government, governmental subdivision or agency, business trust, estate, trust, partnership or association or any other entity.
(Source: P.A. 78-777.) [Formerly Ill. Rev. Stat. 17 §5911.]

250/2.10. Receives or receiving, defined.

§2.10. "Receives" or "receiving" means acquiring possession or control.
(Source: P.A. 78-777.) [Formerly Ill. Rev. Stat. 17 §5912.]

250/2.11. Record of charge form, defined.

§2.11. "Record of charge form" means any document submitted or intended to be submitted to an issuer as evidence of a credit transaction for which the issuer has agreed to reimburse persons providing money, goods, property, services or other things of value.
(Source: P.A. 78-777.) [Formerly Ill. Rev. Stat. 17 §5913.]

250/2.12. Revoked credit card or debit card, defined.

§2.12. "Revoked credit card or debit card" means a credit card or debit card which is no longer valid because permission to use it has been suspended or terminated by the issuer.
(Source: P.A. 84-486.) [Formerly Ill. Rev. Stat. 17 §5914.]

250/2.13. Sale, defined.

§2.13. "Sale" means any delivery for value.
(Source: P.A. 78-777.) [Formerly Ill. Rev. Stat. 17 §5915.]

250/2.14. Electronic fund transfer terminal, defined.

§2.14. "Electronic fund transfer terminal" means any machine or device that, when properly activated, will perform any of the following services:

(a) Dispense money as a debit to the cardholder's account; or

(b) Print the cardholder's account balances on a statement; or

(c) Transfer funds between a cardholder's accounts; or

(d) Accept payments on a cardholder's loan; or

(e) Dispense cash advances on an open end credit or a revolving charge agreement; or

(f) Accept deposits to a customer's account; or

(g) Receive inquiries of verification of checks and dispense information that verifies that funds are available to cover such checks; or

(h) Cause money to be transferred electronically from a cardholder's account to an account held by any business, firm, retail merchant, corporation, or any other organization.
(Source: P.A. 84-486.) [Formerly Ill. Rev. Stat. 17 §5915.1.]

250/2.15. Debit card, defined.

§2.15. "Debit card" means any instrument or device, known by any name, issued with or without fee by an issuer for the use of the cardholder in obtaining money, goods, services, and anything else of value, payment of which is made against funds previously deposited by the cardholder. A debit card which also can be used to obtain money, goods, services and anything else of value on credit shall not be considered a debit card when it is being used to obtain money, goods, services or anything else of value on credit.
(Source: P.A. 84-486.) [Formerly Ill. Rev. Stat. 17 §5915.2.]

250/2.16. Electronic funds transfer system, defined.

§2.16. "Electronic funds transfer system", hereafter referred to as "EFT System," means that system whereby funds are transferred electronically from a cardholder's account to any other account.
(Source: P.A. 84-486.) [Formerly Ill. Rev. Stat. 17 §5915.3.]

250/3. False statement made for purpose of procuring card; penalty.

§3. A person who makes or causes to be made, either directly or indirectly, any false statement in writing, knowing it to be false and with intent that it be relied on, respecting his identity, his address or his employment, or that of any other person, firm or corporation, for the purpose of procuring the issuance of a credit card or debit card, is guilty of a Class A misdemeanor.
(Source: P.A. 84-486.) [Formerly Ill. Rev. Stat. 17 §5916.]

250/4. Receiving card of another; penalties.

§4. A person who receives a credit card or debit card from the person, possession, custody or control of another without the cardholder's consent or who, with knowledge that it has been so acquired receives the credit card or debit card, with intent to use it or to sell it, or to transfer it to a person other than the issuer or the cardholder is guilty of a Class A misdemeanor. A person who has in his possession or under his control 2 or more such credit cards or debit cards each issued to different cardholders other than himself is presumed to have violated this Section.

A person who, in any 12-month period, violates this Section with respect to 3 or more credit cards or debit cards each issued to different cardholders other than himself is guilty of a Class 4 felony.
(Source: P.A. 84-486.) [Formerly Ill. Rev. Stat. 17 §5917.]

250/5. Receiving lost or mislaid card; penalty.

§5. A person who receives a credit card or debit card that he knows to have been lost or mislaid and who retains possession with intent to use it or to sell it or to transfer it to a person other than the issuer or the cardholder is guilty of a Class B misdemeanor.

A person who, in a single transaction, violates this Section with respect to 3 or more credit cards or debit cards each issued to different cardholders other than himself is guilty of a Class A misdemeanor.
(Source: P.A. 84-486.) [Formerly Ill. Rev. Stat. 17 §5918.]

250/6. Selling or purchasing card without issuer's consent; penalty.

§6. A person other than the issuer who sells a credit card or debit card, without the consent of the issuer, is guilty of a Class A misdemeanor.

A person who purchases a credit card or debit card from a person other than the issuer, without the consent of the issuer, is guilty of a Class A misdemeanor.

A person who, in a single transaction, makes a sale or purchase prohibited by this Section with respect to 3 or more credit cards or debit cards each issued to different cardholders is guilty of a Class 4 felony.
(Source: P.A. 84-486.) [Formerly Ill. Rev. Stat. 17 §5919.]

250/7. Obtaining control over card as security for debt with intent to defraud; penalty.

§7. A person who, with intent to defraud either the issuer, or a person providing money, goods, property, services or anything else of value, or any other person, obtains control over a credit card or debit card as security for debt or transfers, conveys or gives control over a credit card or debit card as security for debt, is guilty of a Class A misdemeanor.
(Source: P.A. 84-486.) [Formerly Ill. Rev. Stat. 17 §5920.]

250/8. Prohibited uses; penalties.

§8. A person who, with intent to defraud either the issuer, or a person providing money, goods, property, services or anything else of value, or any other person, (i) uses, for the purpose of obtaining money, goods, property, services or anything else of value a credit card or debit card obtained or retained in violation of this Act or without the cardholder's consent, or a credit card or debit card which he knows is counterfeited, or forged, or expired, or revoked, or (ii) obtains or attempts to obtain money, goods, property, services or anything else of value by representing without the consent of the cardholder that he is the holder of a specified card or by representing that he is the holder of a card and such card has not in fact been issued, is guilty of a Class A misdemeanor if the value of all money, goods, property, services and other things of value obtained or sought in violation of this Section does not exceed $300 in any 6-month period; and is guilty of a Class 4 felony if such value exceeds $300 in any 6-month period. Knowledge of revocation shall be presumed to have been received by a cardholder 4 days after it has been mailed to him at the address set forth on the credit card or debit card or at his last known address by registered or certified mail, return receipt requested, and, if the address is more than 500 miles from the place of mailing, by air mail. If the address is located outside the United States, Puerto Rico, the Virgin Islands, the Canal Zone and

Canada, notice shall be presumed to have been received 10 days after mailing by registered or certified mail.
(Source: P.A. 84-486.) [Formerly Ill. Rev. Stat. 17 §5921.]

250/9. Use of credit card to defraud; allowing use by another; penalties.
§9. A cardholder who uses a credit card or debit card issued to him or allows another person to use a credit card or debit card issued to him with intent to defraud the issuer, or a person providing money, goods, property, services or anything else of value, or any other person, is guilty of a Class A misdemeanor if the value of all money, goods, property, services or other things of value does not exceed $150 in any 6-month period; and is guilty of a Class 4 felony if the value exceeds $150 in any 6-month period.
(Source: P.A. 84-486.) [Formerly Ill. Rev. Stat. 17 §5922.]

250/10. Person furnishing money, goods, etc. with intent to defraud; penalties.
§10. A person who is authorized by an issuer to furnish money, goods, property, services or anything else of value upon presentation of a credit card or debit card by the cardholder, or any agent or employee of such person, who, with intent to defraud the issuer or the cardholder, furnishes money, goods, property, services or anything else of value upon presentation of a credit card or debit card obtained or retained in violation of this Act or a credit card or debit card which he knows is counterfeited, or forged, or expired, or revoked is guilty of a Class A misdemeanor, if the value furnished in violation of this Section does not exceed $150 in any 6-month period; and is guilty of a Class 4 felony if such value exceeds $150 in any 6-month period.
(Source: P.A. 84-486.) [Formerly Ill. Rev. Stat. 17 §5923.]

250/11. Persons failing to furnish money, goods, etc. with intent to defraud; punishment.
§11. A person who is authorized by an issuer to furnish money, goods, property, services or anything else of value upon presentation of a credit card or debit card by the cardholder, or any agent or employee of such person, who, with intent to defraud the issuer or the cardholder, fails to furnish money, goods, property, services or anything else of value which he represents in writing to the issuer that he has furnished is guilty of a Class A misdemeanor if the difference between the value of all money, goods, property, services and anything else of value actually furnished and the value represented to the issuer to have been furnished does not exceed $150 in any 6-month period; and is guilty of a Class 4 felony if such difference exceeds $150 in any 6-month period.
(Source: P.A. 84-486.) [Formerly Ill. Rev. Stat. 17 §5924.]

250/12. Utilization of account number or code; utilization or possession of record of charge form; penalties.
§12. A person who, with intent to defraud either an issuer, or a person providing money, goods, property, services or anything else of value, or any other person, utilizes an account number or code or enters information on a record of charge form for the purpose of obtaining money, goods, property, services or anything else of value is guilty of a Class A misdemeanor if the value of the money, goods, property, services and other things of value obtained does not exceed $150 in any 6-month period; and is guilty of a Class 4 felony if such value exceeds $150 in any 6-month period.

A person who, with intent to defraud either an issuer or a person providing money, goods, property, services or anything else of value, or any other person, possesses, without the consent of the issuer or purported issuer, record of charge forms bearing the printed impression of a credit card or debit card, is guilty of a Class A misdemeanor. Possession of such record of charge forms by a person

other than the issuer or a person authorized by the issuer to possess record of charge forms is prima facie evidence of the intent to defraud.
(Source: P.A. 84-486.) [Formerly Ill. Rev. Stat. 17 §5925.]

250/13. Receiving money, goods, etc., obtained in violation of this Act; punishment.

§13. A person who receives money, goods, property, services or anything else of value obtained in violation of this Act, knowing that it was so obtained or under such circumstances as would reasonably induce him to believe that it was so obtained is guilty of a Class A misdemeanor if the value of all money, goods, property, services and other things of value obtained does not exceed $150 in any 6-month period; and is guilty of a Class 4 felony if the value exceeds $150 in any 6-month period.
(Source: P.A. 78-777.) [Formerly Ill. Rev. Stat. 17 §5926.]

250/14. Person other than cardholder signing card with intent to defraud; penalty.

§14. A person other than the cardholder or a person authorized by him who, with intent to defraud either the issuer, or a person providing money, goods, property, services or anything else of value, or any other person, signs a credit card or debit card is guilty of a Class A misdemeanor.
(Source: P.A. 84-486.) [Formerly Ill. Rev. Stat. 17 §5927.]

250/15. Altering card; possession of altered card; penalty.

§15. A person who, with intent to defraud either a purported issuer, or a person providing money, goods, property, services or anything else of value, or any other person, alters a credit card or debit card or a purported credit card or debit card, or possesses a credit card or debit card or a purported credit card or debit card with knowledge that the same has been altered, is guilty of a Class 4 felony. The possession by a person other than the issuer of 2 or more credit cards or debit cards which have been altered is prima facie evidence that the person intended to defraud or that he knew the credit cards or debit cards to have been so altered.
(Source: P.A. 84-486.) [Formerly Ill. Rev. Stat. 17 §5928.]

250/16. Counterfeiting purported card; possession of counterfeited card; penalties.

§16. A person who, with intent to defraud either a purported issuer, or a person providing money, goods, property, services or anything else of value, or any other person, counterfeits a purported credit card or debit card or possesses a purported credit card or debit card with knowledge that the card has been counterfeited, is guilty of a Class 3 felony. The possession by a person other than the purported issuer of 2 or more credit cards or debit cards which have been counterfeited is prima facie evidence that that person intended to defraud or that he knew the credit cards or debit cards to have been so counterfeited.
(Source: P.A. 84-486.) [Formerly Ill. Rev. Stat. 17 §5929.]

250/17. Possession of incomplete card or machinery, plates, etc.; penalty.

§17. A person other than the cardholder possessing an incomplete credit card or debit card, with intent to complete it without the consent of the issuer or a person possessing, with knowledge of its character, machinery, plates or any other contrivance designed to reproduce instruments purporting to be credit cards or debit cards of an issuer who has not consented to the preparation of such credit cards or debit cards, is guilty of a Class 3 felony. A person other than the cardholder or issuer who possesses 2 or more incomplete credit cards

or debit cards is presumed to possess those cards without the consent of the issuer.
(Source: P.A. 84-486.) [Formerly Ill. Rev. Stat. 17 §5930.]

250/17.01. Prohibited deposits.

§17.01. Prohibited deposits. (a) A person who, with intent to defraud the issuer or any person providing value or any other person, deposits into his account or any account, via an electronic fund transfer terminal, a check, draft, money order, or any other such document, knowing such document to be false, fictitious, forged, altered, counterfeit, or not his lawful or legal property, violates this subsection (a) and is guilty of a Class 4 felony.

(b) A person who receives value as a result of a false, fictitious, forged, altered, or counterfeit check, draft, money order or any other such document having been deposited into an account via an electronic fund transfer terminal, knowing at the time of receipt of the value that the document so deposited was false, fictitious, forged, altered, counterfeit or not his lawful or legal property, violates this subsection (b) and is guilty of a Class 4 felony.
(Source: P.A. 84-486.) [Formerly Ill. Rev. Stat. 17 §5930.1.]

250/17.02. Fraudulent use of electronic transmission.

§17.02. Fraudulent use of electronic transmission. (a) Any person who, with intent to defraud the issuer, the cardholder or any other person, intercepts, taps or alters electronic information between an electronic fund transfer terminal and the issuer, or originates electronic information to an electronic fund transfer terminal or to the issuer, via any line, wire or any other means of electronic transmission, at any junction, terminal, or device, or at any location within the EFT System, for the purpose of obtaining value, violates this subsection (a) and is guilty of a Class 4 felony.

(b) Any person who, with intent to defraud the issuer, cardholder, or any other person, intercepts, taps or alters electronic information between an electronic fund transfer terminal and the issuer, or originates electronic information to an electronic fund transfer terminal or to the issuer, via any line, wire or other means of electronic transmission, at any junction, terminal, or device, or at any location within the EFT System, and thereby causes funds to be transferred from one account to any other account, violates this subsection (b) and is guilty of a Class 4 felony.
(Source: P.A. 84-486.) [Formerly Ill. Rev. Stat. 17 §5930.2.]

250/17.03. Payment of charges without the furnishing of money, goods, services, or anything of value.

§17.03. Payment of charges without the furnishing of money, goods, services, or anything of value. (a) No person shall process, deposit, negotiate, or obtain payment of a credit card charge through a retail seller's account with a financial institution or through a retail seller's agreement with a financial institution, card issuer, or organization of financial institutions or card issuers if that retail seller did not furnish or agree to furnish the money, goods, services, or anything of value that is the subject of the credit card charge.

(b) No retail seller shall permit any person to process, deposit, negotiate, or obtain payment of a credit card charge through the retail seller's account with a financial institution or the retail seller's agreement with a financial institution, card issuer, or organization of financial institutions or card issuers if that retail seller did not furnish or agree to furnish the money, goods, services, or anything of value that is the subject of the credit card charge.

(c) Subsections (a) and (b) do not apply to any of the following:

(1) A person who furnishes goods or services on the business premises of a general merchandise retail seller and who processes, deposits, negotiates, or

obtains payment of a credit card charge through that general merchandise retail seller's account or agreement.

(2) A general merchandise retail seller who permits a person described in paragraph (1) to process, deposit, negotiate, or obtain payment of a credit card charge through that general merchandise retail seller's account or agreement.

(3) A franchisee who furnishes the cardholder with money, goods, services, or anything of value that is provided in whole or in part by the franchisor and who processes, deposits, negotiates, or obtains payment of a credit card charge through that franchisor's account or agreement.

(4) A franchisor who permits a franchisee described in paragraph (3) to process, deposit, negotiate, or obtain payment of a credit card charge through that franchisor's account or agreement.

(5) The credit card issuer or a financial institution or a parent, subsidiary, or affiliate of the card issuer or financial institution.

(6) A person who processes, deposits, negotiates, or obtains payment of less than $500 of credit card charges in any one year period through a retail seller's account or agreement. The person shall have the burden of producing evidence that the person transacted less than $500 in credit card charges during any one year period.

(7) A telecommunications carrier that includes charges of other parties in its billings to its subscribers and those other parties whose charges are included in the billings of the telecommunications carrier to its subscribers.

(d) Any person injured by a violation of this Section may bring an action for the recovery of damages, equitable relief, and reasonable attorney's fees and costs.

(e) Any person who violates this Section is guilty of a business offense and shall be fined $10,000 for each offense. Each occurrence in which a person processes, deposits, negotiates, or otherwise seeks to obtain payment of a credit card charge in violation of subsection (a) constitutes a separate offense.

(f) The penalties and remedies provided in this Section are in addition to any other remedies or penalties provided by law.

(g) As used in this Section:

(1) "Retail seller" has the same meaning as in Section 2.4 of the Retail Installment Sales Act.

(2) "Franchisor" and "franchisee" have the same meanings as in Section 3 of the Franchise Disclosure Act of 1987.

(3) "Telecommunications carrier" has the same meaning as in Section 13-202 of the Public Utilities Act.

(Added by P.A. 87-1150, §1, eff. 9/17/92.)
[Formerly Ill. Rev. Stat. 17 §5930.3.]

250/18. Consequences of presumption established by this Act.

§18. When this Act establishes a presumption with respect to any fact which is an element of a crime, it has the following consequences:

(a) when there is sufficient evidence of the facts which give rise to the presumption to go to the jury, the issue of the existence of the presumed fact must be submitted to the jury, unless the court is satisfied that the evidence as a whole clearly negates the presumed fact; and

(b) when the issue of the existence of the presumed fact is submitted to the jury, the court shall charge that while the presumed fact must, on all the evidence, be proved beyond a reasonable doubt, the law declares that the jury may regard the facts giving rise to the presumption as sufficient evidence of the presumed fact.

(Source: P.A. 78-777.) [Formerly Ill. Rev. Stat. 17 §5931.]

250/19. Punishment for subsequent convictions.

§19. Any person convicted of a second or subsequent offense under this Act is guilty of a Class 3 felony.

For purposes of this Section, an offense is considered a second or subsequent offense if, prior to his conviction of the offense, the offender has at any time been convicted under this Act, or any prior Act, or under any law of the United States or of any State relating to credit card or debit card offenses.
(Source: P.A. 84-486.) [Formerly Ill. Rev. Stat. 17 §5932.]

250/20. Effect of invalid provisions.

§20. If any provision of this Act or its application to any person or circumstances is held invalid, the invalidity shall not affect other provisions or applications of the Act which can be given effect without the invalid provision or application, and to this end the provisions of this Act are declared to be severable.
(Source: P.A. 78-777.) [Formerly Ill. Rev. Stat. 17 §5933.]

250/24. Act prohibiting frauds relating to communications services.

§24. Nothing contained in this Act shall be construed to repeal, amend, or otherwise affect "An Act relating to defrauding persons of lawful monetary charges for telecommunications services, and to provide penalties for the violation thereof", approved August 14, 1961, as amended [720 ILCS 365/0.01 et seq.].
(Source: P.A. 78-777.) [Formerly Ill. Rev. Stat. 17 §5937.]

CRIMINAL JURISPRUDENCE ACT [USE OF "PAWNER'S SOCIETY"]

255/220a. Name containing the words "Pawner's Society".

§220a. No person, firm, copartnership, or corporation (except corporations organized and doing business under "An Act to provide for the incorporation, management and regulation of pawners' societies and limiting the rate of compensation to be paid for advances, storage and insurance on pawns and pledges and to allow the loaning of money upon personal property," approved March 29, 1899, in force July 1, 1899, as amended) shall use a name which contains therein the words "Pawners' Society." Any person, firm, copartnership or corporation violating the provisions of this section shall be guilty of a petty offense for each day such person, firm, copartnership or corporation continues to use a name which contains such words and fined not less than $5, nor more than $100.
(Source: P.A. 77-2379.) [Formerly Ill. Rev. Stat. 17 §4568.]

CRIMINAL JURISPRUDENCE ACT [FRAUDULENT CONVEYANCE OF REAL AND PERSONAL PROPERTY]

260/121. Fraudulent conveyance of land; penalty.

§121. Any person, after once selling, bartering or disposing of any tract or tracts of land, town lot or lots, or executing any bond or agreement for the sale of any lands, or town lot or lots, who shall again knowingly and fraudulently sell, barter or dispose of the same tract or tracts of land, or town lot or lots, or any parts thereof, or shall knowingly and fraudulently execute any bond or

agreement to sell or barter, or dispose of the same land, or lot or lots, or any part thereof, to any other person for a valuable consideration, shall be guilty of a Class 3 felony.
(Source: P.A. 77-2370.) [Formerly Ill. Rev. Stat. 30 §201.]

260/122. Fraudulent conveyance of real or personal property; penalty.
§122. Every person who is a party to any fraudulent conveyance of any lands, tenements or hereditaments, goods or chattels, or any right or interest issuing out of the same, or to any bond, action, judgment or enforcement thereof; contract or conveyance had, made or contrived, with intent to deceive and defraud others, or to defeat, hinder or delay creditors or others of their just debts, damages or demands, or who, being a party as above stated, at any time wittingly and willingly puts in use, avow, maintain, justify or defend the same or any of them as true, and done, had or made in good faith, or upon good consideration, or sells, aliens or assigns any of the lands, tenements, hereditaments, goods, chattels or other things before mentioned, to him conveyed as above stated, or any part thereof, is guilty of a business offense and fined not exceeding $1,000.
(Source: P.A. 84-546.) [Formerly Ill. Rev. Stat. 30 §202.]

260/123. Officer falsely certifying acknowledgment of conveyance; penalty.
§123. If any officer authorized to take the proof and acknowledgment of any conveyance of real or personal property, or other instrument, wilfully certifies that such conveyance or other instrument was duly proven or acknowledged by any party thereto, when no such acknowledgment or proof was made, or was not made at the time it was certified to have been made, with intent to injure or defraud, or to enable any other person to injure or defraud, he shall be guilty of a Class 4 felony.
(Source: P.A. 77-2370.) [Formerly Ill. Rev. Stat. 30 §203.]

CRIMINAL JURISPRUDENCE ACT
[CORPORATE NAME FALSELY ASSUMED]

265/220. Corporate name falsely assumed; penalty.
§220. If any company, association or person puts forth any sign or advertisement, and therein assumes, for the purpose of soliciting business, a corporate name, not being incorporated, such company, association or person commits a petty offense and shall be deemed guilty of an additional petty offense for each day he or it shall continue to so offend.

Nothing contained herein prohibits any corporation, company, association or person from using any divisional designation or trade name in conjunction with its corporate name or assumed name (pursuant to Section 4.05 of the "Business Corporation Act of 1983") or, if it is a member of a partnership or joint venture from doing partnership or joint venture business under the partnership or joint venture name. The name under which such joint venture or partnership does business may differ from the names of the members. Business may not be conducted or transacted under that joint venture or partnership name, however, unless all provisions of "An Act in relation to the use of an assumed name in the conduct or transaction of business in this State", approved July 17, 1941, as now or hereafter amended, have been complied with. Nothing in this Section permits a foreign corporation to do business in this State without complying with all Illinois laws regulating the doing of business by foreign corporations. No foreign corporation may conduct or transact business in this State as a member of a partnership or joint venture which violates any Illinois law regulating or pertaining to the doing of business by foreign corporations in Illinois.

The provisions of this Act shall not apply to limited partnerships formed under the Revised Uniform Limited Partnership Act.
(Source: P.A. 84-1412.) [Formerly Ill. Rev. Stat. 32 §211.1.]

CRIMINAL JURISPRUDENCE ACT [FRAUDULENT STOCK CERTIFICATE]

270/119. Fraudulent stock certificate; penalty.

§119. Every president, cashier, treasurer, secretary or other officer, and every agent, attorney, servant or employee of any bank, railroad, manufacturing or other corporation, and every other person who shall, knowingly and designedly, and with intent to defraud any person, bank, railroad, manufacturing or other corporation, issue, sell, transfer, assign or pledge, or cause or procure to be issued, sold, transferred, assigned or pledged, any false, fraudulent or simulated certificate or other evidence of ownership of any share or shares of the capital stock of any bank, railroad, manufacturing or other corporation, shall be guilty of a Class 3 felony.
(Source: P.A. 77-2381.) [Formerly Ill. Rev. Stat. 32 §439.41.]

270/120. Signing fraudulent stock certificate; penalty.

§120. Every president, cashier, treasurer, secretary or other officer, and every agent of any bank, railroad, manufacturing or other corporation, who shall wilfully and designedly sign, with intent to issue, sell, pledge, or cause to be issued, sold or pledged, any false, fraudulent or simulated certificate or other evidence of the ownership or transfer of any share or shares of the capital stock of such corporation, or any instrument purporting to be a certificate or other evidence of such ownership or transfer, the signing, issuing, selling or pledging of which by such president, cashier, treasurer or other officer or agent, shall not be authorized by the charter and by-laws of such corporations, or by some amendment thereof, shall be guilty of a Class 3 felony.
(Source: P.A. 77-2381.) [Formerly Ill. Rev. Stat. 32 §439.42.]

CRIMINAL JURISPRUDENCE ACT [VIOLATIONS OF INSURANCE CODE]

(See also 720 ILCS 5/45-1 et seq. as added by P.A. 87-1134, §1, eff. 1/1/93.)

275/118. *(Repealed by P.A. 87-1134, §2, eff. 1/1/93.)*

(Source: P.A. 86-1284.) [Formerly Ill. Rev. Stat. 73 §1101.]

275/119. Investigation of insurance violations.

§119. (1) Whenever the Director of Insurance has cause to believe that a person has engaged in, or is engaging in, any act, activity or practice which constitutes a business offense, misdemeanor or felony violation of the Illinois Insurance Code or related insurance laws, he shall designate appropriate investigators or agents to investigate such violations. For purposes of carrying out investigations under this Section, the Department of Insurance shall be deemed a criminal justice agency under all federal and State laws and regulations, and as such shall have access to any information which concerns or relates to a violation of the Illinois Insurance Code or related insurance laws and which is available to criminal justice agencies.

(2) The Director of Insurance is empowered to transmit or receive written or oral information relating to possible violations of the insurance laws of this State received by or from any other criminal justice agencies, whether Federal, state or local, if, in the opinion of the Director, such transmittal is appropriate and may further the effective prevention of criminal activities.

(3) The Department of Insurance's papers, documents, reports, or evidence relevant to the subject of an investigation under this Section shall not be subject to public inspection for so long as the Department deems reasonably necessary to complete the investigation, to protect the person investigated from unwarranted injury, or to be in the public interest. Further, such papers, documents, reports, or evidence relevant to the subject of an investigation under this Section shall not be subject to subpoena until opened for public inspection by the Department, unless the Department consents, or until, after notice to the Department and a hearing, the court determines the Department would not be unnecessarily hindered by such subpoena. No officer, agent or employee of the Department shall be subject to subpoena in civil actions by any court of this State to testify concerning any matter of which they have knowledge pursuant to a pending insurance fraud investigation by the Department.

(4) No insurer, or employees or agents of any insurer, shall be subject to civil liability for libel or otherwise by virtue of furnishing information required by the insurance laws of this State or required by the Department of Insurance as a result of its investigation. No cause of action shall exist and no liability may be imposed, either civil or criminal, against the State, the Director, any officer, agent or employee of the Department of Insurance, or individuals employed or retained by the Director, for any act or omission by them in the performance of any power or duty authorized by this Section, unless such act or omission was performed in bad faith and with intent to injure a particular person.

(5) The powers vested in the Director by this Section are additional to any and all other powers and remedies vested in the Director by law, and nothing herein shall be construed as requiring that the Director shall employ the powers conferred herein instead of or as a condition precedent to the exercise of any other power or remedy vested in the Director. The Director may establish systems and procedures for carrying out investigations under this Section as are necessary to avoid the impairment or compromise of his authority under this Section or any other law relating to the regulation of insurance.

(Source: P.A. 85-762.) [Formerly Ill. Rev. Stat. 73 §1102.]

CRIMINAL JURISPRUDENCE ACT [INHERITANCE FRAUD]

280/94. Fraudulent representation of infant as heir.

§94. Every person who shall fraudulently produce an infant, falsely pretending it to have been born of parents whose child would be entitled to a share of any personal estate, or to inherit any real estate, with the intent of intercepting the inheritance of any such real estate, or the distribution of any such personal property from any person lawfully entitled thereto, shall be guilty of a Class 3 felony.

(Source: P.A. 77-2830.) [Formerly Ill. Rev. Stat. 110½ §501.]

CRIMINAL JURISPRUDENCE ACT [INJURING OR ALTERING UTILITY METER]

285/117. Injuring, altering, etc. utility meter; penalty.

§117. Any person, who, with intent to injure or defraud any company, body corporate, copartnership or individual, shall injure, alter, obstruct or prevent the action of any meter provided for the purpose of measuring and registering the quantity of gas, water or electric current consumed by or at any burner, orifice or place, or supplied to any lamp, motor, machine or appliance, or shall cause or procure or aid the injuring or altering of any such meter or the obstruction or prevention of its action, or shall make or cause to be made with any gas pipe, water pipe or electrical conductor any connection so as to conduct or supply illumination or inflammable gas, water or electric current to any burner or orifice or lamp or motor or other machine or appliance from which such gas, water or electricity may be consumed or utilized without passing through or being registered by a meter or without the consent or acquiescence of the company, municipal corporation, body corporate, copartnership or individual furnishing or transmitting such gas, water or electric current through such gas pipe, water pipe or electrical conductor, shall be guilty of a Class B misdemeanor.

(Source: P.A. 77-2590.) [Formerly Ill. Rev. Stat. 111⅔ §381.]

285/117a. Tampering with service-measuring device.

§117a. Any person, who, with the intent to defraud, tampers with, alters, obstructs or prevents the action of any meter, register or other counting device which is a part of any mechanical or electrical machine, equipment or device which measures service, without the consent of the owner of such machine, equipment or device, shall be guilty of a Class B misdemeanor.

(Source: P.A. 77-2590.) [Formerly Ill. Rev. Stat. 111⅔ §382.]

DECEPTIVE SALE OF GOLD AND SILVER ACT

290/1. Deceptive marking—Sale of gold, etc. articles; penalty.

§1. Whoever makes for sale, or sells, or offers to sell or dispose of, or has in his or her possession with intent to sell or dispose of, any article or articles construed in whole or in part, of gold or any alloy or imitation thereof, having thereon or on any box, package, cover, wrapper or other thing enclosing or encasing such article or articles for sale, any stamp, brand, engraving, printed label, trade mark, imprint or other mark, indicating or designed, or intended to indicate, that the gold, alloy or imitation thereof, in such article or articles, is different from or better than the actual kind and quality of such gold, alloy or imitation, shall be guilty of a petty offense and shall be fined in any sum not less than $50 nor more than $100.

(Source: P.A. 77-2250.) [Formerly Ill. Rev. Stat. 121½ §157.16.]

290/1a. Short title.

§1a. Short title. This Act may be cited as the Deceptive Sale of Gold and Silver Act.

(Source: P.A. 86-1324.) [Formerly Ill. Rev. Stat. 121½ §157.16a.]

290/2. Deceptive marking—Sale of silver, etc. articles; penalty.

§2. Whoever makes for sale, sells or offers to sell or dispose of or has in his or her possession, with intent to sell or dispose of, any article or articles constructed in whole or in part of silver or any alloy or imitation thereof, having thereon—or on any box, package, cover, wrapper or other thing enclosing or encasing such article or articles for sale—any stamp, brand, engraving, printed label, trademark, imprint or other mark, containing the words "sterling" or "sterling silver," referring, or designed or intended to refer, to the silver, alloy or imitation thereof in such article or articles, when such silver, alloy or imitation thereof shall contain less than nine hundred and twenty-five one-thousandths thereof of pure silver, shall be guilty of a petty offense and shall be fined in any sum not less than $50 nor more than $100.
(Source: P.A. 77-2250.) [Formerly Ill. Rev. Stat. 121½ §157.17.]

290/3. False use of "coin" or "coin silver"; penalty.

§3. Whoever makes for sale, sells or offers to sell or dispose of or has in his or her possession, with intent to sell or dispose of, any article or articles constructed in whole or in part of silver or any alloy or imitation thereof, having thereon—or on any box, package, cover, wrapper or other thing enclosing or encasing such article or articles for sale—any stamp, brand, engraving, printed label, trademark, imprint, or other mark, containing the words "coin" or "coin silver," referring to or designed or intended to refer to, the silver, alloy or imitation thereof, in such article or articles, when such silver, alloy or imitation shall contain less than nine-tenths thereof pure silver, shall be guilty of a petty offense and shall be fined in any sum not less than $50 and not more than $100.
(Source: P.A. 77-2250.) [Formerly Ill. Rev. Stat. 121½ §157.18.]

DECEPTIVE ADVERTISING ACT

Sec.

295/1a. Deceptive advertising; penalty.

§1a. Any person, firm, corporation or association or agent or employee thereof, who, with intent to sell, purchase, or in any wise dispose of, or to contract with reference to merchandise, securities, real estate, service, employment, money, credit or anything offered by such person, firm, corporation or association, or agent or employee thereof, directly or indirectly, to the public for sale, purchase, loan, distribution, or the hire of personal services, or with intent to increase the consumption of or to contract with reference to any merchandise, real estate, securities, money, credit, loan, service or employment, or to induce the public in any manner to enter into any obligation relating thereto, or to acquire title thereto, or an interest therein, or to make any loan, makes, publishes, disseminates, circulates, or places before the public, or causes, directly or indirectly, to be made, published, disseminated, circulated, or placed before the public, in this State, in a newspaper, magazine, or other publication, or in the form of a book, notice, handbill, poster, sign, bill, circular, pamphlet, letter, placard, card, label, or over any radio or television station, or in any other way similar or dissimilar to the foregoing, an advertisement, announcement, or statement of any sort regarding merchandise, securities, real estate, money, credit, service, employment, or anything so offered for use, purchase, loan or sale, or the interest, terms or conditions upon which such loan will be made to the public, which advertisement contains any assertion, representation or

statement of fact which is untrue, misleading or deceptive, shall be guilty of a Class A misdemeanor.
(Source: P.A. 77-2830.) [Formerly Ill. Rev. Stat. 121½ §157.21a.]

295/1b. False advertised price; injunction; penalty.
§1b. Any person, firm or corporation offering for sale merchandise, commodities or service by making, publishing, disseminating, circulating or placing before the public within this State in any manner an advertisement of merchandise, commodities, or service, with the intent, design or purpose not to sell the merchandise, commodities, or service so advertised at the price stated therein, or otherwise communicated, or with intent not to sell the merchandise, commodities, or service so advertised, may be enjoined from such advertising upon application for injunctive relief by the state's attorney or attorney general, and shall also be guilty of a Class A misdemeanor.
(Source: P.A. 83-346.) [Formerly Ill. Rev. Stat. 121½ §157.21b.]

295/1c. Real estate advertisements; requirements; penalty.
§1c. Any person, firm or corporation who makes, publishes, disseminates, circulates or places before the public, or causes, directly or indirectly to be made, published, disseminated, circulated or placed before the public, in this State, in a newspaper, magazine or other publication published in this State, or in the form of a book, notice, handbill, poster, sign, bill, circular, pamphlet, letter, placard, card, or label distributed in this State, or over any radio or television station located in this State or in any other way in this State similar or dissimilar to the foregoing, an advertisement, announcement, statement or representation of any kind to the public relating to the sale, offering for sale, purchase, use or lease of any real estate in a subdivision located outside the State of Illinois may be enjoined from such activity upon application for injunctive relief by the state's attorney or attorney general and shall also be guilty of a Class A misdemeanor unless such advertisement, announcement, statement or representation contains or is accompanied by a clear, concise statement of the proximity of such real estate in common units of measurement to public schools, public highways, fresh water supply, public sewers, electric power, stores and shops, and telephone service or contains a statement that one or more of such facilities are not readily available, and name those not available.
(Source: P.A. 83-346.) [Formerly Ill. Rev. Stat. 121½ §157.21c.]

295/1d. Publisher, etc. acting in good faith; application.
§1d. This Act shall not apply to any medium for the printing, publishing, or disseminating of advertising, or any owner, agent or employee thereof, nor to any advertising agency or owner, agent or employee thereof, nor to any radio or television station, or owner, agent, or employee thereof, for printing, publishing, or disseminating, or causing to be printed, published, or disseminated, such advertisement in good faith and without knowledge of the deceptive character thereof.
(Source: Laws 1965, p. 2646.) [Formerly Ill. Rev. Stat. 121½ §157.21d.]

295/1e. Short title.
§1e. Short title. This Act may be cited as the Deceptive Advertising Act.
(Source: P.A. 86-1324.) [Formerly Ill. Rev. Stat. 121½ §157.21e.]

DEROGATORY STATEMENTS ABOUT BANKS ACT

Sec.

300/0.01. Short title.

§0.01. Short title. This Act may be cited as the Derogatory Statements About Banks Act.

(Source: P.A. 86-1324.) [Formerly Ill. Rev. Stat. 17 §900.]

300/1. Statements derogatory to the financial condition of bank.

§1. Any person who shall willfully and maliciously make, circulate, or transmit to another or others, any statements, rumor or suggestion, written, printed or by word of mouth, which is directly or by inference derogatory to the financial condition, with intent to affect the solvency or financial standing of any corporation doing a banking or trust business in this State, or any building and loan association or federal savings and loan association doing business in this State, or who shall counsel, aid, procure or induce another to start, transmit or circulate any such statement, rumor or suggestion, shall be guilty of a Class A misdemeanor: However, the truth of said statement, established by the maker thereof, shall be a complete defense in any prosecution under the provisions of this Act.

(Source: P.A. 77-2830.) [Formerly Ill. Rev. Stat. 17 §901.]

GASOLINE PRICE ADVERTISING ACT

305/0.01. Short title.

§0.01. Short title. This Act may be cited as the Gasoline Price Advertising Act.

(Source: P.A. 86-1324.) [Formerly Ill. Rev. Stat. 121½ §860.]

305/1. Requirements on advertisement of gasoline price.

§1. No person, firm or corporation owning or operating a service station shall advertise or hold out or state to the public the per gallon price of gasoline, upon any sign on the premises of such station, unless such price includes all taxes, and unless the price, as so advertised, corresponds with the price appearing on the pump from which such gasoline is dispensed. Also, the identity of the product must be included with the price in any such advertisement, holding out or statement to the public.

(Source: P.A. 80-992.) [Formerly Ill. Rev. Stat. 121½ §861.]

305/2. Penalty.

§2. Any person who violates Section 1 of this Act shall be guilty of a petty offense.

(Source: P.A. 80-992.) [Formerly Ill. Rev. Stat. 121½ §862.]

GOVERNMENTAL UNECONOMIC PRACTICES ACT

310/0.01. Short title.

§0.01. Short title. This Act may be cited as the Governmental Uneconomic Practices Act.

(Source: P.A. 86-1324.) [Formerly Ill. Rev. Stat. 121½ §205.9.]

310/1. State prohibited from selling merchandise, etc. to officers and employees.

§1. It is unlawful for the State of Illinois, any political subdivision thereof, or any municipality therein, or any officer, agent or employee of the State of Illinois, any political subdivision thereof or any municipality therein, to sell to or procure for sale or have in its or his possession or under its or his control for sale to any officer, agent or employee of the State or any political subdivision thereof or municipality therein any article, material, product or merchandise of whatsoever nature, excepting meals, public services and such specialized appliances and paraphernalia as may be required for the safety or health of such officers, agents or employees.

The provisions of this section shall not apply to the State, any political subdivision thereof or municipality therein, nor to any officer, agent or employee of the State, or of any such subdivision or municipality while engaged in any recreational, health, welfare, relief, safety or educational activities furnished by the State, or any such political subdivision or municipality.
(Source: Laws 1941, p. 1118.) [Formerly Ill. Rev. Stat. 121½ §206.]

310/2. Penalty.

§2. Any person violating any of the provisions of this Act is guilty of a Class B misdemeanor.
(Source: P.A. 77-2258.) [Formerly Ill. Rev. Stat. 121½ §207.]

HORSE MUTILATION ACT

315/0.01. Short title.

§0.01. Short title. This Act may be cited as the Horse Mutilation Act.
(Source: P.A. 86-1324.) [Formerly Ill. Rev. Stat. 8 §108m.]

315/1. Shortening horse's tail; penalty.

§1. Whoever cuts the solid part of the tail of any horse in the operation known as docking, or by any other operation performed for the purpose of shortening the tail, and whoever shall cause the same to be done, or assist in doing such cutting, unless the same is proved to be a benefit to the horse, shall be guilty of a Class A misdemeanor.
(Source: P.A. 77-2830.) [Formerly Ill. Rev. Stat. 8 §109.]

HORSE RACING FALSE ENTRIES ACT

320/0.01. Short title.

§0.01. Short title. This Act may be cited as the Horse Racing False Entries Act.
(Source: P.A. 86-1324.) [Formerly Ill. Rev. Stat. 8 §33.90.]

320/1. Horse entered under false name or out of proper class.

§1. That in order to encourage the breeding of and improvement in trotting, running and pacing horses in the State of Illinois, it is hereby made unlawful for any person or persons knowingly to enter or cause to be entered for competition, or knowingly to compete with any horse, mare, gelding, colt or filly

under any other than its true name or out of its proper class for any purse, prize, premium, stake or sweepstakes offered or given by any agricultural or other society, association, person or persons in the State of Illinois where such prize, purse, premium, stake or sweepstakes is to be decided by a contest of speed.
(Source: Laws 1895, p. 3.) [Formerly Ill. Rev. Stat. 8 §34.]

320/2. Penalty.

§2. Any person or persons who are guilty of a violation of section one of this act shall be guilty of a Class 4 felony.
(Source: P.A. 77-2666.) [Formerly Ill. Rev. Stat. 8 §35.]

320/3. Regulation of name change.

§3. The name of any horse, mare, gelding, colt or filly, for the purpose of entry for competition or performance in any contest of speed, shall be the name under which said horse has publicly performed, and shall not be changed after having once so performed or contested for a prize, purse, premium, stake or sweepstakes, except as provided by the code of printed rules of the society or association under which the contest is advertised to be conducted.
(Source: Laws 1895, p. 3.) [Formerly Ill. Rev. Stat. 8 §36.]

320/4. Official records received as evidence.

§4. It is further provided that the official records shall be received in all courts as evidence upon the trial of any person under the provisions of this act.
(Source: Laws 1895, p. 3.) [Formerly Ill. Rev. Stat. 8 §37.]

INSURANCE CLAIMS FOR EXCESSIVE CHARGES ACT

Sec.

325/1. Short title.

§1. Short title. This Act may be cited as the Insurance Claims For Excessive Charges Act.
(Source: P.A. 87-327.) [Formerly Ill. Rev. Stat. 73 §1701.]

325/5. Prohibitions.

§5. Prohibitions. (a) A person who sells goods or services commits an offense if:

(1) the person advertises or promises to provide the good or service and to pay:

(A) all or part of any applicable insurance deductible; or

(B) a rebate in an amount equal to all or part of any applicable insurance deductible;

(2) the good or service is paid for by the consumer from proceeds of a property or casualty insurance policy; and

(3) the person knowingly charges an amount for the good or service that exceeds the usual and customary charge by the person for the good or service by an amount equal to or greater than all or part of the applicable insurance deductible paid by the person to an insurer on behalf of an insured or remitted to an insured by the person as a rebate.

(b) A person who is insured under a property or casualty insurance policy commits an offense if the person:

(1) submits a claim under the policy based on charges that are in violation of subsection (a) of this Section; or

(2) knowingly allows a claim in violation of subsection (a) of this Section to be submitted, unless the person promptly notifies the insurer of the excessive charges.
(Source: P.A. 87-327.) [Formerly Ill. Rev. Stat. 73 §1705.]

325/10. Penalty.

§10. Penalty. A person who violates this Act is guilty of a Class A misdemeanor.
(Source: P.A. 87-327.) [Formerly Ill. Rev. Stat. 73 §1710.]

325/15. Effective date.

§15. Effective date. This Act takes effect January 1, 1992.
(Source: P.A. 87-327.) [Formerly Ill. Rev. Stat. 73 §1715.]

LOAN ADVERTISING TO BANKRUPTS ACT

330/0.01. Short title.

§0.01. Short title. This Act may be cited as the Loan Advertising to Bankrupts Act.
(Source: P.A. 86-1324.) [Formerly Ill. Rev. Stat. 121½ §157.24.]

330/1. Solicitation of bankrupt persons.

§1. No person engaged in the business of making loans or of selling any property or services under installment contracts or charge agreements may include in any solicitation of or advertisement for such business any language stating or implying that a loan or extension of credit will be made to a person who has been adjudged a bankrupt.
(Source: Laws 1967, p. 3546.) [Formerly Ill. Rev. Stat. 121½ §157.25.]

330/2. Penalty.

§2. Any person violating this Act shall be guilty of a business offense and shall be fined not more than $1,000.
(Source: P.A. 77-2251.) [Formerly Ill. Rev. Stat. 121½ §157.26.]

MARKS AND SERIAL NUMBERS ACT

335/1. Removal, alteration, etc., of manufacturer's serial number.

§1. Any person who removes, alters, defaces, covers or destroys the manufacturers' serial number or any other manufacturers' number or distinguishing identification mark upon any machine or other article of merchandise, other than a motor vehicle as defined in Section 1-146 of The Illinois Vehicle Code, for the purpose of concealing or destroying the identity of such machine or other article of merchandise shall be guilty of a Class B misdemeanor.
(Source: P.A. 78-255.) [Formerly Ill. Rev. Stat. 121½ §157.13.]

335/2. Short title.

§2. Short title. This Act may be cited as the Marks and Serial Numbers Act.
(Source: P.A. 86-1324.) [Formerly Ill. Rev. Stat. 121½ §157.13a.]

SALE OF MAPS ACT

340/0.01. Short title.

§0.01. Short title. This Act may be cited as the Sale of Maps Act.
(Source: P.A. 86-1324.) [Formerly Ill. Rev. Stat. 124 §200.]

340/1. Sale of current State publications and maps prohibited.

§1. The sale of current Illinois publications or highway maps published by the Secretary of State is prohibited except where provided by law.
(Source: P.A. 80-494.) [Formerly Ill. Rev. Stat. 124 §201.]

340/2. Penalty.

§2. Violation of this Act shall constitute a class B misdemeanor.
(Source: P.A. 80-494.) [Formerly Ill. Rev. Stat. 124 §202.]

SALE OR PLEDGE OF GOODS BY MINORS ACT

345/0.01. Short title.

§0.01. Short title. This Act may be cited as the Sale or Pledge of Goods by Minors Act.
(Source: P.A. 86-1324.) [Formerly Ill. Rev. Stat. 23 §2365.9.]

345/1. Unlawful for junk dealer, pawn broker, or second hand dealer to purchase from minor.

§1. It shall be unlawful for any junk dealer, pawn broker, or any second hand dealer, either directly or indirectly, to purchase or receive by way of barter or exchange, or otherwise, anything of value, or to receive on deposit or pledge anything of value, as security for a loan of money, from any person, either male or female, under the age of their legal majorities respectively.
(Source: Laws 1911, p. 294.) [Formerly Ill. Rev. Stat. 23 §2366.]

345/2. Violations.

§2. Any person violating the provisions of section 1 of this act [720 ILCS 345/1] shall, upon conviction, be guilty of a petty offense.
(Source: P.A. 77-2352.) [Formerly Ill. Rev. Stat. 23 §2367.]

SALE PRICE AD ACT

350/0.01. Short title.

§0.01. Short title. This Act may be cited as the Sale Price Ad Act.
(Source: P.A. 86-1324.) [Formerly Ill. Rev. Stat. 121½ §850.]

350/1. Definitions.

§1. As used in this Act:

"Seller" means any person or legal entity that is in the business of selling consumer goods to the public.

"Consumer goods" means any machine, appliance, clothing, or like product bought for personal, family or household purposes.

"Advertise" or "Advertising" means a notice in a newspaper, magazine, pamphlet or flyer; an announcement on television, cable television, or radio; and any other method of communicating to the public.

(Source: P.A. 79-732.) [Formerly Ill. Rev. Stat. 121½ §851.]

350/2. Incidental services—Advertised price to include cost, or statement to appear that services are furnished at extra cost.

§2. Whenever a seller advertises that consumers goods are for sale and that advertisement states the price of the consumer goods the stated price must include all services incidental to the proper use of the goods by the purchaser, or the ad must state clearly that such services will be furnished at extra cost.

(Source: P.A. 79-732.) [Formerly Ill. Rev. Stat. 121½ §852.]

350/3. Advertisements for goods at reduced prices must include extra charges for services.

§3. Whenever a seller advertises that consumer goods are for sale without stating a price, but with words such as "prices reduced", "⅓ off", "50% off" or words of similar meaning, such ad shall clearly state whether services incidental to the proper use of the goods will require an extra charge.

(Source: P.A. 79-732.) [Formerly Ill. Rev. Stat. 121½ §853.]

350/4. Violations.

§4. Violation of this Act is a business offense with a fine not to exceed $25.

(Source: P.A. 79-732.) [Formerly Ill. Rev. Stat. 121½ §854.]

STALLION AND JACK PEDIGREE ACT

355/0.01. Short title.

§0.01. Short title. This Act may be cited as the Stallion and Jack Pedigree Act.

(Source: P.A. 86-1324.) [Formerly Ill. Rev. Stat. 8 §32.9.]

355/1. Misrepresenting the pedigree or breeding of stallions or jacks.

§1. Any person, being the owner or keeper of any stallion or jack kept for public service, who shall misrepresent the pedigree or breeding of any such stallion or jack, or who shall represent that such animal, so kept for public service, is registered, when in fact it is not registered in a published volume of a society for the registry of standard and purebred animals, or who shall post or publish, or cause to be posted or published, any false pedigree or breeding of such animal, shall be guilty of a petty offense, and for the second or any subsequent offense shall be guilty of a Class B misdemeanor.

(Source: P.A. 77-2664.) [Formerly Ill. Rev. Stat. 8 §33.]

TELEPHONE LINE INTERFERENCE ACT

360/1. Injury to telephone or telegraph wires; interference with messages.

§1. Any person who wilfully and maliciously displaces, removes, injures or destroys any telegraph or telephone line, wire, cable, pole or conduit, belonging to another, or the material or property appurtenant thereto, or maliciously and wilfully cuts, breaks, taps, or makes any connection with any telegraph or telephone line, wire, cable or instrument belonging to another, or maliciously and wilfully reads, takes or copies any message, communication or report intended for another passing over any such telegraph line, wire or cable, in this State; or who wilfully and maliciously prevents, obstructs or delays by any means or contrivance whatsoever, the sending, transmission, conveyance or delivery, in this State of any message, communication or report by or through any telegraph or telephone line, wire or cable; or who uses any apparatus to unlawfully do or cause to be done any of the acts hereinbefore mentioned; or who aids, agrees with, employs or conspires with any person or persons to unlawfully do, or permit or cause to be done, any of the acts hereinbefore mentioned, shall be deemed guilty of a Class A misdemeanor.
(Source: P.A. 77-2615.) [Formerly Ill. Rev. Stat. 134 §15a.]

360/1.1. Short title.

§1.1. Short title. This Act may be cited as the Telephone Line Interference Act.
(Source: P.A. 86-1324.) [Formerly Ill. Rev. Stat. 134 §15a.1.]

TELEPHONE CHARGE FRAUD ACT

Sec.

365/0.01. Short title.

§0.01. Short title. This Act may be cited as the Telephone Charge Fraud Act.
(Source: P.A. 86-1324.) [Formerly Ill. Rev. Stat. 134 §15b.9.]

365/1. Services obtained with intent to defraud.

§1. Any individual, corporation, or other person, who, with intent to defraud or to aid and abet another to defraud any individual, corporation, or other person, of the lawful charge, in whole or in part, for any telecommunications service, shall obtain, or attempt to obtain, or aid and abet another to obtain or to attempt to obtain, any telecommunications service:

(a) by charging such service to an existing telephone number or credit card number without the authority of the subscriber thereto or the legitimate holder thereof, or,

(b) charging such service to a nonexistent, false, fictitious, or counterfeit telephone number or credit card number or to a suspended, terminated, expired, cancelled, or revoked telephone number or credit card number, or,

(c) by use of a code, prearranged scheme, or other similar stratagem or device whereby said person, in effect, sends or receives information, or,

(d) by installing, rearranging, or tampering with any facilities or equipment, whether physically, inductively, acoustically, electronically, or,

(e) by publishing the number or code of an existing, canceled, revoked or nonexistent telephone number, credit number or other credit device or method of numbering or coding which is employed in the issuance of telephone numbers, credit numbers or other credit devices which may be used to avoid the payment of any lawful telephone toll charge, or,

(f) by publishing plans, diagrams or methods for the construction, assembly or usage of any device, instrument or gadget which may be used to avoid the payment of any lawful telephone toll charge, or,

(g) by any other trick, stratagem, impersonation, false pretense, false representation, false statement, contrivance, device, or means, shall be deemed guilty of a Class A Misdemeanor.

As used in this Section "publish" means the communication or dissemination of information to any one or more persons, either orally, in person, or by telephone, radio or television or in writing of any kind, including, without limitation, a letter or memorandum, circular or handbill, newspaper or magazine article or book.

(Source: P.A. 78-853.) [Formerly Ill. Rev. Stat. 134 §15c.]

TELEPHONE COIN BOX TAMPERING ACT

370/0.01. Short title.

§0.01. Short title. This Act may be cited as the Telephone Coin Box Tampering Act.

(Source: P.A. 86-1324.) [Formerly Ill. Rev. Stat. 134 §16.01.]

370/1. Penalty.

§1. Any person who inserts or attempts to insert into the coin box or money receptacle or lock or coin return mechanism of any telephone, or into the material or property appurtenant thereto, any wire, pin, hook, pick, string, cord, paper, cloth, slug, disc, key, or other implement, substance, or object with the intent to defraud the owner of said telephone by obtaining from said telephone, or the material or property appurtenant thereto, a legal tender coin or coins of the United States or who aids, employs or conspires with any person or persons to do or permit or cause to be done any of the acts hereinbefore mentioned, shall be guilty of a Class B misdemeanor.

(Source: P.A. 77-2618.) [Formerly Ill. Rev. Stat. 134 §16.1.]

370/2. Prima facie proof of wrongful intent.

§2. Proof that any of the acts mentioned in Section 1 hereof [720 ILCS 370/1] was done without the lawful authority of the owner of such telephone shall be prima facie proof of the wrongful intent mentioned in Section 1 hereof.

(Source: Laws 1957, p. 222.) [Formerly Ill. Rev. Stat. 134 §16.2.]

TICKET SCALPING ACT

375/0.01. Short title.

§0.01. Short title. This Act may be cited as the Ticket Scalping Act.

(Source: P.A. 86-1324.) [Formerly Ill. Rev. Stat. 121½ §157.30.]

375/1. Sale, barter or exchange of tickets at place other than box office.

§1. It is unlawful for any person, firm or corporation, owner, lessee, manager, trustee, or any of their employees or agents, owning, conducting,

managing or operating any theater, circus, baseball park, place of public entertainment or amusement where tickets of admission are sold for any such places of amusement or public entertainment to sell or permit the sale, barter or exchange of such admission tickets at any other place than in the box office or on the premises of such theater, circus, baseball park, place of public entertainment or amusement, but nothing herein prevents such theater, circus, baseball park, place of public entertainment or amusement from placing any of its admission tickets for sale at any other place at the same price such admission tickets are sold by such theater, circus, baseball park or other place of public entertainment or amusement at its box office or on the premises of such places, at the same advertised price or printed rate thereof.
(Source: Laws 1923, p. 322.) [Formerly Ill. Rev. Stat. 121½ §157.31.]

375/1.5. Sale of ticket for price greater than price printed on ticket.

§1.5. (a) Except as otherwise provided in subsection (b) of this Section and in Section 4 [720 ILCS 375/4], it is unlawful for any person, persons, firm or corporation to sell tickets for baseball games, football games, hockey games, theatre entertainments, or any other amusement for a price more than the price printed upon the face of said ticket, and the price of said ticket shall correspond with the same price shown at the box office or the office of original distribution.

(b) This Act does not apply to the sale of tickets of admission to a sporting event, theater, musical performance, or place of public entertainment or amusement of any kind for a price in excess of the printed box office ticket price by a ticket broker who meets all of the following requirements:

(1) The ticket broker must engage in the sale of tickets on a regular and ongoing basis.

(2) The ticket broker must operate from one or more fixed locations.

(3) The ticket broker and his employees must not engage in the practice of selling, or attempting to sell, tickets for any event while sitting or standing near the facility at which the event is to be held or is being held.

(4) The ticket broker must comply with all requirements of the Retailers' Occupation Tax Act [35 ILCS 120/1 et seq.] and all other applicable federal, State and local laws in connection with his ticket selling activities.
(Source: P.A. 87-383; 87-895.) [Formerly Ill. Rev. Stat. 121½ §157.32.]

375/2. Penalty.

§2. (a) Whoever violates any of the provisions of Section 1 ½ of this Act [720 ILCS 375/1.5] shall be guilty of a Class A misdemeanor and may be fined up to $5,000.00 for each offense and whoever violates any other provision of this Act may be enjoined and be required to make restitution to all injured consumers upon application for injunctive relief by the State's Attorney or Attorney General and shall also be guilty of a Class A misdemeanor, and any owner, lessee, manager or trustee convicted under this Act shall, in addition to the penalty herein provided, forfeit the license of such theatre, circus, baseball park, place of public entertainment or amusement so granted and the same shall be revoked by the authorities granting the same.

(b) Tickets sold or offered for sale by a person, firm or corporation in violation of Section 1 ½ of this Act may be confiscated by a court on motion of the Attorney General, a State's Attorney, the sponsor of the event for which the tickets are being sold, or the owner or operator of the facility at which the event is to be held, and may be donated by order of the court to an appropriate organization as defined under Section 2 of the Charitable Games Act [230 ILCS 30/2].

(c) The Attorney General, a State's Attorney, the sponsor of an event for which tickets are being sold, or the owner or operator of the facility at which an event is to be held may seek an injunction restraining any person, firm or corporation from selling or offering for sale tickets in violation of the provisions

of this Act. In addition, on motion of the Attorney General, a State's Attorney, the sponsor of an event for which tickets are being sold, or the owner or operator of the facility at which an event is to be held, a court may permanently enjoin a person, firm or corporation found guilty of violating Section 1 ½ of this Act from engaging in the offer or sale of tickets.
(Source: P.A. 86-1210.) [Formerly Ill. Rev. Stat. 121½ §157.33.]

375/3. Civil action by person overcharged for tickets.

§3. Whoever, upon the purchase of such admission tickets as herein provided, feels himself aggrieved or injured by paying for such tickets any sum in excess of the advertised price or printed rate, or any sum in excess of the price originally charged at the box office or place where such admission tickets usually are sold by the management of any such place of entertainment or amusement, has, irrespective of the penalties herein provided, a right of action in his name and against such person, firm, corporation, owner, lessee, manager, trustee, or any of their agents or employees owning, conducting, managing or operating any such theater, circus, baseball park or place of public entertainment or amusement, to recover for each ticket for which an overcharge was made contrary to the provisions of this Act, a sum of $100, which may be recovered in a civil action before the circuit court in this State.
(Source: P.A. 84-1103.) [Formerly Ill. Rev. Stat. 121½ §157.34.]

375/4. Collection of service charges.

§4. Nothing contained in this Act was ever intended to prohibit nor shall ever be deemed to prohibit a ticket seller, with consent of the sponsor of such baseball game, football game, hockey game, theatre entertainment or other amusement, from collecting a reasonable service charge, in addition to the printed box office ticket price, from a ticket purchaser in return for service actually rendered.
(Source: P.A. 80-1245.) [Formerly Ill. Rev. Stat. 121½ §157.35.]

TITLE PAGE ACT

Sec.

380/1. Sale of publications without cover, title page or other identification mark.

§1. Any person who knowingly sells, offers or exposes for sale (except in bulk as waste paper) any newspaper, magazine, periodical or other publication, except a rare book, manuscript or educational text, from which the cover or title page has been removed, or from which the title, trade name, trade mark or other identification mark has been removed or obliterated, is guilty of a petty offense.
(Source: P.A. 77-2830.) [Formerly Ill. Rev. Stat. 121½ §157.14.]

380/1a. Short title.

§1a. Short title. This Act may be cited as the Title Page Act.
(Source: P.A. 86-1324.) [Formerly Ill. Rev. Stat. 121½ §157.14a.]

380/2. Penalty for violations.

§2. Whoever violates any of the provisions of this Act shall be guilty of a petty offense and fined not less than $25 nor more than $100.
(Source: P.A. 77-2249.) [Formerly Ill. Rev. Stat. 121½ §157.15.]

UNECONOMIC PRACTICES ACT

385/0.01. Short title.

§0.01. Short title. This Act may be cited as the Uneconomic Practices Act.
(Source: P.A. 86-1324.) [Formerly Ill. Rev. Stat. 121½ §203.9.]

385/1. Sale of articles not in regular course of trade; exceptions.

§1. No person, firm or corporation engaged in any business enterprise in this state shall, by any method or procedure, directly or indirectly, by itself or through a subsidiary agency owned or controlled in whole or in part by such person, firm or corporation, sell or procure for sale or have in its possession or under its control for sale to its employees or any person, any article, material, product or merchandise of whatsoever nature not of his or its own production or not handled in his or its regular course of trade, excepting meals, cigarettes and tobacco, and excepting such specialized appliances and paraphernalia as may be required in said business enterprise for the safety or health of its employees. The provisions of this section shall not apply to associations organized under "An Act to provide for the incorporation of cooperative associations for pecuniary profit," filed July 8, 1915, as amended [805 ILCS 310/1 et seq.], or to associations organized under "An Act in relation to Agricultural Cooperative Associations and Societies," approved June 21, 1923, as amended [805 ILCS 315/1 et seq.].
(Source: Laws 1941, p. 1119.) [Formerly Ill. Rev. Stat. 121½ §204.]

385/2. Penalty for violations.

§2. Any person, firm or corporation violating the provisions of this act shall be deemed guilty of a business offense and upon conviction thereof shall be punished for the first offense by a fine of not less than one hundred dollars nor more than five hundred dollars, and for a second or subsequent offense by a fine of not less than five hundred dollars nor more than one thousand dollars. Each act done, prohibited by this act, shall constitute a separate violation and offense hereunder.
(Source: P.A. 77-2257.) [Formerly Ill. Rev. Stat. 121½ §205.]

USE OF UNIVERSITY STATIONERY ACT

390/0.01. Short title.

§0.01. Short title. This Act may be cited as the Use of University Stationery Act.
(Source: P.A. 86-1324.) [Formerly Ill. Rev. Stat. 38 §70.]

390/1. Prohibition of use.

§1. No person, firm or corporation shall use the official stationery or seal or a facsimile thereof, of any State supported university, college or other institution of higher education or any organization thereof unless approved in writing in advance by the university, college or institution of higher education affected, for any private promotional scheme wherein it is made to appear that the organization or university, college or other institution of higher education is endorsing the private promotional scheme.
(Source: Laws 1965, p. 782.) [Formerly Ill. Rev. Stat. 38 §70-1.]

390/2. Sentence.

§2. Sentence. A violation of this Act is a petty offense.
(Source: P. A. 77-2641.) [Formerly Ill. Rev. Stat. 38 §70-2.]

VIDEO MOVIE SALES AND RENTALS ACT

395/1. Short title.

§1. This Act shall be known and may be cited as the Video Movie Sales and Rentals Act.
(Source: P.A. 84-593.) [Formerly Ill. Rev. Stat. 121½ §1351.]

395/2. Definitions.

§2. As used in this Act, unless the context otherwise requires, the following terms have the meanings ascribed to them in this Section:

(a) "Video movie" means a videotape or video disc copy of a motion picture film.

(b) "Person" means an individual, corporation, partnership, or any other legal or commercial entity.

(c) "Official rating" means an official rating of the Motion Picture Association of America.
(Source: P.A. 84-593.) [Formerly Ill. Rev. Stat. 121½ §1352.]

395/3. Official rating must be displayed.

§3. (a) A person may not sell at retail or rent, or attempt to sell at retail or rent, a video movie in this State unless the official rating of the motion picture from which it is copied is clearly displayed on the outside of any cassette, case, jacket, or other covering of the video movie.

(b) Subsection (a) of this Section does not apply to any video movie of a motion picture which:

(1) Has not been given an official rating; or

(2) Has been altered in any way subsequent to receiving an official rating.
(Source: P.A. 84-593.) [Formerly Ill. Rev. Stat. 121½ §1353.]

395/4. Violations.

§4. Any person who sells or rents, or attempts to sell or rent, a video movie in violation of this Act shall be guilty of a Class C misdemeanor.
(Source: P.A. 84-593.) [Formerly Ill. Rev. Stat. 121½ §1354.]

WILD PLANT CONSERVATION ACT

400/0.01. Short title.

§0.01. Short title. This Act may be cited as the Wild Plant Conservation Act.
(Source: P.A. 86-1324.) [Formerly Ill. Rev. Stat. 5 §230.]

400/1. Sale of plants gathered from public or private lands.

§1. Any person, firm or corporation who knowingly buys, sells, offers or exposes for sale any blood root (Sanguinaria Canadensis), lady slipper (Cyprepedium Parviflorum and Cyprepedium Hirsutum), columbine (Aquilegia Canadensis), trillum (Trillium Grandiflorum and Trillum Sessile), lotus (Nelumbo Lutes), or gentian (Gentiana Crinta and Gentiana Andrewsii), or any part thereof, dug, pulled up or gathered from any public or private land, unless in the case of private land the owner or person lawfully occupying such land gives his consent in writing thereto, is guilty of petty offense.
(Source: P.A. 77-2494.) [Formerly Ill. Rev. Stat. 5 §231.]

400/2. Time limit for prosecutions.

§2. All prosecutions under this Act shall be commenced within six months from the time such offense was committed and not afterwards.
(Source: Laws 1923, p. 5.) [Formerly Ill. Rev. Stat. 5 §232.]

OFFENSES AGAINST THE PUBLIC

ABANDONED REFRIGERATOR ACT

Sec.

505/0.01. Short title.

§0.01. Short title. This Act may be cited as the Abandoned Refrigerator Act.
(Source: P.A. 86-1324.) [Formerly Ill. Rev. Stat. 23 §2355.9.]

505/1. Abandonment of refrigerator, etc. in place accessible to children.

§1. Whoever abandons or discards in any place accessible to children any refrigerator, icebox or ice chest, of a capacity of one and one-half cubic feet or more, which has an attached lid or door which may be opened or fastened shut by means of an attached latch, or who, being the owner, lessee, or manager of such place, knowingly permits such abandoned or discarded refrigerator, icebox or ice chest to remain there in such condition, shall be guilty of a Class C misdemeanor.
(Source: P.A. 77-2347.) [Formerly Ill. Rev. Stat. 23 §2356.]

ILLINOIS ABORTION LAW OF 1975

Sec.

510/1. Legislative intent.

§1. It is the intention of the General Assembly of the State of Illinois to reasonably regulate abortion in conformance with the decisions of the United

States Supreme Court of January 22, 1973. Without in any way restricting the right of privacy of a woman or the right of a woman to an abortion under those decisions, the General Assembly of the State of Illinois do solemnly declare and find in reaffirmation of the longstanding policy of this State, that the unborn child is a human being from the time of conception and is, therefore, a legal person for purposes of the unborn child's right to life and is entitled to the right to life from conception under the laws and Constitution of this State. Further, the General Assembly finds and declares that longstanding policy of this State to protect the right to life of the unborn child from conception by prohibiting abortion unless necessary to preserve the life of the mother is impermissible only because of the decisions of the United States Supreme Court and that, therefore, if those decisions of the United States Supreme Court are ever reversed or modified or the United States Constitution is amended to allow protection of the unborn then the former policy of this State to prohibit abortions unless necessary for the preservation of the mother's life shall be reinstated.

It is the further intention of the General Assembly to assure and protect the woman's health and the integrity of the woman's decision whether or not to continue to bear a child, to protect the valid and compelling state interest in the infant and unborn child, to assure the integrity of marital and familial relations and the rights and interests of persons who participate in such relations, and to gather data for establishing criteria for medical decisions. The General Assembly finds as fact, upon hearings and public disclosures, that these rights and interests are not secure in the economic and social context in which abortion is presently performed.

(Source: P.A. 81-1078.) [Formerly Ill. Rev. Stat. 38 §81-21.]

510/2. Definitions.

§2. Unless the language or context clearly indicates a different meaning is intended, the following words or phrases for the purpose of this Law shall be given the meaning ascribed to them:

(1) "Viability" means that stage of fetal development when, in the medical judgment of the attending physician based on the particular facts of the case before him, there is a reasonable likelihood of sustained survival of the fetus outside the womb, with or without artificial support.

(2) "Physician" means any person licensed to practice medicine in all its branches under the Illinois Medical Practice Act of 1987, as amended [225 ILCS 60/1 et seq.].

(3) "Department" means the Department of Public Health, State of Illinois.

(4) "Abortion" means the use of any instrument, medicine, drug or any other substance or device to terminate the pregnancy of a woman known to be pregnant with an intention other than to increase the probability of a live birth, to preserve the life or health of the child after live birth, or to remove a dead fetus.

(5) "Fertilization" and "conception" each mean the fertilization of a human ovum by a human sperm, which shall be deemed to have occurred at the time when it is known a spermatozoon has penetrated the cell membrane of the ovum.

(6) "Fetus" and "unborn child" each mean an individual organism of the species homo sapiens from fertilization until live birth.

(7) "Abortifacient" means any instrument, medicine, drug, or any other substance or device which is known to cause fetal death when employed in the usual and customary use for which it is manufactured, whether or not the fetus is known to exist when such substance or device is employed.

(8) "Born alive", "live born", and "live birth", when applied to an individual organism of the species homo sapiens, each mean he or she was completely expelled or extracted from his or her mother and after such separation breathed

or showed evidence of any of the following: beating of the heart, pulsation of the umbilical cord, or definite movement of voluntary muscles, irrespective of the duration of pregnancy and whether or not the umbilical cord has been cut or the placenta is attached.
(Source: P.A. 85-1209.) [Formerly Ill. Rev. Stat. 38 §81-22.]

510/3.1. Medical judgment.
§3.1. Medical Judgment. No abortion shall be performed except by a physician after either (a) he determines that, in his best clinical judgment, the abortion is necessary, or (b) he receives a written statement or oral communication by another physician, hereinafter called the "referring physician", certifying that in the referring physician's best clinical judgment the abortion is necessary. Any person who intentionally or knowingly performs an abortion contrary to the requirements of Section 3.1 commits a Class 2 felony.
(Source: P.A. 83-1128.) [Formerly Ill. Rev. Stat. 38 §81-23.1.]

510/5. Life and health of mother.
§5. (1) When the fetus is viable no abortion shall be performed unless in the medical judgment of the attending or referring physician, based on the particular facts of the case before him, it is necessary to preserve the life or health of the mother. Intentional, knowing, or reckless failure to conform to the requirements of subsection (1) of Section 5 is a Class 2 felony.
(2) When the fetus is viable the physician shall certify in writing, on a form prescribed by the Department under Section 10 of this Law [720 ILCS 510/10], the medical indications which, in his medical judgment based on the particular facts of the case before him, warrant performance of the abortion to preserve the life or health of the mother.
(Source: P.A. 83-1128.) [Formerly Ill. Rev. Stat. 38 §81-25.]

510/6. Life and health of fetus; method of abortion employed.
§6. (1) (a) Any physician who intentionally performs an abortion when, in his medical judgment based on the particular facts of the case before him, there is a reasonable likelihood of sustained survival of the fetus outside the womb, with or without artificial support, shall utilize that method of abortion which, of those he knows to be available, is in his medical judgment most likely to preserve the life and health of the fetus.
(b) The physician shall certify in writing, on a form prescribed by the Department under Section 10 of this Act [720 ILCS 510/10], the available methods considered and the reasons for choosing the method employed.
(c) Any physician who intentionally, knowingly, or recklessly violates the provisions of Section 6(1)(a) commits a Class 3 felony.
(2) (a) No abortion shall be performed or induced when the fetus is viable unless there is in attendance a physician other than the physician performing or inducing the abortion who shall take control of and provide immediate medical care for any child born alive as a result of the abortion. This requirement shall not apply when, in the medical judgment of the physician performing or inducing the abortion based on the particular facts of the case before him, there exists a medical emergency; in such a case, the physician shall describe the basis of this judgment on the form prescribed by Section 10 of this Act. Any physician who intentionally performs or induces such an abortion and who intentionally, knowingly, or recklessly fails to arrange for the attendance of such a second physician in violation of Section 6(2)(a) commits a Class 3 felony.
(b) Subsequent to the abortion, if a child is born alive, the physician required by Section 6(2)(a) to be in attendance shall exercise the same degree of professional skill, care and diligence to preserve the life and health of the child as would be required of a physician providing immediate medical care to a child

born alive in the course of a pregnancy termination which was not an abortion. Any such physician who intentionally, knowingly, or recklessly violates Section 6(2)(b) commits a Class 3 felony.

(3) The law of this State shall not be construed to imply that any living individual organism of the species homo sapiens who has been born alive is not an individual under the "Criminal Code of 1961," approved July 28, 1961, as amended [720 ILCS 5/1-1 et seq.].

(4) (a) Any physician who intentionally performs an abortion when, in his medical judgment based on the particular facts of the case before him, there is a reasonable possibility of sustained survival of the fetus outside the womb, with or without artificial support, shall utilize that method of abortion which, of those he knows to be available, is in his medical judgment most likely to preserve the life and health of the fetus.

(b) The physician shall certify in writing, on a form prescribed by the Department under Section 10 of this Act, the available methods considered and the reasons for choosing the method employed.

(c) Any physician who intentionally, knowingly, or recklessly violates the provisions of Section 6(4)(a) commits a Class 3 felony.

(5) Nothing in Section 6 requires a physician to employ a method of abortion which, in the medical judgment of the physician performing the abortion based on the particular facts of the case before him, would increase medical risk to the mother.

(6) When the fetus is viable and when there exists reasonable medical certainty (a) that the particular method of abortion to be employed will cause organic pain to the fetus, and (b) that use of an anesthetic or analgesic would abolish or alleviate organic pain to the fetus caused by the particular method of abortion to be employed, then the physician who is to perform the abortion or his agent or the referring physician or his agent shall inform the woman upon whom the abortion is to be performed that such an anesthetic or analgesic is available, if he knows it to be available, for use to abolish or alleviate organic pain caused to the fetus by the particular method of abortion to be employed. Any person who performs an abortion with knowledge that any such reasonable medical certainty exists and that such an anesthetic or analgesic is available, and intentionally fails to so inform the woman or to ascertain that the woman has been so informed commits a Class B misdemeanor. The foregoing requirements of subsection (6) of Section 6 shall not apply (a) when in the medical judgment of the physician who is to perform the abortion or the referring physician based upon the particular facts of the case before him: (i) there exists a medical emergency, or (ii) the administration of such an anesthetic or analgesic would decrease a possibility of sustained survival of the fetus apart from the body of the mother, with or without artificial support, or (b) when the physician who is to perform the abortion administers an anesthetic or an analgesic to the woman or the fetus and he knows there exists reasonable medical certainty that such use will abolish organic pain caused to the fetus during the course of the abortion.

(7) No person shall sell or experiment upon a fetus produced by the fertilization of a human ovum by a human sperm unless such experimentation is therapeutic to the fetus thereby produced. Intentional violation of this section is a Class A misdemeanor. Nothing in this subsection (7) is intended to prohibit the performance of in vitro fertilization.

(8) No person shall intentionally perform an abortion with knowledge that the pregnant woman is seeking the abortion solely on account of the sex of the fetus. Nothing in Section 6(8) shall be construed to proscribe the performance of an abortion on account of the sex of the fetus because of a genetic disorder linked to that sex. If the application of Section 6(8) to the period of pregnancy

prior to viability is held invalid, then such invalidity shall not affect its application to the period of pregnancy subsequent to viability.
(Source: P.A. 84-1001.) [Formerly Ill. Rev. Stat. 38 §81-26.]

510/10. Report of abortions.

§10. A report of each abortion performed shall be made to the Department on forms prescribed by it. Such report forms shall not identify the patient by name, but by an individual number to be noted in the patient's permanent record in the possession of the physician, and shall include information concerning:

(1) Identification of the physician who performed the abortion and the facility where the abortion was performed and a patient identification number;

(2) State in which the patient resides;

(3) Patient's date of birth, race and marital status;

(4) Number of prior pregnancies;

(5) Date of last menstrual period;

(6) Type of abortion procedure performed;

(7) Complications and whether the abortion resulted in a live birth;

(8) The date the abortion was performed;

(9) Medical indications for any abortion performed when the fetus was viable;

(10) The information required by Sections 6(1)(b) and 6(4)(b) of this Act [720 ILCS 510/6], if applicable;

(11) Basis for any medical judgment that a medical emergency existed when required under Sections 6(2)(a) and 6(6) and when required to be reported in accordance with this Section by any provision of this Law; and

(12) The pathologist's test results pursuant to Section 12 of this Act [720 ILCS 510/12].

Such form shall be completed by the hospital or other licensed facility, signed by the physician who performed the abortion or pregnancy termination, and transmitted to the Department not later than 10 days following the end of the month in which the abortion was performed.

In the event that a complication of an abortion occurs or becomes known after submission of such form, a correction using the same patient identification number shall be submitted to the Department within 10 days of its becoming known.

The Department may prescribe rules and regulations regarding the administration of this Law and shall prescribe regulations to secure the confidentiality of the woman's identity in the information to be provided under the "Vital Records Act" [410 ILCS 535/1 et seq.]. All reports received by the Department shall be treated as confidential and the Department shall secure the woman's anonymity. Such reports shall be used only for statistical purposes.

Upon 30 days public notice, the Department is empowered to require reporting of any additional information which, in the sound discretion of the Department, is necessary to develop statistical data relating to the protection of maternal or fetal life or health, or is necessary to enforce the provisions of this Law, or is necessary to develop useful criteria for medical decisions. The Department shall annually report to the General Assembly all statistical data gathered under this Law and its recommendations to further the purpose of this Law.

The requirement for reporting to the General Assembly shall be satisfied by filing copies of the report with the Speaker, the Minority Leader and the Clerk of the House of Representatives and the President, the Minority Leader and the Secretary of the Senate and the Legislative Research Unit, as required by Section 3.1 of "An Act to revise the law in relation to the General Assembly", approved February 25, 1874, as amended [25 ILCS 5/3.1], and filing such

additional copies with the State Government Report Distribution Center for the General Assembly as is required under paragraph (t) of Section 7 of the State Library Act [15 ILCS 320/7].
(Source: P.A. 84-1438.) [Formerly Ill. Rev. Stat. 38 §81-30.]

510/10.1. Complications resulting from abortion; reports.

§10.1. Any physician who diagnoses a woman as having complications resulting from an abortion shall report, within a reasonable period of time, the diagnosis and a summary of her physical symptoms to the Illinois Department of Public Health in accordance with procedures and upon forms required by such Department. The Department of Public Health shall define the complications required to be reported by rule. The complications defined by rule shall be those which, according to contemporary medical standards, are manifested by symptoms with severity equal to or greater than hemorrhaging requiring transfusion, infection, incomplete abortion, or punctured organs. If the physician making the diagnosis of a complication knows the name or location of the facility where the abortion was performed, he shall report such information to the Department of Public Health.

Any physician who intentionally violates this Section shall be subject to revocation of his license pursuant to paragraph (22) of Section 22 of the Medical Practice Act of 1987 [225 ILCS 60/22].
(Source: P.A. 85-1209.) [Formerly Ill. Rev. Stat. 38 §81-30.1.]

510/11. Violations; penalties.

§11. (1) Any person who intentionally violates any provision of this Law commits a Class A misdemeanor unless a specific penalty is otherwise provided. Any person who intentionally falsifies any writing required by this Law commits a Class A misdemeanor.

Intentional, knowing, reckless, or negligent violations of this Law shall constitute unprofessional conduct which causes public harm under Section 22 of the Medical Practice Act of 1987, as amended [225 ILCS 60/22]; Section 25 of the Illinois Nursing Act of 1987, as amended [225 ILCS 65/25], and Section 21 of the Physician Assistant Practice Act of 1987, as amended [225 ILCS 95/21].

Intentional, knowing, reckless or negligent violations of this Law will constitute grounds for refusal, denial, revocation, suspension, or withdrawal of license, certificate, or permit under Section 30 of the Pharmacy Practice Act of 1987, as amended [225 ILCS 85/30]; Section 7 of the "Ambulatory Surgical Treatment Center Act", effective July 19, 1973, as amended [210 ILCS 5/7]; and Section 7 of the "Hospital Licensing Act", approved July 1, 1953, as amended [210 ILCS 85/7].

(2) Any hospital or licensed facility which, or any physician who intentionally, knowingly, or recklessly fails to submit a complete report to the Department in accordance with the provisions of Section 10 of this Law [720 ILCS 510/10] and any person who intentionally, knowingly, recklessly or negligently fails to maintain the confidentiality of any reports required under this Law or reports required by Sections 10.1 or 12 of this Law [720 ILCS 510/10.1 or 510/12] commits a Class B misdemeanor.

(3) Any person who sells any drug, medicine, instrument or other substance which he knows to be an abortifacient and which is in fact an abortifacient, unless upon prescription of a physician, is guilty of a Class B misdemeanor. Any person who prescribes or administers any instrument, medicine, drug or other substance or device, which he knows to be an abortifacient, and which is in fact an abortifacient, and intentionally, knowingly or recklessly fails to inform the person for whom it is prescribed or upon whom it is administered that it is an abortifacient commits a Class C misdemeanor.

(4) Any person who intentionally, knowingly or recklessly performs upon a woman what he represents to that woman to be an abortion when he knows or should know that she is not pregnant commits a Class 2 felony and shall be answerable in civil damages equal to 3 times the amount of proved damages.
(Source: P.A. 85-1209.) [Formerly Ill. Rev. Stat. 38 §81-31.]

510/11.1. Payment or receipt of referral fee prohibited.

§11.1. (a) The payment or receipt of a referral fee in connection with the performance of an abortion is a Class 4 felony.

(b) For purposes of this Section, "referral fee" means the transfer of anything of value between a doctor who performs an abortion or an operator or employee of a clinic at which an abortion is performed and the person who advised the woman receiving the abortion to use the services of that doctor or clinic.
(Source: P.A. 81-1119.) [Formerly Ill. Rev. Stat. 38 §81-31.1.]

510/12. Gross and microscopic analysis of dead fetus and tissue required.

§12. The dead fetus and all tissue removed at the time of abortion shall be submitted for a gross and microscopic analysis and tissue report to a board eligible or certified pathologist as a matter of record in all cases. The results of the analysis and report shall be given to the physician who performed the abortion within 7 days of the abortion and such physician shall report any complications relevant to the woman's medical condition to his patient within 48 hours of receiving a report if possible. Any evidence of live birth or of viability shall be reported within 7 days, if possible, to the Department by the pathologist. Intentional failure of the pathologist to report any evidence of live birth or of viability to the Department is a Class B misdemeanor.
(Source: P.A. 83-1128.) [Formerly Ill. Rev. Stat. 38 §81-32.]

510/12.1. Use of tissues or cells from dead fetus.

§12.1. Nothing in this Act shall prohibit the use of any tissues or cells obtained from a dead fetus or dead premature infant whose death did not result from an induced abortion, for therapeutic purposes or scientific, research, or laboratory experimentation, provided that the written consent to such use is obtained from one of the parents of such fetus or infant.
(Source: P.A. 81-884.) [Formerly Ill. Rev. Stat. 38 §81-32.1.]

510/13. Liability of persons with objections to abortions.

§13. No physician, hospital, ambulatory surgical center, nor employee thereof, shall be required against his or its conscience declared in writing to perform, permit or participate in any abortion, and the failure or refusal to do so shall not be the basis for any civil, criminal, administrative or disciplinary action, proceeding, penalty or punishment. If any request for an abortion is denied, the patient shall be promptly notified.
(Source: P.A. 81-1078.) [Formerly Ill. Rev. Stat. 38 §81-33.]

510/14. Severability; regulations.

§14. (1) If any provision, word, phrase or clause of this Act or the application thereof to any person or circumstance shall be held invalid, such invalidity shall not affect the provisions, words, phrases, clauses or application of this Act which can be given effect without the invalid provision, word, phrase, clause, or application, and to this end the provisions, words, phrases, and clauses of this Act are declared to be severable.

(2) Within 60 days from the time this Section becomes law, the Department shall issue regulations pursuant to Section 10 [720 ILCS 510/10]. Insofar as Section 10 requires registration under the "Vital Records Act" [410 ILCS 535/1 et seq.], it shall not take effect until such regulations are issued. The Depart-

ment shall make available the forms required under Section 10 within 30 days of the time this Section becomes law. No requirement that any person report information to the Department shall become effective until the Department has made available the forms required under Section 10. All other provisions of this amended Law shall take effect immediately upon enactment.
(Source: P.A. 83-1128.) [Formerly Ill. Rev. Stat. 38 §81-34.]

510/15. Short title.

§15. This Act shall be known and may be cited as the "Illinois Abortion Law of 1975".
(Source: P.A. 81-1078.) [Formerly Ill. Rev. Stat. 38 §81-35.]

ILLINOIS ABORTION PARENTAL CONSENT ACT OF 1977

Sec.

515/1. Legislative intent.

§1. Legislative Intent. It is the intent of the General Assembly of the State of Illinois that the rights and responsibilities of parents be respected, that the health and welfare of minors and their unborn children be protected, and that no minor child who has not married shall be allowed to undergo an abortion operation without the consultation and consent of her parents, or a court order as part of the informed consent of the minor child seeking the abortion.
(Source: P.A. 80-1139.) [Formerly Ill. Rev. Stat. 38 §81-51.]

515/2. Title of Act.

§2. Title of Act. This Act shall be known and may be cited as the Illinois Abortion Parental Consent Act of 1977.
(Source: P.A. 80-1139.) [Formerly Ill. Rev. Stat. 38 §81-52.]

515/3. Abortion, defined.

§3. As used in this Act, "abortion" means the use of any instrument, medicine, drug or other substance, whatever, with the intent to procure a miscarriage of any woman, regardless of whether the woman is pregnant or whether a miscarriage is accomplished.
(Source: P.A. 80-1139.) [Formerly Ill. Rev. Stat. 38 §81-53.]

515/4. Abortion performed on minor child; parental consent.

§4. No abortion shall be performed in this State if the woman is under 18 years of age and has not married except:

(1) By a duly licensed, consenting physician in the exercise of his best clinical medical judgment;

(2) After the minor, 48 hours prior to submitting to the abortion, certifies in writing her consent to the abortion and that her consent is informed and freely given and is not the result of coercion; and

(3) After the consent of her parents is secured and certified in writing.

If one of the parents has died, has deserted his or her family, or is not available, consent by the remaining parent is sufficient. If both parents have died, have deserted their family, or are not available, consent of the minor's guardian or other person standing in loco parentis is sufficient.

If such consent is refused or cannot be obtained, consent may be obtained by order of a judge of the circuit court upon a finding, after such hearing as the judge deems necessary, that the pregnant minor fully understands the consequences of an abortion to her and her unborn child. Such a hearing will not require the appointment of a guardian for the minor. Notice of such hearing shall be sent to the parents of the minor at their last known address by registered or certified mail. The procedure shall be handled expeditiously.

The Department of Public Health shall prescribe a written form for such consent. Such form shall be signed by the proper person or persons and given to the physician performing the abortion who shall maintain it in his permanent files.

Nothing in this Section shall be construed as abolishing or limiting any statutory or common law rights of any other person or persons relative to consent to the performance of an abortion for purposes of any civil action or any injunctive relief. This Section does not apply to any abortion performed which is necessary for the preservation of the life of the mother.
(Source: P.A. 80-1139.) [Formerly Ill. Rev. Stat. 38 §81-54.]

515/5. Violation.

§5. Any person who performs an abortion in violation of this Act commits a Class A misdemeanor.
(Source: P.A. 80-1139.) [Formerly Ill. Rev. Stat. 38 §81-55.]

PARENTAL NOTICE OF ABORTION ACT OF 1983

Sec.

520/1. Short title.

§1. Short title. This Act shall be known and may be cited as the Parental Notice of Abortion Act of 1983.
(Source: P.A. 83-890.) [Formerly Ill. Rev. Stat. 38 §81-61.]

520/2. Legislative purpose and findings.

§2. Legislative purpose and findings. (a) It is the intent of the legislature in enacting this parental notice provision to further the important and compelling State interests of: 1) protecting minors against their own immaturity, 2) fostering the family structure and preserving it as a viable social unit, and 3) protecting the rights of parents to rear children who are members of their household.

(b) The legislature finds as fact that: 1) immature minors often lack the ability to make fully informed choices that take account of both immediate and long-range consequences, 2) the medical, emotional and psychological consequences of abortion are serious and can be lasting, particularly when the patient is immature, 3) the capacity to become pregnant and the capacity for mature judgment concerning the wisdom of an abortion are not necessarily related, 4) parents ordinarily possess information essential to a physician's exercise of his best medical judgment concerning the child, and 5) parents who are aware that their minor daughter has had an abortion may better ensure that she receives adequate medical attention after her abortion. The legislature further finds that parental consultation is usually desirable and in the best interests of the minor.
(Source: P.A. 83-890.) [Formerly Ill. Rev. Stat. 38 §81-62.]

520/3. Definitions.

§3. Definitions. For purposes of this Act, the following definitions will apply:

(a) "minor" means any person under the age of 18;

(b) "emancipated minor" means any minor who is or has been married or has by court order otherwise been freed from the care, custody, and control of her parents;

(c) "actual notice" means the giving of notice directly, in person or by telephone;

(d) "abortion" means the use of any instrument, medicine, drug or any other substance or device with intent to terminate the pregnancy of a woman known to be pregnant with intent other than to cause live birth;

(e) "incompetent" means any person who has been adjudged a disabled person and has had a guardian appointed for her as provided under Section 11a-3(a)(1) or Section 11a-3(3) of the Probate Act of 1975 [755 ILCS 5/11a-3].
(Source: P.A. 83-890.) [Formerly Ill. Rev. Stat. 38 §81-63.]

520/4. Notice required.

§4. Notice required. (a) No person shall perform an abortion upon an unemancipated minor or upon an incompetent unless he or his agent has given at least 24 hours actual notice to both parents or to the legal guardian of the minor pregnant woman or incompetent of his intention to perform the abortion or unless he or his agent has received a written statement or oral communication by another physician, hereinafter called the "referring physician", certifying that the referring physician or his agent has given such notice.

(b) If the minor's or incompetent's parents are divorced, or one parent is not available to the person performing the abortion or his agent or the referring physician or his agent in a reasonable time or manner, then notice to the parent with custody or to the parent who is available shall be sufficient. If neither parent nor the legal guardian is available to the person performing the abortion or his agent or the referring physician or his agent within a reasonable time or manner, notice to any adult person standing in loco parentis shall be sufficient.

(c) A minor or incompetent who objects to notice being given her parents or legal guardian under this section may petition, on her own behalf or by next friend, the circuit court of the county in which the minor resides or in which the abortion is to be performed for a waiver of the notice requirement of this section pursuant to the procedures of Section 5 of this Act [720 ILCS 520/5].
(Source: P.A. 83-890.) [Formerly Ill. Rev. Stat. 38 §81-64.]

520/5. Procedure for waiver of notice.

§5. Procedure for waiver of notice. (a) The requirements and procedures under this Act are available to minors and incompetents whether or not they are residents of this State.

(b) The minor or incompetent may participate in proceedings in the court on her own behalf and the court shall appoint a guardian ad litem for her. The court shall advise her that she has a right to court appointed counsel and shall provide her with such counsel upon her request.

(c) Court proceedings under this Section shall be confidential and shall ensure the anonymity of the minor or incompetent. These proceedings shall be given such precedence over other pending matters as is necessary to ensure that the court may reach a decision promptly, but in no case shall the court fail to rule within 48 hours of the time of application, provided that the 48 hour limitation may be extended at the request of the minor or incompetent.

(d) Notice shall be waived if the court finds either:

(i) That the minor or incompetent is mature and well-informed enough to make the abortion decision on her own, or

(ii) That notification of those to whom Section 4 of this Act [720 ILCS 520/4] requires that notice be given would not be in the best interests of the minor or incompetent.

(e) A court that conducts proceedings under this Section shall issue written and specific factual findings and legal conclusions supporting its decision and shall order that a confidential record of the evidence be maintained.

(f) An expedited confidential appeal shall be available, as the Supreme Court provides by rule, to any minor or incompetent to whom the circuit court denies a waiver of notice.

(g) The Supreme Court is respectfully requested to promulgate any rules and regulations necessary to ensure that proceedings under this Act are handled in an expeditious and confidential manner.

(h) No filing fees shall be required of any minor or incompetent who avails herself of the procedures provided by this Section.
(Source: P.A. 83-1128.) [Formerly Ill. Rev. Stat. 38 §81-65.]

520/6. Medical emergency exception.

§6. Medical emergency exception. The requirements of Section 4 of this Act [720 ILCS 520/4] shall not apply when, in the best medical judgment of a physician based on the facts of the case before him, a medical emergency exists that so complicates the pregnancy as to require an immediate abortion. A physician who does not comply with Section 4 of this Act by reason of this exception shall certify in writing the medical indications on which his judgment was based.

A report indicating the basis for any medical judgment that warrants failure to give notice pursuant to this Act shall be filed with the Department of Public Health of the State of Illinois on forms prescribed by the Department. Dissemination of this report shall comply with the reporting and confidentiality requirements of Section 10 of the Illinois Abortion Law of 1975 [720 ILCS 510/10].
(Source: P.A. 83-1128.) [Formerly Ill. Rev. Stat. 38 §81-66.]

520/7. Other exceptions.

§7. Other exceptions. (a) When the parties to whom notice must be given pursuant to Section 4 of this Act [720 ILCS 520/4] have already been notified and those parties accompany the minor or incompetent to the place where the abortion is to be performed, or submit signed notarized statements indicating that they have been notified, the requirements of Section 4 of this Act shall not apply.

(b) Notwithstanding any other provision of this Act, no notice need be given to any father of any minor requesting an abortion when the minor's mother accompanies her to the abortion and submits a notarized statement that she has been notified and, further, states orally to the physician or his agent that she has a reasonable belief that the fetus to be aborted is the child of the minor's father. Where the mother is deceased or otherwise unavailable, the physician or his agent may rely on a similar statement provided by any other adult relative accompanying the minor. Any physician or his agent relying on such a statement in good faith shall not be civilly or criminally liable under any provisions of this Act for failure to give notice. Nothing in subsection (b) shall be construed to limit the alternative and additional right of a minor to seek a waiver of the notice requirement in accordance with Section 5 [720 ILCS 520/5] on the ground that notice would not be in the best interests of the minor because the fetus to be aborted is the child of the minor's father.
(Source: P.A. 83-890.) [Formerly Ill. Rev. Stat. 38 §81-67.]

520/8. Penalty.

§8. Penalty. Any person who intentionally performs an abortion with knowledge that, or with reckless disregard as to whether the person upon whom the abortion is to be performed is an unemancipated minor or an incompetent, and who intentionally, knowingly, or recklessly fails to conform to any requirement of this Act, is guilty of a Class A misdemeanor.

Failure to provide persons with information pursuant to the requirements of this Act is prima facie evidence of failure to obtain informed consent and of interference with family relations in appropriate civil actions. The law of this State shall not be construed to preclude the award of exemplary damages in any appropriate civil action relevant to violations of this Act. Nothing in this Act shall be construed to limit the common law rights of parents.

Such prima facie evidence shall not apply to any issue other than failure to inform the parents or guardian and interference with family relations in appropriate civil actions.

(Source: P.A. 83-890.) [Formerly Ill. Rev. Stat. 38 §81-68.]

520/8.1. Severability.

§8.1. If any provision, word, phrase or clause of this Act or the application thereof to any person or circumstance shall be held invalid, such invalidity shall not affect the provisions, words, phrases, clauses or application of this Act which can be given effect without the invalid provision, word, phrase, clause, or application, and to this end the provisions, words, phrases, and clauses of this Act are declared to be severable.

(Source: P.A. 83-1128.) [Formerly Ill. Rev. Stat. 38 §81-68.1.]

520/9. Repealer.

§9. Section 3.3 of the "Illinois Abortion Law of 1975", veto overridden November 20, 1975, as amended [720 ILCS 510/3.3], is repealed.

(Source: P.A. 83-890.) [Formerly Ill. Rev. Stat. 38 §81-69.]

520/10. Act effective.

§10. This Act takes effect 90 days after it becomes a law.

(Source: P.A. 83-890.) [Formerly Ill. Rev. Stat. 38 §81-70.]

ADOPTION COMPENSATION PROHIBITION ACT

525/0.01. Short title.

§0.01. Short title. This Act may be cited as the Adoption Compensation Prohibition Act.

(Source: P.A. 86-1324.) [Formerly Ill. Rev. Stat. 40 §1700.]

525/1. Receiving compensation for placing out of child prohibited; exception.

§1. No person and no agency, association, corporation, institution, society, or other organization, except a child welfare agency as defined by the Child Care Act of 1969, as now or hereafter amended [225 ILCS 10/1 et seq.], shall request, receive or accept any compensation or thing of value, directly or indirectly, for placing out of a child.

(Source: P.A. 86-820.) [Formerly Ill. Rev. Stat. 40 §1701.]

525/2. Paying compensation for placing out of child prohibited; exception.

§2. No person shall pay or give any compensation or thing of value, directly or indirectly, for placing out of a child to any person or to any agency, association, corporation, institution, society, or other organization except a child welfare agency as defined by the Child Care Act of 1969, as now or hereafter amended [225 ILCS 10/1 et seq.].

(Source: P.A. 86-820.) [Formerly Ill. Rev. Stat. 40 §1702.]

525/3. Placing out, defined.

§3. As used in this Act the term "placing out" means to arrange for the free care of a child in a family other than that of the child's parent, stepparent, grandparent, brother, sister, uncle or aunt or legal guardian, for the purpose of adoption or for the purpose of providing care.

(Source: Laws 1955, p. 1881.) [Formerly Ill. Rev. Stat. 40 §1703.]

525/4. Provisions do not prevent payment of salaries of licensed child welfare agencies or medical expenses.

§4. The provisions of this Act shall not be construed to prevent the payment of salaries or other compensation by a licensed child welfare agency, as that term is defined by the Child Care Act of 1969, as now or hereafter amended [225 ILCS 10/1 et seq.], to the officers or employees thereof; nor shall it be construed to prevent the payment by a person with whom a child has been placed out of reasonable and actual medical fees or hospital charges for services rendered in connection with the birth of such child, if such payment is made to the physician or hospital who or which rendered the services or to the natural mother of the child or to prevent the receipt of such payment by such physician, hospital, or mother.

(Source: P.A. 86-820.) [Formerly Ill. Rev. Stat. 40 §1704.]

525/4.1. Payment of certain expenses.

§4.1. Payment of certain expenses. (a) A person or persons who have filed or intend to file a petition to adopt a child under the Adoption Act shall be permitted to pay the reasonable living expenses of the biological parents of the child sought to be adopted, in addition to those expenses set forth in Section 4, only in accordance with the provisions of this Section.

"Reasonable living expenses" means the reasonable costs of lodging, food, and clothing for the biological parents during the period of the biological mother's pregnancy and for no more than 30 days after the birth of the child. The term does not include expenses for lost wages, gifts, educational expenses, or other similar expenses of the biological parents.

(b) The petitioners may seek leave of the court to pay the reasonable living expenses of the biological parents. They shall be permitted to pay the reasonable living expenses of the biological parents only upon prior order of the circuit court where the petition for adoption will be filed, or if the petition for adoption has been filed in the circuit court where the petition is pending.

(c) Payments under this Section shall be permitted only in those circumstances where there is a demonstrated need for the payment of such expenses to protect the health of the biological parents or the health of the child sought to be adopted.

(d) Payment of their reasonable living expenses, as provided in this Section, shall not obligate the biological parents to place the child for adoption. In the event the biological parents choose not to place the child for adoption, the petitioners shall have no right to seek reimbursement of moneys paid to the biological parents pursuant to a court order under this Section.

(Added by P.A. 87-1129, §3, eff. 1/1/93.)

[Formerly Ill. Rev. Stat. 40 §1704.1.]

525/5. Violations.

§5. Any person, agency, association, corporation, institution, society, or other organization violating the provisions of this Section shall be guilty of illegal placement of children and upon first conviction for an offense under this Act shall be guilty of a Class 4 felony; and upon conviction for any subsequent offense under this Act shall be guilty of a Class 3 felony.
(Source: P.A. 84-170.) [Formerly Ill. Rev. Stat. 40 §1705.]

AERIAL EXHIBITORS SAFETY ACT

530/0.01. Short title.

§0.01. Short title. This Act may be cited as the Aerial Exhibitors Safety Act.
(Source: P.A. 86-1324.) [Formerly Ill. Rev. Stat. 38 §50.]

530/1. Safety device required.

§1. No person shall participate in a public performance or exhibition, or in a private exercise preparatory thereto, on a trapeze, tightrope, wire, rings, ropes, poles, or other aerial apparatus which requires skill, timing or balance and which creates a substantial risk to himself or others of serious injury by a fall from a height in excess of 20 feet, unless a safety net or other safety device of similar purpose and construction is placed between such person and the ground in such manner as to arrest or cushion his fall and minimize the risk of such injury.
(Source: Laws 1963, p. 3453.) [Formerly Ill. Rev. Stat. 38 §50-1.]

530/2. Participation without net not to be authorized or permitted.

§2. No owner, agent, lessee or other person in control of operations of a circus, carnival, fair or other public place of assembly or amusement shall authorize or permit participation in an aerial performance, exhibition or private exercise in violation of Section 1 of this Act [720 ILCS 530/1].
(Source: Laws 1963, p. 3453.) [Formerly Ill. Rev. Stat. 38 §50-2.]

530/3. Sentence.

§3. Sentence. Violation of this Act is a Class A Misdemeanor.
(Source: P.A. 77-2651.) [Formerly Ill. Rev. Stat. 38 §50-3.]

AIR RIFLE ACT

535/0.01. Short title.

§0.01. Short title. This Act may be cited as the Air Rifle Act.
(Source: P.A. 86-1324.) [Formerly Ill. Rev. Stat. 38 §82.]

535/1. Definitions.

§1. As used in this Act:

(1) "Air rifle" means and includes any air gun, air pistol, spring gun, spring pistol, B-B gun, paint ball gun, pellet gun or any implement that is not a firearm which impels a breakable paint ball containing washable marking colors or, a pellet constructed of hard plastic, steel, lead or other hard materials with a force that reasonably is expected to cause bodily harm.

(2) "Municipalities" include cities, villages, incorporated towns and townships.

(3) "Dealer" means any person, copartnership, association or corporation engaged in the business of selling at retail or renting any of the articles included in the definition of "air rifle".

(Source: P.A. 86-349.) [Formerly Ill. Rev. Stat. 38 §82-1.]

535/2. Selling, renting, or transferring to minors.

§2. It is unlawful for any dealer to sell, lend, rent, give or otherwise transfer an air rifle to any person under the age of 13 years where the dealer knows or has cause to believe the person to be under 13 years of age or where such dealer has failed to make reasonable inquiry relative to the age of such person and such person is under 13 years of age.

It is unlawful for any person to sell, give, lend or otherwise transfer any air rifle to any person under 13 years of age except where the relationship of parent and child, guardian and ward or adult instructor and pupil, exists between such person and the person under 13 years of age, or where such person stands in loco parentis to the person under 13 years of age.

(Source: Laws 1965, p. 2977.) [Formerly Ill. Rev. Stat. 38 §82-2.]

535/3. Carrying or discharging air rifles.

§3. It is unlawful for any person under 13 years of age to carry any air rifle on the public streets, roads, highways or public lands within this State, unless such person under 13 years of age carries such rifle unloaded.

It is unlawful for any person to discharge any air rifle from or across any street, sidewalk, road, highway or public land or any public place except on a safely constructed target range.

(Source: Laws 1965, p. 2977.) [Formerly Ill. Rev. Stat. 38 §82-3.]

535/4. Possession; exceptions.

§4. Notwithstanding any provision of this Act, it is lawful for any person under 13 years of age to have in his possession any air rifle if it is:

(1) Kept within his house of residence or other private enclosure;

(2) Used by the person under 13 years of age and he is a duly enrolled member of any club, team or society organized for educational purposes and maintaining as part of its facilities or having written permission to use an indoor or outdoor rifle range under the supervision guidance and instruction of a responsible adult and then only if said air rifle is actually being used in connection with the activities of said club team or society under the supervision of a responsible adult; or

(3) Used in or on any private grounds or residence under circumstances when such air rifle is fired, discharged or operated in such a manner as not to endanger persons or property and then only if it is used in such manner as to prevent the projectile from passing over any grounds or space outside the limits of such grounds or residence.

(Source: Laws 1965, p. 2977.) [Formerly Ill. Rev. Stat. 38 §82-4.]

535/5. Sales; exceptions.

§5. The provisions of this Act do not prohibit sales of air rifles:

(1) By wholesale dealers or jobbers;

(2) To be shipped out of the State;

(3) To be used at a target range operated in accordance with Section 4 of this Act [720 ILCS 535/4] or by members of the Armed Services of the United States or Veterans' organizations.
(Source: Laws 1965, p. 2977.) [Formerly Ill. Rev. Stat. 38 §82-5.]

535/6. Seizure.

§6. The State Police or any sheriff or police officer shall seize, take, remove or cause to be removed at the expense of the owner, any air rifle sold or used in any manner in violation of this Act.
(Source: P.A. 77-577.) [Formerly Ill. Rev. Stat. 38 §82-6.]

535/7. Sentence.

§7. Sentence. Any dealer violating any provision of Section 2 of this Act commits a petty offense.

Any person violating any other provision of this Act commits a petty offense and shall pay a fine not to exceed $50.
(Source: P.A. 77-2815.) [Formerly Ill. Rev. Stat. 38 §82-7.]

535/8. Municipal ordinances.

§8. The provisions of any ordinance enacted by any municipality which impose greater restrictions or limitations in respect to such sale and purchase, use or possession of air rifles as herein defined than are imposed by this Act, are not invalidated nor affected by this Act.
(Source: Laws 1965, p. 2977.) [Formerly Ill. Rev. Stat. 38 §82-8.]

BAIL BOND FALSE STATEMENT ACT

540/0.01. Short title.

§0.01. Short title. This Act may be cited as the Bail Bond False Statement Act.
(Source: P.A. 86-1324.) [Formerly Ill. Rev. Stat. 16 §25.9.]

540/1. False oath by surety.

§1. That any person who in any affidavit, document, schedule or other application to become surety or bail for another on any bail bond or recognizance in any civil or criminal proceeding then pending or about to be started against such other person, having taken a lawful oath or made affirmation, shall swear or affirm wilfully, corruptly and falsely as to the ownership or liens or incumbrances upon or the value of any real or personal property alleged to be owned by the person proposed as surety or bail, the financial worth or standing of such person proposed as surety or bail, or as to the number or total penalties of all other bonds or recognizances signed by and standing against said proposed surety or bail, or any person who, having taken a lawful oath or made affirmation, shall testify wilfully, corruptly and falsely as to any of said matters for the purpose of inducing the approval of any such bail bond or recognizance; or for the purpose of justifying on any such bail bond or recognizance, or who shall suborn any other person to so swear, affirm or testify as aforesaid, shall be deemed and adjudged guilty of perjury or subornation of perjury (as the case may be) and punished accordingly.
(Source: Laws 1917, p. 215.) [Formerly Ill. Rev. Stat. 16 §26.]

BOARDING AIRCRAFT WITH WEAPON ACT

545/0.01. Short title.

§0.01. Short title. This Act may be cited as the Boarding Aircraft With Weapon Act.
(Source: P.A. 86-1324.) [Formerly Ill. Rev. Stat. 38 §84-0.1.]

545/1. Boarding aircraft.

§1. It is unlawful for any person to board or attempt to board any commercial or charter aircraft, having in his possession any firearm, explosive of any type or other lethal or dangerous weapon.
(Source: P.A. 76-1895.) [Formerly Ill. Rev. Stat. 38 §84-1.]

545/2. Application of Act.

§2. This Act does not apply to any person authorized by either the Federal government or any State government to carry firearms but such person so exempted from the provisions of this Act shall notify the commander of any aircraft he is about to board that he does possess a firearm and show identification satisfactory to the aircraft commander that he is authorized to carry such firearm.
(Source: P.A. 76-1895.) [Formerly Ill. Rev. Stat. 38 §84-2.]

545/3. Person purchasing ticket thereby consents to search of person.

§3. Any person purchasing a ticket to board any commercial or charter aircraft shall by such purchase consent to a search of his person or personal belongings by the company selling the ticket to him. Such person may refuse to submit to a search of his person or personal belongings by the aircraft company but the person refusing may be denied the right to board such commercial or charter aircraft at the discretion of the carrier. Such refusal shall create no inference of unlawful conduct.
(Source: P.A. 76-1895.) [Formerly Ill. Rev. Stat. 38 §84-3.]

545/4. Evidence of criminal activity.

§4. Any evidence of criminal activity found during a search made pursuant to this Act shall be admissible in legal proceedings for the sole purpose of supporting a charge of violation of this Act and is inadmissible as evidence in any legal proceeding for any other purpose, except in the prosecution of offenses related to weapons as set out in Article 24 of the Criminal Code of 1961 [720 ILCS 5/24-1 et seq.].
(Source: P.A. 82-662.) [Formerly Ill. Rev. Stat. 38 §84-4.]

545/6. Airline company; liability.

§6. No action may be brought against any commercial or charter airline company operating in this State, for the refusal of such company to permit a person to board any aircraft where such person refused to be searched as set out in Section 3 of this Act [720 ILCS 545/3].
(Source: P.A. 77-956.) [Formerly Ill. Rev. Stat. 38 §84-6.]

545/7. Sentence.

§7. Sentence. Violation of this Act is a Class A misdemeanor.
(Source: P.A. 82-662.) [Formerly Ill. Rev. Stat. 38 §84-7.]

CANNABIS CONTROL ACT

Sec.

550/1. Legislative declaration.

§1. The General Assembly recognizes that (1) the current state of scientific and medical knowledge concerning the effects of cannabis makes it necessary to acknowledge the physical, psychological and sociological damage which is incumbent upon its use; and (2) the use of cannabis occupies the unusual position of being widely used and pervasive among the citizens of Illinois despite its harmful effects; and (3) previous legislation enacted to control or forbid the use of cannabis has often unnecessarily and unrealistically drawn a large segment of our population within the criminal justice system without succeeding in deterring the expansion of cannabis use. It is, therefore, the intent of the General Assembly, in the interest of the health and welfare of the citizens of Illinois, to establish a reasonable penalty system which is responsive to the current state of knowledge concerning cannabis and which directs the greatest efforts of law enforcement agencies toward the commercial traffickers and large-scale purveyors of cannabis. To this end, this Act provides wide latitude in the sentencing discretion of the courts and establishes penalties in a sharply rising progression based on the amount of substances containing cannabis involved in each case.

(Source: P.A. 77-758.) [Formerly Ill. Rev. Stat. 56½ §701.]

550/2. Short title.

§2. This Act shall be known and may be cited as the "Cannabis Control Act".

(Source: P.A. 77-758.) [Formerly Ill. Rev. Stat. 56½ §702.]

550/3. Definitions.

§3. As used in this Act, unless the context otherwise requires:

(a) "Cannabis" includes marihuana, hashish and other substances which are identified as including any parts of the plant Cannabis Sativa, whether growing or not; the seeds thereof, the resin extracted from any part of such plant; and any compound, manufacture, salt, derivative, mixture, or preparation of such plant, its seeds, or resin, including tetrahydrocannabinol (THC) and all other cannabinol derivatives, including its naturally occurring or synthetically produced ingredients, whether produced directly or indirectly by extraction, or independently by means of chemical synthesis or by a combination of extraction and chemical synthesis; but shall not include the mature stalks of such plant, fiber produced from such stalks, oil or cake made from the seeds of such plant, any other compound, manufacture, salt, derivative, mixture, or preparation of such mature stalks (except the resin extracted therefrom), fiber, oil or cake, or the sterilized seed of such plant which is incapable of germination.

(b) "Casual delivery" means the delivery of not more than 10 grams of any substance containing cannabis without consideration.

(c) "Department" means the Illinois Department of Alcoholism and Substance Abuse of the State of Illinois or its successor agency.

(d) "Deliver" or "delivery" means the actual, constructive or attempted transfer of possession of cannabis, with or without consideration, whether or not there is an agency relationship.

(e) "Department of State Police" means the Department of State Police of the State of Illinois or its successor agency.

(f) "Director" means the Director of the Department of State Police or his designated agent.

(g) "Local authorities" means a duly organized State, county, or municipal peace unit or police force.

(h) "Manufacture" means the production, preparation, propagation, compounding, conversion or processing of cannabis, either directly or indirectly, by extraction from substances of natural origin, or independently by means of chemical synthesis, or by a combination of extraction and chemical synthesis, and includes any packaging or repackaging of cannabis or labeling of its container, except that this term does not include the preparation, compounding, packaging, or labeling of cannabis as an incident to lawful research, teaching, or chemical analysis and not for sale.

(i) "Person" means any individual, corporation, government or governmental subdivision or agency, business trust, estate, trust, partnership or association, or any other entity.

(j) "Produce" or "production" means planting, cultivating, tending or harvesting.

(k) "State" includes the State of Illinois and any state, district, commonwealth, territory, insular possession thereof, and any area subject to the legal authority of the United States of America.

(*l*) "Subsequent offense" means an offense under this Act, the offender of which, prior to his conviction of the offense, has at any time been convicted under this Act or under any laws of the United States or of any state relating to cannabis, or any controlled substance as defined in the Illinois Controlled Substances Act [720 ILCS 570/100 et seq.].

(Source: P.A. 84-25.) [Formerly Ill. Rev. Stat. 56½ §703.]

550/4. Violations; possession of cannabis.

§4. It is unlawful for any person knowingly to possess cannabis. Any person who violates this section with respect to:

(a) not more than 2.5 grams of any substance containing cannabis is guilty of a Class C misdemeanor;

(b) more than 2.5 grams but not more than 10 grams of any substance containing cannabis is guilty of a Class B misdemeanor;

(c) more than 10 grams but not more than 30 grams of any substance containing cannabis is guilty of a Class A misdemeanor; provided, that if any offense under this subsection (c) is a subsequent offense, the offender shall be guilty of a Class 4 felony;

(d) more than 30 grams but not more than 500 grams of any substance containing cannabis is guilty of a Class 4 felony; provided that if any offense under this subsection (d) is a subsequent offense, the offender shall be guilty of a Class 3 felony;

(e) more than 500 grams of any substance containing cannabis is guilty of a Class 3 felony.

(Source: P.A. 78-255.) [Formerly Ill. Rev. Stat. 56½ §704.]

550/5. Violations; manufacture or delivery of cannabis.

§5. It is unlawful for any person knowingly to manufacture, deliver, or possess with intent to deliver, or manufacture, cannabis. Any person who violates this section with respect to:

(a) not more than 2.5 grams of any substance containing cannabis is guilty of a Class B misdemeanor;

(b) more than 2.5 grams but not more than 10 grams of any substance containing cannabis is guilty of a Class A misdemeanor;

(c) more than 10 grams but not more than 30 grams of any substance containing cannabis is guilty of a Class 4 felony;

(d) more than 30 grams but not more than 500 grams of any substance containing cannabis is guilty of a Class 3 felony for which a fine not to exceed $50,000 may be imposed;

(e) more than 500 grams of any substance containing cannabis is guilty of a Class 2 felony for which a fine not to exceed $100,000 may be imposed.

(Source: P.A. 83-778.) [Formerly Ill. Rev. Stat. 56½ §705.]

550/5.1. Cannabis trafficking.

§5.1. Cannabis Trafficking. (a) Except for purposes authorized by this Act, any person who knowingly brings or causes to be brought into this State for the purpose of manufacture or delivery or with the intent to manufacture or deliver 2,500 grams or more of cannabis in this State or any other state or country is guilty of cannabis trafficking.

(b) A person convicted of cannabis trafficking shall be sentenced to a term of imprisonment not less than twice the minimum term and fined an amount as authorized by subsection (e) of Section 5 of this Act [720 ILCS 550/5], based upon the amount of cannabis brought or caused to be brought into this State, and not more than twice the maximum term of imprisonment and fined twice the amount as authorized by subsection (e) of Section 5 of this Act, based upon the amount of cannabis brought or caused to be brought into this State.

(Source: P.A. 85-1388.) [Formerly Ill. Rev. Stat. 56½ §705.1.]

550/5.2. Delivery of cannabis on school grounds.

§5.2. Delivery of cannabis on school grounds. (a) Any person who violates subsection (e) of Section 5 [720 ILCS 550/5] in any school, on the real property comprising any school, or any conveyance owned, leased or contracted by a school to transport students to or from school or a school related activity, or on any public way within 1,000 feet of the real property comprising any school, or any conveyance owned, leased or contracted by a school to transport students to or from school or a school related activity, is guilty of a Class 1 felony, the fine for which shall not exceed $200,000;

(b) Any person who violates subsection (d) of Section 5 in any school, on the real property comprising any school, or any conveyance owned, leased or contracted by a school to transport students to or from school or a school related activity, or on any public way within 1,000 feet of the real property comprising any school, or any conveyance owned, leased or contracted by a school to transport students to or from school or a school related activity, is guilty of a Class 2 felony, the fine for which shall not exceed $100,000;

(c) Any person who violates subsection (c) of Section 5 in any school, on the real property comprising any school, or any conveyance owned, leased or contracted by a school to transport students to or from school or a school related activity, or on any public way within 1,000 feet of the real property comprising any school, or any conveyance owned, leased or contracted by a school to transport students to or from school or a school related activity, is guilty of a Class 3 felony, the fine for which shall not exceed $50,000;

(d) Any person who violates subsection (b) of Section 5 in any school, on the real property comprising any school, or any conveyance owned, leased or contracted by a school to transport students to or from school or a school related activity, or on any public way within 1,000 feet of the real property comprising any school, or any conveyance owned, leased or contracted by a school to transport students to or from school or a school related activity, is guilty of a Class 4 felony, the fine for which shall not exceed $25,000;

(e) Any person who violates subsection (a) of Section 5 in any school, on the real property comprising any school, or any conveyance owned, leased or contracted by a school to transport students to or from school or a school related activity, on any public way within 1,000 feet of the real property comprising any school, or any conveyance owned, leased or contracted by a school to transport students to or from school or a school related activity, is guilty of a Class A misdemeanor.

(Source: P.A. 87-544.) [Formerly Ill. Rev. Stat. 56½ §705.2.]

550/6. Delivery of cannabis as possession.

§6. Any delivery of cannabis which is a casual delivery shall be treated in all respects as possession of cannabis for purposes of penalties.

(Source: P.A. 77-758.) [Formerly Ill. Rev. Stat. 56½ §706.]

550/7. Delivery to or possession, manufacture, or delivery by persons under 18 years of age.

§7. (a) Any person who is at least 18 years of age who violates Section 5 of this Act [720 ILCS 550/5] by delivering cannabis to a person under 18 years of age who is at least 3 years his junior may be sentenced to imprisonment for a term up to twice the maximum term otherwise authorized by Section 5.

(b) Any person under 18 years of age who violates Section 4 or 5 of this Act [720 ILCS 550/4 or 550/5] may be treated by the court in accordance with the Juvenile Court Act of 1987 [705 ILCS 405/1-1 et seq.].

(Source: P.A. 85-1209.) [Formerly Ill. Rev. Stat. 56½ §707.]

550/8. Production or possession of cannabis sativa plant; penalties.

§8. It is unlawful for any person knowingly to produce the cannabis sativa plant or to possess such plants unless production or possession has been authorized pursuant to the provisions of Section 11 of the Act [720 ILCS 550/11]. Any person who violates this Section with respect to production or possession of:

(a) Not more than 5 plants is guilty of a Class A misdemeanor.

(b) More than 5, but not more than 20 plants, is guilty of a Class 4 felony.

(c) More than 20, but not more than 50 plants, is guilty of a Class 3 felony.

(d) More than 50 plants is guilty of a Class 2 felony for which a fine not to exceed $100,000 may be imposed and for which liability for the cost of conducting the investigation and eradicating such plants may be assessed. Compensation for expenses incurred in the enforcement of this provision shall be transmitted to and deposited in the treasurer's office at the level of government represented by the Illinois law enforcement agency whose officers or employees conducted the investigation or caused the arrest or arrests leading to the prosecution, to be subsequently made available to that law enforcement agency as expendable receipts for use in the enforcement of laws regulating controlled substances and cannabis. If such seizure was made by a combination of law

enforcement personnel representing different levels of government, the court levying the assessment shall determine the allocation of such assessment. The proceeds of assessment awarded to the State treasury shall be deposited in a special fund known as the Drug Traffic Prevention Fund.
(Source: P.A. 84-1233.) [Formerly Ill. Rev. Stat. 56½ §708.]

550/9. Calculated criminal cannabis conspiracy.

§9. (a) Any person who engages in a calculated criminal cannabis conspiracy, as defined in subsection (b), is guilty of a Class 3 felony, and fined not more than $200,000 and shall be subject to the forfeitures prescribed in subsection (c); except that, if any person engages in such offense after one or more prior convictions under this Section, Section 4 (d), Section 5 (d), Section 8 (d) [720 ILCS 550/4, 550/5, 550/8] or any law of the United States or of any State relating to cannabis, or controlled substances as defined in the Illinois Controlled Substances Act [720 ILCS 570/100 et seq.], in addition to the fine and forfeiture authorized above, he shall be guilty of a Class 1 felony for which an offender may not be sentenced to death.

(b) For purposes of this section, a person engages in a calculated criminal cannabis conspiracy when:

(1) he violates Section 4 (d), 4 (e), 5 (d), 5 (e), 8 (c) or 8 (d) of this Act; and

(2) such violation is a part of a conspiracy undertaken or carried on with 2 or more other persons; and

(3) he obtains anything of value greater than $500 from, or organizes, directs or finances such violation or conspiracy.

(c) Any person who is convicted under this Section of engaging in a calculated criminal cannabis conspiracy shall forfeit to the State of Illinois:

(1) the receipts obtained by him in such conspiracy; and

(2) any of his interests in, claims against, receipts from, or property or rights of any kind affording a source of influence over, such conspiracy.

(d) The circuit court may enter such injunctions, restraining orders, directions, or prohibitions, or take such other actions, including the acceptance of satisfactory performance bonds, in connection with any property, claim, receipt, right or other interest subject to forfeiture under this Section, as it deems proper.
(Source: P.A. 84-1233.) [Formerly Ill. Rev. Stat. 56½ §709.]

550/10. First offenders.

§10. (a) Whenever any person who has not previously been convicted of, or placed on probation or court supervision for, any offense under this Act or any law of the United States or of any State relating to cannabis, or controlled substances as defined in the Illinois Controlled Substances Act [720 ILCS 570/100 et seq.], pleads guilty to or is found guilty of violating Sections 4 (a), 4 (b), 4 (c), 5 (a), 5 (b), 5 (c) or 8 of this Act [720 ILCS 550/4, 550/5 or 550/8], the court may, without entering a judgment and with the consent of such person, sentence him to probation.

(b) When a person is placed on probation, the court shall enter an order specifying the period of probation, in accordance with subsection (b) of Section 5-6-2 of the "Unified Code of Corrections", approved July 26, 1972, as amended [730 ILCS 5/5-6-2], and shall defer further proceedings in the case until the conclusion of the period or until the filing of a petition alleging violation of a term or condition of probation.

(c) The court may, in addition to other conditions, require that the person:

(1) make a report to and appear in person before or participate with the court or such courts, person, or social service agency as directed by the court in the order of probation;

(2) pay a fine and costs;

(3) work or pursue a course of study or vocational training;

(4) undergo medical or psychiatric treatment; or treatment for drug addiction or alcoholism;

(5) attend or reside in a facility established for the instruction or residence of defendants on probation;

(6) support his dependents;

(7) refrain from possessing a firearm or other dangerous weapon;

(8) and in addition, if a minor:

(i) reside with his parents or in a foster home;

(ii) attend school;

(iii) attend a non-residential program for youth;

(iv) contribute to his own support at home or in a foster home.

(d) Upon violation of a term or condition of probation, the court may enter a judgment on its original finding of guilt and proceed as otherwise provided.

(e) Upon fulfillment of the terms and conditions of probation, the court shall discharge such person and dismiss the proceedings against him.

(f) A disposition of probation is considered to be a conviction for the purposes of imposing the conditions of probation and for appeal, however, discharge and dismissal under this Section is not a conviction for purposes of disqualification or disabilities imposed by law upon conviction of a crime (including the additional penalty imposed for subsequent offenses under Section 4 (c), 4 (d), 5 (c) or 5 (d) of this Act).

(g) Discharge and dismissal under this Section or under Section 410 of the Illinois Controlled Substances Act [720 ILCS 570/410] may occur only once with respect to any person.

(Source: P.A. 80-1202.) [Formerly Ill. Rev. Stat. 56½ §710.]

550/10.1. Fines.

§10.1. (a) Whenever any person pleads guilty to, is found guilty of or is placed on supervision for an offense under this Act, a fine may be levied in addition to any other penalty imposed by the court.

(b) In determining whether to impose a fine under this Section and the amount, time for payment and method of payment of any fine so imposed, the court shall

(1) consider the defendant's income, regardless of source, the defendant's earning capacity and the defendant's financial resources, as well as the nature of the burden the fine will impose on the defendant and any person legally or financially dependent upon the defendant;

(2) consider the proof received at trial, or as a result of a plea of guilty, concerning the full street value of the cannabis seized and any profits or other proceeds derived by the defendant from the violation of this Act;

(3) take into account any other pertinent equitable considerations; and

(4) give primary consideration to the need to deprive the defendant of illegally obtained profits or other proceeds from the offense.

For the purpose of paragraph (2) of this subsection, "street value" shall be determined by the court on the basis of testimony of law enforcement personnel and the defendant as to the amount seized and such testimony as may be required by the court as to the current street value of the cannabis seized.

(c) As a condition of a fine, the court may require that payment be made in specified installments or within a specified period of time, but such period shall not be greater than the maximum applicable term of probation or imprisonment, whichever is greater. Unless otherwise specified, payment of a fine shall be due immediately.

(d) If a fine for a violation of this Act is imposed on an organization, it is the duty of each individual authorized to make disbursements of the assets of the organization to pay the fine from assets of the organization.

(e) (1) A defendant who has been sentenced to pay a fine, and who has paid part but not all of such fine, may petition the court for an extension of the time for payment or modification of the method of payment.

(2) The court may grant a petition made pursuant to this subsection if it finds that

(i) the circumstances that warranted payment by the time or method specified no longer exist; or

(ii) it is otherwise unjust to require payment of the fine by the time or method specified.

(Source: P.A. 83-778.) [Formerly Ill. Rev. Stat. 56½ §710.1.]

550/10.2. Fines; disbursement.

§10.2. (a) Twelve and one-half percent of all amounts collected as fines pursuant to the provisions of this Act shall be paid into the Youth Drug Abuse Prevention Fund, which is hereby created in the State treasury, to be used by the Department of Alcoholism and Substance Abuse for the funding of programs and services for drug-abuse treatment, and prevention and education services, for juveniles.

(b) Eighty-seven and one-half percent of the proceeds of all fines received under the provisions of this Act shall be transmitted to and deposited in the treasurer's office at the level of government as follows:

(1) If such seizure was made by a combination of law enforcement personnel representing differing units of local government, the court levying the fine shall equitably allocate 50% of the fine among these units of local government and shall allocate 37½% to the county general corporate fund. In the event that the seizure was made by law enforcement personnel representing a unit of local government from a municipality where the number of inhabitants exceeds 2 million in population, the court levying the fine shall allocate 87½% of the fine to that unit of local government. If the seizure was made by a combination of law enforcement personnel representing differing units of local government, and at least one of those units represents a municipality where the number of inhabitants exceeds 2 million in population, the court shall equitably allocate 87½% of the proceeds of the fines received among the differing units of local government.

(2) If such seizure was made by State law enforcement personnel, then the court shall allocate 37½% to the State treasury and 50% to the county general corporate fund.

(3) If a State law enforcement agency in combination with a law enforcement agency or agencies of a unit or units of local government conducted the seizure, the court shall equitably allocate 37½% of the fines to or among the law enforcement agency or agencies of the unit or units of local government which conducted the seizure and shall allocate 50% to the county general corporate fund.

(c) The proceeds of all fines allocated to the law enforcement agency or agencies of the unit or units of local government pursuant to subsection (b) shall be made available to that law enforcement agency as expendable receipts for use in the enforcement of laws regulating controlled substances and cannabis. The proceeds of fines awarded to the State treasury shall be deposited in a special fund known as the Drug Traffic Prevention Fund. Monies from this fund may be used by the Department of State Police for use in the enforcement of laws regulating controlled substances and cannabis; to satisfy funding provisions of the Intergovernmental Drug Laws Enforcement Act [30 ILCS 715/1 et seq.]; to defray costs and expenses associated with returning violators of this Act and the Illinois Controlled Substances Act [720 ILCS 570/100 et seq.] only, as provided in such Acts, when punishment of the crime shall be confinement

of the criminal in the penitentiary; and all other monies shall be paid into the general revenue fund in the State treasury.
(Source: P.A. 87-342.) [Formerly Ill. Rev. Stat. 56½ §710.2.]

550/10.3. Additional assessment; amount and payment.

§10.3. (a) Every person convicted of a violation of this Act, and every person placed on probation, conditional discharge, supervision or probation under Section 10 of this Act [720 ILCS 550/10], shall be assessed for each offense a sum fixed at:

(1) $3,000 for a Class X felony;
(2) $2,000 for a Class 1 felony;
(3) $1,000 for a Class 2 felony;
(4) $500 for a Class 3 or Class 4 felony;
(5) $300 for a Class A misdemeanor;
(6) $200 for a Class B or Class C misdemeanor.

(b) The assessment under this Section is in addition to and not in lieu of any fines, restitution costs, forfeitures or other assessments authorized or required by law.

(c) As a condition of the assessment, the court may require that payment be made in specified installments or within a specified period of time. If the assessment is not paid within the period of probation, conditional discharge or supervision to which the defendant was originally sentenced, the court may extend the period of probation, conditional discharge or supervision pursuant to Section 5-6-2 or 5-6-3.1 of the Unified Code of Corrections [730 ILCS 5/5-6-2 or 5/5-6-3.1], as applicable, until the assessment is paid or until successful completion of public or community service set forth in subsection (e) or the successful completion of the substance abuse intervention or treatment program set forth in subsection (f). If a term of probation, conditional discharge or supervision is not imposed, the assessment shall be payable upon judgment or as directed by the court.

(d) If an assessment for a violation of this Act is imposed on an organization, it is the duty of each individual authorized to make disbursements of the assets of the organization to pay the assessment from assets of the organization.

(e) A defendant who has been ordered to pay an assessment may petition the court to convert all or part of the assessment into court-approved public or community service. One hour of public or community service shall be equivalent to $4 of assessment. The performance of this public or community service shall be a condition of the probation, conditional discharge or supervision and shall be in addition to the performance of any other period of public or community service ordered by the court or required by law.

(f) The court may suspend the collection of the assessment imposed under this Section; provided the defendant agrees to enter a substance abuse intervention or treatment program approved by the court; and further provided that the defendant agrees to pay for all or some portion of the costs associated with the intervention or treatment program. In this case, the collection of the assessment imposed under this Section shall be suspended during the defendant's participation in the approved intervention or treatment program. Upon successful completion of the program, the defendant may apply to the court to reduce the assessment imposed under this Section by any amount actually paid by the defendant for his participation in the program. The court shall not reduce the penalty under this subsection unless the defendant establishes to the satisfaction of the court that he has successfully completed the intervention or treatment program. If the defendant's participation is for any reason terminated before his successful completion of the intervention or treatment program, collection of the entire assessment imposed under this Section shall be enforced. Nothing in this Section shall be deemed to affect or suspend any other fines, restitution costs, forfeitures or assessments imposed under this or any other Act.

(g) The court shall not impose more than one assessment per complaint, indictment or information. If the person is convicted of more than one offense in a complaint, indictment or information, the assessment shall be based on the highest class offense for which the person is convicted.

(h) All moneys collected under this Section shall be forwarded by the clerk of the circuit court to the State Treasurer for deposit in the Drug Treatment Fund and expended as provided in Section 411.2 of the Illinois Controlled Substances Act [720 ILCS 570/411.2].

(Source: P.A. 87-772.) [Formerly Ill. Rev. Stat. 56½ §710.3.]

550/11. Research with cannabis.

§11. (a) The Department, with the written approval of the Department of State Police, may authorize the possession, production, manufacture and delivery of substances containing cannabis by persons engaged in research and when such authorization is requested by a physician licensed to practice medicine in all its branches, such authorization shall issue without unnecessary delay where the Department finds that such physician licensed to practice medicine in all its branches has certified that such possession, production, manufacture or delivery of such substance is necessary for the treatment of glaucoma, the side effects of chemotherapy or radiation therapy in cancer patients or such other procedure certified to be medically necessary; such authorization shall be, upon such terms and conditions as may be consistent with the public health and safety. To the extent of the applicable authorization, persons are exempt from prosecution in this State for possession, production, manufacture or delivery of cannabis.

(b) Persons registered under Federal law to conduct research with cannabis may conduct research with cannabis including, but not limited to treatment by a physician licensed to practice medicine in all its branches for glaucoma, the side effects of chemotherapy or radiation therapy in cancer patients or such other procedure which is medically necessary within this State upon furnishing evidence of that Federal registration and notification of the scope and purpose of such research to the Department and to the Department of State Police of that Federal registration.

(c) Persons authorized to engage in research may be authorized by the Department to protect the privacy of individuals who are the subjects of such research by withholding from all persons not connected with the conduct of the research the names and other identifying characteristics of such individuals. Persons who are given this authorization shall not be compelled in any civil, criminal, administrative, legislative or other proceeding to identify the individuals who are the subjects of research for which the authorization was granted, except to the extent necessary to permit the Department to determine whether the research is being conducted in accordance with the authorization.

(Source: P.A. 84-25.) [Formerly Ill. Rev. Stat. 56½ §711.]

550/12. Forfeiture of property.

§12. (a) The following are subject to forfeiture:

(1) all substances containing cannabis which have been produced, manufactured, delivered, or possessed in violation of this Act;

(2) all raw materials, products and equipment of any kind which are produced, delivered, or possessed in connection with any substance containing cannabis in violation of this Act;

(3) all conveyances, including aircraft, vehicles or vessels, which are used, or intended for use, to transport, or in any manner to facilitate the transporta-

tion, sale, receipt, possession, or concealment of property described in paragraph (1) or (2) that constitutes a felony violation of the Act, but:

(i) no conveyance used by any person as a common carrier in the transaction of business as a common carrier is subject to forfeiture under this Section unless it appears that the owner or other person in charge of the conveyance is a consenting party or privy to a violation of this Act;

(ii) no conveyance is subject to forfeiture under this Section by reason of any act or omission which the owner proves to have been committed or omitted without his knowledge or consent;

(iii) a forfeiture of a conveyance encumbered by a bona fide security interest is subject to the interest of the secured party if he neither had knowledge of nor consented to the act or omission;

(4) all money, things of value, books, records, and research products and materials including formulas, microfilm, tapes, and data which are used, or intended for use in a felony violation of this Act;

(5) everything of value furnished or intended to be furnished by any person in exchange for a substance in violation of this Act, all proceeds traceable to such an exchange, and all moneys, negotiable instruments, and securities used, or intended to be used, to commit or in any manner to facilitate any felony violation of this Act.

(b) Property subject to forfeiture under this Act may be seized by the Director or any peace officer upon process or seizure warrant issued by any court having jurisdiction over the property. Seizure by the Director or any peace officer without process may be made:

(1) if the property subject to seizure has been the subject of a prior judgment in favor of the State in a criminal proceeding or in an injunction or forfeiture proceeding based upon this Act or the Drug Asset Forfeiture Procedure Act [725 ILCS 150/1 et seq.];

(2) if there is probable cause to believe that the property is directly or indirectly dangerous to health or safety;

(3) if there is probable cause to believe that the property is subject to forfeiture under this Act and the property is seized under circumstances in which a warrantless seizure or arrest would be reasonable; or

(4) in accordance with the Code of Criminal Procedure of 1963 [725 ILCS 5/100-1 et seq.].

(c) In the event of seizure pursuant to subsection (b), forfeiture proceedings shall be instituted in accordance with the Drug Asset Forfeiture Procedure Act.

(d) Property taken or detained under this Section shall not be subject to replevin, but is deemed to be in the custody of the Director subject only to the order and judgments of the circuit court having jurisdiction over the forfeiture proceedings and the decisions of the State's Attorney under the Drug Asset Forfeiture Procedure Act. When property is seized under this Act, the seizing agency shall promptly conduct an inventory of the seized property, estimate the property's value, and shall forward a copy of the inventory of seized property and the estimate of the property's value to the Director. Upon receiving notice of seizure, the Director may:

(1) place the property under seal;

(2) remove the property to a place designated by him;

(3) keep the property in the possession of the seizing agency;

(4) remove the property to a storage area for safekeeping or, if the property is a negotiable instrument or money and is not needed for evidentiary purposes, deposit it in an interest bearing account;

(5) place the property under constructive seizure by posting notice of pending forfeiture on it, by giving notice of pending forfeiture to its owners and

interest holders, or by filing notice of pending forfeiture in any appropriate public record relating to the property; or

(6) provide for another agency or custodian, including an owner, secured party, or lienholder, to take custody of the property upon the terms and conditions set by the Director.

(e) No disposition may be made of property under seal until the time for taking an appeal has elapsed or until all appeals have been concluded unless a court, upon application therefor, orders the sale of perishable substances and the deposit of the proceeds of the sale with the court.

(f) When property is forfeited under this Act the Director shall sell all such property unless such property is required by law to be destroyed or is harmful to the public, and shall distribute the proceeds of the sale, together with any moneys forfeited or seized, in accordance with subsection (g). However, upon the application of the seizing agency or prosecutor who was responsible for the investigation, arrest or arrests and prosecution which lead to the forfeiture, the Director may return any item of forfeited property to the seizing agency or prosecutor for official use in the enforcement of laws relating to cannabis or controlled substances, if the agency or prosecutor can demonstrate that the item requested would be useful to the agency or prosecutor in their enforcement efforts. When any real property returned to the seizing agency is sold by the agency or its unit of government, the proceeds of the sale shall be delivered to the Director and distributed in accordance with subsection (g).

(g) All monies and the sale proceeds of all other property forfeited and seized under this Act shall be distributed as follows:

(1) 65% shall be distributed to the metropolitan enforcement group, local, municipal, county, or state law enforcement agency or agencies which conducted or participated in the investigation resulting in the forfeiture. The distribution shall bear a reasonable relationship to the degree of direct participation of the law enforcement agency in the effort resulting in the forfeiture, taking into account the total value of the property forfeited and the total law enforcement effort with respect to the violation of the law upon which the forfeiture is based. Amounts distributed to the agency or agencies shall be used for the enforcement of laws governing cannabis and controlled substances, except that amounts distributed to the Secretary of State shall be deposited into the Secretary of State Evidence Fund to be used as provided in Section 2-115 of the Illinois Vehicle Code [625 ILCS 5/2-115].

(2) (i) 12.5% shall be distributed to the Office of the State's Attorney of the county in which the prosecution resulting in the forfeiture was instituted, deposited in a special fund in the county treasury and appropriated to the State's Attorney for use in the enforcement of laws governing cannabis and controlled substances. In counties over 3,000,000 population, 25% will be distributed to a special fund in the county treasury and appropriated to the State's Attorneys Office for use in the enforcement of laws governing cannabis and controlled substances. If the prosecution is undertaken solely by the Attorney General, the portion provided hereunder shall be distributed to the Attorney General for use in the enforcement of laws governing cannabis and controlled substances.

(ii) 12.5% shall be distributed to the Office of the State's Attorneys Appellate Prosecutor and deposited in the Narcotics Profit Forfeiture Fund of that Office to be used for additional expenses incurred in the investigation, prosecution and appeal of cases arising under laws governing cannabis and controlled substances. The Office of the State's Attorneys Appellate Prosecutor shall not receive distribution from cases brought in counties with over 3,000,000 population.

(3) 10% shall be retained by the Department of State Police for expenses related to the administration and sale of seized and forfeited property.
(Chgd. by P.A. 87-993, §1, eff. 9/1/92.)
(Source: P.A. 86-1382; 86-1475; 87-614.) [Formerly Ill. Rev. Stat. 56½ §712.]

550/13. Injunctions.

§13. (a) In addition to any other remedies the Director is authorized to file a complaint and apply to any circuit court for, and such circuit court may upon hearing and for cause shown, grant a temporary restraining order or a preliminary or permanent injunction, without bond, restraining any person from violating this Act whether or not there exists another adequate remedy.

(b) A conviction or acquittal, under the laws of the United States or of any State relating to Cannabis for the same act is a bar to prosecution in this State.
(Source: P.A. 83-342.) [Formerly Ill. Rev. Stat. 56½ §713.]

550/14. Cooperation with federal and state agencies.

§14. (a)* The Director shall cooperate with Federal and other State agencies in discharging his responsibilities concerning traffic in cannabis and in suppressing the use of cannabis. To this end he may:

(1) arrange for the exchange of information among governmental officials concerning the use of cannabis;

(2) coordinate and cooperate in training programs concerning cannabis law enforcement at local and State levels;

(3) cooperate with the Bureau of Narcotics and Dangerous Drugs, United States Department of Justice, or its successor agency; and

(4) conduct programs of eradication aimed at destroying wild illicit growth of plant species from which cannabis may be extracted.

**So in original. No subsec. (b) has been enacted.*
(Source: P.A. 77-758.) [Formerly Ill. Rev. Stat. 56½ §714.]

550/15. Research on cannabis.

§15. The Department shall encourage research on cannabis. In connection with the research, and in furtherance of the purposes of this Act, it may:

(1) establish methods to assess accurately the effect of cannabis;

(2) make studies and undertake programs of research to:

(i) develop new or improved approaches, techniques, systems, equipment and devices to strengthen the enforcement of this Act;

(ii) determine patterns of use of cannabis and its social effects; and

(iii) improve methods for preventing, predicting, understanding, and dealing with the use of cannabis;

(3) enter into contracts with public agencies, educational institutions, and private organizations or individuals for the purpose of conducting research, demonstrations, or special projects which relate to the use of cannabis.
(Source: P.A. 83-969.) [Formerly Ill. Rev. Stat. 56½ §715.]

550/15.1. Cannabis derivative designated, rescheduled or deleted as controlled substance under federal law.

§15.1. (a) If any cannabis derivative is designated or rescheduled as a controlled substance under federal law and notice thereof is given to the Department, the Department shall similarly control the substance under the Illinois Controlled Substances Act [720 ILCS 570/100 et seq.] after the expiration of 30 days from publication in the Federal Register of a final order designating a substance as a controlled substance or rescheduling a substance unless within that 30 day period the Department objects, or a party adversely affected files with the Department substantial written objections to inclusion or rescheduling. In that case, the Department shall publish the reasons for objection or the substantial written objections and afford all interested parties an opportunity to be heard. At the conclusion of the hearing, the Department shall publish its decision, by means of a rule, which shall be final unless altered by statute. Upon publication of objections by the Department, similar control under the Illinois Controlled Substances Act whether by inclusion or rescheduling is suspended until the Department publishes its ruling.

(b) If any cannabis derivative is deleted as a controlled substance under Federal law and notice thereof is given to the Department, the Department shall similarly control the substance under this Act after the expiration of 30 days from publication in the Federal Register of a final order deleting a substance as a controlled substance or rescheduling a substance unless within that 30 day period the Department objects, or a party adversely affected files with the Department substantial written objections to inclusion or rescheduling. In that case, the Department shall publish the reasons for objection or the substantial written objections and afford all interested parties an opportunity to be heard. At the conclusion of the hearing, the Department shall publish its decision, by means of a rule, which shall be final unless altered by statute. Upon publication of objections by the Department, similar control under this Act whether by inclusion or rescheduling is suspended until the Department publishes its ruling.

(c) Cannabis derivatives are deemed to be regulated under this Act until such time as those derivatives are scheduled as provided for under the Illinois Controlled Substances Act. Following such scheduling, those derivatives shall be excepted from this Act and shall be regulated pursuant to the Illinois Controlled Substances Act. At such time that any derivative is deleted from schedules provided for under the Illinois Controlled Substance Act, that derivative shall be regulated pursuant to this Act.

(Source: P.A. 84-1313; 84-1362.) [Formerly Ill. Rev. Stat. 56½ §715.1.]

550/16. Negation of exemptions or exceptions.

§16. It is not necessary for the State to negate any exemption or exception in this Act in any complaint, information, indictment or other pleading or in any trial, hearing, or other proceeding under this Act. The burden of proof of any exemption or exception is upon the person claiming it.

(Source: P.A. 77-758.) [Formerly Ill. Rev. Stat. 56½ §716.]

550/16.1. Affirmative defense.

§16.1. In any prosecution for any violation of this Act, it shall be an affirmative defense that the substance possessed by the defendant was regulated as a controlled substance under the Illinois Controlled Substances Act [720 ILCS 570/100 et seq.]. In order to raise this affirmative defense, the defendant shall give notice thereof to the State not less than 7 days prior to trial.

(Source: P.A. 84-1313; 84-1362.) [Formerly Ill. Rev. Stat. 56½ §716.1.]

550/17. Enforcement.

§17. It is hereby made the duty of the Department of State Police, all peace officers within the State and of all State's attorneys, to enforce all provisions of this Act and to cooperate with all agencies charged with the enforcement of the laws of the United States, of this State, and of all other states, relating to cannabis.

(Source: P.A. 84-25.) [Formerly Ill. Rev. Stat. 56½ §717.]

550/18. Savings clause.

§18. Prosecution for any violation of law occurring prior to the effective date of this Act is not affected or abated by this Act. If the offense being prosecuted would be a violation of this Act, and has not reached the sentencing stage or a final adjudication, then for purposes of penalty the penalties under this Act

apply if they are less than under the prior law upon which the prosecution was commenced.
(Source: P.A. 77-758.) [Formerly Ill. Rev. Stat. 56½ §718.]

550/19. Severability.
§19. If any provision of this Act or the application thereof to any person or circumstance is held invalid, such invalidity shall not affect other provisions or applications of the Act which can be given effect without the invalid provision or application, and to this end the provisions of this Act are declared severable.
(Source: P.A. 77-758.) [Formerly Ill. Rev. Stat. 56½ §719.]

CHILD CURFEW ACT

555/0.01. Short title.
§0.01. Short title. This Act may be cited as the Child Curfew Act.
(Source: P.A. 86-1324.) [Formerly Ill. Rev. Stat. 23 §2370.9.]

555/1. Curfew; violations.
§1. (a) It is unlawful for a person less than 17 years of age to be present at or upon any public assembly, building, place, street or highway at the following times unless accompanied and supervised by a parent, legal guardian or other responsible companion at least 18 years of age approved by a parent or legal guardian or unless engaged in a business or occupation which the laws of this State authorize a person less than 17 years of age to perform:
1. Between 12:01 a. m. and 6:00 a. m. Saturday;
2. Between 12:01 a. m. and 6:00 a. m. Sunday; and
3. Between 11:00 p. m. on Sunday to Thursday, inclusive, and 6:00 a. m. on the following day.

(b) It is unlawful for a parent, legal guardian or other person to knowingly permit a person in his custody or control to violate subparagraph (a) of this Section.
(c) A person convicted of a violation of any provision of this Section shall be guilty of a petty offense and shall be fined not less than $10 nor more than $100.
(Source: P.A. 79-159.) [Formerly Ill. Rev. Stat. 23 §2371.]

555/2. Exercise of legislative or regulatory authority by municipalities.
§2. County, municipal and other local boards and bodies authorized to adopt local police laws and regulations under the constitution and laws of this State may exercise legislative or regulatory authority over this subject matter by ordinance or resolution incorporating the substance of this Act or increasing the requirements thereof or otherwise not in conflict with this Act.
(Source: Laws 1963, p. 3323.) [Formerly Ill. Rev. Stat. 23 §2372.]

ILLINOIS CLEAN PUBLIC ELEVATOR AIR ACT

560/1. Short title.
§1. This Act shall be known and may be cited as the "Illinois Clean Public Elevator Air Act".
(Source: P.A. 86-367.) [Formerly Ill. Rev. Stat. 111½ §7651.]

560/2. Findings.

§2. The General Assembly finds that smoking on elevators is a fire hazard and a danger to public safety and that tobacco smoke is annoying, harmful and dangerous to human beings and a hazard to public health.
(Source: P.A. 86-367.) [Formerly Ill. Rev. Stat. 111½ §7652.]

560/3. Smoking not allowed.

§3. No person shall smoke or possess a lighted cigarette, cigar, pipe or any other form of tobacco or similar substance used for smoking on any elevator in this State.
(Source: P.A. 86-367.) [Formerly Ill. Rev. Stat. 111½ §7653.]

560/4. Penalties.

§4. Any person who violates the provisions of this Act is guilty of a petty offense punishable by a fine of not less than $25 nor more than $250.
(Source: P.A. 86-367.) [Formerly Ill. Rev. Stat. 111½ §7654.]

CONTAINER LABEL OBLITERATION ACT

565/0.01. Short title.

§0.01. Short title. This Act may be cited as the Container Label Obliteration Act.
(Source: P.A. 86-1324.) [Formerly Ill. Rev. Stat. 38 §50-30.]

565/1. Obliterated containers.

§1. No person shall sell or offer for sale any product, article or substance in a container on which any statement of weight, quantity, quality, grade, ingredients or identification of the manufacturer, supplier or processor is obliterated by any other labeling unless such other labeling correctly restates any such obliterated statement.

This Section does not apply to any obliteration which is done in order to comply with Section 2 of this Act [720 ILCS 565/2].
(Source: Laws 1965, p. 2469.) [Formerly Ill. Rev. Stat. 38 §50-31.]

565/2. Used containers.

§2. No person shall utilize any used container for the purpose of sale of any product, article or substance unless the original marks of identification, weight, grade, quality and quantity have first been obliterated.
(Source: Laws 1965, p. 2469.) [Formerly Ill. Rev. Stat. 38 §50-32.]

565/3. Sentence.

§3. Sentence. Violation of any provision of this Act is a business offense for which a fine shall be imposed not to exceed $1,000.
(Source: P.A. 77-2652.) [Formerly Ill. Rev. Stat. 38 §50-33.]

565/4. Construction of Act.

§4. This Act shall not be construed as permitting the use of any containers or labels in a manner prohibited by any other law.
(Source: Laws 1965, p. 2469.) [Formerly Ill. Rev. Stat. 38 §50-34.]

ILLINOIS CONTROLLED SUBSTANCES ACT

ARTICLE I. INTENT, TITLE, AND DEFINITIONS

570/100. Legislative intent.

§100. Legislative intent. It is the intent of the General Assembly, recognizing the rising incidence in the abuse of drugs and other dangerous substances and its resultant damage to the peace, health, and welfare of the citizens of Illinois, to provide a system of control over the distribution and use of controlled substances which will more effectively: (1) limit access of such substances only to those persons who have demonstrated an appropriate sense of responsibility and have a lawful and legitimate reason to possess them; (2) deter the unlawful and destructive abuse of controlled substances; (3) penalize most heavily the illicit traffickers or profiteers of controlled substances, who propagate and perpetuate the abuse of such substances with reckless disregard for its consumptive consequences upon every element of society; (4) acknowledge the functional and consequential differences between the various types of controlled substances and provide for correspondingly different degrees of control over each of the various types; (5) unify where feasible and codify the efforts of this state to conform with the regulatory systems of the Federal government and other states to establish national coordination of efforts to control the abuse of controlled substances; and (6) provide law enforcement authorities with the necessary resources to make this system efficacious.

It is not the intent of the General Assembly to treat the unlawful user or occasional petty distributor of controlled substances with the same severity as the large-scale, unlawful purveyors and traffickers of controlled substances. To this end, guidelines have been provided, along with a wide latitude in sentencing discretion, to enable the sentencing court to order penalties in each case which are appropriate for the purposes of this Act.

(Source: P.A. 77-757.) [Formerly Ill. Rev. Stat. 56½ §1100.]

570/101. Short title.

§101. This Act shall be known as and may be cited as the "Illinois Controlled Substances Act."

(Source: P.A. 77-757.) [Formerly Ill. Rev. Stat. 56½ §1101.]

570/102. Definitions.

§102. As used in this Act, unless the context otherwise requires:

(a) "Addict" means any person who habitually uses any drug, chemical, substance or dangerous drug other than alcohol so as to endanger the public morals, health, safety or welfare or who is so far addicted to the use of a dangerous drug or controlled substance other than alcohol as to have lost the power of self control with reference to his addiction.

(b) "Administer" means the direct application of a controlled substance, whether by injection, inhalation, ingestion, or any other means, to the body of a patient or research subject by:

(1) a practitioner (or, in his presence, by his authorized agent), or

(2) the patient or research subject at the lawful direction of the practitioner.

(c) "Agent" means an authorized person who acts on behalf of or at the direction of a manufacturer, distributor, or dispenser. It does not include a common or contract carrier, public warehouseman or employee of the carrier or warehouseman.

(c-1) "Anabolic Steroids" means any drug or hormonal substance, chemically and pharmacologically related to testosterone (other than estrogens, progestins, and corticosteroids) that promotes muscle growth, and includes:

(i) boldenone,
(ii) chlorotestosterone,
(iii) chostebol,
(iv) dehydrochlormethyltestosterone,
(v) dihydrotestosterone,
(vi) drostanolone,
(vii) ethylestrenol,
(viii) fluoxymesterone,
(ix) formebulone,
(x) mesterolone,
(xi) methandienone,
(xii) methandranone,
(xiii) methandriol,
(xiv) methandrostenolone,
(xv) methenolone,
(xvi) methyltestosterone,
(xvii) mibolerone,
(xviii) nandrolone,
(xix) norethandrolone,
(xx) oxandrolone,
(xxi) oxymesterone,
(xxii) oxymetholone,
(xxiii) stanolone,
(xxiv) stanozolol,
(xxv) testolactone,
(xxvi) testosterone,
(xxvii) trenbolone, and
(xxviii) any salt, ester, or isomer of a drug or substance described or listed in this paragraph, if that salt, ester, or isomer promotes muscle growth.

Any person who is otherwise lawfully in possession of an anabolic steroid, or who otherwise lawfully manufactures, distributes, dispenses, delivers, or possesses with intent to deliver an anabolic steroid, which anabolic steroid is expressly intended for and lawfully allowed to be administered through implants to livestock or other nonhuman species, and which is approved by the Secretary of Health and Human Services for such administration, and which the person intends to administer or have administered through such implants, shall not be considered to be in unauthorized possession or to unlawfully manufacture, distribute, dispense, deliver, or possess with intent to deliver such anabolic steroid for purposes of this Act.

(d) "Administration" means the Drug Enforcement Administration, United States Department of Justice, or its successor agency.

(e) "Control" means to add a drug or other substance, or immediate precursor, to a Schedule under Article II of this Act [720 ILCS 570/201 et seq.] whether by transfer from another Schedule or otherwise.

(f) "Controlled Substance" means a drug, substance, or immediate precursor in the Schedules of Article II of this Act.

(g) "Counterfeit substance" means a controlled substance, which, or the container or labeling of which, without authorization bears the trademark, trade name, or other identifying mark, imprint, number or device, or any likeness thereof, of a manufacturer, distributor, or dispenser other than the person who in fact manufactured, distributed, or dispensed the substance.

(h) "Deliver" or "delivery" means the actual, constructive or attempted transfer of possession of a controlled substance, with or without consideration, whether or not there is an agency relationship.

(i) "Department" means the Illinois Department of Alcoholism and Substance Abuse of the State of Illinois or its successor agency.

(j) "Department of State Police" means the Department of State Police of the State of Illinois or its successor agency.

(k) "Department of Corrections" means the Department of Corrections of the State of Illinois or its successor agency.

(*l*) "Department of Professional Regulation" means the Department of Professional Regulation of the State of Illinois or its successor agency.

(m) "Depressant" or "stimulant substance" means:

(1) a drug which contains any quantity of (i) barbituric acid or any of the salts of barbituric acid which has been designated as habit forming under section 502 (d) of the Federal Food, Drug, and Cosmetic Act (21 U.S.C. 352 (d)); or

(2) a drug which contains any quantity of (i) amphetamine or methamphetamine and any of their optical isomers; (ii) any salt of amphetamine or methamphetamine or any salt of an optical isomer of amphetamine; or (iii) any substance which the Department, after investigation, has found to be, and by rule designated as, habit forming because of its depressant or stimulant effect on the central nervous system; or

(3) lysergic acid diethylamide; or

(4) any drug which contains any quantity of a substance which the Department, after investigation, has found to have, and by rule designated as having, a potential for abuse because of its depressant or stimulant effect on the central nervous system or its hallucinogenic effect.

(n) "Designated product" means any narcotic drug, amphetamine, phenmetrazine, methamphetamine, gluthethimide, pentazocine or cannabis product listed in Schedule II and also means a controlled substance listed in Schedule II which is determined and designated by the Department or its successor agency to be such a product. A designated product shall only be dispensed upon an official prescription blank.

(*o*) "Director" means the Director of the Department of State Police or the Department of Professional Regulation or his designated agents.

(p) "Dispense" means to deliver a controlled substance to an ultimate user or research subject by or pursuant to the lawful order of a practitioner, including the prescribing, administering, packaging, labeling, or compounding necessary to prepare the substance for that delivery.

(q) "Dispenser" means a practitioner who dispenses.

(r) "Distribute" means to deliver, other than by administering or dispensing, a controlled substance.

(s) "Distributor" means a person who distributes.

(t) "Drug" means (1) substances recognized as drugs in the official United States Pharmacopoeia, Official Homeopathic Pharmacopoeia of the United States, or official National Formulary, or any supplement to any of them; (2) substances intended for use in diagnosis, cure, mitigation, treatment, or prevention of disease in man or animals; (3) substances (other than food) intended to affect the structure of any function of the body of man or animals and (4) substances intended for use as a component of any article specified in clause (1), (2), or (3) of this subsection. It does not include devices or their components, parts, or accessories.

(u) "Good Faith" means the prescribing or dispensing of a controlled substance by a practitioner in the regular course of professional treatment to or for any person who is under his treatment for a pathology or condition other than that individual's physical or psychological dependence upon or addiction to a controlled substance, except as provided herein: and application of the term to a pharmacist shall mean the dispensing of a controlled substance pursuant to the prescriber's order which in the professional judgment of the pharmacist is lawful. The pharmacist shall be guided by accepted professional standards including, but not limited to the following, in making the judgment:

(1) lack of consistency of doctor-patient relationship,

(2) frequency of prescriptions for same drug by one prescriber for large numbers of patients,

(3) quantities beyond those normally prescribed,

(4) unusual dosages,

(5) unusual geographic distances between patient, pharmacist and prescriber,

(6) consistent prescribing of habit-forming drugs.

(v) "Immediate precursor" means a substance:

(1) which the Department has found to be and by rule designated as being a principal compound used, or produced primarily for use, in the manufacture of a controlled substance;

(2) which is an immediate chemical intermediary used or likely to be used in the manufacture of such controlled substance; and

(3) the control of which is necessary to prevent, curtail or limit the manufacture of such controlled substance.

(w) "Instructional Activities" means the acts of teaching, educating or instructing by practitioners using controlled substances within educational facilities approved by the State Board of Education or its successor agency.

(x) "Local authorities" means a duly organized State, County or Municipal peace unit or police force.

(y) "Look-alike substance" means a substance, other than a controlled substance which (1) by overall dosage unit appearance, including shape, color, size, markings or lack thereof, taste, consistency, or any other identifying physical characteristic of the substance, would lead a reasonable person to believe that the substance is a controlled substance, or (2) is expressly or impliedly represented to be a controlled substance or is distributed under circumstances which would lead a reasonable person to believe that the substance is a controlled substance. For the purpose of determining whether the representations made or the circumstances of the distribution would lead a reasonable person to believe the substance to be a controlled substance under this clause (2) of subsection (y), the court or other authority may consider the following factors in addition to any other factor that may be relevant:

(a) Statements made by the owner or person in control of the substance concerning its nature, use or effect;

(b) Statements made to the buyer or recipient that the substance may be resold for profit;

(c) Whether the substance is packaged in a manner normally used for the illegal distribution of controlled substances;

(d) Whether the distribution or attempted distribution included an exchange of or demand for money or other property as consideration, and whether the amount of the consideration was substantially greater than the reasonable retail market value of the substance.

Clause (1) of this subsection (y) shall not apply to a noncontrolled substance in its finished dosage form that was initially introduced into commerce prior to the initial introduction into commerce of a controlled substance in its finished dosage form which it may substantially resemble.

Nothing in this subsection (y) prohibits the dispensing or distributing of noncontrolled substances by persons authorized to dispense and distribute controlled substances under this Act, provided that such action would be deemed to be carried out in good faith under subsection (u) if the substances involved were controlled substances.

Nothing in this subsection (y) or in this Act prohibits the manufacture, preparation, propagation, compounding, processing, packaging, advertising or distribution of a drug or drugs by any person registered pursuant to Section 510 of the Federal Food, Drug, and Cosmetic Act (21 U.S.C. 360).

(y-1) "Mail-order pharmacy" means a pharmacy that is located in a state of the United States, other than Illinois, that delivers, dispenses or distributes, through the United States Postal Service or other common carrier, to Illinois residents, any substance which requires a prescription.

(z) "Manufacture" means the production, preparation, propagation, compounding, conversion or processing of a controlled substance, either directly or indirectly, by extraction from substances of natural origin, or independently by means of chemical synthesis, or by a combination of extraction and chemical synthesis, and includes any packaging or repackaging of the substance or labeling of its container, except that this term does not include:

(1) by an ultimate user, the preparation or compounding of a controlled substance for his own use; or

(2) by a practitioner, or his authorized agent under his supervision, the preparation, compounding, packaging, or labeling of a controlled substance:

(a) as an incident to his administering or dispensing of a controlled substance in the course of his professional practice; or

(b) as an incident to lawful research, teaching or chemical analysis and not for sale.

(aa) "Narcotic drug" means any of the following, whether produced directly or indirectly by extraction from substances of natural origin, or independently by means of chemical synthesis, or by a combination of extraction and chemical synthesis:

(1) opium and opiate, and any salt, compound, derivative, or preparation of opium or opiate;

(2) any salt, compound, isomer, derivative, or preparation thereof which is chemically equivalent or identical with any of the substances referred to in clause (1), but not including the isoquinoline alkaloids of opium;

(3) opium poppy and poppy straw;

(4) coca leaves and any salts, compound, isomer, salt of an isomer, derivative, or preparation of coca leaves including cocaine or ecgonine, and any salt, compound, isomer, derivative, or preparation thereof which is chemically equivalent or identical with any of these substances, but not including decocainized coca leaves or extractions of coca leaves which do not contain cocaine or ecgonine (for the purpose of this paragraph, the term "isomer" includes optical, positional and geometric isomers).

(bb) "Nurse" means a registered nurse licensed under The Illinois Nursing Act of 1987 [225 ILCS 65/1 et seq.].

(cc) "Official prescription blanks" means the triplicate prescription forms supplied to practitioners by the Department for prescribing Schedule II Designated Product controlled substances.

(dd) "Opiate" means any substance having an addiction forming or addiction sustaining liability similar to morphine or being capable of conversion into a drug having addiction forming or addiction sustaining liability.

(ee) "Opium poppy" means the plant of the species Papaver somniferum L., except its seeds.

(ff) "Parole and Pardon Board" means the Parole and Pardon Board of the State of Illinois or its successor agency.

(gg) "Person" means any individual, corporation, mail-order pharmacy, government or governmental subdivision or agency, business trust, estate, trust, partnership or association, or any other entity.

(hh) "Pharmacist" means any person who holds a certificate of registration as a registered pharmacist, a local registered pharmacist or a registered assistant pharmacist under the Pharmacy Practice Act of 1987 [225 ILCS 85/1 et seq.].

(ii) "Pharmacy" means any store, ship or other place in which pharmacy is authorized to be practiced under the Pharmacy Practice Act of 1987.

(jj) "Poppy straw" means all parts, except the seeds, of the opium poppy, after mowing.

(kk) "Practitioner" means a physician, dentist, podiatrist, veterinarian, scientific investigator, pharmacist, licensed practical nurse, registered nurse, hospital, laboratory, or pharmacy, or other person licensed, registered, or otherwise lawfully permitted by the United States or this State to distribute, dispense, conduct research with respect to, administer or use in teaching or chemical analysis, a controlled substance in the course of professional practice or research.

(*ll*) "Pre-printed prescription" means a written prescription upon which the designated drug has been indicated prior to the time of issuance.

(mm) "Prescriber" means a physician, dentist, podiatrist or veterinarian who issues a prescription.

(nn) "Prescription" means a lawful written or verbal order of a physician, dentist, podiatrist or veterinarian for any controlled substance.

(oo) "Production" or "produce" means manufacture, planting, cultivating, growing, or harvesting of a controlled substance.

(pp) "Registrant" means every person who is required to register under Section 302 of this Act [720 ILCS 570/302].

(qq) "Registry number" means the number assigned to each person authorized to handle controlled substances under the laws of the United States and of this State.

(rr) "State" includes the State of Illinois and any state, district, commonwealth, territory, insular possession thereof, and any area subject to the legal authority of the United States of America.

(ss) "Ultimate user" means a person who lawfully possesses a controlled substance for his own use or for the use of a member of his household or for administering to an animal owned by him or by a member of his household.
(Source: P.A. 87-754.) [Formerly Ill. Rev. Stat. 56½ §1102.]

570/103. Authority of certain Acts.

§103. Nothing in this Act limits the lawful authority granted by the Medical Practice Act of 1987 [225 ILCS 60/1 et seq.], The Illinois Nursing Act of 1987 [225 ILCS 65/1 et seq.] or the Pharmacy Practice Act of 1987 [225 ILCS 85/1 et seq.].
(Source: P.A. 85-1209.) [Formerly Ill. Rev. Stat. 56½ §1103.]

ARTICLE II. SCHEDULES OF CONTROLLED SUBSTANCES

Sec.

570/201. Execution of article.

§201. (a) The Department shall carry out the provisions of this Article. The Department or its successor agency may add substances to or delete or reschedule all controlled substances in the Schedules of Sections 204, 206, 208, 210 and 212 of this Act [720 ILCS 570/204, 570/206, 570/208, 570/210 and 570/212] and shall determine "designated products" as required under Sections 308, 309, 311 and 312 of this Act [720 ILCS 570/308, 570/309, 570/311 and 570/312]. In making a determination regarding the addition, deletion, or rescheduling of a substance, the Department shall consider the following:

(1) the actual or relative potential for abuse;

(2) the scientific evidence of its pharmacological effect, if known;

(3) the state of current scientific knowledge regarding the substance;

(4) the history and current pattern of abuse;

(5) the scope, duration, and significance of abuse;

(6) the risk to the public health;

(7) the potential of the substance to produce psychological or physiological dependence;

(8) whether the substance is an immediate precursor of a substance already controlled under this Article;

(9) the immediate harmful effect in terms of potentially fatal dosage; and

(10) the long-range effects in terms of permanent health impairment.

(b) In making a determination regarding a "designated product," the Department shall consider the above criteria, and in addition shall consider whether use of the official prescription blank is required to control significant actual illicit traffic of the substance.

After considering the factors enumerated in subsection (a) or in the case of making a determination of a "designated product," the additional factors of subsection (b), the Department shall publish its determination. If, within 30 days from such publication, a party adversely affected files with the Department substantial written objections to inclusion, rescheduling, or deletion of a substance, or to a determination of a "designated product," the Department shall publish the substantial written objections and afford all interested parties an opportunity to be heard. At the conclusion of the hearing, the Department shall make findings with respect thereto and issue a rule controlling the substance if the Department has determined that the substance has a potential for abuse and submits to the General Assembly a written report of its findings with respect thereto. Each such rule adding, deleting or rescheduling a controlled substance or determining a "designated product" shall then be submitted to the General Assembly, in the form of a proposed law amending this Act, and unless the proposed law is adopted by the General Assembly and enacted into law within 2 years after the Department has issued the rule, such rule shall expire and have no further force and effect.

The requirement for reporting to the General Assembly shall be satisfied by filing copies of the report with the Speaker, the minority Leader and the Clerk of the House of Representatives and the President, the Minority Leader and the Secretary of the Senate and the Legislative Research Unit, as required by Section 3.1 of "An Act to revise the law in relation to the General Assembly", approved February 25, 1874, as amended [25 ILCS 5/3.1], and filing such additional copies with the State Government Report Distribution Center for the General Assembly as is required under paragraph (t) of Section 7 of the State Library Act [15 ILCS 320/7].

(c) If the Department designates a substance as an immediate precursor, substances which are precursors of the controlled precursor shall not be subject to control solely because they are precursors of the controlled precursor.

(d) If any substance is designated, rescheduled, or deleted as a controlled substance under Federal law and notice thereof is given to the Department, the Department shall similarly control the substance under this Act after the expiration of 30 days from publication in the Federal Register of a final order designating a substance as a controlled substance or rescheduling or deleting a substance, unless within that 30 day period the Department objects, or a party adversely affected files with the Department substantial written objections objecting to inclusion, rescheduling, or deletion. In that case, the Department shall publish the reasons for objection or the substantial written objections and afford all interested parties an opportunity to be heard. At the conclusion of the hearing, the Department shall publish its decision, by means of a rule, which shall be final unless altered by statute. Upon publication of objections by the Department, similar control under this Act whether by inclusion, rescheduling or deletion is stayed until the Department publishes its ruling.

(e) The Department shall by rule exclude any non-narcotic substances from a schedule if such substance may, under the Federal Food, Drug, and Cosmetic Act [21 U.S.C. §301 et seq.], be lawfully sold over the counter without a prescription.

(f) Dextromethorphan shall not be deemed to be included in any schedule by reason of enactment of this title unless controlled after the date of such enactment pursuant to the foregoing provisions of this section.

(g) Authority to control under this section does not extend to distilled spirits, wine, malt beverages, or tobacco as those terms are defined or used in The Liquor Control Act [235 ILCS 5/1-1 et seq.] and the Tobacco Products Tax Act [repealed].

(Source: P.A. 84-1438.) [Formerly Ill. Rev. Stat. 56½ §1201.]

570/202. Designation of controlled substances by name.

§202. The controlled substances listed or to be listed in the schedules in sections 204, 206, 208, 210 and 212 [720 ILCS 570/204, 570/206, 570/208, 570/210 and 570/212] are included by whatever official, common, usual, chemical, or trade name designated.

(Source: P.A. 77-757.) [Formerly Ill. Rev. Stat. 56½ §1202.]

570/203. Criteria; Schedule I.

§203. The Department shall issue a rule scheduling a substance in Schedule I if it finds that:

(1) the substance has high potential for abuse; and

(2) the substance has no currently accepted medical use in treatment in the United States or lacks accepted safety for use in treatment under medical supervision.

(Source: P.A. 83-969.) [Formerly Ill. Rev. Stat. 56½ §1203.]

570/204. Enumeration; Schedule I.

§204. (a) The controlled substances listed in this Section are included in Schedule I.

(b) Unless specifically excepted or unless listed in another schedule, any of the following opiates, including their isomers, esters, ethers, salts, and salts of isomers, esters, and ethers, whenever the existence of such isomers, esters, ethers and salts is possible within the specific chemical designation:

(1) Acetylmethadol;

(1.1) Acetyl-alpha-methylfentanyl;

(2) Allylprodine;

(3) Alphacetylmethadol;
(4) Alphameprodine;
(5) Alphamethadol;
(6) Alpha-methylfentanyl (N-(1-alpha-methyl-beta-phenyl) ethyl-4-piperidyl) propionanilide; 1-(1-methyl-2-phenylethyl)-4-(N-propanilido) piperidine;
(6.1) Alpha-methylthiofentanyl;
(7) 1-methyl-4-phenyl-4-proprionoxypiperidine (MPPP);
(7.1) 1-(2-phenylethyl)-4-phenyl-4-acetyloxypiperidine (PEPAP);
(8) Benzethidine;
(9) Betacetylmethadol;
(9.1) Beta-hydroxyfentanyl;
(10) Betameprodine;
(11) Betamethadol;
(12) Betaprodine;
(13) Clonitazene;
(14) Dextromoramide;
(15) Diampromide;
(16) Diethylthiambutene;
(17) Difenoxin;
(18) Dimenoxadol;
(19) Dimepheptanol;
(20) Dimethylthiambutene;
(21) Dioxaphetylbutyrate;
(22) Dipipanone;
(23) Ethylmethylthiambutene;
(24) Etonitazene;
(25) Etoxeridine;
(26) Furethidine;
(27) Hydroxpethidine;
(28) Ketobemidone;
(29) Levomoramide;
(30) Levophenacylmorphan;
(31) 3-Methylfentanyl;
(31.1) 3-Methylthiofentanyl;
(32) Morpheridine;
(33) Noracymethadol;
(34) Norlevorphanol;
(35) Normethadone;
(36) Norpipanone;
(36.1) Para-fluorofentanyl;
(37) Phenadoxone;
(38) Phenampromide;
(39) Phenomorphan;
(40) Phenoperidine;
(41) Piritramide;
(42) Proheptazine;
(43) Properidine;
(44) Propiram;
(45) Racemoramide;
(45.1) Thiofentanyl;
(46) Tilidine;
(47) Trimeperidine.

(c) Unless specifically excepted or unless listed in another schedule, any of the following opium derivatives, its salts, isomers and salts of isomers, whenever the existence of such salts, isomers and salts of isomers is possible within the specific chemical designation:

(1) Acetorphine;
(2) Acetyldihydrocodeine;
(3) Benzylmorphine;
(4) Codeine methylbromide;
(5) Codeine-N-Oxide;
(6) Cyprenorphine;
(7) Desomorphine;
(8) Diacetyldihydromorphine (Dihydroheroin);
(9) Dihydromorphine;
(10) Drotebanol;
(11) Etorphine (except hydrochloride salt);
(12) Heroin;
(13) Hydromorphinol;
(14) Methyldesorphine;
(15) Methyldihydromorphine;
(16) Morphine methylbromide;
(17) Morphine methylsulfonate;
(18) Morphine-N-Oxide;
(19) Myrophine;
(20) Nicocodeine;
(21) Nicomorphine;
(22) Normorphine;
(23) Pholcodine;
(24) Thebacon.

(d) Unless specifically excepted or unless listed in another schedule, any material, compound, mixture, or preparation which contains any quantity of the following hallucinogenic substances, or which contains any of its salts, isomers and salts of isomers, whenever the existence of such salts, isomers, and salts of isomers is possible within the specific chemical designation (for the purposes of this paragraph only, the term "isomer" includes the optical, position and geometric isomers):

(1) 3,4-methylenedioxyamphetamine (alpha-methyl,3,4-methylenedioxyphenethylamine, methylenedioxyamphetamine, MDA);
(2) 3,4-methylenedioxymethamphetamine (MDMA);
(3) 3-methoxy-4,5-methylenedioxyamphetamine, (MMDA);
(4) 3,4,5-trimethoxyamphetamine (TMA);
(5) 5-hydroxydimethyltryptamine (Bufotenine);
(6) Diethyltryptamine (DET);
(7) Dimethyltryptamine (DMT);
(8) 4-methyl-2,5-dimethoxyamphetamine (DOM, STP);
(9) Ibogaine;
(10) Lysergic acid diethylamide;
(11) 3,4,5-trimethoxyphenethylamine (Mescaline);
(12) Peyote;
(13) N-ethyl-3-piperidyl benzilate (JB 318);
(14) N-methyl-3-piperidyl benzilate;
(15) Parahexyl; some trade or other names: 3-Hexyl-1-hydroxy-7,8,9,10-tetrahydro-6,6,9-trimethyl-6H-dibenzo (b,d) pyran; Synhexyl;
(16) Psilocybin;
(17) Psilocyn;
(18) Alpha-methyltryptamine (AMT);
(19) 2,5-dimethoxyamphetamine (2,5-dimethoxy-a-methylphenethylamine; 2,5-DMA);

(20) 4-bromo-2,5-dimethoxyamphetamine (4-bromo-2,5-dimethoxy-a-methylphenethylamine; 4-bromo-2,5-DMA);

(21) 4-methoxyamphetamine (4-methoxy-a-methylphenethylamine; paramethoxyamphetamine; PMA);

(22) Thiophene analog of phencyclidine (TPCP);

(23) Ethylamine analog of phencyclidine. Some trade or other names: N-ethyl-1-phenylcyclohexylamine, (1-phenylcyclohexyl) ethylamine, N-(1-phenylcyclohexyl) ethylamine, cyclohexamine, PCE;

(24) Pyrrolidine analog of phencyclidine. Some trade or other names: 1-(1-phenylcyclohexyl) pyrrolidine, PCPy, PHP.

(e) Unless specifically excepted or unless listed in another schedule, any material, compound, mixture, or preparation which contains any quantity of the following substances having a depressant effect on the central nervous system, including its salts, isomers, and salts of isomers whenever the existence of such salts, isomers, and salts of isomers is possible within the specific chemical designation:

(1) mecloqualone; and

(2) methaqualone.

(f) Unless specifically excepted or unless listed in another schedule, any material, compound, mixture, or preparation which contains any quantity of the following substances having a stimulant effect on the central nervous system, including its salts, isomers, and salts of isomers:

(1) Fenethylline;

(2) N-ethylamphetamine.

(Source: P.A. 85-1209; 85-1260; 85-1440.) [Formerly Ill. Rev. Stat. 56½ §1204.]

570/205. Criteria; Schedule II.

§205. The Department shall issue a rule scheduling a substance in Schedule II if it finds that:

(1) the substance has high potential for abuse;

(2) the substance has currently accepted medical use in treatment in the United States, or currently accepted medical use with severe restrictions; and

(3) the abuse of the substance may lead to severe psychological or physiological dependence.

(Source: P.A. 83-969.) [Formerly Ill. Rev. Stat. 56½ §1205.]

570/206. Enumeration; Schedule II.

§206. (a) The controlled substances listed in this Section are included in Schedule II.

(b) Unless specifically excepted or unless listed in another schedule, any of the following substances whether produced directly or indirectly by extraction from substances of vegetable origin, or independently by means of chemical synthesis, or by combination of extraction and chemical synthesis:

(1) Opium and opiates, and any salt, compound, derivative or preparation of opium or opiate, excluding apomorphine, dextrorphan, nalbuphine, nalmefene, naloxone, and naltrexone, and their respective salts, but including the following:

(i) Raw Opium;

(ii) Opium extracts;

(iii) Opium fluid extracts;

(iv) Powdered opium;

(v) Granulated opium;

(vi) Tincture of opium;

(vii) Codeine;

(viii) Ethylmorphine;

(ix) Etorphine Hydrochloride;

(x) Hydrocodone;
(xi) Hydromorphone;
(xii) Metopon;
(xiii) Morphine;
(xiv) Oxycodone;
(xv) Oxymorphone;
(xvi) Thebaine.

(2) Any salt, compound, isomer, derivative or preparation thereof which is chemically equivalent or identical with any of the substances referred to in subparagraph (1), but not including the isoquinoline alkaloids of opium;

(3) Opium poppy and poppy straw;

(4) Coca leaves and any salt, compound, isomer, salt of an isomer, derivative, or preparation of coca leaves including cocaine or ecgonine, and any salt, compound, isomer, derivative, or preparation thereof which is chemically equivalent or identical with any of these substances, but not including decocainized coca leaves or extractions of coca leaves which do not contain cocaine or ecgonine (for the purpose of this paragraph, the term "isomer" includes optical, positional and geometric isomers);

(5) Concentrate of poppy straw (the crude extract of poppy straw in either liquid, solid or powder form which contains the phenanthrine alkaloids of the opium poppy).

(c) Unless specifically excepted or unless listed in another schedule any of the following opiates, including their isomers, esters, ethers, salts, and salts of isomers, whenever the existence of these isomers, esters, ethers and salts is possible within the specific chemical designation, dextrorphan excepted:

(1) Alfentanil;
(2) Alphaprodine;
(3) Anileridine;
(4) Bezitramide;
(5) Bulk Dextropropoxyphene (non-dosage forms);
(6) Dihydrocodeine;
(7) Diphenoxylate;
(8) Fentanyl;
(9) Sufentanil;
(10) Isomethadone;
(11) Levomethorphan;
(12) Levorphanol (Levorphan);
(13) Metazocine;
(14) Methadone;
(15) Methadone-Intermediate, 4-cyano-2-dimethylamino-4,4-diphenyl-1-butane;
(16) Moramide-Intermediate, 2-methyl-3-morpholino-1,1-diphenyl-propane-carboxylic acid;
(17) Pethidine (meperidine);
(18) Pethidine-Intermediate-A, 4-cyano-1-methyl-4-phenylpiperidine;
(19) Pethidine-Intermediate-B, ethyl-4-phenylpiperidine-4-carboxylate; ethyl-4-phenylpiperidine-4-carboxylate;
(20) Pethidine-Intermediate-C, 1-methyl-4-phenyl-piperidine-4-carboxylic acid;
(21) Phenazocine;
(22) Piminodine;
(23) Racemethorphan;
(24) Racemorphan.

(d) Unless specifically excepted or unless listed in another schedule, any material, compound, mixture, or preparation which contains any quantity of the following substances having a stimulant effect on the central nervous system:

(1) Amphetamine, its salts, optical isomers, and salts of its optical isomers;
(2) Methamphetamine, its salts, isomers, and salts of its isomers;
(3) Phenmetrazine and its salts;
(4) Methylphenidate.

(e) Unless specifically excepted or unless listed in another schedule, any material, compound, mixture, or preparation which contains any quantity of the following substances having a depressant effect on the central nervous system, including its salts, isomers, and salts of isomers whenever the existence of such salts, isomers, and salts of isomers is possible within the specific chemical designation:

(1) Amobarbital;
(2) Secobarbital;
(3) Pentobarbital;
(4) Pentazocine;
(5) Phencyclidine;
(6) Gluthethimide;
(7) Dronabinol (synthetic).

(f) Unless specifically excepted or unless listed in another schedule, any material, compound, mixture, or preparation which contains any quantity of the following substances:

(1) Immediate precursor to amphetamine and methamphetamine:
(i)* Phenylacetone
Some trade or other names: phenyl-2-propanone; P2P; benzyl methyl ketone; methyl benzyl ketone.

**So in original. No subsec. (ii) has been enacted.*

(2) Immediate precursors to phencyclidine:
(i) 1-phenylcyclohexylamine;
(ii) 1-piperidinocyclohexanecarbonitrile (PCC).
(3) Nabilone.

(Source: P.A. 85-1209; 85-1260; 85-1440.) [Formerly Ill. Rev. Stat. 56½ §1206.]

570/207. Criteria; Schedule III.

§207. The Department shall issue a rule scheduling a substance in Schedule III if it finds that:

(1) the substance has a potential for abuse less than the substances listed in Schedule I and II;

(2) the substance has currently accepted medical use in treatment in the United States; and

(3) abuse of the substance may lead to moderate or low physiological dependence or high psychological dependence.

(Source: P.A. 83-969.) [Formerly Ill. Rev. Stat. 56½ §1207.]

570/208. Enumeration; Schedule III.

§208. (a) The controlled substances listed in this Section are included in Schedule III.

(b) Unless specifically excepted or unless listed in another schedule, any material, compound, mixture, or preparation which contains any quantity of the following substances having a stimulant effect on the central nervous system, including its salts, isomers (whether optical position, or geometric), and salts of such isomers whenever the existence of such salts, isomers, and salts of isomers is possible within the specific chemical designation;

(1) Those compounds, mixtures, or preparations in dosage unit form containing any stimulant substances listed in Schedule II which compounds, mixtures, or preparations were listed on August 25, 1971, as excepted compounds under Title 21, Code of Federal Regulations, Section 308.32, and any other drug of the quantitative composition shown in that list for those drugs or

which is the same except that it contains a lesser quantity of controlled substances;

(2) Benzphetamine;

(3) Chlorphentermine;

(4) Clortermine;

(5) Phendimetrazine.

(c) Unless specifically excepted or unless listed in another schedule, any material, compound, mixture, or preparation which contains any quantity of the following substances having a potential for abuse associated with a depressant effect on the central nervous system:

(1) Any compound, mixture, or preparation containing amobarbital, secobarbital, pentobarbital or any salt thereof and one or more other active medicinal ingredients which are not listed in any schedule;

(2) Any suppository dosage form containing amobarbital, secobarbital, pentobarbital or any salt of any of these drugs and approved by the Federal Food and Drug Administration for marketing only as a suppository;

(3) Any substance which contains any quantity of a derivative of barbituric acid, or any salt thereof:

(4) Chlorhexadol;

(5) Methyprylon;

(6) Sulfondiethylmethane;

(7) Sulfonethylmethane;

(8) Sulfonmethane;

(9) Lysergic acid;

(10) Lysergic acid amide;

(11) Any material, compound, mixture or preparation containing not more than 12.5 milligrams of pentazocine or any of its salts, per 325 milligrams of aspirin;

(12) Any material, compound, mixture or preparation containing not more than 12.5 milligrams of pentazocine or any of its salts, per 325 milligrams of acetaminophen;

(13) Any material, compound, mixture or preparation containing not more than 50 milligrams of pentazocine or any of its salts plus naloxone HCl USP 0.5 milligrams, per dosage unit;

(14) Preparations containing both tiletamine and zolazepam.

(d) Nalorphine.

(e) Unless specifically excepted or unless listed in another schedule, any material, compound, mixture, or preparation containing limited quantities of any of the following narcotic drugs, or their salts calculated as the free anhydrous base or alkaloid, as set forth below:

(1) not more than 1.8 grams of codeine per 100 milliliters or not more than 90 milligrams per dosage unit, with an equal or greater quantity of an isoquinoline alkaloid of opium;

(2) not more than 1.8 grams of codeine per 100 milliliters or not more than 90 milligrams per dosage unit, with one or more active non-narcotic ingredients in recognized therapeutic amounts;

(3) not more than 300 milligrams of dihydrocodeinone per 100 milliliters or not more than 15 milligrams per dosage unit, with a fourfold or greater quantity of an isoquinoline alkaloid of opium;

(4) not more than 300 milligrams of dihydrocodeinone per 100 milliliters or not more than 15 milligrams per dosage unit, with one or more active, non-narcotic ingredients in recognized therapeutic amounts;

(5) not more than 1.8 grams of dihydrocodeine per 100 milliliters or not more than 90 milligrams per dosage unit, with one or more active, non-narcotic ingredients in recognized therapeutic amounts;

(6) not more than 300 milligrams of ethylmorphine per 100 milliliters or not more than 15 milligrams per dosage unit, with one or more active, non-narcotic ingredients in recognized therapeutic amounts;

(7) not more than 500 milligrams of opium per 100 milliliters or per 100 grams, or not more than 25 milligrams per dosage unit, with one or more active, non-narcotic ingredients in recognized therapeutic amounts;

(8) not more than 50 milligrams of morphine per 100 milliliters or per 100 grams with one or more active, non-narcotic ingredients in recognized therapeutic amounts.

(f) Anabolic steroids.

(g) The Department may except by rule any compound, mixture, or preparation containing any stimulant or depressant substance listed in subsection (b) from the application of all or any part of this Act if the compound, mixture, or preparation contains one or more active medicinal ingredients not having a stimulant or depressant effect on the central nervous system, and if the admixtures are included therein in combinations, quantity, proportion, or concentration that vitiate the potential for abuse of the substances which have a stimulant or depressant effect on the central nervous system.
(Source: P.A. 87-754.) [Formerly Ill. Rev. Stat. 56½ §1208.]

570/209. Criteria; Schedule IV.

§209. The Department shall issue a rule scheduling a substance in Schedule IV if it finds that:

(1) the substance has a low potential for abuse relative to substances in Schedule III;

(2) the substance has currently accepted medical use in treatment in the United States; and

(3) abuse of the substance may lead to limited physiological dependence or psychological dependence relative to the substances in Schedule III.
(Source: P.A. 83-969.) [Formerly Ill. Rev. Stat. 56½ §1209.]

570/210. Enumeration; Schedule IV.

§210. (a) The controlled substances listed in this Section are included in Schedule IV.

(b) Unless specifically excepted or unless listed in another schedule, any material, compound, mixture, or preparation containing limited quantities of any of the following narcotic drugs, or their salts calculated as the free anhydrous base or alkaloid, as set forth below:

(1) Not more than 1 milligram of difenoxin (DEA Drug Code No. 9618) and not less than 25 micrograms of atropine sulfate per dosage unit.

(2) Dextropropoxyphene (Alpha-(+)-4-dimethylamino-1, 2-diphenyl-3-methyl-2-propionoxybutane).

(c) Unless specifically excepted or unless listed in another schedule, any material, compound, mixture, or preparation which contains any quantity of the following substances having a potential for abuse associated with a depressant effect on the central nervous system:

(1) Alprazolam;
(2) Barbital;
(3) Chloral Betaine;
(4) Chloral Hydrate;
(5) Chlordiazepoxide;
(6) Clonazepam;
(7) Clorazepate;
(8) Diazepam;
(9) Ethchlorvynol;
(10) Ethinamate;

(11) Flurazepam;
(12) Halazepam;
(13) Lorazepam;
(14) Mebutamate;
(15) Meprobamate;
(16) Methohexital;
(17) Methylphenobarbital (Mephobarbital);
(18) Oxazepam;
(19) Paraldehyde;
(20) Petrichloral;
(21) Phenobarbital;
(22) Prazepam;
(23) Temazepam;
(24) Triazolam.

(d) Any material, compound, mixture, or preparation which contains any quantity of the following substances, including its salts, isomers (whether optical, position, or geometric), and salts of such isomers, whenever the existence of such salts, isomers and salts of isomers is possible:

(1)* Fenfluramine.

**So in original. No subsec. (2) has been enacted.*

(e) Unless specifically excepted or unless listed in another schedule any material, compound, mixture, or preparation which contains any quantity of the following substances having a stimulant effect on the central nervous system, including its salts, isomers (whether optical, position or geometric), and salts of such isomers whenever the existence of such salts, isomers, and salts of isomers is possible within the specific chemical designation:

(1) Diethylpropion;
(2) Mazindol;
(3) Phentermine;
(4) Pemoline (including organometallic complexes and chelates thereof);
(5) Pipradrol;
(6) SPA((-)-1-dimethylamino-1, 2-diphenylethane).

(f) The Department may except by rule any compound, mixture, or preparation containing any depressant substance listed in subsection (b) from the application of all or any part of this Act if the compound, mixture, or preparation contains one or more active medicinal ingredients not having a depressant effect on the central nervous system, and if the admixtures are included therein in combinations, quantity, proportion, or concentration that vitiate the potential for abuse of the substances which have a depressant effect on the central nervous system.

(Source: P.A. 84-874.) [Formerly Ill. Rev. Stat. 56½ §1210.]

570/211. Criteria; Schedule V.

§211. The Department shall issue a rule scheduling a substance in Schedule V if it finds that:

(1) the substance has low potential for abuse relative to the controlled substances listed in Schedule IV;

(2) the substance has currently accepted medical use in treatment in the United States; and

(3) abuse of the substance may lead to limited physiological dependence or psychological dependence relative to the substances in Schedule IV.

(Source: P.A. 83-969.) [Formerly Ill. Rev. Stat. 56½ §1211.]

570/212. Enumeration; Schedule V.

§212. (a) The controlled substances listed in this section are included in Schedule V.

(b) Any compound, mixture, or preparation containing limited quantities of any of the following narcotic drugs, or their salts calculated as the free anhydrous base or alkaloid which also contains one or more non-narcotic active medicinal ingredients in sufficient proportion to confer upon the compound, mixture, or preparation, valuable medicinal qualities other than those possessed by the narcotic drug alone as set forth below:

(1) not more than 200 milligrams of codeine, or any of its salts, per 100 milliliters or per 100 grams;

(2) not more than 100 milligrams of dihydrocodeine; or any of its salts, per 100 milliliters or per 100 grams;

(3) not more than 100 milligrams of ethylmorphine, or any of its salts, per 100 milliliters or per 100 grams;

(4) not more than 2.5 milligrams of diphenoxylate and not less than 25 micrograms of atropine sulfate per dosage unit;

(5) not more than 100 milligrams of opium per 100 milliliters or per 100 grams;

(6) not more than 0.5 milligram of difenoxin (DEA Drug Code No. 9618) and not less than 25 micrograms of atropine sulfate per dosage unit.

(c) Buprenorphine.

(d) Propylhexedrine, except that preparations containing propylhexedrine which may be lawfully sold over the counter without a prescription under the Federal Food, Drug and Cosmetic Act, as now or hereafter amended (21 U.S.C. 301 et seq.), and are included in Title 21, Part 1308, Section 22 of the Code of Federal Regulations, as now or hereafter amended, are exempted from scheduling herein.

(e) Any compound, mixture or preparation which contains any quantity of any controlled substance when such compound, mixture or preparation is not otherwise controlled in Schedules I, II, III or IV.

(Source: P.A. 86-848.) [Formerly Ill. Rev. Stat. 56½ §1212.]

570/213. Revision and republication of Schedules.

§213. The Department shall revise and republish the Schedules semi-annually for two years from the effective date of this Act, and thereafter annually. If the Department fails to republish the Schedules, the last published Schedules shall remain in full force and effect.

(Source: P.A. 83-969.) [Formerly Ill. Rev. Stat. 56½ §1213.]

570/214. Non-narcotic substances excluded.

§214. The non-narcotic substances excluded from all schedules of the Federal Controlled Substances Act (21 U.S.C. 801 et seq.) pursuant to Section 1308.22 of the Code of Federal regulations (21 C.F.R. 1308.22), are excluded from all schedules of this Act.

(Source: P.A. 80-472.) [Formerly Ill. Rev. Stat. 56½ §1214.]

570/215. Excepted compounds.

§215. Excepted Compounds. The compounds in the form excepted from application of certain specified sections of the Federal Controlled Substances Act (21 U.S.C. 801 et seq.), the Federal Controlled Substances Import and Export Act (21 U.S.C. 951 et seq.) and the Code of Federal Regulations, pursuant to Section 1308.32 of the Code of Federal Regulations (21 C.F.R. 1308.32) are excepted from the application of Sections 312 and 313 of this Act [720 ILCS 570/312 and 570/313].

(Source: P.A. 80-472.) [Formerly Ill. Rev. Stat. 56½ §1215.]

ARTICLE III. REGISTRATION AND CONTROL OF MANUFACTURE, DISTRIBUTION AND DISPENSING

570/301. Promulgation of rules.

§301. The Department of Professional Regulation shall promulgate rules and charge reasonable fees relating to the registration and control of the manufacture, distribution, and dispensing of controlled substances within this State.

(Source: P.A. 85-1209.) [Formerly Ill. Rev. Stat. 56½ §1301.]

570/302. Registration; regulation exemptions.

§302. (a) Every person who manufactures, distributes, or dispenses any controlled substances, or engages in chemical analysis, and instructional activities which utilize controlled substances, within this State or who proposes to engage in the manufacture, distribution, or dispensing of any controlled substance, or to engage in chemical analysis, and instructional activities which utilize controlled substances, within this State, must obtain a registration issued by the Department of Professional Regulation in accordance with its rules. The rules shall include, but not be limited to, setting the expiration date and renewal period for each registration under this Act. The Department, and any facility or service licensed by the Department, shall be exempt from the regulation requirements of this Section.

(b) Persons registered by the Department of Professional Regulation under this Act to manufacture, distribute, or dispense controlled substances may possess, manufacture, distribute, or dispense those substances to the extent authorized by their registration and in conformity with the other provisions of this Article.

(c) The following persons need not register and may lawfully possess controlled substances under this Act:

(1) an agent or employee of any registered manufacturer, distributor, or dispenser of any controlled substance if he is acting in the usual course of his employer's lawful business or employment;

(2) a common or contract carrier or warehouseman, or an agent or employee thereof, whose possession of any controlled substance is in the usual lawful course of such business or employment;

(3) an ultimate user or a person in possession of any controlled substance pursuant to a lawful prescription of a practitioner or in lawful possession of a Schedule V substance;

(4) officers and employees of this State or of the United States while acting in the lawful course of their official duties which requires possession of controlled substances;

(5) a registered pharmacist who is employed in, or the owner of, a pharmacy licensed under this Act and the Federal Controlled Substances Act [21 U.S.C. §801 et seq.], at the licensed location, or if he is acting in the usual course of his lawful profession, business, or employment.

(d) A separate registration is required at each place of business or professional practice where the applicant manufactures, distributes, or dispenses controlled substances. Persons are required to obtain a separate registration for each place of business or professional practice where controlled substances are located or stored. A separate registration is not required for every location at which a controlled substance may be prescribed.

(e) The Department of Professional Regulation or the Department of State Police may inspect the controlled premises, as defined in Section 502 of this Act [720 ILCS 570/502], of a registrant or applicant for registration in accordance with this Act and the rules promulgated hereunder and with regard to persons licensed by the Department, in accordance with Section 8-102 of the Illinois Alcoholism and Other Drug Dependency Act [20 ILCS 305/8-102] and the rules and regulations promulgated thereunder.

(Source: P.A. 87-711.) [Formerly Ill. Rev. Stat. 56½ §1302.]

570/303. Registration; public interest.

§303. (a) The Department of Professional Regulation shall register an applicant to manufacture, distribute or dispense controlled substances included in Sections 204, 206, 208, 210 and 212 of this Act [720 ILCS 570/204, 570/206, 570/208, 570/210 and 570/212] unless it determines that the issuance of that registration would be inconsistent with the public interest. In determining the public interest, the Department of Professional Regulation shall consider the following:

(1) maintenance of effective controls against diversion of controlled substances into other than lawful medical, scientific, or industrial channels;

(2) compliance with applicable Federal, State and local law;

(3) any convictions of the applicant under any law of the United States or of any State relating to any controlled substance;

(4) past experience in the manufacture or distribution of controlled substances, and the existence in the applicant's establishment of effective controls against diversion;

(5) furnishing by the applicant of false or fraudulent material in any application filed under this Act;

(6) suspension or revocation of the applicant's Federal registration to manufacture, distribute, or dispense controlled substances as authorized by Federal law;

(7) whether the applicant is suitably equipped with the facilities appropriate to carry on the operation described in his application;

(8) whether the applicant is of good moral character or, if the applicant is a partnership, association, corporation or other organization, whether the partners, directors, governing committee and managing officers are of good moral character;

(9) any other factors relevant to and consistent with the public health and safety; and

(10) Evidence from court, medical disciplinary and pharmacy board records and those of State and Federal investigatory bodies that the applicant has not or does not prescribe controlled substances within the provisions of this Act.

(b) No registration shall be granted to or renewed for any person who has within 5 years been convicted of a wilful violation of any law of the United States or any law of any State relating to controlled substances, or who is found to be deficient in any of the matters enumerated in subsections (a)(1) through (a)(8).

(c) Registration under subsection (a) does not entitle a registrant to manufacture, distribute or dispense controlled substances in Schedules I or II other than those specified in the registration.

(d) Practitioners who are registered to dispense any controlled substances in Schedules II through V are authorized to conduct instructional activities with controlled substances in Schedules II through V under the law of this State.

(e) If an applicant for registration is registered under the Federal law to manufacture, distribute or dispense controlled substances, upon filing a completed application for registration in this State and payment of all fees due hereunder, he shall be registered in this State to the same extent as his Federal registration, unless, within 30 days after completing his application in this State, the Department of Professional Regulation notifies the applicant that his application has not been granted. A practitioner who is in compliance with the Federal law with respect to registration to dispense controlled substances in Schedules II through V need only send a current copy of that Federal registration to the Department of Professional Regulation and he shall be deemed in compliance with the registration provisions of this State.

(f) The fee for registration as a manufacturer or wholesale distributor of controlled substances shall be $50.00 per year, except that the fee for registration as a manufacturer or wholesale distributor of controlled substances that may be dispensed without a prescription under this Act shall be $15.00 per year. The expiration date and renewal period for each certificate of registration issued under this Act shall be set by rule.

(Source: P.A. 85-1209.) [Formerly Ill. Rev. Stat. 56½ §1303.]

570/303.1. Registration; payment of fees and fines.

§303.1. Any person who delivers a check or other payment to the Department that is returned to the Department unpaid by the financial institution upon which it is drawn shall pay to the Department, in addition to the amount already owed to the Department, a fine of $50. If the check or other payment was for a renewal or issuance fee and that person practices without paying the renewal fee or issuance fee and the fine due, an additional fine of $100 shall be imposed. The fines imposed by this Section are in addition to any other discipline provided under this Act for unlicensed practice or practice on a nonrenewed license. The Department shall notify the person that payment of fees and fines shall be paid to the Department by certified check or money order within 30 calendar days of the notification. If, after the expiration of 30 days from the date of the notification, the person has failed to submit the necessary remittance, the Department shall automatically terminate the license or certificate or deny the application, without hearing. If, after termination or denial, the person seeks a license or certificate, he or she shall apply to the Department for restoration or issuance of the license or certificate and pay all fees and fines due to the Department. The Department may establish a fee for the processing of an application for restoration of a license or certificate to pay all expenses of processing this application. The Director may waive the fines due under this Section in individual cases where the Director finds that the fines would be unreasonable or unnecessarily burdensome.

(Chgd. by P.A. 87-1031, §2, eff. 1/1/93.)
(Source: P.A. 85-1209.) [Formerly Ill. Rev. Stat. 56½ §1303.1.]

570/304. Registration; suspension or revocation.

§304. (a) A registration under Section 303 [720 ILCS 570/303] to manufacture, distribute, or dispense a controlled substance may be suspended or revoked by the Department of Professional Regulation upon a finding that the registrant:

(1) has furnished any false or fraudulent material information in any application filed under this Act; or

(2) has been convicted of a felony under any law of the United States or any State relating to any controlled substance; or

(3) has had suspended or revoked his Federal registration to manufacture, distribute, or dispense controlled substances; or

(4) has been convicted of bribery, perjury, or other infamous crime under the laws of the United States or of any State; or

(5) has violated any provision of this Act or any rules promulgated hereunder, whether or not he has been convicted of such violation; or

(6) has failed to provide effective controls against the diversion of controlled substances in other than legitimate medical, scientific or industrial channels.

(b) The Department of Professional Regulation may limit revocation or suspension of a registration to the particular controlled substance with respect to which grounds for revocation or suspension exist.

(c) The Department of Professional Regulation shall promptly notify the Administration, the Department and the Department of State Police or their successor agencies, of all orders denying, suspending or revoking registration, all forfeitures of controlled substances, and all final court dispositions, if any, of such denials, suspensions, revocations or forfeitures.

(d) If Federal registration of any registrant is suspended, revoked, refused renewal or refused issuance, then the Department of Professional Regulation shall issue a notice and conduct a hearing in accordance with Section 305 of this Act [720 ILCS 570/305].

(Source: P.A. 85-1209.) [Formerly Ill. Rev. Stat. 56½ §1304.]

570/305. Registration; notice of hearing.

§305. (a) Before denying, refusing renewal of, suspending or revoking a registration, the Department of Professional Regulation shall serve upon the applicant or registrant, by registered mail at the address in the application or registration or by any other means authorized under the Civil Practice Law [735 ILCS 5/2-101 et seq.] or Rules of the Illinois Supreme Court for the service of summons or subpoenas, a notice of hearing to determine why registration should not be denied, refused renewal, suspended or revoked. The notice shall contain a statement of the basis therefor and shall call upon the applicant or registrant to appear before the Department of Professional Regulation at a reasonable time and place. These proceedings shall be conducted in accordance with the provisions of the "Civil Administrative Code of Illinois," Sections 60, 60a, 60b, 60c, 60d, 60e, 60f, 60g, and 60h [20 ILCS 2105/60 to 2105/60h], as those sections now exist or shall be amended from time to time, without regard to any criminal prosecution or other proceeding. Except as authorized in subsection (b), proceedings to refuse renewal or suspend or revoke registration shall not abate the existing registration which shall remain in effect until the Department of Professional Regulation has held the hearing called for in the notice and found that the registration shall no longer remain in effect.

(b) If the Department of Professional Regulation finds that there is an imminent danger to the public health or safety by the continued manufacture, distribution or dispensing of controlled substances by the registrant, the Department of Professional Regulation may, upon the issuance of a written ruling stating the reasons for such finding and without notice or hearing, suspend such registrant. The suspension shall continue in effect for not more than 14 days during which time the registrant shall be given an opportunity to be heard. If after the hearing the Department of Professional Regulation finds that the public health or safety requires the suspension to remain in effect it shall so remain until the ruling is terminated by its own terms or subsequent ruling or is dissolved by a circuit court upon determination that the suspension was wholly without basis in fact and law.

(c) If, after a hearing as provided in subsection (a), the Department of Professional Regulation finds that a registration should be refused renewal, suspended or revoked, a written ruling to that effect shall be entered. The Department of Professional Regulation's ruling shall remain in effect until the ruling is terminated by its own terms or subsequent ruling or is dissolved by a circuit court upon a determination that the refusal to renew suspension or revocation was wholly without basis in fact and law.

(Source: P.A. 85-1209.) [Formerly Ill. Rev. Stat. 56½ §1305.]

570/306. Records and inventories.

§306. (a) Every practitioner and person who is required under this Act to be registered to manufacture, distribute or dispense controlled substances under this Act shall keep records and maintain inventories in conformance with the recordkeeping and inventory requirements of the laws of the United States and with any additional rules and forms issued by the Department of Professional Regulation.

(b) Every practitioner and person who is required under this Act to be registered to manufacture or distribute, or both, controlled substances shall report to the Department, on a quarterly basis the same information contained in the federal Drug Enforcement Agency ARCOS report in a similar format and media acceptable to the federal Drug Enforcement Agency.

(Source: P.A. 85-1209; 86-1342.) [Formerly Ill. Rev. Stat. 56½ §1306.]

570/307. Distribution.

§307. Controlled substances in Schedules I and II shall be distributed by a registrant to another registrant only pursuant to a written order. Compliance with the laws of the United States respecting order forms shall be deemed compliance with this Section.

(Source: P.A. 77-757.) [Formerly Ill. Rev. Stat. 56½ §1307.]

570/308. Prescriptions.

§308. Every practitioner who issues a prescription for a controlled substance in Schedule II, which is a narcotic drug listed in Section 206 of this Act [720 ILCS 570/206]; or which contains any quantity of amphetamine or methamphetamine, their salts, optical isomers or salts of optical isomers; phenmetrazine and its salts; gluthethimide; pentazocine; or which is hereafter determined to be a "designated product," as defined in Section 102 of this Act [720 ILCS 570/102], shall issue such prescription on official prescription blanks which shall be issued by the Department except as otherwise provided in this Act. The prescription blanks issued by the Department shall be in serial numbered groups of 100 blanks, each in triplicate, and shall be furnished upon payment of a reasonable non-refundable application fee to such practitioner and such prescription blanks shall not be transferable. The prescription blanks shall be printed on distinctive paper, serial number of the group being shown on each blank and also each blank being serially numbered. No more than one such prescription group shall in any case be issued or furnished by the Department to the same prescriber at one time.

(Source: P.A. 87-754.) [Formerly Ill. Rev. Stat. 56½ §1308.]

570/309. Issuance of prescriptions.

§309. No person shall issue a prescription for a Schedule II controlled substance, which is a narcotic drug listed in Section 206 of this Act [720 ILCS 570/206]; or which contains any quantity of amphetamine or methamphetamine, their salts, optical isomers or salts of optical isomers; phenmetrazine and its salts; gluthethimide; pentazocine; or which is hereafter

determined to be a "designated product," as defined in Section 102 of this Act [720 ILCS 570/102], other than on the official prescription blank issued by the Department and no person shall fill any such prescription other than on the official prescription blank issued by the Department; provided that in the case of an emergency, epidemic or a sudden or unforeseen accident or calamity, the prescriber may issue a lawful oral prescription or a written prescription on a blank other than the official prescription blank issued by the Department where failure to issue such a prescription might result in loss of life or intense suffering, but such prescription shall have endorsed thereon by the prescriber a statement concerning the accident or calamity, or circumstances constituting the emergency, the cause for which the unofficial blank was used. Within 72 hours after issuing an emergency prescription, the prescribing individual practitioner shall cause a written prescription on the official prescription blank for the emergency quantity prescribed to be delivered to the dispensing pharmacist. The prescription shall have written on its face "Authorization for Emergency Dispensing", and the date of the emergency prescription. The written prescription on the official prescription blank may be delivered to the pharmacist in person or by mail, but if delivered by mail it must be postmarked within the 72-hour period. Upon receipt, the dispensing pharmacist shall attach this prescription to the emergency prescription earlier received, or in the case of an oral prescription, reduced to writing. The dispensing pharmacist shall notify the Department of Alcoholism and Substance Abuse if the prescribing individual practitioner fails to deliver the authorization for emergency dispensing on the official prescription blank to him. Failure of the dispensing pharmacist to do so shall void the authority conferred by this paragraph to dispense without a written prescription on an official prescription blank of a prescribing individual practitioner. All prescriptions on the official blanks shall be written in triplicate and all three copies signed by the prescriber. All prescriptions issued for Schedule II controlled substances shall include both a written and numerical notation of quantity on the face of the prescription. No prescription for a Schedule II controlled substance may be refilled.
(Source: P.A. 84-874.) [Formerly Ill. Rev. Stat. 56½ §1309.]

570/310. Prescription copies.

§310. The official prescription blanks containing the prescriber's copies of official prescriptions issued shall be retained by the prescriber and shall be preserved for 2 years and shall at all times be open to inspection by any officer or employee engaged in the enforcement of this Act. If any official prescription blanks are lost or stolen, such loss shall be reported to the local authorities, the Department, and the Department of State Police as soon as such loss is discovered.
(Source: P.A. 84-1308.) [Formerly Ill. Rev. Stat. 56½ §1310.]

570/311. Prescriptions; original and duplicate.

§311. For all controlled substances covered by Sections 308 and 309 of this Act [720 ILCS 570/308 and 570/309], the original and one copy of the official prescription blank shall be delivered to the person filling the prescription. The duplicate shall be properly endorsed by the person filling the prescription at the time such prescription is filled, with his own signature and the date of filling. The original official prescription blank shall be retained by the person filling the prescription and by the 15th of the month following the month in which the prescription was filled, the duplicate shall be returned to the Department at its principal office. These duplicates, any reproductions of these in any form, any computations of the duplicates, any statistics derived from the duplicates or compilations, and any studies incorporating material from these sources shall

be available for inspection and reproduction by any person whom the Director of the Department of State Police has authorized to do so.
(Source: P.A. 84-25.) [Formerly Ill. Rev. Stat. 56½ §1311.]

570/312. Controlled substances; dispensing.

§312. (a) A practitioner, in good faith, may dispense a Schedule II controlled substance, which is a narcotic drug listed in Section 206 of this Act [720 ILCS 570/206]; or which contains any quantity of amphetamine or methamphetamine, their salts, optical isomers or salts of optical isomers; phenmetrazine and its salts; pentazocine; or which is hereafter determined to be a "designated product," as defined in Section 102 of this Act [720 ILCS 570/102] to any person upon an official prescription form and Schedule III, IV, or V controlled substances to any person upon a written prescription of any practitioner, dated and signed by the person prescribing on the day when issued and bearing the name and address of the patient for whom, or the owner of the animal for which the controlled substance is dispensed, and the full name, address and registry number under the laws of the United States relating to controlled substances of the person prescribing, if he is required by those laws to be registered. If the prescription is for an animal it shall state the species of animal for which it is ordered. The practitioner filling the prescription shall write the date of filling and his own signature on the face of the official prescription form. The official prescription form or the written prescription shall be retained on file by the practitioner who filled it or pharmacy in which the prescription was filled for a period of 2 years, so as to be readily accessible for inspection or removal by any officer or employee engaged in the enforcement of this Act. Whenever the practitioner's or pharmacy's copy of any prescription form is removed by an officer or employee engaged in the enforcement of this Act, for the purpose of investigation or as evidence, such officer or employee shall give to the practitioner or pharmacy a receipt in lieu thereof. A prescription form for a Schedule II controlled substance shall not be filled more than 2 days after the date of issuance. A written prescription for Schedule III, IV or V controlled substances shall not be filled or refilled more than 6 months after the date thereof or refilled more than 5 times unless renewed, in writing, by the practitioner.

(b) In lieu of a written prescription required by this Section, a pharmacist, in good faith, may dispense Schedule III, IV, or V substances to any person upon a lawful oral prescription of a practitioner which oral prescription shall be reduced promptly to writing by the pharmacist and such written memorandum thereof shall be dated on the day when such oral prescription is received by the pharmacist and shall bear the full name and address of the ultimate user for whom, or of the owner of the animal for which the controlled substance is dispensed, and the full name, address, and registry number under the law of the United States relating to controlled substances of the practitioner prescribing if he is required by those laws to be so registered, and the pharmacist filling such oral prescription shall write the date of filling and his own signature on the face of such written memorandum thereof. The written memorandum of the oral prescription shall be retained on file by the proprietor of the pharmacy in which it is filled for a period of not less than two years, so as to be readily accessible for inspection by any officer or employee engaged in the enforcement of this Act in the same manner as a written prescription. The oral prescription and the written memorandum thereof shall not be filled or refilled more than 6 months after the date thereof or be refilled more than 5 times, unless renewed, in writing, by the practitioner.

(c) A controlled substance included in Schedule V shall not be distributed or dispensed other than for a medical purpose and not for the purpose of evading this Act, and then:

(1) only personally by a person registered to dispense a Schedule V controlled substance and then only to his patients, or

(2) only personally by a pharmacist, and then only to a person over 21 years of age who has identified himself to the pharmacist by means of 2 positive documents of identification.

(3) the dispenser shall record the name and address of the purchaser, the name and quantity of the product, the date and time of the sale, and the dispenser's signature.

(4) no person shall purchase or be dispensed more than 120 milliliters or more than 120 grams of any Schedule V substance which contains codeine, dihydrocodeine, or any salts thereof, or ethylmorphine, or any salts thereof, in any 96 hour period. The purchaser shall sign a form, approved by the Department of Professional Regulation, attesting that he has not purchased any Schedule V controlled substances within the immediately preceding 96 hours.

(5) a copy of the records of sale, including all information required by paragraph (3), shall be forwarded to the Department of Professional Regulation at its principal office by the 15th day of the following month.

(6) all records of purchases and sales shall be maintained for not less than 2 years.

(7) no person shall obtain or attempt to obtain within any consecutive 96 hour period any Schedule V substances of more than 120 milliliters or more than 120 grams containing codeine, dihydrocodeine or any of its salts, or ethylmorphine or any of its salts. Any person obtaining any such preparations or combination of preparations in excess of this limitation shall be in unlawful possession of such controlled substance.

(8) a person qualified to dispense controlled substances under this Act and registered thereunder shall at no time maintain or keep in stock a quantity of Schedule V controlled substances defined and listed in Section 212 (b) (1), (2) or (3) [720 ILCS 570/212] in excess of 4.5 liters for each substance; a pharmacy shall at no time maintain or keep in stock a quantity of Schedule V controlled substances as defined in excess of 4.5 liters for each substance, plus the additional quantity of controlled substances necessary to fill the largest number of prescription orders filled by that pharmacy for such controlled substances in any one week in the previous year. These limitations shall not apply to Schedule V controlled substances which Federal law prohibits from being dispensed without a prescription.

(9) no person shall distribute or dispense butyl nitrite for inhalation or other introduction into the human body for euphoric or physical effect.

(d) Every practitioner shall keep a record of controlled substances received by him and a record of all such controlled substances administered, dispensed or professionally used by him otherwise than by prescription. It shall, however, be sufficient compliance with this paragraph if any practitioner utilizing controlled substances listed in Schedules III, IV and V shall keep a record of all those substances dispensed and distributed by him other than those controlled substances which are administered by the direct application of a controlled substance, whether by injection, inhalation, ingestion, or any other means to the body of a patient or research subject. A practitioner who dispenses, other than by administering, a controlled substance in Schedule II, which is a narcotic drug listed in Section 206 of this Act, or which contains any quantity of amphetamine or methamphetamine, their salts, optical isomers or salts of optical isomers, pentazocine, methaqualone, or which is hereafter determined to be a "designated product" as defined in Section 102 of this Act, shall do so only upon the issuance of an official prescription blank; and every practitioner who so dispenses such designated products shall comply with the provisions of Sections 310 and 311 of this Act [720 ILCS 570/310 and 570/311].

(e) Whenever a manufacturer distributes a controlled substance in a package prepared by him, and whenever a wholesale distributor distributes a controlled substance in a package prepared by him or the manufacturer, he shall securely affix to each package in which that substance is contained a label showing in legible English the name and address of the manufacturer, the distributor and the quantity, kind and form of controlled substance contained therein. No person except a pharmacist and only for the purposes of filling a prescription under this Act, shall alter, deface or remove any label so affixed.

(f) Whenever a practitioner dispenses any controlled substance, he shall affix to the container in which such substance is sold or dispensed, a label indicating the date of initial filling, the practitioner's name and address, the serial number of the prescription, the name of the patient, the name of the prescribing practitioner, the directions for use and cautionary statements, if any, contained in any prescription or required by law, the proprietary name or names or the established name of the controlled substance, and the dosage and quantity, except as otherwise authorized by regulation by the Department of Professional Regulation. No person shall alter, deface or remove any label so affixed.

(g) A person to whom or for whose use any controlled substance has been prescribed or dispensed by a practitioner, or other persons authorized under this Act, and the owner of any animal for which such substance has been prescribed or dispensed by a veterinarian, may lawfully possess such substance only in the container in which it was delivered to him by the person dispensing such substance.

(h) The responsibility for the proper prescribing or dispensing of controlled substances is upon the prescriber and the responsibility for the proper filling of a prescription for controlled substance drugs rests with the pharmacist. An order purporting to be a prescription issued to any individual, which is not in the regular course of professional treatment nor part of an authorized methadone maintenance program, nor in legitimate and authorized research instituted by any accredited hospital, educational institution, charitable foundation, or federal, state or local governmental agency, and which is intended to provide that individual with controlled substances sufficient to maintain that individual's or any other individual's physical or psychological addiction, habitual or customary use, dependence, or diversion of that controlled substance is not a prescription within the meaning and intent of this Act; and the person issuing it, shall be subject to the penalties provided for violations of the law relating to controlled substances.

(i) A practitioner shall not preprint or cause to be preprinted a prescription for any controlled substance; nor shall any practitioner issue, fill or cause to be issued or filled, a preprinted prescription for any controlled substance.

(j) No person shall manufacture, dispense, deliver, possess with intent to deliver, prescribe, or administer or cause to be administered under his direction any anabolic steroid, for any use in humans other than the treatment of disease in accordance with the order of a physician for a valid medical purpose in the course of professional practice. The use of anabolic steroids for the purpose of hormonal manipulation that is intended to increase muscle mass, strength or weight without a medical necessity to do so, or for the intended purpose of improving physical appearance or performance in any form of exercise, sport, or game, is not a valid medical purpose or in the course of professional practice.
(Source: P.A. 86-625; 87-754.) [Formerly Ill. Rev. Stat. 56½ §1312.]

570/313. Exemptions; hospitals and institutions.

§313. (a) Controlled substances which are lawfully administered in hospitals or institutions licensed under the "Hospital Licensing Act" [210 ILCS 85/1 et seq.] shall be exempt from the requirements of Sections 308 and 312 [720

ILCS 570/308 and 570/312] except that the prescription for the controlled substance shall be in writing on the patient's record, signed by the prescriber, dated, and shall state the name, and quantity of controlled substances ordered and the quantity actually administered. The records of such prescriptions shall be maintained for two years and shall be available for inspection by officers and employees of the Department of State Police, and the Department of Professional Regulation.

(b) Controlled substances which are lawfully administered and/or dispensed in drug abuse treatment programs licensed by the Department shall be exempt from the requirements of Sections 308 and 312, except that the prescription for such controlled substances shall be issued and authenticated on official prescription logs prepared and supplied by the Department. The official prescription logs issued by the Department shall be printed in triplicate on distinctively marked paper and furnished to programs at reasonable cost. The official prescription logs furnished to the programs shall contain, in preprinted form, such information as the Department may require. The official prescription logs shall be properly endorsed by the physician issuing the order, with his own signature and the date of ordering, and further endorsed by the practitioner actually administering or dispensing the dosage at the time of such administering or dispensing in accordance with requirements issued by the Department. The duplicate copy shall be retained by the program for a period of not less than three years nor more than seven years; the original and triplicate copy shall be returned to the Department at its principal office in accordance with requirements set forth by the Department.

(Source: P.A. 85-1209.) [Formerly Ill. Rev. Stat. 56½ §1313.]

570/314. Dispensing by mail or commercial carriers.

§314. Except when a practitioner shall dispense on behalf of a charitable organization as defined in Section 501 (c) of the Federal "Internal Revenue Act" [26 U.S.C. §501(c)], and then in conformance with other provisions of State and Federal laws relating to the dispensing of controlled substances, no practitioner shall dispense a controlled substance by use of the United States mails or other commercial carriers.

(Source: P.A. 77-757.) [Formerly Ill. Rev. Stat. 56½ §1314.]

570/315. Advertisement of controlled substances.

§315. No controlled substance shall be advertised to the public by name.

(Source: P.A. 77-757.) [Formerly Ill. Rev. Stat. 56½ §1315.]

ARTICLE IV. VIOLATIONS AND PENALTIES

Sec.

570/401. Unauthorized manufacture or delivery.

§401. Except as authorized by this Act, it is unlawful for any person knowingly to manufacture or deliver, or possess with intent to manufacture or deliver, a controlled or counterfeit substance or controlled substance analog. For purposes of this Section, "controlled substance analog" or "analog" means a substance which is intended for human consumption, other than a controlled substance, that has a chemical structure substantially similar to that of a controlled substance in Schedule I or II, or that was specifically designed to produce an effect substantially similar to that of a controlled substance in Schedule I or II. Examples of chemical classes in which controlled substance analogs are found include, but are not limited to, the following: phenethylamines, N-substituted piperidines, morphinans, ecgonines, quinazolinones, substituted indoles, and arylcycloalkylamines. For purposes of this Act, a controlled substance analog shall be treated in the same manner as the controlled substance to which it is substantially similar.

(a) Any person who violates this Section with respect to the following amounts of controlled or counterfeit substances or controlled substance analogs, notwithstanding any of the provisions of subsections (c), (d), (e), (f), (g) or (h) to the contrary, is guilty of a Class X felony and shall be sentenced to a term of imprisonment as provided in this subsection (a) and fined as provided in subsection (b):

(1) (A) not less than 6 years and not more than 30 years with respect to 15 grams or more but less than 100 grams of a substance containing heroin, or an analog thereof;

(B) not less than 9 years and not more than 40 years with respect to 100 grams or more but less than 400 grams of a substance containing heroin, or an analog thereof;

(C) not less than 12 years and not more than 50 years with respect to 400 grams or more but less than 900 grams of a substance containing heroin, or an analog thereof;

(D) not less than 15 years and not more than 60 years with respect to 900 grams or more of any substance containing heroin, or an analog thereof;

(2) (A) not less than 6 years and not more than 30 years with respect to 15 grams or more but less than 100 grams of a substance containing cocaine, or an analog thereof;

(B) not less than 9 years and not more than 40 years with respect to 100 grams or more but less than 400 grams of a substance containing cocaine, or an analog thereof;

(C) not less than 12 years and not more than 50 years with respect to 400 grams or more but less than 900 grams of a substance containing cocaine, or an analog thereof;

(D) not less than 15 years and not more than 60 years with respect to 900 grams or more of any substance containing cocaine, or an analog thereof;

(3) (A) not less than 6 years and not more than 30 years with respect to 15 grams or more but less than 100 grams of a substance containing morphine, or an analog thereof;

(B) not less than 9 years and not more than 40 years with respect to 100 grams or more but less than 400 grams of a substance containing morphine, or an analog thereof;

(C) not less than 12 years and not more than 50 years with respect to 400 grams or more but less than 900 grams of a substance containing morphine, or an analog thereof;

(D) not less than 15 years and not more than 60 years with respect to 900 grams or more of a substance containing morphine, or an analog thereof;

(4) 200 grams or more of any substance containing peyote, or an analog thereof;

(5) 200 grams or more of any substance containing a derivative of barbituric acid or any of the salts of a derivative of barbituric acid, or an analog thereof;

(6) 200 grams or more of any substance containing amphetamine or methamphetamine or any salt of an optical isomer of amphetamine or methamphetamine, or an analog thereof;

(7) (A) not less than 6 years and not more than 30 years with respect to: (i) 15 grams or more but less than 100 grams of a substance containing lysergic acid diethylamide (LSD), or an analog thereof, or (ii) 15 or more objects or 15 or more segregated parts of an object or objects but less than 200 objects or 200 segregated parts of an object or objects containing in them or having upon them any amounts of any substance containing lysergic acid diethylamide (LSD), or an analog thereof;

(B) not less than 9 years and not more than 40 years with respect to: (i) 100 grams or more but less than 400 grams of a substance containing lysergic acid diethylamide (LSD), or an analog thereof, or (ii) 200 or more objects or 200 or more segregated parts of an object or objects but less than 600 objects or less than 600 segregated parts of an object or objects containing in them or having upon them any amount of any substance containing lysergic acid diethylamide (LSD), or an analog thereof;

(C) not less than 12 years and not more than 50 years with respect to: (i) 400 grams or more but less than 900 grams of a substance containing lysergic acid diethylamide (LSD), or an analog thereof, or (ii) 600 or more objects or 600 or more segregated parts of an object or objects but less than 1500 objects or 1500 segregated parts of an object or objects containing in them or having upon them any amount of any substance containing lysergic acid diethylamide (LSD), or an analog thereof;

(D) not less than 15 years and not more than 60 years with respect to: (i) 900 grams or more of any substance containing lysergic acid diethylamide (LSD), or an analog thereof, or (ii) 1500 or more objects or 1500 or more segregated parts of an object or objects containing in them or having upon them any amount of a substance containing lysergic acid diethylamide (LSD), or an analog thereof;

(8) 30 grams or more of any substance containing pentazocine or any of the salts, isomers and salts of isomers of pentazocine, or an analog thereof;

(9) 30 grams or more of any substance containing methaqualone or any of the salts, isomers and salts of isomers of methaqualone, or an analog thereof;

(10) 30 grams or more of any substance containing phencyclidine or any of the salts, isomers and salts of isomers of phencyclidine (PCP), or an analog thereof;

(11) 200 grams or more of any substance containing any other controlled substance classified in Schedules I or II, or an analog thereof, which is not otherwise included in this subsection.

(b) Any person sentenced with respect to violations of paragraph (1), (2), (3) or (7) of subsection (a) involving 100 grams or more of the controlled substance named therein, may in addition to the penalties provided therein, be fined an amount not more than $500,000 or the full street value of the controlled or counterfeit substance or controlled substance analog, whichever is greater. The term "street value" shall have the meaning ascribed in Section 110-5 of the Code of Criminal Procedure of 1963 [725 ILCS 5/110-5]. Any person sentenced with respect to any other provision of subsection (a), may in addition to the penalties provided therein, be fined an amount not to exceed $500,000.

(c) Any person who violates this Section with regard to the following amounts of controlled or counterfeit substances or controlled substance analogs, notwithstanding any of the provisions of subsections (a), (b), (d), (e), (f), (g) or (h) to the contrary, is guilty of a Class 1 felony. The fine for violation of this subsection (c) shall not be more than $250,000:

(1) 10 or more grams but less than 15 grams of any substance containing heroin, or an analog thereof;

(2) 1 gram or more but less than 15 grams of any substance containing cocaine, or an analog thereof;

(3) 10 grams or more but less than 15 grams of any substance containing morphine, or an analog thereof;

(4) 50 grams or more but less than 200 grams of any substance containing peyote, or an analog thereof;

(5) 50 grams or more but less than 200 grams of any substance containing a derivative of barbituric acid or any of the salts of a derivative of barbituric acid, or an analog thereof;

(6) 50 grams or more but less than 200 grams of any substance containing amphetamine or methamphetamine or any salt of an optical isomer of amphetamine or methamphetamine, or an analog thereof;

(7) (i) 5 grams or more but less than 15 grams of any substance containing lysergic acid diethylamide (LSD), or an analog thereof, or (ii) more than 10 objects or more than 10 segregated parts of an object or objects but less than 15 objects or less than 15 segregated parts of an object containing in them or having upon them any amount of any substance containing lysergic acid diethylamide (LSD), or an analog thereof;

(8) 10 grams or more but less than 30 grams of any substance containing pentazocine or any of the salts, isomers and salts of isomers of pentazocine, or an analog thereof;

(9) 10 grams or more but less than 30 grams of any substance containing methaqualone or any of the salts, isomers and salts of isomers of methaqualone, or an analog thereof;

(10) 10 grams or more but less than 30 grams of any substance containing phencyclidine or any of the salts, isomers and salts of isomers of phencyclidine (PCP), or an analog thereof;

(11) 50 grams or more but less than 200 grams of any substance containing a substance classified in Schedules I or II, or an analog thereof, which is not otherwise included in this subsection.

(d) Any person who violates this Section with regard to any other amount of a controlled or counterfeit substance classified in Schedules I or II, or an analog thereof, which is (i) a narcotic drug, or (ii) lysergic acid diethylamide (LSD) or an analog thereof, is guilty of a Class 2 felony. The fine for violation of this subsection (d) shall not be more than $200,000.

(e) Any person who violates this Section with regard to any other amount of a controlled or counterfeit substance classified in Schedule I or II, or an analog thereof, which substance is not included under subsection (d) of this Section, is guilty of a Class 3 felony. The fine for violation of this subsection (e) shall not be more than $150,000.

(f) Any person who violates this Section with regard to any other amount of a controlled or counterfeit substance classified in Schedule III is guilty of a Class 3 felony. The fine for violation of this subsection (f) shall not be more than $125,000.

(g) Any person who violates this Section with regard to any other amount of a controlled or counterfeit substance classified in Schedule IV is guilty of a Class 3 felony. The fine for violation of this subsection (g) shall not be more than $100,000.

(h) Any person who violates this Section with regard to any other amount of a controlled or counterfeit substance classified in Schedule V is guilty of a Class 3 felony. The fine for violation of this subsection (h) shall not be more than $75,000.

(i) This Section does not apply to the manufacture, possession or distribution of a substance in conformance with the provisions of an approved new drug application or an exemption for investigational use within the meaning of Section 505 of the Federal Food, Drug and Cosmetic Act [21 U.S.C. §355].

(Source: P.A. 86-266; 86-442; 86-604; 87-754.) [Formerly Ill. Rev. Stat. 56½ §1401.]

570/401.1. Controlled substance trafficking.

§401.1. Controlled Substance Trafficking. (a) Except for purposes as authorized by this Act, any person who knowingly brings or causes to be brought into this State for the purpose of manufacture or delivery or with the intent to manufacture or deliver a controlled or counterfeit substance in this or any other state or country is guilty of controlled substance trafficking.

(b) A person convicted of controlled substance trafficking shall be sentenced to a term of imprisonment not less than twice the minimum term and fined an amount as authorized by Section 401 of this Act [720 ILCS 570/401], based upon the amount of controlled or counterfeit substance brought or caused to be brought into this State, and not more than twice the maximum term of imprisonment and fined twice the amount as authorized by Section 401 of this Act, based upon the amount of controlled or counterfeit substance brought or caused to be brought into this State.

(c) It shall be a Class 2 felony for which a fine not to exceed $100,000 may be imposed for any person to knowingly use a cellular radio telecommunication device in the furtherance of controlled substance trafficking. This penalty shall be in addition to any other penalties imposed by law.

(Source: P.A. 85-1294; 86-1391.) [Formerly Ill. Rev. Stat. 56½ §1401.1.]

570/402. Unauthorized possession.

§402. Except as otherwise authorized by this Act, it is unlawful for any person knowingly to possess a controlled or counterfeit substance.

(a) Any person who violates this Section with respect to the following controlled or counterfeit substances and amounts, notwithstanding any of the provisions of subsection (c) and (d) to the contrary, is guilty of a Class 1 felony and shall, if sentenced to a term of imprisonment, be sentenced as provided in this subsection (a) and fined as provided in subsection (b):

(1) (A) not less than 4 years and not more than 15 years with respect to 15 grams or more but less than 100 grams of a substance containing heroin;

(B) not less than 6 years and not more than 30 years with respect to 100 grams or more but less than 400 grams of a substance containing heroin;

(C) not less than 8 years and not more than 40 years with respect to 400 grams or more but less than 900 grams of any substance containing heroin;

(D) not less than 10 years and not more than 50 years with respect to 900 grams or more of any substance containing heroin;

(2) (A) not less than 4 years and not more than 15 years with respect to 15 grams or more but less than 100 grams of any substance containing cocaine;

(B) not less than 6 years and not more than 30 years with respect to 100 grams or more but less than 400 grams of any substance containing cocaine;

(C) not less than 8 years and not more than 40 years with respect to 400 grams or more but less than 900 grams of any substance containing cocaine;

(D) not less than 10 years and not more than 50 years with respect to 900 grams or more of any substance containing cocaine;

(3) (A) not less than 4 years and not more than 15 years with respect to 15 grams or more but less than 100 grams of any substance containing morphine;

(B) not less than 6 years and not more than 30 years with respect to 100 grams or more but less than 400 grams of any substance containing morphine;

(C) not less than 8 years and not more than 40 years with respect to 400 grams or more but less than 900 grams of any substance containing morphine;

(D) not less than 10 years and not more than 50 years with respect to 900 grams or more of any substance containing morphine;

(4) 200 grams or more of any substance containing peyote;

(5) 200 grams or more of any substance containing a derivative of barbituric acid or any of the salts of a derivative of barbituric acid;

(6) 200 grams or more of any substance containing amphetamine or methamphetamine or any salt of an optical isomer of amphetamine or methamphetamine;

(7) (A) not less than 4 years and not more than 15 years with respect to: (i) 15 grams or more but less than 100 grams of any substance containing lysergic acid diethylamide (LSD), or an analog thereof, or (ii) 15 or more objects or 15 or more segregated parts of an object or objects but less than 200 objects or 200 segregated parts of an object or objects containing in them or having upon them any amount of any substance containing lysergic acid diethylamide (LSD), or an analog thereof;

(B) not less than 6 years and not more than 30 years with respect to: (i) 100 grams or more but less than 400 grams of any substance containing lysergic acid diethylamide (LSD), or an analog thereof, or (ii) 200 or more objects or 200 or more segregated parts of an object or objects but less than 600 objects or less than 600 segregated parts of an object or objects containing in them or having upon them any amount of any substance containing lysergic acid diethylamide (LSD), or an analog thereof;

(C) not less than 8 years and not more than 40 years with respect to: (i) 400 grams or more but less than 900 grams of any substance containing lysergic acid diethylamide (LSD), or an analog thereof, or (ii) 600 or more objects or 600 or more segregated parts of an object or objects but less than 1500 objects or 1500 segregated parts of an object or objects containing in them or having upon them any amount of any substance containing lysergic acid diethylamide (LSD), or an analog thereof;

(D) not less than 10 years and not more than 50 years with respect to: (i) 900 grams or more of any substance containing lysergic acid diethylamide (LSD), or an analog thereof, or (ii) 1500 or more objects or 1500 or more segregated parts of an object or objects containing in them or having upon them any amount of a substance containing lysergic acid diethylamide (LSD), or an analog thereof;

(8) 30 grams or more of any substance containing pentazocine or any of the salts, isomers and salts of isomers of pentazocine, or an analog thereof;

(9) 30 grams or more of any substance containing methaqualone or any of the salts, isomers and salts of isomers of methaqualone;

(10) 30 grams or more of any substance containing phencyclidine or any of the salts, isomers and salts of isomers of phencyclidine (PCP);

(11) 200 grams or more of any substance containing any substance classified as a narcotic drug in Schedules I or II which is not otherwise included in this subsection.

(b) Any person sentenced with respect to violations of paragraph (1), (2), (3) or (7) of subsection (a) involving 100 grams or more of the controlled substance named therein, may in addition to the penalties provided therein, be fined an amount not to exceed $200,000 or the full street value of the controlled or counterfeit substances, whichever is greater. The term "street value" shall have the meaning ascribed in Section 110-5 of the Code of Criminal Procedure of 1963 [725 ILCS 5/110-5]. Any person sentenced with respect to any other provision of subsection (a), may in addition to the penalties provided therein, be fined an amount not to exceed $200,000.

(c) Any person who violates this Section with regard to an amount of a controlled or counterfeit substance not set forth in subsection (a) or (d) is guilty of a Class 4 felony. The fine for a violation punishable under this subsection (c) shall not be more than $15,000.

(d) Any person who violates this Section with regard to any amount of anabolic steroid is guilty of a Class C misdemeanor for the first offense and a Class B misdemeanor for a subsequent offense committed within 2 years of a prior conviction.

(Source: P.A. 86-266; 86-442; 86-604; 87-754.) [Formerly Ill. Rev. Stat. 56½ §1402.]

570/404. Look-alike substance.

§404. (a) For the purposes of this Section:

(1) "Advertise" means the attempt, by publication, dissemination, solicitation or circulation, to induce directly or indirectly any person to acquire, or enter into an obligation to acquire, any substance within the scope of this Section.

(2) "Distribute" has the meaning ascribed to it in subsection (s) of Section 102 of this Act [720 ILCS 570/102] but as relates to look-alike substances.

(3) "Manufacture" means the producing, preparing, compounding, processing, encapsulating, packaging, repackaging, labeling or relabeling of a look-alike substance.

(b) It is unlawful for any person knowingly to manufacture, distribute, advertise, or possess with intent to manufacture or distribute a look-alike substance. Any person who violates this subsection (b) shall be guilty of a Class 3 felony, the fine for which shall not exceed $150,000.

(c) It is unlawful for any person knowingly to possess a look-alike substance. Any person who violates this subsection (c) is guilty of a petty offense. Any person convicted of a subsequent offense under this subsection (c) shall be guilty of a Class C misdemeanor.

(d) In any prosecution brought under this Section, it is not a defense to a violation of this Section that the defendant believed the look-alike substance actually to be a controlled substance.

(e) Nothing in this Section applies to:

(1) The manufacture, processing, packaging, distribution or sale of noncontrolled substances to licensed medical practitioners for use as placebos in professional practice or research.

(2) Persons acting in the course and legitimate scope of their employment as law enforcement officers.

(3) The retention of production samples of noncontrolled substances produced prior to the effective date of this amendatory Act of 1982, where such samples are required by federal law.

(f) Nothing in this Section or in this Act applies to the lawful manufacture, processing, packaging, advertising or distribution of a drug or drugs by any person registered pursuant to Section 510 of the Federal Food, Drug, and Cosmetic Act (21 U.S.C. 360).

(Source: P.A. 83-1362.) [Formerly Ill. Rev. Stat. 56½ §1404.]

570/405. Calculated criminal drug conspiracy.

§405. (a) Any person who engages in a calculated criminal drug conspiracy, as defined in subsection (b), is guilty of a Class X felony. The fine for violation of this Section shall not be more than $500,000, and the offender shall be subject to the forfeitures prescribed in subsection (c).

(b) For purposes of this section, a person engages in a calculated criminal drug conspiracy when:

(1) he violates any of the provisions of subsections (a) or (c) of Section 401 [720 ILCS 570/401] or subsection (a) of Section 402 [720 ILCS 570/402]; and

(2) such violation is a part of a conspiracy undertaken or carried on with two or more other persons; and

(3) he obtains anything of value greater than $500 from, or organizes, directs or finances such violation or conspiracy.

(c) Any person who is convicted under this section of engaging in a calculated criminal drug conspiracy shall forfeit to the State of Illinois:

(1) the receipts obtained by him in such conspiracy; and

(2) any of his interests in, claims against, receipts from, or property or rights of any kind affording a source of influence over, such conspiracy.

(d) The circuit court may enter such injunctions, restraining orders, directions or prohibitions, or to take such other actions, including the acceptance of satisfactory performance bonds, in connection with any property, claim, receipt, right or other interest subject to forfeiture under this Section, as it deems proper.

(Source: P.A. 87-754.) [Formerly Ill. Rev. Stat. 56½ §1405.]

570/405.1. Elements of offense of criminal drug conspiracy; co-conspirators; sentencing.

§405.1. (a) Elements of the offense. A person commits criminal drug conspiracy when, with the intent that an offense set forth in Section 401, Section 402, or Section 407 of this Act [720 ILCS 570/401, 570/402, or 570407] be committed, he agrees with another to the commission of that offense. No person may be convicted of conspiracy to commit such an offense unless an act in furtherance of such agreement is alleged and proved to have been committed by him or by a co-conspirator.

(b) Co-conspirators. It shall not be a defense to conspiracy that the person or persons with whom the accused is alleged to have conspired:

(1) Has not been prosecuted or convicted, or

(2) Has been convicted of a different offense, or

(3) Is not amenable to justice, or

(4) Has been acquitted, or

(5) Lacked the capacity to commit an offense.

(c) Sentence. A person convicted of criminal drug conspiracy may be fined or imprisoned or both not to exceed the maximum provided for the offense which is the object of the conspiracy.

(Source: P.A. 86-809.) [Formerly Ill. Rev. Stat. 56½ §1405.1.]

570/406. Violations; penalties.

§406. (a) It is unlawful for any person:

(1) who is subject to Article III [720 ILCS 570/301 et seq.] knowingly to distribute or dispense a controlled substance in violation of Sections 308 through 314 of this Act [720 ILCS 570/308 through 570/314]; or

(2) who is a registrant, to manufacture a controlled substance not authorized by his registration, or to distribute or dispense a controlled substance not authorized by his registration to another registrant or other authorized person; or

(3) to refuse or fail to make, keep or furnish any record, notification, order form, statement, invoice or information required under this Act; or

(4) to refuse an entry into any premises for any inspection authorized by this Act; or

(5) knowingly to keep or maintain any store, shop, warehouse, dwelling, building, vehicle, boat, aircraft, or other structure or place, which is resorted to by a person unlawfully possessing controlled substances, or which is used for

possessing, manufacturing, dispensing or distributing controlled substances in violation of this Act.

Any person who violates this subsection (a) is guilty of a Class A misdemeanor for the first offense and a Class 4 felony for each subsequent offense. The fine for each subsequent offense shall not be more than $100,000. In addition, any practitioner who is found guilty of violating this subsection (a) is subject to suspension and revocation of his professional license, in accordance with such procedures as are provided by law for the taking of disciplinary action with regard to the license of said practitioner's profession.

(b) It is unlawful for any person knowingly:

(1) to distribute, as a registrant, a controlled substance classified in Schedule I or II, except pursuant to an order form as required by Section 307 of this Act [720 ILCS 570/307]; or

(2) to use, in the course of the manufacture or distribution of a controlled substance, a registration number which is fictitious, revoked, suspended, or issued to another person; or

(3) to acquire or obtain possession of a controlled substance by misrepresentation, fraud, forgery, deception or subterfuge; or

(4) to furnish false or fraudulent material information in, or omit any material information from, any application, report or other document required to be kept or filed under this Act, or any record required to be kept by this Act; or

(5) to make, distribute or possess any punch, die, plate, stone or other thing designed to print, imprint or reproduce the trademark, trade name or other identifying mark, imprint or device of another, or any likeness of any of the foregoing, upon any controlled substance or container or labeling thereof so as to render the drug a counterfeit substance; or

(6) to possess without authorization, official blank prescription forms or counterfeit prescription forms; or

(7) to issue a prescription or fill any prescription for a controlled substance other than on the appropriate lawful prescription form. However, in the case of any epidemic or a sudden or unforeseen accident or calamity, the prescriber may issue a prescription on a form other than the official prescription form issued by the Department, where failure to issue such a prescription might result in loss of life or intense suffering, but such prescription shall have endorsed thereon, by the prescriber, a statement concerning the accident, calamity or circumstance constituting the emergency, the cause of which the unofficial blank was used.

Any person who violates this subsection (b) is guilty of a Class 4 felony for the first offense and a Class 3 felony for each subsequent offense. The fine for the first offense shall be not more than $100,000. The fine for each subsequent offense shall not be more than $200,000.

(Source: P.A. 85-1287.) [Formerly Ill. Rev. Stat. 56½ §1406.]

570/406.1. Unlawful use of a building.

§406.1. (a) Any person who controls any building and who performs the following act commits the offense of permitting unlawful use of a building:

Knowingly grants, permits or makes the building available for use for the purpose of unlawfully manufacturing or delivering a controlled substance.

(b) Permitting unlawful use of a building is a Class 4 felony.

(Source: P.A. 85-537.) [Formerly Ill. Rev. Stat. 56½ §1406.1.]

570/407. Increased penalties; delivery to person under 18 years of age; unauthorized manufacture or delivery in certain places.

§407. (a) (1) Any person 18 years of age or over who violates any subsection of Section 401 [720 ILCS 570/401] or Subsection (b) of Section 404 [720 ILCS 570/404] by delivering a controlled, counterfeit or look-alike substance to a person under 18 years of age may be sentenced to imprisonment for a term up to twice the maximum term and fined an amount up to twice that amount otherwise authorized by the pertinent subsection of Section 401 and Subsection (b) of Section 404.

(2) Except as provided in paragraph (3) of this subsection, any person who violates:

(A) subsection (c) of Section 401 by delivering or possessing with intent to deliver a controlled, counterfeit, or look-alike substance in or on, or within 1,000 feet of, a truck stop or safety rest area, is guilty of a Class 1 felony, the fine for which shall not exceed $250,000;

(B) subsection (d) of Section 401 by delivering or possessing with intent to deliver a controlled, counterfeit, or look-alike substance in or on, or within 1,000 feet of, a truck stop or safety rest area, is guilty of a Class 2 felony, the fine for which shall not exceed $200,000;

(C) subsection (e) of Section 401 or subsection (b) of Section 404 by delivering or possessing with intent to deliver a controlled, counterfeit, or look-alike substance in or on, or within 1,000 feet of, a truck stop or safety rest area, is guilty of a Class 3 felony, the fine for which shall not exceed $150,000;

(D) subsection (f) of Section 401 by delivering or possessing with intent to deliver a controlled, counterfeit, or look-alike substance in or on, or within 1,000 feet of, a truck stop or safety rest area, is guilty of a Class 3 felony, the fine for which shall not exceed $125,000;

(E) subsection (g) of Section 401 by delivering or possessing with intent to deliver a controlled, counterfeit, or look-alike substance in or on, or within 1,000 feet of, a truck stop or safety rest area, is guilty of a Class 3 felony, the fine for which shall not exceed $100,000;

(F) subsection (h) of Section 401 by delivering or possessing with intent to deliver a controlled, counterfeit, or look-alike substance in or on, or within 1,000 feet of, a truck stop or safety rest area, is guilty of a Class 3 felony, the fine for which shall not exceed $75,000;

(3) Any person who violates paragraph (2) of this subsection (a) by delivering or possessing with intent to deliver a controlled, counterfeit, or look-alike substance in or on, or within 1,000 feet of a truck stop or a safety rest area, following a prior conviction or convictions of paragraph (2) of this subsection (a) may be sentenced to a term of imprisonment up to 2 times the maximum term and fined an amount up to 2 times the amount otherwise authorized by Section 401.

(4) For the purposes of this subsection (a):

(A) "Safety rest area" means a roadside facility removed from the roadway with parking and facilities designed for motorists' rest, comfort, and information needs; and

(B) "Truck stop" means any facility (and its parking areas) used to provide fuel or service, or both, to any commercial motor vehicle as defined in Section 18b-101 of the Illinois Vehicle Code.

(b) Any person who violates:

(1) subsection (c) of Section 401 in any school, or any conveyance owned, leased or contracted by a school to transport students to or from school or a school related activity, or residential property owned, operated and managed by a public housing agency or public park, on the real property comprising any school or residential property owned, operated and managed by a public housing

agency or public park or on any public way within 1,000 feet of the real property comprising any school or residential property owned, operated and managed by a public housing agency or public park is guilty of a Class X felony, the fine for which shall not exceed $500,000;

(2) subsection (d) of Section 401 in any school, or any conveyance owned, leased or contracted by a school to transport students to or from school or a school related activity, or residential property owned, operated and managed by a public housing agency or public park, on the real property comprising any school or residential property owned, operated and managed by a public housing agency or public park or on any public way within 1,000 feet of the real property comprising any school or residential property owned, operated and managed by a public housing agency or public park is guilty of a Class 1 felony, the fine for which shall not exceed $250,000;

(3) subsection (e) of Section 401 or Subsection (b) of Section 404 in any school, or any conveyance owned, leased or contracted by a school to transport students to or from school or a school related activity, or residential property owned, operated and managed by a public housing agency or public park, on the real property comprising any school or residential property owned, operated and managed by a public housing agency or public park or on any public way within 1,000 feet of the real property comprising any school or residential property owned, operated and managed by a public housing agency or public park is guilty of a Class 2 felony, the fine for which shall not exceed $200,000;

(4) subsection (f) of Section 401 in any school, or any conveyance owned, leased or contracted by a school to transport students to or from school or a school related activity, or residential property owned, operated and managed by a public housing agency or public park, on the real property comprising any school or residential property owned, operated and managed by a public housing agency or public park or on any public way within 1,000 feet of the real property comprising any school or residential property owned, operated and managed by a public housing agency or public park is guilty of a Class 2 felony, the fine for which shall not exceed $150,000;

(5) subsection (g) of Section 401 in any school, or any conveyance owned, leased or contracted by a school to transport students to or from school or a school related activity, or residential property owned, operated and managed by a public housing agency or public park, on the real property comprising any school or residential property owned, operated and managed by a public housing agency or public park or on any public way within 1,000 feet of the real property comprising any school or residential property owned, operated and managed by a public housing agency or public park is guilty of a Class 2 felony, the fine for which shall not exceed $125,000;

(6) subsection (h) of Section 401 in any school, or any conveyance owned, leased or contracted by a school to transport students to or from school or a school related activity, or residential property owned, operated and managed by a public housing agency or public park, on the real property comprising any school or residential property owned, operated and managed by a public housing agency or public park or on any public way within 1,000 feet of the real property comprising any school or residential property owned, operated and managed by a public housing agency or public park is guilty of a Class 2 felony, the fine for which shall not exceed $100,000.

(c) Regarding penalties prescribed in subsection (b) for violations committed in a school or on or within 1,000 feet of school property, the time of day, time of year and whether classes were currently in session at the time of the offense is irrelevant.

(Chgd. by P.A. 87-1225, §1, eff. 12/22/92.)

(Source: P.A. 86-946; 87-524; 87-754; 87-895.) [Formerly Ill. Rev. Stat. 56½ §1407.]

570/407.1. Employing a person under 18 years of age to deliver; penalty.

§407.1. Any person 18 years of age or over who violates any subsection of Section 401, Section 404 or Section 405 [720 ILCS 570/401, 570/404 or 570/405] by using, engaging or employing a person under 18 years of age to deliver a controlled, counterfeit or look-alike substance may be sentenced to imprisonment for a term up to twice the maximum amount authorized by the pertinent subsection of Section 401, Section 404 or Section 405.
(Source: P.A. 84-1475.) [Formerly Ill. Rev. Stat. 56½ §1407.1.]

570/407.2. Delivery of a controlled substance to a pregnant woman.

§407.2. Delivery of a controlled substance to a pregnant woman. (a) Any person who violates subsection (a) of Section 401 of this Act [720 ILCS 570/401] by delivering a controlled substance to a woman he knows to be pregnant may be sentenced to imprisonment for a term twice the maximum amount authorized by Section 401 of this Act.

(b) Any person who delivers an amount of a controlled substance set forth in subsections (c) and (d) of Section 401 of this Act to a woman he knows to be pregnant commits a Class 1 felony. The fine for a violation of this subsection (b) shall not be more than $250,000.
(Source: P.A. 86-1459; 87-754.) [Formerly Ill. Rev. Stat. 56½ §1407.2.]

570/408. Second or subsequent offense.

§408. (a) Any person convicted of a second or subsequent offense under this Act may be sentenced to imprisonment for a term up to twice the maximum term otherwise authorized, fined an amount up to twice that otherwise authorized, or both.

(b) For purposes of this Section, an offense is considered a second or subsequent offense, if, prior to his conviction of the offense, the offender has at any time been convicted under this Act or under any law of the United States or of any State relating to controlled substances.
(Source: P.A. 78-255.) [Formerly Ill. Rev. Stat. 56½ §1408.]

570/409. Bar to prosecution.

§409. Except for convictions or acquittals which are the basis for a charge of narcotics racketeering under Section 4 of the Narcotics Profit Forfeiture Act [725 ILCS 175/4], a conviction or acquittal, under the laws of the United States or of any State relating to controlled substances, for the same act is a bar to prosecution in this State.
(Source: P.A. 87-466.) [Formerly Ill. Rev. Stat. 56½ §1409.]

570/410. First offender.

§410. (a) Whenever any person who has not previously been convicted of, or placed on probation or court supervision for any offense under this Act or any law of the United States or of any State relating to cannabis or controlled substances, pleads guilty to or is found guilty of possession of a controlled or counterfeit substance under subsection (c) of Section 402 [720 ILCS 570/402], the court, without entering a judgment and with the consent of such person, may sentence him to probation.

(b) When a person is placed on probation, the court shall enter an order specifying the period of probation, in accordance with subsection (b) of Section 5-6-2 of the Unified Code of Corrections [730 ILCS 5/5-6-2] and shall defer further proceedings in the case until the conclusion of the period or until the filing of a petition alleging violation of a term or condition of probation.

(c) The conditions of probation shall be that the person: (1) not violate any criminal statute of any jurisdiction; and (2) refrain from possessing a firearm or other dangerous weapon.

(d) The court may, in addition to other conditions, require that the person:

(1) make a report to and appear in person before or participate with the court or such courts, person, or social service agency as directed by the court in the order of probation;

(2) pay a fine and costs;

(3) work or pursue a course of study or vocational training;

(4) undergo medical or psychiatric treatment; or treatment or rehabilitation approved by the Illinois Department of Alcoholism and Substance Abuse;

(5) attend or reside in a facility established for the instruction or residence of defendants on probation;

(6) support his dependents;

(7) and in addition, if a minor:

(i) reside with his parents or in a foster home;

(ii) attend school;

(iii) attend a non-residential program for youth;

(iv) contribute to his own support at home or in a foster home.

(e) Upon violation of a term or condition of probation, the court may enter a judgment on its original finding of guilt and proceed as otherwise provided.

(f) Upon fulfillment of the terms and conditions of probation, the court shall discharge the person and dismiss the proceedings against him.

(g) A disposition of probation is considered to be a conviction for the purposes of imposing the conditions of probation and for appeal, however, discharge and dismissal under this Section is not a conviction for purposes of this Act or for purposes of disqualifications or disabilities imposed by law upon conviction of a crime.

(h) There may be only one discharge and dismissal under this Section or Section 10 of the Cannabis Control Act [720 ILCS 550/10] with respect to any person.

(Source: P.A. 86-265; 87-754.) [Formerly Ill. Rev. Stat. 56½ §1410.]

570/411. Sentencing.

§411. In determining the appropriate sentence for any conviction under this Act, the sentencing court may consider the following as indicative of the type of offenses which the legislature deems most damaging to the peace and welfare of the citizens of Illinois and which warrants the most severe penalties:

(1) the unlawful delivery of the most highly toxic controlled substances, as reflected by their inclusion in Schedule I or II of this Act;

(2) offenses involving unusually large quantities of controlled substances, as measured by their wholesale value at the time of the offense;

(3) the unlawful delivery of controlled substances by a non-user to a user of controlled substances;

(4) non-possessory offenses by persons who have no other visible means of support;

(5) offenses involving the large-scale manufacture of controlled substances;

(6) offenses which indicate any immediate involvement whatsoever with organized crime in terms of the controlled substance's manufacture, importation, or volume distribution;

(7) the manufacture for, or the delivery of controlled substances to persons 3 years or more junior to the person(s) convicted under this Act;

(8) the unlawful delivery of anabolic steroids by an athletic trainer, coach, or health club personnel.

Nothing in this section shall be construed as limiting in any way the discretion of the court to impose any sentence authorized by this Act.

(Source: P.A. 87-754.) [Formerly Ill. Rev. Stat. 56½ §1411.]

570/411.1. Fines in addition to other penalties.

§411.1. (a) Whenever any person pleads guilty to, is found guilty of or is placed on supervision for an offense under this Article, a fine may be levied in addition to any other penalty imposed by the court.

(b) In determining whether to impose a fine under this Section and the amount, time for payment and method of payment of any fine so impose, the court shall

(1) consider the defendant's income, regardless of source, the defendant's earning capacity and the defendant's financial resources, as well as the nature of the burden the fine will impose on the defendant and any person legally or financially dependent upon the defendant;

(2) consider the proof received at trial, or as a result of a plea of guilty, concerning the full street value of the controlled substances seized and any profits or other proceeds derived by the defendant from the violation of this Act;

(3) take into account any other pertinent equitable considerations; and

(4) give primary consideration to the need to deprive the defendant of illegally obtained profits or other proceeds from the offense.

For the purpose of paragraph (2) of this subsection, "street value" shall be determined by the court on the basis of testimony of law enforcement personnel and the defendant as to the amount seized and such testimony as may be required by the court as to the current street value of the controlled substances.

(c) As a condition of a fine, the court may require that payment be made in specified installments or within a specified period of time, but such period shall not be greater than the maximum applicable term of probation or imprisonment, whichever is greater. Unless otherwise specified, payment of a fine shall be due immediately.

(d) If a fine for a violation of this Act is imposed on an organization, it is the duty of each individual authorized to make disbursements of the assets of the organization to pay the fine from assets of the organization.

(e) (1) A defendant who has been sentenced to pay a fine, and who has paid part but not all of such fine, may petition the court for an extension of the time for payment or modification of the method of payment.

(2) The court may grant a petition made pursuant to this subsection if it finds that

(i) the circumstances that warranted payment by the time or method specified no longer exist; or

(ii) it is otherwise unjust to require payment of the fine by the time or method specified.

(Source: P.A. 83-778.) [Formerly Ill. Rev. Stat. 56½ §1411.1.]

570/411.2. Additional assessment—Amount and payment; Drug Treatment Fund.

§411.2. (a) Every person convicted of a violation of this Act, and every person placed on probation, conditional discharge, supervision or probation under Section 410 of this Act [720 ILCS 570/410], shall be assessed for each offense a sum fixed at:

(1) $3,000 for a Class X felony;
(2) $2,000 for a Class 1 felony;
(3) $1,000 for a Class 2 felony;
(4) $500 for a Class 3 or Class 4 felony;
(5) $300 for a Class A misdemeanor;
(6) $200 for a Class B or Class C misdemeanor.

(b) The assessment under this Section is in addition to and not in lieu of any fines, restitution costs, forfeitures or other assessments authorized or required by law.

(c) As a condition of the assessment, the court may require that payment be made in specified installments or within a specified period of time. If the assessment is not paid within the period of probation, conditional discharge or supervision to which the defendant was originally sentenced, the court may extend the period of probation, conditional discharge or supervision pursuant to Section 5-6-2 or 5-6-3.1 of the Unified Code of Corrections [730 ILCS 5/5-6-2 or 5/5-6-3.1], as applicable, until the assessment is paid or until successful completion of public or community service set forth in subsection (e) or the successful completion of the substance abuse intervention or treatment program set forth in subsection (f). If a term of probation, conditional discharge or supervision is not imposed, the assessment shall be payable upon judgment or as directed by the court.

(d) If an assessment for a violation of this Act is imposed on an organization, it is the duty of each individual authorized to make disbursements of the assets of the organization to pay the assessment from assets of the organization.

(e) A defendant who has been ordered to pay an assessment may petition the court to convert all or part of the assessment into court-approved public or community service. One hour of public or community service shall be equivalent to $4 of assessment. The performance of this public or community service shall be a condition of the probation, conditional discharge or supervision and shall be in addition to the performance of any other period of public or community service ordered by the court or required by law.

(f) The court may suspend the collection of the assessment imposed under this Section; provided the defendant agrees to enter a substance abuse intervention or treatment program approved by the court; and further provided that the defendant agrees to pay for all or some portion of the costs associated with the intervention or treatment program. In this case, the collection of the assessment imposed under this Section shall be suspended during the defendant's participation in the approved intervention or treatment program. Upon successful completion of the program, the defendant may apply to the court to reduce the assessment imposed under this Section by any amount actually paid by the defendant for his participation in the program. The court shall not reduce the penalty under this subsection unless the defendant establishes to the satisfaction of the court that he has successfully completed the intervention or treatment program. If the defendant's participation is for any reason terminated before his successful completion of the intervention or treatment program, collection of the entire assessment imposed under this Section shall be enforced. Nothing in this Section shall be deemed to affect or suspend any other fines, restitution costs, forfeitures or assessments imposed under this or any other Act.

(g) The court shall not impose more than one assessment per complaint, indictment or information. If the person is convicted of more than one offense in a complaint, indictment or information, the assessment shall be based on the highest class offense for which the person is convicted.

(h) In counties under 3,000,000, all moneys collected under this Section shall be forwarded by the clerk of the circuit court to the State Treasurer for deposit in the Drug Treatment Fund, which is hereby established as a special fund within the State Treasury. The Department of Alcoholism and Substance Abuse may make grants to persons licensed under Section 2-101 of the Illinois Alcoholism and Other Drug Dependency Act [20 ILCS 305/2-101] or to municipalities or counties from funds appropriated to the Department from the Drug Treatment Fund for the treatment of pregnant women who are addicted to alcohol, cannabis or controlled substances and for the needed care of minor, unemancipated children of women undergoing residential drug treatment. If the Department of Alcoholism and Substance Abuse grants funds to a municipality or a county that the Department determines is not experiencing a problem with pregnant women addicted to alcohol, cannabis or controlled substances, or with care for minor, unemancipated children of women undergoing residential drug treatment, or intervention, the funds shall be used for the treatment of any person addicted to alcohol, cannabis or controlled substances. The Department may adopt such rules as it deems appropriate for the administration of such grants.

(i) In counties over 3,000,000, all moneys collected under this Section shall be forwarded to the County Treasurer for deposit into the County Health Fund. The County Treasurer shall, no later than the 15th day of each month, forward to the State Treasurer 30 percent of all moneys collected under this Act and received into the County Health Fund since the prior remittance to the State Treasurer. Funds retained by the County shall be used for the hospitalization of pregnant women who are addicted to alcohol, cannabis or controlled substances or for the needed care of minor, unemancipated children of such women. Funds forwarded to the State Treasurer shall be deposited into the State Drug Treatment Fund maintained by the State Treasurer from which the Department of Alcoholism and Substance Abuse may make grants to persons licensed under Section 2-101 of the Illinois Alcoholism and Other Drug Dependency Act or to municipalities or counties from funds appropriated to the Department from the Drug Treatment Fund, provided that the moneys collected from each county be returned proportionately to the counties through grants to licensees located within the county from which the assessment was received and moneys in the State Drug Treatment Fund shall not supplant other local, State or federal funds. If the Department of Alcoholism and Substance Abuse grants funds to a municipality or county that the Department determines is not experiencing a problem with pregnant women addicted to alcohol, cannabis or controlled substances, or with care for minor, unemancipated children or women undergoing residential drug treatment, the funds shall be used for the treatment of any person addicted to alcohol, cannabis or controlled substances. The Department may adopt such rules as it deems appropriate for the administration of such grants.

(Source: P.A. 87-772.) [Formerly Ill. Rev. Stat. 56½ §1411.2.]

570/412. Penalties as addition to civil penalties.

§412. Any penalty imposed for any violation of this Act is in addition to, and not in lieu of, any civil or administrative penalty or sanction otherwise authorized by this Act or any other law.

(Source: P.A. 77-757.) [Formerly Ill. Rev. Stat. 56½ §1412.]

570/413. Fines collected; disbursement.

§413. (a) Twelve and one-half percent of all amounts collected as fines pursuant to the provisions of this Article shall be paid into the Youth Drug Abuse Prevention Fund, which is hereby created in the State treasury, to be used by the Department for the funding of programs and services for drug-abuse treatment, and prevention and education services, for juveniles.

(b) Eighty-seven and one-half percent of the proceeds of all fines received under the provisions of this Article shall be transmitted to and deposited in the treasurer's office at the level of government as follows:

(1) If such seizure was made by a combination of law enforcement personnel representing differing units of local government, the court levying the fine shall equitably allocate 50% of the fine among these units of local government and shall allocate 37½% to the county general corporate fund. In the event that the seizure was made by law enforcement personnel representing a unit of local government from a municipality where the number of inhabitants exceeds 2 million in population, the court levying the fine shall allocate 87½% of the fine

to that unit of local government. If the seizure was made by a combination of law enforcement personnel representing differing units of local government, and at least one of those units represents a municipality where the number of inhabitants exceeds 2 million in population, the court shall equitably allocate 87½% of the proceeds of the fines received among the differing units of local government.

(2) If such seizure was made by State law enforcement personnel, then the court shall allocate 37½% to the State treasury and 50% to the county general corporate fund.

(3) If a State law enforcement agency in combination with a law enforcement agency or agencies of a unit or units of local government conducted the seizure, the court shall equitably allocate 37½% of the fines to or among the law enforcement agency or agencies of the unit or units of local government which conducted the seizure and shall allocate 50% to the county general corporate fund.

(c) The proceeds of all fines allocated to the law enforcement agency or agencies of the unit or units of local government pursuant to subsection (b) shall be made available to that law enforcement agency as expendable receipts for use in the enforcement of laws regulating controlled substances and cannabis. The proceeds of fines awarded to the State treasury shall be deposited in a special fund known as the Drug Traffic Prevention Fund, except that amounts distributed to the Secretary of State shall be deposited into the Secretary of State Evidence Fund to be used as provided in Section 2-115 of the Illinois Vehicle Code [625 ILCS 5/2-115]. Monies from this fund may be used by the Department of State Police or use in the enforcement of laws regulating controlled substances and cannabis; to satisfy funding provisions of the Intergovernmental Drug Laws Enforcement Act [30 ILCS 715/1 et seq.]; to defray costs and expenses associated with returning violators of the Cannabis Control Act [720 ILCS 550/1 et seq.] and this Act only, as provided in those Acts, when punishment of the crime shall be confinement of the criminal in the penitentiary; and all other monies shall be paid into the general revenue fund in the State treasury.

(Chgd. by P.A. 87-993, §2, eff. 9/1/92.)
(Source: P.A. 87-342.) [Formerly Ill. Rev. Stat. 56½ §1413.]

ARTICLE V. ENFORCEMENT AND ADMINISTRATION OF ACT

Sec.

570/501. Duties of department.

§501. (a) It is hereby made the duty of the Department of Professional Regulation and the Department of State Police, their agents, officers, investigators, of this State to enforce all provisions of this Act, except those specifically delegated, and to cooperate with all agencies charged with the enforcement of the laws of the United States, or of any State, relating to controlled substances. Only an agent, officer, investigator designated by the Director shall (1) for the purpose of inspecting, copying and verifying the correctness of records, reports or other documents required to be kept or made under this Act and otherwise facilitating the execution of the functions of the Department of Professional Regulation or the Department of State Police be authorized, in accordance with this Section to enter controlled premises and to conduct administrative inspections thereof, and of the things specified; (2) execute and serve administrative inspection notices, warrants, subpoenas, and summonses under the authority of this State; any inspection or administrative entry of persons licensed by the Department shall be made in accordance with Section 8-102 of the Illinois Alcoholism and Other Drug Dependency Act [20 ILCS 305/8-102] and the rules and regulations promulgated thereunder.

(b) Such administrative entries and inspections as designated in subsection (a) (1) shall be carried out through agents, officers, investigators and peace officers (hereinafter referred to as "inspectors") designated by the Director. Any such inspector, upon stating his purpose and presenting to the owner, operator or agent in charge of such premises (1) appropriate credentials and (2) a written notice of his inspection authority (which notice in the case of an inspection requiring or in fact supported by, an administrative inspecting warrant shall consist of such warrant), shall have the right to enter such premises and conduct such inspection at reasonable times.

Inspectors appointed by the Director under this Section 501 are conservators of the peace and as such have all the powers possessed by policemen in cities and by sheriffs, except that they may exercise such powers anywhere in the State, in enforcing the duties conferred upon them under this Act.

(c) Except as may otherwise be indicated in an applicable inspection warrant, the inspector shall have the right—

(1) to inspect and copy records, reports and other documents required to be kept or made under this Act;

(2) to inspect, within reasonable limits and in a reasonable manner, controlled premises and all pertinent equipment, finished and unfinished drugs and other substances or materials, containers and labeling found therein, and, all other things therein (including records, files, papers, processes, controls and facilities) appropriate for verification of the records, reports and documents referred to in subsection (1) or otherwise bearing on the provisions of this Act; and

(3) to inventory any stock of any controlled substance.

(d) Except when the owner, operator or agent in charge of the controlled premises so consents in writing, no inspection authorized by this Section shall extend to:

(1) financial data;

(2) sales data other than shipment data; or

(3) pricing data.

Any inspection or administrative entry of persons licensed by the Department shall be made in accordance with Section 8-102 of the Illinois Alcoholism and Other Drug Dependency Act, as now or hereafter amended and the rules and regulations promulgated thereunder.

(e) Any agent, officer, investigator or peace officer designated by the Director may (1) make seizure of property pursuant to the provisions of this Act; and (2) perform such other law enforcement duties as the Director shall designate. It is hereby made the duty of all State's Attorneys to prosecute violations of this Act and institute legal proceedings as authorized under this Act.
(Source: P.A. 85-1209.) [Formerly Ill. Rev. Stat. 56½ §1501.]

570/501.1. Application of Administrative Procedure Act.

§501.1. The Illinois Administrative Procedure Act [5 ILCS 100/1-1 et seq.] is hereby expressly adopted and incorporated herein, but shall apply only to the Department of Professional Regulation, as if all of the provisions of such Act

were included in this Act, except that the provision of paragraph (c) of Section 16 of The Illinois Administrative Procedure Act [5 ILCS 100/10-65], which provides that at hearings the licensee has the right to show compliance with all lawful requirements for retention, or continuation or renewal of the license, is specifically excluded, and for the purposes of this Act the notice required under Section 10 of The Illinois Administrative Procedure Act [5 ILCS 100/10-25] is deemed sufficient when mailed to the last known address of a party.
(Source: P.A. 85-1209.) [Formerly Ill. Rev. Stat. 56½ §1501.1.]

570/502. Administrative inspection warrants.

§502. (a) Issuance and execution of administrative inspection warrants shall be as follows:

(1) a judge of a circuit court upon proper oath or affirmation showing probable cause, may issue warrants for the purpose of conducting administrative inspections authorized by this Act or rules hereunder, and seizures of property appropriate to the inspections. For purposes of the issuance of administrative inspection warrants, probable cause exists upon showing a valid public interest in the effective enforcement of this Act or rules hereunder, sufficient to justify administrative inspection of the controlled premises, as defined in subsection (b), specified in the application for the warrant.

(2) an inspection warrant shall issue only upon an affidavit of any person having knowledge of the facts alleged, sworn to before the circuit judge and establishing the grounds for issuing the inspection warrant. If the circuit judge is satisfied that there is probable cause to believe that grounds for issuance of an inspection warrant exist, he shall issue an inspection warrant identifying the controlled premises to be inspected, the purpose of the inspection, and, if appropriate, the type of property to be inspected or seized, if any. The inspection warrant shall:

(i) state the ground for its issuance and the name of each person whose affidavit has been taken in support thereof;

(ii) be directed to a person authorized by Section 501 [720 ILCS 570/501] to execute it;

(iii) command the person to whom it is directed to inspect the controlled premises identified for the purpose specified and, if appropriate, direct the seizure of the property specified;

(iv) identify the item or types of property to be seized, if any;

(v) direct that it be served at any time of the day or night and designate the circuit court judge to whom it shall be returned.

(3) an inspection warrant issued pursuant to this Section must be executed and returned within 10 days of its date of issuance unless, upon a showing of a need for additional time, the court which issued the inspection warrant orders otherwise. If property is seized pursuant to an inspection warrant, a copy of the inventory of such seized property shall be given to the person from whom or from whose controlled premises the property is taken. If no person is available, the inspection warrant and a copy of the inventory shall be left at such controlled premises. The inventory shall be made under oath by the person executing the warrant.

(4) an inspection warrant shall be returnable before the judge of the circuit court who issued the inspection warrant or any judge named in the inspection warrant or before the circuit court. The judge before whom the return is made shall attach to the inspection warrant a copy of the return and all papers returnable in connection therewith and file them with the clerk of the circuit court in which the inspection warrant was executed.

(5) no warrant shall be quashed nor evidence suppressed because of technical irregularities not affecting the substantial rights of the person responsible for the controlled premises.

(b) The Director may make inspections of controlled premises in accordance with the following provisions:

(1) For purposes of this Section only, "controlled premises" means:

(i) places where persons registered or exempted from registration requirements under this Act keep records required under this Act; and

(ii) places, including but not limited to, areas, buildings, premises, factories, warehouses, establishments and conveyances in which persons registered or exempted from registration requirements under this Act are permitted to possess, manufacture, distribute, dispense, administer, or otherwise dispose of any controlled substance.

(2) When authorized by an inspection warrant issued pursuant to this Act, any agent designated by the Director or any peace officer, upon presenting the inspection warrant to the person designated in the inspection warrant or any other person on the controlled premises, may enter controlled premises for the purpose of conducting the inspection.

(3) When authorized by an inspection warrant any agent designated by the Director may execute the inspection warrant in accordance with its terms.

(4) This section does not prevent the inspection without a warrant of books and records pursuant to an administrative subpoena issued in accordance with "The Civil Administrative Code of Illinois," [20 ILCS 5/1 et seq.] nor does it prevent entries and administrative inspections, including seizures of property, without a warrant:

(i) if the person in charge of the controlled premises consents; or

(ii) in situations presenting imminent danger to health or safety; or

(iii) in situations involving inspection of conveyances if there is reasonable cause to believe that the mobility of the conveyance makes it impracticable to obtain a warrant; or

(iv) in any other exceptional or emergency circumstance where time or opportunity to apply for a warrant is lacking.

(5) An inspection warrant authorized by this Section shall not extend to financial data, sales data, other than shipment data, or pricing data unless the person in charge of the controlled premises consents in writing, provided, however, that records required to be kept under this Act are not included in such financial data, sales data or pricing data.

(Source: P.A. 79-1362.) [Formerly Ill. Rev. Stat. 56½ §1502.]

570/503. Temporary or permanent injunctions.

§503. In addition to any other remedies, the Director is authorized to file a complaint and apply to any circuit court for, and such circuit court may upon hearing and for cause shown, grant a temporary restraining order or a preliminary or permanent injunction, without bond, restraining any person from violating this Act whether or not there exists other judicial remedies.

(Source: P.A. 83-342.) [Formerly Ill. Rev. Stat. 56½ §1503.]

570/504. Cooperation with other agencies.

§504. (a) The Director shall cooperate with Federal and other State agencies in discharging his responsibilities concerning traffic in controlled substances and in suppressing the misuse and abuse of controlled substances. To this end he may:

(1) arrange for the exchange of information among governmental officials concerning the use, misuse and abuse of controlled substances;

(2) coordinate and cooperate in training programs concerning controlled substance law enforcement at local and State levels;

(3) cooperate with the federal Drug Enforcement Administration or its successor agency; and

(4) conduct programs of eradication aimed at destroying wild illicit growth of plant species from which controlled substances may be extracted.

(b) Results, information, and evidence received from the Drug Enforcement Administration relating to the regulatory functions of this Act, including results of inspections conducted by it may be relied and acted upon by the Director in the exercise of his regulatory functions under this Act.
(Source: P.A. 84-874.) [Formerly Ill. Rev. Stat. 56½ §1504.]

570/505. Forfeiture.

§505. (a) The following are subject to forfeiture:

(1) all substances which have been manufactured, distributed, dispensed, or possessed in violation of this Act;

(2) all raw materials, products and equipment of any kind which are used, or intended for use in manufacturing, distributing, dispensing, administering or possessing any substance in violation of this Act;

(3) all conveyances, including aircraft, vehicles or vessels, which are used, or intended for use, to transport, or in any manner to facilitate the transportation, sale, receipt, possession, or concealment of property described in paragraphs (1) and (2), but:

(i) no conveyance used by any person as a common carrier in the transaction of business as a common carrier is subject to forfeiture under this Section unless it appears that the owner or other person in charge of the conveyance is a consenting party or privy to a violation of this Act;

(ii) no conveyance is subject to forfeiture under this Section by reason of any act or omission which the owner proves to have been committed or omitted without his knowledge or consent;

(iii) a forfeiture of a conveyance encumbered by a bona fide security interest is subject to the interest of the secured party if he neither had knowledge of nor consented to the act or omission;

(4) all money, things of value, books, records, and research products and materials including formulas, microfilm, tapes, and data which are used, or intended to be used in violation of this Act;

(5) everything of value furnished, or intended to be furnished, in exchange for a substance in violation of this Act, all proceeds traceable to such an exchange, and all moneys, negotiable instruments, and securities used, or intended to be used, to commit or in any manner to facilitate any violation of this Act;

(6) all real property, including any right, title, and interest (including, but not limited to, any leasehold interest or the beneficial interest in a land trust) in the whole of any lot or tract of land and any appurtenances or improvements, which is used or intended to be used, in any manner or part, to commit, or in any manner to facilitate the commission of, any violation or act that constitutes a violation of Section 401 or 405 of this Act [720 ILCS 570/401 or 570/405] or that is the proceeds of any violation or act that constitutes a violation of Section 401 or 405 of this Act.

(b) Property subject to forfeiture under this Act may be seized by the Director or any peace officer upon process or seizure warrant issued by any court having jurisdiction over the property. Seizure by the Director or any peace officer without process may be made:

(1) if the seizure is incident to inspection under an administrative inspection warrant;

(2) if the property subject to seizure has been the subject of a prior judgment in favor of the State in a criminal proceeding, or in an injunction or forfeiture proceeding based upon this Act or the Drug Asset Forfeiture Procedure Act [725 ILCS 150/1 et seq.];

(3) if there is probable cause to believe that the property is directly or indirectly dangerous to health or safety;

(4) if there is probable cause to believe that the property is subject to forfeiture under this Act and the property is seized under circumstances in which a warrantless seizure or arrest would be reasonable; or

(5) in accordance with the Code of Criminal Procedure of 1963 [725 ILCS 5/100-1 et seq.].

(c) In the event of seizure pursuant to subsection (b), forfeiture proceedings shall be instituted in accordance with the Drug Asset Forfeiture Procedure Act.

(d) Property taken or detained under this Section shall not be subject to replevin, but is deemed to be in the custody of the Director subject only to the order and judgments of the circuit court having jurisdiction over the forfeiture proceedings and the decisions of the State's Attorney under the Drug Asset Forfeiture Procedure Act. When property is seized under this Act, the seizing agency shall promptly conduct an inventory of the seized property and estimate the property's value, and shall forward a copy of the inventory of seized property and the estimate of the property's value to the Director. Upon receiving notice of seizure, the Director may:

(1) place the property under seal;

(2) remove the property to a place designated by the Director;

(3) keep the property in the possession of the seizing agency;

(4) remove the property to a storage area for safekeeping or, if the property is a negotiable instrument or money and is not needed for evidentiary purposes, deposit it in an interest bearing account;

(5) place the property under constructive seizure by posting notice of pending forfeiture on it, by giving notice of pending forfeiture to its owners and interest holders, or by filing notice of pending forfeiture in any appropriate public record relating to the property; or

(6) provide for another agency or custodian, including an owner, secured party, or lienholder, to take custody of the property upon the terms and conditions set by the Director.

(e) If the Department of Professional Regulation suspends or revokes a registration, all controlled substances owned or possessed by the registrant at the time of suspension or the effective date of the revocation order may be placed under seal. No disposition may be made of substances under seal until the time for taking an appeal has elapsed or until all appeals have been concluded unless a court, upon application therefor, orders the sale of perishable substances and the deposit of the proceeds of the sale with the court. Upon a revocation rule becoming final, all substances may be forfeited to the Department of Professional Regulation.

(f) When property is forfeited under this Act the Director shall sell all such property unless such property is required by law to be destroyed or is harmful to the public, and shall distribute the proceeds of the sale, together with any moneys forfeited or seized, in accordance with subsection (g). However, upon the application of the seizing agency or prosecutor who was responsible for the investigation, arrest or arrests and prosecution which lead to the forfeiture, the Director may return any item of forfeited property to the seizing agency or prosecutor for official use in the enforcement of laws relating to cannabis or controlled substances, if the agency or prosecutor can demonstrate that the item requested would be useful to the agency or prosecutor in their enforcement efforts. When any real property returned to the seizing agency is sold by the agency or its unit of government, the proceeds of the sale shall be delivered to the Director and distributed in accordance with subsection (g).

(g) All monies and the sale proceeds of all other property forfeited and seized under this Act shall be distributed as follows:

(1) 65% shall be distributed to the metropolitan enforcement group, local, municipal, county, or state law enforcement agency or agencies which conducted or participated in the investigation resulting in the forfeiture. The distribution shall bear a reasonable relationship to the degree of direct participation of the law enforcement agency in the effort resulting in the forfeiture, taking into account the total value of the property forfeited and the total law enforcement effort with respect to the violation of the law upon which the forfeiture is based. Amounts distributed to the agency or agencies shall be used for the enforcement of laws governing cannabis and controlled substances.

(2) (i) 12.5% shall be distributed to the Office of the State's Attorney of the county in which the prosecution resulting in the forfeiture was instituted, deposited in a special fund in the county treasury and appropriated to the State's Attorney for use in the enforcement of laws governing cannabis and controlled substances. In counties over 3,000,000 population, 25% will be distributed to a special fund in the county treasury and appropriated to the State's Attorneys Office for use in the enforcement of laws governing cannabis and controlled substances. If the prosecution is undertaken solely by the Attorney General, the portion provided hereunder shall be distributed to the Attorney General for use in the enforcement of laws governing cannabis and controlled substances.

(ii) 12.5% shall be distributed to the Office of the State's Attorneys Appellate Prosecutor and deposited in the Narcotics Profit Forfeiture Fund of that office to be used for additional expenses incurred in the investigation, prosecution and appeal of cases arising under laws governing cannabis and controlled substances. The Office of the State's Attorneys Appellate Prosecutor shall not receive distribution from cases brought in counties with over 3,000,000 population.

(3) 10% shall be retained by the Department of State Police for expenses related to the administration and sale of seized and forfeited property.

(h) Species of plants from which controlled substances in Schedules I and II may be derived which have been planted or cultivated in violation of this Act, or of which the owners or cultivators are unknown, or which are wild growths, may be seized and summarily forfeited to the State. The failure, upon demand by the Director or any peace officer, of the person in occupancy or in control of land or premises upon which the species of plants are growing or being stored, to produce registration, or proof that he is the holder thereof, constitutes authority for the seizure and forfeiture of the plants.

(Source: P.A. 86-1382; 86-1475; 87-614.) [Formerly Ill. Rev. Stat. 56½ §1505.]

570/506. Burden of proof of exemptions or exceptions.

§506. It is not necessary for the State to negate any exemption or exception in this Act in any complaint, information, indictment or other pleading or in any trial, hearing, or other proceeding under this Act. The burden of proof of any exemption or exception is upon the person claiming it.

(Source: P.A. 77-757.) [Formerly Ill. Rev. Stat. 56½ §1506.]

570/507. Administrative Review Law; review.

§507. All rulings, final determinations, findings, and conclusions of the Department of State Police, the Department of Professional Regulation, and the Illinois Department of Alcoholism and Substance Abuse of the State of Illinois under this Act are final and conclusive decisions of the matters involved. Any person aggrieved by the decision may obtain review of the decision pursuant to the provisions of the Administrative Review Law, as amended [735 ILCS 5/3-101 et seq.] and the rules adopted pursuant thereto. Pending final decision on such review, the acts, orders and rulings of the Department shall remain in full force and effect unless modified or suspended by order of court

pending final judicial decision. Pending final decision on such review, the acts, orders, sanctions and rulings of the Department of Professional Regulation regarding any registration shall remain in full force and effect, unless stayed by order of court. However, no stay of any decision of the administrative agency shall issue unless the person aggrieved by the decision establishes by a preponderance of the evidence that good cause exists therefor. In determining good cause, the court shall find that the aggrieved party has established a substantial likelihood of prevailing on the merits and that granting the stay will not have an injurious effect on the general public. Good cause shall not be established solely on the basis of hardships resulting from an inability to engage in the registered activity pending a final judicial decision.
(Source: P.A. 85-1209.) [Formerly Ill. Rev. Stat. 56½ §1507.]

570/507.1. Payment of costs for furnishing and certifying records.
§507.1. The Department shall not be required to certify any record to the court or file any answer in court or otherwise appear in any court proceedings under the Administrative Review Law [735 ILCS 5/3-101 et seq.], unless there is filed in the court with the complaint a receipt from the Department acknowledging payment of the costs of furnishing and certifying the record. Exhibits shall be certified without cost. Failure on the part of the plaintiff to file such receipt in court shall be grounds for dismissal of the action.
(Source: P.A. 83-969.) [Formerly Ill. Rev. Stat. 56½ §1507.1.]

570/508. Controlled substances; research.
§508. The Department shall encourage research on controlled substances. In connection with the research, and in furtherance of the purposes of this Act, the Department may:

(1) establish methods to assess accurately the effect of controlled substances and identify and characterize those with potential for abuse;

(2) make studies and undertake programs of research to:

(i) develop new or improved approaches, techniques, systems, equipment and devices to strengthen the enforcement of this Act;

(ii) determine patterns of use, misuse, and abuse of controlled substances and their social effects; and

(iii) improve methods for preventing, predicting, understanding, and dealing with the use, misuse and abuse of controlled substances; and

(3) enter into contracts with public agencies, educational institutions, and private organizations or individuals for the purpose of conducting research, demonstrations, or special projects which relate to the use, misuse and abuse of controlled substances.

(b)* Persons authorized to engage in research may be authorized by the Department to protect the privacy of individuals who are the subjects of such research by withholding from all persons not connected with the conduct of the research the names and other identifying characteristics of such individuals. Persons who are given this authorization shall not be compelled in any civil, criminal, administrative, legislative or other proceeding to identify the individuals who are the subjects of research for which the authorization was granted, except to the extent necessary to permit the Department to determine whether the research is being conducted in accordance with the authorization.
**So in original. No subsec. (a) has been designated.*

(c) The Department may authorize the possession and dispensing of controlled substances by persons engaged in research, upon such terms and conditions as may be consistent with the public health and safety. The Department may also approve research and treatment programs involving the administration of Methadone. The use of Methadone, or any similar controlled substance by any person is prohibited in this State except as approved and authorized by the Department in accordance with its rules and regulations. To the extent of the applicable authorization, persons are exempt from prosecution in this State for possession, manufacture or delivery of controlled substances.

(d) Practitioners registered under Federal law to conduct research with Schedule I substances may conduct research with Schedule I substances within this State upon furnishing evidence of that Federal registration and notification of the scope and purpose of such research to the Department.
(Source: P.A. 83-969.) [Formerly Ill. Rev. Stat. 56½ §1508.]

570/509. Probation or parole; periodic tests.

§509. Whenever any court in this State grants probation to any person that the court has reason to believe is or has been an addict or unlawful possessor of controlled substances, the court shall require, as a condition of probation, that the probationer submit to periodic tests by the Department of Corrections to determine by means of appropriate chemical detection tests whether the probationer is using controlled substances. The court may require as a condition of probation that the probationer enter an approved treatment program, if the court determines that the probationer is addicted to a controlled substance. Whenever the Parole and Pardon Board grants parole to a person whom the Board has reason to believe has been an unlawful possessor or addict of controlled substances, the Board shall require as a condition of parole that the parolee submit to appropriate periodic chemical tests by the Department of Corrections to determine whether the parolee is using controlled substances.
(Source: P.A. 77-757.) [Formerly Ill. Rev. Stat. 56½ §1509.]

ARTICLE VI. APPLICATION AND VALIDITY

Sec.

570/601. Savings clause.

§601. Prosecution for any violation of law occurring prior to the effective date of this Act is not affected or abated by this Act. If the offense being prosecuted would be a violation of this Act, and has not reached the sentencing stage or final adjudication, then for purposes of penalty the penalties under this Act apply if they are less than under the prior law upon which the prosecution was commenced.
(Source: P.A. 77-757.) [Formerly Ill. Rev. Stat. 56½ §1601.]

570/602. Severability.

§602. If any provision of this Act or the application thereof to any person or circumstance is invalid, such invalidation shall not affect other provisions or applications of the Act which can be given effect without the invalid provision or application, and to this end the provisions of this Act are declared to be severable.
(Source: P.A. 77-757.) [Formerly Ill. Rev. Stat. 56½ §1602.]

570/603. Repeals.

§603. The following Acts and parts of Acts are repealed:

(a) The "Uniform Narcotic Drug Act," approved July 11, 1957, as amended [repealed].

(b) The "Drug Abuse Control Act," approved August 17, 1967, as amended [repealed].

(c) "An Act to amend Sections 2-15, 41 (a) and 43 of, and to add Sections 43.1, 43.2, 43.3, 43.4, 43.5, 43.6 and 43.7 to the 'Uniform Drug, Device and Cosmetic Act', approved July 9, 1959, as amended," approved August 11, 1967, as amended [repealed].

(d) "An Act to amend Section 46 of the 'Uniform Drug, Device and Cosmetic Act', approved July 9, 1959, as amended", approved August 18, 1967, as amended [repealed].
(Source: P.A. 77-757.) [Formerly Ill. Rev. Stat. 56½ §1603.]

CRIMINAL JURISPRUDENCE ACT [DISEASED ANIMALS]

575/258. Diseased sheep and other domestic animals; permitting to run at large.

§258. Any person who shall hereafter knowingly and willfully bring or cause to be brought into this state any sheep or other domestic animals infected with contagious disease, or who shall knowingly and willfully suffer or permit sheep or other domestic animals infected with contagious disease to run at large, shall be guilty of a petty offense, and shall be liable in a civil action for all damages occasioned thereby.
(Source: P.A. 77-2680.) [Formerly Ill. Rev. Stat. 8 §191.1.]

CRIMINAL JURISPRUDENCE ACT [COMMON CARRIERS]

580/49. Common carriers.

§49. Whoever, having personal management or control of or over any steamboat or other public conveyance used for the common carriage of persons, is guilty of gross carelessness or neglect in, or in relation to, the conduct, management or control of such steamboat, or other public conveyance, while being so used, for the common carriage of persons, whereby the safety of any person shall be endangered, shall be guilty of a Class 4 felony.
(Source: P.A. 77-2590.) [Formerly Ill. Rev. Stat. 111⅔ §361.]

ILLINOIS DANGEROUS ANIMALS ACT

585/0.1. Definitions.

§0.1. As used in this Act, unless the context otherwise requires:

"Dangerous animal" means a lion, tiger, leopard, ocelot, jaguar, cheetah, margay, mountain lion, lynx, bobcat, jaguarundi, bear, hyena, wolf or coyote, or any poisonous or life-threatening reptile.

"Owner" means any person who (a) has a right of property in a dangerous animal, (b) keeps or harbors a dangerous animal, (c) has a dangerous animal in his care, or (d) acts as custodian of a dangerous animal.

"Person" means any individual, firm, association, partnership, corporation, or other legal entity, any public or private institution, the State of Illinois, or any municipal corporation or political subdivision of the State.
(Source: P.A. 84-28.) [Formerly Ill. Rev. Stat. 8 §240.]

585/1. Possession of dangerous animals.

§1. No person shall have a right of property in, keep, harbor, care for, act as custodian of or maintain in his possession any dangerous animal except at

a properly maintained zoological park, federally licensed exhibit, circus, scientific or educational institution, research laboratory, veterinary hospital or animal refuge in an escape-proof enclosure.
(Source: P.A. 84-28.) [Formerly Ill. Rev. Stat. 8 §241.]

585/2. Attempt to domesticate dangerous animals.

§2. It is no defense to a violation of Section 1 [720 ILCS 585/1] that the person violating such Section has attempted to domesticate the dangerous animal. If there appears to be imminent danger to the public, any dangerous animal found not in compliance with the provisions of this Act shall be subject to seizure and may immediately be placed in an approved facility. Upon the conviction of a person for a violation of Section 1, the animal with regard to which the conviction was obtained shall be confiscated and placed in an approved facility, with the owner thereof to be responsible for all costs connected with the seizure and confiscation of such animal. Approved facilities include, but are not limited to, a zoological park, federally licensed exhibit, humane society, veterinary hospital or animal refuge.
(Source: P.A. 84-28.) [Formerly Ill. Rev. Stat. 8 §242.]

585/3. Violations.

§3. Any person violating this Act shall be guilty of a Class C misdemeanor. Each day of violation constitutes a separate offense.

In the event the person violating this Act is a corporation or partnership, any officer, director, manager or managerial agent of the partnership or corporation who violates this Section or causes the partnership or corporation to violate this Section is guilty of a Class C misdemeanor.
(Source: P.A. 84-28.) [Formerly Ill. Rev. Stat. 8 §243.]

585/4. Short title.

§4. This Act shall be known and may be cited as the "Illinois Dangerous Animals Act".
(Source: P.A. 84-28.) [Formerly Ill. Rev. Stat. 8 §244.]

DISCRIMINATION IN SALE OF REAL ESTATE ACT

Sec.

590/0.01. Short title.

§0.01. Short title. This Act may be cited as the Discrimination in Sale of Real Estate Act.
(Source: P.A. 86-1324.) [Formerly Ill. Rev. Stat. 38 §70-50.]

590/1. Inducements to sell or purchase by reason of race, color, religion, national origin, ancestry, creed, handicap, or sex—Prohibition of solicitation.

§1. Inducements to sell or purchase by reason of race, color, religion, national origin, ancestry, creed, handicap, or sex—Prohibition of Solicitation. It shall be unlawful for any person or corporation knowingly:

(a) To solicit for sale, lease, listing or purchase any residential real estate within the State of Illinois, on the grounds of loss of value due to the present or prospective entry into the vicinity of the property involved of any person or persons of any particular race, color, religion, national origin, ancestry, creed, handicap, or sex.

(b) To distribute or cause to be distributed, written material or statements designed to induce any owner of residential real estate in the State of Illinois to sell or lease his or her property because of any present or prospective changes in the race, color, religion, national origin, ancestry, creed, handicap, or sex, of residents in the vicinity of the property involved.

(c) To intentionally create alarm, among residents of any community, by transmitting in any manner including a telephone call whether or not conversation thereby ensues, with a design to induce any owner of residential real estate in the State of Illinois to sell or lease his or her property because of any present or prospective entry into the vicinity of the property involved of any person or persons of any particular race, color, religion, national origin, ancestry, creed, handicap, or sex.

(d) To solicit any owner of residential property to sell or list such residential property at any time after such person or corporation has notice that such owner does not desire to sell such residential property. For the purpose of this subsection, notice must be provided as follows:

(1) The notice may be given by the owner personally or by a third party in the owner's name, either in the form of an individual notice or a list, provided it complies with this subsection.

(2) Such notice shall be explicit as to whether each owner on the notice seeks to avoid both solicitation for listing and sale, or only for listing, or only for sale, as well as the period of time for which any avoidance is desired. The notice shall be dated and either of the following shall apply: (A) each owner shall have signed the notice or (B) the person or entity preparing the notice shall provide an accompanying affidavit to the effect that all the names on the notice are, in fact, genuine as to the identity of the persons listed and that such persons have requested not to be solicited as indicated.

(3) The individual notice, or notice in the form of a list with the accompanying affidavit, shall be served personally or by certified or registered mail, return receipt requested.

(Source: P.A. 80-338; 80-920; 80-1364.) [Formerly Ill. Rev. Stat. 38 §70-51.]

590/2. Sentence.

§2. Sentence. (a) Any person who violates any provision of this Act commits a Class A misdemeanor, provided that such person has not been convicted of any prior offense under the terms of this Act.

(b) Any person who violates any provision of this Act after having been previously convicted of an offense under this Section, commits a Class 4 felony.

(Source: P.A. 77-2642.) [Formerly Ill. Rev. Stat. 38 §70-52.]

590/3. Report of conviction.

§3. Whenever a person is convicted of any violation of this Act, the clerk of the court shall report such conviction to the Department of Professional Regulation, which shall thereupon revoke any certificate of registration as a real estate broker or real estate salesman held by such person.

(Source: P.A. 85-1209.) [Formerly Ill. Rev. Stat. 38 §70-53.]

DRAFT CARD MUTILATION ACT

Sec.

595/0.01. Short title.

§0.01. Short title. This Act may be cited as the Draft Card Mutilation Act.

(Source: P.A. 86-1324.) [Formerly Ill. Rev. Stat. 38 §90-10.]

595/1. Sentence.

§1. Sentence. A person who knowingly destroys or mutilates a valid registration certificate or any other valid certificate issued under the federal

"Military Selective Service Act of 1967" [50 App. U.S.C. §451 et seq.] commits a Class 4 felony.
(Source: P.A. 77-2648.) [Formerly Ill. Rev. Stat. 38 §90-11.]

DRUG PARAPHERNALIA CONTROL ACT

600/1. Short title.

§1. This Act shall be known and may be cited as the "Drug Paraphernalia Control Act".
(Source: P.A. 82-1032.) [Formerly Ill. Rev. Stat. 56½ §2101.]

600/2. Definitions.

§2. As used in this Act, unless the context otherwise requires:

(a) The term "cannabis" shall have the meaning ascribed to it in Section 3 of the "Cannabis Control Act" [720 ILCS 550/3], as if that definition were incorporated herein.

(b) The term "controlled substance" shall have the meaning ascribed to it in Section 102 of the "Illinois Controlled Substances Act" [720 ILCS 570/102], as if that definition were incorporated herein.

(c) "Deliver" or "delivery" means the actual, constructive or attempted transfer of possession, with or without consideration, whether or not there is an agency relationship.

(d) "Drug paraphernalia" means all equipment, products and materials of any kind which are peculiar to and marketed for use in planting, propagating, cultivating, growing, harvesting, manufacturing, compounding, converting, producing, processing, preparing, testing, analyzing, packaging, repackaging, storing, containing, concealing, injecting, ingesting, inhaling or otherwise introducing into the human body cannabis or a controlled substance in violation of the "Cannabis Control Act" [720 ILCS 550/1 et seq.] or the "Illinois Controlled Substances Act" [720 ILCS 570/100 et seq.]. It includes, but is not limited to:

(1) Kits peculiar to and marketed for use in manufacturing, compounding, converting, producing, processing or preparing cannabis or a controlled substance;

(2) Isomerization devices peculiar to and marketed for use in increasing the potency of any species of plant which is cannabis or a controlled substance;

(3) Testing equipment peculiar to and marketed for private home use in identifying or in analyzing the strength, effectiveness or purity of cannabis or controlled substances;

(4) Diluents and adulterants peculiar to and marketed for cutting cannabis or a controlled substance by private persons;

(5) Objects peculiar to and marketed for use in ingesting, inhaling, or otherwise introducing cannabis, cocaine, hashish, or hashish oil into the human body including, where applicable, the following items:

(A) water pipes;
(B) carburetion tubes and devices;
(C) smoking and carburetion masks;
(D) miniature cocaine spoons and cocaine vials;
(E) carburetor pipes;
(F) electric pipes;

(G) air-driven pipes;
(H) chillums;
(I) bongs;
(J) ice pipes or chillers;
(6) Any item whose purpose, as announced or described by the seller, is for use in violation of this Act.
(Source: P.A. 82-1032.) [Formerly Ill. Rev. Stat. 56½ §2102.]

600/3. Sale of paraphernalia.
§3. (a) Any person who keeps for sale, offers for sale, sells, or delivers for any commercial consideration any item of drug paraphernalia commits a Class 4 felony for which a minimum fine of $1,000 for each such item shall be imposed. Any person 18 years of age or older who sells or delivers for any commercial consideration any item of drug paraphernalia to a person under 18 years of age is guilty of a Class 3 felony.

(b) Any person who sells or delivers for a commercial consideration any item of drug paraphernalia to a woman he knows to be pregnant is guilty of a Class 2 felony.

(c) Any store, place, or premises from which or in which any item of drug paraphernalia is kept for sale, offered for sale, sold, or delivered for any commercial consideration is declared to be a public nuisance.

The State's Attorney of the county in which such a nuisance is located may commence an action in the circuit court, in the name of the People of the State of Illinois, to abate the public nuisance as described in this subsection (c).

Upon being satisfied by affidavits or other sworn evidence that an alleged public nuisance exists, the court may, without bond, enter a temporary restraining order to enjoin any defendant from maintaining the nuisance and may, without bond, enter a preliminary injunction restraining any defendant from removing or interfering with any property used in connection with the public nuisance.

If during the proceedings and hearings upon the merits the existence of the nuisance is established, and it is established that the nuisance was maintained with the intentional, knowing or reckless permission of the owner, or an agent of the owner managing the premises, the court shall enter an order restraining all persons from maintaining or permitting the nuisance and from using the premises for a period of one year thereafter. However an owner, lessee, or other occupant thereof may use the premises if the owner gives bond with sufficient security or surety, in an amount between $5,000 and $10,000 approved by the court, payable to the People of the State of Illinois. The bond shall include a condition that no offense specified in this Act shall be committed at, in, or upon the property described, and a condition that the principal obligor and surety assume responsibility for any fine, costs, or damages incurred by any person resulting from such an offense.
(Source: P.A. 86-271; 86-1459; 86-1466; 87-435; 87-828.) [Formerly Ill. Rev. Stat. 56½ §2103.]

600/4. Applicability of Act.
§4. This Act shall not apply to:

(a) Items marketed for use in the preparation, compounding, packaging, labeling, or other use of cannabis or a controlled substance as an incident to lawful research, teaching, or chemical analysis and not for sale; or

(b) Items marketed for, or historically and customarily used in connection with the planting, propagating, cultivating, growing, harvesting, manufacturing, compounding, converting, producing, processing, preparing, testing, analyzing, packaging, repackaging, storing, containing, concealing, injecting, ingesting, or inhaling of tobacco or any other lawful substance.

Items exempt under this subsection include, but are not limited to, garden hoes, rakes, sickles, baggies, tobacco pipes, and cigarette-rolling papers.

(c) Items listed in Section (2) of this Act [720 ILCS 600/2] which are marketed for decorative purposes, when such items have been rendered completely inoperable or incapable of being used for any illicit purpose prohibited by this Act.

In determining whether or not a particular item is exempt under this subsection, the trier of fact should consider, in addition to all other logically relevant factors, the following:

(1) The general, usual, customary, and historical use to which the item involved has been put;

(2) Expert evidence concerning the ordinary or customary use of the item and the effect of any peculiarity in the design or engineering of the device upon its functioning;

(3) Any written instructions accompanying the delivery of the item concerning the purposes or uses to which the item can or may be put;

(4) Any oral instructions provided by the seller of the item at the time and place of sale or commercial delivery;

(5) Any national or local advertising, concerning the design, purpose or use of the item involved, and the entire context in which such advertising occurs;

(6) The manner, place and circumstances in which the item was displayed for sale, as well as any item or items displayed for sale or otherwise exhibited upon the premises where the sale was made;

(7) Whether the owner or anyone in control of the object is a legitimate supplier of like or related items to the community, such as a licensed distributor or dealer of tobacco products;

(8) The existence and scope of legitimate uses for the object in the community.

(Source: P.A. 82-1032.) [Formerly Ill. Rev. Stat. 56½ §2104.]

600/5. Forfeiture.

§5. (a) All drug paraphernalia is subject to forfeiture.

(b) Property subject to forfeiture under this Act may be seized by any peace officer upon process issued by any court having jurisdiction over the property. Judgments in favor of the State in a criminal or forfeiture proceeding based upon this Act against a person's specific property shall serve as process authorizing a police officer to seize such property without further process.

Seizure by a police officer may be made without process:

(1) If there is probable cause to believe that the property is directly dangerous to health or safety and existing circumstances do not allow reasonable time for the officer to obtain lawful process; or

(2) In accordance with the provisions of The Code of Criminal Procedure of 1963, as amended [725 ILCS 5/100-1 et seq.].

(3) The presence of items which are deemed violative of this Act or are otherwise subject to its forfeiture provisions in an inventory shall not subject the entire inventory to seizure or forfeiture.

(c) Property taken or detained under this Section shall not be subject to replevin, but is deemed to be in the custody of the law enforcement department or agency employing the seizing officer, subject only to the order and judgments of the circuit court having jurisdiction over the forfeiture proceedings. When property is seized under this Act, the chief administrative officer of the seizing department or agency may place the property under seal, or remove the property to a place designated by him.

(d) No disposition may be made of property under seal until the validity of the seizure has been determined in a Circuit Court, unless such court upon application therefor, orders the sale of perishable substances and the deposit of the proceeds of the sale with the clerk of the court. The Circuit Court shall rule on the validity of the seizure within 30 days after the seizure, unless a continuance is obtained by a person from whom the items were seized or a person who otherwise has standing to complain, or by the State for good cause shown. In no event shall a continuance be granted to the State pursuant to this Section extend beyond 30 days. If judgment is entered in favor of the person from whom the property is seized, all seized property shall be returned immediately. Appeals from orders of the Circuit Court shall be heard within 60 days from the date judgment is entered. Judgments in favor of the person entitled to possession of the subject property shall serve as a mandate to the agency holding said property to return same forthwith.

(e) When property is forfeited under this Act the chief administrative officer of the seizing department or agency may retain it for official use, or forward it to the Bureau of Narcotics and Dangerous Drugs, United States Department of Justice, or its successor agency, for disposition.
(Source: P.A. 82-1032.) [Formerly Ill. Rev. Stat. 56½ §2105.]

600/6. Intent of Act.

§6. This Act is intended to be used solely for the suppression of the commercial traffic in items which, within the context of the sale or offering for sale, are clearly and beyond a reasonable doubt marketed for the illegal and unlawful use of cannabis or controlled substances. To this end all reasonable and common-sense inferences shall be drawn in favor of the legitimacy of any transaction or item.
(Source: P.A. 82-1032.) [Formerly Ill. Rev. Stat. 56½ §2106.]

600/7. Effect of Act on local ordinances.

§7. The provisions of any ordinance enacted by any municipality or unit of local government which imposes the same or greater restrictions or limitations upon the availability of drug paraphernalia as defined herein, including the acquisition, sale or delivery of such items, are not invalidated or affected by this Act.
(Source: P.A. 82-1032.) [Formerly Ill. Rev. Stat. 56½ §2107.]

EXCAVATION FENCE ACT

605/0.01. Short title.

§0.01. Short title. This Act may be cited as the Excavation Fence Act.
(Source: P.A. 86-1324.) [Formerly Ill. Rev. Stat. 54 §25.9.]

605/1. Protective covering or fencing required.

§1. Any person, corporation or partnership which either owns, or maintains, or uses, or abandons any open well, cesspool, cistern, quarry, recharging basin, catch basin, sump, excavation for the erection of any building structure or excavation created by the razing or removal of any building structure without covering or surrounding such installation with protective fencing is guilty of a Class C misdemeanor. The provisions of this Act shall not apply during the course of repair, construction, removal or filling of any of the structures or conditions herein described while any worker is present at the location thereof either performing services thereon or as a watchman to guard such location.
(Source: P.A. 81-992.) [Formerly Ill. Rev. Stat. 54 §26.]

FEEDING GARBAGE TO ANIMALS ACT

610/0.01. Short title.

§0.01. Short title. This Act may be cited as the Feeding Garbage to Animals Act.

(Source: P.A. 86-1324.) [Formerly Ill. Rev. Stat. 8 §210.]

610/1. Definitions.

§1. When used in this Act, unless the context otherwise indicates:

"Department" means the Department of Agriculture of the State of Illinois.

"Garbage" means putrescible vegetable waste, animal, poultry, or fish carcasses or parts thereof resulting from the handling, preparation, cooking, or consumption of food, but does not include the contents of the bovine digestive tract. "Garbage" also means the bodies or parts of bodies of animals, poultry or fish.

"Person" means any person, firm, partnership, association, corporation, or other legal entity, any public or private institution, the State of Illinois, or any municipal corporation or political subdivision of the State.

(Source: P.A. 83-760.) [Formerly Ill. Rev. Stat. 8 §211.]

610/1.1. Certain establishments exempt.

§1.1. Establishments licensed under the Illinois Dead Animal Disposal Act [225 ILCS 610/1 et seq.] or under similar laws in other states are exempt from the provisions of this Act.

(Source: P.A. 83-760.) [Formerly Ill. Rev. Stat. 8 §211.1.]

610/2. Farms where swine are kept; feeding garbage prohibited.

§2. No person shall feed or permit the feeding of garbage to swine or any animals or poultry on any farm or any other premises where swine are kept. However, nothing in this Act shall be construed to apply to any person who feeds garbage produced in his own household to animals or poultry kept on the premises where he resides except such garbage if fed to swine shall not contain particles of meat.

(Source: P.A. 76-227.) [Formerly Ill. Rev. Stat. 8 §212.]

610/3. Penalty for violations.

§3. Whoever violates this Act is guilty of a misdemeanor and for the first offense shall be fined not less than $100 nor more than $500 and for a second or subsequent offense shall be fined not less than $200 nor more than $500 or imprisoned in a penal institution other than the penitentiary for not more than 6 months, or both.

(Source: P.A. 76-227.) [Formerly Ill. Rev. Stat. 8 §213.]

610/4. Violators may be enjoined by the Department.

§4. A person violating this Act may be enjoined by the Department from continuing such violation.

(Source: P.A. 76-227.) [Formerly Ill. Rev. Stat. 8 §214.]

610/5. Inspections.

§5. The Department may make reasonable inspections necessary for the enforcement of this Act, and is authorized to enforce, and administer the provisions of this Act.
(Source: P.A. 76-227.) [Formerly Ill. Rev. Stat. 8 §215.]

FIRE EXTINGUISHER SERVICE ACT

615/0.01. Short title.

§0.01. Short title. This Act may be cited as the Fire Extinguisher Service Act.
(Source: P.A. 86-1324.) [Formerly Ill. Rev. Stat. 127½ §60.]

615/1. False representation of service, repair or examination of fire extinguishing equipment.

§1. It is unlawful for any person to represent that a fire extinguisher or fire extinguishing equipment has been serviced, repaired or examined for the purpose of determining whether or not it is in good working condition when in fact no such service, repairing or examination has been performed. Such representations for the purpose of this Act shall mean any mark, symbol, initial or date recorded on the extinguisher or equipment or on anything attached thereto or on any list schedule or in any other place where such service, repair or examination is normally recorded.

Any person who violates the provisions of this Act is guilty of a petty offense.
(Source: P.A. 77-2448.) [Formerly Ill. Rev. Stat. 127½ §61.]

FLAG DESECRATION ACT

620/0.01. Short title.

§0.01. Short title. This Act may be cited as the Flag Desecration Act.
(Source: P.A. 86-1324.) [Formerly Ill. Rev. Stat. 1 §3350.]

620/1. Desecration of flag; penalty.

§1. Any person who (a) for exhibition or display, places or causes to be placed any word, figure, mark, picture, design, drawing, or any advertisement of any nature, upon any flag, standard, color or ensign of the United States or State flag of this State or ensign, (b) exposes or causes to be exposed to public view any such flag, standard, color or ensign, upon which has been printed, painted or otherwise placed, or to which has been attached, appended, affixed, or annexed, any word, figure, mark, picture, design or drawing or any advertisement of any nature, or (c) exposes to public view, manufactures, sells, exposes for sale, gives away, or has in possession for sale or to give away or for use for any purpose, any article or substance, being an article of merchandise, or a receptacle of merchandise or article or thing for carrying or transporting merchandise upon which has been printed, painted, attached, or otherwise placed a representation of any such flag, standard, color, or ensign, to advertise, call attention to, decorate, mark or distinguish the article or substance on which so placed, shall be guilty of a Class C misdemeanor.

Any person who publicly mutilates, defaces, defiles, tramples, or intentionally displays on the ground or floor any such flag, standard, color or ensign shall be guilty of a Class 4 felony.
(Source: P.A. 86-942.) [Formerly Ill. Rev. Stat. 1 §3351.]

620/2. Definitions.

§2. The words flag, standard, color or ensign, as used in this act, shall include any flag, standard, color, ensign or any picture or representation of either thereof, made of any substance or represented on any substance and of any size evidently purporting to be either of said flag, standard, color or ensign of the United States of America, or a picture or a representation of either thereof, upon which shall be shown the colors, the stars, and the stripes, in any number of either thereof, of the flag, colors, standard, or ensign of the United States of America.
(Source: Laws 1907, p. 351.) [Formerly Ill. Rev. Stat. 1 §3352.]

620/4. Prosecution of offenders.

§4. All prosecutions under this Act shall be brought by any person in the name of the People of the State of Illinois, against any person or persons violating any of the provisions of this Act, before any circuit court. The State's Attorneys shall see that this Act is enforced in their respective counties, and shall prosecute all offenders on receiving information of the violation of this Act. Sheriffs, deputy sheriffs, and police officers shall inform against and prosecute all persons whom there is probable cause to believe are guilty of violating this Act. One-half of the amount recovered in any penal action under this Act shall be paid to the person making and filing the complaint in such action, and the remaining ½ to the school fund of the county in which the conviction is obtained.
(Source: Laws 1968, p. 173.) [Formerly Ill. Rev. Stat. 1 §3354.]

620/5. Time limit for prosecutions.

§5. All prosecutions under this act shall be commenced within six months from the time such offense was committed, and not afterwards.
(Source: Laws 1907, p. 351.) [Formerly Ill. Rev. Stat. 1 §3355.]

GRAIN COLORING ACT

625/0.01. Short title.

§0.01. Short title. This Act may be cited as the Grain Coloring Act.
(Source: P.A. 86-1324.) [Formerly Ill. Rev. Stat. 5 §210.]

625/1. Fumigation and grain coloring.

§1. No person shall subject, or cause to be subjected, any barley, wheat or other grain to fumigation, by sulphur, or other material, or to any chemical or coloring process, whereby the color, quality or germ of such grain is affected.
(Source: Laws 1877, p. 91.) [Formerly Ill. Rev. Stat. 5 §211.]

625/2. Selling fumigated or colored grain.

§2. No person shall offer for sale, or procure to be sold, any barley, wheat, or other grain, which shall have been subjected to such fumigation, or other

process, as provided in section one (1) of this act, knowing such barley, wheat, or other grain to have been so subjected.
(Source: Laws 1877, p. 91.) [Formerly Ill. Rev. Stat. 5 §212.]

625/3. Violations.
§3. Any person violating the provisions of this act, shall be guilty of a Class B misdemeanor, and shall also be liable for all damages sustained by any person injured by such violation.
(Source: P.A. 77-2492.) [Formerly Ill. Rev. Stat. 5 §213.]

GUIDE DOG ACCESS ACT

Sec.

630/0.01. Short title.
§0.01. Short title. This Act may be cited as the Guide Dog Access Act.
(Source: P.A. 86-1324.) [Formerly Ill. Rev. Stat. 38 §65.]

630/1. Persons accompanied by guide dog—Right of entry and use of facilities.
§1. When a blind, hearing impaired or physically handicapped person is accompanied by a dog which serves as a guide or leader for such person, neither the blind, hearing impaired or physically handicapped person nor the dog shall be denied the right of entry and use of facilities of any public place of accommodation as defined in Section 5-101 of the "Illinois Human Rights Act" [775 ILCS 5/5-101], if such dog is wearing a harness and such person presents credentials for inspection issued by a school for training guide dogs.
Any violation of this Act is a Class C misdemeanor.
(Source: P.A. 83-93.) [Formerly Ill. Rev. Stat. 38 §65-1.]

HYPODERMIC SYRINGES AND NEEDLES ACT

Sec.

635/0.01. Short title.
§0.01. Short title. This Act may be cited as the Hypodermic Syringes and Needles Act.
(Source: P.A. 86-1324.) [Formerly Ill. Rev. Stat. 38 §22-49.9.]

635/1. Prohibition of possession of instruments adapted for use of cannabis or controlled substances.
§1. No person, not being a physician, dentist, chiropodist or veterinarian licensed under the laws of this State or of the state where he resides, or a registered professional nurse, or a registered embalmer, manufacturer or dealer in embalming supplies, wholesale druggist, manufacturing pharmacist, registered pharmacist, manufacturer of surgical instruments, industrial user, official of any government having possession of the articles hereinafter mentioned by reason of his official duties, nurse or a medical laboratory technician acting under the direction of a physician or dentist, employee of an incorporated hospital acting under the direction of its superintendent or officer in immediate

charge, or a carrier or messenger engaged in the transportation of such articles, or the holder of a permit issued under Section 5 of this Act [720 ILCS 635/5], or a farmer engaged in the use of such instruments on livestock, or a person engaged in chemical, clinical, pharmaceutical or other scientific research, shall have in his possession a hypodermic syringe, hypodermic needle, or any instrument adapted for the use of controlled substances or cannabis by subcutaneous injection.

(Source: P.A. 77-771.) [Formerly Ill. Rev. Stat. 38 §22-50.]

635/2. Exchange or sale of instruments.

§2. No such syringe, needle or instrument shall be delivered or sold to, or exchanged with, any person except a registered pharmacist, physician, dentist, veterinarian, registered embalmer, manufacturer or dealer in embalming supplies, wholesale druggist, manufacturing pharmacist, industrial user, a nurse upon the written order of a physician or dentist, the holder of a permit issued under Section 5 of this Act [720 ILCS 635/5], a registered chiropodist, or an employee of an incorporated hospital upon the written order of its superintendent or officer in immediate charge; provided that the provisions of this Act shall not prohibit the sale, possession or use of hypodermic syringes or hypodermic needles for treatment of livestock or poultry by the owner or keeper thereof or a person engaged in chemical, clinical, pharmaceutical or other scientific research.

(Source: Laws 1955, p. 1408.) [Formerly Ill. Rev. Stat. 38 §22-51.]

635/3. Inspection of records.

§3. A record shall be kept by the person selling such syringe, needle or instrument which shall give the date of the sale, the name and address of the purchaser and a description of the instrument. This record shall at all times be open to inspection by the Department of State Police authorized agents of said Department, and police authorities and police officers of cities, villages and towns.

(Source: P.A. 84-25.) [Formerly Ill. Rev. Stat. 38 §22-52.]

635/4. Violations; penalty.

§4. Whoever violates any provisions of Sections 1, 2, and 3 of this Act [720 ILCS 635/1, 635/2, and 635/3] shall be guilty of a Class A misdemeanor for the first such offense; for a second or any succeeding offense, he shall be guilty of a Class 4 felony.

(Source: P.A. 77-2830.) [Formerly Ill. Rev. Stat. 38 §22-53.]

635/5. Written and oral prescriptions.

§5. A licensed physician may direct a patient under his immediate charge to have in possession any of the instruments specified in Sections 1 and 2 [720 ILCS 635/1 and 635/2] which may be dispensed by a registered pharmacist or assistant registered pharmacist in this state only (1) upon a written prescription of such physician, or (2) upon an oral order of such physician, which order is reduced promptly to writing and filed by the pharmacist, or (3) by refilling any such written or oral prescription if such refilling is authorized by the prescriber either in the original prescription or by oral order which is reduced promptly to writing and filed by the pharmacist in the same manner and under the same conditions as any other prescription issued by a practitioner licensed by law to write prescriptions, or (4) upon a signed statement of the patient, upon proper identification, stating that the prescriptions or instruments specified in Sections 1 and 2 were lost or broken, as the case may be, the name and address of the prescriber, the name and address of the patient and the purpose for which the prescription was ordered; provided, however, that the registered pharmacists or assistant registered pharmacists who deliver or sell any instruments specified in Sections 1 and 2 shall send a copy of such affidavit to the Department of State Police by the 15th of the month following the month in which such instruments were delivered or sold. Such written or oral prescriptions when reduced to writing for instruments specified in Sections 1 and 2 shall contain the date of such prescription, the name and address of the prescriber, the name and address of the patient, the purpose for which the prescription is ordered, the date when dispensed and by whom dispensed.

Provided, however, that a licensed physician or other allied medical practitioner, authorized by the laws of the State of Illinois to prescribe or administer controlled substances or cannabis to humans or animals, may authorize any person or the owner of any animal, to purchase and have in his possession any of the instruments specified in Sections 1 and 2, which may be sold to him without a specific written or oral prescription or order, by any person authorized by the laws of the State of Illinois to sell and dispense controlled substances or cannabis, if such authorization is in the form of a certificate giving the name and address of such licensed physician or other allied medical practitioner, the name, address and signature of the person, or of the owner of the animal, so authorized, the purpose or reason of such authorization, and the date of such certificate and in that event, no other prescription, writing or record shall be required to authorize the possession or sale of such instruments.
(Source: P.A. 84-25.) [Formerly Ill. Rev. Stat. 38 §22-54.]

635/6. Prosecution commenced by information.

§6. Any prosecution under this Act may be commenced by an information as defined in Section 102-12 of the Code of Criminal Procedure of 1963.
(Source: P.A. 77-1849.) [Formerly Ill. Rev. Stat. 38 §22-55.]

IMPROPER SUPERVISION OF CHILDREN ACT

640/0.01. Short title.

§0.01. Short title. This Act may be cited as the Improper Supervision of Children Act.
(Source: P.A. 86-1324.) [Formerly Ill. Rev. Stat. 23 §2368.9.]

640/1. Improper supervision.

§1. Any parent, legal guardian or other person commits improper supervision of a child when he knowingly permits a child in his custody or control under the age of 18 years to associate with known thieves, burglars, felons, narcotic addicts or other persons of ill repute, visit a place of prostitution, commit a lewd act, commit an act tending to break the peace or violate a municipal curfew ordinance.
(Source: Laws 1961, p. 2454.) [Formerly Ill. Rev. Stat. 23 §2369.]

640/2. Penalties.

§2. A person first convicted of improper supervision of a child shall be guilty of a petty offense and shall be fined not to exceed $25. A person so convicted a second time shall be guilty of a petty offense and shall be fined not to exceed $50. A person so convicted a third or subsequent time shall be guilty of a Class B misdemeanor.
(Source: P.A. 77-2354.) [Formerly Ill. Rev. Stat. 23 §2370.]

LEGISLATIVE MISCONDUCT ACT

645/0.01. Short title.

§0.01. Short title. This Act may be cited as the Legislative Misconduct Act.
(Source: P.A. 86-1324.) [Formerly Ill. Rev. Stat. 38 §90-0.1.]

645/1. Acceptance of money.

§1. No member of the General Assembly shall accept or receive, directly or indirectly, any money or other valuable thing, from any corporation, company or person, for any vote or influence he may give or withhold on any bill, resolution or appropriation, or for any other official act.
(Source: Laws 1965, p. 81.) [Formerly Ill. Rev. Stat. 38 §90-1.]

645/2. Sentence.

§2. Sentence. Violation of this Act is a Class 3 felony.
(Source: P.A. 77-2647.) [Formerly Ill. Rev. Stat. 38 §90-2.]

NITROGLYCERIN TRANSPORTATION ACT

650/0.01. Short title.

§0.01. Short title. This Act may be cited as the Nitroglycerin Transportation Act.
(Source: P.A. 86-1324.) [Formerly Ill. Rev. Stat. 127½ §50.]

650/1. Transportation of liquid nitroglycerin.

§1. No person, personally or through an agent, shall transport nitroglycerin in a liquid state on any highway; except this Act shall not prohibit the transportation of desensitized liquid nitroglycerin on any highway.

Any person who violates this Act shall be guilty of a Class B misdemeanor.
(Source: P.A. 77-2273.) [Formerly Ill. Rev. Stat. 127½ §51.]

OUTDOOR LIGHTING INSTALLATION ACT

655/0.01. Short title.

§0.01. Short title. This Act may be cited as the Outdoor Lighting Installation Act.
(Source: P.A. 86-1324.) [Formerly Ill. Rev. Stat. 67½ §120.]

655/1. Lights required at front entrance-way of multiple dwelling.

§1. The owner of every multiple dwelling shall install and maintain a light or lights at or near the outside of the front entrance-way of the building which shall in the aggregate provide not less than 50 watts incandescent illumination for a building with a frontage up to 22 feet and 100 watts incandescent illumination for a building with a frontage in excess of 22 feet, or equivalent illumination and shall be kept burning from sunset every day to sunrise on the day following. In the case of a multiple dwelling with a frontage in excess of 22

feet, the front entrance doors of which have a combined width in excess of 5 feet, there shall be at least 2 lights, one at each side of the entrance way, with an aggregate illumination of 150 watts or equivalent illumination. The owners shall determine the actual location, design and nature of the installation of such light or lights to meet practical, aesthetic and other considerations, so long as the minimum level of illumination is maintained.
(Source: Laws 1967, p. 2071.) [Formerly Ill. Rev. Stat. 67½ §121.]

655/2. Multiple dwelling, defined.

§2. As used in this Act "multiple dwelling" means any dwelling that is either rented, leased, let or hired out, to be occupied, or is occupied as the residence or home of 3 or more families living independently of each other. A "multiple dwelling" shall not be deemed to include a hospital, convent, monastery, asylum or public institution, or a fireproof building used wholly for commercial purposes except for not more than one janitor's apartment and not more than one penthouse occupied by not more than 2 families. However, residential quarters for members or personnel of any hospital staff which are not located in any building primarily used for hospital use, shall be deemed to be a "multiple dwelling".
(Source: Laws 1967, p. 2071.) [Formerly Ill. Rev. Stat. 67½ §122.]

655/3. Violations.

§3. Any violation of this Act by the owner is a Class C misdemeanor for each day and every day such violation occurs.
(Source: P.A. 77-2527.) [Formerly Ill. Rev. Stat. 67½ §123.]

PARTY LINE EMERGENCY ACT

Sec.

660/0.01. Short title.

§0.01. Short title. This Act may be cited as the Party Line Emergency Act.
(Source: P.A. 86-1324.) [Formerly Ill. Rev. Stat. 134 §16.5h.]

660/1. Definitions.

§1. "Party Line" means a subscribers' line telephone circuit, consisting of 2 or more main telephone stations connected therewith, each station with a distinctive ring or telephone number.

"Emergency" means a situation in which property or human life are in jeopardy and the prompt summoning of aid is essential.
(Source: Laws 1959, p. 682.) [Formerly Ill. Rev. Stat. 134 §16.6.]

660/2. Refusing to yield or surrender party line in emergency.

§2. Any person who wilfully refuses to yield or surrender the use of a party line to another person for the purpose of permitting such other person to report a fire or summon police, medical or other aid in case of emergency, is guilty of a Class B misdemeanor.
(Source: P.A. 77-2621.) [Formerly Ill. Rev. Stat. 134 §16.7.]

660/3. Requesting use of party line under pretext of emergency.

§3. Any person who asks for or requests the use of a party line on the pretext that an emergency exists, knowing that no emergency in fact exists, is guilty of a Class C misdemeanor.
(Source: P.A. 77-2621.) [Formerly Ill. Rev. Stat. 134 §16.8.]

660/4. Explanation of this law to be included in telephone directories.

§4. After the 90th day following the effective date of this act, every telephone directory thereafter published for distribution to the members of the general public shall contain a notice which explains this law, such notice to be printed in type which is no smaller than any other type on the same page and to be preceded by the word "WARNING". The provisions of this section shall not apply to those directories distributed solely for business advertising purposes, commonly known as classified directories.

(Source: Laws 1959, p. 682.) [Formerly Ill. Rev. Stat. 134 §16.9.]

PEEPHOLE INSTALLATION ACT

Sec.

665/0.01. Short title.

§0.01. Short title. This Act may be cited as the Peephole Installation Act.

(Source: P.A. 86-1324.) [Formerly Ill. Rev. Stat. 67½ §110.]

665/1. Peepholes required in entrance doors of multiple dwellings.

§1. The owner of every multiple dwelling on which construction is commenced after the effective date of this Act shall provide and maintain peepholes in the entrance door of each housing unit within such multiple dwelling. The peephole must be located so as to enable a person in such housing unit to view from the inside of the entrance door any person immediately outside the entrance door.

(Source: Laws 1967, p. 1803.) [Formerly Ill. Rev. Stat. 67½ §111.]

665/2. Multiple dwelling, defined; applicability of act.

§2. As used in this Act "multiple dwelling" means any dwelling containing 5 or more independent housing units which are rented, leased, let or hired out to the tenant for use as a residence.

This Act shall not apply to hotels, apartment hotels, motels, dormitories, hospitals, convents or public institutions.

(Source: Laws 1967, p. 1803.) [Formerly Ill. Rev. Stat. 67½ §112.]

665/3. Violations; penalty.

§3. Any tenant affected by a violation of this Act by the owner may compel the owner to install such peepholes by bringing an appropriate action in the circuit court. Any violation of this Act by the owner is a petty offense and shall be punished by a fine of not less than $25 nor more than $100 for each housing unit constructed without a peephole in the entrance door. Each day that a violation continues is a separate offense.

(Source: P.A. 79-1362.) [Formerly Ill. Rev. Stat. 67½ §113.]

SALE OF IMMORAL PUBLICATIONS TO CHILDREN ACT

Sec.

670/0.01. Short title.

§0.01. Short title. This Act may be cited as the Sale of Immoral Publications to Children Act.

(Source: P.A. 86-1324.) [Formerly Ill. Rev. Stat. 23 §2362.9.]

670/1. Unlawful to sell certain publications to minors.

§1. It shall be unlawful for any person to sell, lend, give away or show, or have in his possession with intent to sell or give away, or to show or advertise, or otherwise offer for loan, gift or distribution to any minor child any book, pamphlet, magazine, newspaper, story paper or other printed paper devoted to the publication, or principally made up of criminal news, police reports, or accounts of criminal deeds, or pictures and stories of deeds of bloodshed, lust or crime.

(Source: Laws 1889, p. 114.) [Formerly Ill. Rev. Stat. 23 §2363.]

670/2. Unlawful exhibition.

§2. It shall be unlawful to exhibit upon any street or highway, or in any place within the view, or which may be within the view of any minor child, any book, magazine, newspaper, pamphlet, story paper or other paper or publication coming within the description of matters mentioned in the first section of this act, or any of them.

(Source: Laws 1889, p. 114.) [Formerly Ill. Rev. Stat. 23 §2364.]

670/3. Employing minor child.

§3. It shall be unlawful to hire, use or employ any minor child to sell or give away, or in any manner to distribute, or who, having the care, custody or control of any minor child, to permit such child to sell, give away, or in any manner to distribute any book, magazine, pamphlet, newspaper, story paper or publication coming within the description of matters mentioned in the first section of this act, and any person violating any of the provisions of this act shall be guilty of a Class B misdemeanor.

(Source: P.A. 77-2351.) [Formerly Ill. Rev. Stat. 23 §2365.]

SALE OF TOBACCO TO MINORS ACT

675/0.01. Short title.

§0.01. Short title. This Act may be cited as the Sale of Tobacco to Minors Act.

(Source: P.A. 86-1324.) [Formerly Ill. Rev. Stat. 23 §2356.9.]

675/1. Sale of tobacco to any minor prohibited.

§1. No minor under 18 years of age shall buy any cigar, cigarette, smokeless tobacco or tobacco in any of its forms. No person shall sell, buy for, distribute samples of or furnish any cigar, cigarette, smokeless tobacco or tobacco in any of its forms, to any minor under 18 years of age.

For the purpose of this Section, "smokeless tobacco" means any tobacco products that are suitable for dipping or chewing.

(Source: P.A. 85-305; 86-1181.) [Formerly Ill. Rev. Stat. 23 §2357.]

675/2. Penalty.

§2. Any person who violates any provision of this Act is guilty of a petty offense and for the first offense shall be fined not to exceed $100, and for a second or any subsequent offense shall be guilty of a petty offense and fined not to exceed $250.

(Source: P.A. 85-305.) [Formerly Ill. Rev. Stat. 23 §2358.]

SMOKELESS TOBACCO LIMITATION ACT

680/1. Short title.

§1. This Act shall be known and may be cited as the "Smokeless Tobacco Limitation Act".
(Source: P.A. 85-465.) [Formerly Ill. Rev. Stat. 23 §2358-21.]

680/2. Definitions.

§2. For purposes of this Act, the term "smokeless tobacco" means any finely cut, ground, powdered, or leaf tobacco that is intended to be placed in the oral cavity.
(Source: P.A. 85-465.) [Formerly Ill. Rev. Stat. 23 §2358-22.]

680/3. Selling smokeless tobacco product to person under 18 prohibited.

§3. No person shall sell any smokeless tobacco product to any person under the age of 18. Any person who violates this Section shall be guilty of a business offense punishable by a fine of not more than $50 for each violation.
(Source: P.A. 85-465.) [Formerly Ill. Rev. Stat. 23 §2358-23.]

680/4. Distributing smokeless tobacco product to person under 18 prohibited—Penalties.

§4. No person shall distribute or cause to be distributed to any person under the age of 18, without charge or at a nominal cost, any smokeless tobacco product. Any person who violates this Section shall be guilty of a business offense punishable for a first offense by a fine of not less than $100 nor more than $500 and for a second or subsequent offense by a fine of not less than $600 nor more than $3000.
(Source: P.A. 85-465.) [Formerly Ill. Rev. Stat. 23 §2358-24.]

TOBACCO ACCESSORIES AND SMOKING HERBS CONTROL ACT

685/1. Short title.

§1. This Act shall be known and may be cited as the "Tobacco Accessories and Smoking Herbs Control Act".
(Source: P.A. 82-487.) [Formerly Ill. Rev. Stat. 23 §2358-1.]

685/2. Purpose.

§2. Purpose. The sale and possession of marijuana, hashish, cocaine, opium and their derivatives, is not only prohibited by Illinois Law, but the use of these substances has been deemed injurious to the health of the user.

It has further been determined by the Surgeon General of the United States that the use of tobacco is hazardous to human health.

The ready availability of smoking herbs to minors could lead to the use of tobacco and illegal drugs.

It is in the best interests of the citizens of the State of Illinois to seek to prohibit the spread of illegal drugs, tobacco or smoking materials to minors. The prohibition of the sale of tobacco and snuff accessories and smoking herbs to minors would help to curb the usage of illegal drugs and tobacco products, among our youth.
(Source: P.A. 82-487.) [Formerly Ill. Rev. Stat. 23 §2358-2.]

685/3. Definitions.

§3. Definitions. The following definitions shall apply to this Act: (a) "Tobacco accessories" shall mean cigarette papers, pipes, holders of smoking materials of all types, cigarette rolling machines, and other items, designed primarily for the smoking or ingestion of tobacco products or of substances made illegal under any statute or of substances whose sale, gift, barter, or exchange is made unlawful under this Act.

(b) "Smoking herbs" shall mean all substances of plant origin and their derivatives, including but not limited to broom, calea, California poppy, damiana, hops, ginseng, lobelia, jimson weed and other members of the Datura genus, passion flower and wild lettuce, which are processed or sold primarily for use as smoking materials.
(Source: P.A. 82-487.) [Formerly Ill. Rev. Stat. 23 §2358-3.]

685/4. Offenses.

§4. Offenses. (a) Sale to minors. No person shall knowingly sell, barter, exchange, deliver or give away or cause or permit or procure to be sold, bartered, exchanged, delivered, or given away tobacco accessories or smoking herbs to any person under 18 years of age.

(b) Sale of cigarette paper. No person shall knowingly offer, sell, barter, exchange, deliver or give away cigarette paper or cause, permit, or procure cigarette paper to be sold, offered, bartered, exchanged, delivered, or given away except from premises or an establishment where other tobacco products are sold. For purposes of this Section, "tobacco products" means cigarettes, cigars, smokeless tobacco, or tobacco in any of its forms.

(c) Sale of cigarette paper from vending machines. No person shall knowingly offer, sell, barter, exchange, deliver or give away cigarette paper or cause, permit, or procure cigarette paper to be sold, offered, bartered, exchanged, delivered, or given away by use of a vending or coin-operated machine or device. For purposes of this Section, "cigarette paper" shall not include any paper that is incorporated into a product to which a tax stamp must be affixed under the Cigarette Tax Act [35 ILCS 130/1 et seq.] or the Cigarette Use Tax Act [35 ILCS 135/1 et seq.].

(d) Use of identification cards. No person in the furtherance or facilitation of obtaining smoking accessories and smoking herbs shall display or use a false or forged identification card or transfer, alter, or deface an identification card.

(e) Warning to minors. Any person, firm, partnership, company or corporation operating a place of business where tobacco accessories and smoking herbs are sold or offered for sale shall post in a conspicuous place upon the premises a sign upon which there shall be imprinted the following statement, "SALE OF TOBACCO ACCESSORIES AND SMOKING HERBS TO PERSONS UNDER EIGHTEEN YEARS OF AGE OR THE MISREPRESENTATION OF AGE TO PROCURE SUCH A SALE IS PROHIBITED BY LAW". The sign shall be printed on a white card in red letters at least one-half inch in height.
(Source: P.A. 87-153.) [Formerly Ill. Rev. Stat. 23 §2358-4.]

685/5. Penalty.

§5. Penalty. Any person who shall knowingly violate, or shall knowingly cause the violation of any provision of this Act shall be guilty of a Class C misdemeanor.
(Source: P.A. 82-487.) [Formerly Ill. Rev. Stat. 23 §2358-5.]

USE OF INTOXICATING COMPOUNDS ACT

690/0.01. Short title.

§0.01. Short title. This Act may be cited as the Use of Intoxicating Compounds Act.
(Source: P.A. 86-1324.) [Formerly Ill. Rev. Stat. 38 §81.]

690/1. Use of intoxicating compounds.

§1. No person shall breathe, inhale or drink any compound, liquid or chemical containing toluol, hexane, trichloroethylene, acetone, toluene, ethyl acetate, methyl ethyl ketone, trichloroathane, isopropanol, methyl isobutyl ketone, methyl cellosolve acetate, cyclohexanone, or any other substance for the purpose of inducing a condition of intoxication, stupefaction, depression, giddiness, paralysis or irrational behavior, or in any manner changing, distorting or disturbing the auditory, visual or mental processes. For the purposes of this Act, any such condition so induced shall be deemed to be an intoxicated condition.
(Source: Laws 1965, p. 2718.) [Formerly Ill. Rev. Stat. 38 §81-1.]

690/2. Sale of intoxicating compounds.

§2. No person shall knowingly sell or offer for sale, deliver or give to any person under 17 years of age, unless upon written order of such person's parent or guardian, any compound liquid or chemical containing toluol, hexane, trichloroethylene, acetone, toluene, ethyl acetate, methyl ethyl ketone, trichloroathane, isopropanol, methyl isobutyl ketone, methyl cellosolve acetate, cyclohexanone, or any other substance which will induce an intoxicated condition, as defined herein, when the seller, offeror or deliverer knows or has reason to know that such compound is intended for use to induce such condition.
(Source: Laws 1965, p. 2718.) [Formerly Ill. Rev. Stat. 38 §81-2.]

690/3. Prescription of practitioner.

§3. This Act shall not apply to any person who commits any act described herein pursuant to the direction or prescription of a practitioner authorized to so direct or prescribe. For purposes of this Section, practitioner shall mean any person authorized by law to practice medicine in all its branches in this State, to practice dentistry in this State, to practice veterinary medicine in this State, or to practice chiropody in this State.
(Source: P.A. 83-333.) [Formerly Ill. Rev. Stat. 38 §81-3.]

690/4. Sentence.

§4. Sentence. Violation of this Act is a Class C misdemeanor.
(Source: P.A. 77-2643.) [Formerly Ill. Rev. Stat. 38 §81-4.]

This page intentionally left blank.

CHAPTER 725
CRIMINAL PROCEDURE

CODE OF CRIMINAL PROCEDURE OF 1963

TITLE I. GENERAL PROVISIONS

ARTICLE 100. TITLE AND SCOPE

5/100-1. Short title.

§100-1. Short title. This Act shall be known and may be cited as the "Code of Criminal Procedure of 1963".
(Source: Laws 1963, p. 2836.) [Formerly Ill. Rev. Stat. 38 §100-1.]

5/100-2. Scope.

§100-2. Scope. These provisions shall govern the procedure in the courts of Illinois in all criminal proceedings except where provision for a different procedure is specifically provided by law.
(Source: Laws 1963, p. 2836.) [Formerly Ill. Rev. Stat. 38 §100-2.]

ARTICLE 101. GENERAL PURPOSES

5/101-1. General purposes.

§101-1. General purposes. The provisions of this Code shall be construed in accordance with the general purposes hereof, to:

(a) Secure simplicity in procedure;

(b) Ensure fairness of administration including the elimination of unjustifiable delay;

(c) Ensure the effective apprehension and trial of persons accused of crime;

(d) Provide for the just determination of every criminal proceeding by a fair and impartial trial and an adequate review; and

(e) Preserve the public welfare and secure the fundamental human rights of individuals.
(Source: Laws 1963, p. 2836.) [Formerly Ill. Rev. Stat. 38 §101-1.]

ARTICLE 102. GENERAL DEFINITIONS

5/102-1. Meanings of words and phrases.

§102-1. Meanings of words and phrases. For the purposes of this Code, the words and phrases described in this Article have the meanings designated in this Article, except when a particular context clearly requires a different meaning.
(Source: Laws 1963, p. 2836.) [Formerly Ill. Rev. Stat. 38 §102-1.]

5/102-2. Reference to criminal code for words and phrases not described.

§102-2. Reference to criminal code for words and phrases not described. A word or phrase not described in this Code but which is described in Article 2 of the "Criminal Code of 1961", approved July 28, 1961, as heretofore and hereafter amended [720 ILCS 5/2-.5 et seq], shall have the meaning therein described, except when a particular context in this Code clearly requires a different meaning.
(Source: Laws 1963, p. 2836.) [Formerly Ill. Rev. Stat. 38 §102-2.]

5/102-3. Singular term includes plural—Gender.

§102-3. Singular term includes plural—Gender. A singular term shall include the plural and the masculine gender shall include the feminine except when a particular context clearly requires a different meaning.
(Source: Laws 1963, p. 2836.) [Formerly Ill. Rev. Stat. 38 §102-3.]

5/102-4. "Arraignment".

§102-4. "Arraignment". "Arraignment" means the formal act of calling the defendant into open court, informing him of the offense with which he is charged, and asking him whether he is guilty or not guilty.
(Source: Laws 1963, p. 2836.) [Formerly Ill. Rev. Stat. 38 §102-4.]

5/102-5. "Arrest".

§102-5. "Arrest". "Arrest" means the taking of a person into custody.
(Source: Laws 1963, p. 2836.) [Formerly Ill. Rev. Stat. 38 §102-5.]

5/102-6. "Bail".

§102-6. "Bail". "Bail" means the amount of money set by the court which is required to be obligated and secured as provided by law for the release of a person in custody in order that he will appear before the court in which his appearance may be required and that he will comply with such conditions as set forth in the bail bond.
(Source: Laws 1963, p. 2836.) [Formerly Ill. Rev. Stat. 38 §102-6.]

5/102-7. "Bail bond".

§102-7. "Bail bond". "Bail bond" means an undertaking secured by bail entered into by a person in custody by which he binds himself to comply with such conditions as are set forth therein.
(Source: Laws 1963, p. 2836.) [Formerly Ill. Rev. Stat. 38 §102-7.]

5/102-8. "Charge".

§102-8. "Charge". "Charge" means a written statement presented to a court accusing a person of the commission of an offense and includes complaint, information and indictment.
(Source: Laws 1963, p. 2836.) [Formerly Ill. Rev. Stat. 38 §102-8.]

5/102-9. "Complaint".

§102-9. "Complaint". "Complaint" means a verified written statement other than an information or an indictment, presented to a court, which charges the commission of an offense.
(Source: Laws 1963, p. 2836.) [Formerly Ill. Rev. Stat. 38 §102-9.]

5/102-10. "Court".

§102-10. "Court". "Court" means a place where justice is judicially administered and includes a judge thereof.
(Source: P.A. 77-1286.) [Formerly Ill. Rev. Stat. 38 §102-10.]

5/102-11. "Indictment".

§102-11. "Indictment". "Indictment" means a written statement, presented by the Grand Jury to a court, which charges the commission of an offense.
(Source: Laws 1963, p. 2836.) [Formerly Ill. Rev. Stat. 38 §102-11.]

5/102-12. "Information".

§102-12. "Information". "Information" means a verified written statement signed by a State's Attorney, and presented to a court, which charges the commission of an offense.
(Source: Laws 1963, p. 2836.) [Formerly Ill. Rev. Stat. 38 §102-12.]

5/102-13. "Judge".

§102-13. "Judge". "Judge" means a person who is invested by law with the power to perform judicial functions and includes a court when a particular context so requires.
(Source: P.A. 77-1286.) [Formerly Ill. Rev. Stat. 38 §102-13.]

5/102-14. "Judgment".

§102-14. "Judgment". "Judgment" means an adjudication by the court that the defendant is guilty or not guilty and if the adjudication is that the defendant is guilty it includes the sentence pronounced by the court.
(Source: Laws 1963, p. 2836.) [Formerly Ill. Rev. Stat. 38 §102-14.]

5/102-15. "Offense".

§102-15. "Offense". "Offense" means a violation of any penal statute of this State.
(Source: P.A. 76-1796.) [Formerly Ill. Rev. Stat. 38 §102-15.]

5/102-16. "Parole".

§102-16. "Parole". "Parole" means the conditional and revocable release of a committed person under the supervision of a paroling authority.
(Source: P.A. 77-2476.) [Formerly Ill. Rev. Stat. 38 §102-16.]

5/102-17. "Preliminary examination".

§102-17. "Preliminary examination". "Preliminary examination" means a hearing before a judge to determine if there is probable cause to believe that the person accused has committed an offense.
(Source: Laws 1963, p. 2836.) [Formerly Ill. Rev. Stat. 38 §102-17.]

5/102-18. "Probation".

§102-18. "Probation". "Probation" means a sentence or adjudication of conditional and revocable release under the supervision of a probation officer.
(Source: P.A. 77-2476.) [Formerly Ill. Rev. Stat. 38 §102-18.]

5/102-19. "Recognizance".

§102-19. "Recognizance". "Recognizance" means an undertaking without security entered into by a person by which he binds himself to comply with such conditions as are set forth therein and which may provide for the forfeiture of a sum set by the court on failure to comply with the conditions thereof.
(Source: Laws 1963, p. 2836.) [Formerly Ill. Rev. Stat. 38 §102-19.]

5/102-20. "Sentence".

§102-20. "Sentence". "Sentence" is the disposition imposed on the defendant by the court.
(Source: P.A. 77-2476.) [Formerly Ill. Rev. Stat. 38 §102-20.]

5/102-21. Clinical psychologist; court-appointed examiner.

§102-21. Clinical psychologist; court-appointed examiner. (a) "Clinical psychologist" means a psychologist licensed under the Clinical Psychologist Licensing Act [255 ILCS 15/1 et seq.].

(b) "Court-appointed examiner" means a clinical social worker as defined in Section 9 of the Clinical Social Work and Social Work Practice Act [225 ILCS 20/1 et seq.].

(Source: P.A. 87-530.) [Formerly Ill. Rev. Stat. 38 §102-21.]

ARTICLE 103. RIGHTS OF ACCUSED

Sec.

5/103-1. Rights on arrest.

§103-1. Rights on arrest. (a) After an arrest on a warrant the person making the arrest shall inform the person arrested that a warrant has been issued for his arrest and the nature of the offense specified in the warrant.

(b) After an arrest without a warrant the person making the arrest shall inform the person arrested of the nature of the offense on which the arrest is based.

(c) No person arrested for a traffic, regulatory or misdemeanor offense, except in cases involving weapons or a controlled substance, shall be strip searched unless there is reasonable belief that the individual is concealing a weapon or controlled substance.

(d) "Strip search" means having an arrested person remove or arrange some or all of his or her clothing so as to permit a visual inspection of the genitals, buttocks, anus, female breasts or undergarments of such person.

(e) All strip searches conducted under this Section shall be performed by persons of the same sex as the arrested person and on premises where the search cannot be observed by persons not physically conducting the search.

(f) Every peace officer or employee of a police department conducting a strip search shall:

(1) Obtain the written permission of the police commander or an agent thereof designated for the purposes of authorizing a strip search in accordance with this Section.

(2) Prepare a report of the strip search. The report shall include the written authorization required by paragraph (1) of this subsection (f), the name of the person subjected to the search, the names of the persons conducting the search, and the time, date and place of the search. A copy of the report shall be provided to the person subject to the search.

(g) No search of any body cavity other than the mouth shall be conducted without a duly executed search warrant; any warrant authorizing a body cavity search shall specify that the search must be performed under sanitary conditions and conducted either by or under the supervision of a physician licensed to practice medicine in all of its branches in this State.

(h) Any peace officer or employee who knowingly or intentionally fails to comply with any provision of this Section is guilty of official misconduct as provided in Section 103-8; provided however, that nothing contained in this

Section shall preclude prosecution of a peace officer or employee under another section of this Code.

(i) Nothing in this Section shall be construed as limiting any statutory or common law rights of any person for purposes of any civil action or injunctive relief.

(j) The provisions of subsections (c) through (h) of this Section shall not apply when the person is taken into custody by or remanded to the sheriff or correctional institution pursuant to a court order.
(Source: P.A. 81-1509.) [Formerly Ill. Rev. Stat. 38 §103-1.]

5/103-2. Treatment while in custody.

§103-2. Treatment while in custody. (a) On being taken into custody every person shall have the right to remain silent.

(b) No unlawful means of any kind shall be used to obtain a statement, admission or confession from any person in custody.

(c) Persons in custody shall be treated humanely and provided with proper food, shelter and, if required, medical treatment.
(Source: Laws 1963, p. 2836.) [Formerly Ill. Rev. Stat. 38 §103-2.]

5/103-3. Right to communicate with attorney and family; transfers.

§103-3. Right to communicate with attorney and family; transfers. (a) Persons who are arrested shall have the right to communicate with an attorney of their choice and a member of their family by making a reasonable number of telephone calls or in any other reasonable manner. Such communication shall be permitted within a reasonable time after arrival at the first place of custody.

(b) In the event the accused is transferred to a new place of custody his right to communicate with an attorney and a member of his family is renewed.
(Source: Laws 1963, p. 2836.) [Formerly Ill. Rev. Stat. 38 §103-3.]

5/103-4. Right to consult with attorney.

§103-4. Right to consult with attorney. Any person committed, imprisoned or restrained of his liberty for any cause whatever and whether or not such person is charged with an offense shall, except in cases of imminent danger of escape, be allowed to consult with any licensed attorney at law of this State whom such person may desire to see or consult, alone and in private at the place of custody, as many times and for such period each time as is reasonable. When any such person is about to be moved beyond the limits of this State under any pretense whatever the person to be moved shall be entitled to a reasonable delay for the purpose of obtaining counsel and of availing himself of the laws of this State for the security of personal liberty.
(Source: Laws 1963, p. 2836.) [Formerly Ill. Rev. Stat. 38 §103-4.]

5/103-5. Speedy trial.

§103-5. Speedy trial. (a) Every person in custody in this State for an alleged offense shall be tried by the court having jurisdiction within 120 days from the date he was taken into custody unless delay is occasioned by the defendant, by an examination for fitness ordered pursuant to Section 104-13 of this Act, by a fitness hearing, by an adjudication of unfitness to stand trial, by a continuance allowed pursuant to Section 114-4 of this Act after a court's determination of the defendant's physical incapacity for trial, or by an interlocutory appeal.

(b) Every person on bail or recognizance shall be tried by the court having jurisdiction within 160 days from the date defendant demands trial unless delay is occasioned by the defendant, by an examination for fitness ordered pursuant to Section 104-13 of this Act, by a fitness hearing, by an adjudication of unfitness to stand trial, by a continuance allowed pursuant to Section 114-4 of this Act after a court's determination of the defendant's physical incapacity for trial, or by an interlocutory appeal.

For purposes of computing the 160 day period under this subsection, every person who was in custody for an alleged offense and demanded trial and is subsequently released on bail or recognizance and demands trial, shall be given credit for time spent in custody following the making of the demand while in custody. Any demand for trial made under this provision shall be in writing; and in the case of a defendant not in custody, the demand for trial shall include the date of any prior demand made under this provision while the defendant was in custody.

(c) If the court determines that the State has exercised without success due diligence to obtain evidence material to the case and that there are reasonable grounds to believe that such evidence may be obtained at a later day the court may continue the cause on application of the State for not more than an additional 60 days. If the court determines that the State has exercised without success due diligence to obtain results of DNA testing that is material to the case and that there are reasonable grounds to believe that such results may be obtained at a later day, the court may continue the cause on application of the State for not more than an additional 120 days.

(d) Every person not tried in accordance with subsections (a), (b) and (c) of this Section shall be discharged from custody or released from the obligations of his bail or recognizance.

(e) If a person is simultaneously in custody upon more than one charge pending against him in the same county, or simultaneously demands trial upon more than one charge pending against him in the same county, he shall be tried, or adjudged guilty after waiver of trial, upon at least one such charge before expiration relative to any of such pending charges of the period prescribed by subsections (a) and (b) of this Section. Such person shall be tried upon all of the remaining charges thus pending within 160 days from the date on which judgment relative to the first charge thus prosecuted is rendered pursuant to the Unified Code of Corrections [730 ILCS 5/1-1-1 et seq.] or, if such trial upon such first charge is terminated without judgment and there is no subsequent trial of, or adjudication of guilt after waiver of trial of, such first charge within a reasonable time, the person shall be tried upon all of the remaining charges thus pending within 160 days from the date on which such trial is terminated; if either such period of 160 days expires without the commencement of trial of, or adjudication of guilt after waiver of trial of, any of such remaining charges thus pending, such charge or charges shall be dismissed and barred for want of prosecution unless delay is occasioned by the defendant, by an examination for fitness ordered pursuant to Section 104-13 of this Act, by a fitness hearing, by an adjudication of unfitness for trial, by a continuance allowed pursuant to Section 114-4 of this Act after a court's determination of the defendant's physical incapacity for trial, or by an interlocutory appeal; provided, however, that if the court determines that the State has exercised without success due diligence to obtain evidence material to the case and that there are reasonable grounds to believe that such evidence may be obtained at a later day the court may continue the cause on application of the State for not more than an additional 60 days.

(f) Delay occasioned by the defendant shall temporarily suspend for the time of the delay the period within which a person shall be tried as prescribed by subsections (a), (b), or (e) of this Section and on the day of expiration of the delay the said period shall continue at the point at which it was suspended. Where such delay occurs within 21 days of the end of the period within which a person shall be tried as prescribed by subsections (a), (b), or (e) of this Section, the court may continue the cause on application of the State for not more than an additional 21 days beyond the period prescribed by subsections (a), (b), or (e).

This subsection (f) shall become effective on, and apply to persons charged with alleged offenses committed on or after, March 1, 1977.
(Source: P.A. 86-1210; 87-281.) [Formerly Ill. Rev. Stat. 38 §103-5.]

5/103-6. Waiver of jury trial.

§103-6. Waiver of jury trial. Every person accused of an offense shall have the right to a trial by jury unless (i) understandingly waived by defendant in open court or (ii) the offense is an ordinance violation punishable by fine only and the defendant either fails to file a demand for a trial by jury at the time of entering his or her plea of not guilty or fails to pay to the clerk of the circuit court at the time of entering his or her plea of not guilty any jury fee required to be paid to the clerk.
(Source: P.A. 86-1386.) [Formerly Ill. Rev. Stat. 38 §103-6.]

5/103-7. Posting notice of rights.

§103-7. Posting notice of rights. Every sheriff, chief of police or other person who is in charge of any jail, police station or other building where persons under arrest are held in custody pending investigation, bail or other criminal proceedings, shall post in every room, other than cells, of such buildings where persons are held in custody, in conspicuous places where it may be seen and read by persons in custody and others, a poster, printed in large type, containing a verbatim copy in the English language of the provisions of Sections 103-2, 103-3, 103-4, 109-1, 110-2, 110-4, and sub-parts (a) and (b) of Sections 110-7 and 113-3 of this Code. Each person who is in charge of any courthouse or other building in which any trial of an offense is conducted shall post in each room primarily used for such trials and in each room in which defendants are confined or wait, pending trial, in conspicuous places where it may be seen and read by persons in custody and others, a poster, printed in large type, containing a verbatim copy in the English language of the provisions of Sections 103-6, 113-1, 113-4 and 115-1 and of subparts (a) and (b) of Section 113-3 of this Code.
(Source: Laws 1965, p. 2622.) [Formerly Ill. Rev. Stat. 38 §103-7.]

5/103-8. Mandatory duty of officers.

§103-8. Mandatory duty of officers. Any peace officer who intentionally prevents the exercise by an accused of any right conferred by this Article or who intentionally fails to perform any act required of him by this Article shall be guilty of official misconduct and may be punished in accordance with Section 33-3 of the "Criminal Code of 1961" approved July 28, 1961, as heretofore and hereafter amended [720 ILCS 5/33-3].
(Source: Laws 1963, p. 2836.) [Formerly Ill. Rev. Stat. 38 §103-8.]

5/103-9. Bail bondsmen.

§103-9. Bail bondsmen. No bail bondsman from any state may seize or transport unwillingly any person found in this State who is allegedly in violation of a bail bond posted in some other state. The return of any such person to another state may be accomplished only as provided by the laws of this State. Any bail bondsman who violates this Section is fully subject to the criminal and civil penalties provided by the laws of this State for his actions.
(Source: P.A. 84-694.) [Formerly Ill. Rev. Stat. 38 §103-9.]

ARTICLE 104. FITNESS FOR TRIAL, TO PLEAD OR TO BE SENTENCED

Sec.

5/104-10. Presumption of fitness; fitness standard.

§104-10. Presumption of Fitness; Fitness Standard. A defendant is presumed to be fit to stand trial or to plead, and be sentenced. A defendant is unfit if, because of his mental or physical condition, he is unable to understand the nature and purpose of the proceedings against him or to assist in his defense.
(Source: P.A. 81-1217.) [Formerly Ill. Rev. Stat. 38 §104-10.]

5/104-11. Raising issue; burden; fitness motions.

§104-11. Raising Issue; Burden; Fitness Motions. (a) The issue of the defendant's fitness for trial, to plead, or to be sentenced may be raised by the defense, the State or the Court at any appropriate time before a plea is entered or before, during, or after trial. When a bonafide doubt of the defendant's fitness is raised, the court shall order a determination of the issue before proceeding further.

(b) Upon request of the defendant that a qualified expert be appointed to examine him or her to determine prior to trial if a bonafide doubt as to his or her fitness to stand trial may be raised, the court, in its discretion, may order an appropriate examination. However, no order entered pursuant to this subsection shall prevent further proceedings in the case. An expert so appointed shall examine the defendant and make a report as provided in Section 104-15. Upon the filing with the court of a verified statement of services rendered, the court shall enter an order on the county board to pay such expert a reasonable fee stated in the order.

(c) When a bonafide doubt of the defendant's fitness has been raised, the burden of proving that the defendant is fit by a preponderance of the evidence and the burden of going forward with the evidence are on the State. However, the court may call its own witnesses and conduct its own inquiry.

(d) Following a finding of unfitness, the court may hear and rule on any pretrial motion or motions if the defendant's presence is not essential to a fair determination of the issues. A motion may be reheard upon a showing that evidence is available which was not available, due to the defendant's unfitness, when the motion was first decided.
(Source: P.A. 81-1217.) [Formerly Ill. Rev. Stat. 38 §104-11.]

5/104-12. Right to jury.

§104-12. Right to Jury. The issue of the defendant's fitness may be determined in the first instance by the court or by a jury. The defense or the State may demand a jury or the court on its own motion may order a jury. However, when the issue is raised after trial has begun or after conviction but before

sentencing, or when the issue is to be redetermined under Section 104-20 or 104-27, the issue shall be determined by the court.
(Source: P.A. 81-1217.) [Formerly Ill. Rev. Stat. 38 §104-12.]

5/104-13. Fitness examination.

§104-13. Fitness Examination. (a) When the issue of fitness involves the defendant's mental condition, the court shall order an examination of the defendant by one or more licensed physicians, clinical psychologists, or psychiatrists chosen by the court. No physician, clinical psychologist or psychiatrist employed by the Department of Mental Health and Developmental Disabilities shall be ordered to perform, in his official capacity, an examination under this Section.

(b) If the issue of fitness involves the defendant's physical condition, the court shall appoint one or more physicians and in addition, such other experts as it may deem appropriate to examine the defendant and to report to the court regarding the defendant's condition.

(c) An examination ordered under this Section shall be given at the place designated by the person who will conduct the examination, except that if the defendant is being held in custody, the examination shall take place at such location as the court directs. No examinations under this Section shall be ordered to take place at facilities operated by the Department of Mental Health and Developmental Disabilities. If the defendant fails to keep appointments without reasonable cause or if the person conducting the examination reports to the court that diagnosis requires hospitalization or extended observation, the court may order the defendant admitted to an appropriate facility for an examination, other than a screening examination, for not more than 7 days. The court may, upon a showing of good cause, grant an additional 7 days to complete the examination.

(d) Release on bail or on recognizance shall not be revoked and an application therefor shall not be denied on the grounds that an examination has been ordered.

(e) Upon request by the defense and if the defendant is indigent, the court may appoint, in addition to the expert or experts chosen pursuant to subsection (a) of this Section, a qualified expert selected by the defendant to examine him and to make a report as provided in Section 104-15. Upon the filing with the court of a verified statement of services rendered, the court shall enter an order on the county board to pay such expert a reasonable fee stated in the order.
(Source: P.A. 85-971.) [Formerly Ill. Rev. Stat. 38 §104-13.]

5/104-14. Use of statements made during examination or treatment.

§104-14. Use of Statements Made During Examination or Treatment. (a) Statements made by the defendant and information gathered in the course of any examination or treatment ordered under Section 104-13, 104-17 or 104-20 shall not be admissible against the defendant unless he raises the defense of insanity or the defense of drugged or intoxicated condition, in which case they shall be admissible only on the issue of whether he was insane, drugged, or intoxicated. The refusal of the defendant to cooperate in such examinations shall not preclude the raising of the aforesaid defenses but shall preclude the defendant from offering expert evidence or testimony tending to support such defenses if the expert evidence or testimony is based upon the expert's examination of the defendant.

(b) Except as provided in paragraph (a) of this Section, no statement made by the defendant in the course of any examination or treatment ordered under Section 104-13, 104-17 or 104-20 which relates to the crime charged or to other criminal acts shall be disclosed by persons conducting the examination or the treatment, except to members of the examining or treating team, without the informed written consent of the defendant, who is competent at the time of giving such consent.

(c) The court shall advise the defendant of the limitations on the use of any statements made or information gathered in the course of the fitness examination or subsequent treatment as provided in this Section. It shall also advise him that he may refuse to cooperate with the person conducting the examination, but that his refusal may be admissible into evidence on the issue of his mental or physical condition.

(Source: P.A. 81-1217.) [Formerly Ill. Rev. Stat. 38 §104-14.]

5/104-15. Report.

§104-15. Report. (a) The person or persons conducting an examination of the defendant, pursuant to paragraph (a) or (b) of Section 104-13 shall submit a written report to the court, the State, and the defense within 30 days of the date of the order. The report shall include:

(1) A diagnosis and an explanation as to how it was reached and the facts upon which it is based;

(2) A description of the defendant's mental or physical disability, if any; its severity; and an opinion as to whether and to what extent it impairs the defendant's ability to understand the nature and purpose of the proceedings against him or to assist in his defense, or both.

(b) If the report indicates that the defendant is not fit to stand trial or to plead because of a disability, the report shall include an opinion as to the likelihood of the defendant attaining fitness within one year if provided with a course of treatment. If the person or persons preparing the report are unable to form such an opinion, the report shall state the reasons therefor. The report may include a general description of the type of treatment needed and of the least physically restrictive form of treatment therapeutically appropriate.

(c) The report shall indicate what information, if any, contained therein may be harmful to the mental condition of the defendant if made known to him.

(Source: P.A. 81-1217.) [Formerly Ill. Rev. Stat. 38 §104-15.]

5/104-16. Fitness hearing.

§104-16. Fitness Hearing. (a) The court shall conduct a hearing to determine the issue of the defendant's fitness within 45 days of receipt of the final written report of the person or persons conducting the examination or upon conclusion of the matter then pending before it, subject to continuances allowed pursuant to Section 114-4 of this Act.

(b) Subject to the rules of evidence, matters admissible on the issue of the defendant's fitness include, but are not limited to, the following:

(1) The defendant's knowledge and understanding of the charge, the proceedings, the consequences of a plea, judgment or sentence, and the functions of the participants in the trial process;

(2) The defendant's ability to observe, recollect and relate occurrences, especially those concerning the incidents alleged, and to communicate with counsel;

(3) The defendant's social behavior and abilities; orientation as to time and place; recognition of persons, places and things; and performance of motor processes.

(c) The defendant has the right to be present at every hearing on the issue of his fitness. The defendant's presence may be waived only if there is filed with the court a certificate stating that the defendant is physically unable to be present and the reasons therefor. The certificate shall be signed by a licensed physician who, within 7 days, has examined the defendant.

(d) On the basis of the evidence before it, the court or jury shall determine whether the defendant is fit to stand trial or to plead. If it finds that the defendant is unfit, the court or the jury shall determine whether there is substantial probability that the defendant, if provided with a course of treatment, will attain fitness within one year. If the court or the jury finds that there is not a substantial probability, the court shall proceed as provided in Section 104-23. If such probability is found or if the court or the jury is unable to determine whether a substantial probability exists, the court shall order the defendant to undergo treatment for the purpose of rendering him fit. In the event that a defendant is ordered to undergo treatment when there has been no determination as to the probability of his attaining fitness, the court shall conduct a hearing as soon as possible following the receipt of the report filed pursuant to paragraph (d) of Section 104-17, unless the hearing is waived by the defense, and shall make a determination as to whether a substantial probability exists.

(e) An order finding the defendant unfit is a final order for purposes of appeal by the State or the defendant.

(Source: P.A. 81-1217.) [Formerly Ill. Rev. Stat. 38 §104-16.]

5/104-17. Commitment for treatment; treatment plan.

§104-17. Commitment for Treatment; Treatment Plan. (a) If the defendant is eligible to be or has been released on bail or on his own recognizance, the court shall select the least physically restrictive form of treatment therapeutically appropriate and consistent with the treatment plan.

(b) If the defendant's disability is mental, the court may order him placed for treatment in the custody of the Department of Mental Health and Developmental Disabilities, or the court may order him placed in the custody of any other appropriate public or private mental health facility or treatment program which has agreed to provide treatment to the defendant. If the defendant is placed in the custody of the Department of Mental Health and Developmental Disabilities, the defendant shall be placed in a secure setting unless the court determines that there are compelling reasons why such placement is not necessary. During the period of time required to determine the appropriate placement the defendant shall remain in jail. Upon completion of the placement process, the sheriff shall be notified and shall transport the defendant to the designated facility. The placement may be ordered either on an inpatient or an outpatient basis.

(c) If the defendant's disability is physical, the court may order him placed under the supervision of the Department of Rehabilitation Services which shall place and maintain the defendant in a suitable treatment facility or program, or the court may order him placed in an appropriate public or private facility or treatment program which has agreed to provide treatment to the defendant. The placement may be ordered either on an inpatient or an outpatient basis.

(d) The clerk of the circuit court shall transmit to the Department, agency or institution, if any, to which the defendant is remanded for treatment, the following:

(1) a certified copy of the order to undergo treatment;

(2) the county and municipality in which the offense was committed;

(3) the county and municipality in which the arrest took place; and

(4) all additional matters which the Court directs the clerk to transmit.

(e) Within 30 days of entry of an order to undergo treatment, the person supervising the defendant's treatment shall file with the court, the State, and the defense a report assessing the facility's or program's capacity to provide appropriate treatment for the defendant and indicating his opinion as to the probability of the defendant's attaining fitness within a period of one year from the date of the finding of unfitness. If the report indicates that there is a substantial probability that the defendant will attain fitness within the time period, the treatment supervisor shall also file a treatment plan which shall include:

(1) A diagnosis of the defendant's disability;

(2) A description of treatment goals with respect to rendering the defendant fit, a specification of the proposed treatment modalities, and an estimated timetable for attainment of the goals;

(3) An identification of the person in charge of supervising the defendant's treatment.

(Source: P.A. 83-839.) [Formerly Ill. Rev. Stat. 38 §104-17.]

5/104-18. Progress reports.

§104-18. Progress Reports. (a) The treatment supervisor shall submit a written progress report to the court, the State, and the defense:

(1) At least 7 days prior to the date for any hearing on the issue of the defendant's fitness;

(2) Whenever he believes that the defendant has attained fitness;

(3) Whenever he believes that there is not a substantial probability that the defendant will attain fitness, with treatment, within one year from the date of the original finding of unfitness.

(b) The progress report shall contain:

(1) The clinical findings of the treatment supervisor and the facts upon which the findings are based;

(2) The opinion of the treatment supervisor as to whether the defendant has attained fitness or as to whether the defendant is making progress, under treatment, toward attaining fitness within one year from the date of the original finding of unfitness;

(3) If the defendant is receiving medication, information from the prescribing physician indicating the type, the dosage and the effect of the medication on the defendant's appearance, actions and demeanor.

(Source: P.A. 81-1217.) [Formerly Ill. Rev. Stat. 38 §104-18.]

5/104-19. Records.

§104-19. Records. Any report filed of record with the court concerning diagnosis, treatment or treatment plans made pursuant to this Article shall not be placed in the defendant's court record but shall be maintained separately by the clerk of the court and shall be available only to the court or an appellate court, the State and the defense, a facility or program which is providing treatment to the defendant pursuant to an order of the court or such other persons as the court may direct.

(Source: P.A. 81-1217.) [Formerly Ill. Rev. Stat. 38 §104-19.]

5/104-20. Ninety-day hearings; continuing treatment.

§104-20. Ninety-Day Hearings; Continuing Treatment. (a) Upon entry or continuation of any order to undergo treatment, the court shall set a date for hearing to reexamine the issue of the defendant's fitness not more than 90 days thereafter. In addition, whenever the court receives a report from the supervisor of the defendant's treatment pursuant to subparagraph (2) or (3) of paragraph (a) of Section 104-18, the court shall forthwith set the matter for hearing. On the date set or upon conclusion of the matter then pending before it, the court, sitting without a jury, shall conduct a hearing, unless waived by the defense, and shall determine:

(1) Whether the defendant is fit to stand trial or to plead; and if not,

(2) Whether the defendant is making progress under treatment toward attainment of fitness within one year from the date of the original finding of unfitness.

(b) If the court finds the defendant to be fit pursuant to this Section, the court shall set the matter for trial; provided that if the defendant is in need of continued care or treatment and the supervisor of the defendant's treatment agrees to continue to provide it, the court may enter any order it deems appropriate for the continued care or treatment of the defendant by the facility or program pending the conclusion of the criminal proceedings.

(c) If the court finds that the defendant is still unfit but that he is making progress toward attaining fitness, the court may continue or modify its original treatment order entered pursuant to Section 104-17.

(d) If the court finds that the defendant is still unfit and that he is not making progress toward attaining fitness such that there is not a substantial probability that he will attain fitness within one year from the date of the original finding of unfitness, the court shall proceed pursuant to Section 104-23. However, if the defendant is in need of continued care and treatment and the supervisor of the defendant's treatment agrees to continue to provide it, the court may enter any order it deems appropriate for the continued care or treatment by the facility or program pending the conclusion of the criminal proceedings.

(Source: P.A. 81-1217.) [Formerly Ill. Rev. Stat. 38 §104-20.]

5/104-21. Medication.

§104-21. Medication. (a) A defendant who is receiving psychotropic drugs or other medications under medical direction is entitled to a hearing on the issue of his fitness while under medication. If the court finds a defendant. who is receiving such medication to be fit but also finds that it is probable that the defendant will be fit without the use of such medication if he receives or continues in treatment, the court may order the defendant to undergo or to continue treatment within the time limits prescribed by this Article. The court shall not order such defendant to undergo or continue treatment under this Section if the defendant wishes to proceed while under medication, except that the court may make such orders as it deems appropriate under paragraph (b) of this Section.

(b) Whenever a defendant who is receiving medication under medical direction is transferred between a place of custody and a treatment facility or program, a written report from the prescribing physician shall accompany the defendant. The report shall state the type and dosage of the defendant's medication and the duration of the prescription. The chief officer of the place of custody or the treatment supervisor at the facility or program shall insure that such medication is provided according to the directions of the prescribing physician or until superseded by order of a physician who has examined the defendant.

(Source: P.A. 81-1217.) [Formerly Ill. Rev. Stat. 38 §104-21.]

5/104-22. Trial with special provisions and assistance.

§104-22. Trial with special provisions and assistance. (a) On motion of the defendant, the State or on the court's own motion, the court shall determine whether special provisions or assistance will render the defendant fit to stand trial as defined in Section 104-10.

(b) Such special provisions or assistance may include but are not limited to:

(1) Appointment of qualified translators who shall simultaneously translate all testimony at trial into language understood by the defendant.

(2) Appointment of experts qualified to assist a defendant who because of a disability is unable to understand the proceedings or communicate with his or her attorney.

(c) The case may proceed to trial only if the court determines that such provisions or assistance compensate for a defendant's disabilities so as to render the defendant fit as defined in Section 104-10. In such cases the court shall state for the record the following:

(1) The qualifications and experience of the experts or other persons appointed to provide special assistance to the defendant;

(2) The court's reasons for selecting or appointing the particular experts or other persons to provide the special assistance to the defendant;

(3) How the appointment of the particular expert or other persons will serve the goal of rendering the defendant fit in view of the appointee's qualifications and experience, taken in conjunction with the particular disabilities of the defendant; and

(4) Any other factors considered by the court in appointing that individual.

(Source: P.A. 81-1217.) [Formerly Ill. Rev. Stat. 38 §104-22.]

5/104-23. Unfit defendants.

§104-23. Unfit defendants. Cases involving an unfit defendant who demands a discharge hearing or a defendant who cannot become fit to stand trial and for whom no special provisions or assistance can compensate for his disability and render him fit shall proceed in the following manner:

(a) Upon a determination that there is not a substantial probability that the defendant will attain fitness within one year from the original finding of unfitness, a defendant or the attorney for the defendant may move for a discharge hearing pursuant to the provisions of Section 104-25. The discharge hearing shall be held within 120 days of the filing of a motion for a discharge hearing, unless the delay is occasioned by the defendant.

(b) If at any time the court determines that there is not a substantial probability that the defendant will become fit to stand trial or to plead within one year from the date of the original finding of unfitness, or if at the end of one year from that date the court finds the defendant still unfit and for whom no special provisions or assistance can compensate for his disabilities and render him fit, the State shall request the court:

(1) To set the matter for hearing pursuant to Section 104-25 unless a hearing has already been held pursuant to paragraph (a) of this Section; or

(2) To release the defendant from custody and to dismiss with prejudice the charges against him; or

(3) To remand the defendant to the custody of the Department of Mental Health and Developmental Disabilities and order a hearing to be conducted pursuant to the provisions of the Mental Health and Developmental Disabilities Code, as now or hereafter amended. If the defendant is committed to the Department of Mental Health and Developmental Disabilities pursuant to such hearing, the court having jurisdiction over the criminal matter shall dismiss the charges against the defendant, with the leave to reinstate. In such cases the Department of Mental Health and Developmental Disabilities shall notify the court, the State's attorney and the defense attorney upon the discharge of the defendant. A former defendant so committed shall be treated in the same manner as any other civilly committed patient for all purposes including admission, selection of the place of treatment and the treatment modalities, entitlement to rights and privileges, transfer, and discharge. A defendant who is not committed shall be remanded to the court having jurisdiction of the criminal matter for disposition pursuant to subparagraph (1) or (2) of paragraph (b) of this Section.

(c) If the defendant is restored to fitness and the original charges against him are reinstated, the speedy trial provisions of Section 103-5 shall commence to run.

(Source: P.A. 82-577.) [Formerly Ill. Rev. Stat. 38 §104-23.]

5/104-24. Time credit.

§104-24. Time Credit. Time spent in custody pursuant to orders issued under Section 104-17 or 104-20 or pursuant to a commitment to the Department of Mental Health and Developmental Disabilities following a finding of unfitness or incompetency under prior law, shall be credited against any sentence imposed on the defendant in the pending criminal case or in any other case arising out of the same conduct.
(Source: P.A. 81-1217.) [Formerly Ill. Rev. Stat. 38 §104-24.]

5/104-25. Discharge hearing.

§104-25. Discharge hearing. (a) As provided for in paragraph (a) of Section 104-23 and subparagraph (1) of paragraph (b) of Section 104-23 a hearing to determine the sufficiency of the evidence shall be held. Such hearing shall be conducted by the court without a jury. The State and the defendant may introduce evidence relevant to the question of defendant's guilt of the crime charged.

The court may admit hearsay or affidavit evidence on secondary matters such as testimony to establish the chain of possession of physical evidence, laboratory reports, authentication of transcripts taken by official reporters, court and business records, and public documents.

(b) If the evidence does not prove the defendant guilty beyond a reasonable doubt, the court shall enter a judgment of acquittal; however nothing herein shall prevent the State from requesting the court to commit the defendant to the Department of Mental Health and Developmental Disabilities under the provisions of the Mental Health and Developmental Disabilities Code [405 ILCS 5/1-100 et seq.].

(c) If the defendant is found not guilty by reason of insanity, the court shall enter a judgment of acquittal and the proceedings after acquittal by reason of insanity under Section 5-2-4 of the Unified Code of Corrections [730 ILCS 5/5-2-4] shall apply.

(d) If the discharge hearing does not result in an acquittal of the charge the defendant may be remanded for further treatment and the one year time limit set forth in Section 104-23 shall be extended as follows:

(1) If the most serious charge upon which the State sustained its burden of proof was a Class 1 or Class X felony, the treatment period may be extended up to a maximum treatment period of 2 years; if a Class 2, 3, or 4 felony, the treatment period may be extended up to a maximum of 15 months;

(2) If the State sustained its burden of proof on a charge of first degree murder, the treatment period may be extended up to a maximum treatment period of 5 years.

(e) Transcripts of testimony taken at a discharge hearing may be admitted in evidence at a subsequent trial of the case, subject to the rules of evidence, if the witness who gave such testimony is legally unavailable at the time of the subsequent trial.

(f) If the court fails to enter an order of acquittal the defendant may appeal from such judgment in the same manner provided for an appeal from a conviction in a criminal case.

(g) At the expiration of an extended period of treatment ordered pursuant to this Section:

(1) Upon a finding that the defendant is fit or can be rendered fit consistent with Section 104-22, the court may proceed with trial.

(2) If the defendant continues to be unfit to stand trial, the court shall determine whether he or she is subject to involuntary admission under the Mental Health and Developmental Disabilities Code or constitutes a serious threat to the public safety. If so found, the defendant shall be remanded to the Department of Mental Health and Developmental Disabilities or to the Depart-

ment of Rehabilitation Services for further treatment and shall be treated in the same manner as a civilly committed patient for all purposes, except that the original court having jurisdiction over the defendant shall be required to approve any conditional release or discharge of the defendant, for the period of commitment equal to the maximum sentence to which the defendant would have been subject had he or she been convicted in a criminal proceeding. However, if the defendant is remanded to the Department of Mental Health and Developmental Disabilities, the defendant shall be placed in a secure setting unless the court determines that there are compelling reasons why such placement is not necessary.

(3) If the defendant is not committed pursuant to this Section, he or she shall be released.

(4) In no event may the treatment period be extended to exceed the maximum sentence to which a defendant would have been subject had he or she been convicted in a criminal proceeding. For purposes of this Section, the maximum sentence shall be determined by Section 5-8-1 of the "Unified Code of Corrections" [730 ILCS 5/5-8-1], excluding any sentence of natural life.

(Source: P.A. 84-1450.) [Formerly Ill. Rev. Stat. 38 §104-25.]

5/104-26. Disposition of defendants suffering disabilities.

§104-26. Disposition of Defendants suffering disabilities. (a) A defendant convicted following a trial conducted under the provisions of Section 104-22 shall not be sentenced before a written presentence report of investigation is presented to and considered by the court. The presentence report shall be prepared pursuant to Sections 5-3-2, 5-3-3 and 5-3-4 of the Unified Code of Corrections, as now or hereafter amended [730 ILCS 5/5-3-2, 5/5-3-3 and 5/5-3-4], and shall include a physical and mental examination unless the court finds that the reports of prior physical and mental examinations conducted pursuant to this Article are adequate and recent enough so that additional examinations would be unnecessary.

(b) A defendant convicted following a trial under Section 104-22 shall not be subject to the death penalty.

(c) A defendant convicted following a trial under Section 104-22 shall be sentenced according to the procedures and dispositions authorized under the Unified Code of Corrections, as now or hereafter amended [730 ILCS 5/1-1-1 et seq.], subject to the following provisions:

(1) The court shall not impose a sentence of imprisonment upon the offender if the court believes that because of his disability a sentence of imprisonment would not serve the ends of justice and the interests of society and the offender or that because of his disability a sentence of imprisonment would subject the offender to excessive hardship. In addition to any other conditions of a sentence of conditional discharge or probation the court may require that the offender undergo treatment appropriate to his mental or physical condition.

(2) After imposing a sentence of imprisonment upon an offender who has a mental disability, the court may remand him to the custody of the Department of Mental Health and Developmental Disabilities and order a hearing to be conducted pursuant to the provisions of the Mental Health and Developmental Disabilities Code, as now or hereafter amended [405/ILCS 5/1-100 et seq.]. If the offender is committed following such hearing, he shall be treated in the same manner as any other civilly committed patient for all purposes except as provided in this Section. If the defendant is not committed pursuant to such hearing, he shall be remanded to the sentencing court for disposition according to the sentence imposed.

(3) If the court imposes a sentence of imprisonment upon an offender who has a mental disability but does not proceed under subparagraph (2) of paragraph (c) of this Section, it shall order the Department of Corrections to proceed

pursuant to Section 3-8-5 of the Unified Code of Corrections, as now or hereafter amended [730 ILCS 5/3-8-5].

(4) If the court imposes a sentence of imprisonment upon an offender who has a physical disability, it may authorize the Department of Corrections to place the offender in a public or private facility which is able to provide care or treatment for the offender's disability and which agrees to do so.

(5) When an offender is placed with the Department of Mental Health and Developmental Disabilities or another facility pursuant to subparagraph (2) or (4) of this paragraph (c), the Department or private facility shall not discharge or allow the offender to be at large in the community without prior approval of the court. If the defendant is placed in the custody of the Department of Mental Health and Developmental Disabilities, the defendant shall be placed in a secure setting unless the court determines that there are compelling reasons why such placement is not necessary. The offender shall accrue good time and shall be eligible for parole in the same manner as if he were serving his sentence within the Department of Corrections. When the offender no longer requires hospitalization, care, or treatment, the Department of Mental Health and Developmental Disabilities or the facility shall transfer him, if his sentence has not expired, to the Department of Corrections. If an offender is transferred to the Department of Corrections, the Department of Mental Health and Developmental Disabilities shall transfer to the Department of Corrections all related records pertaining to length of custody and treatment services provided during the time the offender was held.

(6) The Department of Corrections shall notify the Department of Mental Health and Developmental Disabilities or a facility in which an offender has been placed pursuant to subparagraph (2) or (4) of paragraph (c) of this Section of the expiration of his sentence. Thereafter, an offender in the Department of Mental Health and Developmental Disabilities shall continue to be treated pursuant to his commitment order and shall be considered a civilly committed patient for all purposes including discharge. An offender who is in a facility pursuant to subparagraph (4) of paragraph (c) of this Section shall be informed by the facility of the expiration of his sentence, and shall either consent to the continuation of his care or treatment by the facility or shall be discharged.

(Source: P.A. 83-839.) [Formerly Ill. Rev. Stat. 38 §104-26.]

5/104-27. Defendants found unfit prior to this Article; reports; appointment of counsel.

§104-27. Defendants Found Unfit Prior to this Article; Reports; Appointment of Counsel. (a) Within 180 days after the effective date of this Article, the Department of Mental Health and Developmental Disabilities shall compile a report on each defendant under its custody who was found unfit or incompetent to stand trial or to be sentenced prior to the effective date of this Article. Each report shall include the defendant's name, indictment and warrant numbers, the county of his commitment, the length of time he has been hospitalized, the date of his last fitness hearing, and a report on his present status as provided in Section 104-18.

(b) The reports shall be forwarded to the Supreme Court which shall distribute copies thereof to the chief judge of the court in which the criminal charges were originally filed, to the state's attorney and the public defender of the same county, and to the defendant's attorney of record, if any. Notice that the report has been delivered shall be given to the defendant.

(c) Upon receipt of the report, the chief judge shall appoint the public defender or other counsel for each defendant who is not represented by counsel and who is indigent pursuant to Section 113-3 of this Act, as now or hereafter amended. The court shall provide the defendant's counsel with a copy of the report.

(Source: P.A. 84-1395.) [Formerly Ill. Rev. Stat. 38 §104-27.]

5/104-28. Disposition of defendants found unfit prior to this Article.

§104-28. Disposition of Defendants Found Unfit Prior to this Article. (a) Upon reviewing the report, the court shall determine whether the defendant has been in the custody of the Department of Mental Health and Developmental Disabilities for a period of time equal to the length of time that the defendant would have been required to serve, less good time, before becoming eligible for parole or mandatory supervised release had he been convicted of the most serious offense charged and had he received the maximum sentence therefor. If the court so finds, it shall dismiss the charges against the defendant, with leave to reinstate. If the defendant has not been committed pursuant to the Mental Health and Developmental Disabilities Code [405 ILCS 5/1-100 et seq.], the court shall order him discharged or shall order a hearing to be conducted forthwith pursuant to the provisions of the Code. If the defendant was committed pursuant to the Code, he shall continue to be treated pursuant to his commitment order and shall be considered a civilly committed patient for all purposes including discharge.

(b) If the court finds that a defendant has been in the custody of the Department of Mental Health and Developmental Disabilities for a period less than that specified in paragraph (a) of this Section, the court shall conduct a hearing pursuant to Section 104-20 forthwith to redetermine the issue of the defendant's fitness to stand trial or to plead. If the defendant is fit, the matter shall be set for trial. If the court finds that the defendant is unfit, it shall proceed pursuant to Section 104-20 or 104-23, provided that a defendant who is still unfit and who has been in the custody of the Department of Mental Health and Developmental Disabilities for a period of more than one year from the date of the finding of unfitness shall be immediately subject to the provisions of Section 104-23.

(Source: P.A. 82-577.) [Formerly Ill. Rev. Stat. 38 §104-28.]

5/104-29. Conflict of Article.

§104-29. In the event of any conflict between this Article and the "Mental Health and Developmental Disabilities Code" [405 ILCS 5/1-100 et seq.], the provisions of this Article shall govern.

(Source: P.A. 81-1217.) [Formerly Ill. Rev. Stat. 38 §104-29.]

5/104-30. Notice to law enforcement agencies regarding release of defendants.

§104-30. Notice to Law Enforcement Agencies Regarding Release of Defendants. (a) Prior to the release by the Department of Mental Health and Developmental Disabilities or the Department of Rehabilitation Services of any person admitted pursuant to any provision of this Article, the Department of Mental Health and Developmental Disabilities or Department of Rehabilitation Services shall give written notice to the Sheriff of the county from which the defendant was admitted. In cases where the arrest of the defendant or the commission of the offense took place in any municipality with a population of more than 25,000 persons, the Department of Mental Health and Developmental Disabilities or Department of Rehabilitation Services shall also give written notice to the proper law enforcement agency for said municipality, provided the municipality has requested such notice in writing.

(b) Where a defendant in the custody of the Department of Mental Health and Developmental Disabilities or Department of Rehabilitation Services under any provision of this Article is released pursuant to an order of court, the clerk of the circuit court shall, after the entry of the order, transmit a certified copy of the order of release to the Department of Mental Health and Developmental Disabilities or Department of Rehabilitation Services, and the Sheriff of the county from which the defendant was admitted. In cases where the arrest of

the defendant or the commission of the offense took place in any municipality with a population of more than 25,000 persons, the Clerk of the circuit court shall also send a certified copy of the order of release to the proper law enforcement agency for said municipality provided the municipality has requested such notice in writing.
(Source: P.A. 82-564.) [Formerly Ill. Rev. Stat. 38 §104-30.]

5/104-31. Defendant's privileges.

§104-31. No defendant placed in a secure setting of the Department of Mental Health and Developmental Disabilities pursuant to the provisions of Sections 104-17, 104-25, or 104-26 shall be permitted outside the facility's housing unit unless escorted or accompanied by personnel of the Department of Mental Health and Developmental Disabilities. Nor shall such defendant be permitted any off-grounds privileges, either with or without escort by personnel of the Department of Mental Health and Developmental Disabilities, or any unsupervised on-ground privileges, unless such off-grounds or unsupervised on-grounds privileges have been approved by specific court order, which order may include such conditions on the defendant as the court may deem appropriate and necessary to reasonably assure the defendant's satisfactory progress in treatment and the safety of the defendant or others.
(Source: P.A. 84-1308.) [Formerly Ill. Rev. Stat. 38 §104-31.]

ARTICLE 106. WITNESS IMMUNITY

Sec.

5/106-1. Granting of immunity.

§106-1. Granting of immunity. In any investigation before a Grand Jury, or trial in any court, the court on motion of the State may order that any material witness be released from all liability to be prosecuted or punished on account of any testimony or other evidence he may be required to produce.
(Source: P.A. 79-1360.) [Formerly Ill. Rev. Stat. 38 §106-1.]

5/106-2. Effect of immunity.

§106-2. Effect of immunity. Such order of immunity shall forever be a bar to prosecution against the witness for any offense shown in whole or in part by such testimony or other evidence except for perjury committed in the giving of such testimony.
(Source: Laws 1963, p. 2836.) [Formerly Ill. Rev. Stat. 38 §106-2.]

5/106-2.5. Use immunity.

§106-2.5. Use immunity. (a) In lieu of the immunity provided in Section 106-2 of this Code, the State's Attorney may make application to the court that a street gang member, who testifies on behalf of a public authority in a civil proceeding brought against a streetgang under the Illinois Streetgang Terrorism Omnibus Prevention Act [740 ILCS 147/1 et seq.], be granted immunity from prosecution in a criminal case as to any information directly or indirectly derived from the production of evidence by the streetgang member. The court shall grant the order of immunity if:

(1) the production of the evidence is necessary to a fair determination of a cause of action under the Illinois Streetgang Terrorism Omnibus Prevention Act; and

(2) The streetgang member has refused or is likely to refuse to produce the evidence on the basis of his or her privilege against self-incrimination.

(b) If a streetgang member refuses, on the basis of his or her privilege against self-incrimination, to produce evidence in an action brought under the Illinois Streetgang Terrorism Omnibus Prevention Act, and the judge informs the streetgang member of an order of immunity issued under this Section, the streetgang member may not refuse to comply with the order on the basis of his or her privilege against self-incrimination.

(c) The production of evidence so compelled under the order, and any information directly or indirectly derived from it, may not be used against the streetgang member in a criminal case, except in a prosecution for perjury, false swearing, or an offense otherwise involving a failure to comply with the order.

(d) Upon request of the streetgang member so compelled, a copy of the evidence produced under the order shall be furnished to him.

(Added by P.A. 87-932, §2-100, eff. 1/1/93.)
[Formerly Ill. Rev. Stat. 38 §106-2.5.]

5/106-3. Refusal to testify.

§106-3. Refusal to testify. Any witness who having been granted immunity refuses to testify or produce other evidence shall be in contempt of court subject to proceedings in accordance to law.

(Source: Laws 1963, p. 2836.) [Formerly Ill. Rev. Stat. 38 §106-3.]

ARTICLE 106B. CHILD VICTIMS OF SEXUAL ABUSE

Sec.

5/106B-1. Testimony of child in sexual abuse case via closed circuit television.

§106B-1. (a) (1) In a proceeding in the prosecution of an offense of criminal sexual assault, aggravated criminal sexual assault, criminal sexual abuse or aggravated criminal sexual abuse, a court may order that the testimony of a child victim under the age of 18 years be taken outside the courtroom and shown in the courtroom by means of a closed circuit television if:

(i) The testimony is taken during the proceeding; and

(ii) The judge determines that testimony by the child victim in the courtroom will result in the child suffering serious emotional distress such that the child cannot reasonably communicate or that the child will suffer severe emotional distress that is likely to cause the child to suffer severe adverse effects.

(2) Only the prosecuting attorney, the attorney for the defendant, and the judge may question the child.

(3) The operators of the closed circuit television shall make every effort to be unobtrusive.

(b) (1) Only the following persons may be in the room with the child when the child testifies by closed circuit television:

(i) The prosecuting attorney;

(ii) The attorney for the defendant;

(iii) The judge;

(iv) The operators of the closed circuit television equipment; and

(v) Any person or persons whose presence, in the opinion of the court, contributes to the well-being of the child, including a person who has dealt with the child in a therapeutic setting concerning the abuse, a parent or guardian of the child, and court security personnel.

(2) During the child's testimony by closed circuit television, the defendant shall be in the courtroom and shall not communicate with the jury if the cause is being heard before a jury.

(3) The defendant shall be allowed to communicate with the persons in the room where the child is testifying by any appropriate electronic method.

(c) The provisions of this Section do not apply if the defendant represents himself pro se.

(d) This Section may not be interpreted to preclude, for purposes of identification of a defendant, the presence of both the victim and the defendant in the courtroom at the same time.

(Source: P.A. 87-345.) [Formerly Ill. Rev. Stat. 38 §106B-1.]

ARTICLE 106C. IMMUNITY IN THE PROSECUTION OF DRUG OFFENSES

5/106C-1. Immunity.

§106C-1. Immunity. During the prosecution of felony violations of the Illinois Controlled Substances Act [720 ILCS 570/100 et seq.], the Cannabis Control Act [720 ILCS 550/1 et seq.], the Cannabis and Controlled Substances Tax Act [35 ILCS 520/1 et seq.], the Drug Paraphernalia Control Act [720 ILCS 600/1 et seq.] or for the offenses of controlled substance trafficking, cannabis trafficking, narcotics racketeering, or money laundering, or during a grand jury proceeding regarding such violations, whenever a witness refuses, on the basis of his privilege against self-incrimination, to testify or provide other information in a proceeding before a circuit court or grand jury of the State of Illinois, and the person presiding over the proceeding communicates to the witness an order issued under this Article, the witness may not refuse to comply with the order on the basis of his privilege against self-incrimination; but no testimony or other information compelled under the order may be used against the witness in any criminal case, except a prosecution for perjury or an offense otherwise involving a failure to comply with the order. An order of immunity granted under this Article does not bar prosecution of the witness, except as specifically provided herein.

(Source: P.A. 87-505; 87-895.) [Formerly Ill. Rev. Stat. 38 §106C-1.]

5/106C-2. Court and grand jury proceedings.

§106C-2. Court and grand jury proceedings. (a) In the case of an individual who has been or may be called to testify or provide other information at any proceeding before any circuit court or grand jury of the State of Illinois, the circuit court for the county in which the proceeding is or may be held shall issue, in accordance with subsection (b) of this Section, upon the request of the State's Attorney or an Assistant State's Attorney he designates for that county or the Attorney General or an Assistant Attorney General he designates, an order requiring that individual to give testimony or provide other information that he refuses to give or provide on the basis of his privilege against self-incrimination, the order to become effective as provided in Section 106C-1 of this Article.

(b) A State's Attorney, or his designated Assistant, or the Attorney General, or his designated Assistant, may request an order under subsection (a) of this Section when in his judgment:

(1) The testimony or other information from the individual may be necessary to the public interest; and

(2) The individual has refused or is likely to refuse to testify or provide other information on the basis of his privilege against self-incrimination.

(Source: P.A. 87-505; 87-895.) [Formerly Ill. Rev. Stat. 38 §106C-2.]

TITLE II. APPREHENSION AND INVESTIGATION

ARTICLE 107. ARREST

5/107-1. Definitions.

§107-1. Definitions. (a) A "warrant of arrest" is a written order from a court directed to a peace officer, or to some other person specifically named, commanding him to arrest a person.

(b) A "summons" is a written order issued by a court which commands a person to appear before a court at a stated time and place.

(c) A "notice to appear" is a written request issued by a peace officer that a person appear before a court at a stated time and place.

(Source: Laws 1963, p. 2836.) [Formerly Ill. Rev. Stat. 38 §107-1.]

5/107-2. Arrest by peace officer.

§107-2. Arrest by Peace Officer. (1) A peace officer may arrest a person when:

(a) He has a warrant commanding that such person be arrested; or

(b) He has reasonable grounds to believe that a warrant for the person's arrest has been issued in this State or in another jurisdiction; or

(c) He has reasonable grounds to believe that the person is committing or has committed an offense.

(2) Whenever a peace officer arrests a person, the officer shall question the arrestee as to whether he or she has any children under the age of 18 living with him or her who may be neglected as a result of the arrest or otherwise. The peace officer shall assist the arrestee in the placement of the children with a relative or other responsible person designated by the arrestee. If the peace officer has reasonable cause to believe that a child may be a neglected child as defined in the Abused and Neglected Child Reporting Act [325 ILCS 5/1 et seq.], he shall report it immediately to the Department of Children and Family Services as provided in that Act.

(3) A peace officer who executes a warrant of arrest in good faith beyond the geographical limitation of the warrant shall not be liable for false arrest.

(Source: P.A. 86-298.) [Formerly Ill. Rev. Stat. 38 §107-2.]

5/107-3. Arrest by private person.

§107-3. Arrest by private person. Any person may arrest another when he has reasonable grounds to believe that an offense other than an ordinance violation is being committed.

(Source: Laws 1963, p. 2836.) [Formerly Ill. Rev. Stat. 38 §107-3.]

5/107-4. Arrest by peace officer from other jurisdiction.

§107-4. Arrest by peace officer from other jurisdiction. (a) As used in this Section:

(1) "State" means any State of the United States and the District of Columbia.

(2) "Peace Officer" means any peace officer or member of any duly organized State, County, or Municipal peace unit or police force of another State.

(3) "Fresh pursuit" means the immediate pursuit of a person who is endeavoring to avoid arrest.

(b) Any peace officer of another State who enters this State in fresh pursuit and continues within this State in fresh pursuit of a person in order to arrest him on the ground that he has committed an offense in the other State has the same authority to arrest and hold the person in custody as peace officers of this State have to arrest and hold a person in custody on the ground that he has committed an offense in this State.

(c) If an arrest is made in this State by a peace officer of another State in accordance with the provisions of this Section he shall without unnecessary delay take the person arrested before the circuit court of the county in which the arrest was made. Such court shall conduct a hearing for the purpose of determining the lawfulness of the arrest. If the court determines that the arrest was lawful it shall commit the person arrested, to await for a reasonable time the issuance of an extradition warrant by the Governor of this State, or admit him to bail for such purpose. If the court determines that the arrest was unlawful it shall discharge the person arrested.

(Source: Laws 1963, p. 2836.) [Formerly Ill. Rev. Stat. 38 §107-4.]

5/107-5. Method of arrest.

§107-5. Method of arrest. (a) An arrest is made by an actual restraint of the person or by his submission to custody.

(b) An arrest may be made on any day and at any time of the day or night.

(c) An arrest may be made anywhere within the jurisdiction of this State.

(d) All necessary and reasonable force may be used to effect an entry into any building or property or part thereof to make an authorized arrest.

(Source: Laws 1963, p. 2836.) [Formerly Ill. Rev. Stat. 38 §107-5.]

5/107-6. Release by officer of person arrested.

§107-6. Release by officer of person arrested. A peace officer who arrests a person without a warrant is authorized to release the person without requiring him to appear before a court when the officer is satisfied that there are no grounds for criminal complaint against the person arrested.

(Source: Laws 1963, p. 2836.) [Formerly Ill. Rev. Stat. 38 §107-6.]

5/107-7. Persons exempt from arrest.

§107-7. Persons exempt from arrest. (a) Electors shall, in all cases except treason, felony or breach of the peace, be privileged from arrest during their attendance at election, and in going to and returning from the same.

(b) Senators and representatives shall, in all cases, except treason, felony or breach of the peace, be privileged from arrest during the session of the General Assembly, and in going to and returning from the same.

(c) The militia shall in all cases, except treason, felony, or breach of the peace, be privileged from arrest during their attendance at musters and elections, and in going to and returning from the same.

(d) Judges, attorneys, clerks, sheriffs, and other court officers shall be privileged from arrest while attending court and while going to and returning from court.

(Source: Laws 1963, p. 2836.) [Formerly Ill. Rev. Stat. 38 §107-7.]

5/107-8. Assisting peace officer.

§107-8. Assisting peace officer. (a) A peace officer making a lawful arrest may command the aid of persons over the age of 18.

(b) A person commanded to aid a peace officer shall have the same authority to arrest as that peace officer.

(c) A person commanded to aid a peace officer shall not be civilly liable for any reasonable conduct in aid of the officer.

(Source: P.A. 80-360.) [Formerly Ill. Rev. Stat. 38 §107-8.]

5/107-9. Issuance of arrest warrant upon complaint.

§107-9. Issuance of arrest warrant upon complaint. (a) When a complaint is presented to a court charging that an offense has been committed it shall examine upon oath or affirmation the complainant or any witnesses.

(b) The complaint shall be in writing and shall:

(1) State the name of the accused if known, and if not known the accused may be designated by any name or description by which he can be identified with reasonable certainty;

(2) State the offense with which the accused is charged;

(3) State the time and place of the offense as definitely as can be done by the complainant; and

(4) Be subscribed and sworn to by the complainant.

(c) A warrant shall be issued by the court for the arrest of the person complained against if it appears from the contents of the complaint and the examination of the complainant or other witnesses, if any, that the person against whom the complaint was made has committed an offense.

(d) The warrant of arrest shall:

(1) Be in writing;

(2) Specify the name, sex and birth date of the person to be arrested or if his name, sex or birth date is unknown, shall designate such person by any name or description by which he can be identified with reasonable certainty;

(3) Set forth the nature of the offense;

(4) State the date when issued and the municipality or county where issued;

(5) Be signed by the judge of the court with the title of his office;

(6) Command that the person against whom the complaint was made be arrested and brought before the court issuing the warrant or if he is absent or unable to act before the nearest or most accessible court in the same county;

(7) Specify the amount of bail; and

(8) Specify any geographical limitation placed on the execution of the warrant, but such limitation shall not be expressed in mileage.

(e) The warrant shall be directed to all peace officers in the State. It shall be executed by the peace officer, or by a private person specially named therein, at any location within the geographic limitation for execution placed on the warrant. If no geographic limitation is placed on the warrant, then it may be executed anywhere in the State.

(f) The warrant may be issued electronically or electromagnetically by use of a facsimile transmission machine and any such warrant shall have the same validity as a written warrant.

(Source: P.A. 86-298; 87-523.) [Formerly Ill. Rev. Stat. 38 §107-9.]

5/107-10. Defective warrant.

§107-10. Defective warrant. A warrant of arrest shall not be quashed or abated nor shall any person in custody for an offense be discharged from such custody because of technical irregularities not affecting the substantial rights of the accused.

(Source: Laws 1963, p. 2836.) [Formerly Ill. Rev. Stat. 38 §107-10.]

5/107-11. When summons may be issued.

§107-11. When summons may be issued. (a) When authorized to issue a warrant of arrest, a court may instead issue a summons.

(b) The summons shall:

(1) Be in writing;

(2) State the name of the person summoned and his or her address, if known;

(3) Set forth the nature of the offense;

(4) State the date when issued and the municipality or county where issued;

(5) Be signed by the judge of the court with the title of his or her office; and

(6) Command the person to appear before a court at a certain time and place.

(c) The summons may be served in the same manner as the summons in a civil action, except that police officers may serve summons for violations of ordinances occurring within their municipalities.

(Source: P.A. 87-574.) [Formerly Ill. Rev. Stat. 38 §107-11.]

5/107-12. Notice to appear.

§107-12. Notice to appear. (a) Whenever a peace officer is authorized to arrest a person without a warrant he may instead issue to such person a notice to appear.

(b) The notice shall:

(1) Be in writing;

(2) State the name of the person and his address, if known;

(3) Set forth the nature of the offense;

(4) Be signed by the officer issuing the notice; and

(5) Request the person to appear before a court at a certain time and place.

(c) Upon failure of the person to appear a summons or warrant of arrest may issue.

(d) In any case in which a person is arrested for a Class C misdemeanor or a petty offense and remanded to the sheriff other than pursuant to a court order, the sheriff may issue such person a notice to appear.

(Source: P.A. 83-693.) [Formerly Ill. Rev. Stat. 38 §107-12.]

5/107-13. Offenses committed by corporations.

§107-13. Offenses committed by corporations. (a) When a corporation is charged with the commission of an offense the court shall issue a summons setting forth the nature of the offense and commanding the corporation to appear before a court at a certain time and place.

(b) The summons for the appearance of a corporation may be served in the manner provided for service of summons upon a corporation in a civil action.

(c) If, after being summoned, the corporation does not appear, a plea of not guilty shall be entered by the court having jurisdiction to try the offense for which the summons was issued, and such court shall proceed to trial and judgment without further process.

(Source: Laws 1963, p. 2836.) [Formerly Ill. Rev. Stat. 38 §107-13.]

5/107-14. Temporary questioning without arrest.

§107-14. Temporary questioning without arrest. A peace officer, after having identified himself as a peace officer, may stop any person in a public place for a reasonable period of time when the officer reasonably infers from the circumstances that the person is committing, is about to commit or has committed an offense as defined in Section 102-15 of this Code, and may demand the name and address of the person and an explanation of his actions. Such detention and temporary questioning will be conducted in the vicinity of where the person was stopped.

(Source: Laws 1968, p. 218.) [Formerly Ill. Rev. Stat. 38 §107-14.]

ARTICLE 108. SEARCH AND SEIZURE

5/108-1. Search without warrant.

§108-1. Search without warrant. (1) When a lawful arrest is effected a peace officer may reasonably search the person arrested and the area within such person's immediate presence for the purpose of:

(a) Protecting the officer from attack; or

(b) Preventing the person from escaping; or

(c) Discovering the fruits of the crime; or

(d) Discovering any instruments, articles, or things which may have been used in the commission of, or which may constitute evidence of, an offense.

(2) No motor vehicle, or driver or passenger of such vehicle, shall be stopped or searched by any law enforcement officer solely on the basis of a violation or suspected violation of Section 12-603.1 of The Illinois Vehicle Code [625 ILCS 5/12-603.1].

(Source: P.A. 85-291.) [Formerly Ill. Rev. Stat. 38 §108-1.]

5/108-1.01. Search during temporary questioning.

§108-1.01. Search during temporary questioning. When a peace officer has stopped a person for temporary questioning pursuant to Section 107-14 of this Code and reasonably suspects that he or another is in danger of attack, he may search the person for weapons. If the officer discovers a weapon, he may take it until the completion of the questioning, at which time he shall either return the weapon, if lawfully possessed, or arrest the person so questioned.

(Source: Laws 1968, p. 218.) [Formerly Ill. Rev. Stat. 38 §108-1.01.]

5/108-2. Custody and disposition of things seized.

§108-2. Custody and disposition of things seized. An inventory of all instruments, articles or things seized on a search without warrant shall be given to the person arrested and a copy thereof delivered to the judge before whom the person arrested is taken, and thereafter, such instruments, articles or things shall be handled and disposed of in accordance with Sections 108-11 and 108-12 of this Code. If the person arrested is released without a charge being preferred against him all instruments, articles or things seized, other than contraband, shall be returned to him upon release.

(Source: Laws 1963, p. 2836.) [Formerly Ill. Rev. Stat. 38 §108-2.]

5/108-3. Grounds for search warrant.

§108-3. Grounds for search warrant. (a) Except as provided in subsection (b), upon the written complaint of any person under oath or affirmation which states facts sufficient to show probable cause and which particularly describes the place or person, or both, to be searched and the things to be seized, any judge may issue a search warrant for the seizure of the following:

(1) Any instruments, articles or things which have been used in the commission of, or which may constitute evidence of, the offense in connection with which the warrant is issued.

(2) Any person who has been kidnaped in violation of the laws of this State, or who has been kidnaped in another jurisdiction and is now concealed within this State, or any human fetus or human corpse.

(b) When the things to be seized are the work product of, or used in the ordinary course of business, and in the possession, custody, or control of any person known to be engaged in the gathering or dissemination of news for the print or broadcast media, no judge may issue a search warrant unless the requirements set forth in subsection (a) are satisfied and there is probable cause to believe that:

(1) such person has committed or is committing a criminal offense; or

(2) the things to be seized will be destroyed or removed from the State if the search warrant is not issued.

(Source: P.A. 81-806.) [Formerly Ill. Rev. Stat. 38 §108-3.]

5/108-4. Issuance of search warrant.

§108-4. Issuance of search warrant. All warrants shall state the time and date of issuance and be the warrants of the judge issuing the same and not the warrants of the court in which he is then sitting and such warrants need not bear the seal of the court or clerk thereof. The complaint on which the warrant is issued need not be filed with the clerk of the court nor with the court if there is no clerk until the warrant has been executed or has been returned "not executed".

The search warrant may be issued electronically or electromagnetically by use of a facsimile transmission machine and any such warrant shall have the same validity as a written search warrant.

(Source: P.A. 87-523.) [Formerly Ill. Rev. Stat. 38 §108-4.]

5/108-5. Persons authorized to execute search warrants.

§108-5. Persons authorized to execute search warrants. The warrant shall be issued in duplicate and shall be directed for execution to all peace officers of the State. However, the judge may direct the warrant to be executed by any person named specially therein.

(Source: Laws 1963, p. 2836.) [Formerly Ill. Rev. Stat. 38 §108-5.]

5/108-6. Execution of search warrants.

§108-6. Execution of search warrants. The warrant shall be executed within 96 hours from the time of issuance. If the warrant is executed the duplicate copy shall be left with any person from whom any instruments, articles or things are seized or if no person is available the copy shall be left at the place from which the instruments, articles or things were seized. Any warrant not executed within such time shall be void and shall be returned to the court of the judge issuing the same as "not executed".

(Source: Laws 1963, p. 2836.) [Formerly Ill. Rev. Stat. 38 §108-6.]

5/108-7. Command of search warrant.

§108-7. Command of search warrant. The warrant shall command the person directed to execute the same to search the place or person particularly described in the warrant and to seize the instruments, articles or things particularly described in the warrant.

(Source: Laws 1963, p. 2836.) [Formerly Ill. Rev. Stat. 38 §108-7.]

5/108-8. Use of force in execution of search warrant.

§108-8. Use of force in execution of search warrant. (a) All necessary and reasonable force may be used to effect an entry into any building or property or part thereof to execute a search warrant.

(b) Upon a finding by the judge issuing the warrant that any of the following exigent circumstances exist, the judge may order the person executing the warrant to make entry without first knocking and announcing his office:

(1) the presence of firearms or explosives in the building in an area where they are accessible to any occupant;

(2) the prior possession of firearms by an occupant of the building within a reasonable period of time;

(3) the presence of surveillance equipment, such as video cameras, or alarm systems, inside or outside of the building;

(4) the presence of steel doors, wooden planking, crossbars, dogs, or other similar means of preventing or impeding entry into the building.

(Source: P.A. 87-522; 87-895.) [Formerly Ill. Rev. Stat. 38 §108-8.]

5/108-9. Detention and search of persons on premises.

§108-9. Detention and search of persons on premises. In the execution of the warrant the person executing the same may reasonably detain to search any person in the place at the time:

(a) To protect himself from attack, or

(b) To prevent the disposal or concealment of any instruments, articles or things particularly described in the warrant.

(Source: Laws 1963, p. 2836.) [Formerly Ill. Rev. Stat. 38 §108-9.]

5/108-10. Return to court of things seized.

§108-10. Return to court of things seized. A return of all instruments, articles or things seized shall be made without unnecessary delay before the judge issuing the warrant or before any judge named in the warrant or before any court of competent jurisdiction. An inventory of any instruments, articles or things seized shall be filed with the return and signed under oath by the officer or person executing the warrant. The judge shall upon request deliver a copy of the inventory to the person from whom or from whose premises the instruments, articles or things were taken and to the applicant for the warrant.

(Source: Laws 1963, p. 2836.) [Formerly Ill. Rev. Stat. 38 §108-10.]

5/108-11. Disposition of things seized.

§108-11. Disposition of things seized. The court before which the instruments, articles or things are returned shall enter an order providing for their custody pending further proceedings.

(Source: P.A. 83-334.) [Formerly Ill. Rev. Stat. 38 §108-11.]

5/108-12. Disposition of obscene material.

§108-12. Disposition of obscene material. In the case of any material seized which is alleged to have been possessed or used or intended to be used contrary to, or is evidence of a violation of, Section 11-20 of the "Criminal Code of 1961", approved July 28, 1961, as heretofore and hereafter amended [720 ILCS 5/11-20], the court before which the material is returned shall, upon written request of any person from whom the material was seized or any person claiming ownership or other right to possession of such material, enter an order providing for a hearing to determine the obscene nature thereof not more than 10 days after such return. If the material is determined to be obscene it shall be held pending further proceedings as provided by Section 108-11 of this Code. If the material is determined not to be obscene it shall be returned to the person from whom or place from which it was seized, or to the person claiming ownership or other right to possession of such material; provided that enough

of the record material may be retained by the State for purposes of appellate proceedings. The decision of the court upon this hearing shall not be admissible as evidence in any other proceeding nor shall it be res judicata of any question in any other proceeding.
(Source: P.A. 83-334.) [Formerly Ill. Rev. Stat. 38 §108-12.]

5/108-13. When warrant may be executed.

§108-13. When warrant may be executed. The warrant may be executed at any time of any day or night.
(Source: Laws 1963, p. 2836.) [Formerly Ill. Rev. Stat. 38 §108-13.]

5/108-14. No warrant quashed for technicality.

§108-14. No warrant quashed for technicality. No warrant shall be quashed nor evidence suppressed because of technical irregularities not affecting the substantial rights of the accused.
(Source: Laws 1963, p. 2836.) [Formerly Ill. Rev. Stat. 38 §108-14.]

ARTICLE 108A. JUDICIAL SUPERVISION OF THE USE OF EAVESDROPPING DEVICES

Sec.

5/108A-1. Authorization for use of eavesdropping device.

§108A-1. Authorization for Use of Eavesdropping Device. The State's Attorney may authorize an application to a circuit judge or an associate judge assigned by the Chief Judge of the circuit for, and such judge may grant in conformity with this Article, an order authorizing or approving the use of an eavesdropping device by a law enforcement officer or agency having the responsibility for the investigation of any felony under Illinois law where any one party to a conversation to be monitored, or previously monitored in the case of an emergency situation as defined in this Article, has consented to such monitoring.

The Chief Judge of the circuit may assign to associate judges the power to issue orders authorizing or approving the use of eavesdropping devices by law enforcement officers or agencies in accordance with this Article. After assignment by the Chief Judge, an associate judge shall have plenary authority to issue such orders without additional authorization for each specific application made to him by the State's Attorney until such time as the associate judge's power is rescinded by the Chief Judge.
(Source: P.A. 86-391.) [Formerly Ill. Rev. Stat. 38 §108A-1.]

5/108A-2. Authorized disclosure or use of information.

§108A-2. Authorized Disclosure or Use of Information. (a) Any law enforcement officer who, by any means authorized in this Article, has obtained knowledge of the contents of any conversation overheard or recorded by use of an eavesdropping device or evidence derived therefrom, may disclose such contents to another law enforcement officer or prosecuting attorney to the extent that such disclosure is appropriate to the proper performance of the official duties of the person making or receiving the disclosure.

(b) Any investigative or law enforcement officer who, by any means authorized in this Article, has obtained knowledge of the contents of any conversation overheard or recorded use of an eavesdropping device or evidence derived therefrom, may use the contents to the extent such use is appropriate to the proper performance of his official duties.

(c) Admissibility into evidence in any judicial, administrative, or legislative proceeding shall be as elsewhere described in this Article.
(Source: P.A. 79-1159.) [Formerly Ill. Rev. Stat. 38 §108A-2.]

5/108A-3. Procedure for obtaining judicial approval of use of eavesdropping device.

§108A-3. Procedure for Obtaining Judicial Approval of Use of Eavesdropping Device. (a) Where any one party to a conversation to occur in the future has consented to the use of an eavesdropping device to overhear or record the conversation, a judge may grant approval to an application to use an eavesdropping device pursuant to the provisions of this section.

Each application for an order authorizing or subsequently approving the use of an eavesdropping device shall be made in writing upon oath or affirmation to a circuit judge, or an associate judge assigned for such purpose pursuant to Section 108A-1 of this Code, and shall state the applicant's authority to make such application. Each application shall include the following:

(1) the identity of the investigative or law enforcement officer making the application and the State's Attorney authorizing the application;

(2) a statement of the facts and circumstances relied upon by the applicant to justify his belief that an order should be issued including: (a) details as to the felony that has been, is being, or is about to be committed; (b) a description of the type of communication sought to be monitored; (c) the identity of the party to the expected conversation consenting to the use of an eavesdropping device; (d) the identity of the person, if known, whose conversations are to be overheard by the eavesdropping device;

(3) a statement of the period of time for which the use of the device is to be maintained or, if the nature of the investigation is such that the authorization for use of the device should not terminate automatically when the described type of communication is overheard or recorded, a description of facts establishing reasonable cause to believe that additional conversations of the same type will occur thereafter;

(4) a statement of the existence of all previous applications known to the individual making the application which have been made to any judge requesting permission to use an eavesdropping device involving the same persons in the present application, and the action taken by the judge on the previous applications;

(5) when the application is for an extension of an order, a statement setting forth the results so far obtained from the use of the eavesdropping device or an explanation of the failure to obtain such results.

(b) The judge may request the applicant to furnish additional testimony, witnesses, or evidence in support of the application.
(Source: P.A. 86-391.) [Formerly Ill. Rev. Stat. 38 §108A-3.]

5/108A-4. Grounds for approval or authorization.

§108A-4. Grounds for Approval or Authorization. The judge may authorize or approve the use of the eavesdropping device where it is found that:

(a) one party to the conversation has or will have consented to the use of the device;

(b) there is reasonable cause for believing that an individual is committing, has committed, or is about to commit a felony under Illinois law;

(c) there is reasonable cause for believing that particular conversations concerning that felony offense will be obtained through such use; and

(d) for any extension authorized, that further use of a device is warranted on similar grounds.

(Source: P.A. 79-1159.) [Formerly Ill. Rev. Stat. 38 §108A-4.]

5/108A-5. Orders authorizing use of an eavesdropping device.

§108A-5. Orders Authorizing Use of an Eavesdropping Device. (a) Each order authorizing or approving the use of an eavesdropping device shall specify:

(1) the identity of the person who has consented to the use of the device to monitor any of his conversations and a requirement that any conversation overheard or received must include this person;

(2) the identity of the other person or persons, if known, who will participate in the conversation;

(3) the period of time in which the use of the device is authorized, including a statement as to whether or not the use shall automatically terminate when the described conversations have been first obtained.

(b) No order entered under this section may authorize or approve the use of any eavesdropping device for any period longer than 10 days. An initial or a subsequent extension, in no case for more than 10 days each, of an order may be granted but only upon application made in accordance with Section 108A-3 and where the court makes the findings required in Section 108A-4.

(Source: P.A. 79-1159.) [Formerly Ill. Rev. Stat. 38 §108A-5.]

5/108A-6. Emergency exception to procedures.

§108A-6. Emergency Exception to Procedures. (a) Notwithstanding any other provisions of this Article, any investigative or law enforcement officer, upon approval of a State's Attorney, or without it if a reasonable effort has been made to contact the appropriate State's Attorney, may use an eavesdropping device in an emergency situation as defined in this Section. Such use must be in accordance with the provisions of this Section and may be allowed only where the officer reasonably believes that an order permitting the use of the device would issue were there a prior hearing.

An emergency situation exists when, without previous notice to the law enforcement officer sufficient to obtain prior judicial approval, the conversation to be overheard or recorded will occur within a short period of time, the use of the device is necessary for the protection of the law enforcement officer or it will occur in a situation involving a clear and present danger of imminent death or great bodily harm to persons resulting from: (1) a kidnapping or the holding of a hostage by force or the threat of the imminent use of force; or (2) the occupation by force or the threat of the imminent use of force of any premises, place, vehicle, vessel or aircraft.

(b) In all such cases, an application for an order approving the previous or continuing use of an eavesdropping device must be made within 48 hours of the commencement of such use. In the absence of such an order, or upon its denial, any continuing use shall immediately terminate.

In order to approve such emergency use, the judge must make a determination (1) that he would have granted an order had the information been before the court prior to the use of the device and (2) that there was an emergency situation as defined in this Section.

(c) In the event that an application for approval under this Section is denied the contents of the conversations overheard or recorded shall be treated as having been obtained in violation of this Article.

(Source: P.A. 86-763.) [Formerly Ill. Rev. Stat. 38 §108A-6.]

5/108A-7. Retention and review of recordings.

§108A-7. Retention and Review of Recordings. (a) The contents of any conversation overheard by any eavesdropping device shall, if possible, be recorded on tape or a comparable device. The recording of the contents of a conversation under this Article shall be done in such a way as will protect the recording from editing or other alterations.

(b) Immediately after the expiration of the period of the order or extension or, where the recording was made in an emergency situation as defined in Section 108A-6, at the time of the request for approval subsequent to the emergency, all such recordings shall be made available to the judge issuing the order or hearing the application for approval of an emergency application.

The judge shall listen to the tapes, determine if the conversations thereon are within his order or were appropriately made in emergency situations, and make a record of such determination to be retained with the tapes.

The recordings shall be sealed under the instructions of the judge and custody shall be where he orders. Such recordings shall not be destroyed except upon order of the judge hearing the application and in any event shall be kept for 10 years if not destroyed upon his order.

Duplicate recordings may be made for any use or disclosure authorized by this Article. The presence of the seal provided for in this Section or a satisfactory explanation for the absence thereof shall be a pre-requisite for the use or disclosure of the contents of the recordings or any evidence derived therefrom.

(c) Applications made and orders granted under this Article shall be sealed by the judge. Custody of the applications and orders shall be wherever the judge requests. Such applications and orders shall be disclosed only upon a showing of good cause before a judge. Such documents shall not be destroyed except on the order of the issuing or denying judge or after the expiration of 10 years time if not destroyed upon his order.

(Source: P.A. 79-1159.) [Formerly Ill. Rev. Stat. 38 §108A-7.]

5/108A-8. Notice to parties overheard.

§108A-8. Notice to Parties Overheard. (a) Within a reasonable time, but not later than 90 days after either the filing of an application for an order of authorization or approval which is denied or not later than 90 days after the termination of the period of an order or extension thereof, the issuing or denying judge shall cause to be served on the persons named in the order or application and such other persons in the recorded conversation as the judge may determine that justice requires be notified, a notice of the transaction involving any requested or completed use of an eavesdropping device which shall include:

(1) notice of the entry of an order, of subsequent approval in an emergency situation, or the denial of an application;

(2) the date of the entry, approval, or denial;

(3) the period of the authorized use of any eavesdropping device; and

(4) notice of whether during the period of eavesdropping devices were or were not used to overhear and record various conversations and whether or not such conversations are recorded.

On an ex parte showing of good cause, the notice required by this subsection may be postponed.

(b) Upon the filing of a motion, the judge may in his discretion make available to such person or his attorney for inspection such portions of the recorded conversations or the applications and orders as the judge determines it would be in the interest of justice to make available.

(c) The contents of any recorded conversation or evidence derived therefrom shall not be received in evidence or otherwise disclosed in any trial, hearing, or other judicial or administrative proceeding unless each party not less than 10 days before such a proceeding has been furnished with a copy of the court order

and accompanying application under which the recording was authorized or approved and has had an opportunity to examine the portion of the tapes to be introduced or relied upon. Such 10 day period may be waived by the judge if he finds that it was not possible to furnish the party with such information within the stated period and that the party will not be materially prejudiced by the delay in receiving such information.
(Source: P.A. 79-1159.) [Formerly Ill. Rev. Stat. 38 §108A-8.]

5/108A-9. Motion to suppress contents of recording, etc.

§108A-9. Motion to Suppress Contents of Recording, etc. (a) Any aggrieved person in any judicial or administrative proceeding may move to suppress the contents of any recorded conversation or evidence derived therefrom on the grounds that:

(1) the conversation was unlawfully overheard and recorded;

(2) the order of authorization or approval under which the device was used or a recording made was improperly granted; or

(3) the recording or interception was not made in conformity with the order of authorization.

(b) Such a motion shall be made before the proceeding unless there was no previous opportunity for such motion. If the motion is granted, the contents shall be treated as having been obtained in violation of this Article. Upon the filing of such a motion, the judge may in his discretion make available to the moving party or his attorney such portions of the recorded conversation or evidence derived therefrom as the judge determines to be in the interests of justice.
(Source: P.A. 79-1159.) [Formerly Ill. Rev. Stat. 38 §108A-9.]

5/108A-10. Appeal by State.

§108A-10. Appeal by State. In addition to any other right to appeal, the State shall have the right to appeal from a denial of an application for an order of authorization or approval and the right to appeal the granting of a motion to suppress.

Where the State appeals, such appeal shall be taken within 30 days after the date the order was denied or motion granted and shall be diligently prosecuted.
(Source: P.A. 79-1159.) [Formerly Ill. Rev. Stat. 38 §108A-10.]

5/108A-11. Reports concerning use of eavesdropping devices.

§108A-11. Reports Concerning Use of Eavesdropping Devices. (a) In January of each year the State's Attorney of each county in which eavesdropping devices were used pursuant to the provisions of this Article shall report to the Department of State Police the following with respect to each application for an order authorizing the use of an eavesdropping device, or an extension thereof, made during the preceding calendar year:

(1) the fact that such an order, extension, or subsequent approval of an emergency was applied for;

(2) the kind of order or extension applied for;

(3) a statement as to whether the order or extension was granted as applied for was modified, or was denied;

(4) the period authorized by the order or extensions in which an eavesdropping device could be used;

(5) the felony specified in the order extension or denied application;

(6) the identity of the applying investigative or law enforcement officer and agency making the application and the State's Attorney authorizing the application; and

(7) the nature of the facilities from which or the place where the eavesdropping device was to be used.

(b) Such report shall also include the following:

(1) a general description of the uses of eavesdropping devices actually made under such order to overheard* or record conversations, including: (a) the approximate nature and frequency of incriminating conversations overheard, (b) the approximate nature and frequency of other conversations overheard, (c) the approximate number of persons whose conversations were overheard, and (d) the approximate nature, amount, and cost of the manpower and other resources used pursuant to the authorization to use an eavesdropping device;

**So in original. Probably should be "overhear".*

(2) the number of arrests resulting from authorized uses of eavesdropping devices and the offenses for which arrests were made;

(3) the number of trials resulting from such uses of eavesdropping devices;

(4) the number of motions to suppress made with respect to such uses, and the number granted or denied; and

(5) the number of convictions resulting from such uses and the offenses for which the convictions were obtained and a general assessment of the importance of the convictions.

(c) In April of each year, the Department of State Police shall transmit to the General Assembly a report including information on the number of applications for orders authorizing the use of eavesdropping devices, the number of orders and extensions granted or denied during the preceding calendar year, and the convictions arising out of such uses.

The requirement for reporting to the General Assembly shall be satisfied by filing copies of the report with the Speaker, the Minority Leader and the Clerk of the House of Representatives and the President, the Minority Leader and the Secretary of the Senate and the Legislative Research Unit, as required by Section 3.1 of "An Act to revise the law in relation to the General Assembly", approved February 25, 1874, as amended [25 ILCS 5/3.1], and filing such additional copies with the State Government Report Distribution Center for the General Assembly as is required under paragraph (t) of Section 7 of the State Library Act [15 ILCS 320/7].

(Source: P.A. 86-391.) [Formerly Ill. Rev. Stat. 38 §108A-11.]

ARTICLE 108B. ELECTRONIC CRIMINAL SURVEILLANCE

Sec.

5/108B-1. Definitions.

§108B-1. Definitions. For the purpose of this Article:

(a) "Aggrieved person" means a person who was a party to any intercepted wire or oral communication or any person against whom the intercept was directed.

(b) "Chief Judge" means, when referring to a judge authorized to receive application for, and to enter orders authorizing, interceptions of private oral communications, the Chief Judge of the Circuit Court wherein the application for order of interception is filed, or a Circuit Judge designated by the Chief Judge to enter these orders. In circuits other than the Cook County Circuit, "Chief Judge" also means, when referring to a judge authorized to receive application for, and to enter orders authorizing, interceptions of private oral communications, an Associate Judge authorized by Supreme Court Rule to try felony cases who is assigned by the Chief Judge to enter these orders. After assignment by the Chief Judge, an Associate Judge shall have plenary authority to issue orders without additional authorization for each specific application made to him by the State's Attorney until the time the Associate Judge's power is rescinded by the Chief Judge.

(c) "Communications common carrier" means any person engaged as a common carrier for hire in the transmission of communications by wire or radio, not including radio broadcasting.

(d) "Contents" includes information obtained from a private oral communication concerning the existence, substance, purport or meaning of the communication, or the identity of a party of the communication.

(e) "Court of competent jurisdiction" means any circuit court.

(f) "Department" means Illinois Department of State Police.

(g) "Director" means Director of the Illinois Department of State Police.

(h) "Electronic criminal surveillance device" or "eavesdropping device" means any device or apparatus, including an induction coil, that can be used to intercept human speech other than:

(1) Any telephone, telegraph or telecommunication instrument, equipment or facility, or any component of it, furnished to the subscriber or user by a communication common carrier in the ordinary course of its business, or purchased by any person and being used by the subscriber, user or person in the ordinary course of his business, or being used by a communications common carrier in the ordinary course of its business, or by an investigative or law enforcement officer in the ordinary course of his duties; or

(2) A hearing aid or similar device being used to correct subnormal hearing to not better than normal.

(i) "Electronic criminal surveillance officer" means any law enforcement officer of the United States or of the State or political subdivision of it, or of another State, or of a political subdivision of it, who is certified by the Illinois Department of State Police to intercept private oral communications.

(j) "In-progress trace" means to determine the origin of a wire communication to a telephone or telegraph instrument, equipment or facility during the course of the communication.

(k) "Intercept" means the aural acquisition of the contents of any oral communication through the use of any electronic criminal surveillance device.

(*l*) "Journalist" means a person engaged in, connected with, or employed by news media, including newspapers, magazines, press associations, news agencies, wire services, radio, television or other similar media, for the purpose of gathering, processing, transmitting, compiling, editing or disseminating news for the general public.

(m) "Law enforcement agency" means any law enforcement agency of the United States, or the State or a political subdivision of it.

(n) "Oral communication" means human speech used to communicate by one party to another, in person, by wire communication or by any other means.

(*o*) "Private oral communication" means a wire or oral communication uttered by a person exhibiting an expectation that the communication is not subject to interception, under circumstances reasonably justifying the expectation. Circumstances that reasonably justify the expectation that a communication is not subject to interception include the use of a cordless telephone or cellular communication device.

(p) "Wire communication" means any human speech used to communicate by one party to another in whole or in part through the use of facilities for the transmission of communications by wire, cable or other like connection between the point of origin and the point of reception furnished or operated by a communications common carrier.

(q) "Privileged communications" means a private oral communication between:

(1) a licensed and practicing physician and a patient within the scope of the profession of the physician;

(2) a licensed and practicing psychologist to a patient within the scope of the profession of the psychologist;

(3) a licensed and practicing attorney-at-law and a client within the scope of the profession of the lawyer;

(4) a practicing clergyman and a confidant within the scope of the profession of the clergyman;

(5) a practicing journalist within the scope of his profession;

(6) spouses within the scope of their marital relationship; or

(7) a licensed and practicing social worker to a client within the scope of the profession of the social worker.

(Source: P.A. 86-391; 86-763; 86-1028; 86-1206; 87-530.) [Formerly Ill. Rev. Stat. 38 §108B-1.]

5/108B-2. Request for application for interception.

§108B-2. Request for application for interception. (a) A State's Attorney may apply for an order authorizing interception of oral communications in accordance with the provisions of this Article.

(b) The head of a law enforcement agency, including, for purposes of this subsection, the acting head of such law enforcement agency if the head of such agency is absent or unable to serve, may request that a State's Attorney apply for an order authorizing interception of oral communications in accordance with the provisions of this Article.

Upon request of a law enforcement agency, the Department may provide technical assistance to such an agency which is authorized to conduct an interception.

(Source: P.A. 85-1203.) [Formerly Ill. Rev. Stat. 38 §108B-2.]

5/108B-2a. Authorized disclosure or use of information.

§108B-2a. Authorized disclosure or use of information. (a) Any law enforcement officer who, by any means authorized in this Article, has obtained knowledge of the contents of any conversation overheard or recorded by use of an eavesdropping device or evidence derived therefrom, may disclose such contents to another law enforcement officer or prosecuting attorney to the extent that such disclosure is appropriate to the proper performance of the official duties of the person making or receiving the disclosure.

(b) Any investigative officer, including any attorney authorized by law to prosecute or participate in the prosecution of offenses enumerated in Section 108B-3 of this Act or law enforcement officer who, by any means authorized in this Article, has obtained knowledge of the contents of any conversation overheard or recorded by use of an eavesdropping device or evidence derived therefrom, may use the contents to the extent such use is appropriate to the proper performance of his official duties.

(c) Admissibility into evidence in any judicial, administrative, or legislative proceeding shall be as elsewhere described in this Article.

(Source: P.A. 85-1203.) [Formerly Ill. Rev. Stat. 38 §108B-2a.]

5/108B-3. Authorization for the interception of private oral communication.

§108B-3. Authorization for the interception of private oral communication. The State's Attorney, or a person designated in writing or by law to act for him and to perform his duties during his absence or disability, may authorize, in writing, an ex parte application to the chief judge of a court of competent jurisdiction for an order authorizing the interception of a private oral communication when no party has consented to the interception and the interception may provide evidence of, or may assist in the apprehension of a person who has committed, is committing or is about to commit, a violation of Section 401, 401.1 (controlled substance trafficking), 405, or 407 of the Illinois Controlled Substances Act [720 ILCS 570/401, 570/401.1, 570/405, or 570/407] or in response to a clear and present danger of imminent death or great bodily harm to persons resulting from: (1) a kidnapping or the holding of a hostage by force or the threat of the imminent use of force; or (2) the occupation by force or the threat of the imminent use of force of any premises, place, vehicle, vessel or aircraft.

(Source: P.A. 86-763.) [Formerly Ill. Rev. Stat. 38 §108B-3.]

5/108B-4. Application for order of interception.

§108B-4. Application for order of interception. (a) Each application for an order of authorization to intercept a private oral communication shall be made in writing upon oath or affirmation and shall include:

(1) The authority of the applicant to make the application;

(2) The identity of the electronic criminal surveillance officer for whom the authority to intercept a private oral communication is sought;

(3) The facts relied upon by the applicant including:

(i) The identity of the particular person, if known, who is committing, is about to commit, or has committed the offense and whose communication is to be intercepted;

(ii) The details as to the particular offense that has been, is being, or is about to be committed;

(iii) The particular type of communication to be intercepted;

(iv) A showing that there is probable cause to believe that the communication will be communicated on the particular wire communication facility involved or at the particular place where the oral communication is to be intercepted;

(v) The character and location of the particular wire communication facilities involved or the particular place where the oral communication is to be intercepted;

(vi) The objective of the investigation;

(vii) A statement of the period of time for which the interception is required to be maintained, and, if the objective of the investigation is such that the authorization for interception should not automatically terminate when the described type of communication has been first obtained, a particular statement of facts establishing probable cause to believe that additional communications of the same type will continue to occur;

(viii) A particular statement of facts showing that other normal investigative procedures with respect to the offense have been tried and have failed, or reasonably appear to be unlikely to succeed if tried, or are too dangerous to employ;

(4) Where the application is for the extension of an order, a statement of facts showing the results obtained from the interception, or a reasonable explanation of the failure to obtain results;

(5) A statement of the facts concerning all previous applications known to the applicant made to any court for authorization to intercept an oral com-

munication involving any of the same facilities or places specified in the application or involving any person whose communication is to be intercepted, and the action taken by the court on each application;

(6) A proposed order of authorization for consideration by the judge; and

(7) Such additional statements of facts in support of the application on which the applicant may rely or as the chief judge may require.

(b) As part of the consideration of that part of an application for which there is no corroborative evidence offered, the chief judge may inquire in camera as to the identity of any informant or request any other additional information concerning the basis upon which the State's Attorney, or the head of the law enforcement agency has relied in making an application or a request for application for the order of authorization which the chief judge finds relevant to the determination of probable cause under this Article.

(Source: P.A. 85-1203.) [Formerly Ill. Rev. Stat. 38 §108B-4.]

5/108B-5. Requirements for order of interception.

§108B-5. Requirements for order of interception. Upon consideration of an application, the chief judge may enter an ex parte order, as requested or as modified, authorizing the interception of a private oral communication, if the chief judge determines on the basis of the application submitted by the applicant, that:

(1) There is probable cause for belief that (a) the person whose communication is to be intercepted is committing, has committed, or is about to commit an offense enumerated in Section 108B-3, or (b) the facilities from which, or the place where, the private oral communication is to be intercepted, is, has been, or is about to be used in connection with the commission of the offense, or is leased to, listed in the name of, or commonly used by, the person; and

(2) There is probable cause for belief that a particular communication concerning such offense may be obtained through the interception; and

(3) Normal investigative procedures with respect to the offense have been tried and have failed or reasonably appear to be unlikely to succeed if tried or too dangerous to employ; and

(4) The electronic criminal surveillance officers to be authorized to supervise the interception of the private oral communication have been certified by the Department.

(b)* In the case of an application, other than for an extension, for an order to intercept a communication of a person or on a wire communication facility that was the subject of a previous order authorizing interception, the application shall be based upon new evidence or information different from and in addition to the evidence or information offered to support the prior order, regardless of whether the evidence was derived from prior interceptions or from other sources.

**So in original. No subsec. (a) has been designated.*

(c) The chief judge may authorize interception of a private oral communication anywhere in the judicial circuit. If the court authorizes the use of an eavesdropping device with respect to a vehicle, watercraft, or aircraft that is within the judicial circuit at the time the order is issued, the order may provide that the interception may continue anywhere within the State if the vehicle, watercraft, or aircraft leaves the judicial circuit.

(Source: P.A. 85-1203.) [Formerly Ill. Rev. Stat. 38 §108B-5.]

5/108B-6. Privileged communications.

§108B-6. Privileged communications. Nothing in this Article shall be construed to authorize the interception, disclosure or use of information obtained from privileged communications.

(Source: P.A. 85-1203.) [Formerly Ill. Rev. Stat. 38 §108B-6.]

5/108B-7. Contents of order for use of eavesdropping device.

§108B-7. Contents of order for use of eavesdropping device. (a) Each order authorizing the interception of a private oral communication shall state:

(1) The chief judge is authorized to issue the order;

(2) The identity of, or a particular description of, the person, if known, whose communications are to be intercepted;

(3) The character and location of the particular wire communication facilities as to which, or the particular place of the communications as to which, authority to intercept is granted;

(4) A particular description of the type of communication to be intercepted and a statement of the particular offense to which it relates;

(5) The identity and certification of the electronic criminal surveillance officers to whom the authority to intercept a private oral communication is given and the identity of the person who authorized the application; and

(6) The period of time during which the interception is authorized, including a statement as to whether or not the interception shall automatically terminate when the described communication has been first obtained.

(b) No order entered under this Section shall authorize the interception of private oral communications for a period of time in excess of that necessary to achieve the objective of the authorization. Every order entered under this Section shall require that the interception begin and terminate as soon as practicable and be conducted in such a manner as to minimize the interception of communications not otherwise subject to interception. No order, other than for an extension, entered under this Section may authorize the interception of private oral communications for any period exceeding 30 days. Extensions of an order may be granted for periods of not more than 30 days. No extension shall be granted unless an application for it is made in accordance with Section 108B-4 and the judge makes the findings required by Section 108B-5 and, where necessary, Section 108B-6.

(c) Whenever an order authorizing an interception is entered, the order shall require reports to be made to the chief judge who issued the order showing what progress has been made toward achievement of the authorized objective and the need for continued interception. The reports shall be made at such intervals as the judge may require.

(d) An order authorizing the interception of a private oral communication shall, upon request of the applicant, direct that a communications common carrier, landlord, owner, building operator, custodian, or other person furnish the applicant forthwith all information, facilities and technical assistance necessary to accomplish the interception unobtrusively and with a minimum of interference with the services that the carrier, owner, building operator, landlord, custodian, or person is affording the person whose communication is to be intercepted. The obligation of a communications common carrier under the order may include conducting an in-progress trace during an interception. Any communications common carrier, landlord, owner, building operator, custodian, or person furnishing the facilities or technical assistance shall be compensated by the applicant at the prevailing rates.

(e) A communications common carrier, landlord, owner, building operator, custodian, or other person who has been provided with an order issued under this Article shall not disclose the existence of the order of interception, or of a device used to accomplish the interception unless:

(1) He is required to do so by legal process; and

(2) He has given prior notification to the State's Attorney, who has authorized the application for the order.

(f) An order authorizing the interception of a private oral communication shall, upon the request of the applicant, authorize the entry into the place or facilities by electronic criminal surveillance officers as often as necessary for the purpose of installing, maintaining or removing an intercepting device where the entry is necessary to conduct or complete the interception. The chief judge who issues the order shall be notified of the fact of each entry prior to entry, if practicable, and, in any case, within 48 hours of entry.

(g) (1) Notwithstanding any provision of this Article, any chief judge of a court of competent jurisdiction to which any application is made under this Article may take any evidence, make any finding, or issue any order to conform the proceedings or the issuance of any order to the Constitution of the United States, or of any law of the United States or to the Constitution of the State of Illinois or to the laws of Illinois.

(2) When the language of this Article is the same or similar to the language of Title III of P.L. 90-351 (82 Stat. 211 et seq., codified at, 18 U.S.C. 2510 et seq.), the courts of this State in construing this Article shall follow the construction given to Federal law by the United States Supreme Court or United States Court of Appeals for the Seventh Circuit.

(Source: P.A. 85-1203.) [Formerly Ill. Rev. Stat. 38 §108B-7.]

5/108B-8. Emergency use of eavesdropping device.

§108B-8. Emergency use of eavesdropping device. (a) Whenever, upon informal application by the State's Attorney, a chief judge of competent jurisdiction determines that:

(1) There may be grounds upon which an order could be issued under this Article;

(2) There is probable cause to believe that an emergency situation exists with respect to the investigation of an offense enumerated in Section 108B-3; and

(3) There is probable cause to believe that a substantial danger to life or limb exists justifying the authorization for immediate interception of a private oral communication before formal application for an order could with due diligence be submitted to him and acted upon; the chief judge may grant oral approval for an interception, without an order, conditioned upon the filing with him, within 48 hours, of an application for an order under Section 108B-4 which shall also recite the oral approval under this Section and be retroactive to the time of the oral approval.

(b) Interception under oral approval under this Section shall immediately terminate when the communication sought is obtained or when the application for an order is denied, whichever is earlier.

(c) In the event no formal application for an order is subsequently made under this Section, the content of any private oral communication intercepted under oral approval under this Section shall be treated as having been obtained in violation of this Article.

(d) In the event no application for an order is made under this Section or an application made under this Section is subsequently denied, the judge shall cause an inventory to be served under Section 108B-11 of this Article and shall require the tape or other recording of the intercepted communication to be delivered to, and sealed by, the judge. The evidence shall be retained by the court, and it shall not be used or disclosed in any legal proceeding, except a civil action brought by an aggrieved person under Section 14-6 of the Criminal Code of 1961, or as otherwise authorized by the order of a court of competent jurisdiction. In addition to other remedies or penalties provided by law, failure to deliver any tape or other recording to the chief judge shall be punishable as contempt by the judge directing the delivery.

(Source: P.A. 85-1203.) [Formerly Ill. Rev. Stat. 38 §108B-8.]

5/108B-9. Recordings, records and custody.

§108B-9. Recordings, records and custody. (a) Any private oral communication intercepted in accordance with this Article shall, if practicable, be recorded by tape or other comparable method. The recording shall, if practicable, be done in such a way as will protect it from editing or other alteration. During an interception, the interception shall be carried out by an electronic criminal surveillance officer, and, if practicable, such officer shall keep a signed, written record, including:

(1) The date and hours of surveillance;

(2) The time and duration of each intercepted communication;

(3) The parties, if known, to each intercepted conversation; and

(4) A summary of the contents of each intercepted communication.

(b) Immediately upon the expiration of the order or its extensions, the tapes and other recordings shall be transferred to the chief judge issuing the order and sealed under his direction. Custody of the tapes, or other recordings, shall be maintained wherever the chief judge directs. They shall not be destroyed except upon an order of a court of competent jurisdiction and in any event shall be kept for 10 years. Duplicate tapes or other recordings may be made for disclosure or use under paragraph (a) of Section 108B-2a of this Article. The presence of the seal provided by this Section, or a satisfactory explanation for its absence, shall be a prerequisite for the disclosure of the contents of any private oral communication, or evidence derived from it, under paragraph (b) of Section 108B-2a of this Article.

(Source: P.A. 86-763.) [Formerly Ill. Rev. Stat. 38 §108B-9.]

5/108B-10. Applications, orders, and custody.

§108B-10. Applications, orders, and custody. (a) Applications made and orders granted under this Article for the interception of private oral communications shall be sealed by the chief judge issuing or denying them and held in custody as the judge shall direct. The applications and orders shall be kept for a period of 10 years. Destruction of the applications and orders prior to the expiration of that period of time may be made only upon the order of a court of competent jurisdiction. Disclosure of the applications and orders may be ordered by a court of competent jurisdiction on a showing of good cause.

(b) The electronic criminal surveillance officer shall retain a copy of applications and orders for the interception of private oral communications. The applications and orders shall be kept for a period of 10 years. Destruction of the applications and orders prior to the expiration of that period of time may be made only upon an order of a court of competent jurisdiction. Disclosure and use of the applications and orders may be made by an electronic criminal surveillance officer only in the proper performance of his official duties.

(c) In addition to any other remedies or penalties provided by law, any violation of this Section shall be punishable as contempt of court.

(Source: P.A. 85-1203.) [Formerly Ill. Rev. Stat. 38 §108B-10.]

5/108B-11. Inventory.

§108B-11. Inventory. (a) Within a reasonable period of time but not later than 90 days after the termination of the period of the order, or its extensions, or the date of the denial of an application made under Section 108B-8, the chief judge issuing or denying the order or extension shall cause an inventory to be served on any person:

(1) Named in the order;

(2) Arrested as a result of the interception of his private oral communication;

(3) Indicted or otherwise charged as a result of the interception of his private oral communication;

(4) Any person whose private oral communication was intercepted and who the judge issuing or denying the order or application may in his discretion determine should be informed in the interest of justice.

(b) The inventory under this Section shall include:

(1) Notice of the entry of the order or the application for an order denied under Section 108B-8;

(2) The date of the entry of the order or the denial of an order applied for under Section 108B-8;

(3) The period of authorized or disapproved interception; and

(4) The fact that during the period a private oral communication was or was not intercepted.

(c) A court of competent jurisdiction, upon filing of a motion, may in its discretion make available to those persons or their attorneys for inspection those portions of the intercepted communications, applications and orders as the court determines to be in the interest of justice.

(d) On an ex parte showing of good cause to a court of competent jurisdiction, the serving of the inventories required by this Section may be postponed for a period not to exceed 12 months.

(Source: P.A. 85-1203.) [Formerly Ill. Rev. Stat. 38 §108B-11.]

5/108B-12. Approval, notice, suppression.

§108B-12. Approval, notice, suppression. (a) If an electronic criminal surveillance officer, while intercepting a private oral communication in accordance with the provision of this Article, intercepts a private oral communication that relates to an offense other than an offense enumerated in Section 108B-3 of the Act, or relates to an offense enumerated in Section 108B-3 but not specified in the order of authorization, the State's Attorney, or a person designated in writing or by law to act for him, may, in order to permit the disclosure or use of the information under Section 108B-2a of this Act, make a motion for an order approving the interception. The chief judge of a court of competent jurisdiction shall enter an order approving the interception if he finds that at the time of the application, there existed probable cause to believe that a person whose private oral communication was intercepted was committing or had committed an offense and the content of the communication relates to that offense, and that the communication was otherwise intercepted in accordance with the provisions of this Article.

(b) An intercepted private oral communication, or evidence derived from it, may not be received in evidence or otherwise disclosed in an official proceeding unless each aggrieved person who is a party in the official proceeding, including any proceeding before a legislative, judicial, administrative or other governmental agency or official authorized to hear evidence under oath or other person taking testimony or depositions in any such proceeding, other than a grand jury, has, not less than 10 days before the official proceeding, been furnished with a copy of the court order, and the accompanying application, under which the interception was authorized or approved. The 10 day period may be waived by the presiding official if he finds that it was not practicable to furnish the person with the information 10 days before the proceeding, and that the person will not be or has not been prejudiced by delay in receiving the information.

(c) An aggrieved person in an official proceeding may make a motion under this Section to suppress the contents of an intercepted private oral communication, or evidence derived from it, on the grounds that:

(1) The communication was unlawfully intercepted;

(2) The order of authorization or approval under which it was intercepted is insufficient on its face; or

(3) The interception was not made in conformity with the order of authorization or approval or at the time of the application there was not probable cause to believe that the aggrieved person was committing or had committed the offense to which the content of the communication relates.

(d) If a motion under this Section duly alleges that the evidence sought to be suppressed in an official proceeding, including a grand jury, has been derived from an unlawfully intercepted private oral communication, and if the aggrieved person who is a party has not been served with notice of the interception under this Section, the opponent of the allegation shall, after conducting a thorough search of its files, affirm or deny the occurrence of the alleged unlawful interception, but no motion shall be considered if the alleged unlawful interception took place more than 5 years before the event to which the evidence relates.

(e) Where a motion is duly made under this Section prior to the appearance of a witness before a grand jury, the opponent of the motion may make such applications and orders as it has available to the chief judge of a court of competent jurisdiction in camera, and if the judge determines that there is no defect in them sufficient on its face to render them invalid, the judge shall inform the witness that he has not been the subject of an unlawful interception. If the judge determines that there is a defect in them sufficient on its face to render them invalid, he shall enter an order prohibiting any question being put to the witness based on the unlawful interception.

(f) Motions under this Section shall be made prior to the official proceeding unless there was no opportunity to make the motion or unless the aggrieved person who is a party was not aware of the grounds for the motion. Motions by co-indictees shall, on motion of the People, be heard in a single consolidated hearing.

(g) A chief judge of a court of competent jurisdiction, upon the filing of a motion by an aggrieved person who is a party under this Section, except before a grand jury, may make available for inspection by the aggrieved person or his attorney such portions of the intercepted communications, applications and orders or the evidence derived from them as the judge determines to be in the interest of justice.

(h) If a motion under this Section is granted, the intercepted private oral communication, and evidence derived from it, may not be received in evidence in an official proceeding, including a grand jury.

(i) In addition to any other right of appeal, the People shall have the right to appeal from an order granting a motion to suppress if the official to whom the order authorizing the interception was granted certifies to the court that the appeal is not taken for purposes of delay. The appeal shall otherwise be taken in accordance with the law.

(Source: P.A. 85-1203.) [Formerly Ill. Rev. Stat. 38 §108B-12.]

5/108B-13. Reports concerning use of eavesdropping devices.

§108B-13. Reports concerning use of eavesdropping devices. (a) Within 30 days after the expiration of an order and each extension thereof authorizing an interception, or within 30 days after the denial of an application or disapproval of an application subsequent to any alleged emergency situation, the State's Attorney shall report to the Department of State Police the following:

(1) the fact that such an order, extension, or subsequent approval of an emergency was applied for;

(2) the kind of order or extension applied for;

(3) a statement as to whether the order or extension was granted as applied for was modified, or was denied;

(4) the period authorized by the order or extensions in which an eavesdropping device could be used;

(5) the offense enumerated in Section 108B-3 which is specified in the order or extension or in the denied application;

(6) the identity of the applying electronic criminal surveillance officer and agency making the application and the State's Attorney authorizing the application; and

(7) the nature of the facilities from which or the place where the eavesdropping device was to be used.

(b) In January of each year the State's Attorney of each county in which an interception occurred pursuant to the provisions of this Article shall report to the Department of State Police the following:

(1) a general description of the uses of eavesdropping devices actually made under such order to overhear or record conversations, including: (a) the approximate nature and frequency of incriminating conversations overheard, (b) the approximate nature and frequency of other conversations overheard, (c) the approximate number of persons whose conversations were overheard, and (d) the approximate nature, amount, and cost of the manpower and other resources used pursuant to the authorization to use an eavesdropping device;

(2) the number of arrests resulting from authorized uses of eavesdropping devices and the offenses for which arrests were made;

(3) the number of trials resulting from such uses of eavesdropping devices;

(4) the number of motions to suppress made with respect to such uses, and the number granted or denied; and

(5) the number of convictions resulting from such uses and the offenses for which the convictions were obtained and a general assessment of the importance of the convictions.

On or before March 1 of each year, the Director of the Department of State Police shall submit to the Governor a report of all intercepts as defined herein conducted pursuant to this Article and terminated during the preceding calendar year. Such report shall include:

(1) the reports of State's Attorneys forwarded to the Director as required in this Section;

(2) the number of Department personnel authorized to possess, install, or operate electronic, mechanical, or other devices;

(3) the number of Department and other law enforcement personnel who participated or engaged in the seizure of intercepts pursuant to this Article during the preceding calendar year;

(4) the number of electronic criminal surveillance officers trained by the Department;

(5) the total cost to the Department of all activities and procedures relating to the seizure of intercepts during the preceding calendar year, including costs of equipment, manpower, and expenses incurred as compensation for use of facilities or technical assistance provided to or by the Department; and

(6) a summary of the use of eavesdropping devices pursuant to orders of interception including (a) the frequency of use in each county, (b) the frequency of use for each crime enumerated in Section 108B-3 of the Code of Criminal Procedure of 1963, as amended, (c) the type and frequency of eavesdropping device use, and (d) the frequency of use by each police department or law enforcement agency of this State.

(d)* In April of each year, the Director of the Department of State Police and the Governor shall each transmit to the General Assembly reports including information on the number of applications for orders authorizing the use of eavesdropping devices, the number of orders and extensions granted or denied during the preceding calendar year, the convictions arising out of such uses, and a summary of the information required by subsections (a) and (b) of this Section.

The requirement for reporting to the General Assembly shall be satisfied by filing copies of the report with the Speaker, the Minority Leader and the Clerk of the House of Representatives and the President, the Minority Leader and the Secretary of the Senate and the Legislative Research Unit, as required by Section 3.1 of the General Assembly Organization Act [25 ILCS 5/3.1], and filing such additional copies with the State Government Report Distribution Center for the General Assembly as is required under paragraph (t) of Section 7 of the State Library Act [15 ILCS 320/7].

**So in original. No subsec. (c) has been designated.*

(Source: P.A. 85-1203; 86-1226; 86-1475.) [Formerly Ill. Rev. Stat. 38 §108B-13.]

5/108B-14. Training.

§108B-14. Training. (a) The Director of the Illinois Department of State Police shall:

(1) Establish a course of training in the legal, practical, and technical aspects of the interception of private oral communications and related investigation and prosecution techniques;

(2) Issue regulations as he finds necessary for the training program;

(3) In cooperation with the Illinois Local Governmental Law Enforcement Officers Training Board, set minimum standards for certification and periodic recertification of electronic criminal surveillance officers as eligible to apply for orders authorizing the interception of private oral communications, to conduct the interceptions, and to use the communications or evidence derived from them in official proceedings; and

(4) In cooperation with the Illinois Local Governmental Law Enforcement Officers Training Board, revoke or suspend the certification of any electronic criminal surveillance officer who has violated any law relating to electronic criminal surveillance, or any of the guidelines established by the Department for conducting electronic criminal surveillance.

(b) The Executive Director of the Illinois Local Governmental Law Enforcement Officers Training Board shall:

(1) Pursuant to the Illinois Police Training Act [50 ILCS 705/1 et seq.], review the course of training prescribed by the Department for the purpose of certification relating to reimbursement of expenses incurred by local law enforcement agencies participating in the electronic criminal surveillance officer training process, and

(2) Assist the Department in establishing minimum standards for certification and periodic recertification of electronic criminal surveillance officers as being eligible to apply for orders authorizing the interception of private oral communications, to conduct the interpretations, and to use the communications or evidence derived from them in official proceedings.

(Source: P.A. 86-763.) [Formerly Ill. Rev. Stat. 38 §108B-14.]

TITLE III. PROCEEDINGS AFTER ARREST

ARTICLE 109. PRELIMINARY EXAMINATION

5/109-1. Person arrested.

§109-1. Person arrested. (a) A person arrested with or without a warrant shall be taken without unnecessary delay before the nearest and most accessible judge in that county, except when such county is a participant in a regional jail authority, in which event such person may be taken to the nearest and most accessible judge, irrespective of the county where such judge presides, and a charge shall be filed. Whenever a person arrested either with or without a warrant is required to be taken before a judge, and such person is in a different building than the building in which the judge is located, a charge may be filed against such person by way of a two-way closed circuit television system, except that a hearing to deny bail to the defendant may not be conducted by way of closed circuit television.

(b) The judge shall:

(1) Inform the defendant of the charge against him and shall provide him with a copy of the charge.

(2) Advise the defendant of his right to counsel and if indigent shall appoint a public defender or licensed attorney at law of this State to represent him in accordance with the provisions of Section 113-3 of this Code.

(3) Schedule a preliminary hearing in appropriate cases; and

(4) Admit the defendant to bail in accordance with the provisions of Article 110 of this Code [725 ILCS 5/110-1 et seq.].

(c) The court may issue an order of protection in accordance with the provisions of Article 112A of this Code [725 ILCS 5/112A-1 et seq.].

(Source: P.A. 85-1209.) [Formerly Ill. Rev. Stat. 38 §109-1.]

5/109-1.1. Care of children of person arrested.

§109-1.1. (1)* Whenever a person arrested either with or without a warrant is taken before a judge as provided for in Sections 107-9(d) (6) and 109-1(a), the judge shall ask the arrestee whether he or she has any children under 18 years old living with him or her who may be neglected as a result of the arrest, incarceration or otherwise. If the judge has reasonable cause to believe that a child may be a neglected child as defined in the Abused and Neglected Child Care Reporting Act [325 ILCS 5/1 et seq.], he shall instruct a probation officer to report it immediately to the Department of Children and Family Services as provided in that Act.

**So in original. No subsec. (2) has been enacted.*

(Source: P.A. 82-228.) [Formerly Ill. Rev. Stat. 38 §109-1.1.]

5/109-2. Person arrested in another county.

§109-2. Person arrested in another county. (a) Any person arrested in a county other than the one in which a warrant for his arrest was issued shall be taken without unnecessary delay before the nearest and most accessible judge in the county where the arrest was made or, if no additional delay is created, before the nearest and most accessible judge in the county from which the warrant was issued. He shall be admitted to bail in the amount specified in the warrant or, for offenses other than felonies, in an amount as set by the judge, and such bail shall be conditioned on his appearing in the court issuing the warrant on a certain date. The judge may hold a hearing to determine if the defendant is the same person as named in the warrant.

(b) Notwithstanding the provisions of subsection (a), any person arrested in a county other than the one in which a warrant for his arrest was issued, may waive the right to be taken before a judge in the county where the arrest was made. If a person so arrested waives such right, the arresting agency shall surrender such person to a law enforcement agency of the county that issued the warrant without unnecessary delay. The provisions of Section 109-1 shall then apply to the person so arrested.

(Source: P.A. 86-298.) [Formerly Ill. Rev. Stat. 38 §109-2.]

5/109-3. Preliminary examination.

§109-3. Preliminary examination. (a) The judge shall hold the defendant to answer to the court having jurisdiction of the offense if from the evidence it appears there is probable cause to believe an offense has been committed by the defendant, as provided in Section 109-3.1 of this Code, if the offense is a felony.

(b) If the defendant waives preliminary examination the judge shall hold him to answer and may, or on the demand of the prosecuting attorney shall, cause the witnesses for the State to be examined. After hearing the testimony if it appears that there is not probable cause to believe the defendant guilty of any offense the judge shall discharge him.

(c) During the examination of any witness or when the defendant is making a statement or testifying the judge may and on the request of the defendant or State shall exclude all other witnesses. He may also cause the witnesses to be kept separate and to be prevented from communicating with each other until all are examined.

(d) If the defendant is held to answer the judge may require any material witness for the State or defendant to enter into a written undertaking to appear at the trial, and may provide for the forfeiture of a sum certain in the event the witness does not appear at the trial. Any witness who refuses to execute a recognizance may be committed by the judge to the custody of the sheriff until trial or further order of the court having jurisdiction of the cause. Any witness who executes a recognizance and fails to comply with its terms shall, in addition to any forfeiture provided in the recognizance, be subject to the penalty provided in Section 32-10 of the "Criminal Code of 1961", approved July 28, 1961, as heretofore and hereafter amended [720 ILCS 5/32-10], for violation of bail bond.

(e) During preliminary hearing or examination the defendant may move for an order of suppression of evidence pursuant to Section 114-11 or 114-12 of this Act or for other reasons, and may move for dismissal of the charge pursuant to Section 114-1 of this Act or for other reasons.

(Source: P.A. 83-644.) [Formerly Ill. Rev. Stat. 38 §109-3.]

5/109-3.1. Persons charged with felonies.

§109-3.1. Persons Charged with Felonies. (a) In any case involving a person charged with a felony in this State, alleged to have been committed on or after January 1, 1984, the provisions of this Section shall apply.

(b) Every person in custody in this State for the alleged commission of a felony shall receive either a preliminary examination as provided in Section 109-3 or an indictment by Grand Jury as provided in Section 111-2, within 30 days from the date he or she was taken into custody. Every person on bail or recognizance for the alleged commission of a felony shall receive either a preliminary examination as provided in Section 109-3 or an indictment by Grand Jury as provided in Section 111-2, within 60 days from the date he or she was arrested. The provisions of this paragraph shall not apply in the following situations:

(1) when delay is occasioned by the defendant; or

(2) when the defendant has been indicted by the Grand Jury on the felony offense for which he or she was initially taken into custody or on an offense arising from the same transaction or conduct of the defendant that was the basis for the felony offense or offenses initially charged; or

(3) when a competency examination is ordered by the court; or

(4) when a competency hearing is held; or

(5) when an adjudication of incompetency for trial has been made; or

(6) when the case has been continued by the court under Section 114-4 of this Code after a determination that the defendant is physically incompetent to stand trial.

(c) Delay occasioned by the defendant shall temporarily suspend, for the time of the delay, the period within which the preliminary examination must

be held. On the day of expiration of the delay the period in question shall continue at the point at which it was suspended.
(Source: P.A. 83-644.) [Formerly Ill. Rev. Stat. 38 §109-3.1.]

ARTICLE 110. BAIL

Sec.

5/110-1. Definitions.

§110-1. Definitions. (a) "Security" is that which is required to be pledged to insure the payment of bail.

(b) "Sureties" encompasses the monetary and nonmonetary requirements set by the court as conditions for release either before or after conviction. "Surety" is one who executes a bail bond and binds himself to pay the bail if the person in custody fails to comply with all conditions of the bail bond.

(c) The phrase "for which a sentence of imprisonment, without conditional and revocable release, shall be imposed by law as a consequence of conviction" means an offense for which a sentence of imprisonment, without probation, periodic imprisonment or conditional discharge, is required by law upon conviction.

(d) "Real and present threat to the physical safety of any person or persons", as used in this Article, includes a threat to the community, person, persons or class of persons.
(Source: P.A. 85-892.) [Formerly Ill. Rev. Stat. 38 §110-1.]

5/110-2. Release on own recognizance.

§110-2. Release on own recognizance. When from all the circumstances the court is of the opinion that the accused will appear as required either before or after conviction and the accused will not pose a danger to any person or the community and that the accused will comply with all conditions of bond, the accused may be released on his own recognizance. A failure to appear as required by such recognizance shall constitute an offense subject to the penalty provided in Section 32-10 of the "Criminal Code of 1961", approved July 28, 1961, as heretofore and hereafter amended [720 ILCS 5/32-10], for violation of the bail bond, and any obligated sum fixed in the recognizance shall be forfeited and collected in accordance with subsection (g) of Section 110-7 of this Code.

This Section shall be liberally construed to effectuate the purpose of relying upon contempt of court proceedings or criminal sanctions instead of financial loss to assure the appearance of the accused, and that the accused will not pose a danger to any person or the community and that the defendant will comply with all conditions of bond. Monetary bail should be set only when it is determined that no other conditions of release will reasonably assure the defendant's appearance in court, that the defendant does not present a danger to any person or the community and that the defendant will comply with all conditions of bond.

The State may appeal any order permitting release by personal recognizance.
(Source: P.A. 86-984.) [Formerly Ill. Rev. Stat. 38 §110-2.]

5/110-3. Issuance of warrant.

§110-3. Issuance of warrant. Upon failure to comply with any condition of a bail bond or recognizance the court having jurisdiction at the time of such failure may, in addition to any other action provided by law, issue a warrant for the arrest of the person at liberty on bail or his own recognizance. The contents of such a warrant shall be the same as required for an arrest warrant issued upon complaint. When a defendant is at liberty on bail or his own recognizance on a felony charge and fails to appear in court as directed, the court shall issue a warrant for the arrest of such person. Such warrant shall be noted with a directive to peace officers to arrest the person and hold such person without bail and to deliver such person before the court for further proceedings. A defendant who is arrested or surrenders within 30 days of the issuance of such warrant shall not be bailable in the case in question unless he shows by the preponderance of the evidence that his failure to appear was not intentional.
(Source: P.A. 86-298; 86-984; 86-1028.) [Formerly Ill. Rev. Stat. 38 §110-3.]

5/110-4. Bailable offenses.

§110-4. Bailable Offenses. (a) All persons shall be bailable before conviction, except the following offenses where the proof is evident or the presumption great that the defendant is guilty of the offense: capital offenses; offenses for which a sentence of life imprisonment may be imposed as a consequence of imprisonment, without conditional and revocable release, shall be imposed by law as a consequence of conviction, where the court after a hearing, determines that the release of the defendant would pose a real and present threat to the physical safety of any person or persons; or stalking or aggravated stalking, where the court, after a hearing, determines that the release of the defendant would pose a real and present threat to the physical safety of the alleged victim of the offense and denial of bail is necessary to prevent fulfillment of the threat upon which the charge is based.

(b) A person seeking release on bail who is charged with a capital offense or an offense for which a sentence of life imprisonment may be imposed shall not be bailable until a hearing is held wherein such person has the burden of demonstrating that the proof of his guilt is not evident and the presumption is not great.

(c) Where it is alleged that bail should be denied to a person upon the grounds that the person presents a real and present threat to the physical safety of any person or persons, the burden of proof of such allegations shall be upon the State.

(d) When it is alleged that bail should be denied to a person charged with stalking or aggravated stalking upon the grounds set forth in Section 110-6.3 of this Code, the burden of proof of those allegations shall be upon the State.
(Source: P.A. 87-870; 87-871.) [Formerly Ill. Rev. Stat. 38 §110-4.]

5/110-5. Determining the amount of bail and conditions of release.

§110-5. Determining the amount of bail and conditions of release. (a) In determining the amount of monetary bail or conditions of release, if any, which will reasonably assure the appearance of a defendant as required or the safety of any other person or the community and the likelihood of compliance by the defendant with all the conditions of bail, the court shall, on the basis of available information, take into account such matters as the nature and circumstances of the offense charged, whether the evidence shows that as part of the offense there was a use of violence or threatened use of violence, whether the offense involved corruption of public officials or employees, whether there was physical harm or threats of physical harm to any public official, public employee, judge, prosecutor, juror or witness, senior citizen, child or handicapped person, whether evidence shows that during the offense or during the arrest the defendant possessed or used a firearm, machine gun, explosive or metal piercing ammunition or explosive bomb device or any military or paramilitary armament, the condition of the victim, any written statement submitted by the victim or proffer or representation by the State regarding the impact which the alleged criminal conduct has had on the victim and the victim's concern, if any, with further contact with the defendant if released on bail, whether the offense was based on racial, religious, sexual orientation or ethnic hatred, the likelihood of the filing of a greater charge, the likelihood of conviction, the sentence applicable upon conviction, the weight of the evidence against such defendant, whether there exists motivation or ability to flee, whether there is any verification as to prior residence, education, or family ties in the local jurisdiction, in another county, state or foreign country, the defendant's employment, financial resources, character and mental condition, past conduct, prior use of alias names or dates of birth, and length of residence in the community, whether a foreign national defendant is lawfully admitted in the United States of America, whether the government of the foreign national maintains an extradition treaty with the United States by which the foreign government will extradite to the United States its national for a trial for a crime allegedly committed in the United States, whether the defendant is currently subject to deportation or exclusion under the immigration laws of the United States, whether the defendant, although a United States citizen, is considered under the law of any foreign state a national of that state for the purposes of extradition or non-extradition to the United States, the amount of unrecovered proceeds lost as a result of the alleged offense, the source of bail funds tendered or sought to be tendered for bail, whether from the totality of the court's consideration, the loss of funds posted or sought to be posted for bail will not deter the defendant from flight, whether the evidence shows that the defendant is engaged in significant possession, manufacture, or delivery of a controlled substance or cannabis, either individually or in consort with others, whether at the time of the offense charged he was on bond or pre-trial release pending trial, probation, periodic imprisonment or conditional discharge pursuant to this Code or the comparable Code of any other state or federal jurisdiction, whether the defendant is on bond or pre-trial release pending the imposition or execution of sentence or appeal of sentence for any offense under the laws of Illinois or any other state or federal jurisdiction, whether the defendant is under parole or mandatory supervised release or work release from the Illinois Department of Corrections or any penal institution or corrections department of any state or federal jurisdiction, the defendant's record of convictions, whether the defendant has been convicted of a misdemeanor or ordinance offense in Illinois or similar offense in other state or federal jurisdiction within the 10 years preceding the current charge or convicted of a felony in Illinois, whether the defendant was convicted of an offense in another state or federal jurisdiction that would be a felony if committed in Illinois within the 20 years preceding the current charge or has been convicted of such felony and released from the penitentiary within 20 years preceding the current charge if a penitentiary sentence was imposed in Illinois or other state or federal jurisdiction, the defendant's records of juvenile adjudication of delinquency in any jurisdiction, any record of appearance or failure to appear by the defendant at court proceedings, whether there was flight to avoid arrest or prosecution, whether the defendant escaped or attempted to escape to avoid arrest, whether the defendant refused to identify himself, or whether there was a refusal by the defendant to be fingerprinted as required by law. Information used by the court in its findings or stated in or offered in connection with this Section may be by way of proffer based upon reliable information offered by the State or defendant. All evidence shall be admissible if it is relevant and reliable regardless of whether it would be admissible under the rules of evidence applicable at criminal trials.

(b) The amount of bail shall be:

(1) Sufficient to assure compliance with the conditions set forth in the bail bond;

(2) Not oppressive;

(3) Considerate of the financial ability of the accused.

(4) When a person is charged with a drug related offense involving possession or delivery of cannabis or possession or delivery of a controlled substance as defined in the Cannabis Control Act [720 ILCS 550/1 et seq.], as amended, or the Illinois Controlled Substances Act [720 ILCS 570/100 et seq.], as amended, the full street value of the drugs seized shall be considered. "Street value" shall be determined by the court on the basis of a proffer by the State based upon reliable information of a law enforcement official contained in a written report as to the amount seized and such proffer may be used by the court as to the current street value of the smallest unit of the drug seized.

(c) When a person is charged with an offense punishable by fine only the amount of the bail shall not exceed double the amount of the maximum penalty.

(d) When a person has been convicted of an offense and only a fine has been imposed the amount of the bail shall not exceed double the amount of the fine.

(e) The State may appeal any order granting bail or setting a given amount for bail.

(Source: P.A. 86-984.) [Formerly Ill. Rev. Stat. 38 §110-5.]

5/110-6. Grant, denial, reduction or increase of bail.

§110-6. (a) Upon verified application by the State or the defendant or on its own motion the court before which the proceeding is pending may increase or reduce the amount of bail or may alter the conditions of the bail bond or grant bail where it has been previously revoked or denied. If bail has been previously revoked pursuant to subsection (f) of this Section or if bail has been denied to the defendant pursuant to subsection (e) of Section 110-6.1 or subsection (e) of Section 110-6.3, the defendant shall be required to present a verified application setting forth in detail any new facts not known or obtainable at the time of the previous revocation or denial of bail proceedings. If the court grants bail where it has been previously revoked or denied, the court shall state on the record of the proceedings the findings of facts and conclusion of law upon which such order is based.

(b) Violation of the conditions of Section 110-10 of this Code or any special conditions of bail as ordered by the court shall constitute grounds for the court to increase the amount of bail, or otherwise alter the conditions of bail, or, where the alleged offense committed on bail is a forcible felony in Illinois or a Class 2 or greater offense under the Controlled Substances Act [720 ILCS 570/100 et seq.] or Cannabis Control Act [720 ILCS 550/1 et seq.], revoke bail pursuant to the appropriate provisions of subsection (e) of this section.

(c) Reasonable notice of such application by the defendant shall be given to the State.

(d) Reasonable notice of such application by the State shall be given to the defendant, except as provided in subsection (e).

(e) Upon verified application by the State stating facts or circumstances constituting a violation or a threatened violation of any of the conditions of the bail bond the court may issue a warrant commanding any peace officer to bring the defendant without unnecessary delay before the court for a hearing on the matters set forth in the application. If the actual court before which the proceeding is pending is absent or otherwise unavailable another court may issue a warrant pursuant to this Section. When the defendant is charged with a felony offense and while free on bail is charged with a subsequent felony offense and is the subject of a proceeding set forth in Section 109-1 or 109-3 of this Code, upon the filing of a verified petition by the State alleging a violation of Section 110-10 (a) (4) of this Code, the court shall without prior notice to the defendant, grant leave to file such application and shall order the transfer of the defendant and the application without unnecessary delay to the court before which the previous felony matter is pending for a hearing as provided in subsection (b) or this subsection of this Section. The defendant shall be held without bond pending transfer to and a hearing before such court. At the conclusion of the hearing based on a violation of the conditions of Section 110-10 of this Code or any special conditions of bail as ordered by the court the court may enter an order increasing the amount of bail or alter the conditions of bail as deemed appropriate.

(f) Where the alleged violation consists of the violation of one or more felony statutes of any jurisdiction which would be a forcible felony in Illinois or a Class 2 or greater offense under the Illinois Controlled Substances Act or Cannabis Control Act and the defendant is on bail for the alleged commission of a felony, the court shall, on the motion of the State or its own motion, revoke bail in accordance with the following provisions:

(1) The court shall hold the defendant without bail pending the hearing on the alleged breach; however, if the defendant is not admitted to bail the hearing shall be commenced within 10 days from the date the defendant is taken into custody or the defendant may not be held any longer without bail, unless delay is occasioned by the defendant. Where defendant occasions the delay, the running of the 10 day period is temporarily suspended and resumes at the termination of the period of delay. Where defendant occasions the delay with 5 or fewer days remaining in the 10 day period, the court may grant a period of up to 5 additional days to the State for good cause shown. The State, however, shall retain the right to proceed to hearing on the alleged violation at any time, upon reasonable notice to the defendant and the court.

(2) At a hearing on the alleged violation the State has the burden of going forward and proving the violation by clear and convincing evidence. The evidence shall be presented in open court with the opportunity to testify, to present witnesses in his behalf, and to cross-examine witnesses if any are called by the State, and representation by counsel and if the defendant is indigent to have counsel appointed for him. The rules of evidence applicable in criminal trials in this State shall not govern the admissibility of evidence at such hearing. Information used by the court in its findings or stated in or offered in connection with hearings for increase or revocation of bail may be by way of proffer based upon reliable information offered by the State or defendant. All evidence shall be admissible if it is relevant and reliable regardless of whether it would be admissible under the rules of evidence applicable at criminal trials. A motion by the defendant to suppress evidence or to suppress a confession shall not be entertained at such a hearing. Evidence that proof may have been obtained as a result of an unlawful search and seizure or through improper interrogation is not relevant to this hearing.

(3) Upon a finding by the court that the State has established by clear and convincing evidence that the defendant has committed a forcible felony or a

Class 2 or greater offense under the Controlled Substances Act or Cannabis Control Act while admitted to bail, the court shall revoke the bail of the defendant and hold the defendant for trial without bail. Neither the finding of the court nor any transcript or other record of the hearing shall be admissible in the State's case in chief, but shall be admissible for impeachment, or as provided in Section 115-10.1 of this Code or in a perjury proceeding.

(4) If the bail of any defendant is revoked pursuant to paragraph (f) (3) of this Section, the defendant may demand and shall be entitled to be brought to trial on the offense with respect to which he was formerly released on bail within 90 days after the date on which his bail was revoked. If the defendant is not brought to trial within the 90 day period required by the preceding sentence, he shall not be held longer without bail. In computing the 90 day period, the court shall omit any period of delay resulting from a continuance granted at the request of the defendant.

(5) If the defendant either is arrested on a warrant issued pursuant to this Code or is arrested for an unrelated offense and it is subsequently discovered that the defendant is a subject of another warrant or warrants issued pursuant to this Code, the defendant shall be transferred promptly to the court which issued such warrant. If, however, the defendant appears initially before a court other than the court which issued such warrant, the non-issuing court shall not alter the amount of bail heretofore set on such warrant unless the court sets forth on the record of proceedings the conclusions of law and facts which are the basis for such altering of another court's bond. The non-issuing court shall not alter another courts bail set on a warrant unless the interests of justice and public safety are served by such action.

(g) The State may appeal any order where the court has increased or reduced the amount of bail or altered the conditions of the bail bond or granted bail where it has previously been revoked.

(Source: P.A. 86-984; 87-870; 87-871.) [Formerly Ill. Rev. Stat. 38 §110-6.]

5/110-6.1. Denial of bail in non-probationable felony offenses.

§110-6.1. Denial of bail in non-probationable felony offenses. (a) Upon verified petition by the State, the court shall hold a hearing to determine whether bail should be denied to a defendant who is charged with a felony offense for which a sentence of imprisonment, without probation, periodic imprisonment or conditional discharge, is required by law upon conviction, when it is alleged that the defendant's admission to bail poses a real and present threat to the physical safety of any person or persons.

(1) A petition may be filed without prior notice to the defendant at the first appearance before a judge, or within the 21 calendar days, except as provided in Section 110-6, after arrest and release of the defendant upon reasonable notice to defendant; provided that while such petition is pending before the court, the defendant if previously released shall not be detained.

(2) The hearing shall be held immediately upon the defendant's appearance before the court, unless for good cause shown the defendant or the State seeks a continuance. A continuance on motion of the defendant may not exceed 5 calendar days, and a continuance on the motion of the State may not exceed 3 calendar days. The defendant may be held in custody during such continuance.

(b) The court may deny bail to the defendant where, after the hearing, it is determined that:

(1) the proof is evident or the presumption great that the defendant has committed an offense for which a sentence of imprisonment, without probation, periodic imprisonment or conditional discharge, must be imposed by law as a consequence of conviction, and

(2) the defendant poses a real and present threat to the physical safety of any person or persons, by conduct which may include, but is not limited to, a

forcible felony, the obstruction of justice, intimidation, injury, physical harm, or an offense under the Illinois Controlled Substances Act [720 ILCS 570/100 et seq.] which is a Class X felony, and

(3) the court finds that no condition or combination of conditions set forth in subsection (b) of Section 110-10 of this Article, can reasonably assure the physical safety of any other person or persons.

(c) Conduct of the hearings.

(1) The hearing on the defendant's culpability and dangerousness shall be conducted in accordance with the following provisions:

(A) Information used by the court in its findings or stated in or offered at such hearing may be by way of proffer based upon reliable information offered by the State or by defendant. Defendant has the right to be represented by counsel, and if he is indigent, to have counsel appointed for him. Defendant shall have the opportunity to testify, to present witnesses in his own behalf, and to cross-examine witnesses if any are called by the State. The defendant has the right to present witnesses in his favor. When the ends of justice so require, the court may exercises* its discretion and compel the appearance of a complaining witness. The court shall state on the record reasons for granting a defense request to compel the presence of a complaining witness. Cross-examination of a complaining witness at the pretrial detention hearing for the purpose of impeaching the witness' credibility is insufficient reason to compel the presence of the witness. In deciding whether to compel the appearance of a complaining witness, the court shall be considerate of the emotional and physical well-being of the witness. The pre-trial detention hearing is not to be used for purposes of discovery, and the post arraignment rules of discovery do not apply. The State shall tender to the defendant, prior to the hearing, copies of defendant's criminal history, if any, if available, and any written or recorded statements and the substance of any oral statements made by any person, if relied upon by the State in its petition. The rules concerning the admissibility of evidence in criminal trials do not apply to the presentation and consideration of information at the hearing. At the trial concerning the offense for which the hearing was conducted neither the finding of the court nor any transcript or other record of the hearing shall be admissible in the State's case in chief, but shall be admissible for impeachment, or as provided in Section 115-10.1 of this Code, or in a perjury proceeding.

**So in original. Probably should be "exercise".*

(B) A motion by the defendant to suppress evidence or to suppress a confession shall not be entertained. Evidence that proof may have been obtained as the result of an unlawful search and seizure or through improper interrogation is not relevant to this state of the prosecution.

(2) The facts relied upon by the court to support a finding that the defendant poses a real and present threat to the physical safety of any person or persons shall be supported by clear and convincing evidence presented by the State.

(d) Factors to be considered in making a determination of dangerousness. The court may, in determining whether the defendant poses a real and present threat to the physical safety of any person or persons, consider but shall not be limited to evidence or testimony concerning:

(1) The nature and circumstances of any offense charged, including whether the offense is a crime of violence, involving a weapon.

(2) The history and characteristics of the defendant including:

(A) Any evidence of the defendant's prior criminal history indicative of violent, abusive or assaultive behavior, or lack of such behavior. Such evidence may include testimony or documents received in juvenile proceedings, criminal, quasi-criminal, civil commitment, domestic relations or other proceedings.

(B) Any evidence of the defendant's psychological, psychiatric or other similar social history which tends to indicate a violent, abusive, or assaultive nature, or lack of any such history.

(3) The identity of any person or persons to whose safety the defendant is believed to pose a threat, and the nature of the threat;

(4) Any statements made by, or attributed to the defendant, together with the circumstances surrounding them;

(5) The age and physical condition of any person assaulted by the defendant;

(6) Whether the defendant is known to possess or have access to any weapon or weapons;

(7) Whether, at the time of the current offense or any other offense or arrest, the defendant was on probation, parole, mandatory supervised release or other release from custody pending trial, sentencing, appeal or completion of sentence for an offense under federal or state law;

(8) Any other factors, including those listed in Section 110-5 of this Article deemed by the court to have a reasonable bearing upon the defendant's propensity or reputation for violent, abusive or assaultive behavior, or lack of such behavior.

(e) Detention order. The court shall, in any order for detention:

(1) briefly summarize the evidence of the defendant's culpability and its reasons for concluding that the defendant should be held without bail;

(2) direct that the defendant be committed to the custody of the sheriff for confinement in the county jail pending trial;

(3) direct that the defendant be given a reasonable opportunity for private consultation with counsel, and for communication with others of his choice by visitation, mail and telephone; and

(4) direct that the sheriff deliver the defendant as required for appearances in connection with court proceedings.

(f) If the court enters an order for the detention of the defendant pursuant to subsection (e) of this Section, the defendant shall be brought to trial on the offense for which he is detained within 90 days after the date on which the order for detention was entered. If the defendant is not brought to trial within the 90 day period required by the preceding sentence, he shall not be held longer without bail. In computing the 90 day period, the court shall omit any period of delay resulting from a continuance granted at the request of the defendant.

(g) Rights of the defendant. Any person shall be entitled to appeal any order entered under this Section denying bail to the defendant.

(h) The State may appeal any order entered under this Section denying any motion for denial of bail.

(i) Nothing in this Section shall be construed as modifying or limiting in any way the defendant's presumption of innocence in further criminal proceedings.
(Source: P.A. 85-1209.) [Formerly Ill. Rev. Stat. 38 §110-6.1.]

5/110-6.2. Post-conviction detention.

§110-6.2. Post-conviction Detention. (a) The court shall order that a person who has been found guilty of an offense and who is waiting imposition or execution of sentence be held without bond unless the court finds by clear and convincing evidence that the person is not likely to flee or pose a danger to any other person or the community if released under Sections 110-5 and 110-10 of this Act.

(b) The court shall order that person who has been found guilty of an offense and sentenced to a term of imprisonment shall be held without bond unless the court finds by clear and convincing evidence that:

(1) the person is not likely to flee or pose a danger to the safety of any other person or the community if released on bond pending appeal; and

(2) that the appeal is not for purpose of delay and raises a substantial question of law or fact likely to result in reversal or an order for a new trial.
(Source: P.A. 86-984.) [Formerly Ill. Rev. Stat. 38 §110-6.2.]

5/110-6.3. Denial of bail in stalking and aggravated stalking offenses.

§110-6.3. Denial of bail in stalking and aggravated stalking offenses. (a) Upon verified petition by the State, the court shall hold a hearing to determine whether bail should be denied to a defendant who is charged with stalking or aggravated stalking, when it is alleged that the defendant's admission to bail poses a real and present threat to the physical safety of the alleged victim of the offense, and denial of release on bail or personal recognizance is necessary to prevent fulfillment of the threat upon which the charge is based.

(1) A petition may be filed without prior notice to the defendant at the first appearance before a judge, or within 21 calendar days, except as provided in Section 110-6, after arrest and release of the defendant upon reasonable notice to defendant; provided that while the petition is pending before the court, the defendant if previously released shall not be detained.

(2) The hearing shall be held immediately upon the defendant's appearance before the court, unless for good cause shown the defendant or the State seeks a continuance. A continuance on motion of the defendant may not exceed 5 calendar days, and the defendant may be held in custody during the continuance. A continuance on the motion of the State may not exceed 3 calendar days; however, the defendant may be held in custody during the continuance under this provision if the defendant has been previously found to have violated an order of protection or has been previously convicted of, or granted court supervision for, any of the offenses set forth in Sections 12-2, 12-3.2, 12-4, 12-4.1, 12-7.3, 12-7.4, 12-13, 12-14, 12-15 or 12-16 of the Criminal Code of 1961 [720 ILCS 5/12-2, 5/12-3.2, 5/12-4, 5/12-4.1, 5/12-7.3, 5/12-7.4, 5/12-13, 5/12-14, 5/12-15 or 5/12-16], against the same person as the alleged victim of the stalking or aggravated stalking offense.

(b) The court may deny bail to the defendant when, after the hearing, it is determined that:

(1) the proof is evident or the presumption great that the defendant has committed the offense of stalking or aggravated stalking; and

(2) the defendant poses a real and present threat to the physical safety of the alleged victim of the offense; and

(3) the denial of release on bail or personal recognizance is necessary to prevent fulfillment of the threat upon which the charge is based; and

(4) the court finds that no condition or combination of conditions set forth in subsection (b) of Section 110-10 of this Code, including mental health treatment at a community mental health center, hospital, or facility of the Department of Mental Health and Developmental Disabilities, can reasonably assure the physical safety of the alleged victim of the offense.

(c) Conduct of the hearings.

(1) The hearing on the defendant's culpability and threat to the alleged victim of the offense shall be conducted in accordance with the following provisions:

(A) Information used by the court in its findings or stated in or offered at the hearing may be by way of proffer based upon reliable information offered by the State or by defendant. Defendant has the right to be represented by counsel, and if he is indigent, to have counsel appointed for him. Defendant shall have the opportunity to testify, to present witnesses in his own behalf, and to cross-examine witnesses if any are called by the State. The defendant has the right to present witnesses in his favor. When the ends of justice so require, the court may exercise its discretion and compel the appearance of a complaining witness. The court shall state on the record reasons for granting a defense request to compel the presence of a complaining witness. Cross-examination of a complaining witness at the pretrial detention hearing for the purpose of impeaching the witness' credibility is insufficient reason to compel the presence of the witness. In deciding whether to compel the appearance of a complaining witness, the court shall be considerate of the emotional and physical well-being of the witness. The pretrial detention hearing is not to be used for the purposes of discovery, and the post arraignment rules of discovery do not apply. The State shall tender to the defendant, prior to the hearing, copies of defendant's criminal history, if any, if available, and any written or recorded statements and the substance of any oral statements made by any person, if relied upon by the State. The rules concerning the admissibility of evidence in criminal trials do not apply to the presentation and consideration of information at the hearing. At the trial concerning the offense for which the hearing was conducted neither the finding of the court nor any transcript or other record of the hearing shall be admissible in the State's case in chief, but shall be admissible for impeachment, or as provided in Section 115-10.1 of this Code, or in a perjury proceeding.

(B) A motion by the defendant to suppress evidence or to suppress a confession shall not be entertained. Evidence that proof may have been obtained as the result of an unlawful search and seizure or through improper interrogation is not relevant to this state of the prosecution.

(2) The facts relied upon by the court to support a finding that:

(A) the defendant poses a real and present threat to the physical safety of the alleged victim of the offense; and

(B) the denial of release on bail or personal recognizance is necessary to prevent fulfillment of the threat upon which the charge is based;

shall be supported by clear and convincing evidence presented by the State.

(d) Factors to be considered in making a determination of the threat to the alleged victim of the offense. The court may, in determining whether the defendant poses, at the time of the hearing, a real and present threat to the physical safety of the alleged victim of the offense, consider but shall not be limited to evidence or testimony concerning:

(1) The nature and circumstances of the offense charged;

(2) The history and characteristics of the defendant including:

(A) Any evidence of the defendant's prior criminal history indicative of violent, abusive or assaultive behavior, or lack of that behavior. The evidence may include testimony or documents received in juvenile proceedings, criminal, quasi-criminal, civil commitment, domestic relations or other proceedings;

(B) Any evidence of the defendant's psychological, psychiatric or other similar social history that tends to indicate a violent, abusive, or assaultive nature, or lack of any such history.

(3) The nature of the threat which is the basis of the charge against the defendant;

(4) Any statements made by, or attributed to the defendant, together with the circumstances surrounding them;

(5) The age and physical condition of any person assaulted by the defendant;

(6) Whether the defendant is known to possess or have access to any weapon or weapons;

(7) Whether, at the time of the current offense or any other offense or arrest, the defendant was on probation, parole, mandatory supervised release or other release from custody pending trial, sentencing, appeal or completion of sentence for an offense under federal or state law;

(8) Any other factors, including those listed in Section 110-5 of this Code, deemed by the court to have a reasonable bearing upon the defendant's propen-

sity or reputation for violent, abusive or assaultive behavior, or lack of that behavior.

(e) The court shall, in any order denying bail to a person charged with stalking or aggravated stalking:

(1) briefly summarize the evidence of the defendant's culpability and its reasons for concluding that the defendant should be held without bail;

(2) direct that the defendant be committed to the custody of the sheriff for confinement in the county jail pending trial;

(3) direct that the defendant be given a reasonable opportunity for private consultation with counsel, and for communication with others of his choice by visitation, mail and telephone; and

(4) direct that the sheriff deliver the defendant as required for appearances in connection with court proceedings.

(f) If the court enters an order for the detention of the defendant under subsection (e) of this Section, the defendant shall be brought to trial on the offense for which he is detained within 90 days after the date on which the order for detention was entered. If the defendant is not brought to trial within the 90 day period required by this subsection (f), he shall not be held longer without bail. In computing the 90 day period, the court shall omit any period of delay resulting from a continuance granted at the request of the defendant. The court shall immediately notify the alleged victim of the offense that the defendant has been admitted to bail under this subsection.

(g) Any person shall be entitled to appeal any order entered under this Section denying bail to the defendant.

(h) The State may appeal any order entered under this Section denying any motion for denial of bail.

(i) Nothing in this Section shall be construed as modifying or limiting in any way the defendant's presumption of innocence in further criminal proceedings.
(Source: P.A. 87-870; 87-871.) [Formerly Ill. Rev. Stat. 38 §110-6.3.]

5/110-7. Deposit of bail security.

§110-7. Deposit of Bail Security. (a) The person for whom bail has been set shall execute the bail bond and deposit with the clerk of the court before which the proceeding is pending a sum of money equal to 10% of the bail, but in no event shall such deposit be less than $25. The clerk of the court shall provide a space on each form for a person other than the accused who has provided the money for the posting of bail to so indicate and a space signed by an accused who has executed the bail bond indicating whether a person other than the accused has provided the money for the posting of bail. The form shall also include a written notice to such person who has provided the defendant with the money for the posting of bail indicating that if the defendant fails to comply with the conditions of the bail bond, the court shall enter an order declaring the bail to be forfeited and that the bail may be used to pay costs, attorney's fees, fines or other purposes authorized by the court. When a person for whom bail has been set is charged with an offense under the "Illinois Controlled Substances Act" [720 ILCS 570/100 et seq.] which is a Class X felony, the court may require the defendant to deposit a sum equal to 100% of the bail. Where any person is charged with a forcible felony while free on bail and is the subject of proceedings under Section 109-3 of this Code the judge conducting the preliminary examination may also conduct a hearing upon the application of the State pursuant to the provisions of Section 110-6 of this Code to increase or revoke the bail for that person's prior alleged offense.

(b) Upon depositing this sum the person shall be released from custody subject to the conditions of the bail bond.

(c) Once bail has been given and a charge is pending or is thereafter filed in or transferred to a court of competent jurisdiction the latter court shall continue the original bail in that court subject to the provisions of Section 110-6 of this Code.

(d) After conviction the court may order that the original bail stand as bail pending appeal or deny, increase or reduce bail subject to the provisions of Section 110-6.2.

(e) After the entry of an order by the trial court allowing or denying bail pending appeal either party may apply to the reviewing court having jurisdiction or to a justice thereof sitting in vacation for an order increasing or decreasing the amount of bail or allowing or denying bail pending appeal subject to the provisions of Section 110-6.2.

(f) When the conditions of the bail bond have been performed and the accused has been discharged from all obligations in the cause the clerk of the court shall return to the accused or to the defendant's designee by an assignment executed at the time the bail amount is deposited, unless the court orders otherwise, 90% of the sum which had been deposited and shall retain as bail bond costs 10% of the amount deposited. However, in no event shall the amount retained by the clerk as bail bond costs be less than $5. Bail bond deposited by or on behalf of a defendant in one case may be used, in the court's discretion, to satisfy financial obligations of that same defendant incurred in a different case due to a fine, court costs, restitution or fees of the defendant's attorney of record. The court shall not order bail bond deposited by or on behalf of a defendant in one case to be used to satisfy financial obligations of that same defendant in a different case until the bail bond is first used to satisfy court costs in the case in which the bail bond has been deposited.

At the request of the defendant the court may order such 90% of defendant's bail deposit, or whatever amount is repayable to defendant from such deposit, to be paid to defendant's attorney of record.

(g) If the accused does not comply with the conditions of the bail bond the court having jurisdiction shall enter an order declaring the bail to be forfeited. Notice of such order of forfeiture shall be mailed forthwith to the accused at his last known address. If the accused does not appear and surrender to the court having jurisdiction within 30 days from the date of the forfeiture or within such period satisfy the court that appearance and surrender by the accused is impossible and without his fault the court shall enter judgment for the State if the charge for which the bond was given was a felony or misdemeanor, or if the charge was quasi-criminal or traffic, judgment for the political subdivision of the State which prosecuted the case, against the accused for the amount of the bail and costs of the court proceedings. The deposit made in accordance with paragraph (a) shall be applied to the payment of costs. If any amount of such deposit remains after the payment of costs it shall be applied to payment of the judgment and transferred to the treasury of the municipal corporation wherein the bond was taken if the offense was a violation of any penal ordinance of a political subdivision of this State, or to the treasury of the county wherein the bond was taken if the offense was a violation of any penal statute of this State. The balance of the judgment may be enforced and collected in the same manner as a judgment entered in a civil action.

(h) After a judgment for a fine and court costs or either is entered in the prosecution of a cause in which a deposit had been made in accordance with paragraph (a) the balance of such deposit, after deduction of bail bond costs, shall be applied to the payment of the judgment.

(Source: P.A. 86-337; 86-984; 86-1028.) [Formerly Ill. Rev. Stat. 38 §110-7.]

5/110-8. Cash, stocks, bonds and real estate as security for bail.

§110-8. Cash, stocks, bonds and real estate as security for bail. (a) In lieu of the bail deposit provided for in Section 110-7 of this Code any person for whom bail has been set may execute the bail bond with or without sureties which bond may be secured:

(1) By a deposit, with the clerk of the court, of an amount equal to the required bail, of cash, or stocks and bonds in which trustees are authorized to invest trust funds under the laws of this State; or

(2) By real estate situated in this State with unencumbered equity not exempt owned by the accused or sureties worth double the amount of bail set in the bond.

(b) If the bail bond is secured by stocks and bonds the accused or sureties shall file with the bond a sworn schedule which shall be approved by the court and shall contain:

(1) A list of the stocks and bonds deposited describing each in sufficient detail that it may be identified;

(2) The market value of each stock and bond;

(3) The total market value of the stocks and bonds listed;

(4) A statement that the affiant is the sole owner of the stocks and bonds listed and they are not exempt from the enforcement of a judgment thereon;

(5) A statement that such stocks and bonds have not previously been used or accepted as bail in this State during the 12 months preceding the date of the bail bond; and

(6) A statement that such stocks and bonds are security for the appearance of the accused in accordance with the conditions of the bail bond.

(c) If the bail bond is secured by real estate the accused or sureties shall file with the bond a sworn schedule which shall contain:

(1) A legal description of the real estate;

(2) A description of any and all encumbrances on the real estate including the amount of each and the holder thereof;

(3) The market value of the unencumbered equity owned by the affiant;

(4) A statement that the affiant is the sole owner of such unencumbered equity and that it is not exempt from the enforcement of a judgment thereon;

(5) A statement that the real estate has not previously been used or accepted as bail in this State during the 12 months preceding the date of the bail bond; and

(6) A statement that the real estate is security for the appearance of the accused in accordance with the conditions of the bail bond.

(d) The sworn schedule shall constitute a material part of the bail bond. The affiant commits perjury if in the sworn schedule he makes a false statement which he does not believe to be true. He shall be prosecuted and punished accordingly, or, he may be punished for contempt.

(e) A certified copy of the bail bond and schedule of real estate shall be filed immediately in the office of the registrar of titles or recorder of the county in which the real estate is situated and the State shall have a lien on such real estate from the time such copies are filed in the office of the registrar of titles or recorder. The registrar of titles or recorder shall enter, index and record (or register as the case may be) such bail bonds and schedules without requiring any advance fee, which fee shall be taxed as costs in the proceeding and paid out of such costs when collected.

(f) When the conditions of the bail bond have been performed and the accused has been discharged from his obligations in the cause, the clerk of the court shall return to him or his sureties the deposit of any cash, stocks or bonds. If the bail bond has been secured by real estate the clerk of the court shall forthwith notify in writing the registrar of titles or recorder and the lien of the bail bond on the real estate shall be discharged.

(g) If the accused does not comply with the conditions of the bail bond the court having jurisdiction shall enter an order declaring the bail to be forfeited.

Notice of such order of forfeiture shall be mailed forthwith by the clerk of the court to the accused and his sureties at their last known address. If the accused does not appear and surrender to the court having jurisdiction within 30 days from the date of the forfeiture or within such period satisfy the court that appearance and surrender by the accused is impossible and without his fault the court shall enter judgment for the State against the accused and his sureties for the amount of the bail and costs of the proceedings.

(h) When judgment is entered in favor of the State on any bail bond given for a felony or misdemeanor, or judgement for a political subdivision of the state on any bail bond given for a quasi-criminal or traffic offense, the State's Attorney or political subdivision's attorney shall forthwith obtain a certified copy of the judgment and deliver same to the sheriff to be enforced by levy on the cash, stocks or bonds deposited with the clerk of the court and the real estate described in the bail bond schedule. The cash shall be used to satisfy the judgment and costs and paid into the treasury of the municipal corporation wherein the bail bond was taken if the offense was a violation of any penal ordinance of a political subdivision of this State, or into the treasury of the county wherein the bail bond was taken if the offense was a violation of any penal statute of this State. The stocks, bonds and real estate shall be sold in the same manner as in sales for the enforcement of a judgment in civil actions and the proceeds of such sale shall be used to satisfy all court costs, prior encumbrances, if any, and from the balance a sufficient amount to satisfy the judgment shall be paid into the treasury of the municipal corporation wherein the bail bond was taken if the offense was a violation of any penal ordinance of a political subdivision of this State, or into the treasury of the county wherein the bail bond was taken if the offense was a violation of any penal statute of this State. The balance shall be returned to the owner. The real estate so sold may be redeemed in the same manner as real estate may be redeemed after judicial sales or sales for the enforcement of judgments in civil actions.

(i) No stocks, bonds or real estate may be used or accepted as bail bond security in this State more than once in any 12 month period.
(Source: P.A. 84-546.) [Formerly Ill. Rev. Stat. 38 §110-8.]

5/110-9. Taking of bail by peace officer.

§110-9. Taking of bail by peace officer. When bail has been set by a judicial officer for a particular offense or offender any sheriff or other peace officer may take bail in accordance with the provisions of Section 110-7 or 110-8 of this Code and release the offender to appear in accordance with the conditions of the bail bond, the Notice to Appear or the Summons. The officer shall give a receipt to the offender for the bail so taken and within a reasonable time deposit such bail with the clerk of the court having jurisdiction of the offense.
(Source: Laws 1963, p. 2836.) [Formerly Ill. Rev. Stat. 38 §110-9.]

5/110-10. Conditions of bail bond.

§110-10. Conditions of bail bond. (a) If a person is released prior to conviction, either upon payment of bail security or on his or her own recognizance, the conditions of the bail bond shall be that he or she will:

(1) Appear to answer the charge in the court having jurisdiction on a day certain and thereafter as ordered by the court until discharged or final order of the court;

(2) Submit himself or herself to the orders and process of the court;

(3) Not depart this State without leave of the court; and

(4) Not violate any criminal statute of any jurisdiction.

(b) The court may impose other conditions, such as the following, if the court finds that such conditions are reasonably necessary to assure the defendant's appearance in court, protect the public from the defendant, or prevent the defendant's unlawful interference with the orderly administration of justice:

(1) Report to or appear in person before such person or agency as the court may direct;

(2) Refrain from possessing a firearm or other dangerous weapon;

(3) Refrain from approaching or communicating with particular persons or classes of persons;

(4) Refrain from going to certain described geographical areas or premises;

(5) Refrain from engaging in certain activities or indulging in intoxicating liquors or in certain drugs;

(6) Undergo treatment for drug addiction or alcoholism;

(7) Undergo medical or psychiatric treatment;

(8) Work or pursue a course of study or vocational training;

(9) Attend or reside in a facility designated by the court;

(10) Support his or her dependents;

(11) If a minor resides with his or her parents or in a foster home, attend school, attend a non-residential program for youths, and contribute to his or her own support at home or in a foster home;

(12) Observe any curfew ordered by the court;

(13) Remain in the custody of such designated person or organization agreeing to supervise his release. Such third party custodian shall be responsible for notifying the court if the defendant fails to observe the conditions of release which the custodian has agreed to monitor, and shall be subject to contempt of court for failure so to notify the court;

(14) Be placed under direct supervision of the Pretrial Services Agency, Probation Department or Court Services Department in a pretrial bond home supervision capacity with or without the use of an approved electronic monitoring device subject to Article 8A of Chapter V of the Unified Code of Corrections [730 ILCS 5/5-8A-1 et seq.]; or

(14.1) The court shall impose upon a defendant who is charged with any alcohol, cannabis or controlled substance violation and is placed under direct supervision of the Pretrial Services Agency, Probation Department or Court Services Department in a pretrial bond home supervision capacity with the use of an approved monitoring device, as a condition of such bail bond, a fee not to exceed $5 for each day of such bail supervision ordered by the court, unless after determining the inability of the defendant to pay the fee, the court assesses a lesser fee or no fee as the case may be. The fee shall be collected by the clerk of the circuit court. The clerk of the circuit court shall pay all monies collected from this fee to the county treasurer for deposit in the substance abuse services fund under Section 5-1086.1 of the Counties Code [55 ILCS 5/5-1086.1].

(14.2) The court shall impose upon all defendants, other than those defendants subject to paragraph (14.1) above, placed under direct supervision of the Pretrial Services Agency, Probation Department or Court Services Department in a pretrial bond home supervision capacity with the use of an approved monitoring device, as a condition of such bail bond, a fee not to exceed $5 for each day of such bail supervision ordered by the court, unless after determining the inability of the defendant to pay the fee, the court assesses a lesser fee or no fee as the case may be. The fee shall be collected by the clerk of the circuit court. The clerk of the circuit court shall pay all monies collected from this fee to the county treasurer who shall use the monies collected to defray the costs of corrections. The county treasurer shall deposit the fee collected in the county working cash fund under Section 6-27001 of the Counties Code [55 ILCS 5/6-27001].

(15) Comply with the terms and conditions of an order of protection issued by the court under the Illinois Domestic Violence Act of 1986.

(16) Such other reasonable conditions as the court may impose.

(c) When a person is charged with an offense under Section 12-13, 12-14, 12-15 or 12-16 of the "Criminal Code of 1961" [720 ILCS 5/12-13, 5/12-14, 5/12-15 or 5/12-16], involving a victim who is a minor under 18 years of age living in the same household with the defendant at the time of the offense, in granting bail or releasing the defendant on his own recognizance, the judge shall impose conditions to restrict the defendant's access to the victim which may include, but are not limited to conditions that he will:

1. Vacate the Household.
2. Make payment of temporary support to his dependents.
3. Refrain from contact or communication with the child victim, except as ordered by the court.

(d) When a person is charged with a criminal offense and the victim is a family or household member as defined in Article 112A, conditions shall be imposed at the time of the defendant's release on bond that restrict the defendant's access to the victim. Unless provided otherwise by the court, the restrictions shall include requirements that the defendant do the following:

(1) refrain from contact or communication with the victim for a minimum period of 72 hours following the defendant's release; and

(2) refrain from entering or remaining at the victim's residence for a minimum period of 72 hours following the defendant's release.

(e) Local law enforcement agencies shall develop standardized bond forms for use in cases involving family or household members as defined in Article 112A, including specific conditions of bond as provided in subsection (d). Failure of any law enforcement department to develop or use those forms shall in no way limit the applicability and enforcement of subsections (d) and (f).

(f) If the defendant is admitted to bail after conviction the conditions of the bail bond shall be that he will, in addition to the conditions set forth in subsections (a) and (b) hereof:

(1) Duly prosecute his appeal;

(2) Appear at such time and place as the court may direct;

(3) Not depart this State without leave of the court;

(4) Comply with such other reasonable conditions as the court may impose; and,

(5) If the judgment is affirmed or the cause reversed and remanded for a new trial, forthwith surrender to the officer from whose custody he was bailed.

(Chgd. by P.A. 87-1186, §1, eff. 1/1/93.)
(Source: P.A. 86-1281; 87-805.) [Formerly Ill. Rev. Stat. 38 §110-10.]

5/110-11. Bail on a new trial.

§110-11. Bail on a new trial. If the judgment of conviction is reversed and the cause remanded for a new trial the trial court may order that the bail stand pending such trial, or reduce or increase bail.
(Source: Laws 1963, p. 2836.) [Formerly Ill. Rev. Stat. 38 §110-11.]

5/110-12. Notice of change of address.

§110-12. Notice of change of address. A person who has been admitted to bail shall give written notice to the clerk of the court before which the proceeding is pending of any change in his address within 24 hours after such change.
(Source: Laws 1963, p. 2836.) [Formerly Ill. Rev. Stat. 38 §110-12.]

5/110-13. Persons prohibited from furnishing bail security.

§110-13. Persons prohibited from furnishing bail security. No attorney at law practicing in this State and no official authorized to admit another to bail or to accept bail shall furnish any part of any security for bail in any criminal action or any proceeding nor shall any such person act as surety for any accused admitted to bail.
(Source: Laws 1963, p. 2836.) [Formerly Ill. Rev. Stat. 38 §110-13.]

5/110-14. Credit for incarceration on bailable offense.

§110-14. Credit for Incarceration on Bailable Offense. Any person incarcerated on a bailable offense who does not supply bail and against whom a fine is levied on conviction of such offense shall be allowed a credit of $5 for each day so incarcerated upon application of the defendant. The clerk of the court shall notify the defendant in writing of this provision of the Act at the time he is convicted. However, in no case shall the amount so allowed or credited exceed the amount of the fine.

(Source: P.A. 80-666.) [Formerly Ill. Rev. Stat. 38 §110-14.]

5/110-15. Applicability of provisions for giving and taking bail.

§110-15. Applicability of Provisions for Giving and Taking Bail. The provisions of Sections 110-7 and 110-8 of this Code are exclusive of other provisions of law for the giving, taking, or enforcement of bail. In all cases where a person is admitted to bail the provisions of Sections 110-7 and 110-8 of this Code shall be applicable.

However, the Supreme Court may, by rule or order, prescribe a uniform schedule of amounts of bail in specified traffic and conservation cases, quasi-criminal offenses, and misdemeanors. Such uniform schedule may provide that the cash deposit provisions of Section 110-7 shall not apply to bail amounts established for alleged violations punishable by fine alone, and the schedule may further provide that in specified traffic cases a valid Illinois chauffeur's or operator's license must be deposited, in addition to 10% of the amount of the bail specified in the schedule.

(Source: Laws 1967, p. 2969.) [Formerly Ill. Rev. Stat. 38 §110-15.]

5/110-16. Bail bond—Forfeiture in same case or absents self during trial—Not bailable.

§110-16. Bail Bond—Forfeiture in Same Case or Absents Self During Trial—Not Bailable. If a person admitted to bail on a felony charge forfeits his bond and fails to appear in court during the 30 days immediately after such forfeiture, on being taken into custody thereafter he shall not be bailable in the case in question, unless the court finds that his absence was not for the purpose of obstructing justice or avoiding prosecution.

(Source: P.A. 77-1447.) [Formerly Ill. Rev. Stat. 38 §110-16.]

5/110-17. Unclaimed bail deposits.

§110-17. Unclaimed Bail Deposits. Notwithstanding the provisions of the Uniform Disposition of Unclaimed Property Act, any sum of money deposited by any person to secure his release from custody which remains unclaimed by the person entitled to its return for 3 years after the conditions of the bail bond have been performed and the accused has been discharged from all obligations in the cause shall be presumed to be abandoned.

(a) The clerk of the circuit court, as soon thereafter as practicable, shall cause notice to be published once, in English, in a newspaper or newspapers of general circulation in the county wherein the deposit of bond was received.

(b) The published notice shall be entitled "Notice of Persons Appearing to be Owners of Abandoned Property" and shall contain:

(1) The names, in alphabetical order, of persons to whom the notice is directed.

(2) A statement that information concerning the amount of the property may be obtained by any persons possessing an interest in the property by making an inquiry at the office of the clerk of the circuit court at a location designated by him.

(3) A statement that if proof of claim is not presented by the owner to the clerk of the circuit court and if the owner's right to receive the property is not

established to the satisfaction of the clerk of the court within 65 days from the date of the published notice, the abandoned property will be placed in the custody of the treasurer of the county, not later than 85 days after such publication, to whom all further claims must thereafter be directed. If the claim is established as aforesaid and after deducting an amount not to exceed $20 to cover the cost of notice publication and related clerical expenses, the clerk of the court shall make payment to the person entitled thereto.

(4) The clerk of the circuit court is not required to publish in such notice any items of less than $100 unless he deems such publication in the public interest.

(c) Any clerk of the circuit court who has caused notice to be published as provided by this Section shall, within 20 days after the time specified in this Section for claiming the property from the clerk of the court, pay or deliver to the treasurer of the county having jurisdiction of the offense, whether the bond was taken there or any other county, all sums deposited as specified in this section less such amounts as may have been returned to the persons whose rights to receive the sums deposited have been established to the satisfaction of the clerk of the circuit court. Any clerk of the circuit court who transfers such sums to the county treasury including sums deposited by persons whose names are not required to be set forth in the published notice aforesaid, is relieved of all liability for such sums as have been transferred as unclaimed bail deposits or any claim which then exists or which thereafter may arise or be made in respect to such sums.

(d) The treasurer of the county shall keep just and true accounts of all moneys paid into the treasury, and if any person appears within 5 years after the deposit of moneys by the clerk of the circuit court and claims any money paid into the treasury, he shall file a claim therefor on the form prescribed by the treasurer of the county who shall consider any claim filed under this Act and who may, in his discretion, hold a hearing and receive evidence concerning it. The treasurer of the county shall prepare a finding and the decision in writing on each hearing, stating the substance of any evidence heard by him, his findings of fact in respect thereto, and the reasons for his decision. The decision shall be a public record.

(e) All claims which are not filed within the 5 year period shall be forever barred.

(Source: P.A. 85-768.) [Formerly Ill. Rev. Stat. 38 §110-17.]

5/110-18. Reimbursement.

§110-18. Reimbursement. The sheriff of each county shall certify to the treasurer of each county the number of days that persons had been detained in the custody of the sheriff without a bond being set as a result of an order entered pursuant to Section 110-6.1 of this Code. The county treasurer shall, no later than January 1, annually certify to the Supreme Court the number of days that persons had been detained without bond during the twelve-month period ending November 30. The Supreme Court shall reimburse, from funds appropriated to it by the General Assembly for such purposes, the treasurer of each county an amount of money for deposit in the county general revenue fund at a rate of $50 per day for each day that persons were detained in custody without bail as a result of an order entered pursuant to Section 110-6.1 of this Code.

(Source: P.A. 85-892.) [Formerly Ill. Rev. Stat. 38 §110-18.]

TITLE IV. PROCEEDINGS TO COMMENCE PROSECUTION

ARTICLE 111. CHARGING AN OFFENSE

Sec.

5/111-1. Methods of prosecution.

§111-1. Methods of prosecution. When authorized by law a prosecution may be commenced by:

(a) A complaint;

(b) An information;

(c) An indictment.

Upon commencement of a prosecution for a violation of Section 11-501 of The Illinois Vehicle Code [625 ILCS 5/11-501], or a similar provision of a local ordinance, or Section 9-3 of the Criminal Code of 1961, as amended [720 ILCS 5/9-3], relating to the offense of reckless homicide, the victims of these offenses shall have all the rights under this Section as they do in Section 4 of the Bill of Rights for Victims and Witnesses of Violent Crime Act [725 ILCS 120/4].

For the purposes of this Section "victim" shall mean an individual who has suffered personal injury as a result of the commission of a violation of Section 11-501 of The Illinois Vehicle Code, or a similar provision of a local ordinance, or Section 9-3 of the Criminal Code of 1961, as amended, relating to the offense of reckless homicide. In regard to a violation of Section 9-3 of the Criminal Code of 1961, as amended, relating to the offense of reckless homicide, "victim" shall also include, but not be limited to, spouse, guardian, parent, or other family member.

(Source: P.A. 84-272.) [Formerly Ill. Rev. Stat. 38 §111-1.]

5/111-2. Commencement of prosecutions.

§111-2. Commencement of prosecutions. (a) All prosecutions of felonies shall be by information or by indictment. No prosecution may be pursued by information unless a preliminary hearing has been held or waived in accordance with Section 109-3 and at that hearing probable cause to believe the defendant committed an offense was found, and the provisions of Section 109-3.1 of this Code have been complied with.

(b) All other prosecutions may be by indictment, information or complaint.

(c) Upon the filing of an information or indictment in open court charging the defendant with the commission of a sex offense defined in any Section of Article 11 of the Criminal Code of 1961, as amended [720 ILCS 5/11-6 et seq.], and a minor as defined in Section 1-3 of the Juvenile Court Act of 1987, as amended [705 ILCS 405/1-3], is alleged to be the victim of the commission of the acts of the defendant in the commission of such offense, the court may appoint a guardian ad litem for the minor as provided in Section 2-17, 3-19, 4-16 or 5-17 of the Juvenile Court Act of 1987 [705 ILCS 405/2-17, 405/3-19, 405/4-16 or 405/5-17].

(d) Upon the filing of an information or indictment in open court, the court shall immediately issue a warrant for the arrest of each person charged with an offense directed to a peace officer or some other person specifically named commanding him to arrest such person.

(e) When the offense is bailable, the judge shall endorse on the warrant the amount of bail required by the order of the court, and if the court orders the process returnable forthwith, the warrant shall require that the accused be arrested and brought immediately into court.

(f) Where the prosecution of a felony is by information or complaint after preliminary hearing, or after a waiver of preliminary hearing in accordance with paragraph (a) of this Section, such prosecution may be for all offenses, arising from the same transaction or conduct of a defendant even though the complaint or complaints filed at the preliminary hearing charged only one or some of the offenses arising from that transaction or conduct.
(Source: P.A. 85-1209.) [Formerly Ill. Rev. Stat. 38 §111-2.]

5/111-3. Form of charge.

§111-3. Form of charge. (a) A charge shall be in writing and allege the commission of an offense by:

(1) Stating the name of the offense;

(2) Citing the statutory provision alleged to have been violated;

(3) Setting forth the nature and elements of the offense charged;

(4) Stating the date and county of the offense as definitely as can be done; and

(5) Stating the name of the accused, if known, and if not known, designate the accused by any name or description by which he can be identified with reasonable certainty.

(b) An indictment shall be signed by the foreman of the Grand Jury and an information shall be signed by the State's Attorney and sworn to by him or another. A complaint shall be sworn to and signed by the complainant; Provided, however, that when a citation is issued on a Uniform Traffic Ticket or Uniform Conservation Ticket (in a form prescribed by the Conference of Chief Circuit Judges and filed with the Supreme Court), the copy of such Uniform Ticket which is filed with the circuit court constitutes a complaint to which the defendant may plead, unless he specifically requests that a verified complaint be filed.

(c) When the State seeks an enhanced sentence because of a prior conviction, the charge shall also state the intention to seek an enhanced sentence and shall state such prior conviction so as to give notice to the defendant. However, the fact of such prior conviction and the State's intention to seek an enhanced sentence are not elements of the offense and may not be disclosed to the jury during trial unless otherwise permitted by issues properly raised during such trial. For the purposes of this Section, "enhanced sentence" means a sentence which is increased by a prior conviction from one classification of offense to another higher level classification of offense set forth in Section 5-5-1 of the "Unified Code of Corrections", approved July 26, 1972, as amended [730 ILCS 5/5-5-1]; it does not include an increase in the sentence applied within the same level of classification of offense.

(d) At any time prior to trial, the State on motion shall be permitted to amend the charge, whether brought by indictment, information or complaint, to make the charge comply with subsection (c) of this Section.

(e) The provisions of Article 33B of the Criminal Code of 1961, as amended [720 ILCS 5/33B-1 et seq.], shall not be affected by this Section.
(Source: P.A. 86-964.) [Formerly Ill. Rev. Stat. 38 §111-3.]

5/111-4. Joinder of offenses and defendants.

§111-4. Joinder of offenses and defendants. (a) Two or more offenses may be charged in the same indictment, information or complaint in a separate count for each offense if the offenses charged, whether felonies or misdemeanors or both, are based on the same act or on 2 or more acts which are part of the same comprehensive transaction.

(b) Two or more defendants may be charged in the same indictment, information or complaint if they are alleged to have participated in the same act or in the same comprehensive transaction out of which the offense or offenses arose. Such defendants may be charged in one or more counts together or separately and all of the defendants need not be charged in each count.

(c) Two or more acts or transactions in violation of any provision or provisions of Sections 8A-2, 8A-3, 8A-4, 8A-4A and 8A-5 of the Illinois Public Aid Code [305 ILCS 5/8A-2, 5/8A-3, 5/8A-4, 5/8A-4A and 5/8A-5], Sections 16-1, 16-2, 16-3, 16-5, 16-7, 16-8, 16-10, 16A-3, 16B-2, 16C-2, 17-1, 17-6, 17-7, 17-8, 17-9 or 17-10 of the Criminal Code of 1961 [720 ILCS 5/16-1, 5/16-2, 5/16-3, 5/16-5, 5/16-7, 5/16-8, 5/16-10, 5/16A-3, 5/16B-2, 5/16C-2, 5/17-1, 5/17-6, 5/17-7, 5/17-8, 5/17-9 or 5/17-10] and Section 118 of Division I of the Criminal Jurisprudence Act [720 ILCS 275/118], may be charged as a single offense in a single count of the same indictment, information or complaint, if such acts or transactions by one or more defendants are in furtherance of a single intention and design and if the property, labor or services obtained are of the same person or are of several persons having a common interest in such property, labor or services. In such a charge, the period between the dates of the first and the final such acts or transactions may be alleged as the date of the offense and, if any such act or transaction by any defendant was committed in the county where the prosecution was commenced, such county may be alleged as the county of the offense.
(Source: P.A. 87-805.) [Formerly Ill. Rev. Stat. 38 §111-4.]

5/111-5. Formal defects in a charge.

§111-5. Formal defects in a charge. An indictment, information or complaint which charges the commission of an offense in accordance with Section 111-3 of this Code shall not be dismissed and may be amended on motion by the State's Attorney or defendant at any time because of formal defects, including:

(a) Any miswriting, misspelling or grammatical error;

(b) Any misjoinder of the parties defendant;

(c) Any misjoinder of the offense charged;

(d) The presence of any unnecessary allegation;

(e) The failure to negative any exception, any excuse or proviso contained in the statute defining the offense; or

(f) The use of alternative or disjunctive allegations as to the acts, means, intents or results charged.
(Source: Laws 1963, p. 2836.) [Formerly Ill. Rev. Stat. 38 §111-5.]

5/111-6. Bill of particulars.

§111-6. Bill of particulars. When an indictment, information or complaint charges an offense in accordance with the provisions of Section 111-3 of this Code but fails to specify the particulars of the offense sufficiently to enable the defendant to prepare his defense the court may, on written motion of the defendant, require the State's Attorney to furnish the defendant with a Bill of Particulars containing such particulars as may be necessary for the preparation of the defense. At the trial of the cause the State's evidence shall be confined to the particulars of the bill.
(Source: Laws 1963, p. 2836.) [Formerly Ill. Rev. Stat. 38 §111-6.]

5/111-7. Loss of charge.

§111-7. Loss of charge. When an indictment, information or complaint which has been returned or presented to a court as authorized by law has

become illegible or cannot be produced at the arraignment or trial the defendant may be arraigned and tried on a copy thereof certified by the clerk of the court.
(Source: Laws 1963, p. 2836.) [Formerly Ill. Rev. Stat. 38 §111-7.]

5/111-8. Orders of protection to prohibit domestic violence.

§111-8. Orders of protection to prohibit domestic violence. (a) Whenever a violation of Section 9-1, 9-2, 9-3, 10-4, 10-5, 11-15, 11-15.1 11-20a, 12-1, 12-2, 12-3, 12-4, 12-4.1 12-5, 12-6, 12-11, 12-13, 12-14, 12-15 or 12-16 of the Criminal Code of 1961, as now or hereafter amended [720 ILCS 5/9-1, 5/9-2, 5/9-3, 5/10-4, 5/10-5, 5/11-15, 5/11-15.1, 5/11-20a, 5/12-1, 5/12-2, 5/12-3, 5/12-4, 5/12-4.1, 5/12-5, 5/12-6, 5/12-11, 5/12-13, 5/12-14, 5/12-15 or 5/12-16], is alleged in an information, complaint or indictment on file, and the alleged offender and victim are family or household members, as defined in the Illinois Domestic Violence Act, as now or hereafter amended [750 ILCS 60/101 et seq.], the People through the respective State's Attorneys may by separate petition and upon notice to the defendant, except as provided in subsection (c) herein, request the court to issue an order of protection.

(b) In addition to any other remedies specified in Section 208 of the Illinois Domestic Violence Act, as now or hereafter amended [see 750 ILCS 60/214], the order may direct the defendant to initiate no contact with the alleged victim or victims who are family or household members and to refrain from entering the residence, school or place of business of the alleged victim or victims.

(c) The court may grant emergency relief without notice upon a showing of immediate and present danger of abuse to the victim or minor children of the victim and may enter a temporary order pending notice and full hearing on the matter.
(Source: P.A. 83-1067.) [Formerly Ill. Rev. Stat. 38 §111-8.]

ARTICLE 112. GRAND JURY

Sec.

5/112-1. Selection and qualification.

§112-1. Selection and qualification. The grand jurors shall be summoned, drawn, qualified and certified according to law.
(Source: Laws 1963, p. 2836.) [Formerly Ill. Rev. Stat. 38 §112-1.]

5/112-2. Impaneling the Grand Jury.

§112-2. Impaneling the Grand Jury. (a) The Grand Jury shall consist of 16 persons, 12 of whom shall be necessary to constitute a quorum.

(b) The Grand Jury shall be impaneled, sworn and instructed as to its duties by the court. The court shall select and swear one of the grand jurors to serve as foreman.

(c) Before the Grand Jury shall enter upon the discharge of their duties the following oath shall be administered to the jurors:

"You and each of you do solemnly swear (or affirm, as the case may be), that you will diligently inquire into and true presentment make of all such matters and things as shall be given you in charge, or shall otherwise come to your knowledge, touching the present service; you shall present no person through malice, hatred or ill-will; nor shall you leave any unpresented through fear,

favor, affection, or for any fee or reward, or for any hope or promise thereof; but in all of your presentments, you shall present the truth, the whole truth, and nothing but the truth, according to the best of your skill and understanding; so help you God."
(Source: P.A. 85-690.) [Formerly Ill. Rev. Stat. 38 §112-2.]

5/112-3. Duration of Grand Jury.

§112-3. Duration of Grand Jury. (a) In counties with a population in excess of 1,000,000 a Grand Jury shall be convened, impaneled and sworn, and shall commence the performance of its duties for an indeterminate period, on the first Monday of each month. In such counties a Grand Jury shall serve until discharged by the court, except that no Grand Jury shall serve in excess of 18 months and not more than 6 Grand Juries shall sit at the same time.

(b) In all other counties the Grand Jury shall be called and sit at such times and for such periods as the circuit court may order on its own motion or that of the State's Attorney; provided, that no Grand Jury shall sit for a period in excess of 18 months and, provided further, that no more than one Grand Jury shall sit at the same time.

(c) At any time for cause shown the court may excuse a grand juror either temporarily or permanently and, if permanently, may impanel another person in place of the grand juror excused.
(Source: Laws 1967, p. 2824.) [Formerly Ill. Rev. Stat. 38 §112-3.]

5/112-4. Duties of Grand Jury and State's Attorney.

§112-4. Duties of Grand Jury and State's Attorney. (a) The Grand Jury shall hear all evidence presented by the State's Attorney.

(b) The Grand Jury has the right to subpoena and question any person against whom the State's Attorney is seeking a Bill of Indictment, or any other person, and to obtain and examine any documents or transcripts relevant to the matter being prosecuted by the State's Attorney. Prior to the commencement of its duties and, again, before the consideration of each matter or charge before the Grand Jury, the State's Attorney shall inform the Grand Jury of these rights. In cases where the initial charge has been commenced by information or complaint and a finding of no probable cause has resulted as to any offense charged therein, the Grand Jury shall be informed of the finding entered at the preliminary hearing and further advised that such finding shall not bar the State from initiating new charges by indictment, information or complaint if the State's Attorney has reasonable grounds to believe that the evidence available at that time is sufficient to establish probable cause. In such cases, the Grand Jury shall be further advised that it has the right to subpoena and question any witness who testified at the preliminary hearing, or who is believed to have knowledge of such offense, and of its right to obtain and examine the testimony heard at the preliminary hearing, either through the production of a transcript of the proceedings, or through the verbatim testimony of the court reporter who attended the preliminary hearing. The State's Attorney shall file an affidavit as part of the Grand Jury record indicating whether the jurors were advised of such previous findings of no probable cause and of their rights based upon such previous finding.

Any person subpoenaed who is already charged with an offense or against whom the State's Attorney is seeking a Bill of Indictment shall have the right to be accompanied by counsel who shall advise him of his rights during the proceedings but may not participate in any other way. Before any testimony is given by such a person, he shall be informed that he has the right to refuse to answer any question that will tend to incriminate him, that anything he says may be used against him in a court of law, that he has the right to be accompanied and advised of his rights by counsel, and that he will have counsel appointed for him if he cannot afford one.

(c) The foreman shall preside over all hearings and swear all witnesses. Except where otherwise provided by this Article, the foreman may delegate duties to other grand jurors and determine rules of procedure.

(d) If 9 grand jurors concur that the evidence before them constitutes probable cause that a person has committed an offense the State's Attorney shall prepare a Bill of Indictment charging that person with such offense. The foreman shall sign each Bill of Indictment which shall be returned in open court.

(e) When the evidence presented to the Grand Jury does not warrant the return of a Bill of Indictment, the State's Attorney may prepare a written memorandum to such effect, entitled, "No Bill".

(Source: P.A. 85-690.) [Formerly Ill. Rev. Stat. 38 §112-4.]

5/112-4.1. Right of counsel.

§112-4.1. Any person appearing before the grand jury shall have the right to be accompanied by counsel who shall advise him of his rights but shall not participate in any other way.

(Source: P.A. 81-1112.) [Formerly Ill. Rev. Stat. 38 §112-4.1.]

5/112-5. Duties of others.

§112-5. Duties of others. (a) The clerk of the court shall keep such records of Bills of Indictments and No Bills as may be prescribed by Rule of the Supreme Court.

(b) The court may appoint an investigator or investigators on petition showing good cause for same and signed by the foreman and 8 other grand jurors. The duties and tenure of appointment of such investigator or investigators shall be determined by the court.

(Source: P.A. 85-690.) [Formerly Ill. Rev. Stat. 38 §112-5.]

5/112-6. Secrecy of proceedings.

§112-6. Secrecy of proceedings. (a) Only the State's Attorney, his reporter and any other person authorized by the court or by law may attend the sessions of the Grand Jury. Only the grand jurors shall be present during the deliberations and vote of the Grand Jury. If no reporter is assigned by the State's Attorney to attend the sessions of the Grand Jury, the court shall appoint such reporter.

(b) Matters other than the deliberations and vote of any grand juror shall not be disclosed by the State's Attorney, except as otherwise provided for in subsection (c). The court may direct that a Bill of Indictment be kept secret until the defendant is in custody or has given bail and in either event the clerk shall seal the Bill of Indictment and no person shall disclose the finding of the Bill of Indictment except when necessary for the issuance and execution of a warrant.

(c) (1) Disclosure otherwise prohibited by this Section of matters occurring before the Grand Jury, other than its deliberations and the vote of any grand juror, may be made to:

a. a State's Attorney for use in the performance of such State's Attorney's duty; and

b. such government personnel as are deemed necessary by the State's Attorney in the performance of such State's Attorney's duty to enforce State criminal law.

(2) Any person to whom matters are disclosed under paragraph (1) of this subsection (c) shall not use the Grand Jury material for any purpose other than assisting the State's Attorney in the performance of such State's Attorney's duty to enforce State criminal law. The State's Attorney shall promptly provide the court, before which was impaneled the Grand Jury whose material has been disclosed, with the names of the persons to whom such disclosure has been made.

(3) Disclosure otherwise prohibited by this Section of matters occurring before the Grand Jury may also be made when the court, preliminary to or in connection with a judicial proceeding, directs such in the interests of justice or when a law so directs.

(d) Any grand juror or officer of the court who discloses, other than to his attorney, matters occurring before the Grand Jury other than in accordance with the provisions of this subsection or Section 112-7 shall be punished as a contempt of court, subject to proceedings in accordance to law.
(Source: P.A. 85-690.) [Formerly Ill. Rev. Stat. 38 §112-6.]

5/112-7. Transcript.

§112-7. A transcript shall be made of all questions asked of and answers given by witnesses before the grand jury.
(Source: P.A. 79-669.) [Formerly Ill. Rev. Stat. 38 §112-7.]

ARTICLE 112A. DOMESTIC VIOLENCE: ORDER OF PROTECTION

5/112A-1. Construction.

§112A-1. Construction. This Article shall be interpreted in accordance with the purposes and rules of construction set forth in Section 102 of the Illinois Domestic Violence Act of 1986 [750 ILCS 60/102]. Each of the provisions of the Illinois Domestic Violence Act of 1986 [750 ILCS 60/101 et seq.] which are included in this Article shall govern the issuance, recording and enforcement of orders of protection in criminal proceedings.
(Source: P.A. 84-1305.) [Formerly Ill. Rev. Stat. 38 §112A-1.]

5/112A-2. Commencement of actions.

§112A-2. Commencement of Actions. (a) Actions for orders of protection are commenced in conjunction with a delinquency petition or a criminal prosecution by filing a petition for an order of protection, under the same case number as the delinquency petition or the criminal prosecution, to be granted during pre-trial release of a defendant, with any dispositional order issued under Section 5-23 of the Juvenile Court Act of 1987 [705 ILCS 405/5-23], or as a condition of release, supervision, conditional discharge, probation, periodic imprisonment, parole or mandatory supervised release, or in conjunction with imprisonment or a bond forfeiture warrant, provided that:

(i) the violation is alleged in an information, complaint, indictment or delinquency petition on file, and the alleged offender and victim are family or household members; and

(ii) the petition, which is filed by the State's Attorney, names a victim of the alleged crime as a petitioner.

(b) Withdrawal or dismissal of any petition for an order of protection prior to adjudication where the petitioner is represented by the state shall operate as a dismissal without prejudice.

(c) Voluntary dismissal or withdrawal of any delinquency petition or criminal prosecution or a finding of not guilty shall not require dismissal of the action for the order of protection; instead, in the discretion of the State's Attorney, it may be treated as an independent action and, if necessary and appropriate, transferred to a different court or division. Dismissal of any delinquency petition or criminal prosecution shall not affect the validity of any previously issued order of protection, and thereafter subsection (b) of Section 112A-20 shall be inapplicable to that order.

(Chgd. by P.A. 87-1186, §1, eff. 1/1/93.)
(Source: P.A. 86-1300; 87-443.) [Formerly Ill. Rev. Stat. 38 §112A-2.]

5/112A-3. Definitions.

§112A-3. Definitions. For the purposes of this Article, the following terms shall have the following meanings:

(1) "Abuse" means physical abuse, harassment, intimidation of a dependent, interference with personal liberty or willful deprivation but does not include reasonable direction of a minor child by a parent or person in loco parentis.

(2) "Domestic violence" means abuse as described in paragraph (1).

(3) "Family or household members" include spouses, former spouses, parents, children, stepchildren and other persons related by blood or by present or prior marriage, persons who share or formerly shared a common dwelling, persons who have or allegedly have a child in common, persons who share or allegedly share a blood relationship through a child, persons who have or have had a dating or engagement relationship, and persons with disabilities and their personal assistants. For purposes of this paragraph, neither a casual acquaintanceship nor ordinary fraternization between 2 individuals in business or social contexts shall be deemed to constitute a dating relationship.

(4) "Harassment" means knowing conduct which is not necessary to accomplish a purpose which is reasonable under the circumstances; would cause a reasonable person emotional distress; and does cause emotional distress to the petitioner. Unless the presumption is rebutted by a preponderance of the evidence, the following types of conduct shall be presumed to cause emotional distress:

(i) creating a disturbance at petitioner's place of employment or school;

(ii) repeatedly telephoning petitioner's place of employment, home or residence;

(iii) repeatedly following petitioner about in a public place or places;

(iv) repeatedly keeping petitioner under surveillance by remaining present outside his or her home, school, place of employment, vehicle or other place occupied by petitioner or by peering in petitioner's windows;

(v) improperly concealing a minor child from petitioner, repeatedly threatening to improperly remove a minor child of petitioner's from the jurisdiction or from the physical care of petitioner, repeatedly threatening to conceal a minor child from petitioner, or making a single such threat following an actual or attempted improper removal or concealment, unless respondent was fleeing from an incident or pattern of domestic violence; or

(vi) threatening physical force, confinement or restraint on one or more occasions.

(5) "Interference with personal liberty" means committing or threatening physical abuse, harassment, intimidation or willful deprivation so as to compel another to engage in conduct from which she or he has a right to abstain or to refrain from conduct in which she or he has a right to engage.

(6) "Intimidation of a dependent" means subjecting a person who is dependent because of age, health or disability to participation in or the witnessing of: physical force against another or physical confinement or restraint of another which constitutes physical abuse as defined in this Article, regardless of whether the abused person is a family or household member.

(7) "Order of protection" means an emergency order, interim order or plenary order, granted pursuant to this Article, which includes any or all of the remedies authorized by Section 112A-14 of this Code.

(8) "Petitioner" may mean not only any named petitioner for the order of protection and any named victim of abuse on whose behalf the petition is brought, but also any other person protected by this Article.

(9) "Physical abuse" includes sexual abuse and means any of the following:

(i) knowing or reckless use of physical force, confinement or restraint;

(ii) knowing, repeated and unnecessary sleep deprivation; or

(iii) knowing or reckless conduct which creates an immediate risk of physical harm.

(10) "Willful deprivation" means wilfully denying a person who because of age, health or disability requires medication, medical care, shelter, accessible shelter or services, food, therapeutic device, or other physical assistance, and thereby exposing that person to the risk of physical, mental or emotional harm, except with regard to medical care and treatment when such dependent person has expressed the intent to forgo such medical care or treatment. This paragraph does not create any new affirmative duty to provide support to dependent persons.

(Chgd. by P.A. 87-1186, §1, eff. 1/1/93.)
(Source: P.A. 85-293.) [Formerly Ill. Rev. Stat. 38 §112A-3.]

5/112A-4. Persons protected by this Article.

§112A-4. Persons Protected By This Article. (a) The following persons are protected by this Article:

(i) any person abused by a family or household member;

(ii) any minor child or dependent adult in the care of such person; and

(iii) any person residing or employed at a private home or public shelter which is housing an abused family or household member.

(b) A petition for an order of protection may be filed only by a person who has been abused by a family or household member or by any person on behalf of a minor child or an adult who has been abused by a family or household member and who, because of age, health, disability, or inaccessibility, cannot file the petition. However, any petition properly filed under this Article may seek protection for any additional persons protected by this Article.

(Chgd. by P.A. 87-1186, §1, eff. 1/1/93.)
(Source: P.A. 84-1305.) [Formerly Ill. Rev. Stat. 38 §112A-4.]

5/112A-5. Pleading; non-disclosure of address.

§112A-5. Pleading; non-disclosure of address. (a) A petition for an order of protection shall be in writing and verified or accompanied by affidavit and shall allege that petitioner has been abused by respondent, who is a family or household member. The petition shall further set forth whether there is any other pending action between the parties. During the pendency of this proceeding, each party has a continuing duty to inform the court of any subsequent proceeding for an order of protection in this or any other state.

(b) If the petition states that disclosure of petitioner's address would risk abuse of petitioner or any member of petitioner's family or household or reveal the confidential address of a shelter for domestic violence victims, that address may be omitted from all documents filed with the court. If disclosure is necessary to determine jurisdiction or consider any venue issue, it shall be made orally and in camera. If petitioner has not disclosed an address under this subsection, petitioner shall designate an alternative address at which respondent may serve notice of any motions.

(Chgd. by P.A. 87-1186, §1, eff. 1/1/93.)
(Source: P.A. 84-1305.) [Formerly Ill. Rev. Stat. 38 §112A-5.]

5/112A-6. Application of rules of civil procedure.

§112A-6. Application of rules of civil procedure. (a)* Any proceeding to obtain, modify, reopen or appeal an order of protection, whether commenced alone or in conjunction with a civil or criminal proceeding, shall be governed by the rules of civil procedure of this State. The standard of proof in such a proceeding is proof by a preponderance of the evidence, whether the proceeding is heard in criminal or civil court. The Code of Civil Procedure [735 ILCS 5/1-101 et seq.] and Supreme Court and local court rules applicable to civil proceedings, as now or hereafter amended, shall apply, except as otherwise provided by law. Civil law on venue and on penalties for untrue statements shall not apply to order of protection proceedings heard in Criminal Court.

**So in original. No subsec. (b) has been enacted.*
(Chgd. by P.A. 87-1186, §1, eff. 1/1/93.)
(Source: P.A. 84-1305.) [Formerly Ill. Rev. Stat. 38 §112A-6.]

5/112A-7. Trial by jury.

§112A-7. Trial by jury. There shall be no right to trial by jury in any proceeding to obtain, modify, vacate or extend any order of protection under this Article. However, nothing in this Section shall deny any existing right to trial by jury in a criminal proceeding.

(Chgd. by P.A. 87-1186, §1, eff. 1/1/93.)
(Source: P.A. 87-895.) [Formerly Ill. Rev. Stat. 38 §112A-7.]

5/112A-8. Subject matter jurisdiction.

§112A-8. Subject matter jurisdiction. Each of the circuit courts shall have the power to issue orders of protection.

(Source: P.A. 84-1305.) [Formerly Ill. Rev. Stat. 38 §112A-8.]

5/112A-9. Jurisdiction over persons.

§112A-9. Jurisdiction over persons. In child custody proceedings, the court's personal jurisdiction is determined by this State's Uniform Child Custody Jurisdiction Act, as now or hereafter amended [750 ILCS 35/1 et seq.]. Otherwise, the courts of this State have jurisdiction to bind (i) State residents, and (ii) non-residents having minimum contacts with this State, to the extent permitted by the long-arm statute, Section 2-209 of the Code of Civil Procedure, as now or hereafter amended [735 ILCS 5/2-209].

(Source: P.A. 84-1305.) [Formerly Ill. Rev. Stat. 38 §112A-9.]

5/112A-10. Process.

§112A-10. Process. (a) Summons. Any action for an order of protection, whether commenced alone or in conjunction with another proceeding, is a distinct cause of action and requires that a separate summons be issued and served, except that in pending criminal cases, the summons may be delivered to respondent in open court. The summons shall be in the form prescribed by Supreme Court Rule 101(d), except that it shall require respondent to answer or appear within 7 days, and shall be accompanied by the petition for the order of protection, any supporting affidavits, if any, and any emergency order of protection that has been issued. The enforcement of an order of protection under Section 112A-23 shall not be affected by the lack of service or delivery, provided the requirements of subsection (a) of that Section are otherwise met.

(b) Fees. No fee shall be charged for service of summons.

(c) Expedited service. The summons shall be served by the sheriff or other law enforcement officer at the earliest time and shall take precedence over other summonses except those of a similar emergency nature. Special process servers may be appointed at any time, and their designation shall not affect the responsibilities and authority of the sheriff or other official process servers. Process shall not be served in court.

(d) Remedies Requiring Actual Notice. The counseling, payment of support, payments of shelter services, and payment of losses remedies provided by paragraphs 4, 12, 13, and 16 of subsection (b) of Section 112A-14 may be granted only if respondent has been personally served with process, has answered or has made a general appearance.

(e) Remedies upon constructive notice. Service of process on a member of respondent's household or by publication, in accordance with Sections 2-203, 2-206 and 2-207 of the Code of Civil Procedure [735 ILCS 5/2-203, 5/2-206 and 5/2-207], as now or hereafter amended, shall be adequate for the remedies provided by paragraphs 1, 2, 3, 5, 6, 7, 8, 9, 10, 11, 14, 15, and 17 of subsection (b) of Section 112A-14, but only if: (i) petitioner has made all reasonable efforts to accomplish actual service of process personally upon respondent, but respondent cannot be found to effect such service; and (ii) petitioner files an affidavit or presents sworn testimony as to those efforts.

(f) Default. A plenary order of protection may be entered by default (1) for any of the remedies sought in the petition, if respondent has been served with documents in accordance with subsection (a) and if respondent then fails to appear on the specified return date or on any subsequent hearing date agreed to by the parties or set by the court; or (2) for any of the remedies provided under subsection (e), if the defendant fails to answer or appear in accordance with the date set in the publication notice or the return date indicated on the service of a household member.

(Chgd. by P.A. 87-1186, §1, eff. 1/1/93.)

(Source: P.A. 84-1305.) [Formerly Ill. Rev. Stat. 38 §112A-10.]

5/112A-11. Service of notice of hearings.

§112A-11. Service of Notice of Hearings. A party presenting a petition or motion to the court shall provide the other parties with written notice of the date, time and place of the hearing thereon, together with a copy of any petition, motion or accompanying affidavit not yet served upon that party, and shall file proof of that service, in accordance with Supreme Court Rules 11 and 12, unless notice is excused by Section 112A-17 of this Article, or by the Code of Civil Procedure [735 ILCS 5/1-101 et seq.], Supreme Court Rules or local rules.

(Source: P.A. 84-1305.) [Formerly Ill. Rev. Stat. 38 §112A-11.]

5/112A-12. Hearings.

§112A-12. Hearings. (a) A petition for an order of protection shall be treated as an expedited proceeding, and no court shall transfer or otherwise decline to decide all or part of such petition, except as otherwise provided herein. Nothing in this Section shall prevent the court from reserving issues when jurisdiction or notice requirements are not met.

(b) A criminal court may decline to decide contested issues of physical care, custody, visitation, or family support unless a decision on one or more of those contested issues is necessary to avoid the risk of abuse, neglect, removal from the state or concealment within the state of the child or of separation of the child from the primary caretaker.

(c) The court shall transfer to the appropriate court or division any issue it has declined to decide. Any court may transfer any matter which must be tried by jury to a more appropriate calendar or division.

(d) If the court transfers or otherwise declines to decide any issue, judgment on that issue shall be expressly reserved and ruling on other issues shall not be delayed or declined.

(Chgd. by P.A. 87-1186, §1, eff. 1/1/93.)
(Source: P.A. 84-1305.) [Formerly Ill. Rev. Stat. 38 §112A-12.]

5/112A-13. Continuances.

§112A-13. Continuances. (a) Petitions for Emergency Orders. Petitions for emergency remedies shall be granted or denied in accordance with the standards of Section 217 [750 ILCS 60/217], regardless of respondent's presence in court or appearance.

(b) Petitions for Interim and Plenary Orders. Any action for an order of protection is an expedited proceeding. Continuances should be granted only for good cause shown and kept to the minimum reasonable duration, taking into account the reasons for the continuance. If the continuance is necessary for some, but not all, of the remedies requested, hearing on those other remedies shall not be delayed.

(Source: P.A. 84-1305.) [Formerly Ill. Rev. Stat. 38 §112A-13.]

5/112A-14. Order of protection; remedies.

§112A-14. Order of protection; remedies. (a) Issuance of order. If the court finds that petitioner has been abused by a family or household member, as defined in this Article, an order of protection prohibiting such abuse shall issue; provided that petitioner must also satisfy the requirements of one of the following Sections, as appropriate: Section 112A-17 on emergency orders, Section 112A-18 on interim orders, or Section 112A-19 on plenary orders. Petitioner shall not be denied an order of protection because petitioner or respondent is a minor. The court, when determining whether or not to issue an order of protection, shall not require physical manifestations of abuse on the person of the victim. Modification and extension of prior orders of protection shall be in accordance with this Article.

(b) Remedies and standards. The remedies to be included in an order of protection shall be determined in accordance with this Section and one of the following Sections, as appropriate: Section 112A-17 on emergency orders, Section 112A-18 on interim orders, and Section 112A-19 on plenary orders. The remedies listed in this subsection shall be in addition to other civil or criminal remedies available to petitioner.

(1) Prohibition of abuse. Prohibit respondent's harassment, interference with personal liberty, intimidation of a dependent, physical abuse or willful deprivation, as defined in this Article, if such abuse has occurred or otherwise appears likely to occur if not prohibited.

(2) Grant of exclusive possession of residence. Prohibit respondent from entering or remaining in any residence or household of the petitioner, including one owned or leased by respondent, if petitioner has a right to occupancy thereof. The grant of exclusive possession of the residence shall not affect title to real property, nor shall the court be limited by the standard set forth in Section 701 of the Illinois Marriage and Dissolution of Marriage Act [750 ILCS 5/701].

(A) Right to occupancy. A party has a right to occupancy of a residence or household if it is solely or jointly owned or leased by that party, that party's spouse, a person with a legal duty to support that party or a minor child in that party's care, or by any person or entity other than the opposing party that authorizes that party's occupancy (e.g., a domestic violence shelter). Standards set forth in subparagraph (B) shall not preclude equitable relief.

(B) Presumption of hardships. If petitioner and respondent each has the right to occupancy of a residence or household, the court shall balance (i) the hardships to respondent and any minor child or dependent adult in respondent's care resulting from entry of this remedy with (ii) the hardships to petitioner and any minor child or dependent adult in petitioner's care resulting from continued exposure to the risk of abuse (should petitioner remain at the residence or household) or from loss of possession of the residence or household (should petitioner leave to avoid the risk of abuse). When determining the balance of hardships, the court shall also take into account the accessibility of the residence or household. Hardships need not be balanced if respondent does not have a right to occupancy.

The balance of hardships is presumed to favor possession by petitioner unless the presumption is rebutted by a preponderance of the evidence, showing that the hardships to respondent substantially outweigh the hardships to petitioner and any minor child or dependent adult in petitioner's care. The court, on the request of petitioner or on its own motion, may order respondent to provide suitable, accessible, alternate housing for petitioner instead of excluding respondent from a mutual residence or household.

(3) Stay away order and additional prohibitions. Order respondent to stay away from petitioner or any other person protected by the order of protection, or prohibit respondent from entering or remaining present at petitioner's school, place of employment, or other specified places at times when petitioner is present, or both, if reasonable, given the balance of hardships. Hardships need not be balanced for the court to enter a stay away order or prohibit entry if respondent has no right to enter the premises.

If an order of protection grants petitioner exclusive possession of the residence, or prohibits respondent from entering the residence, or orders respondent to stay away from petitioner or other protected persons, then the court may allow respondent access to the residence to remove items of clothing and personal adornment used exclusively by respondent, medications, and other items as the court directs. The right to access shall be exercised on only one occasion as the court directs and in the presence of an agreed-upon adult third party or law enforcement officer.

(4) Counseling. Require or recommend the respondent to undergo counseling for a specified duration with a social worker, psychologist, clinical psychologist, psychiatrist, family service agency, alcohol or substance abuse program, mental health center guidance counselor, agency providing services to elders, program designed for domestic violence abusers or any other guidance service the court deems appropriate.

(5) Physical care and possession of the minor child. In order to protect the minor child from abuse, neglect, or unwarranted separation from the person who has been the minor child's primary caretaker, or to otherwise protect the well-being of the minor child, the court may do either or both of the following:

(i) grant petitioner physical care or possession of the minor child, or both, or (ii) order respondent to return a minor child to, or not remove a minor child from, the physical care of a parent or person in loco parentis.

If a court finds, after a hearing, that respondent has committed abuse (as defined in Section 112A-3) of a minor child, there shall be a rebuttable presumption that awarding physical care to respondent would not be in the minor child's best interest.

(6) Temporary legal custody. Award temporary legal custody to petitioner in accordance with this Section, the Illinois Marriage and Dissolution of Marriage Act [750 ILCS 5/101 et seq.], the Illinois Parentage Act of 1984 [750 ILCS 45/1 et seq.], and this State's Uniform Child Custody Jurisdiction Act [750 ILCS 35/1 et seq.].

If a court finds, after a hearing, that respondent has committed abuse (as defined in Section 112A-3) of a minor child, there shall be a rebuttable presumption that awarding temporary legal custody to respondent would not be in the child's best interest.

(7) Visitation. Determine the visitation rights, if any, of respondent in any case in which the court awards physical care or temporary legal custody of a minor child to petitioner. The court shall restrict or deny respondent's visitation with a minor child if the court finds that respondent has done or is likely to do any of the following: (i) abuse or endanger the minor child during visitation; (ii) use the visitation as an opportunity to abuse or harass petitioner or petitioner's family or household members; (iii) improperly conceal or detain the minor child; or (iv) otherwise act in a manner that is not in the best interests of the minor child. The court shall not be limited by the standards set forth in Section 607.1 of the Illinois Marriage and Dissolution of Marriage Act [750 ILCS 5/607.1]. If the court grants visitation, the order shall specify dates and times for the visitation to take place or other specific parameters or conditions that are appropriate. No order for visitation shall refer merely to the term "reasonable visitation".

Petitioner may deny respondent access to the minor child if, when respondent arrives for visitation, respondent is under the influence of drugs or alcohol and constitutes a threat to the safety and well-being of petitioner or petitioner's minor children or is behaving in a violent or abusive manner.

If necessary to protect any member of petitioner's family or household from future abuse, respondent shall be prohibited from coming to petitioner's residence to meet the minor child for visitation, and the parties shall submit to the court their recommendations for reasonable alternative arrangements for visitation. A person may be approved to supervise visitation only after filing an affidavit accepting that responsibility and acknowledging accountability to the court.

(8) Removal or concealment of minor child. Prohibit respondent from removing a minor child from the State or concealing the child within the State.

(9) Order to appear. Order the respondent to appear in court, alone or with a minor child, to prevent abuse, neglect, removal or concealment of the child, to return the child to the custody or care of the petitioner or to permit any court-ordered interview or examination of the child or the respondent.

(10) Possession of personal property. Grant petitioner exclusive possession of personal property and, if respondent has possession or control, direct respondent to promptly make it available to petitioner, if:

(i) petitioner, but not respondent, owns the property; or

(ii) the parties own the property jointly; sharing it would risk abuse of petitioner by respondent or is impracticable; and the balance of hardships favors temporary possession by petitioner.

If petitioner's sole claim to ownership of the property is that it is marital property, the court may award petitioner temporary possession thereof under the standards of subparagraph (ii) of this paragraph only if a proper proceeding has been filed under the Illinois Marriage and Dissolution of Marriage Act, as now or hereafter amended.

No order under this provision shall affect title to property.

(11) Protection of property. Forbid the respondent from taking, transferring, encumbering, concealing, damaging or otherwise disposing of any real or personal property, except as explicitly authorized by the court, if:

(i) petitioner, but not respondent, owns the property; or

(ii) the parties own the property jointly, and the balance of hardships favors granting this remedy.

If petitioner's sole claim to ownership of the property is that it is marital property, the court may grant petitioner relief under subparagraph (ii) of this paragraph only if a proper proceeding has been filed under the Illinois Marriage and Dissolution of Marriage Act, as now or hereafter amended.

The court may further prohibit respondent from improperly using the financial or other resources of an aged member of the family or household for the profit or advantage of respondent or of any other person.

(12) Order for payment of support. Order respondent to pay temporary support for the petitioner or any child in the petitioner's care or custody, when the respondent has a legal obligation to support that person, in accordance with the Illinois Marriage and Dissolution of Marriage Act, which shall govern, among other matters, the amount of support, payment through the clerk and withholding of income to secure payment. An order for child support may be granted to a petitioner with lawful physical care or custody of a child, or an order or agreement for physical care or custody, prior to entry of an order for legal custody. Such a support order shall expire upon entry of a valid order granting legal custody to another, unless otherwise provided in the custody order.

(13) Order for payment of losses. Order respondent to pay petitioner for losses suffered as a direct result of the abuse. Such losses shall include, but not be limited to, medical expenses, lost earnings or other support, repair or replacement of property damaged or taken, reasonable attorney's fees, court costs and moving or other travel expenses, including additional reasonable expenses for temporary shelter and restaurant meals.

(i) Losses affecting family needs. If a party is entitled to seek maintenance, child support or property distribution from the other party under the Illinois Marriage and Dissolution of Marriage Act, as now or hereafter amended, the court may order respondent to reimburse petitioner's actual losses, to the extent that such reimbursement would be "appropriate temporary relief", as authorized by subsection (a)(3) of Section 501 of that Act [750 ILCS 5/501].

(ii) Recovery of expenses. In the case of an improper concealment or removal of a minor child, the court may order respondent to pay the reasonable expenses incurred or to be incurred in the search for and recovery of the minor child, including but not limited to legal fees, court costs, private investigator fees, and travel costs.

(14) Prohibition of entry. Prohibit the respondent from entering or remaining in the residence or household while the respondent is under the influence of alcohol or drugs and constitutes a threat to the safety and well-being of the petitioner or the petitioner's children.

(15) Prohibition of access to records. If an order of protection prohibits respondent from having contact with the minor child, or if petitioner's address is omitted under subsection (b) of Section 112A-5, or if necessary to prevent abuse or wrongful removal or concealment of a minor child, the order shall deny

respondent access to, and prohibit respondent from inspecting, obtaining, or attempting to inspect or obtain, school or any other records of the minor child who is in the care of petitioner.

(16) Order for payment of shelter services. Order respondent to reimburse a shelter providing temporary housing and counseling services to the petitioner for the cost of the services, as certified by the shelter and deemed reasonable by the court.

(17) Order for injunctive relief. Enter injunctive relief necessary or appropriate to prevent further abuse of a family or household member or to effectuate one of the granted remedies, if supported by the balance of hardships. If the harm to be prevented by the injunction is abuse or any other harm that one of the remedies listed in paragraphs (1) through (16) of this subsection is designed to prevent, no further evidence is necessary to establish that the harm is an irreparable injury.

(c) Relevant factors; findings:

(1) In determining whether to grant a specific remedy, other than payment of support, the court shall consider relevant factors, including but not limited to the following:

(i) the nature, frequency, severity, pattern and consequences of the respondent's past abuse of the petitioner or any family or household member, including the concealment of his or her location in order to evade service of process or notice, and the likelihood of danger of future abuse to petitioner or any member of petitioner's or respondent's family or household; and

(ii) the danger that any minor child will be abused or neglected or improperly removed from the jurisdiction, improperly concealed within the State or improperly separated from the child's primary caretaker.

(2) In comparing relative hardships resulting to the parties from loss of possession of the family home, the court shall consider relevant factors, including but not limited to the following:

(i) availability, accessibility, cost, safety, adequacy, location and other characteristics of alternate housing for each party and any minor child or dependent adult in the party's care;

(ii) the effect on the party's employment; and

(iii) the effect on the relationship of the party, and any minor child or dependent adult in the party's care, to family, school, church and community.

(3) Subject to the exceptions set forth in paragraph (4) of this subsection, the court shall make its findings in an official record or in writing, and shall at a minimum set forth the following:

(i) That the court has considered the applicable relevant factors described in paragraphs (1) and (2) of this subsection.

(ii) Whether the conduct or actions of respondent, unless prohibited, will likely cause irreparable harm or continued abuse.

(iii) Whether it is necessary to grant the requested relief in order to protect petitioner or other alleged abused persons.

(4) For purposes of issuing an ex parte emergency order of protection, the court, as an alternative to or as a supplement to making the findings described in paragraphs (c)(3)(i) through (c)(3)(iii) of this subsection, may use the following procedure:

When a verified petition for an emergency order of protection in accordance with the requirements of Sections 112A-5 and 112A-17 is presented to the court, the court shall examine petitioner on oath or affirmation. An emergency order of protection shall be issued by the court if it appears from the contents of the petition and the examination of petitioner that the averments are sufficient to indicate abuse by respondent and to support the granting of relief under the issuance of the emergency order of protection.

(5) Never married parties. No rights or responsibilities for a minor child born outside of marriage attach to a putative father until a father and child relationship has been established under the Illinois Parentage Act of 1984. Absent such an adjudication, no putative father shall be granted temporary custody of the minor child, visitation with the minor child, or physical care and possession of the minor child, nor shall an order of payment for support of the minor child be entered.

(d) Balance of hardships; findings. If the court finds that the balance of hardships does not support the granting of a remedy governed by paragraph (2), (3), (10), (11) or (16) of subsection (b) of this Section, which may require such balancing, the court's findings shall so indicate and shall include a finding as to whether granting the remedy will result in hardship to respondent that would substantially outweigh the hardship to petitioner from denial of the remedy. The findings shall be an official record or in writing.

(e) Denial of Remedies. Denial of any remedy shall not be based, in whole or in part, on evidence that:

(1) Respondent has cause for use of force, unless that cause satisfies the standards for justifiable use of force provided by Article VII of the Criminal Code of 1961 [720 ILCS 5/7-1 et seq.];

(2) Respondent was voluntarily intoxicated;

(3) Petitioner acted in self-defense or defense of another, provided that, if petitioner utilized force, such force was justifiable under Article VII of the Criminal Code of 1961;

(4) Petitioner did not act in self-defense or defense of another;

(5) Petitioner left the residence or household to avoid further abuse by respondent;

(6) Petitioner did not leave the residence or household to avoid further abuse by respondent;

(7) Conduct by any family or household member excused the abuse by respondent, unless that same conduct would have excused such abuse if the parties had not been family or household members.

(Chgd. by P.A. 87-1186, §1, eff. 1/1/93.)

(Source: P.A. 87-743.) [Formerly Ill. Rev. Stat. 38 §112A-14.]

5/112A-15. Mutual orders of protection; correlative separate orders.

§112A-15. Mutual orders of protection; correlative separate orders. Mutual orders of protection are prohibited. Correlative separate orders of protection undermine the purposes of this Article. If separate orders of protection in a criminal or delinquency case are sought, there must be compliance with Section 112A-2. Nothing in this Section prohibits a party from seeking a civil order of protection.

If correlative separate orders of protection result after being sought in separate criminal or delinquency actions in accordance with Section 112A-2, that fact shall not be a sufficient basis to deny any remedy to either petitioner or to prove that the parties are equally at fault or equally endangered.

(Chgd. by P.A. 87-1186, §1, eff. 1/1/93.)

(Source: P.A. 84-1305.) [Formerly Ill. Rev. Stat. 38 §112A-15.]

5/112A-16. Accountability for actions of others.

§112A-16. Accountability for Actions of Others. For the purposes of issuing an order of protection, deciding what remedies should be included and enforcing the order, Article 5 of the Criminal Code of 1961 [720 ILCS 5/5-1 et seq.] shall govern whether respondent is legally accountable for the conduct of another person.

(Source: P.A. 84-1305.) [Formerly Ill. Rev. Stat. 38 §112A-16.]

5/112A-17. Emergency order of protection.

§112A-17. Emergency order of protection. (a) Prerequisites. An emergency order of protection shall issue if petitioner satisfies the requirements of this subsection for one or more of the requested remedies. For each remedy requested, petitioner shall establish that:

(1) The court has jurisdiction under Section 112A-9;

(2) The requirements of Section 112A-14 are satisfied; and

(3) There is good cause to grant the remedy, regardless of prior service of process or of notice upon the respondent, because:

(i) For the remedies of "prohibition of abuse" described in Section 112A-14 (b)(1), "stay away order and additional prohibitions" described in Section 112A-14 (b)(3), "removal or concealment of minor child" described in Section 112A-14 (b)(8), "order to appear" described in Section 112A-14 (b)(9), "physical care and possession of the minor child" described in Section 112A-14 (b)(5), "protection of property" described Section 112A-14 (b)(11), "prohibition of entry" described in Section 112A-14 (b)(14), "prohibition of access to records" described in Section 112A-14 (b)(15), and "injunctive relief" described in Section 112A-14 (b)(16), the harm which that remedy is intended to prevent would be likely to occur if the respondent were given any prior notice, or greater notice than was actually given, of the petitioner's efforts to obtain judicial relief;

(ii) For the remedy of "grant of exclusive possession of residence" described in Section 112A-14 (b)(2), the immediate danger of further abuse of petitioner by respondent, if petitioner chooses or had chosen to remain in the residence or household while respondent was given any prior notice or greater notice than was actually given of petitioner's efforts to obtain judicial relief, outweighs the hardships to respondent of an emergency order granting petitioner exclusive possession of the residence or household. This remedy shall not be denied because petitioner has or could obtain temporary shelter elsewhere while prior notice is given to respondent, unless the hardships to respondent from exclusion from the home substantially outweigh those to petitioner.

(iii) For the remedy of "possession of personal property" described in Section 112A-14 (b)(10), improper disposition of the personal property would be likely to occur if respondent were given any prior notice, or greater notice than was actually given, of petitioner's efforts to obtain judicial relief, or petitioner has an immediate and pressing need for possession of that property.

An emergency order may not include the counseling, legal custody, payment of support or monetary compensation remedies.

(b) Appearance by Respondent.

If respondent appears in court for this hearing for an emergency order, he or she may elect to file a general appearance and testify. Any resulting order may be an emergency order, governed by this Section. Notwithstanding the requirements of this Section, if all requirements of Section 112A-18 have been met, the Court may issue a 30-day interim order.

(c) Emergency orders: court holidays and evenings.

(1) Prerequisites. When the court is unavailable at the close of business, the petitioner may file a petition for a 21-day emergency order before any available circuit judge or associate judge who may grant relief under this Article. If the judge finds that there is an immediate and present danger of abuse to petitioner and that petitioner has satisfied the prerequisites set forth in subsection (a) of Section 112A-17, that judge may issue an emergency order of protection.

(2) Certification and transfer. Any order issued under this Section and any documentation in support thereof shall be certified on the next court day to the appropriate court. The clerk of that court shall immediately assign a case number, file the petition, order and other documents with the court and enter the order of record and file it with the sheriff for service, in accordance with

Section 112A-22. Filing the petition shall commence proceedings for further relief, under Section 112A-2. Failure to comply with the requirements of this subsection shall not affect the validity of the order.
(Chgd. by P.A. 87-1186, §1, eff. 1/1/93.)
(Source: P.A. 84-1305.) [Formerly Ill. Rev. Stat. 38 §112A-17.]

5/112A-18. 30-day interim order of protection.

§112A-18. 30-Day interim order of protection. (a) Prerequisites. An interim order of protection shall issue if petitioner has served notice of the hearing for that order on respondent, in accordance with Section 112A-11, and satisfies the requirements of this subsection for one or more of the requested remedies. For each remedy requested, petitioner shall establish that:

(1) The court has jurisdiction under Section 112A-9;

(2) The requirements of Section 112A-14 are satisfied; and

(3) A general appearance was made or filed by or for respondent; or process was served on respondent in the manner required by Section 112A-10; or the petitioner is diligently attempting to complete the required service of process.

An interim order may not include the counseling, payment of support or monetary compensation remedies, unless the respondent has filed a general appearance or has been personally served.

(b) Appearance by respondent. If respondent appears in court for this hearing for an interim order, he or she may elect to file a general appearance and testify. Any resulting order may be an interim order, governed by this Section. Notwithstanding the requirements of this Section, if all requirements of Section 112A-19 have been met, the Court may issue a plenary order of protection.
(Chgd. by P.A. 87-1186, §1, eff. 1/1/93.)
(Source: P.A. 84-1305.) [Formerly Ill. Rev. Stat. 38 §112A-18.]

5/112A-19. Plenary order of protection.

§112A-19. Plenary Order of Protection. A plenary order of protection shall issue if petitioner has served notice of the hearing for that order on respondent, in accordance with Section 112A-11, and satisfies the requirements of this Section for one or more of the requested remedies. For each remedy requested, petitioner must establish that:

(1) The court has jurisdiction under Section 112A-9;

(2) The requirements of Section 112A-14 are satisfied; and

(3) A general appearance was made or filed by or for respondent or process was served on respondent in the manner required by Section 112A-10; and

(4) Respondent has answered or is in default.
(Source: P.A. 84-1305.) [Formerly Ill. Rev. Stat. 38 §112A-19.]

5/112A-20. Duration and extension of orders.

§112A-20. Duration and extension of orders. (a) Duration of emergency and interim orders. Unless re-opened or extended or voided by entry of an order of greater duration:

(1) Emergency orders issued under Section 112A-17 shall be effective for not less than 14 days nor more than 21 days;

(2) Interim orders shall be effective for up to 30 days.

(b) Duration of plenary orders. Except as otherwise provided in this Section, a plenary order of protection shall be valid for a fixed period of time not to exceed 2 years. A plenary order of protection entered in conjunction with a criminal prosecution shall remain in effect as follows:

(1) if entered during pre-trial release, until disposition, withdrawal, or dismissal of the underlying charge; if, however, the case is continued as an independent cause of action, the order's duration may be for a fixed period of time not to exceed 2 years;

(2) if in effect in conjunction with a bond forfeiture warrant, until final disposition or an additional period of time not exceeding 2 years; no order of protection, however, shall be terminated by a dismissal that is accompanied by the issuance of a bond forfeiture warrant;

(3) until expiration of any supervision, conditional discharge, probation, periodic imprisonment, parole or mandatory supervised release and for an additional period of time thereafter not exceeding 2 years; or

(4) until the date set by the court for expiration of any sentence of imprisonment and subsequent parole or mandatory supervised release and for an additional period of time thereafter not exceeding 2 years.

(c) Computation of time. The duration of an order of protection shall not be reduced by the duration of any prior order of protection.

(d) Law enforcement records. When a plenary order of protection expires upon the occurrence of a specified event, rather than upon a specified date as provided in subsection (b), no expiration date shall be entered in Department of State Police records. To remove the plenary order from those records, either party shall request the clerk of the court to file a certified copy of an order stating that the specified event has occurred or that the plenary order has been vacated or modified with the sheriff, and the sheriff shall direct that law enforcement records shall be promptly corrected in accordance with the filed order.

(e) Extension of Orders. Any emergency, interim or plenary order of protection may be extended one or more times, as required, provided that the requirements of Section 112A-17, 112A-18 or 112A-19, as appropriate, are satisfied.

If the motion for extension is uncontested and petitioner seeks no modification of the order, the order may be extended on the basis of petitioner's motion or affidavit stating that there has been no material change in relevant circumstances since entry of the order and stating the reason for the requested extension. Extensions may be granted only in open court and not under the provisions of Section 112A-17(c), which applies only when the court is unavailable at the close of business or on a court holiday.

(f) Termination date. Any order of protection which would expire on a court holiday shall instead expire at the close of the next court business day.

(g) Statement of purpose. The practice of dismissing or suspending a criminal prosecution in exchange for issuing an order of protection undermines the purposes of this Article. This Section shall not be construed as encouraging that practice.

(Chgd. by P.A. 87-1186, §1, eff. 1/1/93.)
(Source: P.A. 84-1305.) [Formerly Ill. Rev. Stat. 38 §112A-20.]

5/112A-21. Contents of orders.

§112A-21. Contents of orders. (a) Any order of protection shall describe, in reasonable detail and not by reference to any other document, the following:

(1) Each remedy granted by the court, in reasonable detail and not by reference to any other document, so that respondent may clearly understand what he or she must do or refrain from doing. Pre-printed form orders of protection shall include the definitions of the types of abuse, as provided in Section 112A-3. Remedies set forth in preprinted form orders shall be numbered consistently with and corresponding to the numerical sequence of remedies listed in Section 112A-14 (at least as of the date the form orders are printed).

(2) The reason for denial of petitioner's request for any remedy listed in Section 112A-14.

(b) An order of protection shall further state the following:

(1) The name of each petitioner that the court finds was abused by respondent, and that respondent is a member of the family or household of each such

petitioner, and the name of each other person protected by the order and that such person is protected by this Act.

(2) For any remedy requested by petitioner on which the court has declined to rule, that that remedy is reserved.

(3) The date and time the order of protection was issued, whether it is an emergency, interim or plenary order and the duration of the order.

(4) The date, time and place for any scheduled hearing for extension of that order of protection or for another order of greater duration or scope.

(5) For each remedy in an emergency order of protection, the reason for entering that remedy without prior notice to respondent or greater notice than was actually given.

(6) For emergency and interim orders of protection, that respondent may petition the court, in accordance with Section 112A-24, to re-open that order if he or she did not receive actual prior notice of the hearing, in accordance with Section 112A-11, and alleges that he or she had a meritorious defense to the order or that the order or any of its remedies was not authorized by this Article.

(c) Any order of protection shall include the following notice, printed in conspicuous type: "Any knowing violation of an order of protection forbidding physical abuse, harassment, intimidation, interference with personal liberty, willful deprivation, or entering or remaining present at specified places when the protected person is present, or granting exclusive possession of the residence or household, or granting a stay away order is a Class A misdemeanor. Grant of exclusive possession of the residence or household shall constitute notice forbidding trespass to land. Any knowing violation of an order awarding legal custody or physical care of a child or prohibiting removal or concealment of a child may be a Class 4 felony. Any willful violation of any order is contempt of court. Any violation may result in fine or imprisonment."

(Chgd. by P.A. 87-1186, §1, eff. 1/1/93.)
(Source: P.A. 84-1305; 86-1300.) [Formerly Ill. Rev. Stat. 38 §112A-21.]

5/112A-22. Notice of orders.

§112A-22. Notice of orders. (a) Entry and issuance. Upon issuance of any order of protection, the clerk shall immediately (i) enter the order on the record and file it in accordance with the circuit court procedures and (ii) provide a file stamped copy of the order to respondent, if present, and to petitioner.

(b) Filing with sheriff. The clerk of the issuing judge shall, or the petitioner may, on the same day that an order of protection is issued, file a copy of that order with the sheriff or other law enforcement officials charged with maintaining Department of State Police records or charged with serving the order upon respondent.

(c) Service by sheriff. Unless respondent was present in court when the order was issued, the sheriff, other law enforcement official or special process server shall promptly serve that order upon respondent and file proof of such service, in the manner provided for service of process in civil proceedings. If process has not yet been served upon the respondent, it shall be served with the order.

(d) Extensions, modifications and revocations. Any order extending, modifying or revoking any order of protection shall be promptly recorded, issued and served as provided in this Section.

(Chgd. by P.A. 87-1186, §1, eff. 1/1/93.)
(Source: P.A. 84-1305.) [Formerly Ill. Rev. Stat. 38 §112A-22.]

5/112A-23. Enforcement of orders of protection.

§112A-23. Enforcement of orders of protection. (a) When violation is crime. A violation of any order of protection, whether issued in a civil, quasi-criminal proceeding, may be enforced by a criminal court when:

(1) The respondent commits the crime of violation of an order of protection pursuant to Section 12-30 of the Criminal Code of 1961 [720 ILCS 5/12-30], by having knowingly violated remedies described in paragraphs (1), (2), (3), or (14) of subsection (b) of Section 112A-14 or any other remedy when the act constitutes a crime against the protected parties as defined by the Criminal Code of 1961 [720 ILCS 5/1-1 et seq.]. Prosecution for a violation of an order of protection shall not bar concurrent prosecution for any other crime, including any crime that may have been committed at the time of the violation of the order of protection; or

(2) The respondent commits the crime of child abduction pursuant to Section 10-5 of the Criminal Code of 1961 [720 ILCS 5/10-5], by having knowingly violated remedies described in paragraphs (5), (6) or (8) of subsection (b) of Section 112A-14.

(b) When violation is contempt of court. A violation of any valid Illinois order of protection, whether issued in a civil or criminal proceeding, may be enforced through civil or criminal contempt procedures, as appropriate, by any court with jurisdiction, regardless where the act or acts which violated the order of protection were committed, to the extent consistent with the venue provisions of this Article. Nothing in this Article shall preclude any Illinois court from enforcing any valid order of protection issued in another state. Illinois courts may enforce orders of protection through both criminal prosecution and contempt proceedings, unless the action which is second in time is barred by collateral estoppel or the constitutional prohibition against double jeopardy.

(1) In a contempt proceeding where the petition for a rule to show cause sets forth facts evidencing an immediate danger that the respondent will flee the jurisdiction, conceal a child, or inflict physical abuse on the petitioner or minor children or on dependent adults in petitioner's care, the court may order the attachment of the respondent without prior service of the rule to show cause or the petition for a rule to show cause. Bond shall be set unless specifically denied in writing.

(2) A petition for a rule to show cause for violation of an order of protection shall be treated as an expedited proceeding.

(c) Violation of custody or support orders. A violation of remedies described in paragraphs (5), (6), (8), or (9) of subsection (b) of Section 112A-14 may be enforced by any remedy provided by Section 611 of the Illinois Marriage and Dissolution of Marriage Act [750 ILCS 5/611]. The court may enforce any order for support issued under paragraph (12) of subsection (b) of Section 112A-14 in the manner provided for under Articles V and VII of the Illinois Marriage and Dissolution of Marriage Act [750 ILCS 5/501 et seq. and 5/701 et seq.].

(d) Actual knowledge. An order of protection may be enforced pursuant to this Section if the respondent violates the order after respondent has actual knowledge of its contents as shown through one of the following means:

(1) By service, delivery, or notice under Section 112A-10.

(2) By notice under Section 112A-11.

(3) By service of an order of protection under Section 112A-22.

(4) By other means demonstrating actual knowledge of the contents of the order.

(e) The enforcement of an order of protection in civil or criminal court shall not be affected by either of the following:

(1) The existence of a separate, correlative order entered under Section 112A-15.

(2) Any finding or order entered in a conjoined criminal proceeding.

(f) Circumstances. The court, when determining whether or not a violation of an order of protection has occurred, shall not require physical manifestations of abuse on the person of the victim.

(g) Penalties.

(1) Except as provided in paragraph (3) of this subsection, where the court finds the commission of a crime or contempt of court under subsections (a) or (b) of this Section, the penalty shall be the penalty that generally applies in such criminal or contempt proceedings, and may include one or more of the following: incarceration, payment of restitution, a fine, payment of attorneys' fees and costs, or community service.

(2) The court shall hear and take into account evidence of any factors in aggravation or mitigation before deciding an appropriate penalty under paragraph (1) of this subsection.

(3) To the extent permitted by law, the court is encouraged to:

(i) increase the penalty for the knowing violation of any order of protection over any penalty previously imposed by any court for respondent's violation of any order of protection or penal statute involving petitioner as victim and respondent as defendant;

(ii) impose a minimum penalty of 24 hours imprisonment for respondent's first violation of any order of protection; and

(iii) impose a minimum penalty of 48 hours imprisonment for respondent's second or subsequent violation of an order of protection.

unless the court explicitly finds that an increased penalty or that period of imprisonment would be manifestly unjust.

(4) In addition to any other penalties imposed for a violation of an order of protection, a criminal court may consider evidence of any violations of an order of protection:

(i) to increase, revoke or modify the bail bond on an underlying criminal charge pursuant to Section 110-6;

(ii) to revoke or modify an order of probation, conditional discharge or supervision, pursuant to Section 5-6-4 of the Unified Code of Corrections [730 ILCS 5/5-6-4];

(iii) to revoke or modify a sentence of periodic imprisonment, pursuant to Section 5-7-2 of the Unified Code of Corrections [730 ILCS 5/5-7-2].

(Chgd. by P.A. 87-1186, §1, eff. 1/1/93.)

(Source: P.A. 86-1300; 87-743.) [Formerly Ill. Rev. Stat. 38 §112A-23.]

5/112A-24. Modification and re-opening of orders.

§112A-24. Modification and re-opening of orders. (a) Except as otherwise provided in this Section, upon motion by petitioner, the court may modify an emergency, interim, or plenary order of protection:

(1) If respondent has abused petitioner since the hearing for that order, by adding or altering one or more remedies, as authorized by Section 112A-14; and

(2) Otherwise, by adding any remedy authorized by Section 112A-14 which was:

(i) reserved in that order of protection;

(ii) not requested for inclusion in that order of protection; or

(iii) denied on procedural grounds, but not on the merits.

(b) Upon motion by petitioner or respondent, the court may modify any prior order of protection's remedy for custody, visitation or payment of support in accordance with the relevant provisions of the Illinois Marriage and Dissolution of Marriage Act [750 ILCS 5/101 et seq.].

(c) After 30 days following the entry of a plenary order of protection, a court may modify that order only when changes in the applicable law or facts since that plenary order was entered warrant a modification of its terms.

(d) Upon 2 days notice to petitioner, in accordance with Section 112A-11, or such shorter notice as the court may prescribe, a respondent subject to an emergency or interim order of protection issued under this Article may appear and petition the court to re-hear the original or amended petition. Any petition to re-hear shall be verified and shall allege the following:

(1) that respondent did not receive prior notice of the initial hearing in which the emergency or interim order was entered, in accordance with Sections 112A-11 and 112A-17; and

(2) that respondent had a meritorious defense to the order or any of its remedies or that the order or any of its remedies was not authorized under this Article.

(e) If the emergency or interim order granted petitioner exclusive possession of the residence and the petition of respondent seeks to re-open or vacate that grant, the court shall set a date for hearing within 14 days on all issues relating to exclusive possession. Under no circumstances shall a court continue a hearing concerning exclusive possession beyond the 14th day except by agreement of the parties. Other issues raised by the pleadings may be consolidated for the hearing if neither party nor the court objects.

(f) This Section does not limit the means, otherwise available by law, for vacating or modifying orders of protection.

(Chgd. by P.A. 87-1186, §1, eff. 1/1/93.)
(Source: P.A. 85-293.) [Formerly Ill. Rev. Stat. 38 §112A-24.]

5/112A-25. Immunity from prosecution.

§112A-25. Immunity from Prosecution. Any individual or organization acting in good faith to report the abuse of any person 60 years of age or older or to do any of the following in complying with the provisions of this Article shall not be subject to criminal prosecution or civil liability as a result of such action: providing any information to the appropriate law enforcement agency, providing that the giving of any information does not violate any privilege of confidentiality under law; assisting in any investigation; assisting in the preparation of any materials for distribution under this Article; or by providing services ordered under an order of protection.

(Source: P.A. 84-1305 incorporating 84-1232; 84-1438.) [Formerly Ill. Rev. Stat. 38 §112A-25.]

5/112A-26. Arrest without warrant.

§112A-26. Arrest without warrant. (a) Any law enforcement officer may make an arrest without warrant if the officer has probable cause to believe that the person has committed or is committing any crime, including but not limited to violation of an order of protection, under Section 12-30 of the Criminal Code of 1961 [720 ILCS 5/12-30], even if the crime was not committed in the presence of the officer.

(b) The law enforcement officer may verify the existence of an order of protection by telephone or radio communication with his or her law enforcement agency or by referring to the copy of the order provided by petitioner or respondent.

(Added by P.A. 87-1186, §1, eff. 1/1/93.)
[Formerly Ill. Rev. Stat. 38 §112A-26.]

5/112A-27. Law enforcement policies.

§112A-27. Law enforcement policies. Every law enforcement agency shall develop, adopt, and implement written policies regarding arrest procedures for domestic violence incidents consistent with the provisions of this Article. In developing these policies, each law enforcement agency is encouraged to consult with community organizations and other law enforcement agencies with expertise in recognizing and handling domestic violence incidents.

(Added by P.A. 87-1186, §1, eff. 1/1/93.)
[Formerly Ill. Rev. Stat. 38 §112A-27.]

5/112A-28. Data maintenance by law enforcement agencies.

§112A-28. Data maintenance by law enforcement agencies. (a) All sheriffs shall furnish to the Department of State Police, daily, in the form and detail the Department requires, copies of any recorded orders of protection issued by the court and transmitted to the sheriff by the clerk of the court pursuant to subsection (b) of Section 112A-22 of this Act. Each order of protection shall be entered in the Law Enforcement Automated Data System on the same day it is issued by the court.

(b) The Department of State Police shall maintain a complete and systematic record and index of all valid and recorded orders of protection issued pursuant to this Act. The data shall be used to inform all dispatchers and law enforcement officers at the scene of an alleged incident of abuse or violation of an order of protection of any recorded prior incident of abuse involving the abused party and the effective dates and terms of any recorded order of protection.

(c) The data, records and transmittals required under this Section shall pertain to any valid emergency, interim or plenary order of protection, whether issued in a civil or criminal proceeding.

(Added by P.A. 87-1186, §1, eff. 1/1/93.)
[Formerly Ill. Rev. Stat. 38 §112A-28.]

5/112A-29. Reports by law enforcement officers.

§112A-29. Reports by law enforcement officers. (a) Every law enforcement officer investigating an alleged incident of abuse between family or household members shall make a written police report of any bona fide allegation and the disposition of such investigation. The police report shall include the victim's statements as to the frequency and severity of prior incidents of abuse by the same family or household member and the number of prior calls for police assistance to prevent such further abuse.

(b) Every police report completed pursuant to this Section shall be recorded and compiled as a domestic crime within the meaning of Section 5.1 of the Criminal Identification Act [20 ILCS 2630/5.1].

(Added by P.A. 87-1186, §1, eff. 1/1/93.)
[Formerly Ill. Rev. Stat. 38 §112A-29.]

5/112A-30. Assistance by law enforcement officers.

§5/112A-30. Assistance by law enforcement officers. (a) Whenever a law enforcement officer has reason to believe that a person has been abused by a family or household member, the officer shall immediately use all reasonable means to prevent further abuse, including:

(1) Arresting the abusing party, where appropriate;

(3)* Accompanying the victim of abuse to his or her place of residence for a reasonable period of time to remove necessary personal belongings and possessions;

**So in original. No subsec. (2) has been enacted.*

(4) Offering the victim of abuse immediate and adequate information (written in a language appropriate for the victim or in Braille or communicated in appropriate sign language), which shall include a summary of the procedures and relief available to victims of abuse under subsection (c) of Section 112A-17 and the officer's name and badge number;

(5) Providing the victim with one referral to an accessible service agency;

(6) Advising the victim of abuse about seeking medical attention and preserving evidence (specifically including photographs of injury or damage and damaged clothing or other property); and

(7) Providing or arranging accessible transportation for the victim of abuse (and, at the victim's request, any minors or dependents in the victim's care) to

a medical facility for treatment of injuries or to a nearby place of shelter or safety; or, after the close of court business hours, providing or arranging for transportation for the victim (and, at the victim's request, any minors or dependents in the victim's care) to the nearest available circuit judge or associate judge so the victim may file a petition for an emergency order of protection under subsection (c) of Section 112A-17. When a victim of abuse chooses to leave the scene of the offense, it shall be presumed that it is in the best interests of any minors or dependents in the victim's care to remain with the victim or a person designated by the victim, rather than to remain with the abusing party.

(b) Whenever a law enforcement officer does not exercise arrest powers or otherwise initiate criminal proceedings, the officer shall:

(1) Make a police report of the investigation of any bona fide allegation of an incident of abuse and the disposition of the investigation, in accordance with subsection (a) of Section 112A-29;

(2) Inform the victim of abuse of the victim's right to request that a criminal proceeding be initiated where appropriate, including specific times and places for meeting with the State's Attorney's office, a warrant officer, or other official in accordance with local procedure; and

(3) Advise the victim of the importance of seeking medical attention and preserving evidence (specifically including photographs of injury or damage and damaged clothing or other property).

(Added by P.A. 87-1186, §1, eff. 1/1/93.)
[Formerly Ill. Rev. Stat. 38 §112A-30.]

5/112A-31. Limited law enforcement liability.

§112A-31. Limited law enforcement liability. Any act of omission or commission by any law enforcement officer acting in good faith in rendering emergency assistance or otherwise enforcing this Article shall not impose civil liability upon the law enforcement officer or his or her supervisor or employer, unless the act is a result of willful or wanton misconduct.

(Added by P.A. 87-1186, §1, eff. 1/1/93.)
[Formerly Ill. Rev. Stat. 38 §112A-31.]

TITLE V. PROCEEDINGS PRIOR TO TRIAL

ARTICLE 113. ARRAIGNMENT

Sec.

5/113-1. Procedure on arraignment.

§113-1. Procedure on arraignment. Before any person is tried for the commission of an offense he shall be called into open court, informed of the charge against him, and called upon to plead thereto. If the defendant so requests the formal charge shall be read to him before he is required to plead. An entry of the arraignment shall be made of record.

(Source: Laws 1963, p. 2836.) [Formerly Ill. Rev. Stat. 38 §113-1.]

5/113-2. Joint defendants.

§113-2. Joint defendants. Defendants who are jointly charged may be arraigned separately or together in the discretion of the court.

(Source: Laws 1963, p. 2836.) [Formerly Ill. Rev. Stat. 38 §113-2.]

5/113-3. Counsel for defendant, court appointed.

§113-3. (a) Every person charged with an offense shall be allowed counsel before pleading to the charge. If the defendant desires counsel and has been unable to obtain same before arraignment the court shall recess court or continue the cause for a reasonable time to permit defendant to obtain counsel and consult with him before pleading to the charge. If the accused is a dissolved corporation, and is not represented by counsel, the court may, in the interest of justice, appoint as counsel a licensed attorney of this State.

(b) In all cases, except where the penalty is a fine only, if the court determines that the defendant is indigent and desires counsel, the Public Defender shall be appointed as counsel. If there is no Public Defender in the county or if the defendant requests counsel other than the Public Defender and the court finds that the rights of the defendant will be prejudiced by the appointment of the Public Defender, the court shall appoint as counsel a licensed attorney at law of this State, except that in a county having a population of 1,000,000 or more the Public Defender shall be appointed as counsel in all misdemeanor cases where the defendant is indigent and desires counsel unless the case involves multiple defendants, in which case the court may appoint counsel other than the Public Defender for the additional defendants. The court shall require an affidavit signed by any defendant who requests court-appointed counsel. Such affidavit shall be in the form established by the Supreme Court containing sufficient information to ascertain the assets and liabilities of that defendant. The Court may direct the Clerk of the Circuit Court to assist the defendant in the completion of the affidavit. Any person who knowingly files such affidavit containing false information concerning his assets and liabilities shall be liable to the county where the case, in which such false affidavit is filed, is pending for the reasonable value of the services rendered by the public defender or other court-appointed counsel in the case to the extent that such services were unjustly or falsely procured.

(c) Upon the filing with the court of a verified statement of services rendered the court shall order the county treasurer of the county of trial to pay counsel other than the Public Defender a reasonable fee. The court shall consider all relevant circumstances, including but not limited to the time spent while court is in session, other time spent in representing the defendant, and expenses reasonably incurred by counsel. In counties with a population greater than 2,000,000, the court shall order the county treasurer of the county of trial to pay counsel other than the Public Defender a reasonable fee stated in the order and based upon a rate of compensation of not more than $40 for each hour spent while court is in session and not more than $30 for each hour otherwise spent representing a defendant, and such compensation shall not exceed $150 for each defendant represented in misdemeanor cases and $1250 in felony cases, in addition to expenses reasonably incurred as hereinafter in this Section provided, except that, in extraordinary circumstances, payment in excess of the limits herein stated may be made if the trial court certifies that such payment is necessary to provide fair compensation for protracted representation. A trial court may entertain the filing of this verified statement before the termination of the cause, and may order the provisional payment of sums during the pendency of the cause.

(d) In capital cases, in addition to counsel, if the court determines that the defendant is indigent the court may, upon the filing with the court of a verified statement of services rendered, order the county treasurer of the county of trial to pay necessary expert witnesses for defendant reasonable compensation stated in the order not to exceed $250 for each defendant.

(e) If the court in any county having a population greater than 1,000,000 determines that the defendant is indigent the court may, upon the filing with

the court of a verified statement of such expenses, order the county treasurer of the county of trial, in such counties having a population greater than 1,000,000 to pay the general expenses of the trial incurred by the defendant not to exceed $50 for each defendant.
(Source: P.A. 85-1344.) [Formerly Ill. Rev. Stat. 38 §113-3.]

5/113-3.1. Payment for court-appointed counsel.

§113-3.1. Payment for Court-Appointed Counsel. (a) Whenever under Section 113-3 of this Code, Rule 607 of the Illinois Supreme Court, or Section 18 of the Illinois Parentage Act of 1984, as now or hereafter amended [750 ILCS 45/1 et seq.], the court appoints counsel to represent a defendant, the court may order the defendant to pay to the Clerk of the Circuit Court a reasonable sum to reimburse either the county or the State for such representation. In a hearing to determine the amount of the payment, the court shall consider the affidavit prepared by the defendant under Section 113-3 of this Code and any other information pertaining to the defendant's financial circumstances which may be submitted by the parties. Such hearing shall be conducted on the court's own motion or on motion of the State's Attorney at any time after the appointment of counsel but no later than 90 days after the entry of a final order disposing of the case at the trial level.

(b) Any sum ordered paid under this Section may not exceed $500 for a defendant charged with a misdemeanor, $5,000 for a defendant charged with a felony, or $2,500 for a defendant who is appealing a conviction of any class offense.

(c) The method of any payment required under this Section shall be as specified by the Court. Any sum deposited as money bond with the Clerk of the Circuit Court under Section 110-7 of this Code may be used in the court's discretion in whole or in part to comply with any payment order entered in accordance with paragraph (a) of this Section. The court may give special consideration to the interests of relatives or other third parties who may have posted a money bond on the behalf of the defendant to secure his release. At any time prior to full payment of any payment order the court on its own motion or the motion of any party may reduce, increase, or suspend the ordered payment, or modify the method of payment, as the interest of fairness may require. No increase, suspension, or reduction may be ordered without a hearing and notice to all parties.

(d) The Supreme Court or the circuit courts may provide by rule for procedures for the enforcement of orders entered under this Section. Such rules may provide for the assessment of all costs, including attorneys' fees which are required for the enforcement of orders entered under this Section when the court in an enforcement proceeding has first found that the defendant has willfully refused to pay. The Clerk of the Circuit Court shall keep records and make reports to the court concerning funds paid under this Section in whatever manner the court directs.

(e) Whenever an order is entered under this Section for the reimbursement of the State due to the appointment of the State Appellate Defender as counsel on appeal, the order shall provide that the Clerk of the Circuit Court shall retain all funds paid pursuant to such order until the full amount of the sum ordered to be paid by the defendant has been paid. When no balance remains due on such order, the Clerk of the Circuit Court shall inform the court of this fact and the court shall promptly order the Clerk of the Circuit Court to pay to the State Treasurer all of the sum paid.

(f) The Clerk of the Circuit Court shall retain all funds under this Section paid for the reimbursement of the county, and shall inform the court when no balance remains due on an order entered hereunder. The Clerk of the Circuit Court shall make payments of funds collected under this Section to the County Treasurer in whatever manner and at whatever point as the court may direct.

(g) A defendant who fails to obey any order of court entered under this Section may be punished for contempt of court. Any arrearage in payments may be reduced to judgment in the court's discretion and collected by any means authorized for the collection of money judgments under the law of this State.
(Source: P.A. 86-666.) [Formerly Ill. Rev. Stat. 38 §113-3.1.]

5/113-4. Plea.

§113-4. Plea. (a) When called upon to plead at arraignment the defendant shall be furnished with a copy of the charge and shall plead guilty, guilty but mentally ill, or not guilty.

(b) If the defendant stands mute a plea of not guilty shall be entered for him and the trial shall proceed on such plea.

(c) If the defendant pleads guilty such plea shall not be accepted until the court shall have fully explained to the defendant the consequences of such plea and the maximum penalty provided by law for the offense which may be imposed by the court. After such explanation if the defendant understandingly persists in his plea it shall be accepted by the court and recorded.

(d) If the defendant pleads guilty but mentally ill, the court shall not accept such a plea until the defendant has undergone examination by a clinical psychologist or psychiatrist and the judge has examined the psychiatric or psychological report or reports, held a hearing on the issue of the defendant's mental condition and is satisfied that there is a factual basis that the defendant was mentally ill at the time of the offense to which the plea is entered.

(e) If a defendant pleads not guilty, the court shall advise him at that time or at any later court date on which he is present that if he escapes from custody or is released on bond and fails to appear in court when required by the court that his failure to appear would constitute a waiver of his right to confront the witnesses against him and trial could proceed in his absence.
(Source: P.A. 82-553.) [Formerly Ill. Rev. Stat. 38 §113-4.]

5/113-4.1. Plea of nolo contendere.

§113-4.1. Plea of nolo contendere. A defendant who is charged with a violation of the Illinois Income Tax Act [35 ILCS 5/101 et seq.] may plead not guilty, guilty or, with the consent of the court, nolo contendere. The court may refuse to accept a plea of guilty, and shall not accept such plea or a plea of nolo contendere without first addressing the defendant personally and determining that the plea is made voluntarily with understanding of the nature of the charge and the consequences of the plea. If a defendant refuses to plead or if the court refuses to accept a plea of guilty or if a defendant corporation fails to appear, the court shall enter a plea of not guilty. The court shall not enter a judgment upon a plea of guilty unless it is satisfied that there is a factual basis for the plea.
(Source: P.A. 78-267.) [Formerly Ill. Rev. Stat. 38 §113-4.1.]

5/113-5. Plea and waiver of jury by person under 18.

§113-5. Plea and Waiver of Jury by Person under 18. No person under the age of 18 years shall be permitted to plead guilty, guilty but mentally ill or waive trial by jury in any case except where the penalty is by fine only unless he is represented by counsel in open court.
(Source: P.A. 82-553.) [Formerly Ill. Rev. Stat. 38 §113-5.]

5/113-6. Effect of failure to arraign and irregularity of arraignment.

§113-6. Effect of failure to arraign and irregularity of arraignment. Neither a failure to arraign nor an irregularity in the arraignment shall effect the validity of any proceeding in the cause if the defendant pleads to the charge or proceeds to trial without objecting to such failure or irregularity.
(Source: Laws 1963, p. 2836.) [Formerly Ill. Rev. Stat. 38 §113-6.]

ARTICLE 114. PRE-TRIAL MOTIONS

5/114-1. Motion to dismiss charge.

§114-1. Motion to dismiss charge. (a) Upon the written motion of the defendant made prior to trial before or after a plea has been entered the court may dismiss the indictment, information or complaint upon any of the following grounds:

(1) The defendant has not been placed on trial in compliance with Section 103-5 of this Code;

(2) The prosecution of the offense is barred by Sections 3-3 through 3-8 of the "Criminal Code of 1961", approved July 28, 1961, as heretofore and hereafter amended [720 ILCS 5/3-3 through 5/3-8];

(3) The defendant has received immunity from prosecution for the offense charged;

(4) The indictment was returned by a Grand Jury which was improperly selected and which results in substantial injustice to the defendant;

(5) The indictment was returned by a Grand Jury which acted contrary to Article 112 of this Code [725 ILCS 5/112-1 et seq.] and which results in substantial injustice to the defendant;

(6) The court in which the charge has been filed does not have jurisdiction;

(7) The county is an improper place of trial;

(8) The charge does not state an offense;

(9) The indictment is based solely upon the testimony of an incompetent witness;

(10) The defendant is misnamed in the charge and the misnomer results in substantial injustice to the defendant.

(11) The requirements of Section 109-3.1 have not been complied with.

(b) The court shall require any motion to dismiss to be filed within a reasonable time after the defendant has been arraigned. Any motion not filed within such time or an extension thereof shall not be considered by the court and the grounds therefor, except as to subsections (a) (6) and (a) (8) of this Section, are waived.

(c) If the motion presents only an issue of law the court shall determine it without the necessity of further pleadings. If the motion alleges facts not of record in the case the State shall file an answer admitting or denying each of the factual allegations of the motion.

(d) When an issue of fact is presented by a motion to dismiss and the answer of the State the court shall conduct a hearing and determine the issues.

(e) Dismissal of the charge upon the grounds set forth in subsections (a) (4) through (a) (11) of this Section shall not prevent the return of a new indictment or the filing of a new charge and upon such dismissal the court may order that the defendant be held in custody or if he had been previously released on bail that his bail be continued for a specified time pending the return of a new indictment or the filing of a new charge.

(f) If the court determines that the motion to dismiss based upon the grounds set forth in subsections (a) (6) and (a) (7) is well founded it may, instead of dismissal, order the cause transferred to a court of competent jurisdiction or to a proper place of trial.

(Source: P.A. 83-644.) [Formerly Ill. Rev. Stat. 38 §114-1.]

5/114-2. Motion for a bill of particulars.

§114-2. Motion for a bill of particulars. (a) A written motion for a bill of particulars shall be filed before or within a reasonable time after arraignment and shall specify the particulars of the offense necessary to enable the defendant to prepare his defense.

(b) A bill of particulars may be amended at any time before trial subject to such conditions as justice may require.

(Source: Laws 1963, p. 2836.) [Formerly Ill. Rev. Stat. 38 §114-2.]

5/114-3. Motion to discharge jury panel.

§114-3. Motion to discharge jury panel. (a) Any objection to the manner in which a jury panel has been selected or drawn shall be raised by a motion to discharge the jury panel prior to the voir dire examination. For good cause shown the court may entertain the motion after the voir dire has begun but such motion shall not be heard after a jury has been sworn to hear the cause.

(b) The motion shall be in writing supported by affidavit and shall state facts which show that the jury panel was improperly selected or drawn.

(c) If the motion states facts which show that the jury panel has been improperly selected or drawn it shall be the duty of the court to conduct a hearing. The burden of proving that the jury panel was improperly selected or drawn shall be upon the movant.

(d) If the court finds that the jury panel was improperly selected or drawn the court shall order the jury panel discharged and the selection or drawing of a new panel in the manner provided by law.

(Source: Laws 1963, p. 2836.) [Formerly Ill. Rev. Stat. 38 §114-3.]

5/114-4. Motion for continuance.

§114-4. Motion for continuance. (a) The defendant or the State may move for a continuance. If the motion is made more than 30 days after arraignment the court shall require that it be in writing and supported by affidavit.

(b) A written motion for continuance made by defendant more than 30 days after arraignment may be granted when:

(1) Counsel for the defendant is ill, has died, or is held to trial in another cause; or

(2) Counsel for the defendant has been unable to prepare for trial because of illness or because he has been held to trial in another cause; or

(3) A material witness is unavailable and the defense will be prejudiced by the absence of his testimony; however, this shall not be a ground for continuance if the State will stipulate that the testimony of the witness would be as alleged; or

(4) The defendant cannot stand trial because of physical or mental incompetency; or

(5) Pre-trial publicity concerning the case has caused a prejudice against defendant on the part of the community; or

(6) The amendment of a charge or a bill of particulars has taken the defendant by surprise and he cannot fairly defend against such an amendment without a continuance.

(c) A written motion for continuance made by the State more than 30 days after arraignment may be granted when:

(1) The prosecutor assigned to the case is ill, has died, or is held to trial in another cause; or

(2) A material witness is unavailable and the prosecution will be prejudiced by the absence of his testimony; however this shall not be a ground for continuance if the defendant will stipulate that the testimony of the witness would be as alleged; or

(3) Pre-trial publicity concerning the case has caused a prejudice against the prosecution on the part of the community.

(d) The court may upon the written motion of either party or upon the court's own motion order a continuance for grounds not stated in subsections (b) and (c) of this Section if he finds that the interests of justice so require.

(e) All motions for continuance are addressed to the discretion of the trial court and shall be considered in the light of the diligence shown on the part of the movant. Where 1 year has expired since the filing of an information or indictments, filed after January 1, 1980, if the court finds that the State has failed to use due diligence in bringing the case to trial, the court may, after a hearing had on the cause, on its own motion, dismiss the information or indictment. Any demand that the defendant had made for a speedy trial under Section 103-5 of this code shall not abate if the State files a new information or the grand jury reindicts in the cause.

After a hearing has been held upon the issue of the State's diligence and the court has found that the State has failed to use due diligence in pursuing the prosecution, the court may not dismiss the indictment or information without granting the State one more court date upon which to proceed. Such date shall be not less than 14 nor more than 30 days from the date of the court's finding. If the State is not prepared to proceed upon that date, the court shall dismiss the indictment or information, as provided in this Section.

(f) After trial has begun a reasonably brief continuance may be granted to either side in the interests of justice.

(g) During the time the General Assembly is in session, the court shall, on motion of either party or on its own motion, grant a continuance where the party or his attorney is a member of either house of the General Assembly whose presence is necessary for the full, fair trial of the cause and, in the case of an attorney, where the attorney was retained by the party before the cause was set for trial.

(h) This Section shall be construed to the end that criminal cases are tried with due diligence consonant with the rights of the defendant and the State to a speedy, fair and impartial trial.

(i) Physical incapacity of a defendant may be grounds for a continuance at any time. If, upon written motion of the defendant or the State or upon the court's own motion, and after presentation of affidavits or evidence, the court determines that the defendant is physically unable to appear in court or to assist in his defense, or that such appearance would endanger his health or result in substantial prejudice, a continuance shall be granted. If such continuance precedes the appearance of counsel for such defendant the court shall simultaneously appoint counsel in the manner prescribed by Section 113-3 of this Act. Such continuance shall suspend the provisions of Section 103-5 of this Act, which periods of time limitation shall commence anew when the court, after presentation of additional affidavits or evidence, has determined that such physical incapacity has been substantially removed.

(j) In actions arising out of building code violations or violations of municipal ordinances caused by the failure of a building or structure to conform to the minimum standards of health and safety, the court shall grant a continuance only upon a written motion by the party seeking the continuance specifying the reason why such continuance should be granted.

(k) In prosecutions for violations of Section 10-1, 10-2, 12-13, 12-14, 12-15 or 12-16 of the "Criminal Code of 1961" [720 ILCS 5/10-1, 5/10-2, 5/12-13, 5/12-14, 5/12-15 or 5/12-16] involving a victim or witness who is a minor under 18 years of age, the court shall, in ruling on any motion or other request for a delay or continuance of proceedings, consider and give weight to the adverse impact the delay or continuance may have on the well-being of a child or witness.

(*l*) The court shall consider the age of the victim and the condition of the victim's health when ruling on a motion for a continuance.

(Source: P.A. 86-876.) [Formerly Ill. Rev. Stat. 38 §114-4.]

5/114-5. Substitution of judge.

§114-5. Substitution of judge. (a) Within 10 days after a cause involving only one defendant has been placed on the trial call of a judge the defendant may move the court in writing for a substitution of that judge on the ground that such judge is so prejudiced against him that he cannot receive a fair trial. Upon the filing of such a motion the court shall proceed no further in the cause but shall transfer it to another judge not named in the motion. The defendant may name only one judge as prejudiced, pursuant to this subsection; provided, however, that in a case in which the offense charged is a Class X felony or may be punished by death or life imprisonment, the defendant may name two judges as prejudiced.

(b) Within 24 hours after a motion is made for substitution of judge in a cause with multiple defendants each defendant shall have the right to move in accordance with subsection (a) of this Section for a substitution of one judge. The total number of judges named as prejudiced by all defendants shall not exceed the total number of defendants. The first motion for substitution of judge in a cause with multiple defendants shall be made within 10 days after the cause has been placed on the trial call of a judge.

(c) Within 10 days after a cause has been placed on the trial call of a judge the State may move the court in writing for a substitution of that judge on the ground that such judge is prejudiced against the State. Upon the filing of such a motion the court shall proceed no further in the cause but shall transfer it to another judge not named in the motion. The State may name only one judge as prejudiced, pursuant to this subsection.

(d) In addition to the provisions of subsections (a), (b) and (c) of this Section the State or any defendant may move at any time for substitution of judge for cause, supported by affidavit. Upon the filing of such motion a hearing shall be conducted as soon as possible after its filing by a judge not named in the motion; provided, however, that the judge named in the motion need not testify, but may submit an affidavit if the judge wishes. If the motion is allowed, the case shall be assigned to a judge not named in the motion. If the motion is denied the case shall be assigned back to the judge named in the motion.

(Source: P.A. 84-1428.) [Formerly Ill. Rev. Stat. 38 §114-5.]

5/114-6. Change of place of trial.

§114-6. Change of place of trial. (a) A defendant may move the court for a change of place of trial on the ground that there exists in the county in which the charge is pending such prejudice against him on the part of the inhabitants that he cannot receive a fair trial in such county.

(b) The motion shall be in writing and supported by affidavit which shall state facts showing the nature of the prejudice alleged. The State may file counter-affidavits. The court shall conduct a hearing and determine the merits of the motion.

(c) If the court determines that there exists in the county where the prosecution is pending such prejudice against the defendant that he cannot receive a fair trial it shall transfer the cause to the circuit court in any county where a fair trial may be had.

(d) In all cases of change of place of trial the clerk of the court from which the change is granted shall immediately prepare a full transcript of the record and proceedings in the case, and of the petition, affidavits and order for the change of place of trial, and transmit the same, together with all papers filed in the case, including the indictment and recognizances of the defendant and all witnesses, to the proper court. If the change is granted to a part but not all of several defendants, a certified copy of the indictment or information, and of the other papers in the case, shall be transmitted to the court to which the change of place of trial is ordered, and such certified copies shall stand as the originals. Such transcript and papers may be transmitted by mail, or in such other way as the court may direct.

(e) When the applicant is in custody or confined in jail, the court shall enter an order directed to the sheriff or other officer having custody of the applicant, to remove his body to the common jail of the county to which the place of trial is changed, and there deliver him to the keeper of the jail, together with the warrant by virtue of which he is confined or held in custody, not more than 3 days next before the day upon which the trial is to commence in the court; and the sheriff shall obey such order and shall endorse on such warrant of commitment the reason of the change of custody, and shall deliver such warrant, with the body of the prisoner, to the keeper of the jail of the proper county, who shall receive the same and give to the sheriff a receipt therefor, and shall take charge of and keep the prisoner in the same manner as if he had originally been committed to his custody.

(f) When the place of trial is changed in any criminal case, the parties and witnesses, and all others who may have entered recognizances to attend the trial of such cause, having notice of the change of place of trial, must attend at the time and place at which the trial is to be had according to such change, and a failure to do so shall operate as a forfeiture of the recognizance.

(g) When the place of trial is changed the State's attorney shall have all the witnesses on the part of the prosecution recognized to appear at the court to which the change is ordered on the day upon which the trial is to commence.

(h) Upon the termination of any trial, when a change of place of trial has been obtained, the clerk of the court in which the trial is had shall submit a certified statement of all costs, fees, charges, claims and expenses resulting from such change of place of trial and necessarily incurred in connection with or incident to the trial of the case, or any appeal therefrom, or required in executing any and all orders of the court made in the case, but shall not include charges for the use of the courtroom or the facilities thereof, nor shall it include fees or salaries paid to employees of the county in which the trial is held, unless it is made necessary by reason of such trial, and when so certified, the items thereof shall be paid by the county in which such indictment or information was found to the officers and persons entitled thereto. All fines imposed and collected in the county where the trial is had, shall be paid over to the county in which the indictment or information was found.

(Source: P.A. 82-280.) [Formerly Ill. Rev. Stat. 38 §114-6.]

5/114-7. Joinder of related prosecutions.

§114-7. Joinder of related prosecutions. The court may order 2 or more charges to be tried together if the offenses and the defendants could have been joined in a single charge. The procedure shall be the same as if the prosecution were under a single charge.

(Source: Laws 1963, p. 2836.) [Formerly Ill. Rev. Stat. 38 §114-7.]

5/114-8. Motion for severance.

§114-8. Motion for severance. If it appears that a defendant or the State is prejudiced by a joinder of related prosecutions or defendants in a single charge or by joinder of separate charges or defendants for trial the court may order separate trials, grant a severance of defendants, or provide any other relief as justice may require.
(Source: Laws 1963, p. 2836.) [Formerly Ill. Rev. Stat. 38 §114-8.]

5/114-9. Motion for a list of witnesses.

§114-9. Motion for a list of witnesses. (a) On motion of the defendant the court shall order the State to furnish the defense with a list of prosecution witnesses and their last known addresses, except the home address of any peace officer witness shall not be required to be so furnished, the address of his assignment station being sufficient for the purposes of this statute.

(b) The court may permit witnesses not named in an original or amended list to testify when the names of the additional witnesses were not known and could not have been obtained by the exercise of due diligence prior to trial.

(c) The requirements of subsection (a) of this Section shall not apply to rebuttal witnesses.
(Source: P.A. 77-1428.) [Formerly Ill. Rev. Stat. 38 §114-9.]

5/114-10. Motion to produce confession.

§114-10. Motion to produce confession. (a) On motion of a defendant in any criminal case made prior to trial the court shall order the State to furnish the defendant with a copy of any written confession made to any law enforcement officer of this State or any other State and a list of the witnesses to its making and acknowledgment. If the defendant has made an oral confession a list of the witnesses to its making shall be furnished.

(b) The list of witnesses may upon notice and motion be amended by the State prior to trial.

(c) No such confession shall be received in evidence which has not been furnished in compliance with subsection (a) of this Section unless the court is satisfied that the prosecutor was unaware of the existence of such confession prior to trial and that he could not have become aware of such in the exercise of due diligence.
(Source: Laws 1963, p. 2836.) [Formerly Ill. Rev. Stat. 38 §114-10.]

5/114-11. Motion to suppress confession.

§114-11. Motion to Suppress Confession. (a) Prior to the trial of any criminal case a defendant may move to suppress as evidence any confession given by him on the ground that it was not voluntary.

(b) The motion shall be in writing and state facts showing wherein the confession is involuntary.

(c) If the allegations of the motion state facts which, if true, show that the confession was not voluntarily made the court shall conduct a hearing into the merits of the motion.

(d) The burden of going forward with the evidence and the burden of proving that a confession was voluntary shall be on the State. Objection to the failure of the State to call all material witnesses on the issue of whether the confession was voluntary must be made in the trial court.

(e) The motion shall be made only before a court with jurisdiction to try the offense.

(f) The issue of the admissibility of the confession shall not be submitted to the jury. The circumstances surrounding the making of the confession may be submitted to the jury as bearing upon the credibility or the weight to be given to the confession.

(g) The motion shall be made before trial unless opportunity therefor did not exist or the defendant was not aware of the grounds for the motion. If the motion is made during trial, and the court determines that the motion is not untimely, and the court conducts a hearing on the merits and enters an order suppressing the confession, the court shall terminate the trial with respect to every defendant who was a party to the hearing and who was within the scope of the order of suppression, without further proceedings, unless the State files a written notice that there will be no interlocutory appeal from such order of suppression. In the event of such termination, the court shall proceed with the trial of other defendants not thus affected. Such termination of trial shall be proper and shall not bar subsequent prosecution of the identical charges and defendants; however, if after such termination the State fails to prosecute the interlocutory appeal until a determination of the merits of the appeal by the reviewing court, the termination shall be improper within the meaning of subparagraph (a) (3) of Section 3-4 of the "Criminal Code of 1961", approved July 28, 1961, as amended, and subsequent prosecution of such defendants upon such charges shall be barred.

(Source: P.A. 76-1096.) [Formerly Ill. Rev. Stat. 38 §114-11.]

5/114-12. Motion to suppress evidence illegally seized.

§114-12. Motion to Suppress Evidence Illegally Seized. (a) A defendant aggrieved by an unlawful search and seizure may move the court for the return of property and to suppress as evidence anything so obtained on the ground that:

(1) The search and seizure without a warrant was illegal; or

(2) The search and seizure with a warrant was illegal because the warrant is insufficient on its face; the evidence seized is not that described in the warrant; there was not probable cause for the issuance of the warrant; or, the warrant was illegally executed.

(b) The motion shall be in writing and state facts showing wherein the search and seizure were unlawful. The judge shall receive evidence on any issue of fact necessary to determine the motion and the burden of proving that the search and seizure were unlawful shall be on the defendant. If the motion is granted the property shall be restored, unless otherwise subject to lawful detention, and it shall not be admissible in evidence against the movant at any trial.

(1) If a defendant seeks to suppress evidence because of the conduct of a peace officer in obtaining the evidence, the State may urge that the peace officer's conduct was taken in a reasonable and objective good faith belief that the conduct was proper and that the evidence discovered should not be suppressed if otherwise admissible. The court shall not suppress evidence which is otherwise admissible in a criminal proceeding if the court determines that the evidence was seized by a peace officer who acted in good faith.

(2) "Good faith" means whenever a peace officer obtains evidence:

(i) pursuant to a search or an arrest warrant obtained from a neutral and detached judge, which warrant is free from obvious defects other than non-deliberate errors in preparation and contains no material misrepresentation by any agent of the State, and the officer reasonably believed the warrant to be valid; or

(ii) pursuant to a warrantless search incident to an arrest for violation of a statute or local ordinance which is later declared unconstitutional or otherwise invalidated.

(3) This amendatory Act of 1987 shall not be construed to limit the enforcement of any appropriate civil remedy or criminal sanction in actions pursuant to other provisions of law against any individual or government entity found to have conducted an unreasonable search or seizure.

(4) This amendatory Act of 1987 does not apply to unlawful electronic eavesdropping or wiretapping.

(c) The motion shall be made before trial unless opportunity therefor did not exist or the defendant was not aware of the grounds for the motion. If the motion is made during trial, and the court determines that the motion is not untimely, and the court conducts a hearing on the merits and enters an order suppressing the evidence, the court shall terminate the trial with respect to every defendant who was a party to the hearing and who was within the scope of the order of suppression, without further proceedings, unless the State files a written notice that there will be no interlocutory appeal from such order of suppression. In the event of such termination, the court shall proceed with the trial of other defendants not thus affected. Such termination of trial shall be proper and shall not bar subsequent prosecution of the identical charges and defendants; however, if after such termination the State fails to prosecute the interlocutory appeal until a determination of the merits of the appeal by the reviewing court, the termination shall be improper within the meaning of subparagraph (a) (3) of Section 3-4 of the "Criminal Code of 1961", approved July 28, 1961, as amended [720 ILCS 5/3-4], and subsequent prosecution of such defendants upon such charges shall be barred.

(d) The motion shall be made only before a court with jurisdiction to try the offense.

(e) The order or judgment granting or denying the motion shall state the findings of facts and conclusions of law upon which the order or judgment is based.

(Source: P.A. 85-388.) [Formerly Ill. Rev. Stat. 38 §114-12.]

5/114-13. Discovery in criminal cases.

§114-13. Discovery in criminal cases. Discovery procedures in criminal cases shall be in accordance with Supreme Court Rules.

(Source: Laws 1963, p. 2836.) [Formerly Ill. Rev. Stat. 38 §114-13.]

TITLE VI. PROCEEDINGS AT TRIAL

ARTICLE 115. TRIAL

5/115-1. Method of trial.

§115-1. Method of Trial. All prosecutions except on a plea of guilty or guilty but mentally ill shall be tried by the court and a jury unless the defendant waives a jury trial in writing.
(Source: P.A. 87-410.) [Formerly Ill. Rev. Stat. 38 §115-1.]

5/115-2. Pleas of guilty and guilty but mentally ill.

§115-2. Pleas of Guilty and guilty but mentally ill. (a) Before or during trial a plea of guilty may be accepted when:

(1) The defendant enters a plea of guilty in open court;

(2) The court has informed the defendant of the consequences of his plea and of the maximum penalty provided by law which may be imposed upon acceptance of such plea.

Upon acceptance of a plea of guilty the court shall determine the factual basis for the plea.

(b) Before or during trial a plea of guilty but mentally ill may be accepted by the court when:

(1) the defendant has undergone an examination by a clinical psychologist or psychiatrist and has waived his right to trial; and

(2) the judge has examined the psychiatric or psychological report or reports; and

(3) the judge has held a hearing, at which either party may present evidence, on the issue of the defendant's mental health and, at the conclusion of such hearing, is satisfied that there is a factual basis that the defendant was mentally ill at the time of the offense to which the plea is entered.
(Source: P.A. 82-553.) [Formerly Ill. Rev. Stat. 38 §115-2.]

5/115-3. Trial by the Court.

§115-3. Trial by the Court. (a) A trial shall be conducted in the presence of the defendant unless he waives the right to be present.

(b) Upon conclusion of the trial the court shall enter a general finding, except that, when the affirmative defense of insanity has been presented during the trial and acquittal is based solely upon the defense of insanity, the court shall enter a finding of not guilty by reason of insanity. In the event of a finding of not guilty by reason of insanity, a hearing shall be held pursuant to the Mental Health and Developmental Disabilities Code [405 ILCS 5/1-100 et seq.] to determine whether the defendant is subject to involuntary admission.

(c) When the defendant has asserted a defense of insanity, the court may find the defendant guilty but mentally ill if, after hearing all of the evidence, the court finds that:

(1) the State has proven beyond a reasonable doubt that the defendant is guilty of the offense charged; and

(2) the defendant has failed to prove his insanity as required in subsection (b) of Section 3-2 of the Criminal Code of 1961, as amended [720 ILCS 5/3-2], and subsections (a), (b) and (e) of Section 6-2 of the Criminal Code of 1961, as amended [720 ILCS 5/6-2]; and

(3) the defendant has proven by a preponderance of the evidence that he was mentally ill, as defined in subsections (c) and (d) of Section 6-2 of the Criminal Code of 1961, as amended, at the time of the offense.
(Source: P.A. 86-392.) [Formerly Ill. Rev. Stat. 38 §115-3.]

5/115-4. Trial by court and jury.

§115-4. Trial by Court and Jury. (a) Questions of law shall be decided by the court and questions of fact by the jury.

(b) The jury shall consist of 12 members.

(c) Upon request the parties shall be furnished with a list of prospective jurors with their addresses if known.

(d) Each party may challenge jurors for cause. If a prospective juror has a physical impairment, the court shall consider such prospective juror's ability to perceive and appreciate the evidence when considering a challenge for cause.

(e) A defendant tried alone shall be allowed 20 peremptory challenges in a capital case, 10 in a case in which the punishment may be imprisonment in the penitentiary, and 5 in all other cases; except that, in a single trial of more than one defendant, each defendant shall be allowed 12 peremptory challenges in a capital case, 6 in a case in which the punishment may be imprisonment in the penitentiary, and 3 in all other cases. If several charges against a defendant or defendants are consolidated for trial, each defendant shall be allowed peremptory challenges upon one charge only, which single charge shall be the charge against that defendant authorizing the greatest maximum penalty. The State shall be allowed the same number of peremptory challenges as all of the defendants.

(f) After examination by the court the jurors may be examined, passed upon, accepted and tendered by opposing counsel as provided by Supreme Court rules.

(g) After the jury is impaneled and sworn the court may direct the selection of 2 alternate jurors who shall take the same oath as the regular jurors. Each party shall have one additional peremptory challenge for each alternate juror. If before the final submission of a cause a member of the jury dies or is discharged he shall be replaced by an alternate juror in the order of selection.

(h) A trial by the court and jury shall be conducted in the presence of the defendant unless he waives the right to be present.

(i) After arguments of counsel the court shall instruct the jury as to the law.

(j) Unless the affirmative defense of insanity has been presented during the trial, the jury shall return a general verdict as to each offense charged. When the affirmative defense of insanity has been presented during the trial, the court shall provide the jury not only with general verdict forms but also with a special verdict form of not guilty by reason of insanity, as to each offense charged, and in such event the court shall separately instruct the jury that a special verdict of not guilty by reason of insanity may be returned instead of a general verdict but such special verdict requires a unanimous finding by the jury that the defendant committed the acts charged but at the time of the commission of those acts the defendant was insane. In the event of a verdict of not guilty by reason of insanity, a hearing shall be held pursuant to the Mental Health and Developmental Disabilities Code [405 ILCS 5/1-100 et seq.] to determine whether the defendant is subject to involuntary admission. When the affirmative defense of insanity has been presented during the trial, the court, where warranted by the evidence, shall also provide the jury with a special verdict form of guilty but mentally ill, as to each offense charged and shall separately instruct the jury that a special verdict of guilty but mentally ill may be returned instead of a general verdict, but that such special verdict requires a unanimous finding by the jury that: (1) the State has proven beyond a reasonable doubt that the defendant is guilty of the offense charged; and (2) the defendant has failed to prove his insanity as required in subsection (b) of Section 3-2 of the Criminal Code of 1961, as amended [720 ILCS 5/3-2], and subsections (a), (b) and (e) of Section 6-2 of the Criminal Code of 1961 [720 ILCS 5/6-2], as amended; and (3) the defendant has proven by a preponderance of the evidence that he was mentally ill, as defined in subsections (c) and (d) of Section 6-2 of the Criminal Code of 1961, as amended, at the time of the offense.

(k) When, at the close of the State's evidence or at the close of all of the evidence, the evidence is insufficient to support a finding or verdict of guilty the court may and on motion of the defendant shall make a finding or direct the jury to return a verdict of not guilty, enter a judgment of acquittal and discharge the defendant.

(*l*) When the jury retires to consider its verdict an officer of the court shall be appointed to keep them together and to prevent conversation between the jurors and others; however, if any juror is deaf, the jury may be accompanied by and may communicate with a court-appointed interpreter during its deliberations. Upon agreement between the State and defendant or his counsel the jury may seal and deliver its verdict to the clerk of the court, separate, and then return such verdict in open court at its next session.

(m) In the trial of a capital or other offense, any juror who is a member of a panel or jury which has been impaneled and sworn as a panel or as a jury shall be permitted to separate from other such jurors during every period of adjournment to a later day, until final submission of the cause to the jury for determination, except that no such separation shall be permitted in any trial after the court, upon motion by the defendant or the State or upon its own motion, finds a probability that prejudice to the defendant or to the State will result from such separation.

(n) The members of the jury shall be entitled to take notes during the trial, and the sheriff of the county in which the jury is sitting shall provide them with writing materials for this purpose. Such notes shall remain confidential, and shall be destroyed by the sheriff after the verdict has been returned or a mistrial declared.

(*o*) A defendant tried by the court and jury shall only be found guilty, guilty but mentally ill, not guilty or not guilty by reason of insanity, upon the unanimous verdict of the jury.

(Source: P.A. 86-392.) [Formerly Ill. Rev. Stat. 38 §115-4.]

5/115-4.1. Absence of defendant.

§115-4.1. Absence of defendant. (a) When a defendant after arrest and an initial court appearance for a non-capital felony, fails to appear for trial, at the request of the State and after the State has affirmatively proven through substantial evidence that the defendant is willfully avoiding trial, the court may commence trial in the absence of the defendant. Absence of a defendant as specified in this Section shall not be a bar to indictment of a defendant, return of information against a defendant, or arraignment of a defendant for the charge for which bail has been granted. If a defendant fails to appear at arraignment, the court may enter a plea of "not guilty" on his behalf. If a defendant absents himself before trial on a capital felony, trial may proceed as specified in this Section provided that the State certifies that it will not seek a death sentence following conviction. Trial in the defendant's absence shall be by jury unless the defendant had previously waived trial by jury. The absent defendant must be represented by retained or appointed counsel. The court, at the conclusion of all of the proceedings, may order the clerk of the circuit court to pay counsel such sum as the court deems reasonable, from any bond monies which were posted by the defendant with the clerk, after the clerk has first deducted all court costs. If trial had previously commenced in the presence of the defendant and the defendant willfully absents himself for two successive court days, the court shall proceed to trial. All procedural rights guaranteed by the United States Constitution, Constitution of the State of Illinois, statutes of the State of Illinois, and rules of court shall apply to the proceedings the same as if the defendant were present in court and had not either forfeited his bail bond or escaped from custody. The court may set the case for a trial which may be conducted under this Section despite the failure of the defendant to appear at the hearing at which the trial date is set. When such trial date is set the clerk shall send to the defendant, by certified mail at his last known address indicated on his bond slip, notice of the new date which has been set for trial. Such notification shall be required when the defendant was not personally present in open court at the time when the case was set for trial.

(b) The absence of a defendant from a trial conducted pursuant to this Section does not operate as a bar to concluding the trial, to a judgment of conviction resulting therefrom, or to a final disposition of the trial in favor of the defendant.

(c) Upon a verdict of not guilty, the court shall enter judgment for the defendant. Upon a verdict of guilty, the court shall set a date for the hearing of post-trial motions and shall hear such motion in the absence of the defendant. If post-trial motions are denied, the court shall proceed to conduct a sentencing hearing and to impose a sentence upon the defendant.

(d) A defendant who is absent for part of the proceedings of trial, post-trial motions, or sentencing, does not thereby forfeit his right to be present at all remaining proceedings.

(e) When a defendant who in his absence has been either convicted or sentenced or both convicted and sentenced appears before the court, he must be granted a new trial or new sentencing hearing if the defendant can establish that his failure to appear in court was both without his fault and due to circumstances beyond his control. A hearing with notice to the State's Attorney on the defendant's request for a new trial or a new sentencing hearing must be held before any such request may be granted. At any such hearing both the defendant and the State may present evidence.

(f) If the court grants only the defendant's request for a new sentencing hearing, then a new sentencing hearing shall be held in accordance with the provisions of the Unified Code of Corrections. At any such hearing, both the defendant and the State may offer evidence of the defendant's conduct during his period of absence from the court. The court may impose any sentence authorized by the Unified Code of Corrections and is not in any way limited or restricted by any sentence previously imposed.

(g) A defendant whose motion under paragraph (e) for a new trial or new sentencing hearing has been denied may file a notice of appeal therefrom. Such notice may also include a request for review of the judgment and sentence not vacated by the trial court.

(Source: P.A. 84-945.) [Formerly Ill. Rev. Stat. 38 §115-4.1.]

5/115-5. Business records as evidence.

§115-5. Business records as evidence. (a) Any writing or record, whether in the form of an entry in a book or otherwise, made as a memorandum or record of any act, transaction, occurrence, or event, shall be admissible as evidence of such act, transaction, occurrence, or event, if made in regular course of any business, and if it was the regular course of such business to make such memorandum or record at the time of such act, transaction, occurrence, or event or within a reasonable time thereafter.

All other circumstances of the making of such writing or record, including lack of personal knowledge by the entrant or maker, may be shown to affect its weight, but such circumstances shall not affect its admissibility.

The term "business," as used in this Section, includes business, profession, occupation, and calling of every kind.

(b) If any business, institution, member of a profession or calling, or any department or agency of government, in the regular course of business or activity has kept or recorded any memorandum, writing, entry, print, representation or combination thereof, of any act, transaction, occurrence, or event, and in the regular course of business has caused any or all of the same to be recorded, copied, or reproduced by any photographic, photostatic, microfilm, micro-card, miniature photographic, or other process which accurately reproduces or forms a durable medium for so reproducing the original, the original may be destroyed in the regular course of business unless its preservation is required by law. Such reproduction, when satisfactorily identified, is as admissible in evidence as the original itself in any proceeding whether the original is in existence or not and an enlargement or facsimile of such reproduction is likewise admissible in evidence if the original reproduction is in existence and available for inspection under direction of court. The introduction of a reproduced record, enlargement, or facsimile does not preclude admission of the original. This Section shall not be construed to exclude from evidence any document or copy thereof which is otherwise admissible under the rules of evidence.

(c) No writing or record made in the regular course of any business shall become admissible as evidence by the application of this Section if:

(1) Such writing or record has been made by anyone in the regular course of any form of hospital or medical business; or

(2) Such writing or record has been made by anyone during an investigation of an alleged offense or during any investigation relating to pending or anticipated litigation of any kind.

(Source: Laws 1967, p. 2838.) [Formerly Ill. Rev. Stat. 38 §115-5.]

5/115-5.1. Coroner's medical or laboratory examiner records as evidence.

§115-5.1. In any civil or criminal action the records of the coroner's medical or laboratory examiner summarizing and detailing the performance of his or her official duties in performing medical examinations upon deceased persons or autopsies, or both, and kept in the ordinary course of business of the coroner's office, duly certified by the county coroner or chief supervisory coroner's pathologist or medical examiner, shall be received as competent evidence in any court of this State, to the extent permitted by this Section. These reports, specifically including but not limited to the pathologist's protocol, autopsy reports and toxicological reports, shall be public documents and thereby may be admissible as prima facie evidence of the facts, findings, opinions, diagnoses and conditions stated therein.

A duly certified coroner's protocol or autopsy report, or both, complying with the requirements of this Section may be duly admitted into evidence as an exception to the hearsay rule as prima facie proof of the cause of death of the person to whom it relates. The records referred to in this Section shall be limited to the records of the results of post-mortem examinations of the findings of autopsy and toxicological laboratory examinations.

Persons who prepare reports or records offered in evidence hereunder may be subpoenaed as witnesses in civil or criminal cases upon the request of either party to the cause. However, if such person is dead, the county coroner or a duly authorized official of the coroner's office may testify to the fact that the examining pathologist, toxicologist or other medical or laboratory examiner is deceased and that the offered report or record was prepared by such deceased person. The witness must further attest that the medical report or record was prepared in the ordinary and usual course of the deceased person's duty or employment in conformity with the provisions of this Section.

(Source: P.A. 82-783.) [Formerly Ill. Rev. Stat. 38 §115-5.1.]

5/115-6. Appointment of psychiatrist or clinical psychologist.

§115-6. Appointment of Psychiatrist or Clinical Psychologist. If the defendant has given notice that he may rely upon the defense of insanity as defined in Section 6-2 of the Criminal Code of 1961 [720 ILCS 5/6-2] or the defendant indicates that he intends to plead guilty but mentally ill or the defense of intoxicated or drugged condition as defined in Section 6-3 of the Criminal Code of 1961 [720 ILCS 5/6-3] or if the facts and circumstances of the case justify a

reasonable belief that the aforesaid defenses may be raised, the Court shall, on motion of the State, order the defendant to submit to examination by at least one clinical psychologist or psychiatrist, to be named by the prosecuting attorney. The Court shall also order the defendant to submit to an examination by one neurologist, one clinical psychologist and one electroencephalographer to be named by the prosecuting attorney if the State asks for one or more of such additional examinations. The Court may order additional examinations if the Court finds that additional examinations by additional experts will be of substantial value in the determination of issues of insanity or drugged conditions. The reports of such experts shall be made available to the defense. Any statements made by defendant to such experts shall not be admissible against the defendant unless he raises the defense of insanity or the defense of drugged condition, in which case they shall be admissible only on the issue of whether he was insane or drugged. The refusal of the defendant to cooperate in such examinations shall not automatically preclude the raising of the aforesaid defenses but shall preclude the defendant from offering expert evidence or testimony tending to support such defenses if the expert evidence or testimony is based upon the expert's examination of the defendant. If the Court, after a hearing, determines to its satisfaction that the defendant's refusal to cooperate was unreasonable it may, in its sound discretion, bar any or all evidence upon the defense asserted.
(Source: P.A. 82-553.) [Formerly Ill. Rev. Stat. 38 §115-6.]

5/115-7. Reputation of rape victim as evidence.

§115-7. a. In prosecutions for aggravated criminal sexual assault, criminal sexual assault, aggravated criminal sexual abuse, criminal sexual abuse, or criminal transmission of HIV; and in prosecutions for battery and aggravated battery, when the commission of the offense involves sexual penetration or sexual conduct as defined in Section 12-12 of the Criminal Code of 1961; and with the trial or retrial of the offenses formerly known as rape, deviate sexual assault, indecent liberties with a child, and aggravated indecent liberties with a child, the prior sexual activity or the reputation of the alleged victim is inadmissible except as evidence concerning the past sexual conduct of the alleged victim with the accused.

b. No evidence admissible under this Section shall be introduced unless ruled admissible by the trial judge after an offer of proof has been made at a hearing to be held in camera in order to determine whether the defense has evidence to impeach the witness in the event that prior sexual activity with the defendant is denied. Such offer of proof shall include reasonably specific information as to the date, time and place of the past sexual conduct between the alleged victim and the defendant. Unless the court finds that reasonably specific information as to date, time or place, or some combination thereof, has been offered as to prior sexual activity with the defendant, counsel for the defendant shall be ordered to refrain from inquiring into prior sexual activity between the alleged victim and the defendant.
(Chgd. by P.A. 87-1068, §1, eff. 1/1/93.)
(Source: P.A. 85-837.) [Formerly Ill. Rev. Stat. 38 §115-7.]

5/115-7.1. Court may not order mental examination of sex victim.

§115-7.1. Court may not order mental examination of sex victim. Except where explicitly authorized by this Code or by the Rules of the Supreme Court of Illinois, no court may require or order a witness who is the victim of an alleged sex offense to submit to or undergo either a psychiatric or psychological examination.
(Source: P.A. 83-289.) [Formerly Ill. Rev. Stat. 38 §115-7.1.]

5/115-7.2. Evidence relating to post-traumatic stress syndrome.

§115-7.2. In a prosecution for an illegal sexual act perpetrated upon a victim, including but not limited to prosecutions for violations of Sections 12-13 through 12-16 of the Criminal Code of 1961 [720 ILCS 5/12-13 through 5/12-16], or ritualized abuse of a child under Section 12-33 of the Criminal Code of 1961 [720 ILCS 5/12-33], testimony by an expert, qualified by the court relating to any recognized and accepted form of post-traumatic stress syndrome shall be admissible as evidence.

(Chgd. by P.A. 87-1167, §2, eff. 1/1/93.)
(Source: P.A. 85-1279.) [Formerly Ill. Rev. Stat. 38 §115-7.2.]

5/115-8. Presence during trial; waiver of right.

§115-8 A defendant may waive his right to be present during trial. However, upon motion of the State's Attorney made prior to or during trial, the court shall order the defendant to present himself in open court for the purpose of identification.

(Source: P.A. 77-1426.) [Formerly Ill. Rev. Stat. 38 §115-8.]

5/115-9. Photograph as evidence.

§115-9. (a) In a prosecution for theft, retail theft, deceptive practice, robbery, armed robbery, burglary or residential burglary, the court shall receive as competent evidence, a photograph of property over which the accused is alleged to have exerted unauthorized control or to have otherwise obtained unlawfully, if the photograph:

(1) will serve the purpose of demonstrating the nature of the property; and

(2) is otherwise admissible into evidence under all other rules of law governing the admissibility of photographs into evidence. The fact that it is impractical to introduce into evidence the actual property for any reason, including its size, weight, or unavailability, need not be established for the court to find a photograph of that property to be competent evidence. If a photograph is found to be competent evidence under this subsection, it is admissible into evidence in place of the property and to the same extent as the property itself.

(b) A law enforcement agency that is holding as evidence property over which a person is alleged to have exerted unauthorized control or to have otherwise obtained unlawfully, shall return that property to its owner if:

(1) the property has been photographed in a manner that will serve the purpose of demonstrating the nature of the property, and if these photographs are filed with or retained by the law enforcement agency in place of the property;

(2) receipt for the property is obtained from the owner upon delivery by the law enforcement agency;

(3) the prosecuting attorney who is prosecuting a case that involves the property furnishes the law enforcement agency with a written request for return of the property to its owner; and

(4) the property may be lawfully possessed by the owner.

(c) Notwithstanding the provisions of subsection (b) of this Section a court may, if a motion so requesting is filed by defendant before expiration of the time period specified in subsection (d) of this Section, order the law enforcement agency to hold such property as evidence pending completion of trial.

(d) The time period during which the defendant may file a motion with the court for retention of the property as evidence shall be as follows:

(1) if the property was being displayed, held, stored or offered for sale to the public by a person or entity holding a Retailers Occupation Tax Number issued by the State of Illinois, the time period shall expire 14 days after the arrest of the defendant;

(2) for all other property, the time period shall expire 30 days after the filing of an information or indictment, or in the case of misdemeanor charges within 30 days after the filing of a complaint.
(Source: P.A. 83-1362.) [Formerly Ill. Rev. Stat. 38 §115-9.]

5/115-10. Prosecution for sexual act upon a minor; evidence as exception to hearsay rule.

§115-10. (a) In a prosecution for a sexual act perpetrated upon a child under the age of 13, including but not limited to prosecutions for violations of Sections 12-13 through 12-16 of the Criminal Code of 1961 [720 ILCS 5/12-13 through 5/12-16], the following evidence shall be admitted as an exception to the hearsay rule:

(1) testimony by such child of an out of court statement made by such child that he or she complained of such act to another; and

(2) testimony of an out of court statement made by such child describing any complaint of such act or matter or detail pertaining to any act which is an element of an offense which is the subject of a prosecution for a sexual act perpetrated upon a child.

(b) Such testimony shall only be admitted if:

(1) The court finds in a hearing conducted outside the presence of the jury that the time, content, and circumstances of the statement provide sufficient safeguards of reliability; and

(2) The child either:

(A) Testifies at the proceeding; or

(B) Is unavailable as a witness and there is corroborative evidence of the act which is the subject of the statement.

(c) If a statement is admitted pursuant to this Section, the court shall instruct the jury that it is for the jury to determine the weight and credibility to be given the statement and that, in making the determination, it shall consider the age and maturity of the child, the nature of the statement, the circumstances under which the statement was made, and any other relevant factor.

(d) The proponent of the statement shall give the adverse party reasonable notice of his intention to offer the statement and the particulars of the statement.
(Source: P.A. 85-837.) [Formerly Ill. Rev. Stat. 38 §115-10.]

5/115-10.1. Admissibility of prior inconsistent statements.

§115-10.1. Admissibility of Prior Inconsistent Statements. In all criminal cases, evidence of a statement made by a witness is not made inadmissible by the hearsay rule if

(a) the statement is inconsistent with his testimony at the hearing or trial, and

(b) the witness is subject to cross-examination concerning the statement, and

(c) the statement—

(1) was made under oath at a trial, hearing, or other proceeding, or

(2) narrates, describes, or explains an event or condition of which the witness had personal knowledge, and

(A) the statement is proved to have been written or signed by the witness, or

(B) the witness acknowledged under oath the making of the statement either in his testimony at the hearing or trial in which the admission into evidence of the prior statement is being sought, or at a trial, hearing, or other proceeding, or

(C) the statement is proved to have been accurately recorded by a tape recorder, videotape recording, or any other similar electronic means of sound recording.

Nothing in this Section shall render a prior inconsistent statement inadmissible for purposes of impeachment because such statement was not recorded or otherwise fails to meet the criteria set forth herein.
(Source: P.A. 83-1042.) [Formerly Ill. Rev. Stat. 38 §115-10.1.]

5/115-11. Persons having no direct interest; exclusion from proceedings where victim is a minor.

§115-11. In a prosecution for a criminal offense defined in Article 11 [720 ILCS 5/11-6 et seq.] or in Section 12-13, 12-14, 12-15 or 12-16 of the "Criminal Code of 1961" [720 ILCS 5/12-13, 5/12-14, 5/12-15 or 5/12-16], where the alleged victim of the offense is a minor under 18 years of age, the court may exclude from the proceedings while the victim is testifying, all persons, who, in the opinion of the court, do not have a direct interest in the case, except the media.
(Source: P.A. 85-196.) [Formerly Ill. Rev. Stat. 38 §115-11.]

5/115-11.1. Use of "rape".

§115-11.1. Use of "Rape". The use of the word "rape", "rapist", or any derivative of "rape" by any victim, witness, State's Attorney, defense attorney, judge or other court personnel in any prosecutions of offenses in Sections 12-13 through 12-16 of the Criminal Code of 1961, as amended [720 ILCS 5/12-13 through 5/12-16], is not inadmissible.
(Source: P.A. 83-1117.) [Formerly Ill. Rev. Stat. 38 §115-11.1.]

5/115-12. Substantive admissibility of prior identification.

§115-12. Substantive Admissibility of Prior Identification. A statement is not rendered inadmissible by the hearsay rule if (a) the declarant testifies at the trial or hearing, and (b) the declarant is subject to cross-examination concerning the statement, and (c) the statement is one of identification of a person made after perceiving him.
(Source: P.A. 83-367.) [Formerly Ill. Rev. Stat. 38 §115-12.]

5/115-13. Statements admitted as an exception to the hearsay rule.

§115-13. In a prosecution for violation of Section 12-13, 12-14, 12-15 or 12-16 of the "Criminal Code of 1961" [720 ILCS 5/12-13, 5/12-14, 5/12-15 or 5/12-16], statements made by the victim to medical personnel for purposes of medical diagnosis or treatment including descriptions of the cause of symptom, pain or sensations, or the inception or general character of the cause or external source thereof insofar as reasonably pertinent to diagnosis or treatment shall be admitted as an exception to the hearsay rule.
(Source: P.A. 85-767.) [Formerly Ill. Rev. Stat. 38 §115-13.]

5/115-14. Witness competency.

§115-14. Witness Competency. (a) Every person, irrespective of age, is qualified to be a witness and no person is disqualified to testify to any matter, except as provided in subsection (b).

(b) A person is disqualified to be a witness if he or she is:

(1) Incapable of expressing himself or herself concerning the matter so as to be understood, either directly or through interpretation by one who can understand him or her; or

(2) Incapable of understanding the duty of a witness to tell the truth.

(c) A party may move the court prior to a witness' testimony being received in evidence, requesting that the court make a determination if a witness is competent to testify. The hearing shall be conducted outside the presence of the jury and the burden of proof shall be on the moving party.
(Source: P.A. 85-1190.) [Formerly Ill. Rev. Stat. 38 §115-14.]

ARTICLE 116. POST-TRIAL MOTIONS

5/116-1. Motion for new trial.

§116-1. Motion for new trial. (a) Following a verdict or finding of guilty the court may grant the defendant a new trial.

(b) A written motion for a new trial shall be filed by the defendant within 30 days following the entry of a finding or the return of a verdict. Reasonable notice of the motion shall be served upon the State.

(c) The motion for a new trial shall specify the grounds therefor.
(Source: Laws 1963, p. 2836.) [Formerly Ill. Rev. Stat. 38 §116-1.]

5/116-2. Motion in arrest of judgment.

§116-2. Motion in arrest of judgment. (a) A written motion in arrest of judgment shall be filed by the defendant within 30 days following the entry of a verdict or finding of guilty. Reasonable notice of the motion shall be served upon the State.

(b) The court shall grant the motion when:

(1) The indictment, information or complaint does not charge an offense, or

(2) The court is without jurisdiction of the cause.

(c) A motion in arrest of judgment attacking the indictment, information, or complaint on the ground that it does not charge an offense shall be denied if the indictment, information or complaint apprised the accused of the precise offense charged with sufficient specificity to prepare his defense and allow pleading a resulting conviction as a bar to future prosecution out of the same conduct.
(Source: P.A. 86-391.) [Formerly Ill. Rev. Stat. 38 §116-2.]

[TITLE VII. PROCEEDINGS AFTER TRIAL]

ARTICLE 119. EXECUTION OF SENTENCE

5/119-5. Execution of death sentence.

§119-5. Execution of Death Sentence. (a) (1) A defendant sentenced to death shall be executed by an intravenous administration of a lethal quantity of an ultrashort-acting barbiturate in combination with a chemical paralytic agent and potassium chloride or other equally effective substances sufficient to cause death until death is pronounced by a licensed physician according to accepted standards of medical practice.

(2) If the execution of the sentence of death as provided in paragraph (1) is held illegal or unconstitutional by a reviewing court of competent jurisdiction, the sentence of death shall be carried out by electrocution.

(b) In pronouncing the sentence of death the court shall set the date of the execution which shall be not less than 60 nor more than 90 days from the date sentence is pronounced.

(c) A sentence of death shall be executed at a Department of Corrections facility.

(d) The warden of the penitentiary shall supervise such execution, which shall be conducted in the presence of 6 witnesses who shall certify the execution of the sentence. The certification shall be filed with the clerk of the court that imposed the sentence.

(e) The identity of executioners and other persons who participate or perform ancillary functions in an execution and information contained in records that would identify those persons shall remain confidential, shall not be subject to disclosure, and shall not be admissible as evidence or be discoverable in any action of any kind in any court or before any tribunal, board, agency, or person. In order to protect the confidentiality of persons participating in an execution, the Director of Corrections may direct that the Department make payments in cash for such services.

(f) The amendatory changes to this Section made by this amendatory Act of 1991 [P.A. 87-353] are severable under Section 1.31 of the Statute on Statutes [5 ILCS 70/1.31].

(Chgd. by P.A. 87-1198, §3, eff. 9/25/92.)
(Source: P.A. 87-353.) [Formerly Ill. Rev. Stat. 38 §119-5.]

ARTICLE 121. APPEAL BY DEFENDANT

5/121-1. Application of article.

§121-1. Application of article. Unless otherwise provided by Rules of the Supreme Court this Article shall govern review in all criminal cases.
(Source: Laws 1963, p. 2836.) [Formerly Ill. Rev. Stat. 38 §121-1.]

5/121-13. Pauper appeals.

§121-13. Pauper Appeals. (a) In any case wherein the defendant was convicted of a felony, if the court determines that the defendant desires counsel on appeal but is indigent the Public Defender or the State Appellate Defender shall be appointed as counsel, unless with the consent of the defendant and for good cause shown, the court may appoint counsel other than the Public Defender or the State Appellate Defender.

(b) In any case wherein the defendant was convicted of a felony and a sentence of death was not imposed in the trial court the reviewing court, upon petition of the defendant's counsel made not more frequently than every 60 days after appointment, shall determine a reasonable amount to be allowed an indigent defendant's counsel other than the Public Defender or the State Appellate Defender for compensation and reimbursement of expenditures necessarily incurred in the prosecution of the appeal or review proceedings. The compensation shall not exceed $1500 in each case, except that, in extraordinary circumstances, payment in excess of the limits herein stated may be made if the reviewing court certifies that the payment is necessary to provide fair compensation for protracted representation. The reviewing court shall enter an order directing the county treasurer of the county where the case was tried to pay the amount allowed by the court. The reviewing court may order the provisional payment of sums during the pendency of the cause.

(c) In any case in which a sentence of death was imposed in the trial court, the Supreme Court, upon written petition of the defendant's counsel made not more than every 60 days after appointment, shall determine reasonable compensation for an indigent defendant's attorneys on appeal. The compensation shall not exceed $2,000 in each case, except that, in extraordinary circumstances, payment in excess of the limits herein stated may be made if the reviewing court certifies that the payment is necessary to provide fair compensation for protracted representation. The Supreme Court shall enter an order directing the county treasurer of the county where the case was tried to pay compensation and reimburse expenditures necessarily incurred in the prosecution of the appeal or review proceedings. The Supreme Court may order the provisional payment of sums during the pendency of the cause.
(Source: P.A. 86-318; 87-580.) [Formerly Ill. Rev. Stat. 38 §121-13.]

ARTICLE 122. POST-CONVICTION HEARING

5/122-1. Petition in the trial court.

§122-1. Petition in the trial court. Any person imprisoned in the penitentiary who asserts that in the proceedings which resulted in his conviction there was a substantial denial of his rights under the Constitution of the United States or of the State of Illinois or both may institute a proceeding under this Article. The proceeding shall be commenced by filing with the clerk of the court in which the conviction took place a petition (together with a copy thereof) verified by affidavit. Petitioner shall also serve another copy upon the State's Attorney by any of the methods provided in Rule 7 of the Supreme Court. The clerk shall docket the petition for consideration by the court pursuant to Section 122-2.1 upon his receipt thereof and bring the same promptly to the attention of the court. No proceedings under this Article shall be commenced more than 6 months after the denial of a petition for leave to appeal or the date for filing such a petition if none is filed or issuance of the opinion from the Illinois Supreme Court or 6 months after the date of the order denying certiorari by the United States Supreme Court or the date for filing such a petition if none is filed or 3 years from the date of conviction, whichever is later, unless the petitioner alleges facts showing that the delay was not due to his culpable negligence.
(Source: P.A. 86-1210; 87-580.) [Formerly Ill. Rev. Stat. 38 §122-1.]

5/122-2. Contents of petition.

§122-2. Contents of petition. The petition shall identify the proceeding in which the petitioner was convicted, give the date of the rendition of the final judgment complained of, and clearly set forth the respects in which petitioner's constitutional rights were violated. The petition shall have attached thereto affidavits, records, or other evidence supporting its allegations or shall state why the same are not attached. The petition shall identify any previous proceedings that the petitioner may have taken to secure relief from his conviction. Argument and citations and discussion of authorities shall be omitted from the petition.
(Source: Laws 1963, p. 2836.) [Formerly Ill. Rev. Stat. 38 §122-2.]

5/122-2.1. Examination of petition.

§122-2.1. (a) Within 90 days after the filing and docketing of each petition, the court shall examine such petition and enter an order thereon pursuant to this Section.

(1) If the petitioner is under sentence of death and is without counsel and alleges that he is without means to procure counsel, he shall state whether or not he wishes counsel to be appointed to represent him. If appointment of counsel is so requested, the court shall appoint counsel if satisfied that the petitioner has no means to procure counsel.

(2) If the petitioner is sentenced to imprisonment and the court determines the petition is frivolous or is patently without merit, it shall dismiss the petition in a written order, specifying the findings of fact and conclusions of law it made

in reaching its decision. Such order of dismissal is a final judgment and shall be served upon the petitioner by certified mail within 10 days of its entry.

(b) If the petition is not dismissed pursuant to this Section, the court shall order the petition to be docketed for further consideration in accordance with Sections 122-4 through 122-6.

(c) In considering a petition pursuant to this Section, the court may examine the court file of the proceeding in which the petitioner was convicted, any action taken by an appellate court in such proceeding and any transcripts of such proceeding.

(Chgd. by P.A. 87-904, §1, eff. 1/1/93.)
(Source: P.A. 86-655.) [Formerly Ill. Rev. Stat. 38 §122-2.1.]

5/122-3. Waiver of claims.

§122-3. Waiver of claims. Any claim of substantial denial of constitutional rights not raised in the original or an amended petition is waived.
(Source: Laws 1963, p. 2836.) [Formerly Ill. Rev. Stat. 38 §122-3.]

5/122-4. Pauper petitions.

§122-4. Pauper Petitions. If the petition is not dismissed pursuant to Section 122-2.1, and alleges that the petitioner is unable to pay the costs of the proceeding, the court may order that the petitioner be permitted to proceed as a poor person and order a transcript of the proceedings delivered to petitioner in accordance with Rule of the Supreme Court. If the petitioner is without counsel and alleges that he is without means to procure counsel, he shall state whether or not he wishes counsel to be appointed to represent him. If appointment of counsel is so requested, and the petition is not dismissed pursuant to Section 122-2.1, the court shall appoint counsel if satisfied that the petitioner has no means to procure counsel.

A Circuit Court or the Illinois Supreme Court may appoint the State Appellate Defender to provide post-conviction representation in a case in which the defendant is sentenced to death. Any attorney assigned by the Office of the State Appellate Defender to provide post-conviction representation for indigent defendants in cases in which a sentence of death was imposed in the trial court may, from time to time submit bills and time sheets to the Office of the State Appellate Defender for payment of services rendered and the Office of the State Appellate Defender shall pay bills from funds appropriated for this purpose in accordance with rules promulgated by the State Appellate Defender.

The court, at the conclusion of the proceedings upon receipt of a petition by the appointed counsel, shall determine a reasonable amount to be allowed an indigent defendant's counsel other than the Public Defender or the State Appellate Defender for compensation and reimbursement of expenditures necessarily incurred in the proceedings. The compensation shall not exceed $500 in each case, except that, in extraordinary circumstances, payment in excess of the limits herein stated may be made if the trial court certifies that the payment is necessary to provide fair compensation for protracted representation, and the amount is approved by the chief judge of the circuit. The court shall enter an order directing the county treasurer of the county where the case was tried to pay the amount thereby allowed by the court. The court may order the provisional payment of sums during the pendency of the cause.
(Source: P.A. 87-580.) [Formerly Ill. Rev. Stat. 38 §122-4.]

5/122-5. Proceedings on petition.

§122-5. Proceedings on petition. Within 30 days after the making of an order pursuant to subsection (b) of Section 122-2.1, or within such further time as the court may set, the State shall answer or move to dismiss. In the event that a motion to dismiss is filed and denied, the State must file an answer within 20 days after such denial. No other or further pleadings shall be filed except as

the court may order on its own motion or on that of either party. The court may in its discretion grant leave, at any stage of the proceeding prior to entry of judgment, to withdraw the petition. The court may in its discretion make such order as to amendment of the petition or any other pleading, or as to pleading over, or filing further pleadings, or extending the time of filing any pleading other than the original petition, as shall be appropriate, just and reasonable and as is generally provided in civil cases.
(Source: P.A. 83-942.) [Formerly Ill. Rev. Stat. 38 §122-5.]

5/122-6. Disposition in trial court.

§122-6. Disposition in trial court. The court may receive proof by affidavits, depositions, oral testimony, or other evidence. In its discretion the court may order the petitioner brought before the court for the hearing. If the court finds in favor of the petitioner, it shall enter an appropriate order with respect to the judgment or sentence in the former proceedings and such supplementary orders as to rearraignment, retrial, custody, bail or discharge as may be necessary and proper.
(Source: Laws 1963, p. 2836.) [Formerly Ill. Rev. Stat. 38 §122-6.]

5/122-7. Review.

§122-7. Any final judgment entered upon such petition shall be reviewed in a manner pursuant to the rules of the Supreme Court.
(Source: P.A. 79-917.) [Formerly Ill. Rev. Stat. 38 §122-7.]

5/122-8. Different judge to consider.

§122-8. Different Judge to Consider. All proceedings under this Article shall be conducted and all petitions shall be considered by a judge who was not involved in the original proceeding which resulted in conviction.
(Source: P.A. 83-942.) [Formerly Ill. Rev. Stat. 38 §122-8.]

TITLE VIII. MISCELLANEOUS

ARTICLE 125. CONSTRUCTION AND EFFECTIVE DATE

5/125-1. Effect of headings.

§125-1. Effect of headings. Section, Article and Title headings contained herein shall not be deemed to govern, limit, modify or in any manner affect the scope, meaning or intent of the provisions of any Section, Article or Title hereof.
(Source: Laws 1963, p. 2836.) [Formerly Ill. Rev. Stat. 38 §125-1.]

5/125-2. Partial invalidity.

§125-2. Partial invalidity. The invalidity of any provision of this Code shall not affect the validity of the remainder of this Code.
(Source: Laws 1963, p. 2836.) [Formerly Ill. Rev. Stat. 38 §125-2.]

5/125-3. Savings provisions.

§125-3. Savings provisions. (a) The provisions of Sections 2, 3 and 4 of "An Act to revise the law in relation to the construction of the statutes", approved March 5, 1874, as heretofore and hereafter amended [5 ILCS 70/2, 70/3 and 70/4], shall apply in all construction of this Code.

(b) In any case pending on or after the effective date of this Code involving an offense committed prior to such date the procedural provisions of this Code shall govern insofar as they are justly applicable and their application does not introduce confusion or delay.

(c) Provisions of this Code according a defense or mitigation shall apply with the consent of the defendant.

(d) Provisions of this Code governing the treatment, eligibility, release or discharge of prisoners, probationers and parolees shall apply to persons under sentence for offenses committed prior to the effective date of this Code except that the minimum or maximum period of their detention or supervision shall in no case be increased.

(Source: Laws 1963, p. 2836.) [Formerly Ill. Rev. Stat. 38 §125-3.]

5/125-4. Effective date.

§125-4. Effective date. This Code shall take effect January 1, 1964.

(Source: Laws 1963, p. 2836.) [Formerly Ill. Rev. Stat. 38 §125-4.]

ARTICLE 126. REPEAL

5/126-1. Repeal.

§126-1. Repeal. The following Acts and parts of Acts are repealed:

Section 229 and 274 of Division I, Sections 7, 12 and 13 of Division II, Sections 1, 2, 3, 4, 5, 6, 7a and 16a of Division III, Sections 3, 4, 5, 6, 7 and 8 of Division VI, all of Division VII, all of Division VIII, Section 3 of Division X, Sections 1, 2, 3, 4, 5, 6, 7, 9, 10 and 11 of Division XI, all of Division XII, Sections 1, 2, 2a, 3, 4, 5, 8, 8a, 11, 12, 13, 14, 15, 16, 17 and 18 of Division XIII, Sections 1, 2, 3, 3a, 4, 5, 7, 14, 18 and 19 of Division XIV, all of Division XV and Sections 350-A, 350-B and 350-C of "An Act to revise the law in relation to criminal jurisprudence", approved March 27, 1874, as amended;

"An Act to bar certain prosecutions for violations of criminal laws of this State", approved July 22, 1959;

"An Act in relation to the punishment of criminals", approved June 23, 1883, as amended;

"An Act in relation to the punishment and parole of habitual criminals", approved April 11, 1957;

"An Act to bar certain actions for want of prosecution", approved July 8, 1957, as amended;

"An Act providing that persons arrested for certain offenses shall be furnished with a copy of the information or complaint upon which they are charged", approved July 8, 1933;

"An Act in relation to the holding of persons in custody without their being able to notify their families or to have legal assistance", approved May 14, 1951;

"An Act to regulate the granting of continuances in criminal cases", approved June 26, 1885, as amended;

Sections 1, 2, 3, 4, 5, 6.1, 7, 8, 15, 16 and 17 of "An Act providing for a system of probation, for the appointment and compensation of probation officers, and authorizing the suspension of final judgment and the imposition of sentence upon persons found guilty of certain defined crimes and offenses, and legalizing their ultimate discharge without punishment", approved June 10, 1911, as amended;

Sections 1, 1a, 2, 3, 3.1, 3a, 9, 9.1 and 16 of "An Act to revise the law in relation to the fixing of the punishment and the sentence and commitment of persons convicted of crime or offenses, and providing for a system of parole", approved June 25, 1917, as amended; and

"An Act to provide a remedy for persons convicted and imprisoned in the penitentiary, who assert that rights guaranteed to them by the Constitution of

the United States or the State of Illinois, or both, have been denied or violated, in proceedings in which they were convicted", approved August 4, 1949.
(Source: Laws 1963, p. 2836.) [Formerly Ill. Rev. Stat. 38 §126-1.]

STATE APPELLATE DEFENDER ACT

105/1. Short title.

§1. Short title. This Act may be cited as the "State Appellate Defender Act".
(Source: P.A. 77-2633.) [Formerly Ill. Rev. Stat. 38 §208-1.]

105/2. Definitions.

§2. Definitions. In this Act, unless the context clearly requires a different meaning, the following definitions apply:

(1) "Commission" means the State Appellate Defender Commission; and

(2) "State Appellate Defender", when used with reference to representation under this Act, includes Deputy Defender and Assistant Appellate Defender.
(Source: P.A. 77-2633.) [Formerly Ill. Rev. Stat. 38 §208-2.]

105/3. Creation of office.

§3. Creation of office. There is created the office of State Appellate Defender as an agency of state government.
(Source: P.A. 77-2633.) [Formerly Ill. Rev. Stat. 38 §208-3.]

105/4. Commission.

§4. Commission. (a) There is created the State Appellate Defender Commission, to consist of 9 members appointed as follows:

(1) A chairman appointed by the Governor;

(2) One member appointed by the Supreme Court;

(3) One member appointed by each of the 5 Appellate Courts;

(4) One member appointed by the Supreme Court from a panel of 3 persons nominated by the Illinois State Bar Association;

(5) One member appointed by the Governor from a panel of 3 persons nominated by the Illinois Public Defender Association.

All appointments shall be filed with the Secretary of State by the appointing authority.

The terms of the original members shall be as follows:

One one year term and until a successor is appointed and qualified;
One 2 year term and until a successor is appointed and qualified;
One 3 year term and until a successor is appointed and qualified;
2 4 year terms and until a successor is appointed and qualified;
2 5 year terms and until a successor is appointed and qualified;
2 6 year terms and until a successor is appointed and qualified.

Thereafter all terms shall be for 6 years and until a successor is appointed and qualified. The Chairman, at the first meeting of the Commission, shall conduct a drawing by lot to determine the length of each original member's term.

(b) No member may serve more than one full 6 year term. Vacancies in the membership of the commission are filled in the same manner as original appointments. Appointment to fill vacancies occurring before the expiration of a term are for the remainder of the unexpired term.

(c) Members of the commission shall elect a vice-chairman and secretary from the membership of the commission. The commission shall meet once every six months. The chairman shall determine the time and place of meetings. Additional meetings may be held upon petition to the chairman by four or more members of the commission or upon the call of the Chairman after seven days written notice to the members.

(d) Members of the commission are not entitled to receive compensation. Members of the commission shall receive reimbursement for actual expenses incurred in the performance of their duties.

(e) Four members of the commission constitutes a quorum.

(Source: P.A. 77-2633.) [Formerly Ill. Rev. Stat. 38 §208-4.]

105/5. Powers of Supreme Court.

§5. Powers of Supreme Court. (a) The Supreme Court shall by a vote of a majority of the judges thereof appoint the State Appellate Defender for a four-year term and until his successor is appointed and qualified. No person may be appointed to or hold the office of State Appellate Defender who is not an attorney licensed to practice law in this state. The State Appellate Defender shall devote full time to the duties of his office and may not engage in the private practice of law.

(b) The Supreme Court may remove the State Appellate Defender only for cause and after a hearing. The Supreme Court may hold such hearing on its own motion or upon a motion by the commission and may adopt rules establishing other procedures for such hearing.

(Source: P.A. 77-2633.) [Formerly Ill. Rev. Stat. 38 §208-5.]

105/6. Powers and duties of commission.

§6. Powers and Duties of Commission. (a) The commission shall advise the State Appellate Defender and may, subject to rules of the Supreme Court, recommend policies for the operation of the office of State Appellate Defender.

(b) The commission shall approve or modify an operational budget submitted to it by the State Appellate Defender and set the number of employees each year.

(c) The commission may recommend to the Supreme Court the removal of the State Appellate Defender if the commission has reasonable grounds for making such recommendation.

(d) The commission shall exercise such other powers and duties as the Supreme Court by rule may provide.

(e) The State Appellate Defender shall submit reports to the commission on the operation of his office at each semi-annual meeting. He shall submit a comprehensive report to the commission at the end of each fiscal year. The commission may require the State Appellate Defender to submit additional or amended reports on any phase of the operation of his office.

(Source: P.A. 77-2633.) [Formerly Ill. Rev. Stat. 38 §208-6.]

105/7. Oath of office.

§7. Oath of office. The State Appellate Defender shall take the oath of office provided by law before entering into the duties of his office.

(Source: P.A. 77-2633.) [Formerly Ill. Rev. Stat. 38 §208-7.]

105/8. Salary.

§8. Salary. The State Appellate Defender is entitled to receive an annual salary of not less than $30,000.00 per year.

(Source: P.A. 77-2633.) [Formerly Ill. Rev. Stat. 38 §208-8.]

105/9. Organization of office.

§9. Organization of office. (a) The State Appellate Defender shall establish an office in each judicial district.

(b) The State Appellate Defender shall appoint a deputy defender for each judicial district who shall serve as the administrator of the district office. Each such appointment shall be approved by a majority of the appellate court judges of the judicial district. Each deputy defender must be an attorney licensed to practice law in this state. Deputy defenders shall serve at the pleasure of the State Appellate Defender.

(c) The staff of the State Appellate Defender may consist of additional attorneys licensed to practice law in this state to serve as assistant appellate defenders, and administrative, investigative, secretarial, and clerical employees necessary to discharge the duties of the office.

(d) Deputy Defenders shall employ, with the approval of the State Appellate Defender, assistant appellate defenders, investigators, secretaries, clerks, and other employees under their direct supervision.

(e) Attorneys employed by the State Appellate Defender or by a Deputy Defender shall devote full time to their duties, except as provided in Section 9.1 [725 ILCS 105/9.1], and may not engage in the private practice of law.

(f) The State Appellate Defender shall establish and supervise training programs for his employees.

(g) The State Appellate Defender shall promulgate regulations, instructions, and orders, consistent with this Act, further defining the organization of his office and the duties of his employees.

(Source: P.A. 83-771.) [Formerly Ill. Rev. Stat. 38 §208-9.]

105/9.1. Two individuals may share one attorney or staff position.

§9.1. Two individuals may share one attorney or staff position. For purposes of this Section, "shared position" means a position in which 2 individuals share the salary and employee benefits. For purposes of seniority, each individual shall receive credit at a rate equal to the percentage of time employed in a shared position. Attorneys sharing a position may not engage in the private practice of law.

(Source: P.A. 83-771.) [Formerly Ill. Rev. Stat. 38 §208-9.1.]

105/10. Powers and duties of State Appellate Defender.

§10. Powers and duties of State Appellate Defender. (a) The State Appellate Defender shall represent indigent persons on appeal in criminal and delinquent minor proceedings, when appointed to do so by a court under a Supreme Court Rule or law of this State.

(b) The State Appellate Defender shall submit a budget for the approval of the State Appellate Defender Commission.

(c) The State Appellate Defender may:

(1) maintain a panel of private attorneys available to serve as counsel on a case basis;

(2) establish programs, alone or in conjunction with law schools, for the purpose of utilizing volunteer law students as legal assistants;

(3) cooperate and consult with state agencies, professional associations, and other groups concerning the causes of criminal conduct, the rehabilitation and correction of persons charged with and convicted of crime, the administration of criminal justice, and, in counties of less than 1,000,000 population, study, design, develop and implement model systems for the delivery of trial level defender services, and make an annual report to the General Assembly;

(4) provide investigative services to appointed counsel and county public defenders.

The requirement for reporting to the General Assembly shall be satisfied by filing copies of the report with the Speaker, the Minority Leader and the Clerk of the House of Representatives and the President, the Minority Leader and the Secretary of the Senate and the Legislative Research Unit, as required by Section 3.1 of the General Assembly Organization Act [25 ILCS 5/3.1] and filing such additional copies with the State Government Report Distribution Center for the General Assembly as is required under paragraph (t) of Section 7 of the State Library Act [15 ILCS 320/7].
(Source: P.A. 86-1210; 87-435; 87-580; 87-614.) [Formerly Ill. Rev. Stat. 38 §208-10.]

105/11. Recovery of funds.
§11. Recovery of funds. (a) The State Appellate Defender may, on behalf of the state, recover payment or reimbursement, as the case may be, from each person who has received legal assistance under this Act, to which he was not entitled and for which he refuses to pay or reimburse. Suit must be brought within three (3) years from the date the aid was received.

(b) Amounts recovered under this section are paid into the state general fund.
(Source: P.A. 77-2633.) [Formerly Ill. Rev. Stat. 38 §208-11.]

ARREST AND CONVICTION OF OUT OF STATE MURDERERS ACT

Sec.

110/0.01. Short title.
§0.01. Short title. This Act may be cited as the Arrest and Conviction of Out of State Murderers Act.
(Source: P.A. 86-1324.) [Formerly Ill. Rev. Stat. 60 §50.]

110/1. Payment of expenses for arrest and conviction.
§1. Whenever any citizen of this state, or any minor child residing with its parents or guardian in this state, shall heretofore have been, or shall hereafter be, by fraudulent pretenses, enticed or kidnapped and taken out of this state into any other state, and by such enticer or kidnapper or his confederates murdered, and the relatives or parents or guardian of such person, shall have pursued or shall pursue such criminal and procured his arrest and conviction of such crime under the laws of such other state, the reasonable expense incurred in procuring such arrest and conviction in such other state, shall be paid out of the treasury of this state as follows:

Any person making claim under the provision of this act shall file a statement of the claim with the several items thereof with the State Comptroller, which claim shall be verified by the oath of the claimant and by record or other satisfactory proof of the conviction of the criminal, and by such other proof as the nature of the case will admit, and such claim and the proofs shall be considered by the governor, Comptroller and attorney general, who shall examine said claim and proof and may require other proof if they judge necessary; and upon being satisfied that said claim or any of the items thereof was incurred in the prosecution of such criminal in such other state, and was a just and reasonable expense for that purpose, they shall allow the same for such an amount as they judge just and reasonable, and shall so certify to the Comptroller, who shall thereupon draw his warrant in favor of the claimant on the treasurer for the amount so allowed: Provided, no more than $3,500 shall be allowed in any one case.
(Source: P.A. 78-592.) [Formerly Ill. Rev. Stat. 60 §51.]

BILL OF RIGHTS FOR CHILDREN

115/1. Short title.

§1. Short title. This Act shall be known and may be cited as the Bill of Rights for Children.
(Source: P.A. 86-862.) [Formerly Ill. Rev. Stat. 38 §1351.]

115/2. Purposes.

§2. Purposes. The purpose of this Act is to ensure the fair and compassionate treatment of children involved in the criminal justice system by affording certain basic rights and considerations to these children.
(Source: P.A. 86-862.) [Formerly Ill. Rev. Stat. 38 §1352.]

115/3. Rights to present child impact statement.

§3. Rights to present child impact statement. In any case where a defendant has been convicted of a violent crime involving a child or a juvenile has been adjudicated a delinquent for any offense defined in Sections 12-13 through 12-16 of the Criminal Code of 1961 [720 ILCS 5/12-13 through 5/12-16], except those in which both parties have agreed to the imposition of a specific sentence, and a parent or legal guardian of the child involved is present in the courtroom at the time of the sentencing or the disposition hearing, the parent or legal guardian upon his or her request shall have the right to address the court regarding the impact which the defendant's criminal conduct or the juvenile's delinquent conduct has had upon the child. If the parent or legal guardian chooses to exercise this right, the impact statement must have been prepared in writing in conjunction with the Office of the State's Attorney prior to the initial hearing or sentencing, before it can be presented orally at the sentencing hearing. The court shall consider any statements made by the parent or legal guardian, along with all other appropriate factors in determining the sentence of the defendant or disposition of such juvenile.

This Section shall apply to any child victims of any offense defined in Sections 12-13 through 12-16 of the Criminal Code of 1961 during any dispositional hearing under Section 5-22 of the Juvenile Court Act of 1987 [705 ILCS 405/5-22] which takes place pursuant to an adjudication of delinquency for any such offense.
(Source: P.A. 86-862.) [Formerly Ill. Rev. Stat. 38 §1353.]

115/4. Rights or responsibilities unaffected.

§4. This Act does not limit any rights or responsibilities otherwise enjoyed by or imposed upon victims or witnesses of violent crime, nor does it grant any person a cause of action for damages which does not otherwise exist.
(Source: P.A. 86-862.) [Formerly Ill. Rev. Stat. 38 §1354.]

BILL OF RIGHTS FOR VICTIMS AND WITNESSES OF VIOLENT CRIME ACT

120/1. Short title.

§1. This Article I shall be known and may be cited as the "Bill of Rights for Victims and Witnesses of Violent Crime Act".
(Source: P.A. 83-1432.) [Formerly Ill. Rev. Stat. 38 §1401.]

120/2. Purpose.

§2. The purpose of this Act is to ensure the fair and compassionate treatment of victims and witnesses of violent crime and to increase the effectiveness of the criminal justice system by affording certain basic rights and considerations to the victims and witnesses of violent crime who are essential to prosecution.
(Source: P.A. 83-1432.) [Formerly Ill. Rev. Stat. 38 §1402.]

120/3. Definitions.

§3. The terms used in this Act, unless the context clearly requires otherwise, shall have the following meanings:

(a) "Victim" means (1) a person physically injured in this State as a result of a violent crime perpetrated or attempted against that person or (2) a person who suffers injury to or loss of property as a result of a violent crime perpetrated or attempted against that person or (3) the spouse, parent, child or sibling of a person killed as a result of a violent crime perpetrated against the person killed or the spouse, parent, child or sibling of any person granted rights under this Act who is physically or mentally incapable of exercising such rights, except where the spouse, parent, child or sibling is also the defendant or prisoner or (4) any person against whom a violent crime has been committed or (5) any person who has suffered personal injury as a result of a violation of Section 11-501 of The Illinois Vehicle Code [625 ILCS 5/11-501], or of a similar provision of a local ordinance, or of Section 9-3 of the Criminal Code of 1961, as amended [720 ILCS 5/9-3];

(b) "Witness" means any person who personally observed the commission of a violent crime and who will testify on behalf of the State of Illinois in the criminal prosecution of the violent crime;

(c) "Violent Crime" means any felony in which force or threat of force was used against the victim or any misdemeanor which results in death or great bodily harm to the victim or any violation of Section 9-3 of the Criminal Code of 1961, as amended, or Section 11-501 of The Illinois Vehicle Code, or a similar provision of a local ordinance, if the violation resulted in personal injury or death. For the purposes of this paragraph, "personal injury" shall include any injury requiring immediate professional attention in either a doctor's office or medical facility;

(d) "Sentencing Hearing" means any hearing where a sentence is imposed by the court on a convicted defendant and includes hearings conducted pursuant to Sections 5-6-4, 5-6-4.1, 5-7-2 and 5-7-7 of the Unified Code of Corrections [730 ILCS 5/5-6-4, 5/5-6-4.1, 5/5-7-2 and 5/5-7-7].
(Source: P.A. 84-1308; 84-1426.) [Formerly Ill. Rev. Stat. 38 §1403.]

120/4. Rights of victims.

§4. Rights of victims. Victims shall have the following rights:

(1) Upon specific request by the victim, to be informed by law enforcement authorities investigating the case of the status of the investigation, except where the State's Attorney determines that disclosure of such information would unreasonably interfere with the investigation, until such time as the alleged assailant is apprehended or the investigation is closed;

(2) To be notified by the Office of the State's Attorney of the filing of an information, the return of an indictment by which a prosecution for any violent crime is commenced, or the filing of a petition to adjudicate a minor as a

delinquent for any offense defined in Sections 12-13 through 12-16 of the Criminal Code of 1961 [720 ILCS 5/12-13 through 5/12-16];

(3) Upon specific request by the victim, to be informed by the Office of the State's Attorney within a reasonable time, of the release of the defendant on bail or personal recognizance or the release from detention of a minor who has been detained for any offense defined in Sections 12-13 through 12-16 of the Criminal Code of 1961;

(4) Upon specific request by the victim to have the details of any plea or verdict of a defendant, or any adjudication of a juvenile as a delinquent for any offense defined in Sections 12-13 through 12-16 of the Criminal Code of 1961 explained by the Office of the State's Attorney in nontechnical language;

(5) To be notified by the Office of the State's Attorney, of the date, time, and place of any hearing in the case. Notice shall be given a reasonable amount of time in advance when the victim's presence is required at the hearing. Whenever possible, notice shall also be given in advance when the victim's presence is not required, and the victim shall be notified of the cancellation of any scheduled hearing in sufficient time to prevent an unnecessary appearance in court. Notice of any sentencing hearing shall include notice of the right to make a victim impact statement as provided by law. The victim, as defined in subsections (a)(1), (a)(2), (a)(4), and (a)(5) of Section 3 of this Act [725 ILCS 120/3], shall have the right to be present in court at all times during the trial of the defendant, unless the prosecuting attorney objects or a judge has ordered the victim excluded or removed from the courtroom for the same causes and in the same manner as the rules of court or law provide for the exclusion or removal of the defendant;

(6) Upon specific request by the victim, to be notified by the office of the State's Attorney before the office of the State's Attorney makes any offer of a plea bargain to the defendant or enters into negotiations with the defendant concerning a possible plea bargain;

(7) Upon specific request by the victim, to be notified by the Office of the State's Attorney of the ultimate disposition of the cases arising from an indictment or an information, or a petition to have a juvenile adjudicated as a delinquent for any offense defined in Sections 12-13 through 12-16 of the Criminal Code of 1961;

(8) Upon specific request by the victim, to be notified by the Office of the State's Attorney of any appeal taken by the defendant or the State and of the date, time and place of any hearing concerning the appeal. Whenever possible, notice of the hearing shall be given in advance;

(9) Upon specific request by the victim to be notified by the Office of the State's Attorney of any petition for post-conviction review filed by the defendant under Article 122 of the Code of Criminal Procedure of 1963 [725 ILCS 5/122-1 et seq.], and of the date, time and place of any hearing concerning the petition. Whenever possible, notice of the hearing shall be given in advance;

(10) Upon specific request by the victim, to be informed by the Prisoner Review Board of the prisoner's final discharge, or by the custodian of the discharge of an individual who was adjudicated a delinquent for any offense defined in Sections 12-13 through 12-16 of the Criminal Code of 1961, from State custody and by the Sheriff of the appropriate county of any such person's final discharge from county custody. Upon specific request by the victim, to be informed by the Prisoner Review Board of the prisoner's release on furlough; and where feasible to be informed at least 7 days prior to a prisoner's furlough of the times and date of such furlough. Upon specific request by the victim, the State's Attorney shall notify the victim once of the times and dates of release of a prisoner sentenced to periodic imprisonment. Such request shall include the mailing address and telephone number of the victim making the request;

(11) Upon specific request, where the defendant has been committed to the Department of Mental Health and Developmental Disabilities pursuant to Section 5-2-4 or any other provision of the Unified Code of Corrections [730 ILCS 5/5-2-4], to be notified by the releasing authority of the defendant's discharge from State custody;

(12) To be informed by the Office of the State's Attorney, law enforcement authorities or victim advocate personnel of social services and financial assistance available for victims of violent crime, including information on how to apply for these services and assistance;

(13) To have any stolen or other personal property held by law enforcement authorities for evidentiary or other purposes returned as expeditiously as possible, pursuant to the procedures set out in Section 115-9 of the Code of Criminal Procedure of 1963 [725 ILCS 5/115-9];

(14) To be provided with appropriate employer intercession services by the State's Attorney or victim advocate personnel to ensure that employers of victims will cooperate with the criminal justice system in order to minimize an employee's loss of pay and other benefits resulting from court appearances;

(15) To be provided, whenever possible, a secure waiting area during court proceedings that does not require victims to be in close proximity to defendants or juveniles accused of an offense defined in Sections 12-13 through 12-16 of the Criminal Code of 1961, and their families and friends;

(16) To be provided, where necessary, with the services of a translator;

(17) In the event of an escape from State custody, the Department of Corrections immediately shall notify the Prisoner Review Board of the escape and the Prisoner Review Board shall notify the victim. Such notification shall be based upon the most recent information as to the victim's residence or other location available to the Board. Where no such information is available, the Board shall make all reasonable efforts to obtain such information and make such notification. When the escapee is apprehended, the Department of Corrections immediately shall notify the Prisoner Review Board and the Board shall notify the victim;

(18) The victim of the violent crime for which the prisoner has been sentenced shall receive reasonable written notice not less than 15 days prior to the parole hearing and may submit, in writing, on film, video tape or other electronic means or in the form of a recording or in person at the parole hearing, information for consideration by the Prisoner Review Board. The victim shall be notified within 7 days after the prisoner has been granted parole and shall be informed of the right to inspect the registry of parole decisions, established under subsection (g) of Section 3-3-5 of the Unified Code of Corrections [730 ILCS 5/3-3-5]. The provisions of this paragraph (18) are subject to the Open Parole Hearings Act;

(19) In the case of the death of a person, which death occurred in the same transaction or occurrence in which acts occurred for which a defendant is charged with an offense, the spouse, parent, child or sibling of the decedent shall be notified by the Office of the State's Attorney and law enforcement authorities of the date of the trial of the person or persons allegedly responsible for the death;

(20) To be provided by the office of the State's Attorney with a written explanation, in nontechnical language, of the victim's rights under this Act;

(21) To retain an attorney, at the victim's own expense, who, upon written notice filed with the clerk of the court and State's Attorney, is to receive copies of all notices, motions and court orders filed thereafter in the case, in the same manner as if the victim were a named party in the case;

(22) To be informed at the sentencing hearing of the minimum amount of time during which the defendant may actually be physically imprisoned. The

minimum actual imprisonment of a defendant shall be computed by subtracting any good conduct credit and good conduct credit for meritorious service for which the defendant may be eligible from the sentence set in accordance with Sections 5-8-1, 5-8-2, and 5-8-3 of the Unified Code of Corrections [730 ILCS 5/5-8-1, 5/5-8-2, and 5/5-8-3]; and

(23) Upon request by the victim, to have the State's Attorney forward a copy of any statement presented under Section 6 to the Prisoner Review Board to be considered by the Board in making its determination under subsection (b) of Section 3-3-8 of the Unified Code of Corrections [730 ILCS 5/3-3-8].

(24) If a statement is presented under Section 6 [725 ILCS 120/6], to be informed by Prisoner Review Board of any order of discharge entered by the Board pursuant to Section 3-3-8 of the Unified Code of Corrections.
(Source: P.A. 86-263; 86-567; 86-1028; 87-224.) [Formerly Ill. Rev. Stat. 38 §1404.]

120/5. Rights of witnesses.

§5. Rights of Witnesses. Witnesses as defined in subsection (b) of Section 3 of this Act [725 ILCS 120/3] shall have the following rights:

(1) To be notified by the Office of the State's Attorney of all court proceedings at which the witness' presence is required in a reasonable amount of time prior to the proceeding, and to be notified of the cancellation of any scheduled court proceeding in sufficient time to prevent an unnecessary appearance in court, where possible;

(2) To be provided with appropriate employer intercession services by the Office of State's Attorney or the victim advocate personnel to ensure that employers of witnesses will cooperate with the criminal justice system in order to minimize an employee's loss of pay and other benefits resulting from court appearances;

(3) To be provided, whenever possible, a secure waiting area during court proceedings that does not require witnesses to be in close proximity to defendants and their families and friends;

(4) To be provided, where necessary, with the services of a translator.
(Source: P.A. 84-187.) [Formerly Ill. Rev. Stat. 38 §1405.]

120/6. Rights to present victim impact statement.

§6. Rights to present victim impact statement. In any case where a defendant has been convicted of a violent crime or a juvenile has been adjudicated a delinquent for any offense defined in Sections 12-13 through 12-16 of the Criminal Code of 1961 [720 ILCS 5/12-13 through 5/12-16], except those in which both parties have agreed to the imposition of a specific sentence, and a victim of the violent crime is present in the courtroom at the time of the sentencing or the disposition hearing, the victim upon his or her request shall have the right to address the court regarding the impact which the defendant's criminal conduct or the juvenile's delinquent conduct has had upon the victim. If the victim chooses to exercise this right, the impact statement must have been prepared in writing in conjunction with the Office of the State's Attorney prior to the initial hearing or sentencing, before it can be presented orally at the sentencing hearing. The court shall consider any statements made by the victim, along with all other appropriate factors in determining the sentence of the defendant or disposition of such juvenile.

This Section shall apply to any victims of any offense defined in Sections 12-13 through 12-16 of the Criminal Code of 1961 during any dispositional hearing under Section 5-22 of the Juvenile Court Act of 1987 [705 ILCS 405/5-22] which takes place pursuant to an adjudication of delinquency for any such offense.
(Source: P.A. 85-1209.) [Formerly Ill. Rev. Stat. 38 §1406.]

120/7. Responsibilities of victims and witnesses.

§7. Responsibilities of victims and witnesses. Victims and witnesses shall have the following responsibilities to aid in the prosecution of violent crime:

(a) To make a timely report of the violent crime;

(b) To cooperate with law enforcement authorities throughout the investigation, prosecution, and trial;

(c) To testify at trial;

(d) To notify law enforcement authorities of any change of address.

(Source: P.A. 83-1499.) [Formerly Ill. Rev. Stat. 38 §1407.]

120/9. Rights or responsibilities unaffected.

§9. This Act does not limit any rights or responsibilities otherwise enjoyed by or imposed upon victims or witnesses of violent crime, nor does it grant any person a cause of action for damages which does not otherwise exist.

(Source: P.A. 84-187.) [Formerly Ill. Rev. Stat. 38 §1408.]

CRIMINAL JURISPRUDENCE ACT [INDICTMENT]

125/8(Div.XI). Instrument destroyed or withheld.

§8(Div.XI). When an instrument, which is the subject of an indictment, has been destroyed or withheld by the act or procurement of the defendant, and the fact of such destruction or withholding is alleged in the indictment and established on trial, the accused shall not be acquitted on account of any misdescription of the instrument so withheld or destroyed.

(Source: Laws 1874, p. 348.) [Formerly Ill. Rev. Stat. 38 §150-1.]

[WITNESSES IN GENERAL]

125/6(Div.XII). Disqualifications removed.

§6(Div.XII). No person shall be disqualified as a witness in any criminal case or proceeding by reason of his or her interest in the event of the same, as a party or otherwise, or by reason of his or her having been convicted of any crime; but such interest or conviction may be shown for the purpose of affecting the credibility of the witness: Provided, however, that a defendant in any criminal case or proceeding shall only at his or her own request be deemed a competent witness, and the person's neglect to testify shall not create any presumption against the person, nor shall the court permit any reference or comment to be made to or upon such neglect.

In all criminal cases, husband and wife may testify for or against each other: provided, that neither may testify as to any communication or admission made by either of them to the other or as to any conversation between them during marriage, except in cases where either is charged with an offense against the person or property of the other, or in case of spouse abandonment, or where the interests of their child or children or of any child or children in either spouse's care, custody or control are directly involved, or where either is charged under Section 12-13, 12-14, 12-15, or 12-16 of the Criminal Code of 1961 [720 ILCS 5/12-13, 5/12-14, 5/12-15, or 5/12-16] and the victim is a minor under 18 years

of age in either spouse's care, custody or control at the time of the offense, or as to matters in which either has acted as agent of the other.
(Source: P.A. 85-499.) [Formerly Ill. Rev. Stat. 38 §155-1.]

125/7(Div.XII). Subpoenas.
§7(Div.XII). It shall be the duty of the clerk of the court to issue subpoenas, either on the part of the people or of the accused, directed to the sheriff or coroner of any county of this state. And every witness who shall be duly subpoenaed, and shall neglect or refuse to attend any court, pursuant to the requisitions of such subpoena, shall be proceeded against and punished for contempt of the court. Any attachments against witnesses who live in a different county from that where such subpoena is returnable, may be served in the same manner as warrants are directed to be served out of the county from which they issue.
(Source: P.A. 84-551.) [Formerly Ill. Rev. Stat. 38 §155-2.]

125/8(Div.XII). Witness to crime; employer may not discharge for loss of time.
§8(Div.XII). No employer shall discharge or terminate, or threaten to discharge or terminate, from his employment, or otherwise punish or penalize any employee of his who is a witness to a crime, because of time lost from regular employment resulting from his attendance at any proceeding pursuant to subpoena issued in any criminal proceeding relative to such crime. Any employer who shall knowingly or intentionally violate this section shall be proceeded against and punished for contempt of court. This section shall not be construed as requiring an employer to pay an employee for time lost resulting from attendance at any proceeding.
(Source: P.A. 81-808.) [Formerly Ill. Rev. Stat. 38 §155-3.]

[LIE DETECTOR TESTS]

125/8b(Div.XII). Restraints on court.
§8b(Div.XII). In the course of any criminal trial the court shall not require, request or suggest that the defendant submit to a polygraphic detection deception test, commonly known as a lie detector test to questioning under the effect of thiopental sodium or to any other test or questioning by means of any mechanical device or chemical substance.
(Source: Laws 1961, p. 2462.) [Formerly Ill. Rev. Stat. 38 §155-11.]

[CRIMINAL COSTS AND LIEN]

130/13. Judgment; costs.
§13. When any person is convicted of an offense under any statute, or at common law, the court shall enter judgment that the offender pay the costs of the prosecution. Such costs shall include reasonable costs incurred by the Sheriff for serving any arrest warrants, for picking up the offender from a county other than the one in which he was convicted, and for picking up the offender from any location outside the State of Illinois pursuant either to his extradition or to his waiver of extradition.
(Source: P.A. 85-645.) [Formerly Ill. Rev. Stat. 38 §180-3.]

130/15. Judgment lien on real and personal property.
§15. The property, real and personal, of every person who shall be convicted of any offense, shall be bound, and a lien is hereby created on the property, both

real and personal, of every such offender, not exempt from the enforcement of a judgment or attachment, from the time of finding the indictment at least so far as will be sufficient to pay the fine and costs of prosecution. The clerk of the court in which the conviction is had shall upon the expiration of 30 days after judgment is entered issue a certified copy of the judgment for any fine that remains unpaid, and all costs of conviction remaining unpaid; in which certified copy of the judgment shall be stated the day on which the arrest was made, or indictment found, as the case may be. Enforcement of the judgment may be directed to the proper officer of any county in this state. The officer to whom such certified copy of the judgment is delivered shall levy the same upon all the estate, real and personal, of the defendant (not exempt from enforcement,) possessed by him or her on the day of the arrest or finding the indictment, as stated in the certified copy of the judgment and any such property subsequently acquired; and the property so levied upon shall be advertised and sold in the same manner as in civil cases, with the like rights to all parties that may be interested therein. It shall be no objection to the selling of any property under such judgment, that the defendant is in custody for the fine or costs, or both.
(Source: P.A. 83-346.) [Formerly Ill. Rev. Stat. 38 §180-4.]

[CRIMINAL BREACH OF PEACE]

135/1. Conservators of the peace; preservation.

§1. All courts are conservators of the peace, and shall cause to be kept all laws made for the preservation of the peace, and may require persons to give security to keep the peace, or for their good behavior, or both, as provided by this act.
(Source: P.A. 83-334.) [Formerly Ill. Rev. Stat. 38 §200-1.]

135/2. Complaint; examination.

§2. When complaint is made to any such judge that a person has threatened or is about to commit an offense against the person or property of another, the court shall examine on oath the complaint, and any witness who may be produced, and reduce the complaint to writing, and cause it to be subscribed and sworn to by the complainant.

The complaint may be issued electronically or electromagnetically by use of a facsimile transmission machine and any such complaint shall have the same validity as a written complaint.
(Source: P.A. 87-523.) [Formerly Ill. Rev. Stat. 38 §200-2.]

135/3. Issuance of warrant.

§3. If the court is satisfied that there is danger that such offense will be committed, the court shall issue a warrant requiring the proper officer to whom it is directed forthwith to apprehend the person complained of, and bring him before the court having jurisdiction in the premises.

The warrant may be issued electronically or electromagnetically by use of a facsimile transmission machine and any such warrant shall have the same validity as a written warrant.
(Source: P.A. 87-523.) [Formerly Ill. Rev. Stat. 38 §200-3.]

135/4. Examination before the court.

§4. When the person complained of is brought before the court if the charge is controverted the testimony produced on behalf of the plaintiff and defendant shall be heard.
(Source: P.A. 83-334.) [Formerly Ill. Rev. Stat. 38 §200-4.]

135/5. Judgment against complainant.

§5. If it appears that there is no just reason to fear the commission of the offense, the defendant shall be discharged; and if the court is of the opinion that the prosecution was commenced maliciously without probable cause, the court may enter judgment against the complainant for the costs of the prosecution.
(Source: P.A. 83-334.) [Formerly Ill. Rev. Stat. 38 §200-5.]

135/6. Recognizance.

§6. If, however, there is just reason to fear the commission of such offense, the defendant shall be required to give a recognizance, with sufficient security, in such sum as the court may direct, to keep the peace towards all people of this state, and especially towards the person against whom or whose property there is reason to fear the offense may be committed, for such time, not exceeding 12 months, as the court may order. But he shall not be bound over to the next court unless he is also charged with some other offense for which he ought to be held to answer at such court.
(Source: P.A. 83-334.) [Formerly Ill. Rev. Stat. 38 §200-6.]

135/7. Commitment or discharge.

§7. If the person so ordered to recognize complies with the order, he or she shall be discharged; but if he or she refuses or neglects, the court shall commit him or her to jail during the period for which he or she was required to give security, or until he or she so recognizes, stating in the warrant the cause of commitment, with the sum and time for which the security was required.
(Source: P.A. 86-1475.) [Formerly Ill. Rev. Stat. 38 §200-7.]

135/8. Cost of prosecution.

§8. When a person is required to give security to keep the peace, or for his or her good behavior, the court may further order that the costs of the prosecution, or any part thereof, shall be paid by such person, who shall stand committed until the costs are paid, or he or she is otherwise legally discharged.
(Source: P.A. 83-334.) [Formerly Ill. Rev. Stat. 38 §200-8.]

135/13. Discharge on giving security.

§13. A person committed for not finding sureties, or refusing to recognize as required by the court, may be discharged on giving such security as was required.
(Source: P.A. 83-334.) [Formerly Ill. Rev. Stat. 38 §200-13.]

135/14. Filing of recognizance.

§14. Every recognizance taken in pursuance of the foregoing provisions shall be filed of record by the clerk and upon a breach of the condition the same shall be prosecuted by the State's Attorney.
(Source: Laws 1965, p. 40.) [Formerly Ill. Rev. Stat. 38 §200-14.]

135/15. Unnecessary to show conviction.

§15. In proceeding upon a recognizance it shall not be necessary to show a conviction of the defendant of an offense against the person or property of another.
(Source: R.S. 1874, p. 348.) [Formerly Ill. Rev. Stat. 38 §200-15.]

135/16. Breach of peace.

§16. A person who, in the presence of a court, commits or threatens to commit an offense against the person or property of another, may be ordered, without process, to enter into a recognizance to keep the peace for a period not exceeding 12 months, and in case of refusal be committed as in other cases.
(Source: P.A. 83-334.) [Formerly Ill. Rev. Stat. 38 §200-16.]

135/17. Remittance.

§17. When, upon an action brought upon a recognizance, the penalty thereof is adjudged forfeited, the court may, on the petition of any defendant, remit such portion of it as the circumstances of the case render just and reasonable.
(Source: P.A. 83-334.) [Formerly Ill. Rev. Stat. 38 §200-17.]

135/18. Surrender of principal to sheriff.

§18. The sureties of any person bound to keep the peace may, at any time, surrender their principal to the sheriff of the county in which the principal was bound, under the same rules and regulations governing the surrender of the principal in other criminal cases.
(Source: R.S. 1874, p. 348.) [Formerly Ill. Rev. Stat. 38 §200-18.]

135/19. Principal may recognize anew.

§19. The person so surrendered may recognize anew, with sufficient sureties, before any court, for the residue of the time, and shall thereupon be discharged.
(Source: P.A. 83-334.) [Formerly Ill. Rev. Stat. 38 §200-19.]

135/20. Amendment to conformance.

§20. No proceeding to prevent a breach of the peace shall be dismissed on account of any informality or insufficiency in the complaint, or any process or proceeding, but the same may be amended, by order of the court, to conform to the facts in the case.
(Source: P.A. 83-1362.) [Formerly Ill. Rev. Stat. 38 §200-20.]

CRIMINAL PROCEEDING INTERPRETER ACT

Sec.

140/0.01. Short title.

§0.01. Short title. This Act may be cited as the Criminal Proceeding Interpreter Act.
(Source: P.A. 86-1324.) [Formerly Ill. Rev. Stat. 38 §165-10.]

140/1. Appointment.

§1. Whenever any person accused of committing a felony or misdemeanor is to be tried in any court of this State, the court shall upon its own motion or that of defense or prosecution determine whether the accused is capable of understanding the English language and is capable of expressing himself in the English language so as to be understood directly by counsel, court or jury. If the court finds the accused incapable of so understanding or so expressing himself,

the court shall appoint an interpreter for the accused whom he can understand and who can understand him.
(Source: P.A. 77-1527.) [Formerly Ill. Rev. Stat. 38 §165-11.]

140/2. Order of appointment.

§2. The court shall enter an order of its appointment of the interpreter who shall be sworn to truly interpret or translate all questions propounded or answers given as directed by the court.
(Source: P.A. 77-1527.) [Formerly Ill. Rev. Stat. 38 §165-12.]

140/3. Payment of fees.

§3. The court shall determine a reasonable fee for all such interpreter services which shall be paid out of the general county funds.
(Source: P.A. 77-1527.) [Formerly Ill. Rev. Stat. 38 §165-13.]

CRIMINAL VICTIMS' ASSET DISCOVERY ACT

(Chgd. by P.A. 87-1157, §1, eff. 9/18/92.)

145/1. Short title.

§1. Short title. This Act may be cited as the Criminal Victims' Asset Discovery Act.
(Chgd. by P.A. 87-1157, §1, eff. 9/18/92.)
(Source: P.A. 81-906.) [Formerly Ill. Rev. Stat. 70 §401.]

145/2. Definitions.

§2. Definitions. The following words and phrases when used in this Act shall, for the purposes of this Act, have the meanings respectively ascribed to them except when the context requires otherwise.
(Source: P.A. 81-906.) [Formerly Ill. Rev. Stat. 70 §402.]

145/2.1. Person, defined.

§2.1. "Person" means every natural person, firm, partnership, association, corporation or other legal entity.
(Source: P.A. 81-906.) [Formerly Ill. Rev. Stat. 70 §402.1.]

145/2.2. *(Repealed by P.A. 87-1157, §4, eff. 9/18/92.)*
(Source: P.A. 81-906.) [Formerly Ill. Rev. Stat. 70 §402.2.]

145/2.3. Victim, defined.

§2.3. "Victim" means a person killed or physically injured in this State as a result of a crime perpetrated or attempted against that person.
(Source: P.A. 81-906.) [Formerly Ill. Rev. Stat. 70 §402.3.]

145/3. Deposition; assets of criminal.

§3. Deposition; assets of criminal. (a) Any person who has been convicted of first degree murder or a Class X felony in this State or who has been found not guilty by reason of insanity or guilty but mentally ill of first degree murder or a Class X felony, involving a victim as described in Section 2.3 [725 ILCS 145/2.3], or any other person who has reasonable grounds to know of any assets of the person convicted of first degree murder or a Class X felony, or who has been found not guilty by reason of insanity or guilty but mentally ill of first degree murder or a Class X felony, may be deposed by the victim or the victim's legal representative concerning those assets.

(b) Upon written request of the victim, the Department of Corrections shall disclose to the victim any assets of the person convicted of first degree murder or a Class X felony, or found not guilty by reason of insanity or guilty but mentally ill of first degree murder or a Class X felony, known by the Department.

(c) The victim may seek attachment against the property of the person convicted of first degree murder or a Class X felony, or found not guilty by reason of insanity or guilty but mentally ill of first degree murder or a Class X felony, against him or her.

(Chgd. by P.A. 87-1157, §1, eff. 9/18/92.)

(Source: P.A. 86-706.) [Formerly Ill. Rev. Stat. 70 §403.]

145/4 to 145/14. *(Repealed by P.A. 87-1157, §4, eff. 9/18/92.)*

(Sources: P.A. 81-906; 84-1029; 86-706.) [Formerly Ill. Rev. Stat. 70 §§404 to 414.]

DRUG ASSET FORFEITURE PROCEDURE ACT

Sec.

150/1. Short title.

§1. Short Title. This Act shall be known and may be cited as the Drug Asset Forfeiture Procedure Act.

(Source: P.A. 86-1382.) [Formerly Ill. Rev. Stat. 56½ §1671.]

150/2. Legislative declaration.

§2. Legislative Declaration. The General Assembly finds that the civil forfeiture of property which is used or intended to be used in, is attributable to or facilitates the manufacture, sale, transportation, distribution, possession or use of substances in certain violations of the Illinois Controlled Substances Act [720 ILCS 570/100 et seq.] or the Cannabis Control Act [720 ILCS 550/1 et seq.], will have a significant beneficial effect in deterring the rising incidence of the abuse and trafficking of such substances within this State. While forfeiture may secure for State and local units of government some resources for deterring drug abuse and drug trafficking, forfeiture is not intended to be an alternative means of funding the administration of criminal justice. The General Assembly further finds that the federal narcotics civil forfeiture statute upon which this Act is based has been very successful in deterring the use and distribution of controlled substances within this State and throughout the country. It is therefore the intent of the General Assembly that the forfeiture provisions of this Act be construed in light of the federal forfeiture provisions contained in 21 U.S.C. 881 as interpreted by the federal courts, except to the extent that the provisions of this Act expressly differ therefrom.

(Source: P.A. 86-1382; 87-614.) [Formerly Ill. Rev. Stat. 56½ §1672.]

150/3. Applicability.

§3. Applicability. The provisions of this Act are applicable to all property forfeitable under the Illinois Controlled Substances Act [720 ILCS 570/100 et seq.] or the Cannabis Control Act [720 ILCS 550/1 et seq.].
(Source: P.A. 86-1382.) [Formerly Ill. Rev. Stat. 56½ §1673.]

150/4. Notice to owner or interest holder.

§4. Notice to Owner or Interest Holder. (A) Whenever notice of pending forfeiture or service of an in rem complaint is required under the provisions of this Act, such notice or service shall be given as follows:

(1) If the owner's or interest holder's name and current address are known, then by either personal service or mailing a copy of the notice by certified mail, return receipt requested, to that address. For purposes of notice under this Section, if a person has been arrested for the conduct giving rise to the forfeiture, then the address provided to the arresting agency at the time of arrest shall be deemed to be that person's known address. Provided, however, if an owner or interest holder's address changes prior to the effective date of the notice of pending forfeiture, the owner or interest holder shall promptly notify the seizing agency of the change in address or, if the owner or interest holder's address changes subsequent to the effective date of the notice of pending forfeiture, the owner or interest holder shall promptly notify the State's Attorney of the change in address; or

(2) If the property seized is a conveyance, to the address reflected in the office of the agency or official in which title or interest to the conveyance is required by law to be recorded, then by mailing a copy of the notice by certified mail, return receipt requested, to that address; or

(3) If the owner's or interest holder's address is not known, and is not on record as provided in paragraph (2), then by publication for 3 successive weeks in a newspaper of general circulation in the county in which the seizure occurred.

(B) Notice served under this Act is effective upon personal service, the last date of publication, or the mailing of written notice, whichever is earlier.
(Source: P.A. 86-1382; 87-614.) [Formerly Ill. Rev. Stat. 56½ §1674.]

150/5. Notice to state's attorney.

§5. Notice to State's Attorney. The law enforcement agency seizing property for forfeiture under the Illinois Controlled Substances Act [720 ILCS 570/100 et seq.] or the Cannabis Control Act [720 ILCS 550/1 et seq.] shall, within 52 days of seizure, notify the State's Attorney for the county in which an act or omission giving rise to the forfeiture occurred or in which the property was seized of the seizure of the property and the facts and circumstances giving rise to the seizure and shall provide the State's Attorney with the inventory of the property and its estimated value. When the property seized for forfeiture is a vehicle, the law enforcement agency seizing the property shall immediately notify the Secretary of State that forfeiture proceedings are pending regarding such vehicle.
(Source: P.A. 86-1382.) [Formerly Ill. Rev. Stat. 56½ §1675.]

150/6. Non-judicial forfeiture.

§6. Non-Judicial Forfeiture. If non-real property that exceeds $20,000 in value excluding the value of any conveyance, or if real property is seized under the provisions of the Illinois Controlled Substances Act [720 ILCS 570/100 et seq.] or the Cannabis Control Act [720 ILCS 550/1 et seq.], the State's Attorney shall institute judicial in rem forfeiture proceedings as described in Section 9 of this Act [725 ILCS 150/9] within 45 days from receipt of notice of seizure from the seizing agency under Section 5 of this Act [725 ILCS 150/5]. However, if non-real property that does not exceed $20,000 in value excluding the value of any conveyance is seized, the following procedure shall be used:

(A) If, after review of the facts surrounding the seizure, the State's Attorney is of the opinion that the seized property is subject to forfeiture, then within 45 days of the receipt of notice of seizure from the seizing agency, the State's Attorney shall cause notice of pending forfeiture to be given to the owner of the property and all known interest holders of the property in accordance with Section 4 of this Act [725 ILCS 150/4].

(B) The notice of pending forfeiture must include a description of the property, the estimated value of the property, the date and place of seizure, the conduct giving rise to forfeiture or the violation of law alleged, and a summary of procedures and procedural rights applicable to the forfeiture action.

(C) (1) Any person claiming an interest in property which is the subject of notice under subsection (A) of Section 6 of this Act, may, within 45 days after the effective date of notice as described in Section 4 of this Act, file a verified claim with the State's Attorney expressing his or her interest in the property. The claim must set forth:

(i) the caption of the proceedings as set forth on the notice of pending forfeiture and the name of the claimant;

(ii) the address at which the claimant will accept mail;

(iii) the nature and extent of the claimant's interest in the property;

(iv) the date, identity of the transferor, and circumstances of the claimant's acquisition of the interest in the property;

(v) the name and address of all other persons known to have an interest in the property;

(vi) the specific provision of law relied on in asserting the property is not subject to forfeiture;

(vii) all essential facts supporting each assertion; and

(viii) the relief sought.

(2) If a claimant files the claim and deposits with the State's Attorney a cost bond, in the form of a cashier's check payable to the clerk of the court, in the sum of 10 percent of the reasonable value of the property as alleged by the State's Attorney or the sum of $100, whichever is greater, upon condition that, in the case of forfeiture, the claimant must pay all costs and expenses of forfeiture proceedings, then the State's Attorney shall institute judicial in rem forfeiture proceedings and deposit the cost bond with the clerk of the court as described in Section 9 of this Act within 45 days after receipt of the claim and cost bond. In lieu of a cost bond, a person claiming interest in the seized property may file, under penalty of perjury, an indigency affidavit.

(3) If none of the seized property is forfeited in the judicial in rem proceeding, the clerk of the court shall return to the claimant, unless the court orders otherwise, 90% of the sum which has been deposited and shall retain as costs 10% of the money deposited. If any of the seized property is forfeited under the judicial forfeiture proceeding, the clerk of the court shall transfer 90% of the sum which has been deposited to the State's Attorney prosecuting the civil forfeiture to be applied to the costs of prosecution and the clerk shall retain as costs 10% of the sum deposited.

(D) If no claim is filed or bond given within the 45 day period as described in subsection (C) of Section 6 of this Act, the State's Attorney shall declare the property forfeited and shall promptly notify the owner and all known interest holders of the property and the Director of the Illinois Department of State Police of the declaration of forfeiture and the Director shall dispose of the property in accordance with law.

(Source: P.A. 86-1382; 87-614.) [Formerly Ill. Rev. Stat. 56½ §1676.]

150/7. Presumptions.

§7. Presumptions. The following situations shall give rise to a presumption that the property described therein was furnished or intended to be furnished in exchange for a substance in violation of the Illinois Controlled Substances Act [720 ILCS 570/100 et seq.] or the Cannabis Control Act [720 ILCS 550/1 et seq.], or is the proceeds of such an exchange, and therefore forfeitable under this Act, such presumptions being rebuttable by a preponderance of the evidence:

(1) All moneys, coin, or currency found in close proximity to forfeitable substances, to forfeitable drug manufacturing or distributing paraphernalia, or to forfeitable records of the importation, manufacture or distribution of substances;

(2) All property acquired or caused to be acquired by a person either between the dates of occurrence of two or more acts in felony violation of the Illinois Controlled Substances Act or the Cannabis Control Act, or an act committed in another state, territory or country which would be punishable as a felony under either the Illinois Controlled Substances Act or the Cannabis Control Act, committed by that person within 5 years of each other, or all property acquired by such person within a reasonable amount of time after the commission of such acts if:

(a) At least one of the above acts was committed after the effective date of this Act; and

(b) At least one of the acts is or was punishable as a Class X, Class 1, or Class 2 felony; and

(c) There was no likely source for such property other than a violation of the above Acts.

(Source: P.A. 86-1382.) [Formerly Ill. Rev. Stat. 56½ §1677.]

150/8. Exemptions from forfeiture.

§8. Exemptions from forfeiture. A property interest is exempt from forfeiture under this Section if its owner or interest holder establishes by a preponderance of evidence that the owner or interest holder:

(A) (i) in the case of personal property, is not legally accountable for the conduct giving rise to the forfeiture, did not acquiesce in it, and did not know and could not reasonably have known of the conduct or that the conduct was likely to occur, or

(ii) in the case of real property, is not legally accountable for the conduct giving rise to the forfeiture, or did not solicit, conspire, or attempt to commit the conduct giving rise to the forfeiture; and

(B) had not acquired and did not stand to acquire substantial proceeds from the conduct giving rise to its forfeiture other than as an interest holder in an arms length commercial transaction; and

(C) with respect to conveyances, did not hold the property jointly or in common with a person whose conduct gave rise to the forfeiture; and

(D) does not hold the property for the benefit of or as nominee for any person whose conduct gave rise to its forfeiture, and, if the owner or interest holder acquired the interest through any such person, the owner or interest holder acquired it as a bona fide purchaser for value without knowingly taking part in the conduct giving rise to the forfeiture; and

(E) that the owner or interest holder acquired the interest:

(i) before the commencement of the conduct giving rise to its forfeiture and the person whose conduct gave rise to its forfeiture did not have the authority to convey the interest to a bona fide purchaser for value at the time of the conduct; or

(ii) after the commencement of the conduct giving rise to its forfeiture, and the owner or interest holder acquired the interest as a mortgagee, secured creditor, lienholder, or bona fide purchaser for value without knowledge of the conduct which gave rise to the forfeiture; and

(a) in the case of personal property, without knowledge of the seizure of the property for forfeiture; or

(b) in the case of real estate, before the filing in the office of the Recorder of Deeds of the county in which the real estate is located of a notice of seizure for forfeiture or a lis pendens notice.

(Source: P.A. 86-1382.) [Formerly Ill. Rev. Stat. 56½ §1678.]

150/9. Judicial in rem procedures.

§9. Judicial in rem procedures. If property seized under the provisions of the Illinois Controlled Substances Act [720 ILCS 570/100 et seq.] or the Cannabis Control Act [720 ILCS 550/1 et seq.] is non-real property that exceeds $20,000 in value excluding the value of any conveyance, or is real property, or a claimant has filed a claim and a cost bond under subsection (C) of Section 6 of this Act, the following judicial in rem procedures shall apply:

(A) If, after a review of the facts surrounding the seizure, the State's Attorney is of the opinion that the seized property is subject to forfeiture, then within 45 days of the receipt of notice of seizure by the seizing agency or the filing of the claim and cost bond, whichever is later, the State's Attorney shall institute judicial forfeiture proceedings by filing a verified complaint for forfeiture and, if the claimant has filed a claim and cost bond, by depositing the cost bond with the clerk of the court. When authorized by law, a forfeiture must be ordered by a court on an action in rem brought by a State's Attorney under a verified complaint for forfeiture.

(B) During the probable cause portion of the judicial in rem proceeding wherein the State presents its case-in-chief, the court must receive and consider, among other things, all relevant hearsay evidence and information. The laws of evidence relating to civil actions shall apply to all other portions of the judicial in rem proceeding.

(C) Only an owner of or interest holder in the property may file an answer asserting a claim against the property in the action in rem. For purposes of this Section, the owner or interest holder shall be referred to as claimant.

(D) The answer must be signed by the owner or interest holder under penalty of perjury and must set forth:

(i) the caption of the proceedings as set forth on the notice of pending forfeiture and the name of the claimant;

(ii) the address at which the claimant will accept mail;

(iii) the nature and extent of the claimant's interest in the property;

(iv) the date, identity of transferor, and circumstances of the claimant's acquisition of the interest in the property;

(v) the name and address of all other persons known to have an interest in the property;

(vi) the specific provisions of Section 8 of this Act [725 ILCS 150/8] relied on in asserting it is not subject to forfeiture;

(vii) all essential facts supporting each assertion; and

(viii) the precise relief sought.

(E) The answer must be filed with the court within 45 days after service of the civil in rem complaint.

(F) The hearing must be held within 60 days after filing of the answer unless continued for good cause and must be by the court without a jury.

(G) The state shall show the existence of probable cause for forfeiture of the property. If the State shows probable cause, the claimant has the burden of showing by a preponderance of the evidence that the claimant's interest in the property is not subject to forfeiture.

(H) If the State does not show existence of probable cause or a claimant has established by a preponderance of evidence that the claimant has an interest that is exempt under Section 8 of this Act, the court shall order the interest in the property returned or conveyed to the claimant and shall order all other property forfeited to the State. If the State does show existence of probable cause and the claimant does not establish by a preponderance of evidence that the claimant has an interest that is exempt under Section 8 of this Act, the court shall order all property forfeited to the State.

(I) A defendant convicted in any criminal proceeding is precluded from later denying the essential allegations of the criminal offense of which the defendant was convicted in any proceeding under this Act regardless of the pendency of an appeal from that conviction. However, evidence of the pendency of an appeal is admissible.

(J) An acquittal or dismissal in a criminal proceeding shall not preclude civil proceedings under this Act; however, for good cause shown, on a motion by the State's Attorney, the court may stay civil forfeiture proceedings during the criminal trial for a related criminal indictment or information alleging a violation of the Illinois Controlled Substances Act or the Cannabis Control Act. Such a stay shall not be available pending an appeal. Property subject to forfeiture under the Illinois Controlled Substances Act or the Cannabis Control Act shall not be subject to return or release by a court exercising jurisdiction over a criminal case involving the seizure of such property unless such return or release is consented to by the State's Attorney.

(K) All property declared forfeited under this Act vests in this State on the commission of the conduct giving rise to forfeiture together with the proceeds of the property after that time. Any such property or proceeds subsequently transferred to any person remain subject to forfeiture and thereafter shall be ordered forfeited unless the transferee claims and establishes in a hearing under the provisions of this Act that the transferee's interest is exempt under Section 8 of this Act.

(L) A civil action under this Act must be commenced within 5 years after the last conduct giving rise to forfeiture became known or should have become known or 5 years after the forfeitable property is discovered, whichever is later, excluding any time during which either the property or claimant is out of the State or in confinement or during which criminal proceedings relating to the same conduct are in progress.

(Source: P.A. 86-1382; 87-614.) [Formerly Ill. Rev. Stat. 56½ §1679.]

150/10. Stay of time periods.

§10. Stay of time periods. If property is seized for evidence and for forfeiture, the time periods for instituting judicial and non-judicial forfeiture proceedings shall not begin until the property is no longer necessary for evidence.

(Source: P.A. 86-1382.) [Formerly Ill. Rev. Stat. 56½ §1680.]

150/11. Settlement of claims.

§11. Settlement of Claims. Notwithstanding other provisions of this Act, the State's Attorney and a claimant of seized property may enter into an agreed-upon settlement concerning the seized property in such an amount and upon such terms as are set out in writing in a settlement agreement.

(Source: P.A. 86-1382.) [Formerly Ill. Rev. Stat. 56½ §1681.]

150/12. Property which constitutes attorney's fees.

§12. Nothing in this Act shall apply to property which constitutes reasonable bona fide attorney's fees paid to an attorney for services rendered or to be rendered in the forfeiture proceeding or criminal proceeding relating directly thereto where such property was paid before its seizure, before the issuance of

any seizure warrant or court order prohibiting transfer of the property and where the attorney, at the time he or she received the property did not know that it was property subject to forfeiture under this Act.
(Source: P.A. 86-1382.) [Formerly Ill. Rev. Stat. 56½ §1682.]

150/13. Construction.

§13. Construction. It shall be the intent of the General Assembly that the forfeiture provisions of this Act be liberally construed so as to effect their remedial purpose. The forfeiture of property and other remedies hereunder shall be considered to be in addition, and not exclusive of any sentence or other remedy provided by law.
(Source: P.A. 86-1382.) [Formerly Ill. Rev. Stat. 56½ §1683.]

150/14. Judicial review.

§14. Judicial Review. If property has been declared forfeited under Section 6 of this Act [725 ILCS 150/6], any person who has an interest in the property declared forfeited may, within 30 days of the effective date of the notice of the declaration of forfeiture, file a claim and cost bond as described in subsection (C) of Section 6 of this Act. If a claim and cost bond is filed under this Section, then the procedures described in Section 9 of this Act shall apply.
(Source: P.A. 87-614.) [Formerly Ill. Rev. Stat. 56½ §1684.]

FEDERAL PRISONER PRODUCTION EXPENSE ACT

Sec.

155/0.01. Short title.

§0.01. Short title. This Act may be cited as the Federal Prisoner Production Expense Act.
(Source: P.A. 86-1324.) [Formerly Ill. Rev. Stat. 38 §156-10.]

155/1. Production and return.

§1. Whenever a federal prisoner in the custody of the Attorney General of the United States or his authorized representative has been produced in a court of this State for prosecution of a criminal charge pending against such federal prisoner in such court, the costs and expenses of producing and returning such prisoner shall be paid out of the state treasury, on the certificate of the Governor and warrant of the State Comptroller, if the prosecution of such charge results in a sentence of imprisonment exceeding one year; and in all other cases such costs and expenses shall be paid out of the county treasury in the county wherein the offense charged was allegedly committed. Such costs and expenses shall include the cost of necessary travel in producing and returning such prisoner. The necessary travel expenses allowed shall be the same, as near as may be, as the amounts for travel allowed pursuant to the rules and regulations of the Illinois Department of Central Management Services. Before such accounts shall be certified by the Governor, or paid by the county, they shall be verified by affidavit, and certified to by the state's attorney of the county wherein the offense charged was allegedly committed, and submitted therewith shall be documentary evidence of the authority for such travel by the prisoner and his custodians.
(Source: P.A. 82-789.) [Formerly Ill. Rev. Stat. 38 §156-11.]

FINES PAID TO SOCIETIES ACT

Sec.

160/0.01. Short title.

§0.01. Short title. This Act may be cited as the Fines Paid to Societies Act.
(Source: P.A. 86-1324.) [Formerly Ill. Rev. Stat. 23 §2410.]

160/1. Fines paid to society for prevention of cruelty to children—Disposition.

§1. All fines, paid in money, imposed through the agency of any humane society or society for the prevention of cruelty to children under the laws of the State of Illinois, shall, when collected, be paid into the treasury of such society, to be applied towards its support.
(Source: P.A. 78-905.) [Formerly Ill. Rev. Stat. 23 §2411.]

160/2. Fines paid under ordinances to societies incorporated in State.

§2. All fines paid in money imposed through the agency of any humane society (or society for the prevention of cruelty to children) under the laws or ordinances of any city, town or village, within the State of Illinois, may, when collected, be paid into the treasury of such society. Such society named in this Act must, however, be incorporated under and by virtue of the laws of the State of Illinois.
(Source: P.A. 78-905.) [Formerly Ill. Rev. Stat. 23 §2412.]

FIREARM SEIZURE ACT

165/0.01. Short title.

§0.01. Short title. This Act may be cited as the Firearm Seizure Act.
(Source: P.A. 86-1324.) [Formerly Ill. Rev. Stat. 38 §161.]

165/1. Examination of complainant and witnesses.

§1. When a complaint is made to any circuit court that a person possessing a firearm or firearms has threatened to use a firearm illegally, the court shall examine on oath such complainant, and any witnesses which may be produced, reduce the complaint to writing and have it subscribed and sworn to by the complainant. If the court is satisfied that there is any danger of such illegal use of firearms, it shall issue a warrant requiring the apprehension of such person, hereafter referred to as the defendant, for appearance before the court. Such warrant shall also authorize the seizure of any firearm in the possession of the defendant.
(Source: Laws 1965, p. 2693.) [Formerly Ill. Rev. Stat. 38 §161-1.]

165/2. Order for production of firearms; safekeeping and return of firearms.

§2. When the defendant is brought before the court, if the charge is controverted the testimony produced on both sides shall be heard. When it appears to the court that the defendant has threatened to use any firearm illegally, and it appears to the court that the surrender of such firearm would serve to keep the peace, the court shall order any firearm taken from the defendant to be kept by the State for safekeeping during a stated period of time not to exceed one year. The firearm or firearms shall be returned to the defendant at the end of the stated period. If such firearm was not seized when the defendant was brought before the court, the defendant may be ordered by the court to produce such firearm for safekeeping as provided above, and upon failure to produce

such weapon within a time period established by the court, the defendant may be punished by the court as a contempt.
(Source: Laws 1965, p. 2693.) [Formerly Ill. Rev. Stat. 38 §161-2.]

165/3. Costs of prosecution.

§3. If, however, it should appear to the court that the complaint is unfounded, the defendant shall be dismissed. When, in addition, the court is of the opinion that the proceeding was commenced maliciously without probable cause, it may enter judgment against the complainant for the costs of the prosecution.
(Source: P.A. 84-547.) [Formerly Ill. Rev. Stat. 38 §161-3.]

165/4. Recognizance; surrender of firearms.

§4. In lieu of requiring the surrender of any firearm, the court may require the defendant to give a recognizance as provided in Division V of "An Act to revise the law in relation to criminal jurisprudence".
(Source: Laws 1965, p. 2693.) [Formerly Ill. Rev. Stat. 38 §161-4.]

165/5. Nature of proceedings.

§5. Any action brought under this Act is a civil action, governed by the Civil Practice Law as now or hereafter amended [735 ILCS 5/2-101 et seq.] and by the Supreme Court Rules as now or hereafter adopted in relation to that Law. Appeals may be taken as in other civil cases.
(Source: P.A. 82-783.) [Formerly Ill. Rev. Stat. 38 §161-5.]

FUGITIVE APPREHENSION REWARD ACT

170/0.01. Short title.

§0.01. Short title. This Act may be cited as the Fugitive Apprehension Reward Act.
(Source: P.A. 86-1324.) [Formerly Ill. Rev. Stat. 60 §11.9.]

170/12. Reward by Governor for apprehension of criminal.

§12. If any person charged with, or convicted of treason, first degree murder, criminal sexual assault, aggravated criminal sexual assault, robbery, burglary, arson, theft, forgery, counterfeiting or kidnapping, shall break prison, escape or flee from justice or abscond or secrete himself in such cases it shall be lawful for the Governor, if he shall judge it necessary, to offer any reward not exceeding $1,000, for apprehending and delivering such person into the custody of such sheriff or other officer as he may direct. The person so apprehending or delivering any such persons as aforesaid and producing to the Governor the receipt of the sheriff or other proper officer, for the body, it shall be lawful for the Governor to certify the amount of such claim to the State Comptroller, who shall issue his warrant on the treasurer for the same.
(Source: P.A. 84-1450.) [Formerly Ill. Rev. Stat. 60 §12.]

170/13. Reward by county board for apprehension of criminal.

§13. It shall be lawful for the county board of any county, by an order to be entered upon its records, to fix upon a sum not exceeding $1,000 as a reward to be paid to any person who shall hereafter pursue and apprehend, beyond the

limits of the county where the offense shall have been committed, any person guilty of any felony or other high crime, which reward shall be paid by the county where the offense was committed, on the conviction of the criminal: Provided, nevertheless, that said reward shall not disqualify the person entitled thereto from being a witness.
(Source: R.S. 1874, p. 543.) [Formerly Ill. Rev. Stat. 60 §13.]

170/14. Expenses defrayed by county board.
§14. It shall be lawful for the county board of any county to enter an order upon their records, allowing to any person who shall have aided or assisted in the pursuit or arrest of any person suspected or accused of any felony, or other high crime, committed in their county, such reasonable sum as said county board shall deem just, to defray the expenses of the person in aiding or assisting in the pursuit or arrest of such offender in making such pursuit or arrest; which sum so allowed shall be paid out of the county treasury in the same manner that other county expenses are paid.
(Source: R.S. 1874, p. 543.) [Formerly Ill. Rev. Stat. 60 §14.]

170/15. Reward by county board for horse thief.
§15. The county boards of the respective counties may offer rewards not exceeding $1,000 each, for the pursuit, arrest, detection or conviction of any person guilty of stealing any horse, mare, colt, mule, ass, or neat cattle, or any other property exceeding $50 in value.
(Source: R.S. 1874, p. 543.) [Formerly Ill. Rev. Stat. 60 §15.]

170/16. County boards authorized to levy taxes to pay rewards and disbursements.
§16. For the purpose of providing a fund for the payment of said rewards and disbursements, the said county boards are hereby authorized to levy a tax, annually, of such amounts as to them may seem necessary, for the purpose herein contemplated; said taxes to be levied and collected in the same manner as other taxes for county purposes are by law authorized to be levied and collected.
(Source: R.S. 1874, p. 543.) [Formerly Ill. Rev. Stat. 60 §16.]

170/17. Payment for expenses.
§17. When any person shall pursue any person charged with felony, for whom no reward shall have been offered, or in any case where a reward has been offered and the pursuit shall be unsuccessful, the party pursuing may make out his bill for all necessary expenses, which shall not exceed $1 for each man per day, and present the same to the county board, and it shall be the duty of the said board to allow said account, (if satisfied of its correctness and propriety) and pay the same out of said fund: Provided, when a reward is paid, no expenses shall be allowed, and the expenses of more than five persons shall never be paid in the same case, and only such shall be paid, in any case, as the county board shall see fit to allow.
(Source: R.S. 1874, p. 543.) [Formerly Ill. Rev. Stat. 60 §17.]

NARCOTICS PROFIT FORFEITURE ACT

Sec.

175/1. Short title.

§1. This Act shall be known and may be cited as the Narcotics Profit Forfeiture Act.
(Source: P.A. 82-940.) [Formerly Ill. Rev. Stat. 56½ §1651.]

175/2. Legislative declaration.

§2. Legislative Declaration. Narcotics racketeering is a far-reaching and extremely profitable criminal enterprise. Racketeering schemes persist despite the threat of prosecution and the actual prosecution and imprisonment of individual participants because existing sanctions do not effectively reach the money and other assets generated by such schemes. It is therefore necessary to supplement existing sanctions by mandating forfeiture of money and other assets generated by narcotics racketeering activities. Forfeiture diminishes the financial incentives which encourage and sustain narcotics racketeering, and secures for the People of the State of Illinois assets to be used for enforcement of laws governing narcotics activity.
(Source: P.A. 82-940.) [Formerly Ill. Rev. Stat. 56½ §1652.]

175/3. Definitions.

§3. Definitions. (a) "Narcotics activity" means:

1. Any conduct punishable as a felony under the Cannabis Control Act [720 ILCS 550/1 et seq.] or the Illinois Controlled Substances Act [720 ILCS 570/100 et seq.], or

2. Any conduct punishable, by imprisonment for more than one year, as an offense against the law of the United States or any State, concerning narcotics, controlled substances, dangerous drugs, or any substance or things scheduled or listed under the Cannabis Control Act or the Illinois Controlled Substances Act.

(b) "Pattern of narcotics activity" means 2 or more acts of narcotics activity of which at least 2 such acts were committed within 5 years of each other. At least one of those acts of narcotics activity must have been committed after the effective date of this Act and at least one of such acts shall be or shall have been punishable as a Class X, Class 1 or Class 2 felony.

(c) "Person" includes any individual or entity capable of holding a legal or beneficial interest in property.

(d) "Enterprise" includes any individual, partnership, corporation, association, or other entity, or group of individuals associated in fact, although not a legal entity.
(Source: P.A. 82-940.) [Formerly Ill. Rev. Stat. 56½ §1653.]

175/4. Narcotics racketeering.

§4. A person commits narcotics racketeering when he:

(a) Receives income knowing such income to be derived, directly or indirectly, from a pattern of narcotics activity in which he participated, or for which he is accountable under Section 5-2 of the Criminal Code of 1961 [720 ILCS 5/5-2]; or

(b) Receives income, knowing such income to be derived, directly or indirectly, from a pattern of narcotics activity in which he participated, or for which he is accountable under Section 5-2 of the Criminal Code of 1961, and he uses or invests, directly or indirectly, any part of such income, or the proceeds of such income, in acquisition of any interest in, or the establishment or operation of, any enterprise doing business in the State of Illinois; or

(c) Knowingly, through a pattern of narcotics activity in which he participated, or for which he is accountable under Section 5-2 of the Criminal Code of 1961, acquires or maintains, directly or indirectly, any interest in or contract of any enterprise which is engaged in, or the activities of which affect, business in the State of Illinois; or

(d) Being a person employed by or associated with any enterprise doing business in the State of Illinois, he knowingly conducts or participates, directly or indirectly, in the conduct of such enterprise's affairs through a pattern of narcotics activity in which he participated, or for which he is accountable under Section 5-2 of the Criminal Code of 1961.

(Source: P.A. 82-940.) [Formerly Ill. Rev. Stat. 56½ §1654.]

175/5. Penalty.

§5. (a) A person who commits the offense of narcotics racketeering shall:

(1) be guilty of a Class 1 felony; and

(2) be subject to a fine of up to $250,000.

A person who commits the offense of narcotics racketeering or who violates Section 3 of the Drug Paraphernalia Control Act [720 ILCS 600/3] shall forfeit to the State of Illinois: (A) any profits or proceeds and any property or property interest he has acquired or maintained in violation of this Act or Section 3 of the Drug Paraphernalia Control Act or has used to facilitate a violation of this Act that the court determines, after a forfeiture hearing, under subsection (b) of this Section to have been acquired or maintained as a result of narcotics racketeering or violating Section 3 of the Drug Paraphernalia Control Act, or used to facilitate narcotics racketeering; and (B) any interest in, security of, claim against, or property or contractual right of any kind affording a source of influence over, any enterprise which he has established, operated, controlled, conducted, or participated in the conduct of, in violation of this Act or Section 3 of the Drug Paraphernalia Control Act, that the court determines, after a forfeiture hearing, under subsection (b) of this Section to have been acquired or maintained as a result of narcotics racketeering or violating Section 3 of the Drug Paraphernalia Control Act or used to facilitate narcotics racketeering.

(b) The court shall, upon petition by the Attorney General or State's Attorney, at any time subsequent to the filing of an information or return of an indictment, conduct a hearing to determine whether any property or property interest is subject to forfeiture under this Act. At the forfeiture hearing the people shall have the burden of establishing, by a preponderance of the evidence, that property or property interests are subject to forfeiture under this Act. There is a rebuttable presumption at such hearing that any property or property interest of a person charged by information or indictment with narcotics racketeering or who is convicted of a violation of Section 3 of the Drug Paraphernalia Control Act is subject to forfeiture under this Section if the State establishes by a preponderance of the evidence that:

(1) such property or property interest was acquired by such person during the period of the violation of this Act or Section 3 of the Drug Paraphernalia Control Act or within a reasonable time after such period; and

(2) there was no likely source for such property or property interest other than the violation of this Act or Section 3 of the Drug Paraphernalia Control Act.

(c) In an action brought by the People of the State of Illinois under this Act, wherein any restraining order, injunction or prohibition or any other action in connection with any property or property interest subject to forfeiture under this Act is sought, the circuit court which shall preside over the trial of the person or persons charged with narcotics racketeering as defined in Section 4 of this Act [725 ILCS 175/4] or violating Section 3 of the Drug Paraphernalia Control Act shall first determine whether there is probable cause to believe that the person or persons so charged has committed the offense of narcotics racketeering as defined in Section 4 of this Act or a violation of Section 3 of the Drug Paraphernalia Control Act and whether the property or property interest is subject to forfeiture pursuant to this Act.

In order to make such a determination, prior to entering any such order, the court shall conduct a hearing without a jury, wherein the People shall establish that there is: (i) probable cause that the person or persons so charged have committed the offense of narcotics racketeering or violating Section 3 of the Drug Paraphernalia Control Act and (ii) probable cause that any property or property interest may be subject to forfeiture pursuant to this Act. Such hearing may be conducted simultaneously with a preliminary hearing, if the prosecution is commenced by information or complaint, or by motion of the People, at any stage in the proceedings. The court may accept a finding of probable cause at a preliminary hearing following the filing of an information charging the offense of narcotics racketeering as defined in Section 4 of this Act or the return of an indictment by a grand jury charging the offense of narcotics racketeering as defined in Section 4 of this Act or after a charge is filed for violating Section 3 of the Drug Paraphernalia Control Act as sufficient evidence of probable cause as provided in item (i) above.

Upon such a finding, the circuit court shall enter such restraining order, injunction or prohibition, or shall take such other action in connection with any such property or property interest subject to forfeiture under this Act, as is necessary to insure that such property is not removed from the jurisdiction of the court, concealed, destroyed or otherwise disposed of by the owner of that property or property interest prior to a forfeiture hearing under subsection (b) of this Section. The Attorney General or State's Attorney shall file a certified copy of such restraining order, injunction or other prohibition with the recorder of deeds or registrar of titles of each county where any such property of the defendant may be located. No such injunction, restraining order or other prohibition shall affect the rights of any bona fide purchaser, mortgagee, judgment creditor or other lien holder arising prior to the date of such filing.

The court may, at any time, upon verified petition by the defendant, conduct a hearing to release all or portions of any such property or interest which the court previously determined to be subject to forfeiture or subject to any restraining order, injunction, or prohibition or other action. The court may release such property to the defendant for good cause shown and within the sound discretion of the court.

(d) Prosecution under this Act may be commenced by the Attorney General or a State's Attorney.

(e) Upon an order of forfeiture being entered pursuant to subsection (b) of this Section, the court shall authorize the Attorney General to seize any property or property interest declared forfeited under this Act and under such terms and conditions as the court shall deem proper. Any property or property interest that has been the subject of an entered restraining order, injunction or prohibition or any other action filed under subsection (c) shall be forfeited unless the claimant can show by a preponderance of the evidence that the property or property interest has not been acquired or maintained as a result of narcotics racketeering or has not been used to facilitate narcotics racketeering.

(f) The Attorney General or his designee is authorized to sell all property forfeited and seized pursuant to this Act, unless such property is required by law to be destroyed or is harmful to the public, and, after the deduction of all requisite expenses of administration and sale, shall distribute the proceeds of such sale, along with any moneys forfeited or seized, in accordance with subsection (g) or (h), whichever is applicable.

(g) All monies and the sale proceeds of all other property forfeited and seized pursuant to this Act shall be distributed as follows:

(1) An amount equal to 50% shall be distributed to the unit of local government whose officers or employees conducted the investigation into narcotics racketeering and caused the arrest or arrests and prosecution leading to the forfeiture. Amounts distributed to units of local government shall be used for enforcement of laws governing narcotics activity. In the event, however, that the investigation, arrest or arrests and prosecution leading to the forfeiture were undertaken solely by a State agency, the portion provided hereunder shall be paid into the Drug Traffic Prevention Fund in the State treasury to be used for enforcement of laws governing narcotics activity.

(2) An amount equal to 12.5% shall be distributed to the county in which the prosecution resulting in the forfeiture was instituted, deposited in a special fund in the county treasury and appropriated to the State's Attorney for use in the enforcement of laws governing narcotics activity.

An amount equal to 12.5% shall be distributed to the Office of the State's Attorneys Appellate Prosecutor and deposited in the Narcotics Profit Forfeiture Fund, which is hereby created in the State treasury, to be used by the Office of the State's Attorneys Appellate Prosecutor for additional expenses incurred in prosecuting appeals arising under this Act. Any amounts remaining in the Fund after all additional expenses have been paid shall be used by the Office to reduce the participating county contributions to the Office on a pro-rated basis as determined by the board of governors of the Office of the State's Attorneys Appellate Prosecutor based on the populations of the participating counties.

(3) An amount equal to 25% shall be paid into the Drug Traffic Prevention Fund in the State treasury to be used by the Department of State Police for funding Metropolitan Enforcement Groups created pursuant to the Intergovernmental Drug Laws Enforcement Act [30 ILCS 715/1 et seq.]. Any amounts remaining in the Fund after full funding of Metropolitan Enforcement Groups shall be used for enforcement, by the State or any unit of local government, of laws governing narcotics activity.

(h) Where the investigation or indictment for the offense of narcotics racketeering or a violation of Section 3 of the Drug Paraphernalia Control Act has occurred under the provisions of the Statewide Grand Jury Act, all monies and the sale proceeds of all other property shall be distributed as follows:

(1) 60% shall be distributed to the metropolitan enforcement group, local, municipal, county, or State law enforcement agency or agencies which conducted or participated in the investigation resulting in the forfeiture. The distribution shall bear a reasonable relationship to the degree of direct participation of the law enforcement agency in the effort resulting in the forfeiture, taking into account the total value of the property forfeited and the total law enforcement effort with respect to the violation of the law on which the forfeiture is based. Amounts distributed to the agency or agencies shall be used for the enforcement of laws governing cannabis and controlled substances.

(2) 25% shall be distributed by the Attorney General as grants to drug education, treatment and prevention programs licensed or approved by the Illinois Department of Alcoholism and Substance Abuse. In making these grants, the Attorney General shall take into account the plans and service priorities of, and the needs identified by, the Department of Alcoholism and Substance Abuse.

(3) 15% shall be distributed to the Attorney General and the State's Attorney, if any, participating in the prosecution resulting in the forfeiture. The distribution shall bear a reasonable relationship to the degree of direct participation in the prosecution of the offense, taking into account the total value of the property forfeited and the total amount of time spent in preparing and

presenting the case, the complexity of the case and other similar factors. Amounts distributed to the Attorney General under this paragraph shall be retained in a fund held by the State Treasurer as ex-officio custodian to be designated as the Statewide Grand Jury Prosecution Fund and paid out upon the direction of the Attorney General for expenses incurred in criminal prosecutions arising under the Statewide Grand Jury Act [725 ILCS 215/1 et seq.]. Amounts distributed to a State's Attorney shall be deposited in a special fund in the county treasury and appropriated to the State's Attorney for use in the enforcement of laws governing narcotics activity.

(i) All monies deposited pursuant to this Act in the Drug Traffic Prevention Fund established under Section 5-9-1.2 of the Unified Code of Corrections [730 ILCS 5/5-9-1.2] are appropriated, on a continuing basis, to the Department of State Police to be used for funding Metropolitan Enforcement Groups created pursuant to the Intergovernmental Drug Laws Enforcement Act or otherwise for the enforcement of laws governing narcotics activity.

(Chgd. by P.A. 87-1013, §1, eff. 9/3/92.)

(Source: P.A. 86-271; 86-350; 86-1475; 87-435; 87-466; 87-895.) [Formerly Ill. Rev. Stat. 56½ §1655.]

175/5.1. Imposing fines for guilty sentencing.

§5.1. (a) Whenever any person pleads guilty to, is found guilty of or is placed on supervision for an offense under this Act, a fine may be levied in addition to any other penalty imposed by the court.

(b) In determining whether to impose a fine under this Section and the amount, time for payment and method of payment of any fine so imposed, the court shall

(1) consider the defendant's income, regardless of source, the defendant's earning capacity and the defendant's financial resources, as well as the nature of the burden the fine will impose on the defendant and any person legally or financially dependent upon the defendant;

(2) consider the proof received at trial, or as a result of a plea of guilty, concerning the full street value of the controlled substances, cannabis or the drug paraphernalia seized and any profits or other proceeds derived by the defendant from the violation of this Act;

(3) take into account any other pertinent equitable considerations; and

(4) give primary consideration to the need to deprive the defendant of illegally obtained profits or other proceeds from the offense.

For the purpose of paragraph (2) of this subsection, "street value" shall be determined by the court on the basis of testimony of law enforcement personnel and the defendant as to the amount seized and such testimony as may be required by the court as to the current street value of the cannabis, controlled substances or drug paraphernalia seized.

(c) As a condition of a fine, the court may require that payment be made in specified installments or within a specified period of time, but such period shall not be greater than the maximum applicable term of probation or imprisonment, whichever is greater. Unless otherwise specified, payment of a fine shall be due immediately.

(d) If a fine for a violation of this Act is imposed on an organization, it is the duty of each individual authorized to make disbursements of the assets of the organization to pay the fine from assets of the organization.

(e) (1) A defendant who has been sentenced to pay a fine, and who has paid part but not all of such fine, may petition the court for an extension of the time for payment or modification of the method of payment.

(2) The court may grant a petition made pursuant to this subsection if it finds that

(i) the circumstances that warranted payment by the time or method specified no longer exist; or

(ii) it is otherwise unjust to require payment of the fine by the time or method specified.

(Source: P.A. 86-271.) [Formerly Ill. Rev. Stat. 56½ §1655.1.]

175/5.2. Fines collected; disbursement.

§5.2. (a) Twelve and one-half percent of all amounts collected as fines pursuant to the provisions of this Act shall be paid into the Youth Drug Abuse Prevention Fund, which is hereby created in the State treasury, to be used by the Department of Alcoholism and Substance Abuse for the funding of programs and services for drug-abuse treatment, and prevention and education services, for juveniles.

(b) Eighty-seven and one-half percent of the proceeds of all fines received under the provisions of this Act shall be transmitted to and deposited in the treasurer's office at the level of government as follows:

(1) If such seizure was made by a combination of law enforcement personnel representing differing units of local government, the court levying the fine shall equitably allocate 50% of the fine among these units of local government and shall allocate 37½% to the county general corporate fund. In the event that the seizure was made by law enforcement personnel representing a unit of local government from a municipality where the number of inhabitants exceeds 2 million in population, the court levying the fine shall allocate 87½% of the fine to that unit of local government. If the seizure was made by a combination of law enforcement personnel representing differing units of local government, and at least one of those units represents a municipality where the number of inhabitants exceeds 2 million in population, the court shall equitably allocate 87½% of the proceeds of the fines received among the differing units of local government.

(2) If such seizure was made by State law enforcement personnel, then the court shall allocate 37½% to the State treasury and 50% to the county general corporate fund.

(3) If a State law enforcement agency in combination with a law enforcement agency or agencies of a unit or units of local government conducted the seizure, the court shall equitably allocate 37½% of the fines to or among the law enforcement agency or agencies of the unit or units of local government which conducted the seizure and shall allocate 50% to the county general corporate fund.

(c) The proceeds of all fines allocated to the law enforcement agency or agencies of the unit or units of local government pursuant to subsection (b) shall be made available to that law enforcement agency as expendable receipts for use in the enforcement of laws regulating controlled substances and cannabis. The proceeds of fines awarded to the State treasury shall be deposited in a special fund known as the Drug Traffic Prevention Fund. Monies from this fund may be used by the Department of State Police for use in the enforcement of laws regulating controlled substances and cannabis; to satisfy funding provisions of the Intergovernmental Drug Laws Enforcement Act [30 ILCS 715/1 et seq.]; to defray costs and expenses associated with returning violators of the Cannabis Control Act [720 ILCS 550/1 et seq.] and the Illinois Controlled Substances Act [720 ILCS 570/100 et seq.] only, as provided in those Acts, when punishment of the crime shall be confinement of the criminal in the penitentiary; and all other monies shall be paid into the general revenue fund in the State treasury.

(Source: P.A. 87-342.) [Formerly Ill. Rev. Stat. 56½ §1655.2.]

175/6. Jurisdiction of circuit courts.

§6. (a) The circuit courts of the State shall have jurisdiction to prevent and restrain violations of this Act by issuing appropriate orders, including, but not limited to: ordering any person to divest himself of any interest, direct or indirect, in any enterprise; imposing reasonable restriction on the future activities or investment of any person, including, but not limited to, prohibiting any person from engaging in the same type of endeavor as the enterprise engaged in, the activities of which affect business in the State of Illinois; or ordering dissolution or reorganization of any enterprise, making due provisions for the rights of innocent persons.

(b) The Attorney General or the State's Attorney may institute proceedings under this Section. In any action brought by the State of Illinois under this Section, the court shall proceed as soon as practicable to the hearing and determination thereof. Pending that determination thereof, the court may at any time enter such temporary restraining orders, preliminary or permanent injunctions, or prohibitions, or take such other actions including the acceptance of satisfactory performance bonds by a defendant, as it shall deem proper.

(c) Any person injured in his business, person or property by reason of a violation of this Act may sue the violator therefor in any appropriate circuit court and shall recover threefold the damages he sustains and the cost of the action, including a reasonable attorney's fee.

(d) A final judgment entered in favor of the People of the State of Illinois in any criminal proceeding brought under this Act shall estop the defendant in the criminal case from denying the essential allegations of the criminal offense in any subsequent civil proceeding brought under this Act.

(Source: P.A. 84-545.) [Formerly Ill. Rev. Stat. 56½ §1656.]

175/7. Institution of proceedings.

§7. Any civil action or proceeding under this Act against any person may be instituted in the circuit court for any county in which such person resides, is found, has an agent, transacts his affairs, or in which property that is the subject of these proceedings is located.

(Source: P.A. 82-940.) [Formerly Ill. Rev. Stat. 56½ §1657.]

175/8. Legislative intent.

§8. It is the intent of the General Assembly that this Act be liberally construed so as to effect the purposes of this Act and be construed in accordance with similar provisions contained in Title IX of the Organized Crime Control Act of 1970, as amended (18 U.S.C. 1961-1968).

(Source: P.A. 82-940.) [Formerly Ill. Rev. Stat. 56½ §1658.]

175/9. Severability.

§9. If any provision of this Act or the application thereof to any person or circumstance is invalid, such invalidation shall not affect other provisions or applications of the Act which can be given effect without the invalid provision or application, and to this end the provisions of this Act are declared to be severable.

(Source: P.A. 82-940.) [Formerly Ill. Rev. Stat. 56½ §1659.]

175/11. Effective date.

§11. This Act takes effect upon becoming law.

(Source: P.A. 82-940.) [Formerly Ill. Rev. Stat. 56½ §1660.]

PARK ORDINANCE VIOLATION PROCEDURE ACT

Sec.

180/0.01. Short title.

§0.01. Short title. This Act may be cited as the Park Ordinance Violation Procedure Act.
(Source: P.A. 86-1324.) [Formerly Ill. Rev. Stat. 105 §330h.]

180/1. Violation of park ordinance.

§1. In all actions for the violation of any ordinance of any board of public park commissioners, organized under any general or special law of this state, the first process shall be a summons. However a warrant for the arrest of the offender may issue in the first instance upon the affidavit of any person that any such ordinance has been violated, and that the person making the complaint has reasonable grounds to believe the party charged is guilty thereof; and any person arrested upon such warrant shall, without unnecessary delay, be taken before the proper judicial officer in the county within which is situated the park system under the control of any such board of public park commissioners, to be tried for the alleged offense. Any person upon whom any fine or penalty shall be imposed may, upon the order of the court before whom the conviction is had, be committed to the county jail or the city prison, house of correction, or other place in said county, provided by such public park commissioners, or as may be designated by them, for the incarceration of such offenders until such fine, penalty and costs shall be fully paid. However no such imprisonment shall exceed six months for any one offense. Every person so committed shall be required to work at such labor as his or her strength will permit, within and without such prison, house of correction or other place provided for the incarceration of such offenders, as aforesaid, not to exceed ten hours each working day; and for such work the person so employed or worked shall be allowed, exclusive of his or her board, the sum of fifty cents for each day's work on account of such fine and costs.
(Source: P.A. 77-1297.) [Formerly Ill. Rev. Stat. 105 §331.]

PRETRIAL SERVICES ACT

Sec.

185/0.01. Short title.

§0.01. Short title. This Act may be cited as the Pretrial Services Act.
(Source: P.A. 86-1324.) [Formerly Ill. Rev. Stat. 38 §300.]

185/1. Pretrial services agency.

§1. Each circuit court shall establish a pretrial services agency to provide the court with accurate background data regarding the pretrial release of persons charged with felonies and effective supervision of compliance with the terms and conditions imposed on release.
(Source: P.A. 84-1449.) [Formerly Ill. Rev. Stat. 38 §301.]

185/2. Supervision.

§2. Pretrial services agencies may be independent divisions of the circuit courts accountable to the chief judge or his designee for program activities. The agencies shall be supervised by a director appointed by the chief judge and removable for cause. The chief judge or his designee shall have the authority to hire, terminate or discipline agency personnel on recommendation of the program director.
(Source: P.A. 84-1449.) [Formerly Ill. Rev. Stat. 38 §302.]

185/3. Functions.

§3. The functions of the pretrial services agency shall be assigned to the Department of Probation and Court Services or other arm of the court where the volume of criminal proceedings does not justify the establishment of a separate division.
(Source: P.A. 84-1449.) [Formerly Ill. Rev. Stat. 38 §303.]

185/4. Personnel.

§4. All pretrial services agency personnel shall be full-time employees supervised by the director and, except for secretarial staff, subject to the hiring and training requirements established by the Supreme Court as provided in "An Act providing for a system of probation, for the appointment and compensation of probation officers, and authorizing the suspension of final judgment and the imposition of sentence upon persons found guilty of certain defined crimes and offenses, and legalizing their ultimate discharge without punishment", approved June 10, 1911, as amended [730 ILCS 110/0.01 et seq.].
(Source: P.A. 84-1449.) [Formerly Ill. Rev. Stat. 38 §304.]

185/5. Compensation.

§5. The compensation for pretrial services agency personnel shall be commensurate with salaries and other benefits accorded probation department employees.
(Source: P.A. 84-1449.) [Formerly Ill. Rev. Stat. 38 §305.]

185/6. Volunteer groups.

§6. Volunteer groups and individuals may be assigned such interviewing and verification as may be determined by the director.
(Source: P.A. 84-1449.) [Formerly Ill. Rev. Stat. 38 §306.]

185/7. Duties.

§7. Pretrial services agencies shall perform the following duties for the circuit court:

(a) Interview and assemble verified information and data concerning the community ties, employment, residency, criminal record, and social background of arrested persons who are to be, or have been, presented in court for first appearance on felony charges, to assist the court in determining the appropriate terms and conditions of pretrial release;

(b) Submit written reports of those investigations to the court along with such findings and recommendations, if any, as may be necessary to assess:

(1) the need for financial security to assure the defendant's appearance at later proceedings; and

(2) appropriate conditions which shall be imposed to protect against the risks of nonappearance and commission of new offenses or other interference with the orderly administration of justice before trial;

(c) Supervise compliance with pretrial release conditions, and promptly report violations of those conditions to the court and prosecutor to assure effective enforcement;

(d) Cooperate with the court and all other criminal justice agencies in the development of programs to minimize unnecessary pretrial detention and protect the public against breaches of pretrial release conditions; and

(e) Monitor the local operations of the pretrial release system and maintain accurate and comprehensive records of program activities.
(Source: P.A. 84-1449.) [Formerly Ill. Rev. Stat. 38 §307.]

185/8. Additional services.

§8. In addition to the foregoing, pretrial services agencies may with the approval of the chief judge provide one or more of the following services to the circuit court:

(a) Supervise compliance with the terms and conditions imposed by the courts for appeal bonds; and

(b) Assist in such other pretrial services activities as may be delegated to the agency by the court.
(Source: P.A. 84-1449.) [Formerly Ill. Rev. Stat. 38 §308.]

185/9. Authority to interview and process.

§9. Pretrial services agencies shall have standing court authority to interview and process all persons charged with non-capital felonies either before or after first appearance if the person is in custody. The chief judge and director of the pretrial services agency may establish interviewing priorities where resources do not permit total coverage, but no other criteria shall be employed to exclude categories of offenses or offenders from program operations.
(Source: P.A. 84-1449.) [Formerly Ill. Rev. Stat. 38 §309.]

185/10. Assessment of benefits of agency intervention.

§10. The chief judge and director of the pretrial services agency shall continuously assess the benefits of agency intervention before or after the first appearance of accused persons. In determining the best allocation of available resources, consideration shall be given to current release practices of first appearance judges in misdemeanor and lesser felony cases; the logistics of pre-first appearance intervention where decentralized detention facilities are utilized; the availability of verification resources for pre-first appearance intervention; and the ultimate goal of prompt and informed determinations of pretrial release conditions.
(Source: P.A. 84-1449.) [Formerly Ill. Rev. Stat. 38 §310.]

185/11. Inquiry of defendant.

§11. No person shall be interviewed by a pretrial services agency unless he or she has first been apprised of the identity and purpose of the interviewer, the scope of the interview, the right to secure legal advice, and the right to refuse cooperation. Inquiry of the defendant shall carefully exclude questions concerning the details of the current charge. Statements made by the defendant during the interview, or evidence derived therefrom, are admissible in evidence only when the court is considering the imposition of pretrial or posttrial conditions to bail or recognizance, or when considering the modification of a prior release order.

(Source: P.A. 84-1449.) [Formerly Ill. Rev. Stat. 38 §311.]

185/12. Interviews.

§12. Interviews shall be individually conducted by agency personnel in facilities or locations which assure an adequate opportunity for discussion, consistent with security needs.

The chief judge or his designee shall maintain a continuous liaison between the agency director and the sheriff, or other affected law enforcement agencies, to assure that pretrial services interviewers have prompt access consistent with security and law enforcement needs to all prisoners after booking.

(Source: P.A. 84-1449.) [Formerly Ill. Rev. Stat. 38 §312.]

185/13. Recorded information.

§13. Information received from the arrested person as a result of the agency interview shall be recorded on uniform interview forms.

(Source: P.A. 84-1449.) [Formerly Ill. Rev. Stat. 38 §313.]

185/14. Verification of required information.

§14. The pretrial services agency shall, after interviewing arrestees, immediately verify and supplement the information required by the uniform interview form before submitting its report to the court. Minimum verification shall include the interviewee's prior criminal record, residency, and employment circumstances. The chief judge or his designee shall assist the program director in establishing and maintaining cooperation with the circuit clerk and law enforcement information systems to assure the prompt verification of prior criminal records.

(Source: P.A. 84-1449.) [Formerly Ill. Rev. Stat. 38 §314.]

185/15. Verified and supplemental information.

§15. Verified and supplemental information assembled by the pretrial services agency shall be recorded on a uniform reporting form established by the Supreme Court.

(Source: P.A. 84-1449.) [Formerly Ill. Rev. Stat. 38 §315.]

185/16. Submitted reports.

§16. Pretrial services agencies interviewing arrested persons shall submit a report of their information and findings to the court in all cases where the individual remains in custody at the completion of the verification process, and in such additional cases where the agency believes that additional or modified conditions are appropriate and shall be imposed on earlier release orders.

(Source: P.A. 84-1449.) [Formerly Ill. Rev. Stat. 38 §316.]

185/17. Format of reports.

§17. Reports shall be in writing, signed by an authorized representative of the pretrial services agency, and prepared on the uniform reporting form. Copies of the report shall be provided to all parties and counsel of record.

(Source: P.A. 84-1449.) [Formerly Ill. Rev. Stat. 38 §317.]

185/18. Representative present at hearings.

§18. A representative of the pretrial services agency shall where feasible be present or otherwise available to the court at the first appearance or such later hearings at which the agency report is to be considered by the court. At such hearings, the factual findings, conclusions and recommendations in the written report may be challenged by the interviewee, his or her counsel, or the prosecuting attorney, by the presentation of any relevant evidence.
(Source: P.A. 85-405.) [Formerly Ill. Rev. Stat. 38 §318.]

185/19. Written reports on factual findings.

§19. Written reports under Section 17 [725 ILCS 185/17] shall set forth all factual findings on which any recommendation and conclusions contained therein are based together with the source of each fact, and shall contain information and data relevant to the following issues:

(a) The need for financial security to assure the defendant's appearance for later court proceedings; and

(b) Appropriate conditions imposed to protect against the risk of nonappearance and commission of new offenses or other interference with the orderly administration of justice before trial.
(Source: P.A. 84-1449.) [Formerly Ill. Rev. Stat. 38 §319.]

185/20. Preparing and presenting written reports.

§20. In preparing and presenting its written reports under Section 17 and 19 [725 ILCS 185/17 and 185/19], pretrial services agencies shall in appropriate cases include specific recommendations for the setting, increase, or decrease of bail; the release of the interviewee on his own recognizance in sums certain; and the imposition of pretrial conditions to bail or recognizance designed to minimize the risks of nonappearance, the commission of new offenses while awaiting trial, and other potential interference with the orderly administration of justice. In establishing objective internal criteria of any such recommendation policies, the agency may utilize so-called "point scales" for evaluating the aforementioned risks, but no interviewee shall be considered as ineligible for particular agency recommendations by sole reference to such procedures.
(Source: P.A. 84-1449.) [Formerly Ill. Rev. Stat. 38 §320.]

185/21. Completed reports referred to the judge.

§21. Pretrial services agency reports completed following the first appearance shall be immediately referred to the judge who there presided; to any judge to whom the proceedings have been assigned for next hearing or trial; or in the event of their unavailability to a judge or group of judges designated for that purpose by the chief judge of the circuit. At the request of the court, or any party or counsel to the action, a hearing shall be scheduled with appropriate notice to review the interviewee's release or detention status. At the hearing, the factual findings, conclusions, and recommendations in the report may be challenged by the interviewee, his or her counsel, or the prosecuting attorney, by the presentation of any relevant evidence.
(Source: P.A. 85-405.) [Formerly Ill. Rev. Stat. 38 §321.]

185/22. Uniform release order.

§22. If so ordered by the court, the pretrial services agency shall prepare and submit for the court's approval and signature a uniform release order on the uniform form established by the Supreme Court in all cases where an interviewee may be released from custody under conditions contained in an agency report. Such conditions shall become part of the conditions of the bail bond. A copy of the uniform release order shall be provided to the defendant and defendant's attorney of record, and the prosecutor.
(Source: P.A. 84-1449.) [Formerly Ill. Rev. Stat. 38 §322.]

185/23. Reporting non-compliance.

§23. Pretrial services agencies shall have primary responsibility for reporting non-compliance by interviewees with the terms and conditions of pretrial release specified in the uniform release order entered under Section 22 [725 ILCS 185/22], including but not limited to appearances as required for later court proceedings and the commission of new offenses as evidenced by the filing of formal charges.
(Source: P.A. 84-1449.) [Formerly Ill. Rev. Stat. 38 §323.]

185/24. Delegated functions.

§24. Where functions of the pretrial services agency have been delegated to a probation department or other arm of the court under Section 3 [725 ILCS 185/3], their records shall be segregated from other records. Two years after the date of the first interview with a pretrial services agency representative, the defendant may apply to the chief circuit judge, or a judge designated by the chief circuit judge for these purposes, for an order expunging from the records of the pretrial services agency all files pertaining to the defendant.
(Source: P.A. 84-1449.) [Formerly Ill. Rev. Stat. 38 §324.]

185/25. Written notification of court appearance obligations.

§25. The agency shall provide written notification to supervised persons of court appearance obligations, and may require their periodic reporting by letter, telephone or personal appearance to verify such compliance.
(Source: P.A. 84-1449.) [Formerly Ill. Rev. Stat. 38 §325.]

185/26. Monitoring of arrest records.

§26. Agency personnel shall regularly monitor the arrest records of local law enforcement agencies to determine whether any supervised person has been formally charged with the commission of a new offense in violation of the uniform release order. In such event, the agency shall prepare a formal report of that fact and present same to the court. A copy shall be provided to the prosecuting officer.
(Source: P.A. 84-1449.) [Formerly Ill. Rev. Stat. 38 §326.]

185/27. Monitoring conduct of supervised persons.

§27. In addition to the supervisory duties set forth in Sections 25 and 26 [725 ILCS 185/25 and 185/26], the pretrial services agency shall continuously monitor the conduct and circumstances of supervised persons before trial and submit reports to the court, defendant and defendant's attorney of record, and prosecuting officer whenever:

(a) Apparent violations of other conditions imposed by the court under the uniform release order have occurred; or

(b) Modification of the uniform release order and conditions thereof are deemed in the best interests of either the accused or the community.
(Source: P.A. 84-1449.) [Formerly Ill. Rev. Stat. 38 §327.]

185/28. Providing information to law enforcement authorities.

§28. Whenever an arrest warrant, summons or other process is issued to compel the appearance of supervised persons before the court under Sections 25, 26 or 27 [725 ILCS 185/25, 185/26 or 185/27], the pretrial services agency shall provide such information to law enforcement authorities as may be necessary to insure immediate execution of the process.
(Source: P.A. 84-1449.) [Formerly Ill. Rev. Stat. 38 §328.]

185/29. Supervisory services.

§29. Pretrial services agencies shall, with the approval of the chief judge, offer supervisory services to similar programs operating in Illinois and other jurisdictions.
(Source: P.A. 84-1449.) [Formerly Ill. Rev. Stat. 38 §329.]

185/30. Maintaining records and statistics.

§30. Records and statistics shall be maintained by pretrial services agencies of their operations and effect upon the criminal justice system, with monthly reports submitted to the circuit court and the Supreme Court on a uniform statistical form developed by the Supreme Court.
(Source: P.A. 84-1449.) [Formerly Ill. Rev. Stat. 38 §330.]

185/31. Access to unreleased information and records; confidentiality.

§31. Information and records maintained by the pretrial services agency which has not been disclosed in open court during a court proceeding shall not be released by the pretrial services agency to any individual or organization, other than any employee of a Probation and Court Service Department, without the express permission of the interviewed or supervised person at or near the time the information is to be released. An individual shall have access to all information and records about himself or herself maintained by or collected by the pretrial services agency. The principle of confidentiality shall not bar a pretrial services agency from making its data available for research purposes to qualified personnel, provided that no records or other information shall be made available in which individuals interviewed or supervised are identified or from which their identities are ascertainable.
(Source: P.A. 84-1449.) [Formerly Ill. Rev. Stat. 38 §331.]

185/32. Provision of adequate facilities.

§32. Pretrial services agencies shall be provided by the circuit court with adequate facilities and supportive services, including secretarial staffs or pools, to assure maximum utilization of resources and effective service to the court.
(Source: P.A. 84-1449.) [Formerly Ill. Rev. Stat. 38 §332.]

185/33. Monthly reimbursement for expenses.

§33. The Supreme Court shall pay from funds appropriated to it for this purpose 100% of all approved costs for pretrial services, including pretrial services officers, necessary support personnel, travel costs reasonably related to the delivery of pretrial services, space costs, equipment, telecommunications, postage, commodities, printing and contractual services. Costs shall be reimbursed monthly, based on a plan and budget approved by the Supreme Court. No department may be reimbursed for costs which exceed or are not provided for in the approved plan and budget.
(Source: P.A. 84-1449.) [Formerly Ill. Rev. Stat. 38 §333.]

PRIVACY OF CHILD VICTIMS OF CRIMINAL SEXUAL OFFENSES ACT

Sec.

190/1. Short title.

§1. This Act shall be known and may be cited as the "Privacy of Child Victims of Criminal Sexual Offenses Act".
(Source: P.A. 84-1428.) [Formerly Ill. Rev. Stat. 38 §1451.]

190/2. Definition.

§2. As used in this Act, "Child" means any person under 18 years of age.
(Source: P.A. 84-1428.) [Formerly Ill. Rev. Stat. 38 §1452.]

190/3. Confidentiality of law enforcement and court records.

§3. Confidentiality of Law Enforcement and Court Records. Notwithstanding any other law to the contrary, inspection and copying of law enforcement records maintained by any law enforcement agency or circuit court records maintained by any circuit clerk relating to any investigation or proceeding pertaining to a criminal sexual offense, by any person, except a judge, state's attorney, assistant state's attorney, psychologist, psychiatrist, social worker, doctor, parent, defendant or defendant's attorney in any criminal proceeding or investigation related thereto, shall be restricted to exclude the identity of any child who is a victim of such criminal sexual offense or alleged criminal sexual offense. A court may for the child's protection and for good cause shown, prohibit any person or agency present in court from further disclosing the child's identity.

When a criminal sexual offense is committed or alleged to have been committed by a school district employee on the premises under the jurisdiction of a public school district or during an official school sponsored activity, a copy of the law enforcement records maintained by any law enforcement agency or circuit court records maintained by any circuit clerk relating to the investigation of the offense or alleged offense shall be made available for inspection and copying by the superintendent of schools of the district. The superintendent shall be restricted from specifically revealing the name of the victim without written consent of the victim or victim's parent or guardian.

A court may prohibit such disclosure only after giving notice and a hearing to all affected parties. In determining whether to prohibit disclosure of the minor's identity the court shall consider:

(a) the best interest of the child; and

(b) whether such nondisclosure would further a compelling State interest.
(Source: P.A. 87-553.) [Formerly Ill. Rev. Stat. 38 §1453.]

QUASI-CRIMINAL AND MISDEMEANOR BAIL ACT

195/0.01. Short title.

§0.01. Short title. This Act may be cited as the Quasi-criminal and Misdemeanor Bail Act.
(Source: P.A. 86-1324.) [Formerly Ill. Rev. Stat. 16 §80.]

195/1. Bail; place of payment.

§1. Whenever in any circuit there shall be in force a rule or order of the Supreme Court establishing a uniform schedule prescribing the amounts of bail for specified conservation cases, traffic cases, quasi-criminal offenses and misdemeanors, any general superintendent, chief, captain, lieutenant, or sergeant of police, or other police officer, the sheriff, the circuit clerk, and any deputy sheriff or deputy circuit clerk designated by the Circuit Court for the purpose, are authorized to let to bail any person charged with a quasi-criminal offense or misdemeanor and to accept and receipt for bonds or cash bail in accordance with regulations established by rule or order of the Supreme Court. Unless otherwise provided by Supreme Court Rule, no such bail may be posted or accepted in any place other than a police station, sheriff's office or jail, or other county, municipal or other building housing governmental units, or a division headquarters building of the Illinois State Police. Bonds and cash so received shall be delivered to the office of the circuit clerk or that of his designated deputy as provided by regulation. Such cash and securities so received shall be delivered to the office of such clerk or deputy clerk within at least 48 hours of receipt or within the time set for the accused's appearance in court whichever is earliest.

In all cases where a person is admitted to bail under a uniform schedule prescribing the amount of bail for specified conservation cases, traffic cases, quasi-criminal offenses and misdemeanors the provisions of Section 110-15 of the "Code of Criminal Procedure of 1963", approved August 14, 1963, as amended by the 75th General Assembly [725 ILCS 5/110-15] shall be applicable.
(Source: P.A. 80-897.) [Formerly Ill. Rev. Stat. 16 §81.]

195/2. Conditions of bail.

§2. The conditions of the bail bond or deposit of cash bail shall be that the accused will appear to answer the charge in court at a time and place specified in the bond and thereafter as ordered by the court until discharged on final order of the court and to submit himself to the orders and process of the court. The accused shall be furnished with an official receipt on a form prescribed by rule of court for any cash or other security deposited, and shall receive a copy of the bond specifying the time and place of his court appearance.

Upon performance of the conditions of the bond, the bond shall be null and void and any cash bail or other security shall be returned to the accused.
(Source: Laws 1963, p. 2652.) [Formerly Ill. Rev. Stat. 16 §82.]

195/3. Person has right to be brought before judge in lieu of making bond or depositing bail.

§3. In lieu of making bond or depositing cash bail as provided in this Act or the deposit of other security authorized by law, any accused person has the right to be brought without unnecessary delay before the nearest or most accessible judge of the circuit to be dealt with according to law.
(Source: P.A. 77-1248.) [Formerly Ill. Rev. Stat. 16 §83.]

195/4. Guilty pleas and trial waivers.

§4. Whenever in any circuit there shall be in force a uniform schedule prescribing the amounts of fines, penalties, forfeitures and costs on pleas of guilty in specified minor conservation and traffic offenses, any circuit clerk or deputy circuit clerk is authorized to receive written appearances, pleas of guilty and waivers of trial and to accept and receipt for payments, in satisfaction of the judgment to be entered upon the plea, in accordance with the uniform schedule. The accused shall be furnished with an official receipt on a form prescribed by such uniform schedule for the purpose for any fine paid pursuant to this section.
(Source: Laws 1967, p. 2949.) [Formerly Ill. Rev. Stat. 16 §84.]

195/5. Violations.

§5. Any person authorized to accept bail or pleas of guilty by this Act who violates any provision of this Act is guilty of a Class B misdemeanor.
(Source: P.A. 77-2319.) [Formerly Ill. Rev. Stat. 16 §85.]

SEX OFFENSE VICTIM POLYGRAPH ACT

Sec.

200/0.01. Short title.

§0.01. Short title. This Act may be cited as the Sex Offense Victim Polygraph Act.

(Source: P.A. 86-1324.) [Formerly Ill. Rev. Stat. 38 §1550.]

200/1. Lie detector tests.

§1. Lie Detector Tests. (a) No law enforcement officer, State's Attorney or other official shall require an alleged victim of an offense described in Sections 12-13 through 12-16 of the Criminal Code of 1961, as amended [720 ILCS 5/12-13 through 5/12-16], to submit to a polygraph examination or any form of a mechanical or electrical lie detector test as a condition for proceeding with the investigation, charging or prosecution of such offense, and such test shall be administered to such victim solely at the victim's request.

(b) A victim's refusal to submit to a polygraph or any form of a mechanical or electrical lie detector test shall not mitigate against the investigation, charging or prosecution of the pending case as originally charged.

(Source: P.A. 85-664.) [Formerly Ill. Rev. Stat. 38 §1551.]

SEXUALLY DANGEROUS PERSONS ACT

Sec.

205/0.01. Short title.

§0.01. Short title. This Act may be cited as the Sexually Dangerous Persons Act.

(Source: P.A. 86-132.) [Formerly Ill. Rev. Stat. 38 §105-0.01.]

205/1.01. Sexually dangerous persons; definition.

§1.01. As used in this Act:

All persons suffering from a mental disorder, which mental disorder has existed for a period of not less than one year, immediately prior to the filing of the petition hereinafter provided for, coupled with criminal propensities to the commission of sex offenses, and who have demonstrated propensities toward acts of sexual assault or acts of sexual molestation of children, are hereby declared sexually dangerous persons.

(Source: Laws 1955, p. 1144.) [Formerly Ill. Rev. Stat. 38 §105-1.01.]

205/2. Jurisdiction.

§2. Jurisdiction of proceedings under this Act is vested in the circuit courts in this State, for the purpose of conducting hearings for commitment and detention of such persons, as hereinafter provided.

(Source: Laws 1965, p. 3462.) [Formerly Ill. Rev. Stat. 38 §105-2.]

205/3. Petition.

§3. When any person is charged with a criminal offense and it shall appear to the Attorney General or to the State's Attorney of the county wherein such

person is so charged, that such person is a sexually dangerous person, within the meaning of this Act, then the Attorney General or State's Attorney of such county may file with the clerk of the court in the same proceeding wherein such person stands charged with criminal offense, a petition in writing setting forth facts tending to show that the person named is a sexually dangerous person.
(Source: Laws 1955, p. 1144.) [Formerly Ill. Rev. Stat. 38 §105-3.]

205/3.01. Civil nature of proceedings.
§3.01. The proceedings under this Act shall be civil in nature, however, the burden of proof required to commit a defendant to confinement as a sexually dangerous person shall be the standard of proof required in a criminal proceedings of proof beyond a reasonable doubt. The provisions of the Civil Practice Law, and all existing and future amendments of that Law and modifications thereof [735 ILCS 5/2-101 et seq.] and the Supreme Court Rules now or hereafter adopted in relation to that Law shall apply to all proceedings hereunder except as otherwise provided in this Act.
(Source: P.A. 82-783.) [Formerly Ill. Rev. Stat. 38 §105-3.01.]

205/4. Personal examination by psychiatrists.
§4. After the filing of the petition, the court shall appoint two qualified psychiatrists to make a personal examination of such alleged sexually dangerous person, to ascertain whether such person is sexually dangerous, and the psychiatrists shall file with the court a report in writing of the result of their examination, a copy of which shall be delivered to the respondent.
(Source: Laws 1955, p. 1144.) [Formerly Ill. Rev. Stat. 38 §105-4.]

205/4.01. Qualified psychiatrist, definition.
§4.01. "Qualified psychiatrist" means a reputable physician licensed in Illinois to practice medicine in all its branches, who has specialized in the diagnosis and treatment of mental and nervous disorders for a period of not less than 5 years.
(Source: Laws 1959, p. 1685.) [Formerly Ill. Rev. Stat. 38 §105-4.01.]

205/4.02. Cost of psychiatric examinations.
§4.02. In counties of less than 500,000 inhabitants the cost of the psychiatric examination required by Section 4 [725 ILCS 205/4] is a charge against and shall be paid out of the general fund of the county in which the proceeding is brought.
(Source: Laws 1959, p. 1685.) [Formerly Ill. Rev. Stat. 38 §105-4.02.]

205/5. Right to jury trial.
§5. The respondent in any proceedings under this Act shall have the right to demand a trial by jury and to be represented by counsel. At the hearing on the petition it shall be competent to introduce evidence of the commission by the respondent of any number of crimes together with whatever punishments, if any, were inflicted.
(Source: Laws 1955, p. 1144.) [Formerly Ill. Rev. Stat. 38 §105-5.]

205/8. Director of Corrections; guardian.
§8. If the respondent is found to be a sexually dangerous person then the court shall appoint the Director of Corrections guardian of the person found to be sexually dangerous and such person shall stand committed to the custody of such guardian. The Director of Corrections as guardian shall keep safely the person so committed until the person has recovered and is released as hereinafter provided. The Director of Corrections as guardian shall provide care and treatment for the person committed to him designed to effect recovery. The Director may place that ward in any facility in the Department of Corrections or portion thereof set aside for the care and treatment of sexually dangerous

persons. The Department of Corrections may also request another state Department or Agency to examine such patient and upon such request, such Department or Agency shall make such examination and the Department of Corrections may, with the consent of the chief executive officer of such other Department or Agency, thereupon place such patient in the care and treatment of such other Department or Agency.
(Source: P.A. 77-2477.) [Formerly Ill. Rev. Stat. 38 §105-8.]

205/9. Application showing recovery.

§9. An application in writing setting forth facts showing that such sexually dangerous person or criminal sexual psychopathic person has recovered may be filed before the committing court. Upon receipt thereof, the clerk of the court shall cause a copy of the application to be sent to the Director of the Department of Corrections. The Director shall then cause to be prepared and sent to the court a socio-psychiatric report concerning the applicant. The report shall be prepared by the psychiatrist, sociologist, psychologist and warden of, or assigned to, the institution wherein such applicant is confined. The court shall set a date for the hearing upon such application and shall consider the report so prepared under the direction of the Director of the Department of Corrections and any other relevant information submitted by or on behalf of such applicant. If the patient is found to be no longer dangerous, the court shall order that he be discharged. If the court finds that the patient appears no longer to be dangerous but that it is impossible to determine with certainty under conditions of institutional care that such person has fully recovered, the court shall enter an order permitting such person to go at large subject to such conditions and such supervision by the Director as in the opinion of the court will adequately protect the public. In the event the person violates any of the conditions of such order, the court shall revoke such conditional release and recommit the person pursuant to Section 5-6-4 of the Unified Code of Corrections [730 ILCS 5/5-6-4] under the terms of the original commitment. Upon an order of discharge every outstanding information and indictment, the basis of which was the reason for the present detention, shall be quashed.
(Source: P.A. 77-2477.) [Formerly Ill. Rev. Stat. 38 §105-9.]

205/10. Conditional release.

§10. Whenever the Director finds that any person committed to him under this Act as now or hereafter amended, appears no longer to be dangerous but that it is impossible to determine with certainty under conditions of institutional care that such person has fully recovered, the Director of the Department of Corrections may petition the committing court for an order authorizing the conditional release of any person committed to him under this Act and the court may enter an order permitting such person to go at large subject to such conditions and such supervision by the Director as in the opinion of the court will adequately protect the public. In the event the person violates any of the conditions of such order, the court shall revoke such conditional release and re-commit the person pursuant to Section 5-6-4 of the Unified Code of Corrections [730 ILCS 5/5-6-4] under the terms of the original commitment.
(Source: P.A. 77-2477.) [Formerly Ill. Rev. Stat. 38 §105-10.]

205/11. Invalidity.

§11. If any provision of this Act, or the application of any provision to any person or circumstance, is held invalid, the remainder of the Act, and the application of such provision to other persons or circumstances, shall not be affected thereby.
(Source: Laws 1955, p. 1144.) [Formerly Ill. Rev. Stat. 38 §105-11.]

205/12. Custody transferred.

§12. Persons heretofore committed to the Department of Public Safety are deemed transferred and committed to the custody of the Director of Corrections.
(Source: P.A. 76-451.) [Formerly Ill. Rev. Stat. 38 §105-12.]

STATE'S ATTORNEYS APPELLATE PROSECUTOR'S ACT

210/1. Short title.

§1. This Act may be cited as the State's Attorneys Appellate Prosecutor's Act.
(Source: P.A. 84-1062.) [Formerly Ill. Rev. Stat. 14 §201.]

210/2. Definitions.

§2. In this Act, unless the context clearly requires a different meaning, the following definitions apply:

(1) "Board" means the board of governors of the Office of the State's Attorneys Appellate Prosecutor;

(2) "Member" means a member of the board;

(3) "Director" means the Director of the Office of the State's Attorneys Appellate Prosecutor; and

(4) "District" means a judicial district as defined in "An Act establishing the Judicial Districts", approved May 13, 1963, as now or hereafter amended [705 ILCS 20/0.01 et seq.];

(5) "State" means the State of Illinois; and

(6) "Office" means the Office of the State's Attorneys Appellate Prosecutor.
(Source: P.A. 84-1062.) [Formerly Ill. Rev. Stat. 14 §202.]

210/3. Creation of office; board members.

§3. There is created the Office of the State's Attorneys Appellate Prosecutor as an agency of state government.

(a) The Office of the State's Attorneys Appellate Prosecutor shall be governed by a board of governors which shall consist of 10 members as follows:

(1) Eight State's Attorneys, 2 to be elected from each District containing less than 3,000,000 inhabitants;

(2) The State's Attorney of Cook County; and

(3) One State's Attorney to be appointed by the other 9 members.

(b) Voting for elected members shall be by District with each of the State's Attorneys voting from their respective district. Each board member must be duly elected or appointed and serving as State's Attorney in the district from which he was elected or appointed.

(c) Members shall serve for a term of one year commencing on the first day of July and until their successors are duly elected or appointed and qualified.

(d) An annual election of members of the board shall be held during the month of June, and the board shall certify the results to the Secretary of State.

(e) The board shall promulgate rules of procedure for the election of its members and the conduct of its meetings and shall elect a Chairman and a Vice-Chairman and such other officers as it deems appropriate. The board shall meet at least once every 3 months, and in addition thereto as directed by the Chairman, or upon the special call of any 5 members of the board, in writing, sent to the Chairman, designating the time and place of the meeting.

(f) Five members of the board shall constitute a quorum for the purpose of transacting business.

(g) Members of the board shall serve without compensation, but shall be reimbursed for necessary expenses incurred in the performance of their duties.

(h) A position shall be vacated by either a member's resignation, removal or inability to serve as State's Attorney.

(i) Vacancies on the board of elected members shall be filled within 30 days of the occurrence of the vacancy by a special election held by the State's Attorneys in the district where the vacancy occurred. Vacancies on the board of the appointed member shall be filled within 30 days of the occurrence of the vacancy by a special election by the members. A member elected or appointed to fill such position shall serve for the unexpired term of the member whom he is succeeding. Any member may be re-elected or re-appointed for additional terms.

(Source: P.A. 84-1062.) [Formerly Ill. Rev. Stat. 14 §203.]

210/4. Powers and duties of board.

§4. The board and the Office have the powers and duties enumerated in Sections 4.01 through 4.10 [725 ILCS 210/4.01 through 210/4.10].

(Source: P.A. 84-1062.) [Formerly Ill. Rev. Stat. 14 §204.]

210/4.01. Appellate cases; services to county; tax objections.

§4.01. The Office and all attorneys employed thereby may represent the People of the State of Illinois on appeal in all cases which emanate from a district containing less than 3,000,000 inhabitants, when requested to do so and at the direction of the State's Attorney, otherwise responsible for prosecuting the appeal, and may, with the advice and consent of the State's Attorney prepare, file and argue such appellate briefs in the Illinois Appellate Court. The Office may also assist County State's Attorneys in the discharge of their duties under the Illinois Controlled Substances Act [720 ILCS 570/100 et seq.], the Narcotics Profit Forfeiture Act [725 ILCS 175/1 et seq.], and the Illinois Public Labor Relations Act [5 ILCS 315/1 et seq.], including negotiations conducted on behalf of a county or pursuant to an intergovernmental agreement as well as in the

trial and appeal of said cases and of tax objections, and the counties which use services relating to labor relations shall reimburse the Office on pro-rated shares as determined by the board based upon the population and number of labor relations cases of the participating counties.
(Source: P.A. 85-617.) [Formerly Ill. Rev. Stat. 14 §204.01.]

210/4.02. Director of board; appointment.
§4.02. The board shall appoint a Director.
(Source: P.A. 84-1062.) [Formerly Ill. Rev. Stat. 14 §204.02.]

210/4.03. Board shall advise the Director and establish policies.
§4.03. The board shall advise the Director and shall establish policies for the operation of the Office.
(Source: P.A. 84-1062.) [Formerly Ill. Rev. Stat. 14 §204.03.]

210/4.04. Establishment of offices; districts with less than 3,000,000 inhabitants.
§4.04. The board shall establish an Office in each district containing less than 3,000,000 inhabitants.
(Source: P.A. 84-1062.) [Formerly Ill. Rev. Stat. 14 §204.04.]

210/4.05. Budget; number of employees.
§4.05. The board shall approve or modify an annual budget submitted to it by the Director and establish the number of employees.
(Source: P.A. 84-1062.) [Formerly Ill. Rev. Stat. 14 §204.05.]

210/4.06. Annual report submitted to General Assembly and Governor.
§4.06. The board shall submit an annual report to the General Assembly and Governor regarding the operation of the Office of the State's Attorneys Appellate Prosecutor.

The requirement for reporting to the General Assembly shall be satisfied by filing copies of the report with the Speaker, the Minority Leader and the Clerk of the House of Representatives and the President, the Minority Leader and the Secretary of the Senate and the Legislative Research Unit, as required by Section 3.1 of "An Act to revise the law in relation to the General Assembly", approved February 25, 1874, as amended [25 ILCS 5/3.1], and filing such additional copies with the State Government Report Distribution Center for the General Assembly as is required under paragraph (t) of Section 7 of the State Library Act [15 ILCS 320/7].
(Source: P.A. 84-1438.) [Formerly Ill. Rev. Stat. 14 §204.06.]

210/4.07. Accepting and expending gifts and services.
§4.07. The Office may accept and expend monies, gifts, grants and services from any public or private source; contract or enter into agreements with educational institutions or any Illinois county, the state of Illinois or federal agencies.
(Source: P.A. 84-1062.) [Formerly Ill. Rev. Stat. 14 §204.07.]

210/4.08. Establishment of programs using law students as legal assistants and interns.
§4.08. The Office may establish programs, alone or in conjunction with law schools, for the purpose of utilizing law students as legal assistants and interns.
(Source: P.A. 84-1062.) [Formerly Ill. Rev. Stat. 14 §204.08.]

210/4.09. Rules and regulations.
§4.09. The board shall provide for such rules and regulations as may be required for the administration of this Act.
(Source: P.A. 84-1062.) [Formerly Ill. Rev. Stat. 14 §204.09.]

210/4.10. Money from training programs and publications to be deposited in the Continuing Legal Education Trust Fund.

§4.10. The Office may conduct and charge tuition for training programs for State's Attorneys, Assistant State's Attorneys and other law enforcement officers. The Office shall conduct training programs for Illinois state's attorneys, assistant state's attorneys and law enforcement officers on techniques and methods of eliminating or reducing the trauma of testifying in criminal proceedings for children who serve as witnesses in such proceedings. In addition, the Office may publish, disseminate and sell publications and newsletters which digest current Appellate and Supreme Court cases and legislative developments of importance to prosecutors and law enforcement officials. The moneys collected by the Office from the programs and publications provided for in this Section shall be deposited in the Continuing Legal Education Trust Fund, which special fund is hereby created in the State Treasury. In addition, such gifts or grants of money as the Office may secure from any public or private source for the purposes described in this Section shall be deposited in the Continuing Legal Education Trust Fund. The General Assembly shall make appropriations from the Continuing Legal Education Trust Fund for the expenses of the Office incident to conducting the programs and publishing the materials provided for in this Section.

(Source: P.A. 84-1340.) [Formerly Ill. Rev. Stat. 14 §204.10.]

210/5. Director and attorneys to take oath of office.

§5. The Director and all attorneys employed by the Office of the State's Attorneys Appellate Prosecutor shall take the oath of office in like manner as Assistant State's Attorneys.

(Source: P.A. 84-1062.) [Formerly Ill. Rev. Stat. 14 §205.]

210/6. Organization of office.

§6. The Office is to be organized in the following manner:

(a) The staff of the Office of the State's Attorneys Appellate Prosecutor shall consist of a Director, 4 Deputy Directors, Staff Attorneys and such other administrative, secretarial and clerical employees as may be necessary.

(b) The Director and all Office Attorneys must be licensed to practice law in the State of Illinois. Staff Attorneys and Deputy Directors hired by the Director, with the concurrence of the board, shall devote full time to their duties and may not engage in the private practice of law, except as provided in Section 7.02 [725 ILCS 210/7.02].

(c) The Director and such other employees as may be hired hereunder shall not be subject to the provisions of the Illinois Personnel Code [20 ILCS 415/1 et seq.].

(Source: P.A. 84-1062.) [Formerly Ill. Rev. Stat. 14 §206.]

210/7. Powers and duties.

§7. The Director has the powers and duties enumerated in Sections 7.01 through 7.06 [725 ILCS 210/7.01 through 210/7.06].

(Source: P.A. 81-1057.) [Formerly Ill. Rev. Stat. 14 §207.]

210/7.01. Director; appointment.

§7.01. The Director shall be appointed by and serve at the pleasure of the board.

(Source: P.A. 84-1062.) [Formerly Ill. Rev. Stat. 14 §207.01.]

210/7.02. Employees; hiring and compensation.

§7.02. The Director may, with the concurrence of the board, hire such employees, including part-time employees, as are necessary to carry out Office duties, and the Director shall establish rates of compensation therefor within

the limits of the appropriations made by the General Assembly and such other funds as may be available. All Attorneys hired as part-time employees who devote 50% or more of their time to Office duties are prohibited from the private practice of law.
(Source: P.A. 84-1062.) [Formerly Ill. Rev. Stat. 14 §207.02.]

210/7.03. Organization of office; duties of employees.

§7.03. The Director may, with the concurrence of the board, promulgate regulations, instructions and orders consistent with this Act further defining the organization of the Office and duties of the employees.
(Source: P.A. 84-1062.) [Formerly Ill. Rev. Stat. 14 §207.03.]

210/7.04. Reports submitted by Director.

§7.04. The Director shall submit reports to the board on the operation of his office at each meeting. The Director shall submit a comprehensive report to the board at the end of each fiscal year, and the board may require the Director to submit additional or amended reports on any phase of the operation of his office.
(Source: P.A. 84-1062.) [Formerly Ill. Rev. Stat. 14 §207.04.]

210/7.05. Annual budget.

§7.05. The Director shall submit an annual budget for the approval of the board.
(Source: P.A. 84-1062.) [Formerly Ill. Rev. Stat. 14 §207.05.]

210/7.06. Investigators.

§7.06. The Director may hire no more than 12 investigators to provide investigative services in criminal cases and tax objection cases for staff counsel and county state's attorneys. Investigators may be authorized by the board to carry tear gas gun projectors or bombs, pistols, revolvers, stun guns, tasers or other firearms.

Subject to the qualifications set forth below, investigators shall be peace officers and shall have all the powers possessed by policemen in cities and by sheriffs; provided, that investigators shall exercise such powers anywhere in the State only after contact and in cooperation with the appropriate local law enforcement agencies.

No investigator shall have peace officer status or exercise police powers unless he or she successfully completes the basic police training course mandated and approved by the Illinois Local Governmental Law Enforcement Officers Training Board or such board waives the training requirement by reason of the investigator's prior law enforcement experience or training or both.

The board shall not waive the training requirement unless the investigator has had a minimum of 5 years experience as a sworn officer of a local, state or federal law enforcement agency, 2 of which shall have been in an investigatory capacity.
(Source: P.A. 86-9; 87-677.) [Formerly Ill. Rev. Stat. 14 §207.06.]

210/8. State's attorneys' right to prosecute appeals.

§8. Nothing herein contained shall be construed to abrogate or diminish the rights of State's Attorneys to prosecute appeals in any case.
(Source: P.A. 80-1stSS-1; 80-1stSS-3.) [Formerly Ill. Rev. Stat. 14 §208.]

210/9. State's Attorneys Appellate Prosecutor's County Fund.

§9. There is created a special fund in the State Treasury designated as the State's Attorneys Appellate Prosecutor's County Fund. It shall be funded from contributions collected from the counties in the program, other than moneys received from the counties for the programs and publications authorized by Section 4.10 of this Act [725 ILCS 210/4.10]. The contributions shall be based

on pro rated shares as determined by the board based on the populations of the participating counties. This fund is to be used exclusively for the expenses of the Office.
(Source: P.A. 84-1062.) [Formerly Ill. Rev. Stat. 14 §209.]

210/9.01. Expenses.
§9.01. The General Assembly shall appropriate money for the expenses of the Office, other than the expenses of the Office incident to the programs and publications authorized by Section 4.10 of this Act, one-third from the State's Attorneys Appellate Prosecutor's County Fund and two-thirds from the General Revenue Fund, except for employees in the collective bargaining unit, for which all personal services expenses shall be paid from the General Revenue Fund.
(Source: P.A. 86-332.) [Formerly Ill. Rev. Stat. 14 §209.01.]

210/9.02. Allocation of county shares of expenses.
§9.02. Within 30 days after the appropriation becomes law, the board shall allocate the county shares of the expenses to the participating counties in proportion to population.
(Source: P.A. 84-1062.) [Formerly Ill. Rev. Stat. 14 §209.02.]

210/9.03. Unobligated balance remaining in fund at end of fiscal year.
§9.03. If there is an unobligated balance remaining in the State's Attorneys Appellate Prosecutor's County Fund at the end of a fiscal year, that sum shall be rolled over for use in the ensuing fiscal year, and shall be considered by the board in allocating the county shares of the expenses to the participating counties.
(Source: P.A. 86-332.) [Formerly Ill. Rev. Stat. 14 §209.03.]

210/9.04. Reallocation of contributions when county elects to participate following allocation.
§9.04. If a county wishes to elect to participate in the program after the county shares of the expenses have been allocated to the participating counties, the board may permit such participation and reallocate the contributions. The board shall give proportionate refunds or credits based on population as may be required.
(Source: P.A. 84-1062.) [Formerly Ill. Rev. Stat. 14 §209.04.]

210/9.05. Population determination.
§9.05. For the purposes of Sections 9 through 9.04 [725 ILCS 210/9 through 210/9.04], population shall be determined by the last available federal census.
(Source: P.A. 80-1stSS-1; 80-1stSS-3.) [Formerly Ill. Rev. Stat. 14 §209.05.]

210/10. Participation in program in succeeding years.
§10. A county that is participating in the program will be deemed to have elected to participate in the succeeding fiscal year unless it notifies the board in writing at least 90 days before the beginning of the fiscal year.
(Source: P.A. 84-1062.) [Formerly Ill. Rev. Stat. 14 §210.]

210/11. Applicability of Illinois Administrative Procedure Act.
§11. The provisions of the "Illinois Administrative Procedure Act", as now or hereafter amended [5 ILCS 100/1-1 et seq.], are hereby expressly adopted and incorporated herein as though a part of this Act, and shall apply to all administrative rules and procedures of the Office of the State's Attorneys Appellate Prosecutor under this Act.
(Source: P.A. 84-1062.) [Formerly Ill. Rev. Stat. 14 §211.]

STATEWIDE GRAND JURY ACT

215/1. Short title.

§1. This Act shall be known and may be cited as the Statewide Grand Jury Act.
(Source: P.A. 87-466.) [Formerly Ill. Rev. Stat. 38 §1701.]

215/2. Findings.

§2. County grand juries and State's Attorneys have always had and shall continue to have primary responsibility for investigating, indicting and prosecuting persons who violate the criminal laws of the State of Illinois. However, in recent years certain criminal enterprises have developed that require investigation, indictment and prosecution on a statewide or multicounty level. These enterprises exist as a result of the allure of profitability that cannabis and controlled substance trafficking and narcotics racketeering present. In order to weaken or eliminate these enterprises, the profit must be removed. State statutes exist that can accomplish that goal. Among them are the offense of money laundering, the Cannabis and Controlled Substances Tax Act [35 ILCS 520/1 et seq.], and the Narcotics Profit Forfeiture Act [725 ILCS 175/1 et seq.]. Local prosecutors need investigative personnel and specialized training to attack and eliminate these profits. In light of the transitory and complex nature of conduct which constitutes the offenses of cannabis and controlled substance trafficking and narcotics racketeering, and the many diverse property interests which may be acquired directly or indirectly as a result of such an offense, and the many places said illegally obtained property may be located, it is the purpose of this Act to create a limited, multicounty Statewide Grand Jury with authority to investigate, indict and prosecute narcotic activity, including cannabis and controlled substance trafficking, narcotics racketeering, money laundering and the Cannabis and Controlled Substances Tax Act.
(Source: P.A. 87-466.) [Formerly Ill. Rev. Stat. 38 §1702.]

215/3. Appointment of judge.

§3. Written application for the appointment of a Circuit Judge to convene and preside over a Statewide Grand Jury, with jurisdiction extending throughout the State, shall be made to the Chief Justice of the Supreme Court. Upon such written application, the Chief Justice of the Supreme Court shall appoint a Circuit Judge from the circuit where the Statewide Grand Jury is being sought to be convened, who shall make a determination that the convening of a Statewide Grand Jury is necessary.

In such application the Attorney General shall state that the convening of a Statewide Grand Jury is necessary because of an alleged offense or offenses set forth in this Section involving more than one county of the state and identifying any such offense alleged; and

(a) that he believes that the grand jury function for the investigation and indictment of the offense or offenses cannot effectively be performed by a county grand jury together with his reasons for such belief, and

(b) (1) that each State's Attorney with jurisdiction over an offense or offenses to be investigated has consented to the impaneling of the Statewide Grand Jury, or

(2) if one or more of the State's Attorneys having jurisdiction over an offense or offenses to be investigated fails to consent to the impaneling of the Statewide Grand Jury, the Attorney General shall set forth good cause for impaneling the Statewide Grand Jury. If the Circuit Judge determines that the convening of a Statewide Grand Jury is necessary, he shall convene and impanel the Statewide Grand Jury with jurisdiction extending throughout the State to investigate and return indictments:

(a) For violations of the Illinois Controlled Substances Act [720 ILCS 570/100 et seq.], the Cannabis Control Act [720 ILCS 550/1 et seq.], the Narcotics Profit Forfeiture Act [725 ILCS 175/1 et seq.], the Cannabis and Controlled Substances Tax Act [35 ILCS 520/1 et seq.], and any other criminal offense committed in the course of such a violation, and for the offense of money laundering; provided that the violation or offense involves Acts occurring in more than one county of this State; and

(b) For the offenses of perjury, subornation of perjury, communicating with jurors and witnesses, harassment of jurors and witnesses, as they relate to matters before the Statewide Grand Jury.

(Source: P.A. 87-466.) [Formerly Ill. Rev. Stat. 38 §1703.]

215/4. Venue.

§4. (a) The presiding judge of the Statewide Grand Jury will receive recommendations from the Attorney General as to the county in which the Grand Jury will sit. Prior to making the recommendations, the Attorney General shall obtain the permission of the local State's Attorney to use his or her county for the site of the Statewide Grand Jury. Upon receiving the Attorney General's recommendations, the presiding judge will choose one of those recommended locations as the site where the Grand Jury shall sit.

Any indictment by a Statewide Grand Jury shall be returned to the Circuit Judge presiding over the Statewide Grand Jury and shall include a finding as to the county or counties in which the alleged offense was committed. Thereupon, the judge shall, by order, designate the county of venue for the purpose of trial. The judge may also, by order, direct the consolidation of an indictment returned by a county grand jury with an indictment returned by the Statewide Grand Jury and set venue for trial.

(b) Venue for purposes of trial for the offense of narcotics racketeering shall be proper in any county where:

(1) Cannabis or a controlled substance which is the basis for the charge of narcotics racketeering was used; acquired; transferred or distributed to, from or through; or any county where any act was performed to further the use; acquisition, transfer or distribution of said cannabis or controlled substance; or

(2) Any money, property, property interest, or any other asset generated by narcotics activities was acquired, used, sold, transferred or distributed to, from or through; or,

(3) Any enterprise interest obtained as a result of narcotics racketeering was acquired, used, transferred or distributed to, from or through, or where any activity was conducted by the enterprise or any conduct to further the interests of such an enterprise.

(c) Venue for purposes of trial for the offense of money laundering shall be proper in any county where any part of a financial transaction in criminally derived property took place, or in any county where any money or monetary interest which is the basis for the offense, was acquired, used, sold, transferred or distributed to, from, or through.

(d) A person who commits the offense of cannabis trafficking or controlled substance trafficking may be tried in any county.
(Source: P.A. 87-466.) [Formerly Ill. Rev. Stat. 38 §1704.]

215/5. Establishment of Statewide Grand Jury.

§5. A Statewide Grand Jury shall be called and shall sit at such times and for such periods, and subject to the same procedures, as grand juries in counties having not more than 1,000,000 inhabitants, except as otherwise provided in this Act.
(Source: P.A. 87-466.) [Formerly Ill. Rev. Stat. 38 §1705.]

215/6. Powers and duties of Statewide Grand Jury.

§6. Except as otherwise provided in this Act, a Statewide Grand Jury shall have the same powers and duties, shall be selected in the same manner, shall be served by county personnel in the same manner, and shall follow the same procedures, as other grand juries in the county in which the Statewide Grand Jury sits.

A Statewide Grand Jury may, at the discretion of the presiding judge, draw jurors from counties adjoining the one in which it is to sit. Personnel of adjoining counties shall assist the Statewide Grand Jury in drawing such jurors from their respective counties in the same manner as they would assist in the selection of grand jurors sitting in their own county.
(Source: P.A. 87-466.) [Formerly Ill. Rev. Stat. 38 §1706.]

215/7. Powers and duties of Attorney General.

§7. The Attorney General or his assistant shall attend each Statewide Grand Jury, and shall prosecute any indictment returned by it, unless the State's Attorney of the country* of venue for the indictment consents to prosecute the indictment. The Attorney General or his assistant shall have the same powers and duties in relation to a Statewide Grand Jury that a State's Attorney has in relation to a county grand jury, except as otherwise provided in this Act.

**So in original. Probably should be "county".*

(Source: P.A. 87-466.) [Formerly Ill. Rev. Stat. 38 §1707.]

215/8. Costs.

§8. The costs of impaneling a Statewide Grand Jury, and the costs and expenses incurred in the performance of its functions and duties, shall be paid by the county in which it sits. The county shall be reimbursed for such costs and expenses by the State out of funds appropriated to the Attorney General for that purpose.
(Source: P.A. 87-466.) [Formerly Ill. Rev. Stat. 38 §1708.]

215/9. Jurisdiction of Statewide Grand Jury; limitations.

§9. No provision of this Act shall be construed as limiting the jurisdiction of county grand juries or State's Attorneys, nor shall an investigation by a Statewide Grand Jury be deemed to preempt an investigation by any other grand jury or agency having jurisdiction over the same subject matter.
(Source: P.A. 87-466.) [Formerly Ill. Rev. Stat. 38 §1709.]

215/10. Rights and duties of State's Attorney.

§10. The Attorney General shall, at the earliest opportunity, upon initiation of Grand Jury action, consult with and advise the State's Attorney of any county involved in a Statewide Grand Jury narcotics investigation. Further, the State's Attorney may attend the Grand Jury proceedings or the trial of any party being investigated or indicted by the Statewide Grand Jury, and may assist in the prosecution, which in his or her judgment, is in the interest of the people of his or her county. Prior to granting transactional immunity to any witness before the Statewide Grand Jury, any State's Attorney with jurisdiction over the offense or offenses being investigated by the Statewide Grand Jury must

consent to the granting of immunity to the witness. Prior to granting use immunity to any witness before the Statewide Grand Jury, the Attorney General shall consult with any State's Attorney with jurisdiction over the offense or offenses being investigated by the Statewide Grand Jury.
(Source: P.A. 87-466.) [Formerly Ill. Rev. Stat. 38 §1710.]

UNIFORM ACT TO SECURE THE ATTENDANCE OF WITNESSES FROM WITHIN OR WITHOUT A STATE IN CRIMINAL PROCEEDINGS

Sec.

220/1. Definitions.

§1. "Witness" as used in this Act shall include a person whose testimony is desired in any proceeding or investigation by a grand jury or in a criminal action, prosecution or proceeding.

The word "summons" shall include a subpoena (both subpoena ad testificandum and subpoena duces tecum), order or other notice requiring the appearance of a witness.
(Source: Laws 1965, p. 2694.) [Formerly Ill. Rev. Stat. 38 §156-1.]

220/2. Summoning witness in this State to testify in another state.

§2. Summoning witness in this state to testify in another state. If a judge of a court of record in any state which by its laws has made provision for commanding persons within that state to attend and testify in this state certifies under the seal of such court that there is a criminal prosecution pending in such court, or that a grand jury investigation has commenced or is about to commence, that a person being within this state is a material witness in such prosecution, or grand jury investigation, and his presence will be required for a specified number of days, upon presentation of such certificate to any judge of a court in the county in which such person is, such judge shall fix a time and place for a hearing, and shall make an order directing the witness to appear at a time and place certain for the hearing.

If at a hearing the judge determines that the witness is material and necessary, that it will not cause undue hardship to the witness to be compelled to attend and testify in the prosecution or a grand jury investigation in the other state, and that the laws of the state in which the prosecution is pending, or grand jury investigation has commenced or is about to commence (and of any other state through which the witness may be required to pass by ordinary course of travel), will give to him protection from arrest and the service of civil and criminal process, he shall issue a summons, with a copy of the certificate attached, directing the witness to attend and testify in the court where the prosecution is pending, or where a grand jury investigation has commenced or is about to commence at a time and place specified in the summons. In any such hearing the certificate shall be prima facie evidence of all the facts stated therein.

If said certificate recommends that the witness be taken into immediate custody and delivered to an officer of the requesting state to assure his attendance in the requesting state, such judge may, in lieu of notification of the hearing, direct that such witness be forthwith brought before him for said hearing; and the judge at the hearing being satisfied of the desirability of such custody and delivery, for which determination the certificate shall be prima facie proof of such desirability may, in lieu of issuing subpoena or summons, order that said witness be forthwith taken into custody and delivered to an officer of the requesting state.

If the witness, who is summoned as above provided, after being paid or tendered by some properly authorized person the sum of 10 cents a mile for each mile by the ordinary travel route to and from the court where the prosecution is pending and five dollars for each day that he is required to travel and attend as a witness, fails without good cause to attend and testify as directed in the summons, he shall be punished in the manner provided for the punishment of any witness who disobeys a summons issued from a court in this state.

(Source: Laws 1967, p. 3804.) [Formerly Ill. Rev. Stat. 38 §156-2.]

220/3. Witness from another state summoned to testify in this State.

§3. Witness from another state summoned to testify in this State. If a person in any state, which by its laws has made provision for commanding persons within its borders to attend and testify in criminal prosecutions, or grand jury investigations commenced or about to commence, in this state, is a material witness in a prosecution pending in a court in this state, or in a grand jury investigation which has commenced or is about to commence, a judge of such court may issue a certificate under the seal of the court stating these facts and specifying the number of days the witness will be required. Said certificate may include a recommendation that the witness be taken into immediate custody and delivered to an officer of this state to assure his attendance in this state. This certificate shall be presented to a judge of a court of record in the county in which the witness is found.

If the witness is summoned to attend and testify in this state he shall be tendered the sum of 10 cents a mile for each mile by the ordinary traveled route to and from the court where the prosecution is pending, and 5 dollars for each day that he is required to travel and attend as a witness. A witness who has appeared in accordance with the provisions of the summons shall not be required to remain within this state a longer period of time than the period mentioned in the certificate, unless otherwise ordered by the court. If such witness, after coming into this state, fails without good cause to attend and testify as directed in the summons, he shall be punished in the manner provided for the punishment of any witness who disobeys a summons issued from a court in this state.

(Source: Laws 1967, p. 3804.) [Formerly Ill. Rev. Stat. 38 §156-3.]

220/4. Exemption from arrest and service of process.

§4. Exemption from arrest and service of process. If a person comes into this state in obedience to a summons directing him to attend and testify in this state he shall not, while in this state pursuant to such summons be subject to arrest or the service of process, civil or criminal, in connection with matters which arose before his entrance into this state under the summons.

If a person passes through this state while going to another state in obedience to a summons to attend and testify in that state or while returning therefrom, he shall not while so passing through this state be subject to arrest or the service of process, civil or criminal, in connection with matters which arose before his entrance into this state under the summons.

(Source: Laws 1959, p. 2147.) [Formerly Ill. Rev. Stat. 38 §156-4.]

220/5. Uniformity of interpretation.

§5. Uniformity of interpretation. This act shall be so interpreted and construed as to effectuate its general purpose to make uniform the law of the states which enact it.

(Source: Laws 1959, p. 2147.) [Formerly Ill. Rev. Stat. 38 §156-5.]

220/6. Short title.

§6. Short title. This Act may be cited as the Uniform Act to Secure the Attendance of Witnesses from Within or Without a State in Criminal Proceedings.
(Source: Laws 1959, p. 2147.) [Formerly Ill. Rev. Stat. 38 §156-6.]

UNIFORM CRIMINAL EXTRADITION ACT

225/1. Definitions.

§1. Definitions. Where appearing in this Act, the term "Governor" includes any person performing the functions of Governor by authority of the law of this State. The term "Executive Authority" includes the Governor, and any person performing the functions of Governor in a state other than this State, and the term "State", referring to a state other than this State, includes any other state or territory, organized or unorganized, of the United States of America.
(Source: Laws 1955, p. 1982.) [Formerly Ill. Rev. Stat. 60 §18.]

225/2. Fugitives from justice: duty of Governor.

§2. Fugitives from Justice: Duty of Governor. Subject to the provisions of this Act, the provisions of the Constitution of the United States controlling, and any and all acts of Congress enacted in pursuance thereof, it is the duty of the Governor of this State to have arrested and delivered up to the Executive Authority of any other state of the United States any person charged in that State with treason, felony, or other crime, who has fled from justice and is found in this State.
(Source: Laws 1955, p. 1982.) [Formerly Ill. Rev. Stat. 60 §19.]

225/3. Form of demand.

§3. Form of Demand. No demand for the extradition of a person charged with crime in another state shall be recognized by the Governor unless in writing alleging, except in cases arising under Section 6 [725 ILCS 225/6], that the accused was present in the demanding state at the time of the commission of the alleged crime, and that thereafter he fled from the state, and accompanied by a copy of an indictment found or by information supported by affidavit in the state having jurisdiction of the crime, or by a copy of an affidavit made before a magistrate there, together with a copy of any warrant which was issued thereupon; or by a copy of a judgment of conviction or of a sentence imposed in execution thereof, together with a statement by the Executive Authority of the demanding state that the person claimed has escaped from confinement or has broken the terms of his bail, probation or parole. The indictment, information, or affidavit made before the magistrate must substantially charge the person demanded with having committed a crime under the law of that state; and the copy of indictment, information, affidavit, judgment of conviction or sentence must be authenticated by the Executive Authority making the demand.
(Source: Laws 1955, p. 1982.) [Formerly Ill. Rev. Stat. 60 §20.]

225/4. Governor may investigate case.

§4. Governor May Investigate Case. When a demand shall be made upon the Governor of this State by the Executive Authority of another state for the surrender of a person so charged with crime, the Governor may call upon the Attorney-General or any prosecuting officer in this State to investigate or assist in investigating the demand, and to report to him the situation and circumstances of the person so demanded, and whether he ought to be surrendered.
(Source: Laws 1955, p. 1982.) [Formerly Ill. Rev. Stat. 60 §21.]

225/5. Extradition of persons imprisoned or awaiting trial in another state or who have left the demanding state under compulsion.

§5. Extradition of Persons Imprisoned or Awaiting Trial in Another State or Who Have Left the Demanding State Under Compulsion. When it is desired to have returned to this State a person charged in this State with a crime, and such person is imprisoned or is held under criminal proceedings then pending against him in another state, the Governor of this State may agree with the Executive Authority of such other state for the extradition of such person before the conclusion of such proceedings or his term of sentence in such other state, upon condition that such person be returned to such other state at the expense of this State as soon as the prosecution in this State is terminated.

The Governor of this State may also surrender on demand of the Executive Authority of any other state any person in this State who is charged in the manner provided in Section 23 of this Act [725 ILCS 225/23] with having violated the laws of the state whose Executive Authority is making the demand, even though such person left the demanding state involuntarily.
(Source: Laws 1955, p. 1982.) [Formerly Ill. Rev. Stat. 60 §22.]

225/6. Extradition of persons not present in demanding state at time of commission of crime.

§6. Extradition of Persons Not Present in Demanding State at Time of Commission of Crime. The Governor of this State may also surrender, on demand of the Executive Authority of any other state, any person in this State charged in such other state in the manner provided in Section 3 [725 ILCS 225/3] with committing an act in this State, or in a third state, intentionally resulting in a crime in the state whose Executive Authority is making the demand.
(Source: Laws 1955, p. 1982.) [Formerly Ill. Rev. Stat. 60 §23.]

225/7. Issue of Governor's warrant of arrest; its recitals.

§7. Issue of Governor's Warrant of Arrest; Its Recitals. If the Governor decides that the demand should be complied with, he shall sign a warrant of arrest, which shall be sealed with the state seal, and be directed to any peace officer or other person whom he may think fit to entrust with the execution thereof. The warrant must substantially recite the facts necessary to the validity of its issuance.

(Source: Laws 1955, p. 1982.) [Formerly Ill. Rev. Stat. 60 §24.]

225/8. Manner and place of execution.

§8. Manner and Place of Execution. Such warrant shall authorize the peace officer or other person to whom directed to arrest the accused at any time and any place where he may be found within the state and to command the aid of all peace officers or other persons in the execution of the warrant, and to deliver the accused, subject to the provisions of this Act to the duly authorized agent of the demanding state.

(Source: Laws 1955, p. 1982.) [Formerly Ill. Rev. Stat. 60 §25.]

225/9. Authority of arresting officer.

§9. Authority of Arresting Officer. Every such peace officer or other person empowered to make the arrest, shall have the same authority, in arresting the accused, to command assistance therein, as peace officers have by law in the execution of any criminal process directed to them, with like penalties against those who refuse their assistance.

(Source: Laws 1955, p. 1982.) [Formerly Ill. Rev. Stat. 60 §26.]

225/10. Rights of accused person: application for relief by habeas corpus: appeals.

§10. Rights of Accused Person: Application for relief by Habeas Corpus: Appeals. No person arrested upon such warrant shall be delivered over to the agent whom the Executive Authority demanding him shall have appointed to receive him unless he shall first be taken forthwith before a judge of the circuit court of the county wherein he is arrested who shall inform him of the demand made for his surrender and of the crime with which he is charged, and that he has the right to demand and procure within a reasonable time and opportunity, not less than 24 hours, legal counsel; and if the prisoner or his counsel shall state that he or they desire to test the legality of his arrest, the judge of such court shall fix a reasonable time to be allowed him within which to apply for relief by habeas corpus. When such relief is applied for, notice thereof, and of the time and place of hearing thereon, shall be given to the prosecuting officer of the county in which the arrest is made and in which the accused is in custody, and to the agent of the demanding state.

Either party may take an appeal from the judgment or order of the circuit court, as in other civil cases.

(Source: P.A. 81-243.) [Formerly Ill. Rev. Stat. 60 §27.]

225/11. Penalty for non-compliance with preceding section.

§11. Penalty for non-compliance with preceding section. Any officer who shall deliver to the agent for extradition of the demanding state a person in his custody under the Governor's warrant, in wilful disobedience to the last section [725 ILCS 225/10], shall be guilty of a Class B misdemeanor.

(Source: P.A. 77-2517.) [Formerly Ill. Rev. Stat. 60 §28.]

225/12. Confinement in jail when necessary.

§12. Confinement in Jail When Necessary. The officer or persons executing the Governor's warrant of arrest, or the agent of the demanding state to whom the prisoner may have been delivered may, when necessary, confine the prisoner in the jail of any county or city through which he may pass; and the keeper of such jail must receive and safely keep the prisoner until the officer or person having charge of him is ready to proceed on his route, such officer or person being chargeable with the expense of keeping.

The officer or agent of a demanding state to whom a prisoner may have been delivered following extradition proceedings in another state, or to whom a prisoner may have been delivered after waiving extradition in such other state, and who is passing through this state with such a prisoner for the purpose of immediately returning such prisoner to the demanding state may, when necessary, confine the prisoner in the jail of any county or city through which he may pass; and the keeper of such jail must receive and safely keep the prisoner until the officer or agent having charge of him is ready to proceed on his route, such officer or agent, however, being chargeable with the expense of keeping; provided, however, that such officer or agent shall produce and show to the keeper of such jail satisfactory written evidence of the fact that he is actually transporting such prisoner to the demanding state after a requisition by the Executive Authority of such demanding state. Such prisoner shall not be entitled to demand a new requisition while in this State.
(Source: Laws 1955, p. 1982.) [Formerly Ill. Rev. Stat. 60 §29.]

225/13. Arrest prior to requisition.

§13. Arrest Prior to Requisition. Whenever any person within this State shall be charged on the oath of any credible person before any judge of this State with the commission of any crime in any other state and, except in cases arising under Section 6 [725 ILCS 225/6], with having fled from justice, or with having been convicted of a crime in that state and having escaped from confinement, or having broken the terms of his bail, probation or parole, or whenever complaint shall have been made before any judge in this State setting forth on the affidavit of any credible person in another state that a crime has been committed in such other state and that the accused has been charged in such state with the commission of the crime, and, except in cases arising under Section 6, has fled from justice, or with having been convicted of a crime in that state and having escaped from confinement, or having broken the terms of his bail, probation or parole and is believed to be in this State, the judge shall issue a warrant directed to any peace officer commanding him to apprehend the person named therein, wherever he may be found in this State, and to bring him before the same or any other judge or court who or which may be available in or convenient of access to the place where the arrest may be made, to answer the charge or complaint and affidavit, and a certified copy of the sworn charge or complaint and affidavit upon which the warrant is issued shall be attached to the warrant.
(Source: P.A. 77-1256.) [Formerly Ill. Rev. Stat. 60 §30.]

225/14. Arrest without a warrant.

§14. Arrest Without a Warrant. The arrest of a person may be lawfully made also by any peace officer or a private person, without a warrant upon reasonable information that the accused stands charged in the courts of a state with a crime punishable by death or imprisonment for a term exceeding one year, but when so arrested the accused must be taken before a judge with all practicable speed and complaint must be made against him under oath setting forth the ground for the arrest as in the preceding Section; and thereafter his answer shall be heard as if he had been arrested on a warrant.
(Source: P.A. 77-1256.) [Formerly Ill. Rev. Stat. 60 §31.]

225/15. Commitment to await requisition—Bail.

§15. Commitment to await requisition—Bail. If from the examination before the judge it appears that the person held is the person charged with having committed the crime alleged and, except in cases arising under Section 6 [725 ILCS 225/6], that he has fled from justice, the judge must, by a warrant reciting the accusation, commit him to the county jail for such a time not exceeding 30 days and specified in the warrant, as will enable the arrest of the accused to be made under a warrant of the Governor on a requisition of the Executive Authority of the state having jurisdiction of the offense, unless the accused give bail as provided in the next section, or until he shall be legally discharged.
(Source: P.A. 77-1256.) [Formerly Ill. Rev. Stat. 60 §32.]

225/16. Bail—In what cases—Conditions of bond.

§16. Bail—In What Cases—Conditions of Bond. Unless the offense with which the prisoner is charged is shown to be an offense punishable by death or life imprisonment under the laws of the state in which it was committed, a judge in this State may admit the person arrested to bail by bond, with sufficient sureties, and in such sum as he deems proper, conditioned for his appearance before him at a time specified in such bond, and for his surrender, to be arrested upon the warrant of the Governor of this State.
(Source: P.A. 77-1256.) [Formerly Ill. Rev. Stat. 60 §33.]

225/17. Extension of time of commitment—Adjournment.

§17. Extension of Time of Commitment—Adjournment. If the accused is not arrested under warrant of the Governor by the expiration of the time specified in the warrant or bond, a judge may discharge him or may recommit him for a further period not to exceed 60 days, or a judge may again take bail for his appearance and surrender, as provided in Section 16 [725 ILCS 225/16] but within a period not to exceed 60 days after the date of such new bond.
(Source: P.A. 77-1256.) [Formerly Ill. Rev. Stat. 60 §34.]

225/18. Forfeiture of bail.

§18. Forfeiture of Bail. If the prisoner is admitted to bail, and fails to appear and surrender himself according to the conditions of his bond, the judge, by proper order, shall declare the bond forfeited and order his immediate arrest without warrant if he be within this State. Recovery may be had on such bond in the name of the state as in the case of other bonds given by the accused in criminal proceedings within this State.
(Source: P.A. 77-1256.) [Formerly Ill. Rev. Stat. 60 §35.]

225/19. Persons under criminal prosecution in this State at time of requisition.

§19. Persons Under Criminal Prosecution in This State at Time of Requisition. If a criminal prosecution has been instituted against such person under the laws of this State and is still pending the Governor, in his discretion, either may surrender him on demand of the Executive Authority of another state or hold him until he has been tried and discharged or convicted and punished in this State.
(Source: Laws 1955, p. 1982.) [Formerly Ill. Rev. Stat. 60 §36.]

225/20. Guilt or innocence of the accused, when inquired into.

§20. Guilt or Innocence of the Accused, when Inquired into. The guilt or innocence of the accused as to the crime of which he is charged may not be inquired into by the Governor or in any proceeding after the demand for extradition accompanied by a charge of crime in legal form as above provided shall have been presented to the Governor, except as it may be involved in identifying the person held as the person charged with the crime.
(Source: Laws 1955, p. 1982.) [Formerly Ill. Rev. Stat. 60 §37.]

225/21. Governor may recall warrant or issue alias.

§21. Governor May Recall Warrant or Issue Alias. The Governor may recall his warrant of arrest or may issue another warrant whenever he deems proper.
(Source: Laws 1955, p. 1982.) [Formerly Ill. Rev. Stat. 60 §38.]

225/22. Fugitives from this state; duty of Governors.

§22. Fugitives from This State; Duty of Governors. Whenever the Governor of this State shall demand a person charged with crime or with escaping from confinement or breaking the terms of his bail, probation or parole in this State, from the Executive Authority of any other state, or from the chief justice or an associate justice of the Supreme Court of the District of Columbia authorized to receive such demand under the laws of the United States, he shall issue a warrant under the seal of this State, to some agent, commanding him to receive the person so charged if delivered to him and convey him to the proper officer of the county in this State in which the offense was committed.
(Source: Laws 1955, p. 1982.) [Formerly Ill. Rev. Stat. 60 §39.]

225/23. Application for issuance of requisition—By whom made—Contents.

§23. Application for issuance of requisition—By whom made—Contents. I. When the return to this State of a person charged with crime in this State is required, the prosecuting attorney shall present to the Governor his written application for a requisition for the return of the person charged, in which application shall be stated the name of the person so charged, the crime charged against him, the approximate time, place and circumstances of its commission, the state in which he is believed to be, including the location of the accused therein at the time the application is made and certifying that, in the opinion of the said prosecuting attorney the ends of justice require the arrest and return of the accused to this State for trial and that the proceeding is not instituted to enforce a private claim.

II. When the return to this State is required of a person who has been convicted of a crime in this State and has escaped from confinement or broken the terms of his bail, probation or parole, the prosecuting attorney of the county in which the offense was committed, the parole and pardon board, or the warden of the institution or sheriff of the county, from which escape was made, shall present to the Governor a written application for a requisition for the return of such person, in which application shall be stated the name of the person, the crime of which he was convicted, the circumstances of his escape from confinement or of the breach of the terms of his bail, probation or parole, the state in which he is believed to be, including the location of the person therein at the time application is made.

III. The application shall be verified by affidavit, shall be executed in duplicate and shall be accompanied by two certified copies of the indictment returned, or information and affidavit filed, or of the complaint made to the judge, stating the offense with which the accused is charged, or of the judgment of conviction or of the sentence. The prosecuting officer, parole and pardon board, warden or sheriff may also attach such further affidavits and other documents in duplicate as he shall deem proper to be submitted with such application. One copy of the application, with the action of the Governor indicated by endorsement thereon, and one of the certified copies of the indictment, complaint, information, and affidavits, or of the judgment of conviction or of the sentence shall be filed in the office of the Secretary of State to remain of record in that office. The other copies of all papers shall be forwarded with the Governor's requisition.
(Source: P.A. 77-1256.) [Formerly Ill. Rev. Stat. 60 §40.]

225/24. Costs and expenses.

§24. Costs and expenses. When the punishment of the crime shall be the confinement of the criminal in the penitentiary, the expenses shall be paid out of the state treasury, on the certificate of the Governor and warrant of the State Comptroller; and in all other cases they shall be paid out of the county treasury in the county wherein the crime is alleged to have been committed. The expenses shall be the fees paid to the officers of the asylum state, and all necessary travel in returning such fugitives. The necessary travel expenses allowed shall be the same, as near as may be, as the amounts for travel allowed pursuant to the rules and regulations of the Illinois Department of Central Management Services. Before such accounts shall be certified by the Governor, or paid by the county, they shall be verified by affidavit, and certified to by the state's attorney of the county wherein the crime is alleged to have been committed, and submitted therewith shall be the agent's authority or a certified copy of the waiver of extradition.
(Source: P.A. 82-789.) [Formerly Ill. Rev. Stat. 60 §41.]

225/24.1. Transportation of released prisoners.

§24.1. Transportation of released prisoners. (a) Whenever a person is brought into this State on an extradition warrant or upon waiver of extradition to be tried for an offense within this State and is subsequently released from custody without being convicted of the offense for which he was brought into this State to be tried, it shall be the duty of the peace officer, sheriff or other official from whom he was released from custody to provide or offer the person transportation to the nearest public transportation facility if the municipality or county in which he was held does not have a public transportation facility.

(b) As used in this Section:

(1) "Public transportation facility" means a terminal or other place where one may obtain public transportation; and

(2) "Public transportation" means the transportation or conveyance of persons by means available to the general public, except for transportation by automobiles not used for conveyance of the general public as passengers.
(Source: P.A. 86-1263.) [Formerly Ill. Rev. Stat. 60 §41.1.]

225/25. Immunity from service of process in certain civil actions.

§25. Immunity from Service of Process in Certain Civil Actions. A person brought into this State by, or after waiver of, extradition based on a criminal charge shall not be subject to service of personal process in civil actions arising out of the same facts as the criminal proceeding to answer which he is being or has been returned, until he has been convicted in the criminal proceeding, or, if acquitted, until he has had reasonable opportunity to return to the state from which he was extradited.
(Source: Laws 1955, p. 1982.) [Formerly Ill. Rev. Stat. 60 §42.]

225/26. Written waiver of extradition proceedings.

§26. Written waiver of extradition proceedings. Any person arrested in this State charged with having committed any crime in another state or alleged to have escaped from confinement, or broken the terms of his bail, probation or parole may waive the issuance and service of the warrant provided for in Sections 7 and 8 [725 ILCS 225/7 and 225/8] and all other procedure incidental to extradition proceedings, by executing or subscribing in the presence of a judge of the circuit court a writing which states that he consents to return to the demanding state; provided, however, that before such waiver shall be executed or subscribed by such person it shall be the duty of such judge to inform such person of his rights to the issuance and service of a warrant of extradition and to obtain a relief by habeas corpus as provided for in Section 10 [725 ILCS 225/10].

If and when such consent has been duly executed it shall forthwith be forwarded to the office of the Governor of this State and filed therein. The judge shall direct the officer having such person in custody to deliver forthwith such person to the duly accredited agent or agents of the demanding state, and shall deliver or cause to be delivered to such agent or agents a copy of such consent; provided, however, that nothing in this Section shall be deemed to limit the rights of the accused person to return voluntarily and without formality to the demanding state, nor shall this waiver procedure be deemed to be an exclusive procedure or to limit the powers, rights or duties of the officers of the demanding state or of this State.

(Source: P.A. 81-243.) [Formerly Ill. Rev. Stat. 60 §43.]

225/27. Non-waiver by this State.

§27. Non-Waiver by This State. Nothing in this Act contained shall be deemed to constitute a waiver by this State of its right, power or privilege to try such demanded person for crime committed within this State, or of its right, power or privilege to regain custody of such person by extradition proceedings or otherwise for the purpose of trial, sentence or punishment for any crime committed within this State, nor shall any proceedings had under this Act which result in, or fail to result in, extradition be deemed a waiver by this State of any of its rights, privileges or jurisdiction in any way whatsoever.

(Source: Laws 1955, p. 1982.) [Formerly Ill. Rev. Stat. 60 §44.]

225/28. No right of asylum. No immunity from other criminal prosecutions while in this State.

§28. No Right of Asylum. No Immunity from Other Criminal Prosecutions While in This State. After a person has been brought back to this State by, or after waiver of extradition proceedings, he may be tried in this State for other crimes which he may be charged with having committed here as well as that specified in the requisition for his extradition.

(Source: Laws 1955, p. 1982.) [Formerly Ill. Rev. Stat. 60 §45.]

225/29. Interpretation.

§29. Interpretation. The provisions of this Act shall be so interpreted and construed as to effectuate its general purposes to make uniform the law of those states which enact it.

(Source: Laws 1955, p. 1982.) [Formerly Ill. Rev. Stat. 60 §46.]

225/30. Constitutionality.

§30. Constitutionality. If any provision of this Act or the application thereof to any person or circumstances is held invalid, such invalidity shall not affect other provisions or applications of the act which can be given effect without the invalid provision or application, and to this end the provisions of this Act are declared to be severable.

(Source: Laws 1955, p. 1982.) [Formerly Ill. Rev. Stat. 60 §47.]

225/32. Short title.

§32. Short title. This Act may be cited as the Uniform Criminal Extradition Act.

(Source: Laws 1955, p. 1982.) [Formerly Ill. Rev. Stat. 60 §49.]

UNIFORM RENDITION OF ACCUSED PERSONS ACT

Sec.

230/1. Arrest of accused person illegally in State.

§1. Arrest of Accused Person Illegally in State. (a) If a person who has been charged with crime in another state and released from custody prior to final judgment, including the final disposition of any appeal, is alleged to have violated the terms and conditions of his release, and is present in this State, a designated agent of the court, judge, or magistrate which authorized the release may request the issuance of a warrant for the arrest of the person and an order authorizing his return to the demanding court, judge, or magistrate. Before the warrant is issued, the designated agent must file with the circuit court the following documents:

(1) an affidavit stating the name and whereabouts of the person whose removal is sought, the crime with which the person was charged, the time and place of the crime charged, and the status of the proceedings against him;

(2) a certified copy of the order or other document specifying the terms and conditions under which the person was released from custody; and

(3) a certified copy of an order of the demanding court, judge, or magistrate stating the manner in which the terms and the conditions of the release have been violated and designating the affiant its agent for seeking removal of the person.

(b) Upon initially determining that the affiant is a designated agent of the demanding court, judge, or magistrate, and that there is probable cause for believing that the person whose removal is sought has violated the terms or conditions of his release, the circuit court shall issue a warrant to a law enforcement officer of this State for the person's arrest.

(c) The circuit court shall notify the State's Attorney of its action and shall direct him to investigate the case to ascertain the validity of the affidavits and documents required by subsection (a) and the identity and authority of the affiant.

(Source: P.A. 77-1282.) [Formerly Ill. Rev. Stat. 38 §157-21.]

230/2. Hearing and right to counsel.

§2. Hearing and Right to Counsel. (a) The person whose removal is sought shall be brought before the circuit court immediately upon arrest pursuant to the warrant; whereupon such circuit court shall set a time and place for hearing, and shall advise the person of his right to have the assistance of counsel, to confront the witnesses against him, and to produce evidence in his own behalf at the hearing.

(b) The person whose removal is sought may at this time in writing waive the hearing and agree to be returned to the demanding court, judge or magistrate. If a waiver is executed, the circuit court shall issue an order pursuant to Section 3 of this Act [725 ILCS 230/3].

(c) The circuit court may impose conditions of release authorized by the laws of this State which will reasonably assure the appearance at the hearing of the person whose removal is sought.

(Source: P.A. 77-1282.) [Formerly Ill. Rev. Stat. 38 §157-22.]

230/3. Order of return to demanding court.

§3. Order of return to Demanding Court. The State's Attorney shall appear at the hearing and report to the circuit court the results of his investigation. If the circuit court finds that the affiant is a designated agent of the demanding court, judge, or magistrate and that the person whose removal is sought was released from custody by the demanding court, judge or magistrate and that

the person has violated the terms or conditions of his release, the circuit court shall issue an order authorizing the return of the person to the custody of the demanding court, judge, or magistrate forthwith.
(Source: P.A. 77-1282.) [Formerly Ill. Rev. Stat. 38 §157-23.]

230/4. Severability.

§4. Severability. If any provision of this Act or the application thereof to any person or circumstance is held invalid, the invalidity does not affect other provisions or applications of the Act which can be given effect without the invalid provision or application, and to this end the provisions of this Act are severable.
(Source: P.A. 76-1189.) [Formerly Ill. Rev. Stat. 38 §157-24.]

230/5. Uniformity of interpretation.

§5. Uniformity of Interpretation. This Act shall be so construed as to effectuate its general purpose to make uniform the law of those states which enact it.
(Source: P.A. 76-1189.) [Formerly Ill. Rev. Stat. 38 §157-25.]

230/6. Short title.

§6. Short Title. This Act may be cited as the Uniform Rendition of Accused Persons Act.
(Source: P.A. 76-1189.) [Formerly Ill. Rev. Stat. 38 §157-26.]

UNIFORM RENDITION OF PRISONERS AS WITNESSES IN CRIMINAL PROCEEDINGS ACT

Sec.

235/1. Definitions.

§1. Definitions. As used in this act,

(a) "Witness" means a person who is confined in a penal institution in any state and whose testimony is desired in another state in any criminal proceeding or investigation by a grand jury or in any criminal action before a court.

(b) "Penal institution" includes a jail, prison, penitentiary, house of correction, or other place of penal detention.

(c) "State" includes any state of the United States, the District of Columbia, the Commonwealth of Puerto Rico, and any territory of the United States.
(Source: Laws 1963, p. 2171.) [Formerly Ill. Rev. Stat. 38 §157-1.]

235/2. Summoning witness in this State to testify in another state.

§2. Summoning Witness in this State to Testify in Another State. A judge of a state court of record in another state, which by its laws has made provision for commanding persons confined in penal institutions within that state to attend and testify in this state, may certify (1) that there is a criminal proceeding or investigation by a grand jury or a criminal action pending in the court, (2) that a person who is confined in a penal institution in this state may be a material witness in the proceeding, investigation, or action, and (3) that his presence will be required during a specified time. Upon presentation of the

certificate to any judge having jurisdiction over the person confined, and upon notice to the Attorney General, the judge in this state shall fix a time and place for a hearing and shall make an order directed to the person having custody of the prisoner requiring that the prisoner be produced before him at the hearing.
(Source: Laws 1963, p. 2171.) [Formerly Ill. Rev. Stat. 38 §157-2.]

235/3. Court order.

§3. Court order. If at the hearing the judge determines (1) that the witness may be material and necessary, (2) that his attending and testifying are not adverse to the interests of this State or to the health or legal rights of the witness, (3) that the laws of the state in which he is requested to testify will give him protection from arrest and the service of civil and criminal process because of any act committed prior to his arrival in the state under the order, and (4) that as a practical matter the possibility is negligible that the witness may be subject to arrest or to the service of civil or criminal process in any state through which he will be required to pass, the judge shall issue an order, with a copy of the certificate attached, (a) directing the witness to attend and testify, (b) directing the person having custody of the witness to produce him, in the court where the criminal action is pending, or where the grand jury investigation is pending, at a time and place specified in the order, and (c) prescribing such conditions as the judge shall determine.
(Source: Laws 1963, p. 2171.) [Formerly Ill. Rev. Stat. 38 §157-3.]

235/4. Terms and conditions.

§4. Terms and Conditions. The order to the witness and to the person having custody of the witness shall provide for the return of the witness at the conclusion of his testimony, proper safeguards on his custody, and proper financial reimbursement or prepayment by the requesting jurisdiction for all expenses incurred in the production and return of the witness, and may prescribe such other conditions as the judge thinks proper or necessary. The order shall not become effective until the judge of the state requesting the witness enters an order directing compliance with the conditions prescribed.
(Source: Laws 1963, p. 2171.) [Formerly Ill. Rev. Stat. 38 §157-4.]

235/5. Exceptions.

§5. Exceptions. This act does not apply to any person in this State confined as mentally ill, in need of mental treatment, or under sentence of death.
(Source: Laws 1963, p. 2171.) [Formerly Ill. Rev. Stat. 38 §157-5.]

235/6. Prisoner from another state summoned to testify in this State.

§6. Prisoner from Another State Summoned to Testify in this State. If a person confined in a penal institution in any other state may be a material witness in a criminal action pending in a court of record or in a grand jury investigation in this State, a judge of the court may certify (1) that there is a criminal proceeding or investigation by a grand jury or a criminal action pending in the court, (2) that a person who is confined in a penal institution in the other state may be a material witness in the proceeding, investigation, or action, and (3) that his presence will be required during a specified time. The certificate shall be presented to a judge of a court of record in the other state having jurisdiction over the prisoner confined, and a notice shall be given to the Attorney General of the state in which the prisoner is confined.
(Source: Laws 1963, p. 2171.) [Formerly Ill. Rev. Stat. 38 §157-6.]

235/7. Compliance.

§7. Compliance. The judge of the court in this state may enter an order directing compliance with the terms and conditions prescribed by the judge of the state in which the witness is confined.
(Source: Laws 1963, p. 2171.) [Formerly Ill. Rev. Stat. 38 §157-7.]

235/8. Exemption from arrest and service of process.

§8. Exemption from Arrest and Service of Process. If a witness from another state comes into or passes through this state under an order directing him to attend and testify in this or another state, he shall not while in this state pursuant to the order be subject to arrest or the service of process, civil or criminal, because of any act committed prior to his arrival in this state under the order.
(Source: Laws 1963, p. 2171.) [Formerly Ill. Rev. Stat. 38 §157-8.]

235/9. Uniformity of interpretation.

§9. Uniformity of Interpretation. This act shall be so construed as to effectuate its general purpose to make uniform the law of those states which enact it.
(Source: Laws 1963, p. 2171.) [Formerly Ill. Rev. Stat. 38 §157-9.]

235/10. Short title.

§10. Short Title. This act may be cited as the "Uniform Rendition of Prisoners as Witnesses in Criminal Proceedings Act".
(Source: Laws 1963, p. 2171.) [Formerly Ill. Rev. Stat. 38 §157-10.]

235/11. Severability clause.

§11. Severability Clause. If any provision of this act or the application thereof to any person or circumstance is held invalid, the invalidity shall not affect other provisions or applications of the act which can be given effect without the invalid provision or application, and to this end the provisions of this act are severable.
(Source: Laws 1963, p. 2171.) [Formerly Ill. Rev. Stat. 38 §157-11.]

VIOLENT CRIME VICTIMS ASSISTANCE ACT

240/1. Short title.

§1. Short title. This Act shall be known and may be cited as the "Violent Crime Victims Assistance Act".
(Source: P.A. 83-908.) [Formerly Ill. Rev. Stat. 70 §501.]

240/2. Legislative findings and intent.

§2. Legislative findings and intent. The General Assembly finds that when crime strikes, the chief concern of criminal justice agencies has been apprehending and dealing with the criminal, and that the victim or witness is frequently forgotten or further victimized by the criminal justice system. Nevertheless, the single most important determinant of whether a case is resolved is the information and assistance provided by the victim or witness.

It is, therefore, the intent of the General Assembly to provide ways of improving attitudes of victims and witnesses toward the criminal justice system and to provide for faster and more complete victim recovery from the effects of crime through the establishment of victim and witness assistance centers.

All services and practices of each center shall further or complement the following goals:

(a) Assist the criminal justice agencies in giving more consideration and personal attention to victims and witnesses of violent crime;

(b) Sensitize law enforcement officials and others who come into contact with crime victims and witnesses;

(c) Attempt to decrease the incidence of unreported crimes;

(d) Assure that victims and witnesses are informed of the progress of the cases in which they are involved;

(e) Encourage public use of the services made available under this Act.

This Act shall be construed to complement the provisions of the "Crime Victims Compensation Act" [740 ILCS 45/1 et seq.] in meeting their common goals, but this Act shall be administered and funded as provided herein.

(Source: P.A. 83-908.) [Formerly Ill. Rev. Stat. 70 §502.]

240/3. Definitions.

§3. Definitions. As used in this Act:

(a) "Advisory Commission" means the Violent Crimes Advisory Commission created in Section 4 of this Act [725 ILCS 240/4];

(b) "Fund" means the Violent Crime Victims Assistance Fund created in Section 10 of this Act [725 ILCS 240/10];

(c) "Agency" or "agencies" means any federal, State, local or private entity which provides, operates or coordinates victim and witness assistance programs.

(Source: P.A. 83-908.) [Formerly Ill. Rev. Stat. 70 §503.]

240/4. Advisory Commission created.

§4. Advisory Commission created. There is created a Violent Crimes Advisory Commission, hereinafter called the Advisory Commission, consisting of 14 members: the Attorney General, or his or her designee who shall serve as Chairperson; the Director of Children and Family Services; 2 members of the House of Representatives, 1 to be appointed by the Speaker of the House and 1 to be appointed by the Minority Leader of the House; 2 members of the Senate, 1 to be appointed by the President of the Senate and 1 to be appointed by the Minority Leader of the Senate; and the following to be appointed by the Attorney General: 1 police officer; 1 State's Attorney from a county in Illinois; 1 health services professional possessing experience and expertise in dealing with the victims of violent crime; and 5 members of the public, one of whom shall be a senior citizen age 60 or over, possessing experience and expertise in dealing with victims of violent crime, including experience with victims of domestic and sexual violence. The members of the Advisory Commission shall be appointed biennially for terms expiring on July 1 of each succeeding odd-numbered year and shall serve until their respective successors are appointed or until termination of their legislative service, whichever first occurs. The members of the Commission shall receive no compensation for their services but shall be reimbursed for necessary expenses incurred in the performance of their duties. Vacancies occurring because of death or resignation shall be filled by the appointing authority for the group in which the vacancy occurs.

Eight members of the Advisory Commission shall constitute a quorum for the transaction of business, and the concurrence of at least 8 members shall be necessary to render a determination, decision or recommendation by the Advisory Committee. In addition to the Attorney General, who shall serve as Chairperson, the Advisory Commission may select such other officers as it deems necessary.

(Source: P.A. 85-1193.) [Formerly Ill. Rev. Stat. 70 §504.]

240/5. Advisory Commission—General responsibilities.

§5. Advisory Commission—General responsibilities. (a) The Advisory Commission shall have the following responsibilities:

(1) To study the operation of all Illinois laws, practices, agencies and organizations which affect victims of crime;

(2) To promote and conduct studies, research, analysis and investigation of matters affecting the interests of crime victims;

(3) To recommend legislation to develop and improve policies which promote the recognition of the legitimate rights, needs and interests of crime victims;

(4) To serve as a clearinghouse for public information relating to crime victims' problems and programs;

(5) To coordinate, monitor and evaluate the activities of programs operating under this Act;

(6) To make any necessary outreach efforts to encourage the development and maintenance of services throughout the State, with special attention to the regions and neighborhoods with the greatest need for victim assistance services;

(7) To perform other activities, in cooperation with the Attorney General, which the Advisory Commission considers useful to the furtherance of the stated legislative intent;

(8) To make an annual report to the General Assembly.

(b) The Advisory Committee may also perform any of the functions enumerated in subparagraph (a) of this section relative to witnesses to crime.

(Source: P.A. 83-908.) [Formerly Ill. Rev. Stat. 70 §505.]

240/6. Attorney General—Organization of programs.

§6. Attorney General—Organization of Programs. During the period between January 1, 1984 and June 30, 1984, the Attorney General, in cooperation with the Advisory Commission, shall establish rules and regulations for the performance of his or her activities under this Act, including procedures for the designation and funding of victims' assistance centers; thereafter, he or she shall:

(a) Adopt and publicize the concept of victim and witness assistance centers, including guidelines for applications, selection and operation of centers;

(b) Receive and, when appropriate, solicit applications from agencies for funding of centers;

(c) Designate agencies and award grants to operate centers;

(d) Accept any grant, including federal grants, or gift to promote the purposes of this Act.

(Source: P.A. 83-908.) [Formerly Ill. Rev. Stat. 70 §506.]

240/7. Administration of Fund.

§7. Administration of Fund. The Attorney General shall administer the disbursement of monies collected by the Fund in accordance with the following procedures.

(a) Any public or private nonprofit agency may apply to the Attorney General for selection and funding as a victim and witness assistance center pursuant to this Act.

(b) The Attorney General shall consider the following factors together with any other circumstances he or she deems appropriate in selecting applicants to receive funds and to be designated as victim and witness assistance centers:

(1) Stated goals of applicants;

(2) Commitment and ability to provide the services described in Section 8 of this Act [725 ILCS 240/8];

(3) Number of people to be served and the needs of the community;

(4) Evidence of community support;

(5) Organizational structure of the agency;

(6) Maximization of volunteers.

(c) After evaluation of all applicants, the Attorney General shall select a number of applicants which the Attorney General deems qualified under this Act for designation to receive funding pursuant to this Act for the establishment and operation of the centers. Funding contracts shall be entered into by the Attorney General with each designated applicant on an annual basis. Dispersal of grant funds shall be made on a semi-annual basis. The Attorney General may impose matching funds requirements on grant recipients. The Attorney General may evaluate each recipient prior to each semi-annual fund dispersal and cancel the remaining term of any contract in which the recipient has failed to meet the contract requirements or for any good cause.

(Source: P.A. 87-743.) [Formerly Ill. Rev. Stat. 70 §507.]

240/8. Centers—Services provided.

§8. Centers—Services provided. (a) Each center shall provide one or more of the following services:

(1) Coordinate volunteers to work with criminal justice agencies to provide direct victim services or to establish community support;

(2) Provide assistance to victims of violent crime and their families in obtaining assistance through other official or community resources;

(3) Provide elderly victims of crime with services appropriate to their special needs;

(4) Provide transportation and/or household assistance to those victims participating in the criminal justice process;

(5) Provide victims of domestic and sexual violence with services appropriate to their special needs;

(6) Provide courthouse reception and guidance, including explanation of unfamiliar procedures and bilingual information;

(7) Provide in-person or telephone hot-line assistance to victims;

(8) Provide special counseling facilities and rehabilitation services to victims;

(9) Provide other services as the Commission shall deem appropriate to further the purposes of this Act;

(10) Provide public education on crime and crime victims;

(11) Provide training and sensitization for persons who work with victims of crime;

(12) Provide special counseling facilities and rehabilitation services for child victims of sex offenses;

(13) When applicable, centers shall enter into written networking agreements to provide for the special needs of child victims of violent crimes.

(b) Such centers may provide one or more of the services enumerated in subparagraph (a) of this section for witnesses of crime.

(Source: P.A. 85-1440.) [Formerly Ill. Rev. Stat. 70 §508.]

240/9. Centers—Accountability to Attorney General.

§9. Centers—Accountability to Attorney General. Each center shall provide the Attorney General periodic reports on the activities of the center. Submission of any such reports as the Attorney General shall require is a prerequisite to renewal of any grant awarded under this Act.

(Source: P.A. 83-908.) [Formerly Ill. Rev. Stat. 70 §509.]

240/10. Violent Crime Victims Assistance Fund.

§10. Violent Crime Victims Assistance Fund. (a) The "Violent Crime Victims Assistance Fund" is created as a special fund in the State Treasury to provide monies for the grants to be awarded under this Act.

In addition to any other permitted use of moneys in the Fund, and notwithstanding any restriction on the use of the Fund, moneys in the Violent Crime Victims Assistance Fund may be transferred to the General Revenue Fund as authorized by this amendatory Act of 1992. The General Assembly finds that an excess of moneys exists in the Fund. On February 1, 1992, the Comptroller shall order transferred and the Treasurer shall transfer $3,850,000 (or such lesser amount as may be on deposit in the Fund and unexpended and unobligated on that date) from the Fund to the General Revenue Fund.

(b) On and after September 18, 1986, there shall be added to each fine imposed upon conviction of any felony or conviction of or disposition of supervision for any misdemeanor, or upon conviction of or disposition of supervision for any offense under the Illinois Vehicle Code [625 ILCS 5/1-100 et seq.], exclusive of offenses enumerated in paragraph (a)(2) of Section 6-204 of that Code [625 ILCS 5/6-204], and exclusive of any offense enumerated in Article VI of Chapter 11 of that Code [625 ILCS 5/11-601 et seq.] relating to restrictions, regulations and limitations on the speed at which a motor vehicle is driven or operated, an additional penalty of $4 for each $40, or fraction thereof, of fine imposed. Such additional amounts shall be assessed by the court and shall be collected by the Clerk of the Circuit Court in addition to the fine and costs in the case. Each such additional penalty collected under this subsection (b) or subsection (c) of this Section shall be remitted by the Clerk of the Circuit Court within one month after receipt to the State Treasurer for deposit into the Violent Crime Victims Assistance Fund, except as provided in subsection (g) of this Section. Such additional penalty shall not be considered a part of the fine for purposes of any reduction made in the fine for time served either before or after sentencing. Not later than March 1 of each year the Clerk of the Circuit Court shall submit to the State Comptroller a report of the amount of funds remitted by him to the State Treasurer under this Section during the preceding calendar year. Except as otherwise provided by Supreme Court Rules, if a court in sentencing an offender levies a gross amount for fine, costs, fees and penalties, the amount of the additional penalty provided for herein shall be computed on the amount remaining after deducting from the gross amount levied all fees of the Circuit Clerk, the State's Attorney and the Sheriff. After deducting from the gross amount levied the fees and additional penalty provided for herein, less any other additional penalties provided by law, the clerk shall remit the net balance remaining to the entity authorized by law to receive the fine imposed in the case. For purposes of this Section "fees of the Circuit Clerk" shall include, if applicable, the fee provided for under Section 27.3a of the Clerks of Courts Act [705 ILCS 105/27.3a] and the fee, if applicable, payable to the county in which the violation occurred pursuant to Section 5-1101 of the Counties Code [55 ILCS 5/5-1101].

(c) When any person is convicted in Illinois on or after August 28, 1986, of an offense listed below, or placed on supervision for such an offense on or after September 18, 1986, the court which enters the conviction or order for supervision, if it does not impose a fine, shall impose, in addition to any other penalty authorized by law, a charge in accordance with the following schedule:

(1) $25, for any crime of violence as defined in subsection (c) of Section 2 of the Crime Victims Compensation Act [740 ILCS 45/2]; and

(2) $20, for any other felony or misdemeanor, excluding any conservation offense.

Such charge shall not be subject to the provisions of Section 110-14 of the Code of Criminal Procedure of 1963 [725 ILCS 5/110-14].

(d) Monies forfeited, and proceeds from the sale of property forfeited and seized, under the forfeiture provisions of Section 11-20.1A of the Criminal Code of 1961 [720 ILCS 5/11-20.1A] shall be accepted for the Violent Crime Victims Assistance Fund.

(e) Investment income which is attributable to the investment of monies in the Violent Crime Victims Assistance Fund shall be credited to that fund for uses specified in this Act. The Treasurer shall provide the Attorney General a monthly status report on the amount of money in the Fund.

(f) Monies from the fund may be granted on and after July 1, 1984.

(g) All amounts and charges imposed under this Section for any violation of Chapters 3, 4, 6, and 11 of the Illinois Vehicle Code [625 ILCS 5/3-100 et seq., 5/4-100, 5/6-100, and 5/11-100], or a similar provision of a local ordinance, or any violation of the Child Passenger Protection Act [625 ILCS 25/1 et seq.], or a similar provision of a local ordinance, shall be collected and disbursed by the circuit clerk as provided under Section 27.5 of the Clerks of Courts Act [705 ILCS 105/27.5].

(Source: P.A. 86-1475; 87-670; 87-838; 87-895.) [Formerly Ill. Rev. Stat. 70 §510.]

240/11. Severability.

§11. Severability. The invalidity of any provision of this Act shall not affect the validity of the remainder of this Act.

(Source: P.A. 83-908.) [Formerly Ill. Rev. Stat. 70 §511.]

WITNESS PROTECTION ACT

Sec.

245/1. Short title.

§1. This Act shall be known and may be cited as the "Witness Protection Act".

(Source: P.A. 77-1772.) [Formerly Ill. Rev. Stat. 38 §155-21.]

245/2. Grants to attorneys; Law Enforcement Commission.

§2. The Illinois Law Enforcement Commission with respect to federal grant moneys received by such Commission prior to January 1, 1983, may make grants prior to April 1, 1983 to the several states attorneys of the State of Illinois. Such grants may be made to any states attorney who applies for funds to provide for protection of witnesses and the families and property of witnesses involved in criminal investigations and prosecutions.

(Source: P.A. 82-1039.) [Formerly Ill. Rev. Stat. 38 §155-22.]

245/3. Salaries and costs.

§3. The protection which may be provided includes, but is not limited to the salaries and related costs of personal guards, protective custody and relocation costs. No such protection may be provided without the written consent of the witness.

(Source: P.A. 77-1772.) [Formerly Ill. Rev. Stat. 38 §155-23.]

245/4. Grants made pursuant to rules and regulations.

§4. All grants made pursuant to this Act shall be made in accordance with this Act and rules and regulations established prior to January 1, 1983 by the Illinois Law Enforcement Commission.

(Source: P.A. 82-1039.) [Formerly Ill. Rev. Stat. 38 §155-24.]

This page intentionally left blank.

CHAPTER 730
CORRECTIONS

UNIFIED CODE OF CORRECTIONS

CHAPTER I. GENERAL PROVISIONS

ARTICLE I. SHORT TITLE, PURPOSES

5/1-1-1. Short title.

§1-1-1. Short title. This Code shall be known and may be cited as the Unified Code of Corrections.
(Source: P.A. 77-2097.) [Formerly Ill. Rev. Stat. 38 §1001-1-1.]

5/1-1-2. Purposes.

§1-1-2. Purposes. The purposes of this Code of Corrections are to:

(a) prescribe sanctions proportionate to the seriousness of the offenses and permit the recognition of differences in rehabilitation possibilities among individual offenders;

(b) forbid and prevent the commission of offenses;

(c) prevent arbitrary or oppressive treatment of persons adjudicated offenders or delinquents; and

(d) restore offenders to useful citizenship.
(Source: P.A. 77-2097.) [Formerly Ill. Rev. Stat. 38 §1001-1-2.]

[CHAPTER II. RESERVED]

CHAPTER III. DEPARTMENT OF CORRECTIONS

ARTICLE 1. DEFINITIONS

5/3-1-1. Meanings of words and phrases.

§3-1-1. Meanings of Words and Phrases. For the purposes of this Chapter, the words and phrases described in this Article have the meanings designated in this Article, except when a particular context clearly requires a different meaning.
(Source: P.A. 77-2097.) [Formerly Ill. Rev. Stat. 38 §1003-1-1.]

5/3-1-2. Definitions.

§3-1-2. Definitions. (a) "Chief Administrative Officer" means the person designated by the Director to exercise the powers and duties of the Department of Corrections in regard to committed persons within a correctional institution or facility, and includes the superintendent of any juvenile institution or facility.

(b) "Commitment" means a judicially determined placement in the custody of the Department of Corrections on the basis of delinquency or conviction.

(c) "Committed Person" is a person committed to the Department, however a committed person shall not be considered to be an employee of the Department of Corrections for any purpose, including eligibility for a pension, benefits, or any other compensation or rights or privileges which may be provided to employees of the Department.

(d) "Correctional Institution or Facility" means any building or part of a building where committed persons are kept in a secured manner.

(e) "Department" means the Department of Corrections of this State.

(f) "Director" means the Director of the Department of Corrections.

(g) "Discharge" means the final termination of a commitment to the Department of Corrections.

(h) "Discipline" means the rules and regulations for the maintenance of order and the protection of persons and property within the institutions and facilities of the Department and their enforcement.

(i) "Escape" means the intentional and unauthorized absence of a committed person from the custody of the Department.

(j) "Furlough" means an authorized leave of absence from the Department of Corrections for a designated purpose and period of time.

(k) "Parole" means the conditional and revocable release of a committed person under the supervision of a parole officer.

(*l*) "Prisoner Review Board" means the Board established in Section 3-3-1(a) [730 ILCS 5/3-3-1], independent of the Department, to review rules and regulations with respect to good time credits, to hear charges brought by the Department against certain prisoners alleged to have violated Department rules with respect to good time credits, to set release dates for certain prisoners sentenced under the law in effect prior to the effective date of this Amendatory Act of 1977, to hear requests and make recommendations to the Governor with respect to pardon, reprieve or commutation, to set conditions for parole and mandatory supervised release and determine whether violations of those conditions justify revocation of parole or release, and to assume all other functions previously exercised by the Illinois Parole and Pardon Board.

(m) Whenever medical treatment, service, counseling, or care is referred to in this Unified Code of Corrections [730 ILCS 5/1-1-1 et seq.], such term may be construed by the Department or Court, within its discretion, to include treatment, service or counseling by a Christian Science practitioner or nursing care appropriate therewith whenever request therefor is made by a person subject to the provisions of this Act.

(n) "Victim" shall have the meaning ascribed to it in subsection (a) of Section 3 of the Bill of Rights for Victims and Witnesses of Violent Crime Act [725 ILCS 120/3].

(Source: P.A. 83-1433; 83-1499.) [Formerly Ill. Rev. Stat. 38 §1003-1-2.]

ARTICLE 2. ORGANIZATION OF DEPARTMENT

5/3-2-1. Consolidation of the Department.

§3-2-1. Consolidation of the Department. This Chapter consolidates in one statute certain powers and duties of the Department of Corrections and deletes inoperative and duplicative statutory provisions with respect to such powers and duties.

(Source: P.A. 77-2097.) [Formerly Ill. Rev. Stat. 38 §1003-2-1.]

5/3-2-2. Powers and duties of the Department.

§3-2-2. Powers and Duties of the Department. In addition to the powers, duties and responsibilities which are otherwise provided by law, the Department shall have the following powers:

(a) To accept persons committed to it by the courts of this State for care, custody, treatment and rehabilitation.

(b) To develop and maintain reception and evaluation units for purposes of analyzing the custody and rehabilitation needs of persons committed to it and to assign such persons to institutions and programs under its control or transfer them to other appropriate agencies. In consultation with the Department of Alcoholism and Substance Abuse, the Department of Corrections shall develop a master plan for the screening and evaluation of persons committed to its custody who have alcohol or drug abuse problems, and for making appropriate treatment available to such persons; the Department shall report to the General Assembly on such plan not later than April 1, 1987. The maintenance and implementation of such plan shall be contingent upon the availability of funds.

(c) To maintain and administer all State correctional institutions and facilities under its control and to establish new ones as needed. Pursuant to its power to establish new institutions and facilities, the Department may, with the written approval of the Governor, authorize the Department of Central Management Services to enter into an agreement of the type described in subsection (d) of Section 67.02 of The Civil Administrative Code of Illinois [20 ILCS 405/67.02]. The Department shall designate those institutions which shall constitute the State Penitentiary System.

Pursuant to its power to establish new institutions and facilities, the Department may authorize the Department of Central Management Services to accept bids from counties and municipalities for the construction, remodeling or conversion of a structure to be leased to the Department of Corrections for the purposes of its serving as a correctional institution or facility. Such construction, remodeling or conversion may be financed with revenue bonds issued pursuant to the Industrial Building Revenue Bond Act [50 ILCS 445/1 et seq.] by the municipality or county. The lease specified in a bid shall be for a term of not less than the time needed to retire any revenue bonds used to finance the project, but not to exceed 40 years. The lease may grant to the State the option to purchase the structure outright.

Upon receipt of the bids, the Department may certify one or more of the bids and shall submit any such bids to the General Assembly for approval. Upon approval of a bid by a constitutional majority of both houses of the General Assembly, pursuant to joint resolution, the Department of Central Management Services may enter into an agreement with the county or municipality pursuant to such bid.

(d) To develop and maintain programs of control, rehabilitation and employment of committed persons within its institutions.

(e) To establish a system of supervision and guidance of committed persons in the community.

(f) To establish in cooperation with the Department of Transportation to supply a sufficient number of prisoners for use by the Department of Transportation to clean up the trash and garbage along State, county, township, or municipal highways as designated by the Department of Transportation. The Department of Corrections, at the request of the Department of Transportation, shall furnish such prisoners at least annually for a period to be agreed upon between the Director of Corrections and the Director of Transportation. The prisoners used on this program shall be selected by the Director of Corrections on whatever basis he deems proper in consideration of their term, behavior and earned eligibility to participate in such program—where they will be outside of the prison facility but still in the custody of the Department of Corrections. Prisoners convicted of first degree murder, or a Class X felony, or armed violence, or aggravated kidnapping, or criminal sexual assault, aggravated criminal sexual abuse or a subsequent conviction for criminal sexual abuse, or forcible detention, or arson, or a prisoner adjudged a Habitual Criminal shall not be eligible for selection to participate in such program. The prisoners shall remain as prisoners in the custody of the Department of Corrections and such Department shall furnish whatever security is necessary. The Department of Transportation shall furnish trucks and equipment for the highway cleanup program and personnel to supervise and direct the program. Neither the Department of Corrections nor the Department of Transportation shall replace any regular employee with a prisoner.

(g) To maintain records of persons committed to it and to establish programs of research, statistics and planning.

(h) To investigate the grievances of any person committed to the Department, to inquire into any alleged misconduct by employees or committed persons, and to investigate the assets of committed persons to implement Section 3-7-6 of this Code [730 ILCS 5/3-7-6]; and for these purposes it may issue subpoenas and compel the attendance of witnesses and the production of writings and papers, and may examine under oath any witnesses who may appear before it; to also investigate alleged violations of a parolee's or releasee's conditions of parole or release; and for this purpose it may issue subpoenas and compel the attendance of witnesses and the production of documents only if there is reason to believe that such procedures would provide evidence that such violations have occurred.

If any person fails to obey a subpoena issued under this subsection, the Director may apply to any circuit court to secure compliance with the subpoena. The failure to comply with the order of the court issued in response thereto shall be punishable as contempt of court.

(i) To appoint and remove the chief administrative officers, and administer programs of training and development of personnel of the Department. Personnel assigned by the Department to be responsible for the custody and control of committed persons or to investigate the alleged misconduct of committed persons or employees or alleged violations of a parolee's or releasee's conditions of parole shall be conservators of the peace for those purposes, and shall have the full power of peace officers outside of the facilities of the Department in the protection, arrest, retaking and reconfining of committed persons or where the exercise of such power is necessary to the investigation of such misconduct or violations.

(j) To cooperate with other departments and agencies and with local communities for the development of standards and programs for better correctional services in this State.

(k) To administer all moneys and properties of the Department.

(*l*) To report annually to the Governor on the committed persons, institutions and programs of the Department.

(m) To make all rules and regulations and exercise all powers and duties vested by law in the Department.

(n) To establish rules and regulations for administering a system of good conduct credits, established in accordance with Section 3-6-3 [730 ILCS 5/3-6-3], subject to review by the Prisoner Review Board.

(*o*) To administer the distribution of funds from the State Treasury to reimburse counties where State penal institutions are located for the payment of assistant state's attorneys' salaries under Section 4-2001 of the Counties Code [55 ILCS 5/4-2001].

(p) To exchange information with the Illinois Department of Public Aid for the purpose of verifying living arrangements and for other purposes directly connected with the administration of this Code and The Illinois Public Aid Code [305 ILCS 5/1-1 et seq.].

(q) To establish a diversion program.

The program shall provide a structured environment for selected technical parole or mandatory supervised release violators and committed persons who have violated the rules governing their conduct while in work release. This program shall not apply to those persons who have committed a new offense while serving on parole or mandatory supervised release or while committed to work release.

Elements of the program shall include, but shall not be limited to, the following:

(1) The staff of a diversion facility shall provide supervision in accordance with required objectives set by the facility.

(2) Participants shall be required to maintain employment.

(3) Each participant shall pay for room and board at the facility on a sliding-scale basis according to the participant's income.

(4) Each participant shall:

(A) provide restitution to victims in accordance with any court order;

(B) provide financial support to his dependents; and

(C) make appropriate payments toward any other court-ordered obligations.

(5) Each participant shall complete community service in addition to employment.

(6) Participants shall take part in such counseling, educational and other programs as the Department may deem appropriate.

(7) Participants shall submit to drug and alcohol screening.

(8) The Department shall promulgate rules governing the administration of the program.

(r) To do all other acts necessary to carry out the provisions of this Chapter.

(Source: P.A. 85-1209; 85-1433; 86-820; 86-1182; 86-1183; 86-1475.) [Formerly Ill. Rev. Stat. 38 §1003-2-2.]

5/3-2-2.1. County Jail Revolving Loan Fund.

§3-2-2.1. In addition to all other powers, duties and responsibilities which are otherwise provided by law, the Department shall administer the County Jail Revolving Loan Fund, a special fund in the State Treasury which is hereby created. The Department shall accept for deposit into such fund any and all grants, loans, subsidies, matching funds, reimbursements, appropriations, transfers of appropriations, income derived from investments, State bond proceeds, proceeds from repayment of loans, or other things of value from the federal or State governments, person, firm or corporation, public or private. Monies in the County Jail Revolving Loan Fund shall be invested in the same manner as provided in "An Act relating to certain investments of public funds by public agencies", approved July 23, 1973, as amended [30 ILCS 235/0.01 et seq.]. A portion of the proceeds from the interest or dividends from such investments may be used to pay administrative costs of the Department incurred in the administration of the fund. The Department shall loan money from the County Jail Revolving Loan Fund to any county for the purpose of constructing a new county jail or remodeling, reconstructing or renovating an existing county jail. The Department shall adopt rules and regulations establishing criteria to be used in determining loan eligibility and the interest rate, if any, to be charged on loaned money from the fund. The eligibility criteria shall include the following factors:

(a) creditworthiness of the county;

(b) ability of the county to borrow money by traditional methods;

(c) evidence of the county's efforts to raise funds in traditional markets; and

(d) the costs of borrowing that the county would encounter in traditional markets.

To be eligible for a loan from the fund, a county must demonstrate it has the ability to make debt service payments and that it has explored all reasonable methods of expanding, constructing, reconstructing or upgrading the county jail facility and the method selected is the least expensive or most practical.

No county may finance more than 75% of the total costs of constructing, reconstructing, upgrading or expanding a county jail facility from the fund. The term of payment for loans authorized by the Department shall be at least 10 years. The Department may impose such other charges or fees as it deems necessary to defray the costs of administering the loans under the fund.

Counties already in the process of upgrading county jail facilities and counties that combine to construct a regional jail facility shall be eligible for loans from the fund.

(Source: P.A. 84-1411.) [Formerly Ill. Rev. Stat. 38 §1003-2-2.1.]

5/3-2-2.2. County Juvenile Detention Center Revolving Loan Fund.

§3-2-2.2. In addition to all other powers, duties and responsibilities otherwise provided by law, the Department shall administer the County Juvenile Detention Center Revolving Loan Fund, a special fund in the State treasury which is hereby created. The Department shall accept for deposit into such fund any and all grants, loans, subsidies, matching funds, reimbursements, appropriations, transfers of appropriations, income derived from investments, State bond proceeds, proceeds from repayment of loans, or other things of value from the federal or State government or any person, firm or public or private corporation. Monies in the County Juvenile Detention Center Revolving Loan Fund shall be invested in the same manner as provided in "An Act relating to certain investments of public funds by public agencies", approved July 23, 1973 [30 ILCS 235/0.01 et seq.]. The Department shall loan money from the County Juvenile Detention Center Revolving Loan Fund to any county for the purpose of constructing a new juvenile detention center or non-secure group home or remodeling, reconstructing or renovating an existing juvenile detention center or non-secure group home. Such facilities shall be administered by the Circuit Court. The Department shall adopt rules and regulations establishing criteria to be used in determining loan eligibility and the interest rate, if any, to be charged on money loaned from the fund. The interest rate shall not exceed 80% of the prime interest rate charged by the largest commercial bank in the State of Illinois at the time that the loan is approved. The eligibility criteria shall include the following factors:

(a) creditworthiness of the county;

(b) ability of the county to borrow money by traditional methods;

(c) evidence of the county's efforts to raise funds in traditional markets;

(d) the costs of borrowing that the county would encounter in traditional markets;

(e) a direct appropriation by the General Assembly; and

(f) approval by the chief judge of the circuit.

To be eligible for a loan from the fund, a county must demonstrate it has the ability to make debt service payments.

No county shall finance more than 75% of the total costs of constructing, reconstructing, upgrading or expanding a facility from the fund. The term of payment for loans authorized by the Department shall be at least 10 years. The Department may impose such other charges or fees as it deems necessary to defray the costs of administering loans from the fund.

No loan shall be granted within three years of the granting of any other loan under this program within the same circuit.

Counties in the process of upgrading county juvenile detention facilities and non-secure group homes on the effective date of this amendatory Act of 1990 and counties that combine to construct a regional facility shall be eligible for loans from the fund.
(Source: P.A. 86-1327.) [Formerly Ill. Rev. Stat. 38 §1003-2-2.2.]

5/3-2-3. Director; appointment; powers and duties.
§3-2-3. Director; Appointment; Powers and Duties. (a) The Department shall be administered by the Director of Corrections who shall be appointed by the Governor in accordance with The Civil Administrative Code of Illinois [20 ILCS 5/1 et seq.].

(b) The Director shall establish such Divisions within the Department in addition to those established under Section 3-2-5 [730 ILCS 5/3-2-5] as shall be desirable and shall assign to the various Divisions the responsibilities and duties placed in the Department by the laws of this State.
(Source: P.A. 77-2097.) [Formerly Ill. Rev. Stat. 38 §1003-2-3.]

5/3-2-3.1. Treaties.
§3-2-3.1. Treaties. If a treaty in effect between the United States and a foreign country provides for the transfer or exchange of convicted offenders to the country of which they are citizens or nationals, the Governor may, on behalf of the State and subject to the terms of the treaty, authorize the Director of Corrections to consent to the transfer or exchange of offenders and take any other action necessary to initiate the participation of this State in the treaty.
(Source: P.A. 83-587.) [Formerly Ill. Rev. Stat. 38 §1003-2-3.1.]

5/3-2-4. Governor to visit.
§3-2-4. Governor to Visit. The Governor shall visit the institutions, facilities and programs of the Department as often as he deems fit, for the purpose of examining into the affairs and conditions of the Department.
(Source: P.A. 77-2097.) [Formerly Ill. Rev. Stat. 38 §1003-2-4.]

5/3-2-5. Organization of the Department.
§3-2-5. Organization of the Department. (a) There shall be an Adult Division within the Department which shall be administered by an Assistant Director appointed by the Governor under The Civil Administrative Code of Illinois [20 ILCS 5/1 et seq.]. The Assistant Director shall be under the direction of the Director. The Adult Division shall be responsible for all persons committed or transferred to the Department under Sections 3-10-7 or 5-8-6 of this Code [730 ILCS 5/3-10-7 or 5/5-8-6].

(b) There shall be a Juvenile Division within the Department which shall be administered by an Assistant Director appointed by the Governor under The Civil Administrative Code of Illinois. The Assistant Director shall be under the direction of the Director. The Juvenile Division shall be responsible for all persons committed to the Juvenile Division of the Department under Section 5-8-6 of this Code or Section 5-10 of the Juvenile Court Act [repealed] or Section 5-33 of the Juvenile Court Act of 1987 [705 ILCS 405/5-33].
(Source: P.A. 85-1209.) [Formerly Ill. Rev. Stat. 38 §1003-2-5.]

5/3-2-6. Advisory Boards.
§3-2-6. Advisory Boards. (a) There shall be an Adult Advisory Board and a Juvenile Advisory Board each composed of 11 persons, one of whom shall be a senior citizen age 60 or over, appointed by the Governor to advise the Director on matters pertaining to adult and juvenile offenders respectively. The members of the Boards shall be qualified for their positions by demonstrated interest in and knowledge of adult and juvenile correctional work and shall not be officials of the State in any other capacity. The members first appointed under

this amendatory Act of 1984 shall serve for a term of 6 years and shall be appointed as soon as possible after the effective date of this amendatory Act of 1984. The members of the Boards now serving shall complete their terms as appointed, and thereafter members shall be appointed by the Governor to terms of 6 years. Any vacancy occurring shall be filled in the same manner for the remainder of the term. The Director of Corrections and the Assistant Directors, Adult and Juvenile Divisions respectively, for the 2 Boards, shall be ex-officio members of the Boards. Each Board shall elect a chairman from among its appointed members. The Director shall serve as secretary of each Board. Members of each Board shall serve without compensation but shall be reimbursed for expenses necessarily incurred in the performance of their duties. Each Board shall meet quarterly and at other times at the call of the chairman. At the request of the Director, the Boards may meet together.

(b) The Boards shall advise the Director concerning policy matters and programs of the Department with regard to the custody, care, study, discipline, training and treatment of persons in the State correctional institutions and for the care and supervision of persons released on parole.

(c) There shall be a Subcommittee on Women Offenders to the Adult Advisory Board. The Subcommittee shall be composed of 3 members of the Adult Advisory Board appointed by the Chairman who shall designate one member as the chairman of the Subcommittee. Members of the Subcommittee shall serve without compensation but shall be reimbursed for expenses necessarily incurred in the performance of their duties. The Subcommittee shall meet no less often than quarterly and at other times at the call of its chairman.

The Subcommittee shall advise the Adult Advisory Board and the Director on all policy matters and programs of the Department with regard to the custody, care, study, discipline, training and treatment of women in the State correctional institutions and for the care and supervision of women released on parole.

(Source: P.A. 85-624.) [Formerly Ill. Rev. Stat. 38 §1003-2-6.]

5/3-2-7. Staff training and development.

§3-2-7. Staff Training and Development. (a) The Department shall train its own personnel and any personnel from local agencies by agreements under Section 3-15-2 [730 ILCS 5/3-15-2].

(b) To develop and train its personnel, the Department may make grants in aid for academic study and training in fields related to corrections. The Department shall establish rules for the conditions and amounts of such grants. The Department may employ any person during his program of studies and may require the person to work for it on completion of his program according to the agreement entered into between the person receiving the grant and the Department.

(Source: P.A. 77-2097.) [Formerly Ill. Rev. Stat. 38 §1003-2-7.]

5/3-2-8. Research and long range planning.

§3-2-8. Research and Long Range Planning. (a) The Department shall establish programs of research, statistics and planning, including the study of its own performance concerning the treatment of juveniles and adult offenders.

(b) The Department may conduct and supervise research into the causes, detection and treatment of criminality, and disseminate such information to the public and to governmental and private agencies.

(c) The Department may establish such joint research and information facilities with governmental and private agencies as it shall determine, and in furtherance thereof may accept financial and other assistance from public or private sources.

(Source: P.A. 77-2097.) [Formerly Ill. Rev. Stat. 38 §1003-2-8.]

5/3-2-9. Financial impact statement.

§3-2-9. Each fiscal year, the Department shall prepare and submit to the clerk of the circuit court a financial impact statement that includes the estimated annual and monthly cost of incarcerating an individual in a Department facility and the estimated construction cost per bed. The estimated annual cost of incarcerating an individual in a Department facility shall be derived by taking the annual expenditures of Adult Division facilities and all administrative costs and dividing the sum of these factors by the average annual inmate population of the facilities. All statements shall be made available to the public for inspection and copying.

(Source: P.A. 87-417.) [Formerly Ill. Rev. Stat. 38 §1003-2-9.]

ARTICLE 3. PAROLE AND PARDON BOARD

5/3-3-1. Establishment and appointment of Prisoner Review Board.

§3-3-1. Establishment and Appointment of Prisoner Review Board. (a) There shall be a Prisoner Review Board independent of the Department of Corrections which shall be:

(1) the paroling authority for persons sentenced under the law in effect prior to the effective date of this amendatory Act of 1977;

(2) the board of review for cases involving the revocation of good conduct credits or a suspension or reduction in the rate of accumulating such credit;

(3) the board of review and recommendation for the exercise of executive clemency by the Governor;

(4) the authority for establishing release dates for certain prisoners sentenced under the law in existence prior to the effective date of this amendatory Act of 1977, in accordance with Section 3-3-2.1 of this Code [730 ILCS 5/3-3-2.1];

(5) the authority for setting conditions for parole and mandatory supervised release under Section 5-8-1(a) of this Code [730 ILCS 5/5-8-1], and determining whether a violation of those conditions warrant revocation of parole or mandatory supervised release or the imposition of other sanctions.

(b) The Board shall consist of 12 persons appointed by the Governor by and with the advice and consent of the Senate. One member of the Board shall be designated by the Governor to be Chairman and shall serve as Chairman at the pleasure of the Governor. The members of the Board shall have had at least 5 years of actual experience in the fields of penology, corrections work, law enforcement, sociology, law, education, social work, medicine, psychology, other behavioral sciences, or a combination thereof. At least 6 members so appointed must have had at least 3 years experience in the field of juvenile matters. No more than 6 Board members may be members of the same political party. Each member of the Board shall serve on a full time basis and shall not hold any other salaried public office, whether elective or appointive. The Chairman of the Board shall receive $35,000 a year, or an amount set by the Compensation Review Board, whichever is greater, and each other member $30,000, or an amount set by the Compensation Review Board, whichever is greater.

(c) The terms of the present members of the Prisoner Review Board shall expire on the effective date of this amendatory Act of 1985, but the incumbent members shall continue to exercise all of the powers and be subject to all the duties of members of the Board until their respective successors are appointed and qualified. The Governor shall appoint 3 members to the Prisoner Review Board whose terms shall expire on the third Monday in January 1987, 4 members whose terms shall expire on the third Monday in January 1989, and 3 members whose terms shall expire on the third Monday in January 1991. The term of one of the members created by this amendatory Act of 1986 shall expire on the third Monday in January 1989 and the term of the other shall expire on the third Monday in January 1991. Their respective successors shall be appointed for terms of 6 years from the third Monday in January of the year of appointment. Each member shall serve until his successor is appointed and qualified. Any member may be removed by the Governor for incompetence, neglect of duty, malfeasance or inability to serve.

(d) The Chairman of the Board shall be its chief executive and administrative officer.

(Source: P.A. 85-1433.) [Formerly Ill. Rev. Stat. 38 §1003-3-1.]

5/3-3-2. Powers and duties.

§3-3-2. Powers and Duties. (a) The Parole and Pardon Board is abolished and the term "Parole and Pardon Board" as used in any law of Illinois, shall read "Prisoner Review Board." After the effective date of this amendatory Act of 1977, the Prisoner Review Board shall provide by rule for the orderly transition of all files, records, and documents of the Parole and Pardon Board and for such other steps as may be necessary to effect an orderly transition and shall:

(1) through a panel of at least 3 members, hear cases of prisoners who were sentenced under the law in effect prior to the effective date of this amendatory Act of 1977, and who are eligible for parole;

(2) through a panel of at least 3 members, determine the conditions of parole and the time of discharge from parole, impose sanctions for violations of parole, and revoke parole for those sentenced under the law in effect prior to this amendatory Act of 1977; provided that the decision to parole and the conditions of parole for all prisoners who were sentenced for first degree murder or who received a minimum sentence of 20 years or more under the law in effect prior to February 1, 1978 shall be determined by a majority vote of the Prisoner Review Board;

(3) through a panel of at least 3 members, determine the conditions of mandatory supervised release and the time of discharge from mandatory supervised release, impose sanctions for violations of mandatory supervised release, and revoke mandatory supervised release for those sentenced under the law in effect after the effective date of this amendatory Act of 1977;

(4) hear by at least 1 member and through a panel of at least 3 members, decide cases brought by the Department of Corrections against a prisoner in the custody of the Department for alleged violation of Department rules with respect to good conduct credits pursuant to Section 3-6-3 of this Code [730 ILCS 5/3-6-3] in which the Department seeks to revoke good conduct credits, if the

amount of time at issue exceeds 30 days or when, during any 12 month period, the cumulative amount of credit revoked exceeds 30 days except where the infraction is committed or discovered within 60 days of scheduled release. In such cases, the Department of Corrections may revoke up to 30 days of good conduct credit. The Board may subsequently approve the revocation of additional good conduct credit, if the Department seeks to revoke good conduct credit in excess of thirty days. However, the Board shall not be empowered to review the Department's decision with respect to the loss of 30 days of good conduct credit for any prisoner or to increase any penalty beyond the length requested by the Department; and*

(5) through a panel of at least 3 members, by majority vote set the release dates for certain prisoners sentenced under the law in existence prior to the effective date of this amendatory Act of 1977, in accordance with Section 3-3-2.1 of this Code [730 ILCS 5/3-3-2.1]; and*

**So in original. Probably "and" should be deleted.*

(6) through a panel of at least 3 members, hear all requests for pardon, reprieve or commutation, and make confidential recommendations to the Governor; and

(7) comply with the requirements of the Open Parole Hearings Act [730 ILCS 105/1 et seq.].

(b) Upon recommendation of the Department the Board may restore good conduct credit previously revoked.

(c) The Board shall cooperate with the Department in promoting an effective system of parole and mandatory supervised release.

(d) The Board shall promulgate rules for the conduct of its work, and the Chairman shall file a copy of such rules and any amendments thereto with the Director and with the Secretary of State.

(e) The Board shall keep records of all of its official actions and shall make them accessible in accordance with law and the rules of the Board.

(f) The Board or one who has allegedly violated the conditions of his parole or mandatory supervised release may require by subpoena the attendance and testimony of witnesses and the production of documentary evidence relating to any matter under investigation or hearing. The Chairman of the Board may sign subpoenas which shall be served by any agent or public official authorized by the Chairman of the Board, or by any person lawfully authorized to serve a subpoena under the laws of the State of Illinois. The attendance of witnesses, and the production of documentary evidence, may be required from any place in the State to a hearing location in the State before the Chairman of the Board or his designated agent or agents or any duly constituted Committee or Subcommittee of the Board. Witnesses so summoned shall be paid the same fees and mileage that are paid witnesses in the circuit courts of the State, and witnesses whose depositions are taken and the persons taking those depositions are each entitled to the same fees as are paid for like services in actions in the circuit courts of the State. Fees and mileage shall be vouchered for payment when the witness is discharged from further attendance.

In case of disobedience to a subpoena, the Board may petition any circuit court of the State for an order requiring the attendance and testimony of witnesses or the production of documentary evidence or both. A copy of such petition shall be served by personal service or by registered or certified mail upon the person who has failed to obey the subpoena, and such person shall be advised in writing that a hearing upon the petition will be requested in a court room to be designated in such notice before the judge hearing motions or extraordinary remedies at a specified time, on a specified date, not less than 10 nor more than 15 days after the deposit of the copy of the written notice and petition in the U.S. mails addressed to the person at his last known address or after the personal service of the copy of the notice and petition upon such person.

The court upon the filing of such a petition, may order the person refusing to obey the subpoena to appear at an investigation or hearing, or to there produce documentary evidence, if so ordered, or to give evidence relative to the subject matter of that investigation or hearing. Any failure to obey such order of the circuit court may be punished by that court as a contempt of court.

Each member of the Board and any hearing officer designated by the Board shall have the power to administer oaths and to take the testimony of persons under oath.

(g) Except under subsection (a) of this Section, a majority of the members then appointed to the Prisoner Review Board shall constitute a quorum for the transaction of all business of the Board.

(h) The Prisoner Review Board shall annually transmit to the Director a detailed report of its work for the preceding calendar year. The annual report shall also be transmitted to the Governor for submission to the Legislature.
(Source: P.A. 87-224.) [Formerly Ill. Rev. Stat. 38 §1003-3-2.]

5/3-3-2.1. Prisoner Review Board—Release Date.

§3-3-2.1. Prisoner Review Board—Release Date. (a) Except as provided in subsection (b), the Prisoner Review Board shall, no later than 7 days following a prisoner's next parole hearing after the effective date of this Amendatory Act of 1977, provide each prisoner sentenced under the law in effect prior to the effective date of this amendatory Act of 1977, with a fixed release date.

(b) No release date under this Section shall be set for any person sentenced to an indeterminate sentence under the law in effect prior to the effective date of this amendatory Act of 1977 in which the minimum term of such sentence is 20 years or more.

(c) The Prisoner Review Board shall notify each eligible offender of his or her release date in a form substantially as follows:

Date of Notice

"To (Name of offender):

Under a recent change in the law you are provided with this choice:

(1) You may remain under your present indeterminate sentence and continue to be eligible for parole; or (2) you may waive your right to parole and accept the release date which has been set for you. From this release date will be deducted any good conduct credit you may earn.

If you accept the release date established by the Board, you will no longer be eligible for parole.

Your release date from prison has been set for: (release date) , subject to a term of mandatory supervised release as provided by law.

If you accumulate the maximum amount of good conduct credit as allowed by law recently enacted, you can be released on:. . . . . , subject to a term of mandatory supervised release as provided by law.

Should you choose not to accept the release date, your next parole hearing will be: .

The Board has based its determination of your release date on the following:

(1) The material that normally would be examined in connection with your parole hearing, as set forth in paragraph (d) of Section 3-3-4 of the Unified Code of Corrections [730 ILCS 5/3-3-4]:

(2) the intent of the court in imposing sentence on you;

(3) the present schedule of sentences for similar offenses provided by Sections 5-8-1 and 5-8-2 of the Unified Code of Corrections, as amended [730 ILCS 5/5-8-1 and 5/5-8-2];

(4) the factors in mitigation and aggravation provided by Sections 5-5-3.1 and 5-5-3.2 of the Unified Code of Corrections, as amended [730 ILCS 5/5-5-3.1 and 5/5-5-3.2];

(5) The rate of accumulating good conduct credits provided by Section 3-6-3 of the Unified Code of Corrections, as amended [730 ILCS 5/3-6-3];

(6) your behavior since commitment.

You now have 60 days in which to decide whether to remain under your indeterminate sentence and continue to be eligible for parole or waive your right to parole and accept the release date established for you by the Board. If you do nothing within 60 days, you will remain under the parole system.

If you accept the release date, you may accumulate good conduct credit at the maximum rate provided under the law recently enacted.

If you feel that the release date set for you is unfair or is not based on complete information required to be considered by the Board, you may request that the Board reconsider the date. In your request you must set forth specific reasons why you feel the Board's release date is unfair and you may submit relevant material in support of your request.

The Department of Corrections is obligated to assist you in that effort, if you ask it to do so.

The Board will notify you within 60 days whether or not it will reconsider its decision. The Board's decision with respect to reconsidering your release date is final and cannot be appealed to any court.

If the Board decides not to reconsider your case you will have 60 days in which to decide whether to accept the release date and waive your right to parole or to continue under the parole system. If you do nothing within 60 days after you receive notification of the Board's decision you will remain under the parole system.

If the Board decides to reconsider its decision with respect to your release date, the Board will schedule a date for reconsideration as soon as practicable, but no later than 60 days from the date it receives your request, and give you at least 30 days notice. You may submit material to the Board which you believe will be helpful in deciding a proper date for your release. The Department of Corrections is obligated to assist you in that effort, if you ask it to do so.

Neither you nor your lawyer has the right to be present on the date of reconsideration, nor the right to call witnesses. However, the Board may ask you or your lawyer to appear or may ask to hear witnesses. The Board will base its determination on the same data on which it made its earlier determination, plus any new information which may be available to it.

When the Board has made its decision you will be informed of the release date. In no event will it be longer than the release date originally determined. From this date you may continue to accumulate good conduct credits at the maximum rate. You will not be able to appeal the Board's decision to a court.

Following the Board's reconsideration and upon being notified of your release date you will have 60 days in which to decide whether to accept the release date and waive your right to parole or to continue under the parole system. If you do nothing within 60 days after notification of the Board's decision you will remain under the parole system."

(d) The Board shall provide each eligible offender with a form substantially as follows:

"I (name of offender) am fully aware of my right to choose between parole eligibility and a fixed release date. I know that if I accept the release date established, I will give up my right to seek parole. I have read and understood the Prisoner Review Board's letter, and I know how and under what circumstances the Board has set my release date. I know that I will be released on that date and will be released earlier if I accumulate good conduct credit. I know that the date set by the Board is final, and can't be appealed to a court.

Fully aware of all the implications, I expressly and knowingly waive my right to seek parole and accept the release date as established by the Prisoner Review Board."

(e) The Board shall use the following information and standards in establishing a release date for each eligible offender who requests that a date be set:

(1) Such information as would be considered in a parole hearing under Section 3-3-4 of this Code;

(2) The intent of the court in imposing the offender's sentence;

(3) The present schedule for similar offenses provided by Sections 5-8-1 and 5-8-2 of this Code;

(4) Factors in aggravation and mitigation of sentence as provided in Sections 5-5-3.1 and 5-5-3.2 of this Code;

(5) The rate of accumulating good conduct credits provided by Section 3-6-3 of this Code;

(6) The offender's behavior since commitment to the Department.

(f) After the release date is set by the Board, the offender can accumulate good conduct credits in accordance with Section 3-6-3 of this Code.

(g) The release date established by the Board shall not be sooner than the earliest date that the offender would have been eligible for release under the sentence imposed on him by the court, less time credit previously earned for good behavior, nor shall it be later than the latest date at which the offender would have been eligible for release under such sentence, less time credit previously earned for good behavior.

(h) (1) Except as provided in subsection (b), each prisoner appearing at his next parole hearing subsequent to the effective date of the amendatory Act of 1977, shall be notified within 7 days of the hearing that he will either be released on parole or that a release date has been set by the Board. The notice and waiver form provided for in subsections (c) and (d) shall be presented to eligible prisoners no later than 7 days following their parole hearing. A written statement of the basis for the decision with regard to the release date set shall be given to such prisoners no later than 14 days following the parole hearing.

(2) Each prisoner upon notification of his release date shall have 60 days to choose whether to remain under the parole system or to accept the release date established by the Board. No release date shall be effective unless the prisoner waives his right to parole in writing. If no choice is made by such prisoner within 60 days from the date of his notification of a release date, such prisoner shall remain under the parole system.

(3) Within the 60 day period as provided in paragraph (2) of this subsection, a prisoner may request that the Board reconsider its decision with regard to such prisoner's release date. No later than 60 days following receipt of such request for reconsideration, the Board shall notify the prisoner as to whether or not it will reconsider such prisoner's release date. No court shall have jurisdiction to review the Board's decision. No prisoner shall be entitled to more than one request for reconsideration of his release date.

(A) If the Board decides not to reconsider the release date, the prisoner shall have 60 days to choose whether to remain under the parole system or to accept the release date established by the Board. No release date shall be effective unless the prisoner waives his right to parole in writing. If no choice is made by such prisoner within 60 days from the date of the notification by the Board refusing to reconsider his release date, such prisoner shall remain under the parole system.

(B) If the Board decides to reconsider its decision with respect to such release date, the Board shall schedule a date for reconsideration as soon as practicable, but no later than 60 days from the date of the prisoner's request, and give such prisoner at least 30 days notice. Such prisoner may submit any relevant material to the Board which would aid in ascertaining a proper release date. The Department of Corrections shall assist any such prisoner if asked to do so.

Neither the prisoner nor his lawyer has the right to be present on the date of reconsideration, nor the right to call witnesses. However, the Board may ask such prisoner or his or her lawyer to appear or may ask to hear witnesses. The Board shall base its determination on the factors specified in subsection (e), plus any new information which may be available to it.

(C) When the Board has made its decision, the prisoner shall be informed of the release date as provided for in subsection (c) no later than 7 days following the reconsideration. In no event shall such release date be longer than the release date originally determined. The decision of the Board is final. No court shall have jurisdiction to review the Board's decision.

Following the Board's reconsideration and its notification to the prisoner of his or her release date, such prisoner shall have 60 days from the date of such notice in which to decide whether to accept the release date and waive his or her right to parole or to continue under the parole system. If such prisoner does nothing within 60 days after notification of the Board's decision, he or she shall remain under the parole system.

(Source: P.A. 80-1387.) [Formerly Ill. Rev. Stat. 38 §1003-3-2.1.]

5/3-3-3. Eligibility for parole or release.

§3-3-3. Eligibility for Parole or Release. (a) Except for those offenders who accept the fixed release date established by the Prisoner Review Board under Section 3-3-2.1 [730 ILCS 5/3-3-2.1], every person serving a term of imprisonment under the law in effect prior to the effective date of this amendatory Act of 1977 shall be eligible for parole when he has served:

(1) the minimum term of an indeterminate sentence less time credit for good behavior, or 20 years less time credit for good behavior, whichever is less; or

(2) 20 years of a life sentence less time credit for good behavior; or

(3) 20 years or one-third of a determinate sentence, whichever is less, less time credit for good behavior.

(b) No person sentenced under this amendatory Act of 1977 or who accepts a release date under Section 3-3-2.1 shall be eligible for parole.

(c) Except for those sentenced to a term of natural life imprisonment, every person sentenced to imprisonment under this amendatory Act of 1977 or given a release date under Section 3-3-2.1 of this Act shall serve the full term of a determinate sentence less time credit for good behavior and shall then be released under the mandatory supervised release provisions of paragraph (d) of Section 5-8-1 of this Code [730 ILCS 5/5-8-1].

(d) No person serving a term of natural life imprisonment may be paroled or released except through executive clemency.

(e) Every person committed to the Juvenile Division under Section 5-10 of the Juvenile Court Act [repealed] or Section 5-33 of the Juvenile Court Act of 1987 [705 ILCS 405/5-33] or Section 5-8-6 of this Code [730 ILCS 5/5-8-6] and confined in the State correctional institutions or facilities if such juvenile has not been tried as an adult shall be eligible for parole without regard to the length of time the person has been confined or whether the person has served any minimum term imposed. However, if a juvenile has been tried as an adult he shall only be eligible for parole or mandatory supervised release as an adult under this Section.

(Source: P.A. 85-1209.) [Formerly Ill. Rev. Stat. 38 §1003-3-3.]

5/3-3-4. Preparation for parole hearing.

§3-3-4. Preparation for Parole Hearing. (a) The Prisoner Review Board shall consider the parole of each eligible person committed to the Adult Division at least 30 days prior to the date he shall first become eligible for parole, and shall consider the parole of each person committed to the Juvenile Division as a delinquent at least 30 days prior to the expiration of the first year of confinement.

(b) A person eligible for parole shall, in advance of his parole hearing, prepare a parole plan in accordance with the rules of the Prisoner Review Board. The person shall be assisted in preparing his parole plan by personnel of the Department and may, for this purpose, be released on furlough under Article 11 [730 ILCS 5/3-11-1 et seq.] or on authorized absence under Section 3-9-4 [730 ILCS 5/3-9-4]. The Department shall also provide assistance in obtaining information and records helpful to the individual for his parole hearing.

(c) The members of the Board shall have access at all reasonable times to any committed person and to his master record file within the Department, and the Department shall furnish such reports to the Board as the Board may require concerning the conduct and character of any such person.

(d) In making its determination of parole, the Board shall consider:

(1) material transmitted to the Department by the clerk of the committing court under Section 5-4-1 or Section 5-10 of the Juvenile Court Act [repealed] or Section 5-33 of the Juvenile Court Act of 1987 [705 ILCS 405/5-33];

(2) the report under Section 3-8-2 or 3-10-2 [730 ILCS 5/3-8-2 or 5/3-10-2];

(3) a report by the Department and any report by the chief administrative officer of the institution or facility;

(4) a parole progress report;

(5) a medical and psychological report, if requested by the Board;

(6) material in writing, or on film, video tape or other electronic means in the form of a recording submitted by the person whose parole is being considered; and

(7) material in writing, or on film, video tape or other electronic means in the form of a recording or testimony submitted by the State's Attorney and the victim pursuant to the Bill of Rights for Victims and Witnesses of Violent Crime Act [725 ILCS 120/1 et seq.].

(e) The prosecuting State's Attorney's office shall receive reasonable written notice not less than 15 days prior to the parole hearing and may submit relevant information in writing, or on film, video tape or other electronic means or in the form of a recording to the Board for its consideration. The State's Attorney may waive the written notice.

(f) The victim of the violent crime for which the prisoner has been sentenced shall receive notice of a parole hearing as provided in paragraph (16) of Section 4 of the Bill of Rights for Victims and Witnesses of Violent Crime Act [725 ILCS 120/4].

(g) Any recording considered under the provisions of subsection (d)(6), (d)(7) or (e) of this Section shall be in the form designated by the Board. Such recording shall be both visual and aural. Every voice on the recording and person present shall be identified and the recording shall contain either a visual or aural statement of the person submitting such recording, the date of the recording and the name of the person whose parole eligibility is being considered. Such recordings, if retained by the Board shall be deemed to be submitted at any subsequent parole hearing if the victim or State's Attorney submits in writing a declaration clearly identifying such recording as representing the present position of the victim or State's Attorney regarding the issues to be considered at the parole hearing.

(Source: P.A. 86-642.) [Formerly Ill. Rev. Stat. 38 §1003-3-4.]

5/3-3-5. Hearing and determination.

§3-3-5. Hearing and Determination. (a) The Prisoner Review Board shall meet as often as need requires to consider the cases of persons eligible for parole. Except as otherwise provided in paragraph (2) of subsection (a) of Section 3-3-2 of this Act [730 ILCS 5/3-3-2], the Prisoner Review Board may meet and order its actions in panels of 3 or more members. The action of a majority of the panel shall be the action of the Board. In consideration of persons committed to the Juvenile Division, the panel shall have at least a majority of members experienced in juvenile matters.

(b) If the person under consideration for parole is in the custody of the Department, at least one member of the Board shall interview him, and a report of that interview shall be available for the Board's consideration. However, in the discretion of the Board, the interview need not be conducted if a psychiatric examination determines that the person could not meaningfully contribute to the Board's consideration. The Board may in its discretion parole a person who is then outside the jurisdiction on his record without an interview. The Board need not hold a hearing or interview a person who is paroled under paragraphs (d) or (e) of this Section or released on Mandatory release under Section 3-3-10 [730 ILCS 5/3-3-10].

(c) The Board shall not parole a person eligible for parole if it determines that:

(1) there is a substantial risk that he will not conform to reasonable conditions of parole; or

(2) his release at that time would deprecate the seriousness of his offense or promote disrespect for the law; or

(3) his release would have a substantially adverse effect on institutional discipline.

(d) A person committed under the Juvenile Court Act [repealed] or the Juvenile Court Act of 1987 [705 ILCS 405/1-1 et seq.] who has not been sooner released shall be paroled on or before his 20th birthday to begin serving a period of parole under Section 3-3-8 [730 ILCS 5/3-3-8].

(e) A person who has served the maximum term of imprisonment imposed at the time of sentencing less time credit for good behavior shall be released on parole to serve a period of parole under Section 5-8-1 [730 ILCS 5/5-8-1].

(f) The Board shall render its decision within a reasonable time after hearing and shall state the basis therefor both in the records of the Board and in written notice to the person on whose application it has acted. In its decision, the Board shall set the person's time for parole, or if it denies parole it shall provide for a rehearing not less frequently than once every 3 years. The Board may, after denying parole to a person originally sentenced or who became eligible for parole between January 1, 1973 and September 30, 1977, schedule a rehearing no later than 3 years from the date of the parole denial, if the Board finds that it is not reasonable to expect that parole would be granted at a hearing prior to the scheduled rehearing date. If the Board shall parole a person, and, if he is not released within 90 days from the effective date of the order granting parole, the matter shall be returned to the Board for review.

(g) The Board shall maintain a registry of decisions in which parole has been granted, which shall include the name and case number of the prisoner, the highest charge for which the prisoner was sentenced, the length of sentence imposed, the date of the sentence, the date of the parole, the basis for the decision of the Board to grant parole and the vote of the Board on any such decisions. The registry shall be made available for public inspection and copying during business hours and shall be a public record pursuant to the provisions of The Freedom of Information Act [5 ILCS 140/1 et seq.].

(h) The Board shall promulgate rules regarding the exercise of its discretion under this Section.

(Source: P.A. 85-1209.) [Formerly Ill. Rev. Stat. 38 §1003-3-5.]

5/3-3-6. Parole or release to warrant or detainer.

§3-3-6. Parole or release to warrant or detainer. (a) If a warrant or detainer is placed against a person by the court, parole agency, or other authority of this or any other jurisdiction, the Prisoner Review Board shall inquire before such person becomes eligible for parole or release whether the authority concerned intends to execute or withdraw the process if the person is released on parole or otherwise.

(b) If the authority notifies the Board that it intends to execute such process when the person is released, the Board shall advise the authority concerned of the sentence or disposition under which the person is held, the time of eligibility for parole or release, any decision of the Board relating to the person and the nature of his or her adjustment during confinement, and shall give reasonable notice to such authority of the person's release date.

(c) The Board may parole or release a person to a warrant or detainer. The Board may provide, as a condition of parole or release, that if the charge or charges on which the warrant or detainer is based are dismissed or satisfied, prior to the expiration of his or her parole term, the authority to whose warrant or detainer he or she was released shall return him to serve the remainder of his or her parole term or such part thereof as the Board may determine subject to paragraph (d) of Section 5-8-1 [730 ILCS 5/5-8-1].

(d) If a person paroled to a warrant or detainer is thereafter sentenced to probation, or released on parole in another jurisdiction prior to the expiration of his or her parole or mandatory supervised release term in this State, the Board may permit him or her to serve the remainder of his or her term, or such part thereof as the Board may determine, in either of the jurisdictions.

(Source: P.A. 83-346.) [Formerly Ill. Rev. Stat. 38 §1003-3-6.]

5/3-3-7. Conditions of parole or mandatory supervised release.

§3-3-7. Conditions of Parole or Mandatory Supervised Release. (a) The conditions of parole or mandatory supervised release shall be such as the Prisoner Review Board deems necessary to assist the subject in leading a law-abiding life. The conditions of every parole and mandatory supervised release are that the subject:

(1) not violate any criminal statute of any jurisdiction during the parole or release term; and

(2) refrain from possessing a firearm or other dangerous weapon.

(b) The Board may in addition to other conditions require that the subject:

(1) work or pursue a course of study or vocational training;

(2) undergo medical or psychiatric treatment, or treatment for drug addiction or alcoholism;

(3) attend or reside in a facility established for the instruction or residence of persons on probation or parole;

(4) support his dependents;

(5) report to an agent of the Department of Corrections;

(6) permit the agent to visit him at his home or elsewhere to the extent necessary to discharge his duties;

(7) comply with the terms and conditions of an order of protection issued pursuant to the Illinois Domestic Violence Act of 1986, enacted by the 84th General Assembly [750 ILCS 60/101 et seq.].

(8) and, in addition, if a minor:

(i) reside with his parents or in a foster home;

(ii) attend school;

(iii) attend a non-residential program for youth;

(iv) contribute to his own support at home or in a foster home.

(c) The conditions under which the parole or mandatory supervised release is to be served shall be communicated to the person in writing prior to his release, and he shall sign the same before release. A signed copy of these conditions, including a copy of an order of protection where one had been issued by the criminal court, shall be retained by the person and another copy forwarded to the officer in charge of his supervision.

(d) After a hearing under Section 3-3-9 [730 ILCS 5/3-3-9], the Prisoner Review Board may modify or enlarge the conditions of parole or mandatory supervised release.

(e) The Department shall inform all offenders committed to the Department of the optional services available to them upon release and shall assist inmates in availing themselves of such optional services upon their release on a voluntary basis.

(Source: P.A. 84-1305.) [Formerly Ill. Rev. Stat. 38 §1003-3-7.]

5/3-3-8. Length of parole and mandatory supervised release; discharge.

§3-3-8. Length of parole and mandatory supervised release; discharge. (a) The length of parole for a person sentenced under the law in effect prior to the effective date of this amendatory Act of 1977 and the length of mandatory supervised release for those sentenced under the law in effect on and after such effective date shall be as set out in Section 5-8-1 [730 ILCS 5/5-8-1] unless sooner terminated under paragraph (b) of this Section. The parole period of a juvenile committed to the Department under the Juvenile Court Act [repealed] or the Juvenile Court Act of 1987 [705 ILCS 405/1-1 et seq.] shall extend until he is 21 years of age unless sooner terminated under paragraph (b) of this Section.

(b) The Prisoner Review Board may enter an order releasing and discharging one from parole or mandatory supervised release, and his commitment to the Department, when it determines that he is likely to remain at liberty without committing another offense.

(c) The order of discharge shall become effective upon entry of the order of the Board. The Board shall notify the clerk of the committing court of the order. Upon receipt of such copy, the clerk shall make an entry on the record judgment that the sentence or commitment has been satisfied pursuant to the order.

(d) Rights of the person discharged under this Section shall be restored under Section 5-5-5 [730 ILCS 5/5-5-5]. This Section is subject to Section 5-33 of the Juvenile Court Act of 1987 [705 ILCS 405/5-33].

(Source: P.A. 85-1209.) [Formerly Ill. Rev. Stat. 38 §1003-3-8.]

5/3-3-9. Violations; changes of conditions; preliminary hearing; revocation of parole or mandatory supervised release; revocation hearing.

§3-3-9. Violations; changes of conditions; preliminary hearing; revocation of parole or mandatory supervised release; revocation hearing. (a) If prior to expiration or termination of the term of parole or mandatory supervised release, a person violates a condition set by the Prisoner Review Board to govern that term, the Board may:

(1) continue the existing term,with or without modifying or enlarging the conditions; or

(2) parole or release the person to a half-way house; or

(3) revoke the parole or mandatory supervised release and reconfine the person for a term computed in the following manner:

(i) (A) For those sentenced under the law in effect prior to this amendatory Act of 1977, the recommitment shall be for any portion of the imposed maximum term of imprisonment or confinement which had not been served at the time of parole and the parole term, less the time elapsed between the parole of the person and the commission of the violation for which parole was revoked;

(B) For those subject to mandatory supervised release under paragraph (d) of Section 5-8-1 of this Code [730 ILCS 5/5-8-1], the recommitment shall be for the total mandatory supervised release term, less the time elapsed between the release of the person and the commission of the violation for which mandatory supervised release is revoked. The Board may also order that a prisoner serve up to one year of the sentence imposed by the court which was not served due to the accumulation of good conduct credit.

(ii) the person shall be given credit against the term of reimprisonment or reconfinement for time spent in custody since he was paroled or released which has not been credited against another sentence or period of confinement;

(iii) persons committed under the Juvenile Court Act [repealed] or the Juvenile Court Act of 1987 [705 ILCS 405/1-1 et seq.] shall be recommitted until the age of 21;

(iv) this Section is subject to the release under supervision and the reparole and rerelease provisions of Section 3-3-10 [730 ILCS 5/3-3-10].

(b) The Board may revoke parole or mandatory supervised release for violation of a condition for the duration of the term and for any further period which is reasonably necessary for the adjudication of matters arising before its expiration. The issuance of a warrant of arrest for an alleged violation of the conditions of parole or mandatory supervised release shall toll the running of the term until the final determination of the charge, but where parole or mandatory supervised release is not revoked that period shall be credited to the term.

(c) A person charged with violating a condition of parole or mandatory supervised release shall have a preliminary hearing before a hearing officer designated by the Board to determine if there is cause to hold the person for a revocation hearing. However, no preliminary hearing need be held when revocation is based upon new criminal charges and a court finds probable cause on the new criminal charges or when the revocation is based upon a new criminal conviction and a certified copy of that conviction is available.

(d) Parole or mandatory supervised release shall not be revoked without written notice to the offender setting forth the violation of parole or mandatory supervised release charged against him.

(e) A hearing on revocation shall be conducted before at least one member of the Prisoner Review Board. The Board may meet and order its actions in panels of 3 or more members. The action of a majority of the panel shall be the action of the Board. In consideration of persons committed to the Juvenile Division, the member hearing the matter and at least a majority of the panel shall be experienced in juvenile matters. A record of the hearing shall be made. At the hearing the offender shall be permitted to:

(1) appear and answer the charge; and

(2) bring witnesses on his behalf.

(f) The Board shall either revoke parole or mandatory supervised release or order the person's term continued with or without modification or enlargement of the conditions.

(g) Parole or mandatory supervised release shall not be revoked for failure to make payments under the conditions of parole or release unless the Board determines that such failure is due to the offender's willful refusal to pay.
(Source: P.A. 85-1209.) [Formerly Ill. Rev. Stat. 38 §1003-3-9.]

5/3-3-10. Eligibility after revocation; release under supervision.

§3-3-10. Eligibility after Revocation; Release under Supervision. (a) A person whose parole or mandatory supervised release has been revoked may be reparoled or rereleased by the Board at any time to the full parole or mandatory supervised release term under Section 3-3-8 [730 ILCS 5/3-3-8], except that the time which the person shall remain subject to the Board shall not exceed (1) the imposed maximum term of imprisonment or confinement and the parole term for those sentenced under the law in effect prior to the effective date of this amendatory Act of 1977 or (2) the term of imprisonment imposed by the court and the mandatory supervised release term for those sentenced under the law in effect on and after such effective date.

(b) If the Board sets no earlier release date:

(1) A person sentenced for any violation of law which occurred before January 1, 1973, shall be released under supervision 6 months prior to the expiration of his maximum sentence of imprisonment less good time credit under Section 3-6-3 [730 ILCS 5/3-6-3];

(2) Any person who has violated the conditions of his parole and been reconfined under Section 3-3-9 [730 ILCS 5/3-3-9] shall be released under supervision 6 months prior to the expiration of the term of his reconfinement under paragraph (a) of Section 3-3-9 less good time credit under Section 3-6-3. This paragraph shall not apply to persons serving terms of mandatory supervised release.

(3) Nothing herein shall require the release of a person who has violated his parole within 6 months of the date when his release under this Section would otherwise be mandatory.

(c) Persons released under this Section shall be subject to Sections 3-3-6, 3-3-7, 3-3-9, 3-14-1, 3-14-2, 3-14-3 and 3-14-4 [730 ILCS 5/3-3-6, 5/3-3-7, 5/3-3-9, 5/3-14-1, 5/3-14-2, 5/3-14-3 and 5/3-14-4].

(Source: P.A. 80-1099.) [Formerly Ill. Rev. Stat. 38 §1003-3-10.]

5/3-3-11. Interstate Parole Reciprocal Agreements.

§3-3-11. Interstate Parole Reciprocal Agreements. (a)* The Governor of this State is hereby authorized and directed to enter into a compact on behalf of this State with any of the United States legally joining therein in the form substantially as follows:

A COMPACT.

Entered into by and among the contracting States, signatories hereto, with the consent of Congress of the United States of America, granted by "An Act granting the consent of Congress to any two or more states to enter into agreements or compacts for cooperative effort and mutual assistance in the prevention of crime and for other purposes" [4 U.S.C. §112].

The contracting States solemnly agree:

(1) That it shall be competent for the duly constituted judicial and administrative authorities of a State party to this compact, (herein called "sending State") to permit any person convicted of an offense within such State and placed on probation or released on parole to reside in any other State party to this compact, (herein called "receiving State") while on probation or parole, if

(a) Such person is in fact a resident of or has his family residing within the receiving State and can obtain employment there;

(b) Though not a resident of the receiving State and not having his family residing there, the receiving State consents to such person's being sent there.

Before granting such permission, opportunity shall be granted to the receiving State to investigate the home and prospective employment of such person.

A resident of the receiving State, within the meaning of this Section, is one who has been an actual inhabitant of such State continuously for more than one year prior to his coming to the sending State and has not resided within the sending State for more than 6 continuous months immediately preceding the commission of the offense for which he has been convicted.

(2) That each receiving State will assume the duties of visitation of and supervision over probationers or parolees of any sending State and in the exercise of those duties will be governed by the same standards that prevail for its own probationers and parolees.

(3) That duly accredited officers of a sending State may at all times enter a receiving State and there apprehend and retake any person on probation or parole. For that purpose no formalities will be required other than establishing the authority of the officer and the identity of the person to be retaken. All legal requirements to obtain extradition of fugitives from justice are hereby expressly waived. The decision of the sending State to retake a person on probation or parole shall be conclusive upon and not reviewable within the receiving State: Provided, however, that if at the time when a State seeks to retake a probationer or parolee there should be pending against him within the receiving State any criminal charge, or he should be suspected of having committed within such State a criminal offense, he shall not be retaken without the consent of the receiving State until discharged from prosecution or from imprisonment for such offense.

(4) That the duly accredited officers of the sending State will be permitted to transport prisoners being retaken through any and all States parties to this compact, without interference.

(5) That the Governor of each State may designate an officer who, acting jointly with like officers of other contracting States, if and when appointed, shall promulgate such rules and regulations as may be deemed necessary to carry out more effectively the terms of this compact.

(6) That this compact shall become operative immediately upon its ratification by any State as between it and any other State or States so ratifying. When ratified it shall have the full force and effect of law within such State. The form of ratification shall be in accordance with the laws of the ratifying State.

(7) That this compact shall continue in force and remain binding upon each ratifying State until renounced by it. The duties and obligations hereunder of a renouncing State shall continue as to parolees or probationers residing therein at the time of withdrawal until retaken or finally discharged by the sending State. Renunciation of this compact shall be by the same authority which ratified it, by sending 6 months notice in writing of its intention to withdraw from the compact.

**So in original. No subsec. (b) has been enacted.*

(Source: P.A. 77-2097.) [Formerly Ill. Rev. Stat. 38 §1003-3-11.]

5/3-3-11.1. State defined.

§3-3-11.1. State defined. As used in Sections 3-3-11 through 3-3-11.3 [730 ILCS 5/3-3-11 through 5/3-3-11.3], unless the context clearly indicates otherwise, the term "State" means any of the several states of the United States and the Commonwealth of Puerto Rico, the Virgin Islands, and the District of Columbia.

(Source: P.A. 77-2097.) [Formerly Ill. Rev. Stat. 38 §1003-3-11.1.]

5/3-3-11.2. Force and effect of compact.

§3-3-11.2. Force and effect of compact. When the Governor of this State shall sign and seal this compact or any compact with any other State, pursuant to the provisions of this Act, such compact or compacts as between the State of Illinois and such other State so signing shall have the force and effect of law immediately upon the enactment by such other State of a law giving it similar effect.

(Source: P.A. 77-2097.) [Formerly Ill. Rev. Stat. 38 §1003-3-11.2.]

5/3-3-11.3. Compacts for crime prevention and correction.

§3-3-11.3. Compacts for Crime Prevention and Correction. The Governor of the State of Illinois is further authorized and empowered to enter into any other agreements or compacts with any of the United States not inconsistent with the laws of this State or of the United States, or the other agreeing States, for co-operative effort and mutual assistance in the prevention of crime and in the

enforcement of the penal laws and policies of the contracting States and to establish agencies, joint or otherwise, as may be deemed desirable for making effective such agreements and compacts. The intent and purpose of this Act is to grant to the Governor of the State of Illinois administrative power and authority if and when conditions of crime make it necessary to bind the State in a cooperative effort to reduce crime and to make the enforcement of the criminal laws of agreeing States more effective, all pursuant to the consent of the Congress of the United States heretofore granted.
(Source: P.A. 77-2097.) [Formerly Ill. Rev. Stat. 38 §1003-3-11.3.]

5/3-3-11.4. Parole or probation violations—Notification of Compact Administrator of sending State.

§3-3-11.4. Where supervision of a parolee or probationer is being administered pursuant to the Interstate Compact for the Supervision of Parolees and Probationers (Section 3-3-11 [730 ILCS 5/3-3-11]), the appropriate judicial or administrative authorities in this State shall notify the Compact Administrator of the sending State whenever, in their view, consideration should be given to retaking or reincarceration for a parole or probation violation. Prior to the giving of any such notification, a hearing shall be held within a reasonable time as to whether there is probable cause to believe that the parolee or probationer has violated a condition of his parole or probation, unless such hearing is waived by the parolee or probationer. The appropriate officer or officers of this State shall as soon as practicable, following termination of any such hearing, report to the sending State, furnish a copy of the hearing record, and make recommendations regarding the disposition to be made of the parolee or probationer.
(Source: P.A. 78-939.) [Formerly Ill. Rev. Stat. 38 §1003-3-11.4.]

5/3-3-12. Parole outside State.

§3-3-12. Parole Outside State. The Prisoner Review Board may assign a non-resident person or a person whose family, relatives, friends or employer reside outside of this State, to a person, firm or company in some state other than Illinois, to serve his parole or mandatory supervised release. An inmate so released shall make regular monthly reports in writing to the Department or supervising authority, obey the rules of the Board, obey the laws of such other state, and in all respects keep faithfully his parole or mandatory supervised release agreement until discharged. Should such person violate his agreement, he shall from the date of such violation be subject to the provisions of Section 3-3-9 [730 ILCS 5/3-3-9].
(Source: P.A. 80-1099.) [Formerly Ill. Rev. Stat. 38 §1003-3-12.]

5/3-3-13. Procedure for executive clemency.

§3-3-13. Procedure for Executive Clemency. (a) Petitions seeking pardon, commutation or reprieve shall be addressed to the Governor and filed with the Prisoner Review Board. The petition shall be in writing and signed by the person under conviction or by a person on his behalf. It shall contain a brief history of the case and the reasons for executive clemency.

(b) Notice of the proposed application shall be given by the Board to the committing court and the state's attorney of the county where the conviction was had.

(c) The Board shall, if requested and upon due notice, give a hearing to each application, allowing representation by counsel, if desired, after which it shall confidentially advise the Governor by a written report of its recommendations which shall be determined by majority vote. The Board shall meet to consider such petitions no less than 4 times each year.

(d) The Governor shall decide each application and communicate his decision to the Board which shall notify the petitioner.

In the event a petitioner who has been convicted of a Class X felony is granted a release, after the Governor has communicated such decision to the Board, the Board shall give written notice to the Sheriff of the county from which the offender was sentenced if such sheriff has requested that such notice be given on a continuing basis. In cases where arrest of the offender or the commission of the offense took place in any municipality with a population of more than 10,000 persons, the Board shall also give written notice to the proper law enforcement agency for said municipality which has requested notice on a continuing basis.
(Source: P.A. 84-1301.) [Formerly Ill. Rev. Stat. 38 §1003-3-13.]

ARTICLE 4. FINANCIAL AND PROPERTY ADMINISTRATION

5/3-4-1. Gifts and grants; special trust funds.

§3-4-1. Gifts and Grants; Special Trust Funds. (a) The Department may accept, receive and use, for and in behalf of the State, any moneys, goods or services given for general purposes of this Chapter by the Federal government or from any other source, public or private, and may comply with such conditions and enter into such agreements upon such covenants, terms and conditions as the Department may deem necessary or desirable if the agreement is not in conflict with State law.

(b) Federal moneys, including reimbursement for services rendered under grant or contract, shall be deposited with the State Treasurer and held and disbursed by him under Section 1 of "An Act in relation to the receipt, custody and disbursement of money allotted by the United States of America or any agency thereof for use in this State", approved July 3, 1939, as now or hereafter amended [15 ILCS 515/0.01].

(c) Other moneys received by the Department, including reimbursement for services rendered under grant or contract, may be deposited in special trust funds established by the Department with the State Treasurer, to be held by him outside the State Treasury as ex officio custodian in banks or savings and loan associations which have been approved by him as State depositories under "AN ACT in relation to State moneys" [15 ILCS 520/0.01 et seq.], and with respect to such moneys, he shall be entitled to the same rights and privileges as are provided by such Act with respect to moneys in the Treasury of the State of Illinois.
(Source: P.A. 83-541.) [Formerly Ill. Rev. Stat. 38 §1003-4-1.]

5/3-4-2. Disposition of property.

§3-4-2. Disposition of Property. (a) The Department may with the consent of the Director of Central Management Services lease its unneeded, unused or unproductive land upon such terms and conditions, as in its judgment are in the best interest of the State; but any such lease shall provide for the cancellation thereof by the Department, upon reasonable notice given by the Department whenever such land may be needed by the Department or any other agency of this State. Land leased by the Department shall not be placed under a land trust.

(b) The Department may transfer any realty under its control to any other department of this State government or to the State Employees Housing Commission, or acquire or accept Federal or other lands, when such transfer or

acquisition is advantageous to the State and approved in writing by the Governor.
(Source: P.A. 83-597.) [Formerly Ill. Rev. Stat. 38 §1003-4-2.]

5/3-4-3. Funds and property of persons committed.

§3-4-3. Funds and Property of Persons Committed. (a) The Department shall establish accounting records with accounts for each person who has or receives money while in an institution or facility of the Department and it shall allow the withdrawal and disbursement of money by the person under rules and regulations of the Department. Any interest or other income from moneys deposited with the Department by a resident of the Juvenile Division in excess of $200 shall accrue to the individual's account, or in balances up to $200 shall accrue to the Residents' Benefit Fund. For an individual in an institution or facility of the Adult Division the interest shall accrue to the Residents' Benefit Fund. The Department shall disburse all moneys so held no later than the person's final discharge from the Department. The Department shall under rules and regulations record and receipt all personal property not allowed to committed persons. The Department shall return such property to the individual no later than the person's release on parole.

(b) Any money held in accounts of committed persons separated from the Department by death, discharge, or unauthorized absence and unclaimed for a period of 1 year thereafter by the person or his legal representative may be expended by the Department for the special benefit of persons committed to the Department. Articles of personal property of persons so separated may be sold or used by the Department if unclaimed for a period of 1 year for the same purpose. Clothing, if unclaimed within 30 days, may be used or disposed of as determined by the Department.

(c) Profits on sales from commissary stores shall be expended by the Department for the special benefit of committed persons which shall include but not be limited to the advancement of inmate payrolls, for the special benefit of employees, and for the advancement or reimbursement of employee travel, provided that amounts expended for employees shall not exceed the amount of profits derived from sales made to employees by such commissaries, as determined by the Department.
(Source: P.A. 84-240.) [Formerly Ill. Rev. Stat. 38 §1003-4-3.]

5/3-4-4. Interstate Corrections Compact.

§3-4-4. Interstate Corrections Compact. (a) The State of Illinois ratifies and approves the following compact:

INTERSTATE CORRECTIONS COMPACT

ARTICLE I
PURPOSE AND POLICY

The party states, desiring by common action to fully utilize and improve their institutional facilities and provide adequate programs for the confinement, treatment and rehabilitation of various types of offenders, declare that it is the policy of each of the party states to provide such facilities and programs on a basis of cooperation with one another, thereby serving the best interests of such offenders and of society and effecting economies in capital expenditures and operational costs. The purpose of this compact is to provide for the mutual development and execution of such programs of cooperation for the confinement, treatment and rehabilitation of offenders with the most economical use of human and material resources.

ARTICLE II
DEFINITIONS

As used in this compact, unless the context clearly requires otherwise:

(a) "State" means a state of the United States; the United States of America; a territory or possession of the United States; the District of Columbia; the commonwealth of Puerto Rico.

(b) "Sending state" means a state party to this compact in which conviction or court commitment was had.

(c) "Receiving state" means a state party to this compact to which an inmate is sent for confinement other than a state in which conviction or court commitment was had.

(d) "Inmate" means a male or female offender who is committed, under sentence to or confined in a penal or correctional institution.

(e) "Institution" means any penal or correctional facility, including but not limited to a facility for the mentally ill or mentally defective, in which inmates as defined in (d) above may lawfully be confined.

ARTICLE III
CONTRACTS

(a) Each party state may make one or more contracts with any one or more of the other party states for the confinement of inmates on behalf of a sending state in institutions situated within receiving states. Any such contract shall provide for:

1. Its duration.
2. Payments to be made to the receiving state by the sending state for inmate maintenance, extraordinary medical and dental expenses, and any participation in or receipt by inmates of rehabilitative or correctional services, facilities, programs or treatment not reasonably included as part of normal maintenance.
3. Participation in programs of inmate employment, if any; the disposition or crediting of any payments received by inmates on account thereof; and the crediting of proceeds from or disposal of any products resulting therefrom.
4. Delivery and retaking of inmates.
5. Such other matters as may be necessary and appropriate to fix the obligations, responsibilities and rights of the sending and receiving states.

(b) The terms and provisions of this compact shall be a part of any contract entered into by the authority of or pursuant thereto, and nothing in any such contract shall be inconsistent therewith.

ARTICLE IV
PROCEDURES AND RIGHTS

(a) Whenever the duly constituted authorities in a state party to this compact, and which has entered into a contract pursuant to Article III, shall decide that confinement in, or transfer of an inmate to, an institution within the territory of another party state is necessary or desirable in order to provide adequate quarters and care or an appropriate program of rehabilitation or treatment, such official may direct that the confinement be within an institution within the territory of such other party state, the receiving state to act in that regard solely as agent for the sending state.

(b) The appropriate officials of any state party to this compact shall have access, at all reasonable times, to any institution in which it has a contractual right to confine inmates for the purpose of inspecting the facilities thereof and visiting such of its inmates as may be confined in the institution.

(c) Inmates confined in an institution pursuant to this compact shall at all times be subject to the jurisdiction of the sending state and may at any time be removed therefrom for transfer to a prison or other institution within the sending state, for transfer to another institution in which the sending state may have a contractual or other right to confine inmates, for release on probation or parole, for discharge, or for any other purpose permitted by the laws of the sending state. However, the sending state shall continue to be obligated to such payments as may be required pursuant to the terms of any contract entered into under the terms of Article III.

(d) Each receiving state shall provide regular reports to each sending state on the inmates of that sending state who are in institutions pursuant to this compact including a conduct record of each inmate and shall certify such record to the official designated by the sending state, in order that each inmate may have official review of his or her record in determining and altering the disposition of the inmate in accordance with the law which may obtain in the sending state and in order that the same may be a source of information for the sending state.

(e) All inmates who may be confined in an institution pursuant to this compact shall be treated in a reasonable and humane manner and shall be treated equally with such similar inmates of the receiving state as may be confined in the same institution. The fact of confinement in a receiving state shall not deprive any inmate so confined of any legal rights which the inmate would have had if confined in an appropriate institution of the sending state.

(f) Any hearing or hearings to which an inmate confined pursuant to this compact may be entitled by the laws of the sending state may be had before the appropriate authorities of the sending state, or of the receiving state if authorized by the sending state. The receiving state shall provide adequate facilities for such hearing as may be conducted by the appropriate officials of a sending state. In the event such hearing or hearings are had before officials of the receiving state, the governing law shall be that of the sending state and a record of the hearing or hearings as prescribed by the sending state shall be made. The record together with any recommendations of the hearing officials shall be transmitted forthwith to the official or officials before whom the hearing would have been had if it had taken place in the sending state. In any and all proceedings had pursuant to the provisions of this paragraph (f), the officials of the receiving state shall act solely as agents of the sending state and no final determination shall be made in any matter except by the appropriate officials of the sending state.

(g) Any inmate confined pursuant to this compact shall be released within the territory of the sending state unless the inmate and the sending and receiving states shall agree upon release in some other place. The sending state shall bear the cost of such return to its territory.

(h) Any inmate confined pursuant to this compact shall have any rights and all rights to participate in and derive any benefits or incur or be relieved of any obligations or have such obligations modified or his status changed on account of any action or proceeding in which he could have participated if confined in any appropriate institution of the sending state located within such state.

(i) The parent, guardian, trustee or other person or persons entitled under the laws of the sending state to act for, advise or otherwise function with respect to any inmate shall not be deprived of or restricted in his exercise of any power in respect of any inmate confined pursuant to the terms of this compact.

ARTICLE V
ACT NOT REVIEWABLE IN RECEIVING STATE: EXTRADITION

(a) Any decision of the sending state in respect of any matter over which it retains jurisdiction pursuant to this compact shall be conclusive upon and not reviewable within the receiving state, but if at the time the sending state seeks to remove an inmate from an institution in the receiving state there is pending against the inmate within such state any criminal charge or if the inmate is formally accused of having committed with* such state a criminal offense, the inmate shall not be returned without the consent of the receiving state until discharged from prosecution or other form of proceeding, imprisonment or detention for such offense. The duly accredited officer of the sending state shall be permitted to transport inmates pursuant to this compact through any and all state** party to this compact without interference.

**So in original. Probably should be "within".*

***So in original. Probably should be "states".*

(b) An inmate who escapes from an institution in which he is confined pursuant to this compact shall be deemed a fugitive from the sending state and from the state in which the institution escaped from is situated. In the case of an escape to a jurisdiction other than the sending or receiving state, the responsibility for institution of extradition or rendition proceedings shall be that of the sending state, but nothing contained herein shall be construed to prevent or affect the activities of officers and agencies of any jurisdiction directed toward the apprehension and return of an escapee.

ARTICLE VI
FEDERAL AID

Any state party to this compact may accept federal aid for use in connection with any institution or program, the use of which is or may be affected by this compact or any contract pursuant thereto. Any inmate in a receiving state pursuant to this compact may participate in any such federally aided program or activity for which the sending and receiving states have made contractual provision. However, if such program or activity is not part of the customary correctional regimen, the express consent of the appropriate official of the sending state shall be required therefor.

ARTICLE VII
ENTRY INTO FORCE

This compact shall enter into force and become effective and binding upon the states so acting when it has been enacted into law by any 2 states. Thereafter, this compact shall enter into force and become effective and binding as to any other of such states upon similar action by such state.

ARTICLE VIII
WITHDRAWAL AND TERMINATION

This compact shall continue in force and remain binding upon a party state until it shall have enacted a statute repealing the compact and providing for the sending of formal written notice of withdrawal from the compact to the appropriate officials of all other party states. An actual withdrawal shall not take effect until one year after the notices provided in the statute have been sent. Such withdrawal shall not relieve the withdrawing state from its obligations assumed hereunder prior to the effective date of withdrawal. Before the effective date of withdrawal, a withdrawal state shall remove to its territory, at its own expense, such inmates as it may have confined pursuant to the provisions of this compact.

ARTICLE IX
OTHER ARRANGEMENTS UNAFFECTED

Nothing contained in this compact shall be construed to abrogate or impair an agreement or other arrangement which a party state may have with a non-party state for the confinement, rehabilitation or treatment of inmates, nor to repeal any other laws of a party state authorizing the making of cooperative institutional arrangements.

ARTICLE X
CONSTRUCTION AND SEVERABILITY

The provisions of this compact shall be liberally construed and shall be severable. If any phrase, clause, sentence or provision of this compact is declared to be contrary to the constitution of any participating state or of the United States or the applicability thereof to any government, agency, person or circumstance is held invalid, the validity of the remainder of this compact and the applicability thereof to any government, agency, person or circumstance shall not be affected thereby. If this compact shall be held contrary to the constitution of any state participating therein, the compact shall remain in full force and effect as to the remaining states and in full force and effect as to the state affected as to all severable matters.

(b) Powers. The Department of Corrections is authorized and directed to do all things necessary or incidental to the carrying out of the compact in every particular.
(Source: P.A. 77-2097.) [Formerly Ill. Rev. Stat. 38 §1003-4-4.]

ARTICLE 5. RECORDS AND REPORTS

5/3-5-1. Master record file.

§3-5-1. Master Record File. (a) The Department shall maintain a master record file on each person committed to it, which shall contain the following information:

(1) all information from the committing court;
(2) reception summary;
(3) evaluation and assignment reports and recommendations;
(4) reports as to program assignment and progress;
(5) reports of disciplinary infractions and disposition;
(6) any parole plan;
(7) any parole reports;
(8) the date and circumstances of final discharge; and any other pertinent data concerning the person's background, conduct, associations and family relationships as may be required by the Department. A current summary index shall be maintained on each file.

(b) All files shall be confidential and access shall be limited to authorized personnel of the Department. Personnel of other correctional, welfare or law enforcement agencies may have access to files under rules and regulations of the Department. The Department shall keep a record of all outside personnel who have access to files, the files reviewed, any file material copied, and the purpose of access. If the Department or the Prisoner Review Board makes a determination under this Code which affects the length of the period of confinement or commitment, the committed person and his counsel shall be advised of factual information relied upon by the Department or Board to make the determination, provided that the Department or Board shall not be required to advise a person committed to the Juvenile Division any such information which in the opinion of the Department or Board would be detrimental to his treatment or rehabilitation.

(c) The master file shall be maintained at a place convenient to its use by personnel of the Department in charge of the person. When custody of a person is transferred from the Department to another department or agency, a summary of the file shall be forwarded to the receiving agency with such other information required by law or requested by the agency under rules and regulations of the Department.

(d) The master file of a person no longer in the custody of the Department shall be placed on inactive status and its use shall be restricted subject to rules and regulations of the Department.

(e) All public agencies may make available to the Department on request any factual data not otherwise privileged as a matter of law in their possession in respect to individuals committed to the Department.
(Source: P.A. 80-1099.) [Formerly Ill. Rev. Stat. 38 §1003-5-1.]

5/3-5-2. Institutional record.

§3-5-2. Institutional Record. The Department shall maintain records of the examination, assignment, transfer, discipline of committed persons and what grievances, if any, are made in each of its institutions, facilities and programs. The record shall contain the name of the persons involved, the time, date, place and purpose of the procedure, the decision and basis therefor, and any review of the decision made.
(Source: P.A. 77-2097.) [Formerly Ill. Rev. Stat. 38 §1003-5-2.]

5/3-5-3. Annual and other reports.

§3-5-3. Annual and other Reports. (a) The Director shall make an annual report to the Governor under Section 25 of The Civil Administrative Code of Illinois [20 ILCS 5/25], concerning the state and condition of all persons committed to the Department, its institutions, facilities and programs, of all moneys expended and received, and on what accounts expended and received. The report may also include an abstract of all reports made to the Department by individual institutions, facilities or programs during the preceding year.

(b) The Director shall make an annual report to the Governor and to the State Legislature on any inadequacies in the institutions, facilities or programs of the Department and also such amendments to the laws of the State which in his judgment are necessary in order to best advance the purposes of this Code.

(c) The Director may require such reports from division administrators, chief administrative officers and other personnel as he deems necessary for the administration of the Department.

(d) The Department of Corrections shall, by January 1, 1990, January 1, 1991, and every 2 years thereafter, transmit to the Governor and the General Assembly a 5 year long range planning document for adult female offenders under the Department's supervision. The document shall detail how the Department plans to meet the housing, educational/training, Correctional Industries and programming needs of the escalating adult female offender population.
(Source: P.A. 86-1001.) [Formerly Ill. Rev. Stat. 38 §1003-5-3.]

5/3-5-3.1. Report to General Assembly.

§3-5-3.1. As used in this Section, "facility" includes any facility of the Adult Division and any facility of the Juvenile Division of the Department of Corrections.

The Department of Corrections shall, by January 1st, April 1st, July 1st, and October 1st of each year, transmit to the General Assembly, a report which shall include the following information reflecting the period ending fifteen days prior to the submission of the report: 1) the number of residents in all Department facilities indicating the number of residents in each listed facility; 2) a classification of each facility's residents by the nature of the offense for which each

resident was committed to the Department; 3) the number of residents in maximum, medium, and minimum security facilities indicating the classification of each facility's residents by the nature of the offense for which each resident was committed to the Department; 4) the educational and vocational programs provided at each facility and the number of residents participating in each such program; 5) the present capacity levels in each facility; 6) the projected capacity of each facility six months and one year following each reporting date; 7) the ratio of the security guards to residents in each facility; 8) the ratio of total employees to residents in each facility; 9) the number of residents in each facility that are single-celled and the number in each facility that are double-celled; 10) information indicating the distribution of residents in each facility by the allocated floor space per resident; 11) a status of all capital projects currently funded by the Department, location of each capital project, the projected on-line dates for each capital project, including phase-in dates and full occupancy dates; 12) the projected adult prison and Juvenile Division facility populations for each of the succeeding twelve months following each reporting date, indicating all assumptions built into such population estimates; 13) the projected exits and projected admissions in each facility for each of the succeeding twelve months following each reporting date, indicating all assumptions built into such population estimate; and 14) the locations of all Department-operated or contractually operated community correctional centers, including the present capacity and population levels at each facility.
(Source: P.A. 85-252.) [Formerly Ill. Rev. Stat. 38 §1003-5-3.1.]

ARTICLE 6. INSTITUTIONS; FACILITIES; AND PROGRAMS

Sec.

5/3-6-1. Institutions; facilities; and programs.

§3-6-1. Institutions; Facilities; and Programs. (a) The Department shall designate those institutions and facilities which shall be maintained for persons assigned as adults and as juveniles.

(b) The types, number and population of institutions and facilities shall be determined by the needs of committed persons for treatment and the public for protection. All institutions and programs shall conform to the minimum standards under this Chapter.
(Source: P.A. 77-2097.) [Formerly Ill. Rev. Stat. 38 §1003-6-1.]

5/3-6-2. Institutions and facility administration.

§3-6-2. Institutions and Facility Administration. (a) Each institution and facility of the Department shall be administered by a chief administrative officer appointed by the Director. A chief administrative officer shall be responsible for all persons assigned to the institution or facility. The chief administrative officer shall administer the programs of the Department for the custody and treatment of such persons.

(b) The chief administrative officer shall have such assistants as the Department may assign.

(c) The Director or Assistant Director shall have the emergency powers to temporarily transfer individuals without formal procedures to any State, county, municipal or regional correctional or detention institution or facility in the State, subject to the acceptance of such receiving institution or facility, or to designate any reasonably secure place in the State as such an institution or facility and to make transfers thereto. However, transfers made under emergency powers shall be reviewed as soon as practicable under Article 8 [730 ILCS 5/3-8-1 et seq.], and shall be subject to Section 1-7 of the Juvenile Court Act of 1987 [705 ILCS 405/1-7]. This Section shall not apply to transfers to the Department of Mental Health and Developmental Disabilities which are provided for under Section 3-8-5 or Section 3-10-5 [730 ILCS 5/3-8-5 or 5/3-10-5].

(d) The Department shall provide educational programs for all committed persons so that all persons have an opportunity to attain the achievement level equivalent to the completion of the twelfth grade in the public school system in this State. Other higher levels of attainment shall be encouraged and professional instruction shall be maintained wherever possible. The Department may establish programs of mandatory education and may establish rules and regulations for the administration of such programs.

(e) A person committed to the Department who becomes in need of medical or surgical treatment but is incapable of giving consent thereto shall receive such medical or surgical treatment by the chief administrative officer consenting on the person's behalf. Before the chief administrative officer consents, he or she shall obtain the advice of one or more physicians licensed to practice medicine in all its branches in this State. If such physician or physicians advise:

(1) that immediate medical or surgical treatment is required relative to a condition threatening to cause death, damage or impairment to bodily functions, or disfigurement; and

(2) that the person is not capable of giving consent to such treatment; the chief administrative officer may give consent for such medical or surgical treatment, and such consent shall be deemed to be the consent of the person for all purposes, including, but not limited to, the authority of a physician to give such treatment.

(f) In the event that the person requires medical care and treatment at a place other than the institution or facility, the person may be removed therefrom under conditions prescribed by the Department.

(g) Any person having sole custody of a child at the time of commitment or any woman giving birth to a child after her commitment, may arrange through the Department of Children and Family Services for suitable placement of the child outside of the Department of Corrections. The Director of the Department of Corrections may determine that there are special reasons why the child should continue in the custody of the mother until the child is 6 years old.

(h) The Department may provide Family Responsibility Services which may consist of, but not be limited to the following:

(1) family advocacy counseling;

(2) parent self-help group;

(3) parenting skills training;

(4) parent and child overnight program;

(5) parent and child reunification counseling, either separately or together, preceding the inmate's release; and

(6) a prerelease reunification staffing involving the family advocate, the inmate and the child's counselor, or both and the inmate.

(i) Prior to the release of any inmate who has a documented history of intravenous drug use, and upon the receipt of that inmate's written informed consent, the Department shall provide for the testing of such inmate for infection with human immunodeficiency virus (HIV) and any other identified causative agent of acquired immunodeficiency syndrome (AIDS). The testing provided under this subsection shall consist of an enzyme-linked immunosorbent assay (ELISA) test or such other test as may be approved by the Illinois Department of Public Health. If the test result is positive, the Western Blot

Assay or more reliable confirmatory test shall be administered. All inmates tested in accordance with the provisions of this subsection shall be provided with pre-test and post-test counseling. Notwithstanding any provision of this subsection to the contrary, the Department shall not be required to conduct the testing and counseling required by this subsection unless sufficient funds to cover all costs of such testing and counseling are appropriated for that purpose by the General Assembly.

(Source: P.A. 86-661; 86-918; 86-1028; 86-1380.) [Formerly Ill. Rev. Stat. 38 §1003-6-2.]

5/3-6-3. Rules and regulations for early release.

§3-6-3. Rules and Regulations for Early Release. (a) (1) The Department of Corrections shall prescribe rules and regulations for the early release on account of good conduct of persons committed to the Department which shall be subject to review by the Prisoner Review Board.

(2) Such rules and regulations shall provide that the prisoner shall receive one day of good conduct credit for each day of service in prison other than where a sentence of "natural life" has been imposed. Each day of good conduct credit shall reduce by one day the inmate's period of incarceration set by the court.

(3) Such rules and regulations shall also provide that the Director may award up to 180 days additional good conduct credit for meritorious service in specific instances as the Director deems proper; except that the additional 90 days of good conduct credit for meritorious service provided by this amendatory Act of 1990 shall not be awarded to any prisoner who is serving a sentence for conviction of first degree murder, reckless homicide while under the influence of alcohol or any other drug, aggravated kidnapping, kidnapping, aggravated criminal sexual assault, criminal sexual assault, deviate sexual assault, aggravated criminal sexual abuse, aggravated indecent liberties with a child, indecent liberties with a child, child pornography, heinous battery, aggravated battery of a spouse, aggravated battery of a spouse with a firearm, aggravated battery of a child, endangering the life or health of a child, cruelty to a child, or narcotic racketeering.

(4) Such rules and regulations shall also provide that the good conduct credit accumulated and retained under paragraph (2) of subsection (a) of this Section by any inmate during specific periods of time in which such inmate is engaged full-time in educational programs provided by the Department under this paragraph (4) and achieves a goal of improved literacy or has satisfactorily completed other academic or vocational training programs provided by the Department as determined by the standards of the Department of Corrections School District, shall be multiplied by a factor of 1.25. However, no inmate shall be eligible for the additional good conduct credit under this paragraph (4), if convicted of first degree murder, second degree murder, or a Class X felony. No inmate shall be eligible for the additional good conduct credit under this paragraph (4) if such inmate has engaged in the educational, academic or vocational training programs provided by the Department under this paragraph (4) and has subsequently been convicted of a felony. Educational programs under which good conduct credit may be increased through the achievement of academic goals shall be provided by the Department on the basis of documented professional standards and shall be made available to any inmate seeking admission to such programs within the limits of fiscal resources appropriated by the General Assembly for such purpose. Eligible inmates who are denied immediate admission shall be placed on a waiting list under criteria established by the Department. The inability of any inmate to become engaged in any such educational program by reason of insufficient program resources or for any other reason established under the rules and regulations of the Department shall not be deemed a cause of action under which the Department or any employee or agent of the Department shall be liable for damages to the inmate.

(5) Whenever the Department is to release any inmate earlier than it otherwise would because of a grant of good conduct credit for meritorious service given at any time during the term, the Department shall give reasonable advance notice of such impending release to the State's attorney of the county where the prosecution of the inmate took place.

(b) Whenever a person is or has been committed under several convictions, with separate sentences, such sentences shall be construed under Section 5-8-4 [730 ILCS 5/5-8-4] in granting and forfeiting of good time.

(c) The Department shall prescribe rules and regulations for revoking good conduct credit, or suspending or reducing the rate of accumulation thereof for specific rule violations, during imprisonment. Such rules and regulations shall provide that:

(1) Good conduct credits previously earned shall accumulate on a monthly basis.

(2) No inmate may be penalized more than one year of good conduct credit for any one infraction.

When the Department seeks to revoke, suspend or reduce the rate of accumulation of any good conduct credits for an alleged infraction of its rules, it shall bring charges therefor against the prisoner sought to be so deprived of good conduct credits before the Prisoner Review Board as provided in subparagraph (a)(4) of Section 3-3-2 of this Code [730 ILCS 5/3-3-2], if the amount of credit at issue exceeds 30 days or when during any 12 month period, the cumulative amount of credit revoked exceeds 30 days except where the infraction is committed or discovered within 60 days of scheduled release. In such cases, the Department of Corrections may revoke up to 30 days of good conduct credit. The Board may subsequently approve the revocation of additional good conduct credit, if the Department seeks to revoke good conduct credit in excess of thirty days. However, the Board shall not be empowered to review the Department's decision with respect to the loss of 30 days of good conduct credit within any calendar year for any prisoner or to increase any penalty beyond the length requested by the Department.

The Director of the Department of Corrections, in appropriate cases, may restore up to 30 days good conduct credits which have been revoked, suspended or reduced. Any restoration of good conduct credits in excess of 30 days shall be subject to review by the Prisoner Review Board. However, the Board may not restore good conduct credit in excess of the amount requested by the Director.

Nothing contained in this Section shall prohibit the Prisoner Review Board from ordering, pursuant to Section 3-3-9(a)(3)(i)(B) [730 ILCS 5/3-3-9], that a prisoner serve up to one year of the sentence imposed by the court which was not served due to the accumulation of good conduct credit.

(Source: P.A. 86-1090; 86-1373; 87-435.) [Formerly Ill. Rev. Stat. 38 §1003-6-3.]

5/3-6-4. Enforcement of discipline—Escape.

§3-6-4. Enforcement of Discipline—Escape. (a) A committed person who escapes or attempts to escape from an institution or facility of the Adult Division, or escapes or attempts to escape while in the custody of an employee of the Adult Division, or holds or participates in the holding of any person as a hostage by force, threat or violence, or while participating in any disturbance, demonstration or riot, causes, directs or participates in the destruction of any property is guilty of a Class 2 felony. A committed person who fails to return from furlough or from work and day release is guilty of a Class 3 felony.

(b) If one or more committed persons injures or attempts to injure in a violent manner any employee, officer, guard, other peace officer or any other committed person or damages or attempts to damage any building or workshop, or any appurtenances thereof, or attempts to escape, or disobeys or resists any lawful command, the employees, officers, guards and other peace officers shall use all suitable means to defend themselves, to enforce the observance of discipline, to secure the persons of the offenders, and prevent such attempted violence or escape; and said employees, officers, guards, or other peace officers, or any of them, shall, in the attempt to prevent the escape of any such person, or in attempting to retake any such person who has escaped, or in attempting to prevent or suppress violence by a committed person against another person, a riot, revolt, mutiny or insurrection, be justified in the use of force, including force likely to cause death or great bodily harm under Section 7-8 of the Criminal Code of 1961 [720 ILCS 5/7-8] which he reasonably believed necessary.

As used in this Section, "peace officer" means any officer or member of any duly organized State, county or municipal police unit or police force.
(Source: P.A. 82-705.) [Formerly Ill. Rev. Stat. 38 §1003-6-4.]

5/3-6-5. Crimes committed by persons confined by the Department.

§3-6-5. Crimes Committed by Persons Confined by the Department. When any person is charged with committing an offense while confined by the Department, cognizance thereof shall be taken by the circuit court of the county wherein such crime was committed. Such court shall adjudicate and sentence the person charged with such crime in the same manner and subject to the same rules and limitations as are now established by law in relation to other persons charged with crime. The expense of prosecution shall be paid by the Department.
(Source: P.A. 77-2097.) [Formerly Ill. Rev. Stat. 38 §1003-6-5.]

5/3-6-6. Computer assisted literacy program.

§3-6-6. Computer assisted literacy program. (a) The Director, with the approval of and acting through the Department of Central Management Services, shall enter into an agreement with a major international manufacturer of computers by which that manufacturer (i) shall loan to the Department and install in a correctional facility equipment to implement a computer assisted literacy pilot program and (ii) shall aid in the implementation of that pilot program. The configuration of the computer equipment utilized in the pilot program shall be similar to that installed in other correctional facilities. The Director and the manufacturer shall designate the correctional facility in which the pilot program shall be established.

(b) The computer assisted literacy pilot program shall be conducted for not less than 6 months. The Department shall establish criteria for evaluating the pilot program, based on criteria used in other states for evaluating computer assisted literacy programs in correctional facilities in those states.

(c) The computer assisted literacy pilot program instructor shall submit periodic reports to the Director concerning utilization of the pilot program, benefits of the pilot program, and progress made by committed persons participating in the pilot program. The Director shall promptly forward these reports to the General Assembly.

(d) Not later than 6 months after the conclusion of the computer assisted literacy pilot program, the Director shall report the results of the pilot program to the General Assembly. The General Assembly shall thereupon evaluate the effectiveness of the pilot program.

(e) After the conclusion of the computer assisted literacy pilot program, the Department, with the approval of and acting through the Department of Central Management Services, may purchase the equipment utilized in the pilot program, subject to the availability of monies appropriated to the Department for that purpose.
(Source: P.A. 87-635.) [Formerly Ill. Rev. Stat. 38 §1003-6-6.]

ARTICLE 7. FACILITIES

5/3-7-1. Administrative regulations.

§3-7-1. Administrative Regulations. The Department shall promulgate Rules and Regulations in conformity with this Code.
(Source: P.A. 77-2097.) [Formerly Ill. Rev. Stat. 38 §1003-7-1.]

5/3-7-2. Facilities.

§3-7-2. Facilities. (a) All institutions and facilities of the Department shall provide every committed person with access to toilet facilities, barber facilities, bathing facilities at least once each week, a library of legal materials and published materials including newspapers and magazines approved by the Director.

(b) All institutions and facilities of the Department shall provide every committed person access to a radio or television system unless the chief administrative officer determines that such access is to be denied for disciplinary reasons.

(c) All institutions and facilities of the Department shall provide facilities for every committed person to leave his cell for at least one hour each day unless the chief administrative officer determines that it would be harmful or dangerous to the security or safety of the institution or facility.

(d) All institutions and facilities of the Department shall provide every committed person with a wholesome and nutritional diet at regularly scheduled hours, drinking water, clothing adequate for the season, bedding, soap and towels and medical and dental care.

(e) All institutions and facilities of the Department shall permit every committed person to send and receive an unlimited number of uncensored letters, provided, however, that the Director may order that mail be inspected and read for reasons of the security, safety or morale of the institution or facility. Each week, the Department shall provide to every committed person postage for at least 3 first-class letters weighing one ounce or less.

(f) All of the institutions and facilities of the Department shall permit every committed person to receive visitors, except in case of abuse of the visiting privilege or when the chief administrative officer determines that such visiting would be harmful or dangerous to the security, safety or morale of the institution or facility. Clergy, religious chaplain and attorney visiting privileges shall be as broad as the security of the institution or facility will allow.

(g) All institutions and facilities of the Department shall permit religious ministrations and sacraments to be available to every committed person, but attendance at religious services shall not be required.
(Source: P.A. 81-346.) [Formerly Ill. Rev. Stat. 38 §1003-7-2.]

5/3-7-2a. Commissary selling prices.

§3-7-2a. If a facility maintains a commissary or commissaries, the selling prices for all goods shall be sufficient to cover the costs of the goods and an additional charge of from 3% through 10%. A compliance audit of all commissaries and the distribution of commissary funds shall be included in the regular compliance audit of the Department conducted by the Auditor General in accordance with the Illinois State Auditing Act [30 ILCS 5/1-1 et seq.].

Items purchased for sale at any such commissary shall be purchased, wherever possible, at wholesale costs.
(Source: P.A. 82-652.) [Formerly Ill. Rev. Stat. 38 §1003-7-2a.]

5/3-7-2b. Prior notice to General Assembly.
§3-7-2b. Prior notice to General Assembly. Prior to the selection of any site for the construction of any correctional facility, work release center, community correctional center or any facility used for such purposes, the Governor shall provide prior timely notice to the President of the Senate, Speaker of the House, Senate Minority Leader and House Minority Leader. Such notice shall precede any public announcement or announcement to private individuals.
(Source: P.A. 83-942.) [Formerly Ill. Rev. Stat. 38 §1003-7-2b.]

5/3-7-3. Institutional safety and sanitation.
§3-7-3. Institutional Safety and Sanitation. (a) Standards of sanitation and safety for all institutions and facilities shall be established and enforced by the Department. All buildings and facilities shall be cleaned regularly and properly maintained. Ventilation of air and heat adequate to the climate and season shall be provided.

(b) All new, remodeled and newly designated institutions or facilities shall provide at least 50 square feet of cell, room or dormitory floor space.
(Source: P.A. 83-942.) [Formerly Ill. Rev. Stat. 38 §1003-7-3.]

5/3-7-4. Protection of persons.
§3-7-4. Protection of Persons. The Department shall establish rules and regulations for the protection of the person and property of employees of the Department and every committed person.
(Source: P.A. 77-2097.) [Formerly Ill. Rev. Stat. 38 §1003-7-4.]

5/3-7-5. Energy conservation program.
§3-7-5. The Department shall implement a comprehensive energy conservation program at all correctional institutions and facilities in the State, for the purpose of conserving energy in any and all forms and to ultimately reduce expenditures in such regard. The Department may request the Capital Development Board to provide personnel and services in connection with the inspection of the institutions and facilities and the making of specific recommendations for current expenditures for improvement and ultimate cost reduction.
(Source: P.A. 81-558.) [Formerly Ill. Rev. Stat. 38 §1003-7-5.]

5/3-7-6. Recovery of expenses incurred.
§3-7-6. The Director shall, when reasonably able, require convicted persons committed to Department correctional institutions or facilities to reimburse the Department for the expenses incurred by their incarceration to the extent of their ability to pay for such expenses. The Attorney General, upon authorization of the Director, shall institute actions in the name of the people of the State of Illinois to recover from convicted persons committed to Department correctional institutions or facilities the expenses incurred by their confinement.
(Source: P.A. 85-736; 86-1320.) [Formerly Ill. Rev. Stat. 38 §1003-7-6.]

5/3-7-7. Establishment of rules; services to committed persons.
§3-7-7. The Department shall establish rules governing the provision of mental health services to committed persons. Such rules shall provide, among other matters, that a committed person who is diagnosed as suffering from a mental illness or developmental disability shall have access to treatment as determined necessary by a qualified mental health or developmental disability professional of the Department, and that mental health records be disclosed

only for purposes authorized by Department rule or the Unified Code of Corrections [730 ILCS 5/1-1-1 et seq.] or as otherwise authorized by law.
(Source: P.A. 86-1403.) [Formerly Ill. Rev. Stat. 38 §1003-7-7.]

ARTICLE 8. ADULT INSTITUTIONAL PROCEDURES

Sec.

5/3-8-1. Receiving procedures.

§3-8-1. Receiving Procedures. (a) The Department shall establish one or more receiving stations for committed persons and for persons transferred under Section 3-10-11 [730 ILCS 5/3-10-11] and shall advise the sheriffs of the several counties of the location of such stations. In the execution of the mittimus or order for the commitment or transfer of a person to the Department, the sheriff shall deliver such person to the nearest receiving station of the Department. The sheriff shall also convey with such person at the time of delivery, the items under Section 5-4-1 [730 ILCS 5/5-4-1], and a record of the person's time, his behavior and conduct while under the sheriff's custody.

(b) The Department shall verify the identity of the person delivered before accepting custody and shall require delivery of the items under paragraph (a) of this Section or a statement of the reason why they cannot be delivered.

(c) The Department shall inventory and issue a receipt to such person for all money and other personal property not permitted to the possession of such person.

(Source: P.A. 78-255.) [Formerly Ill. Rev. Stat. 38 §1003-8-1.]

5/3-8-2. Social evaluation.

§3-8-2. Social Evaluation. (a) A social evaluation shall be made of a committed person's medical, psychological, educational and vocational condition and history, including the use of alcohol and other drugs, the circumstances of his offense, and such other information as the Department may determine. The committed person shall be assigned to an institution or facility in so far as practicable in accordance with the social evaluation. Recommendations shall be made for medical, dental, psychiatric, psychological and social service treatment.

(b) A record of the social evaluation shall be entered in the committed person's master record file and shall be forwarded to the institution or facility to which the person is assigned.

(c) Upon admission to a correctional institution each committed person shall be given a physical examination [, and if]. *If* he is suspected of having a communicable disease[, he shall be quarantined until he is known to be free from such disease.] *that in the judgment of the Department medical personnel requires medical isolation, the committed person shall remain in medical isolation until it is no longer deemed medically necessary.*

(Chgd. by P.A. 87-1256, §3, eff. 7/1/93. Matter in brackets eff. only until 7/1/93. Matter in italics eff. 7/1/93.)

(Source: P.A. 84-1475.) [Formerly Ill. Rev. Stat. 38 §1003-8-2.]

5/3-8-3. Program assignments.

§3-8-3. Program Assignments. (a) Work, education and other program assignments shall be made in so far as practicable in accordance with the social evaluation.

(b) The Director shall establish procedures for making and reviewing program assignments.

(Source: P.A. 77-2097.) [Formerly Ill. Rev. Stat. 38 §1003-8-3.]

5/3-8-4. Intradivisional transfers.

§3-8-4. Intradivisional Transfers. (a) After the initial assignments under Sections 3-8-2 and 3-8-3 [730 ILCS 5/3-8-2 and 5/3-8-3], all transfers of committed persons to another institution or facility shall be reviewed and approved by a person or persons designated by the Director. A record of each transfer and the reasons therefor shall be included in the person's master record file.

(b) Transfers to facilities for psychiatric treatment and care within the Department shall be made only after prior psychiatric examination and certification to the Director that such transfer is required. Persons in facilities for psychiatric treatment and care within the Department shall be reexamined at least every 6 months. Persons found to no longer require psychiatric treatment and care shall be transferred to other facilities of the Department.

(Source: P.A. 77-2097.) [Formerly Ill. Rev. Stat. 38 §1003-8-4.]

5/3-8-5. Transfer to Department of Mental Health and Developmental Disabilities.

§3-8-5. Transfer to Department of Mental Health and Developmental Disabilities. (a) The Department shall cause inquiry and examination at periodic intervals to ascertain whether any person committed to it may be subject to involuntary admission, as defined in Section 1-119 of the Mental Health and Developmental Disabilities Code [405 ILCS 5/1-119], or meets the standard for judicial admission as defined in Section 4-500 of the Mental Health and Developmental Disabilities Code [405 ILCS 5/4-500], or is an addict, alcoholic or intoxicated person as defined in the Illinois Alcoholism and Other Drug Dependency Act [20 ILCS 305/1-101 et seq.]. The Department may provide special psychiatric or psychological or other counseling or treatment to such persons in a separate institution within the Department, or the Director of the Department of Corrections may transfer such persons other than addicts, alcoholics or intoxicated persons to the Department of Mental Health and Developmental Disabilities for observation, diagnosis and treatment, subject to the approval of the Director of the Department of Mental Health and Developmental Disabilities, for a period of not more than 6 months, if the person consents in writing to the transfer. The person shall be advised of his right not to consent, and if he does not consent, such transfer may be effected only by commitment under paragraphs (c) and (d) of this Section.

(b) The person's spouse, guardian or nearest relative and his attorney of record shall be advised of their right to object, and if objection is made, such transfer may be effected only by commitment under paragraph (c) of this Section. Notices of such transfer shall be mailed to such person's spouse, guardian or nearest relative and to the attorney of record marked for delivery to addressee only at his last known address by certified mail with return receipt requested together with written notification of the manner and time within which he may object thereto.

(c) If a committed person does not consent to his transfer to the Department of Mental Health and Developmental Disabilities or if a person objects under paragraph (b) of this Section, or if the Department of Mental Health and Developmental Disabilities determines that a transferred person requires commitment to the Department of Mental Health and Developmental Disabilities for more than 6 months, or if the person's sentence will expire within 6 months, the Director of the Department of Corrections shall file a petition in the circuit court of the county in which the correctional institution or facility is located requesting the transfer of such person to the Department of Mental Health and Developmental Disabilities. A certificate of a psychiatrist, clinical psychologist or, if admission to a developmental disability facility is sought, of a physician that the person is in need of commitment to the Department of Mental Health and Developmental Disabilities for treatment or habilitation shall be attached to the petition. Copies of the petition shall be furnished to the named person and to the state's attorneys of the county in which the correctional institution or facility is located and the county in which the named person was committed to the Department of Corrections.

(d) The court shall set a date for a hearing on the petition within the time limit set forth in the Mental Health and Developmental Disabilities Code. The hearing shall be conducted in the manner prescribed by the Mental Health and Developmental Disabilities Code [405 ILCS 5/1-100 et seq.]. If the person is found to be in need of commitment to the Department of Mental Health and Developmental Disabilities for treatment or habilitation, the court may commit him to that Department.

(e) Nothing in this Section shall limit the right of the Director or the chief administrative officer of any institution or facility to utilize the emergency admission provisions of the Mental Health and Developmental Disabilities Code with respect to any person in his custody or care. The transfer of a person to an institution or facility of the Department of Mental Health and Developmental Disabilities under paragraph (a) of this Section does not discharge the person from the control of the Department.

(Source: P.A. 85-965; 86-1403.) [Formerly Ill. Rev. Stat. 38 §1003-8-5.]

5/3-8-6. Return and release from Department of Mental Health and Developmental Disabilities.

§3-8-6. Return and Release from Department of Mental Health and Developmental Disabilities. (a) The Department of Mental Health and Developmental Disabilities shall return to the Department of Corrections any person committed to it under Section 3-8-5 [730 ILCS 5/3-8-5], whose sentence has not expired and whom the Department of Mental Health and Developmental Disabilities deems no longer subject to involuntary admission, or no longer meets the standard for judicial admission.

(b) If a person returned to the Department of Corrections under paragraph (a) of this Section is eligible for parole and has not had a parole hearing within the preceding 6 months, he shall have a parole hearing within 45 days after his return.

(c) The Department of Corrections shall notify the Director of Mental Health and Developmental Disabilities of the expiration of the sentence of any person transferred to the Department of Mental Health and Developmental Disabilities under Section 3-8-5. If the Department of Mental Health and Developmental Disabilities determines that a person transferred to it under paragraph (a) of Section 3-8-5 requires further hospitalization, it shall file a petition for the involuntary or judicial admission of such person under the Mental Health and Developmental Disabilities Code [405 ILCS 5/1-100 et seq.].

(d) The Department of Mental Health and Developmental Disabilities shall release under the Mental Health and Developmental Disabilities Code, any person transferred to it under paragraph (c) of Section 3-8-5, whose sentence and parole term have expired and whom the Department of Mental Health and Developmental Disabilities deems no longer subject to involuntary admission, or no longer meets the standard for judicial admission.

(Source: P.A. 83-969.) [Formerly Ill. Rev. Stat. 38 §1003-8-6.]

5/3-8-7. Disciplinary procedures.

§3-8-7. Disciplinary Procedures. (a) All disciplinary action shall be consistent with this Chapter. Committed persons shall be informed of rules of behavior and conduct, the penalties for violation thereof, and the disciplinary procedure by which such penalties may be imposed. Such rules, penalties and procedures shall be posted and issued to the persons committed.

(b) (1) Corporal punishment and disciplinary restrictions on diet, medical or sanitary facilities, clothing, bedding, mail or access to legal materials are prohibited, as are reductions in the frequency of use of toilets, washbowls and showers.

(2) Disciplinary restrictions on visitations, work, education or program assignments, and the use of the prison's library shall be related as closely as practicable to abuse of such privileges or facilities. This paragraph shall not apply to segregation or isolation of persons for purposes of institutional control.

(3) No person in the Adult Division may be placed in solitary confinement for disciplinary reasons for more than 15 consecutive days or more than 30 days out of any 45 day period except in cases of violence or attempted violence committed against another person or property when an additional period of isolation for disciplinary reasons is approved by the chief administrative officer.

(c) Review of disciplinary action imposed under this Section shall be provided by means of the grievance procedure under Section 3-8-8 [730 ILCS 5/3-8-8]. A written report of the infraction shall be filed with the chief administrative officer within 72 hours of the occurrence of the infraction or the discovery of it and such report shall be placed in the file of the institution or facility. No disciplinary proceeding shall be commenced more than 8 calendar days after the infraction or the discovery of it unless the committed person is unable or unavailable for any reason to participate in the disciplinary proceeding.

(d) All institutions and facilities of the Adult Division shall establish, subject to the approval of the Director, procedures for hearing disciplinary cases except those that may involve the imposition of disciplinary isolation; the loss of good time credit under Section 3-6-3 [730 ILCS 5/3-6-3] or eligibility to earn good time credit; or a change in work, education, or other program assignment of more than 7 days duration.

(e) In disciplinary cases which may involve the imposition of disciplinary isolation, the loss of good time credit or eligibility to earn good time credit, or a change in work, education, or other program assignment of more than 7 days duration, the Director shall establish disciplinary procedures consistent with the following principles:

(1) Any person or persons who initiate a disciplinary charge against a person shall not determine the disposition of the charge. The Director may establish one or more disciplinary boards to hear and determine charges. To the extent possible, a person representing the counseling staff of the institution or facility shall participate in determining the disposition of the disciplinary case.

(2) Any committed person charged with a violation of Department rules of behavior shall be given notice of the charge including a statement of the misconduct alleged and of the rules this conduct is alleged to violate.

(3) Any person charged with a violation of rules is entitled to a hearing on that charge at which time he shall have an opportunity to appear before and address the person or persons deciding the charge.

(4) The person or persons determining the disposition of the charge may also summon to testify any witnesses or other persons with relevant knowledge of the incident. The person charged may be permitted to question any person so summoned.

(5) If the charge is sustained, the person charged is entitled to a written statement of the decision by the persons determining the disposition of the charge which shall include the basis for the decision and the disciplinary action, if any, to be imposed.

(6) A change in work, education, or other program assignment shall not be used for disciplinary purposes except as provided in paragraph (b) of this Section and then only after review and approval under Section 3-8-3 [730 ILCS 5/3-8-3].

(Source: P.A. 80-1099.) [Formerly Ill. Rev. Stat. 38 §1003-8-7.]

5/3-8-8. Grievances.

§3-8-8. Grievances. (a) The Director shall establish procedures to review the grievances of committed persons. The Director may establish one or more administrative review boards within the Department to review grievances. A committed person's right to file grievances shall not be restricted. Such procedure shall provide for the review of grievances by a person or persons other than the person or persons directly responsible for the conditions or actions against which the grievance is made.

(b) Such procedures shall provide that a record of such grievance and any decision made with respect to it shall be preserved for a period of one year.

(c) Such procedures shall allow committed persons to communicate grievances directly to the Director or some person designated by the Director outside of the institution or facility where the person is confined.

(d) All committed persons shall be informed of the grievance procedures established by the Department and they shall be available to all committed persons.

(e) Discipline shall not be imposed because of use of the grievance procedure.

(Source: P.A. 77-2097.) [Formerly Ill. Rev. Stat. 38 §1003-8-8.]

5/3-8-9. Agreement on detainers.

§3-8-9. Agreement on Detainers. (a) The Agreement on Detainers is hereby enacted into law and entered into by this State with all other jurisdictions legally joining therein in the form substantially as follows:

ARTICLE I

The party states find that charges outstanding against a prisoner, detainers based on untried indictments, informations or complaints, and difficulties in securing speedy trial of persons already incarcerated in other jurisdictions, produce uncertainties which obstruct programs of prisoner treatment and rehabilitation. Accordingly, it is the policy of the party states and the purpose of this agreement to encourage the expeditious and orderly disposition of such charges and determination of the proper status of any and all detainers based on untried indictments, informations or complaints. The party states also find that proceedings with reference to such charges and detainers, when emanating from another jurisdiction, cannot properly be had in the absence of cooperative procedures. It is the further purpose of this agreement to provide such cooperative procedures.

ARTICLE II

As used in this agreement:

(a) "State" shall mean a state of the United States; the United States of America; a territory or possession of the United States; the District of Columbia; the Commonwealth of Puerto Rico.

(b) "Sending state" shall mean a state in which a prisoner is incarcerated at the time that he initiates a request for final disposition pursuant to Article III hereof or at the time that a request for custody or availability is initiated pursuant to Article IV hereof.

(c) "Receiving state" shall mean the state in which trial is to be had on an indictment, information or complaint pursuant to Article III or Article IV hereof.

ARTICLE III

(a) Whenever a person has entered upon a term of imprisonment in a penal or correctional institution of a party state, and whenever during the continuance of the term of imprisonment there is pending in any other party state any untried indictment, information or complaint on the basis of which a detainer has been lodged against the prisoner, he shall be brought to trial within 180 days after he shall have caused to be delivered to the prosecuting officer and the appropriate court of the prosecuting officer's jurisdiction written notice of the place of his imprisonment and his request for a final disposition to be made of the indictment, information or complaint: provided that for a good cause shown in open court, the prisoner or his counsel being present, the court having jurisdiction of the matter may grant any necessary or reasonable continuance. The request of the prisoner shall be accompanied by a certificate of the appropriate official having custody of the prisoner, stating the term of commitment under which the prisoner is being held, the time already served, the time remaining to be served on the sentence, the amount of good time earned, the time of parole eligibility of the prisoner, and any decisions of the state parole agency relating to the prisoner.

(b) The written notice and request for final disposition referred to in paragraph (a) hereof shall be given or sent by the prisoner to the warden, commissioner of corrections or other official having custody of him, who shall promptly forward it together with the certificate to the appropriate prosecuting official and court by registered or certified mail, return receipt requested.

(c) The warden, commissioner of corrections or other official having custody of the prisoner shall promptly inform him of the source and contents of any detainer lodged against him and shall also inform him of his right to make a request for final disposition of the indictment, information or complaint on which the detainer is based.

(d) Any request for final disposition made by a prisoner pursuant to paragraph (a) hereof shall operate as a request for final disposition of all untried indictments, informations or complaints on the basis of which detainers have been lodged against the prisoner from the state to whose prosecuting official the request for final disposition is specifically directed. The warden, commissioner of corrections or other official having custody of the prisoner shall forthwith notify all appropriate prosecuting officers and courts in the several jurisdictions within the state to which the prisoner's request for final disposition is being sent of the proceeding being initiated by the prisoner. Any notification sent pursuant to this paragraph shall be accompanied by copies of the prisoner's written notice, request, and the certificate. If trial is not had on any indictment, information or complaint contemplated hereby prior to the return of the prisoner to the original place of imprisonment, such indictment, information or complaint shall not be of any further force or effect, and the court shall enter an order dismissing the same with prejudice.

(e) Any request for final disposition made by a prisoner pursuant to paragraph (a) hereof shall also be deemed to be a waiver of extradition with respect to any charge or proceeding contemplated thereby or included therein by reason of paragraph (d) hereof, and a waiver of extradition to the receiving state to serve any sentence there imposed upon him, after completion of his term of imprisonment in the sending state. The request for final disposition shall also constitute a consent by the prisoner to the production of his body in any court where his presence may be required in order to effectuate the purposes of this agreement and a further consent voluntarily to be returned to the original place of imprisonment in accordance with the provisions of this agreement. Nothing in this paragraph shall prevent the imposition of a concurrent sentence if otherwise permitted by law.

(f) Escape from custody by the prisoner subsequent to his execution of the request for final disposition referred to in paragraph (a) hereof shall void the request.

ARTICLE IV

(a) The appropriate officer of the jurisdiction in which an untried indictment, information or complaint is pending shall be entitled to have a prisoner against whom he has lodged a detainer and who is serving a term of imprisonment in any party state made available in accordance with Article V (a) hereof upon presentation of a written request for temporary custody or availability to the appropriate authorities of the state in which the prisoner is incarcerated: provided that the court having jurisdiction of such indictment, information or complaint shall have duly approved, recorded and transmitted the request: and provided further that there shall be a period of 30 days after receipt by the appropriate authorities before the request be honored, within which period the governor of the sending state may disapprove the request for temporary custody or availability, either upon his own motion or upon motion of the prisoner.

(b) Upon receipt of the officer's written request as provided in paragraph (a) hereof, the appropriate authorities having the prisoner in custody shall furnish the officer with a certificate stating the term of commitment under which the prisoner is being held, the time already served, the time remaining to be served on the sentence, the amount of good time earned, the time of parole eligibility of the prisoner, and any decisions of the state parole agency relating to the prisoner. Said authorities simultaneously shall furnish all other officers and appropriate courts in the receiving state who have lodged detainers against the prisoner with similar certificates and with notices informing them of the request for custody or availability and of the reasons therefor.

(c) In respect of any proceeding made possible by this Article, trial shall be commenced within 120 days of the arrival of the prisoner in the receiving state, but for good cause shown in open court, the prisoner or his counsel being present, the court having jurisdiction of the matter may grant any necessary or reasonable continuance.

(d) Nothing contained in this Article shall be construed to deprive any prisoner of any right which he may have to contest the legality of his delivery as provided in paragraph (a) hereof, but such delivery may not be opposed or denied on the ground that the executive authority of the sending state has not affirmatively consented to or ordered such delivery.

(e) If trial is not had on any indictment, information or complaint contemplated hereby prior to the prisoner's being returned to the original place of imprisonment pursuant to Article V (e) hereof, such indictment, information or complaint shall not be of any further force or effect, and the court shall enter an order dismissing the same with prejudice.

ARTICLE V

(a) In response to a request made under Article III or Article IV hereof, the appropriate authority in a sending state shall offer to deliver temporary custody of such prisoner to the appropriate authority in the state where such indictment, information or complaint is pending against such person in order that speedy and efficient prosecution may be had. If the request for final disposition is made by the prisoner, the offer of temporary custody shall accompany the written notice provided for in Article III of this agreement. In the case of a federal prisoner, the appropriate authority in the receiving state shall be entitled to temporary custody as provided by this agreement or to the prisoner's presence in federal custody at the place for trial, whichever custodial arrangement may be approved by the custodian.

(b) The officer or other representative of a state accepting an offer of temporary custody shall present the following upon demand:

(1) Proper identification and evidence of his authority to act for the state into whose temporary custody the prisoner is to be given.

(2) A duly certified copy of the indictment, information or complaint on the basis of which the detainer has been lodged and on the basis of which the request for temporary custody of the prisoner has been made.

(c) If the appropriate authority shall refuse or fail to accept temporary custody of said person, or in the event that an action on the indictment, information or complaint on the basis of which the detainer has been lodged is not brought to trial within the period provided in Article III or Article IV hereof, the appropriate court of the jurisdiction where the indictment, information or complaint has been pending shall enter an order dismissing the same with prejudice, and any detainer based thereon shall cease to be of any force or effect.

(d) The temporary custody referred to in this agreement shall be only for the purpose of permitting prosecution on the charge or charges contained in one or more untried indictments, informations or complaints which form the basis of the detainer or detainers or for prosecution on any other charge or charges arising out of the same transaction. Except for his attendance at court and while being transported to or from any place at which his presence may be required, the prisoner shall be held in a suitable jail or other facility regularly used for persons awaiting prosecution.

(e) At the earliest practicable time consonant with the purposes of this agreement, the prisoner shall be returned to the sending state.

(f) During the continuance of temporary custody or while the prisoner is otherwise being made available for trial as required by this agreement, time being served on the sentence shall continue to run but good time shall be earned by the prisoner only if, and to the extent that, the law and practice of the jurisdiction which imposed the sentence may allow.

(g) For all purposes other than that for which temporary custody as provided in this agreement is exercised, the prisoner shall be deemed to remain in the custody of and subject to the jurisdiction of the sending state and any escape from the temporary custody may be dealt with in the same manner as an escape from the original place of imprisonment or in any other manner permitted by law.

(h) From the time that a party state receives custody of a prisoner pursuant to this agreement until such prisoner is returned to the territory and custody of the sending state, the state in which the one or more untried indictments, informations or complaints are pending or in which trial is being had shall be responsible for the prisoner and shall also pay all costs of transporting, caring for, keeping and returning the prisoner. The provisions of this paragraph shall govern unless the states concerned shall have entered into a supplementary agreement providing for a different allocation of costs and responsibilities as between or among themselves. Nothing herein contained shall be construed to alter or affect any internal relationship among the departments, agencies and officers of and in the government of a party state, or between a party state and its subdivisions, as to the payment of costs, or responsibilities therefor.

ARTICLE VI

(a) In determining the duration and expiration dates of the time periods provided in Articles III and IV of this agreement, the running of said time periods shall be tolled whenever and for as long as the prisoner is unable to stand trial, as determined by the court having jurisdiction of the matter.

(b) No provision of this agreement, and no remedy made available by this agreement, shall apply to any person who is adjudged to be mentally ill.

ARTICLE VII

Each state party to this agreement shall designate an officer who, acting jointly with like officers of other party states, shall promulgate rules and regulations to carry out more effectively the terms and provisions of this agreement, and who shall provide, within and without the state, information necessary to the effective operation of this agreement.

ARTICLE VIII

This agreement shall enter into full force and effect as to a party state when such state has enacted the same into law. A state party to this agreement may withdraw herefrom by enacting a statute repealing the same. However, the withdrawal of any state shall not affect the status of any proceedings already initiated by inmates or by state officers at the time such withdrawal takes effect, nor shall it affect their rights in respect thereof.

ARTICLE IX

This agreement shall be liberally construed so as to effectuate its purposes. The provisions of this agreement shall be severable and if any phrase, clause, sentence or provision of this agreement is declared to be contrary to the constitution of any party state or of the United States or the applicability thereof to any government, agency, person or circumstance is held invalid, the validity of the remainder of this agreement and the applicability thereof to any government, agency, person or circumstance shall not be affected thereby. If this agreement shall be held contrary to the constitution of any state party hereto, the agreement shall remain in full force and effect as to the remaining states and in full force and effect as to the state affected as to all severable matters.

(b) "Appropriate court" as used in this Section with reference to the courts of this State means circuit courts.

(c) All courts, departments, agencies, officers and employees of this State and its political subdivisions are hereby directed to enforce the Agreement on Detainers and to cooperate with one another and with other party states in enforcing the agreement and effectuating its purpose.

(d) Section 3-6-4 [730 ILCS 5/3-6-4] shall apply to offenders while in the custody of another state under this Section.

(e) It shall be lawful and mandatory upon the chief administrative officer or other official in charge of a penal or correctional institution in this State to give over the person of any inmate thereof whenever so required by the operation of the Agreement on Detainers.

(f) The Director of the Department of Corrections shall be the officer designated under Article VII of the Agreement on Detainers.

(g) Copies of this act shall, upon its approval, be transmitted to the governor of each state, the attorney general and the administrator of general services of the United States, and the council of State Governments.
(Source: P.A. 77-2097.) [Formerly Ill. Rev. Stat. 38 §1003-8-9.]

5/3-8-10. Intrastate detainers.

§3-8-10. Intrastate Detainers. Except for persons sentenced to death, subsection (b), (c) and (e) of Section 103-5 of the Code of Criminal Procedure of 1963 [725 ILCS 5/103-5] shall also apply to persons committed to any institution or facility or program of the Illinois Department of Corrections who have untried complaints, charges or indictments pending in any county of this State, and such person shall include in the demand under subsection (b), a statement of the place of present commitment, the term, and length of the remaining term, the charges pending against him or her to be tried and the county of the charges, and the demand shall be addressed to the state's attorney of the county where he or she is charged with a copy to the clerk of that court and a copy to the chief administrative officer of the Department of Corrections institution or facility to which he or she is committed. The state's attorney shall then procure the presence of the defendant for trial in his county by habeas corpus. Additional time may be granted by the court for the process of bringing and serving an order of habeas corpus ad prosequendum. In the event that the person is not brought to trial within the allotted time, then the charge for which he or she has requested a speedy trial shall be dismissed.
(Source: P.A. 83-346.) [Formerly Ill. Rev. Stat. 38 §1003-8-10.]

ARTICLE 9. PROGRAMS OF THE JUVENILE DIVISION

5/3-9-1. Educational programs.

§3-9-1. Educational Programs. (a) All institutions or facilities housing persons of such age as to be subject to compulsory school attendance shall establish an educational program to provide such persons the opportunity to attain an elementary and secondary school education equivalent to the completion of the twelfth grade in the public school systems of this State; and, in furtherance thereof, shall utilize assistance from local public school districts and State agencies in established curricula and staffing such program.

(b) All institutions or facilities housing persons not subject to compulsory school attendance shall make available programs and training to provide such persons an opportunity to attain an elementary and secondary school education equivalent to the completion of the twelfth grade in the public school systems of this State; and, in furtherance thereof, such institutions or facilities may utilize assistance from local public school districts and State agencies in creating curricula and staffing the program.

(c) The Department of Corrections shall develop and establish a suicide reduction program in all institutions or facilities housing persons committed to the Juvenile Division. The program shall be designed to increase the life coping skills and self esteem of juvenile offenders and to decrease their propensity to commit self destructive acts.
(Source: P.A. 85-736.) [Formerly Ill. Rev. Stat. 38 §1003-9-1.]

5/3-9-2. Work training programs.

§3-9-2. Work Training Programs. (a) The Juvenile Division, in conjunction with the private sector, may establish and offer work training to develop work habits and equip persons committed to it with marketable skills to aid in their community placement upon release. Committed persons participating in this program shall be paid wages similar to those of comparable jobs in the surrounding community. A portion of the wages earned shall go to the Juvenile Division to pay part of the committed person's room and board, a portion shall be deposited into the Violent Crime Victim's Assistance Fund to assist victims of crime, and the remainder shall be placed into a savings account for the committed person which shall be given to the committed person upon release. The Department shall promulgate rules to regulate the distribution of the wages earned.

(b) The Juvenile Division may establish programs of incentive by achievement, participation in which shall be on a voluntary basis, to sell goods or services to the public with the net earnings distributed to the program participants subject to rules of the Department.

(Source: P.A. 87-199.) [Formerly Ill. Rev. Stat. 38 §1003-9-2.]

5/3-9-3. Day release.

§3-9-3. Day Release. (a) The Department may institute day release programs for persons committed to the Juvenile Division and shall establish rules and regulations therefor.

(b) The Department may arrange with local schools, public or private agencies or persons approved by the Department for the release of persons committed to the Juvenile Division on a daily basis to the custody of such schools, agencies or persons for participation in programs or activities.

(Source: P.A. 77-2097.) [Formerly Ill. Rev. Stat. 38 §1003-9-3.]

5/3-9-4. Authorized absence.

§3-9-4. Authorized Absence. The Department may extend the limits of the place of confinement of a person committed to the Juvenile Division so that he may leave such place on authorized absence. Whether or not such person is to be accompanied shall be determined by the chief administrative officer of the institution or facility from which such authorized absence is granted. An authorized absence may be granted for a period of time determined by the Department and any purpose approved by the Department.

(Source: P.A. 77-2097.) [Formerly Ill. Rev. Stat. 38 §1003-9-4.]

5/3-9-5. Minimum standards.

§3-9-5. Minimum Standards. The minimum standards under Article 7 [730 ILCS 5/3-7-1 et seq.] shall apply to all institutions and facilities under the authority of the Juvenile Division.

(Source: P.A. 77-2097.) [Formerly Ill. Rev. Stat. 38 §1003-9-5.]

5/3-9-6. Unauthorized absence.

§3-9-6. Unauthorized Absence. Whenever a person committed to the Juvenile Division of the Department of Corrections absconds or absents himself or herself without authority to do so, from any facility or program to which he or she is assigned, he or she may be held in custody for return to the proper correctional official by the authorities or whomsoever directed, when an order is certified by the Director or a person duly designated by the Director, with the seal of the Department of Corrections attached. The person so designated by the Director with such seal attached may be one or more persons and the appointment shall be made as a ministerial one with no recordation or notice necessary as to the designated appointees. The order shall be directed to all sheriffs, coroners, police officers, keepers or custodians of jails or other deten-

tion facilities whether in or out of the State of Illinois, or to any particular person named in the order.
(Source: P.A. 83-346.) [Formerly Ill. Rev. Stat. 38 §1003-9-6.]

5/3-9-7. Sexual abuse counseling programs.
§3-9-7. Sexual Abuse Counseling Programs. The Juvenile Division shall establish and offer sexual abuse counseling to both victims of sexual abuse and sexual offenders in as many facilities as necessary to insure sexual abuse counseling throughout the State.
(Source: P.A. 87-444.) [Formerly Ill. Rev. Stat. 38 §1003-9-7.]

ARTICLE 10. JUVENILE PROCEDURES

Sec.

5/3-10-1. Receiving procedures.
§3-10-1. Receiving Procedures. The receiving procedures under Section 3-8-1 [730 ILCS 5/3-8-1] shall be applicable to institutions and facilities of the Juvenile Division.
(Source: P.A. 77-2097.) [Formerly Ill. Rev. Stat. 38 §1003-10-1.]

5/3-10-2. Examination of persons committed to the Juvenile Division.
§3-10-2. Examination of Persons Committed to the Juvenile Division. (a) A person committed to the Juvenile Division shall be examined in regard to his medical, psychological, social, educational and vocational condition and history, including the use of alcohol and other drugs, the circumstances of his offense and any other information as the Department may determine.

(b) Based on its examination, the Department may exercise the following powers in developing a treatment program of any person committed to the Juvenile Division:

(1) Require participation by him in vocational, physical, educational and corrective training and activities to return him to the community.

(2) Place him in any institution or facility of the Juvenile Division.

(3) Order replacement or referral to the Parole and Pardon Board as often as it deems desirable. The Department shall refer the person to the Parole and Pardon Board as required under Section 3-3-4 [730 ILCS 5/3-3-4].

(4) Enter into agreements with the Director of the Department of Mental Health and Developmental Disabilities, the Director of Children and Family Services, and the Director of the Department of Alcoholism and Substance Abuse, with courts having probation officers and with private agencies or institutions for separate care or special treatment of persons subject to the control of the Department.

(c) The Department shall make periodic reexamination of all persons under the control of the Juvenile Division to determine whether existing orders in individual cases should be modified or continued. This examination shall be made with respect to every person at least once annually.

(d) A record of the treatment decision including any modification thereof and the reason therefor, shall be part of the committed person's master record file.

(e) The Department shall by certified mail, return receipt requested, notify the parent, guardian or nearest relative of any person committed to the Juvenile Division of his physical location and any change thereof.

(Source: P.A. 83-969.) [Formerly Ill. Rev. Stat. 38 §1003-10-2.]

5/3-10-3. Program Assignment.

§3-10-3. Program Assignment. (a) The chief administrative officer of each institution or facility of the Juvenile Division shall designate a person or persons to classify and assign juveniles to programs in the institution or facility.

(b) The program assignment of persons assigned to institutions or facilities of the Juvenile Division shall be made on the following basis:

(1) As soon as practicable after he is received, and in any case no later than the expiration of the first 30 days, his file shall be studied and he shall be interviewed and a determination made as to the program of education, employment, training, treatment, care and custody appropriate for him. A record of such program assignment shall be made and shall be a part of his master record file. A staff member shall be designated for each person as his staff counselor.

(2) The program assignment shall be reviewed at least once every 3 months and he shall be interviewed if it is deemed desirable or if he so requests. After review, such changes in his program of education, employment, training, treatment, care and custody may be made as is considered necessary or desirable and a record thereof made a part of his file. If he requests a change in his program and such request is denied, the basis for denial shall be given to him and a written statement thereof shall be made a part of his file.

(c) The Department may promulgate rules and regulations governing the administration of treatment programs within institutions and facilities of the Department.

(Source: P.A. 77-2097.) [Formerly Ill. Rev. Stat. 38 §1003-10-3.]

5/3-10-4. Intradivisional transfers.

§3-10-4. Intradivisional Transfers. (a) The transfer of committed persons between institutions or facilities of the Juvenile Division shall be under this Section, except that emergency transfers shall be under Section 3-6-2 [730 ILCS 5/3-6-2].

(b) The chief administrative officer of an institution or facility desiring to transfer a committed person to another institution or facility shall notify the Assistant Director of the Juvenile Division or his delegate of the basis for the transfer. The Assistant Director or his delegate shall approve or deny such request.

(c) If a transfer request is made by a committed person or his parent, guardian or nearest relative, the chief administrative officer of the institution or facility from which the transfer is requested shall notify the Assistant Director of the Juvenile Division or his delegate of the request, the reasons therefor and his recommendation. The Assistant Director or his delegate shall either grant the request or if he denies the request he shall advise the person or his parent, guardian or nearest relative of the basis for the denial.

(Source: P.A. 77-2097.) [Formerly Ill. Rev. Stat. 38 §1003-10-4.]

5/3-10-5. Transfers to the Department of Mental Health and Developmental Disabilities.

§3-10-5. Transfers to the Department of Mental Health and Developmental Disabilities. (a) If a person committed to the Juvenile Division meets the standard for admission of a minor to a mental health facility or is suitable for admission to a developmental disability facility, as these terms are used in the Mental Health and Developmental Disabilities Code [405 ILCS 5/1-100 et seq.], the Department may transfer the person to an appropriate State hospital or institution of the Department of Mental Health and Developmental Disabilities for a period not to exceed 6 months, if the person consents in writing to the transfer. The person shall be advised of his right not to consent, and if he does not consent, the transfer may be effected only by commitment under paragraph (e) of this Section.

(b) The parent, guardian or nearest relative and the attorney of record shall be advised of his right to object. If an objection is made, the transfer may be effected only by commitment under paragraph (e) of this Section. Notice of the transfer shall be mailed to the person's parent, guardian or nearest relative marked for delivery to addressee only at his last known address by certified mail with return receipt requested together with written notification of the manner and time within which he may object to the transfer. Objection to the transfer must be made by the parent, guardian or nearest relative within 15 days of receipt of the notification of transfer, by written notice of the objection to the Assistant Director or chief administrative officer of the institution or facility of the Department where the person was confined.

(c) If a person committed to the Department under the Juvenile Court Act [repealed] or the Juvenile Court Act of 1987 [705 ILCS 405/1-1 et seq.] is committed to a hospital or facility of the Department of Mental Health and Developmental Disabilities under this Section, the Assistant Director of the Juvenile Division shall so notify the committing juvenile court.

(d) Nothing in this Section shall limit the right of the Assistant Director of the Juvenile Division or the chief administrative officer of any institution or facility to utilize the emergency admission provisions of the Mental Health and Developmental Disabilities Code with respect to any person in his custody or care. The transfer of a person to an institution or facility of the Department of Mental Health and Developmental Disabilities under paragraph (a) of this Section does not discharge the person from the control of the Department.

(e) If the person does not consent to his transfer to the Department of Mental Health and Developmental Disabilities or if a person objects under paragraph (b) of this Section, or if the Department of Mental Health and Developmental Disabilities determines that a transferred person requires admission to the Department of Mental Health and Developmental Disabilities for more than 6 months for any reason, the Assistant Director of the Juvenile Division shall file a petition in the circuit court of the county in which the institution or facility is located requesting admission of the person to the Department of Mental Health and Developmental Disabilities. A certificate of a clinical psychologist, licensed clinical social worker who is a qualified examiner as defined in Section 1-122 of the Mental Health and Development Disabilities Code, or psychiatrist, or, if admission to a developmental disability facility is sought, of a physician that the person is in need of commitment to the Department of Mental Health and Developmental Disabilities for treatment or habilitation shall be attached to the petition. Copies of the petition shall be furnished to the named person, his parent, or guardian or nearest relative, the committing court, and to the state's attorneys of the county in which the institution or facility of the Juvenile Division from which the person was transferred is located and the county from which the named person was committed to the Department of Corrections.

(f) The court shall set a date for a hearing on the petition within the time limit set forth in the Mental Health and Developmental Disabilities Code. The hearing shall be conducted in the manner prescribed by the Mental Health and Developmental Disabilities Code. If the person is found to be in need of commitment to the Department of Mental Health and Developmental Disabilities for treatment or habilitation, the court may commit him to that Department.

(g) In the event that a person committed to the Department under the Juvenile Court Act or the Juvenile Court Act of 1987 is committed to facilities of the Department of Mental Health and Developmental Disabilities under paragraph (e) of this Section, the Assistant Director shall petition the committing juvenile court for an order terminating the Assistant Director's custody.
(Chgd. by P.A. 87-1158, §1, eff. 9/18/92.)
(Source: P.A. 85-1209.) [Formerly Ill. Rev. Stat. 38 §1003-10-5.]

5/3-10-6. Return and release from Department of Mental Health and Developmental Disabilities.

§3-10-6. Return and Release from Department of Mental Health and Developmental Disabilities. (a) The Department of Mental Health and Developmental Disabilities shall return to the Juvenile Division any person committed to a facility of the Department under paragraph (a) of Section 3-10-5 [730 ILCS 5/3-10-5] when the person no longer meets the standard for admission of a minor to a mental health facility, or is suitable for administrative admission to a developmental disability facility.

(b) If a person returned to the Juvenile Division under paragraph (a) of this Section has not had a parole hearing within the preceding 6 months, he shall have a parole hearing within 45 days after his return.

(c) The Juvenile Division shall notify the Director of the Department of Mental Health and Developmental Disabilities of the expiration of the commitment or sentence of any person transferred to the Department of Mental Health and Developmental Disabilities under Section 3-10-5. If the Department of Mental Health and Developmental Disabilities determines that such person transferred to it under paragraph (a) of Section 3-10-5 requires further hospitalization, it shall file a petition for commitment of such person under the Mental Health and Developmental Disabilities Code [405 ILCS 5/1-100 et seq.].

(d) The Department of Mental Health and Developmental Disabilities shall release under the Mental Health and Developmental Disabilities Code, any person transferred to it pursuant to paragraph (c) of Section 3-10-5, whose sentence has expired and whom it deems no longer meets the standard for admission of a minor to a mental health facility, or is suitable for administrative admission to a developmental disability facility. A person committed to the Department of Corrections under the Juvenile Court Act [repealed] or the Juvenile Court Act of 1987 [705 ILCS 405/1-1 et seq.] and transferred to the Department of Mental Health and Developmental Disabilities under paragraph (c) of Section 3-10-5 shall be released to the committing juvenile court when the Department of Mental Health and Developmental Disabilities determines that he no longer requires hospitalization for treatment.
(Source: P.A. 85-1209.) [Formerly Ill. Rev. Stat. 38 §1003-10-6.]

5/3-10-7. Interdivisional transfers.

§3-10-7. Interdivisional Transfers. (a) In any case where a minor was originally prosecuted under the provisions of the Criminal Code of 1961, as amended [720 ILCS 5/1-1 et seq.], and sentenced under the provisions of this Act pursuant to Section 2-7 of the Juvenile Court Act [repealed] or Section 5-4 of the Juvenile Court Act of 1987 [705 ILCS 405/5-4] and committed to the Juvenile Division under Section 5-8-6 [730 ILCS 5/5-8-6], the Department of Corrections shall, within 30 days of the date that the minor reaches the age of 17, send formal notification to the sentencing court and the State's Attorney of the county from which the minor was sentenced indicating the day upon which the minor offender will achieve the age of 17. Within 90 days of receipt of that notice, the sentencing court shall conduct a hearing, pursuant to the provisions of subsection (c) of this Section to determine whether or not the minor shall continue to remain under the auspices of the Juvenile Division or be transferred to the Adult Division of the Department of Corrections.

The minor shall be served with notice of the date of the hearing, shall be present at the hearing, and has the right to counsel at the hearing. The minor, with the consent of his or her counsel or guardian may waive his presence at hearing.

(b) Unless sooner paroled under Section 3-3-3 [730 ILCS 5/3-3-3], the confinement of a minor person committed for an indeterminate sentence in a criminal proceeding shall terminate at the expiration of the maximum term of imprisonment, and he shall thereupon be released to serve a period of parole under Section 5-8-1 [730 ILCS 5/5-8-1], but if the maximum term of imprisonment does not expire until after his 21st birthday, he shall continue to be subject to the control and custody of the Department, and on his 21st birthday, he shall be transferred to the Adult Division. If such person is on parole on his 21st birthday, his parole supervision may be transferred to the Adult Division.

(c) Any interdivisional transfer hearing conducted pursuant to subsection (a) of this Section shall consider all available information which may bear upon the issue of transfer. All evidence helpful to the court in determining the question of transfer, including oral and written reports containing hearsay, may be relied upon to the extent of its probative value, even though not competent for the purposes of an adjudicatory hearing. The court shall consider, along with any other relevant matter, the following:

1. The nature of the offense for which the minor was found guilty and the length of the sentence the minor has to serve and the record and previous history of the minor.

2. The record of the minor's adjustment within the Department of Corrections' Juvenile Division, including, but not limited to, reports from the minor's counselor, any escapes, attempted escapes or violent or disruptive conduct on the part of the minor, any tickets received by the minor, summaries of classes attended by the minor, and any record of work performed by the minor while in the institution.

3. The relative maturity of the minor based upon the physical, psychological and emotional development of the minor.

4. The record of the rehabilitative progress of the minor and an assessment of the vocational potential of the minor.

5. An assessment of the necessity for transfer of the minor, including, but not limited to, the availability of space within the Department of Corrections, the disciplinary and security problem which the minor has presented to the Juvenile Division and the practicability of maintaining the minor in a juvenile facility, whether resources have been exhausted within the Juvenile Division of the Department of Corrections, the availability of rehabilitative and vocational programs within the Department of Corrections, and the anticipated ability of the minor to adjust to confinement within an adult institution based upon the minor's physical size and maturity.

All relevant factors considered under this subsection need not be resolved against the juvenile in order to justify such transfer. Access to social records, probation reports or any other reports which are considered by the court for the purpose of transfer shall be made available to counsel for the juvenile at least 30 days prior to the date of the transfer hearing. The Sentencing Court, upon granting a transfer order, shall accompany such order with a statement of reasons.

(d) Whenever the Director or his designee determines that the interests of safety, security and discipline require the transfer to the Adult Division of a person 17 years or older who was prosecuted under the provisions of the

Criminal Code of 1961, as amended, and sentenced under the provisions of this Act pursuant to Section 2-7 of the Juvenile Court Act or Section 5-4 of the Juvenile Court Act of 1987 and committed to the Juvenile Division under Section 5-8-6, the Director or his designee may authorize the emergency transfer of such person, unless the transfer of the person is governed by subsection (e) of this Section. The sentencing court shall be provided notice of any emergency transfer no later than 3 days after the emergency transfer. Upon motion brought within 60 days of the emergency transfer by the sentencing court or any party, the sentencing court may conduct a hearing pursuant to the provisions of subsection (c) of this Section in order to determine whether the person shall remain confined in the Adult Division.

(e) The Director or his designee may authorize the permanent transfer to the Adult Division of any person 18 years or older who was prosecuted under the provisions of the Criminal Code of 1961, as amended, and sentenced under the provisions of this Act pursuant to Section 2-7 of the Juvenile Court Act or Section 5-4 of the Juvenile Court Act of 1987 and committed to the Juvenile Division under Section 5-8-6 of this Act. The Director or his designee shall be governed by the following factors in determining whether to authorize the permanent transfer of the person to the Adult Division:

1. The nature of the offense for which the person was found guilty and the length of the sentence the person has to serve and the record and previous history of the person.

2. The record of the person's adjustment within the Department of Corrections' Juvenile Division, including, but not limited to, reports from the person's counselor, any escapes, attempted escapes or violent or disruptive conduct on the part of the person, any tickets received by the person, summaries of classes attended by the person, and any record of work performed by the person while in the institution.

3. The relative maturity of the person based upon the physical, psychological and emotional development of the person.

4. The record of the rehabilitative progress of the person and an assessment of the vocational potential of the person.

5. An assessment of the necessity for transfer of the person, including, but not limited to, the availability of space within the Department of Corrections, the disciplinary and security problem which the person has presented to the Juvenile Division and the practicability of maintaining the person in a juvenile facility, whether resources have been exhausted within the Juvenile Division of the Department of Corrections, the availability of rehabilitative and vocational programs within the Department of Corrections, and the anticipated ability of the person to adjust to confinement within an adult institution based upon the person's physical size and maturity.

(Source: P.A. 85-1209.) [Formerly Ill. Rev. Stat. 38 §1003-10-7.]

5/3-10-8. Discipline.

§3-10-8. Discipline. (a) (1) Corporal punishment and disciplinary restrictions on diet, medical or sanitary facilities, clothing, bedding or mail are prohibited, as are reductions in the frequency of use of toilets, washbowls and showers.

(2) Disciplinary restrictions on visitation, work, education or program assignments, the use of toilets, washbowls and showers shall be related as closely as practicable to abuse of such privileges or facilities. This paragraph shall not apply to segregation or isolation of persons for purposes of institutional control.

(3) No person committed to the Juvenile Division may be isolated for disciplinary reasons for more than 7 consecutive days nor more than 15 days out of any 30 day period except in cases of violence or attempted violence committed against another person or property when an additional period of

isolation for disciplinary reasons is approved by the chief administrative officer. A person who has been isolated for 24 hours or more shall be interviewed daily by his staff counselor or other staff member.

(b) The Juvenile Division shall establish rules and regulations governing disciplinary practices, the penalties for violation thereof, and the disciplinary procedure by which such penalties may be imposed. The rules of behavior shall be made known to each committed person, and the discipline shall be suited to the infraction and fairly applied.

(c) All disciplinary action imposed upon persons in institutions and facilities of the Juvenile Division shall be consistent with this Section and Department rules and regulations adopted hereunder.

(d) Disciplinary action imposed under this Section shall be reviewed by the grievance procedure under Section 3-8-8 [730 ILCS 5/3-8-8].

(e) A written report of any infraction for which discipline is imposed shall be filed with the chief administrative officer within 72 hours of the occurrence of the infraction or the discovery of it and such report shall be placed in the file of the institution or facility.

(f) All institutions and facilities of the Juvenile Division shall establish, subject to the approval of the Director, procedures for disciplinary cases except those that may involve the imposition of disciplinary isolation; delay in referral to the Parole and Pardon Board or a change in work, education or other program assignment of more than 7 days duration.

(g) In disciplinary cases which may involve the imposition of disciplinary isolation, delay in referral to the Parole and Pardon Board, or a change in work, education or other program assignment of more than 7 days duration, the Director shall establish disciplinary procedures consistent with the following principles:

(1) Any person or persons who initiate a disciplinary charge against a person shall not decide the charge. To the extent possible, a person representing the counseling staff of the institution or facility shall participate in deciding the disciplinary case.

(2) Any committed person charged with a violation of Department rules of behavior shall be given notice of the charge including a statement of the misconduct alleged and of the rules this conduct is alleged to violate.

(3) Any person charged with a violation of rules is entitled to a hearing on that charge at which time he shall have an opportunity to appear before and address the person or persons deciding the charge.

(4) The person or persons deciding the charge may also summon to testify any witnesses or other persons with relevant knowledge of the incident. The person charged may be permitted to question any person so summoned.

(5) If the charge is sustained, the person charged is entitled to a written statement of the decision by the persons deciding the charge which shall include the basis for the decision and the disciplinary action, if any, to be imposed.

(6) A change in work, education, or other program assignment shall not be used for disciplinary purposes except as provided in paragraph (a) of the Section and then only after review and approval under Section 3-10-3 [730 ILCS 5/3-10-3].

(Source: P.A. 80-1099.) [Formerly Ill. Rev. Stat. 38 §1003-10-8.]

5/3-10-9. Grievances.

§3-10-9. Grievances. The procedures for grievances of the Juvenile Division shall be governed under Section 3-8-8 [730 ILCS 5/3-8-8].

(Source: P.A. 77-2097.) [Formerly Ill. Rev. Stat. 38 §1003-10-9.]

5/3-10-10. Assistance to committed persons.

§3-10-10. Assistance to Committed Persons. A person committed to the Juvenile Division shall be furnished with staff assistance in the exercise of any rights and privileges granted him under this Code. Such person shall be informed of his right to assistance by his staff counselor or other staff member.
(Source: P.A. 77-2097.) [Formerly Ill. Rev. Stat. 38 §1003-10-10.]

5/3-10-11. Transfers from Department of Children and Family Services.

§3-10-11. Transfers from Department of Children and Family Services. (a) If a minor is adjudicated a delinquent under the Juvenile Court Act [repealed] or the Juvenile Court Act of 1987 [705 ILCS 405/1-1 et seq.] and placed with the Department of Children and Family Services, and the Department of Children and Family Services determines that it lacks adequate facilities to care for and rehabilitate such minor, it may transfer the minor to the Juvenile Division of the Department of Corrections provided that:

(1) the juvenile court that adjudicated the minor a delinquent orders the transfer after a hearing with opportunity to the minor to be heard and defend; and

(2) the Assistant Director of the Department of Corrections, Juvenile Division, is made a party to the action; and

(3) notice of such transfer is given to the minor's parent, guardian or nearest relative.

(b) Guardianship of a minor transferred under this Section shall remain with the Department of Children and Family Services.
(Source: P.A. 85-1209.) [Formerly Ill. Rev. Stat. 38 §1003-10-11.]

5/3-10-12. Institution or facility of Juvenile Division as Juvenile Detention Facility.

§3-10-12. The Director of the Department of Corrections may authorize the use of any institution or facility of the Juvenile Division as a Juvenile Detention Facility for the confinement of minors under 16 years of age in the custody or detained by the Sheriff of any County or the police department of any city when said juvenile is being held for appearance before a Juvenile Court or by Order of Court or for other legal reason, when there is no Juvenile Detention facility available or there are no other arrangements suitable for the confinement of juveniles. The Director of the Department of Corrections may certify that suitable facilities and personnel are available at the appropriate institution or facility for the confinement of such minors and this certification shall be filed with the Clerk of the Circuit Court of the County. The Director of the Department of Corrections may withdraw or withhold certification at any time. Upon the filing of the certificate in a county the authorities of the county may then use those facilities and set forth in the certificate under the terms and conditions therein for the above purpose. Juveniles confined, by the Department of Corrections, under this Section, must be kept separate from adjudicated delinquents.
(Source: P.A. 78-878.) [Formerly Ill. Rev. Stat. 38 §1003-10-12.]

ARTICLE 11. FURLOUGHS

5/3-11-1. Furloughs.

§3-11-1. Furloughs. (a) The Department may extend the limits of the place of confinement of a committed person under prescribed conditions, so that he may leave such place on a furlough. Whether or not such person is to be accompanied on furlough shall be determined by the chief administrative officer. The Department may make an appropriate charge for the necessary expenses of accompanying a person on furlough. Such furloughs may be granted for a period of time not to exceed 14 days, for any of the following purposes:

(1) to visit a spouse, child (including a stepchild or adopted child), parent (including a stepparent or foster parent), grandparent (including stepgrandparent) or brother or sister who is seriously ill or to attend the funeral of any such person; or

(2) to obtain medical, psychiatric or psychological services when adequate services are not otherwise available; or

(3) to make contacts for employment; or

(4) to secure a residence upon release on parole or discharge; or

(5) to visit such person's family; or

(6) to appear before various educational panels, study groups, educational units, and other groups whose purpose is obtaining an understanding of the results, causes and prevention of crime and criminality, including appearances on television and radio programs.

(b) Furloughs may be granted for any period of time under paragraph 13 of Section 55a of The Civil Administrative Code of Illinois [20 ILCS 2605/55a].

(c) In any case where the person furloughed is not to be accompanied on furlough, the Department of Corrections shall give prior notice of the intended furlough to the State's Attorney of the county from which the offender was sentenced originally, the State's Attorney of the county where the furlough is to occur, and to the Sheriff of the county where the furlough is to occur. Said prior notice is to be in writing except in situations where the reason for the furlough is of such an emergency nature that previous written notice would not be possible. In such cases, oral notice of the furlough shall occur.

(Source: P.A. 86-820.) [Formerly Ill. Rev. Stat. 38 §1003-11-1.]

ARTICLE 12. CORRECTIONAL EMPLOYMENT PROGRAMS

Sec.

5/3-12-1. Useful employment.

§3-12-1. Useful Employment. The Department shall, in so far as possible, employ at useful work committed persons confined in institutions and facilities of the Department, who are over the age of compulsory school attendance, physically capable of such employment, and not otherwise occupied in programs of the Department. Such employment shall equip such persons with marketable skills, promote habits of work and responsibility and contribute to the expense of the employment program and the committed person's cost of incarceration.

(Source: P.A. 86-450.) [Formerly Ill. Rev. Stat. 38 §1003-12-1.]

5/3-12-2. Types of employment.

§3-12-2. Types of Employment. (a) The Department may establish, maintain, train and employ committed persons in industries for the production of articles, materials or supplies for resale to authorized purchasers. It may also employ committed persons on public works, buildings and property, the conservation of natural resources of the State, anti-pollution or environmental control projects, or for other public purposes, for the maintenance of the Department's buildings and properties and for the production of food or other necessities for its programs. The Department may establish, maintain and employ committed persons in the production of vehicle registration plates. A committed person's labor shall not be sold, contracted or hired out by the Department except under this Article and under Section 3-9-2 [730 ILCS 5/3-9-2].

(b) Works of art, literature, handicraft or other items produced by committed persons as an avocation and not as a product of a work program of the Department may be sold to the public under rules and regulations established by the Department. The cost of selling such products may be deducted from the proceeds, and the balance shall be credited to the person's account under Section 3-4-3 [730 ILCS 5/3-4-3].

(Source: P.A. 86-450.) [Formerly Ill. Rev. Stat. 38 §1003-12-2.]

5/3-12-3. Vocational training.

§3-12-3. Vocational Training. The Department shall maintain programs of training in various vocations and trades in connection with its employment programs and shall also provide opportunities for training outside working hours.

(Source: P.A. 77-2097.) [Formerly Ill. Rev. Stat. 38 §1003-12-3.]

5/3-12-3a. Contracts, leases and business agreements.

§3-12-3a. (a) Contracts, leases and business agreements. The Department may enter into a contract, lease or any other type of business agreement, not to exceed 20 years, with any private corporation, partnership, person or other business entity for the purpose of utilizing committed persons in the manufacture of goods or wares, in the provision of services or for any other business or commercial enterprise deemed by the Department to be consistent with proper training and rehabilitation of committed persons.

(b) The Department shall be permitted to construct buildings on State property for the purposes identified in subsection (a) and to lease for a period not to exceed 20 years any building or portion thereof on State property for the purposes identified in subsection (a).

(c) Any contract, lease or other business agreement referenced in subsection (a), shall include a provision requiring that all committed persons assigned receive in connection with their assignment such vocational training and/or apprenticeship programs as the Department deems appropriate.

(d) Committed persons assigned in accordance with this Section shall be compensated in accordance with the provisions of Section 3-12-5 [730 ILCS 5/3-12-5].

(Source: P.A. 86-450.) [Formerly Ill. Rev. Stat. 38 §1003-12-3a.]

5/3-12-4. Hours and conditions.

§3-12-4. Hours and Conditions. The Department shall make rules and regulations governing the hours and conditions of labor for committed persons and shall require a medical examination of all persons to determine their physical capacity to work.

(Source: P.A. 77-2097.) [Formerly Ill. Rev. Stat. 38 §1003-12-4.]

5/3-12-5. Compensation.

§3-12-5. Compensation. Persons performing a work assignment under subsection (a) of Section 3-12-2 [730 ILCS 5/3-12-2] may receive wages under rules and regulations of the Department. In determining rates of compensation, the Department shall consider the effort, skill and economic value of the work performed. Compensation may be given to persons who participate in other programs of the Department. Of the compensation earned pursuant to this Section, a portion, as determined by the Department, shall be used to offset the cost of the committed person's incarceration. All other wages shall be deposited in the individual's account under rules and regulations of the Department.
(Source: P.A. 86-450.) [Formerly Ill. Rev. Stat. 38 §1003-12-5.]

5/3-12-6. Industrial production; location; assignment.

§3-12-6. Industrial Production; Location; Assignment. The Department shall establish or cause to be established industrial production at its institutions and facilities to secure the most practical and efficient use of labor. The office for coordinating such industrial production shall be located in Springfield. It shall assign its personnel to direct the production of goods and shall employ committed persons assigned by the chief administrative officer. The Department may also direct such vocational programs as the institution or facility may require as a part of the employment program.
(Source: P.A. 80-728.) [Formerly Ill. Rev. Stat. 38 §1003-12-6.]

5/3-12-7. Purchasers; allocation.

§3-12-7. Purchasers; Allocation. (a) The State, its political units, its agencies and public institutions shall purchase from the Department all articles, materials, industry related services, food stuffs, and supplies required by them which are produced or manufactured by persons confined in institutions and facilities of the Department. The Secretary of State may purchase from the Department vehicle registration plates produced by persons confined in institutions and facilities of the Department. The Secretary shall determine reasonable specifications and prices of such vehicle registration plates as agreed upon with the Department. Not-for-profit corporations chartered in Illinois or other States may purchase such goods and services. Units of the Federal government and units of government in other States may also purchase such goods and services. All entities which contract with the State, its political units, its agencies, its public institutions or not-for-profit corporations chartered in Illinois, may purchase goods or services from the Department which are used in the performance of such contracts. Nothing shall prohibit the Department from bidding on portions of a State contract which are subcontracted by the primary contractor. The public may purchase crushed limestone and lime dust for agricultural and horticultural purposes and hardwood. The Department may also sell grain from its agricultural operations on the open market. All other articles, materials, industry related services, food stuffs and supplies which are produced or manufactured by persons confined in institutions and facilities of the Department shall be available for sale on the open market.

(b) Allocation of goods shall be made in the following manner:

(1) first, for needs of the Department;

(2) second, for the State, its agencies and public institutions;

(3) third, for those political subdivisions of the State and their agencies in which the producing institution or facility of the Department is located;

(4) fourth, for other political subdivisions of the State and their agencies and public institutions;

(5) fifth, for sale on the open market;

(6) sixth, for not for profit corporations chartered in Illinois;

(7) seventh, for units of government in other states;

(8) eighth, for units of the Federal government;
(9) ninth, for not-for-profit organizations chartered in other states;
(10) tenth, all other permitted purchasers.

(c) Exemption from required purchases shall be on certification of the Department that the items requested are not then available.
(Source: P.A. 86-450.) [Formerly Ill. Rev. Stat. 38 §1003-12-7.]

5/3-12-8. Purchase and control of supplies.

§3-12-8. Purchase and Control of Supplies. The Department may enter into contracts for the purchase of raw materials required for industrial production and shall have charge of articles, materials and supplies manufactured for sale to purchasers.
(Source: P.A. 77-2097.) [Formerly Ill. Rev. Stat. 38 §1003-12-8.]

5/3-12-9. Sale and lease of goods.

§3-12-9. Sale and Lease of Goods. (a) The Department shall establish procedures and issue regulations governing the sale and lease of goods. It shall issue a list of all goods available for sale and lease and shall issue certificates to any required purchasers under Section 3-12-7 [730 ILCS 5/3-12-7] where the goods requested are not currently available.

(b) Prices shall be determined by the Department as near to the usual market price for such items as possible and shall be uniform for all purchasers.

(c) Any disagreement between the Department and an authorized purchaser or lessee which cannot be resolved between the parties shall be submitted to arbitration. A board of 3 arbitrators shall be chosen: one by the Department; one by the purchaser; and one by the other 2 arbitrators. The decision of the arbitrators shall be final. The arbitrators shall receive no compensation but expenses shall be shared by the parties on an equal basis.
(Source: P.A. 84-1041.) [Formerly Ill. Rev. Stat. 38 §1003-12-9.]

5/3-12-10. Contracts null and void.

§3-12-10. Contracts Null and Void. Any contract or agreement violating this Article is null and void. The Attorney General of this State may bring legal action to challenge the validity of any contract agreement which he believes to be in violation of this Article.
(Source: P.A. 77-2097.) [Formerly Ill. Rev. Stat. 38 §1003-12-10.]

5/3-12-11. Report to the General Assembly.

§3-12-11. Report to the General Assembly. By November 1st of each year, the Department shall furnish to the General Assembly a report with respect to the following factors for the preceding fiscal year:

(a) A balance sheet;
(b) A financial statement, including profit or loss figures;
(c) The number and location of industries;
(d) The quantity of each good produced;
(e) The cost of materials and labor;
(f) Sales and actual receipts, by purchaser and in total;
(g) The average length of time between the receipt of orders and delivery;
(h) The average length of time between delivery and receipt of payment;
(i) The number of residents employed in each facility and industry, the number of vacancies occurring throughout the year, whether or not they have been subsequently filled, and the reasons for such vacancies; and
(j) Beginning on November 1, 1981, recidivism and employment statistics on former resident employees.
(Source: P.A. 81-1507.) [Formerly Ill. Rev. Stat. 38 §1003-12-11.]

5/3-12-11a. Food production facilities.

§3-12-11a. The Department shall establish, operate and maintain food production facilities whereby the Department shall employ committed persons to grow or produce as much food as is practicable for consumption within its institutions.

(Source: P.A. 85-306.) [Formerly Ill. Rev. Stat. 38 §1003-12-11a.]

5/3-12-12. Food processing facilities; provision of food for institutions of the Department.

§3-12-12. The Department shall establish, operate and maintain food processing facilities and provide food for its institutions and for the institutions of the Department of Mental Health and Developmental Disabilities.

(Source: P.A. 80-728.) [Formerly Ill. Rev. Stat. 38 §1003-12-12.]

5/3-12-13. Sale of property.

§3-12-13. Sale of Property. Whenever a responsible officer of the Correctional Industries Division of the Department seeks to dispose of property pursuant to the "State Property Control Act" [30 ILCS 605/1 et seq.], proceeds received by the Administrator under that Act from the sale of property under the control of the Division of Correctional Industries of the Department shall be deposited into the Working Capital Revolving Fund of the Correction Industries Division if such property was originally purchased with funds therefrom.

(Source: P.A. 81-1507.) [Formerly Ill. Rev. Stat. 38 §1003-12-13.]

5/3-12-14. Recycling and refuse sorting program.

§3-12-14. Recycling and Refuse Sorting Program. The Department shall establish and operate a recycling and refuse sorting program in which committed persons shall be employed. The Department shall promulgate rules and regulations to establish guidelines for the program. The Department shall report to the General Assembly as to the progress of this Recycling and Refuse Sorting Program.

(Source: P.A. 87-647.) [Formerly Ill. Rev. Stat. 38 §1003-12-14.]

ARTICLE 13. WORK AND DAY RELEASE

Sec.

5/3-13-1. Establishment.

§3-13-1. Establishment. The Department shall establish and maintain work and day release programs and facilities for persons committed to the Department. The Department may establish work and day release programs for nonviolent pregnant female offenders and nonviolent female offenders and their children under the age of 6.

(Source: P.A. 86-1380.) [Formerly Ill. Rev. Stat. 38 §1003-13-1.]

5/3-13-2. Purposes.

§3-13-2. Purposes. The Department may allow a committed person to leave an institution or facility during reasonable hours where such release would assist the individual's rehabilitation and would not cause undue risk to the public for any of the following purposes:

(1) work; or

(2) conduct a business or other self-employed occupation including housekeeping or attending to family needs; or

(3) attend an educational institution, including vocational education; or

(4) obtain medical or psychological treatment, including treatment for drug addiction or alcoholism; or

(5) other purposes directly related to programs of the Department.

(Source: P.A. 77-2097.) [Formerly Ill. Rev. Stat. 38 §1003-13-2.]

5/3-13-3. Record of release status.

§3-13-3. Record of Release Status. The fact and circumstances of release status shall be entered in the master record file of each person placed on work or day release.

(Source: P.A. 77-2097.) [Formerly Ill. Rev. Stat. 38 §1003-13-3.]

5/3-13-4. Rules and sanctions.

§3-13-4. Rules and Sanctions. (a) The Department shall establish rules governing release status and shall provide written copies of such rules to both the committed person on work or day release and to the employer or other person responsible for the individual. Such employer or other responsible person shall agree to abide by such rules, notify the Department of any violation thereof by the individual on release status, and notify the Department of the discharge of the person from work or other programs.

(b) If a committed person violates any rule, the Department may impose sanctions appropriate to the violation. The Department shall provide sanctions for unauthorized absences which shall include prosecution for escape under Section 3-6-4 [730 ILCS 5/3-6-4].

(c) An order certified by the Director, Assistant Director Adult Division, or the Supervisor of the Apprehension Unit, or a person duly designated by him or her, with the seal of the Department of Corrections attached and directed to all sheriffs, coroners, police officers, or to any particular persons named in the order shall be sufficient warrant for the officer or person named therein to arrest and deliver the violator to the proper correctional official. Such order shall be executed the same as criminal processes.

In the event that a work-releasee is arrested for another crime, the sheriff or police officer shall hold the releasee in custody until he notifies the nearest Office of Field Services or any of the above-named persons designated in this Section to certify the particular process or warrant.

(d) Not less than 15 days prior to any person being placed in a work release facility, the Department of Corrections shall provide to the State's Attorney and Sheriff of the county in which the work release center is located, relevant identifying information concerning the person to be placed in the work release facility. Such information shall include, but not be limited to, such identifying information as name, age, physical description, photograph, the offense, and the sentence for which the person is serving time in the Department of Corrections, and like information. The Department of Corrections shall, in addition, give written notice not less than 15 days prior to the placement to the State's Attorney of the county from which the offender was originally sentenced.

(Source: P.A. 83-346.) [Formerly Ill. Rev. Stat. 38 §1003-13-4.]

5/3-13-5. Wages and working conditions.

§3-13-5. Wages and Working Conditions. A person on work release shall not be required to work for less than the prevailing wage or under worse than prevailing working conditions in the area.
(Source: P.A. 77-2097.) [Formerly Ill. Rev. Stat. 38 §1003-13-5.]

5/3-13-6. Expenses; disposition of wages.

§3-13-6. Expenses; Disposition of Wages. (a) The Department shall establish reasonable fees for the costs of maintenance, transportation, and incidental expenses for those released for employment purposes. Advances of moneys as required by persons prior to receiving their first paycheck may be made by the Department under rules and regulations established by it.

(b) Compensation paid on account of any person's employment shall be credited to the individual's account in a bank or other financial institution determined by the Department.

(c) Any earnings after deduction of costs by the Department shall be sent to any legal dependents of the individual, if he shall direct, or to the appropriate agency if such dependents are receiving public assistance or are residents of a State hospital, State school, or foster care facility provided by the State. The surplus shall be deposited in his account for distribution at his direction according to rules and regulations of the Department.
(Source: P.A. 77-2097.) [Formerly Ill. Rev. Stat. 38 §1003-13-6.]

ARTICLE 14. PAROLE AND AFTER-CARE

Sec.

5/3-14-1. Release from the institution.

§3-14-1. Release from the Institution. (a) Upon release of a person on parole, mandatory release, final discharge or pardon the Department shall return all property held for him, provide him with suitable clothing and procure necessary transportation for him to his designated place of residence and employment. It may provide such person with a grant of money for travel and expenses which may be paid in installments. The amount of the money grant shall be determined by the Department.

The Department of Corrections may establish and maintain, in any institution it administers, revolving funds to be known as "Travel and Allowances Revolving Funds". These revolving funds shall be used for advancing travel and expense allowances to committed, paroled, and discharged prisoners. The moneys paid into such revolving funds shall be from appropriations to the Department for Committed, Paroled, and Discharged Prisoners.

(b) The Department shall, not later than January 1, 1986, enter into a written agreement with the Illinois Department of Public Aid which shall provide for interagency procedures to process and expedite applications for benefits authorized by the Illinois Public Aid Code [305 ILCS 5/1-1 et seq.] which are filed by or on behalf of persons scheduled for discharge from facilities operated by the Department.

(c) Except as otherwise provided in this Code, the Department shall establish procedures to provide written notification of any release of any person who has been convicted of a Class X felony to the sheriff of the county from which the offender was sentenced, and to the sheriff of the county in which the commission of the offense took place, at the written request of the sheriff from the county in which the commission of the offense took place. Except as otherwise provided in this Code, the Department shall establish procedures to provide written notification to the proper law enforcement agency for any municipality with a population of more than 25,000 persons, of any release of any person who has been convicted of a Class X felony where the arrest of the offender or the commission of the offense took place in such municipality, at the written request of the appropriate law enforcement agency.

(d) Upon the release of a committed person on parole, mandatory supervised release, final discharge or pardon, the Department shall provide such person with information concerning programs and services of the Illinois Department of Public Health to ascertain whether such person has been exposed to the human immunodeficiency virus (HIV) or any identified causative agent of Acquired Immunodeficiency Syndrome (AIDS).

(Source: P.A. 86-765.) [Formerly Ill. Rev. Stat. 38 §1003-14-1.]

5/3-14-2. Supervision on parole, mandatory supervised release and release by statute.

§3-14-2. Supervision on Parole, Mandatory Supervised Release and Release by Statute. (a) The Department shall retain custody of all persons placed on parole or mandatory supervised release or released pursuant to Section 3-3-10 of this Code [730 ILCS 5/3-3-10] and shall supervise such persons during their parole or release period in accord with the conditions set by the Prisoner Review Board. Such conditions shall include referral to an alcohol or drug abuse treatment program, as appropriate, if such person has previously been identified as having an alcohol or drug abuse problem. Such conditions may include that the person use an approved electronic monitoring device subject to Article 8A of Chapter V [730 ILCS 5/5-8A-1 et seq.].

(b) The Department shall assign personnel to assist persons eligible for parole in preparing a parole plan. Such Department personnel shall make a report of their efforts and findings to the Prisoner Review Board prior to its consideration of the case of such eligible person.

(c) A copy of the conditions of his parole or release shall be signed by the parolee or releasee and given to him and to his supervising officer who shall report on his progress under the rules and regulations of the Prisoner Review Board. The supervising officer shall report violations to the Prisoner Review Board and shall have the full power of peace officers in the arrest and retaking of any parolees or releasees or the officer may request the Department to issue a warrant for the arrest of any parolee or releasee who has allegedly violated his parole or release conditions. If the parolee or releasee commits an act that constitutes a felony using a firearm or knife, the officer shall request the Department to issue a warrant and the Department shall issue the warrant and the officer or the Department shall file a violation report with notice of charges with the Prisoner Review Board. A sheriff or other peace officer may detain an alleged parole or release violator until a warrant for his return to the Department can be issued. The parolee or releasee may be delivered to any secure place until he can be transported to the Department.

(d) The supervising officer shall regularly advise and consult with the parolee or releasee, assist him in adjusting to community life, inform him of the restoration of his rights on successful completion of sentence under Section 5-5-5 [730 ILCS 5/5-5-5].

(e) Supervising officers shall receive specialized training in the special needs of female releasees or parolees including the family reunification process.

(f) The supervising officer shall keep such records as the Prisoner Review Board or Department may require. All records shall be entered in the master file of the individual.

(Source: P.A. 86-661; 86-1281; 87-855.) [Formerly Ill. Rev. Stat. 38 §1003-14-2.]

5/3-14-3. Parole services.

§3-14-3. Parole Services. To assist parolees or releasees, the Department shall provide employment counseling and job placement services, and may in addition to other services provide the following:

(1) assistance in residential placement;

(2) family and individual counseling and treatment placement;

(3) financial counseling;

(4) vocational and educational counseling and placement; and

(5) referral services to any other State or local agencies. The Department may purchase necessary services for a parolee or releasee if they are otherwise unavailable and the parolee or releasee is unable to pay for them. It may assess all or part of the costs of such services to a parolee or releasee in accordance with his ability to pay for them.

(Source: P.A. 84-669.) [Formerly Ill. Rev. Stat. 38 §1003-14-3.]

5/3-14-4. Half-way houses.

§3-14-4. Half-way Houses. (a) The Department may establish and maintain half-way houses for the residence of persons on parole or mandatory release. Such half-way houses shall be maintained apart from security institutions, except that the Director of Corrections is authorized to designate that any work or day release facility, or any portion thereof, may be used as a half-way house for the residence of persons on parole or mandatory supervised release.

(b) For those persons to be placed in a half-way house directly upon release from an institution on parole or mandatory supervised release status, not less than 15 days prior to the placement of such a person in such a half-way house, the Department of Corrections shall give written notice to the State's Attorney and the Sheriff of the county in which the half-way house is located of the identity of the person to be placed in that program. Such identifying information shall include, but not be limited to, the name of the individual, age, physical description, photograph, the crime for which the person was originally sentenced to the Department of Corrections, and like information. The notice shall be given in all cases, except when placement of an emergency nature is necessary. In such emergency cases, oral notice shall be given to the appropriate parties within 24 hours with written notice to follow within 5 days.

(c) Persons on parole or mandatory supervised release status who have been previously released to the community, but who are not currently residing in a half-way house, may be placed in a half-way house upon the oral notification of the parties within 24 hours as indicated in subsection (b) of this Section. Such oral notification shall be followed with written notification within 5 days.

(Source: P.A. 82-717.) [Formerly Ill. Rev. Stat. 38 §1003-14-4.]

5/3-14-5. Mental health treatment; stalking and aggravated stalking.

§3-14-5. Mental Health treatment; stalking and aggravated stalking. For defendants found guilty of stalking or aggravated stalking and sentenced to the custody of the Department of Corrections, the court may order the Prisoner Review Board to consider requiring the defendant to undergo mental health treatment by a mental health professional or at a community mental health center, hospital, or facility of thc Department of Mental Health and Developmental Disabilities as a condition of parole or mandatory supervised release.

(Source: P.A. 87-870; 87-871.) [Formerly Ill. Rev. Stat. 38 §1003-14-5.]

ARTICLE 15. FIELD SERVICES

Sec.

5/3-15-1. Purpose.

§3-15-1. Purpose. The Department shall establish and provide post release treatment programs for juvenile offenders committed to the Department and released by the Prisoner Review Board.
(Source: P.A. 80-1099.) [Formerly Ill. Rev. Stat. 38 §1003-15-1.]

5/3-15-2. Standards and assistance to local jails and detention and shelter care facilities.

§3-15-2. Standards and Assistance to Local Jails and Detention and Shelter Care Facilities. (a) The Department shall establish for the operation of county and municipal jails and houses of correction, and county juvenile detention and shelter care facilities established pursuant to the "County Shelter Care and Detention Home Act" [55 ILCS 75/1 et seq.], minimum standards for the physical condition of such institutions and for the treatment of inmates with respect to their health and safety and the security of the community.

Such standards shall not apply to county shelter care facilities which were in operation prior to January 1, 1980. Such standards shall not seek to mandate minimum floor space requirements for each inmate housed in cells and detention rooms in county and municipal jails and houses of correction. However, no more than two inmates may be housed in a single cell or detention room.

(b) At least once each year, the Department may inspect each such facility for compliance with the standards established and the results of such inspection shall be made available by the Department for public inspection. If any detention, shelter care or correctional facility does not comply with the standards established, the Director of Corrections shall give notice to the county board and the sheriff or the corporate authorities of the municipality, as the case may be, of such noncompliance, specifying the particular standards that have not been met by such facility. If the facility is not in compliance with such standards when six months have elapsed from the giving of such notice, the Director of Corrections may petition the appropriate court for an order requiring such facility to comply with the standards established by the Department or for other appropriate relief.

(c) The Department may provide consultation services for the design, construction, programs and administration of detention, shelter care, and correctional facilities and services for children and adults operated by counties and municipalities and may make studies and surveys of the programs and the administration of such facilities. Personnel of the Department shall be admitted to these facilities as required for such purposes. The Department may develop and administer programs of grants-in-aid for correctional services in cooperation with local agencies. The Department may provide courses of training for the personnel of such institutions and conduct pilot projects in the institutions.

(d) The Department is authorized to issue reimbursement grants for counties, municipalities or public building commissions for the purpose of meeting minimum correctional facilities standards set by the Department under this Section. Grants may be issued only for projects that were completed after July 1, 1980 and initiated prior to January 1, 1987.

(1) Grants for regional correctional facilities shall not exceed 90% of the project costs or $7,000,000, whichever is less.

(2) Grants for correctional facilities by a single county, municipality or public building commission shall not exceed 75% of the proposed project costs or $4,000,000, whichever is less.

(3) As used in this subsection (d), "project" means only that part of a facility that is constructed for jail, correctional or detention purposes and does not include other areas of multi-purpose buildings.

Construction or renovation grants are authorized to be issued by the Capital Development Board from capital development bond funds after application by

a county or counties, municipality or municipalities or public building commission or commissions and approval of a construction or renovation grant by the Department for projects initiated after January 1, 1987.
(Source: P.A. 87-860.) [Formerly Ill. Rev. Stat. 38 §1003-15-2.]

5/3-15-3. Standards and procedures; mental health and developmental disability services.

§3-15-3. The Department may by rule establish standards and procedures for the provision of mental health and developmental disability services to mentally ill and developmentally disabled persons confined in a local jail or juvenile detention facility as set forth under Section 3-7-7 of this Code.
(Source: P.A. 86-1403.) [Formerly Ill. Rev. Stat. 38 §1003-15-3.]

CHAPTER V. SENTENCING

ARTICLE 1. GENERAL DEFINITIONS

5/5-1-1. Meanings of words and phrases.

§5-1-1. Meanings of Words and Phrases. For the purposes of this Chapter, the words and phrases described in this Article have the meanings designated in this Article, except when a particular context clearly requires a different meaning.
(Source: P.A. 77-2097.) [Formerly Ill. Rev. Stat. 38 §1005-1-1.]

5/5-1-2. Business Offense.

§5-1-2. Business Offense. "Business Offense" means a petty offense for which the fine is in excess of $500.
(Source: P.A. 77-2097.) [Formerly Ill. Rev. Stat. 38 §1005-1-2.]

5/5-1-3. Charge.

§5-1-3. Charge. "Charge" means a written statement presented to a court accusing a person of the commission of an offense and includes complaint, information and indictment.
(Source: P.A. 77-2097.) [Formerly Ill. Rev. Stat. 38 §1005-1-3.]

5/5-1-4. Conditional discharge.

§5-1-4. Conditional discharge. "Conditional Discharge" means a sentence or disposition of conditional and revocable release without probationary supervision but under such conditions as may be imposed by the court.
(Source: P.A. 78-1297.) [Formerly Ill. Rev. Stat. 38 §1005-1-4.]

5/5-1-5. Conviction.

§5-1-5. Conviction. "Conviction" means a judgment of conviction or sentence entered upon a plea of guilty or upon a verdict or finding of guilty of an offense, rendered by a legally constituted jury or by a court of competent jurisdiction authorized to try the case without a jury.
(Source: P.A. 77-2097.) [Formerly Ill. Rev. Stat. 38 §1005-1-5.]

5/5-1-6. Court.

§5-1-6. Court. "Court" means a circuit court of Illinois and includes a judge thereof.
(Source: P.A. 77-2097.) [Formerly Ill. Rev. Stat. 38 §1005-1-6.]

5/5-1-7. Defendant.

§5-1-7. Defendant. "Defendant" means a person charged with an offense.
(Source: P.A. 77-2097.) [Formerly Ill. Rev. Stat. 38 §1005-1-7.]

5/5-1-8. Defendant in need of mental treatment.

§5-1-8. Defendant in Need of Mental Treatment. "Defendant in need of mental treatment" means any defendant afflicted with a mental disorder, not including a person who is mentally retarded, if that defendant, as a result of such mental disorder, is reasonably expected at the time of determination or within a reasonable time thereafter to intentionally or unintentionally physically injure himself or other persons, or is unable to care for himself so as to guard himself from physical injury or to provide for his own physical needs.
(Source: P.A. 77-2097.) [Formerly Ill. Rev. Stat. 38 §1005-1-8.]

5/5-1-9. Felony.

§5-1-9. Felony. "Felony" means an offense for which a sentence to death or to a term of imprisonment in a penitentiary for one year or more is provided.
(Source: P.A. 77-2097.) [Formerly Ill. Rev. Stat. 38 §1005-1-9.]

5/5-1-10. Imprisonment.

§5-1-10. Imprisonment. "Imprisonment" means incarceration in a correctional institution under a sentence of imprisonment and does not include "periodic imprisonment" under Article 7 [730 ILCS 5/5-7-1 et seq.].
(Source: P.A. 77-2097.) [Formerly Ill. Rev. Stat. 38 §1005-1-10.]

5/5-1-11. Insanity.

§5-1-11. Insanity. "Insanity" means the lack of a substantial capacity either to appreciate the criminality of one's conduct or to conform one's conduct to the requirements of the law as a result of mental disorder or mental defect.
(Source: P.A. 77-2097.) [Formerly Ill. Rev. Stat. 38 §1005-1-11.]

5/5-1-12. Judgment.

§5-1-12. Judgment. "Judgment" means an adjudication by the court that the defendant is guilty or not guilty, and if the adjudication is that the defendant is guilty, it includes the sentence pronounced by the court.
(Source: P.A. 77-2097.) [Formerly Ill. Rev. Stat. 38 §1005-1-12.]

5/5-1-13. Mentally retarded.

§5-1-13. Mentally Retarded. "Mentally retarded and mental retardation" mean sub-average general intellectual functioning generally originating during the developmental period and associated with impairment in adaptive behavior

reflected in delayed maturation or reduced learning ability or inadequate social adjustment.
(Source: P.A. 77-2097.) [Formerly Ill. Rev. Stat. 38 §1005-1-13.]

5/5-1-14. Misdemeanor.
§5-1-14. Misdemeanor. "Misdemeanor" means any offense for which a sentence to a term of imprisonment in other than a penitentiary for less than one year may be imposed.
(Source: P.A. 77-2097.) [Formerly Ill. Rev. Stat. 38 §1005-1-14.]

5/5-1-15. Offense.
§5-1-15. Offense. "Offense" means conduct for which a sentence to a term of imprisonment or to a fine is provided by any law of this State or by any law, local law or ordinance of a political subdivision of this State, or by any order, rule or regulation of any governmental instrumentality authorized by law to adopt the same.
(Source: P.A. 77-2097.) [Formerly Ill. Rev. Stat. 38 §1005-1-15.]

5/5-1-16. Parole.
§5-1-16. Parole. "Parole" means the conditional and revocable release of a committed person under the supervision of a parole officer.
(Source: P.A. 78-939.) [Formerly Ill. Rev. Stat. 38 §1005-1-16.]

5/5-1-17. Petty offense.
§5-1-17. Petty Offense. "Petty offense" means any offense for which a sentence to a fine only is provided.
(Source: P.A. 77-2097.) [Formerly Ill. Rev. Stat. 38 §1005-1-17.]

5/5-1-18. Probation.
§5-1-18. Probation. "Probation" means a sentence or disposition of conditional and revocable release under the supervision of a probation officer.
(Source: P.A. 78-939.) [Formerly Ill. Rev. Stat. 38 §1005-1-18.]

5/5-1-18.1. Public or community service.
§5-1-18.1. "Public or community service" means uncompensated labor for a non-profit organization or public body whose purpose is to enhance physical or mental stability, environmental quality or the social welfare and which agrees to accept public or community service from offenders and to report on the progress of the public or community service to the court.
(Source: P.A. 85-449.) [Formerly Ill. Rev. Stat. 38 §1005-1-18.1.]

5/5-1-18.2. Site.
§5-1-18.2. "Site" means non-profit organization or public body agreeing to accept community service from offenders and to report on the progress of ordered public or community service to the court or its delegate.
(Source: P.A. 85-449.) [Formerly Ill. Rev. Stat. 38 §1005-1-18.2.]

5/5-1-19. Sentence.
§5-1-19. Sentence. "Sentence" is the disposition imposed by the court on a convicted defendant.
(Source: P.A. 77-2097.) [Formerly Ill. Rev. Stat. 38 §1005-1-19.]

5/5-1-20. State.
§5-1-20. State. "State" or "this State" means the State of Illinois.
(Source: P.A. 77-2097.) [Formerly Ill. Rev. Stat. 38 §1005-1-20.]

5/5-1-21. Supervision.
§5-1-21. Supervision. "Supervision" means a disposition of conditional and revocable release without probationary supervision, but under such conditions

and reporting requirements as are imposed by the court, at the successful conclusion of which disposition the defendant is discharged and a judgment dismissing the charges is entered.
(Source: P.A. 79-1334.) [Formerly Ill. Rev. Stat. 38 §1005-1-21.]

5/5-1-22. Victim.

§5-1-22. Victim. "Victim" shall have the meaning ascribed to it in subsection (a) of Section 3 of the Bill of Rights for Victims and Witnesses of Violent Crime Act [725 ILCS 120/3].
(Source: P.A. 83-1499.) [Formerly Ill. Rev. Stat. 38 §1005-1-22.]

ARTICLE 2. DIVERSION FOR SPECIALIZED TREATMENT

5/5-2-3. Fitness to be executed.

§5-2-3. Fitness to be Executed. (a) A person is unfit to be executed if because of a mental condition he is unable to understand the nature and purpose of such sentence.

(b) The question of fitness to be executed may be raised after pronouncement of the death sentence. The procedure for raising and deciding the question shall be the same as that provided for raising and deciding the question of fitness to stand trial subject to the following specific provisions:

(1) the question shall be raised by motion filed in the sentencing court;

(2) the question shall be decided by the court;

(3) the burden of proving that the offender is unfit to be executed is on the offender;

(4) if the offender is found unfit to be executed, he shall be remanded to the custody of the Department of Corrections until he becomes fit to be executed.
(Source: P.A. 77-2097.) [Formerly Ill. Rev. Stat. 38 §1005-2-3.]

5/5-2-4. Proceedings after acquittal by reason of insanity.

§5-2-4. Proceedings after Acquittal by Reason of Insanity. (a) After a finding or verdict of not guilty by reason of insanity under Sections 104-25, 115-3 or 115-4 of The Code of Criminal Procedure of 1963 [725 ILCS 5/104-25, 5/115-3 or 5/115-4], the defendant shall be ordered to the Department of Mental Health and Developmental Disabilities for an evaluation as to whether he is subject to involuntary admission or in need of mental health services. The order shall specify whether the evaluation shall be conducted on an inpatient or outpatient basis. If the evaluation is to be conducted on an inpatient basis, the defendant shall be placed in a secure setting unless the Court determines that there are compelling reasons why such placement is not necessary. After the evaluation and during the period of time required to determine the appropriate placement, the defendant shall remain in jail. Upon completion of the placement process the sheriff shall be notified and shall transport the defendant to the designated facility.

The Department shall provide the Court with a report of its evaluation within 30 days of the date of this order. The Court shall hold a hearing as provided under the Mental Health and Developmental Disabilities Code [405 ILCS 5/1-100 et seq.] to determine if the individual is: (a) subject to involuntary admission; (b) in need of mental health services on an inpatient basis; (c) in need of mental health services on an outpatient basis; (d) a person not in need of mental health services. The Court shall enter its findings.

If the defendant is found to be subject to involuntary admission or in need of mental health services on an inpatient care basis, the Court shall order the defendant to the Department of Mental Health and Developmental Disabilities. The defendant shall be placed in a secure setting unless the Court determines that there are compelling reasons why such placement is not necessary. Such defendants placed in a secure setting shall not be permitted outside the facility's housing unit unless escorted or accompanied by personnel of the Department of Mental Health and Developmental Disabilities or with the prior approval of the Court for unsupervised on-grounds privileges as provided herein. If the defendant is found to be in need of mental health services, but not on an inpatient care basis, the Court shall conditionally release the defendant, under such conditions as set forth in this Section as will reasonably assure the defendant's satisfactory progress in treatment or rehabilitation and the safety of the defendant or others. If the Court finds the person not in need of mental health services, then the Court shall order the defendant discharged from custody.

(1)* Definitions: For the purposes of this Section:

(A) "Subject to involuntary admission" means: A defendant has been found not guilty by reason of insanity; and

(i) who is mentally ill and who because of his mental illness is reasonably expected to inflict serious physical harm upon himself or another in the near future; or

(ii) who is mentally ill and who because of his illness is unable to provide for his basic physical needs so as to guard himself from serious harm.

(B) "In need of mental health services on an inpatient basis" means: a defendant who has been found not guilty by reason of insanity who is not subject to involuntary admission but who is reasonably expected to inflict serious physical harm upon himself or another and who would benefit from inpatient care or is in need of inpatient care.

(C) "In need of mental health services on an outpatient basis" means: a defendant who has been found not guilty by reason of insanity who is not subject to involuntary admission or in need of mental health services on an inpatient basis, but is in need of outpatient care, drug and/or alcohol rehabilitation programs, community adjustment programs, individual, group, or family therapy, or chemotherapy.

(D) "Conditional Release" means: the release from the custody of either the Department of Mental Health and Developmental Disabilities or the custody of the Court of a person who has been found not guilty by reason of insanity under such conditions as the court may impose which reasonably assure the defendant's satisfactory progress in treatment or habilitation and the safety of the defendant and others. The Court shall consider such terms and conditions which may include, but need not be limited to, outpatient care, alcoholic and drug rehabilitation programs, community adjustment programs, individual, group, family, and chemotherapy, periodic checks with the legal authorities and/or the Department of Mental Health and Developmental Disabilities. The person or facility rendering the outpatient care shall be required to periodically report to the Court on the progress of the Defendant. Such conditional release shall be for a period of five years, unless the defendant, the person or facility rendering the treatment, therapy, program or outpatient care, or the State's attorney petitions the Court for an extension of the conditional release period for an additional three years. Upon receipt of such a petition, the Court shall hold a hearing consistent with the provisions of this paragraph (a) and paragraph (f) of this Section, shall determine whether the defendant should continue to be subject to the terms of conditional release, and shall enter an order either extending the defendant's period of conditional release for a single additional three year period or discharging the defendant. In no event shall the defendant's period of conditional release exceed eight years. These provisions for extension of conditional release shall only apply to defendants conditionally released on or after July 1, 1979. However the extension provisions of this amendatory Act of 1984 apply only to defendants charged with a forcible felony.

**So in original. No subsec. (2) has been enacted.*

(b) If the Court finds the defendant subject to involuntary admission or in need of mental health services on an inpatient basis, the admission, detention, care, treatment or habilitation, review proceedings, and discharge of the defendant after such order shall be under the Mental Health and Developmental Disabilities Code, except that the initial order for admission of a defendant acquitted of a felony by reason of insanity shall be for an indefinite period of time. Such period of commitment shall not exceed the maximum length of time that the defendant would have been required to serve, less credit for good behavior, before becoming eligible for release had he been convicted of and received the maximum sentence for the most serious crime for which he has been acquitted by reason of insanity. The Court shall determine the maximum period of commitment by an appropriate order. During this period of time, the defendant shall not be permitted to be in the community in any manner, including but not limited to off-grounds privileges, with or without escort by personnel of the Department of Mental Health and Developmental Disabilities, unsupervised on-grounds privileges, discharge or conditional or temporary release, except by a plan as provided in this Section. In no event shall a defendant's continued unauthorized absence be a basis for discharge. Not more than 30 days after admission and every 60 days thereafter so long as the initial order remains in effect, the facility director shall file a treatment plan with the court. Such plan shall include an evaluation of the defendant's progress and the extent to which he is benefiting from treatment. Such plan may also include unsupervised on-grounds privileges, off-grounds privileges (with or without escort by personnel of the Department of Mental Health and Developmental Disabilities), home visits and participation in work programs, but only where such privileges have been approved by specific court order, which order may include such conditions on the defendant as the Court may deem appropriate and necessary to reasonably assure the defendant's satisfactory progress in treatment and the safety of the defendant and others.

(c) Every defendant acquitted of a felony by reason of insanity and subsequently found to be subject to involuntary admission or in need of mental health services shall be represented by counsel in all proceedings under this Section and under the Mental Health and Developmental Disabilities Code.

(1) The court shall appoint as counsel the public defender or an attorney licensed by this State.

(2) Upon filing with the court of a verified statement of legal services rendered by the private attorney appointed pursuant to paragraph (1) of this subsection, the court shall determine a reasonable fee for such services. If the defendant is unable to pay the fee, the court shall enter an order upon the State to pay the entire fee or such amount as the defendant is unable to pay from funds appropriated by the General Assembly for that purpose.

(d) When the facility director determines that:

(1) the defendant is no longer subject to involuntary admission or in need of mental health services on an inpatient basis; and

(2) the defendant may be conditionally released because he or she is still in need of mental health services or that the defendant may be discharged as not in need of any mental health services; or

(3) the defendant no longer requires placement in a secure setting; the facility director shall give written notice to the Court, State's Attorney and defense attorney. Such notice shall set forth in detail the basis for the recom-

mendation of the facility director, and specify clearly the recommendations, if any, of the facility director, concerning conditional release. Within 30 days of the notification by the facility director, the Court shall set a hearing and make a finding as to whether the defendant is:

(i) subject to involuntary admission; or

(ii) in need of mental health services in the form of inpatient care; or

(iii) in need of mental health services but not subject to involuntary admission or inpatient care; or

(iv) no longer in need of mental health services; or

(v) no longer requires placement in a secure setting.

Upon finding by the Court, the Court shall enter its findings and such appropriate order as provided in subsection (a) of this Section.

(e) A defendant admitted pursuant to this Section, or any person on his behalf, may file a petition for transfer to a non-secure setting within the Department of Mental Health and Developmental Disabilities or discharge or conditional release under the standards of this Section in the court which rendered the verdict. Upon receipt of a petition for transfer to a non-secure setting or discharge or conditional release, the court shall set a hearing to be held within 30 days. Thereafter, no new petition may be filed for 60 days without leave of the court.

(f) The court shall direct that notice of the time and place of the hearing be served upon the defendant, the facility director, the State's Attorney, and the defendant's attorney. If requested by either the State or the defense or if the Court feels it is appropriate, an impartial examination of the defendant by a psychiatrist or clinical psychologist as defined in Section 1-103 of the Mental Health and Developmental Disabilities Code [405 ILCS 5/1-103] who is not in the employ of the Department of Mental Health and Developmental Disabilities shall be ordered, and the report considered at the time of the hearing.

(g) The findings of the court shall be established by clear and convincing evidence. The burden of proof and the burden of going forth with the evidence rest with the State when a hearing is held to review the determination of the facility director that the defendant should be transferred to a non-secure setting, discharged or conditionally released. The burden of proof and the burden of going forth with the evidence rest on the defendant when a hearing is held to review a petition filed by or on behalf of such defendant. The evidence shall be presented in open court with the right of confrontation and cross-examination.

(h) If the court finds that the defendant is no longer in need of mental health services it shall order the facility director to discharge the defendant. If the Court finds that the defendant is in need of mental health services, and no longer in need of inpatient care, it shall order the facility director to release the defendant under such conditions as the Court deems appropriate and as provided by this Section. Such conditional release shall be imposed for a period of five years and shall be subject to later modification by the court as provided by this Section. If the court finds that the defendant is subject to involuntary admission or in need of mental health services on an inpatient basis, it shall order the facility director not to discharge or release the defendant in accordance with paragraph (b) of this Section.

(i) If within the period of the defendant's conditional release, the court determines, after hearing evidence, that the defendant has not fulfilled the conditions of release, the court shall order a hearing to be held consistent with the provisions of paragraph (f) and (g) of this section. At such hearing, if the court finds that the defendant is subject to involuntary admission or in need of mental health services on an inpatient basis, it shall enter an order remanding him or her to the Department of Mental Health and Developmental Disabilities or other facility. If the defendant is remanded to the Department of Mental Health and Developmental Disabilities, he or she shall be placed in a secure setting unless the court determines that there are compelling reasons that such placement is not necessary. If the court finds that the defendant continues to be in need of mental health services but not on an inpatient basis, it may modify the conditions of the original release in order to reasonably assure the defendant's satisfactory progress in treatment and his or her safety and the safety of others. In no event shall such conditional release be longer than eight years. Nothing in this Section shall limit a court's contempt powers or any other powers of a court.

(j) An order of admission under this Section does not affect the remedy of habeas corpus.

(k) In the event of a conflict between this Section and the Mental Health and Developmental Disabilities Code or the Mental Health and Developmental Disabilities Confidentiality Act [740 ILCS 110/1 et seq.], the provisions of this Section shall govern.

(*l*) This amendatory Act shall apply to all persons who have been found not guilty by reason of insanity and who are presently committed to the Department of Mental Health and Developmental Disabilities.

(m) The Clerk of the court shall, after the entry of an order of transfer to a non-secure setting of the Department of Mental Health and Developmental Disabilities or discharge or conditional release, transmit a certified copy of the order to the Department of Mental Health and Developmental Disabilities, and the sheriff of the county from which the defendant was admitted. In cases where the arrest of the defendant or the commission of the offense took place in any municipality with a population of more than 25,000 persons, the Clerk of the court shall also transmit a certified copy of the order of discharge or conditional release to the proper law enforcement agency for said municipality provided the municipality has requested such notice in writing.

(Source: P.A. 83-1449.) [Formerly Ill. Rev. Stat. 38 §1005-2-4.]

5/5-2-5. Testimony of clinical psychologist as an expert witness.

§5-2-5. In any issue of determination of fitness of a defendant to plead, to stand trial, to be sentenced or to be executed, or in any issue related to insanity or to mental illness, a clinical psychologist as defined in paragraph (a) of Section 102-21 of the Code of Criminal Procedure of 1963 shall be deemed qualified to testify as an expert witness in the form of his opinion about the issue of fitness or insanity or mental illness and shall not be restricted to testifying with regard to test results only.

(Source: P.A. 82-553.) [Formerly Ill. Rev. Stat. 38 §1005-2-5.]

5/5-2-6. Sentencing and treatment of defendant found guilty but mentally ill.

§5-2-6. Sentencing and Treatment of Defendant Found Guilty but Mentally Ill. (a) After a plea or verdict of guilty but mentally ill under Sections 115-2, 115-3 or 115-4 of the Code of Criminal Procedure of 1963 [725 ILCS 5/115-2, 5/115-3 or 5/115-4], the court shall order a presentence investigation and report pursuant to Sections 5-3-1 and 5-3-2 of this Act [730 ILCS 5/5-3-1 and 5/5-3-2], and shall set a date for a sentencing hearing. The court may impose any sentence upon the defendant which could be imposed pursuant to law upon a defendant who had been convicted of the same offense without a finding of mental illness.

(b) If the court imposes a sentence of imprisonment upon a defendant who has been found guilty but mentally ill, the defendant shall be committed to the Department of Corrections, which shall cause periodic inquiry and examination to be made concerning the nature, extent, continuance, and treatment of the defendant's mental illness. The Department of Corrections shall provide such psychiatric, psychological, or other counseling and treatment for the defendant as it determines necessary.

(c) The Department of Corrections may transfer the defendant's custody to the Department of Mental Health and Developmental Disabilities in accordance with the provisions of Section 3-8-5 of this Act [730 ILCS 5/3-8-5].

(d)(1) The Department of Mental Health and Developmental Disabilities shall return to the Department of Corrections any person committed to it pursuant to this Section whose sentence has not expired and whom the Department of Mental Health and Developmental Disabilities deems no longer requires hospitalization for mental treatment, mental retardation, or addiction.

(2) The Department of Corrections shall notify the Director of Mental Health and Developmental Disabilities of the expiration of the sentence of any person transferred to the Department of Mental Health and Developmental Disabilities under this Section. If the Department of Mental Health and Developmental Disabilities determines that any such person requires further hospitalization, it shall file an appropriate petition for involuntary commitment pursuant to the Mental Health and Developmental Disabilities Code [405 ILCS 5/1-100 et seq.].

(e)(1) All persons found guilty but mentally ill, whether by plea or by verdict, who are placed on probation or sentenced to a term of periodic imprisonment or a period of conditional discharge shall be required to submit to a course of mental treatment prescribed by the sentencing court.

(2) The course of treatment prescribed by the court shall reasonably assure the defendant's satisfactory progress in treatment or habilitation and for the safety of the defendant and others. The court shall consider terms, conditions and supervision which may include, but need not be limited to, notification and discharge of the person to the custody of his family, community adjustment programs, periodic checks with legal authorities and outpatient care and utilization of local mental health or developmental disabilities facilities.

(3) Failure to continue treatment, except by agreement with the treating person or agency and the court, shall be a basis for the institution of probation revocation proceedings.

(4) The period of probation shall be in accordance with Section 5-6-2 of this Act [730 ILCS 5/5-6-2] and shall not be shortened without receipt and consideration of such psychiatric or psychological report or reports as the court may require.
(Source: P.A. 82-553.) [Formerly Ill. Rev. Stat. 38 §1005-2-6.]

ARTICLE 3. PRESENTENCE PROCEDURE

Sec.

5/5-3-1. Presentence investigation.

§5-3-1. Presentence Investigation. A defendant shall not be sentenced for a felony before a written presentence report of investigation is presented to and considered by the court.

However, the court need not order a presentence report of investigation where both parties agree to the imposition of a specific sentence, provided there is a finding made for the record as to the defendant's history of delinquency or criminality, including any previous sentence to a term of probation, periodic imprisonment, conditional discharge, or imprisonment.

The court may order a presentence investigation of any defendant.
(Source: P.A. 80-1099.) [Formerly Ill. Rev. Stat. 38 §1005-3-1.]

5/5-3-2. Presentence report.

§5-3-2. Presentence Report. (a) In felony cases, the presentence report shall set forth:

(1) the defendant's history of delinquency or criminality, physical and mental history and condition, family situation and background, economic status, education, occupation and personal habits;

(2) information about special resources within the community which might be available to assist the defendant's rehabilitation, including treatment centers, residential facilities, vocational training services, correctional manpower programs, employment opportunities, special educational programs, alcohol and drug abuse programming, psychiatric and marriage counseling, and other programs and facilities which could aid the defendant's successful reintegration into society;

(3) the effect the offense committed has had upon the victim or victims thereof, and any compensatory benefit that various sentencing alternatives would confer on such victim or victims;

(4) information concerning the defendant's status since arrest, including his record if released on his own recognizance, or the defendant's achievement record if released on a conditional pre-trial supervision program;

(5) when appropriate, a plan, based upon the personal, economic and social adjustment needs of the defendant, utilizing public and private community resources as an alternative to institutional sentencing; and

(6) any other matters that the investigatory officer deems relevant or the court directs to be included.

(b) The investigation shall include a physical and mental examination of the defendant when so ordered by the court. If the court determines that such an examination should be made, it shall issue an order that the defendant submit to examination at such time and place as designated by the court and that such examination be conducted by a physician, psychologist or psychiatrist designated by the court. Such an examination may be conducted in a court clinic if so ordered by the court. The cost of such examination shall be paid by the county in which the trial is held.

(c) In misdemeanor, business offense or petty offense cases, except as specified in subsection (d) of this Section, when a presentence report has been ordered by the court, such presentence report shall contain information on the defendant's history of delinquency or criminality and shall further contain only those matters listed in any of paragraphs (1) through (6) of subsection (a) or in subsection (b) of this Section as are specified by the court in its order for the report.

(d) In cases under Section 12-15 and Section 12-30 of the Criminal Code of 1961, as amended [720 ILCS 5/12-15 and 5/12-30], the presentence report shall set forth information about alcohol, drug abuse, psychiatric, and marriage counseling or other treatment programs and facilities, information on the defendant's history of delinquency or criminality, and shall contain those additional matters listed in any of paragraphs (1) through (6) of subsection (a) or in subsection (b) of this Section as are specified by the court.

(e) Nothing in this Section shall cause the defendant to be held without bail or to have his bail revoked for the purpose of preparing the presentence report or making an examination.

(Source: P.A. 86-391.) [Formerly Ill. Rev. Stat. 38 §1005-3-2.]

5/5-3-3. Presentence commitment for study.

§5-3-3. Presentence Commitment for Study. (a) In felony cases where the court is of the opinion that imprisonment may be appropriate but desires more information as a basis for determining the sentence than has been or may be provided by a presentence report under Section 5-3-1 [730 ILCS 5/5-3-1], the court may commit for a period not exceeding 60 days a convicted person to the custody of the court clinic or the Department of Corrections if the Department has certified to the court that it can examine such persons under this Section.

(b) The Department or court clinic shall conduct a study of the person and shall, pursuant to the court's request, inquire into such matters as his previous delinquency or criminal experience, his social background, his capabilities and his mental, emotional and physical health and the rehabilitative resources of programs adaptable to his needs and any other matters that the court directs.

(c) At the expiration of the commitment or the sooner completion of the ordered studies, the person shall be returned to the court for sentencing with a written report of the results of the study. The report shall be filed of record under Section 5-3-4 [730 ILCS 5/5-3-4].

(d) The time for which the defendant was committed for study shall be credited against any sentence imposed.

(Source: P.A. 77-2097.) [Formerly Ill. Rev. Stat. 38 §1005-3-3.]

5/5-3-4. Disclosure of reports.

§5-3-4. Disclosure of Reports. (a) Any report made pursuant to this Article or Section 5-22 of the Juvenile Court Act of 1987 [705 ILCS 405/5-22] shall be filed of record with the court in a sealed envelope.

(b) Presentence reports shall be open for inspection only as follows:

(1) to the sentencing court;

(2) to the state's attorney and the defendant's attorney at least 3 days prior to the imposition of sentence, unless such 3 day requirement is waived;

(3) to an appellate court in which the conviction or sentence is subject to review;

(4) to any department, agency or institution to which the defendant is committed;

(5) to any probation department of whom courtesy probation is requested;

(6) to any probation department assigned by a court of lawful jurisdiction to conduct a presentence report;

(7) to any other person only as ordered by the court.

(c) Presentence reports shall be filed of record with the court within 30 days of a verdict or finding of guilty for any offense involving an illegal sexual act perpetrated upon victim, including but not limited to offenses for violations of Article 12 of the Criminal Code of 1961 [720 ILCS 5/12-1 et seq.].

(d) A complaint, information or indictment shall not be quashed or dismissed nor shall any person in custody for an offense be discharged from custody because of noncompliance with subsection (c) of this Section.

(Chgd. by P.A. 87-900, §1, eff. 1/1/93.)
(Source: P.A. 86-391.) [Formerly Ill. Rev. Stat. 38 §1005-3-4.]

ARTICLE 4. SENTENCING

5/5-4-1. Sentencing hearing.

§5-4-1. Sentencing Hearing. (a) Except when the death penalty is sought under hearing procedures otherwise specified, after a determination of guilt, a hearing shall be held to impose the sentence. However, prior to the imposition of sentence on an individual being sentenced for an offense based upon a charge for a violation of Section 11-501 of The Illinois Vehicle Code [625 ILCS 5/11-501] or a similar provision of a local ordinance, the individual must undergo a professional evaluation to determine if an alcohol or other drug abuse problem exists and the extent of such a problem. Programs conducting these evaluations shall be licensed by the Department of Alcoholism and Substance Abuse. However, if the individual is not a resident of Illinois, the court may, in its discretion, accept an evaluation from a program in the state of such individual's residence. The court may in its sentencing order approve an eligible defendant for placement in a Department of Corrections impact incarceration program as provided in Section 5-8-1.1 [730 ILCS 5/5-8-1.1]. At the hearing the court shall:

(1) consider the evidence, if any, received upon the trial;

(2) consider any presentence reports;

(3) consider the financial impact of incarceration based on the financial impact statement filed with the clerk of the court by the Department of Corrections;

(4) consider evidence and information offered by the parties in aggravation and mitigation;

(5) hear arguments as to sentencing alternatives;

(6) afford the defendant the opportunity to make a statement in his own behalf;

(7) afford the victim of a violent crime or a violation of Section 11-501 of the Illinois Vehicle Code, or a similar provision of a local ordinance, committed by the defendant the opportunity to make a statement concerning the impact on the victim and to offer evidence in aggravation or mitigation; provided that the statement and evidence offered in aggravation or mitigation must first be prepared in writing in conjunction with the State's Attorney before it may be presented orally at the hearing. Any sworn testimony offered by the victim is subject to the defendant's right to cross-examine. All statements and evidence offered under this paragraph (7) shall become part of the record of the court; and

(8) in cases of reckless homicide afford the victim's spouse, guardians, parents or other immediate family members an opportunity to make oral statements.

(b) All sentences shall be imposed by the judge based upon his independent assessment of the elements specified above and any agreement as to sentence reached by the parties. The judge who presided at the trial or the judge who accepted the plea of guilty shall impose the sentence unless he is no longer sitting as a judge in that court. Where the judge does not impose sentence at the same time on all defendants who are convicted as a result of being involved in the same offense, the defendant or the State's attorney may advise the sentencing court of the disposition of any other defendants who have been sentenced.

(c) In imposing a sentence for a violent crime or for an offense of operating or being in physical control of a vehicle while under the influence of alcohol, any other drug or any combination thereof, or a similar provision of a local ordinance, when such offense resulted in the personal injury to someone other than the defendant, the trial judge shall specify on the record the particular evidence, information, factors in mitigation and aggravation or other reasons that led to his sentencing determination. The full verbatim record of the sentencing hearing shall be filed with the clerk of the court and shall be a public record.

(d) When the defendant is committed to the Department of Corrections, the State's Attorney shall and counsel for the defendant may file a statement with the clerk of the court to be transmitted to the department, agency or institution to which the defendant is committed to furnish such department, agency or institution with the facts and circumstances of the offense for which the person was committed together with all other factual information accessible to them in regard to the person prior to his commitment relative to his habits, associates, disposition and reputation and any other facts and circumstances which may aid such department, agency or institution during its custody of such person. The clerk shall within 10 days after receiving any such statements transmit a copy to such department, agency or institution and a copy to the other party, provided, however, that this shall not be cause for delay in conveying the person to the department, agency or institution to which he has been committed.

(e) The clerk of the court shall transmit to the department, agency or institution, if any, to which the defendant is committed, the following:

(1) the sentence imposed;

(2) any statement by the court of the basis for imposing the sentence;

(3) any presentence reports;

(4) the number of days, if any, which the defendant has been in custody and for which he is entitled to credit against the sentence, which information shall be provided to the clerk by the sheriff;

(5) all statements filed under subsection (d) of this Section;

(6) any medical or mental health records or summaries of the defendant;

(7) the municipality where the arrest of the offender or the commission of the offense has occurred, where such municipality has a population of more than 25,000 persons;

(8) all statements made and evidence offered under paragraph (7) of subsection (a) of this Section; and

(9) all additional matters which the court directs the clerk to transmit.

(Source: P.A. 86-1182; 86-1183; 87-417.) [Formerly Ill. Rev. Stat. 38 §1005-4-1.]

5/5-4-2. Multiple offenses.

§5-4-2. Multiple Offenses. (a) After conviction and before sentencing, the defendant shall be permitted, subject to the approval of the State's Attorney, to plead guilty to other offenses he has committed which are within the same county. If the defendant is not formally charged with such offenses, an information shall be filed on the basis of the defendant's admission of guilt. Submission of such a plea shall constitute a waiver of all objections which the defendant might otherwise have to the charge. If such a plea is tendered and accepted, the court shall sentence the defendant for all offenses in one hearing under Section 5-8-4 [730 ILCS 5/5-8-4].

(b) A defendant convicted, charged, or held in custody in a county other than that in which any other charge is pending against him may state in writing or in court that he desires to plead guilty, to waive trial in the county in which the charge is pending and to consent to disposition of the case in the county in which he is held, convicted or charged, subject to the approval of the state's attorney for each county. Upon receiving notification from the sentencing court, the clerk of the court in which the charge is pending shall transmit the papers in the proceeding or certified copies thereof to the clerk of the court in which the defendant desires to plead guilty. Thereafter, the prosecution shall continue in that county. If after the proceeding has been transferred, the defendant pleads not guilty, the proceeding shall be restored to the docket of the court where the charge was pending.

(Source: P.A. 77-2097.) [Formerly Ill. Rev. Stat. 38 §1005-4-2.]

5/5-4-3. Sexual offenses; genetic marker groupings determined from blood samples.

§5-4-3. (a) Any person convicted of, or who received a disposition of court supervision for, a sexual offense or attempt of a sexual offense or institutionalized as a sexually dangerous person under the Sexually Dangerous Persons Act [725 ILCS 205/0.01 et seq.] shall, regardless of the sentence imposed, be required to submit specimens of blood to the Illinois Department of State Police in accordance with the provisions of this Section, provided such person is:

(1) convicted of a sexual offense or attempt of a sexual offense on or after the effective date of this amendatory Act of 1989, and sentenced to a term of imprisonment, periodic imprisonment, fine, probation, conditional discharge or any other form of sentence, or given a disposition of court supervision for the offense, or

(2) ordered institutionalized as a sexually dangerous person on or after the effective date of this amendatory Act of 1989, or

(3) convicted of a sexual offense or attempt of a sexual offense before the effective date of this amendatory Act of 1989 and is presently confined as a result of such conviction in any State correctional facility or county jail or is presently serving a sentence of probation, conditional discharge or periodic imprisonment as a result of such conviction, or

(4) presently institutionalized as a sexually dangerous person or presently institutionalized as a person found guilty but mentally ill of a sexual offense or attempt of a sexual offense.

(b) Any person required by paragraphs (a)(1) and (a)(2) to provide specimens of blood shall be ordered by the court to have specimens of blood collected within 45 days after sentencing at a collection site designated by the Illinois Department of State Police.

(c) Any person required by paragraphs (a)(3) and (a)(4) to provide specimens of blood shall be required to provide such samples prior to final discharge, parole, or release at a collection site designated by the Illinois Department of State Police.

(d) The Illinois Department of State Police shall provide all equipment and instructions necessary for the collection of blood samples. The collection of samples shall be performed in a medically approved manner. Only a physician authorized to practice medicine, a registered nurse or other qualified person approved by the Illinois Department of Public Health may withdraw blood for the purposes of this Act. The samples shall thereafter be forwarded to the Illinois Department of State Police, Division of Forensic Services and Identification, for analysis and categorizing into genetic marker groupings.

(e) The genetic marker groupings shall be maintained by the Illinois Department of State Police, Division of Forensic Services and Identification.

(f) The genetic marker grouping analysis information obtained pursuant to this Act shall be confidential and shall be released only to peace officers of the United States, of other states or territories, of the insular possessions of the United States, of foreign countries duly authorized to receive the same, to all peace officers of the State of Illinois and to all prosecutorial agencies.

(g) For the purposes of this Section, "sexual offense" means any violation of Sections 11-11, 12-13, 12-14, 12-15 or 12-16 of the Criminal Code of 1961 [720 ILCS 5/11-11, 5/12-13, 5/12-14, 5/12-15 or 5/12-16], or any former statute of this State which defined a felony sexual offense.

(h) The Illinois Department of State Police shall be the State central repository for all genetic marker grouping analysis information obtained pursuant to this Act. The Illinois Department of State Police may promulgate rules for the form and manner of the collection of blood samples and other procedures for the operation of this Act. The provisions of the Administrative Review Law [735 ILCS 5/3-101 et seq.] shall apply to all actions taken under the rules so promulgated.

(i) A person ordered by the court to provide a blood specimen shall cooperate with the collection of the specimen and any deliberate act by that person intended to impede, delay or stop the collection of the blood specimen shall be punishable as contempt of court.

(Chgd. by P.A. 87-963, §2, eff. 8/28/92.)

(Source: P.A. 86-881.) [Formerly Ill. Rev. Stat. 38 §1005-4-3.]

5/5-4-3.1. Sentencing hearing for sex offenses.

§5-4-3.1. Sentencing Hearing for Sex Offenses. (a) Except for good cause shown by written motion, any person adjudged guilty of any offense involving an illegal sexual act perpetrated upon a victim, including but not limited to offenses for violations of Article 12 of the Criminal Code of 1961 [720 ILCS 5/12-1 et seq.], shall be sentenced within 45 days of a verdict or finding of guilt for the offense.

(b) The court shall set the sentencing date at the time the verdict or finding of guilt is entered by the court.

(c) Any motion for continuance shall be in writing and supported by affidavit and in compliance with Section 114-4 of the Code of Criminal Procedure of 1963 [725 ILCS 5/114-4], and the victim shall be notified of the date and time of hearing and shall be provided an opportunity to address the court on the impact the continuance may have on the victim's well-being.

(d) A complaint, information or indictment shall not be quashed or dismissed, nor shall any person in custody for an offense be discharged from custody because of non-compliance with this Section.

(Added by P.A. 87-900, §1, eff. 1/1/93.)

[Formerly Ill. Rev. Stat. 38 §1005-4-3.1.]

ARTICLE 5. AUTHORIZED DISPOSITIONS

Sec.

5/5-5-1. Classification of offenses.

§5-5-1. Classification of Offenses. (a) The provisions of this Article shall govern the classification of all offenses for sentencing purposes.

(b) Felonies are classified, for the purpose of sentencing, as follows:

(1) First degree murder (as a separate class of felony);

(2) Class X felonies;

(3) Class 1 felonies;

(4) Class 2 felonies;

(5) Class 3 felonies; and

(6) Class 4 felonies.

(c) Misdemeanors are classified, for the purpose of sentencing, as follows:

(1) Class A misdemeanors;

(2) Class B misdemeanors; and

(3) Class C misdemeanors.

(d) Petty offenses and business offenses are not classified.

(Source: P.A. 84-1450.) [Formerly Ill. Rev. Stat. 38 §1005-5-1.]

5/5-5-2. Unclassified offenses.

§5-5-2. Unclassified Offenses. (a) The particular classification of each felony is specified in the law defining the felony. Any unclassified offense which is declared by law to be a felony or which provides a sentence to a term of imprisonment for one year or more shall be a Class 4 felony.

(b) The particular classification of each misdemeanor is specified in the law or ordinance defining the misdemeanor.

(1) Any offense not so classified which provides a sentence to a term of imprisonment of less than one year but in excess of 6 months shall be a Class A misdemeanor.

(2) Any offense not so classified which provides a sentence to a term of imprisonment of 6 months or less but in excess of 30 days shall be a Class B misdemeanor.

(3) Any offense not so classified which provides a sentence to a term of imprisonment of 30 days or less shall be a Class C misdemeanor.

(c) Any unclassified offense which does not provide for a sentence of imprisonment shall be a petty offense or a business offense.

(Source: P.A. 80-1099.) [Formerly Ill. Rev. Stat. 38 §1005-5-2.]

5/5-5-3. Disposition.

§5-5-3. Disposition. (a) Every person convicted of an offense shall be sentenced as provided in this Section.

(b) The following options shall be appropriate dispositions, alone or in combination, for all felonies and misdemeanors other than those identified in subsection (c) of this Section:

(1) A period of probation;

(2) A term of periodic imprisonment;

(3) A term of conditional discharge;

(4) A term of imprisonment;

(5) An order directing the offender to clean up and repair the damage, if the offender was convicted under paragraph (h) of Section 21-1 of the Criminal Code of 1961 [720 ILCS 5/21-1];

(6) A fine; or

(7) An order directing the offender to make restitution to the victim under Section 5-5-6 of this Code [730 ILCS 5/5-5-6].

Whenever an individual is sentenced for an offense based upon an arrest for a violation of Section 11-501 of the Illinois Vehicle Code [625 ILCS 5/11-501], or a similar provision of a local ordinance, and the professional evaluation recommends remedial or rehabilitative treatment or education, neither the treatment nor the education shall be the sole disposition and either or both may be imposed only in conjunction with another disposition. The court shall monitor compliance with any remedial education or treatment recommendations contained in the professional evaluation. Programs conducting alcohol or other drug evaluation or remedial education must be licensed by the Department of Alcoholism and Substance Abuse. However, if the individual is not a resident of Illinois, the court may accept an alcohol or other drug evaluation or remedial education program in the state of such individual's residence. Programs providing treatment must be licensed under existing applicable alcoholism and drug treatment licensure standards.

In addition to any other fine or penalty required by law, any individual convicted of a violation of Section 11-501 of the Illinois Vehicle Code or a similar provision of local ordinance, whose operation of a motor vehicle while in violation of Section 11-501 or such ordinance proximately caused an incident resulting in an appropriate emergency response, shall be required to make restitution to a public agency for the costs of that emergency response. Such restitution shall not exceed $500 per public agency for each such emergency response. For the purpose of this paragraph, emergency response shall mean any incident requiring a response by: a police officer as defined under Section 1-162 of the Illinois Vehicle Code [625 ILCS 5/1-162]; a fireman carried on the rolls of a regularly constituted fire department; and an ambulance as defined under Section 4.05 of the Emergency Medical Services (EMS) Systems Act [210 ILCS 50/4.05].

Neither a fine nor restitution shall be the sole disposition for a felony and either or both may be imposed only in conjunction with another disposition.

(c)(1) When a defendant is found guilty of first degree murder the State may either seek a sentence of imprisonment under Section 5-8-1 of this Code [730 ILCS 5/5-8-1], or where appropriate seek a sentence of death under Section 9-1 of the Criminal Code of 1961 [720 ILCS 5/9-1].

(2) A period of probation, a term of periodic imprisonment or conditional discharge shall not be imposed for the following offenses. The court shall sentence the offender to not less than the minimum term of imprisonment set forth in this Code for the following offenses, and may order a fine or restitution or both in conjunction with such term of imprisonment:

(A) First degree murder where the death penalty is not imposed;

(B) Attempted first degree murder;

(C) A Class X felony;

(D) A violation of Section 401.1 or 407 of the Illinois Controlled Substances Act [720 ILCS 570/401.1 or 570/407], or a violation of subdivision (c)(2) of Section 401 of that Act [720 ILCS 570/401] which relates to more than 5 grams of a substance containing cocaine or an analog thereof;

(E) A violation of Section 5.1 or 9 of the Cannabis Control Act [720 ILCS 550/5.1 or 550/9];

(F) A Class 2 or greater felony if the offender had been convicted of a Class 2 or greater felony within 10 years of the date on which he committed the offense for which he is being sentenced;

(G) Residential burglary;

(H) Criminal sexual assault, except as otherwise provided in subsection (e) of this Section;

(I) Aggravated battery of a senior citizen;

(J) A forcible felony if the offense was related to the activities of an organized gang. For the purposes of this paragraph, "organized gang" means an association of 5 or more persons, with an established hierarchy, that encourages members of the association to perpetrate crimes or provides support to the members of the association who do commit crimes.

(3) A minimum term of imprisonment of not less than 48 consecutive hours or 10 days of community service as may be determined by the court shall be imposed for a second or subsequent violation committed within 5 years of a previous violation of Section 11-501 of the Illinois Vehicle Code or a similar provision of a local ordinance.

(4) A minimum term of imprisonment of not less than 7 consecutive days or 30 days of community service shall be imposed for a violation of paragraph (c) of Section 6-303 of the Illinois Vehicle Code [625 ILCS 5/6-303].

(5) The court may sentence an offender convicted of a business offense or a petty offense or a corporation or unincorporated association convicted of any offense to:

(A) A period of conditional discharge;

(B) A fine;

(C) Make restitution to the victim under Section 5-5-6 of this Code.

(6) In no case shall an offender be eligible for a disposition of probation or conditional discharge for a Class 1 felony committed while he was serving a term of probation or conditional discharge for a felony.

(7) When a defendant is adjudged a habitual criminal under Article 33B of the Criminal Code of 1961 [720 ILCS 5/33B-1 et seq.], the court shall sentence the defendant to a term of natural life imprisonment.

(8) When a defendant, over the age of 21 years, is convicted of a Class 1 or Class 2 felony, after having twice been convicted of any Class 2 or greater Class felonies in Illinois, and such charges are separately brought and tried and arise out of different series of acts, such defendant shall be sentenced as a Class X offender. This paragraph shall not apply unless (1) the first felony was committed after the effective date of this amendatory Act of 1977; and (2) the second felony was committed after conviction on the first; and (3) the third felony was committed after conviction on the second.

(9) A defendant convicted of a second or subsequent offense of ritualized abuse of a child may be sentenced to a term of natural life imprisonment.

(d) In any case in which a sentence originally imposed is vacated, the case shall be remanded to the trial court. The trial court shall hold a hearing under Section 5-4-1 of the Unified Code of Corrections [730 ILCS 5/5-4-1] which may include evidence of the defendant's life, moral character and occupation during the time since the original sentence was passed. The trial court shall then impose sentence upon the defendant. The trial court may impose any sentence which could have been imposed at the original trial subject to Section 5-5-4 of the Unified Code of Corrections [730 ILCS 5/5-5-4].

(e) In cases where prosecution for criminal sexual assault or aggravated criminal sexual abuse under Section 12-13 or 12-16 of the Criminal Code of 1961 [720 ILCS 5/12-13 or 5/12-16] results in conviction of a defendant who was a family member of the victim at the time of the commission of the offense, the court shall consider the safety and welfare of the victim and may impose a sentence of probation only where:

(1) the court finds (A) or (B) or both are appropriate:

(A) the defendant is willing to undergo a court approved counseling program for a minimum duration of 2 years; or

(B) the defendant is willing to participate in a court approved plan including but not limited to the defendant's:

(i) removal from the household;

(ii) restricted contact with the victim;

(iii) continued financial support of the family;

(iv) restitution for harm done to the victim; and

(v) such other measures that the court may deem appropriate; and

(2) the court orders the defendant to pay for the victim's counseling services, to the extent that the court finds, after considering the defendant's income and assets, that the defendant is financially capable of paying for such services, if the victim was under 18 years of age at the time the offense was committed and requires counseling as a result of the offense.

Probation may be revoked or modified pursuant to Section 5-6-4 [730 ILCS 5/5-6-4]; except where the court determines at the hearing that the defendant violated a condition of his or her probation restricting contact with the victim or other family members or commits another offense with the victim or other family members, the court shall revoke the defendant's probation and impose a term of imprisonment.

For the purposes of this Section, "family member" and "victim" shall have the meanings ascribed to them in Section 12-12 of the Criminal Code of 1961 [720 ILCS 5/12-12].

(f) This Article shall not deprive a court in other proceedings to order a forfeiture of property, to suspend or cancel a license, to remove a person from office, or to impose any other civil penalty.

(g) Whenever a defendant is convicted of an offense under Sections 11-14, 11-15, 11-15.1, 11-16, 11-17, 11-18, 11-18.1, 11-19, 11-19.1, 11-19.2, 12-13, 12-14, 12-15 or 12-16 of the Criminal Code of 1961 [720 ILCS 5/11-14, 5/11-15, 5/11-15.1, 5/11-16, 5/11-17, 5/11-18, 5/11-18.1, 5/11-19, 5/11-19.1, 5/11-19.2,

5/12-13, 5/12-14, 5/12-15 or 5/12-16], the defendant shall undergo medical testing to determine whether the defendant has any sexually transmissible disease, including a test for infection with human immunodeficiency virus (HIV) or any other identified causative agent of acquired immunodeficiency syndrome (AIDS). Any such medical test shall be performed only by appropriately licensed medical practitioners and may include an analysis of any bodily fluids as well as an examination of the defendant's person. Except as otherwise provided by law, the results of such test shall be kept strictly confidential by all medical personnel involved in the testing and must be personally delivered in a sealed envelope to the judge of the court in which the conviction was entered for the judge's inspection in camera. Acting in accordance with the best interests of the victim and the public, the judge shall have the discretion to determine to whom, if anyone, the results of the testing may be revealed. The court shall notify the defendant of a positive test showing an infection with the human immunodeficiency virus (HIV). The court shall provide information on the availability of HIV testing and counseling at Department of Public Health facilities to all parties to whom the results of the testing are revealed and shall direct the State's Attorney to provide the information to the victim when possible. A State's Attorney may petition the court to obtain the results of any HIV test administered under this Section, and the court shall grant the disclosure if the State's Attorney shows it is relevant in order to prosecute a charge of criminal transmission of HIV under Section 12-16.2 of the Criminal Code of 1961 against the defendant. The court shall order that the cost of any such test shall be paid by the county and may be taxed as costs against the convicted defendant.

(h) Whenever a defendant is convicted of an offense under Section 1 or 2 of the Hypodermic Syringes and Needles Act [720 ILCS 635/1 or 635/2], the defendant shall undergo medical testing to determine whether the defendant has been exposed to human immunodeficiency virus (HIV) or any other identified causative agent of acquired immunodeficiency syndrome (AIDS). Except as otherwise provided by law, the results of such test shall be kept strictly confidential by all medical personnel involved in the testing and must be personally delivered in a sealed envelope to the judge of the court in which the conviction was entered for the judge's inspection in camera. Acting in accordance with the best interests of the public, the judge shall have the discretion to determine to whom, if anyone, the results of the testing may be revealed. The court shall notify the defendant of a positive test showing an infection with the human immunodeficiency virus (HIV). The court shall provide information on the availability of HIV testing and couseling at Department of Public Health facilities to all parties to whom the results of the testing are revealed and shall direct the State's Attorney to provide the information to the victim when possible. A State's Attorney may petition the court to obtain the results of any HIV test adminstered under this Section, and the court shall grant the disclosure if the State's Attorney shows it is relevant in order to prosecute a charge of criminal transmission of HIV under Section 12-16.2 of the Criminal Code of 1961 against the defendant. The court shall order that the cost of any such test shall be paid by the county and may be taxed as costs against the convicted defendant.

(i) All fines and penalties imposed under this Section for any violation of Chapters 3, 4, 6, and 11 of the Illinois Vehicle Code [625 ILCS 5/3-100 et seq., 5/4-100 et seq., 5/6-100 et seq., and 5/11-100 et seq.], or a similar provision of a local ordinance, and any violation of the Child Passenger Protection Act [625 ILCS 25/1 et seq.], or a similar provision of a local ordinance, shall be collected and disbursed by the circuit clerk as provided under Section 27.5 of the Clerks of Courts Act [705 ILCS 105/27.5].

(Chgd. by P.A. 87-1167, §3, eff. 1/1/93; P.A. 87-1190, §1, eff. 9/24/92.)

(Source: P.A. 86-581; 86-863; 86-1028; 86-1470; 87-435; 87-670.) [Formerly Ill. Rev. Stat. 38 §1005-5-3.]

5/5-5-3.1. Factors in mitigation.

§5-5-3.1. Factors in Mitigation. (a) The following grounds shall be accorded weight in favor of withholding or minimizing a sentence of imprisonment:

(1) the defendant's criminal conduct neither caused nor threatened serious physical harm to another;

(2) the defendant did not contemplate that his criminal conduct would cause or threaten serious physical harm to another;

(3) the defendant acted under a strong provocation;

(4) there were substantial grounds tending to excuse or justify the defendant's criminal conduct, though failing to establish a defense;

(5) the defendant's criminal conduct was induced or facilitated by someone other than the defendant;

(6) the defendant has compensated or will compensate the victim of his criminal conduct for the damage or injury that he sustained;

(7) the defendant has no history of prior delinquency or criminal activity or has led a law-abiding life for a substantial period of time before the commission of the present crime;

(8) the defendant's criminal conduct was the result of circumstances unlikely to recur;

(9) the character and attitudes of the defendant indicate that he is unlikely to commit another crime;

(10) the defendant is particularly likely to comply with the terms of a period of probation;

(11) the imprisonment of the defendant would entail excessive hardship to his dependents;

(12) the imprisonment of the defendant would endanger his or her medical condition.

(13) the defendant was mentally retarded as defined in Section 5-1-13 of this Code [730 ILCS 5/5-1-13].

(b) If the court, having due regard for the character of the offender, the nature and circumstances of the offense and the public interest finds that a sentence of imprisonment is the most appropriate disposition of the offender, or where other provisions of this Code mandate the imprisonment of the offender, the grounds listed in paragraph (a) of this subsection shall be considered as factors in mitigation of the term imposed.

(Source: P.A. 86-903.) [Formerly Ill. Rev. Stat. 38 §1005-5-3.1.]

5/5-5-3.2. Factors in aggravation.

§5-5-3.2. Factors in Aggravation. (a) The following factors shall be accorded weight in favor of imposing a term of imprisonment or may be considered by the court as reasons to impose a more severe sentence under Section 5-8-1 [730 ILCS 5/5-8-1]:

(1) the defendant's conduct caused or threatened serious harm;

(2) the defendant received compensation for committing the offense;

(3) the defendant has a history of prior delinquency or criminal activity;

(4) the defendant, by the duties of his office or by his position, was obliged to prevent the particular offense committed or to bring the offenders committing it to justice;

(5) the defendant held public office at the time of the offense, and the offense related to the conduct of that office;

(6) the defendant utilized his professional reputation or position in the community to commit the offense, or to afford him an easier means of committing it;

(7) the sentence is necessary to deter others from committing the same crime;

(8) the defendant committed the offense against a person 60 years of age or older or such person's property;

(9) the defendant committed the offense against a person who is physically handicapped or such person's property;

(10) the defendant committed the offense against a person or a person's property because of such person's race, color, creed, religion, ancestry, gender, sexual orientation, physical or mental disability, or national origin. For the purposes of this Section, "sexual orientation" means heterosexuality, homosexuality, or bisexuality;

(11) the offense took place in a place of worship or on the grounds of a place of worship, immediately prior to, during or immediately following worship services. For purposes of this subparagraph, "place of worship" shall mean any church, synagogue or other building, structure or place used primarily for religious worship;

(12) the defendant was convicted of a felony committed while he was released on bail or his own recognizance pending trial for a prior felony and was convicted of such prior felony, or the defendant was convicted of a felony committed while he was serving a period of probation or conditional discharge for a prior felony;

(13) the defendant committed or attempted to commit a felony while he was wearing a bulletproof vest. For the purposes of this paragraph (13), a bulletproof vest is any device which is designed for the purpose of protecting the wearer from bullets, shot or other lethal projectiles;

(14) the defendant held a position of trust or supervision such as, but not limited to, family member as defined in Section 12-12 of the Criminal Code of 1961 [720 ILCS 5/12-12], teacher, scout leader, baby sitter, or day care worker, in relation to a victim under 18 years of age, and the defendant committed an offense in violation of Section 11-6, 11-11, 11-15.1, 11-19.1, 11-19.2, 11-20.1, 12-13, 12-14, 12-15 or 12-16 of the Criminal Code of 1961 [720 ILCS 5/11-6, 5/11-11, 5/11-15.1, 5/11-19.1, 5/11-19.2, 5/11-20.1, 5/12-13, 5/12-14, 5/12-15 or 5/12-16] against that victim.

(b) The following factors may be considered by the court as reasons to impose an extended term sentence under Section 5-8-2 [730 ILCS 5/5-8-2] upon any offender:

(1) When a defendant is convicted of any felony, after having been previously convicted in Illinois or any other jurisdiction of the same or similar class felony or greater class felony, when such conviction has occurred within 10 years after the previous conviction, excluding time spent in custody, and such charges are separately brought and tried and arise out of different series of acts; or

(2) When a defendant is convicted of any felony and the court finds that the offense was accompanied by exceptionally brutal or heinous behavior indicative of wanton cruelty; or

(3) When a defendant is convicted of voluntary manslaughter, second degree murder, involuntary manslaughter or reckless homicide in which the defendant has been convicted of causing the death of more than one individual; or

(4) When a defendant is convicted of any felony committed against:

(i) a person under 12 years of age at the time of the offense or such person's property;

(ii) a person 60 years of age or older at the time of the offense or such person's property; or

(iii) a person physically handicapped at the time of the offense or such person's property; or

(5) In the case of a defendant convicted of aggravated criminal sexual assault or criminal sexual assault, when the court finds that aggravated criminal sexual assault or criminal sexual assault was also committed on the same victim by one or more other individuals, and the defendant voluntarily participated in the crime with the knowledge of the participation of the others in the crime, and the commission of the crime was part of a single course of conduct during which there was no substantial change in the nature of the criminal objective; or

(6) When a defendant is convicted of any felony and the offense involved any of the following types of specific misconduct committed as part of a ceremony, rite, initiation, observance, performance, practice or activity of any actual or ostensible religious, fraternal, or social group:

(i) the brutalizing or torturing of humans or animals;

(ii) the theft of human corpses;

(iii) the kidnapping of humans;

(iv) the desecration of any cemetery, religious, fraternal, business, governmental, educational, or other building or property; or

(v) ritualized abuse of a child; or

(7) When a defendant is convicted of first degree murder, after having been previously convicted in Illinois of any offense listed under paragraph (c)(2) of Section 5-5-3 [730 ILCS 5/5-5-3], when such conviction has occurred within 10 years after the previous conviction, excluding time spent in custody, and such charges are separately brought and tried and arise out of different series of acts.

(c) The court may impose an extended term sentence under Section 5-8-2 upon any offender who was convicted of aggravated criminal sexual assault where the victim was under 18 years of age at the time of the commission of the offense.

(Chgd. by P.A. 87-921, §2; 87-1067, §1; 87-1167, §3, eff. 1/1/93.)

(Source: P.A. 86-820; 86-865; 86-1418; 87-440; 87-805; 87-895.) [Formerly Ill. Rev. Stat. 38 §1005-5-3.2.]

5/5-5-4. Resentences.

§5-5-4. Resentences. Where a conviction or sentence has been set aside on direct review or on collateral attack, the court shall not impose a new sentence for the same offense or for a different offense based on the same conduct which is more severe than the prior sentence less the portion of the prior sentence previously satisfied unless the more severe sentence is based upon conduct on the part of the defendant occurring after the original sentencing.

(Source: P.A. 77-2097.) [Formerly Ill. Rev. Stat. 38 §1005-5-4.]

5/5-5-4.1. Appeal.

§5-5-4.1. Appeal. The defendant has the right of appeal in all cases from sentences entered on conviction of first degree murder or any other Class of felony.

(Source: P.A. 84-1450.) [Formerly Ill. Rev. Stat. 38 §1005-5-4.1.]

5/5-5-4.2. Statewide sentence equalization procedures.

§5-5-4.2. Statewide Sentence Equalization Procedures. The Supreme Court may by rule, not inconsistent with law, prescribe such practices and procedures as will promote a uniformity and parity of sentences within and among the various circuit courts and appellate court districts.

(Source: P.A. 80-1099.) [Formerly Ill. Rev. Stat. 38 §1005-5-4.2.]

5/5-5-4.3. Duties of Department of Corrections.

§5-5-4.3. Duties of Department of Corrections. (a) The Department of Corrections shall publish an annual report beginning not less than 18 months after the effective date of this amendatory Act of 1977 and not later than April 30 of each year which shall be made available to trial and appellate court judges for their use in imposing or reviewing sentences under this Code and to other interested parties upon a showing of need. That report shall set forth the following data:

(1) The range, frequency, distribution and average of terms of imprisonment imposed on offenders committed to the Department of Corrections, by offense:

(2) The range, frequency, distribution and average of terms actually served in prison by offenders committed to the Department of Corrections, by offense:

(3) The number of instances in which an offender was committed to the Department of Corrections pursuant to Sections 5-8-1, 5-8-2 and 5-8-4 of this Code [730 ILCS 5/5-8-1, 5/5-8-2 and 5/5-8-4], by offense, and the range, frequency, distribution and average of sentences imposed pursuant to those provisions, by offense; and

(4) Such other information which the Department can provide which might be requested by the court to assist it in imposing sentences.

(b) All data required to be disseminated by this Section shall be set forth for a period of not less than the preceding 5 years, insofar as possible.

(c) All data required to be disseminated by this Section shall conform fully to all state and federal laws and resolutions concerning the security, privacy and confidentiality of such materials.

(Source: P.A. 84-240.) [Formerly Ill. Rev. Stat. 38 §1005-5-4.3.]

5/5-5-5. Loss and restoration of rights.

§5-5-5. Loss and Restoration of Rights. (a) Conviction and disposition shall not entail the loss by the defendant of any civil rights, except under this Section and Sections 29-6 and 29-10 of The Election Code, as now or hereafter amended [10 ILCS 5/29-6 and 5/29-10].

(b) A person convicted of a felony shall be ineligible to hold an office created by the Constitution of this State until the completion of his sentence.

(c) A person sentenced to imprisonment shall lose his right to vote until released from imprisonment.

(d) On completion of sentence of imprisonment or upon discharge from probation, conditional discharge or periodic imprisonment, or at any time thereafter, all license rights and privileges granted under the authority of this State which have been revoked or suspended because of conviction of an offense shall be restored unless the authority having jurisdiction of such license rights finds after investigation and hearing that restoration is not in the public interest. This paragraph (d) shall not apply to the suspension or revocation of a license to operate a motor vehicle under the Illinois Vehicle Code [625 ILCS 5/1-100 et seq.].

(e) Upon a person's discharge from incarceration or parole, or upon a person's discharge from probation or at any time thereafter, the committing court may enter an order certifying that the sentence has been satisfactorily completed when the court believes it would assist in the rehabilitation of the person and be consistent with the public welfare. Such order may be entered upon the motion of the defendant or the State or upon the court's own motion.

(f) Upon entry of the order, the court shall issue to the person in whose favor the order has been entered a certificate stating that his behavior after conviction has warranted the issuance of the order.

(g) This Section shall not affect the right of a defendant to collaterally attack his conviction or to rely on it in bar of subsequent proceedings for the same offense.

(Source: P.A. 86-558.) [Formerly Ill. Rev. Stat. 38 §1005-5-5.]

5/5-5-6. Restitution.

§5-5-6. In all convictions for offenses in violation of the Criminal Code of 1961 [720 ILCS 5/1-1 et seq.] committed against any person 65 years of age or older in which the person received any injury to their person or damage to their real or personal property as a result of the criminal act of the defendant, and in cases where the defendant is convicted of looting under Section 42-1 of the Criminal Code of 1961 [720 ILCS 5/42-1], the court shall order restitution as provided in this Section. In all other cases the court shall at the sentence hearing determine whether restitution is an appropriate sentence to be imposed on each defendant convicted of an offense. If the court determines that an order directing the offender to make restitution is appropriate the offender may be sentenced to make restitution which shall be determined by the Court as hereinafter set forth:

(a) At the sentence hearing, the court shall determine whether the property may be restored in kind to the possession of the owner or the person entitled to possession thereof; or whether the defendant is possessed of sufficient skill to repair and restore property damaged; or whether the defendant should be required to make restitution in cash, for out-of-pocket expenses, damages, losses, or injuries found to have been proximately caused by the conduct of the defendant or another for whom the defendant is legally accountable under the provisions of Article V of the Criminal Code of 1961 [720 ILCS 5/5-1 et seq.].

(b) In fixing the amount of restitution to be paid in cash, the court shall allow credit for property returned in kind, for property damages ordered to be repaired by the defendant, and for property ordered to be restored by the defendant; and after granting the credit, the court shall assess the actual out-of-pocket expenses, losses, damages, and injuries suffered by the victim named in the charge and any other victims who may also have suffered out-of-pocket expenses, losses, damages, and injuries proximately caused by the same criminal conduct of the defendant, and insurance carriers who have indemnified the named victim or other victims for the out-of-pocket expenses, losses, damages, or injuries, provided that in no event shall restitution be ordered to be paid on account of pain and suffering. If a defendant fails to pay restitution in the manner or within the time period specified by the court, the court may enter an order directing the sheriff to seize any real or personal property of a defendant to the extent necessary to satisfy the order of restitution and dispose of the property by public sale. All proceeds from such sale in excess of the amount of restitution plus court costs and the costs of the sheriff in conducting the sale shall be paid to the defendant.

(c) In cases where more than one defendant is accountable for the same criminal conduct that results in out-of-pocket expenses, losses, damages, or injuries, each defendant shall be ordered to pay restitution in the amount of the total actual out-of-pocket expenses, losses, damages, or injuries to the victim proximately caused by the conduct of all of the defendants who are legally accountable for the offense.

(1) In no event shall the victim be entitled to recover restitution in excess of the actual out-of-pocket expenses, losses, damages, or injuries, proximately caused by the conduct of all of the defendants.

(2) As between the defendants, the court may apportion the restitution that is payable in proportion to each co-defendant's culpability in the commission of the offense.

(3) In the absence of a specific order apportioning the restitution, each defendant shall bear his pro rata share of the restitution.

(4) As between the defendants, each defendant shall be entitled to a pro rata reduction in the total restitution required to be paid to the victim for amounts of restitution actually paid by co-defendants, and defendants who shall have

paid more than their pro rata share shall be entitled to refunds to be computed by the court as additional amounts are paid by co-defendants.

(d) In instances where a defendant has more than one criminal charge pending against him in a single case, or more than one case, and the defendant stands convicted of one or more charges, a plea agreement negotiated by the State's Attorney and the defendants may require the defendant to make restitution to victims of charges that have been dismissed or which it is contemplated will be dismissed under the terms of the plea agreement, and under the agreement, the court may impose a sentence of restitution on the charge or charges of which the defendant has been convicted that would require the defendant to make restitution to victims of other offenses as provided in the plea agreement.

(e) The court may require the defendant to apply the balance of the cash bond, after payment of court costs, and any fine that may be imposed to the payment of restitution.

(f) Taking into consideration the ability of the defendant to pay, the court shall determine whether restitution shall be paid in a single payment or in installments, and shall fix a period of time not in excess of 5 years within which payment of restitution is to be paid in full. If the defendant is ordered to pay restitution and the court orders that restitution is to be paid over a period greater than 6 months, the court shall order that the defendant make monthly payments; the court may waive this requirement of monthly payments only if there is a specific finding of good cause for waiver.

(g) The court shall, after determining that the defendant has the ability to pay, require the defendant to pay for the victim's counseling services if:

(1) the defendant was convicted of an offense under Sections 11-19.2, 11-20.1, 12-13, 12-14, 12-15 or 12-16 of the Criminal Code of 1961 [720 ILCS 5/11-19.2, 5/11-20.1, 5/12-13, 5/12-14, 5/12-15 or 5/12-16], or was charged with such an offense and the charge was reduced to another charge as a result of a plea agreement under subsection (d) of this Section, and

(2) the victim was under 18 years of age at the time the offense was committed and requires counseling as a result of the offense.

The payments shall be made by the defendant to the clerk of the circuit court and transmitted by the clerk to the appropriate person or agency as directed by the court. The order may require such payments to be made for a period not to exceed 5 years after sentencing.

(h) The judge may enter an order of withholding to collect the amount of restitution owed in accordance with Part 8 of Article XII of the Code of Civil Procedure [735 ILCS 5/12-801 et seq.].

(i) A sentence of restitution may be modified or revoked by the court if the offender commits another offense, or the offender fails to make restitution as ordered by the court, but no sentence to make restitution shall be revoked unless the court shall find that the offender has had the financial ability to make restitution, and he has wilfully refused to do so. If the court shall find that the defendant has failed to make restitution and that the failure is not wilful, the court may impose an additional period of time within which to make restitution. The length of the additional period shall not be more than 2 years. The court shall retain all of the incidents of the original sentence, including the authority to modify or enlarge the conditions, and to revoke or further modify the sentence if the conditions of payment are violated during the additional period.

(j) The procedure upon the filing of a Petition to Revoke a sentence to make restitution shall be the same as the procedures set forth in Section 5-6-4 of this Code [730 ILCS 5/5-6-4] governing violation, modification, or revocation of Probation, of Conditional Discharge, or of Supervision.

(k) Nothing contained in this Section shall preclude the right of any party to proceed in a civil action to recover for any damages incurred due to the criminal misconduct of the defendant.

(*l*) Restitution ordered under this Section shall not be subject to disbursement by the circuit clerk under Section 27.5 of the Clerks of Courts Act [705 ILCS 105/27.5].

(m) A restitution order under this Section is a judgment lien in favor of the victim that:

(1) Attaches to the property of the person subject to the order;

(2) May be perfected in the same manner as provided in Part 3 of Article 9 of the Uniform Commercial Code [810 ILCS 5/9-301 et seq.];

(3) May be enforced to satisfy any payment that is delinquent under the restitution order by the person in whose favor the order is issued or the person's assignee; and

(4) Expires in the same manner as a judgment lien created in a civil proceeding.

When a restitution order is issued under this Section, the issuing court shall send a certified copy of the order to the clerk of the circuit court in the county where the charge was filed. Upon receiving the order, the clerk shall enter and index the order in the circuit court judgment docket.

(n) An order of restitution under this Section does not bar a civil action for:

(1) Damages that the court did not require the person to pay to the victim under the restitution order but arise from an injury or property damages that is the basis of restitution ordered by the court; and

(2) Other damages suffered by the victim.

Regardless of whether restitution is required under this Section as a condition of a sentence, the restitution order is not discharged by the completion of the sentence imposed for the offense.

A restitution order under this Section is not discharged by the liquidation of a person's estate by a receiver. A restitution order under this Section may be enforced in the same manner as judgment liens are enforced under Article XII of the Code of Civil Procedure [735 ILCS 5/12-101 et seq.].
(Chgd. by P.A. 87-1170, §2, eff. 1/1/93; P.A. 87-1230, §6, eff. 7/1/93.)
(Source: P.A. 87-204; 87-609; 87-610; 87-670; 87-895.) [Formerly Ill. Rev. Stat. 38 §1005-5-6.]

5/5-5-7. Performing public or community service.

§5-5-7. Neither the State, any local government, probation department, public or community service program or site, nor any official or employee thereof acting in the course of their official duties shall be liable for any injury or loss a person might receive while performing public or community service as ordered by the court, nor shall they be liable for any tortious acts of any person performing public or community service, except for wilful, wanton misconduct or gross negligence on the part of such governmental unit, official or employee.
(Source: P.A. 85-449.) [Formerly Ill. Rev. Stat. 38 §1005-5-7.]

5/5-5-8. Person assigned to public or community service program.

§5-5-8. No person assigned to a public or community service program shall be considered an employee for any purpose, nor shall the county board be obligated to provide any compensation to such person.
(Source: P.A. 85-449.) [Formerly Ill. Rev. Stat. 38 §1005-5-8.]

5/5-5-9. Community service.

§5-5-9. Community service. When a defendant is ordered by the court to perform community service as a condition of his or her sentence, the court in its discretion may appoint a non-profit organization to administer a program of community service relating to cleaning up the community, repairing damage, and painting buildings or other structures defaced. The non-profit organization

approved by the court may determine dates and locations of the defendant's service, procure necessary cleaning or other utensils for defendant to use in performing community service, choose sites to be repainted or cleaned, and provide supervision of the defendant's activities. A defendant participating in the program shall be given reasonable rest periods as determined by the non-profit organization with the approval of the court. The county sheriff or municipal law enforcement agency may provide one or more peace officers to supervise the program. A defendant who fails to successfully complete the community service program established in this Section shall be subject to resentencing as provided in this Chapter V.
(Added by P.A. 87-907, §1, eff. 1/1/93.)
[Formerly Ill. Rev. Stat. 38 §1005-5-9.]

ARTICLE 6. SENTENCES OF PROBATION AND CONDITIONAL DISCHARGE

5/5-6-1. Sentences of probation and of conditional discharge and disposition of supervision.

§5-6-1. Sentences of Probation and of Conditional Discharge and Disposition of Supervision. (a) Except where specifically prohibited by other provisions of this Code, the court shall impose a sentence of probation or conditional discharge upon an offender unless, having regard to the nature and circumstance of the offense, and to the history, character and condition of the offender, the court is of the opinion that:

(1) his imprisonment or periodic imprisonment is necessary for the protection of the public; or

(2) probation or conditional discharge would deprecate the seriousness of the offender's conduct and would be inconsistent with the ends of justice.

(b) The court may impose a sentence of conditional discharge for an offense if the court is of the opinion that neither a sentence of imprisonment nor of periodic imprisonment nor of probation supervision is appropriate.

(c) The court may, upon a plea of guilty or a stipulation by the defendant of the facts supporting the charge or a finding of guilt, defer further proceedings and the imposition of a sentence, and enter an order for supervision of the defendant if the defendant is not charged with a felony and having regard for the circumstances of the offense, and the history, character and condition of the offender, the court is of the opinion that:

(1) the offender is not likely to commit further crimes;

(2) the defendant and the public would be best served if the defendant were not to receive a criminal record; and

(3) in the best interests of justice an order of supervision is more appropriate than a sentence otherwise permitted under this Code.

(d) The provisions of paragraph (c) shall not apply to a defendant charged with violating Section 11-501 of the Illinois Vehicle Code [625 ILCS 5/11-501] or a similar provision of a local ordinance or a violation of Section 5-401.3 of The Illinois Vehicle Code [625 ILCS 5/5-401.3] if said defendant has within 10 years prior to the date of the current offense for violations of Section 11-501 of the Illinois Vehicle Code or a similar provision of a local ordinance or has within 5 years prior to the date of the current offense for a violation of Section 5-401.3 of the Illinois Vehicle Code been:

(1) convicted for a violation of Section 11-501 of the Illinois Vehicle Code or a similar provision of a local ordinance or a violation of Section 5-401.3 of the Illinois Vehicle Code; or

(2) assigned supervision for a violation of Section 11-501 of the Illinois Vehicle Code or a similar provision of a local ordinance or a violation of Section 5-401.3 of the Illinois Vehicle Code; or

(3) pleaded guilty to or stipulated to the facts supporting a charge or a finding of guilty to a violation of Section 11-503 of the Illinois Vehicle Code [625 ILCS 5/11-503] or a similar provision of a local ordinance, and the plea or stipulation was the result of a plea agreement.

The court shall consider the statement of the prosecuting authority with regard to the standards set forth in this Section.

(e) The provisions of paragraph (c) shall not apply to a defendant charged with violating Section 16A-3 of the Criminal Code of 1961 [720 ILCS 5/16A-3] if said defendant has within the last 5 years been:

(1) convicted for a violation of Section 16A-3 of the Criminal Code of 1961; or

(2) assigned supervision for a violation of Section 16A-3 of the Criminal Code of 1961.

The court shall consider the statement of the prosecuting authority with regard to the standards set forth in this Section.

(f) The provisions of paragraph (c) shall not apply to a defendant charged with violating Sections 15-111, 15-112, 15-301, paragraph (b) of Section 6-104, or Section 11-605 of the Illinois Vehicle Code [625 ILCS 5/15-111, 5/15-112, 5/15-301, 5/6-104, or 5/11-605] or a similar provision of a local ordinance.

(g) The provisions of paragraph (c) shall not apply to a defendant charged with violating Section 3-707, 3-708 or 3-710 of the Illinois Vehicle Code [625 ILCS 5/3-707, 5/3-708 or 5/3-710] or a similar provision of a local ordinance if the defendant has within the last 5 years been:

(1) convicted for a violation of Section 3-707, 3-708 or 3-710 of the Illinois Vehicle Code or a similar provision of a local ordinance; or

(2) assigned supervision for a violation of Section 3-707, 3-708 or 3-710 of The Illinois Vehicle Code or a similar provision of a local ordinance.

The court shall consider the statement of the prosecuting authority with regard to the standards set forth in this Section.

(h) The provisions of paragraph (c) shall not apply to a defendant charged with a violation of Section 12-3.2 or 12-15 of the Criminal Code of 1961 [720 ILCS 5/12-3.2 or 5/12-15] if said defendant has within the last 5 years been:

(1) convicted for a violation of Section 12-3.2 or 12-15 of the Criminal Code of 1961; or

(2) assigned supervision for a violation of Section 12-3.2 or 12-15 of the Criminal Code of 1961.

(Chgd. by P.A. 87-1074, §1, eff. 1/1/93.)

(Source: P.A. 86-149; 86-929; 86-979; 86-1005; 86-1012; 86-1475.) [Formerly Ill. Rev. Stat. 38 §1005-6-1.]

5/5-6-2. Incidents of probation and of conditional discharge.

§5-6-2. Incidents of Probation and of Conditional Discharge. (a) When an offender is sentenced to probation or conditional discharge, the court shall impose a period under paragraph (b) of this Section, and shall specify the conditions under Section 5-6-3 [730 ILCS 5/5-6-3].

(b) Unless terminated sooner as provided in paragraph (c) of this Section or extended pursuant to paragraph (e) of this Section, the period of probation or conditional discharge shall be as follows:

(1) for a Class 1 or Class 2 felony, not to exceed 4 years;

(2) for a Class 3 or Class 4 felony, not to exceed 30 months;

(3) for a misdemeanor, not to exceed 2 years;

(4) for a petty offense, not to exceed 6 months.

Multiple terms of probation imposed at the same time shall run concurrently.

(c) The court may at any time terminate probation or conditional discharge if warranted by the conduct of the offender and the ends of justice, as provided in Section 5-6-4 [730 ILCS 5/5-6-4].

(d) Upon the expiration or termination of the period of probation or of conditional discharge, the court shall enter an order discharging the offender.

(e) The court may extend any period of probation or conditional discharge beyond the limits set forth in paragraph (b) of this Section upon a violation of a condition of the probation or conditional discharge, or for the payment of an assessment required by Section 10.3 of the Cannabis Control Act [720 ILCS 550/10.3] or Section 411.2 of the Illinois Controlled Substances Act [720 ILCS 570/411.2].

(Source: P.A. 86-929; 87-772; 87-895.) [Formerly Ill. Rev. Stat. 38 §1005-6-2.]

5/5-6-3. Conditions of probation and of conditional discharge.

§5-6-3. Conditions of Probation and of Conditional Discharge. (a) The conditions of probation and of conditional discharge shall be that the person:

(1) not violate any criminal statute of any jurisdiction;

(2) report to or appear in person before such person or agency as directed by the court;

(3) refrain from possessing a firearm or other dangerous weapon;

(4) not leave the State without the consent of the court or, in circumstances in which the reason for the absence is of such an emergency nature that prior consent by the court is not possible, without the prior notification and approval of the person's probation officer; and

(5) permit the probation officer to visit him at his home or elsewhere to the extent necessary to discharge his duties.

(b) The Court may in addition to other reasonable conditions relating to the nature of the offense or the rehabilitation of the defendant as determined for each defendant in the proper discretion of the Court require that the person:

(1) serve a term of periodic imprisonment under Article 7 [730 ILCS 5/5-7-1 et seq.] for a period not to exceed that specified in paragraph (d) of Section 5-7-1 [730 ILCS 5/5-7-1];

(2) pay a fine and costs;

(3) work or pursue a course of study or vocational training;

(4) undergo medical, psychological or psychiatric treatment; or treatment for drug addiction or alcoholism;

(5) attend or reside in a facility established for the instruction or residence of defendants on probation;

(6) support his dependents;

(7) and in addition, if a minor:

(i) reside with his parents or in a foster home;

(ii) attend school;

(iii) attend a non-residential program for youth;

(iv) contribute to his own support at home or in a foster home;

(8) make restitution as provided in Section 5-5-6 of this Code [730 ILCS 5/5-5-6];

(9) perform some reasonable public or community service;

(10) serve a term of home confinement. In addition to any other applicable condition of probation or conditional discharge, the conditions of home confinement shall be that the offender:

(i) remain within the interior premises of the place designated for his confinement during the hours designated by the court;

(ii) admit any person or agent designated by the court into the offender's place of confinement at any time for purposes of verifying the offender's compliance with the conditions of his confinement; and

(iii) if further deemed necessary by the court or the Probation or Court Services Department, be placed on an approved electronic monitoring device, subject to Article 8A of Chapter V [730 ILCS 5/5-8A-1 et seq.];

(iv) for persons convicted of any alcohol, cannabis or controlled substance violation who are placed on an approved monitoring device as a condition of probation or conditional discharge, the court shall impose a fee not to exceed $5 for each day of the use of the device, unless after determining the inability of the offender to pay the fee, the court assesses a lesser fee or no fee as the case may be. The fee shall be collected by the clerk of the circuit court. The clerk of the circuit court shall pay all monies collected from this fee to the county treasurer for deposit in the substance abuse services fund under Section 5-1086.1 of the Counties Code [55 ILCS 5/5-1086.1]; and

(v) for persons convicted of offenses other than those referenced in clause (iv) above and who are placed on an approved monitoring device as a condition of probation or conditional discharge, the court shall impose a fee not to exceed $5 for each day of the use of the device, unless after determining the inability of the defendant to pay the fee, the court assesses a lesser fee or no fee as the case may be. The fee shall be imposed in addition to the fee imposed under subsection (i) of Section 5-6-3. The fee shall be collected by the clerk of the circuit court. The clerk of the circuit court shall pay all monies collected from this fee to the county treasurer who shall use the monies collected to defray the costs of corrections. The county treasurer shall deposit the fee collected in the county working cash fund under Section 6-27001 of the Counties Code [55 ILCS 5/6-27001].

(11) comply with the terms and conditions of an order of protection issued by the court pursuant to the Illinois Domestic Violence Act of 1986, as now or hereafter amended [750 ILCS 60/101 et seq.]. A copy of the order of protection shall be transmitted to the probation officer or agency having responsibility for the case;

(12) reimburse any "local anti-crime program" as defined in Section 7 of the Anti-Crime Advisory Council Act [20 ILCS 3910/7] for any reasonable expenses incurred by the program on the offender's case, not to exceed the maximum amount of the fine authorized for the offense for which the defendant was sentenced;

(13) contribute a reasonable sum of money, not to exceed the maximum amount of the fine authorized for the offense for which the defendant was sentenced, to a "local anti-crime program", as defined in Section 7 of the Anti-Crime Advisory Council Act;

(14) refrain from entering into a designated geographic area except upon such terms as the court finds appropriate. Such terms may include consideration of the purpose of the entry, the time of day, other persons accompanying the defendant, and advance approval by a probation officer, if the defendant has been placed on probation or advance approval by the court, if the defendant was placed on conditional discharge;

(15) refrain from having any contact, directly or indirectly, with certain specified persons or particular types of persons, including but not limited to members of street gangs and drug users or dealers.

(c) The court may as a condition of probation or of conditional discharge require that a person under 18 years of age found guilty of any alcohol, cannabis or controlled substance violation, refrain from acquiring a driver's license during the period of probation or conditional discharge. If such person is in possession of a permit or license, the court may require that the minor refrain from driving or operating any motor vehicle during the period of probation or conditional discharge, except as may be necessary in the course of the minor's lawful employment.

(d) An offender sentenced to probation or to conditional discharge shall be given a certificate setting forth the conditions thereof.

(e) The court shall not require as a condition of the sentence of probation or conditional discharge that the offender be committed to a period of imprisonment in excess of 6 months.

Persons committed to imprisonment as a condition of probation or conditional discharge shall not be committed to the Department of Corrections.

(f) The court may combine a sentence of periodic imprisonment under Article 7 with a sentence of probation or conditional discharge.

(g) An offender sentenced to probation or to conditional discharge and who during the term of either undergoes mandatory drug or alcohol testing, or both, or is assigned to be placed on an approved electronic monitoring device, may be ordered to pay all costs incidental to such mandatory drug or alcohol testing, or both, and all costs incidental to such approved electronic monitoring in accordance with the defendant's ability to pay those costs. The county board with the concurrence of the Chief Judge of the judicial circuit in which the county is located may establish reasonable fees for the cost of maintenance, testing, and incidental expenses related to the mandatory drug or alcohol testing, or both, and all costs incidental to approved electronic monitoring, involved in a successful probation program for the county. The concurrence of the Chief Judge shall be in the form of an administrative order.

(h) Jurisdiction over an offender may be transferred from the sentencing court to the court of another circuit with the concurrence of both courts. Further transfers or retransfers of jurisdiction are also authorized in the same manner. The court to which jurisdiction has been transferred shall have the same powers as the sentencing court.

(i) The court shall impose upon an offender sentenced to probation after January 1, 1989 or to conditional discharge after January 1, 1992, as a condition of such probation or conditional discharge, a fee not to exceed $25 for each month of probation or conditional discharge supervision ordered by the court, unless after determining the inability of the person sentenced to probation or conditional discharge to pay the fee, the court assesses a lesser fee. The fee shall be imposed only upon an offender who is actively supervised by the probation and court services department. The fee shall be collected by the clerk of the circuit court. The clerk of the circuit court shall pay all monies collected from this fee to the county treasurer for deposit in the probation and court services fund under Section 15.1 of the Probation and Probation Officers Act [730 ILCS 110/15.1].

(j) All fines and costs imposed under this Section for any violation of Chapters 3, 4, 6, and 11 of the Illinois Vehicle Code [625 ILCS 5/3-100 et seq., 5/4-100 et seq., 5/6-100 et seq., and 5/11-100 et seq.], or a similar provision of a local ordinance, and any violation of the Child Passenger Protection Act [625 ILCS 25/1 et seq.], or a similar provision of a local ordinance, shall be collected and disbursed by the circuit clerk as provided under Section 27.5 of the Clerks of Courts Act [705 ILCS 105/27.5].

(Chgd. by P.A. 87-1198, §4, eff. 9/25/92.)

(Source: P.A. 86-308; 86-856; 86-1012; 86-1028; 86-1281; 86-1320; 87-435; 87-609; 87-610; 87-670; 87-805; 87-895.) [Formerly Ill. Rev. Stat. 38 §1005-6-3.]

5/5-6-3.1. Incidents and conditions of supervision.

§5-6-3.1. Incidents and Conditions of Supervision. (a) When a defendant is placed on supervision, the court shall enter an order for supervision specifying the period of such supervision, and shall defer further proceedings in the case until the conclusion of the period.

(b) The period of supervision shall be reasonable under all of the circumstances of the case, but may not be longer than 2 years, unless the defendant has failed to pay the assessment required by Section 10.3 of the Cannabis Control Act [720 ILCS 550/10.3] or Section 411.2 of the Illinois Controlled Substances Act [720 ILCS 570/411.2], in which case the court may extend supervision beyond 2 years.

(c) The court may in addition to other reasonable conditions relating to the nature of the offense or the rehabilitation of the defendant as determined for each defendant in the proper discretion of the court require that the person:

(1) make a report to and appear in person before or participate with the court or such courts, person, or social service agency as directed by the court in the order of supervision;

(2) pay a fine and costs;

(3) work or pursue a course of study or vocational training;

(4) undergo medical, psychological or psychiatric treatment; or treatment for drug addiction or alcoholism;

(5) attend or reside in a facility established for the instruction or residence of defendants on probation;

(6) support his dependents;

(7) refrain from possessing a firearm or other dangerous weapon;

(8) and in addition, if a minor:

(i) reside with his parents or in a foster home;

(ii) attend school;

(iii) attend a non-residential program for youth;

(iv) contribute to his own support at home or in a foster home; and

(9) make restitution or reparation in an amount not to exceed actual loss or damage to property and pecuniary loss. The court shall determine the amount and conditions of payment;

(10) perform some reasonable public or community service;

(11) comply with the terms and conditions of an order of protection issued by the court pursuant to the Illinois Domestic Violence Act of 1986 [750 ILCS 60/101 et seq.]. If the court has ordered the defendant to make a report and appear in person under paragraph (1) of this subsection, a copy of the order of protection shall be transmitted to the person or agency so designated by the court;

(12) reimburse any "local anti-crime program" as defined in Section 7 of the Anti-Crime Advisory Council Act [20 ILCS 3910/7] for any reasonable expenses incurred by the program on the offender's case, not to exceed the maximum amount of the fine authorized for the offense for which the defendant was sentenced;

(13) contribute a reasonable sum of money, not to exceed the maximum amount of the fine authorized for the offense for which the defendant was sentenced, to a "local anti-crime program", as defined in Section 7 of the Anti-Crime Advisory Council Act;

(14) refrain from entering into a designated geographic area except upon such terms as the court finds appropriate. Such terms may include consideration of the purpose of the entry, the time of day, other persons accompanying the defendant, and advance approval by a probation officer;

(15) refrain from having any contact, directly or indirectly, with certain specified persons or particular types of person, including but not limited to members of street gangs and drug users or dealers.

(d) The court shall defer entering any judgment on the charges until the conclusion of the supervision.

(e) At the conclusion of the period of supervision, if the court determines that the defendant has successfully complied with all of the conditions of supervision, the court shall discharge the defendant and enter a judgment dismissing the charges.

(f) Discharge and dismissal upon a successful conclusion of a disposition of supervision shall be deemed without adjudication of guilt and shall not be termed a conviction for purposes of disqualification or disabilities imposed by law upon conviction of a crime. Two years after the discharge and dismissal under this Section, unless the disposition of supervision was for a violation of Sections 3-707, 3-708, 3-710, 5-401.3, 11-501, or 11-503 of the Illinois Vehicle Code [625 ILCS 5/3-707, 5/3-708, 5/3-710, 5/5-401.3, 5/11-501, or 5/11-503] or a similar provision of a local ordinance, or for a violation of Sections 12-3.2, 12-15 or 16A-3 of the Criminal Code of 1961 [720 ILCS 5/12-3.2, 5/12-15 or 5/16A-3], in which case it shall be 5 years after discharge and dismissal, a person may have his record of arrest sealed or expunged as may be provided by law. However, any defendant placed on supervision before January 1, 1980, may move for sealing or expungement of his arrest record, as provided by law, at any time after discharge and dismissal under this Section.

(g) A defendant placed on supervision and who during the period of supervision undergoes mandatory drug or alcohol testing, or both, or is assigned to be placed on an approved electronic monitoring device, may be ordered to pay the costs incidental to such mandatory drug or alcohol testing, or both, and costs incidental to such approved electronic monitoring in accordance with the defendant's ability to pay those costs. The county board with the concurrence of the Chief Judge of the judicial circuit in which the county is located may establish reasonable fees for the cost of maintenance, testing, and incidental expenses related to the mandatory drug or alcohol testing, or both, and all costs incidental to approved electronic monitoring, of all offenders placed on supervision. The concurrence of the Chief Judge shall be in the form of an administrative order.

(h) A disposition of supervision is a final order for the purposes of appeal.

(i) The court shall impose upon a defendant placed on supervision after January 1, 1992, as a condition of supervision, a fee not to exceed $25 for each month of supervision ordered by the court, unless after determining the inability of the person placed on supervision to pay the fee, the court assesses a lesser fee. The fee shall be imposed only upon a defendant who is actively supervised by the probation and court services department. The fee shall be collected by the clerk of the circuit court. The clerk of the circuit court shall pay all monies collected from this fee to the county treasurer for deposit in the probation and court services fund pursuant to Section 15.1 of the Probation and Probation Officers Act [730 ILCS 110/15.1].

(j) All fines and costs imposed under this Section for any violation of Chapters 3, 4, 6, and 11 of the Illinois Vehicle Code [625 ILCS 5/3-100 et seq., 5/4-100 et seq., 5/6-100 et seq., and 5/11-100 et seq.], or a similar provision of a local ordinance, and any violation of the Child Passenger Protection Act [625 ILCS 25/1 et seq.], or a similar provision of a local ordinance, shall be collected and disbursed by the circuit clerk as provided under Section 27.5 of the Clerks of Courts Act [705 ILCS 105/27.5].

(Source: P.A. 86-1012; 86-1300; 86-1320; 86-1475; 87-548; 87-609; 87-610; 87-670; 87-772; 87-895.) [Formerly Ill. Rev. Stat. 38 §1005-6-3.1.]

5/5-6-3.2. Probation Challenge Program.

§5-6-3.2. (a) In counties with populations of 2,000,000 or more inhabitants, the court may, after consideration of the factors set forth in paragraph (c), require as a condition of probation that a person participate in the Probation Challenge Program. Upon imposing such condition on the person, the court shall provide the person with the address of the Program's offices and the name of the Counselor Supervisor of the Program, and require that the person present himself to the Counselor Supervisor at such address by the close of office hours on the immediately succeeding day during which the Program maintains regular office hours. The clerk of the court shall promptly notify the Counselor Supervisor of each person who has been required to participate in the Program as a condition of his probation and the date on which such condition was imposed. Whether a person is eligible for entry into the Program is a judicial determination.

(b) The condition that the person participate in the Probation Challenge Program includes the specific conditions that the person present himself to the Counselor Supervisor of such Program pursuant to paragraph (a), that the person punctually appear for all meetings scheduled between him and any personnel of such Program, and that the person strictly comply with all rules prescribed by the Board of City College of Chicago pursuant to Section 12 of the Probation Challenge Program Act [730 ILCS 120/12]. Violation of any of the specific conditions set forth in this paragraph shall not be grounds for revocation of probation, except where such violation has resulted in the person's expulsion from the Program.

(c) In determining whether to require that a person participate in the Probation Challenge Program as a condition of his probation, the court should consider

(1) Whether the person demonstrates a desire to avoid future conduct of the type which resulted in his being sentenced to a term of probation;

(2) Whether the type of assistance offered by the Probation Challenge Program is best suited to the person's needs;

(3) Whether the person appears, in light of his age and history, to be a likely candidate for rehabilitation;

(4) Whether the person has access to the economic resources, and is exposed to the type of social influences, which would enable him to attain the types of goals established for clients of the Probation Challenge Program without his participating in the Program;

(5) Whether the person demonstrates potential for accomplishing the types of goals which would be established for him were he a client of the Probation Challenge Program; and

(6) The need for limiting the number of participants in the Probation Challenge Program to a level which can be efficiently managed by the personnel of such Program.

(d) Participation by a person in the Probation Challenge Program shall be for the duration of the person's term of probation. In the event the person successfully attains all the goals which have been established for him by his counselor and instructor in the Probation Challenge Program, the court may, on its own motion, on the motion of the person's probation officer or at the request of the person, terminate the person's probation if, in the opinion of the court, such action would best serve the interests of the person and the ends of justice.

(e) A person shall be expelled from the Probation Challenge Program upon his violating for the fourth time any of the conditions set forth in paragraph (b). A person who has been expelled from the Probation Challenge Program shall

not subsequently participate in such Program absent compelling reasons in favor of such subsequent participation.
(Source: P.A. 84-1426.) [Formerly Ill. Rev. Stat. 38 §1005-6-3.2.]

5/5-6-4. Violation, modification or revocation of probation, of conditional discharge or supervision—Hearing.

§5-6-4. Violation, Modification or Revocation of Probation, of Conditional Discharge or Supervision—Hearing. (a) Except in cases where conditional discharge or supervision was imposed for a petty offense as defined in Section 5-1-17 [730 ILCS 5/5-1-17], when a petition is filed charging a violation of a condition, the court may:

(1) in the case of probation violations, order the issuance of a notice to the offender to be present by the County Probation Department or such other agency designated by the court to handle probation matters; and in the case of conditional discharge or supervision violations, such notice to the offender shall be issued by the Circuit Court Clerk;

(2) order a summons to the offender to be present for hearing; or

(3) order a warrant for the offender's arrest where there is danger of his fleeing the jurisdiction or causing serious harm to others or when the offender fails to answer a summons or notice from the clerk of the court.

Personal service of the petition for violation of probation or the issuance of such warrant, summons or notice shall toll the period of probation, conditional discharge or supervision until the final determination of the charge, and the term of probation, conditional discharge or supervision shall not run until the hearing and disposition of the petition for violation.

(b) The court shall conduct a hearing of the alleged violation. The court shall admit the offender to bail pending the hearing unless the alleged violation is itself a criminal offense in which case the offender shall be admitted to bail on such terms as are provided in the Code of Criminal Procedure of 1963, as amended [725 ILCS 5/100-1 et seq.]. In any case where an offender remains incarcerated only as a result of his alleged violation of the court's earlier order of probation, supervision, or conditional discharge, such hearing shall be held within 14 days of the onset of said incarceration, unless the alleged violation is the commission of another offense by the offender during the period of probation, supervision or conditional discharge in which case such hearing shall be held within the time limits described in Section 103-5 of the Code of Criminal Procedure of 1963, as amended [725 ILCS 5/103-5].

(c) The State has the burden of going forward with the evidence and proving the violation by the preponderance of the evidence. The evidence shall be presented in open court with the right of confrontation, cross-examination, and representation by counsel.

(d) Probation, conditional discharge, periodic imprisonment and supervision shall not be revoked for failure to comply with conditions of a sentence or supervision, which imposes financial obligations upon the offender unless such failure is due to his willful refusal to pay.

(e) If the court finds that the offender has violated a condition at any time prior to the expiration or termination of the period, it may continue him on the existing sentence, with or without modifying or enlarging the conditions, or may impose any other sentence that was available under Section 5-5-3 [730 ILCS 5/5-5-3] at the time of initial sentencing.

(f) The conditions of probation, of conditional discharge and of supervision may be modified by the court on motion of the probation officer or on its own motion or at the request of the offender after notice and a hearing.

(g) A judgment revoking supervision, probation or conditional discharge is a final appealable order.

(h) Resentencing after revocation of probation, conditional discharge or supervision shall be under Article 4 [730 ILCS 5/5-4-1 et seq.]. Time served on probation, conditional discharge or supervision shall not be credited by the court against a sentence of imprisonment or periodic imprisonment unless the court orders otherwise.
(Source: P.A. 85-628.) [Formerly Ill. Rev. Stat. 38 §1005-6-4.]

5/5-6-4.1. Violation, modification or revocation of conditional discharge or supervision—Hearing.

§5-6-4.1. Violation, Modification or Revocation of Conditional Discharge or Supervision—Hearing. (a) In cases where a defendant was placed upon supervision or conditional discharge for the commission of a petty offense, upon the oral or written motion of the State, or on the court's own motion, which charges that a violation of a condition of that conditional discharge or supervision has occurred, the court may:

(1) Conduct a hearing instanter if the offender is present in court;

(2) Order the issuance by the court clerk of a notice to the offender to be present for a hearing for violation;

(3) Order summons to the offender to be present; or

(4) Order a warrant for the offender's arrest.

The oral motion, if the defendant is present, or the issuance of such warrant, summons or notice shall toll the period of conditional discharge or supervision until the final determination of the charge, and the term of conditional discharge or supervision shall not run until the hearing and disposition of the petition for violation.

(b) The Court shall admit the offender to bail pending the hearing.

(c) The State has the burden of going forward with the evidence and proving the violation by the preponderance of the evidence. The evidence shall be presented in open court with the right of confrontation, cross-examination, and representation by counsel.

(d) Conditional discharge or supervision shall not be revoked for failure to comply with the conditions of the discharge or supervision which imposed financial obligations upon the offender unless such failure is due to his wilful refusal to pay.

(e) If the court finds that the offender has violated a condition at any time prior to the expiration or termination of the period, it may continue him on the existing sentence or supervision with or without modifying or enlarging the conditions, or may impose any other sentence that was available under Section 5-5-3 [730 ILCS 5/5-5-3] at the time of initial sentencing.

(f) The conditions of conditional discharge and of supervision may be modified by the court on motion of the probation officer or on its own motion or at the request of the offender after notice to the defendant and a hearing.

(g) A judgment revoking supervision is a final appealable order.

(h) Resentencing after revocation of conditional discharge or of supervision shall be under Article 4 [730 ILCS 5/5-4-1 et seq.]. Time served on conditional discharge or supervision shall be credited by the court against a sentence of imprisonment or periodic imprisonment unless the court orders otherwise.
(Source: P.A. 81-815.) [Formerly Ill. Rev. Stat. 38 §1005-6-4.1.]

ARTICLE 7. SENTENCE OF PERIODIC IMPRISONMENT

Sec.

5/5-7-1. Sentence of periodic imprisonment.

§5-7-1. Sentence of Periodic Imprisonment. (a) A sentence of periodic imprisonment is a sentence of imprisonment during which the committed person may be released for periods of time during the day or night or for periods of days, or both, or if convicted of a felony, other than first degree murder, a Class X or Class 1 felony, committed to any county, municipal, or regional correctional or detention institution or facility in this State for such periods of time as the court may direct. Unless the court orders otherwise, the particular times and conditions of release shall be determined by the Department of Corrections, the sheriff, or the Superintendent of the house of corrections, who is administering the program.

(b) A sentence of periodic imprisonment may be imposed to permit the defendant to:

(1) seek employment;

(2) work;

(3) conduct a business or other self-employed occupation including housekeeping;

(4) attend to family needs;

(5) attend an educational institution, including vocational education;

(6) obtain medical or psychological treatment;

(7) perform work duties at a county, municipal, or regional correctional or detention institution or facility;

(8) continue to reside at home with or without supervision involving the use of an approved electronic monitoring device, subject to Article 8A of Chapter V [730 ILCS 5/5-8A-1 et seq.]; or

(9) for any other purpose determined by the court.

(c) Except where prohibited by other provisions of this Code, the court may impose a sentence of periodic imprisonment for a felony or misdemeanor on a person who is 17 years of age or older. The court shall not impose a sentence of periodic imprisonment if it imposes a sentence of imprisonment upon the defendant in excess of 90 days.

(d) A sentence of periodic imprisonment shall be for a definite term of from 3 to 4 years for a Class 1 felony, 18 to 30 months for a Class 2 felony, and up to 18 months, or the longest sentence of imprisonment that could be imposed for the offense, whichever is less, for all other offenses; however, no person shall be sentenced to a term of periodic imprisonment longer than one year if he is committed to a county correctional institution or facility, and in conjunction with that sentence participate in a county work release program comparable to the work and day release program provided for in Article 13 of the Unified Code of Corrections [730 ILCS 5/3-13-1] in State facilities. The term of the sentence shall be calculated upon the basis of the duration of its term rather than upon the basis of the actual days spent in confinement. No sentence of periodic imprisonment shall be subject to the good time credit provisions of Section 3-6-3 of this Code [730 ILCS 5/3-6-3].

(e) When the court imposes a sentence of periodic imprisonment, it shall state:

(1) the term of such sentence;

(2) the days or parts of days which the defendant is to be confined;

(3) the conditions.

(f) The court may issue an order of protection pursuant to the Illinois Domestic Violence Act of 1986 [750 ILCS 60/101 et seq.] as a condition of a sentence of periodic imprisonment. The Illinois Domestic Violence Act of 1986 shall govern the issuance, enforcement and recording of orders of protection issued under this Section. A copy of the order of protection shall be transmitted to the person or agency having responsibility for the case.

(g) An offender sentenced to periodic imprisonment, and who during the term of either undergoes mandatory drug or alcohol testing, or both, or is assigned to be placed on an approved electronic monitoring device, may be ordered to pay the costs incidental to such mandatory drug or alcohol testing, or both, and costs incidental to such approved electronic monitoring in accordance with the defendant's ability to pay those costs. The county board with the concurrence of the Chief Judge of the judicial circuit in which the county is located may establish reasonable fees for the cost of maintenance, testing, and incidental expenses related to the mandatory drug or alcohol testing, or both, and all costs incidental to approved electronic monitoring, of all offenders with a sentence of periodic imprisonment. The concurrence of the Chief Judge shall be in the form of an administrative order.

(h) All fees and costs imposed under this Section for any violation of Chapters 3, 4, 6, and 11 of the Illinois Vehicle Code [625 ILCS 5/3-100 et seq., 5/4-100 et seq., 5/6-100 et seq., and 5/11-100 et seq.] , or a similar provision of a local ordinance, and any violation of the Child Passenger Protection Act [625 ILCS 25/1 et seq.], or a similar provision of a local ordinance, shall be collected and disbursed by the circuit clerk as provided under Section 27.5 of the Clerks of Courts Act [705 ILCS 105/27.5].

(Source: P.A. 86-328; 86-1281; 86-1320; 86-1475; 87-670.) [Formerly Ill. Rev. Stat. 38 §1005-7-1.]

5/5-7-2. Modification and revocation.

§5-7-2. Modification and Revocation. (a) A sentence of periodic imprisonment may be modified or revoked by the court if:

(1) the offender commits another offense; or

(2) the offender violates any of the conditions of the sentence; or

(3) the offender violates any rule or regulation of the institution, agency or Department to which he has been committed.

(b) If the offender violates the order of periodic imprisonment, the Department of Corrections, the sheriff, or the superintendent of the house of corrections shall report such violation to the court.

(c) The court shall not modify or revoke a sentence of periodic imprisonment unless the offender has been given written notice and afforded a hearing under Section 5-6-4 [730 ILCS 5/5-6-4]. If the offender is incarcerated as a result of his alleged violation of the court's prior order, such hearing shall be held within 14 days of the onset of said incarceration. Where a sentence of periodic imprisonment is revoked, the court may impose any other sentence that was available at the time of initial sentencing. That part of the term under paragraph (d) of Section 5-7-1 [730 ILCS 5/5-7-1] which has been served under the sentence of periodic imprisonment shall be credited against a sentence of imprisonment.

(Source: P.A. 80-1099.) [Formerly Ill. Rev. Stat. 38 §1005-7-2.]

5/5-7-3. Commitment.

§5-7-3. Commitment. (a) Commitment under a sentence of periodic imprisonment for a misdemeanor shall be to the sheriff or the superintendent of the house of corrections or workhouse.

(b) Commitment under a sentence of periodic imprisonment for a felony may be under paragraph (a) of this Section or to the Department of Corrections if the Director of the Department has certified that appropriate facilities and personnel are available to administer sentences of periodic imprisonment.

(c) The Director of the Department of Corrections may certify that an appropriate institution has the facilities and personnel to administer periodic imprisonment. Such certification shall be filed with the clerk of the circuit court from which commitments to such institution will be accepted. Any such certification may be revoked by filing a notice of revocation with such clerk.

(d) The sheriff of any county may certify that an appropriate institution has the facilities and personnel to administer periodic imprisonment. Such certification shall be filed with the clerk of the circuit court from which commitments to such institution will be accepted. Any such certification may be revoked by filing a notice of revocation with such clerk.

(e) If the sheriff to whose custody a defendant is committed for a term of periodic imprisonment certifies an institution under subsection (d), the sheriff may contract, subject to the approval of the county board, with a certified institution for the housing of the offender in that institution, and while so placed the offender shall be subject to the court's terms of imprisonment. The cost of maintenance of such offender shall be paid by the county in which he was committed.

(f) Neither the State, any unit of local government or the sheriff of the county to whose custody a defendant is committed, nor any officer or employee thereof acting in the course of their official duties shall be liable for any injury or loss which a person might suffer while residing at a certified institution, nor shall they be liable for any tortious acts of any offender housed at the certified institution, or for any tortious acts of an officer or employee of such institution, except for wilful and wanton misconduct or gross negligence on the part of such governmental unit, officer or employee.

(Source: P.A. 85-1433.) [Formerly Ill. Rev. Stat. 38 §1005-7-3.]

5/5-7-4. Continuation of employment.

§5-7-4. Continuation of Employment. If the offender has been regularly employed, the Department of Corrections, the sheriff, the superintendent of the house of correction or workhouse, or the probation officer shall arrange for a continuation of such employment. If the offender has not been regularly employed, every reasonable effort shall be made to secure employment for such person, and any person for whom employment is secured shall be paid a fair and reasonable wage and shall not be required to work more than 8 hours per day, nor more than 48 hours per week.

(Source: P.A. 77-2097.) [Formerly Ill. Rev. Stat. 38 §1005-7-4.]

5/5-7-5. Arrangement between sheriffs for employment.

§5-7-5. Arrangement between Sheriffs for Employment. The court may authorize the sheriff to whose custody a defendant is committed, to arrange with another sheriff for the employment of the offender in the latter's county, and while so employed to be in the latter sheriff's custody but in other respects to be and continue subject to the commitment. The cost of maintenance of such offender shall be paid by the county in which he was committed. The Department of Corrections may transfer an offender committed to it to another institution or facility of the Department subject to the approval of the committing court.

(Source: P.A. 77-2097.) [Formerly Ill. Rev. Stat. 38 §1005-7-5.]

5/5-7-6. Duty of clerk of court or the Department of Correction; collection and disposition of compensation.

§5-7-6. Duty of Clerk of Court or the Department of Correction; Collection and Disposition of Compensation. (a) Every gainfully employed offender shall be responsible for managing his earnings. The clerk of the circuit court shall have only those responsibilities regarding an offender's earnings as are set forth in this Section.

Every offender, including offenders who are sentenced to periodic imprisonment for weekends only, gainfully employed is liable for the cost of his board at the rate of $12.00 per day or 50% of his rate of daily earnings, whichever is less. If he is necessarily absent from the institution at mealtime he shall, for a reasonable charge, be furnished with lunch to carry to work. Each week, on a day designated by the clerk of the circuit court, every offender shall pay the clerk for his board. Failure to pay the clerk on the day designated shall result in the termination of the offender's release.

By order of the court, all or a portion of the earnings of employed offenders shall be turned over to the clerk to be distributed for the following purposes, in the order stated:

(1) the board of the offender;

(2) necessary travel expenses to and from work and other incidental expenses of the offender, where those expenses are incurred by the administrator of the offender's imprisonment;

(3) support of the offender's dependents, if any.

(b) If the offender has one or more dependents who are recipients of financial assistance pursuant to The Illinois Public Aid Code [305 ILCS 5/1-1 et seq.], or who are residents of a State hospital, State school or foster care facility provided by the State, the court shall order the offender to turn over all or a portion of his earnings to the clerk who shall, after making the deductions provided for under paragraph (a), distribute those earnings to the appropriate agency as reimbursement for the cost of care of such dependents. The order shall permit the Illinois Department of Public Aid or the local governmental unit, as the case may be, to request the clerk that subsequent payments be made directly to the dependents, or to some agency or person in their behalf, upon removal of the dependents from the public aid rolls; and upon such direction and removal of the recipients from the public aid rolls, the Illinois Department of Public Aid or the local governmental unit, as the case requires, shall give written notice of such action to the court. Payments received by the Illinois Department of Public Aid or by governmental units in behalf of recipients of public aid shall be deposited into the General Revenue Fund of the State Treasury or General Assistance Fund of the governmental unit, under Section 10-19 of The Illinois Public Aid Code [305 ILCS 5/10-19].

(c) The clerk of the circuit court shall keep individual accounts of all money collected by him as required by this Article. He shall deposit all moneys as trustee in a depository designated by the county board and shall make payments required by the court's order from such trustee account. Such accounts shall be subject to audit in the same manner as accounts of the county are audited.

(d) If an institution or the Department of Corrections certifies to the court that it can administer this Section with respect to persons committed to it under this Article, the clerk of the court shall be relieved of its duties under this Section and they shall be assumed by such institution or the Department.

(Source: P.A. 84-230.) [Formerly Ill. Rev. Stat. 38 §1005-7-6.]

5/5-7-7. Jurisdiction.

§5-7-7. Jurisdiction. The court which committed the offender to periodic imprisonment shall retain jurisdiction over him during the term of commitment and may order a diminution of the term if his conduct, diligence and general attitude merit such diminution.

(Source: P.A. 77-2097.) [Formerly Ill. Rev. Stat. 38 §1005-7-7.]

5/5-7-8. Subsequent sentences.

§5-7-8. Subsequent Sentences. (a) The service of a sentence of imprisonment shall satisfy any sentence of periodic imprisonment which was imposed on an offender for an offense committed prior to the imposition of the sentence. An offender who is serving a sentence of periodic imprisonment at the time a sentence of imprisonment is imposed shall be delivered to the custody of the Department of Corrections to commence service of the sentence immediately.

(b) If a sentence of imprisonment under Section 5-8-3 [730 ILCS 5/5-8-3] is imposed on an offender who is under a previously imposed sentence of periodic imprisonment, such person shall commence service of the sentence immediately. Where such sentence is for a term in excess of 90 days, the service of such sentence shall satisfy the sentence of periodic imprisonment.

(Source: P.A. 82-717.) [Formerly Ill. Rev. Stat. 38 §1005-7-8.]

ARTICLE 8. IMPRISONMENT

Sec.

5/5-8-1. Sentence of imprisonment for felony.

§5-8-1. Sentence of Imprisonment for Felony. (a) Except as otherwise provided in the statute defining the offense, a sentence of imprisonment for a felony shall be a determinate sentence set by the court under this Section, according to the following limitations:

(1) for first degree murder,

(a) a term shall be not less than 20 years and not more than 60 years, or

(b) if the court finds that the murder was accompanied by exceptionally brutal or heinous behavior indicative of wanton cruelty or, except as set forth in subsection (a)(1)(c) of this Section, that any of the aggravating factors listed in subsection (b) of Section 9-1 of the Criminal Code of 1961 [720 ILCS 5/9-1] are present, the court may sentence the defendant to a term of natural life imprisonment, or

(c) if the defendant,

(i) has previously been convicted of first degree murder under any state or federal law, or

(ii) is found guilty of murdering more than one victim, or

(iii) is found guilty of murdering a peace officer or fireman when the peace officer or fireman was killed in the course of performing his official duties, or to prevent the peace officer or fireman from performing his official duties, or in retaliation for the peace officer or fireman performing his official duties, and the defendant knew or should have known that the murdered individual was a peace officer or fireman, or

(iv) is found guilty of murdering an employee of an institution or facility of the Department of Corrections, or any similar local correctional agency, when the employee was killed in the course of performing his official duties, or to prevent the employee from performing his official duties, or in retaliation for the employee performing his official duties, the court shall sentence the defendant to a term of natural life imprisonment;

(2) for a person adjudged a habitual criminal under Article 33B of the Criminal Code of 1961 [720 ILCS 5/33B-1 et seq.], as amended, the sentence shall be a term of natural life imprisonment.

(3) except as otherwise provided in the statute defining the offense, for a Class X felony, the sentence shall be not less than 6 years and not more than 30 years;

(4) for a Class 1 felony, the sentence shall be not less than 4 years and not more than 15 years;

(5) for a Class 2 felony, the sentence shall be not less than 3 years and not more than 7 years;

(6) for a Class 3 felony, the sentence shall be not less than 2 years and not more than 5 years;

(7) for a Class 4 felony, the sentence shall be not less than 1 year and not more than 3 years.

(b) The sentencing judge in each felony conviction shall set forth his reasons for imposing the particular sentence he enters in the case, as provided in Section 5-4-1 of this Code [730 ILCS 5/5-4-1]. Those reasons may include any mitigating or aggravating factors specified in this Code, or the lack of any such circumstances, as well as any other such factors as the judge shall set forth on the record that are consistent with the purposes and principles of sentencing set out in this Code.

(c) A motion to reduce a sentence may be made, or the court may reduce a sentence without motion, within 30 days after the sentence is imposed. However, the court may not increase a sentence once it is imposed.

If a motion to reduce a sentence is timely filed within 30 days after the sentence is imposed, the proponent of the motion shall exercise due diligence in seeking a determination on the motion and the court shall thereafter decide such motion within a reasonable time.

If a motion to reduce a sentence is timely filed within 30 days after the sentence is imposed, then for purposes of perfecting an appeal, a final judgment shall not be considered to have been entered until the motion to reduce a sentence has been decided by order entered by the trial court.

A motion to reduce a sentence shall not be considered to have been timely filed unless it is filed with the circuit court clerk within 30 days after the sentence is imposed together with a notice of motion, which notice of motion shall set the motion on the court's calendar on a date certain within a reasonable time after the date of filing.

(d) Except where a term of natural life is imposed, every sentence shall include as though written therein a term in addition to the term of imprisonment. For those sentenced under the law in effect prior to February 1, 1978, such term shall be identified as a parole term. For those sentenced on or after February 1, 1978, such term shall be identified as a mandatory supervised release term. Subject to earlier termination under Section 3-3-8 [730 ILCS 5/3-3-8], the parole or mandatory supervised release term shall be as follows:

(1) for first degree murder or a Class X felony, 3 years;

(2) for a Class 1 felony or a Class 2 felony, 2 years;

(3) for a Class 3 felony or a Class 4 felony, 1 year.

(e) A defendant who has a previous and unexpired sentence of imprisonment imposed by another state or by any district court of the United States and who, after sentence for a crime in Illinois, must return to serve the unexpired prior sentence may have his sentence by the Illinois court ordered to be concurrent with the prior sentence in the other state. The court may order that any time served on the unexpired portion of the sentence in the other state, prior to his return to Illinois, shall be credited on his Illinois sentence. The other state shall be furnished with a copy of the order imposing sentence which shall provide that, when the offender is released from confinement of the other state, whether by parole or by termination of sentence, the offender shall be transferred by the Sheriff of the committing county to the Illinois Department of Corrections. The court shall cause the Department of Corrections to be notified of such sentence at the time of commitment and to be provided with copies of all records regarding the sentence.

(f) A defendant who has a previous and unexpired sentence of imprisonment imposed by an Illinois circuit court for a crime in this State and who is subsequently sentenced to a term of imprisonment by another state or by any district court of the United States and who has served a term of imprisonment imposed by the other state or district court of the United States, and must return to serve the unexpired prior sentence imposed by the Illinois Circuit Court may apply to the court which imposed sentence to have his sentence reduced.

The circuit court may order that any time served on the sentence imposed by the other state or district court of the United States be credited on his Illinois sentence. Such application for reduction of a sentence under this subsection (f) shall be made within 30 days after the defendant has completed the sentence imposed by the other state or district court of the United States.

(Chgd. by P.A. 87-921, §2, eff. 1/1/93.)

(Source: P.A. 85-1209; 85-1440.) [Formerly Ill. Rev. Stat. 38 §1005-8-1.]

5/5-8-1.1. Impact incarceration.

§5-8-1.1. Impact incarceration. (a) The Department may establish and operate an impact incarceration program for youthful offenders. If the court finds under Section 5-4-1 [730 ILCS 5/5-4-1] that an offender sentenced to a term of imprisonment for a felony may meet the eligibility requirements of the Department, the court may in its sentencing order approve the offender for placement in the impact incarceration program conditioned upon his acceptance in the program by the Department. Notwithstanding the sentencing provisions of this Code, the sentencing order also shall provide that if the Department accepts the offender in the program and determines that the offender has successfully completed the impact incarceration program, the sentence shall be reduced to time considered served upon certification to the court by the Department that the offender has successfully completed the program. In the event the offender is not accepted for placement in the impact incarceration program or the offender does not successfully complete the program, his term of imprisonment shall be as set forth by the court in its sentencing order.

(b) In order to be eligible to participate in the impact incarceration program, the committed person shall meet all of the following requirements:

(1) The person must be not less than 17 years of age nor more than 29 years of age.

(2) The person has never served a sentence of imprisonment for a felony in an adult correctional facility.

(3) The person has not been convicted of a Class X felony, first or second degree murder, armed violence, aggravated kidnapping, criminal sexual assault, aggravated criminal sexual abuse or a subsequent conviction for criminal sexual abuse, forcible detention, or arson.

(4) The person has been sentenced to a term of imprisonment of 5 years or less.

(5) The person must be physically able to participate in strenuous physical activities or labor.

(6) The person must not have any mental disorder or disability that would prevent participation in the impact incarceration program.

(7) The person has consented in writing to participation in the impact incarceration program and to the terms and conditions thereof.

(8) The person was recommended and approved for placement in the impact incarceration program in the court's sentencing order.

The Department may also consider, among other matters, whether the committed person has any outstanding detainers or warrants, whether the committed person has a history of escaping or absconding, whether participation in the impact incarceration program may pose a risk to the safety or security of any person and whether space is available.

(c) The impact incarceration program shall include, among other matters, mandatory physical training and labor, military formation and drills, regimented activities, uniformity of dress and appearance, education and counseling, including drug counseling where appropriate.

(d) Privileges including visitation, commissary, receipt and retention of property and publications and access to television, radio and a library may be suspended or restricted, notwithstanding provisions to the contrary in this Code.

(e) Committed persons participating in the impact incarceration program shall adhere to all Department rules and all requirements of the program. Committed persons shall be informed of rules of behavior and conduct. Disciplinary procedures required by this Code or by Department rule are not applicable except in those instances in which the Department seeks to revoke good time.

(f) Participation in the impact incarceration program shall be for a period of 120 to 180 days. The period of time a committed person shall serve in the impact incarceration program shall not be reduced by the accumulation of good time.

(g) The committed person shall serve a term of mandatory supervised release as set forth in subsection (d) of Section 5-8-1 [730 ILCS 5/5-8-1].

(h) A committed person may be removed from the program for a violation of the terms or conditions of the program or in the event he is for any reason unable to participate. The Department shall promulgate rules and regulations governing conduct which could result in removal from the program or in a determination that the committed person has not successfully completed the program. Committed persons shall have access to such rules, which shall provide that a committed person shall receive notice and have the opportunity to appear before and address one or more hearing officers. A committed person may be transferred to any of the Department's facilities prior to the hearing.

(i) The Department may terminate the impact incarceration program at any time.

(j) The Department shall report to the Governor and the General Assembly on or before September 30th of each year on the impact incarceration program, including the composition of the program by the offenders, by county of commitment, sentence, age, offense and race.

(k) The Department of Corrections shall consider the affirmative action plan approved by the Department of Human Rights in hiring staff at the impact incarceration facilities. The Department shall report to the Director of Human Rights on or before April 1 of each year on the sex, race and national origin of persons employed at each impact incarceration facility.

(Subsec. (k) added by P.A. 86-1182, §1, eff. 8/20/90. See other subsec. (k) below.)

(k) The Department of Corrections shall consider the affirmative action plan approved by the Department of Human Rights in hiring staff at the impact incarceration facilities. The Department shall report to the Director of Human Rights on or before April 1 of the year on the sex, race and national origin of persons employed at each impact incarceration facility.

(Subsec. (k) added by P.A. 86-1183, §1, eff. 8/20/90. See other subsec. (k) above.)

(Source: P.A. 86-1182; 86-1183.) [Formerly Ill. Rev. Stat. 38 §1005-8-1.1.]

5/5-8-2. Extended term.

§5-8-2. Extended Term. (a) A judge shall not sentence an offender to a term of imprisonment in excess of the maximum sentence authorized by Section 5-8-1 [730 ILCS 5/5-8-1] for the class of the most serious offense of which the offender was convicted unless the factors in aggravation set forth in paragraph (b) of Section 5-5-3.2 [730 ILCS 5/5-5-3.2] were found to be present. Where the judge finds that such factors were present, he may sentence an offender to the following:

(1) for first degree murder, a term shall be not less than 60 years and not more than 100 years;

(2) for a Class X felony, a term shall be not less than 30 years and not more than 60 years;

(3) for a Class 1 felony, a term shall be not less than 15 years and not more than 30 years;

(4) for a Class 2 felony, a term shall be not less than 7 years and not more than 14 years;

(5) for a Class 3 felony, a term shall not be less than 5 years and not more than 10 years;

(6) for a Class 4 felony, a term shall be not less than 3 years and not more than 6 years.

(b) If the conviction was by plea, it shall appear on the record that the plea was entered with the defendant's knowledge that a sentence under this Section was a possibility. If it does not so appear on the record, the defendant shall not be subject to such a sentence unless he is first given an opportunity to withdraw his plea without prejudice.
(Source: P.A. 85-902.) [Formerly Ill. Rev. Stat. 38 §1005-8-2.]

5/5-8-3. Sentence of imprisonment for misdemeanor.

§5-8-3. Sentence of Imprisonment for Misdemeanor. (a) A sentence of imprisonment for a misdemeanor shall be for a determinate term according to the following limitations:

(1) for a Class A misdemeanor, for any term less than one year;

(2) for a Class B misdemeanor, for not more than 6 months;

(3) for a Class C misdemeanor, for not more than 30 days.

(b) The good behavioral allowance shall be determined under Section 3 of the Misdemeanant Good Behavior Allowance Act [730 ILCS 130/3].
(Source: P.A. 81-1050.) [Formerly Ill. Rev. Stat. 38 §1005-8-3.]

5/5-8-4. Concurrent and consecutive terms of imprisonment.

§5-8-4. Concurrent and Consecutive Terms of Imprisonment. (a) When multiple sentences of imprisonment are imposed on a defendant at the same time, or when a term of imprisonment is imposed on a defendant who is already subject to sentence in this State or in another state, or for a sentence imposed by any district court of the United States, the sentences shall run concurrently or consecutively as determined by the court. When a term of imprisonment is imposed on a defendant by an Illinois circuit court and the defendant is subsequently sentenced to a term of imprisonment by another state or by a district court of the United States, the Illinois circuit court which imposed the sentence may order that the Illinois sentence be made concurrent with the sentence imposed by the other state or district court of the United States. The defendant must apply to the circuit court within 30 days after the defendant's sentence imposed by the other state or district of the United States is finalized. The court shall not impose consecutive sentences for offenses which were committed as part of a single course of conduct during which there was no substantial change in the nature of the criminal objective, unless, one of the offenses for which defendant was convicted was a Class X or Class 1 felony and the defendant inflicted severe bodily injury, or where the defendant was convicted of a violation of Section 12-13 or 12-14 of the Criminal Code of 1961 [720 ILCS 5/12-13 or 5/12-14], in which event the court shall enter sentences to run consecutively. Sentences shall run concurrently unless otherwise specified by the court.

(b) The court shall not impose a consecutive sentence except as provided for in subsection (a) unless, having regard to the nature and circumstances of the offense and the history and character of the defendant, it is of the opinion that such a term is required to protect the public from further criminal conduct by the defendant, the basis for which the court shall set forth in the record.

(c) (1) For sentences imposed under law in effect prior to February 1, 1978 the aggregate maximum of consecutive sentences shall not exceed the maximum term authorized under Section 5-8-1 [730 ILCS 5/5-8-1] for the 2 most serious felonies involved. The aggregate minimum period of consecutive sentences shall not exceed the highest minimum term authorized under Section 5-8-1 for the 2 most serious felonies involved. When sentenced only for misdemeanors, a defendant shall not be consecutively sentenced to more than the maximum for one Class A misdemeanor.

(2) For sentences imposed under the law in effect on or after February 1, 1978, the aggregate of consecutive sentences shall not exceed the sum of the maximum terms authorized under Section 5-8-2 [730 ILCS 5/5-8-2] for the 2 most serious felonies involved. When sentenced only for misdemeanors, a defendant shall not be consecutively sentenced to more than the maximum for one Class A misdemeanor.

(d) An offender serving a sentence for a misdemeanor who is convicted of a felony and sentenced to imprisonment shall be transferred to the Department of Corrections, and the misdemeanor sentence shall be merged in and run concurrently with the felony sentence.

(e) In determining the manner in which consecutive sentences of imprisonment, one or more of which is for a felony, will be served, the Department of Corrections shall treat the offender as though he had been committed for a single term with the following incidents:

(1) the maximum period of a term of imprisonment shall consist of the aggregate of the maximums of the imposed indeterminate terms, if any, plus the aggregate of the imposed determinate sentences for felonies plus the aggregate of the imposed determinate sentences for misdemeanors subject to paragraph (c) of this Section;

(2) the parole or mandatory supervised release term shall be as provided in paragraph (e) of Section 5-8-1 of this Code for the most serious of the offenses involved;

(3) the minimum period of imprisonment shall be the aggregate of the minimum and determinate periods of imprisonment imposed by the court, subject to paragraph (c) of this Section; and

(4) the offender shall be awarded credit against the aggregate maximum term and the aggregate minimum term of imprisonment for all time served in an institution since the commission of the offense or offenses and as a consequence thereof at the rate specified in Section 3-6-3 of this Code [730 ILCS 5/3-6-3].

(f) A sentence of an offender committed to the Department of Corrections at the time of the commission of the offense shall be served consecutive to the sentence under which he is held by the Department of Corrections. However, in case such offender shall be sentenced to punishment by death, the sentence shall be executed at such time as the court may fix without regard to the sentence under which such offender may be held by the Department.

(g) A sentence under Section 3-6-4 [730 ILCS 5/3-6-4] for escape or attempted escape shall be served consecutive to the terms under which the offender is held by the Department of Corrections.

(h) If a person charged with a felony commits a separate felony while on pre-trial release or in pretrial detention in a county jail facility or county detention facility, the sentences imposed upon conviction of these felonies shall be served consecutively regardless of the order in which the judgments of conviction are entered.

(i) If a person admitted to bail following conviction of a felony commits a separate felony while free on bond or if a person detained in a county jail facility or county detention facility following conviction of a felony commits a separate felony while in detention, any sentence following conviction of the separate felony shall be consecutive to that of the original sentence for which the defendant was on bond or detained.

(Source: P.A. 85-1440.) [Formerly Ill. Rev. Stat. 38 §1005-8-4.]

5/5-8-5. Commitment of the offender.

§5-8-5. Commitment of the Offender. Upon rendition of judgment after pronouncement of a sentence of periodic imprisonment, imprisonment, or death, the court shall commit the offender to the custody of the sheriff or to the Department of Corrections. A sheriff in executing an order for commitment to the Department of Corrections shall convey such offender to the nearest receiving station designated by the Department of Corrections. The court may commit the offender to the custody of the Attorney General of the United States under Section 5-8-6 [730 ILCS 5/5-8-6] when a sentence for a State offense provides that such sentence is to run concurrently with a previous and unexpired federal sentence. The expense of conveying a person committed by the juvenile court or an offender convicted of a felony shall be paid by the State. The expenses in all other cases shall be paid by the county of the committing court.

(Source: P.A. 84-551.) [Formerly Ill. Rev. Stat. 38 §1005-8-5.]

5/5-8-6. Place of confinement.

§5-8-6. Place of Confinement. (a) Offenders sentenced to a term of imprisonment for a felony shall be committed to the penitentiary system of the Department of Corrections. However, such sentence shall not limit the powers of the Department of Children and Family Services in relation to any child under the age of one year in the sole custody of a person so sentenced, nor in relation to any child delivered by a female so sentenced while she is so confined as a consequence of such sentence. A person sentenced for a felony may be assigned by the Department of Corrections to any of its institutions, facilities or programs.

(b) Offenders sentenced to a term of imprisonment for less than one year shall be committed to the custody of the sheriff. A person committed to the Department of Corrections, prior to July 14, 1983, for less than one year may be assigned by the Department to any of its institutions, facilities or programs.

(c) All offenders under 17 years of age when sentenced to imprisonment shall be committed to the Juvenile Division of the Department of Corrections and the court in its order of commitment shall set a definite term. Such order of commitment shall be the sentence of the court which may be amended by the court while jurisdiction is retained; and such sentence shall apply whenever the offender sentenced is in the control and custody of the Adult Division of the Department of Corrections. The provisions of Section 3-3-3 [730 ILCS 5/3-3-3] shall be a part of such commitment as fully as though written in the order of commitment. The committing court shall retain jurisdiction of the subject matter and the person until he or she reaches the age of 21 unless earlier discharged. However, the Juvenile Division of the Department of Corrections shall, after a juvenile has reached 17 years of age, petition the court to conduct a hearing pursuant to subsection (c) of Section 3-10-7 of this Code [730 ILCS 5/3-10-7].

(d) No defendant shall be committed to the Department of Corrections for the recovery of a fine or costs.

(e) When a court sentences a defendant to a term of imprisonment concurrent with a previous and unexpired sentence of imprisonment imposed by any district court of the United States, it may commit the offender to the custody of the Attorney General of the United States. The Attorney General of the United States, or the authorized representative of the Attorney General of the United States, shall be furnished with the warrant of commitment from the court imposing sentence, which warrant of commitment shall provide that, when the offender is released from federal confinement, whether by parole or by termination of sentence, the offender shall be transferred by the Sheriff of the committing county to the Department of Corrections. The court shall cause the Department to be notified of such sentence at the time of commitment and to be provided with copies of all records regarding the sentence.

(Source: P.A. 83-1362.) [Formerly Ill. Rev. Stat. 38 §1005-8-6.]

5/5-8-7. Calculation of term of imprisonment.

§5-8-7. Calculation of Term of Imprisonment. (a) A sentence of imprisonment shall commence on the date on which the offender is received by the Department or the institution at which the sentence is to be served.

(b) The offender shall be given credit on the determinate sentence or maximum term and the minimum period of imprisonment for time spent in custody as a result of the offense for which the sentence was imposed, at the rate specified in Section 3-6-3 of this Code [730 ILCS 5/3-6-3].

(c) An offender arrested on one charge and prosecuted on another charge for conduct which occurred prior to his arrest shall be given credit on the determinate sentence or maximum term and the minimum term of imprisonment for time spent in custody under the former charge not credited against another sentence.

(Source: P.A. 80-1099.) [Formerly Ill. Rev. Stat. 38 §1005-8-7.]

ARTICLE 8A. ELECTRONIC HOME DETENTION

Sec.

5/5-8A-1. Title.

§5-8A-1. Title. This Article shall be known and may be cited as the Electronic Home Detention Law.

(Source: P.A. 86-1281.) [Formerly Ill. Rev. Stat. 38 §1005-8A-1.]

5/5-8A-2. Definitions.

§5-8A-2. Definitions. As used in this Article:

(A) "Approved electronic monitoring device" means a device approved by the supervising authority which is primarily intended to record or transmit information as to the defendants presence or nonpresence in the home.

An approved electronic monitoring device may record or transmit: oral or wire communications or an auditory sound; visual images; or information regarding the offender's activities while inside the offender's home. These devices are subject to the required consent as set forth in Section 5-8A-5 of this Article [730 ILCS 5/5-8A-5].

An approved electronic monitoring device may be used to record a conversation between the participant and the monitoring device, or the participant and the person supervising the participant solely for the purpose of identification and not for the purpose of eavesdropping or conducting any other illegally intrusive monitoring.

(B) "Home detention" means the confinement of a person convicted or charged with an offense to his or her place of residence under the terms and conditions established by the supervising authority.

(C) "Participant" means an inmate or offender placed into an electronic monitoring program.

(D) "Supervising authority" means the Department of Corrections, probation supervisory authority, sheriff, superintendent of municipal house of corrections or any other officer or agency charged with authorizing and supervising home detention.

(Source: P.A. 86-1281.) [Formerly Ill. Rev. Stat. 38 §1005-8A-2.]

5/5-8A-3. Application.

§5-8A-3. Application. A person charged with or convicted of first degree murder, escape, or any Class X or Class 1 felony, except residential burglary, may not be placed in an electronic home detention program, except for bond pending trial or appeal or while on parole or mandatory supervised release. Applications for electronic home detention may include, but will not be limited to the following:

(1) pretrial or pre-adjudicatory detention;
(2) probation;
(3) conditional discharge;
(4) periodic imprisonment;
(5) parole or mandatory supervised release;
(6) work release; or
(7) furlough.

(Source: P.A. 86-1281; 87-148; 87-860; 87-890.) [Formerly Ill. Rev. Stat. 38 §1005-8A-3.]

5/5-8A-4. Program description.

§5-8A-4. Program description. The supervising authority may promulgate rules that prescribe reasonable guidelines under which an electronic home detention program shall operate. These rules shall include but not be limited to the following:

(A) The participant shall remain within the interior premises or within the property boundaries of his or her residence at all times during the hours designated by the supervising authority. Such instances of approved absences from the home may include but are not limited to the following:

(1) working or employment approved by the court or traveling to or from approved employment;

(2) unemployed and seeking employment approved for the participant by the court;

(3) undergoing medical, psychiatric, mental health treatment, counseling, or other treatment programs approved for the participant by the court;

(4) attending an educational institution or a program approved for the participant by the court;

(5) attending a regularly scheduled religious service at a place of worship;

(6) participating in community work release or community service programs approved for the participant by the supervising authority; or

(7) for another compelling reason consistent with the public interest, as approved by the supervising authority.

(B) The participant shall admit any person or agent designated by the supervising authority into his or her residence at any time for purposes of verifying the participant's compliance with the conditions of his or her detention.

(C) The participant shall make the necessary arrangements to allow for any person or agent designated by the supervising authority to visit the participant's place of education or employment at any time, based upon the approval of the educational institution employer or both, for the purpose of verifying the participant's compliance with the conditions of his or her detention.

(D) The participant shall acknowledge and participate with the approved electronic monitoring device as designated by the supervising authority at any time for the purpose of verifying the participant's compliance with the conditions of his or her detention.

(E) The participant shall maintain the following:

(1) a working telephone in the participant's home;

(2) a monitoring device in the participant's home, or on the participant's person, or both; and

(3) a monitoring device in the participant's home and on the participant's person in the absence of a telephone.

(F) The participant shall obtain approval from the supervising authority before the participant changes residence or the schedule described in subsection (A) of Section 5-8A-4.

(G) The participant shall not commit another crime during the period of home detention ordered by the Court.

(H) Notice to the participant that violation of the order for home detention may subject the participant to prosecution for the crime of escape.

(I) The participant shall abide by other conditions as set by the supervising authority.

(Source: P.A. 86-1281.) [Formerly Ill. Rev. Stat. 38 §1005-8A-4.]

5/5-8A-5. Consent of the participant.

§5-8A-5. Consent of the participant. Before entering an order for commitment for electronic home detention, the supervising authority shall inform the participant and other persons residing in the home of the nature and extent of the approved electronic monitoring devices by doing the following:

(A) Securing the written consent of the participant in the program to comply with the rules and regulations of the program as stipulated in subsections (A) through (I) of Section 5-8A-4 [730 ILCS 5/5-8A-4].

(B) Securing the written consent of other persons residing in the home of the participant at the time of the order or commitment for electronic home detention is entered and acknowledge the nature and extent of approved electronic monitoring devices.

(C) Insure that the approved electronic devices be minimally intrusive upon the privacy of the participant and other persons residing in the home while remaining in compliance with subsections (B) through (D) of Section 5-8A-4.

(Source: P.A. 86-1281; 87-860; 87-890.) [Formerly Ill. Rev. Stat. 38 §1005-8A-5.]

ARTICLE 9. FINES

Sec.

5/5-9-1. Authorized fines.

§5-9-1. Authorized fines. (a) An offender may be sentenced to pay a fine which shall not exceed for each offense:

(1) for a felony, $10,000 or the amount specified in the offense, whichever is greater, or where the offender is a corporation, $50,000 or the amount specified in the offense, whichever is greater;

(2) for a Class A misdemeanor, $1,000 or the amount specified in the offense, whichever is greater;

(3) for a Class B or Class C misdemeanor, $500;

(4) for a petty offense, $500 or the amount specified in the offense, whichever is less;

(5) for a business offense, the amount specified in the statute defining that offense.

(b) A fine may be imposed in addition to a sentence of conditional discharge, probation, periodic imprisonment, or imprisonment.

(c) There shall be added to every fine imposed in sentencing for a criminal or traffic offense, except an offense relating to parking or registration, or offense by a pedestrian, an additional penalty of $4 for each $40, or fraction thereof, of fine imposed. The additional penalty of $4 for each $40, or fraction thereof, of fine imposed, if not otherwise assessed, shall also be added to every fine imposed upon a plea of guilty, stipulation of facts or findings of guilty, resulting in a judgment of conviction, or order of supervision in criminal, traffic, local ordinance, county ordinance, and conservation cases (except parking, registration, or pedestrian violations), or upon a sentence of probation without entry of judgment under Section 10 of the Cannabis Control Act [720 ILCS 550/10] or Section 410 of the Controlled Substances Act [720 ILCS 570/410].

Such additional amounts shall be assessed by the court imposing the fine and shall be collected by the Circuit Clerk in addition to the fine and costs in the case. Each such additional penalty shall be remitted by the Circuit Clerk within one month after receipt to the State Treasurer for deposit into the Traffic and Criminal Conviction Surcharge Fund, unless the fine, costs or additional amounts are subject to disbursement by the circuit clerk under Section 27.5 of the Clerks of Courts Act [705 ILCS 105/27.5]. Such additional penalty shall not be considered a part of the fine for purposes of any reduction in the fine for time served either before or after sentencing. Not later than March 1 of each year the Circuit Clerk shall submit a report of the amount of funds remitted to the State Treasurer under this subsection (c) during the preceding calendar year. Except as otherwise provided by Supreme Court Rules, if a court in imposing a fine against an offender levies a gross amount for fine, costs, fees and penalties, the amount of the additional penalty provided for herein shall be computed on the amount remaining after deducting from the gross amount levied all fees of the Circuit Clerk, the State's Attorney and the Sheriff. After deducting from the gross amount levied the fees and additional penalty provided for herein, less any other additional penalties provided by law, the clerk shall remit the net balance remaining to the entity authorized by law to receive the fine imposed in the case. For purposes of this Section "fees of the Circuit Clerk" shall include, if applicable, the fee provided for under Section 27.3a of the Clerks of Courts Act [705 ILCS 105/27.3a] and the fee, if applicable, payable to the county in which the violation occurred pursuant to Section 5-1101 of the Counties Code [55 ILCS 5/5-1101].

The Circuit Clerk may accept payment of fines and costs by credit card from an offender who has been convicted of a traffic offense, petty offense or misdemeanor and may charge the service fee permitted where fines and costs are paid by credit card provided for in Section 27.3b of the Clerks of Courts Act.

(d) In determining the amount and method of payment of a fine, except for those fines established for violations of Chapter 15 of the Illinois Vehicle Code [625 ILCS 5/15-100 et seq.], the court shall consider:

(1) the financial resources and future ability of the offender to pay the fine; and

(2) whether the fine will prevent the offender from making court ordered restitution or reparation to the victim of the offense; and

(3) in a case where the accused is a dissolved corporation and the court has appointed counsel to represent the corporation, the costs incurred either by the county or the State for such representation.

(e) The court may order the fine to be paid forthwith or within a specified period of time or in installments.

(f) All fines, costs and additional amounts imposed under this Section for any violation of Chapters 3, 4, 6, and 11 of the Illinois Vehicle Code [625 ILCS 5/3-100 et seq., 5/4-100 et seq., 5/6-100 et seq., and 5/11-100 et seq.], or a similar provision of a local ordinance, and any violation of the Child Passenger Protection Act [625 ILCS 25/1 et seq.], or a similar provision of a local ordinance, shall be collected and disbursed by the circuit clerk as provided under Section 27.5 of the Clerks of Courts Act.

(Source: P.A. 86-555; 86-1005; 86-1028; 86-1475; 87-670.) [Formerly Ill. Rev. Stat. 38 §1005-9-1.]

5/5-9-1.1. Fines for drug related offenses.

§5-9-1.1. When a person has been adjudged guilty of a drug related offense involving possession or delivery of cannabis or possession or delivery of a controlled substance as defined in the Cannabis Control Act, as amended [720 ILCS 550/1 et seq.], or the Illinois Controlled Substances Act, as amended [720 ILCS 570/100 et seq.], in addition to any other penalty imposed, a fine shall be levied by the court at not less than the full street value of the cannabis or controlled substances seized.

"Street value" shall be determined by the court on the basis of testimony of law enforcement personnel and the defendant as to the amount seized and such testimony as may be required by the court as to the current street value of the cannabis or controlled substance seized.

(Source: P.A. 82-449.) [Formerly Ill. Rev. Stat. 38 §1005-9-1.1.]

5/5-9-1.2. Proceeds of fines.

§5-9-1.2. (a) Twelve and one-half percent of all amounts collected as fines pursuant to Section 5-9-1.1 [730 ILCS 5/5-9-1.1] shall be paid into the Youth Drug Abuse Prevention Fund, which is hereby created in the State treasury, to be used by the Department of Alcoholism and Substance Abuse for the funding of programs and services for drug-abuse treatment, and prevention and education services, for juveniles.

(b) Eighty-seven and one-half percent of the proceeds of all fines received pursuant to Section 5-9-1.1 shall be transmitted to and deposited in the treasurer's office at the level of government as follows:

(1) If such seizure was made by a combination of law enforcement personnel representing differing units of local government, the court levying the fine shall equitably allocate 50% of the fine among these units of local government and shall allocate 37½% to the county general corporate fund. In the event that the seizure was made by law enforcement personnel representing a unit of local government from a municipality where the number of inhabitants exceeds 2 million in population, the court levying the fine shall allocate 87½% of the fine to that unit of local government. If the seizure was made by a combination of law enforcement personnel representing differing units of local government, and at least one of those units represents a municipality where the number of inhabitants exceeds 2 million in population, the court shall equitably allocate 87½% of the proceeds of the fines received among the differing units of local government.

(2) If such seizure was made by State law enforcement personnel, then the court shall allocate 37½% to the State treasury and 50% to the county general corporate fund.

(3) If a State law enforcement agency in combination with a law enforcement agency or agencies of a unit or units of local government conducted the seizure, the court shall equitably allocate 37½% of the fines to or among the law enforcement agency or agencies of the unit or units of local government which conducted the seizure and shall allocate 50% to the county general corporate fund.

(c) The proceeds of all fines allocated to the law enforcement agency or agencies of the unit or units of local government pursuant to subsection (b) shall be made available to that law enforcement agency as expendable receipts for use in the enforcement of laws regulating controlled substances and cannabis. The proceeds of fines awarded to the State treasury shall be deposited in a special fund known as the Drug Traffic Prevention Fund. Monies from this fund may be used by the Department of State Police for use in the enforcement of laws regulating controlled substances and cannabis; to satisfy funding provisions of the Intergovernmental Drug Laws Enforcement Act [30 ILCS 715/1 et seq.]; to defray costs and expenses associated with returning violators of the Cannabis Control Act [720 ILCS 550/1 et seq.] and the Illinois Controlled Substances Act [720 ILCS 570/100 et seq.] only, as provided in those Acts, when punishment of the crime shall be confinement of the criminal in the penitentiary; and all other monies shall be paid into the general revenue fund in the State treasury.

(Source: P.A. 87-342.) [Formerly Ill. Rev. Stat. 38 §1005-9-1.2.]

5/5-9-1.3. Guilty of a felony under Section 16-1, 16-9 or 17-1.

§5-9-1.3. When a person has been adjudged guilty of a felony under §16-1, 16-9 or 17-1 of the Criminal Code of 1961 [720 ILCS 5/16-1, repealed or 5/17-1], a fine may be levied by the court in an amount which is the greater of $10,000 or twice the value of the property which is the subject of the offense.

(Source: P.A. 85-660.) [Formerly Ill. Rev. Stat. 38 §1005-9-1.3.]

5/5-9-1.4. Crime laboratory.

§5-9-1.4. (a) "Crime laboratory" means any not-for-profit laboratory registered with the Drug Enforcement Administration of the United States Department of Justice, substantially funded by a unit or combination of units of local government or the State of Illinois, which regularly employs at least one person engaged in the analysis of controlled substances, cannabis or steroids for criminal justice agencies in criminal matters and provides testimony with respect to such examinations.

(b) When a person has been adjudged guilty of an offense in violation of the Cannabis Control Act [720 ILCS 550/1 et seq.] , the Illinois Controlled Substances Act [720 ILCS 570/100 et seq.] or the Steroid Control Act [repealed], in addition to any other disposition, penalty or fine imposed, a criminal laboratory analysis fee of $50 for each offense for which he was convicted shall be levied by the court. Any person placed on probation pursuant to Section 10 of the Cannabis Control Act [720 ILCS 550/10], Section 410 of the Illinois Controlled Substances Act [720 ILCS 570/410] or Section 10 of the Steroid Control Act [repealed] or placed on supervision for a violation of the Cannabis Control Act, the Illinois Controlled Substances Act or the Steroid Control Act shall be assessed a criminal laboratory analysis fee of $50 for each such offense for which he was charged. Upon verified petition of the person, the court may suspend payment of all or part of the fee if it finds that the person does not have the ability to pay the fee.

(c) In addition to any other disposition made pursuant to the provisions of the Juvenile Court Act of 1987 [705 ILCS 405/1-1 et seq.], any minor adjudicated delinquent for an offense which if committed by an adult would constitute a violation of the Cannabis Control Act, the Illinois Controlled Substances Act or the Steroid Control Act shall be assessed a criminal laboratory analysis fee of $50 for each adjudication. Upon verified petition of the minor, the court may suspend payment of all or part of the fee if it finds that the minor does not have the ability to pay the fee. The parent, guardian or legal custodian of the minor may pay some or all of such fee on the minor's behalf.

(d) All criminal laboratory analysis fees provided for by this Section shall be collected by the clerk of the court and forwarded to the appropriate crime laboratory fund as provided in subsection (f).

(e) Crime laboratory funds shall be established as follows:

(1) Any unit of local government which maintains a crime laboratory may establish a crime laboratory fund within the office of the county or municipal treasurer.

(2) Any combination of units of local government which maintains a crime laboratory may establish a crime laboratory fund within the office of the treasurer of the county where the crime laboratory is situated.

(3) The State Crime Laboratory Fund is hereby created as a special fund in the State Treasury.

(f) The analysis fee provided for in subsections (b) and (c) of this Section shall be forwarded to the office of the treasurer of the unit of local government that performed the analysis if that unit of local government has established a crime laboratory fund, or to the State Crime Laboratory Fund if the analysis was performed by a laboratory operated by the Illinois State Police. If the analysis was performed by a crime laboratory funded by a combination of units of local government, the analysis fee shall be forwarded to the treasurer of the county where the crime laboratory is situated if a crime laboratory fund has been established in that county. If the unit of local government or combination of units of local government has not established a crime laboratory fund, then the analysis fee shall be forwarded to the State Crime Laboratory Fund. The clerk of the circuit court may retain the amount of $5 from each collected analysis fee to offset administrative costs incurred in carrying out the clerk's responsibilities under this Section.

(g) Fees deposited into a crime laboratory fund created pursuant to paragraphs (1) or (2) of subsection (e) of this Section shall be in addition to any allocations made pursuant to existing law and shall be designated for the exclusive use of the crime laboratory. These uses may include, but are not limited to, the following:

(1) costs incurred in providing analysis for controlled substances in connection with criminal investigations conducted within this State;

(2) purchase and maintenance of equipment for use in performing analyses; and

(3) continuing education, training and professional development of forensic scientists regularly employed by these laboratories.

(h) Fees deposited in the State Crime Laboratory Fund created pursuant to paragraph (3) of subsection (d) of this Section shall be used by State crime laboratories as designated by the Director of State Police. These funds shall be in addition to any allocations made pursuant to existing law and shall be designated for the exclusive use of State crime laboratories. These uses may include those enumerated in subsection (g) of this Section.

(Source: P.A. 86-1399; 86-1475.) [Formerly Ill. Rev. Stat. 38 §1005-9-1.4.]

5/5-9-1.5. Domestic violence fine.

§5-9-1.5. Domestic violence fine. In addition to any other penalty imposed, a fine of $100 shall be imposed upon any person who pleads guilty or no contest to or who is convicted of murder, voluntary manslaughter, involuntary manslaughter, burglary, residential burglary, criminal trespass to residence, criminal trespass to vehicle, criminal trespass to land, criminal damage to property, telephone harassment, kidnapping, aggravated kidnapping, unlawful restraint, forcible detention, child abduction, indecent solicitation of a child, sexual relations between siblings, exploitation of a child, child pornography, assault, aggravated assault, battery, aggravated battery, heinous battery, aggravated battery of a child, domestic battery, reckless conduct, intimidation, criminal sexual assault, aggravated criminal sexual assault, criminal sexual abuse, aggravated criminal sexual abuse, violation of an order of protection, disorderly conduct, endangering the life or health of a child, child abandonment, contributing to dependency or neglect of child, or cruelty to children and others; provided that the offender and victim are family or household members as defined in Section 103 of the Illinois Domestic Violence Act of 1986 [750 ILCS 60/103]. Upon request of the victim or the victim's representative, the court shall determine whether the fine will impose an undue burden on the victim of the offense. For purposes of this paragraph, the defendant may not be considered the victim's representative. If the court finds that the fine would impose an undue burden on the victim, the court may reduce or waive the fine. The court shall order that the defendant may not use funds belonging solely to the victim of the offense for payment of the fine. The circuit clerk shall remit each fine within one month of its receipt to the State Treasurer for deposit as follows: (i) for sexual assault, as defined in Section 5-9-1.7, when the offender and victim are family members, one-half to the Domestic Violence Shelter and Service Fund, and one-half to the Sexual Assault Services Fund; (ii) for the remaining offenses to the Domestic Violence Shelter and Service Fund.

(Chgd. by P.A. 87-1072, §2, eff. 1/1/93.)

(Source: P.A. 87-791.) [Formerly Ill. Rev. Stat. 38 §1005-9-1.5.]

5/5-9-1.6. Fine for domestic battery.

§5-9-1.6. Fine for Domestic Battery. There shall be added to every penalty imposed in sentencing for the offense of domestic battery an additional fine in the amount of $10 to be imposed upon a plea of guilty, stipulation of facts or finding of guilty resulting in a judgment of conviction or order of supervision.

Such additional amount shall be assessed by the court imposing sentence and shall be collected by the Circuit Clerk in addition to the fine, if any, and costs in the case. Each such additional penalty shall be remitted by the Circuit

Clerk within one month after receipt to the State Treasurer for deposit into the Domestic Violence Shelter and Service Fund. The Circuit Clerk shall retain 10% of such penalty to cover the costs incurred in administering and enforcing this Section. Such additional penalty shall not be considered a part of the fine for purposes of any reduction in the fine for time served either before or after sentencing.

Not later than March 1 of each year the Clerk of the Circuit Court shall submit to the State Comptroller a report of the amount of funds remitted by him to the State Treasurer under this Section during the preceding calendar year. Except as otherwise provided by Supreme Court Rules, if a court in sentencing an offender levies a gross amount for fine, costs, fees and penalties, the amount of the additional penalty provided for herein shall be collected from the amount remaining after deducting from the gross amount levied all fees of the Circuit Clerk, the State's Attorney and the Sheriff. After deducting from the gross amount levied the fees and additional penalty provided for herein, less any other additional penalties provided by law, the clerk shall remit the net balance remaining to the entity authorized by law to receive the fine imposed in the case. For purposes of this Section "fees of the Circuit Clerk" shall include, if applicable, the fee provided for under Section 27.3a of the Clerks of Courts Act [705 ILCS 105/27.3a] and the fee, if applicable, payable to the county in which the violation occurred under Section 5-1101 of the Counties Code [55 ILCS 5/5-1101].

(Source: P.A. 87-480; 87-895.) [Formerly Ill. Rev. Stat. 38 §1005-9-1.6.]

5/5-9-1.7. Child pornography fines.

§5-9-1.7. Child pornography fines. One hundred percent of the fines in excess of $10,000 collected for violations of Section 11-20.1 of the Criminal Code of 1961 [720 ILCS 5/11-20.1] shall be deposited into the Child Sexual Abuse Fund that is created in the State Treasury. Moneys in the Fund shall be for the use of the Department of Children and Family Services for grants to private entities giving treatment and counseling to victims of child sexual abuse.

(Added by P.A. 87-1070, §2, eff. 9/13/92.) [Formerly Ill. Rev. Stat. 38 §1005-9-1.7.]

(See other §5/5-9-1.7 below.)

5/5-9-1.7. Sexual assault fines.

§5-9-1.7. Sexual assault fines. (a) Definitions. The terms used in this Section shall have the following meanings ascribed to them:

(1) "Sexual assault" means the commission or attempted commission of the following: criminal sexual assault, aggravated criminal sexual assault, criminal sexual abuse, aggravated criminal sexual abuse, indecent solicitation of a child, public indecency, sexual relations within families, soliciting for a juvenile prostitute, keeping a place of juvenile prostitution, patronizing a juvenile prostitute, juvenile pimping, exploitation of a child, obscenity, child pornography, or harmful material, as those offenses are defined in the Criminal Code of 1961 [720 ILCS 5/1-1 et seq.].

(2) "Family member" shall have the meaning ascribed to it in Section 12-12 of the Criminal Code of 1961 [720 ILCS 5/12-12].

(3) "Sexual assault organization" means any not-for-profit organization providing comprehensive, community-based services to victims of sexual assault. "Community-based services" include, but are not limited to, direct crisis intervention through a 24-hour response, medical and legal advocacy, counseling, information and referral services, training, and community education.

(b) Sexual assault fine; collection by clerk.

(1) In addition to any other penalty imposed, a fine of $100 shall be imposed upon any person who pleads guilty or who is convicted of, or who receives a disposition of court supervision for, a sexual assault or attempt of a sexual

assault. Upon request of the victim or the victim's representative, the court shall determine whether the fine will impose an undue burden on the victim of the offense. For purposes of this paragraph, the defendant may not be considered the victim's representative. If the court finds that the fine would impose an undue burden on the victim, the court may reduce or waive the fine. The court shall order that the defendant may not use funds belonging solely to the victim of the offense for payment of the fine.

(2) Sexual assault fines shall be assessed by the court imposing the sentence and shall be collected by the circuit clerk. The circuit clerk shall retain 10% of the penalty to cover the costs involved in administering and enforcing this Section. The circuit clerk shall remit the remainder of each fine within one month of its receipt to the State Treasurer for deposit as follows:

(i) for family member offenders, one-half to the Sexual Assault Services Fund, and one-half to the Domestic Violence Shelter and Service Fund; and

(ii) for other than family member offenders, the full amount to the Sexual Assault Services Fund.

(c) Sexual Assault Services Fund; administration. There is created a Sexual Assault Services Fund. Moneys deposited into the Fund under this Section shall be appropriated to the Department of Public Health. Upon appropriation of moneys from the Sexual Assault Services Fund, the Department of Public Health shall make grants of these moneys from the Fund to sexual assault organizations with whom the Department has contracts for the purpose of providing community-based services to victims of sexual assault. Grants made under this Section are in addition to, and are not substitutes for, other grants authorized and made by the Department.

(Added by P.A. 87-1072, §2, eff. 1/1/93.) [Formerly Ill. Rev. Stat. 38 §1005-9-1.7.]
(See other §5/5-9-1.7 above.)

5/5-9-2. Revocation of a fine.

§5-9-2. Revocation of a Fine. Except as to fines established for violations of Chapter 15 of the Illinois Vehicle Code [625 ILCS 5/15-101 et seq.], the court, upon good cause shown, may revoke the fine or the unpaid portion or may modify the method of payment.

(Source: P.A. 87-396.) [Formerly Ill. Rev. Stat. 38 §1005-9-2.]

5/5-9-3. Default.

§5-9-3. Default. (a) An offender who defaults in the payment of a fine or in any installment may be held in contempt and imprisoned for nonpayment. The court may issue a summons for his appearance or a warrant of arrest.

(b) Unless the offender shows that his default was not due to his intentional refusal to pay, or not due to a failure on his part to make a good faith effort to pay, the court may order the offender imprisoned for a term not to exceed 6 months if the fine was for a felony, or 30 days if the fine was for a misdemeanor, a petty offense or a business offense. Payment of the fine at any time will entitle the offender to be released, but imprisonment under this Section shall not satisfy the payment of the fine.

(c) If it appears that the default in the payment of a fine is not intentional under paragraph (b) of this Section, the court may enter an order allowing the offender additional time for payment, reducing the amount of the fine or of each installment, or revoking the fine or the unpaid portion.

(d) When a fine is imposed on a corporation or unincorporated organization or association, it is the duty of the person or persons authorized to make disbursement of assets, and their superiors, to pay the fine from assets of the corporation or unincorporated organization or association. The failure of such persons to do so shall render them subject to proceedings under paragraphs (a) and (b) of this Section.

(e) A default in the payment of a fine or any installment may be collected by any means authorized for the collection of money judgments rendered in favor of the State.
(Source: P.A. 78-255.) [Formerly Ill. Rev. Stat. 38 §1005-9-3.]

5/5-9-4. Order of withholding.
§5-9-4. Order of Withholding. The court may enter an order of withholding to collect the amount of a fine imposed on an offender in accordance with Part 8 of Article XII of the Code of Civil Procedure [735 ILCS 5/12-801 et seq.].
(Source: P.A. 87-609.) [Formerly Ill. Rev. Stat. 38 §1005-9-4.]

[CHAPTER VI. RESERVED FOR ORGANIZATION OF PROBATION SERVICES]

[CHAPTER VII. RESERVED]

CHAPTER VIII. MISCELLANEOUS

ARTICLE 1. CUMULATIVE EFFECT

5/8-1-1. Cumulative powers.
§8-1-1. Cumulative powers. The provisions of this Code shall be cumulative in effect and if any provision is inconsistent with another provision of this Code or with any other Act not expressly repealed by Section 8-5-1 [730 ILCS 5/8-5-1], it shall be considered as an alternative or additional power and not as a limitation upon any other power granted to or possessed by the Department of Corrections.
(Source: P.A. 78-939.) [Formerly Ill. Rev. Stat. 38 §1008-1-1.]

5/8-1-2. Powers of State agencies.
§8-1-2. Powers of State Agencies. The provisions of this Code do not impair, alter, modify or repeal any of the jurisdiction or powers possessed by any department, board, commission, or officer of the State government immediately prior to the effective date of this Code.
(Source: P.A. 77-2097.) [Formerly Ill. Rev. Stat. 38 §1008-1-2.]

ARTICLE 2. SAVINGS PROVISIONS

5/8-2-1. Saving clause.
§8-2-1. Saving Clause. The repeal of Acts or parts of Acts enumerated in Section 8-5-1 [730 ILCS 5/8-5-1] does not: (1) affect any offense committed, act done, prosecution pending, penalty, punishment or forfeiture incurred, or rights, powers or remedies accrued under any law in effect immediately prior to the effective date of this Code; (2) impair, avoid, or affect any grant or conveyance made or right acquired or cause of action then existing under any such repealed Act or amendment thereto; (3) affect or impair the validity of any bail or other bond or other obligation issued or sold and constituting a valid obligation of the issuing authority immediately prior to the effective date of this Code; (4) the validity of any contract; or (5) the validity of any tax levied under

any law in effect prior to the effective date of this Code. The repeal of any validating Act or part thereof shall not avoid the effect of the validation. No Act repealed by Section 8-5-1 shall repeal any Act or part thereof which embraces the same or a similar subject matter as the Act repealed.
(Source: P.A. 78-255.) [Formerly Ill. Rev. Stat. 38 §1008-2-1.]

5/8-2-2. Continuation of prior law.

§8-2-2. Continuation of prior law. The provisions of this Code insofar as they are the same or substantially the same as those of any prior statute, shall be construed as a continuation of such prior statute and not as a new enactment.

If in any other statute reference is made to an Act of the General Assembly, or a Section of such an Act, which is continued in this Code such reference shall be held to refer to the Act or Section thereof so continued in this Code.
(Source: P.A. 77-2097.) [Formerly Ill. Rev. Stat. 38 §1008-2-2.]

5/8-2-3. Existing indebtedness.

§8-2-3. Existing indebtedness. Any bond or other evidence of indebtedness issued under the provisions of any Act repealed by this Code which is outstanding and unpaid on the effective date of this Code shall be amortized and retired by taxation or revenue in the manner provided by the Act under which such indebtedness was incurred, notwithstanding the repeal of such Act.

However, the provisions of this Section shall not be construed to prevent the refunding of any such indebtedness under the provisions of this Code or as may be otherwise provided by law.
(Source: P.A. 77-2097.) [Formerly Ill. Rev. Stat. 38 §1008-2-3.]

5/8-2-4. Prosecutions continued; applicable sentencing provisions.

§8-2-4. Prosecutions Continued; Applicable Sentencing Provisions. (a) Prosecution for any violation of law occurring prior to January 1, 1973, is not affected or abated by the Unified Code of Corrections. If the offense being prosecuted has not reached the sentencing stage or a final adjudication by January 1, 1973, then for purposes of sentencing the sentences under the Unified Code of Corrections [730 ILCS 5/1-1-1 et seq.] apply if they are less than under the prior law upon which the prosecution was commenced.

(b) Prosecution for any violation of law occurring before the effective date of this amendatory Act of 1977 is not affected or abated by this amendatory Act of 1977. If the defendant has not been sentenced before the effective date of this amendatory Act of 1977, he shall have the right to elect to be sentenced under the law as it existed at the time of his offense or under the law in effect on and after the effective date of this amendatory Act of 1977. If a sentence has been imposed before the effective date of this amendatory Act of 1977, the defendant shall not have the right of election even though his case has not been finally adjudicated on appeal; however, where eligible, he shall have the rights provided by Section 3-3-2.1 of this Code [730 ILCS 5/3-3-2.1].
(Source: P.A. 80-1099.) [Formerly Ill. Rev. Stat. 38 §1008-2-4.]

ARTICLE 3. CHAPTER, ARTICLE OR SECTION HEADINGS—EFFECT—REFERENCES THERETO

Sec.

5/8-3-1. Chapter, article or section headings—Effect.

§8-3-1. Chapter, Article or Section Headings—Effect. Chapter, Article or Section headings contained in this Code shall not be deemed to govern, limit, modify or in any manner affect the scope, meaning or intent of the provisions of any Chapter, Article or Section hereof.
(Source: P.A. 77-2097.) [Formerly Ill. Rev. Stat. 38 §1008-3-1.]

5/8-3-2. References to headings.

§8-3-2. References to headings. Where, in this Code, reference is made to a Section, Article or Chapter by its number and no Act is specified, the reference is to the correspondingly numbered Section, Article or Chapter of this Code. Where reference is made to "this Chapter" or "this Article" or "this Section" and no Act is specified, the reference is to the Chapter, Article or Section of this Code in which the reference appears. If any Section, Article or Chapter of this Code is hereafter amended, the reference shall thereafter be treated and considered as a reference to the Section, Article or Chapter as so amended.
(Source: P.A. 77-2097.) [Formerly Ill. Rev. Stat. 38 §1008-3-2.]

ARTICLE 4. SEVERABILITY

Sec.

5/8-4-1. Severability of invalid provisions.

§8-4-1. Severability of invalid provisions. If any provision of this Code or application thereof to any person or circumstance is held invalid, such invalidity does not affect other provisions or applications of this Code which can be given effect without the invalid application or provision, and to this end the provisions of this Code are declared to be severable.
(Source: P.A. 77-2097.) [Formerly Ill. Rev. Stat. 38 §1008-4-1.]

ARTICLE 5. REPEAL

Sec.

5/8-5-1. Repeals.

§8-5-1. Repeals. The following Acts and parts of Acts are repealed:

The "Juvenile Offenders Act", approved June 30, 1953, as amended.

"An Act relating to the establishment, operation and maintenance of the Illinois Industrial School for Boys and to repeal an Act named therein", approved June 30, 1953.

"An Act in relation to the Illinois State Training School for Boys", approved May 10, 1901, as amended.

"An Act in relation to the Illinois State Training School for Girls, and to repeal an Act named therein", approved June 30, 1953.

"An Act to establish and provide for a State Reformatory for Women", approved June 30, 1927, as amended.

Section 1-7 of the "Criminal Code of 1961", approved July 28, 1961, as amended.

Section 38a of the "Uniform Narcotic Drug Act", approved July 11, 1957, as amended.

Sections 104-1, 104-2, 104-3, 113-7, 117-1, 117-2, 117-3, 118-1, 118-2, 119-1, 119-2, 119-3, 119-4, 123-1, 123-2, 123-3, 123-4, 123-6, 123-7, and 124-2 of the "Code of Criminal Procedure of 1963", approved August 14, 1963, as amended.

"An Act authorizing the Governor to enter into certain reciprocal agreements with other states", approved January 7, 1936, as amended.

"An Act in relation to the employment of persons committed to a county jail, house of correction or workhouse", approved July 17, 1959, as amended.

"An Act in relation to imprisonment for nonpayment of a fine imposed for violation of an ordinance, resolution, rule or regulation of a political entity", approved August 13, 1963.

"An Act to regulate the manner of applying for pardons, reprieves and commutations", approved May 31, 1879.

"An Act in relation to pardons and the commutation of sentences", approved June 5, 1897, as amended.

"An Act in relation to the penitentiary at Joliet, to be entitled, 'An Act to provide for the management of the Illinois State Penitentiary at Joliet'", approved June 16, 1871, as amended.

"An Act to regulate the labor of convicts of the penitentiary of the State", approved March 25, 1874, as amended.

"An Act in relation to certain rights of persons convicted of crime", approved June 26, 1925, as amended.

"An Act in relation to merger of certain sentences", approved July 9, 1957.

"An Act to secure the clergymen of all denominations free access to the penitentiary at Joliet and all other penal, reformatory and charitable institutions in the State of Illinois", approved March 28, 1874, as amended.

"An Act to give to the authorities of penitentiaries, in the State of Illinois, police powers on grounds owned or leased by the State in connection with said penitentiaries", approved May 30, 1881.

"An Act to regulate the employment of convicts and prisoners in penal and reformatory institutions and regulating the disposition of the products of convict or prison labor", approved May 11, 1903, as amended.

"An Act authorizing the employment of inmates in the penal and reformatory institutions of the State for manufacturing materials and machinery used in the construction and maintenance of State highways", approved May 18, 1905, as amended.

"An Act to authorize the employment of convicts and prisoners in the penal and reformatory institutions of the State of Illinois in the preparation of road building materials and in working on the public roads, etc.", approved June 28, 1913, as amended.

"An Act in relation to the Illinois State penitentiary", approved June 30, 1933, as amended.

"An Act concerning furloughs for qualified inmates of the State prison system for certain purposes", approved July 31, 1969.

"An Act for the identification of habitual criminals", approved April 15, 1889, as amended.

"An Act to revise the law in relation to the fixing of the punishment and the sentence and commitment of persons convicted of crime or offenses, and providing for a system of parole", approved June 25, 1917, as amended.

"An Act in relation to the Illinois State Farm", approved June 27, 1923, as amended.

Sections 5.11a, 6.05, 55a.1, 55a.2, 55b, 55c, 55c.1, 55d, 55e, 55f, 55g, 55h of "The Civil Administrative Code of Illinois", approved March 7, 1917, as amended.

"An Act relating to the establishment, maintenance and operation of certain transitional institutions by the Department of Corrections", approved August 16, 1963, as amended.

"An Act to establish a professional apprentice system within the Department of Corrections", approved August 16, 1963, as amended.

"An Act ratifying and approving the Interstate corrections compact and providing for the administration thereof", approved August 4, 1971.

Public Act No. 77-358.
Public Act No. 77-359.
Public Act No. 77-365.
Public Act No. 77-366.
Public Act No. 77-367.
Public Act No. 77-368.
Public Act No. 77-432.

Public Act No. 77-448.
Public Act No. 77-449.
Public Act No. 77-451.
Public Act No. 77-453.
Public Act No. 77-454.
Public Act No. 77-455.
Public Act No. 77-458.
Public Act No. 77-651.
Public Act No. 77-661.
Public Act No. 77-768.
Public Act No. 77-1425.

(Source: P.A. 77-2097; 77-2827; 78-255.) [Formerly Ill. Rev. Stat. 38 §1008-5-1.]

ARTICLE 6. EFFECTIVE DATE

5/8-6-1. Effective date.

§8-6-1. Effective Date. This Act shall take effect January 1, 1973.

(Source: P.A. 77-2097.) [Formerly Ill. Rev. Stat. 38 §1008-6-1.]

OPEN PAROLE HEARINGS ACT

105/1. Short title.

§1. Short title. This Act may be cited as the Open Parole Hearings Act.

(Source: P.A. 87-224.) [Formerly Ill. Rev. Stat. 38 §1651.]

105/5. Definitions.

§5. Definitions. As used in this Act:

(a) "Applicant" means an inmate who is being considered for parole by the Prisoner Review Board.

(b) "Board" means the Prisoner Review Board as established in Section 3-3-1 of the Unified Code of Corrections [730 ILCS 5/3-3-1].

(c) "Parolee" means a person subject to parole revocation proceedings.

(d) "Parole hearing" means the formal hearing and determination of an inmate being considered for release from incarceration on* community supervision.

**So in original. Probably should be "or".*

(e) "Parole or mandatory supervised release revocation hearing" means the formal hearing and determination of allegations that a parolee or mandatory supervised releasee has violated the conditions of his or her release agreement.

(f) "Victim" means a victim or witness of a violent crime as defined in subsection (a) of Section 3 of the Bill of Rights for Victims and Witnesses of Violent Crime Act [725 ILCS 120/3].

(g) "Violent crime" means a crime defined in subsection (c) of Section 3 of the Bill of Rights for Victims and Witnesses of Violent Crime Act.

(Source: P.A. 87-224.) [Formerly Ill. Rev. Stat. 38 §1655.]

105/10. Victim's statements.

§10. Victim's statements. (a) Upon request of the victim, the State's Attorney shall forward a copy of any statement presented at the time of trial to the Prisoner Review Board to be considered at the time of a parole hearing.

(b) The victim may enter a statement either oral, written, on video tape, or other electronic means in the form and manner described by the Prisoner Review Board to be considered at the time of a parole consideration hearing.
(Source: P.A. 87-224.) [Formerly Ill. Rev. Stat. 38 §1660.]

105/15. Open hearings.

§15. Open hearings. (a) The Board may restrict the number of individuals allowed to attend parole or parole revocation hearings in accordance with physical limitations, security requirements of the hearing facilities or those giving repetitive or cumulative testimony.

(b) The Board may deny admission or continued attendance at parole or parole revocation hearings to individuals who:

(1) threaten or present danger to the security of the institution in which the hearing is being held;

(2) threaten or present a danger to other attendees or participants; or

(3) disrupt the hearing.

(c) Upon formal action of a majority of the Board members present, the Board may close parole and parole revocation hearings in order to:

(1) deliberate upon the oral testimony and any other relevant information received from applicants, parolees, victims, or others; or

(2) provide applicants and parolees the opportunity to challenge information other than that which if the person's identity were to be exposed would possibly subject them to bodily harm or death, which they believe detrimental to their parole determination hearing or revocation proceedings.
(Source: P.A. 87-224.) [Formerly Ill. Rev. Stat. 38 §1665.]

105/20. Finality of Board decisions.

§20. Finality of Board decisions. A Board decision concerning parole or parole revocation shall be final at the time the decision is delivered to the inmate, subject to any rehearing granted under Board rules.
(Source: P.A. 87-224.) [Formerly Ill. Rev. Stat. 38 §1670.]

105/25. Notification of future parole hearings.

§25. Notification of future parole hearings. (a) The Board shall notify the State's Attorney of the committing county of the pending hearing and the victim of all forthcoming parole hearings at least 15 days in advance. Written notification shall contain:

(1) notification of the place of the hearing;

(2) the date and approximate time of the hearing;

(3) their right to enter a statement, to appear in person, and to submit other information by video tape, tape recording, or other electronic means in the form and manner described by the Board.

Notification to the victims shall be at the last known address of the victim. It shall be the responsibility of the victim to notify the board of any changes in address and name.

(b) However, at any time the victim may request by a written certified statement that the Prisoner Review Board stop sending notice under this Section.

(d)* No later than 7 days after a parole hearing the Board shall send notice of its decision to the State's Attorney and victim. If parole is denied, the Board shall within a reasonable period of time notify the victim of the month and year of the next scheduled hearing.

**So in original. No subsec. (c) has been enacted.*

(Source: P.A. 87-224.) [Formerly Ill. Rev. Stat. 38 §1675.]

105/30. Board rules.

§30. Board rules. Within 90 days of the effective date of this Act, the Board may develop rules in accordance with this Act.
(Source: P.A. 87-224.) [Formerly Ill. Rev. Stat. 38 §1680.]

105/35. Victim impact statements.

§35. Victim impact statements. (a) The Board shall receive and consider victim impact statements.

(b) Written victim impact statements shall not be considered public documents under provisions of the Freedom of Information Act [5 ILCS 140/1 et seq.].

(c) The inmate or his attorney shall be informed of the existence of a victim impact statement and its contents under provisions of Board rules. This shall not be construed to permit disclosure to an inmate of any information which might result in the risk of threats or physical harm to a victim or complaining witness.

(d) The inmate shall be given the opportunity to answer a victim impact statement, either orally or in writing.

(e) All written victim impact statements shall be part of the applicant's or parolee's parole file.
(Source: P.A. 87-224.) [Formerly Ill. Rev. Stat. 38 §1685.]

PROBATION AND PROBATION OFFICERS ACT

Sec.

110/0.01. Short title.

§0.01. Short title. This Act may be cited as the Probation and Probation Officers Act.
(Source: P.A. 86-1324.) [Formerly Ill. Rev. Stat. 38 §204-1a.9.]

110/9b. Definitions.

§9b. For the purposes of this Act, the words and phrases described in this Section have the meanings designated in this Section, except when a particular context clearly requires a different meaning.

(1) "Division" means the Division of Probation Services of the Supreme Court.

(2) "Department" means a probation or court services department that provides probation or court services and such other related services assigned to it by the circuit court or by law.

(3) "Probation Officer" means a person employed full time in a probation or court services department providing services to a court under this Act or the Juvenile Court Act of 1987 [705 ILCS 405/1-1 et seq]. A probation officer includes detention staff, non-secure group home staff and management personnel who meet minimum standards established by the Supreme Court and who are hired under the direction of the circuit court. These probation officers are

judicial employees designated on a circuit wide or county basis and compensated by the appropriate county board or boards.

(4) "Basic Services" means the number of personnel determined by the Division as necessary to comply with adult, juvenile, and detention services workload standards and to operate authorized programs of intensive probation supervision, public or community service, intake services, secure detention services, non-secure group home services and home confinement.

(5) "New or Expanded Services" means personnel necessary to operate pretrial programs, victim and restitution programs, psychological services, drunk driving programs, specialized caseloads, community resource coordination programs, and other programs designed to generally improve the quality of probation and court services.

(6) "Individualized Services and Programs" means individualized services provided through purchase of service agreements with individuals, specialists, and local public or private agencies providing non-residential services for the rehabilitation of adult and juvenile offenders as an alternative to local or state incarceration.

(Source: P.A. 86-639; 86-1327.) [Formerly Ill. Rev. Stat. 38 §204-1b.]

110/10. Probation officers to take oath.

§10. Before entering upon the duties of his office, each probation officer shall take and subscribe to an oath before the county clerk of his county to support the constitution and laws of the United States and of the State of Illinois, and faithfully to perform the duties of his office.

(Source: P.A. 84-692.) [Formerly Ill. Rev. Stat. 38 §204-2.]

110/11. Probationer arrested by officer for violation of condition of probation.

§11. Probation officers, in the exercise of their official duties, and sheriffs and police officers, may, anywhere within the state, arrest on view any probationer found by them violating any of the conditions of his or her probation, and it shall be the duty of the officer making such arrest immediately to take the probationer before the court having jurisdiction over him or her for further order.

(Source: P.A. 83-341.) [Formerly Ill. Rev. Stat. 38 §204-3.]

110/12. Duties of probation officers.

§12. The duties of probation officers shall be:

(1) To investigate as required by section 5-3-1 of the "Unified Code of Corrections", approved July 26, 1972, as amended [730 ILCS 5/5-3-1], the case of any person to be placed on probation. Full opportunity shall be afforded a probation officer to confer with the person under investigation when such person is in custody.

(2) To notify the court of any previous conviction for crime or previous probation of any defendant invoking the provisions of this act.

(3) All reports and notifications required in this Act to be made by probation officers shall be in writing and shall be filed by the clerk in the respective cases.

(4) To preserve complete and accurate records of cases investigated, including a description of the person investigated, the action of the court with respect to his case and his probation, the subsequent history of such person, if he becomes a probationer, during the continuance of his probation, which records shall be open to inspection by any judge or by any probation officer pursuant to order of court, but shall not be a public record, and its contents shall not be divulged otherwise than as above provided, except upon order of court.

(5) To take charge of and watch over all persons placed on probation under such regulations and for such terms as may be prescribed by the court, and

giving to each probationer full instructions as to the terms of his release upon probation and requiring from him such periodical reports as shall keep the officer informed as to his conduct.

(6) To develop and operate programs of reasonable public or community service for any persons ordered by the court to perform public or community service, providing, however, that no probation officer or any employee of a probation office acting in the course of his official duties shall be liable for any tortious acts of any person performing public or community service except for wilful misconduct or gross negligence on the part of the probation officer or employee.

(7) When any person on probation removes from the county where his offense was committed, it shall be the duty of the officer under whose care he was placed to report the facts to the probation officer in the county to which the probationer has removed; and it shall thereupon become the duty of such probation officer to take charge of and watch over said probationer the same as if the case originated in that county; and for that purpose he shall have the same power and authority over said probationer as if he had been originally placed in said officer's charge; and such officer shall be required to report in writing every 6 months, or more frequently upon request the results of his supervision to the probation officer in whose charge the said probationer was originally placed by the court.

(8) To authorize travel permits to individuals under their supervision unless otherwise ordered by the court.

(9) To perform such other duties as are provided for in this act or by rules of court and such incidental duties as may be implied from those expressly required.

(Source: P.A. 86-639.) [Formerly Ill. Rev. Stat. 38 §204-4.]

110/13. Chief probation officer or director of the court services department—Supervisory powers and duties; assistants.

§13. It shall be the duty of the director of the court services department or the chief probation officer, appointed as provided in this act, to supervise and control the work of all subordinate court services or probation officers under his or her jurisdiction subject to the general administrative and supervisory authority of the Chief Circuit Judge or another judge designated by the Chief Circuit Judge, and to control and supervise, as herein provided, the conduct of probationers to such extent as the court may direct.

The Chief Circuit Judge or another judge designated by the Chief Circuit Judge to have general administrative and supervisory authority over the director of the court services department or the chief probation officer, or may authorize the director or chief probation officer to appoint all subordinate court services department or probation officers who shall serve at the pleasure of the director or chief probation officer. In addition to the authority to discharge such subordinate officers, the director or chief probation officer may impose lesser disciplinary sanctions as the circumstances warrant in the judgment of the director or chief probation officer. Any disciplinary action taken by the director or chief probation officer shall be in accordance with any state or federal laws that may be applicable.

It shall be the duty of the county board to furnish suitable rooms and accommodations, equipment and supplies for said probation officers and clerical assistants in that jurisdiction, and for the keeping of the records, equipment and supplies of the office. The number of clerical assistants shall be determined by the Chief Circuit Judge or another judge designated by the Chief Circuit Judge to have general administrative and supervisory authority over the director of the court services department or the chief probation officer and shall

be appointed by the director or chief probation officer. Salaries of said clerical assistants shall be fixed by the county board.
(Source: P.A. 86-639.) [Formerly Ill. Rev. Stat. 38 §204-5.]

110/13a. Appointment of officers under Juvenile Court Act.

§13a. The appointment of officers to probation or court services departments under the Juvenile Court Act of 1987 [705 ILCS 405/1-1 et seq.] shall be in accordance with the provisions of this Act.
(Source: P.A. 85-1209.) [Formerly Ill. Rev. Stat. 38 §204-5a.]

110/14. Salary and expenses of probation officers.

§14. The amount of compensation to be paid any court services or probation officer, including a director of a court services department or a chief probation officer appointed by any circuit court, shall be determined by the county boards of the several counties in which such officers, respectively, are appointed, and shall be paid by the county treasurer on the warrant of the county comptroller or other person authorized to issue warrants on the county treasurer; and such salary and reimbursement for expenses of such chiefs and probation officers serving throughout such circuit or probation officer district shall be apportioned between such counties on the basis of their population as determined by the last national census, and the respective portions thereof shall be paid by the county treasurer upon warrants issued by the Chief Circuit Judge. All such expenses after being certified by the Chief Circuit Judge, and approved by the board of such county, shall be paid by the county treasurer on warrant by the proper county officer. No probation officer receiving compensation from any public funds under the provisions of this Act shall receive any compensation, gift or gratuity whatsoever from any person, firm or corporation for doing or refraining from doing any official act in any way connected with any proceeding then pending or about to be instituted in any court with which the probation officer has to do. Any probation officer receiving compensation from any public funds under this Act, who receives any compensation, gift or gratuity whatever from any person, firm or corporation for doing or refraining from doing any official act in any way connected with any proceeding then pending or about to be instituted in any court with which the probation officer has to do, is guilty of a misdemeanor, and shall be punished accordingly, and shall be immediately removed.
(Source: P.A. 84-692.) [Formerly Ill. Rev. Stat. 38 §204-6.]

110/15. Division of Probation Services established; funds; costs.

§15. (1) The Supreme Court of Illinois may establish a Division of Probation Services whose purpose shall be the development, establishment, promulgation, and enforcement of uniform standards for probation services in this State, and to otherwise carry out the intent of this Act. The Division may:

(a) establish qualifications for chief probation officers and other probation and court services personnel as to hiring, promotion, and training.

(b) make available, on a timely basis, lists of those applicants whose qualifications meet the regulations referred to herein, including on said lists all candidates found qualified.

(c) establish a means of verifying the conditions for reimbursement under this Act and develop criteria for approved costs for reimbursement.

(d) develop standards and approve employee compensation schedules for probation and court services departments.

(e) employ sufficient personnel in the Division to carry out the functions of the Division.

(f) establish a system of training and establish standards for personnel orientation and training.

(g) develop standards for a system of record keeping for cases and programs, gather statistics, establish a system of uniform forms, and develop research for planning of Probation Services.

(h) develop standards to assure adequate support personnel, office space, equipment and supplies, travel expenses, and other essential items necessary for Probation and Court Services Departments to carry out their duties.

(i) review and approve annual plans submitted by Probation and Court Services Departments.

(j) monitor and evaluate all programs operated by Probation and Court Services Departments, and may include in the program evaluation criteria such factors as the percentage of Probation sentences for felons convicted of Probationable offenses.

(k) seek the cooperation of local and State government and private agencies to improve the quality of probation and court services.

(*l*) where appropriate, establish programs and corresponding standards designed to generally improve the quality of probation and court services and reduce the rate of adult or juvenile offenders committed to the Department of Corrections.

(m) establish such other standards and regulations and do all acts necessary to carry out the intent and purposes of this Act.

The State of Illinois shall provide for the costs of personnel, travel, equipment, telecommunications, postage, commodities, printing, space, contractual services and other related costs necessary to carry out the intent of this Act.

(2) (a) The chief judge of each circuit shall provide full-time probation services for all counties within the circuit, in a manner consistent with the annual probation plan, the standards, policies, and regulations established by the Supreme Court. A probation district of two or more counties within a circuit may be created for the purposes of providing full-time probation services. Every county or group of counties within a circuit shall maintain a probation department which shall be under the authority of the Chief Judge of the circuit or some other judge designated by the Chief Judge. The Chief Judge, through the Probation and Court Services Department shall submit annual plans to the Division for probation and related services.

(b) The Chief Judge of each circuit shall appoint the Chief Probation Officer and all other probation officers for his or her circuit from lists of qualified applicants supplied by the Supreme Court. Candidates for chief managing officer and other probation officer positions must apply with both the Chief Judge of the circuit and the Supreme Court.

(3) A Probation and Court Service Department shall apply to the Supreme Court for funds for basic services, and may apply for funds for new and expanded programs or Individualized Services and Programs. Costs shall be reimbursed monthly based on a plan and budget approved by the Supreme Court. No Department may be reimbursed for costs which exceed or are not provided for in the approved annual plan and budget. After the effective date of this amendatory Act of 1985, each county must provide basic services in accordance with the annual plan and standards created by the division. No department may receive funds for new or expanded programs or individualized services and programs unless they are in compliance with standards as enumerated in paragraph (h) of subsection (1) of this Section, the annual plan, and standards for basic services.

(4) The Division shall reimburse the county or counties for probation services as follows:

(a) 100% of the salary of all chief managing officers designated as such by the Chief Judge and the division.

(b) 100% of the salary for all probation officer and supervisor positions approved for reimbursement by the division after April 1, 1984, to meet workload standards and to implement intensive probation supervision programs and other basic services as defined in this Act.

(c) 100% of the salary for all secure detention personnel and non-secure group home personnel approved for reimbursement after December 1, 1990. Allocation of such positions will be based on comparative need considering capacity, staff/resident ratio, physical plant and program.

(d) $1,000 per month for salaries for the remaining probation officer positions engaged in basic services and new or expanded services. All such positions shall be approved by the division in accordance with this Act and division standards.

(e) 100% of the travel expenses in accordance with Division standards for all Probation positions approved under paragraph (b) of subsection 4 of this Section.

(f) If the amount of funds reimbursed to the county under paragraphs (a) through (e) of subsection 4 of this Section on an annual basis is less than the amount the county had received during the 12 month period immediately prior to the effective date of this amendatory Act of 1985, then the Division shall reimburse the amount of the difference to the county. The effect of paragraph (b) of subsection 7 of this Section shall be considered in implementing this supplemental reimbursement provision.

(5) The Division shall provide funds beginning on April 1, 1987 for the counties to provide Individualized Services and Programs as provided in Section 16 of this Act [730 ILCS 110/16].

(6) A Probation and Court Services Department in order to be eligible for the reimbursement must submit to the Supreme Court an application containing such information and in such a form and by such dates as the Supreme Court may require. Departments to be eligible for funding must satisfy the following conditions:

(a) The Department shall have on file with the Supreme Court an annual Probation plan for continuing, improved, and new Probation and Court Services Programs approved by the Supreme Court or its designee. This plan shall indicate the manner in which Probation and Court Services will be delivered and improved, consistent with the minimum standards and regulations for Probation and Court Services, as established by the Supreme Court. In counties with more than one Probation and Court Services Department eligible to receive funds, all Departments within that county must submit plans which are approved by the Supreme Court.

(b) The annual probation plan shall seek to generally improve the quality of probation services and to reduce the commitment of adult and juvenile offenders to the Department of Corrections and shall require, when appropriate, coordination with the Department of Corrections and the Department of Children and Family Services in the development and use of community resources, information systems, case review and permanency planning systems to avoid the duplication of services.

(c) The Department shall be in compliance with standards developed by the Supreme Court for basic, new and expanded services, training, personnel hiring and promotion.

(7) No statement shall be verified by the Supreme Court or its designee or vouchered by the Comptroller unless each of the following conditions have been met:

(a) The probation officer is a full-time employee appointed by the Chief Judge to provide probation services.

(b) The probation officer, in order to be eligible for State reimbursement, is receiving a salary of at least $17,000 per year.

(c) The probation officer is appointed or was reappointed in accordance with minimum qualifications or criteria established by the Supreme Court; however, all probation officers appointed prior to January 1, 1978, shall be exempted from the minimum requirements established by the Supreme Court. Payments shall be made to counties employing these exempted probation officers as long as they are employed in the position held on the effective date of this amendatory Act of 1985. Promotions shall be governed by minimum qualifications established by the Supreme Court.

(d) The Department has an established compensation schedule approved by the Supreme Court. The compensation schedule shall include salary ranges with necessary increments to compensate each employee. The increments shall, within the salary ranges, be based on such factors as bona fide occupational qualifications, performance, and length of service. Each position in the Department shall be placed on the compensation schedule according to job duties and responsibilities of such position. The policy and procedures of the compensation schedule shall be made available to each employee.

(8) In order to obtain full reimbursement of all approved costs, each Department must continue to employ at least the same number of probation officers and probation managers as were authorized for employment for the fiscal year which includes January 1, 1985. This number shall be designated as the base amount of the Department. No positions approved by the Division under paragraph (b) of subsection 4 will be included in the base amount. In the event that the Department employs fewer Probation officers and Probation managers than the base amount for a period of 90 days, funding received by the Department under subsection 4 of this Section may be reduced on a monthly basis by the amount of the current salaries of any positions below the base amount.

(9) Before the 15th day of each month, the treasurer of any county which has a Probation and Court Services Department, or the treasurer of the most populous county, in the case of a Probation or Court Services Department funded by more than one county, shall submit an itemized statement of all approved costs incurred in the delivery of Basic Probation and Court Services under this Act to the Supreme Court. The treasurer may also submit an itemized statement of all approved costs incurred in the delivery of new and expanded Probation and Court Services as well as Individualized Services and Programs. The Supreme Court or its designee shall verify compliance with this Section and shall examine and audit the monthly statement and, upon finding them to be correct, shall forward them to the Comptroller for payment to the county treasurer. In the case of payment to a treasurer of a county which is the most populous of counties sharing the salary and expenses of a Probation and Court Services Department, the treasurer shall divide the money between the counties in a manner that reflects each county's share of the cost incurred by the Department.

(10) The county treasurer must certify that funds received under this Section shall be used solely to maintain and improve Probation and Court Services. The county or circuit shall remain in compliance with all standards, policies and regulations established by the Supreme Court. If at any time the Supreme Court determines that a county or circuit is not in compliance, the Supreme Court shall immediately notify the Chief Judge, county board chairman and the Director of Court Services Chief Probation Officer. If after 90 days of written notice the noncompliance still exists, the Supreme Court shall be required to reduce the amount of monthly reimbursement by 10%. An additional 10% reduction of monthly reimbursement shall occur for each consecutive month of noncompliance. Except as provided in subsection 5 of Section 15,

funding to counties shall commence on April 1, 1986. Funds received under this Act shall be used to provide for Probation Department expenses including those required under Section 13 of this Act [730 ILCS 110/13].

(11) The respective counties shall be responsible for capital and space costs, fringe benefits, clerical costs, equipment, telecommunications, postage, commodities and printing.

(12) Probation officers shall be considered peace officers in the exercise of their official duties. Probation officers, sheriffs and police officers may, anywhere within the State, arrest any probationer who is in violation of any of the conditions of his probation, and it shall be the duty of the officer making such arrest to take said probationer before the Court having jurisdiction over him for further order.

(Source: P.A. 86-639; 86-1327.) [Formerly Ill. Rev. Stat. 38 §204-7.]

110/15.1. Probation and court services fund.

§15.1. (a) The county treasurer in each county shall establish a probation and court services fund consisting of fees collected pursuant to subsection (i) of Section 5-6-3 and subsection (i) of Section 5-6-3.1 of the Unified Code of Corrections, as amended [730 ILCS 5/5-6-3 and 5/5-6-3.1]. The county treasurer shall disburse monies from the fund only at the direction of the chief judge of the circuit court in such circuit where the county is located. The county treasurer of each county shall, on or before January 10 of each year, submit an annual report to the Supreme Court.

(b) Monies in the probation and court services fund shall be appropriated by the county board to be used within the county where collected in accordance with policies and guidelines approved by the Supreme Court for the costs of operating the probation and court services department or departments; however, monies in the probation and court services fund shall not be used for the payment of salaries of probation and court services personnel.

(c) Monies expended from the probation and court services fund shall be used to supplement, not supplant, county appropriations for probation and court services.

(d) Interest earned on monies deposited in a probation and court services fund may be used by the county for its ordinary and contingent expenditures.

(Source: P.A. 86-640; 87-609; 87-610.) [Formerly Ill. Rev. Stat. 38 §204-7.1.]

110/16. Legislative policy; local plans.

§16. (1) The purpose of the Section is to encourage the development of a coordinated justice system. It is the legislative policy of the State to more effectively protect society, to promote efficiency and economy in the delivery of services to offenders and to encourage utilization of appropriate sentencing alternatives to imprisonment in State operated institutions. This Section shall be construed to support the development of local individualized programs which will:

(a) Provide a continuum of sanctions to increase sentencing options to the judiciary of the State;

(b) Enable the Courts to utilize programs which enhance the offender's ability to become a contributing member to his or her community and which will increase the benefits to victims and the communities through restitution;

(c) Increase sentencing alternatives for less serious felony offenders and delinquent juveniles in order to reserve prisons and jail beds for serious violent offenders.

(2) Any local plan for implementation of individualized services and programs may include but are not limited to the following:

(a) Direct offender services—those services applied directly to offenders, including job readiness, educational, vocational, drug or alcohol treatment services; and

(b) Nonresidential rehabilitation programs—those programs which comprise a coordinated network within the justice system which expand sentencing options for the judiciary, including drunk driver diversion programs, public services employment, restitution collection; and

(c) Emergency services—including detoxification, emergency shelter and support; and

(d) Assessment and evaluation services—reports or diagnostic recommendations to provide the justice system with accurate individualized case information, including mental health, drug, alcohol, and living situation information; and

(e) Residential alternative sentencing programs—those programs which provide expanded sentencing options for less serious felony offenders and delinquent juveniles, including mother and child unification programs.

The local plan must be directed in such a manner as to emphasize an individualized approach to servicing offenders in a strong community based system including probation as the broker of services.

The local plan shall be limited to services and shall not include costs for:

(a) capital expenditures;

(b) renovations or remodeling;

(c) personnel costs for Probation.

(3) A county may make application to the Supreme Court for funds to provide for Individualized Services and Programs. The Department shall be in compliance with all standards and regulations established by the Division for the delivery of basic Services and application shall be part of the Department's annual Probation plan and shall set forth the following:

(a) a statement of objectives for which said funds shall be used;

(b) a statement of service needs based upon persons under supervision of the Department;

(c) a statement of the type of services and programs to provide for the individual needs of offenders;

(d) a budget indicating the costs of each service or program to be funded under the plan;

(e) a summary of contracts and service agreements indicating the treatment goals and number of offenders to be served by each service provider; and

(f) a statement indicating that the individualized services and programs will not be duplicating existing services and programs.

Funds for this plan shall not supplant existing county funded programs. The allocation of payments for adult and juvenile services under the local plan shall be based on the proportionate adult and juvenile workload of the department or departments covered by the local plan.

(4) A county or group of counties shall be eligible to apply for an amount of funding not to exceed the same proportionate share of total appropriations for Individualized Services and Programs as the county or group of counties received of total State reimbursements under subsection 4 of Section 15 of this Act [730 ILCS 110/15] or previous Probation subsidy programs in the prior State fiscal year. However the Supreme Court may waive this limitation to encourage the participation of rural counties.

The Supreme Court shall forward Individualized Services and Programs allocations to the county treasurer as provided in Section 15 of this Act. Each county shall receive, maintain, and appropriate said funds in a separate line item account of the probation department budget. In addition, the Supreme Court shall, upon approval of the annual plan, forward 20% of the approved

Individualized Services and Programs allocations to the county treasurer to be deposited in said line item account. Subsequent allocations shall be made to the county on a monthly basis.

It shall be the responsibility of the county through the probation budget and in accordance with county policy and procedure to make payments for Individualized Services and Programs.

At the end of the State of Illinois fiscal year, the county shall promptly return any uncommitted and unused funds from this account.

(5) The Supreme Court shall be responsible for the following:

(a) The Supreme Court may review each Individualized Services and Programs plan for compliance with standards established for such plans. A plan may be approved as submitted, approved with modifications, or rejected. No plan shall be considered for approval if the circuit or county is not in full compliance with all regulations, standards and guidelines pertaining to the delivery of basic probation services as established by the Supreme Court.

(b) The Supreme Court shall monitor on a continual basis and shall evaluate annually both the program and its fiscal activities in all counties receiving an allocation under Individualized Services and Programs. Any program or service which has not met the goals and objectives of its contract or service agreement shall be subject to denial for funding in subsequent years. The Supreme Court shall evaluate the effectiveness of Individualized Services and Programs in each circuit or county. In determining the future funding for Individualized Services and Programs under this Act, such evaluation shall include, as a primary indicator of success, an increased or maintained percentage of probation sentences for felons convicted of probationable offenses.

(c) Any Individualized Services and Programs allocations not applied for and approved by the Supreme Court shall be available for redistribution to approved plans for the remainder of that fiscal year. Any county that invests local moneys in the Individualized Services and Programs shall be given first consideration for any redistribution of allocations.

(Source: P.A. 86-639.) [Formerly Ill. Rev. Stat. 38 §204-8.]

PROBATION COMMUNITY SERVICE ACT

Sec.

115/0.01. Short title.

§0.01. Short title. This Act may be cited as the Probation Community Service Act.

(Source: P.A. 86-1324.) [Formerly Ill. Rev. Stat. 38 §204a.]

115/1. Public or community service programs.

§1. (a) "Public or Community Service" means uncompensated labor for a non-profit organization or public body whose purpose is to enhance physical, or mental stability, environmental quality or the social welfare and which agrees to accept public or community service from offenders and to report on the progress of the public or community service to the court.

(b) "Site" means non-profit organization or public body agreeing to accept community service from offenders and to report on the progress of ordered public or community service to the court or its delegate.

(c) The county boards of the several counties in this State are authorized to establish and operate agencies to develop and supervise programs of public or community service for those persons placed by the court on probation, conditional discharge, or supervision.

(d) The programs shall be developed in cooperation with the circuit courts for the respective counties developing such programs and shall conform with any law restricting the use of public or community service.

(e) Neither the State, any local government, probation department, public or community service program or site, nor any official or employee thereof acting in the course of their official duties shall be liable for any injury or loss a person might receive while performing public or community service as ordered by the court, nor shall they be liable for any tortious acts of any person performing public or community service, except for wilful, wanton misconduct or gross negligence on the part of such governmental unit, official or employee.

(f) No person assigned to a public or community service program shall be considered an employee for any purpose, nor shall the county board be obligated to provide any compensation to such person.

(Source: P.A. 85-449.) [Formerly Ill. Rev. Stat. 38 §204a-1.]

PROBATION CHALLENGE PROGRAM ACT

Sec.

120/1. Short title.

§1. This Article shall be known as the Probation Challenge Program Act.

(Source: P.A. 84-1426.) [Formerly Ill. Rev. Stat. 38 §1501.]

120/2. Purpose.

§2. The purpose of this Act is to provide an intensive program of educational instruction, as well as social and vocational counseling, to certain convicted criminal defendants in an effort to afford them a realistic opportunity to employ their latent talents and abilities and become contributing members of the society in which they live.

(Source: P.A. 84-1426.) [Formerly Ill. Rev. Stat. 38 §1502.]

120/3. Definitions.

§3. For the purposes of this Act, the following words have the meanings ascribed to them in this Section.

(1) "Board" refers to the Board of City College of Chicago District 508.

(2) "Client" refers to a person whose participation in the Program has been required as a condition of probation pursuant to the Unified Code of Corrections [730 ILCS 5/1-1-1 et seq.].

(3) "Program" refers to the Probation Challenge Program.

(Source: P.A. 84-1426.) [Formerly Ill. Rev. Stat. 38 §1503.]

120/4. Probation Challenge Program created.

§4. There is created in each county having a population of 2,000,000 or more inhabitants, for the purpose of operating on an experimental basis, a Probation Challenge Program. The State shall bear the costs necessary to carry out the functions of the Program.

(Source: P.A. 84-1426.) [Formerly Ill. Rev. Stat. 38 §1504.]

120/5. Program governed by Board of City College of Chicago.

§5. The Program shall be governed by the Board of City College of Chicago. The Board shall prescribe such rules as may be necessary to assure the efficient and effective operation of the Program, including but not limited to rules establishing qualifications for Program employees.
(Source: P.A. 84-1426.) [Formerly Ill. Rev. Stat. 38 §1505.]

120/6. Provision of facilities.

§6. To the fullest extent practicable, the Board shall provide for the utilization of the facilities of community colleges within each county having a population of 2,000,000 or more inhabitants in the administration of this Act.
(Source: P.A. 84-1426.) [Formerly Ill. Rev. Stat. 38 §1506.]

120/7. Program Director; duties.

§7. The Board shall appoint a Program Director who shall act as a chief operating officer and shall devote his full time to supervising the overall operation and fiscal affairs of the Program. The Program Director's duties as supervisor of the Program include but are not limited to the hiring of an Educational Coordinator, a Counselor Supervisor, a Psychologist and an Administrator for the Program, and acting as a liaison between the Program and the county Adult Probation Department in an effort to foster cooperation between the Program and such Department in accomplishing the purposes of this Act and to avoid the Program's duplicating services already being adequately provided by such Department.
(Source: P.A. 84-1426.) [Formerly Ill. Rev. Stat. 38 §1507.]

120/8. Employees; duties.

§8. (a) The Educational Coordinator shall be responsible for the overall planning, development and operation of the educational training of clients of the Program and the hiring and supervision of instructors for the Program.

(b) The Counselor Supervisor shall be responsible for the hiring and supervision of counselors for the Program and for initially meeting with new clients of the Program.

(c) The Program Psychologist shall be responsible for conducting an educational and psychological evaluation of all clients upon their entering the Program and upon his receiving requests for such evaluations from the Educational Coordinator or Counselor Supervisor, and for making recommendations to educational or counseling personnel based upon those evaluations.

(d) The Administrator shall be responsible for supervising the daily business affairs of the Program, including but not limited to the hiring and management of clerical personnel, the maintenance of all records, books and accounts of the Program, and the procurement of office and other necessary space, supplies and equipment.
(Source: P.A. 84-1426.) [Formerly Ill. Rev. Stat. 38 §1508.]

120/9. Salaries.

§9. The salaries of the Program Director and all supervisors and employees of the Program shall be determined by the Board.
(Source: P.A. 84-1426.) [Formerly Ill. Rev. Stat. 38 §1509.]

120/10. Initial meeting with client.

§10. At his initial meeting with the client, the Counselor Supervisor shall arrange meetings between the client and the Educational Coordinator and between the client and a counselor whom the Counselor Supervisor shall assign to the client. The Counselor Supervisor shall also arrange a private meeting between the client and the Program Psychologist.

At his initial meeting with the client, the Educational Coordinator shall arrange a meeting between the client and an instructor whom the Educational Coordinator shall assign to the client.

The client's failure to punctually appear at any meeting scheduled between him and any personnel of the Program shall be promptly reported by the person with whom the client was to meet to the client's probation officer and to the court which required the client's participation in the Program.

(Source: P.A. 84-1426.) [Formerly Ill. Rev. Stat. 38 §1510.]

120/11. Duties of counselor and instructor.

§11. (a) The duties of a counselor as to a client are

(1) To become as thoroughly familiar as is practicable with the client, utilizing all available sources of information, including but not limited to consultations with the Program Psychologist and the client's instructor, examination of the records of the judicial proceeding the disposition of which required the client's participation in the Program, and consultation with any available court personnel involved with the client;

(2) To assist the client in establishing vocational and social goals to be accomplished by the client as the result of the client's participation in the Program, which goals shall include the client's successfully procuring and retaining employment;

(3) To establish a weekly schedule for meetings with the client in compliance with the rules prescribed pursuant to Section 12 [730 ILCS 120/12];

(4) To provide advice, counseling and supervision to the client, with due regard for the particular social and economic circumstances surrounding that client's case, in an effort to fully and efficiently assist the client in accomplishing the goals which have been established for him;

(5) To keep such records as the Counselor Supervisor may require of each client's progress in attaining the goals which have been established for him;

(6) To assist each client in establishing such contacts with businesses and social and civic organizations as the counselor deems will best enable the client to accomplish the goals which have been established for him; and

(7) To perform such other functions as the Board may by regulation require.

(b) The duties of an instructor as to a client are

(1) To become as thoroughly familiar as is practicable with the client through consultation with the client's counselor and the Program Psychologist and utilization of all other available sources of information which would be of use to the instructor in helping the client to attain his educational goals;

(2) To assist each client in establishing educational goals to be accomplished by the client as a result of the client's participation in the Program, which goals shall include the client's earning a General Education Diploma;

(3) To establish a weekly schedule of instruction for the client in compliance with the rules prescribed pursuant to Section 12 [730 ILCS 120/12];

(4) To provide each client with individualized instruction in subjects which shall include but need not be limited to English, history, reading, mathematics, science and ethics;

(5) To keep such records as the Educational Coordinator may require of each client's progress in attaining the educational goals which have been established for him; and

(6) To perform such other functions as the Board may by regulation require.

(Source: P.A. 84-1426.) [Formerly Ill. Rev. Stat. 38 §1511.]

120/12. Rules regarding client performance.

§12. The Board shall promulgate rules governing client performance in the Program. Those rules shall include but need not be limited to requirements that

(1) The client meet with his counselor for at least 3 hours each week during his participation in the Program;

(2) The client meet with his instructor for at least 9 hours each week during his participation in the Program;

(3) The client meet, during his participation in the Program, for at least 2 hours each week with other clients, under the supervision of their respective counselors, for the purpose of conducting general discussion groups; and

(4) The client cooperate with his probation officer or any other agent designated by the court to monitor the client's compliance with the conditions of his probation.

(Source: P.A. 84-1426.) [Formerly Ill. Rev. Stat. 38 §1512.]

120/13. Client's counselor and instructor; joint report.

§13. (a) Each client's instructor and counselor shall meet together as often as is necessary for the purpose of exchanging information and ideas which may be of use in assisting the client in attaining the goals which have been established for him.

(b) Each client's counselor and instructor shall, at the end of every 3-month period during which the client participates in the Program, jointly prepare and file with the county Adult Probation Department and court which required the client's participation in the Program a report evaluating the client's progress in the Program. Such report shall include a determination as to whether continued participation in the Program by the client would be beneficial to the client and the public interest.

(Source: P.A. 84-1426.) [Formerly Ill. Rev. Stat. 38 §1513.]

120/14. Confidentiality of client's files.

§14. All files of the Program regarding a client shall be confidential. Access to such files shall be limited to personnel of the Program, personnel of the court which required the client's participation in the Program, the county Adult Probation Department and other persons and entities to whom the Board may by rule grant such access.

(Source: P.A. 84-1426.) [Formerly Ill. Rev. Stat. 38 §1514.]

COUNTY JAIL ACT

125/0.01. Short title.

§0.01. Short title. This Act may be cited as the County Jail Act.
(Source: P.A. 86-1324.) [Formerly Ill. Rev. Stat. 75 §100.]

125/1. Facilities required.

§1. There shall be kept and maintained in good and sufficient condition and repair, one or more jail facilities for the use of each county within this State. However, this requirement may be satisfied by a single jail facility jointly maintained and used by 2 or more counties. It shall be unlawful to build a jail within 200 feet of any building used exclusively for school purposes.
(Source: P.A. 83-1073.) [Formerly Ill. Rev. Stat. 75 §101.]

125/2. Sheriff to be warden.

§2. The Sheriff of each county in this State shall be the warden of the jail of the county, and have the custody of all prisoners in the jail, except when otherwise provided in the "County Department of Corrections Act" [repealed].
(Source: P.A. 83-1073.) [Formerly Ill. Rev. Stat. 75 §102.]

125/2.1. New jail.

§2.1. New jail. The sheriff of each county in this State shall be the warden of any new jail facility constructed or otherwise acquired in the county and shall have the custody of all prisoners in that facility, except when otherwise provided in Division 3-15 of the Counties Code [55 ILCS 5/3-15001 et seq.].
(Source: P.A. 87-645.) [Formerly Ill. Rev. Stat. 75 §102.1.]

125/3. Appointment of superintendent of jail.

§3. The Sheriff may appoint a superintendent of the jail, and remove him at his pleasure, for whose conduct and training, he shall be responsible. The Sheriff shall also be responsible for the hiring and training of all personnel necessary to operate and maintain the jail.
(Source: P.A. 83-1073.) [Formerly Ill. Rev. Stat. 75 §103.]

125/4. Duty to receive and confine persons committed.

§4. The Warden of the jail shall receive and confine in such jail, until discharged by due course of law, all persons committed to such jail by any competent authority.

When there is no county jail facility operating in a county, arresting agencies shall be responsible for delivering persons arrested to an adjoining county jail facility, if the adjoining county has entered into a written agreement with the committing county allowing for the maintenance of prisoners in the adjoining county.
(Source: P.A. 86-570.) [Formerly Ill. Rev. Stat. 75 §104.]

125/5. Costs of maintaining persons committed.

§5. All costs of maintaining persons committed for violations of Illinois law, shall be the responsibility of the county. All costs of maintaining persons committed under any ordinance or resolution of a unit of local government, including medical costs, is the responsibility of the unit of local government enacting the ordinance or resolution, and arresting the person.
(Source: P.A. 83-1073.) [Formerly Ill. Rev. Stat. 75 §105.]

125/6. Permanent calendar.

§6. The warden of the jail shall keep an exact permanent calendar of all persons committed to jail, registering the name, place of abode, time, cause and authority of their commitment, and the time and manner of their discharge.
(Source: P.A. 83-1073.) [Formerly Ill. Rev. Stat. 75 §106.]

125/7. Monthly list of prisoners.

§7. On the first day of each month, the warden of the jail of the county shall prepare a list of all prisoners in his custody, specifying the causes for which and the persons by whom they were committed, and make available to the court his calendar of prisoners.
(Source: P.A. 83-1073.) [Formerly Ill. Rev. Stat. 75 §107.]

125/8. Coroner to be warden if Sheriff imprisoned.

§8. The Sheriff may be imprisoned in the jail of his county, and for the time he is so imprisoned, the coroner shall be warden of the jail, and perform all the duties of the sheriff in regard thereto, and shall, by himself and his sureties, be answerable for the faithful discharge of his duties as such warden.
(Source: P.A. 83-1073.) [Formerly Ill. Rev. Stat. 75 §108.]

125/9. Confinement in jail in another county.

§9. When there is no jail or other penal institution in a county, or the jail or other penal institution of the county is insufficient, the sheriff may commit any person in his custody, either on civil or criminal process, to the nearest sufficient jail of another county, and the warden of the jail of such county shall receive and confine such prisoner, until removed by order of the court having jurisdiction of the offense, or discharged by due course of law.
(Source: P.A. 83-1073.) [Formerly Ill. Rev. Stat. 75 §109.]

125/10. Confinement in jail in another county; payment of expenses.

§10. Whenever a prisoner is committed to the jail of one county for a criminal offense committed or charged to have been committed in another, or is transferred to another county for safe keeping or trial, the county in which the crime was committed, or charged to have been committed, shall pay the expenses of the keeping of such prisoner. In civil suits, the plaintiff or defendant shall pay the expenses, in the same manner as if the imprisonment had taken place in the same county where the suit was commenced.
(Source: P.A. 83-1073.) [Formerly Ill. Rev. Stat. 75 §110.]

125/11. Segregation and classification of prisoners.

§11. Debtors and witnesses shall not be confined in the same room with other prisoners; male and female prisoners shall not be kept in the same room; minors shall be kept separate from those previously convicted of a felony or other infamous crime; and persons charged with an offense shall not be confined in the same cell as those convicted of a crime. The confinement of those persons convicted of a misdemeanor or felony shall be in accordance with a classification system developed and implemented by the local jail authority.
(Chgd. by P.A. 87-899, eff. 1/1/93.)
(Source: P.A. 85-164.) [Formerly Ill. Rev. Stat. 75 §111.]

125/12. Notice of insufficiency of jail.

§12. Whenever the Warden of the jail of any county deems such jail insufficient to secure the prisoners confined therein, he shall give notice thereof to the county board.
(Source: P.A. 83-1073.) [Formerly Ill. Rev. Stat. 75 §112.]

125/13. Person charged with high crime; employment of guard.

§13. Whenever the Warden of any jail shall have in his custody any person charged with a capital offense or other high crime, and there is no jail in his county, or the jail is insufficient, he may, with the advice of the judge of the circuit court of such county, employ a sufficient guard, not exceeding 3 persons, for the guarding and safe keeping of such prisoner in his own county. The expense of such guard shall be audited and paid as other county expenses.
(Source: P.A. 83-1073.) [Formerly Ill. Rev. Stat. 75 §113.]

125/14. Endangerment of prisoners; removal.

§14. At any time, in the opinion of the Warden, the lives or health of the prisoners are endangered, to such a degree as to render their removal necessary, the Warden may cause the prisoners to be removed to some suitable place within the county, or to the jail of some convenient county, where they may be confined until they can be safely returned to the place whence they were removed. No prisoner charged with a felony shall be removed by the warden to a Mental Health or Developmental Disabilities facility as defined in the Mental Health and Developmental Disabilities Code [405 ILCS 5/1-100 et seq.], except as specifically authorized by Article 104 of the Code of Criminal Procedure of 1963 [725 ILCS 5/104-10 et seq.], or the Mental Health and Developmental Disabilities Code. Any place to which the prisoners are so removed shall, during their imprisonment there, be deemed, as to such prisoners, a prison of the county in which they were originally confined; but, they shall be under the care, government and direction of the Warden of the jail of the county in which they are confined.

(Source: P.A. 83-1073.) [Formerly Ill. Rev. Stat. 75 §114.]

125/15. Provision of food and water.

§15. The Warden of the jail shall furnish each prisoner daily with as much clean water as may be necessary for drink and personal cleanliness, and serve him three times a day with wholesome food, well cooked and in sufficient quantity. The Warden of the jail in counties of the first and second class shall procure at the expense of the county, all necessary foods and provisions for the support of the prisoners confined in the jail, and shall employ suitable persons to prepare and serve the food for the prisoners, or otherwise provide suitable food service.

(Source: P.A. 83-1073.) [Formerly Ill. Rev. Stat. 75 §115.]

125/16. Alcoholic beverages and controlled substances prohibited.

§16. The Warden of the jail or other person shall not permit any prisoner to send for or have any alcoholic beverages or controlled substances except when prescribed by a physician as medicine.

(Source: P.A. 83-1073.) [Formerly Ill. Rev. Stat. 75 §116.]

125/17. Provision of bedding, clothing, etc.; medical costs.

§17. The Warden of the jail shall furnish necessary bedding, clothing, fuel and medical aid for all prisoners under his charge, and keep an accurate account of the same. When medical or hospital services are required by any person held in custody, the county, private hospital, physician or any public agency which provides such services shall be entitled to obtain reimbursement from the county for the cost of such services. To the extent that such person is reasonably able to pay for such care, including reimbursement from any insurance program or from other medical benefit programs available to such person, he or she shall reimburse the county or arresting authority. If such person has already been determined eligible for medical assistance under The Illinois Public Aid Code [305 ILCS 5/1-1 et seq.] at the time the person is initially detained pending trial, the cost of such services, to the extent such cost exceeds $2,500, shall be reimbursed by the Department of Public Aid under that Code. A reimbursement under any public or private program authorized by this Section shall be paid to the county or arresting authority to the same extent as would have been obtained had the services been rendered in a non-custodial environment.

An arresting authority shall be responsible for any incurred medical expenses relating to the arrestee until such time as the arrestee is placed in the custody of the sheriff. However, the arresting authority shall not be so responsible if the arrest was made pursuant to a request by the sheriff.

For the purposes of this Section, "arresting authority" means a unit of local government, other than a county, which employs peace officers and whose peace officers have made the arrest of a person. For the purposes of this Section, "medical expenses relating to the arrestee" means only those expenses incurred for medical care or treatment provided to an arrestee on account of an injury suffered by the arrestee during the course of his arrest; the term does not include any expenses incurred for medical care or treatment provided to an arrestee on account of a health condition of the arrestee which existed prior to the time of his arrest.
(Source: P.A. 86-794.) [Formerly Ill. Rev. Stat. 75 §117.]

125/18. Condition of jail.
§18. The Warden shall keep and maintain the jail in a clean and healthful condition.
(Source: P.A. 83-1073.) [Formerly Ill. Rev. Stat. 75 §118.]

125/19. Personal cleanliness.
§19. The Warden of the jail shall see that strict attention is constantly paid to the personal cleanliness of all prisoners confined in the jail.
(Source: P.A. 83-1073.) [Formerly Ill. Rev. Stat. 75 §119.]

125/20. Payment of costs; reimbursement by convicted persons.
§20. The cost and expense of keeping, maintaining and furnishing the jail of each county, and of keeping and maintaining the prisoner thereof, except as otherwise provided by law, shall be paid from the county treasury, the account therefor being first settled and allowed by the county board.

The county board may require convicted persons confined in its jail to reimburse the county for the expenses incurred by their incarceration to the extent of their ability to pay for such expenses. The State's Attorney of the county in which such jail is located may, if requested by the County Board, institute civil actions in the circuit court of the county in which the jail is located to recover from such convicted confined persons the expenses incurred by their confinement. Such funds recovered shall be paid into the county treasury.
(Source: P.A. 83-1073.) [Formerly Ill. Rev. Stat. 75 §120.]

125/21. Confinement in jail in another county; payment of expenses; reimbursement by convicted persons.
§21. Whenever a prisoner is committed to the jail of one county for a criminal offense committed or charged to have been committed in another, or is transferred to another county for safekeeping or trial, the county in which the crime was committed, or charged to have been committed, shall pay the expenses of the keeping of such prisoner. In civil suits, the plaintiff or defendant shall pay the expenses, in the same manner as if the imprisonment had taken place in the same county where the suit was commenced.

The County Board of the county in which the crime was committed, may require convicted prisoners transferred from such county to reimburse the county for the expenses incurred by their incarceration to the extent of their ability to pay for such expenses. The State's Attorney of the county which incurred the expenses, if authorized by the County Board, may institute civil actions in the circuit court of such county to recover from such convicted confined persons the expenses incurred by their confinement. Such expenses recovered shall be paid into the county treasury.
(Source: P.A. 83-1073.) [Formerly Ill. Rev. Stat. 75 §121.]

125/22. Grand jury inspection; report to court.
§22. It shall be the duty of the grand jury, or a committee of not less than three of its members, at least once every twelve months, to visit the jail and

examine its condition and the treatment of the prisoners, and make report thereof to the court and particularly whether any of the provisions of this Act have been violated or neglected, and the causes of such violation or neglect. In counties where twelve months have passed since the last grand jury term, the chief judge of the Circuit Court shall appoint a committee of citizens to visit the jail, examine its condition and treatment of prisoners and make a report.
(Source: P.A. 83-1073.) [Formerly Ill. Rev. Stat. 75 §122.]

125/23. Circuit court to ensure performance of grand jury duty; report.
§23. The circuit courts of the respective counties shall see that the grand jury or committee of citizens performs the duty imposed upon it by the preceding section, and the report being made, a copy thereof shall be transmitted by the clerk of the court to the county clerk, who shall lay the same before the county board at its next meeting.
(Source: P.A. 83-1073.) [Formerly Ill. Rev. Stat. 75 §123.]

125/25. Failure of Sheriff or superintendent to comply with Act.
§25. Any Sheriff or superintendent of the jail who shall fail or refuse to comply with the provisions of this Act shall be guilty of a petty offense and fined not exceeding $100.
(Source: P.A. 83-1073.) [Formerly Ill. Rev. Stat. 75 §125.]

COUNTY JAIL GOOD BEHAVIOR ALLOWANCE ACT

Sec.

130/1. Short title.
§1. This Act shall be known and may be cited as the "County Jail Good Behavior Allowance Act".
(Source: P.A. 83-1073.) [Formerly Ill. Rev. Stat. 75 §30.]

130/2. Definitions.
§2. For the purposes of this Act:

"Good behavior" means the compliance by a person with all rules and regulations of the institution and all laws of the State while confined in a county jail.

"Good behavior allowance" means the number of days awarded in diminution of sentence as a reward for good behavior.

"Date of sentence" means and includes the date of the calendar month on which the person commences to serve the sentence. If the sentence commences at midnight, date of sentence shall be the date of the day occurring one minute after midnight.

"Warden" means any sheriff or other police official charged with the duty of supervising and maintaining the confinement of prisoners.
(Source: P.A. 85-836.) [Formerly Ill. Rev. Stat. 75 §31.]

130/3. Rate; exceptions.
§3. The good behavior of any person who commences a sentence of confinement in a county jail for a fixed term of imprisonment after January 1, 1987 shall entitle such person to a good behavior allowance, except that: (1) a person who inflicted physical harm upon another person in committing the offense for which he is confined shall receive no good behavior allowance; and (2) a person sentenced for an offense for which the law provides a mandatory minimum sentence shall not receive any portion of a good behavior allowance that would

reduce the sentence below the mandatory minimum. The good behavior allowance provided for in this Section shall not apply to individuals sentenced for a felony to probation or conditional discharge where a condition of such probation or conditional discharge is that the individual serve a sentence of periodic imprisonment or to individuals sentenced under an order of court for civil contempt.

Such good behavior allowance shall be cumulative and awarded as provided in this Section.

The good behavior allowance rate shall be cumulative and awarded on the following basis:

The prisoner shall receive one day of good behavior allowance for each day of service of sentence in the county jail, and one day of good behavior allowance for each day of incarceration in the county jail before sentencing for the offense that he or she is currently serving sentence but was unable to post bail before sentencing, except that a prisoner serving a sentence of periodic imprisonment under Section 5-7-1 of the Unified Code of Corrections [730 ILCS 5/5-7-1] shall only be eligible to receive good behavior allowance if authorized by the sentencing judge. Each day of good behavior allowance shall reduce by one day the prisoner's period of incarceration set by the court. For the purpose of calculating a prisoner's good behavior allowance, a fractional part of a day shall not be calculated as a day of service of sentence in the county jail unless the fractional part of the day is over 12 hours in which case a whole day shall be credited on the good behavior allowance.

If consecutive sentences are served and the time served amounts to a total of one year or more, the good behavior allowance shall be calculated on a continuous basis throughout the entire time served beginning on the first date of sentence or incarceration, as the case may be.

(Chgd. by P.A. 87-1198, §5, eff. 9/25/92.)
(Source: P.A. 85-1209.) [Formerly Ill. Rev. Stat. 75 §32.]

130/3.1. Uniform rules and regulations.

§3.1. (a) Within 3 months after the effective date of this amendatory Act of 1986, the wardens who supervise institutions under this Act shall meet and agree upon uniform rules and regulations for behavior and conduct, penalties, and the awarding, denying and revocation of good behavior allowance, in such institutions; and such rules and regulations shall be immediately promulgated and consistent with the provisions of this Act. Interim rules shall be provided by each warden consistent with the provision of this Act and shall be effective until the promulgation of uniform rules. All disciplinary action shall be consistent with the provisions of this Act. Committed persons shall be informed of rules of behavior and conduct, the penalties for violation thereof, and the disciplinary procedure by which such penalties may be imposed. Any rules, penalties and procedures shall be posted and made available to the committed persons.

(b) Whenever a person is alleged to have violated a rule of behavior, a written report of the infraction shall be filed with the warden within 72 hours of the occurrence of the infraction or the discovery of it, and such report shall be placed in the file of the institution or facility. No disciplinary proceeding shall be commenced more than 8 days after the infraction or the discovery of it, unless the committed person is unable or unavailable for any reason to participate in the disciplinary proceeding.

(c) All or any of the good behavior allowance earned may be revoked by the warden, unless he initiates the charge, and in that case by the disciplinary board, for violations of rules of behavior at any time prior to discharge from the institution, consistent with the provisions of this Act.

(d) In disciplinary cases that may involve the loss of good behavior allowance or eligibility to earn good behavior allowance, the warden shall establish disciplinary procedures consistent with the following principles:

(1) The warden may establish one or more disciplinary boards, made up of one or more persons, to hear and determine charges. Any person who initiates a disciplinary charge against a committed person shall not serve on the disciplinary board that will determine the disposition of the charge. In those cases in which the charge was initiated by the warden, he shall establish a disciplinary board which will have the authority to impose any appropriate discipline.

(2) Any committed person charged with a violation of rules of behavior shall be given notice of the charge, including a statement of the misconduct alleged and of the rules this conduct is alleged to violate, no less than 24 hours before the disciplinary hearing.

(3) Any committed person charged with a violation of rules is entitled to a hearing on that charge, at which time he shall have an opportunity to appear before and address the warden or disciplinary board deciding the charge.

(4) The person or persons determining the disposition of the charge may also summon to testify any witnesses or other persons with relevant knowledge of the incident. The person charged may be permitted to question any person so summoned.

(5) If the charge is sustained, the person charged is entitled to a written statement, within 14 days after the hearing, of the decision by the warden or the disciplinary board which determined the disposition of the charge, and the statement shall include the basis for the decision and the disciplinary action, if any, to be imposed.

(6) The warden may impose the discipline recommended by the disciplinary board, or may reduce the discipline recommended; however, no committed person may be penalized more than 30 days of good behavior allowance for any one infraction.

(7) The warden, in appropriate cases, may restore good behavior allowance that has been revoked, suspended or reduced.

(Source: P.A. 84-1411.) [Formerly Ill. Rev. Stat. 75 §32.1.]

ILLINOIS PRISON INSPECTION ACT

135/1. Short title.

§1. This Act shall be known as the Illinois Prison Inspection Act.

(Source: P.A. 80-367.) [Formerly Ill. Rev. Stat. 38 §1101.]

135/2. Purpose.

§2. The purpose of this Act is to establish a procedure for the periodic inspection of state operated prison facilities with regard to sanitary conditions and medical facilities.

(Source: P.A. 80-367.) [Formerly Ill. Rev. Stat. 38 §1102.]

135/3. Annual inspections.

§3. The Illinois Department of Public Health may, with the cooperation of the Department of Corrections, inspect all institutional facilities of the Department of Corrections used to incarcerate committed persons and report to the

Director of Corrections as to the sanitary conditions and needs of the institutions and the medical facilities and services available.
(Source: P.A. 87-860.) [Formerly Ill. Rev. Stat. 38 §1103.]

135/4. Inspectors qualifications.

§4. All persons examining prison facilities shall have a familiarity with the prison standards promulgated by the federal and State governments and shall have a working knowledge of prison and institutional architecture and construction.
(Source: P.A. 80-367.) [Formerly Ill. Rev. Stat. 38 §1104.]

135/5. Notification prior to visitation.

§5. The Department of Public Health shall notify, at least 5 days prior to any intended examining visitation, the chairman of the Penal Subcommittee of the Committee to Visit and Examine State Institutions.

Inspections shall be made in the company of a designated representative of the Director of Corrections.

The report required by Section 3 of this Act [730 ILCS 135/3] shall be submitted only to the Director of Corrections, and shall be so submitted within 30 days of the completion of the examining visitation.
(Source: P.A. 80-367.) [Formerly Ill. Rev. Stat. 38 §1105.]

135/6. Minimum standards.

§6. The Department of Public Health shall establish by regulation minimum standards for water supply, sewage and solid waste disposal, food service sanitation, rodent and insect control, water hazards, first aid, and communicable disease control. The Department shall conduct public hearings on all such proposed standards and all amendments thereto. At least 20 days notice of the public hearings shall be given by the Department in such manner as the Department considers adequate to bring the hearings to the attention of all persons and State agencies interested in the standards. Written notice of any such public hearing shall be given by the Department to the Director of Corrections and to those who file a written request for a notice of any such hearings. Hearings shall be conducted by the Director of the Department of Public Health or a hearing officer designated in writing by the Director.

The Department shall develop the standards in cooperation with the Department of Corrections and shall consult with the Director of Corrections before adopting or amending the standards.
(Source: P.A. 81-646.) [Formerly Ill. Rev. Stat. 38 §1106.]

PRIVATE CORRECTIONAL FACILITY MORATORIUM ACT

Sec.

140/1. Short title.

§1. Short title. This Act shall be known and may be cited as the Private Correctional Facility Moratorium Act.
(Source: P.A. 86-1412.) [Formerly Ill. Rev. Stat. 38 §1581.]

140/2. Legislative findings.

§2. Legislative findings. The General Assembly hereby finds and declares that the management and operation of a correctional facility or institution involves functions that are inherently governmental. The imposition of punishment on errant citizens through incarceration requires the State to exercise its

coercive police powers over individuals and is thus distinguishable from privatization in other areas of government. It is further found that issues of liability, accountability and cost warrant a prohibition of the ownership, operation or management of correctional facilities by for-profit private contractors.
(Source: P.A. 86-1412.) [Formerly Ill. Rev. Stat. 38 §1582.]

140/3. Certain contracts prohibited.

§3. Certain contracts prohibited. After the effective date of this Act, the State shall not contract with a private contractor or private vendor for the provision of services relating to the operation of a correctional facility or the incarceration of persons in the custody of the Department of Corrections; however, this Act does not apply to State work release centers operated in whole or part by private contractors or to contracts for ancillary services, including medical services, educational services, repair and maintenance contracts, or other services not directly related to the ownership, management or operation of security services in a correctional facility.
(Source: P.A. 86-1412.) [Formerly Ill. Rev. Stat. 38 §1583.]

140/4. Applicability.

§4. Applicability. In case of any conflict between this Act and any other law, this Act shall control.
(Source: P.A. 86-1412.) [Formerly Ill. Rev. Stat. 38 §1584.]

ILLINOIS SUBSTANCE ABUSE TREATMENT PROGRAM

145/1. Short title.

§1. Short Title. This Act shall be known and may be cited as the Illinois Substance Abuse Treatment Program.
(Source: P.A. 86-1320.) [Formerly Ill. Rev. Stat. 38 §1531.]

145/2. Purpose.

§2. Purpose. The Substance Abuse Treatment Program shall be established as a one year pilot project to be instituted within the Illinois Department of Corrections in an effort to assist inmates in their rehabilitation from illicit drug and alcohol abuse.
(Source: P.A. 86-1320.) [Formerly Ill. Rev. Stat. 38 §1532.]

145/3. Program.

§3. Program. The program shall include a thirty day treatment program of highly structured activities to instruct the substance abuser in healthy living skills, dynamics of substance abuse patterns and personalities, and to aid the abuser in a personal inventory of patterns. Peer counselors shall be active in providing support and assistance to the inmates participating in this program. Peer counselors must have successfully graduated from the program demonstrating exceptional participation and healthy leadership ability. Inmates who successfully complete all assignments within the program will be considered graduates. Each graduate will be awarded a Certificate of Achievement and a Guides for Better Living Certificate.
(Source: P.A. 86-1320.) [Formerly Ill. Rev. Stat. 38 §1533.]

145/4. Power of Department.

§4. Power of Department. The Department of Corrections shall have the authority to promulgate such rules and regulations as the Director deems necessary to carry out the purposes of this Act.
(Source: P.A. 86-1320.) [Formerly Ill. Rev. Stat. 38 §1534.]

145/5. Funding.

§5. Funding. The Funding for this program shall be from funds appropriated to the Department of Corrections for this purpose.
(Source: P.A. 86-1320.) [Formerly Ill. Rev. Stat. 38 §1535.]

CHILD SEX OFFENDER REGISTRATION ACT

(Chgd. by P.A. 87-1064, §2, eff. 1/1/93.)

150/1. Short title.

§1. Short title. This Article shall be known and may be cited as the Child Sex Offender Registration Act.
(Chgd. by P.A. 87-1064, §1, eff. 1/1/93.)
(Source: P.A. 84-1279.) [Formerly Ill. Rev. Stat. 38 §221.]

150/2. Definitions.

§2. Definitions. As used in this Article, the following definitions apply:

(A) "Child sex offender" includes any person who, after July 1, 1986, is convicted a second or subsequent time for any of the sex offenses or attempts to commit any of the offenses set forth in subsection (B) of this Section or any person who after the effective date of this amendatory Act of 1992 is convicted for any of the sex offenses or attempts to commit any of the offenses set forth in subsection (B) of this Section. Upon conviction the court shall certify that the person is a "child sex offender" and shall include the certification in the order of commitment. Convictions that result from or are connected with the same act, or result from offenses committed at the same time, shall be counted for the purpose of this Article as one conviction. Any conviction set aside pursuant to law is not a conviction for purposes of this Article.

(B) As used in this Section, "sex offense" means:

(1) A violation of any of the following Sections of the Criminal Code of 1961 [720 ILCS 5/1-1 et seq.] when the victim is under 18 years of age:

12-13 (criminal sexual assault),
12-14 (aggravated criminal sexual assault),
12-15 (criminal sexual abuse when the offense is a felony),
12-16 (aggravated criminal sexual abuse).

(2) A violation of any former law of this State substantially equivalent to any offense listed in subsection (B)(1) of this Section.

(C) A conviction before the effective date of this amendatory Act of 1992, for an offense of the law of another state that is substantially equivalent to any offense listed in subsection (B)(1) of this Section shall constitute a first conviction for the purpose of this Article.

(D) As used in this Article, "law enforcement agency having jurisdiction" means the Chief of Police in the municipality in which the offender expects to reside upon his discharge, parole or release, or the Sheriff of the county, in the event no Police Chief exists or if the offender intends to reside in an unincorporated area.
(Chgd. by P.A. 87-1064, §1, eff. 1/1/93.)
(Source: P.A. 87-457.) [Formerly Ill. Rev. Stat. 38 §222.]

150/3. Duty to register.

§3. Duty to register. Any child sex offender shall within 30 days of his coming into any county in which he resides or is temporarily domiciled for more than 30 days, register with the chief of police of the municipality in which he resides, or in the event no police chief exists or if he resides in an unincorporated area he shall register with the sheriff of the county.
(Chgd. by P.A. 87-1064, §1, eff. 1/1/93.)
(Source: P.A. 84-1279.) [Formerly Ill. Rev. Stat. 38 §223.]

150/4. Discharge of child sex offender from penal institution; duties of official in charge.

§4. Discharge of child sex offender from penal institution; duties of official in charge. Any child sex offender, as defined by this Article, who is discharged or paroled from a prison, hospital or other institution or facility where he was confined because of a conviction of one of the offenses defined in subsection (B) of Section 2 of this Article [730 ILCS 150/2], shall prior to discharge, parole or release, be informed of his duty to register under this Article, by the facility in which he was confined.

The facility shall require the person to read and sign such form as may be required by the Department of State Police stating that the duty to register and the procedure for registration has been explained to him. The facility shall obtain the address where the person expects to reside upon his discharge, parole or release and shall report the address to the Department of State Police. The facility shall give one copy of the form to the person and shall send two copies to the Department of State Police which shall forward one copy to the law enforcement agency having jurisdiction where the person expects to reside upon his discharge, parole or release.
(Chgd. by P.A. 87-1064, §1, eff. 1/1/93.)
(Source: P.A. 84-1279.) [Formerly Ill. Rev. Stat. 38 §224.]

150/5. Release of child sex offender; duties of the Court.

§5. Release of child sex offender; duties of the Court. Any child sex offender, as defined by this Article, who is released on probation or discharged upon payment of a fine because of the commission or attempt to commit one of the offenses defined in subsection (B) of Section 2 of this Article [730 ILCS 150/2], shall, prior to such release be informed of his duty to register under this Article by the Court in which he was convicted. The Court shall require the person to read and sign such form as may be required by the Department of State Police stating that the duty to register and the procedure for registration has been explained to him. The Court shall obtain the address where the person expects to reside upon his release, and shall report the address to the Department of State Police. The Court shall give one copy of the form to the person and shall send two copies to the Department of State Police which shall forward one copy to the law enforcement agency having jurisdiction where the person expects to reside upon his release.
(Chgd. by P.A. 87-1064, §1, eff. 1/1/93.)
(Source: P.A. 84-1279.) [Formerly Ill. Rev. Stat. 38 §225.]

150/6. Change of address; duty to inform.

§6. Change of address; duty to inform. If any person required to register under this Article changes his residence address, he shall inform the law enforcement agency with whom he last registered of his new address, in writing, within 10 days. The law enforcement agency shall, within 3 days of receipt, forward the information to the Department of State Police and to the law enforcement agency having jurisdiction of the new place of residence.
(Source: P.A. 84-1279.) [Formerly Ill. Rev. Stat. 38 §226.]

150/7. Duration of registration.

§7. Duration of registration. Any person required to register under this Article shall be required to register for a period of 10 years after conviction if not confined to a penal institution, hospital or any other institution or facility, and if confined, for a period of 10 years after parole, discharge or release from any such facility. Liability for registration terminates at the expiration of 10 years from the date of conviction if not confined to a penal institution, hospital or any other institution or facility and if confined, at the expiration of 10 years from the date of parole, discharge or release from any such facility, providing such convicted child sex offender does not, during that period, again become liable to register under the provisions of this Article.
(Chgd. by P.A. 87-1064, §1, eff. 1/1/93.)
(Source: P.A. 84-1279.) [Formerly Ill. Rev. Stat. 38 §227.]

150/8. Registration requirements.

§8. Registration Requirements. Registration as required by this Article shall consist of a statement in writing signed by the person giving the information that is required by the Department of State Police, which may include the fingerprints and photograph of the person. Within 3 days, the registering law enforcement agency shall forward the statement and any other required information to the Department of State Police and the Department shall enter the information into the Law Enforcement Agencies Data System (LEADS) as provided in Sections 6 and 7 of the Intergovernmental Missing Child Recovery Act of 1984 [325 ILCS 40/6 and 40/7].
(Chgd. by P.A. 87-1065, §2, eff. 9/13/92.)
(Source: P.A. 84-1279.) [Formerly Ill. Rev. Stat. 38 §228.]

150/9. Public inspection of registration data prohibited.

§9. Public inspection of registration data prohibited. The statements or any other information required by this Article shall not be open to inspection by the public, or by any person other than by a law enforcement officer or other individual as may be authorized by law. It is a Class B misdemeanor to permit the unauthorized release of any information required by this Article.
(Source: P.A. 84-1279.) [Formerly Ill. Rev. Stat. 38 §229.]

150/10. Penalty.

§10. Penalty. Any person who is required to register under this Article who violates any of the provisions thereof is guilty of a Class A misdemeanor.
(Source: P.A. 84-1279.) [Formerly Ill. Rev. Stat. 38 §230.]

PRISONER INTERCHANGE ACT

Sec.

155/0.01. Short title.

§0.01. Short title. This Act may be cited as the Prisoner Interchange Act.
(Source: P.A. 86-1324.) [Formerly Ill. Rev. Stat. 75 §60.]

155/1. Recommitment—Authority; records.

§1. The warden or superintendent of any penal institution in any county, township, city, village or incorporated town to which prisoners have been committed for imprisonment for conviction of misdemeanors or for nonpayment of fines for violation of state law, ordinance, resolution, rule or regulation of a township, city, village or incorporated town may recommit such prisoners to confinement in any other penal institution in the county in which, by contract or otherwise, such prisoners may be held, but only with the consent of the warden or superintendent of the other penal institution. In making such recommitment the warden or superintendent shall take into consideration the nature of the offense, the character of the offender, whether the offender should be held under maximum security conditions and any other condition pertinent to such decision. The warden or superintendent may recommit prisoners committed to his institution to be confined in another penal institution in which he may hold prisoners when in his judgment, such recommitment will be beneficial to the welfare or rehabilitation of the prisoner or is desirable to relieve overcrowding in any such penal institution.

Appropriate records of such recommitments shall be kept by the wardens or superintendents of both penal institutions. Such recommitments shall not operate to lengthen or shorten the term of imprisonment of prisoners.
(Source: Laws 1965, p. 472.) [Formerly Ill. Rev. Stat. 75 §61.]

INDUSTRIAL SCHOOLS FOR GIRLS ACT

160/0.01. Short title.

§0.01. Short title. This Act may be cited as the Industrial Schools for Girls Act.
(Source: P.A. 86-1324.) [Formerly Ill. Rev. Stat. 122 §645.9.]

160/1. Incorporation.

§1. Any seven or more persons, residents of this state, a majority of whom are women, who may organize, or have organized, under the general laws of the state, relating to corporations, for the purpose of establishing, maintaining and carrying on an Industrial School for Girls, shall have under the corporate names assumed, all the powers, rights and privileges of corporations of this state, not for pecuniary profit, and shall be, and hereby are exempted from all state and local taxes: Provided, however, that any persons organized, or who may hereafter organize as above set forth, desiring to avail themselves of the provisions of this act, shall first obtain the consent of the Governor thereto, in writing, which consent must be filed in the office of the Secretary of State.
(Source: Laws 1879, p. 309.) [Formerly Ill. Rev. Stat. 122 §646.]

160/1a. Commitment in accordance with Juvenile Court Act.

§1a. Dependent and neglected girls committed to an industrial school for girls shall be committed in accordance with the provisions of the Juvenile Court Act of 1987 [705 ILCS 405/1-1 et seq.].
(Source: P.A. 85-1209.) [Formerly Ill. Rev. Stat. 122 §646a.]

160/2. Purpose; maintenance.

§2. The object of Industrial Schools for Girls shall be to provide a home and proper training for such girls as may be committed to their charge; and they shall be maintained by voluntary contributions, excepting as hereinafter provided.
(Source: Laws 1879, p. 309.) [Formerly Ill. Rev. Stat. 122 §647.]

160/8. Conveyance fees.

§8. The fees for conveying a dependent girl to an Industrial School for Girls, shall be the same as for conveying a juvenile offender to the Reform School for Juvenile Offenders, at Pontiac, in this state, and they shall be paid by the counties from which such dependent girls are sent, unless they are paid by the parent or guardian.
(Source: Laws 1879, p. 309.) [Formerly Ill. Rev. Stat. 122 §653.]

160/9. Payment of expenses.

§9. For the tuition, maintenance and care of dependent and neglected girls committed to an industrial school for girls, the county from which they are sent may pay to the industrial school for girls, to which they may be committed, such amount of money per month as may be necessary for each dependent or neglected girl under the age of 18 years so committed; and upon the proper officer rendering proper accounts therefor, monthly, the county board shall allow and order the same paid out of the county treasury. However, no charges shall be made against any county by any industrial school for girls on account of any dependent or neglected girl in the care thereof, who has been by such school put out to a trade or employment in the manner hereinafter provided. Payments by the county to industrial schools for girls under this section shall qualify for partial reimbursement from the State in the manner and to the extent provided in Sections 6-7 through 6-11 of the Juvenile Court Act of 1987 [705 ILCS 405/6-7 through 405/6-11].
(Source: P.A. 85-1209.) [Formerly Ill. Rev. Stat. 122 §654.]

160/10. Duties of officers and trustees.

§10. The officers and trustees of any Industrial School for Girls in this state, shall receive into such school all girls committed thereto under the provisions of this act, and shall have the exclusive custody, care and guardianship of such girls. They shall provide for their support and comfort; instruct them in such branches of useful knowledge as may be suited to their years and capacities, and shall cause them to be taught in domestic avocations, such as sewing, knitting, and housekeeping in all its departments. And for the purpose of their education and training, and that they may assist in their own support, they shall be required to pursue such tasks suitable to their years and sex, as may be prescribed by such officers and trustees.
(Source: Laws 1879, p. 309.) [Formerly Ill. Rev. Stat. 122 §655.]

160/11. Placement in private home; adoption.

§11. Any girl committed under the provisions of this act to an Industrial School for Girls may, by the officers and trustees of said school, be placed in the home of any good citizen upon such terms and for such purpose and time, not beyond her minority, as may be agreed upon, or she may be given to any suitable person of good character who will adopt her. The officers and trustees shall have a supervising care over such girl to see that she is properly treated and cared

for; and in case such girl is cruelly treated, or is neglected, or the terms upon which she was committed to the care and protection of any person are not observed, or in case such care and protection shall for any reason cease, then such officers and trustees shall take and receive such girl again into the custody, care and protection of the industrial school.
(Source: Laws 1951, p. 1203.) [Formerly Ill. Rev. Stat. 122 §656.]

160/12. Restriction on admissions.
§12. No imbecile, or idiot girl, or one incapacitated for labor, nor any girl having any infectious, contagious or incurable disease, shall be committed or received into any industrial school for girls in this state.
(Source: Laws 1879, p. 309.) [Formerly Ill. Rev. Stat. 122 §657.]

160/13. Discharge.
§13. Any girl committed to an Industrial School for Girls, under the provisions of this act, may be discharged therefrom at any time, in accordance with the rules thereof, when in the judgment of the officers and trustees, the good of the girl or the good of the school, would be promoted by such discharge, and the Governor may at any time order the discharge of any girl committed to an industrial school under the provisions of this act.
(Source: Laws 1879, p. 309.) [Formerly Ill. Rev. Stat. 122 §658.]

160/14. Inspection, etc. by Department of Children and Family Services.
§14. All industrial schools for girls in this state shall be subject to the same visitation, inspection and supervision of the Department of Children and Family Services, as the charitable and penal institutions of the state, and avoiding as far as practicable, sectarianism, suitable provisions shall be made for the moral and religious instruction of the inmates of all such schools. No such industrial school shall receive an appropriation from the state for any purpose, and any school receiving an appropriation from the state shall not have the benefit of this act.
(Source: Laws 1963, p. 1049.) [Formerly Ill. Rev. Stat. 122 §659.]

160/15. Court-ordered discharge.
§15. The court which committed any girl to a training school under this Act may order the discharge of the girl or her restoration to her parents upon a showing that the welfare of the girl will be best promoted by her discharge from the school. The president of the school where the girl is confined must be notified of the application for discharge and may appear and resist the same.
Appeals may be taken from all final orders made by the court under this Act as in other cases.
(Source: P.A. 76-1378.) [Formerly Ill. Rev. Stat. 122 §660.]

TRAINING SCHOOLS FOR BOYS ACT

Sec.

165/0.01. Short title.

§0.01. Short title. This Act may be cited as the Training Schools for Boys Act.

(Source: P.A. 86-1324.) [Formerly Ill. Rev. Stat. 122 §660.9.]

165/1. Incorporation.

§1. Any seven or more persons, residents of this state, who may organize, or have organized, under the general laws of the state, relating to corporations, for the purpose of establishing, maintaining and carrying on a training school for boys, shall have, under the corporate name assumed, all the powers, rights and privileges of corporations of this state, not for pecuniary profit: Provided, however, that any persons organized, or who may hereafter organize as above set forth desiring to avail themselves of the provisions of this act, shall first obtain the consent of the Governor thereto, in writing, which consent must be filed in the office of the Secretary of State.

(Source: Laws 1883, p. 168.) [Formerly Ill. Rev. Stat. 122 §661.]

165/1a. Commitment in accordance with Juvenile Court Act.

§1a. Any dependent and neglected boys committed to a training school for boys shall be committed in accordance with the provisions of the Juvenile Court Act of 1987 [705 ILCS 405/1-1 et seq.].

(Source: P.A. 85-1209.) [Formerly Ill. Rev. Stat. 122 §661a.]

165/2. Purpose; maintenance.

§2. The object of training schools for boys shall be to provide a home and proper training school for such boys as may be committed to their charge; and they shall be maintained by voluntary contributions, excepting as hereinafter provided.

(Source: Laws 1883, p. 168.) [Formerly Ill. Rev. Stat. 122 §662.]

165/8. Conveyance fees.

§8. The fees for conveying a dependent boy to a training school for boys shall be the same as for conveying a juvenile offender to the reform school for juvenile offenders at Pontiac, in this state, and they shall be paid by the counties from which such dependent boys are sent, unless they are paid by the parent or guardian.

(Source: Laws 1883, p. 168.) [Formerly Ill. Rev. Stat. 122 §668.]

165/9. Payment of expenses.

§9. For clothing, tuition, maintenance and care of dependent and neglected boys, the county from which they are sent may pay the training school for boys to which they may be committed, as follows: For each dependent such amount of money per month as may be necessary, but no boy shall be committed whose age is over 17 years; and upon the proper officer rendering proper accounts therefor, monthly, the county board shall allow and order the same paid out of the county treasury. However, no charge shall be made against any county by any training school for boys on account of any dependent or neglected boy in the care thereof who has been by such school put out to trade or employment, or for adoption, after he has been, and as long as he remains so put out. Payments by the county to training schools for boys under this Section qualify for partial reimbursement from the State as provided in Sections 6-7 through 6-11 of the Juvenile Court Act of 1987 [705 ILCS 405/6-7 through 405/6-11].

(Source: P.A. 85-1209.) [Formerly Ill. Rev. Stat. 122 §669.]

165/10. Duties of officers and managers.

§10. The officers and managers of any training school for boys in this state shall receive into such school all boys not idiotic and not afflicted with a

contagious disease committed thereto under the provisions of this act, shall have the exclusive custody, care and guardianship of such boys, shall provide for their support and comfort, instruct them in such branches of useful knowledge as may be suited to their years and capacities, and shall cause them to be taught or trained in some trade or industrial pursuit. And for the purpose of their education and training, and that they may assist in their own support, they shall be required to perform such tasks suitable to their years and sex as may be prescribed by such officers and managers, and as may be reasonable and proper.
(Source: Laws 1883, p. 168.) [Formerly Ill. Rev. Stat. 122 §670.]

165/11. Placement in private home; adoption.

§11. Any boy committed under the provisions of this act to a training school for boys may, by the officers and managers of said school, be placed in the home of any good citizen, upon such terms and for such purpose and time, not beyond his minority, as may be agreed upon, or he may be given to any suitable person of good character who will adopt him. The officers and managers shall have a supervising care over such boy after he shall be so put out to see that he is properly treated and cared for; and, in case such boy is cruelly treated, or is neglected, or the terms upon which he shall have been put out to any person be not observed, then such officers and managers shall take such boy again into the custody, care and protection of the training school. And the officers and managers may reclaim any boy so put out, without the consent of the person to whom the boy was so put out, whenever, in the judgment of said officers and managers, the boy shall be cruelly treated, neglected in training, proper instruction or otherwise, or not properly cared for.
(Source: Laws 1951, p. 1203.) [Formerly Ill. Rev. Stat. 122 §671.]

165/12. Discharge.

§12. Any boy committed to a training school for boys, under the provisions of this act, may be discharged therefrom at any time in accordance with the rules thereof when, in the judgment of the officers and managers, the good of the boy or the good of the school would be promoted by such discharge, and the Governor may at any time order the discharge of any boy committed to a training school under the provisions of this act.
(Source: Laws 1883, p. 168.) [Formerly Ill. Rev. Stat. 122 §672.]

165/13. Inspection, etc. by Department of Children and Family Services.

§13. All training schools for boys in this state organized under this act shall be subject to the same visitation, inspection and supervision of the Department of Children and Family Services as the charitable institutions of the state.
(Source: Laws 1963, p. 1052.) [Formerly Ill. Rev. Stat. 122 §673.]

165/14. Court-ordered discharge.

§14. The court committing any boy to a training school under this act has power after making such commitment, upon proper showing, to order the discharge of the boy or his restoration to his parents. The court also has power to make all orders relative to boys committed by the court in order to apply the benefits of this act to the boys. Appeals may be taken from all final orders made by the court under this act as in other cases.
(Source: P.A. 76-1377.) [Formerly Ill. Rev. Stat. 122 §674.]

ALTERNATIVE SENTENCING JOB TRAINING ACT

170/1. Short title.

§1. Short title. This Act may be cited as the Alternative Sentencing Job Training Act.
(Source: P.A. 87-648.) [Formerly Ill. Rev. Stat. 38 §1541-1.]

170/5. Finding.

§5. Finding. The Legislature finds that throughout the State there are areas in which overcrowding in county jails exist* as well as similar problems in the State correctional facilities, at the same time, many communities have a problem with deteriorating housing that with adequate repair and restoration could be used as housing for the homeless and low income families as transitional accommodations.
**So in original. Probably should be "exists".*
(Source: P.A. 87-648.) [Formerly Ill. Rev. Stat. 38 §1541-5.]

170/10. Authority.

§10. Authority. The Department of Corrections may enter into joint contracts with county, units of local government and non-profit housing development corporations to develop job training programs to rehabilitate houses. These rehabilitated houses may be used as transitional housing for homeless and low income citizens in areas where there exists severe housing shortages or deterioration of housing in a community.
(Source: P.A. 87-648.) [Formerly Ill. Rev. Stat. 38 §1541-10.]

170/15. Administrative rules; violent crime offenders ineligible.

§15. Administrative rules; violent crime offenders ineligible. The Director of the Department of Corrections and the Director of Labor shall develop by rule the criteria for selection of the participants of the program in conjunction with and approval by the sentencing court. Violent crime offenders are not eligible to participate in the program.
(Source: P.A. 87-648.) [Formerly Ill. Rev. Stat. 38 §1541-15.]

This page intentionally left blank.

CHAPTER 735
CIVIL PROCEDURE

CODE OF CIVIL PROCEDURE

ARTICLE X. HABEAS CORPUS

5/10-101. Action commenced by plaintiff.

§10-101. Action commenced by plaintiff. In all proceedings commenced under Article X of this Act, the name of the person seeking the relief afforded by this Article shall be set out as plaintiff without the use of the phrase "People ex rel." or "People on the relation of".
(Source: P.A. 82-280.) [Formerly Ill. Rev. Stat. 110 §10-101.]

5/10-102. Who may file.

§10-102. Who may file. Every person imprisoned or otherwise restrained of his or her liberty, except as herein otherwise provided, may apply for habeas corpus in the manner provided in Article X of this Act, to obtain relief from such imprisonment or restraint, if it prove to be unlawful.
(Source: P.A. 82-280.) [Formerly Ill. Rev. Stat. 110 §10-102.]

5/10-103. Application.

§10-103. Application. Application for the relief shall be made to the Supreme Court or to the circuit court of the county in which the person in whose behalf the application is made, is imprisoned or restrained, or to the circuit court of the county from which such person was sentenced or committed.

Application shall be made by complaint signed by the person for whose relief it is intended, or by some person in his or her behalf, and verified by affidavit.
(Source: P.A. 82-280.) [Formerly Ill. Rev. Stat. 110 §10-103.]

5/10-104. Substance of complaint.

§10-104. Substance of complaint. The complaint shall state in substance:

1. That the person in whose behalf the relief is applied for is imprisoned or restrained of his or her liberty, and the place where—naming all the parties if they are known, or describing them if they are not known.

2. The cause or pretense of the restraint, according to the best knowledge and belief of the applicant, and that such person is not committed or detained by virtue of any process, or judgment, specified in Section 10-123 of this Act.

3. If the commitment or restraint is by virtue of any warrant or process, a copy thereof shall be annexed, or it shall be stated that by reason of such prisoner being removed or concealed before application, a demand of such copy could not be made, or that such demand was made, and the legal fees therefor tendered to the officer or person having such prisoner in his or her custody, and that such copy was refused.
(Source: P.A. 82-280.) [Formerly Ill. Rev. Stat. 110 §10-104.]

5/10-105. Copy of process.

§10-105. Copy of process. Any sheriff or other officer or person having custody of any prisoner committed on any civil or criminal process of any court who shall neglect to give such prisoner a copy of the process or order of commitment by which he or she is imprisoned within 6 hours after demand made by the prisoner, or any one on behalf of the prisoner, shall forfeit to the prisoner or party affected not exceeding $500. This Section shall not apply to the Illinois Department of Corrections.
(Source: P.A. 85-907.) [Formerly Ill. Rev. Stat. 110 §10-105.]

5/10-106. Grant of relief—Penalty.

§10-106. Grant of relief—Penalty. Unless it shall appear from the complaint itself, or from the documents thereto annexed, that the party can neither be discharged, admitted to bail nor otherwise relieved, the court shall forthwith award relief by habeas corpus. Any judge empowered to grant relief by habeas corpus who shall corruptly refuse to grant the relief when legally applied for in a case where it may lawfully be granted, or who shall for the purpose of oppression unreasonably delay the granting of such relief shall, for every such offense, forfeit to the prisoner or party affected a sum not exceeding $1,000.
(Source: P.A. 83-707.) [Formerly Ill. Rev. Stat. 110 §10-106.]

5/10-107. Form of orders.

§10-107. Form of orders. If the relief is allowed by an order of a court it shall be certified by the clerk under the seal of the court; if by a judge, it shall be under the judge's signature, and shall be directed to the person in whose custody or under whose restraint the prisoner is, and may be substantially in the following form: The People of the State of Illinois, to the Sheriff of .... county (or, "to A B," as the case may be):

You are hereby commanded to have the body of C D, imprisoned and detained by you, together with the time and cause of such imprisonment and detention by whatsoever name C D is called or charged, before .... court of .... County (or before E F, judge of, etc.), at, etc., immediately after being served with a certified copy of this order, to be dealt with according to law; and you are to deliver a certified copy of this order with a return thereon of your performance in carrying out this order.
(Source: P.A. 83-707.) [Formerly Ill. Rev. Stat. 110 §10-107.]

5/10-108. Indorsement.

§10-108. Indorsement. With the intent that no officer or person to whom such order is directed may pretend ignorance thereof, every such order shall be indorsed with these words: "By the habeas corpus law."
(Source: P.A. 82-280.) [Formerly Ill. Rev. Stat. 110 §10-108.]

5/10-109. Subpoena—Service.

§10-109. Subpoena—Service. When the party has been committed upon a criminal charge, unless the court deems it unnecessary, a subpoena shall also be issued to summon the witnesses whose names have been endorsed upon the warrant of commitment, to appear before such court at the time and place when and where such order of habeas corpus is returnable, and it shall be the duty of the sheriff, or other officer to whom the subpoena is issued, to serve the same, if it is possible, in time to enable such witnesses to attend.
(Source: P.A. 82-280.) [Formerly Ill. Rev. Stat. 110 §10-109.]

5/10-110. Service of order.

§10-110. Service of order. The habeas corpus order may be served by the sheriff, coroner or any person appointed for that purpose by the court which entered the order; if served by a person not an officer, he or she shall have the same power, and be liable to the same penalty for non-performance of his or her duty, as though he or she were sheriff.
(Source: P.A. 83-707.) [Formerly Ill. Rev. Stat. 110 §10-110.]

5/10-111. Manner of service.

§10-111. Manner of service. Service shall be made by leaving a copy of the order with the person to whom it is directed, or with any of his or her under officers who may be at the place where the prisoner is detained; or if he or she can not be found, or has not the person imprisoned or restrained in custody, the service may be made upon any person who has the person in custody with the same effect as though he or she had been made a defendant therein.
(Source: P.A. 82-280.) [Formerly Ill. Rev. Stat. 110 §10-111.]

5/10-112. Expense involved.

§10-112. Expense involved. When the person confined or restrained is in the custody of a civil officer, the court entering the order shall certify thereon the sum to be paid for the expense of bringing the person from the place of imprisonment, not exceeding 10 cents per mile, and the officer shall not be bound to obey it unless the sum so certified is paid or tendered to him or her, and security is given to pay the charges of carrying the party back if he or she should be remanded. If the court is satisfied that the party so confined or restrained is a poor person and unable to pay such expense, then the court shall so state in the order, and in such case no tender or payment of expenses need be made or security given but the officer shall be bound to obey such order.
(Source: P.A. 82-280.) [Formerly Ill. Rev. Stat. 110 §10-112.]

5/10-113. Form of return.

§10-113. Form of return. The officer or person upon whom such order is served shall state in his or her return, plainly and unequivocally:

1. Whether he or she has or has not the party in his or her custody or control, or under his or her restraint, and if he or she has not, whether he or she has had the party in his or her custody or control, or under his or her restraint, at any and what time prior or subsequent to the date of the order.
2. If he or she has the party in his or her custody or control, or under his or her restraint, the authority and true cause of such imprisonment or restraint, setting forth the same in detail.

3. If the party is detained by virtue of any order, warrant or other written authority, a copy thereof shall be attached to the return, and the original shall be produced and exhibited on the return of the order to the court before whom the same is returnable.

4. If the person upon whom the order is served has had the party in his or her custody or control or under his or her restraint, at any time prior or subsequent to the date of the order but has transferred such custody or restraint to another, the return shall state particularly to whom, at what time, for what cause and by what authority such transfer took place. The return shall be signed by the person making the same, and except where such person is a sworn public officer and makes the return in his or her official capacity, it shall be verified by oath.

(Source: P.A. 82-280.) [Formerly Ill. Rev. Stat. 110 §10-113.]

5/10-114. Bringing of body.

§10-114. Bringing of body. The officer or person making the return, shall, at the same time, bring the body of the party, if in his or her custody or power or under his or her restraint, according to the command of the order unless prevented by the sickness or infirmity of the party.

(Source: P.A. 82-280.) [Formerly Ill. Rev. Stat. 110 §10-114.]

5/10-115. Sickness or infirmity.

§10-115. Sickness or infirmity. When, from the sickness or infirmity of the party, he or she cannot without danger, be brought to the place designated for the return of the order, that fact shall be stated in the return, and if it is proved to the satisfaction of the judge, he or she may proceed to the jail or other place where the party is confined, and there make an examination, or the judge may adjourn the same to such other time, or make such other order in the case as law and justice require.

(Source: P.A. 82-280.) [Formerly Ill. Rev. Stat. 110 §10-115.]

5/10-116. Neglect to obey order.

§10-116. Neglect to obey order. If the officer or person upon whom such order is served refuses or neglects to obey the same, by producing the party named in the order and making a full and explicit return thereto within the time required by Article X of this Act, and no sufficient excuse is shown for such refusal or neglect, the court before whom the order is returnable, upon proof of the service thereof, shall enforce obedience by attachment as for contempt, and the officer or person so refusing or neglecting shall forfeit to the party a sum not exceeding $500, and be incapable of holding office.

(Source: P.A. 82-280.) [Formerly Ill. Rev. Stat. 110 §10-116.]

5/10-117. Order in case of neglect.

§10-117. Order in case of neglect. The court may also, at the same time or afterwards, enter an order to the sheriff or other person to whom such attachment is directed, commanding him or her to bring forthwith before the court the party for whose benefit the habeas corpus order was entered, who shall thereafter remain in the custody of such sheriff, or other person, until the party is discharged, bailed or remanded, as the court directs.

(Source: P.A. 82-280.) [Formerly Ill. Rev. Stat. 110 §10-117.]

5/10-118. Proceedings in case of emergency.

§10-118. Proceedings in case of emergency. Whenever it appears by the complaint, or by affidavit, that any one is illegally held in custody or restraint, and that there is good reason to believe that such person will be taken out of the jurisdiction of the court in which the application for a habeas corpus is made, or will suffer some irreparable injury before compliance with the order can be

enforced, the court may enter an order directed to the sheriff or other proper officer, commanding him or her to take the prisoner thus held in custody or restraint, and forthwith bring him or her before the court to be dealt with according to law. The court may also, if it is deemed necessary, order the apprehension of the person charged with causing the illegal restraint. The officer shall execute the order by bringing the person therein named before the court, and the like return and proceedings shall be had as in other orders of habeas corpus.
(Source: P.A. 83-707.) [Formerly Ill. Rev. Stat. 110 §10-118.]

5/10-119. Examination.
§10-119. Examination. Upon the return of an order of habeas corpus, the court shall, without delay, proceed to examine the cause of the imprisonment or restraint, but the examination may be adjourned from time to time as circumstances require.
(Source: P.A. 82-280.) [Formerly Ill. Rev. Stat. 110 §10-119.]

5/10-120. Denial of allegations in return.
§10-120. Denial of allegations in return. The party imprisoned or restrained may file a reply to the return and deny any of the material facts set forth in the return, and may allege any other facts that may be material in the case, which denial or allegation shall be on oath; and the court shall proceed promptly to examine the cause of the imprisonment or restraint, hear the evidence produced by any person interested or authorized to appear, both in support of such imprisonment or restraint and against it, and thereupon shall determine the matter according to law.
(Source: P.A. 82-280.) [Formerly Ill. Rev. Stat. 110 §10-120.]

5/10-121. Seeking wrong remedy not fatal.
§10-121. Seeking wrong remedy not fatal. Where relief is sought under Article X of this Act and the court determines, on motion directed to the pleadings, or on motion for summary judgment or upon trial, that the plaintiff has pleaded or established facts which entitle the plaintiff to relief but that the plaintiff has sought the wrong remedy, the court shall permit the pleadings to be amended, on just and reasonable terms, and the court shall grant the relief to which the plaintiff is entitled on the amended pleadings or upon the evidence. In considering whether a proposed amendment is just and reasonable, the court shall consider the right of the defendant to assert additional defenses, to demand a trial by jury, to plead a counterclaim or third party complaint, and to order the plaintiff to take additional steps which were not required under the pleadings as previously filed.
(Source: P.A. 82-280.) [Formerly Ill. Rev. Stat. 110 §10-121.]

5/10-122. Amendments.
§10-122. Amendments. The return, as well as any denial or allegation, may be amended at any time by leave of the court.
(Source: P.A. 82-280.) [Formerly Ill. Rev. Stat. 110 §10-122.]

5/10-123. When prisoner not entitled to discharge.
§10-123. When prisoner not entitled to discharge. No person shall be discharged under the provisions of this Act, if he or she is in custody:

1. By virtue of process of any court of the United States, in a case where such court has exclusive jurisdiction; or,
2. By virtue of a final judgment of any circuit court, or of any proceeding for the enforcement of such judgment, unless the time during which such party may be legally detained has expired; or,

3. For any treason, felony or other crime committed in any other state or territory of the United States, for which such person ought, by the Constitution and laws of the United States, to be delivered to the executive power of such state or territory.
(Source: P.A. 82-280.) [Formerly Ill. Rev. Stat. 110 §10-123.]

5/10-124. Causes for discharge when in custody on process of court.
§10-124. Causes for discharge when in custody on process of court. If it appears that the prisoner is in custody by virtue of process from any court legally constituted, he or she may be discharged only for one or more of the following causes:

1. Where the court has exceeded the limit of its jurisdiction, either as to the matter, place, sum or person.
2. Where, though the original imprisonment was lawful, nevertheless, by some act, omission or event which has subsequently taken place, the party has become entitled to be discharged.
3. Where the process is defective in some substantial form required by law.
4. Where the process, though in proper form, has been issued in a case or under circumstances where the law does not allow process to issue or orders to be entered for imprisonment or arrest.
5. Where, although in proper form, the process has been issued in a case or under circumstances unauthorized to issue or execute the same, or where the person having the custody of the prisoner under such process is not the person empowered by law to detain him or her.
6. Where the process appears to have been obtained by false pretense or bribery.
7. Where there is no general law, nor any judgment or order of a court to authorize the process if in a civil action, nor any conviction if in a criminal proceeding. No court, on the return of a habeas corpus, shall, in any other matter, inquire into the legality or justice of a judgment of a court legally constituted.

(Source: P.A. 82-280.) [Formerly Ill. Rev. Stat. 110 §10-124.]

5/10-125. New commitment.
§10-125. New commitment. In all cases where the imprisonment is for a criminal, or supposed criminal matter, if it appears to the court that there is sufficient legal cause for the commitment of the prisoner, although such commitment may have been informally made, or without due authority, or the process may have been executed by a person not duly authorized, the court shall make a new commitment in proper form, and direct it to the proper officer, or admit the party to bail if the case is bailable. The court shall also, when necessary, take the recognizance of all material witnesses against the prisoner, as in other cases. The recognizances shall be in the form provided by law, and returned as other recognizances. If any judge shall neglect or refuse to bind any such prisoner or witness by recognizance, or to return a recognizance when taken as hereinabove stated, he or she shall be guilty of a Class A misdemeanor in office, and be proceeded against accordingly.
(Source: P.A. 82-280.) [Formerly Ill. Rev. Stat. 110 §10-125.]

5/10-126. Remand.
§10-126. Remand. When any prisoner brought up on a habeas corpus is remanded to prison, it shall be the duty of the court remanding the prisoner to deliver to the sheriff, or other person to whose custody the prisoner is remanded, an order in writing, stating the cause of remanding the prisoner. If such prisoner obtains a second order of habeas corpus, it shall be the duty of such sheriff, or other person to whom the same is directed, to return therewith the order above

stated; and if it appears that the prisoner was remanded for an offense adjudged not bailable, it shall be taken and received as conclusive, and the prisoner shall be remanded without further proceedings.
(Source: P.A. 82-280.) [Formerly Ill. Rev. Stat. 110 §10-126.]

5/10-127. Grant of habeas corpus.

§10-127. Grant of habeas corpus. It is not lawful for any court, on a second order of habeas corpus obtained by such prisoner, to discharge the prisoner, if he or she is clearly and specifically charged in the warrant of commitment with a criminal offense; but the court shall, on the return of such second order, have power only to admit such prisoner to bail where the offense is bailable by law, or remand him or her to prison where the offense is not bailable, or being bailable, where such prisoner fails to give the bail required.
(Source: P.A. 82-280.) [Formerly Ill. Rev. Stat. 110 §10-127.]

5/10-128. Person discharged again imprisoned.

§10-128. Person discharged again imprisoned. No person who has been discharged by order of the court on a habeas corpus, shall be again imprisoned, restrained or kept in custody for the same cause, unless he or she is afterwards indicted for the same offense, nor unless by the legal order or process of the court wherein he or she is bound by recognizance to appear. The following shall not be deemed to be the same cause:

1. If, after a discharge for a defect of proof, or any material defect in the commitment, in a criminal case, the prisoner is again arrested on sufficient proof, and committed by legal process for the same offense.
2. If, in a civil action, the party has been discharged for any illegality in the judgment or process, and is afterwards imprisoned by legal process for the same cause of action.
3. Generally, whenever the discharge is ordered on account of the non-observance of any of the forms required by law, the party may be a second time imprisoned if the cause is legal and the forms required by law observed.

(Source: P.A. 82-280.) [Formerly Ill. Rev. Stat. 110 §10-128.]

5/10-129. Penalty for rearrest of person discharged.

§10-129. Penalty for rearrest of person discharged. Any person who, knowing that another has been discharged by order of a competent court on a habeas corpus, shall, contrary to the provisions of Article X of this Act, arrest or detain him or her again for the same cause which was shown on the return to such order, shall forfeit $500 for the first offense, and $1,000 for every subsequent offense.
(Source: P.A. 82-280.) [Formerly Ill. Rev. Stat. 110 §10-129.]

5/10-130. Prisoner not to be removed from county.

§10-130. Prisoner not to be removed from county. To prevent any person from avoiding or delaying his or her trial, it shall not be lawful to remove any prisoner on habeas corpus under Article X of this Act out of the county in which he or she is confined, within 15 days next preceding the first day of the calendar month in which such person ought to be tried unless it is done to convey him or her into the county where the offense with which he or she stands charged is properly cognizable.
(Source: P.A. 82-280.) [Formerly Ill. Rev. Stat. 110 §10-130.]

5/10-131. Custody not to be changed.

§10-131. Custody not to be changed. Any person being committed to any prison, or in the custody of any sheriff or other officer or person for any criminal or supposed criminal matter, shall not be removed therefrom into any other prison or custody, unless it is done by habeas corpus order or some other legal

process or when it is expressly allowed by law. If any person removes, or causes to be removed any prisoner so committed, except as above provided, he or she shall forfeit to the party affected a sum not exceeding $300.
(Source: P.A. 83-707.) [Formerly Ill. Rev. Stat. 110 §10-131.]

5/10-132. Avoidance of order—Punishment.

§10-132. Avoidance of order—Punishment. Any one having a person in his or her custody, or under his or her restraint, power or control, for whose relief an order of habeas corpus is entered, who, with intent to avoid the effect of such order, transfers such person to the custody or places him or her under the control of another, or conceals him or her, or changes the place of his or her confinement, with intent to avoid the operation of such order, or with intent to remove him or her out of the State, shall, for every such offense, be guilty of a Class 4 felony. In any prosecution for the penalty incurred under this Section it shall not be necessary to show that the order of habeas corpus had been entered at the time of the removal, transfer or concealment therein mentioned, if it is proven that the acts therein forbidden were done with the intent to avoid the operation of such order.
(Source: P.A. 83-707.) [Formerly Ill. Rev. Stat. 110 §10-132.]

5/10-133. Penalties—How recovered.

§10-133. Penalties—How recovered. All the pecuniary forfeitures incurred under this Act shall inure to the use of the party for whose benefit the order of habeas corpus was entered, and shall be sued for and recovered with costs, by the Attorney General or State's Attorney, in the name of the State, by complaint; and the amount, when recovered, shall, without any deduction, be paid to the party entitled thereto.
(Source: P.A. 82-280.) [Formerly Ill. Rev. Stat. 110 §10-133.]

5/10-134. No bar to civil damages.

§10-134. No bar to civil damages. The recovery of the penalties shall be no bar to a civil action for damages.
(Source: P.A. 82-280.) [Formerly Ill. Rev. Stat. 110 §10-134.]

5/10-135. Habeas corpus to testify.

§10-135. Habeas corpus to testify. The several courts having authority to grant relief by habeas corpus, may enter orders, when necessary, to bring before them any prisoner to testify, or to be surrendered in discharge of bail, or for trial upon any criminal charge lawfully pending in the same court or to testify in a criminal proceeding in another state as provided for by Section 2 of the "Uniform Act to secure the attendance of witnesses from within or without a state in criminal proceedings", approved July 23, 1959, as heretofore or hereafter amended [725 ILCS 220/2]; and the order may be directed to any county in the State, and there be served and returned by any officer to whom it is directed.
(Source: P.A. 82-280.) [Formerly Ill. Rev. Stat. 110 §10-135.]

5/10-136. Prisoner remanded or punished.

§10-136. Prisoner remanded or punished. After a prisoner has given his or her testimony, or been surrendered, or his or her bail discharged, or he or she has been tried for the crime with which he or she is charged, he or she shall be returned to the jail or other place of confinement from which he or she was taken for that purpose. If such prisoner is convicted of a crime punishable with death or imprisonment in the penitentiary, he or she may be punished accordingly; but in any case where the prisoner has been taken from the penitentiary, and his or her punishment is by imprisonment, the time of such imprisonment shall

not commence to run until the expiration of the time of service under any former sentence.
(Source: P.A. 82-280.) [Formerly Ill. Rev. Stat. 110 §10-136.]

5/10-137. Contempt—Discharge.

§10-137. Contempt—Discharge. Any person imprisoned for any contempt of court for the non-performance of any order or judgment for the payment of money, is entitled to relief by habeas corpus, and if it appears, on full examination of such person and such witnesses, and other evidence as may be adduced, that he or she is unable to comply with such order or judgment, or to endure the confinement, and that all persons interested in the order or judgment have had reasonable notice of the time and place of trial, the court may discharge him or her from imprisonment, but no such discharge shall operate to release the lien of such order or judgment, but the same may be enforced against the property of such person as other orders and judgments are enforced in civil cases.
(Source: P.A. 82-280.) [Formerly Ill. Rev. Stat. 110 §10-137.]

This page intentionally left blank.

CHAPTER 740
CIVIL LIABILITIES

ILLINOIS ANTITRUST ACT

10/1. Short title.

§1. This Act shall be known and may be cited as the Illinois Antitrust Act.
(Source: Laws 1965, p. 1943.) [Formerly Ill. Rev. Stat. 38 §60-1.]

10/2. Purpose of Act.

§2. The purpose of this Act is to promote the unhampered growth of commerce and industry throughout the State by prohibiting restraints of trade which are secured through monopolistic or oligarchic practices and which act or tend to act to decrease competition between and among persons engaged in commerce and trade, whether in manufacturing, distribution, financing, and service industries or in related for-profit pursuits.
(Source: Laws 1965, p. 1943.) [Formerly Ill. Rev. Stat. 38 §60-2.]

10/3. Violations.

§3. Every person shall be deemed to have committed a violation of this Act who shall:

(1) Make any contract with, or engage in any combination or conspiracy with, any other person who is, or but for a prior agreement would be, a competitor of such person:

a. for the purpose or with the effect of fixing, controlling, or maintaining the price or rate charged for any commodity sold or bought by the parties thereto, or the fee charged or paid for any service performed or received by the parties thereto;

b. fixing, controlling, maintaining, limiting, or discontinuing the production, manufacture, mining, sale or supply of any commodity, or the sale or supply of any service, for the purpose or with the effect stated in paragraph a. of subsection (1);

c. allocating or dividing customers, territories, supplies, sales, or markets, functional or geographical, for any commodity or service; or

(2) By contract, combination, or conspiracy with one or more other persons unreasonably restrain trade or commerce; or

(3) Establish, maintain, use, or attempt to acquire monopoly power over any substantial part of trade or commerce of this State for the purpose of excluding competition or of controlling, fixing, or maintaining prices in such trade or commerce; or

(4) Lease or make a sale or contract for sale of goods, wares, merchandise, machinery, supplies, or other commodities, or services (including master antenna television service), whether patented or unpatented, for use, consumption, enjoyment, or resale, or fix a price charged thereof, or discount from, or rebate upon, such price, on the condition, agreement, or understanding that the lessee or purchaser thereof shall not use or deal in the goods, wares, merchandise, machinery, supplies, or other commodity or service (including cable television service or cable television relay service), of a competitor or competitors of the lessor or seller, where the effect of such lease, sale or contract for such sale or such condition, agreement, or understanding may be to substantially lessen competition or tend to create a monopoly in any line of commerce; or

(5) Being an employee, officer or agent of any foreign government, or an employee, officer or agent of a corporation or other entity which does business with or seeks to do business with any foreign government or instrumentality thereof; enforce, attempt to enforce, agree to or take action to forward the aims of, any discriminatory practice by the foreign government which is based on race, color, creed, national ancestry or sex or on ethnic or religious grounds, where such conduct, course of conduct, or agreement takes place in whole or in part within the United States and affects business in this State.

(Source: P.A. 82-219.) [Formerly Ill. Rev. Stat. 38 §60-3.]

10/4. Definitions.

§4. As used in this Act, unless the context otherwise requires:

"Trade or commerce" includes all economic activity involving or relating to any commodity or service.

"Commodity" shall mean any kind of real or personal property.

"Service" shall mean any activity, not covered by the definition of "commodity," which is performed in whole or in part for the purpose of financial gain.

"Service" shall not be deemed to include labor which is performed by natural persons as employees of others.

"Person" shall mean any natural person, or any corporation, partnership, or association of persons.

(Source: P.A. 83-516.) [Formerly Ill. Rev. Stat. 38 §60-4.]

10/5. Exceptions.

§5. No provisions of this Act shall be construed to make illegal:

(1) the activities of any labor organization or of individual members thereof which are directed solely to labor objectives which are legitimate under the laws of either the State of Illinois or the United States;

(2) the activities of any agricultural or horticultural cooperative organization, whether incorporated or unincorporated, or of individual members thereof, which are directed solely to objectives of such cooperative organizations which are legitimate under the laws of either the State of Illinois or the United States;

(3) the activities of any public utility or telecommunications carrier, as defined in Sections 3-105 and 13-202 of the Public Utilities Act [220 ILCS 5/3-105 and 5/13-202] to the extent that such activities are subject to the jurisdiction of the Illinois Commerce Commission, or to the activities of telephone mutual concerns referred to in Section 13-202 of the Public Utilities Act to the extent such activities relate to the providing and maintenance of telephone service to owners and customers;

(4) the activities (including, but not limited to, the making of or participating in joint underwriting or joint reinsurance arrangement) of any insurer, insurance agent, insurance broker, independent insurance adjuster or rating organization to the extent that such activities are subject to regulation by the

Director of Insurance of this State under, or are permitted or are authorized by, the Insurance Code [215 ILCS 5/1 et seq.] or any other law of this State;

(5) the religious and charitable activities of any not-for-profit corporation, trust or organization established exclusively for religious or charitable purposes, or for both purposes;

(6) the activities of any not-for-profit corporation organized to provide telephone service on a mutual or co-operative basis or electrification on a co-operative basis, to the extent such activities relate to the marketing and distribution of telephone or electrical service to owners and customers;

(7) the activities engaged in by securities dealers who are (i) licensed by the State of Illinois or (ii) members of the National Association of Securities Dealers or (iii) members of any National Securities Exchange registered with the Securities and Exchange Commission under the Securities Exchange Act of 1934, as amended [15 U.S.C. §78a et seq.], in the course of their business of offering, selling, buying and selling, or otherwise trading in or underwriting securities, as agent, broker, or principal, and activities of any National Securities Exchange so registered, including the establishment of commission rates and schedules of charges;

(8) the activities of any board of trade designated as a "contract market" by the Secretary of Agriculture of the United States pursuant to Section 5 of the Commodity Exchange Act, as amended [7 U.S.C. §7];

(9) the activities of any motor carrier, rail carrier, or common carrier by pipeline, as defined in The Illinois Commercial Transportation Law of The Illinois Vehicle Code, as amended [625 ILCS 5/18c-1101 et seq.], to the extent that such activities are permitted or authorized by the Act or are subject to regulation by the Illinois Commerce Commission;

(10) the activities of any state or national bank to the extent that such activities are regulated or supervised by officers of the state or federal government under the banking laws of this State or the United States;

(11) the activities of any state or federal savings and loan association to the extent that such activities are regulated or supervised by officers of the state or federal government under the savings and loan laws of this State or the United States;

(12) the activities of any bona fide not-for-profit association, society or board, of attorneys, practitioners of medicine, architects, engineers, land surveyors or real estate brokers licensed and regulated by an agency of the State of Illinois, in recommending schedules of suggested fees, rates or commissions for use solely as guidelines in determining charges for professional and technical services;

(13) Conduct involving trade or commerce (other than import trade or import commerce) with foreign nations unless:

(a) such conduct has a direct, substantial, and reasonably foreseeable effect:

(i) on trade or commerce which is not trade or commerce with foreign nations, or on import trade or import commerce with foreign nations; or

(ii) on export trade or export commerce with foreign nations of a person engaged in such trade or commerce in the United States; and

(b) such effect gives rise to a claim under the provisions of this Act, other than this subsection (13).

(c) If this Act applies to conduct referred to in this subsection (13) only because of the provisions of paragraph (a)(ii), then this Act shall apply to such conduct only for injury to export business in the United States which affects this State; or

(14) the activities of a unit of local government or school district and the activities of the employees, agents and officers of a unit of local government or school district.

(Source: P.A. 85-553.) [Formerly Ill. Rev. Stat. 38 §60-5.]

10/6. Punishment for violation; prosecution.

§6. Every person who shall knowingly do any of the acts prohibited by subsections (1) and (4) of Section 3 of this Act [740 ILCS 10/3] commits a Class 4 felony and shall be punished by a fine not to exceed $1,000,000 if a corporation, or, if any other person, $100,000.

(1) The Attorney General, with such assistance as he may from time to time require of the State's Attorneys in the several counties shall investigate suspected criminal violations of this Act and shall commence and try all prosecutions under this Act. Prosecutions under this Act may be commenced by complaint, information, or indictment. With respect to the commencement and trial of such prosecutions, the Attorney General shall have all of the powers and duties vested by law in State's Attorneys with respect to criminal prosecutions generally.

(2) A prosecution for any offense in violation of Section 6 of this Act must be commenced within 4 years after the commission thereof.

(3) The Attorney General shall not commence prosecutions under this Act against any defendant who, at the time, is a defendant with regard to any current pending complaint, information or indictment filed by the United States for violation, or alleged violation, of the Federal Anti-Trust Statutes (including but not being limited, Act of July 2, 1890, Ch. 647, 26 U.S.Stat. 209, 15 U.S.C., Secs. 1-7; Act of Oct. 15, 1914, Ch. 323, 38 U.S.Stat. 730, 15 U.S.C. Secs. 12-27, 44; Act of August 17, 1937, Ch. 690, Title VIII, 50 U.S.Stat. 693, 15 U.S.C. Sec. 1; Act of July 7, 1955, Ch. 281, 69 U.S.Stat. 282, 15 U.S.C. Secs. 1-3; Act of May 26, 1938, Ch. 283, 52 U.S.Stat. 446, 15 U.S.C. Sec. 13-C; and any similar Acts passed in the future) involving substantially the same subject matter.
(Source: P.A. 83-238.) [Formerly Ill. Rev. Stat. 38 §60-6.]

10/7. Civil actions.

§7. The following civil actions and remedies are authorized under this Act:

(1) The Attorney General, with such assistance as he may from time to time require of the State's Attorneys in the several counties, shall bring suit in the Circuit Court to prevent and restrain violations of Section 3 of this Act [740 ILCS 10/3]. In such a proceeding, the court shall determine whether a violation has been committed, and shall enter such judgment as it considers necessary to remove the effects of any violation which it finds, and to prevent such violation from continuing or from being renewed in the future. The court, in its discretion, may exercise all powers necessary for this purpose, including, but not limited to, injunction, divestiture of property, divorcement of business units, dissolution of domestic corporations or associations, and suspension or termination of the right of foreign corporations or associations to do business in the State of Illinois.

(2) Any person who has been injured in his business or property, or is threatened with such injury, by a violation of Section 3 of this Act may maintain an action in the Circuit Court for damages, or for an injunction, or both, against any person who has committed such violation. If, in an action for an injunction, the court issues an injunction, the plaintiff shall be awarded costs and reasonable attorney's fees. In an action for damages, if injury is found to be due to a violation of subsections (1) or (4) of Section 3 of this Act, the person injured shall be awarded 3 times the amount of actual damages resulting from that violation, together with costs and reasonable attorney's fees. If injury is found to be due to a violation of subsections (2) or (3) of Section 3 of this Act, the person injured shall recover the actual damages caused by the violation, together with costs and reasonable attorney's fees, and if it is shown that such violation was willful, the court may, in its discretion, increase the amount recovered as damages up to a total of 3 times the amount of actual damages. This State, counties, municipalities, townships and any political subdivision organized under the

authority of this State, and the United States, are considered a person having standing to bring an action under this subsection. The Attorney General may bring an action on behalf of this State, counties, municipalities, townships and other political subdivisions organized under the authority of this State to recover the damages under this subsection or by any comparable Federal law.

No provision of this Act shall deny any person who is an indirect purchaser the right to sue for damages. Provided, however, that in any case in which claims are asserted against a defendant by both direct and indirect purchasers, the court shall take all steps necessary to avoid duplicate liability for the same injury including transfer and consolidation of all actions. Provided further that no person other than the Attorney General of this State shall be authorized to maintain a class action in any court of this State for indirect purchasers asserting claims under this Act.

Beginning January 1, 1970, a file setting out the names of all special assistant attorneys general retained to prosecute antitrust matters and containing all terms and conditions of any arrangement or agreement regarding fees or compensation made between any such special assistant attorney general and the office of the Attorney General shall be maintained in the office of the Attorney General, open during all business hours to public inspection.

Any action for damages under this subsection is forever barred unless commenced within 4 years after the cause of action accrued, except that, whenever any action is brought by the Attorney General for a violation of this Act, the running of the foregoing statute of limitations, with respect to every private right of action for damages under the subsection which is based in whole or in part on any matter complained of in the action by the Attorney General, shall be suspended during the pendency thereof, and for one year thereafter. No cause of action barred under existing law on July 21, 1965 shall be revived by this Act. In any action for damages under this subsection the court may, in its discretion, award reasonable fees to the prevailing defendant upon a finding that the plaintiff acted in bad faith, vexatiously, wantonly or for oppressive reasons.

(3) Upon a finding that any domestic or foreign corporation organized or operating under the laws of this State has been engaged in conduct prohibited by Section 3 of this Act, or the terms of any injunction issued under this Act, a circuit court may, upon petition of the Attorney General, order the revocation, forfeiture or suspension of the charter, franchise, certificate of authority or privileges of any corporation operating under the laws of this State, or the dissolution of any such corporation.

(4) In lieu of any criminal penalty otherwise prescribed for a violation of this Act, and in addition to any action under this Act or any Federal antitrust law, the Attorney General may bring an action in the name and on behalf of the people of the State against any person, trustee, director, manager or other officer or agent of a corporation, or against a corporation, domestic or foreign, to recover a penalty not to exceed $100,000 from every corporation or $50,000 from every other person for any act herein declared illegal. The action must be brought within 4 years after the commission of the act upon which it is based. Nothing in this subsection shall impair the right of any person to bring an action under subsection (2) of this Section.

(Source: P.A. 83-1362.) [Formerly Ill. Rev. Stat. 38 §60-7.]

10/7.1. Personal service of process.

§7.1. Personal service of any process in an action under this Act may be made upon any person outside the state if such person has engaged in conduct in violation of this Act in this State. Such persons shall be deemed to have thereby submitted themselves to the jurisdiction of the courts of this state within the meaning of this section.

(Source: P.A. 76-208.) [Formerly Ill. Rev. Stat. 38 §60-7.1.]

10/7.2. Investigation.

§7.2. Whenever it appears to the Attorney General that any person has engaged in, is engaging in, or is about to engage in any act or practice prohibited by this Act, or that any person has assisted or participated in any agreement or combination of the nature described herein, he may, in his discretion, conduct an investigation as he deems necessary in connection with the matter and has the authority prior to the commencement of any civil or criminal action as provided for in the Act to subpoena witnesses, compel their attendance, examine them under oath, or require the production of any books, documents, records, writings or tangible things hereafter referred to as "documentary material" which the Attorney General deems relevant or material to his investigation, for inspection, reproducing or copying under such terms and conditions as hereafter set forth. Any subpoena issued by the Attorney General shall contain the following information:

(a) The statute and section thereof, the alleged violation of which is under investigation and the general subject matter of the investigation.

(b) The date and place at which time the person is required to appear or produce documentary material in his possession, custody or control in the office of the Attorney General located in Springfield or Chicago. Said date shall not be less than 10 days from date of service of the subpoena.

(c) Where documentary material is required to be produced, the same shall be described by class so as to clearly indicate the material demanded.

The Attorney General is hereby authorized, and may so elect, to require the production, pursuant to this section, of documentary material prior to the taking of any testimony of the person subpoenaed, in which event, said documentary material shall be made available for inspection and copying during normal business hours at the principal place of business of the person served, or at such other time and place, as may be agreed upon by the person served and the Attorney General. When documentary material is demanded by subpoena, said subpoena shall not:

(i) Contain any requirement which would be unreasonable or improper if contained in a subpoena duces tecum issued by a court of this State; or

(ii) Require the disclosure of any documentary material which would be privileged, or which for any other reason would not be required by a subpoena duces tecum issued by a court of this State.

(d) The production of documentary material in response to a subpoena served pursuant to this Section shall be made under a sworn certificate, in such form as the subpoena designates, by the person, if a natural person, to whom the demand is directed or, if not a natural person, by a person or persons having knowledge of the facts and circumstances relating to such production, to the effect that all of the documentary material required by the demand and in the possession, custody, or control of the person to whom the demand is directed has been produced and made available to the custodian.

While in the possession of the Attorney General and under such reasonable terms and conditions as the Attorney General shall prescribe: (A) documentary material shall be available for examination by the person who produced such material or by any duly authorized representative of such person, and (B) transcript of oral testimony shall be available for examination by the person who produced such testimony, or his counsel.

Except as otherwise provided in this Section, no documentary material or transcripts of oral testimony, or copies thereof, in the possession of the Attorney General shall be available for examination by any individual other than an authorized employee of the Attorney General or other law enforcement officials without the consent of the person who produced such material or transcripts.

(e) No person shall, with intent to avoid, evade, prevent, or obstruct compliance in whole or in part by any person with any duly served subpoena of the Attorney General under this Act, knowingly remove from any place, conceal, withhold, destroy, mutilate, alter, or by any other means falsify any documentary material that is the subject of such subpoena. A violation of this subsection is a Class A misdemeanor. The Attorney General, with such assistance as he may from time to time require of the State's Attorneys in the several counties, shall investigate suspected violations of this subsection and shall commence and try all prosecutions under this subsection.
(Source: P.A. 81-1051.) [Formerly Ill. Rev. Stat. 38 §60-7.2.]

10/7.3. Subpoena of Attorney General.

§7.3. Service of a subpoena of the Attorney General as provided herein may be made by (a) Delivery of a duly executed copy thereof to the person served, or if a person is not a natural person, to the principal place of business of the person to be served, or (b) Mailing by certified mail, return receipt requested, a duly executed copy thereof addressed to the person to be served at his principal place of business in this State, or, if said person has no place of business in the State, to his principal office.
(Source: P.A. 76-208.) [Formerly Ill. Rev. Stat. 38 §60-7.3.]

10/7.4. Examination of witnesses by Attorney General.

§7.4. The examination of all witnesses under this section shall be conducted by the Attorney General or by an assistant attorney general designated by him before an officer authorized to administer oaths in this State. The testimony shall be taken stenographically or by a sound recording device and shall be transcribed.

The Attorney General or his designated assistant conducting the examination shall exclude from the place where the examination is held all persons except the person being examined, his counsel, the officer before whom the testimony is to be taken, and any stenographer taking such testimony. Any person compelled to appear under a demand for oral testimony pursuant to this Act may be accompanied, represented, and advised by counsel. The examination shall be conducted in a manner consistent with the Illinois Civil Practice Law [735 ILCS 5/2-101 et seq.] and Illinois Supreme Court Rules. If such person refuses to answer any question, the Attorney General or his designated assistant conducting the examination may petition the Circuit Court pursuant to Section 7.6 of this Act [740 ILCS 10/7.6] for an order compelling such person to answer such question.
(Source: P.A. 83-1539.) [Formerly Ill. Rev. Stat. 38 §60-7.4.]

10/7.5. Fees and mileage for persons subpoenaed.

§7.5. All persons served with a subpoena by the Attorney General under this Act shall be paid the same fees and mileage as paid witnesses in the courts of this State.
(Source: P.A. 76-208.) [Formerly Ill. Rev. Stat. 38 §60-7.5.]

10/7.6. Failure to obey subpoena.

§7.6. In the event a witness served with a subpoena by the Attorney General under this Act fails or refuses to obey same or produce documentary material as provided herein, or to give testimony, relevant or material, to the investigation being conducted, the Attorney General may petition the Circuit Court of Sangamon or Cook County, or the county wherein the witness resides for an order requiring said witness to attend and testify or produce the documentary material demanded; thereafter, any failure or refusal on the part of the witness to obey such order of court may be punishable by the court as a contempt thereof.
(Source: P.A. 76-208.) [Formerly Ill. Rev. Stat. 38 §60-7.6.]

10/7.7. Incriminating testimony.

§7.7. In any investigation brought by the Attorney General pursuant to this Act, no individual shall be excused from attending, testifying or producing documentary material, objects or tangible things in obedience to a subpoena or under order of the court on the ground that the testimony or evidence required of him may tend to incriminate him or subject him to any penalty. No individual shall be criminally prosecuted or subjected to any criminal penalty for or on account of any testimony given by him in any investigation brought by the Attorney General pursuant to this Act; provided no individual so testifying shall be exempt from prosecution or punishment for perjury committed in so testifying.
(Source: P.A. 81-1051.) [Formerly Ill. Rev. Stat. 38 §60-7.7.]

10/7.8. Action for damages.

§7.8. The Attorney General may bring an action on behalf of this State, counties, municipalities, townships and other political subdivisions organized under the authority of this State in Federal Court to recover damages provided for under any comparable provision of Federal law; provided, however, this shall not impair the authority of any such county, municipality, township or political subdivision to bring such action on its own behalf nor impair its authority to engage its own counsel in connection therewith.
(Source: P.A. 76-208.) [Formerly Ill. Rev. Stat. 38 §60-7.8.]

10/7.9. Barred actions.

§7.9. No action under this Act shall be barred on the grounds that the activities or conduct complained of in any way affects or involves interstate or foreign commerce.
(Source: P.A. 76-208.) [Formerly Ill. Rev. Stat. 38 §60-7.9.]

10/8. Prima facie evidence in action for damages.

§8. A final judgment or order rendered in any civil or criminal proceeding brought by the Attorney General under this Act to the effect that a defendant has violated this Act shall be prima facie evidence against such defendant in any action for damages brought by any other party against such defendant under subsection (2) of Section 7 of this Act [740 ILCS 10/7], as to all matters respecting which said judgment or order would be an estoppel as between the parties thereto: Provided, that this Section shall not apply to civil consent judgments or orders entered before any testimony has been taken.
(Source: P.A. 79-1365.) [Formerly Ill. Rev. Stat. 38 §60-8.]

10/9. Conspiracy at common law.

§9. No contract, combination, conspiracy, or other act which violates this Act shall constitute or be deemed a conspiracy at common law.
(Source: Laws 1965, p. 1943.) [Formerly Ill. Rev. Stat. 38 §60-9.]

10/11. Federal antitrust law; construction.

§11. When the wording of this Act is identical or similar to that of a federal antitrust law, the courts of this State shall use the construction of the federal law by the federal courts as a guide in construing this Act. However, this Act shall not be construed to restrict the exercise by units of local government or school districts of powers granted, either expressly or by necessary implication, by Illinois statute or the Illinois Constitution.
(Source: P.A. 83-929.) [Formerly Ill. Rev. Stat. 38 §60-11.]

CRIME VICTIMS COMPENSATION ACT

Sec.

45/1. Short title.

§1. This Act shall be known and may be cited as the "Crime Victims Compensation Act".
(Source: P.A. 78-359.) [Formerly Ill. Rev. Stat. 70 §71.]

45/2. Definitions.

§2. Definitions. As used in this Act, unless the context otherwise requires:

(a) "Applicant" means any person who applies for compensation under this Act or any person the Court of Claims finds is entitled to compensation, including the guardian of a minor or of a person under legal disability. It includes any person who was a dependent of a deceased victim of a crime of violence for his support at the time of the death of that victim.

(b) "Court of Claims" means the Court of Claims created by the Court of Claims Act [705 ILCS 505/1 et seq.].

(c) "Crime of violence" means and includes any offense defined in Sections 9-1, 9-2, 9-3, 10-1, 10-2, 11-11, 11-19.2, 11-20.1, 12-1, 12-2, 12-3, 12-3.2, 12-4, 12-4.1, 12-5, 12-13, 12-14, 12-15, 12-16, 12-30, 20-1 or 20-1.1 of the Criminal Code of 1961 [720 ILCS 5/9-1, 5/9-2, 5/9-3, 5/10-1, 5/10-2, 5/11-11, 5/11-19.2, 5/11-20.1, 5/12-1, 5/12-2, 5/12-3, 5/12-3.2, 5/12-4, 5/12-4.1, 5/12-5, 5/12-13, 5/12-14, 5/12-15, 5/12-16, 5/12-30, 5/20-1 or 5/20-1.1], and driving under the influence of intoxicating liquor or narcotic drugs as defined in Section 11-501 of the Illinois Vehicle Code [625 ILCS 5/11-501], and if none of the said offenses occurred during a civil riot, insurrection or rebellion. "Crime of violence" does not include any other offense or accident involving a motor vehicle except those vehicle offenses specifically provided for in this paragraph. "Crime of violence" does include all of the offenses specifically provided for in this paragraph that occur within this State but are subject to federal jurisdiction.

(d) "Victim" means (1) a person killed or injured in this State as a result of a crime of violence perpetrated or attempted against him, (2) the parent of a child killed or injured in this State as a result of a crime of violence perpetrated or attempted against the child, (3) a person killed or injured in this State while attempting to assist a person against whom a crime of violence is being perpetrated or attempted, if that attempt of assistance would be expected of a reasonable man under the circumstances, (4) a person killed or injured in this State while assisting a law enforcement official apprehend a person who has perpetrated a crime of violence or prevent the perpetration of any such crime if that assistance was in response to the express request of the law enforcement official, (5) a child who personally witnessed a violent crime perpetrated or attempted against a relative, or (6) an Illinois resident who is a victim of a "crime of violence" as defined in this Act except, if the crime occurred outside this State, the resident has the same rights under this Act as if the crime had occurred in this State upon a showing that the state, territory, country, or political subdivision of a country in which the crime occurred does not have a compensation of victims of crimes law for which that Illinois resident is eligible.

(e) "Dependent" means a relative of a deceased victim who was wholly or partially dependent upon the victim's income at the time of his death and shall include the child of a victim born after his death.

(f) "Relative" means a spouse, parent, grandparent, stepfather, stepmother, child, grandchild, brother, brother-in-law, sister, sister-in-law, half brother, half sister, spouse's parent, nephew, niece, uncle or aunt.

(g) "Child" means an unmarried son or daughter who is under 18 years of age and includes a stepchild, an adopted child or an illegitimate child.

(h) "Pecuniary loss" means, in the case of injury, appropriate medical expenses and hospital expenses including expenses of a medical examination, medically required nursing care expenses, appropriate psychiatric care or psychiatric counseling expenses, expenses for care or counseling by a licensed clinical psychologist or licensed clinical social worker and expenses for treatment by Christian Science practitioners and nursing care appropriate thereto; prosthetic appliances, eyeglasses, and hearing aids necessary or damaged as a result of the crime; replacement services loss, to a maximum of $1000 per month; dependents replacement services loss, to a maximum of $1000 per month; loss of tuition paid to attend grammar school or high school when the victim had been enrolled as a full-time student prior to the injury, or college or graduate school when the victim had been enrolled as a full-time day or night student prior to the injury when the victim becomes unable to continue attendance at school as a result of the crime of violence perpetrated against him; loss of earnings, loss of future earnings because of disability resulting from the injury, and, in addition, in the case of death, funeral and burial expenses to a maximum of $3000 and loss of support of the dependents of the victim. Loss of future earnings shall be reduced by any income from substitute work actually performed by the victim or by income he would have earned in available appropriate substitute work he was capable of performing but unreasonably failed to undertake. Loss of earnings, loss of future earnings and loss of support shall be determined on the basis of the victim's average net monthly earnings for the 6 months immediately preceding the date of the injury or on $1000 per month, whichever is less. If a divorced or legally separated applicant is claiming loss of support for a minor child of the deceased, the amount of support for each child shall be based either on the amount of support the minor child received pursuant to the judgment for the 6 months prior to the date of the deceased victim's injury or death, or, if the subject of pending litigation filed by or on behalf of the divorced or legally separated applicant prior to the injury or death, on the result of that litigation. Pecuniary loss does not include pain and suffering or property loss or damage.

(i) "Replacement services loss" means expenses reasonably incurred in obtaining ordinary and necessary services in lieu of those the permanently injured person would have performed, not for income, but for the benefit of himself or his family, if he had not been permanently injured.

(j) "Dependents replacement services loss" means loss reasonably incurred by dependents after a victim's death in obtaining ordinary and necessary services in lieu of those the victim would have performed, not for income, but for their benefit, if he had not been fatally injured.

(Chgd. by P.A. 87-1186, §4, eff. 1/1/93.)

(Source: P.A. 86-1009; 87-520; 87-530; 87-895.) [Formerly Ill. Rev. Stat. 70 §72.]

45/3.1. Powers and duties—Court of Claims.

§3.1. In addition to other powers and duties set forth in the Court of Claims Act [705 ILCS 505/1 et seq.] and this Act, the Court of Claims shall have power to issue subpoenas, to administer oaths, to conduct hearings required by this Act and to promulgate all rules necessary thereto, and to prepare an annual report.
(Source: P.A. 81-1013.) [Formerly Ill. Rev. Stat. 70 §73.1.]

45/4.1. Powers and duties—Attorney General.

§4.1. In addition to other powers and duties set forth in this Act and other powers exercised by the Attorney General, the Attorney General shall promulgate rules necessary for him to carry out his duties under this Act, investigate all claims and prepare and present a report of each applicant's claim to the Court of Claims prior to the issuance of an order by the Court of Claims, prescribe and furnish all applications, notices of intent to file a claim and other forms required to be filed in the office of the Attorney General by the terms of this Act, and represent the interests of the State of Illinois in any hearing before the Court of Claims.
(Source: P.A. 81-1013.) [Formerly Ill. Rev. Stat. 70 §74.1.]

45/5.1. Notice of Act.

§5.1. (a) Every hospital licensed under the laws of this State shall display prominently in its emergency room posters giving notification of the existence and general provisions of this Act. Such posters shall be provided by the Attorney General.

(b) Any law enforcement agency that investigates an offense committed in this State shall inform the victim of the offense or his dependents concerning the availability of an award of compensation and advise such persons that any information concerning this Act and the filing of a claim may be obtained from the office of the Attorney General.
(Source: P.A. 81-1013.) [Formerly Ill. Rev. Stat. 70 §75.1.]

45/6.1. Conditions for compensation.

§6.1. A person is entitled to compensation under this Act if:

(a) Within one year of the occurrence of the crime upon which the claim is based, he files an application, under oath, with the Court of Claims and on a form prescribed in accordance with Section 7.1 [740 ILCS 45/7.1] furnished by the Attorney General. If the person entitled to compensation is under 18 years of age or under other legal disability at the time of the occurrence or becomes legally disabled as a result of the occurrence, he may file the application required by this subsection within one year after he attains the age of 18 years or the disability is removed, as the case may be. Upon good cause shown, the Court of Claims may extend the time for filing the application for a period not exceeding one year. The Court of Claims may by general orders provide for the extensions of time to file applications.

(b) The appropriate law enforcement officials were notified within 72 hours of the perpetration of the crime allegedly causing the death or injury to the victim or, in the event such notification was made more than 72 hours after the perpetration of the crime, the applicant establishes that such notice was timely under the circumstances.

(c) The applicant has cooperated fully with law enforcement officials in the apprehension and prosecution of the assailant.

(d) The applicant is not the offender or an accomplice of the offender and the award would not unjustly benefit the offender or his accomplice.

(e) The injury to or death of the victim was not substantially attributable to his own wrongful act and was not substantially provoked by the victim.
(Source: P.A. 86-1009; 86-1221.) [Formerly Ill. Rev. Stat. 70 §76.1.]

45/7.1. Application for compensation; contents.

§7.1. (a) The application shall set out:

(1) the name and address of the victim;

(2) if the victim is deceased, the name and address of the applicant and his relationship to the victim, the names and addresses of other persons dependent on the victim for their support and the extent to which each is so dependent, and other persons who may be entitled to compensation for a pecuniary loss;

(3) the date and nature of the crime on which the application for compensation is based;

(4) the date and place where and the law enforcement officials to whom notification of the crime was given;

(5) the nature and extent of the injuries sustained by the victim, and the names and addresses of those giving medical and hospitalization treatment to the victim;

(6) the pecuniary loss to the applicant and to such other persons as are specified under item (2) resulting from the injury or death;

(7) the amount of benefits, payments, or awards, if any, payable under:

(a) the Workers' Compensation Act [820 ILCS 305/1 et seq.],

(b) the Dram Shop Act [235 ILCS 5/1-1 et seq.],

(c) any claim, demand, or cause of action based upon the crime-related injury or death,

(d) the Federal Medicare program,

(e) the State Public Aid program,

(f) Social Security Administration burial benefits,

(g) Veterans administration burial benefits,

(h) life, health, accident or liability insurance,

(i) the Criminal Victims' Escrow Account Act [725 ILCS 145/1 et seq.], or

(j) from any other source.

(8) releases authorizing the surrender to the Court of Claims or Attorney General of reports, documents and other information relating to the matters specified under this Act and rules promulgated in accordance with the Act.

(9) such other information as the Court of Claims or the Attorney General reasonably requires.

(b) The Attorney General may require that materials substantiating the facts stated in the application be submitted with that application.

(c) An applicant, on his own motion, may file an amended application or additional substantiating materials to correct inadvertent errors or omissions at any time before the original application has been disposed of by the Court of Claims. In either case, the filing of additional information or of an amended application shall be considered for the purpose of this Act to have been filed at the same time as the original application.

(Source: P.A. 82-956.) [Formerly Ill. Rev. Stat. 70 §77.1.]

45/8.1. Substantiation of claim.

§8.1. If an applicant does not submit all materials substantiating his claim as requested of him by the Attorney General, the Attorney General shall notify the applicant in writing of the specific additional items of information or materials required and that he has 30 days in which to furnish those items to the Attorney General. The Attorney General shall report an applicant's failure to comply within 30 days of the foregoing notice to the Court of Claims. No award of compensation shall be made for any portion of the applicant's claim that is not substantiated by the applicant. An applicant may request an extension of time from the Attorney General prior to the expiration of the 30 day period.

(Source: P.A. 81-1013.) [Formerly Ill. Rev. Stat. 70 §78.1.]

45/9.1. Matters considered by Court of Claims.

§9.1. In determining whether an applicant is entitled to compensation, the Court of Claims shall consider the facts stated in the application and other material and information submitted and the report of the Attorney General. However, the Court of Claims need not consider whether or not the alleged assailant has been apprehended.
(Source: P.A. 81-1013.) [Formerly Ill. Rev. Stat. 70 §79.1.]

45/10.1. Factors upon which amount of compensation is based.

§10.1. The amount of compensation to which an applicant and other persons is entitled shall be based on the following factors:

(a) a victim may be compensated for his pecuniary loss;

(b) a dependent may be compensated for loss of support;

(c) any person related to the victim, even though not dependent upon the victim for his support, may be compensated for reasonable funeral, medical and hospital expenses of the victim to the extent to which he has paid or become obligated to pay such expenses and only after compensation for reasonable funeral, medical and hospital expenses of the victim have been awarded may compensation be made for reasonable expenses of the victim incurred for psychological treatment of a mental or emotional condition caused or aggravated by the crime;

(d) an award shall be reduced or denied according to the extent to which the victim's acts or conduct provoked or contributed to his injury or death, or the extent to which any prior criminal conviction or conduct of the victim may have directly or indirectly contributed to the injury or death of the victim;

(e) an award shall be reduced by the amount of benefits, payments or awards payable under those sources which are required to be listed under item (7) of Section 7.1(a) [740 ILCS 45/7.1] and any other sources except annuities, pension plans, Federal Social Security payments payable to dependents of the victim and the net proceeds of the first $25,000 of life insurance that would inure to the benefit of the applicant, which the applicant or any other person dependent for the support of a deceased victim, as the case may be, has received or to which he is entitled as a result of injury to or death of the victim.

(f) A final award shall not exceed $10,000 for a crime committed prior to September 22, 1979, $15,000 for a crime committed on or after September 22, 1979 and prior to January 1, 1986, or $25,000 for a crime committed on or after January 1, 1986. If the total pecuniary loss is greater than the maximum amount allowed, the award shall be divided in proportion to the amount of actual loss among those entitled to compensation;

(g) compensation under this Act is a secondary source of compensation and the applicant must show that he has exhausted the benefits reasonably available under the Criminal Victims' Escrow Account Act [725 ILCS 145/1 et seq.] or any governmental or medical or health insurance programs, including, but not limited to Workers' Compensation, the Federal Medicare program, the State Public Aid program, Social Security Administration burial benefits, Veterans Administration burial benefits, and life, health, accident or liability insurance.
(Source: P.A. 86-1009; 87-605.) [Formerly Ill. Rev. Stat. 70 §80.1.]

45/11.1. Manner of payment.

§11.1. The Court of Claims may provide for the payment of an award in a lump sum or in installments.
(Source: P.A. 81-1013.) [Formerly Ill. Rev. Stat. 70 §81.1.]

45/12. Fees.

§12. No fee may be charged to the applicant in any proceeding under this Act except as provided in this Act. If the applicant is represented by counsel or

some other duly authorized agent in making application under this Act or in any further proceedings provided for in this Act, that counsel or agent may receive no payment for his services in preparing or presenting the application before the Court of Claims. He may, however, charge fees to the applicant for representing him at a hearing provided for in this Act but only in such an amount as the Court of Claims determines to be reasonable.
(Source: P.A. 78-359.) [Formerly Ill. Rev. Stat. 70 §82.]

45/12.1. Awards.
§12.1. The Court of Claims may, without a hearing, make an award to a person who has filed an application or any other person it finds is entitled to compensation, including the guardian or conservator of a minor or incompetent, based upon the application, the other information and materials submitted with the application, and the report of the Attorney General.
(Source: P.A. 81-1013.) [Formerly Ill. Rev. Stat. 70 §82.1.]

45/13.1. Hearings.
§13.1. (a) A hearing before a Commissioner of the Court of Claims shall be held for those claims in which:
(1) the Court of Claims on its own motion sets a hearing;
(2) the Attorney General petitions the Court of Claims for a hearing;
(3) a claim has been disposed of without a hearing and an applicant has been denied compensation or has been awarded compensation which he thinks is inadequate and he petitions the Court of Claims for a hearing within 30 days of the date of issuance of the order sought to be reviewed. The petition shall set forth the reasons for which review is sought and a recitation of any additional evidence the applicant desires to present to the Court. A copy of the petition shall be provided to the Attorney General.
(b) At hearings held under this Act before Commissioners of the Court of Claims, any statement, document, information or matter may be received in evidence if in the opinion of the Court or its Commissioner such evidence would contribute to a determination of the claim, regardless of whether such evidence would be admissible in a court of law.
(Source: P.A. 83-298.) [Formerly Ill. Rev. Stat. 70 §83.1.]

45/14.1. Public or closed hearings.
§14.1. (a) Hearings shall be open to the public unless the Court of Claims determines that a closed hearing should be held because:
(1) the alleged assailant has not been brought to trial and a public hearing would adversely affect either his apprehension or his trial;
(2) the offense allegedly perpetrated against the victim is one defined in Section 12-13 or 12-14 of the "Criminal Code of 1961" [720 ILCS 5/12-13 or 5/12-14] and the interests of the victim or of persons dependent on his support require that the public be excluded from the hearing;
(3) the victim or the alleged assailant is a minor; or
(4) the interests of justice would be frustrated, rather than furthered, if the hearing were open to the public.
(b) A transcript shall be kept of the hearings held before the Court of Claims. No part of the transcript of any hearing before the Court of Claims may be used for any purpose in a criminal proceeding except in the prosecution of a person alleged to have perjured himself in his testimony before the Court of Claims. A copy of the transcript may be furnished to the applicant upon his written request to the court reporter, accompanied by payment of a charge established by the Court of Claims in accordance with the prevailing commercial charge for a duplicate transcript. Where the interests of justice require, the Court of Claims

may refuse to disclose the names of victims or other material in the transcript by which the identity of the victim could be discovered.
(Source: P.A. 83-1067.) [Formerly Ill. Rev. Stat. 70 §84.1.]

45/15. Disposition without hearing; orders.

§15. When disposition is made without a hearing or at the conclusion of a hearing held under this Act, the Court of Claims shall enter an order stating (1) its findings of fact, (2) its decision as to whether or not compensation is due under this Act, (3) the amount of compensation, if any, which is due under this Act, (4) whether disbursement of the compensation awarded is to be made in a lump sum or in periodic payments, and (5) the person or persons to whom the compensation should be paid.
(Source: P.A. 81-1013.) [Formerly Ill. Rev. Stat. 70 §85.]

45/16. Modification of dispositions.

§16. The Court of Claims, on its own motion or upon the written request of any applicant, may modify an award of compensation made under this Act or reconsider a denial of compensation. No hearing need be held, however, unless the written request states facts which were not known to the applicant or by the exercise of reasonable diligence could not have been ascertained by him at the time of the entry of the order sought to be modified and which would have directly affected the determination of whether or not compensation should be awarded and, if so, the amount of that compensation.
(Source: P.A. 81-1013.) [Formerly Ill. Rev. Stat. 70 §86.]

45/17. Subrogation.

§17. (a) The Court of Claims may award compensation on the condition that the applicant subrogate to the State his rights to collect damages from the assailant or any third party who may be liable in damages to the applicant. In such a case the Attorney General may, on behalf of the State, bring an action against an assailant or third party for money damages, but must first notify the applicant and give him an opportunity to participate in the prosecution of the action. The excess of the amount recovered in such action over the amount of the compensation offered and accepted or awarded under this Act plus costs of the action and attorneys' fees actually incurred shall be paid to the applicant.

(b) Nothing in this Act affects the right of the applicant to seek civil damages from the assailant and any other party, but that applicant must give written notice to the Attorney General of the making of a claim or the filing of an action for such damages. Failure to notify the Attorney General of such claims and actions at the time they are instituted or at the time an application is filed is a willful omission of fact and the applicant thereby becomes subject to the provisions of Section 20 of this Act [740 ILCS 45/20].

(c) The State has a charge for the amount of compensation paid under this Act upon all claims or causes of action against an assailant and any other party to recover for the injuries or death of a victim which were the basis for that payment of compensation. At the time compensation is ordered to be paid under this Act, the Court of Claims shall give written notice of this charge to the applicant. The charge attaches to any verdict or judgment entered and to any money or property which is recovered on account of the claim or cause of action against the assailant or any other party after the notice is given. On petition filed by the Attorney General on behalf of the State or by the applicant, the circuit court, on written notice to all interested parties, shall adjudicate the right of the parties and enforce the charge. This subsection does not affect the priority of a lien under "AN ACT creating attorney's lien and for enforcement of same", filed June 16, 1909, as amended [770 ILCS 5/0.01 et seq.].

(d) Where compensation is awarded under this Act and the person receiving same also receives any sum required to be, and that has not been deducted under Section 10.1 [740 ILCS 45/10.1], he shall refund to the State the amount of compensation paid to him which would have been deducted at the time the award was made.
(Source: P.A. 84-545.) [Formerly Ill. Rev. Stat. 70 §87.]

45/18. Claims against awards of compensation.

§18. (a) An award is not subject to enforcement, attachment, garnishment, or other process, except that an award is not exempt from a claim of a creditor to the extent that he or she provided products, services, or accommodations the costs of which are included in the award.

(b) An assignment or agreement to assign a right to compensation for loss accruing in the future is unenforceable, except:

(1) an assignment of a right to compensation for work loss to secure payment of maintenance or child support; or (2) an assignment of a right to compensation to the extent of the cost of products, services, or accommodations necessitated by the injury or death on which the claim is based and are provided or to be provided by the assignee.

(c) The court may order that all or a portion of an award be paid jointly to the applicant and another person to the extent that such other person has provided products, services or accommodations, the costs of which are included in the award.
(Source: P.A. 83-346.) [Formerly Ill. Rev. Stat. 70 §88.]

45/20. Willful misstatements or omissions.

§20. (a) In addition to any other civil liability or criminal penalties provided by law, a person who the Court of Claims finds has willfully misstated or omitted facts relevant to the determination of whether compensation is due under this Act or of the amount of that compensation, whether in making application for compensation or in the further proceedings provided for in this Act, shall be denied compensation under this Act.

(b) A person who is convicted of having willfully misstated or omitted facts relevant to the determination of whether compensation is due under this Act or of the amount of that compensation, whether in making application for compensation or in the further proceedings provided for in this Act, shall be guilty of a Class A misdemeanor.
(Source: P.A. 81-1013.) [Formerly Ill. Rev. Stat. 70 §90.]

ILLINOIS STREETGANG TERRORISM OMNIBUS PREVENTION ACT

Sec.

147/1. Short title.

§1. Short title. This Article may be cited as the Illinois Streetgang Terrorism Omnibus Prevention Act.
(Added by P.A. 87-932, §2-1, eff. 1/1/93.)

147/5. Legislative findings.

§5. Legislative findings. (a) The General Assembly hereby finds and declares that it is the right of every person, regardless of race, color, creed, religion, national origin, sex, age, or disability, to be secure and protected from fear, intimidation, and physical harm caused by the activities of violent groups and individuals. It is not the intent of this Act to interfere with the exercise of the constitutionally protected rights of freedom of expression and association. The General Assembly hereby recognizes the constitutional right of every citizen to harbor and express beliefs on any lawful subject whatsoever, to lawfully associate with others who share similar beliefs, to petition lawfully constituted authority for a redress of perceived grievances, and to participate in the electoral process.

(b) The General Assembly finds, however, that urban, suburban, and rural communities, neighborhoods and schools throughout the State are being terrorized and plundered by streetgangs. The General Assembly finds that there are now several hundred streetgangs operating in Illinois, and that while their terrorism is most widespread in urban areas, streetgangs are spreading into suburban and rural areas of Illinois.

(c) The General Assembly further finds that streetgangs are often controlled by criminally sophisticated adults who take advantage of our youth by intimidating and coercing them into membership by employing them as drug couriers and runners, and by using them to commit brutal crimes against persons and property to further the financial benefit to and dominance of the streetgang.

(d) These streetgangs' activities present a clear and present danger to public order and safety and are not constitutionally protected. No society is or should be required to endure such activities without redress. Accordingly, it is the intent of the General Assembly in enacting this Act to create a civil remedy against streetgangs and their members that focuses upon patterns of criminal gang activity and upon the organized nature of streetgangs, which together have been the chief source of their success.

(Added by P.A. 87-932, §2-5, eff. 1/1/93.)

147/10. Definitions.

§10. Definitions. "Course or pattern of criminal activity" means 2 or more gang-related criminal offenses committed in whole or in part within this State when:

(1) at least one such offense was committed after the effective date of this Act;

(2) both offenses were committed within 5 years of each other; and

(3) at least one offense involved the solicitation to commit, conspiracy to commit, attempt to commit, or commission of any offense defined as a felony or forcible felony under the Criminal Code of 1961 [720 ILCS 5/1-1 et seq.].

"Designee of State's Attorney" or "designee" means any attorney for a public authority who has recieved written permission from the State's Attorney to file or join in a civil action authorized by this Act.

"Public authority" means any unit of local government or school district created or established under the Constitution or laws of this State.

"State's Attorney" means the State's Attorney of any county where an offense constituting a part of a course or pattern of gang-related criminal activity has occurred or has been committed.

"Streetgang" or "gang" means any combination, confederation, alliance, network, conspiracy, understanding, or other similar conjoining, in law or in fact, of 3 or more persons:

(1)(i) that, through its membership or through the agency of any member and at the direction, order, solicitation, or request of any conspirator who is a leader, officer, director, organizer, or other governing or policy making person or authority in the conspiracy, or by any agent, representative, or deputy of any such person or authority engages in a course or pattern of criminal activity; or (ii) that, through its membership or through the agency of any member engages in a course or pattern of criminal activity.

(2) For purposes of this Act, it shall not be necessary to show that a particular conspiracy, combination, or conjoining of persons possesses, acknowledges, or is known by any common name, insignia, flag, means of recognition, secret signal or code, creed, belief, structure, leadership or command structure, method of operation or criminal enterprise, concentration or specialty, membership, age, or other qualifications, initiation rites, geographical or territorial situs or boundary or location, or other unifying mark, manner, protocol or method of expressing or indicating membership when the conspiracy's existence, in law or in fact, can be demonstrated by a preponderance of other competent evidence. However, any evidence reasonably tending to show or demonstrate, in law or in fact, the existence of or membership in any conspiracy, confederation, or other association described herein, or probative of the existence of or membership in any such association, shall be admissible in any action or proceeding brought under this Act.

"Streetgang member" or "gang member" means any person who actually and in fact belongs to a gang, and any person who knowingly acts in the capacity of an agent for or accessory to, or is legally accountable for, or voluntarily associates himself with a course or pattern of gang-related criminal activity, whether in a preparatory, executory, or cover-up phase of any activity, or who knowingly performs, aids, or abets any such activity.

"Streetgang related" or "gang-related" means any criminal activity, enterprise, pursuit, or undertaking directed by, ordered by, authorized by, consented to, agreed to, requested by, acquiesced in, or ratified by any gang leader, officer, or governing or policy-making person or authority, or by any agent, representative, or deputy of any such officer, person, or authority:

(1) with the intent to increase the gang's size, membership, prestige, dominance, or control in any geographical area; or

(2) with the intent to provide the gang with any advantage in, or any control or dominance over any criminal market sector, including but not limited to, the manufacture, delivery, or sale of controlled substances or cannabis; arson or arson-for-hire; traffic in stolen property or stolen credit cards; traffic in prostitution, obscenity, or pornography; or that involves robbery, burglary, or theft; or

(3) with the intent to exact revenge or retribution for the gang or any member of the gang; or

(4) with the intent to obstruct justice, or intimidate or eliminate any witness against the gang or any member of the gang; or

(5) with the intent to otherwise directly or indirectly cause any benefit, aggrandizement, gain, profit or other advantage whatsoever to or for the gang, its reputation, influence, or membership.

(Added by P.A. 87-932, §2-10, eff. 1/1/93.)

147/15. Creation of civil cause of action.

§15. Creation of civil cause of action. (a) A civil cause of action is hereby created in favor of any public authority expending money, allocating or reallocating police, firefighting, emergency or other personnel or resources, or otherwise incurring any loss, deprivation, or injury, or sustaining any damage, impairment, or harm whatsoever, proximately caused by any course or pattern of criminal activity.

(b) The cause of action created by this Act shall lie against:

(1) any streetgang in whose name, for whose benefit, on whose behalf, or under whose direction the act was committed; and

(2) any gang officer or director who causes, orders, suggests, authorizes, consents to, agrees to, requests, acquiesces in, or ratifies any such act; and

(3) any gang member who, in the furtherance of or in connection with, any gang-related activity, commits any such act; and

(4) any gang officer, director, leader, or member.

(c) The cause of action authorized by this Act shall be brought by the State's Attorney or attorneys, or by his or their designees. This cause of action shall be in addition to any other civil or criminal proceeding authorized by the laws of this State or by federal law, and shall not be construed as requiring the State's Attorney or his designee to elect a civil, rather than criminal remedy, or as replacing any other cause of action. Liability of the gang, its officers, directors, leaders, and members shall be joint and severable subject only to the apportionment and allocation of punitive damage authorized under Section 35 of this Act [740 ILCS 147/35].

(Added by P.A. 87-932, §2-15, eff. 1/1/93.)

147/20. Commencement of action.

§20. Commencement of action. (a) An action may be commenced under this Act by the filing of a verified complaint as in civil cases.

(b) A complaint filed under this Act, and all other ancillary or collateral matters arising therefrom, including matter relating to discovery, motions, trial, and the perfection or execution of judgments shall be subject to the Code of Civil Procedure [735 ILCS 5/1-101 et seq.], except as may be otherwise provided in this Act, or except as the court may otherwise order upon motion of the State's Attorney or his designee in matters relating to immunity or the physical safety of witnesses.

(c) The complaint shall name each complaining State's Attorney or his designee, and the public authority represented by him or by them.

(d) The complaint shall also name as defendants the gang, all known gang officers, and any gang members specifically identified or alleged in the complaint as having participated in a course or pattern of gang-related criminal activity. The complaint may also name, as a class of defendants, all unknown gang members.

(e) When, at any point prior to trial, other specific gang officers or members become known, the complaint may be amended to include any such person as a named defendant.

(Added by P.A. 87-932, §2-20, eff. 1/1/93.)

147/25. Venue.

§25. Venue. (a) In an action brought under this Act, venue shall lie in any county where an act charged in the complaint as part of a course or pattern of gang-related criminal activity was committed.

(b) It shall not be necessary for all offenses necessary to establishing a course or pattern of criminal activity to have occcured in any one county where the State's Attorneys of several counties, or their designees, each complaining of any offense, elected to join in a complaint. In such instance, it shall be sufficient that the complaint, taken as a whole, alleges a course or pattern of gang-related criminal activity, and each count of any such joint complaint shall be considered as cumulative to other counts for purposes of alleging or demonstrating such a course or pattern of activity.

(c) Where a course or pattern of activity is alleged to have been committed or to have occurred in more than one county, the State's Attorney of each such county, or their designees, may join their several causes of action in a single complaint, which may be filed in any such county agreed to by or among them, but no such joinder shall be had without the consent of the State's Attorney having jurisdiction over each offense alleged as part of the course or pattern of activity.
(Added by P.A. 87-932, §2-25, eff. 1/1/93.)

147/30. Service of process.

§30. Service of process. (a) All streetgangs and streetgang members engaged in a course or pattern of gang-related criminal activity within this State impliedly consent to service of process upon them as set forth in this Section, or as may be otherwise authorized by the Code of Civil Procedure [735 ILCS 5/1-101 et seq.].

(b) Service of process upon a streetgang may be had by leaving a copy of the complaint and summons directed to any officer of such gang, commanding the gang to appear and answer the complaint or otherwise plead at a time and place certain:

(1) with any gang officer; or

(2) with any individual member of the gang simultaneously named therein; or

(3) in the manner provided for service upon a voluntary unincorporated association in a civil action; or

(4) in the manner provided for service by publication in a civil action; or

(5) with any parent, legal guardian, or legal custodian of any persons charged with a gang-related offense when any person sued civilly under this Act is under 18 years of age and is also charged criminally or as a delinquent minor; or

(6) with the director of any agency or department of this State who is the legal guardian, guardianship administrator, or custodian of any person sued under this Act; or

(7) with the probation or parole officer of any person sued under this Act; or

(8) with such other person or agent as the court may, upon petition of the State's Attorney or his designee, authorize as appropriate and reasonable under all of the circumstances.

(c) If after being summoned a streetgang does not appear, the court shall enter an answer for the streetgang neither affirming nor denying the allegations of the complaint but demanding strict proof thereof, and proceed to trial and judgment without further process.

(d) When any person is named as a defendant streetgang member in any complaint, or subsequently becomes known and is added or joined as a named defendant, service of process may be had as authorized or provided for in the Code of Civil Procedure for service of process in a civil case.

(e) Unknown gang members may be sued as a class and designated as such in the caption of any complaint filed under this Act. Service of process upon unknown members may be made in the manner prescribed for provision of notice to members of a class in a class action, or as the court may direct for providing the best service and notice practicable under the circumstances which shall include individual, personal, or other service upon all members who can be identified and located through reasonable effort.
(Added by P.A. 87-932, §2-30, eff. 1/1/93.)

147/35. Injunctive relief, damages, costs, and fees.

§35. Injunctive relief, damages, costs, and fees. (a) In any action brought under this Act, and upon the verified application of the State's Attorney or his designee, the circuit court may at any time enter such restraining orders, injunctions, or other prohibitions, or order such other relief as it deems proper, including but not limited to ordering any person to divest himself of any involvment or interest, direct or indirect, in any illegal streetgang activity and imposing other reasonable restrictions on the future illegal activities of any defendant.

(b) A final judgement in favor of a public authority under this Act shall entitle it to recover compensatory damages for all damages, losses, impairments, or other harm proximately caused, together with the costs of the suit and reasonable attorneys' fees. Punitive damages may be assessed against any streetgang, against any streetgang officer or member found guilty of actual participation in or to be legally accountable for a course or pattern of criminal activity under this Act.

(Added by P.A. 87-932, §2-35, eff. 1/1/93.)

This page intentionally left blank.

CHAPTER 750
FAMILIES

ILLINOIS DOMESTIC VIOLENCE ACT OF 1986

ARTICLE I. GENERAL PROVISIONS

60/101. Short title.

§101. Short Title. This Act shall be known and may be cited as the "Illinois Domestic Violence Act of 1986".
(Source: P.A. 84-1305.) [Formerly Ill. Rev. Stat. 40 §2311-1.]

60/102. Purposes; rules of construction.

§102. Purposes; rules of construction. This Act shall be liberally construed and applied to promote its underlying purposes, which are to:

(1) Recognize domestic violence as a serious crime against the individual and society which produces family disharmony in thousands of Illinois families, promotes a pattern of escalating violence which frequently culminates in intra-family homicide, and creates an emotional atmosphere that is not conducive to healthy childhood development;

(2) Recognize domestic violence against high risk adults with disabilities, who are particularly vulnerable due to impairments in ability to seek or obtain protection, as a serious problem which takes on many forms, including physical abuse, sexual abuse, neglect, and exploitation, and facilitate accessibility of remedies under the Act in order to provide immediate and effective assistance and protection.

(3) Recognize that the legal system has ineffectively dealt with family violence in the past, allowing abusers to escape effective prosecution or financial liability, and has not adequately acknowledged the criminal nature of domestic violence; that, although many laws have changed, in practice there is still widespread failure to appropriately protect and assist victims;

(4) Support the efforts of victims of domestic violence to avoid further abuse by promptly entering and diligently enforcing court orders which prohibit abuse and, when necessary, reduce the abuser's access to the victim and address any related issues of child custody and economic support, so that victims are not trapped in abusive situations by fear of retaliation, loss of a child, financial dependence, or loss of accessible housing or services;

(5) Clarify the responsibilities and support the efforts of law enforcement officers to provide immediate, effective assistance and protection for victims of domestic violence, recognizing that law enforcement officers often become the secondary victims of domestic violence, as evidenced by the high rates of police injuries and deaths that occur in response to domestic violence calls; and

(6) Expand the civil and criminal remedies for victims of domestic violence; including, when necessary, the remedies which effect physical separation of the parties to prevent further abuse.
(Chgd. by P.A. 87-1186, §3, eff. 1/1/93.)
(Source: P.A. 86-542.) [Formerly Ill. Rev. Stat. 40 §2311-2.]

60/103. Definitions.

§103. Definitions. For the purposes of this Act, the following terms shall have the following meanings:

(1) "Abuse" means physical abuse, harassment, intimidation of a dependent, interference with personal liberty or willful deprivation but does not include reasonable direction of a minor child by a parent or person in loco parentis.

(2) "Adult with disabilities" means an elder adult with disabilities or a high-risk adult with disabilities. A person may be an adult with disabilities for purposes of this Act even though he or she has never been adjudicated an incompetent adult. However, no court proceeding may be initiated or continued on behalf of an adult with disabilities over that adult's objection, unless such proceeding is approved by his or her legal guardian, if any.

(3) "Domestic violence" means abuse as defined in paragraph (1).

(4) "Elder adult with disabilities" means an adult prevented by advanced age from taking appropriate action to protect himself or herself from abuse by a family or household member.

(5) "Exploitation" means the illegal, including tortious, use of a high-risk adult with disabilities or of the assets or resources of a high-risk adult with disabilities. Exploitation includes, but is not limited to, the misappropriation of assets or resources of a high-risk adult with disabilities by undue influence, by breach of a fiduciary relationship, by fraud, deception, or extortion, or the use of such assets or resources in a manner contrary to law.

(6) "Family or household members" include spouses, former spouses, parents, children, stepchildren and other persons related by blood or by present or prior marriage, persons who share or formerly shared a common dwelling, persons who have or allegedly have a child in common, persons who share or allegedly share a blood relationship through a child, persons who have or have had a dating or engagement relationship, and persons with disabilities and their personal assistants. For purposes of this paragraph, neither a casual acquaintanceship nor ordinary fraternization between 2 individuals in business or social contexts shall be deemed to constitute a dating relationship. In the case of a high-risk adult with disabilities, "family or household members" includes any person who has the responsibility for a high-risk adult as a result of a family relationship or who has assumed responsibility for all or a portion of the care of a high-risk adult with disabilities voluntarily, or by express or implied contract, or by court order.

(7) "Harassment" means knowing conduct which is not necessary to accomplish a purpose that is reasonable under the circumstances; would cause a reasonable person emotional distress; and does cause emotional distress to the petitioner. Unless the presumption is rebutted by a preponderance of the evidence, the following types of conduct shall be presumed to cause emotional distress:

(i) creating a disturbance at petitioner's place of employment or school;

(ii) repeatedly telephoning petitioner's place of employment, home or residence;

(iii) repeatedly following petitioner about in a public place or places;

(iv) repeatedly keeping petitioner under surveillance by remaining present outside his or her home, school, place of employment, vehicle or other place occupied by petitioner or by peering in petitioner's windows;

(v) improperly concealing a minor child from petitioner, repeatedly threatening to improperly remove a minor child of petitioner's from the jurisdiction or from the physical care of petitioner, repeatedly threatening to conceal a minor child from petitioner, or making a single such threat following an actual or attempted improper removal or concealment, unless respondent was fleeing an incident or pattern of domestic violence; or

(vi) threatening physical force, confinement or restraint on one or more occasions.

(8) "High-risk adult with disabilities" means a person aged 18 or over whose physical or mental disability impairs his or her ability to seek or obtain protection from abuse, neglect, or exploitation.

(9) "Interference with personal liberty" means committing or threatening physical abuse, harassment, intimidation or willful deprivation so as to compel another to engage in conduct from which she or he has a right to abstain or to refrain from conduct in which she or he has a right to engage.

(10) "Intimidation of a dependent" means subjecting a person who is dependent because of age, health or disability to participation in or the witnessing of: physical force against another or physical confinement or restraint of another which constitutes physical abuse as defined in this Act, regardless of whether the abused person is a family or household member.

(11) (A) "Neglect" means the failure to exercise that degree of care toward a high-risk adult with disabilities which a reasonable person would exercise under the circumstances and includes but is not limited to:

(i) the failure to take reasonable steps to protect a high-risk adult with disabilities from acts of abuse;

(ii) the repeated, careless imposition of unreasonable confinement;

(iii) the failure to provide food, shelter, clothing, and personal hygiene to a high-risk adult with disabilities who requires such assistance;

(iv) the failure to provide medical and rehabilitative care for the physical and mental health needs of a high-risk adult with disabilities; or

(v) the failure to protect a high-risk adult with disabilities from health and safety hazards.

(B) Nothing in this subsection (10) shall be construed to impose a requirement that assistance be provided to a high-risk adult with disabilities over his or her objection in the absence of a court order, nor to create any new affirmative duty to provide support to a high-risk adult with disabilities.

(12) "Order of protection" means an emergency order, interim order or plenary order, granted pursuant to this Act, which includes any or all of the remedies authorized by Section 214 of this Act [750 ILCS 60/214].

(13) "Petitioner" may mean not only any named petitioner for the order of protection and any named victim of abuse on whose behalf the petition is brought, but also any other person protected by this Act.

(14) "Physical abuse" includes sexual abuse and means any of the following:

(i) knowing or reckless use of physical force, confinement or restraint;

(ii) knowing, repeated and unnecessary sleep deprivation; or

(iii) knowing or reckless conduct which creates an immediate risk of physical harm.

(15) "Willful deprivation" means wilfully denying a person who because of age, health or disability requires medication, medical care, shelter, accessible shelter or services, food, therapeutic device, or other physical assistance, and thereby exposing that person to the risk of physical, mental or emotional harm, except with regard to medical care or treatment when the dependent person has expressed an intent to forgo such medical care or treatment. This paragraph does not create any new affirmative duty to provide support to dependent persons.

(Chgd. by P.A. 87-1186, §3, eff. 1/1/93.)
(Source: P.A. 86-542.) [Formerly Ill. Rev. Stat. 40 §2311-3.]

ARTICLE II. ORDERS OF PROTECTION

Sec.

60/201. Persons protected by this Act.

§201. Persons protected by this Act. (a) The following persons are protected by this Act:

(i) any person abused by a family or household member;

(ii) any high-risk adult with disabilities who is abused, neglected, or exploited by a family or household member;

(iii) any minor child or dependent adult in the care of such person; and

(iv) any person residing or employed at a private home or public shelter which is housing an abused family or household member.

(b) A petition for an order of protection may be filed only: (i) by a person who has been abused by a family or household member or by any person on behalf of a minor child or an adult who has been abused by a family or household member and who, because of age, health, disability, or inaccessibility, cannot file the petition, or (ii) by any person on behalf of a high-risk adult with disabilities who has been abused, neglected, or exploited by a family or household member. However, any petition properly filed under this Act may seek protection for any additional persons protected by this Act.

(Chgd. by P.A. 87-1186, §3, eff. 1/1/93.)
(Source: P.A. 86-542.) [Formerly Ill. Rev. Stat. 40 §2312-1.]

60/201.1. Access of high-risk adults.

§201.1. Access of high-risk adults. No person shall obstruct or impede the access of a high-risk adult with disabilities to any agency or organization authorized to file a petition for an order of protection under Section 201 of this Act [750 ILCS 60/201] for the purpose of a private visit relating to legal rights, entitlements, claims and services under this Act and Section 1 of "An Act in relation to domestic relations and domestic violence shelters and service programs", approved September 24, 1981, as now or hereafter amended [20 ILCS 2210/0.01 et seq.]. If a person does so obstruct or impede such access of a high-risk adult with disabilities, local law enforcement agencies shall take all appropriate action to assist the party seeking access in petitioning for a search warrant or an ex parte injunctive order. Such warrant or order may issue upon a showing of probable cause to believe that the high-risk adult with disabilities is the

subject of abuse, neglect, or exploitation which constitutes a criminal offense or that any other criminal offense is occurring which affects the interests or welfare of the high-risk adult with disabilities. When, from the personal observations of a law enforcement officer, it appears probable that delay of entry in order to obtain a warrant or order would cause the high-risk adult with disabilities to be in imminent danger of death or great bodily harm, entry may be made by the law enforcement officer after an announcement of the officer's authority and purpose.
(Source: P.A. 86-542.) [Formerly Ill. Rev. Stat. 40 §2312-1.1.]

60/202. Commencement of action; filing fees; dismissal.
§202. Commencement of action; filing fees; dismissal. (a) How to commence action. Actions for orders of protection are commenced:

(1) Independently: By filing a petition for an order of protection in any civil court, unless specific courts are designated by local rule or order.

(2) In conjunction with another civil proceeding: By filing a petition for an order of protection under the same case number as another civil proceeding involving the parties, including but not limited to: (i) any proceeding under the Illinois Marriage and Dissolution of Marriage Act [750 ILCS 5/101 et seq.], Illinois Parentage Act of 1984 [750 ILCS 45/1 et seq.], Nonsupport of Spouse and Children Act [750 ILCS 15/1 et seq.], Revised Uniform Reciprocal Enforcement of Support Act [750 ILCS 20/1 et seq.] or an action for nonsupport brought under Article 10 of the Illinois Public Aid Code [305 ILCS 5/10-1 et seq.], provided that a petitioner and the respondent are a party to or the subject of that proceeding or (ii) a guardianship proceeding under the Probate Act of 1975 [755 ILCS 5/1-1 et seq.], or a proceeding for involuntary commitment under the Mental Health and Developmental Disabilities Code [405 ILCS 5/1-100 et seq.], or any proceeding, other than a delinquency petition, under the Juvenile Court Act of 1987 [705 ILCS 405/1-1 et seq.], provided that a petitioner or the respondent is a party to or the subject of such proceeding.

(3) In conjunction with a delinquency petition or a criminal prosecution: By filing a petition for an order of protection, under the same case number as the delinquency petition or criminal prosecution, to be granted during pre-trial release of a defendant, with any dispositional order issued under Section 5-23 of the Juvenile Court Act of 1987 [705 ILCS 405/5-23] or as a condition of release, supervision, conditional discharge, probation, periodic imprisonment, parole or mandatory supervised release, or in conjunction with imprisonment or a bond forfeiture warrant; provided that:

(i) the violation is alleged in an information, complaint, indictment or delinquency petition on file, and the alleged offender and victim are family or household members or persons protected by this Act; and

(ii) the petition, which is filed by the State's Attorney, names a victim of the alleged crime as a petitioner.

(b) Filing and service fees. No fee shall be charged for filing or service by the sheriff of a petition in an action commenced under this Section.

(c) Dismissal and consolidation. Withdrawal or dismissal of any petition for an order of protection prior to adjudication where the petitioner is represented by the State shall operate as a dismissal without prejudice. No action for an order of protection shall be dismissed because the respondent is being prosecuted for a crime against the petitioner. An independent action may be consolidated with another civil proceeding, as provided by paragraph (2) of subsection (a) of this Section. For any action commenced under paragraph (2) or (3) of subsection (a) of this Section, dismissal of the conjoined case (or a finding of not guilty) shall not require dismissal of the action for the order of protection; instead, it may be treated as an independent action and, if necessary and appropriate, transferred to a different court or division. Dismissal of any conjoined case shall not affect the validity of any previously issued order of protection, and thereafter subsections (b)(1) and (b)(2) of Section 220 [750 ILCS 60/220] shall be inapplicable to such order.

(d) Pro se petitions. The court shall provide, through the office of the clerk of the court, simplified forms and clerical assistance to help with the writing and filing of a petition under this Section by any person not represented by counsel. In addition, that assistance may be provided by the state's attorney.
(Chgd. by P.A. 87-1186, §3, eff. 1/1/93.)
(Source: P.A. 85-1209; 86-1300.) [Formerly Ill. Rev. Stat. 40 §2312-2.]

60/203. Pleading; non-disclosure of address.

§203. Pleading; non-disclosure of address. (a) A petition for an order of protection shall be in writing and verified or accompanied by affidavit and shall allege that petitioner has been abused by respondent, who is a family or household member. The petition shall further set forth whether there is any other pending action between the parties. During the pendency of this proceeding, each party has a continuing duty to inform the court of any subsequent proceeding for an order of protection in this or any other state.

(b) If the petition states that disclosure of petitioner's address would risk abuse of petitioner or any member of petitioner's family or household or reveal the confidential address of a shelter for domestic violence victims, that address may be omitted from all documents filed with the court. If disclosure is necessary to determine jurisdiction or consider any venue issue, it shall be made orally and in camera. If petitioner has not disclosed an address under this subsection, petitioner shall designate an alternative address at which respondent may serve notice of any motions.
(Chgd. by P.A. 87-1186, §3, eff. 1/1/93.)
(Source: P.A. 84-1305.) [Formerly Ill. Rev. Stat. 40 §2312-3.]

60/204. Petitions of indigent persons.

§204. Petitions of indigent persons. (a) Emergency petitions. A petition for an emergency order of protection shall be filed without payment of the filing fee, if any, or without a prior court order waiving or deferring that fee, if accompanied by an affidavit, in compliance with Illinois Supreme Court Rule 298, stating that petitioner lacks the funds to pay filing fees. At the hearing for that emergency order, the court shall determine petitioner's eligibility for waiver or deferral of court costs.

(b) Other petitions. A petition for a 30-day interim order or a plenary order of protection may be filed without payment of the filing fee, if any, only if accompanied by a court order waiving or deferring that fee. Application for such an order shall be in accordance with Illinois Supreme Court Rule 298.

(c) Denial of petitions. A decision to deny indigent status shall not be based, in whole or in part, on any of the following factors:

(i) Petitioner is the sole or joint owner of his or her residence;

(ii) Petitioner is the sole or joint owner of a single automobile worth less than $5,000; or

(iii) Petitioner receives income, if that income is less than 125% of the official poverty threshold set by the U.S. Office of Management and Budget.

(d) Deferral of costs. If petitioner is not eligible for waiver of court costs, the court may nevertheless defer payment of filing and service fees upon evidence that:

(i) Petitioner seeks an order of protection to deter future abuse and lacks immediate resources to pay filing and service fees; and

(ii) either petitioner or respondent will have the means to pay deferred court costs prior to entry of a final order.

(e) Income of alleged abuser. The income of the family or household member alleged to be abusing the petitioner shall not be considered in determining petitioner's eligibility for waiver of court costs. However, such waiver shall not diminish the court's authority to order payment of court costs by the abusive party.
(Chgd. by P.A. 87-1186, §3, eff. 1/1/93.)
(Source: P.A. 84-1305.) [Formerly Ill. Rev. Stat. 40 §2312-4.]

60/205. Application of rules of civil procedure; domestic abuse advocates.

§205. Application of rules of civil procedure; Domestic abuse advocates. (a) Any proceeding to obtain, modify, reopen or appeal an order of protection, whether commenced alone or in conjunction with a civil or criminal proceeding, shall be governed by the rules of civil procedure of this State. The standard of proof in such a proceeding is proof by a preponderance of the evidence, whether the proceeding is heard in criminal or civil court. The Code of Civil Procedure [735 ILCS 5/1-101 et seq.] and Supreme Court and local court rules applicable to civil proceedings, as now or hereafter amended, shall apply, except as otherwise provided by law.

(b) (1) In all circuit court proceedings under this Act, domestic abuse advocates shall be allowed to attend and sit at counsel table and confer with the victim, unless otherwise directed by the court.

(2) In criminal proceedings in circuit courts, domestic abuse advocates shall be allowed to accompany the victim and confer with the victim, unless otherwise directed by the court.

(3) Court administrators shall allow domestic abuse advocates to assist victims of domestic violence in the preparation of petitions for orders of protection.

(4) Domestic abuse advocates are not engaged in the unauthorized practice of law when providing assistance of the types specified in this subsection (b).
(Chgd. by P.A. 87-1186, §3, eff. 1/1/93; P.A. 87-1255, §2, eff. 1/7/93.)
(Source: P.A. 84-1305.) [Formerly Ill. Rev. Stat. 40 §2312-5.]

60/206. Trial by jury.

§206. Trial by jury. There shall be no right to trial by jury in any proceeding to obtain, modify, vacate or extend any order of protection under this Act. However, nothing in this Section shall deny any existing right to trial by jury in a criminal proceeding.
(Chgd. by P.A. 87-1186, §3, eff. 1/1/93.)
(Source: P.A. 84-1305.) [Formerly Ill. Rev. Stat. 40 §2312-6.]

60/207. Subject matter jurisdiction.

§207. Subject matter jurisdiction. Each of the circuit courts shall have the power to issue orders of protection.
(Source: P.A. 84-1305.) [Formerly Ill. Rev. Stat. 40 §2312-7.]

60/208. Jurisdiction over persons.

§208. Jurisdiction over persons. In child custody proceedings, the court's personal jurisdiction is determined by this State's Uniform Child Custody Jurisdiction Act, as now or hereafter amended [750 ILCS 35/1 et seq.]. Otherwise, the courts of this State have jurisdiction to bind (i) State residents and (ii) non-residents having minimum contacts with this State, to the extent permitted by the long-arm statute, Section 2-209 of the Code of Civil Procedure, as now or hereafter amended [735 ILCS 5/2-209].
(Source: P.A. 84-1305.) [Formerly Ill. Rev. Stat. 40 §2312-8.]

60/209. Venue.

§209. Venue. (a) Filing. A petition for an order of protection may be filed in any county where (i) petitioner resides, (ii) respondent resides, (iii) the alleged abuse occurred or (iv) the petitioner is temporarily located if petitioner left petitioner's residence to avoid further abuse and could not obtain safe, accessible, and adequate temporary housing in the county of that residence.

(b) Exclusive Possession. With respect to requests for exclusive possession of the residence under this Act, venue is proper only in the county where the residence is located, except in the following circumstances:

(1) If a request for exclusive possession of the residence is made under this Act in conjunction with a proceeding under the Illinois Marriage and Dissolution of Marriage Act [750 ILCS 5/101 et seq.], venue is proper in the county or judicial circuit where the residence is located or in a contiguous county or judicial circuit.

(2) If a request for exclusive possession of the residence is made under this Act in any other proceeding, provided the petitioner meets the requirements of item (iv) of subsection (a), venue is proper in the county or judicial circuit where the residence is located or in a contiguous county or judicial circuit. In such case, however, if the court is not located in the county where the residence is located, it may grant exclusive possession of the residence under subdivision (b)(2) of Section 214 [750 ILCS 60/214] only in an emergency order under Section 217 [750 ILCS 60/217], and such grant may be extended thereafter beyond the maximum initial period only by a court located in the county where the residence is located.

(c) Inconvenient forum. If an order of protection is issued by a court in a county in which neither of the parties resides, the court may balance hardships to the parties and accordingly transfer any proceeding to extend, modify, re-open, vacate or enforce any such order to a county wherein a party resides.

(d) Objection. Objection to venue is waived if not made within such time as respondent's response is due, except as otherwise provided in subsection (b). In no event shall venue be deemed jurisdictional.

(Chgd. by P.A. 87-1186, §3, eff. 1/1/93.)
(Source: P.A. 86-966.) [Formerly Ill. Rev. Stat. 40 §2312-9.]

60/210. Process.

§210. Process. (a) Summons. Any action for an order of protection, whether commenced alone or in conjunction with another proceeding, is a distinct cause of action and requires that a separate summons be issued and served, except that in pending cases the following methods may be used:

(1) By delivery of the summons to respondent personally in open court in pending civil or criminal cases.

(2) By notice in accordance with Section 210.1 in civil cases in which the defendant has filed a general appearance.

The summons shall be in the form prescribed by Supreme Court Rule 101(d), except that it shall require respondent to answer or appear within 7 days. Attachments to the summons or notice shall include the petition for order of protection and supporting affidavits, if any, and any emergency order of protection that has been issued. The enforcement of an order of protection under Section 223 shall not be affected by the lack of service, delivery, or notice, provided the requirements of subsection (d) of that Section are otherwise met.

(b) Fees. No fee shall be charged for service of summons in any action commenced in conjunction with (i) another civil proceeding, if the summons for both proceedings are filed together or (ii) any criminal proceeding.

(c) Expedited service. The summons shall be served by the sheriff or other law enforcement officer at the earliest time and shall take precedence over other summonses except those of a similar emergency nature. Special process servers may be appointed at any time, and their designation shall not affect the responsibilities and authority of the sheriff or other official process servers.

(d) Remedies requiring actual notice. The counseling, payment of support, payment of shelter services, and payment of losses remedies provided by paragraphs 4, 12, 13, and 16 of subsection (b) of Section 214 [750 ILCS 60/214] may be granted only if respondent has been personally served with process, has answered or has made a general appearance.

(e) Remedies upon constructive notice. Service of process on a member of respondent's household or by publication shall be adequate for the remedies provided by paragraphs 1, 2, 3, 5, 6, 7, 8, 9, 10, 11, 14, 15, and 17 of subsection (b) of Section 214, but only if: (i) petitioner has made all reasonable efforts to accomplish actual service of process personally upon respondent, but respondent cannot be found to effect such service and (ii) petitioner files an affidavit or presents sworn testimony as to those efforts.

(f) Default. A plenary order of protection may be entered by default as follows:

(1) For any of the remedies sought in the petition, if respondent has been served or given notice in accordance with subsection (a) and if respondent then fails to appear as directed or fails to appear on any subsequent appearance or hearing date agreed to by the parties or set by the court; or

(2) For any of the remedies provided in accordance with subsection (e), if respondent fails to answer or appear in accordance with the date set in the publication notice or the return date indicated on the service of a household member.

(Chgd. by P.A. 87-1186, §3, eff. 1/1/93.)
(Source: P.A. 84-1305.) [Formerly Ill. Rev. Stat. 40 §2312-10.]

60/210.1. Service of notice in conjunction with a pending civil case.

§210.1. Service of notice in conjunction with a pending civil case. (a) Notice. When an action for an order of protection is sought in conjunction with a pending civil case in which the court has obtained jurisdiction over respondent, and respondent has filed a general appearance, then a separate summons need not issue. Original notice of a hearing on a petition for an order of protection may be given, and the documents served, in accordance with Illinois Supreme Court Rules 11 and 12. When, however, an emergency order of protection is sought in such a case on an ex parte application, then the procedure set forth in subsection (a) of Section 210 (other than in subsection (a)(2)) shall be followed. If an order of protection is issued using the notice provisions of this Section, then the order of protection or extensions of that order may survive the disposition of the main civil case. The enforcement of any order of protection under Section 223 shall not be affected by the lack of notice under this Section, provided the requirements of subsection (d) of that Section are otherwise met.

(b) Default. The form of notice described in subsection (a) shall include the following language directed to the respondent:

A 2-year plenary order of protection may be entered by default for any of the remedies sought in the petition if you fail to appear on the specified hearing date or on any subsequent hearing date agreed to by the parties or set by the court.

(c) Party to give notice. Notice in the pending civil case shall be given (i) by either party under this Section, with respect to extensions, modifications, hearings, or other relief pertinent to an order of protection, in accordance with Illinois Supreme Court Rules 11 and 12 or (ii) by the respondent as provided in subsection (c) of Section 224.

(Added by P.A. 87-1186, §3, eff. 1/1/93.)
[Formerly Ill. Rev. Stat. 40 §2312-10.1.]

60/211. Service of notice of hearings.

§211. Service of notice of hearings. Except as provided in Sections 210 and 210.1 [750 ILCS 60/210 and 60/210.1], notice of hearings on petitions or motions shall be served in accordance with Supreme Court Rules 11 and 12, unless notice is excused by Section 217 of this Act [750 ILCS 60/217], or by the Code of Civil Procedure [735 ILCS 5/1-101 et seq.], Supreme Court Rules, or local rules, as now or hereafter amended.

(Chgd. by P.A. 87-1186, §3, eff. 1/1/93.)
(Source: P.A. 84-1305.) [Formerly Ill. Rev. Stat. 40 §2312-11.]

60/212. Hearings.

§212. Hearings. (a) A petition for an order of protection shall be treated as an expedited proceeding, and no court shall transfer or otherwise decline to decide all or part of such petition except as otherwise provided herein. Nothing in this Section shall prevent the court from reserving issues when jurisdiction or notice requirements are not met.

(b) Any court or a division thereof which ordinarily does not decide matters of child custody and family support may decline to decide contested issues of physical care, custody, visitation, or family support unless a decision on one or more of those contested issues is necessary to avoid the risk of abuse, neglect, removal from the state or concealment within the state of the child or of separation of the child from the primary caretaker. If the court or division thereof has declined to decide any or all of these issues, then it shall transfer all undecided issues to the appropriate court or division. In the event of such a transfer, a government attorney involved in the criminal prosecution may, but need not, continue to offer counsel to petitioner on transferred matters.

(c) If the court transfers or otherwise declines to decide any issue, judgment on that issue shall be expressly reserved and ruling on other issues shall not be delayed or declined.

(Chgd. by P.A. 87-1186, §3, eff. 1/1/93.)
(Source: P.A. 84-1305.) [Formerly Ill. Rev. Stat. 40 §2312-12.]

60/213. Continuances.

§213. Continuances. (a) Petitions for emergency orders. Petitions for emergency remedies shall be granted or denied in accordance with the standards of Section 217 [750 ILCS 60/217], regardless of respondent's appearance or presence in court.

(b) Petitions for interim and plenary orders. Any action for an order of protection is an expedited proceeding. Continuances should be granted only for good cause shown and kept to the minimum reasonable duration, taking into account the reasons for the continuance. If the continuance is necessary for some, but not all, of the remedies requested, hearing on those other remedies shall not be delayed.

(Chgd. by P.A. 87-1186, §3, eff. 1/1/93.)
(Source: P.A. 84-1305.) [Formerly Ill. Rev. Stat. 40 §2312-13.]

60/213.1. Hearsay exception.

§213.1. Hearsay exception. In an action for an order of protection on behalf of a high-risk adult with disabilities, a finding of lack of capacity to testify shall not render inadmissible any statement as long as the reliability of the statement is ensured by circumstances bringing it within the scope of a hearsay exception. The following evidence shall be admitted as an exception to the hearsay rule whether or not the declarant is available as a witness:

(1) A statement relating to a startling event or condition made spontaneously while the declarant was under the contemporaneous or continuing stress of excitement caused by the event or condition.

(2) A statement made for the purpose of obtaining, receiving, or promoting medical diagnosis or treatment, including psychotherapy, and describing medical history, or past or present symptoms, pain, or sensations, or the inception or general character of the cause or external source thereof insofar as reasonably pertinent to diagnosis or treatment. For purposes of obtaining a protective order, the identity of any person inflicting abuse or neglect as defined in this Act shall be deemed reasonably pertinent to diagnosis or treatment.

(3) A statement not specifically covered by any of the foregoing exceptions but having equivalent circumstantial guarantees of trustworthiness, if the court determines that (A) the statement is offered as evidence of a material fact, and (B) the statement is more probative on the point for which it is offered than any other evidence which the proponent can procure through reasonable efforts.

Circumstantial guarantees of trustworthiness include:

(1) the credibility of the witness who testifies the statement was made;

(2) assurance of the declarant's personal knowledge of the event;

(3) the declarant's interest or bias and the presence or absence of capacity or motive to fabricate;

(4) the presence or absence of suggestiveness or prompting at the time the statement was made;

(5) whether the declarant has ever reaffirmed or recanted the statement; and

(6) corroboration by physical evidence or behavioral changes in the declarant.

The record shall reflect the court's findings of fact and conclusions of law as to the trustworthiness requirement.

A statement shall not be admitted under the exception set forth in this Section unless its proponent gives written notice stating his or her intention to offer the statement and the particulars of it to the adverse party sufficiently in advance of offering the statement to provide the adverse party with a fair opportunity to prepare to meet the statement.
(Source: P.A. 86-542.) [Formerly Ill. Rev. Stat. 40 §2312-13.1.]

60/213.2. Waiver of privilege.

§213.2. Waiver of privilege. When the subject of any proceeding under this Act is a high-risk adult with disabilities for whom no guardian has been appointed, no party other than the high-risk adult or the attorney for the high-risk adult shall be entitled to invoke or waive a common law or statutory privilege on behalf of the high-risk adult which results in the exclusion of evidence.
(Source: P.A. 86-542.) [Formerly Ill. Rev. Stat. 40 §2312-13.2.]

60/213.3. Independent counsel; temporary substitute guardian.

§213.3. Independent counsel; temporary substitute guardian. If the petitioner is a high-risk adult with disabilities for whom a guardian has been appointed, the court shall appoint independent counsel other than a guardian ad litem and, may appoint a temporary substitute guardian under the provisions of Article XIa of the Probate Act of 1975 [755 ILCS 5/11a-1 et seq.]. The court shall appoint a temporary substitute guardian if the guardian is named as a respondent in a petition under this Act.
(Source: P.A. 86-542.) [Formerly Ill. Rev. Stat. 40 §2312-13.3.]

60/214. Order of protection; remedies.

§214. Order of protection; remedies. (a) Issuance of order. If the court finds that petitioner has been abused by a family or household member or that petitioner is a high-risk adult who has been abused, neglected, or exploited, as defined in this Act, an order of protection prohibiting the abuse, neglect, or exploitation shall issue; provided that petitioner must also satisfy the requirements of one of the following Sections, as appropriate: Section 217 [750 ILCS 60/217] on emergency orders, Section 218 [750 ILCS 60/218] on interim orders, or Section 219 [750 ILCS 60/219] on plenary orders. Petitioner shall not be denied an order of protection because petitioner or respondent is a minor. The court, when determining whether or not to issue an order of protection, shall not require physical manifestations of abuse on the person of the victim. Modification and extension of prior orders of protection shall be in accordance with this Act.

(b) Remedies and standards. The remedies to be included in an order of protection shall be determined in accordance with this Section and one of the following Sections, as appropriate: Section 217 on emergency orders, Section 218 on interim orders, and Section 219 on plenary orders. The remedies listed in this subsection shall be in addition to other civil or criminal remedies available to petitioner.

(1) Prohibition of abuse, neglect, or exploitation. Prohibit respondent's harassment, interference with personal liberty, intimidation of a dependent, physical abuse, or willful deprivation, neglect or exploitation, as defined in this Act, or stalking of the petitioner, as defined in Section 12-7.3 of the Criminal Code of 1961 [720 ILCS 5/12-7.3], if such abuse, neglect, exploitation, or stalking has occurred or otherwise appears likely to occur if not prohibited.

(2) Grant of exclusive possession of residence. Prohibit respondent from entering or remaining in any residence or household of the petitioner, including one owned or leased by respondent, if petitioner has a right to occupancy thereof. The grant of exclusive possession of the residence shall not affect title to real property, nor shall the court be limited by the standard set forth in Section 701 of the Illinois Marriage and Dissolution of Marriage Act.

(A) Right to occupancy. A party has a right to occupancy of a residence or household if it is solely or jointly owned or leased by that party, that party's spouse, a person with a legal duty to support that party or a minor child in that party's care, or by any person or entity other than the opposing party that authorizes that party's occupancy (e.g., a domestic violence shelter). Standards set forth in subparagraph (B) shall not preclude equitable relief.

(B) Presumption of hardships. If petitioner and respondent each has the right to occupancy of a residence or household, the court shall balance (i) the hardships to respondent and any minor child or dependent adult in respondent's care resulting from entry of this remedy with (ii) the hardships to petitioner and any minor child or dependent adult in petitioner's care resulting from continued exposure to the risk of abuse (should petitioner remain at the residence or household) or from loss of possession of the residence or household (should petitioner leave to avoid the risk of abuse). When determining the balance of hardships, the court shall also take into account the accessibility of the residence or household. Hardships need not be balanced if respondent does not have a right to occupancy.

The balance of hardships is presumed to favor possession by petitioner unless the presumption is rebutted by a preponderance of the evidence, showing that the hardships to respondent substantially outweigh the hardships to petitioner and any minor child or dependent adult in petitioner's care. The court, on the request of petitioner or on its own motion, may order respondent to provide suitable, accessible, alternate housing for petitioner instead of excluding respondent from a mutual residence or household.

(3) Stay away order and additional prohibitions. Order respondent to stay away from petitioner or any other person protected by the order of protection, or prohibit respondent from entering or remaining present at petitioner's school, place of employment, or other specified places at times when petitioner is

present, or both, if reasonable, given the balance of hardships. Hardships need not be balanced for the court to enter a stay away order or prohibit entry if respondent has no right to enter the premises.

If an order of protection grants petitioner exclusive possession of the residence, or prohibits respondent from entering the residence, or orders respondent to stay away from petitioner or other protected persons, then the court may allow respondent access to the residence to remove items of clothing and personal adornment used exclusively by respondent, medications, and other items as the court directs. The right to access shall be exercised on only one occasion as the court directs and in the presence of an agreed-upon adult third party or law enforcement officer.

(4) Counseling. Require or recommend the respondent to undergo counseling for a specified duration with a social worker, psychologist, clinical psychologist, psychiatrist, family service agency, alcohol or substance abuse program, mental health center guidance counselor, agency providing services to elders, program designed for domestic violence abusers or any other guidance service the court deems appropriate.

(5) Physical care and possession of the minor child. In order to protect the minor child from abuse, neglect, or unwarranted separation from the person who has been the minor child's primary caretaker, or to otherwise protect the well-being of the minor child, the court may do either or both of the following: (i) grant petitioner physical care or possession of the minor child, or both, or (ii) order respondent to return a minor child to, or not remove a minor child from, the physical care of a parent or person in loco parentis.

If a court finds, after a hearing, that respondent has committed abuse (as defined in Section 103) of a minor child, there shall be a rebuttable presumption that awarding physical care to respondent would not be in the minor child's best interest.

(6) Temporary legal custody. Award temporary legal custody to petitioner in accordance with this Section, the Illinois Marriage and Dissolution of Marriage Act [750 ILCS 5/101 et seq.], the Illinois Parentage Act of 1984 [750 ILCS 45/1 et seq.], and this State's Uniform Child Custody Jurisdiction Act [750 ILCS 35/1 et seq.].

If a court finds, after a hearing, that respondent has committed abuse (as defined in Section 103) of a minor child, there shall be a rebuttable presumption that awarding temporary legal custody to respondent would not be in the child's best interest.

(7) Visitation. Determine the visitation rights, if any, of respondent in any case in which the court awards physical care or temporary legal custody of a minor child to petitioner. The court shall restrict or deny respondent's visitation with a minor child if the court finds that respondent has done or is likely to do any of the following: (i) abuse or endanger the minor child during visitation; (ii) use the visitation as an opportunity to abuse or harass petitioner or petitioner's family or household members; (iii) improperly conceal or detain the minor child; or (iv) otherwise act in a manner that is not in the best interests of the minor child. The court shall not be limited by the standards set forth in Section 607.1 of the Illinois Marriage and Dissolution of Marriage Act. If the court grants visitation, the order shall specify dates and times for the visitation to take place or other specific parameters or conditions that are appropriate. No order for visitation shall refer merely to the term "reasonable visitation".

Petitioner may deny respondent access to the minor child if, when respondent arrives for visitation, respondent is under the influence of drugs or alcohol and constitutes a threat to the safety and well-being of petitioner or petitioner's minor children or is behaving in a violent or abusive manner.

If necessary to protect any member of petitioner's family or household from future abuse, respondent shall be prohibited from coming to petitioner's residence to meet the minor child for visitation, and the parties shall submit to the court their recommendations for reasonable alternative arrangements for visitation. A person may be approved to supervise visitation only after filing an affidavit accepting that responsibility and acknowledging accountability to the court.

(8) Removal or concealment of minor child. Prohibit respondent from removing a minor child from the State or concealing the child within the State.

(9) Order to appear. Order the respondent to appear in court, alone or with a minor child, to prevent abuse, neglect, removal or concealment of the child, to return the child to the custody or care of the petitioner or to permit any court-ordered interview or examination of the child or the respondent.

(10) Possession of personal property. Grant petitioner exclusive possession of personal property and, if respondent has possession or control, direct respondent to promptly make it available to petitioner, if:

(i) petitioner, but not respondent, owns the property; or

(ii) the parties own the property jointly; sharing it would risk abuse of petitioner by respondent or is impracticable; and the balance of hardships favors temporary possession by petitioner.

If petitioner's sole claim to ownership of the property is that it is marital property, the court may award petitioner temporary possession thereof under the standards of subparagraph (ii) of this paragraph only if a proper proceeding has been filed under the Illinois Marriage and Dissolution of Marriage Act, as now or hereafter amended.

No order under this provision shall affect title to property.

(11) Protection of property. Forbid the respondent from taking, transferring, encumbering, concealing, damaging or otherwise disposing of any real or personal property, except as explicitly authorized by the court, if:

(i) petitioner, but not respondent, owns the property; or

(ii) the parties own the property jointly, and the balance of hardships favors granting this remedy.

If petitioner's sole claim to ownership of the property is that it is marital property, the court may grant petitioner relief under subparagraph (ii) of this paragraph only if a proper proceeding has been filed under the Illinois Marriage and Dissolution of Marriage Act, as now or hereafter amended.

The court may further prohibit respondent from improperly using the financial or other resources of an aged member of the family or household for the profit or advantage of respondent or of any other person.

(12) Order for payment of support. Order respondent to pay temporary support for the petitioner or any child in the petitioner's care or custody, when the respondent has a legal obligation to support that person, in accordance with the Illinois Marriage and Dissolution of Marriage Act, which shall govern, among other matters, the amount of support, payment through the clerk and withholding of income to secure payment. An order for child support may be granted to a petitioner with lawful physical care or custody of a child, or an order or agreement for physical care or custody, prior to entry of an order for legal custody. Such a support order shall expire upon entry of a valid order granting legal custody to another, unless otherwise provided in the custody order.

(13) Order for payment of losses. Order respondent to pay petitioner for losses suffered as a direct result of the abuse, neglect, or exploitation. Such losses shall include, but not be limited to, medical expenses, lost earnings or other support, repair or replacement of property damaged or taken, reasonable

attorney's fees, court costs and moving or other travel expenses, including additional reasonable expenses for temporary shelter and restaurant meals.

(i) Losses affecting family needs. If a party is entitled to seek maintenance, child support or property distribution from the other party under the Illinois Marriage and Dissolution of Marriage Act, as now or hereafter amended, the court may order respondent to reimburse petitioner's actual losses, to the extent that such reimbursement would be "appropriate temporary relief", as authorized by subsection (a)(3) of Section 501 of that Act [750 ILCS 5/501].

(ii) Recovery of expenses. In the case of an improper concealment or removal of a minor child, the court may order respondent to pay the reasonable expenses incurred or to be incurred in the search for and recovery of the minor child, including but not limited to legal fees, court costs, private investigator fees, and travel costs.

(14) Prohibition of entry. Prohibit the respondent from entering or remaining in the residence or household while the respondent is under the influence of alcohol or drugs and constitutes a threat to the safety and well-being of the petitioner or the petitioner's children.

(15) Prohibition of access to records. If an order of protection prohibits respondent from having contact with the minor child, or if petitioner's address is omitted under subsection (b) of Section 203, or if necessary to prevent abuse or wrongful removal or concealment of a minor child, the order shall deny respondent access to, and prohibit respondent from inspecting, obtaining, or attempting to inspect or obtain, school or any other records of the minor child who is in the care of petitioner.

(16) Order for payment of shelter services. Order respondent to reimburse a shelter providing temporary housing and counseling services to the petitioner for the cost of the services, as certified by the shelter and deemed reasonable by the court.

(17) Order for injunctive relief. Enter injunctive relief necessary or appropriate to prevent further abuse of a family or household member or further abuse, neglect, or exploitation of a high-risk adult with disabilities or to effectuate one of the granted remedies, if supported by the balance of hardships. If the harm to be prevented by the injunction is abuse or any other harm that one of the remedies listed in paragraphs (1) through (16) of this subsection is designed to prevent, no further evidence is necessary that the harm is an irreparable injury.

(c) Relevant factors; findings.

(1) In determining whether to grant a specific remedy, other than payment of support, the court shall consider relevant factors, including but not limited to the following:

(i) the nature, frequency, severity, pattern and consequences of the respondent's past abuse, neglect or exploitation of the petitioner or any family or household member, including the concealment of his or her location in order to evade service of process or notice, and the likelihood of danger of future abuse, neglect, or exploitation to petitioner or any member of petitioner's or respondent's family or household; and

(ii) the danger that any minor child will be abused or neglected or improperly removed from the jurisdiction, improperly concealed within the State or improperly separated from the child's primary caretaker.

(2) In comparing relative hardships resulting to the parties from loss of possession of the family home, the court shall consider relevant factors, including but not limited to the following:

(i) availability, accessibility, cost, safety, adequacy, location and other characteristics of alternate housing for each party and any minor child or dependent adult in the party's care;

(ii) the effect on the party's employment; and

(iii) the effect on the relationship of the party, and any minor child or dependent adult in the party's care, to family, school, church and community.

(3) Subject to the exceptions set forth in paragraph (4) of this subsection, the court shall make its findings in an official record or in writing, and shall at a minimum set forth the following:

(i) That the court has considered the applicable relevant factors described in paragraphs (1) and (2) of this subsection.

(ii) Whether the conduct or actions of respondent, unless prohibited, will likely cause irreparable harm or continued abuse.

(iii) Whether it is necessary to grant the requested relief in order to protect petitioner or other alleged abused persons.

(4) For purposes of issuing an ex parte emergency order of protection, the court, as an alternative to or as a supplement to making the findings described in paragraphs (c)(3)(i) through (c)(3)(iii) of this subsection, may use the following procedure:

When a verified petition for an emergency order of protection in accordance with the requirements of Sections 203 and 217 is presented to the court, the court shall examine petitioner on oath or affirmation. An emergency order of protection shall be issued by the court if it appears from the contents of the petition and the examination of petitioner that the averments are sufficient to indicate abuse by respondent and to support the granting of relief under the issuance of the emergency order of protection.

(5) Never married parties. No rights or responsibilities for a minor child born outside of marriage attach to a putative father until a father and child relationship has been established under the Illinois Parentage Act of 1984. Absent such an adjudication, no putative father shall be granted temporary custody of the minor child, visitation with the minor child, or physical care and possession of the minor child, nor shall an order of payment for support of the minor child be entered.

(d) Balance of hardships; findings. If the court finds that the balance of hardships does not support the granting of a remedy governed by paragraph (2), (3), (10), (11), or (16) of subsection (b) of this Section, which may require such balancing, the court's findings shall so indicate and shall include a finding as to whether granting the remedy will result in hardship to respondent that would substantially outweigh the hardship to petitioner from denial of the remedy. The findings shall be an official record or in writing.

(e) Denial of remedies. Denial of any remedy shall not be based, in whole or in part, on evidence that:

(1) Respondent has cause for any use of force, unless that cause satisfies the standards for justifiable use of force provided by Article VII of the Criminal Code of 1961 [720 ILCS 5/7-1 et seq.];

(2) Respondent was voluntarily intoxicated;

(3) Petitioner acted in self-defense or defense of another, provided that, if petitioner utilized force, such force was justifiable under Article VII of the Criminal Code of 1961;

(4) Petitioner did not act in self-defense or defense of another;

(5) Petitioner left the residence or household to avoid further abuse, neglect, or exploitation by respondent;

(6) Petitioner did not leave the residence or household to avoid further abuse, neglect, or exploitation by respondent;

(7) Conduct by any family or household member excused the abuse, neglect, or exploitation by respondent, unless that same conduct would have excused such abuse, neglect, or exploitation if the parties had not been family or household members.

(Chgd. by P.A. 87-1186, §3, eff. 1/1/93.)

(Source: P.A. 86-542; 86-966; 86-1028; 87-743; 87-870; 87-871.) [Formerly Ill. Rev. Stat. 40 §2312-14.]

60/215. Mutual orders of protection; correlative separate orders.

§215. Mutual orders of protection; correlative separate orders. Mutual orders of protection are prohibited. Correlative separate orders of protection undermine the purposes of this Act and are prohibited unless both parties have properly filed written pleadings, proved past abuse by the other party, given prior written notice to the other party unless excused under Section 217 [750 ILCS 60/217], satisfied all prerequisites for the type of order and each remedy granted, and otherwise complied with this Act. In these cases, the court shall hear relevant evidence, make findings, and issue separate orders in accordance with Sections 214 and 221 [750 ILCS 60/214 and 60/221]. The fact that correlative separate orders are issued shall not be a sufficient basis to deny any remedy to petitioner or to prove that the parties are equally at fault or equally endangered.

(Chgd. by P.A. 87-1186, §3, eff. 1/1/93.)
(Source: P.A. 84-1305.) [Formerly Ill. Rev. Stat. 40 §2312-15.]

60/216. Accountability for actions of others.

§216. Accountability for Actions of Others. For the purposes of issuing an order of protection, deciding what remedies should be included and enforcing the order, Article 5 of the Criminal Code of 1961 [720 ILCS 5/5-1 et seq.] shall govern whether respondent is legally accountable for the conduct of another person.

(Source: P.A. 84-1305.) [Formerly Ill. Rev. Stat. 40 §2312-16.]

60/217. Emergency order of protection.

§217. Emergency order of protection. (a) Prerequisites. An emergency order of protection shall issue if petitioner satisfies the requirements of this subsection for one or more of the requested remedies. For each remedy requested, petitioner shall establish that:

(1) The court has jurisdiction under Section 208 [750 ILCS 60/208];

(2) The requirements of Section 214 [750 ILCS 60/214] are satisfied; and

(3) There is good cause to grant the remedy, regardless of prior service of process or of notice upon the respondent, because:

(i) For the remedies of "prohibition of abuse" described in Section 214(b)(1), "stay away order and additional prohibitions" described in Section 214(b)(3), "removal or concealment of minor child" described in Section 214(b)(8), "order to appear" described in Section 214(b)(9), "physical care and possession of the minor child" described in Section 214(b)(5), "protection of property" described in Section 214(b)(11), "prohibition of entry" described in Section 214(b)(14), "prohibition of access to records" described in Section 214(b)(15), and "injunctive relief" described in Section 214(b)(16), the harm which that remedy is intended to prevent would be likely to occur if the respondent were given any prior notice, or greater notice than was actually given, of the petitioner's efforts to obtain judicial relief;

(ii) For the remedy of "grant of exclusive possession of residence" described in Section 214(b)(2), the immediate danger of further abuse of petitioner by respondent, if petitioner chooses or had chosen to remain in the residence or household while respondent was given any prior notice or greater notice than was actually given of petitioner's efforts to obtain judicial relief, outweighs the hardships to respondent of an emergency order granting petitioner exclusive possession of the residence or household. This remedy shall not be denied because petitioner has or could obtain temporary shelter elsewhere while prior notice is given to respondent, unless the hardships to respondent from exclusion from the home substantially outweigh those to petitioner;

(iii) For the remedy of "possession of personal property" described in Section 214(b)(10), improper disposition of the personal property would be likely to occur if respondent were given any prior notice, or greater notice than was actually given, of petitioner's efforts to obtain judicial relief, or petitioner has an immediate and pressing need for possession of that property.

An emergency order may not include the counseling, legal custody, payment of support or monetary compensation remedies.

(b) Appearance by respondent. If respondent appears in court for this hearing for an emergency order, he or she may elect to file a general appearance and testify. Any resulting order may be an emergency order, governed by this Section. Notwithstanding the requirements of this Section, if all requirements of Section 218 [750 ILCS 60/218] have been met, the court may issue a 30-day interim order.

(c) Emergency orders: court holidays and evenings.

(1) Prerequisites. When the court is unavailable at the close of business, the petitioner may file a petition for a 21-day emergency order before any available circuit judge or associate judge who may grant relief under this Act. If the judge finds that there is an immediate and present danger of abuse to petitioner and that petitioner has satisfied the prerequisites set forth in subsection (a) of Section 217, that judge may issue an emergency order of protection.

(2) Certification and transfer. Any order issued under this Section and any documentation in support thereof shall be certified on the next court day to the appropriate court. The clerk of that court shall immediately assign a case number, file the petition, order and other documents with the court, and enter the order of record and file it with the sheriff for service, in accordance with Section 222 [750 ILCS 60/222]. Filing the petition shall commence proceedings for further relief under Section 202 [750 ILCS 60/202]. Failure to comply with the requirements of this subsection shall not affect the validity of the order.

(Chgd. by P.A. 87-1186, §3, eff. 1/1/93.)

(Source: P.A. 86-966.) [Formerly Ill. Rev. Stat. 40 §2312-17.]

60/218. 30-Day interim order of protection.

§218. 30-Day interim order of protection. (a) Prerequisites. An interim order of protection shall issue if petitioner has served notice of the hearing for that order on respondent, in accordance with Section 211 [750 ILCS 60/211], and satisfies the requirements of this subsection for one or more of the requested remedies. For each remedy requested, petitioner shall establish that:

(1) The court has jurisdiction under Section 208 [750 ILCS 60/208];

(2) The requirements of Section 214 [750 ILCS 60/214]are satisfied; and

(3) A general appearance was made or filed by or for respondent; or process was served on respondent in the manner required by Section 210 [750 ILCS 60/210]; or the petitioner is diligently attempting to complete the required service of process.

An interim order may not include the counseling, payment of support or monetary compensation remedies, unless the respondent has filed a general appearance or has been personally served.

(b) Appearance by respondent. If respondent appears in court for this hearing for an interim order, he or she may elect to file a general appearance and testify. Any resulting order may be an interim order, governed by this Section. Notwithstanding the requirements of this Section, if all requirements of Section 219 [750 ILCS 60/219] have been met, the Court may issue a plenary order of protection.

(Chgd. by P.A. 87-1186, §3, eff. 1/1/93.)

(Source: P.A. 84-1305.) [Formerly Ill. Rev. Stat. 40 §2312-18.]

60/219. Plenary order of protection.

§219. Plenary Order of Protection. A plenary order of protection shall issue if petitioner has served notice of the hearing for that order on respondent, in accordance with Section 211 [750 ILCS 60/211], and satisfies the requirements of this Section for one or more of the requested remedies. For each remedy requested, petitioner must establish that:

(1) The court has jurisdiction under Section 208 [750 ILCS 60/208];

(2) The requirements of Section 214 [750 ILCS 60/214] are satisfied; and

(3) A general appearance was made or filed by or for respondent or process was served on respondent in the manner required by Section 210 [750 ILCS 60/210]; and

(4) Respondent has answered or is in default.

(Source: P.A. 84-1305.) [Formerly Ill. Rev. Stat. 40 §2312-19.]

60/220. Duration and extension of orders.

§220. Duration and extension of orders. (a) Duration of emergency and interim orders. Unless re-opened or extended or voided by entry of an order of greater duration:

(1) Emergency orders issued under Section 217 [750 ILCS 60/217] shall be effective for not less than 14 nor more than 21 days;

(2) Interim orders shall be effective for up to 30 days.

(b) Duration of plenary orders. Except as otherwise provided in this Section, a plenary order of protection shall be valid for a fixed period of time, not to exceed two years.

(1) A plenary order of protection entered in conjunction with another civil proceeding shall remain in effect as follows:

(i) if entered as preliminary relief in that other proceeding, until entry of final judgment in that other proceeding;

(ii) if incorporated into the final judgment in that other proceeding, until the order of protection is vacated or modified; or

(iii) if incorporated in an order for involuntary commitment, until termination of both the involuntary commitment and any voluntary commitment, or for a fixed period of time not exceeding 2 years.

(2) A plenary order of protection entered in conjunction with a criminal prosecution shall remain in effect as follows:

(i) if entered during pre-trial release, until disposition, withdrawal, or dismissal of the underlying charge; if, however, the case is continued as an independent cause of action, the order's duration may be for a fixed period of time not to exceed 2 years;

(ii) if in effect in conjunction with a bond forfeiture warrant, until final disposition or an additional period of time not exceeding 2 years; no order of protection, however, shall be terminated by a dismissal that is accompanied by the issuance of a bond forfeiture warrant;

(iii) until expiration of any supervision, conditional discharge, probation, periodic imprisonment, parole or mandatory supervised release and for an additional period of time thereafter not exceeding 2 years; or

(iv) until the date set by the court for expiration of any sentence of imprisonment and subsequent parole or mandatory supervised release and for an additional period of time thereafter not exceeding 2 years.

(c) Computation of time. The duration of an order of protection shall not be reduced by the duration of any prior order of protection.

(d) Law enforcement records. When a plenary order of protection expires upon the occurrence of a specified event, rather than upon a specified date as provided in subsection (b), no expiration date shall be entered in Department of State Police records. To remove the plenary order from those records, either party shall request the clerk of the court to file a certified copy of an order stating that the specified event has occurred or that the plenary order has been vacated or modified with the Sheriff, and the Sheriff shall direct that law enforcement records shall be promptly corrected in accordance with the filed order.

(e) Extension of orders. Any emergency, interim or plenary order may be extended one or more times, as required, provided that the requirements of Section 217, 218 or 219 [750 ILCS 60/217, 60/218 or 60/219], as appropriate, are satisfied. If the motion for extension is uncontested and petitioner seeks no modification of the order, the order may be extended on the basis of petitioner's motion or affidavit stating that there has been no material change in relevant circumstances since entry of the order and stating the reason for the requested extension. Extensions may be granted only in open court and not under the provisions of subsection (c) of Section 217, which applies only when the court is unavailable at the close of business or on a court holiday.

(f) Termination date. Any order of protection which would expire on a court holiday shall instead expire at the close of the next court business day.

(g) Statement of purpose. The practice of dismissing or suspending a criminal prosecution in exchange for the issuance of an order of protection undermines the purposes of this Act. This Section shall not be construed as encouraging that practice.

(Chgd. by P.A. 87-1186, §3, eff. 1/1/93.)
(Source: P.A. 86-966.) [Formerly Ill. Rev. Stat. 40 §2312-20.]

60/221. Contents of orders.

§221. Contents of orders. (a) Any order of protection shall describe the following:

(1) Each remedy granted by the court, in reasonable detail and not by reference to any other document, so that respondent may clearly understand what he or she must do or refrain from doing. Pre-printed form orders of protection shall include the definitions of the types of abuse, neglect, and exploitation, as provided in Section 103 [750 ILCS 60/103]. Remedies set forth in pre-printed form orders shall be numbered consistently with and corresponding to the numerical sequence of remedies listed in Section 214 [750 ILCS 60/214] (at least as of the date the form orders are printed).

(2) The reason for denial of petitioner's request for any remedy listed in Section 214.

(b) An order of protection shall further state the following:

(1) The name of each petitioner that the court finds was abused, neglected, or exploited by respondent, and that respondent is a member of the family or household of each such petitioner, and the name of each other person protected by the order and that such person is protected by this Act.

(2) For any remedy requested by petitioner on which the court has declined to rule, that that remedy is reserved.

(3) The date and time the order of protection was issued, whether it is an emergency, interim or plenary order and the duration of the order.

(4) The date, time and place for any scheduled hearing for extension of that order of protection or for another order of greater duration or scope.

(5) For each remedy in an emergency order of protection, the reason for entering that remedy without prior notice to respondent or greater notice than was actually given.

(6) For emergency and interim orders of protection, that respondent may petition the court, in accordance with Section 224 [750 ILCS 60/224], to re-open that order if he or she did not receive actual prior notice of the hearing, in accordance with Section 211 [750 ILCS 60/211], and alleges that he or she had a meritorious defense to the order or that the order or any of its remedies was not authorized by this Act.

(c) Any order of protection shall include the following notice, printed in conspicuous type: "Any knowing violation of an order of protection forbidding physical abuse, neglect, exploitation, harassment, intimidation, interference with personal liberty, willful deprivation, or entering or remaining present at specified places when the protected person is present, or granting exclusive possession of the residence or household, or granting a stay away order is a Class A misdemeanor. Grant of exclusive possession of the residence or household shall constitute notice forbidding trespass to land. Any knowing violation of an order awarding legal custody or physical care of a child or prohibiting removal or concealment of a child may be a Class 4 felony. Any willful violation of any order is contempt of court. Any violation may result in fine or imprisonment."

(Chgd. by P.A. 87-1186, §3, eff. 1/1/93.)

(Source: P.A. 86-542; 86-1300.) [Formerly Ill. Rev. Stat. 40 §2312-21.]

60/222. Notice of orders.

§222. Notice of orders. (a) Entry and issuance. Upon issuance of any order of protection, the clerk shall immediately (i) enter the order on the record and file it in accordance with the circuit court procedures and (ii) provide a file stamped copy of the order to respondent, if present, and to petitioner.

(b) Filing with sheriff. The clerk of the issuing judge shall, or the petitioner may, on the same day that an order of protection is issued, file a certified copy of that order with the sheriff or other law enforcement officials charged with maintaining Department of State Police records or charged with serving the order upon respondent.

(c) Service by sheriff. Unless respondent was present in court when the order was issued, the sheriff, other law enforcement official or special process server shall promptly serve that order upon respondent and file proof of such service, in the manner provided for service of process in civil proceedings. If process has not yet been served upon the respondent, it shall be served with the order. A single fee may be charged for service of an order obtained in civil court, or for service of such an order together with process, unless waived or deferred under Section 210 [750 ILCS 60/210].

(d) Extensions, modifications and revocations. Any order extending, modifying or revoking any order of protection shall be promptly recorded, issued and served as provided in this Section.

(e) Notice to schools. Upon request and at the expense of the petitioner, the clerk of the issuing judge shall file a certified copy of an order of protection with the private school or schools or the principal office of the school district or districts in which any children of the petitioner are enrolled.

(f) Disclosure by schools. A private school may prohibit the disclosure by any school employee to any person against whom the school has received a certified copy of an order of protection the location or address of the petitioner for the order of protection. The school shall maintain the copy of the order of protection in the records of the child or children enrolled in the school whose parent is the petitioner of an order of protection. A public school district may prohibit disclosure in accordance with Section 10-22.3c or 34-18.6a of the School Code [105 ILCS 5/10-22.3c or 5/34-18.6a].

(Chgd. by P.A. 87-1186, §3, eff. 1/1/93.)

(Source: P.A. 87-437.) [Formerly Ill. Rev. Stat. 40 §2312-22.]

60/223. Enforcement of orders of protection.

§223. Enforcement of orders of protection. (a) When violation is crime. A violation of any order of protection, whether issued in a civil or criminal proceeding, may be enforced by a criminal court when:

(1) The respondent commits the crime of violation of order of protection pursuant to Section 12-30 of the Criminal Code of 1961 [720 ILCS 5/12-30], by having knowingly violated remedies described in paragraphs (1), (2), (3), or (14) of subsection (b) of Section 214 of this Act [750 ILCS 60/214] or any other remedy when the act constitutes a crime against the protected parties as defined by the

Criminal Code of 1961 [720 ILCS 5/1-1 et seq.]. Prosecution for a violation of an order of protection shall not bar concurrent prosecution for any other crime, including any crime that may have been committed at the time of the violation of the order of protection; or

(2) The respondent commits the crime of child abduction pursuant to Section 10-5 of the Criminal Code of 1961 [720 ILCS 5/10-5], by having knowingly violated remedies described in paragraphs (5), (6) or (8) of subsection (b) of Section 214 of this Act.

(b) When violation is contempt of court. A violation of any valid Illinois order of protection, whether issued in a civil or criminal proceeding, may be enforced through civil or criminal contempt procedures, as appropriate, by any court with jurisdiction, regardless where the act or acts which violated the order of protection were committed, to the extent consistent with the venue provisions of this Act. Nothing in this Act shall preclude any Illinois court from enforcing any valid order of protection issued in another state. Illinois courts may enforce orders of protection through both criminal prosecution and contempt proceedings, unless the action which is second in time is barred by collateral estoppel or the constitutional prohibition against double jeopardy.

(1) In a contempt proceeding where the petition for a rule to show cause sets forth facts evidencing an immediate danger that the respondent will flee the jurisdiction, conceal a child, or inflict physical abuse on the petitioner or minor children or on dependent adults in petitioner's care, the court may order the attachment of the respondent without prior service of the rule to show cause or the petition for a rule to show cause. Bond shall be set unless specifically denied in writing.

(2) A petition for a rule to show cause for violation of an order of protection shall be treated as an expedited proceeding.

(c) Violation of custody or support orders. A violation of remedies described in paragraphs (5), (6), (8), or (9) of subsection (b) of Section 214 of this Act may be enforced by any remedy provided by Section 611 of the Illinois Marriage and Dissolution of Marriage Act [750 ILCS 5/611]. The court may enforce any order for support issued under paragraph (12) of subsection (b) of Section 214 in the manner provided for under Articles V and VII of the Illinois Marriage and Dissolution of Marriage Act [750 ILCS 5/501 et seq. and 5/701 et seq.].

(d) Actual knowledge. An order of protection may be enforced pursuant to this Section if the respondent violates the order after the respondent has actual knowledge of its contents as shown through one of the following means:

(1) By service, delivery, or notice under Section 210 [750 ILCS 60/210].

(2) By notice under Section 210.1 or 211 [750 ILCS 60/210.1 or 60/211].

(3) By service of an order of protection under Section 222 [750 ILCS 60/222].

(4) By other means demonstrating actual knowledge of the contents of the order.

(e) The enforcement of an order of protection in civil or criminal court shall not be affected by either of the following:

(1) The existence of a separate, correlative order, entered under Section 215 [750 ILCS 60/215].

(2) Any finding or order entered in a conjoined criminal proceeding.

(f) Circumstances. The court, when determining whether or not a violation of an order of protection has occurred, shall not require physical manifestations of abuse on the person of the victim.

(g) Penalties.

(1) Except as provided in paragraph (3) of this subsection, where the court finds the commission of a crime or contempt of court under subsections (a) or (b) of this Section, the penalty shall be the penalty that generally applies in such criminal or contempt proceedings, and may include one or more of the

following: incarceration, payment of restitution, a fine, payment of attorneys' fees and costs, or community service.

(2) The court shall hear and take into account evidence of any factors in aggravation or mitigation before deciding an appropriate penalty under paragraph (1) of this subsection.

(3) To the extent permitted by law, the court is encouraged to:

(i) increase the penalty for the knowing violation of any order of protection over any penalty previously imposed by any court for respondent's violation of any order of protection or penal statute involving petitioner as victim and respondent as defendant;

(ii) impose a minimum penalty of 24 hours imprisonment for respondent's first violation of any order of protection; and

(iii) impose a minimum penalty of 48 hours imprisonment for respondent's second or subsequent violation of an order of protection

unless the court explicitly finds that an increased penalty or that period of imprisonment would be manifestly unjust.

(4) In addition to any other penalties imposed for a violation of an order of protection, a criminal court may consider evidence of any violations of an order of protection:

(i) to increase, revoke or modify the bail bond on an underlying criminal charge pursuant to Section 110-6 of the Code of Criminal Procedure of 1963 [725 ILCS 5/110-6];

(ii) to revoke or modify an order of probation, conditional discharge or supervision, pursuant to Section 5-6-4 of the Unified Code of Corrections [730 ILCS 5/5-6-4];

(iii) to revoke or modify a sentence of periodic imprisonment, pursuant to Section 5-7-2 of the Unified Code of Corrections [730 ILCS 5/5-7-2].

(Chgd. by P.A. 87-1186, §3, eff. 1/1/93.)
(Source: P.A. 86-1300; 87-743.) [Formerly Ill. Rev. Stat. 40 §2312-23.]

60/223.1. Order of protection; status.

§223.1. Order of protection; status. Whenever relief is sought under this Act, the court, before granting relief, shall determine whether any order of protection has previously been entered in the instant proceeding or any other proceeding in which any party, or a child of any party, or both, if relevant, has been designated as either a respondent or a protected person.

(Source: P.A. 87-743.) [Formerly Ill. Rev. Stat. 40 §2312-23.1.]

60/224. Modification and re-opening of orders.

§224. Modification and re-opening of orders. (a) Except as otherwise provided in this Section, upon motion by petitioner, the court may modify an emergency, interim, or plenary order of protection:

(1) If respondent has abused petitioner since the hearing for that order, by adding or altering one or more remedies, as authorized by Section 214 [750 ILCS 60/214]; and

(2) Otherwise, by adding any remedy authorized by Section 214 which was:

(i) reserved in that order of protection;

(ii) not requested for inclusion in that order of protection; or

(iii) denied on procedural grounds, but not on the merits.

(b) Upon motion by petitioner or respondent, the court may modify any prior order of protection's remedy for custody, visitation or payment of support in accordance with the relevant provisions of the Illinois Marriage and Dissolution of Marriage Act [750 ILCS 5/101 et seq.]. Each order of protection shall be entered in the Law Enforcement Automated Data System on the same day it is issued by the court.

(c) After 30 days following entry of a plenary order of protection, a court may modify that order only when changes in the applicable law or facts since that plenary order was entered warrant a modification of its terms.

(d) Upon 2 days' notice to petitioner, in accordance with Section 211 of this Act [750 ILCS 60/211], or such shorter notice as the court may prescribe, a respondent subject to an emergency or interim order of protection issued under this Act may appear and petition the court to re-hear the original or amended petition. Any petition to re-hear shall be verified and shall allege the following:

(1) that respondent did not receive prior notice of the initial hearing in which the emergency, interim, or plenary order was entered under Sections 211 and 217 [750 ILCS 60/211 and 60/217]; and

(2) that respondent had a meritorious defense to the order or any of its remedies or that the order or any of its remedies was not authorized by this Act.

(e) In the event that the emergency or interim order granted petitioner exclusive possession and the petition of respondent seeks to re-open or vacate that grant, the court shall set a date for hearing within 14 days on all issues relating to exclusive possession. Under no circumstances shall a court continue a hearing concerning exclusive possession beyond the 14th day, except by agreement of the parties. Other issues raised by the pleadings may be consolidated for the hearing if neither party nor the court objects.

(f) This Section does not limit the means, otherwise available by law, for vacating or modifying orders of protection.

(Chgd. by P.A. 87-1186, §3, eff. 1/1/93.)
(Source: P.A. 84-1305.) [Formerly Ill. Rev. Stat. 40 §2312-24.]

60/225. Immunity from prosecution.

§225. Immunity from prosecution. Any individual or organization acting in good faith to report the abuse of any person 60 years of age or older or to do any of the following in complying with the provisions of this Act shall not be subject to criminal prosecution or civil liability as a result of such action: providing any information to the appropriate law enforcement agency, providing that the giving of any information does not violate any privilege of confidentiality under law; assisting in any investigation; assisting in the preparation of any materials for distribution under this Act; or by providing services ordered under an order of protection.

Any individual, agency, or organization acting in good faith to report or investigate alleged abuse, neglect, or exploitation of a high-risk adult with disabilities, to testify in any proceeding on behalf of a high-risk adult with disabilities, to take photographs or perform an examination, or to perform any other act in compliance with the provisions of this Act shall not be the subject of criminal prosecution, civil liability, or other penalty, sanction, restriction, or retaliation as a result of such action.

(Chgd. by P.A. 87-1186, §3, eff. 1/1/93.)
(Source: P.A. 86-542.) [Formerly Ill. Rev. Stat. 40 §2312-25.]

60/226. Untrue statements.

§226. Untrue statements. Allegations and denials, made without reasonable cause and found to be untrue, shall subject the party pleading them to the payment of reasonable expenses actually incurred by the other party by reason of the untrue pleading, together with a reasonable attorney's fee, to be summarily taxed by the court upon motion made within 30 days of the judgment or dismissal, as provided in Supreme Court Rule 137. The court may direct that a copy of an order entered under this Section be provided to the State's Attorney so that he or she may determine whether to prosecute for perjury. This Section shall not apply to proceedings heard in Criminal Court or to criminal contempt of court proceedings, whether heard in Civil or Criminal Court.

(Chgd. by P.A. 87-1186, §3, eff. 1/1/93.)
(Source: P.A. 84-1305.) [Formerly Ill. Rev. Stat. 40 §2312-26.]

60/227. Privileged communications between domestic violence counselors and victims.

§227. Privileged communications between domestic violence counselors and victims. (a) As used in this Section:

(1) "Domestic violence program" means any unit of local government, organization, or association whose major purpose is to provide one or more of the following: information, crisis intervention, emergency shelter, referral, counseling, advocacy, or emotional support to victims of domestic violence.

(2) "Domestic violence advocate or counselor" means any person (A) who has undergone a minimum of forty hours of training in domestic violence advocacy, crisis intervention, and related areas, and (B) who provides services to victims through a domestic violence program either on an employed or volunteer basis.

(3) "Confidential communication" means any communication between an alleged victim of domestic violence and a domestic violence advocate or counselor in the course of providing information, counseling, or advocacy. The term includes all records kept by the advocate or counselor or by the domestic violence program in the course of providing services to an alleged victim concerning the alleged victim and the services provided. The confidential nature of the communication is not waived by the presence at the time of the communication of any additional persons, including but not limited to an interpreter, to further express the interests of the domestic violence victim or by the advocate's or counselor's disclosure to such an additional person with the consent of the victim when reasonably necessary to accomplish the purpose for which the advocate or counselor is consulted.

(4) "Domestic violence victim" means any person who consults a domestic violence counselor for the purpose of securing advice, counseling or assistance related to one or more alleged incidents of domestic violence.

(5) "Domestic violence" means abuse as defined in the Illinois Domestic Violence Act.

(b) No domestic violence advocate or counselor shall disclose any confidential communication or be examined as a witness in any civil or criminal case or proceeding or in any legislative or administrative proceeding without the written consent of the domestic violence victim except (1) in accordance with the provisions of the Abused and Neglected Child Reporting Act [325 ILCS 5/1 et seq.] or (2) in cases where failure to disclose is likely to result in an imminent risk of serious bodily harm or death of the victim or another person.

(c) A domestic violence advocate or counselor who knowingly discloses any confidential communication in violation of this Act commits a Class A misdemeanor.

(d) When a domestic violence victim is deceased or has been adjudged incompetent by a court of competent jurisdiction, the guardian of the domestic violence victim or the executor or administrator of the estate of the domestic violence victim may waive the privilege established by this Section, except where the guardian, executor or administrator of the estate has been charged with a violent crime against the domestic violence victim or has had an Order of Protection entered against him or her at the request of or on behalf of the domestic violence victim or otherwise has an interest adverse to that of the domestic violence victim with respect to the waiver of the privilege. In that case, the court shall appoint an attorney for the estate of the domestic violence victim.

(e) A minor may knowingly waive the privilege established by this Section. Where a minor is, in the opinion of the court, incapable of knowingly waiving the privilege, the parent or guardian of the minor may waive the privilege on behalf of the minor, except where such parent or guardian has been charged with a violent crime against the minor or has had an Order of Protection entered against him or her on request of or on behalf of the minor or otherwise has any interest adverse to that of the minor with respect to the waiver of the privilege. In that case, the court shall appoint an attorney for the minor child who shall be compensated in accordance with Section 506 of the Illinois Marriage and Dissolution of Marriage Act.

(f) Nothing in this Section shall be construed to limit in any way any privilege that might otherwise exist under statute or common law.

(g) The assertion of any privilege under this Section shall not result in an inference unfavorable to the State's cause or to the cause of the domestic violence victim.

(Chgd. by P.A. 87-1186, §3, eff. 1/1/93.)
(Source: P.A. 84-1305.) [Formerly Ill. Rev. Stat. 40 §2312-27.]

60/227.1. Other privileged information.

§227.1. Other privileged information. Except as otherwise provided in this Section, no court or administrative or legislative body shall compel any person or domestic violence program to disclose the location of any domestic violence program or the identity of any domestic violence advocate or counselor in any civil or criminal case or proceeding or in any administrative or legislative proceeding. A court may compel disclosure of the location of a domestic violence program or the identity of a domestic violence advocate or counselor if the court finds, following a hearing, that there is clear and convincing evidence that failure to disclose would be likely to result in an imminent risk of serious bodily harm or death to a domestic violence victim or another person. If the court makes such a finding, then disclosure shall take place in camera, under a restrictive protective order that does not frustrate the purposes of compelling the disclosure, and the information disclosed shall not be made a part of the written record of the case.

(Added by P.A. 87-1186, §3, eff. 1/1/93.)
[Formerly Ill. Rev. Stat. 40 §2312-27.1.]

ARTICLE III. LAW ENFORCEMENT RESPONSIBILITIES

60/301. Arrest without warrant.

§301. Arrest without warrant. (a) Any law enforcement officer may make an arrest without warrant if the officer has probable cause to believe that the person has committed or is committing any crime, including but not limited to violation of an order of protection, under Section 12-30 of the Criminal Code of 1961 [720 ILCS 5/12-30], even if the crime was not committed in the presence of the officer.

(b) The law enforcement officer may verify the existence of an order of protection by telephone or radio communication with his or her law enforcement agency or by referring to the copy of the order provided by the petitioner or respondent.

(Source: P.A. 84-1305.) [Formerly Ill. Rev. Stat. 40 §2313-1.]

60/301.1. Law enforcement policies.

§301.1. Law enforcement policies. Every law enforcement agency shall develop, adopt, and implement written policies regarding arrest procedures for domestic violence incidents consistent with the provisions of this Act. In

developing these policies, each law enforcement agency is encouraged to consult with community organizations and other law enforcement agencies with expertise in recognizing and handling domestic violence incidents.
(Added by P.A. 87-1186, §3, eff. 1/1/93.)
[Formerly Ill. Rev. Stat. 40 §2313-1.1.]

60/302. Data maintenance by law enforcement agencies.

§302. Data maintenance by law enforcement agencies. (a) All sheriffs shall furnish to the Department of State Police, on the same day as received, in the form and detail the Department requires, copies of any recorded emergency, interim, or plenary orders of protection issued by the court and transmitted to the sheriff by the clerk of the court pursuant to subsection (b) of Section 222 of this Act [750 ILCS 60/222]. Each order of protection shall be entered in the Law Enforcement Automated Data System on the same day it is issued by the court.

(b) The Department of State Police shall maintain a complete and systematic record and index of all valid and recorded orders of protection issued pursuant to this Act. The data shall be used to inform all dispatchers and law enforcement officers at the scene of an alleged incident of abuse, neglect, or exploitation or violation of an order of protection of any recorded prior incident of abuse, neglect, or exploitation involving the abused, neglected, or exploited party and the effective dates and terms of any recorded order of protection.

(c) The data, records and transmittals required under this Section shall pertain to any valid emergency, interim or plenary order of protection, whether issued in a civil or criminal proceeding.
(Chgd. by P.A. 87-1186, §3, eff. 1/1/93.)
(Source: P.A. 86-542.) [Formerly Ill. Rev. Stat. 40 §2313-2.]

60/303. Reports by law enforcement officers.

§303. Reports by law enforcement officers. (a) Every law enforcement officer investigating an alleged incident of abuse, neglect, or exploitation between family or household members shall make a written police report of any bona fide allegation and the disposition of such investigation. The police report shall include the victim's statements as to the frequency and severity of prior incidents of abuse, neglect, or exploitation by the same family or household member and the number of prior calls for police assistance to prevent such further abuse, neglect, or exploitation.

(b) Every police report completed pursuant to this Section shall be recorded and compiled as a domestic crime within the meaning of Section 5.1 of the Criminal Identification Act [20 ILCS 2630/5.1].
(Chgd. by P.A. 87-1186, §3, eff. 1/1/93.)
(Source: P.A. 86-542.) [Formerly Ill. Rev. Stat. 40 §2313-3.]

60/304. Assistance by law enforcement officers.

§304. Assistance by law enforcement officers. (a) Whenever a law enforcement officer has reason to believe that a person has been abused, neglected, or exploited by a family or household member, the officer shall immediately use all reasonable means to prevent further abuse, neglect, or exploitation, including:

(1) Arresting the abusing, neglecting and exploiting party, where appropriate;

(3)* Accompanying the victim of abuse, neglect, or exploitation to his or her place of residence for a reasonable period of time to remove necessary personal belongings and possessions;

**So in original. No subsec. (2) has been enacted.*

(4) Offering the victim of abuse, neglect, or exploitation immediate and adequate information (written in a language appropriate for the victim or in

Braille or communicated in appropriate sign language), which shall include a summary of the procedures and relief available to victims of abuse under subsection (c) of Section 217 [750 ILCS 60/217] and the officer's name and badge number;

(5) Providing the victim with one referral to an accessible service agency;

(6) Advising the victim of abuse about seeking medical attention and preserving evidence (specifically including photographs of injury or damage and damaged clothing or other property); and

(7) Providing or arranging accessible transportation for the victim of abuse (and, at the victim's request, any minors or dependents in the victim's care) to a medical facility for treatment of injuries or to a nearby place of shelter or safety; or, after the close of court business hours, providing or arranging for transportation for the victim (and, at the victim's request, any minors or dependents in the victim's care) to the nearest available circuit judge or associate judge so the victim may file a petition for an emergency order of protection under subsection (c) of Section 217. When a victim of abuse chooses to leave the scene of the offense, it shall be presumed that it is in the best interests of any minors or dependents in the victim's care to remain with the victim or a person designated by the victim, rather than to remain with the abusing party.

(b) Whenever a law enforcement officer does not exercise arrest powers or otherwise initiate criminal proceedings, the officer shall:

(1) Make a police report of the investigation of any bona fide allegation of an incident of abuse, neglect, or exploitation and the disposition of the investigation, in accordance with subsection (a) of Section 303 [750 ILCS 60/303];

(2) Inform the victim of abuse* neglect, or exploitation of the victim's right to request that a criminal proceeding be initiated where appropriate, including specific times and places for meeting with the State's Attorney's office, a warrant officer, or other official in accordance with local procedure; and

So in original. Probably should be "abuse,".

(3) Advise the victim of the importance of seeking medical attention and preserving evidence (specifically including photographs of injury or damage and damaged clothing or other property).

(Chgd. by P.A. 87-1186, §3, eff. 1/1/93.)
(Source: P.A. 86-542.) [Formerly Ill. Rev. Stat. 40 §2313-4.]

60/305. Limited law enforcement liability.

§305. Limited law enforcement liability. Any act of omission or commission by any law enforcement officer acting in good faith in rendering emergency assistance or otherwise enforcing this Act shall not impose civil liability upon the law enforcement officer or his or her supervisor or employer, unless the act is a result of willful or wanton misconduct.

(Source: P.A. 84-1305.) [Formerly Ill. Rev. Stat. 40 §2313-5.]

60/306. Domestic Violence Training and Curriculum Task Force.

§306. Domestic Violence Training and Curriculum Task Force. (a) Creation of the Task Force. There is hereby created within the Illinois Local Governmental Law Enforcement Officers Training Board a Domestic Violence Training and Curriculum Task Force. The Task Force shall be composed of the Directors, or their designees, of the Department on Aging, Department of Children and Family Services, Department of State Police, Office of the State's Attorneys' Appellate Prosecutor, the Executive Directors, or their designees, of the Illinois Criminal Justice Information Authority and the Local Governmental Law Enforcement Officers Training Board, the Attorney General, or his or her designee, the Chief Justice of the Illinois Supreme Court, or his or her designee, and 6 persons appointed by the Governor, 2 of whom shall be representative of domestic violence victims and 2 of whom shall be representative of sexual assault victims, and one each who shall be representative of police chiefs and county sheriffs in Illinois. The first meeting of the Task Force shall be held within 60 days of the effective date of this amendatory Act of 1992. At its first meeting, the Task Force shall select a chairperson from among its members.

(b) Scope and Functions. The Domestic Violence Training and Curriculum Task Force shall:

(1) gather and review current curricula and training programs utilized by law enforcement officers, prosecutors, and the judiciary on domestic violence;

(2) develop a model coordinated response protocol to incidents of domestic violence;

(3) recommend a regionally based system for providing training to, and coordinating the activities of, law enforcement officers, prosecutors, and the judiciary; and

(4) provide a plan for implementation.

(c) Meetings. The Task Force shall meet at least quarterly, and at such other times at the call of the chairperson of the Task Force.

(d) Reporting Requirements. On or before September 1, 1993, the Task Force shall make a written report to the Governor and the General Assembly concerning it findings and recommendations for administrative or legislative changes.

(e) This Section is repealed on September 1, 1994.

(Added by P.A. 87-1255, §2, eff. 1/7/93 only until 9/1/94.)
[Formerly Ill. Rev. Stat. 40 §2313-6.]

ARTICLE IV. RESPONSIBILITIES OF HEALTH CARE PROFESSION

60/401. Information to abuse victims required of health care professionals.

§401. Any person who is licensed, certified or otherwise authorized by the law of this State to administer health care in the ordinary course of business or practice of a profession shall offer to a person suspected to be a victim of abuse immediate and adequate information regarding services available to victims of abuse.

Any person who is licensed, certified or otherwise authorized by the law of this State to administer health care in the ordinary course of business, or practice of a profession and who in good faith offers to a person suspected to be a victim of abuse information regarding services available to victims of abuse shall not be civilly liable for any act or omission of the agency providing those services to the victims of abuse or for the inadequacy of those services provided by the agency.

(Source: P.A. 87-436.) [Formerly Ill. Rev. Stat. 40 §2314-1.]

This page intentionally left blank.

CHAPTER 815
BUSINESS TRANSACTIONS

LOANS AND CREDIT

CREDIT CARD ISSUANCE ACT

140/0.01. Short title.

§0.01. Short title. This Act may be cited as the Credit Card Issuance Act.
(Source: P.A. 86-1324.) [Formerly Ill. Rev. Stat. 17 §6000.]

140/1. Definitions.

§1. As used in this Act: (a) "Credit card" has the meaning set forth in Section 2.03 of the Illinois Credit Card and Debit Card Act [720 ILCS 250/2.03], but does not include "debit card" as defined in Section 2.15 of the Illinois Credit Card and Debit Card Act [720 ILCS 250/2.15], which can also be used to obtain money, goods, services and anything else of value on credit, nor shall it include any negotiable instrument as defined in the Uniform Commercial Code, as now or hereafter amended [810 ILCS 5/1-101 et seq.]; (b) "merchant credit card agreement" means a written agreement between a seller of goods, services or both, and the issuer of a credit card to any other party, pursuant to which the seller is obligated to accept credit cards; and (c) "credit card transaction" means a purchase and sale of goods, services or both, in which a seller, pursuant to a merchant credit card agreement, is obligated to accept a credit card and does accept the credit card in connection with such purchase and sale.
(Source: P.A. 86-427; 86-952.) [Formerly Ill. Rev. Stat. 17 §6001.]

140/1a. Discriminatory denial of credit card.

§1a. No person may be denied a credit card, upon proper application therefor, solely on account of unlawful discrimination, as defined and prohibited in Section 4-103 of the Illinois Human Rights Act [775 ILCS 5/4-103]. No question requesting any information concerning an applicant's marital status shall appear on any credit card application except in connection with an application for a joint account.
(Source: P.A. 81-1216.) [Formerly Ill. Rev. Stat. 17 §6002.]

140/1b. Applications for credit cards; contents.

§1b. All credit card applications shall contain the following words verbatim:

a. No applicant may be denied a credit card on account of race, color, religion, national origin, ancestry, age (between 40 and 70), sex, marital status, physical or mental handicap unrelated to the ability to pay or unfavorable discharge from military service.

b. The applicant may request the reason for rejection of his or her application for a credit card.

c. No person need reapply for a credit card solely because of a change in marital status unless the change in marital status has caused a deterioration in the person's financial position.

d. A person may hold a credit card in any name permitted by law that he or she regularly uses and is generally known by, so long as no fraud is intended thereby.

(Source: P.A. 81-1216.) [Formerly Ill. Rev. Stat. 17 §6003.]

140/1c. Applications conforming to federal law; compliance with Act.

§1c. Notwithstanding the provisions of Sections 1a and 1b [815 ILCS 140/1a and 140/1b], credit card applications which conform to the requirements of the Federal Equal Credit Opportunity Act [15 U.S.C. §1691 et seq.], amendments thereto, and any regulations issued or which may be issued thereunder shall be deemed to be in compliance with this Act.

(Source: P.A. 80-898.) [Formerly Ill. Rev. Stat. 17 §6004.]

140/2. Liability of seller to issuer of credit card.

§2. Except to the extent provided in a merchant credit card agreement, a seller shall not be liable to the issuer of a credit card, or to any other party to a merchant credit card agreement or that party's agent or representative, for loss or damage to the issuer or other party resulting from a failure of the holder or user of the credit card to pay any obligation arising from a credit card transaction, provided that the seller has fully performed its obligation under the merchant credit card agreement and has not breached any of its obligations to the purchaser in the credit card transaction.

(Source: P.A. 76-1333.) [Formerly Ill. Rev. Stat. 17 §6005.]

140/3. Rejection of application for credit card; explanation.

§3. In every case where an applicant for a credit card is rejected by a credit card issuer, the applicant, upon request, shall be informed of the reasons for such rejection. Failure to comply with this section is a civil rights violation under Section 4-103 of the Illinois Human Rights Act [775 ILCS 5/4-103].

(Source: P.A. 81-1216.) [Formerly Ill. Rev. Stat. 17 §6006.]

140/4. Consideration of financial status in determination to issue credit card.

§4. A credit card issuer shall, when requested, consider the financial status of a married couple when making a determination as to whether to issue a credit card.

A credit card issuer shall, upon request by an applicant, consider such person's financial status when making a determination as to whether to issue such person a credit card as an individual.

(Source: P.A. 78-839.) [Formerly Ill. Rev. Stat. 17 §6007.]

140/5. Change in marital status.

§5. No credit card issuer shall require a person to reapply for credit solely because of a change in marital status. Nothing in this section shall prevent a credit card issuer from requiring notification of any name change.

(Source: P.A. 79-600.) [Formerly Ill. Rev. Stat. 17 §6008.]

140/6. Information disclosed on billing statement.

§6. (a) Except as provided in Sections 25, 25.1 and 29.2 of the "Retail Installment Sales Act" [815 ILCS 405/25, 405/25.1 and 405/29.2], relating to sellers or holders under a retail charge agreement and in subsection (c), a credit card issuer shall disclose, either on an application for a credit card or on literature accompanying the application, on or with any credit card account solicitation, and on each periodic billing statement mailed to a card holder, the following: (1) the annual percentage rate or rates of interest applicable to the account, or if the rate is variable, that fact, and the rate as of a specified date or the index from which the rate is determined; (2) the annualized membership and/or participation fee or charge, if any; (3) the grace period, which is defined as the period within which any credit extended under such credit plan must be repaid to avoid incurring an interest charge represented in terms of an annual percentage rate of interest, and if no such period is offered such fact shall be clearly stated; (4) transaction fees, if assessed, for the use of the credit card account, including, but not limited to a late payment charge, minimum finance charge and over the limit charge. The term "solicitation" means written material mailed or any other solicitation in a written form which constitutes an application for, or a written offer which allows a person to open a credit card account without completing an application. Information required to be disclosed under item (2) of subsection (a) of this Section may be disclosed on literature accompanying the periodic billing statement.

(b) Each credit card solicitation, application and periodic billing statement or literature accompanying the periodic billing statement mailed or otherwise presented to Illinois residents shall contain the following statement, verbatim, in bold face type:

"Residents of Illinois may contact the Illinois Commissioner of Banks and Trust Companies for comparative information on interest rates, charges, fees and grace periods."

The Commissioner of Banks and Trust Companies shall prescribe an address or telephone number to be printed next to the statement. Such address or telephone number shall be the means by which the public can contact the Commissioner of Banks and Trust Companies to obtain the information declared to be available in the statement. Any solicitation or distribution of periodic billing statements violating this Act shall be treated as a single violation regardless of the number of solicitations or statements distributed.

(c) No application, literature accompanying the application, account solicitation, periodic billing statement or literature accompanying the periodic billing statement sent by or on behalf of an issuer to residents of this State with respect to charge cards shall be required to set forth the information specified in items (1) and (3) of subsection (a) of this Section. As used in this subsection, the term "charge card" means any card, plate or other credit device pursuant to which the charge card issuer extends credit which is not subject to a finance charge and with which the charge card holder cannot automatically access credit that is repayable in installments.

(Source: P.A. 85-1028.) [Formerly Ill. Rev. Stat. 17 §6009.]

140/7. Filing of terms with Commissioner of Banks and Trust Companies.

§7. (a) If a credit card issuer issues cards to residents of Illinois as determined by the address to which the cards are sent or addresses solicitations to residents of Illinois as determined by the address to which solicitations are sent or otherwise distributes solicitations within the State of Illinois, then such credit card issuer shall file with the Commissioner of Banks and Trust Companies, on forms prescribed by the Commissioner, within 60 days of the effective date of this Amendatory Act of 1987, a statement of its current annual percentage rate or rates for credit card accounts, any membership or participation fees, the number of days allowed for a grace period and any transaction fees which are required to be disclosed under Section 6 of this Act [815 ILCS 140/6] which are then being generally offered.

(b) If a card issuer changes any of the annual percentage rate or rates, membership or participation fees, the number of days for the grace period or transaction fees it shall file said changes with the Commissioner of Banks and Trust Companies within 30 days after the effective date of said change. A credit

card issuer, may, at its option and without disclosure to the Commissioner of Banks and Trust Companies, waive any fee or charges or impose no annual percentage rate of interest when a payment is received after the expiration of the grace period.
(Source: P.A. 86-427.) [Formerly Ill. Rev. Stat. 17 §6010.]

140/7.1. Certain credit card transaction form required.

§7.1. Certain credit card transaction form required. (a) Any person, firm, partnership, association or corporation which issues forms used for credit card transactions between the credit card holder and seller, shall only issue such credit card forms, except for such forms utilized for a special purpose incidental but related to the actual purchase and sale agreement including but not limited to shipping, delivery or installment of purchased merchandise or special orders, which:

(1) are carbonless; or

(2) are carbonized backed forms that may be retained for recordkeeping purposes of the seller, the seller's agent or sub-contractor, the issuer or the customer; or

(3) after the transaction is complete, do not render a separate piece of paper, carbon or otherwise, which readily identifies the cardholder by complete name or account number, other than those necessary for use by the seller, the seller's agent or sub-contractor, credit card holder and issuer to complete the credit card transaction; or

(4) has a perforated or split carbon, half of which is disposable, and upon completion of the transaction the disposable portion of the carbon renders only half of the cardholder's name and account number.

(b) Any person, firm, partnership, association or corporation which accepts credit cards used for credit card transactions between the credit card holder and seller, shall only use credit card forms, except for such forms utilized for a special purpose incidental but related to the actual purchase and sale agreement including but not limited to shipping, delivery or installment of purchased merchandise or special orders, which:

(1) are carbonless; or

(2) are carbonized backed forms that may be retained for recordkeeping purposes of the seller, the seller's agent or sub-contractor, the issuer or the customer; or

(3) after the transaction is complete, do not render a separate piece of paper, carbon or otherwise, which readily identifies the cardholder by complete name or account number, other than those necessary for use by the seller, the seller's agent or sub-contractor, credit card holder and issuer to complete the credit card transaction; or

(4) has a perforated or split carbon, half of which is disposable, and upon completion of the transaction the disposable portion of the carbon renders only half of the cardholder's name and account number.

No person, firm, partnership, association or corporation which accepts credit cards for the transaction of business shall be deemed to have violated the provisions of this subsection, if such person, firm, partnership, association or corporation shows by a preponderance of evidence that the violation was not intentional and resulted from bona fide error made notwithstanding the maintenance of procedures reasonably adopted to avoid such error.

(c) A violation of subsection (a) of this Section is a business offense punishable by a fine of not less than $750 nor more than $1,000. A violation of subsection (b) of this Section constitutes a business offense punishable by a fine of $501, if a first offense by a person; and punishable by a fine of not less than $501, nor more than $1,000 if such offense is a second or subsequent offense by such person.
(Source: P.A. 86-781.) [Formerly Ill. Rev. Stat. 17 §6010.1.]

140/8. Enforcement by Attorney General.

§8. The Attorney General of this State may bring an action in the name of the State against any person to restrain and prevent any violation of this Act and to enforce and collect any penalty provided hereunder. In the enforcement of this Act, the Attorney General may accept an assurance of discontinuance of any act or practice deemed in violation of this Act from any person engaging in, or who has engaged in, that act or practice. Failure to perform the terms of any such assurance constitutes prima facie proof of a violation of this Act.
(Source: P.A. 86-781.) [Formerly Ill. Rev. Stat. 17 §6011.]

140/9. Penalty for violation of this Act.

§9. (a) Any credit card issuer who knowingly violates this Act is guilty of a Class A misdemeanor.

(b) No credit card issuer who violates this Act, except as a result of an accident or bona fide error of computation, may recover interest, annualized membership fee or participation fee or charge, late payment charges, minimum finance charges and over the limit charges in connection with any credit card issued.

(c) If a credit card issuer, as required pursuant to federal law, makes disclosures of all information required to be disclosed under subsection (a) of Section 6 of this Act [815 ILCS 140/6] in connection with application forms, solicitations or periodic billing statements, the credit card issuer shall be deemed to have complied with the requirements of subsection (a) of Section 6 of this Act.
(Source: P.A. 86-427.) [Formerly Ill. Rev. Stat. 17 §6012.]

CREDIT CARD LIABILITY ACT

Sec.

145/0.01. Short title.

§0.01. Short title. This Act may be cited as the Credit Card Liability Act.
(Source: P.A. 86-1324.) [Formerly Ill. Rev. Stat. 17 §6100.]

145/1. Unsolicited credit cards; liability contingent upon indication of acceptance; burden of proof in action.

§1. (a) No person in whose name a credit card is issued without his having requested or applied for the card or for the extension of the credit or establishment of a charge account which that card evidences is liable to the issuer of the card for any purchases made or other amounts owing by a use of that card from which he or a member of his family or household derive no benefit unless he has indicated his acceptance of the card by signing or using the card or by permitting or authorizing use of the card by another. A mere failure to destroy or return an unsolicited card is not such an indication. As used in this Act, "credit card" has the meaning ascribed to it in Section 2.03 of the Illinois Credit Card Act [720 ILCS 250/2.03], except that it does not include a card issued by any telephone company that is subject to supervision or regulation by the Illinois Commerce Commission or other public authority.

(b) When an action is brought by an issuer against the person named on the card, the burden of proving the request, application, authorization, permission, use or benefit as set forth in Section 1 hereof shall be upon plaintiff if put in issue by defendant. In the event of judgment for defendant, the court shall allow defendant a reasonable attorney's fee, to be taxed as costs.
(Source: P.A. 78-777.) [Formerly Ill. Rev. Stat. 17 §6101.]

145/2. Requested or accepted credit cards; liability contingent upon notice; burden of proof in action.

§2. (a) Notwithstanding that a person in whose name a credit card has been issued has requested or applied for such card or has indicated his acceptance of an unsolicited credit card, as provided in Section 1 hereof [815 ILCS 145/1], such person shall not be liable to the issuer unless the card issuer has given notice to such person of his potential liability, on the card or within two years preceding such use, and has provided such person with an addressed notification requiring no postage to be paid by such person which may be mailed in the event of the loss, theft, or possible unauthorized use of the credit card, and such person shall not be liable for any amount in excess of the applicable amount hereinafter set forth, resulting from unauthorized use of that card prior to notification to the card issuer of the loss, theft, or possible unauthorized use of that card:

Card without a signature panel $25.00
Card with a signature panel $50.00

After the holder of the credit card gives notice to the issuer that a credit card is lost or stolen he is not liable for any amount resulting from unauthorized use of the card.

(b) When an action is brought by an issuer against the person named on a card, issuance of which has been requested, applied for, solicited or accepted and defendant puts in issue any transaction arising from the use of such card, the burden of proving benefit, authorization, use or permission by defendant as to such transaction shall be upon plaintiff. In the event defendant prevails with respect to any transaction so put in issue, the court may enter as a credit against any judgment for plaintiff, or as a judgment for defendant, a reasonable attorney's fee for services in connection with the transaction in respect of which the defendant prevails.
(Source: P.A. 77-1637.) [Formerly Ill. Rev. Stat. 17 §6102.]

UNSOLICITED CREDIT CARD ACT OF 1977

150/1. Short title.

§1. This Act may be cited as the Unsolicited Credit Card Act of 1977.
(Source: P.A. 86-1475.) [Formerly Ill. Rev. Stat. 17 §6201.]

150/2. Definitions.

§2. As used in this Act, the following words have the meaning ascribed to them in this Section:

"Financial institution" means any bank, insurance company, credit union, savings and loan association, investment trust or other depository of money or medium of savings or collective investment.

"Credit card" means any instrument or device, whether known as a credit card, credit plate, charge plate or any other name, issued with or without fee by an issuer for the use of the cardholder in obtaining money, goods, services or anything else of value on credit or in consideration of an undertaking or guaranty by the issuer of the payment of a check drawn by the cardholder. Automated cards, issued by financial institutions to and for the use of only the

customers of such financial institutions, to be used in conjunction with or without computer facilities to allow such customers to make deposits and withdrawals to or from checking or savings accounts, cash checks, pay loan installments and utility bills or transfer funds between various accounts shall not be considered credit cards for the purposes of this Act provided they do not permit cash loan advances or by agreement permit overdraft checking services.
(Source: P.A. 81-1509.) [Formerly Ill. Rev. Stat. 17 §6202.]

150/3. Issuance of credit card; restriction.

§3. No financial institution or other person or corporation doing business in this State shall issue any person a credit card, regardless of whether such credit card is to be used for personal, family, household, agricultural, business or commercial purposes, except (1) in response to a request or application therefor; or (2) as a renewal of, or in substitution for, an accepted credit card whether such card is issued by the same or a successor card issuer.
(Source: P.A. 80-531.) [Formerly Ill. Rev. Stat. 17 §6203.]

150/4. Violations; penalty.

§4. Any person, corporation or financial institution who violates the provisions of this Act shall be guilty of a business offense, and may be fined an amount not to exceed $500.
(Source: P.A. 80-531.) [Formerly Ill. Rev. Stat. 17 §6204.]

150/5. Liabilities of issuers under prior law unaffected.

§5. Nothing in this Act shall in any way alter or diminish the liabilities of credit card issuers as heretofore existent under the laws of the United States or the State of Illinois.
(Source: P.A. 80-531.) [Formerly Ill. Rev. Stat. 17 §6205.]

This page intentionally left blank.

SUPREME COURT DISTRICTS

The State is divided into five Judicial Districts for the election of Justices of the Supreme Court.

The counties composing each district are given below.

FIRST JUDICIAL DISTRICT

The county of Cook.

SECOND JUDICIAL DISTRICT

The counties of Boone, Carroll, DeKalb, DuPage, Jo Daviess, Kane, Kendall, Lake, Lee, McHenry, Ogle, Stephenson and Winnebago.

THIRD JUDICIAL DISTRICT

The counties of Bureau, Fulton, Grundy, Hancock, Henderson, Henry, Iroquois, Kankakee, Knox, LaSalle, Marshall, McDonough, Mercer, Peoria, Putnam, Rock Island, Stark, Tazewell, Warren, Whiteside and Will.

FOURTH JUDICIAL DISTRICT

The counties of Adams, Brown, Calhoun, Cass, Champaign, Clark, Coles, Cumberland, DeWitt, Douglas, Edgar, Ford, Greene, Jersey, Livingston, Logan, Macon, Macoupin, Mason, McLean, Menard, Morgan, Moultrie, Piatt, Pike, Sangamon, Schuyler, Scott, Vermilion and Woodford.

FIFTH JUDICIAL DISTRICT

The counties of Alexander, Bond, Christian, Clay, Clinton, Crawford, Edwards, Effingham, Fayette, Franklin, Gallatin, Hamilton, Hardin, Jackson, Jasper, Jefferson, Johnson, Lawrence, Madison, Marion, Massac, Monroe, Montgomery, Perry, Pope, Pulaski, Randolph, Richland, Saline, Shelby, St. Clair, Union, Wabash, Washington, Wayne, White and Williamson.

ILLINOIS SUPREME COURT RULES

ARTICLE IV. RULES ON CRIMINAL PROCEEDINGS IN THE TRIAL COURT

PART A. WAIVERS AND PLEAS

Rule 401. Waiver of counsel

(a) Waiver of counsel. Any waiver of counsel shall be in open court. The court shall not permit a waiver of counsel by a person accused of an offense punishable by imprisonment without first, by addressing the defendant personally in open Court, informing him of and determining that he understands the following:

(1) the nature of the charge;

(2) the minimum and maximum sentence prescribed by law, including, when applicable, the penalty to which the defendant may be subjected because of prior convictions or consecutive sentences; and

(3) that he has a right to counsel and, if he is indigent, to have counsel appointed for him by the court.

(b) Transcript. The proceedings required by this rule to be in open court shall be taken verbatim, and upon order of the trial court transcribed, filed and made a part of the common law record.

Rule 402. Pleas of guilty

In hearings on pleas of guilty, there must be substantial compliance with the following:

(a) Admonitions to defendant. The court shall not accept a plea of guilty without first, by addressing the defendant personally in open court, informing him of and determining that he understands the following:

(1) the nature of the charge;

(2) the minimum and maximum sentence prescribed by law, including, when applicable, the penalty to which the defendant may be subjected because of prior convictions or consecutive sentences;

(3) that the defendant has the right to plead not guilty, or to persist in that plea if it has already been made, or to plead guilty; and

(4) that if he pleads guilty there will not be a trial of any kind, so that by pleading guilty he waives the right to a trial by jury and the right to be confronted with the witnesses against him.

(b) Determining whether the plea is voluntary. The court shall not accept a plea of guilty without first determining that the plea is voluntary. If the tendered plea is the result of a plea agreement, the agreement shall be stated in open court. The court, by questioning the defendant personally in open court, shall confirm the terms of the plea agreement, or that there is no agreement, and shall determine whether any force or threats or any promises, apart from a plea agreement, were used to obtain the plea.

(c) Determining factual basis for plea. The court shall not enter final judgment on a plea of guilty without first determining that there is a factual basis for the plea.

(d) Plea discussions and agreements. When there is a plea discussion or plea agreement, the following provisions, in addition to the preceding paragraphs of this rule, shall apply:

(1) The trial judge shall not initiate plea discussions.

(2) If a tentative plea agreement has been reached by the parties which contemplates entry of a plea of guilty in the expectation that a specified sentence will be imposed or that other charges before the court will be dismissed, the trial judge may permit, upon request of the parties, the disclosure to him of the tentative agreement and the reasons therefor in advance of the tender of the plea. At the same time he may also receive, with the consent of the defendant, evidence in aggravation or mitigation. The judge may then indicate to the parties whether he will concur in the proposed disposition; and if he has not yet received evidence in aggravation or mitigation, he may indicate that his concurrence is conditional on that evidence being consistent with the representations made to him. If he has indicated his concurrence or conditional concurrence, he shall so state in open court at the time the agreement is stated as required by paragraph (b) of this rule. If the defendant thereupon pleads guilty, but the trial judge later withdraws his concurrence or conditional concurrence, he shall so advise the parties and then call upon the defendant either to affirm or to withdraw his plea of guilty. If the defendant thereupon withdraws his plea, the trial judge shall recuse himself.

(3) If the parties have not sought or the trial judge has declined to give his concurrence or conditional concurrence to a plea agreement he shall inform the defendant in open court at the time the agreement is stated as required by paragraph (b) of this rule that the court is not bound by the plea agreement, and that if the defendant persists in his plea the disposition may be different from that contemplated by the plea agreement.

(e) Transcript. In cases in which the defendant is charged with a crime punishable by imprisonment in the penitentiary, the proceedings required by this rule to be in open court shall be taken verbatim, and upon order of the trial court transcribed, filed, and made a part of the common law record.

(f) Plea discussions, plea agreements, pleas of guilty inadmissible under certain circumstances. If a plea discussion does not result in a plea

of guilty, or if a plea of guilty is not accepted or is withdrawn, or if judgment on a plea of guilty is reversed on direct or collateral review, neither the plea discussion nor any resulting agreement, plea, or judgment shall be admissible against the defendant in any criminal proceeding.
(Chgd. by Illinois Supreme Court, 1/5/81, eff. 2/1/81.)

Rule 403. Pleas and waivers by person under eighteen

A person under the age of 18 years shall not, except in cases in which the penalty is by fine only, be permitted to enter a plea of guilty or to waive trial by jury, unless he is represented by counsel in open court. (Chgd. by Illinois Supreme Court, 7/9/83, eff. 10/1/83.)

Rules 404 to 410. *(Reserved.)*

PART B. DISCOVERY

Rule 411. Applicability of discovery rules

These rules shall be applied in all criminal cases wherein the accused is charged with an offense for which, upon conviction, he might be imprisoned in the penitentiary. They shall become applicable following indictment or information and shall not be operative prior to or in the course of any preliminary hearing.

Rule 412. Disclosure to accused

(a) Except as is otherwise provided in these rules as to matters not subject to disclosure and protective orders, the State shall, upon written motion of defense counsel, disclose to defense counsel the following material and information within its possession or control:

(i) the names and last known addresses of persons whom the State intends to call as witnesses, together with their relevant written or recorded statements, memoranda containing substantially verbatim reports of their oral statements, and a list of memoranda reporting or summarizing their oral statements. Upon written motion of defense counsel memoranda reporting or summarizing oral statements shall be examined by the court *in camera* and if found to be substantially verbatim reports of oral statements shall be disclosed to defense counsel;

(ii) any written or recorded statements and the substance of any oral statements made by the accused or by a codefendant, and a list of witnesses to the making and acknowledgement of such statements;

(iii) a transcript of those portions of grand jury minutes containing testimony of the accused and relevant testimony of persons whom the prosecuting attorney intends to call as witnesses at the hearing or trial;

(iv) any reports or statements of experts, made in connection with the particular case, including results of physical or mental examinations and of scientific tests, experiments, or comparisons, and a statement of qualifications of the expert;

(v) any books, papers, documents, photographs or tangible objects which the prosecuting attorney intends to use in the hearing or trial or which were obtained from or belong to the accused; and

(vi) any record of prior criminal convictions, which may be used for impeachment, of persons whom the State intends to call as witnesses at the hearing or trial.

If the State has obtained from the defendant pursuant to Rule 413(d) information regarding defenses the defendant intends to make, it shall provide to defendant not less than 7 days before the date set for the hearing or trial, or at such other time as the court may direct, the names and addresses of witnesses the state intends to call in rebuttal, together with the information required to be disclosed in connection with other witnesses by subdivisions (i), (iii), and (vi), above, and a specific statement as to the substance of the testimony such witnesses shall give at the trial of the cause.

(b) The State shall inform defense counsel if there has been any electronic surveillance (including wiretapping) of conversations to which the accused was a party, or of his premises.

(c) Except as is otherwise provided in these rules as to protective orders, the State shall disclose to defense counsel any material or information within its possession or control which tends to negate the guilt of the accused as to the offense charged or would tend to reduce his punishment therefor.

(d) The State shall perform its obligations under this rule as soon as practicable following the filing of a motion by defense counsel.

(e) The State may perform these obligations in any manner mutually agreeable to itself and defense counsel or by:

(i) notifying defense counsel that material and information, described in general terms, may be inspected, obtained, tested, copied, or photographed, during specified reasonable times; and

(ii) making available to defense counsel at the time specified such material and information, and suitable facilities or other arrangements for inspection, testing, copying, and photographing of such material and information.

(f) The State should ensure that a flow of information is maintained between the various investigative personnel and its office sufficient to place within its possession or control all material and information relevant to the accused and the offense charged.

(g) Upon defense counsel's request and designation of material or information which would be discoverable if in the possession or control of the State and which is in the possession or control of other governmental personnel, the State shall use diligent good-faith efforts to cause such material to be made available to defense counsel; and if the State's efforts are unsuccessful and such material or other governmental personnel are subject to the jurisdiction of the court, the court shall issue suitable subpoenas or orders to cause such material to be made available to defense counsel.

(h) Discretionary disclosures. Upon a showing of materiality to the preparation of the defense, and if the request is reasonable, the court in its discretion may require disclosure to defense counsel of relevant material and information not covered by this rule.

(i) Denial of disclosure. The court may deny disclosure authorized by this rule and Rule 413 if it finds that there is a substantial risk to any person of physical harm, intimidation, bribery, economic reprisals, or unnecessary annoyance or embarrassment resulting from such disclosure which outweighs any usefulness of the disclosure to counsel.

(j) Matters not subject to disclosure.

(i) *Work product.* Disclosure under this rule and Rule 413 shall not be required of legal research or of records, correspondence, reports or memoranda to the extent that they contain the opinions, theories or conclusions of the State or members of its legal or investigative staffs, or of defense counsel or his staff.

(ii) *Informants.* Disclosure of an informant's identity shall not be required where his identity is a prosecution secret and a failure to disclose will not infringe the constitutional rights of the accused. Disclosure shall not be denied hereunder of the identity of witnesses to be produced at a hearing or trial.

(iii) *National security.* Disclosure shall not be required where it involves a substantial risk of grave prejudice to national security and where a failure to disclose will not infringe the constitutional rights of the accused. Disclosure shall not thus be denied hereunder regarding witnesses or material to be produced at a hearing or trial.

Rule 413. Disclosure to prosecution

(a) The person of the accused. Notwithstanding the initiation of judicial proceedings, and subject to constitutional limitations, a judicial officer may require the accused, among other things, to:

(i) appear in a line-up;

(ii) speak for identification by witnesses to an offense;

(iii) be fingerprinted;

(iv) pose for photographs not involving reenactment of a scene;

(v) try on articles of clothing;

(vi) permit the taking of specimens of material under his fingernails;

(vii) permit the taking of samples of his blood, hair and other materials of his body which involve no unreasonable intrusion thereof;

(viii) provide a sample of his handwriting; and

(ix) submit to a reasonable physical or medical inspection of his body.

(b) Whenever the personal appearance of the accused is required for the foregoing purposes, reasonable notice of the time and place of such appearance shall be given by the State to the accused and his counsel, who shall have the right to be present. Provision may be made for appearances for such purposes in an order admitting the accused to bail or providing for his release.

(c) Medical and scientific reports. Subject to constitutional limitations, the trial court shall, on written motion, require that the State be informed of, and permitted to inspect and copy or photograph, any reports or results, or testimony relative thereto, of physical or mental examinations or of scientific tests, experiments or comparisons, or any other reports or statements of experts which defense counsel has in his possession or control, including a statement of the qualifications of such experts, except that those portions of reports containing statements made by the defendant may be withheld if defense counsel does not intend to use any of the material contained in the report at a hearing or trial.

(d) Defenses. Subject to constitutional limitations and within a reasonable time after the filing of a written motion by the State, defense counsel shall inform the State of any defenses which he intends to make at a hearing or trial and shall furnish the State with the following material and information within his possession or control:

(i) The names and last known addresses of persons he intends to call as witnesses together with their relevant written or recorded statements, including memoranda reporting or summarizing their oral statements, any record of prior criminal convictions known to him; and

(ii) any books, papers, documents, photographs, or tangible objects he intends to use as evidence or for impeachment at a hearing or trial;

(iii) and if the defendant intends to prove an alibi, specific information as to the place where he maintains he was at the time of the alleged offense.

(e) Additional disclosure. Upon a showing of materiality, and if the request is reasonable, the court in its discretion may require disclosure to the State of relevant material and information not covered by this rule.

Rule 414. Evidence depositions

(a) If it appears to the court in which a criminal charge is pending that the deposition of any person other than the defendant is necessary for the preservation of relevant testimony because of the substantial possibility it would be unavailable at the time of hearing or trial, the court may, upon motion and notice to both parties and their counsel, order the taking of such person's deposition under oral examination or written questions for use as evidence at a hearing or trial.

(b) The taking of depositions shall be in accordance with rules providing for the taking of depositions in civil cases, and the order for the taking of a deposition may provide that any designated books, papers, documents or tangible objects, not privileged, be produced at the same time and place.

(c) If a witness is committed for failure to execute a recognizance to appear to testify at a hearing or trial, the court on written motion of the witness and upon notice to the State and defense counsel may order that his deposition be taken, and after the deposition has been subscribed, the court may discharge the witness.

(d) Rule 207—Signing and Filing Depositions — shall apply to the signing and filing of depositions taken pursuant to this rule.

(e) The defendant and defense counsel shall have the right to confront and cross-examine any witness whose deposition is taken. The defendant and defense counsel may waive such right in writing, filed with the clerk of the court.

(f) If the defendant is indigent, all costs of taking depositions shall be paid by the county wherein the criminal charge is initiated. If the defendant is not indigent the costs shall be allocated as in civil cases.

Rule 415. Regulation of discovery

(a) Investigations not to be impeded. Except as is otherwise provided as to matters not subject to disclosure and protective orders, neither the counsel for the parties nor other prosecution or defense personnel shall advise persons having relevant material or information (except the accused) to refrain from discussing the case with opposing counsel or showing opposing counsel any relevant material, nor shall they otherwise impede opposing counsel's investigation of the case.

(b) Continuing duty to disclose. If, subsequent to compliance with these rules or orders pursuant thereto, a party discovers additional material or information which is subject to disclosure, he shall promptly notify the other party or his counsel of the existence of such additional material, and if the additional material or information is discovered during trial, the court shall also be notified.

(c) Custody of materials. Any materials furnished to an attorney pursuant to these rules shall remain in his exclusive custody and be used only for the purposes of conducting his side of the case, and shall be subject to such other terms and conditions as the court may provide.

(d) Protective orders. Upon a showing of cause, the court may at any time order that specified disclosures be restricted or deferred, or make such other order as is appropriate provided that all material and information to which a party is entitled must be disclosed in time to permit counsel to make beneficial use thereof.

(e) Excision. When some parts of certain material are discoverable under these rules, and other parts not discoverable, as much of the material should be disclosed as is consistent with the rules. Excision of certain material and disclosure of the balance is preferable to withholding the whole. Material excised pursuant to judicial order shall be sealed, impounded and preserved in the records of the court, to be made available to the reviewing court in the event of an appeal.

(f) In camera proceedings. Upon request of any person, the court may permit any showing of cause for denial or regulation of disclosures, or portion of such showing, to be made *in camera.* A record shall be made of such proceedings. If the court enters an order granting relief following a showing *in camera,* the entire record of such showing shall be sealed, impounded, and preserved in the records of the court, to be made available to the reviewing court in the event of an appeal.

(g) Sanctions.

(i) If at any time during the course of the proceedings it is brought to the attention of the court that a party has failed to comply with an applicable discovery rule or an order issued pursuant thereto, the court may order such party to permit the discovery of material and information not previously disclosed, grant a continuance, exclude such evidence, or enter such other order as it deems just under the circumstances.

(ii) Wilful violation by counsel of an applicable discovery rule or an order issued pursuant thereto may subject counsel to appropriate sanctions by the court.

Rules 416 to 430. *(Reserved.)*

PART C. TRIALS

Rule 431. Voir dire examination

In criminal cases, the *voir dire* examination of jurors shall be conducted in accordance with Rule 234.

Rule 432. Opening statements

Opening statements in criminal cases are governed by Rule 235.

Rule 433. Impeachment of witnesses; hostile witnesses

The impeachment of witnesses and the examination of hostile witnesses in criminal cases is governed by Rule 238. (Chgd. by Illinois Supreme Court, 2/19/82, eff. 4/1/82.)

Rule 434. Jury selection

(a) Impanelling juries. In criminal cases the parties shall pass upon and accept the jury in panels of four, commencing with the State, unless the court, in its discretion, directs otherwise, and alternate jurors shall be passed upon separately.

(b) Names and addresses of prospective jurors. Upon request the parties shall be furnished with a list of prospective jurors with their addresses if known.

(c) Challenging prospective jurors for cause. Each party may challenge jurors for cause. If a prospective juror has a physical impairment, the court shall consider such prospective juror's ability to perceive and appreciate the evidence when considering a challenge for cause.

(d) Peremptory challenges. A defendant tried alone shall be allowed 14 peremptory challenges in a capital case, 7 in a case in which the punishment may be imprisonment in the penitentiary, and 5 in all other cases; except that, in a single trial of more than one defendant, each defendant shall be allowed 8 peremptory challenges in a capital case, 5 in a case in which the punishment may be imprisonment in the penitentiary, and 3 in all other cases. If several charges against a defendant or defendants are consolidated for trial, each defendant shall be allowed peremptory challenges upon one charge only, which single charge shall be the charge against the defendant authorizing the greatest maximum penalty. The State shall be allowed the same number of peremptory challenges as all of the defendants.

(e) Selection of alternate jurors. After the jury is impanelled and sworn the court may direct the selection of alternate jurors who shall take the same oath as the regular jurors. Each party shall have one additional peremptory challenge for each alternate juror. If before the final submission of a cause a

member of the jury dies or is discharged he shall be replaced by an alternate juror in the order of selection.
(Added by Illinois Supreme Court, 2/19/82, eff. 4/1/82; chgd. by Illinois Supreme Court, 3/27/85, eff. 5/1/85.)

Rules 435 to 450. *(Reserved.)*

Rule 451. Instructions

(a) Use of IPI-Criminal Instructions; requirements of other instructions. Whenever Illinois Pattern Instructions in Criminal Cases (IPI-Criminal) contains an instruction applicable in a criminal case, giving due consideration to the facts and the governing law, and the court determines that the jury should be instructed on the subject, the IPI-Criminal instruction shall be used, unless the court determines that it does not accurately state the law. Whenever IPI-Criminal does not contain an instruction on a subject on which the court determines that the jury should be instructed, the instruction given on that subject should be simple, brief, impartial, and free from argument.

(b) Court's instructions. At any time before or during the trial, the court may direct counsel to prepare designated instructions. Counsel shall comply with the direction and copies of instructions so prepared shall be marked "Court's Instructions." Counsel may object at the conference on instructions to any instruction prepared at the court's direction, regardless of who prepared it, and the court shall rule on these objections as well as objections to other instructions. The grounds of the objections shall be particularly specified.

(c) Section 2–1107 of the Code of Civil Procedure to govern. Instructions in criminal cases shall be tendered, settled, and given in accordance with section 2–1107 of the Code of Civil Procedure [735 ILCS 5/2-1107], but substantial defects are not waived by failure to make timely objections thereto if the interests of justice require.

(d) Procedure. The court shall be provided an original and a copy of each instruction, and a copy shall be delivered to each opposing counsel. In addition to numbering the copies and indicating who tendered them, as required by section 2–1107 of the Code of Civil Procedure, the copy shall contain a notation substantially as follows:

"IPI-Criminal No. ____" or "IPI-Criminal No. ____ Modified" or "Not in IPI-Criminal"

as the case may be. All objections made at the conference and the rulings thereon shall be shown in the report of proceedings.
(Chgd. by Illinois Supreme Court, 2/19/82, eff. 4/1/82; 5/28/82, eff. 7/1/82.)

Rules 452 to 470. *(Reserved.)*

PART D. POST-CONVICTION PROCEEDINGS

Rule 471. Transcripts for poor persons bringing post-conviction proceedings

If a petition filed under the provisions of article 122 of the Code of Criminal Procedure of 1963 [725 ILCS 5/122-1 et seq.], dealing with post-conviction hearings, alleges that the petitioner is unable to pay the costs of the proceeding, the trial court may order that the petitioner be permitted to proceed as a poor person and order a transcript of the proceedings resulting in the conviction delivered to petitioner in accordance with paragraph (b) of Rule 607.

Rules 472 to 500. *(Reserved.)*

ARTICLE V. RULES ON TRIAL COURT PROCEEDINGS IN TRAFFIC AND CONSERVATION OFFENSES, ORDINANCE OFFENSES, PETTY OFFENSES, AND CERTAIN MISDEMEANORS—BAIL SCHEDULES

PART A. GENERAL

PART B. BAIL SCHEDULES

PART C. FINES, PENALTIES AND COSTS—10% DEPOSIT STATUTE

PART D. REQUIRED COURT APPEARANCES, FORMS AND PROCEDURES

PART A. GENERAL

Rule 501. Definitions

(a) Bond certificates. Bail security documents which also guarantee payment of judgments for fines, penalties and costs, not to exceed $105 for any single offense or $300 for multiple offenses arising out of the same occurrence (auto bond certificates), or not to exceed $300 for any single offense covered by Rule 526(b)(1) (truck bond certificates), which are issued or guaranteed, in counties other than Cook, by companies or membership associations authorized to do so by the Director of Insurance, State of Illinois, under regulations issued by this court. (Note: Copies of these regulations may be obtained by writing to: Director, Administrative Office of the Illinois Courts, Supreme Court Building, Springfield, IL 62706.) The privilege of issuing bond certificates for use in Cook County shall be governed by rule of the Circuit Court of Cook County. (Note: Copies of the Cook County rule may be obtained by writing to: Office of the Chief Judge, Richard J. Daley Center, Chicago, IL 60602.)

(b) Cash or cash bail. United States currency; traveler's checks issued by major banks or express companies which, alone or in combination with currency, total the exact amount required to be deposited as bail; and negotiable drafts on major credit card companies, under conditions approved by the Administrative Director.

(c) Conservation offense. Any case charging a violation of:

(1) The Fish Code of 1971, effective July 1, 1972, as amended (Ill. Rev. Stat. 1987, ch. 56, par. 1.1 et seq. [515 ILCS 5/1-1 et seq.]);

(2) The Wildlife Code, effective July 1, 1972, as amended (Ill. Rev. Stat. 1987, ch. 61, par. 1.1 et seq. [520 ILCS 5/1.1 et seq.]);

(3) The Boat Registration and Safety Act, approved July 17, 1959, as amended (Ill. Rev. Stat. 1987, ch. 95½, par. 311–1 et seq. [625 ILCS 45/1-1 et seq.]);

(4) The Park District Code, approved July 8, 1947, as amended (Ill. Rev. Stat. 1987, ch. 105, par. 1–1 et seq. [70 ILCS 1205/1-1 et seq.]);

(5) An Act in relation to the creation, maintenance, operation and improvement of the Chicago Park District, approved July 10, 1933, as amended (Ill. Rev. Stat. 1987, ch. 105, par. 333.1 et seq. [70 ILCS 1505/1 et seq.]);

(6) An Act in relation to the acquisition, control, maintenance, improvement and protection of State parks and nature preserves, approved June 26, 1925, as amended (Ill. Rev. Stat. 1987, ch. 105, par. 465 et seq. [20 ILCS 835/1 et seq.]);

(7) An Act in relation to State forests, operation of forest tree nurseries and providing penalties in connection therewith, approved July 2, 1925, as amended (Ill. Rev. Stat. 1987, ch. 96½, par. 5901 et seq. [525 ILCS 40/1 et seq.]);

(8) An Act to provide for the creation of intensive forest fire protection districts, to regulate the burning of combustible materials, to provide penalties for violations and to repeal an Act therein named, approved July 10, 1957, as amended (Ill. Rev. Stat. 1987, ch. 96½, par. 7001 et seq. [425 ILCS 40/1 et seq.]);

(9) The Snowmobile Registration and Safety Act, approved August 27, 1971, as amended (Ill. Rev. Stat. 1987, ch. 95½, par. 601–1 et seq. [625 ILCS 40/1-1 et seq.]);

(10) The Illinois Endangered Species Protection Act, approved August 7, 1972, as amended (Ill. Rev. Stat. 1987, ch. 8, par. 331 et seq. [520 ILCS 10/1 et seq.]);

(11) The Forest Products Transportation Act, approved September 7, 1972, as amended (Ill. Rev. Stat. 1987, ch. 96½, par. 6901 et seq. [225 ILCS 740/1 et seq.]);

(12) The Timber Buyers Licensing Act, approved September 15, 1969, as amended (Ill. Rev. Stat. 1987, ch. 111, par. 701 et seq. [225 ILCS 735/1 et seq.]);

(13) An Act to provide for the creation and management of forest preserve districts in counties having a population of less than 3,000,000, approved June 27, 1913, as amended (Ill. Rev. Stat. 1987, ch. 96½, par. 6301 et seq. [70 ILCS 805/.01 et seq.]);

(14) The Illinois Exotic Weed Act, effective January 1, 1988, as amended (Ill. Rev. Stat. 1987, ch. 5, par. 931 et seq. [525 ILCS 10/1 et seq.]);

(15) An Act to prohibit Harassment of Hunters, Trappers and Fishermen, effective January 1, 1986, as amended (Ill. Rev. Stat. 1987, ch. 61, par. 301 et seq. [720 ILCS 125/1 et seq.]);

(16) An Act to provide for controlled Harvesting and Conservation of Wild American Ginseng, effective January 1, 1986, as amended (Ill. Rev. Stat. 1987, ch. 61, par. 501 et seq. [525 ILCS 20/1 et seq.]);

(17) The All-Terrain Vehicle Safety Act, effective October 1, 1989, as amended (Ill. Rev. Stat. 1987, ch. 95½, par. 1201 et seq. [repealed, eff. 7/13/90]);

(18) The Cave Protection Act, effective January 1, 1986, as amended (Ill. Rev. Stat. 1987, ch. 96½, par. 9501 et seq. [525 ILCS 5/1 et seq.]);

(19) Any regulations, proclamations or ordinances adopted pursuant to any code or act named in this Rule 501(c).

(d) Driver's license. A current driver's license certificate issued by the Secretary of State of Illinois. However, restricted driving permits, judicial driving permits, instruction permits, probationary licenses or temporary licenses issued under chapter 6 of the Illinois Vehicle Code, as amended (Ill. Rev. Stat. 1987, ch. 95½, par. 6–100 et seq. [625 ILCS 5/6-100 et seq.]) shall not be accepted in lieu of or in addition to bail amounts established in Rule 526.

(e) Unit of local government. Any county, municipality, township, special district, or unit designated as a unit of local government by law.

(f) Traffic offense. Any case which charges a violation of any statute, ordinance or regulation relating to the operation or use of motor vehicles, the use of streets and highways by pedestrians or the operation of any other wheeled or tracked vehicle, including cases charging violations under chapter 6 of the Illinois Vehicle Code, as amended (Ill. Rev. Stat. 1987, ch. 95½, par. 6–101 et seq. [625 ILCS 5/6-101 et seq.]), but excluding cases in which a ticket was served by "tie-on," "hang-on," or "appended" methods and cases charging violations of:

(1) Section 9–3(b) of the Criminal Code of 1961, as amended (reckless homicide) (Ill. Rev. Stat. 1987, ch. 38, par. 9–3(b) [720 ILCS 5/9-3(b)]);

(2) Section 12–5 of the Criminal Code of 1961, as amended (reckless conduct) (Ill. Rev. Stat. 1987, ch. 38, par. 12–5 [720 ILCS 5/12-5]);

(3) Article I of chapter 4 of the Illinois Vehicle Code, as amended (anti-theft laws) (Ill. Rev. Stat. 1987, ch. 95½, par. 4–100 et seq. [625 ILCS 5/4-100 et seq.]);

(4) Any charge punishable upon conviction by imprisonment in the penitentiary;

(5) "Jay walking" ordinances of any unit of local government;

(6) Any conservation offense (see Rule 501(c)).

(g) Promise to comply. An option available to residents of other member jurisdictions of the Nonresident Violator Compact of 1977 (Ill. Rev. Stat. 1987, ch. 95½, par. 6–800 et seq. [625 ILCS 5/6-800 et seq.]) to obtain release from custody without bail following arrests on view for minor traffic offenses (see Ill. Rev. Stat. 1987, ch. 95½, par. 6–306.4(a) [625 ILCS 5/6-306.4(a)]) by signing a written promise to comply with the terms of the Uniform Citation and Complaint (Ill. Rev. Stat. 1987, Supp., ch. 95½, par. 6–306.4 [625 ILCS 5/6-306.4]). Residents of Illinois, and nonresidents charged with traffic offenses specified in subsection 6–306.4(b) of the Illinois Vehicle Code, as amended (Ill. Rev. Stat. 1987, ch. 95½, par. 6–306.4(b) [625 ILCS 5/6-306.4(b)]), shall not be released on a promise to comply, but must post bail or secure release in accordance with these rules.

(h) Individual bond. Bonds authorized without security for persons arrested for or charged with offenses covered by Rules 526, 527 and 528 who are unable to secure release from custody under these rules (see Rule 553(d)).
(Chgd. by Illinois Supreme Court, 6/19/89, eff. 8/1/89; 12/7/90, eff. 1/1/91; 6/12/92, eff. 7/1/92.)

Rule 502. Statutory references

Wherever used in this article, "Ill. Rev. Stat. 1987, ch. ___ par. ___" refers to the statutory material appearing in the specified chapter and paragraph of the Illinois Revised Statutes, 1987, State Bar Association edition, and that same material as it may have been or may hereafter be amended or renumbered.
(Chgd. by Illinois Supreme Court, 6/19/89, eff. 8/1/89.)

Rule 503. Multiple charges under these rules

(a) Amount of bail—Hearing date. Police officers should refrain from issuing multiple citations for offenses arising out of the same occurrence. A person arrested and charged with more than one offense arising out of the same occurrence when the bail is established for each such offense under Rule 526, 527 or 528 shall be released from custody as follows:

(1) If bail for each such offense is established by Rule 526, and the accused is eligible for release on each charge by a promise to comply pursuant to section

6–306.4 of the Illinois Vehicle Code, as amended (Ill. Rev. Stat., 1987, ch. 95½, par. 6–306.4 [625 ILCS 5/6-306.4]), he or she may elect to be released by executing the written promise on the complaint copy; a court appearance shall be required on each charge.

(2) In all other cases, the accused shall be released from custody after posting bail on the charge for which the highest bail is required, and, except as provided below, a court appearance shall be required on each charge. Whether a court appearance will be required for any other offenses charged at the same time as an offense requiring bail under Rule 526(b)(1) will be determined without regard to such truck violations. A separate bail shall be required for each case involving truck violations under Rule 526(b)(1) or similar municipal ordinances, and all such charges may be satisfied without a court appearance under Rule 529.

(3) No court appearance shall be required under this rule where all charges are traffic and conservation offenses which may be satisfied without a court appearance under Rule 529 and the accused elects to post separate bail on each such charge.

(4) No court appearance shall be required under this rule where all charges are traffic offenses which may be satisfied without a court appearance under Rule 529, the separate bails required for all such charges do not exceed $300, and the accused has deposited an approved bond certificate in lieu of bail; in such event, if the accused does not appear on the date set for appearance, or any date to which the case(s) may be continued, it shall be presumed he has elected to post separate bails and consented to the entry of *ex parte* judgment on each such charge (see Rule 556(b)).

All such charges, whenever practicable, should be set for hearing on the same day in the same court, to be disposed of at the same time.

(b) New bail—Application of bail and return of balance. After final disposition of a charge for which bail was posted, the court shall set new bail in a single amount to cover any concurrent charges which may be continued for further hearing at a future date. The clerk may apply any cash or security originally posted as bail to payment of any fine, penalties and costs due on the charge for which bail was originally posted or any other charge disposed of at the same time, but shall return any remaining balance to the accused and shall not retain the balance to apply, in whole or in part, to any new bail set by the court, without the consent of the accused.

(Chgd. by Illinois Supreme Court, 6/19/89, eff. 8/1/89; 12/7/90, eff. 1/1/91; 6/12/92, eff. 7/1/92.)

Rule 504. Appearance date

The date set by the arresting officer or the clerk of the circuit court for an accused's appearance in court shall be not less than 14 days but within 49 days after the date of the arrest, whenever practicable. It is the policy of this court that an accused who appears and pleads "not guilty" to an alleged traffic or conservation offense punishable by fine only should be granted a trial on the merits on the appearance date or, if the accused demands a trial by jury, within a reasonable time thereafter. Except as provided in Rule 505, an arresting officer's failure to appear on that date, in and of itself, shall not normally be considered good cause for a continuance. (Chgd. by Illinois Supreme Court, 6/19/89, eff. 8/1/89.)

Rule 505. Notice to accused

When issuing a Uniform Citation and Complaint, a conservation complaint or a Notice to Appear in lieu of either, the officer shall also issue a written notice to the accused in substantially the following form:

AVOID MULTIPLE COURT APPEARANCES

If you intend to plead "not guilty" to this charge, or if, in addition, you intend to demand a trial by jury, so notify the clerk of the court at least 10 days (excluding Saturdays, Sundays or holidays) before the day set for your appearance. A new appearance date will be set, and arrangements will be made to have the arresting officer present on that new date. Failure to notify the clerk of either your intention to plead "not guilty" or your intention to demand a jury trial may result in your having to return to court, if you plead "not guilty" on the date originally set for your court appearance.

Upon timely receipt of notice that the accused intends to plead "not guilty," the clerk shall set a new appearance date not less than 7 days nor more than 49 days after the original appearance date set by the arresting officer, and notify all parties of the new date and the time for appearance. If the accused demands a trial by jury, the trial shall be scheduled within a reasonable period. In order to invoke the right to a speedy trial, the accused if not in custody must file an appropriate, separate demand, as provided in section 103–5 of the Code of Criminal Procedure of 1963, as amended (Ill. Rev. Stat. 1987, ch. 38, par. 103–5 [725 ILCS 5/103-5]). The proper prosecuting attorney shall be served with such separate written demand for speedy trial. If the accused fails to notify the clerk as provided above, the arresting officer's failure to appear on the date originally set for appearance may be considered good cause for a continuance. Any State agency or any unit of local government desiring to be exempt from the requirements of this Rule 505 may apply to the Conference of Chief Circuit Judges for an exemption.
(Chgd. by Illinois Supreme Court, 6/19/89, eff. 8/1/89.)

Rules 506 to 525. *(Reserved.)*

PART B. BAIL SCHEDULES

NOTE: The bail provisions of Rules 526, 527 and 528 do not apply to arrests on warrant. Bail is preset to avoid undue delay in freeing certain persons accused of an offense when, because of the hour or the circumstances, it is not practicable to bring the accused before a judge. When the accused is actually brought before a judge, the bail amounts specified in these rules do not control. Nothing in these rules is intended to limit a peace officer's discretion to issue a Notice to Appear in an appropriate case (Ill. Rev. Stat. 1987, ch. 38, par. 107–12 [725 ILCS 5/107-12]).

Rule 526. Bail schedule—Traffic offenses

(a) Bail in minor traffic offenses. Unless released on a written promise to comply and except as provided in paragraphs (b), (c), (d) and (f) of this rule a person arrested for a traffic offense and personally served by the arresting officer with a Citation and Complaint shall post bail in the amount of $75 in one of the following ways: (1) by depositing, in lieu of such amount, his current Illinois driver's license; or (2) by depositing, in lieu of such amount, an approved bond certificate; or (3) by posting $75 cash bail (see Rule 501(b) for definition of "Cash Bail").

(b) Bail in certain truck offenses.

(1) Persons charged with a violation of section 15–111 of the Illinois Vehicle Code, as amended (truck overweight) (Ill. Rev. Stat. 1991, ch. 95½, par. 15–111 [625 ILCS 5/15-111]), charged with a violation of section 15–112(f) of the Illinois Vehicle Code, as amended (gross weight) (Ill. Rev. Stat. 1991, ch. 95½, par. 15–112(f) [625 ILCS 5/15-112(f)]), or charged with a violation punishable by fine pursuant to sections 15–113.1, 15–113.2 or 15–113.3 of the Illinois Vehicle Code,

as amended (permit moves) (Ill. Rev. Stat. 1991, ch. 95½, par. 15–113.1 et seq. [625 ILCS 5/113.1 et seq.]), shall post cash bail in an amount equal to the amount of the minimum fine fixed by statute, plus penalties and costs. The accused may, in lieu of cash bail, deposit a money order issued by a money transfer service company which has been approved by the Administrative Director under regulations issued by this court. The money order shall be made payable to the clerk of the circuit court of the county in which the violation occurred. When the bail for any offense hereunder does not exceed $300, the accused may, at his option, deposit a truck bond certificate in lieu of bail.

(2) Persons charged with violating section 15–112(h) of the Illinois Vehicle Code, as amended, by refusing to stop and submit a vehicle and load to weighing after being directed to do so by an officer, or with violating section 15–112(h) by removing all or part of the load prior to weighing shall post bail in the amount of $750 (Ill. Rev. Stat. 1991, ch. 95½, par. 15–112(h) [625 ILCS 5/15-112(h)]).

(c) Bail in other traffic offenses (Rules of the Road). Except as provided in paragraph (e) of this rule, persons charged with violations of the following sections of the Illinois Vehicle Code shall post bail in the amount specified:

Illinois Vehicle Code Sec.	Ill. Rev. Stat. 1991 Ch.	Par.	Description	Bail
(1) 11-601	95½	11-601 [625 ILCS 5/11-601]	Speeding, but only when more than 20 mph over the posted limit but not more than 30 mph over the posted limit	$95
			Speeding, but only when more than 30 mph over the posted limit	$105
(2) 11-204	95½	11-204 [625 ILCS 5/11-204]	Fleeing or Attempting to Elude Police Officer	$2,000
(3) 11-204.1	95½	11-204.1 [625 ILCS 5/11-204.1]	Misdemeanor Aggravated Fleeing or Attempting to Elude Police Officer	$2,000
(4) 11-401(a)	95½	11-401(a) [625 ILCS 5/11-401(a)]	Leaving Scene of Accident–Death or Injury	$2,000
(5) 11-501	95½	11-501 [625 ILCS 5/11-501]	Misdemeanor Driving Under Influence of Alcohol or Drugs or with .10 or more Blood or Breath Alcohol Concentration	$3,000
(6) 11-503	95½	11-503 [625 ILCS 5/11-503]	Reckless Driving	$2,000
(7) 11-504	95½	11-504 [625 ILCS 5/11-504]	Drag Racing	$2,000

(d) Bail in other traffic offenses (Vehicle Title & Registration Law). Except as provided in paragraph (e) of this rule, persons charged with violations of the following sections of the Illinois Vehicle Code shall post bail in the amount specified:

Illinois Vehicle Code Sec.	Ill. Rev. Stat. 1991 Ch.	Par.	Description	Bail
(1) 3-707	95½	3-707 [625 ILCS 5/3-707]	Operating Without Insurance	$2,000
(2) 3-708	95½	3-708 [625 ILCS 5/3-708]	Operating When Registration Suspended for Noninsurance	$3,000
(3) 3-710	95½	3-710 [625 ILCS 5/3-710]	Display of False Insurance Card	$2,000

(e) Driver's license or bond certificate in lieu of or in addition to bail. An accused who has a valid Illinois driver's license may deposit his driver's license in lieu of the bail specified in subparagraphs (1), (2), and (6) of Rule 526(c) and subparagraphs (1) and (3) of Rule 526(d). In lieu of posting the cash amount specified in subparagraphs (3), (4), (5) and (7) of Rule 526(c) or subparagraph (2) of Rule 526(d), an accused must post $1,000 bail and his current Illinois driver's license. Persons who do not possess a valid Illinois driver's license shall post bail in the amounts specified in Rule 526(c) or 526(d), except that an accused may deposit an approved bond certificate in lieu of the bail specified in subparagraph (1) of Rule 526(c).

(f) Bail in other traffic offenses (Driver Licensing Law). Persons charged with violations of the following sections of the Illinois Vehicle Code shall post bail in the amount specified:

Illinois Vehicle Code Sec.	Ill. Rev. Stat. 1991 Ch.	Par.	Description	Bail
(1) 6-301	95½ [625 ILCS 5/6-301]	6-301	Unlawful Use of License	$750
(2) 6-303	95½ [625 ILCS 5/6-303]	6-303	Misdemeanor Driving With Suspended or Revoked License	$1,000
(3) 6-304.1	95½ [625 ILCS 5/304.1]	6-304.1	Permitting Driving Under Influence of Alcohol or Drugs	$1,000
(4) 6-101	95½ [625 ILCS 5/6-101]	6-101	Unlicensed Driving, under the following circumstances:	$1,000
See article VI, "Penalties," Illinois Vehicle Code (Ill. Rev. Stat. 1991, ch. 95½, par. 6-601 [625 ILCS 5/6-601]).			(a) All cases other than those charging license expired for less than 6 months (b) License expired less than 6 months (see Rule 526(a))	
(5) 6-507	95½ [625 ILCS 5/6-507]	6-507	Commercial Driver's License	$1,000

(g) Bail for traffic offenses defined by ordinance. Bail for traffic offenses defined by any ordinances of any unit of local government which are similar to those described in this Rule 526 shall be the same amounts as provided for in this rule.
(Chgd. by Illinois Supreme Court, 6/19/89, eff. 8/1/89; 1/11/90, eff. 1/11/90; 12/7/90, eff. 1/1/91; 6/12/92, eff. 7/1/92.)

Rule 527. Bail schedule—Conservation offenses

(a) General. Except as provided in paragraphs (b), (c), (d), (e), (f), (g) and (h) of this Rule 527, a person arrested for a conservation offense and personally served by the arresting officer with a conservation complaint shall post cash bail in the amount of $75.

(b) Bail for specified violations of the Wildlife Code. Persons arrested for a conservation offense listed below and personally served by the arresting officer with a conservation complaint shall post bail in the amount specified:

WILDLIFE CODE

Wildlife Code Sec.	Ill. Rev. Stat. 1987 Ch.	Par.	Description	Bail
1.22	61 [520 ILCS 5/1.22]	1.22	Resistance to Officers	$1,000
2.4	61 [520 ILCS 5/2.4]	2.4	Unlawful Taking or Possession of Birds of Prey	$1,000
2.9	61 [520 ILCS 5/2.9]	2.9	Unlawful Taking or Possession of Wild Turkeys out of Season	$1,000
2.10	61 [520 ILCS 5/2.10]	2.10	Unlawful Taking or Possession of Wild Turkeys out of Season	$1,000
2.16	61 [520 ILCS 5/2.16]	2.16	Unlawful Sale or Barter of Game Birds	$1,000
2.18	61 [520 ILCS 5/2.18]	2.18	Unlawful Taking of Migratory Game Birds	$1,000
2.24	61 [520 ILCS 5/2.24]	2.24	Unlawful Taking or Possessing of Deer out of Season	$1,000
2.25	61 [520 ILCS 5/2.25]	2.25	Unlawful Taking or Possessing of Deer out of Season	$1,000
2.29	61 [520 ILCS 5/2.29]	2.29	Unlawful Sale or Barter of Game Animals	$1,000
2.30	61 [520 ILCS 5/2.30]	2.30	Unlawful Taking of Furbearing Mammals	$1,000
2.33(i)	61 [520 ILCS 5/2.33(i)]	2.33(i)	Unlawful Taking from Vehicle	$1,000
2.33(cc)	61 [520 ILCS 5/2.33(cc)]	2.33(cc)	Possession of Species During Closed Season	$1,000
2.33a(k)	61 [520 ILCS 5/2.33a(k)]	2.33a(k)	Possession of Green Hides	$1,000
2.36	61 [520 ILCS 5/2.36]	2.36	Unlawful Sale and Commercial Possession of Wildlife	$1,000
2.38	61 [520 ILCS 5/2.38]	2.38	Falsification or Misrepresentation	$1,000
3.36	61 [520 ILCS 5/3.36]	3.36	Violations While Under Revocation	$1,000

(c) Bail for specified violations of the Boat Registration and Safety Act. Persons arrested for a conservation offense listed below and personally served by the arresting officer with a conservation complaint shall post bail in the amount specified:

BOAT REGISTRATION AND SAFETY ACT

B.R.S.A. Art.	Sec.	Ill. Rev. Stat. 1987 Ch.	Par.	Description	Bail
II	2-4	95½ [625 ILCS 45/2-4]	312-4	Resistance to Officers	$1,000

IIIA	3A-21	95½ [625 ILCS 45/3A-21]	313A-21	Titling Offenses	$1,000
V	5-1	95½ [625 ILCS 45/5-1]	315-1	Careless Operation of Motorboat	$1,000
V	5-2	95½ [625 ILCS 45/5-2]	315-2	Reckless Operation of Motorboat	$1,000
V	5-16(A)	95½ [625 ILCS 45/5-16(A)]	315-11(A)	Operating Motorboat Under the Influence of Liquors or Drugs	$2,000
XI	11-5	95½ [625 ILCS 45/11A-5]	321A-5	Operating Motorboat During Suspension of Privilege	$1,000

(d) **Bail for specified violations of the Snowmobile Registration and Safety Act.** Persons arrested for a conservation offense listed below and personally served by the arresting officer with a conservation complaint shall post bail in the amount specified:

SNOWMOBILE REGISTRATION AND SAFETY ACT

S.R.S.A.		Ill. Rev. Stat. 1987			
Art.	**Sec.**	**Ch.**	**Par.**	**Description**	**Bail**
II	2-4	95½ [625 ILCS 40/2-4]	602-4	Resistance to Officers	$1,000
III	3-10	95½ [625 ILCS 40/3-10]	603-10	Falsification or Alteration	$1,000
V	5-1B	95½ [625 ILCS 40/5-1(B)]	605-1(B)	Reckless, Negligent or Careless Operation of Snowmobile	$1,000
V	5-1C	95½ [625 ILCS 40/5-1(C)]	605-1(C)	Operating Snowmobile Under the Influence of Liquor or Drugs	$2,000

(e) **Bail for specified violations of the Fish Code of 1971.** Persons arrested for a conservation offense listed below and personally served by the arresting officer with a conservation complaint shall post bail in the amount specified:

FISH CODE OF 1971

Fish Code		Ill. Rev. Stat. 1987			
Art.	**Sec.**	**Ch.**	**Par.**	**Description**	**Bail**
I	1.20	56 [515 ILCS 5/1-200]	1.20	Resistance to Officers	$1,000
III	3.15	56 [515 ILCS 5/10-80]	3.15	Unlawful Taking of Aquatic Life	$1,000
IV	4.1	56 (1988 Supp.) [515 ILCS 5/15-5]	4.1	Failure to Have Required Commercial Fishing License	$1,000
IV	4.1a	56 (1988 Supp.) [515 ILCS 5/15-10]	4.1a	Failure to Have Required Commercial Musselor License	$1,000
IV	4.11	56 (1988 Supp.) [515 ILCS 5/15-50]	4.11	Unlawful Sale and Commercial Possession	$1,000

V	5.19	56 [515 ILCS 5/20-105]	5.19	Violations While Under Revocation	$1,000
V	5.22(h)	56 [515 ILCS 5/20-120]	5.22(h)	Falsification or Misrepresentation	$1,000

(f) Bail for specified violations of the Endangered Species Protection Act. Persons arrested for a conservation offense listed below and personally served by the arresting officer with a conservation complaint shall post bail in the amount specified:

ENDANGERED SPECIES PROTECTION ACT

E.S.P.A. Secs.	Ill. Rev. Stat. 1987 Ch.	Pars.	Description	Bail
331-340	8 [520 ILCS 10/1 et seq.]	331-340	All Offenses	$1,000

(g) Bail for specified violations of the Forest Products Transportation Act. Persons arrested for a conservation offense listed below and personally served by the arresting officer with a conservation complaint shall post bail in the amount specified:

FOREST PRODUCTS TRANSPORTATION ACT

F.P.T.A. Sec.	Ill. Rev. Stat. 1987 Ch.	Par.	Description	Bail
4	96½ [225 ILCS 740/4]	6911	Cutting or Damaging Forest Products Without Consent	$1,000
5	96½ [225 ILCS 740/5]	6912	Transportation of Forest Products Without Consent	$1,000

(h) Bail for specified violations of the Timber Buyers Licensing Act. Persons arrested for a conservation offense listed below and personally served by the arresting officer with a conservation complaint shall post bail in the amount specified:

TIMBER BUYERS LICENSING ACT

T.B.L.A. Sec.	Ill. Rev. Stat. 1987 Ch.	Par.	Description	Bail
3	111 [225 ILCS 735/3]	703	Engaging in Business Without License	$1,000
5	111 [225 ILCS 735/5]	705	Unlawful Activities	$1,000

(Chgd. by Illinois Supreme Court, 6/19/89, eff. 8/1/89; 6/12/92, eff. 7/1/92.)

Rule 528. Bail schedule—Ordinance offenses, petty offenses, business offenses and certain misdemeanors

(a) Offenses punishable by fine not to exceed $500. Bail for offenses (other than traffic or conservation offenses), including ordinance violations, punishable only by a fine which does not exceed $500 shall be $75.

(b) Offenses punishable by fine in excess of $500. Bail for offenses (other than traffic or conservation offenses) punishable only by a fine which exceeds $500 shall be $1,000.

(c) Certain other offenses. Bail for any other offenses, including violation of any ordinance of any unit of local government (other than traffic or conservation offenses) punishable by fine or imprisonment in a penal institution other than the penitentiary, or both, shall be $1,000, except that bail for Class C misdemeanors shall be $75.
(Chgd. by Illinois Supreme Court, 6/12/92, eff. 7/1/92.)

PART C. FINES, PENALTIES AND COSTS— 10% DEPOSIT STATUTE

Rule 529. Fines, penalties and costs on written pleas of guilty in minor traffic and conservation offenses

(a) Traffic offenses. All traffic offenses, except those requiring a court appearance under Rule 551 and those involving offenses set out in Rule 526(b)(1), may be satisfied without a court appearance by a written plea of guilty and payment of fines, penalties and costs, equal to the bail required by Rule 526 unless an order of failure to appear to answer the charge has been entered, in which case the fine, penalties and costs shall be equal to the amount of the required bail, plus $35. Unless otherwise distributed under section 27.5 or 27.6 of the Clerks of Courts Act (Ill. Rev. Stat., ch. 25, pars. 27.5, 27.6 [705 ILCS 105/27.5, 27.6]), the fines, penalties and costs applicable under paragraph (a) of this rule shall be distributed as follows:

(1) The fees of the clerk of the circuit court under sections 27.1, 27.1a, 27.2, 27.2a, 27.3a and 27.3c, as the case may be, of the Clerks of Courts Act (Ill. Rev. Stat., ch. 25, pars. 27.1, 27.1a, 27.2, 27.2a, 27.3a, 27.3c [705 ILCS 105/27.1, 27.1a, 27.2, 27.2a, 27.3a, 27.3c]);

(2) The fee, if any, payable to the county in which the violation occurred, if that county has enacted an ordinance or resolution, pursuant to section 5–1001 of the Counties Code (Ill. Rev. Stat., ch. 34, par. 5–1101), adding such fee to fines imposed for violations of the Illinois Vehicle Code (Ill. Rev. Stat., ch. 95½, par. 1–100 et seq. [625 ILCS 5/1-100]) or similar provisions contained in county or municipal ordinances;

(3) The applicable penalty assessment, if any, payable to the Traffic and Criminal Conviction Surcharge Fund of the State Treasury under Section 5–9–1(c) of the Unified Code of Corrections (Ill. Rev. Stat., ch. 38, par. 1005–9–1(c) [730 ILCS 5/5-9-1(c)]);

(4) The additional penalty, if any, payable to the Drivers Education Fund of the State Treasury under section 16–104a of the Illinois Vehicle Code (Ill. Rev. Stat., ch. 95½, par. 16–104a [625 ILCS 5/16-104a]), for traffic offenses reportable to the Secretary of State under subdivision (a)(2) of section 6–204 of that Code (Ill. Rev. Stat., ch. 95½, par. 6–204(a)(2) [625 ILCS 5/6-204(a)(2)]);

(5) The additional penalty, if any, payable to the Violent Crime Victims Assistance Fund of the State Treasury under section 10 of the Violent Crime Victims Assistance Act (Ill. Rev. Stat., ch. 70, par. 510 [725 ILCS 240/10]);

(6) The amount, if any, to be remitted to the Trauma Center Fund of the State Treasury, under section 16-104b of the Illinois Vehicle Code (Ill. Rev. Stat., ch. 95½, par. 16-104b [625 ILCS 5/16-104b]), for those counties that have not elected to distribute monies under the disbursement formulas in sections 27.5 and 27.6 of the Clerks of Courts Act (Ill. Rev. Stat., ch. 25, pars. 27.5, 27.6 [705 ILCS 105/27.5, 27.6]);

(7) The balance of the bail required by Rule 526 shall be assessed as the fine and remitted to the entity authorized by law to receive the fine imposed in the case.

No other costs shall be assessed in any case which is disposed of on a written plea of guilty without a court appearance under paragraph (a) of Rule 529. A charge of violating section 15–111 or offenses punishable by fine pursuant to sections 15–113.1, 15–113.2 or 15–113.3 of the Illinois Vehicle Code (truck overweight and permit moves) (Ill. Rev. Stat., ch. 95½, pars. 15–111, 15–113.1 through 15–113.3 [625 ILCS 5/15-111, 15-113.1 through 15-113.3]), or similar municipal ordinances, may be satisfied without a court appearance by a written plea of guilty and payment of the minimum fine fixed by statute, plus all applicable penalties and costs (see Rule 526(b)(1)).

(b) Conservation offenses. Conservation offenses for which $75 cash bail is required under Rule 527 may be satisfied without a court appearance by a written plea of guilty and payment of fines, penalties and costs, equal to the cash bail required by Rule 527. The fines, penalties and costs applicable under paragraph (b) of this rule shall be distributed as follows:

(1) The fees of the clerk of the circuit court under sections 27.1, 27.1a, 27.2, 27.2a, 27.3a, and 27.3c, as the case may be, of the Clerks of Courts Act (Ill. Rev. Stat. 1991, ch. 25, pars. 27.1, 27.1a, 27.2, 27.2a, 27.3a, 27.3c [705 ILCS 105/27.1, 27.1a, 27.2, 27.2a, 27.3a, 27.3c]);

(2) The applicable penalty assessment, if any, payable to the Traffic and Criminal Conviction Surcharge Fund of the State Treasury under section 5–9–1(c) of the Unified Code of Corrections (Ill. Rev. Stat. 1991, ch. 38, par. 1005–9–1(c) [730 ILCS 5/5-9-1(c)]);

(3) The additional penalty, if any, payable to the Violent Crime Victims Assistance Fund of the State Treasury under section 10 of the Violent Crime Victims Assistance Act (Ill. Rev. Stat. 1991, ch. 70, par. 510 [725 ILCS 240/10]);

(4) The balance of the bail required by Rule 527 shall be assessed as the fine and remitted to the entity authorized by law to receive the fine imposed in the case.

No other costs shall be assessed in any case which is disposed of on a written plea of guilty without a court appearance under paragraph (b) of this Rule 529.

(c) Supervision on written pleas of guilty. In counties designated by the Conference of Chief Circuit Judges, the circuit court may by rule or order authorize the entry of an order of supervision under section 5–6–3.1 of the Unified Code of Corrections (Ill. Rev. Stat., ch. 38, par. 1005–6–3.1 [730 ILCS 5/5-6-3.1]), for traffic offenses satisfied pursuant to paragraph (a) of this Rule 529 where the accused, upon payment of the fines, penalties and costs provided by law, agrees to attend and successfully complete a traffic safety program approved by the court under standards set by the Conference. The accused shall be responsible for payment of any traffic safety program fees. If the accused fails to file a certificate of successful completion on or before the termination date of the supervision order, the supervision shall be summarily revoked and conviction entered.

(Chgd. by Illinois Supreme Court, 6/19/89, eff. 8/1/89; 12/20/91, eff. 1/1/92; 6/12/92, eff. 7/1/92; 1/20/93, eff. 1/20/93.)

Rule 530. Applicability of 10% cash deposit statute

The 10% cash deposit provision of section 110–7 of the Code of Criminal Procedure of 1963, as amended (Ill. Rev. Stat. 1991, ch. 38, par. 110–7 [725 ILCS 5/110-7]), applies in every case in which the amount of bail under these rules is $750 or more, except those cases involving truck violations under Rule 526(b)(1) or similar municipal ordinances. (Chgd. by Illinois Supreme Court, 6/19/89, eff. 8/1/89; 6/12/92, eff. 7/1/92.)

Rules 531 to 550. *(Reserved.)*

PART D. REQUIRED COURT APPEARANCES, FORMS AND PROCEDURES

Rule 551. Traffic and conservation offenses for which a court appearance is required

A court appearance is required for:

(a) All alleged Class A and Class B misdemeanor violations of the Illinois Vehicle Code, as amended (Ill. Rev. Stat. 1987, ch. 95½, par. 1–100 et seq. [625 ILCS 5/1-100 et seq.]).

(b) All alleged violations of the following specified sections:

Illinois Vehicle Code Sec.	Ill. Rev. Stat. 1988 Supp. Ch.	Par.	Description
3-707	95½ [625 ILCS 5/3-707])	3-707	Operating Without Insurance
3-708	95½ [625 ILCS 5/3-708]	3-708	Operating When Registration Suspended for Noninsurance

Illinois Vehicle Code Sec.	Ill. Rev. Stat. 1987 Ch.	Par.	Description
6-101	95½ [625 ILCS 5/6-101]	6-101	No Valid Driver's License
6-104	95½ [625 ILCS 5/6-104]	6-104	Violation of Classification
6-113	95½ [625 ILCS 5/6-113]	6-113	Operating in Violation of Restricted License or Permit
6-301	95½ [625 ILCS 5/6-301]	6-301	Unlawful Use of License of Permit
11-409	95½ [625 ILCS 5/11-409]	11-409	Making False Report
11-504	95½ [625 ILCS 5/11-504]	11-504	Drag Racing
11-601(b)	95½ [625 ILCS 5/11-601(b)]	11-601(b)	Speeding—Only when more than 85 mph, or more than 30 mph Over the Posted Limit
11-1414(a)	95½ [625 ILCS 5/11-1414(a)]	11-1414(a)	Passed School Bus—Loading or Unloading
15-102	95½ [625 ILCS 5/15-102]	15-102	Vehicle Width
15-103	95½ [625 ILCS 5/15-103]	15-103	Vehicle Height
15-107	95½ [625 ILCS 5/15-107]	15-107	Vehicle Length
15-112(h)	95½ [625 ILCS 5/15-107]	15-112(h)	Refusal to stop and submit vehicle and load to weighing after being directed to do so by an officer, or removal of load prior to weighing
15-301(j)	95½ [625 ILCS 5/15-301(j)]	15-301(j)	Violation of Excess Size or Weight Permit

(c) All alleged violations of the Child Passenger Protection Act, as amended (Ill. Rev. Stat. 1987, ch. 95½, par. 1101 et seq. [625 ILCS 25/1 et seq.]).

(d) Any traffic offense which results in an accident causing the death of any person or injury to any person other than the accused.

(e) Conservation offenses for which more than $75 bail is required under Rule 527, or for which civil penalties are required under section 20.35 of the Fish and Aquatic Life Code, as amended (Ill. Rev. Stat. 1991, ch. 56, par. 20.35 [515 ILCS 20.35]) or section 3.5 of the Wildlife Code, as amended (Ill. Rev. Stat. 1991, ch. 61, par. 3.5 [520 ILCS 5/3.5]).

(f) Offenses arising from multiple charges as provided in Rule 503.

(g) Violation of any ordinance of any unit of local government defining offenses comparable to those specified in subparagraphs (a), (b), (c) and (d) of this Rule 551.

(Chgd. by Illinois Supreme Court, 6/19/89, eff. 8/1/89; 12/7/90, eff. 1/1/91; 6/12/92, eff. 7/1/92.)

Rule 552. Uniform tickets—Processing

Uniform Citation and Complaint forms and conservation complaints shall be in forms which may, from time to time, be approved by the Conference of Chief Circuit Judges and filed with this court. The uniform forms shall be adapted for use by municipalities. The arresting officer shall complete the form or ticket and, within 48 hours after the arrest, shall transmit the portions entitled "Complaint" and "Disposition Report" and, where appropriate, "Report of Conviction," either in person or by mail, to the clerk of the circuit court of the county in which the violation occurred. Each Uniform Citation and Complaint form and conservation complaint shall upon receipt by the clerk be assigned a separate case number, chronologically, including multiple citations issued to the same accused for more than one offense arising out of the same occurrence (see Rule 503(a)). A final disposition noted on the reverse side of the "Complaint" shall be evidence of the judgment in the case. Upon final disposition of each case, the clerk shall execute the "Disposition Report" and promptly forward it to the law enforcement agency that issued the ticket. On a plea or finding of guilty in any traffic case, the clerk shall also execute the "Report of Conviction" portion of the Uniform Citation and Complaint, if and as applicable, and such other reports as required by section 6–204 of the Illinois Vehicle Code, as amended (Ill. Rev. Stat. 1987, ch. 95½, par. 6–204 [625 ILCS 5/6-204]) and promptly forward same to the Secretary of State. This rule does not prohibit the use of electronic or mechanical systems of record keeping, transmitting or reporting. (Chgd. by Illinois Supreme Court, 6/19/89, eff. 8/1/89.)

Rule 553. Posting bail or bond

(a) By whom and where taken. The several circuit clerks, deputy circuit clerks and law enforcement officers designated by name or office by the chief judge of the circuit are authorized to let to bail any person arrested for or charged with an offense covered by Rules 526, 527 and 528. Upon designation by the chief judge of the circuit, bail may be taken in accordance with this article in any county, municipal or other building housing governmental units, police station, sheriff's office or jail, or district headquarters building of the Illinois State Police. Individual bonds under paragraph (d) of this rule may additionally be taken as designated by the chief judge of the circuit.

(b) Copy of bond—Receipt for cash bail. A carbon copy of the bond or an official receipt showing the amount of cash bail posted, specifying the time and place of court appearance, shall be furnished to the accused and shall constitute a receipt for bail. The bond or cash bail, or both, shall be delivered to the office of the circuit clerk of the county in which the violation occurred within 48 hours of receipt or within the time set for the accused's appearance in court, whichever is earlier.

(c) Driver's license or bond certificate. If an accused deposits a driver's license with the arresting officer in lieu of bail or in addition to bail, or deposits a bond certificate, the arresting officer shall note that fact on the accused's copy of the ticket and transmit the driver's license or bond certificate to the clerk within the time provided in paragraph (b) of this rule.

(d) Individual bond. Persons arrested for or charged with an offense covered by Rules 526, 527 and 528 who are unable to secure release from custody under these rules may be released by giving individual bond (in the amount required by this article) by those law enforcement officers designated by name or office by the chief judge of the circuit, except when the accused is (1) unable or unwilling to establish his identity or submit to being fingerprinted as required by law, (2) is charged with an offense punishable by imprisonment and will pose a danger to any person or the community, or (3) elects release on separate bail under Rule 503(a)(3) or 503(a)(4). Persons required to deposit both bail and driver's license under Rule 526(e) may be released on $1,000 individual bond and their current Illinois driver's license. If authorized by the chief judge of the circuit, individual bonds under this paragraph (d) may be executed by signing the citation or complaint agreeing to comply with its conditions.

(e) Alternative procedure in minor cases—Counties other than Cook. In any case arising in counties other than Cook, in which the bail or bond specified by Rule 526, 527 or 528 does not exceed $105, an accused not required to be fingerprinted may place the cash bail or deposit (in the amount required by such rule) in a stamped envelope (to be provided by the arresting officer) addressed to the clerk of the circuit court of the county in which the violation occurred and, in the presence of the arresting officer, deposit that envelope in a United States Government mail box. The accused shall then be released from custody. The appropriate portion(s) of the ticket shall be enclosed with the cash bail or deposit. In rural areas where U.S. government mail boxes are not reasonably available, the accused may elect to deposit with a State Police officer, an enforcement officer of the State Department of Conservation or Secretary of State, or a sheriff or a deputy sheriff the sealed envelope containing the cash bail or deposit, rather than having to accompany the arresting officer to the nearest mail box. In such cases, the officer will mail or deliver the sealed envelopes to the clerk of the circuit court before the end of his current tour of duty.

(Chgd. by Illinois Supreme Court, 6/26/87, eff. 8/1/87; 12/7/90, eff. 1/1/91; 6/12/92, eff. 7/1/92.)

Rule 554. Substitution of cash bail

(a) Not sooner than 10 court days after arrest and not later than 3 court days before the date set for appearance in court, an accused who deposited his driver's license or a bond certificate in lieu of cash bail, or was released on Notice to Appear, promise to comply, or individual bond under Rule 553(d), may recover either his license or bond certificate or further secure his release by substituting cash bail in the amount required by this article with the clerk of the circuit court of the county in which the violation occurred; provided, however, that no driver's license required to be deposited under subparagraph (d) of Rule 526 may be recovered under this rule. The clerk may waive the time limits specified by this rule.

(b) In all cases in which a court appearance is not required under Rule 551, an accused who desires to satisfy the charge but is unwilling to plead guilty may substitute cash bail under paragraph (a) of this rule; in such event, if the accused does not appear on the date set for appearance, or any date to which the case may be continued, it shall be presumed he has consented to the entry of an *ex parte* judgment (see Rule 556(b)).

(Chgd. by Illinois Supreme Court, 6/26/87, eff. 8/1/87.)

Rule 555. Returning bail or documents

(a) Court appearance. A defendant who personally appears in court on the date on which his case is finally disposed of shall, upon payment of any fines, penalties and costs which may be assessed against him upon a plea or finding of guilty, or as a condition of an order of supervision under section 5–6–3.1 of the Unified Code of Corrections, as amended (Ill. Rev. Stat. 1987, ch. 38, par. 1005–6–3.1 [730 ILCS 5/5-6-3.1]), recover unless otherwise provided by law his driver's license (unless revoked or suspended) or the bond certificate deposited by him. Cash bail, or any balance due the defendant, shall be refunded to the defendant by the clerk as soon as practicable after the disposition of the charges.

(b) Written plea of guilty. In any case that can be disposed of on a written plea of guilty without a court appearance under Rule 529, the defendant may submit his written plea of guilty and pay the prescribed fines, penalties and costs to the clerk of the circuit court of the county in which the violation occurred not earlier than 10 court days after arrest, and not later than 3 court days before the date set for appearance, unless the clerk waives these time limits. If cash bail was posted, the clerk shall apply the amount necessary to pay prescribed fines, penalties and costs. If a driver's license or bond certificate was deposited, the full amount of the prescribed fines, penalties and costs must be paid to the clerk. Upon receiving payment in full, the clerk shall unless otherwise provided by law return the driver's license or bond certificate to the defendant. A written plea of guilty may be mailed to the clerk of the circuit court of the county in which the violation occurred. If the plea is accompanied by the full amount of the prescribed fines, penalties and costs, the clerk shall mail to the defendant any driver's license or bond certificate deposited in lieu of bail.

(Chgd. by Illinois Supreme Court, 6/19/89, eff. 8/1/89.)

Rule 556. Procedure if defendant fails to appear

(a) Promise to comply or driver's license deposited. If a person accused of a traffic offense has executed a written promise to comply (see Rule 501(g)), or deposited his driver's license in lieu of or in addition to cash bail or cash deposit and bond, and does not appear on the date set for appearance, or any date to which the case may be continued, the court shall continue the case for a minimum of 30 days and require a notice of the continued court date to be sent to the defendant at his last known address. The clerk shall notify the defendant of the court's order. If the defendant does not appear on the continued court date or, within that period, satisfy the court that his appearance is impossible and without any fault on his part, the court shall enter an order of failure to appear to answer the charge(s). A verified charge may be filed (if none has previously been filed) and a summons or warrant of arrest for the defendant may be issued. Within 21 days after the date to which the case has been continued, the clerk shall notify the Secretary of State of the court's order and forward the defendant's driver's license (if deposited). The Secretary of State shall, in the case of an Illinois licensed driver who has deposited his driver's license, immediately suspend the defendant's driving privileges in accordance with section 6–306.3 of the Illinois Vehicle Code, as amended (Ill. Rev. Stat., 1987, ch. 95½, par. 6–306.3 [625 ILCS 5/6-306.3]); if the defendant is not an Illinois licensed driver or resident the Secretary of State shall notify the appropriate driver's licensing authority pursuant to the Nonresident Violator Compact of 1977, as amended (Ill. Rev. Stat. 1987, ch. 95½, par. 6–800 et seq. [625 ILCS 5/6-800 et seq.]). The clerk of the circuit court shall notify the Secretary of State of the final disposition of the case as provided in Rule 552 when the defendant has appeared and otherwise satisfied his obligations following an order of failure to appear under this paragraph (a).

(b) Court appearance not required—Cash bail posted or bond certificate deposited. In all cases in which a court appearance is not required under Rule 551 and cash bail is posted or a bond certificate deposited, the defendant shall be provided with a statement, in substantially the following form, on the "Complaint" or on the bond form:

"In the event you fail to appear in court to answer to a charge that does not require you to appear in court, you thereby consent to the entry of a judgment against you in the amount of all applicable fines, penalties and costs, and the application of the cash bail or other security you have deposited to their payment and satisfaction."

If the defendant does not appear on the date set for appearance, or any date to which the case may be continued, the court may enter an *ex parte* judgment against the defendant assessing fines, penalties and costs in an amount not to exceed the cash bail required by this article and apply the cash bail or security in payment thereof. (See Rule 529.)

(c) Court appearance required—Cash bail posted or bond certificate deposited. If a defendant fails to appear on the date set for appearance, or any date to which the case may be continued, and a court appearance is required, the court shall enter an order declaring the bail to be forfeited and continue the case for a minimum of 30 days. Notice of such order of forfeiture shall be mailed forthwith to the accused at his last known address. If the accused does not appear on the continued court date or, within that period, satisfy the court that his appearance is impossible and without any fault on his part, the court shall enter judgment in accordance with sections 110–7 and 110–8 of the Code of Criminal Procedure of 1963, as amended (Ill. Rev. Stat. 1987, ch. 38, pars. 110–7, 110–8 [725 ILCS 5/110-7, 110-8]). In addition to forfeiture, a verified charge may be filed and a summons or warrant of arrest may issue.

(d) Individual bonds. In all cases in which a defendant released by giving individual bond under Rule 553(d) fails to appear on the date set for appearance, or any date to which the case may be continued, the court shall enter an order declaring the bond to be forfeited and continue the case for a minimum of 30 days. Notice of such order of forfeiture shall be mailed forthwith to the accused at his last known address. If the accused does not appear on the continued court date or, within that period, satisfy the court that his appearance is impossible and without any fault on his part, the court shall enter judgment in accordance with section 110–8 of the Code of Criminal Procedure of 1963, as amended (Ill. Rev. Stat. 1987, ch. 38, par. 110–8 [725 ILCS 5/110-8]). In addition to forfeiture, a verified charge may be filed and summons or warrant of arrest may issue.
(Chgd. by Illinois Supreme Court, 6/19/89, eff. 8/1/89; 12/7/90, eff. 1/1/91.)

Rules 557 to 600. *(Reserved.)*

ARTICLE VI. APPEALS IN CRIMINAL CASES, POST-CONVICTION CASES, AND JUVENILE COURT PROCEEDINGS

Rule 601. Supersedure of Code of Criminal Procedure of 1963

These rules supersede and replace articles 120 and 121, except sections 121–1 and 121–13 of the Code of Criminal Procedure of 1963 [725 ILCS 5/121-1, 121-13].

Rule 602. Method of review

The only method of review in a criminal case in which judgment was entered on or after January 1, 1964, shall be by appeal. The party appealing shall be known as the appellant and the adverse party as the appellee, but the title of the case shall not be changed. Review of cases in which judgments were entered before January 1, 1964, shall be governed by the time limitations in effect on December 31, 1963, and the procedure shall be as provided by the rules then in effect, or as provided by these rules, at the option of the appellant.

Rule 603. Court to which appeal is taken

Appeals in criminal cases in which a statute of the United States or of this State has been held invalid and appeals by defendants from judgments of the circuit courts imposing sentence of death shall lie directly to the Supreme Court as a matter of right. All other appeals in criminal cases shall be taken to the Appellate Court.

Rule 604. Appeals from certain judgments and orders

(a) Appeals by the State.

(1) *When State may appeal.* In criminal cases the State may appeal only from an order or judgment the substantive effect of which results in dismissing a charge for any of the grounds enumerated in section 114–1 of the Code of Criminal Procedure of 1963 [725 ILCS 5/114-1]; arresting judgment because of a defective indictment, information or complaint; quashing an arrest or search warrant; or suppressing evidence.

(2) *Leave to appeal by State.* The State may petition for leave to appeal under Rule 315(a).

(3) *Release of defendant pending appeal.* A defendant shall not be held in jail or to bail during the pendency of an appeal by the State, or of a petition or appeal by the State under Rule 315(a), unless there are compelling reasons for his continued detention or being held to bail.

(4) *Time appeal pending not counted.* The time during which an appeal by the State is pending is not counted for the purpose of determining whether an accused is entitled to discharge under section 103–5 of the Code of Criminal Procedure of 1963 [725 ILCS 5/103-5].

(b) Appeals when defendant placed under supervision or sentenced to probation, conditional discharge or periodic imprisonment. A defendant who has been placed under supervision or found guilty and sentenced to probation or conditional discharge (see Ill. Rev. Stat. 1981, ch. 38, pars. 1005–6–1 through 1005–6–4 [730 ILCS 5/5-6-1 through 5-6-4]), or to periodic imprisonment (see Ill. Rev. Stat. 1981, ch. 38, pars. 1005–7–1 through 1005–7–8 [730 ILCS 5/5-7-1 through 5-7-8]), may appeal from the judgment and may seek review of the conditions of supervision, or of the finding of guilt or the conditions of the sentence, or both. He may also appeal from an order modifying the conditions of or revoking such an order or sentence.

(c) Appeals from bail orders by defendant before conviction.

(1) *Appealability of order with respect to bail.* Before conviction a defendant may appeal to the Appellate Court from an order setting, modifying, revoking, denying, or refusing to modify bail or the conditions thereof. As a prerequisite to appeal the defendant shall first present to the trial court a written motion for the relief to be sought on appeal. The motion shall be verified by the defendant and shall state the following:

(i) the defendant's financial condition;

(ii) his residence addresses and employment history for the past 10 years;

(iii) his occupation and the name and address of his employer, if he is employed, or his school, if he is in school;

(iv) his family situation; and

(v) any prior criminal record and any other relevant facts.

If the order is entered upon motion of the prosecution, the defendant's verified answer to the motion shall contain the foregoing information.

(2) *Procedure.* The appeal may be taken at any time before conviction by filing a verified motion for review in the Appellate Court. The motion for review shall be accompanied by a verified copy of the motion or answer filed in the trial court and shall state the following:

(i) the court that entered the order;

(ii) the date of the order;

(iii) the crime or crimes charged;

(iv) the amount and condition of bail;

(v) the arguments supporting the motion; and

(vi) the relief sought.

No brief shall be filed. A copy of the motion shall be served upon the opposing party. The State may promptly file an answer.

(3) *Disposition.* Upon receipt of the motion, the clerk shall immediately notify the opposing party by telephone of the filing of the motion, entering the date and time of the notification on the docket, and promptly thereafter present the motion to the court.

(4) *Report of proceedings.* The court, on its own motion or on the motion of any party, may order the court reporter to file in the Appellate Court a report of all proceedings had in the trial court on the question of bail.

(5) *No oral argument.* No oral argument shall be permitted except when ordered on the court's own motion.

(d) Appeal by defendant from a judgment entered upon a plea of guilty. No appeal from a judgment entered upon a plea of guilty shall be taken unless the defendant, within 30 days of the date on which sentence is imposed, files in the trial court a motion to reconsider the sentence, if only the sentence is being challenged, or, if the plea is being challenged, a motion to withdraw his plea of guilty and vacate the judgment. The motion shall be in writing and shall state the grounds therefor. When the motion is based on facts that do not appear of record it shall be supported by affidavit. The motion shall be presented promptly to the trial judge by whom the defendant was sentenced, and if that judge is then not sitting in the court in which the judgment was entered, then to the chief judge of the circuit, or to such other judge as the chief judge shall designate. The trial court shall then determine whether the defendant is represented by counsel, and if the defendant is indigent and desires counsel, the trial court shall appoint counsel. If the defendant is indigent, the trial court shall order a copy of the transcript as provided in Rule 402(e) be furnished the defendant without cost. The defendant's attorney shall file with the trial court a certificate stating that the attorney has consulted with the defendant either by mail or in person to ascertain his contentions of error in the sentence or the entry of the plea of guilty, has examined the trial court file and report of proceedings of the plea of guilty, and has made any amendments to the motion necessary for adequate presentation of any defects in those proceedings. The motion shall be heard promptly, and if allowed, the trial court shall modify the sentence or vacate the judgment and permit the defendant to withdraw his plea of guilty and plead anew. If the motion is denied, a notice of appeal from the judgment and sentence shall be filed within the time allowed in Rule 606, measured from the date of entry of the order denying the motion. Upon appeal any issue not raised by the defendant in the motion to reconsider the sentence or withdraw the plea of guilty and vacate the judgment shall be deemed waived.

(e) Appeal from an order finding defendant unfit to stand trial or be sentenced. The defendant or the State may appeal to the Appellate Court from an order holding the defendant unfit to stand trial or be sentenced.

(f) Appeal from denial of a motion to dismiss on grounds of former jeopardy. The defendant may appeal to the Appellate Court the denial of a motion to dismiss a criminal proceeding on grounds of former jeopardy.

(Chgd. by Illinois Supreme Court, 6/15/82, eff. 7/1/82; 8/9/83, eff. 10/1/83; 4/1/92, eff. 8/1/92.)

Rule 605. Advice to defendant

(a) On judgment and sentence after plea of not guilty. In all cases in which the defendant is found guilty and sentenced to imprisonment, probation or conditional discharge, periodic imprisonment, or to pay a fine, or in which a sentence of probation or conditional discharge has been revoked or the conditions attached to such a sentence have been modified, except in cases in which the judgment and sentence are entered on a plea of guilty, the trial court shall, at the time of imposing sentence or modifying the conditions of the sentence, advise the defendant of his right to appeal, of his right to request the clerk to prepare and file a notice of appeal, and of his right, if indigent, to be furnished, without cost to him, with a transcript of the proceedings at his trial or hearing, and in cases in which the defendant has been convicted of a felony or a Class A misdemeanor or convicted of a lesser offense and sentenced to imprisonment, periodic imprisonment, or to probation or conditional discharge conditioned upon periodic imprisonment, or in which a sentence of probation or conditional discharge has been revoked or the conditions attached to such a sentence have been modified and a sentence or condition of imprisonment or periodic imprisonment imposed, of his right to have counsel appointed on appeal. The trial court shall also advise him that his right to appeal will be preserved only if a notice of appeal is filed in the trial court within 30 days from the date of the sentence.

(b) On judgment and sentence entered on a plea of guilty. In all cases in which a judgment is entered upon a plea of guilty, at the time of imposing sentence, the trial court shall advise the defendant substantially as follows:

(1) That he has a right to appeal;

(2) That prior to taking an appeal he must file in the trial court, within 30 days of the date on which sentence is imposed, a written motion asking to have the trial court reconsider the sentence or to have the judgment vacated and for leave to withdraw his plea of guilty, setting forth his grounds for the motion;

(3) That if the motion is allowed, the sentence will be modified or the plea of guilty, sentence and judgment will be vacated and a trial date will be set on the charges to which the plea of guilty was made;

(4) That upon the request of the State any charges that may have been dismissed as a party of a plea agreement will be reinstated and will also be set for trial;

(5) That if he is indigent, a copy of the transcript of the proceedings at the time of his plea of guilty and sentence will be provided without cost to him and counsel will be appointed to assist him with the preparation of the motions; and

(6) That in any appeal taken from the judgment on the plea of guilty any issue or claim of error not raised in the motion to reconsider the sentence or to vacate the judgment and to withdraw his plea of guilty shall be deemed waived.
(Chgd. by Illinois Supreme Court, 4/1/92, eff. 8/1/92.)

Rule 606. Perfection of appeal

(a) How perfected. In cases in which a death sentence is imposed, an appeal is automatically perfected without any action by the defendant or his counsel. In other cases appeals shall be perfected by filing a notice of appeal with the clerk of the trial court. The notice may be signed by the appellant or his attorney. If the defendant so requests in open court at the time he is advised of his right to appeal or subsequently in writing, the clerk of the trial court shall prepare, sign, and file forthwith a notice of appeal for the defendant. No step in the perfection of the appeal other than the filing of the notice of appeal is jurisdictional.

(b) Time. Except as provided in Rule 604(d), the notice of appeal must be filed with the clerk of the circuit court within 30 days after the entry of the final judgment appealed from or if a motion directed against the judgment is timely filed, within 30 days after the entry of the order disposing of the motion. Within 5 days of its being so filed a copy of the notice of appeal or an amendment of the notice of appeal shall be transmitted by the clerk of the circuit court to the clerk of the court to which the appeal is taken. Except as provided in paragraph (c) below, and in Rule 604(d), no appeal may be taken from a trial court to a reviewing court after the expiration of 30 days from the entry of the order or judgment from which the appeal is taken.

(c) Extension of time in certain circumstances. On motion supported by a showing of reasonable excuse for failing to file a notice of appeal on time filed in the reviewing court within 30 days of the expiration of the time for filing the notice of appeal, or on motion supported by a showing by affidavit that there is merit to the appeal and that the failure to file a notice of appeal on time was not due to appellant's culpable negligence, filed in the reviewing court within six months of the expiration of the time for filing the notice of appeal, in either case accompanied by the proposed notice of appeal, the reviewing court may grant leave to appeal and order the clerk to transmit the notice of appeal to the trial court for filing.

(d) Form of notice of appeal. The notice of appeal shall be substantially in the following form:

In the Circuit Court of the ________ Judicial Court, ____________ County, Illinois.

(or In the Circuit Court of Cook County)

PEOPLE OF THE STATE OF ILLINOIS,

v. No.

____

Notice of Appeal

An appeal is taken from the order or judgment described below.

(1) Court to which appeal is taken: ______________________________

____

(2) Name of appellant and address to which notices shall be sent.
Name: ______________________________
Address: ______________________________

(3) Name and address of appellant's attorney on appeal.
Name:____________________
Address:____________________
If appellant is indigent and has no attorney, does he want one appointed?
____
(4) Date of judgment or order: ____________________
(5) Offense of which convicted:____________________
____
(6) Sentence:____________________
(7) If appeal is not from a conviction, nature of order appealed from:
____

(Signed) ____________________
(May be signed by appellant, attorney for appellant, or clerk of circuit court.)

The notice of appeal may be amended as provided in Rule 303(c)(4).

(e) Copies of notice of appeal to be sent by clerk.

(1) *When defendant is appellant and action is prosecuted by the State.* When the defendant is the appellant and the action was prosecuted by the State, the clerk shall send a copy of the notice of appeal to the State's Attorney of the county in which the judgment was entered and a copy to the Attorney General at his Springfield, Illinois, office.

(2) *When defendant is appellant and the action is prosecuted by a governmental entity other than the State.* If the defendant is the appellant and the action was prosecuted by a governmental entity other than the State for the violation of an ordinance, the copy of the notice of appeal shall be sent to the chief legal officer of the entity (*e.g.*, corporation counsel, city attorney), or if his name and address do not appear of record, then to the chief administrative officer of the entity at his official address.

(3) *When the prosecuting entity is the appellant.* When the State or other prosecuting entity is the appellant a copy of the notice of appeal shall be sent to the defendant and a copy to his counsel.

(f) Docketing. Upon receipt of the copy of the notice of appeal transmitted to the reviewing court pursuant to paragraph (a) of this rule, or the entry of an order granting a motion for leave to appeal under paragraph (c) of this rule, the clerk of the reviewing court shall enter the appeal upon the docket.

(g) Docketing statement; filing fee. Within 14 days after the filing of the notice of appeal and pursuant to notice to the appellee's attorney, the party filing the notice of appeal shall file with the clerk of the reviewing court a docketing statement, together with proof of service thereof, and the required filing fee of $25. The form and contents of the docketing statement shall be as follows:

DOCKET NUMBER IN THE REVIEWING COURT

Case Title (Complete)

Appeal From__________County
Circuit Court No.__________
Date of Notice of Appeal
____
Trial Judge__________
Felony ( ) Misdemeanor ( )
In Custody ( ) Out on Bond ( )

DOCKETING STATEMENT
(CRIMINAL)

Counsel on Appeal
For Appellant(s)
Name: ____________________
Address: ____________________
Telephone: ____________________
Trial Counsel, If
Different
Name: ____________________
Address: ____________________
Telephone: ____________________
Counsel On Appeal
For Appellee(s)
Name: ____________________
Address: ____________________
Telephone: ____________________
Court Reporter(s)
(If more space is
needed, use other
side)
Name: ____________________
Address: ____________________
Telephone: ____________________
Approximate Duration
Of Trial Court Proceedings To Be
Transcribed ____________________
Nature of Case:
( ) Appeal from conviction after trial
( ) Jury trial
( ) Bench trial
( ) Plea of guilty
( ) Post-conviction proceeding
( ) Sentence only
( ) Revocation of probation
( ) Appeal by State
( ) Other (Explain) ____________________
____

General Statement of Issues Proposed To Be Raised (Failure to include an issue in this statement will not result in the waiver of the issue on appeal.)
I, as attorney for the appellant, hereby certify that on ____________________
(Date)
I asked the clerk of the circuit court to prepare the record and on ____________________
(Date)
I made a written request to the court reporter to prepare the transcript.
Date ____________________

____
Appellant's Attorney

I hereby acknowledge receipt of an order for the preparation of a report of proceedings.

____
(Court Reporter or
Supervisor)

____
(Date)

Within 7 days thereafter, appellee's attorney if it is deemed necessary, may file a short responsive statement with the clerk of the reviewing court.

Rule 607. Appeals by poor persons

(a) Appointment of counsel. Upon the imposition of a death sentence, or upon the filing of a notice of appeal in any case in which the defendant has been found guilty of a felony or a Class A misdemeanor, or in which he has been found guilty of a lesser offense and sentenced to imprisonment or periodic imprisonment, or to probation or conditional discharge conditioned upon periodic imprisonment, or in which a sentence of probation or conditional discharge has been revoked or the conditions attached to such a sentence modified and a sentence of imprisonment or periodic imprisonment imposed, and in cases in which the State appeals, the trial court shall determine whether the defendant is represented by counsel on appeal. If not so represented, and the court determines that the defendant is indigent and desires counsel on appeal, the court shall appoint counsel on appeal. When a death sentence has been imposed, the court may appoint two attorneys, one of whom it shall designate as the responsible attorney and the other as assistant attorney for the appeal. Compensation and reimbursement for expenses of appointed attorneys shall be as provided by statute.

(b) Report of proceedings. In any case in which the defendant has been found guilty and sentenced to imprisonment, probation or conditional discharge, or periodic imprisonment, or to pay a fine, or in which a hearing has been held resulting in the revocation of, or modification of the conditions of, probation or conditional discharge, the defendant may petition the court in which he was convicted for a report of the proceedings at his trial or hearing. If the conduct on which the case was based was also the basis for a juvenile proceeding which was dismissed so that the case could proceed, the defendant may include in his petition a request for a report of proceedings in the juvenile proceeding. The petition shall be verified by the petitioner and shall state facts showing that he was at the time of his conviction, or at the time probation or conditional discharge was revoked or its conditions modified, and is at the time of filing the petition, without financial means with which to obtain the report of proceedings. If the judge who imposed sentence or entered the order revoking probation or conditional discharge or modifying the conditions, or in his absence any other judge of the court, finds that the defendant is without financial means with which to obtain the report of proceedings at his trial or hearing, he shall order the court reporter to transcribe an original and copy of his notes. The original and one copy of the report shall be certified by the reporter and filed with the clerk of the trial court as provided below, without charge. The clerk of the trial court shall then, upon written request of the defendant, release the copy of the report of proceedings to the defendant's attorney of record on appeal. In the event no attorney appears of record, the clerk shall, upon written request of the defendant, release the report of proceedings to the defendant, his guardian or custodian. The reporter who prepares a report of proceedings pursuant to an order under this rule shall be paid the same fee for preparing the transcript as is provided by law for the compensation of reporters for preparing transcripts in other cases.

(c) Filing fees excused. If the defendant is represented by court-appointed counsel, the clerk of the reviewing court shall docket the appeal and accept papers for filing without the payment of fees.

(d) Copies of briefs or petitions for leave to appeal. If the defendant is represented by court-appointed counsel, the clerk of the Supreme Court shall accept for filing not less than 12 legible copies of briefs or petitions for leave to appeal or answers thereto; and the clerks of the Appellate Court shall accept for filing not less than 6 legible copies of briefs.

Rule 608. The record on appeal

(a) Designation and contents. Upon the filing of a notice of appeal, and in all cases in which a death sentence is imposed, the clerk of the circuit court shall prepare the record on appeal, which must contain the following:

(1) a cover sheet showing the title of the case;

(2) a certificate of the clerk showing the impaneling of the grand jury if the prosecution was commenced by indictment;

(3) the indictment, information, or complaint;

(4) a transcript of the proceedings at the defendant's arraignment and plea;

(5) all motions, transcript of motion proceedings, and orders entered thereon;

(6) all arrest warrants, search warrants, consent to search forms, eavesdropping orders, and any similar documents;

(7) a transcript of proceedings regarding waiver of counsel and waiver of jury trial, if any;

(8) the report of proceedings, including opening statements by counsel, testimony offered at trial, and objections thereto, offers of proof, arguments and rulings thereon, the instructions offered and given, and the objections and rulings thereon, closing argument of counsel, communications from the jury during deliberations, and responses and supplemental instructions to the jury and objections, arguments and rulings thereon;

(9) in cases in which a sentence of death is imposed, a transcript of all proceedings regarding the selection of the jury. In other cases the court reporter shall take full stenographic notes of the proceedings regarding the selection of the jury, but the notes need not be transcribed unless a party designates that such proceedings be included in the record on appeal;

(10) exhibits offered at trial and sentencing, along with objections, offers of proof, arguments, and rulings thereon; except that physical and demonstrative evidence, other than photographs, which do not fit on a standard size record page shall not be included in the record on appeal unless ordered by a court upon motion of a party or upon the court's own motion;

(11) the verdict of the jury or finding of the court;

(12) post-trial motions, including motions for a new trial, motions in arrest of judgment, motions for judgment notwithstanding the verdict and the testimony, arguments and rulings thereon;

(13) a transcript of proceedings at sentencing, including the presentence investigation report, testimony offered and objections thereto, offers of proof, argument, and rulings thereon, arguments of counsel, and statements by the defendant and the court;

(14) the judgment and sentence; and

(15) the notice of appeal, if any.

Within 14 days after the notice of appeal is filed or after a sentence of death is imposed the appellant and the appellee may file a designation of additional portions of the circuit court record to be included in the record on appeal. Thereupon the clerk shall include those portions in the record on appeal. Additionally, upon motion of a party, the court may allow photographs of exhibits to be filed as a supplemental record on appeal, in lieu of the exhibits themselves, when such photographs accurately depict the exhibits themselves. There is no distinction between the common law record and the report of proceedings, for the purpose of determining what is properly before the reviewing court.

(b) Report of proceedings; time. The report of proceedings contains the testimony and exhibits, the rulings of the trial judge, and all other proceedings before the trial judge, unless the parties designate or stipulate for less. It shall be certified by the reporter or the trial judge and shall be filed in the trial court within 49 days after the filing of the notice of appeal, or, if a death sentence has been imposed, within 49 days from the date of the sentence. The report of proceedings shall be taken as true and correct unless shown to be otherwise and corrected in a manner permitted by Rule 329.

(c) Time for filing record on appeal. The record shall be filed in the reviewing court within 63 days from the date the notice of appeal is filed in the trial court or, if a death sentence has been imposed, within 49 days from the date of the sentence. If more than one appellant appeal from the same judgment or from different judgments in the same cause to the same reviewing court, the trial court may prescribe the time for filing the record in the reviewing court, which shall not be more than 63 days from the date the last notice of appeal is filed. If the time for filing the report of proceedings has been extended, the record on appeal shall be filed within 14 days after the expiration of the extended time.

(d) Extensions of time. The reviewing court or any judge thereof may extend the time for filing, in the trial court, the report of proceedings or agreed statement of facts or for serving a proposed report of proceedings, on notice and motion filed in the reviewing court before the expiration of the original or extended time, or on notice and motion filed within 35 days thereafter. Motions for extensions of time shall be supported by an affidavit showing the necessity for extension, and motions made after expiration of the original or extended time shall be further supported by a showing of reasonable excuse for failure to file the motion earlier.

(Chgd. by Illinois Supreme Court, 2/19/82, eff. 4/1/82.)

Rule 609. Stays

(a) Death sentences. A death sentence shall not be carried out until final order by the Supreme Court.

(b) Imprisonment or confinement. If an appeal is taken from a judgment following which the defendant is sentenced to imprisonment or periodic imprisonment, or to probation or conditional discharge conditioned upon periodic imprisonment, or from an order revoking or modifying the conditions attached to a sentence of probation or conditional discharge and imposing a sentence of imprisonment or periodic imprisonment, the defendant may be admitted to bail and the sentence or condition of imprisonment or periodic imprisonment stayed, with or without bond, by a judge of the trial or reviewing court. Upon motion showing good cause the reviewing court or a judge thereof may revoke the order of the trial court or order that the amount of bail be increased or decreased.

(c) Other cases. On appeals in other cases the judgment or order may be stayed by a judge of the trial or reviewing court, with or without bond. Upon motion showing good cause the reviewing court or a judge thereof may revoke the order of the trial court or order that the amount of bail be increased or decreased.

Rule 610. Motions

Motions in reviewing courts shall be governed by Rule 361, except that in addition to the requirements set forth in Rule 361 every motion for extension of time in a criminal case shall be supported by an affidavit showing the following:

(1) the date on which counsel was engaged or appointed to prosecute the appeal;

(2) the date on which the complete record was filed in the reviewing court;

(3) the reason for the present request for an extension.

The purpose of this rule is the achievement of prompt preparation and disposition of criminal cases in the reviewing courts, and motions for extension of time are looked upon with disfavor.

Rule 611. Oral argument

(a) Sequence and manner of calling. Sequence and manner of calling cases for oral argument is governed by Rule 351, except that oral argument in cases in which a death sentence has been imposed shall be given priority over all other cases, and priority shall be given to appeals in criminal cases over appeals in civil cases.

(b) Other matters. In other respects oral argument is governed by Rule 352.

Rule 612. Procedural matters which are governed by Civil Appeals Rules

The following civil appeals rules apply to criminal appeals insofar as appropriate:

(a) Dismissal of appeals by the trial court: Rule 309.

(b) Appeals to the Supreme Court: Rules 302(b), 315, 316, 317, and 318.

(c) Procedure if no verbatim transcript is available and procedure for an agreed statement of facts: Rule 323(c) and (d).

(d) Preparation and certification of record on appeal by clerk: Rule 324.

(e) Transmission of record on appeal or certificate in lieu of record: Rule 325 (but if the defendant is represented by court-appointed counsel, no fees need be paid to the clerk of the trial court).

(f) Notice of filing: Rule 327.

(g) Amendment of the record on appeal: Rule 329.

(h) Return of record on appeal: Rule 331.

(i) Contents of briefs: Rule 341.

(j) Abstract: Rule 342.

(k) Times for filing and serving briefs: Rule 343.

(*l*) Number of copies and form and method of reproduction of briefs and abstract: Rule 344.

(m) Briefs *amicus curiae:* Rule 345.

(n) Inspection of original exhibits: Rule 363.

(*o*) Appeal to wrong court: Rule 365.

(p) Rehearing in reviewing courts: Rule 367.

(q) Issuance, stay, and recall of mandates from reviewing court: Rule 368.

(r) Process in reviewing courts: Rule 370.

(s) Removing records from the reviewing court: Rule 372.

(t) Constructive date of filing papers in reviewing court: Rule 373.

Rule 613. Mandate of reviewing court

(a) Death cases. If a death sentence is affirmed the Supreme Court shall set the time when the sentence shall be executed. A certified copy of the order of execution shall be authority to the warden or the sheriff of Cook County for execution of the sentence at the time therein specified. If the judgment is reversed or modified the Supreme Court shall direct the trial court to proceed in accordance with the mandate.

(b) Other cases. In all other cases the reviewing court shall direct the appellate or trial court to proceed in accordance with the mandate.

(c) Reversal when appellant is serving sentence. If in a case on appeal the appellant is serving the sentence imposed in the trial court and the judgment is reversed and appellant ordered discharged, the clerk of the reviewing court shall at once mail to the imprisoning officer, certified mail, return receipt requested, a copy of the mandate of the reviewing court. It shall be the duty of the imprisoning officer to release appellant from custody forthwith upon receiving a certified copy of the mandate of the reviewing court. If appellant is serving the sentence and the judgment is reversed and the cause remanded to the trial court for further proceedings, the clerk of the reviewing court shall at once mail to the imprisoning officer, certified mail, return receipt requested, a copy of the mandate of the reviewing court. The imprisoning officer shall forthwith, upon receiving the certified copy of the mandate of the reviewing court, return appellant to the trial court to which the cause was remanded.

(d) Credit for time served pending appeal. In any case in which, pending appeal, an appellant serves any portion of the sentence imposed in the

trial court and the judgment of the trial court is reversed by a reviewing court and a new trial ordered, the appellant shall be given credit in any subsequent sentence for the time served pending appeal.
(Chgd. by Illinois Supreme Court, 6/26/87, eff. 8/1/87.)

Rule 614. Notifying prisoner of affirmance by Appellate Court

When a judgment of conviction of a person incarcerated in a penal institution is affirmed by the Appellate Court, the clerk of that court shall at once mail to the prisoner a copy of the opinion of the court, certified mail, return receipt requested, in an envelope marked, "OFFICIAL LEGAL MAIL–ADDRESSEE MUST ACKNOWLEDGE RECEIPT IN WRITING." The clerk shall note the date of mailing upon the records of the court. (Chgd. by Illinois Supreme Court, 6/26/87, eff. 8/1/87.)

Rule 615. The cause on appeal

(a) Insubstantial and substantial errors on appeal. Any error, defect, irregularity, or variance which does not affect substantial rights shall be disregarded. Plain errors or defects affecting substantial rights may be noticed although they were not brought to the attention of the trial court.

(b) Powers of the reviewing court. On appeal the reviewing court may:

(1) reverse, affirm, or modify the judgment or order from which the appeal is taken;

(2) set aside, affirm, or modify any or all of the proceedings subsequent to or dependent upon the judgment or order from which the appeal is taken;

(3) reduce the degree of the offense of which the appellant was convicted;

(4) reduce the punishment imposed by the trial court; or

(5) order a new trial.

Rules 616 to 650. *(Reserved.)*

Rule 651. Appeals in post-conviction proceedings

(a) Right of appeal. An appeal from a final judgment of the circuit court in any post-conviction proceeding involving a judgment imposing a sentence of death shall lie directly to the Supreme Court as a matter of right. All other appeals from such proceedings shall lie to the Appellate Court in the district in which the circuit court is located.

(b) Notice to petitioner of adverse judgment. Upon the entry of a judgment adverse to a petitioner in a post-conviction proceeding, the clerk of the trial court shall at once mail or deliver to the petitioner a notice in substantially the following form.

"You are hereby notified that on _______ the court entered an order, a copy of which is enclosed herewith. You have a right to appeal. In the case of an appeal from a post-conviction proceeding involving a judgment imposing a sentence of death, the appeal is to the Illinois Supreme Court. In all other cases, the appeal is to the Illinois Appellate Court in the district in which the circuit court is located. If you are indigent, you have a right to a transcript of the record of the post-conviction proceedings and to the appointment of counsel on appeal, both without cost to you. To preserve your right to appeal you must file a notice of appeal in the trial court within 30 days from the date the order was entered."

(c) Record for indigents; appointment of counsel. Upon the timely filing of a notice of appeal in a post-conviction proceeding, if the trial court determines that the petitioner is indigent, it shall order that a transcript of the record of the post-conviction proceedings, including a transcript of the evidence, if any, be prepared and filed with the clerk of the court to which the appeal is taken and shall appoint counsel on appeal, both without cost to the petitioner. The record filed in that court shall contain a showing, which may be made by the certificate of petitioner's attorney, that the attorney has consulted with petitioner either by mail or in person to ascertain his contentions of deprivation of constitutional rights, has examined the record of the proceedings at the trial, and has made any amendments to the petitions filed *pro se* that are necessary for an adequate presentation of petitioner's contentions.

(d) Procedure. The procedure for an appeal in a post-conviction proceeding shall be in accordance with the rules governing criminal appeals, as near as may be.

Rules 652 to 659. *(Reserved.)*

Rule 660. Appeals in cases arising under the Juvenile Court Act

(a) Delinquent minors. Appeals from final judgments in delinquent minor proceedings, except as otherwise specifically provided, shall be governed by the rules applicable to criminal cases.

(b) Other proceedings. In all other proceedings under the Juvenile Court Act, appeals from final judgments shall be governed by the rules applicable to civil cases.

Rule 661. Appeals as poor persons by minors found to be delinquent

Upon the filing of a notice of appeal in any proceeding in which a minor has been found to be delinquent, or in which probation or conditional discharge imposed in such a proceeding has been revoked, appointment of counsel and the provision of a transcript of the adjudicatory and dispositional hearings without cost to the minor shall be governed by Rule 607.

Rule 662. Adjudication of wardship and revocation of probation or conditional discharge

(a) Adjudication of wardship. An appeal may be taken to the Appellate Court from an adjudication of wardship in the event that an order of disposition has not been entered within 90 days of the adjudication of wardship.

(b) Revocation of probation or conditional discharge. An appeal may be taken to the Appellate Court from an order revoking probation or conditional discharge in the event that an order of disposition has not been entered within 90 days from the revocation of probation or conditional discharge.

(c) Procedure. The notice of appeal in appeals under this rule shall be filed within 30 days after the expiration of the 90 days specified in this rule and not thereafter.

Rule 663. Adoption—Appointment of a guardian with power to consent

An appeal may be taken to the Appellate Court from an order of court empowering the guardian of the person of a minor to consent to the adoption of such a minor.

Rules 664 to 700. *(Reserved.)*

INDEX

(Unless otherwise noted, all references are to Chapters 20, 30, 45, 410, 415, 430, 705, 720, 725, 730, 735, 740, 750, and 815 of the Illinois Compiled Statutes. The Illinois Supreme Court Rules are designated with "R" followed by the rule number.)

Department of Corrections - 730 ILCS 5/3-1-1, 5/3-1-2
disabled person - 720 ILCS 5/12-20
domestic violence - 750 ILCS 60/103, 60/227
  order of protection - 725 ILCS 5/112A-3
  shelters - 20 ILCS 2210/1
drug paraphernalia - 720 ILCS 600/2
dwelling - 720 ILCS 5/2-6
eavesdropping - 720 ILCS 5/14-1
elderly person - 720 ILCS 5/12-20
felony - 720 ILCS 5/2-7
firearms - 430 ILCS 65/1.1
Flag Desecration Act - 720 ILCS 620/2
forcible felony - 720 ILCS 5/2-8
gambling - 720 ILCS 5/28-2
hazing - 720 ILCS 120/2
hearing-impaired person - 20 ILCS 305/1-103
Hunter Interference Prohibition Act - 720 ILCS 125/1
Illinois Dangerous Animals Act - 720 ILCS 585/0.1
included offense - 720 ILCS 5/2-9
includes - 720 ILCS 5/2-10
Intergovernmental Drug Laws Enforcement Act - 30 ILCS 715/2 to 2.04
  Department - 30 ILCS 715/2.01
  Director - 30 ILCS 715/2
  drug laws - 30 ILCS 715/2.04
  Metropolitan Enforcement Group (MEG) - 30 ILCS 715/2.02
  unit of local government - 30 ILCS 715/2.03
Interstate Corrections Compact - 730 ILCS 5/3-4-4, Article II
Juvenile Court - 705 ILCS 405/1-3
library materials - 720 ILCS 5/16B-1
litter - 415 ILCS 105/3
mentally retarded person - 720 ILCS 5/2-10.1
misdemeanor - 720 ILCS 5/2-11
narcotics - 725 ILCS 175/3
offense - 720 ILCS 5/2-12, 5/8-6
open parole hearings - 730 ILCS 105/5
parole: state - 730 ILCS 5/3-3-11.1
Party Line Emergency Act - 720 ILCS 660/1
peace officer - 720 ILCS 5/2-13
Peephole Installation Act - 720 ILCS 665/2
penal institution - 720 ILCS 5/2-14
person - 720 ILCS 5/2-14
physically handicapped person - 720 ILCS 5/2-15a
privacy: communications consumer - 720 ILCS 110/2
probation: officer - 730 ILCS 110/9b
Probation Challenge Program - 730 ILCS 120/3
property offenses: deception - 720 ILCS 5/15-4
  obtain - 720 ILCS 5/15-7
  obtains or exerts control - 720 ILCS 5/15-8
  owner - 720 ILCS 5/15-2
  permanently deprive - 720 ILCS 5/15-3
  property - 720 ILCS 5/15-1
  stolen property - 720 ILCS 5/15-6
  threat - 720 ILCS 5/15-5
  value - 720 ILCS 5/15-9
prosecution - 720 ILCS 5/2-16
public employee - 720 ILCS 5/2-17
public officer - 720 ILCS 5/2-18
qualified psychiatrist - 725 ILCS 205/4.01
reasonable belief - 720 ILCS 5/2-19
record of charge form: defined - 720 ILCS 250/2.11
Sale Price Ad Act - 720 ILCS 350/1
sentencing - 730 ILCS 5/5-1-1 to 5-1-22
  business offense - 730 ILCS 5/5-1-2
  charge - 730 ILCS 5/5-1-3
  conditional discharge - 730 ILCS 5/5-1-4
  conviction - 730 ILCS 5/5-1-5
  court - 730 ILCS 5/5-1-6
  defendant - 730 ILCS 5/5-1-7
  defendant in need of mental treatment - 730 ILCS 5/5-1-8
  felony - 730 ILCS 5/5-1-9
  imprisonment - 730 ILCS 5/5-1-10
  insanity - 730 ILCS 5/5-1-11
  judgment - 730 ILCS 5/5-1-12
  mentally retarded - 730 ILCS 5/5-1-13
  misdemeanor - 730 ILCS 5/5-1-14
  offense - 730 ILCS 5/5-1-15
  parole - 730 ILCS 5/5-1-16
  petty offense - 730 ILCS 5/5-1-17
  probation - 730 ILCS 5/5-1-18
  public or community service - 730 ILCS 5/5-1-18.1
  sentence - 730 ILCS 5/5-1-19
  site - 730 ILCS 5/5-1-18.2
  state - 730 ILCS 5/5-1-20
  supervision - 730 ILCS 5/5-1-21
  victim - 730 ILCS 5/5-1-22
sexual offenses - 720 ILCS 5/12-12
sexually dangerous person - 725 ILCS 205/1.01

Air Rifle Act - 720 ILCS 535/0.01
Aircraft Crash Parts Act - 720 ILCS 205/0.01
Alternative Sentencing Job Training Act - 730 ILCS 170/1
Animal Registration Under False Pretenses Act - 720 ILCS 210/0.01
Animal Research and Production Facilities Protection Act - 720 ILCS 215/1
Anti-Crime Advisory Council Act - 730 ILCS 5/5-9-1.4
Appliance Tag Act - 720 ILCS 220/0.01
Arrest and Conviction of Out of State Murderers Act - 725 ILCS 110/0.01
Auction Sales Sign Act - 720 ILCS 225/0.01
Bail Bond False Statement Act - 720 ILCS 540/0.01
Bill of Rights for Children - 725 ILCS 115/1
Bill of Rights for Victims and Witnesses of Violent Crime Act - 725 ILCS 120/1
Boarding Aircraft with Weapon Act - 720 ILCS 545/0.01
Business Use of Military Terms Act - 720 ILCS 230/0.01
Cannabis Control Act - 720 ILCS 550/2
Child Curfew Act - 720 ILCS 555/0.01
Coin Slug Act - 720 ILCS 235/1a
Communications Consumer Privacy Act - 720 ILCS 110/1
Computer Crime Prevention Law - 720 ILCS 5/16D-1
Conditional Sales Protection Act - 720 ILCS 240/0.01
Construction Equipment Identification Defacement Act - 720 ILCS 245/0.01
Container Label Obliteration Act - 720 ILCS 565/0.01
County Jail Act - 730 ILCS 125/0.01
County Jail Good Behavior Allowance Act - 730 ILCS 130/1
Credit Card Issuance Act - 815 ILCS 140/0.01
Crime Victims Compensation Act - 740 ILCS 45/1
Criminal Code of 1961 - 720 ILCS 5/1-1
Criminal Identification Act - 20 ILCS 2630/0.01
Criminal Proceeding Interpreter Act - 725 ILCS 140/0.01
Criminal Victims' Assets Discovery Act - 725 ILCS 145/1
Deceptive Advertising Act - 720 ILCS 295/1e
Deceptive Sale of Gold and Silver Act - 720 ILCS 290/1a
Delivery Container Crime Act - 720 ILCS 5/16E-1
Derogatory Statements About Banks Act - 720 ILCS 300/0.01
Discrimination in Sale of Real Estate Act - 720 ILCS 590/0.01
Domestic Violence Shelters Act - 20 ILCS 2210/0.01
Draft Card Mutilation Act - 720 ILCS 595/0.01
Drug Asset Forfeiture Act - 725 ILCS 150/1
Drug Paraphernalia Control Act - 720 ILCS 600/1
Electronic Home Detention Law - 730 ILCS 5/5-8A-1
Excavation Fence Act - 720 ILCS 605/0.01
Federal Prisoner Production Expense Act - 725 ILCS 220/10
Feeding Garbage to Animals Act - 720 ILCS 610/0.01
Fines Paid to Societies Act - 725 ILCS 160/0.01
Fire Extinguisher Service Act - 720 ILCS 610/0.01
Firearm Owners Identification Card Act - 430 ILCS 65/0.01
Firearm Seizure Act - 725 ILCS 165/0.01
Flag Desecration Act - 720 ILCS 620/0.01
Fugitive Apprehension Reward Act - 725 ILCS 170/0.01
Gasoline Price Advertising Act - 720 ILCS 305/0.01
Governmental Uneconomic Practices Act - 720 ILCS 310/0.01
Grain Coloring Act - 720 ILCS 625/0.01
Guide Dog Access Act - 720 ILCS 630/0.01
Habitual Child Sex Offender Registration Act - 730 ILCS 150/1
Hazing Act - 720 ILCS 120/0.01
Horse Mutilation Act - 720 ILCS 315/0.01
Horse Racing False Entries Act - 720 ILCS 320/0.01
Hunter Interference Prohibition Act - 720 ILCS 125/0.01
Hypodermic Syringes and Needles Act - 720 ILCS 635/0.01

Illinois Abortion Law of 1975 - 720 ILCS 515/1
Illinois Alcoholism and Other Drug Dependency Act - 20 ILCS 305/1-101
Illinois Antitrust Act - 740 ILCS 10/1
Illinois Clean Indoor Air Act - 410 ILCS 80/1
Illinois Clean Public Elevator Air Act - 720 ILCS 560/1
Illinois Controlled Substances Act - 720 ILCS 570/101
Illinois Credit Card and Debit Card Act - 720 ILCS 250/1
Illinois Criminal Justice Information Act - 20 ILCS 3930/1
Illinois Dangerous Animals Act - 720 ILCS 585/0.01
Illinois Domestic Violence Act of 1986 - 750 ILCS 60/101
Illinois Prison Inspection Act - 730 ILCS 135/1
Illinois Public Demonstration Law - 430 ILCS 70/1
Illinois Substance Abuse Treatment Program - 730 ILCS 145/1
Illinois Uniform Conviction Information Act - 20 ILCS 2635/1
Improper Supervision of Children Act - 720 ILCS 640/0.01
Industrial Schools for Girls Act - 730 ILCS 160/0.01
Insurance Claims For Excessive Charges Act - 720 ILCS 325/1
Intergovernmental Drug Laws Enforcement Act - 30 ILCS 715/1
Interstate Agreements on Sexually Dangerous Persons Act - 45 ILCS 20/0.01
Juvenile Court Act of 1987 - 705 ILCS 405/1-1
Legislative Misconduct Act - 720 ILCS 645/0.01
Litter Control Act - 415 ILCS 105/1
Loan Advertising to Bankrupts Act - 720 ILCS 330/0.01
Marks and Serial Numbers Act - 720 ILCS 335/2
Narcotics Profit Forfeiture Act - 725 ILCS 175/1
Neglected Children Offense Act - 720 ILCS 130/0.01
Nitroglycerin Transportation Act - 720 ILCS 650/0.01
Obscene Phone Call Act - 720 ILCS 135/0.01
Open Parole Hearings Act - 730 ILCS 105/1
Outdoor Lighting Installation Act - 720 ILCS 655/0.01
Park Ordinance Violation Procedure Act - 725 ILCS 180/0.01
Party Line Emergency Act - 720 ILCS 660/0.01
Peephole Installation Act - 720 ILCS 665/0.01
Pretrial Services Act - 725 ILCS 185/0.01
Prisoner Interchange Act - 730 ILCS 155/0.01
Privacy of Child Victims of Criminal Sexual Offender Act - 725 ILCS 190/1
Private Correctional Facility Moratorium Act - 730 ILCS 140/1
Probation and Probation Officers Act - 730 ILCS 110/0.01
Probation Challenge Program Act - 730 ILCS 120/1
Probation Community Service Act - 730 ILCS 115/0.01
Quasi-criminal and Misdemeanor Bail Act - 725 ILCS 195/0.01
Sale of Immoral Publications to Children Act - 720 ILCS 670/0.01
Sale of Maps Act - 720 ILCS 340/0.01
Sale of Tobacco to Minors Act - 720 ILCS 675/0.01
Sale or Pledge of Goods by Minors Act - 720 ILCS 345/0.01
Sale Price Ad Act - 720 ILCS 350/0.01
Sex Offense Victim Polygraph Act - 725 ILCS 200/0.01
Sexually Dangerous Persons Act - 725 ILCS 205/1.01
Smokeless Tobacco Limitation Act - 720 ILCS 680/1
Smokeless Tobacco Outdoor Advertising Act - 410 ILCS 75/0.01
Stallion and Jack Pedigree Act - 720 ILCS 355/0.01
State Appellate Defender Act - 725 ILCS 105/1
State's Attorneys Appellate Prosecutor's Act - 725 ILCS 210/1
Statewide Grand Jury Act - 725 ILCS 215/1
Statewide Organized Gang Database Act - 20 ILCS 2640/1
Taxpreparer Disclosure of Information Act - 720 ILCS 140/0.01
Telecommunication Line Tapping Act - 720 ILCS 145/0.01

This page intentionally left blank.

This page intentionally left blank.

GOULD'S QUICK FIND LOCATOR™

HOW TO USE: Bend the edge and follow the arrow to the corresponding black mark.